CASES AND MATERIALS ON
EQUITABLE REMEDIES, RESTITUTION AND DAMAGES

Fifth Edition

By

Robert N. Leavell
Alumni Association Professor of Law, Emeritus
University of Georgia

Jean C. Love
Professor of Law
University of Iowa

Grant S. Nelson
Professor of Law
University of California, Los Angeles

Candace S. Kovacic–Fleischer
Professor of Law
Washington College of Law
The American University

AMERICAN CASEBOOK SERIES®

WEST PUBLISHING CO.
ST. PAUL, MINN., 1994

610 Opperman Drive
P.O. Box 64526
St. Paul, MN 55164–0526
1–800–328–9352

Printed in the United States of America

Library of Congress Cataloging-in-Publication Data

Cases and materials on equitable remedies, restitution and damages / by Robert N. Leavell . . . [et al.]. — 5th ed.

p. cm. — (American casebook series)

Rev. ed. of: Cases and materials on equitable remedies, restitution, and damages / Robert N. Leavell, Jean C. Love, Grant S. Nelson. 4th ed. 1986.

Includes index.

ISBN 0–314–03719–5

1. Equitable remedies—United States—Cases. 2. Restitution—United States—Cases. 3. Damages—United States—Cases. I. Leavell, Robert N. II. Series.

KF9010.A7L43 1994
347.73 ' 77—dc20
[347.30777] 94–18919
CIP

ISBN 0–314–03719–5

TEXT IS PRINTED ON 10% POST CONSUMER RECYCLED PAPER

PRINTED WITH SOY INK™

To Carroll and Deidre.
R.N.L.

To Pat.
J.C.L.

To Judy.
G.S.N.

To Walter and Ilona.
C.S.K–F.

*

Preface to Fifth Edition

In this edition we added three new chapters or subchapters—one on Basic Principles of Damages, the others on equitable defenses and personal injury—in order to make the book a full purpose remedies text. At the same time we retained the book's basic organization, its traditional emphasis and its examination of contemporary issues. We kept many of the discussion-provoking, classic cases, and also added many current cases that we expect will be good teaching vehicles.

We made one organizational change, rearranging the restitution materials. Those materials retain the same comprehensive coverage. There is an introductory chapter that contains cases and materials which explore the fundamentals of all restitutionary remedies, both legal and equitable. The remainder of restitution is dispersed throughout the book to integrate that material with other remedial concepts and to illustrate the uses of the various remedies in a wide variety of factual contexts. Any teacher wishing to teach restitution as a separate unit can still do so by assigning the units titled Restitution in order.

Despite these changes we believe that we have sufficiently preserved the approach and content of the earlier Edition so that the book will seem quite familiar to those teachers now using it. As in prior editions, we have omitted strings of citations, footnotes and dissenting opinions not useful for teaching purposes. We have marked citation and textual deletions with ellipses. We have retained the numbering of footnotes in the original works, and have used asterisks to indicate our footnotes.

We are grateful to our respective law schools and administrations for their substantial encouragement and assistance. We would like to thank the talented students who worked with us on the manuscript, galleys and pageproofs. Finally, we express special gratitude to our families for their support and understanding during the period that we were preparing this edition of the casebook.

ROBERT N. LEAVELL
JEAN C. LOVE
GRANT S. NELSON
CANDACE S. KOVACIC–FLEISCHER

June, 1994

*

Preface to Fifth Edition

Preface to Fourth Edition

The change in the title of the Fourth Edition (from "Equitable Remedies and Restitution" to "Equitable Remedies, Restitution and Damages") reflects the expanded scope of the new edition. Extensive coverage is now given to damages, in addition to the remedies that were previously covered—injunctions, specific performance, declaratory judgments, rescission, reformation and the restitutionary remedies. As a result, the casebook is now suitable for courses in Remedies, Equitable Remedies, Equity, Injunctions, Damages, or Restitution. The new edition is designed for a 3 or 4 hour course in Remedies, but the materials can be used selectively for shorter courses.

The organization of the Fourth Edition is primarily by types of equitable remedies, starting with an expanded chapter on injunctive relief. We believe that this is the preferable organization for a course that focuses on remedies (as opposed to substantive bases for imposing liability). Within each chapter, we frequently cluster the cases by subject matter. At the same time, we often sequence the cases so that the student focuses first on the plaintiff's case for equitable relief, then on the defenses to the remedy, and finally on the nature of the equitable decree. As part of the discussion of the plaintiff's case for equitable relief, we consider the plaintiff's legal remedies (emphasizing damages) because traditionally a plaintiff may obtain equitable relief only upon proof that the legal remedy is inadequate. Tort damages are covered in the chapter on injunctions; breach of contract damages are discussed in the chapter on specific performance; and fraud damages are examined in the chapter on rescission.

The Fourth Edition also develops a theoretical perspective by which remedies may be evaluated. It presents contrasting perspectives on the economic efficiency of damages and equitable remedies. These materials offer an opportunity to discuss important social policy issues raised by the law of remedies.

This edition has been thoroughly updated and it examines such contemporary social issues as the use of contempt to enforce child support decrees, the measure of restitutionary recovery in *Marvin*-type cases, the use of injunctive and legal relief to enforce surrogate mother contracts, and the development of common law remedies for retaliatory discharge and sexual harassment. In addition, it contains completely revised sections on the private enforcement of public nuisance law and the remedial discretion exercised by federal courts in environmental litigation. Finally, remedies for violations of constitutional and civil rights receive expanded coverage in this edition, although the coverage is pervasive throughout the book, rather than concentrated in one chapter (as in the prior edition).

While the casebook has been revised and updated, users of the earlier edition should feel comfortable with the Fourth Edition because it evolved quite naturally from the Third Edition. Neither the fundamental style nor organization of the book has been changed. The book is longer, but that is due primarily to our decision to publish the text in a single-column format. We expect that readers of the Fourth Edition will welcome this modification.

As in prior editions, we have omitted strings of citations, footnotes and dissenting opinions not useful for teaching purposes. We have marked textual deletions with ellipses. Footnotes are ours unless otherwise indicated.

We are grateful to our respective law schools and administrations for their substantial encouragement and assistance. We would like to thank the talented students who worked with us on the manuscript, galleys and page-proofs. Finally, we express special gratitude to our families for their support and understanding during the period that we were preparing this edition of the casebook.

ROBERT N. LEAVELL
JEAN C. LOVE
GRANT S. NELSON

June, 1986

Preface to Third Edition

At the time of the publication of the last Edition the equity and restitution areas were drawing special attention because of developments in the public law area, especially where civil rights are involved. This interest has increased as the courts continue to experiment with such remedies as the injunction, receivers and masters. Recent expressions of a need to return to a focus upon basics in law teaching and in lawyer preparation have added to a "renaissance" in the remedies area. Such statements have come from, among others, Chief Justice Warren Burger; the American Bar Association in its recently published report, "Lawyer Competence: The Role of Law Schools"; the supreme courts of several states, and; the federal courts of appeal in their revisions of standards for both admission and the privilege of continuing in the federal court practice.

One result of these developments is certain to be curriculum adjustment in many law schools, with increased emphasis upon the study of courses such as "Remedies." Especially attractive will be those courses which consider current remedies developments in the public law area and which offer a general examination of traditional legal and equitable remedies in a variety of contexts.

This Edition is organized with those objectives in mind. It retains the coverage of basic remedies materials to be found in the earlier Edition, together with greatly expanded material on damages. The Third Edition contains a substantial amount of new material, including over 100 new cases and dozens of textual notes. Also, a significant new chapter has been added, entitled "Traditional Relief in a Modern Context: Selected Civil Rights Remedies."

Despite these additions we feel we have sufficiently preserved the approach and content of the earlier Edition so that the book will seem quite familiar to those teachers using it now. For example, substantial attention continues to be given to the history of equity, specific performance, injunctions, practicability concerns, reformation, rescission, restitution, enforcement of decrees and law-equity merger problems. Moreover, this expansion in coverage has been accomplished without adding to the length of the book.

We are grateful to our respective law schools and administrations for their substantial encouragement and assistance. We also wish to thank those students who assisted us in the preparation of this Edition.

ROBERT N. LEAVELL
JEAN C. LOVE
GRANT S. NELSON

April, 1980

*

Preface to Second Edition

In the fifteen years since the First Edition the trend to which Professor Van Hecke alluded in his Preface has continued unabated. As a course, Equity finds it difficult to compete at all. Courses in Remedies and Restitution fair somewhat better; however, they are still rather grudgingly given the hours in the single quarter or semester allotted to them.

How this has come about is not easy to understand. Practitioners—and bar examiners—do not appear to have followed the academicians' tendency, and continue to indicate their feeling about the importance of this material in the education of a lawyer. It is due in part to the increasing complexity of several areas of public law, and the need to give more time and classroom hours to them. Recently, courses in environmental law, consumer protection, special problems of the poor, civil rights, and the like, have added to the brisk competition for classroom hours. This latter development, however, should stimulate a renewed interest in the basic course in equitable remedies and restitution.

Indeed, it is when new social demands make special demands upon the growth capacity of the law that the value of an understanding of equity and remedies is most apparent. Teachers with interests in such fields as those just mentioned will recognize the need for a grounding in equitable remedies and related legal remedies such as quasi-contract, and an appreciation of the origin and the creative spirit which infuses them.

Although we generally have followed Professor Van Hecke's organization, we also have found it necessary to add a substantial amount of new material to reflect recent developments. New material is especially evident in Chapter 6, reflecting the increasing use of the injunctive remedy in new and varied contexts. In a few areas we have made important changes in coverage and arrangement. Recent developments with respect to the right to trial by jury in situations involving mixed questions of law and equity require more attention than could be given to them if developed in relation to part of the content of one or more chapters. For this reason we have devoted a short chapter to this and related problems. Secondly, in the interests of keeping the book lean and readily adaptable to use in those courses where the teacher feels the hours allocated to the course are relatively small, we have reduced to very brief note status the material which deals with "Lack of Power and Mistaken Exercise of Power." However, we have sought to emphasize throughout the book the modifications which are taking place in the election of remedies situations, and the general impact upon this area of the merger of law and equity and the modern procedural systems. Finally, we have reduced substantially materials on Bills of Peace and Quieting Title in order to provide for consideration of Receiverships, Masters, Monitors and Sequestration.

We have added to the title the term "Restitution", to make it more descriptive of the book as conceived by Professor Van Hecke. The extensive treatment given by him to quasi-contract, placed alongside the restitutionary material from equity, is continued in the current edition.

The cases and materials have been closely edited. Save in special situations, strings of citations, footnotes and dissenting opinions not useful for teaching purposes have been omitted. Footnotes are ours unless otherwise specified.

We express our appreciation for the permission granted by the publishers and authors of the selections from books and articles reproduced herein. We are also grateful for the assistance and encouragement of our law school administrations and for the valuable contributions of student research.

Finally, to our wives and families we express special gratitude for their patience and understanding during the period we worked on the Second Edition.

ROBERT N. LEAVELL
GRANT S. NELSON

May, 1973

Preface to First Edition

There have been two significant developments in Equity since the publication in 1948 of the Fourth Edition of Cook's Cases and Materials. (1) The status of the course in Equity in the law schools has been increasingly modified to conform to other changes in the curriculum. The modifications have taken these forms: dropping the separate course and distributing parts of the subject matter to other courses, including new courses in Equitable Remedies; retaining the separate course and considerably reducing the number of class-room hours available. (2) Meanwhile, uninhibited by these considerations, the courts and legislatures have continued to improve the equitable and related statutory remedies, so that the flexibility, discretionary concern for the individual situation and capacity for growth of these remedies might enable them to be used more effectively in times of changing conditions and needs. This casebook on Equitable Remedies is an effort to meet these developments.

It is substantially a new book, both in content and arrangement. The areas of substantive equity taught elsewhere in today's curriculum have been largely omitted. The cases and materials here presented, most of them the products of the last fifteen years, hew closely to the equitable and statutory remedies and to their operation, especially in courts where law and equity have been at least administratively merged.

The declaratory judgment cases are distributed for immediate contrast with the handling of comparable problems by the other remedies; the section on Declaratory Judgments is therefore largely a point of reference for the basic literature and statutes. Because the chapter on Jurisdiction seems to become more meaningful after the class has seen the various remedies in operation, it is placed last. However, those who prefer to take Jurisdiction first and to make other changes in the arrangement and order of chapters and sections will incur no appreciable loss.

The cases and materials have been closely edited. Save in special situations, strings of citations, footnotes and dissenting opinions not useful for teaching purposes have been omitted.

I want to thank the teachers of Equity in some forty schools who helpfully responded to my requests for advice and suggestions as to inclusion and exclusion, order and arrangement. I also want record my indebtedness to Mr. W. E. Bondurant, Jr., of the Roswell, New Mexico, Bar, to Mr. John P. Frank, of the Phoenix, Arizona, Bar, to Chief Judge Charles E. Clark, of the U.S. Court of Appeals for the Second Circuit, to Professor J. Francis Paschal, of Duke University, and to the late Professor Edgar N. Durfee, of the University of Michigan, for guidance and counsel.

And, I want to dedicate this book to Mrs. Van Hecke for her encouraging, companionable assistance.

M. T. VAN HECKE

Chapel Hill, North Carolina
December, 1958

Using WESTLAW
to help you understand *Remedies*

Introduction: As a law student, you want to master your courses as completely as possible. Obtaining that mastery is the key to higher levels of performance in law school and better preparedness for the bar exam. Using **WESTLAW** with **West books** is an excellent way to acquire the knowledge and information necessary to understand the legal concepts that you will encounter during law school.

The following examples will show you how to use WESTLAW to quickly retrieve relevant information that will increase your understanding of the many topic areas in Leavell, Love, Nelson and Kovacic-Fleischer's **Equitable Remedies, Restitution and Damages**. All you need is your WESTLAW password and WESTMATE software (if you are going to use WESTLAW from your home computer). To begin, simply type your password, enter a research session identifier and continue with one of the sections below.

I. HOW TO RETRIEVE THE FULL TEXT OF A PRINCIPAL CASE OR NOTE CASE

The principal and note cases in this text are generally not included in full. Reading the entire case, however, may help you understand the court's reasoning and holding, and give you a better grasp of the theories involved. The authors may also provide citations to cases for additional reading to better highlight a point of law. For example, at the top of page 980, the authors cite several cases that show examples of unique personal property entitling a party to specific performance. To see the third case in that list, *Ruddock v. First National Bank*, 559 N.E.2nd 483, 1990, type

find 559 us 483 (*then press* **ENTER**)

*Use the format above to retrieve cases on WESTLAW, e.g., from anywhere in WESTLAW type the word **find** (or **fi**) followed by the **volume number, reporter abbreviation,** and **page number** of the case you wish to view.*

II. HOW TO RETRIEVE LAW REVIEW AND LAW JOURNAL ARTICLES

Often a cited law review or journal article will provide valuable insight into and analysis of a particular issue or topic. Your professor may even suggest or require that you read some of these articles. For example, on page 833, footnote 6, the authors cite an article that gives a general discussion of contract damages, Cooter and Eisenberg, *Damages for Breach of*

Contract, 73 Calif.L.Rev. 1432 (1985). To view this article, first go to the WESTLAW FIND PUBLICATIONS INDEX (to see if the publication is on WESTLAW and to obtain the appropriate citation format) by typing

find pubs (*then press* **ENTER**)

To view publication abbreviations for law reviews and law journals, locate LAW REVIEWS *(it is the last entry)* and type its corresponding page number (and press **ENTER**). To view publications that begin with the letter **C** (for **C**alifornia Law Review) locate the letter **C** and type its corresponding page number (and press **ENTER**). Page ahead (by using the **PAGE DOWN** key or typing **p** then pressing **ENTER**) until you locate **C**alifornia Law Review and its WESTLAW citation format. Combine the abbreviation with the appropriate volume and page, then type

find 73 cal l rev 1432 (*then press* **ENTER**)

Use the format above to retrieve law review and law journal articles on WESTLAW, e.g., from anywhere in WESTLAW type the word find (or fi) followed by the volume number, appropriate law journal or law review abbreviation, and page number of the article you wish to view.

III. HOW TO USE WEST'S TOPIC AND KEY NUMBER SYSTEM TO OBTAIN MORE INFORMATION ABOUT A TOPIC

Cases reported in West Publications are organized in its *topic* and *key number system*. The cases you read on WESTLAW contain paragraphs of information called *headnotes*. The headnotes contain concise statements of law that are designated by *topic* and *key number*. The system is designed to allow you to efficiently retrieve other cases that contain the same topic and key number, meaning that the cases will have similar "on-point" law.

Page forward in any case you are viewing until you find a topic and key number discussing a point of law relevant to your research. Then enter that topic and key number in a case law database to retrieve other cases discussing the same point of law, for example, **Specific Performance** (topic number 358) and **Effect of Delay or Default of Plaintiff** (key number 98).

This example will use the Vermont cases database. You can also determine how the courts in your state (or any other state or federal jurisdiction) have decided this and other issues by using your state case law database, e.g., **tx-cs** (Texas), **mn-cs** (Minnesota), **fl-cs** (Florida), etc. Access the Vermont cases database by typing

db vt-cs (*then press* **ENTER**)*

* You may type **db vt-cs** from anywhere in your WESTLAW research session except from a **find** result. Typing **gb** (go back) then pressing

ENTER will return you from a found document to your previous research location. If you have used FIND more than once in succession, it will be necessary for you to type **gb** more than once.

At the Vermont cases database Enter Query Screen type

358k98 (*then press* **ENTER)**

This will retrieve all cases that contain a headnote classified under West topic **358 (Specific Performance)** under key number **98 (Effect of Delay or Default of Plaintiff).** Pressing **ENTER** will take you to the first page of each retrieved case and then to the topic and key number page(s).

Follow up: Many, but not all of the law review and journal articles referenced in this book are contained in a WESTLAW database. If you have any questions about WESTLAW or the preceding sections, call West Customer Service at 1-800-WESTLAW (1-800-937-8529), or speak to your WESTLAW Academic or student representative.

Summary of Contents

Table of Contents

*

Table of Cases

The principal cases are in bold type. Cases cited or discussed in the text are roman type. References are to pages. Cases cited in principal cases and within other quoted materials are not included.

CASES AND MATERIALS ON

EQUITABLE REMEDIES, RESTITUTION AND DAMAGES

Fifth Edition

*

Chapter 1

INTRODUCTION TO REMEDIES

SECTION 1. SPECIFIC, SUBSTITUTIONARY AND DECLARATORY REMEDIES

Why study remedies? The remedies in litigation are the bottom line for a plaintiff, who might be your client. What the client wants and what that client may be entitled to may be different. As you will see, the remedial rules also reflect our society's values. When will the court order someone to do something and when will the court instead substitute money for the performance? Sometimes the answer is a practical one—it would be impossible to order performance. But in other cases there are values reflected in the decision.

The law of remedies is subdivided into a number of components. One subdivision is the difference between specific, substitutionary and declaratory relief. Specific relief remedies the wrong specifically, for example by returning the thing that was taken or ordering the performance that was expected. Substitutionary relief substitutes money for the specific relief. Declaratory relief tells people what their rights are, but orders no relief.

Another subdivision is equitable and legal relief. Equitable relief is often specific, but can be substitutionary, as in the case of back pay in discrimination cases. Legal relief is usually substitutionary, but can be specific as in the case of legal replevin and ejectment. Equitable relief is recognized by the fact that it is a court order to the defendant to do or not do something. Since it is a court order, if the defendant does not comply, the defendant can be held in contempt. There is normally no jury trial in a proceeding for equitable relief. Legal relief is recognized by the fact that ordinarily it is a judgment order stating that plaintiff is entitled to something. If defendant does not provide that something, the defendant has not violated a court order and is not in contempt. A sheriff will attempt to satisfy the legal judgment by seizing assets, if possible. A jury trial typically is available in an action for legal relief.

SECTION 2. REMEDIES FOR TORTIOUS WRONGS, BREACH OF CONTRACT, UNJUST ENRICHMENT

Although every cause of action will have remedies, this book will focus on remedies for tortious conduct, breach of contract and unjust enrichment. These are basic branches of common law and the remedies for each illustrate a number of basic remedial principles that can be applied to other causes of action as well.

As will be explored, there are basic differences between tort and contract and unjust enrichment. Those differences entail different remedial rules. The law of torts determines the type of conduct society wants to deter. The law of contracts determines those types of promises upon which society can rely. The law of unjust enrichment determines when someone's gain is unjust and restitution is appropriate. The remedial rules in tort want to make the plaintiff whole, as if there had not been a tort. At times those rules will also punish. In contract the remedial rules want to compensate people for breaches of contract without deterring commerce. In unjust enrichment the remedial rules focus on defining a gain and determining whether it should be disgorged.

SECTION 3. HISTORICAL INTRODUCTION TO LAW AND EQUITY

The fact that we continue today to recognize certain substantive and remedial concepts as "equitable" and others "legal" is largely the product of historical accident rather than design. As a result, an analytical insight into the historical development and evolution of equity, as a substantive and procedural companion to the common law, is essential to a proper understanding of the role of equity in our contemporary legal system.

Development of Equity from the Common Law

For our purposes the historical development of equity necessary for an understanding of our Anglo–American legal system begins in England about the year 1200. Until that time, justice for most people was provided by the Saxon courts of the hundred and the shire, and later, by the Norman manorial and other local courts. These courts were administered by people who were usually uneducated and unsophisticated in the law. Consequently, justice was often crude and unwritten. Because it tended to follow local custom, it varied substantially from community to community. *See* W. Walsh, Equity 2 (1930). While this system was extremely rudimentary, it seems to have met society's needs at the time. On the other hand, as one scholar has noted, "another and superior kind of justice was administered where the king * * * or lords were involved, by the king and witan before the [Norman] conquest, by the king and his court thereafter. This, however, was a regular system of law administered for the very great, distinct from the king's justice in special cases affording relief not available in the regular courts. Nevertheless, this regular administration of law by the *Curia Regis* was royal law, based on the same ultimate and superior power in the king to do justice as was the special relief in exceptional cases through the king's prerogative of grace, which later came to be called equity." *Id.* at 2.

It was during the twelfth century that Henry II created a national system of judges and courts to administer legal matters. Gradually the local customary courts were eliminated and the *Curia Regis* was expanded. Access to the king's court was obtained through the issuance of writs by the king's secretary, the chancellor. Writs were issued freely to meet new factual situations whenever justice would be served. In the early development of the king's court, there was no distinction between law and equity. As one scholar pointed out, law and equity "originated in one and the same procedure and existed for a long time, not only side by side, but quite undifferentiated from each other. * * * There was no equity as a separate body of law; for the king's justices felt themselves able to dispense such equity as justice required." Barbour, Some Aspects of Fifteenth Century Chancery, 31 Harv.L.Rev. 834 (1918).

The newly established system flourished. The justices of the courts granted relief freely, whether of a legal or equitable type, as part of the common law. For example, a thirteenth century common law court could be found enforcing specific performance of lease covenants, or enjoining waste by life tenants. *See* W. Walsh, Equity 5–7 (1930). There was little appeal to the king for relief under his prerogative grace, since the courts provided relief for all types of cases.

Gradually, the king's courts asserted ascendency over the local courts. The king's judges rode on circuit throughout the country. Several of the more important writs had the effect of removing from the local courts much of their most important jurisdiction and they became increasingly relegated to dealing with controversies of a relatively trivial nature.

Development of Equity as an Independent Court

WALTER WHEELER COOK, EQUITY, in the Encyclopedia of the Social Sciences, Vol. 5, pp. 584–586 (1931): * "Gradually, however, a hardening process set in which limited the common law to a set of restricted forms of action covering fairly well defined types of cases. This was in large part due to the Provisions of Oxford of 1258, which forbade the chancellor to frame new writs without the consent of the king and Council. Prior to that statute great flexibility in the formation of new writs to meet new situations had existed. The limitation thus put on the powers of the chancellor was to some extent relieved by the 24th chapter of the Statute of Westminister II, which allowed the formation in the Chancery of new writs to meet cases more or less similar to those already provided for; but the hardening process had gone too far and the kinds of relief obtainable had been narrowed too greatly for the common law to meet adequately the needs of a developing society. In most cases, for

* From Equity, by Walter Wheeler Cook. Reprinted with permission of Macmillan Publishing Company from the ENCYCLOPEDIA OF THE SOCIAL SCIENCES, Edwin R.A. Selyman Editor in Chief. Volume 5, pages 584–586. Copyright 1931 and renewed 1959 by the Macmillan Publishing Co.

example, the relief given consisted of damages rather than specific relief. Naturally appeal was once more made to the royal prerogative and duty of administering justice. In the meantime the chancellor had become the chief law member of the Council as well as the most powerful executive officer of state next to the king. These facts and the added fact that the chancellor was usually a great ecclesiastic, learned in the canon and the moral law, brought it about that the petitions to the king or to the Council for justice in cases in which the king's regular tribunals were unable to function effectively began to be referred to the chancellor. Ultimately this became the routine procedure, so that by the middle of the fourteenth century the Chancery had come to be recognized as a separate judicial tribunal or court.

"One striking difference between Chancery as a court and the courts of common law lay in the mode in which cases were begun and carried on, or perhaps better in the theory which was supposed to underlie the process. To initiate a case in a common law court it was necessary to secure from the Chancery office an original writ. This writ, which ran in the name of the king, defined the type of case which the court to which it was addressed was directed to hear and decide and was thus the legal authorization from the king to his court to hear that particular kind of case and no other between the parties specified. In addition, the judgment did not originally command the defendant to do anything but was simply that the plaintiff recover his damages. Failure to satisfy the judgment was therefore not contempt of court. In the case of Chancery, on the other hand, although it came to be regarded as a court, the chancellor continued to speak directly in the name of the king and as the king's representative. On the presentation of the petition, or bill, as it came to be called, a writ was issued in the name of the king, under which the party complained against was directed to appear before the Court of Chancery to answer the complaint and abide by the order that might be made. This order also ran directly in the name of the king; that is, in legal theory it was the direct command of the king to his subject to do or to refrain from doing certain things. It followed that if the defendant disobeyed the order he was in contempt not of the chancellor but of the king and was dealt with accordingly. The statement that 'equity acts *in personam*' is based upon this form of procedure.

"It is probably true that during much of the fourteenth century appeals for justice to the king through the chancellor were in many cases rendered necessary by the inability of the king's ordinary courts of common law to compel obedience from the more wealthy and powerful of the king's subjects in cases in which the complainant was relatively poor. Many of the petitions to the chancellor during this period show this as the chief ground for appealing to the extraordinary powers of the chancellor as the direct representative of the king. Later the emphasis shifted to the inadequacy of the common law remedies to meet the demands of justice in the particular case. Two features demand notice: first, the normal remedy at common law was damages rather than specific relief, although there were of course exceptions. If, for example, someone were wrongfully threatening to cut down valuable shade trees on another's land, the latter aside from any right to use physical force himself to prevent the trespass had at common law no means of preventing the cutting of the trees; all the common law court would do for him was to give him money damages after the trees had been destroyed. Naturally appeal was made to the chancellor for relief. Second, as the common law developed, the mode of trying cases involving disputed questions of fact came to be by jury. Since the jurors were as a rule uneducated men, it became obvious that certain types of issues of fact were not likely to be handled effectively by a jury. This was, for example, thought to be true in cases in which there was a controversy involving more than two sides or one in which the taking of a complicated account was necessary. Appeals to the chancellor were therefore also made in this type of situation, as there was no jury in the Court of Chancery."

The gradual split in the common law court system was solidified in the 15th century with the participation of the chancellor in the creation and support of the doctrine of uses, the forerunner to modern trusts. *See* F. Maitland, Equity 7–22 (1916); W. Walsh, Equity 19 (1930). The doctrine of uses allowed the separation of the legal title to land from the equitable title, transferring the title of the land to a trustee for the "use" of the beneficiary, the *cestui que trust.* The use of the property, with its rents and privileges, would go to the *cestui,* the holder of the equitable title, while the feudal incidents of wardship, marriage, and military tenure would be avoided by the use of the trustees. Further, the use was utilized to avoid the common law prohibitions against gifts of land by will and *inter vivos* transfers except by livery of seisin, transfer of possession, or its equivalent. Prior to the time such uses could be enforced in Chancery, the *cestui* was often powerless against a dishonest trustee because the law courts refused to recognize the use. As one commentator noted, Chancery "gave relief because no remedy at all existed at law. * * * Chancery alone could act in these cases. The Chancellor's court was especially well qualified to act, not only because it was developing a system of law outside of the common law, * * * but also because its procedure *in personam* was exactly adapted to compel specific performance with the terms of the use on the part of the trustee." W. Walsh, Equity 20 (1930).

Inevitably, a period of serious conflict developed between the two court systems. With growing frequency, the courts of equity were encroaching on the traditional powers of the courts of the common law. Cases involving similar fact situations often were resolved in opposite fashions, depending upon whether the case had been brought in law or equity. Consider, for example, the following illustration of the conflict between the two court systems:

> "A typical situation in this struggle was presented by an action at law on a specialty (*e.g.,* bond under seal) which had been obtained from the defendant by 'fraud in the inducement,' such as misrepresentation concerning the value or quality of something sold by plaintiff to defendant on credit where the bond in a large penal sum was given to secure payment of the purchase price. If the defendant had indeed executed the bond, knowing it was a bond, then the kind of fraud by

which he was induced to execute it was not recognized in the law courts as a defense to an action on the bond. Equity, however, did recognize this kind of fraud and would entertain a suit by the debtor against the creditor (obligee on the bond) for a rescission of the bond. If the debtor succeeded in showing the fraud the chancellor would order the obligee to deliver the bond up for cancellation or to give a release of it under seal, on condition that the debtor restore to the creditor whatever benefit he had received in the course of the transaction. Equity would, in short, try to put the parties back into the position they occupied before the fraudulent transaction took place.

"If the debtor discovered the fraud and brought his bill in equity before the creditor got his judgment at law, then the chancellor would enjoin the creditor from pursuing his action at law pending determination of the issue of fraud. If the chancellor found fraud, he would make this temporary injunction a permanent one as part of his final decree. If he found no fraud, he would dissolve the temporary injunction and the creditor would be free to continue prosecuting his action at law. If a judgment at law had already been obtained, effective equitable relief would necessarily involve interference with a law court's judgment." F. James and G. Hazard, Civil Procedure 15–17 (2d ed. 1977).*

The conflict came to a head in the early 1600's. A dispute arose for which the chief spokesmen were Chief Justice Coke of the common law courts and the Lord Chancellor Ellesmere. The question was whether equity could prevent the enforcement of a judgment entered by a court of law by issuing an injunction restraining the party plaintiff in the action at law from enforcing his law judgment. The Chancellor had granted injunctive relief because the law defendant had an equitable defense to the action at law which the common law court refused to consider because it was inappropriate under the common law precedents. The common law judges insisted that the Statute of Praemunire, which prohibited any attack on the judgment of the King's Court, nullified any action by Chancery to interfere with enforcement of the judgments of the law courts. The question cut to the very existence of equity as a credible force in the English legal system. The dispute was referred by the King to an advisory body. On the recommendation of this body, and that of the attorney general, the King decided in favor of the Chancellor. Conceptually, it was said there was no conflict. Since equity was said to act in personam and not in rem, the injunction issued by the court of equity left the law judgment intact. Any enforcement of the law judgment would be valid and an execution sale thereon would result in a proper transfer of title. However, the executing judgment-holder would face the consequences of being held in contempt of court by the Chancellor. This was a practical, if not completely theoretical, victory for Chancery. Even though the legal judgment was technically unaffected by the injunction, the threat of contempt of court was quite likely to stop the legal proceedings. Since the resolution of the Coke–

Ellesmere dispute, the existence and effectiveness of equitable jurisdiction has never been seriously challenged by the common law.

Procedural Unification of Law and Equity

Chancery's victory probably represented its high water mark for at least two reasons. First, equity restricted its jurisdiction voluntarily after its victory by placing increased emphasis on the necessity of an inadequate legal remedy as a condition precedent to its relief. Second, legislation reforming the law courts' jurisdiction often made resort to equity unnecessary. For example, with the enactment of the Statute of Uses, common law recognition was given to uses and jurisdiction over them was placed in the common law courts. As a result, while equity retained jurisdiction over "active" trusts, it no longer was needed to execute inactive uses.

Beginning in the latter part of the eighteenth century, some momentum developed in both England and the United States to accomplish a procedural merger of law and equity. The principal reasons for this are not difficult to understand. The separate development of law and equity courts had resulted in two judicial systems, each with different substantive rules and each having a significantly different system of pleading and procedure. *See* W. Walsh, Equity 36 (1930). Consequently, a party who selected the wrong court was forced to begin again in the correct court, assuming that by his incorrect selection he had not lost his right to do so. Moreover, "equitable defenses could not be set up in law actions; the defendant could establish his defense or other equity only by suit in equity to restrain the plaintiff from prosecuting his action at law, equity taking jurisdiction over the controversy in order that it might be disposed of on equitable principles. All this involved delay, expense, duplication of actions, and the scandal of different results in the same case if brought in one court instead of in the other." *Id.* at 36.

In England, the Judicature Act of 1873 ultimately was the merger vehicle. Under the Act, the Court of Chancery, the Court of Probate, and the Divorce Court were fused together with the common law courts. As a result the English system now has "a High Court with a King's Bench Division, a Chancery Division and a Probate, Divorce and Admiralty Division, and any judge of any Division can adjudicate upon any question whether of equity or of law". H. Hanbury, Modern Equity 20–21 (6th ed. 1952). While procedural merger was thus accomplished, the degree to which there has been a substantive merger is still the subject of disagreement. Some, for example, have stated that any distinction between law and equity is out of date. Perhaps the more accurate view has been stated as follows: "The Judicature Act might be summed up in a few words by saying that its impact on the [procedural] law was immediate and decisive, for it put in the place of the old separate courts of law and equity a composite Supreme Court with jurisdiction in both fields; whereas in the field of substantive law it has had repercussions, the effect of which has been progressive though very gradual, the goal being that fusion of the systems of law and equity to which time brings us nearer, but from which we are still removed by a march of many days." *Id.* at 112.

In the United States, the merger process was both gradual and complex, although the procedural merger was largely achieved before that in England. The United States Constitution as adopted in 1789, together with early amendments, differentiated between law and equity in a variety of contexts. Article III, the Judicial Article, refers to "all cases, in law and equity"; the Eleventh Amendment to any "suit in law or equity"; and the Seventh Amendment to "suits at common law."

At the time the Constitution was adopted, equity jurisdiction was recognized in some of the original states. As of 1787, chancery courts existed "in New York, South Carolina, Maryland, Virginia, and, to an extent, in New Jersey; in Pennsylvania, Delaware and North Carolina, there were no such courts though the common law courts had certain equity powers; in Connecticut and Rhode Island, the Legislature exercised some powers of a Court of Chancery; in Massachusetts and New Hampshire, there were common law courts only having a very few limited powers; Georgia had only common law courts." Warren, New Light on the Federal Judiciary Act of 1789, 37 Harv.L.Rev. 49, 96 (1923). This early American antipathy to equity jurisdiction was due, in part, to the lack of jury trial in equity cases, to abuses by colonial governors while serving as chancellors, and to resentment over the discretionary powers and royalist associations of the English Court of Chancery. *See* A. Scott and S. Simpson, Cases and Materials on Civil Procedure 162–163 (1950).

At the federal level, "congress did not, as no doubt it might have done, create separate national courts of equity and law, but organized only one system of courts in which might be tried cases at law, and cases in equity, according as the same judge happened to be playing the role of common law judge, or of chancellor. But the declaration at law, and the bill in equity retained their distinct names and characteristics, and the case had to be one in law or in equity." McCormick, The Fusion of Law and Equity, 6 N.C.L.Rev. 283, 284 (1928). Moreover, the "law-equity" differentiation in the Constitution resulted in "some expressions in opinions of the courts and in the writings of commentators which might lend color to the view that the Constitution has indelibly impressed the separation of law and equity upon national judicial procedure." *Id.* at 286.

Because of the diversity in the status of equity in the several states, Congress in 1792 provided in effect that the procedure in equity cases in the federal courts should conform to that of the English Court of Chancery, as modified by rules of the United States Supreme Court. This was in sharp contrast to the provision that, in common-law cases, the procedure in the federal courts was to conform to that of the state in which the federal court was sitting. The latter was justified by the relative uniformity of common-law procedure in the state courts. Accordingly, the Supreme Court in 1822 prescribed rules to govern equity procedure in the federal courts. These were revised in 1842 and again in 1912. With respect to the substantive law of equity, the Court ruled in 1851 * that equity cases were to be governed by the doctrine of Swift v. Tyson,** which provided that

* Russell v. Southard, 53 U.S. (12 How.) 139, 13 L.Ed. 927 (1851).

** 41 U.S. (16 Pet.) 1, 10 L.Ed. 865 (1842).

federal courts were not required to apply state common law principles in deciding diversity cases. From that time until 1938,*** the federal courts enunciated their own views of principles of equity jurisprudence, without restriction by the decisions of state courts. Thus, "federal equity" attempted uniformity throughout the United States in its substantive as well as its procedural aspects.

The first major state effort at reform appeared in New York in 1848 with the Field Code, which classified law and equity as one procedural category of civil suits. The substantive rights available under equity were retained; the reform was aimed at improving the procedures and mechanics of the legal process. Within twenty-five years, at least two dozen states enacted statutes or rules similar to the Field Code. *See* C. Clark, Code Pleading 21–31 (2d ed. 1947). In 1938, with the adoption of the Federal Rules of Civil Procedure, the procedural merger of law and equity was largely complete. Rule 2 of the Federal Rules of Civil Procedure states: "There shall be one form of action to be known as 'civil action.'" Today, 46 of the 50 states and the District of Columbia have accomplished such a procedural merger, either through the Field Code approach or through adoption of the Federal Rules.

The four states which have not joined law and equity are Arkansas, Delaware, Mississippi, and Tennessee. For example, the Arkansas statutes provide:

> "27–204—The proceedings in a civil action may be two kinds:
>
> First. At Law.
>
> Second. In Equity.
>
> "27–205—The plaintiff may prosecute his action by equitable proceedings in all cases where courts of chancery, before the adoption of this Code, had jurisdiction, and must so proceed where such jurisdiction was exclusive."

Ark.Stat. §§ 27–204–205. *See also* Del.Code tit. 10 § 341 *et seq.* (1974); Miss. Const. Art. 6, § 159 (1972); Tenn.Code Ann. § 16–11–101 *et seq.* (1980).*

In New Jersey a procedural dichotomy between law and equity persists notwithstanding merger. Even though the Superior Court has both equitable and legal jurisdiction, it continues to be divided into "Law" and "Chancery" divisions. Consequently, "actions in which the plaintiff's primary right or the principal relief sought is equitable * * * shall be brought in the Chancery Division." N.J.Civ.Prac.Rule 4:3–1(a)(1) (1985).

*** Erie R.R. Co. v. Tompkins, 304 U.S. 64, 58 S.Ct. 817, 82 L.Ed. 1188 (1938). See Ruhlin v. New York Life Ins. Co., 304 U.S. 202, 58 S.Ct. 860, 82 L.Ed. 1290 (1938) (*Erie* principle extended to equity cases).

* Although Tennessee adopted procedural rules in 1970 substantially the same as the Federal Rules, separate courts of law and equity remain. *See* Paine, Recent Developments in Tennessee Procedure: The New Tennessee Rules of Civil Procedure, 37 Tenn. L.Rev. 501 (1970). *See also* LeClercq, The Tennessee Court System, 8 Memphis St. L.Rev. 185, 281 (1978).

Law and Equity After Procedural Merger

As a result of the merger process, certain procedures associated with equity have lost much of their uniquely equitable identification. Interpleader is a good example of this phenomenon. Ironically, like many of the early equitable doctrines, interpleader has its roots in the common law. In the 1300's, interpleader was in common usage in the conflicts arising at law under writs of wardship and actions of detinue. The death of a man frequently prompted litigation as to the wardship of any surviving infant children and their inherited properties. The person with custody of the children would be the focus of several claims to the wardship by relatives of the deceased, in response to which the custodian would deliver the children to the court for a determination of the rightful guardian. In actions of detinue, goods or money were often delivered to third party stakeholders upon the completion of a contracted duty. If the stakeholder could not determine whether the duty had been properly discharged, the stakes could be delivered up to the court for proper adjudication. Rogers, Historical Origins of Interpleader, 51 Yale L.J. 924 (1942).

The common law usage of interpleader died with the disuse of wardship and detinue between 1500 and 1800. Chancery stepped in to rescue the discarded common law doctrine. Beginning about 1700, courts of equity adopted the form and name of the common law interpleader procedure. Since equity could effectively enjoin the claiming parties from pursuing their several actions at law, they were forced to interplead among themselves and resolve the issue as to which of the claiming parties had the valid claim to the stakes in question. The procedure became firmly ingrained in equity, the principles of which were set out in the classic statement of the four requirements by Pomeroy in 1883:

> "1. The same thing, debt or duty must be claimed by both or all the parties against whom the relief is demanded; 2. All their adverse titles or claims must be dependent, or be derived from a common source; 3. The person asking the relief must not have or claim any interest in the subject-matter; 4. He must have incurred no independent liability to either of the claimants; that is, he must stand perfectly indifferent between them in the position merely of a stakeholder."

4 J. Pomeroy's Equity Jurisprudence § 1322, at 906 (5th ed. 1941).

Interpleader was codified by the 1938 Federal Rules of Civil Procedure and the 1958 Federal Interpleader Act. These rules and statutes relaxed the traditional equitable requirements and returned interpleader to the courts of law for wide usage in those cases which expose a defendant to multiple claims for the same debt or property. *See* C. Wright, Law of Federal Courts 493–496 (4th ed. 1983).

The procedure for quieting title has evolved by a process somewhat similar to that with respect to interpleader. Originally, the suit to quiet title was brought in equity to preclude a person from filing numerous ejectment actions at law. At that time, the ejectment action did not have conclusive effect, thus allowing for repeated actions by the same party.

Once ejectment actions were afforded res judicata effect, the need for the remedy was extinguished. The term has remained, however, and today it describes at least two forms of suit to vindicate a plaintiff's title claims. One is the bill in equity to remove clouds on title * and the other is the statutory quiet title suit, or suit to determine adverse claims, common in many jurisdictions.** In this instance, however, the remedy in both of these situations seems to have retained some of its original equitable flavor.

Substantive doctrines developed in equity, such as subrogation, the mortgagor's equity of redemption, and promissory estoppel, retain their equitable identification. Certain remedies, such as specific performance, injunctions, mortgage foreclosure by judicial suit and constructive trust, continue to be categorized as "equitable." *** And vestiges of the separate systems of law and equity survive in enforcement procedures. *See* D. Dobbs, Handbook on the Law of Remedies 67 (1973). Specific performance decrees and injunctions, for example, are characteristically in personam orders embodied in a decree signed by the judge who hands it down. The enforcement of such an order is often closely monitored and supervised by the judge who issued it. The contempt power will be used to fine or jail a recalcitrant defendant. By way of contrast, a judge's role in enforcing legal judgments for damages is substantially more limited. Most money judgments are not personal orders to pay and thus not enforceable by the contempt power. Rather, the usual practice is simply to record in the record of the clerk that judgment is entered for the plaintiff for a specified sum. It then remains for the counsel of the judgment creditor to utilize execution to enforce it. Levying execution typically entails finding the assets of the defendant, perfecting a judgment lien thereon, having the sheriff sell them, and applying the proceeds of the sale to satisfy the judgment.

The distinction between the legal or equitable nature of both the substantive law and the remedies involved in a case continues to be of vital importance in determining the right of the parties to a trial by jury. The Seventh Amendment of the Constitution and similar state provisions provide for the right to a jury in actions at law, but not in equity. Whether an action which involves only a single claim is characterized as equitable or legal is ordinarily of critical importance in determining whether a jury trial

* The bill in equity to remove a cloud on title has many limitations and restrictions. Some courts, for example, do not provide relief where the instrument challenged as a cloud on title was void on its face. Some cases make legal title in the plaintiff, as opposed to equitable title, a prerequisite to bringing the suit. Relief has been denied where the cloud on title was based on an oral claim, or where the construction of the instrument was involved rather than its cancellation. The suit is usually unavailable to a plaintiff who is not in possession and has an adequate remedy at law.

** The statutory quiet title actions were created to overcome the limitations on the bill in equity. For an analysis of the various quiet title mechanisms, *see* H. McClintock, Equity § 199 (2d ed. 1948).

*** Such remedies are usually available only when there is no adequate legal remedy. This preference for the legal remedy, of course, can sometimes be explained by the modern judicial inclination to substitute money judgments for the uncertainty and practical problems of enforcing specific in personam relief. More often, however, it represents the historical remains of English Chancery's condition precedent to equitable jurisdiction.

is required. Significant and complex jury trial problems recur when both legal and equitable claims are involved in the same litigation.

Equitable doctrines also have continuing vitality insofar as they inspire judges to consider themselves bound by a higher obligation. Judges often refer to themselves as sitting "as chancellors" and "wearing the hat of the chancellor," especially when dealing with such traditionally equitable defenses and remedies as unclean hands or specific performance. They also continue to express a greater willingness to experiment with innovative remedies when exercising "equitable jurisdiction."

This heritage is in some measure the result of the conduct on the bench of the great chancellors who trained for the church before becoming judges. These men had been students of the Canon Law and were aware of the influence of Roman law and equity upon the growth of the civil law system that prevailed in most of Europe. As judges, they were inclined to deal with the cases before them as the equities required, rather than being bound by stare decisis. Modern judges awarding equitable relief, like the early chancellors, are less constricted in their application of precedents than are their counterparts in law cases.

Note

There are a number of remedies, both legal and equitable, which we mention only incidentally, or not at all. Legal remedies which may play a role in aid of both jurisdiction and satisfaction, such as attachment and garnishment, are left to procedure and other courses. Similarly, we do not discuss the "creditors bill" in equity, which is used to marshal assets and impose equitable liens when garnishment is not adequate.

We do not cover the great "prerogative writs" developed by the law courts. These are "quo warranto," to call into question the charter or grant of privilege under which one purports to act; "mandamus," to compel a public official to discharge the duties of office; "prohibition," to restrain an official from acts not legally appropriate; "certiorari," to remove a matter from a lower court to a higher; and "habeas corpus," which is not used extensively outside the criminal area. These writs often afford the only adequate remedy for controlling improper conduct of public officials. *See* C. Wright, A. Miller & E. Cooper, Federal Practice and Procedure §§ 3932, 1021, 3368 and 3507 (1978). They should be evaluated along with the injunction as a remedy to control such conduct.

The writ of sequestration developed as a remedy which sought to coerce the defendant to obey an outstanding equity decree. When a defendant refused to carry out such an in personam order, the court on the request of the plaintiff appointed sequestrators to take possession of the defendant's chattels and real estate and to obtain the rents and profits. Later development of the remedy permitted sequestrators to sell the chattels to satisfy decrees for the payment of money. There is relatively little coercive use of sequestration today and it is seldom utilized to satisfy equitable decrees because statutes uniformly make execution available as a remedy to enforce equitable decrees for money. Nevertheless, sequestration remains a part of the heritage of remedies to which a court of equity may resort in proper circumstances, and, in some states, also is expressly provided for by statute. *See, e.g.,* V.A.M.S. § 511.340 (1978). *See also* Mo.Rule Civ.Pro. 74.21 (1985). Moreover, Rule 70 of the Federal Rules of

Civil Procedure specifically provides that "if a judgment directs a party to execute a conveyance of land or to deliver deeds or other documents or to perform any other specific act and the party fails to comply within the time specified," the clerk is authorized to issue a writ of sequestration against the property of the disobedient party to coerce obedience to the judgment. *See* C. Wright & A. Miller, Federal Practice and Procedure §§ 3021–3022 (1973). *See generally* H. McClintock, Equity § 18 (2d ed. 1948); W. DeFuniak, Handbook of Modern Equity § 12 (1956).

Another equitable writ of interest is "ne exeat," which issues, *inter alia,* to prevent the removal of a person or property from the court's jurisdiction. It orders an officer to bring the defendant before the Chancellor, where the defendant will be compelled to post bond to assure his or her later appearance. *See, e.g.,* 37 Ga.Code §§ 1401–1406. Because of its extraordinary nature, usually it is available only in special situations where, for example, a strong *prima facie* case of fraud and disposition to leave to avoid process are shown.

Other remedies of lesser significance today are a bill quia timet (to obtain cancellation of an instrument), a bill to preserve evidence, and a writ of assistance (to put the plaintiff in possession after a decree recognizing such a right). It is important to have in mind that any court of general jurisdiction has the power to permit the use of these writs and remedies as part of its inherent equity jurisdiction.

Chapter 2

BASIC PRINCIPLES OF SPECIFIC EQUITABLE REMEDIES

SECTION 1. TYPES OF INJUNCTIONS AND PROCEDURES FOR OBTAINING INJUNCTIVE RELIEF

A. OVERVIEW

D. DOBBS, THE LAW OF REMEDIES

162–164 (2d ed. 1993).*

"Injunction as a Coercive Order

"An injunction is a remedy in the form of an *in personam* order, usually issued by a trial court of general jurisdiction. It directs the defendant to act, or to refrain from acting in a specified way, and it is enforceable by the contempt power. The injunction must be obeyed until it is stayed, dissolved, or reversed, even if it is erroneously issued.

"Any *in personam* order that is enforceable by contempt power is an injunctive order, although more specific names are sometimes used to indicate the factual context to which the injunction belongs. For instance, specific performance is a remedy by which the defendant is ordered to perform a contract and the specific performance order is thus a form of injunction. Reinstatement in a job is a remedy for job discrimination in some cases and the reinstatement order is a form of injunction. Preliminary injunctions and temporary restraining orders are likewise injunctive forms. Even the automatic stay in bankruptcy operates like an injunction.

"An injunction may form the only remedy in a case, or it may be one part of more complex remedies. As the only remedy, the injunction might simply enjoin the defendant's repeated trespass on the plaintiff's land or prohibit infringement of a trademark. * * * Injunctions that forbid future misconduct are also frequently coupled with an award of damages for harms already done.

"Mandatory vs. Prohibitory Injunctions

"*Classification.* Injunctions are sometimes classified as being either mandatory or prohibitory. The prohibitory injunction forbids an act. 'The defendant is hereby enjoined from trespassing upon Blackacre,' is a prohibitory injunction. The mandatory injunction orders an affirmative act or course of conduct. 'The defendant is hereby ordered to remove all boulders he has previously deposited upon Blackacre,' is a mandatory injunction.

"*Formal but not substantive differences.* In both of the examples given above, the defendant's trespass on Blackacre might have been the result of identical acts—deposit of boulders on the plaintiff's land. One of the injunctions, however, addresses the trespass as a continuing trespass or frames the order prohibitively; the other frames the order as a mandatory injunction. In many situations the two kinds of injunctions are different in form, but not in purpose or effect. Courts say that they will ignore the prohibitory locutions and classify the injunction as mandatory if it is 'really' mandatory. This practice calls on standards even less certain than the formal language of the injunction, however. For instance, one court held that an injunction against working for the plaintiff's competitors was mandatory.

"*Reluctance to use mandatory injunctions.* Although the difference between mandatory and prohibitory injunctions is often formal, simply a way of phrasing the order, courts sometimes attach significance to that difference. Sometimes the distinction has a procedural effect discussed later.[11] At other times, courts may be reluctant to award a mandatory injunction because it may be especially intrusive, or more difficult to supervise and enforce. Such intrusions or difficulties, however, usually result, if at all, only because of the injunction's content rather than its mandatory form. Courts are right to weigh intrusion carefully in injunction cases, but the mandatory form of the injunction is not often a good measure of that intrusion and in any event the intrusion effected must be weighed against the intrusion required to provide a suitable remedy.

11. ["Some courts have at times attached an important procedural consequence to the classification of injunctions in these categories. These decisions say that if the injunction is prohibitory, it continues in effect in spite of an appeal, unless it is stayed by order of the trial court or by an appellate judge or pursuant to a statutory provision for stays. Since it continues in effect it must be obeyed even during appeal if the defendant wishes to avoid liability for contempt. On the other hand, if the injunction is classified as mandatory, these courts say that the injunction is stayed 'automatically,' as soon as the defendant perfects an appeal, or that the party enjoined is entitled to obtain a stay from the court as a matter of right.

"In applying this rule, courts have recognized that the character of the injunction is not to be determined merely by the form of words used in writing the order. But the distinction is nevertheless elusive and sometimes whimsical. Even if it provided the bright-line rule needed to determine any such matter as 'automatic' stays, the mandatory-prohibitory line would probably not be the right one. It is probably safer to rely on a stay granted by the judge or appellate judge. Stays obtained in that manner permit judges to estimate the interests of the parties and the public on the basis of the particular case rather than on the basis of a distinction that does not seem to matter much. It also permits judges considering a stay to impose conditions, such as supersedeas bonds, if that is deemed useful."

D. Dobbs, The Law of Remedies 275–276 (2d ed. 1993).]

"Preventive, Reparative and Structural Injunctions

"*Reparative and preventive injunctions.* A second set of classifications for injunctions may be more meaningful. The second set describes injunctions as reparative, preventive, or structural. The reparative injunction requires the defendant to restore the plaintiff to a preexisting entitlement. The mandatory injunction requiring a trespasser to remove the boulders he deposited is in this category. A preventive injunction attempts to prevent the loss of an entitlement in the future. It might be prohibitory, as where the defendant is enjoined not to obstruct ingress into the plaintiff's premises. Of course some injunctive orders both repair and prevent harm.

"The difference between reparative and preventive injunctions is important in presenting evidence and formulating decrees. The reparative injunction goes when the evidence shows that an existing right has been violated but can be repaired or restored effectively. The preventive injunction, on the other hand, is not proper unless the defendant is threatening to commit a wrong in the future. The defendant's past trespass upon the plaintiff's land by dumping boulders on it is not by that act alone threatening to wrong the plaintiff in the future. So a reparative injunction might go to require removal of the boulders, but not a preventive injunction to forbid future trespasses. On the other hand, when demonstrators show intransigent determination to continue trespassing indefinitely, a preventive injunction may be appropriate.

"*Structural injunctions.* Professor Owen Fiss has argued that there is a third type of injunction that belongs in this set. The structural or restructuring injunction attempts to remodel an existing social or political institution to bring it into conformity with constitutional demands. Examples are the injunction that restructures a school system to facilitate equality of educational opportunity, or restructures a prison to eliminate cruel and inhuman punishments. Such injunctions would be simple reparative or preventive injunctions if they merely ordered authorities to carry out or to cease some specific act. However, restructuring injunctions are typically complex and invasive. They are likely to involve the judge in tasks traditionally considered to be non-judicial, that is, less about rights and duties and more about management. For this reason, structural injunctions are likely to be used, as they are now, only as public law remedies for serious and pervasive rights violations."

D. DOBBS, THE LAW OF REMEDIES

184 (2d ed. 1993).*

"Types of Provisional Relief

"*Permanent injunctions.* Injunctions issued after an appropriate trial on the merits are sometimes called permanent injunctions. Permanent injunctions are not necessarily permanent in fact, because they may be modified on motion by either party if circumstances warrant. Some kinds of permanent injunctions are more or less consciously experimental, issued in the expectation that changes will be made, especially where major institutions are restructured to correspond to constitutional architecture.[2] So the permanent injunction is merely one issued after a full trial, and the term merely distinguishes them from temporary injunctive orders issued before a full trial.

"*Preliminary injunctions.* Two kinds of provisional or pre-trial injunctive orders may be issued. The most common is the preliminary injunction. Under the federal scheme and terminology with counterparts in many states, the preliminary injunction is issued only after notice is given to the defendant that the plaintiff will move for such relief, so that the defendant has an opportunity to be heard before the preliminary injunction is issued.[3] The hearing, however, is usually attenuated and much less than due process would require for a full trial. Evidence may be taken by affidavit, for example. The preliminary injunction remains in effect until dissolved or until the permanent injunction is in place or the case dismissed. * * *

"*Temporary restraining orders.* The temporary restraining order, often called a TRO, can put an even greater strain on due process. The TRO is not to be issued unless the plaintiff shows irreparable injury will otherwise result and also 'certifies to the court in writing the efforts, if any, which have been made to give the notice and the reasons supporting his claim that notice should not be required.'[4] In some cases, this rule requires the plaintiff to give notice that he will apply for a TRO, so that the defendant may appear and oppose the order. But it also permits the court to dispense with notice in some cases, so the TRO may be issued *ex parte.* Under this procedure, the defendant is not bound until he receives notice that the order has been issued, but he is put under its constraints without an initial opportunity to present facts or argue his side of the question.

"Unless extended, the TRO must terminate within ten days. It must terminate sooner if the court dissolves it on the defendant's motion. It also terminates when the preliminary injunction hearing is held, at which time the judge may decide to withhold further provisional relief altogether or may substitute the preliminary injunction. The preliminary injunction hearing must be expedited.

"*Other forms of provisional relief.* Provisional relief is not uniquely injunctive or equitable. Courts give provisional relief before trial 'at law' by way of attachment, garnishment, or replevin. Some important security for a plaintiff can be obtained *ex parte* without any judicial process at all, as where the plaintiff files a *lis pendens* notice or a notice of a mechanics' lien."

2. *See* O. Fiss, The Civil Rights Injunction, 36 (1978); § 7.4(4) below.

3. Fed.R.Civ.Proc.Rule 65(a).

4. Rule 65(b) * * *.

FEDERAL RULES OF CIVIL PROCEDURE

RULE 65. INJUNCTIONS

(a) Preliminary Injunction.

(1) *Notice.* No preliminary injunction shall be issued without notice to the adverse party.

(2) *Consolidation of Hearing With Trial on Merits.* Before or after the commencement of the hearing of an application for a preliminary injunction, the court may order the trial of the action on the merits to be advanced and consolidated with the hearing of the application. Even when this consolidation is not ordered, any evidence received upon an application for a preliminary injunction which would be admissible upon the trial on the merits becomes part of the record on the trial and need not be repeated upon the trial. This subdivision (a)(2) shall be so construed and applied as to save to the parties any rights they may have to trial by jury.

(b) Temporary Restraining Order; Notice; Hearing; Duration.

A temporary restraining order may be granted without written or oral notice to the adverse party or his attorney only if (1) it clearly appears from specific facts shown by affidavit or by the verified complaint that immediate and irreparable injury, loss, or damage will result to the applicant before the adverse party or his attorney can be heard in opposition, and (2) the applicant's attorney certifies to the court in writing the efforts, if any, which have been made to give the notice and the reasons supporting his claim that notice should not be required. Every temporary restraining order granted without notice shall be indorsed with the date and hour of issuance; shall be filed forthwith in the clerk's office and entered of record; shall define the injury and state why it is irreparable and why the order was granted without notice; and shall expire by its terms within such time after entry, not to exceed 10 days, as the court fixes, unless within the time so fixed the order, for good cause shown, is extended for a like period or unless the party against whom the order is directed consents that it may be extended for a longer period. The reasons for the extension shall be entered of record. In case a temporary restraining order is granted without notice, the motion for a preliminary injunction shall be set down for hearing at the earliest possible time and takes precedence of all matters except older matters of the same character; and when the motion comes on for hearing the party who obtained the temporary restraining order shall proceed with the application for a preliminary injunction and, if he does not do so, the court shall dissolve the temporary restraining order. On 2 days' notice to the party who obtained the temporary restraining order without notice or on such shorter notice to that party as the court may prescribe, the adverse party may appear and move its dissolution or modification and in that event the court shall proceed to hear and determine such motion as expeditiously as the ends of justice require.

(c) Security.

No restraining order or preliminary injunction shall issue except upon the giving of security by the applicant, in such sum as the court deems proper, for the payment of such costs and damages as may be incurred or suffered by any party who is found to have been wrongfully enjoined or restrained. No such security shall be required of the United States or of an officer or agency thereof.

* * *

(d) Form and Scope of Injunction or Restraining Order.

Every order granting an injunction and every restraining order shall set forth the reasons for its issuance; shall be specific in terms; shall describe in reasonable detail, and not by reference to the complaint or other document, the act or acts sought to be restrained; and is binding only upon the parties to the action, their officers, agents, servants, employees, and attorneys, and upon those persons in active concert or participation with them who receive actual notice of the order by personal service or otherwise.

* * *

B. TEMPORARY RESTRAINING ORDERS

1. Standards for Issuance

CLINTON v. NAGY

United States District Court, Northern District of Ohio, 1974.
411 F.Supp. 1396.

LAMBROS, DISTRICT JUDGE.

Plaintiff, Brenda Clinton, brought this action, through her mother and next friend Johnnie Clinton, seeking the issuance of a temporary restraining order and a preliminary and permanent injunction against defendants John S. Nagy, Commissioner of the Division of Recreation of the City of Cleveland; Robert Maver, Director of the Cleveland Browns Muny Football Association; Charles Hall, Director of Class "F" Muny League teams; and Ralph J. Perk, Mayor of the City of Cleveland. Plaintiff filed the action pursuant to 42 U.S.C.A. § 1983 and seeks to enjoin defendants from depriving her of equal recreational opportunities because of her sex and a declaratory judgment that the policies, customs, and practices of the defendants are in violation of the Constitution and laws of the United States. Notice of a hearing on the motion for temporary relief was afforded defendants, and this matter was heard on Friday, November 1, 1974. The Court granted plaintiff's motion for the temporary restraining order. The Court's ruling therein is set forth with more particularity below.

Plaintiff's claim is that she is a twelve year old female who expressed her interest to her mother and to Mr. William Thomas, coach of the 97th Street Bulldogs football team, in September, 1974, of her desire to play football with Mr. Thomas' team.

The 97th Street Bulldogs football team is licensed by the City as part of the Cleveland Browns Muny Football Association. Plaintiff alleges that neither her mother nor Coach Thomas have any objections to plaintiff's participation on the team. * * * [O]n September 28, 1974 plaintiff was suited and prepared to play with the 97th Street Bulldogs. On that date, and on several subsequent Saturday afternoons, plaintiff was suited and ready to play but was informed by defendant Charles Hall that she would not be permitted to play because she was a female. * * *

Plaintiff, therefore, instituted this suit seeking an order to restrain the defendants from denying her an opportunity to qualify to participate as a member of the 97th Street Bulldogs in the last games of the season, on Saturday, November 2, 1974, and Saturday, November 9, 1974, solely on the basis of her sex. At the hearing on the temporary restraining order, the defendants, through counsel, did not dispute that the reason that plaintiff was not permitted to play with the Bulldogs was because of her sex. The defendants argued, however, that the City's rules and regulations which govern the playing of sports specifically exclude females from participating in contact sports and that such exclusion is lawful because it bears a rational relationship to a legitimate state purpose of providing for the safety and welfare of females.

Accordingly, the sole issue before this Court at the hearing on the motion for a temporary restraining order was whether plaintiff had shown a substantial likelihood of success on the merits of her claim that the defendants should be enjoined from enforcing the City's regulations which exclude females from the opportunity to qualify for participation in Muny league football, a contact sport, because such regulations do not bear a reasonable relationship to any legitimate state purpose. Morris v. Michigan State Board of Education, 472 F.2d 1207 (6th Cir.1973). In this regard, defendants urged that the exclusion of females from contact sports was necessary for their safety and welfare and asserted that the testimony of its medical experts at the hearing on the merits would establish that the rule adopted by the Cleveland Division of Recreation is rationally related to that purpose. Defendants contended that their experts would testify that even at age ten, eleven, or twelve, boys are beginning to develop speed and greater physical stamina at a faster pace than are girls of those ages. * * *

Although the defendants stated, moreover, that the testimony of two medical experts would show that based upon a statistical analysis of variable strengths, males were generally stronger than females, the present action was not brought as a class action seeking to enjoin defendants from refusing to allow females to play football. This action was brought by one named-plaintiff who alleges that she has a right to pursue the opportunity to *qualify* to play football with the Muny leagues. * * *

The plaintiff has cited several recent cases in which courts have struck down school regulations which bar females from participating in school athletics solely on the basis of their sex. Defendants argued, however, that all of those cases have involved the question of whether the school or athletic board had a legitimate state purpose in denying women an equal opportunity to qualify for *non-contact* sports * * *.

* * *

In evaluating the plaintiff's motion for the issuance of a temporary restraining order herein the Court concludes that plaintiff has shown a substantial likelihood of success on the merits of her claim that defendants have precluded her from participating in the Muny League football games because she is a female, and solely because she is a female. Defendants have offered no evidence, nor did defendants indicate that they would present evidence to this Court that Miss Clinton does not possess the qualifications and physical ability required of male members to participate in the league's games. The defendants offered no argument nor did they put forward a factual basis on which this Court could conclude that Miss Brenda Clinton is more susceptible to injury than are the other "Bulldogs." * * *

Defendants argued, however, that even if Brenda were qualified to play as a "Bulldog" the temporary restraining order should not issue because she had made no showing that she would suffer irreparable harm if she were not permitted to play with that team. The Court is unable to concur in defendants' assertion.

Of course, females have not engaged in traditionally male sports, and as a result, in many instances females lack the requisite training to qualify for membership on all-male teams, particularly those teams established for the playing of "contact" sports. Perhaps those who find merit in the more traditional male-female roles may have great difficulty in understanding how a young girl will suffer irreparable harm if she is precluded from engaging in the rough and sometimes even brutal contest of football. Many adults, no doubt, may feel that young girls will in fact suffer great harm, both physically and socially, if they are permitted to participate in "boys'" games. However, football is by its very nature a physically dangerous game, and the threat of injuries to young boys has alarmed many parents in the community for years.

Nevertheless, organized contact sports such as football continue to be played, and those individuals who encourage young men to participate in these sports seem to do so with a sincere belief that although the game is potentially dangerous, the rewards which will be reaped from participation in the game offset the potential dangers. Organized contact sports have generally been thought of as an opportunity and means for a young boy to develop strength of character, leadership qualities and to provide competitive situations through which he will better learn to cope with the demands of the future. Yet, although these are presumably qualities to which we desire all of the young to aspire, the opportunity to qualify to engage in sports activities through which such qualities may be developed has been granted to one class of the young and summarily denied to the other.

It is necessary that we begin to focus on the individual rather than thinking in broad generalities, which have oftentimes resulted in the imposition of irrational barriers, against one class or another. The issue before this Court is whether one young person, Brenda Clinton, who apparently qualifies to play with the 97th Street Bulldogs in every respect except for her sex, should be given the opportunity to participate in the game of football and to develop strength and character in that way in which she, with her mother's approval, believes will be the most valuable to her. The Court concludes that to deprive a qualified twelve year old girl of an opportunity to engage in that activity would cause her to suffer irreparable harm, particularly in light of the fact that there are only two remaining games this season, on November 2, 1974 and November 9, 1974.

The motion for the temporary restraining order is granted. Accordingly, the defendants, their agents, employees, and all persons having actual knowledge of this order are hereby enjoined from prohibiting plaintiff Brenda Clinton from participating as a member of the 97th Street Bulldogs in its football games solely because of her sex. As this Court has already cautioned plaintiff, nothing in this order should be construed as requiring Coach Thomas to put Brenda Clinton into a game, should he determine that she does not qualify on the day of a game or should he deem another member of the team to be better suited to play in the position for which Miss Clinton has qualified.

This matter is set down for a hearing on plaintiff's motion for a preliminary injunction, to be consolidated with a hearing on the merits of her claim for permanent injunctive and declaratory relief on November 26, 1974, at 1:30.

It is so ordered.

NORWALK CORE v. NORWALK BD. OF EDUC.

United States District Court, District of Connecticut, 1968.
298 F.Supp. 203.

TIMBERS, CHIEF JUDGE.

Plaintiffs move for a temporary restraining order to prevent defendant from closing the Nathaniel Ely School, South Norwalk, Connecticut, pending determination of their motion for a preliminary injunction in this class action. Their motion is based on the pleadings, supporting affidavits, briefs and oral argument of counsel on September 3, 1968. After due consideration, the Court holds that plaintiffs' motion for a temporary restraining order should be denied. In addition, pursuant to Rule 65(a)(2), Fed.R.Civ.P., the Court orders that the trial of the action on the merits be advanced and consolidated with the hearing on the motion for a preliminary injunction.

Plaintiff's motion for a temporary restraining order accordingly is denied.

FACTS

Plaintiffs Norwalk Core (Core), Roodner Court Fair Rent Association (Association) and two minor children allege that defendant Norwalk Board of Education (Board), while committed to racial integration in the schools and cognizant of the important advantages of the neighborhood school concept, nevertheless has preserved neighborhood public elementary schools only in middle class and upper middle class white neighborhoods. It is alleged that the Board "has intentionally abandoned or destroyed and permitted to lie unused" public elementary schools in the low income Black and Puerto Rican neighborhoods. This, it is claimed, constitutes a double standard denying the class which plaintiffs claim to represent the right to attend an integrated neighborhood school and compelling them to be transported into white neighborhoods. That the busing operates in one direction only is said to be a denial of equal protection of the law under the guise of racial integration.

Plaintiffs seek a declaratory judgment holding this discriminatory practice unconstitutional; a permanent injunction prohibiting the maintenance of white neighborhood schools without at the same time instituting a Black neighborhood school policy; and a permanent mandatory injunction to compel the Board to produce a Black neighborhood school policy for approval by the Court.

The Board denies all the allegations except those which attribute to it a policy of promoting racial integration * * *.

Plaintiffs, in requesting a temporary restraining order, seek to maintain the status quo as of the time of commencement of this action; such status quo is said to be threatened by the Board's announced plans to discontinue the pre-kindergarten and kindergarten classes at the Nathaniel Ely School prior to the start of the present school year. This decision allegedly was made after commencement of the present action, and is said to be "directly harmful" to plaintiffs' case and an "affirmative move" by the Board to undermine the purposes of the suit. The four and five year old children who would attend Nathaniel Ely are now to be bused, exposed to hazards and disadvantages, and deprived of comfort and self-confidence. Their parents will be deprived of a local forum in which to air their views. * * *

[T]he Board urges that granting of the restraining order would be contrary to recent constitutional doctrine in that it would have the necessary effect of depriving the children of the opportunity to attend an integrated school by compelling them to attend a segregated kindergarten in a building devoid of other school activities.

OPINION

A motion for a temporary restraining order is addressed to the discretion of the Court. It seeks to preserve the status quo pending hearing on the motion for a preliminary injunction and trial on the merits. Although its denial may work injury to the movant, this alone is insufficient to compel its issuance. The movant has no "right" to a temporary restraining order. Instead, the Court must balance the validity of the claims asserted against the nature of the acts to be enjoined, and evaluate the movant's probability of success in the underlying action. Thus, while irreparable injury is a prerequisite, it is not controlling. 7 Moore's Federal Practice ¶ 65.04–.05 (2d ed. 1966).

In the present controversy, plaintiffs are asserting rights against a public instrumentality. At this late date, the temporary restraining order they seek may disrupt the educational policy of the community of Norwalk. As noted in Yakus v. United States, 321 U.S. 414, 440–41 (1944):

> "[W]here an injunction is asked which will adversely affect a public interest for whose impairment, even temporarily, an injunction bond cannot compensate, the court may in the public interest withhold relief until a final determination of the rights of the parties, though the postponement may be burdensome to the plaintiff. * * * This is but another application of the principle, declared in Virginian Ry. Co. v. System Federation, 300 U.S. 515, 552, that 'Courts of equity may, and

frequently do, go much farther both to give and withhold relief in furtherance of the public interest than they are accustomed to go when only private interests are involved.' "

* * *

While, as noted above, irreparable injury, during the pendency of the action, is insufficient by itself to mandate the granting of a temporary restraining order, it is nevertheless "[t]he most significant condition which must be present * * *." Capital City Gas Company v. Phillips Petroleum Company, 373 F.2d 128, 131 (2d Cir.1967). In the present controversy, however, the allegations of irreparable injury focus primarily on the harm which may result if permanent relief is denied. The only claim of injury during the pendency of the action concerns possible damage to the young children incident to being bused and the potential disruption of the academic year if the Nathaniel Ely School is temporarily closed and plaintiffs later are successful. Conversely, it is urged that the order would work no harm to the children who could continue to attend their neighborhood school, nor to the Board which could move the children later if the Board ultimately prevails on the merits.

These claims, however, clearly ignore the adverse consequences of a temporary restraining order on the children themselves: it would continue the de facto economic segregation existing at Nathaniel Ely by compelling Black and Puerto Rican children to attend an unintegrated school. On this motion plaintiffs do not seek to have the Court order the busing of white children into the Nathaniel Ely School during the pendency of the action. This is their ultimate goal; but until it is attained it is difficult to see the "irreparable harm" which will result from placing these young children in a racially integrated environment, albeit one somewhat removed from their home neighborhood. This exposure of young children of all races to the acknowledged benefits of an integrated school is the goal of both sides in the present dispute; the critical difference concerns only the location of this exposure. To deny the exposure in order to preserve a segregated neighborhood school would seem itself to be inconsistent with the relief sought by plaintiffs.

While the issuance of a temporary restraining order "serves as an equitable policing measure to prevent the parties from harming one another during the litigation" and to retain the status quo, Hamilton Watch Co. v. Benrus Watch Co., Inc., 206 F.2d 738, 742 (2d Cir.1963), where as here the alleged disruption of the status quo may be beneficial to both parties and not hinder the effectuation of whatever relief this Court grants in the underlying action, the motion should be denied. * * *

* * *

In denying plaintiffs' present motion the Court wishes to indicate its intended utilization of the procedure of Rule 65(a)(2), Fed.R.Civ.P., should plaintiffs renew their claim on a motion for a preliminary injunction. This will enable the Court to consolidate the trial of the action on the merits with the hearing on the motion for a preliminary injunction, to avoid the repetition of evidence at trial and to expedite final determination of this sensitive issue.[2]

Note

How do the courts use irreparable injury in *Clinton* and *Norwalk Core?* For a discussion of different views on the role of the irreparable injury rule in equitable relief, *compare* D. Laycock, The Death of the Irreparable Injury Rule (1991), and O. Fiss, The Civil Rights Injunction (1978) *with* Rendleman, The Inadequate Remedy at Law Prerequisite for an Injunction, 33 U.Fla.L.Rev. 346 (1981) and E. Yorio, Contract Enforcement: Specific Performance and Injunctions (1989). *See* Professor Dobbs' comments on some of these approaches in Chapter 7, A. 2., *infra*. *See also* D. Dobbs, The Law of Remedies, § 2.5(3) (2d ed. 1993).

2. *Dissolution and Appeal*

HAITIAN REFUGEE CENTER, INC. v. BAKER

United States Court of Appeals, Eleventh Circuit, 1991.
950 F.2d 685.

BY THE COURT:

This matter is before the court on the Appellants' emergency motion seeking a stay of the district court's injunction order pending appeal.

On November 19, 1991, the district court issued a temporary restraining order preventing the defendants from repatriating interdicted Haitians. Following a hearing and briefing on December 3, 1991, the district court issued a preliminary injunction enjoining such repatriation. The court found that the plaintiffs had a substantial likelihood of success on the merits of their claims under the First Amendment and Article 33 of the Convention Relating to the Status of Refugees. Following an expedited appeal, this court dissolved the injunction, holding that the plaintiffs had no enforceable claims under Article 33 and that the First Amendment claim did not support the injunctive relief granted.

This court's mandate issued December 17, 1991, and later that night the district court issued what purports to be another temporary restraining order to enable it to reconsider the plaintiffs' APA claim. In its order dated December 3, 1991, the court had rejected the plaintiffs' APA claim. The present "temporary restraining order," like the previous orders, prevents the defendants from repatriating Haitian interdictees located at Guantanamo Bay Naval Base and on Coast Guard vessels in the Caribbean. The district court denied Appellants' request to stay this order pending appeal.

We must initially decide whether we have jurisdiction. Although a temporary restraining order is not ordinarily appealable, where the order has the effect of a preliminary injunction this court has jurisdiction to review the order and is not bound by the district court's designation of the

2. After a five-day trial, the court denied the request for injunctive relief and dismissed the complaint on the merits. 298 F.Supp. 213 (D.Conn.1969), aff'd, 423 F.2d 121 (2d Cir.1970).

order. *See Sampson v. Murray,* 415 U.S. 61, 86–87 n. 58, 94 S.Ct. 937, 951 n. 58, 39 L.Ed.2d 166 (1974); * * *

In *Connell v. Dulien Steel Products, Inc.,* 240 F.2d 414 (5th Cir.1957), *cert. denied,* 356 U.S. 968, 78 S.Ct. 1008, 2 L.Ed.2d 1074 (1958), the court cited the practical reasons for not ordinarily allowing an appeal from a temporary restraining order. Temporary restraining orders are usually effective for short periods of time that are too brief to allow appeal; they are usually issued without notice to the nonmoving party, thus allowing the trial judge to hear only one side of the case; and the trial court should have an opportunity to have a full presentation of the facts and law before an order is appealable. *Id.* at 418.

In this case, these practical constraints are not present. The "temporary restraining order" issued on December 17, 1991, was issued after the district court had heard from all parties. The plaintiffs' APA claim was included in the complaint before the district court on December 3. The court issued a temporary restraining order on November 19, 1991, in order to consider the plaintiffs' claims for injunctive relief, including the APA claim. Following a full hearing and briefing on the merits, the district court rejected the plaintiffs' APA claim and refused to grant injunctive relief on that claim because it concluded that there was no substantial likelihood that the plaintiffs would succeed on the merits of the claim. * * * The district court has had an opportunity to have full presentation of the merits of this claim. For the foregoing reasons, we conclude that the "temporary restraining order" issued by the district court on December 17, 1991, is in effect a preliminary injunction. We therefore have jurisdiction of the defendants' appeal from the order issuing that injunction.

The parties briefed the merits of the APA claim in the previous appeal to this Court, so the court already has the benefit of full briefing on the claim. Having considered the matter, we conclude that there is a strong likelihood that the defendants will prevail on that claim for the reasons stated by the district court in its original Order Granting Preliminary Injunctive Relief dated December 3, 1991. We conclude that the appellants' motion seeking a stay of that order pending appeal is due to be granted. *See* Fed.R.App.P. 8.

HATCHETT, CIRCUIT JUDGE, dissenting: * * *

Contrary to the majority's holding, the district court is not considering the same APA claim as that previously presented in 91–6060.

The district court makes clear that its previous ruling on the APA claim, which this court earlier refused to review, was based upon the discretion which Congress had delegated to the President; whereas, the district court is now considering the APA claim based on "subordinates" discretion or lack thereof in following program procedures and guidelines." In 91–6060, this court refused to reach the APA claim under any theory; now, through some procedure here before unknown to the law, the majority is able not only to reach the APA claim, but to decide that the claim is without merit even though no hearing has been held and the district court has made no factual findings or legal conclusions.

The district court has scheduled a hearing on the APA claim for 10 a.m. on December 20, 1991, less than fourteen hours from the time the orders in this case will be filed (91–6099). This court should not take the highly unusual and extraordinary step of preventing the district court from hearing the APA claim that the coast guardsmen and immigration officials at Guantanamo Bay, Cuba and on the Coast Guard cutters are not properly interviewing these refugees. * * *

I would dismiss this case because temporary restraining orders are not appealable under the law of this circuit, and the district court has not even made factual findings. Surely, nothing in this record allows this court to hold, as a matter of law, that the low ranking government officials charged with the duty of properly interviewing the refugees are proceeding in accordance with established law.

Note

The Haitian refugee litigation included proceedings in two federal district courts and two courts of appeals. It involved numerous temporary restraining orders, preliminary injunctions and stays. For a chronology of the procedures, *see,* Haitian Centers Council, Inc. v. McNary, 969 F.2d 1326, 1330–34 (2d Cir.1992). There the Second Circuit affirmed in part a preliminary injunction issued by the District Court for the Eastern District of New York prohibiting repatriation of "screened in" Haitians without prior access to attorneys. *Id.* The United States Supreme Court reversed the Second Circuit on the merits. Sale v. Haitian Centers Council, Inc., ___ U.S. ___, 113 S.Ct. 2549, 125 L.Ed.2d 128 (1993).

MILLER v. LEHMAN

United States Court of Appeals, Ninth Circuit, 1983.
736 F.2d 1268.

PER CURIAM:

In Beller v. Middendorf, 632 F.2d 788 (9th Cir.1980), this court held that it was constitutionally permissible for the Navy to discharge appellant James Miller, among others, for homosexuality. On November 16, 1981, when the Supreme Court denied the petition for writ of certiorari in that case, the Navy was free to discharge Miller. According to Miller's allegations, however, the Navy retained him and even gave him the equivalent of a promotion. In December 1982, the Navy finally informed Miller that he would be discharged.

Miller responded by suing in district court for equitable relief, including a temporary restraining order. The district court denied Miller's request. A motions panel of this court then granted Miller an injunction to prevent the Navy from discharging him pending this appeal.

As an initial matter, the Navy argues that we have no jurisdiction over this case because the denial of a temporary restraining order, as a general matter, is not an appealable order. But an exception to this rule allows us to hear an appeal if the "denial of *all* relief was implied in the trial judge's denial of a temporary restraining order." Kimball v. Commandant Twelfth Naval Dist., 423 F.2d 88, 90 (9th Cir.1970). In this case, the district court denied Miller's petition by bare citation of the earlier decision in *Beller.*

The district court thus implied that principles of claim preclusion prevented Miller, one of the losing parties in *Beller,* from receiving any of the relief he requested. Accordingly, the district court's order meets the standard for appealability set forth in *Kimball.*

Turning to the merits of the appeal, we conclude that the district court's application of claim preclusion doctrine was erroneous. *Beller* concerned the constitutionality of certain military regulations. Miller's petition to the district court in this action, however, set forth theories of equitable estoppel, constructive enlistment, and retaliatory discharge. Miller is essentially arguing that, even if the Navy could have discharged him when *Beller* became final, the Navy's conduct since then estops it from discharging him now. In other words, Miller asserts new claims that arose after *Beller* was decided and thus cannot be barred by preclusion principles.

Because the district court applied an erroneous legal standard to Miller's petition for equitable relief, we remand and instruct the district court to issue a temporary restraining order preventing the Navy from discharging Miller. This order shall remain in force until the district court either grants or denies a preliminary injunction. We express no opinion, of course, on how the district court should rule on Miller's request for a preliminary injunction. We merely preserve Miller's right to have that request decided under the proper legal standard.

Notes

1. On occasion, an appeal is allowed from the issuance of a mandatory temporary restraining order. For example, in Adams v. Vance, 570 F.2d 950 (D.C.Cir.1978), the Inupiat Eskimos obtained a temporary restraining order from the district court directing the Secretary of State to object to the International Whaling Commission's proposed ban on hunting bowhead whales, an endangered species. (The Secretary of State, with the approval of the President, had decided that it would be diplomatic to request reconsideration of the ban rather than to file a formal objection.) The court of appeals took jurisdiction over the case for the following reasons:

> "The grant of a temporary restraining order under Rule 65(b), Fed. R.Civ.P., is generally not appealable. However, '[t]he label attached to an order by the trial court is not decisive with regard to whether it falls under Rule 65(a) or Rule 65(b) and the appellate court will look to other factors to determine whether an appeal should be allowed.' Wright & Miller, Federal Practice and Procedure § 2962, at 619 (1973). Here the order was in purpose and effect a mandatory injunction appealable under 28 U.S.C.A. § 1292(a)(1). It did not merely preserve the status quo pending further proceedings, but commanded an unprecedented action irreversibly altering the delicate diplomatic balance in the environmental arena. When an order directs action so potent with consequences so irretrievable, we provide an immediate appeal to protect the rights of the parties." 570 F.2d at 953.*

* The court of appeals vacated the temporary restraining order. As a result, the United States did not formally object to the ban. However, the government was successful in persuading the IWC to permit Alaskan natives to engage in subsistence hunting of a limited number of bowhead whales.

Appeals have also been allowed from the issuance of a temporary restraining order when the order (1) was entered after an adversary hearing, and (2) effectively granted the plaintiff all of the relief which the plaintiff sought. *E.g.*, Commonwealth of Virginia v. Tenneco, Inc., 538 F.2d 1026, 1029–30 (4th Cir.1976) (temporary restraining order restricting supply of gas gave all the relief sought by plaintiff).

2. When a temporary restraining order is issued and is then continued beyond the time permissible under Rule 65, Sampson v. Murray, 415 U.S. 61, 94 S.Ct. 937, 39 L.Ed.2d 166 (1974) indicates that it may be treated as an appealable preliminary injunction:

> "A district court, if it were able to shield its orders from appellate review merely by designating them as temporary restraining orders, rather than as preliminary injunctions, would have virtually unlimited authority over the parties in an injunctive proceeding. In this case, where an adversary hearing has been held, and the court's basis for issuing the order strongly challenged, classification of the potentially unlimited order as a temporary restraining order seems particularly unjustified."

See also, Levesque v. State of Maine, 587 F.2d 78, 79 (1st Cir.1978) (to find that a temporary restraining order operates as a preliminary injunction, "We must find either that a full adversary hearing has been provided or that, in the absence of review, further interlocutory relief is unavailable." *

3. The distinction between final and non-final temporary restraining orders is discussed at greater length in Kimball v. Commandant Twelfth Naval Dist., 423 F.2d 88, 89–90 (9th Cir.1970):

> "In the interests of avoiding uneconomical piecemeal appellate review, it has generally been held that appeal does not lie from the denial of an application for a temporary restraining order. Nevertheless, under certain circumstances the denial of temporary or preliminary relief may decide the merits of a case. In such a situation nothing is gained by requiring an appellant to go through the motions of re-applying for permanent injunctive relief in the trial court. * * *
>
> "Commentators have noted the difficulty that courts have had in characterizing what are final and non-final orders. In general a practical rather than technical construction has been favored.
>
>> 'In the difficult borderline cases, the line between a final and interlocutory order is not always clear. Because of this, the final judgment rule lacks both "finality" and "certainty." Practically every general principle concerning finality is subject to so many competing principles that oftentimes the application of the "proper" rule simply cannot be determined with any degree of certainty. * * *
>>
>> 'However, the Supreme Court has recently stated: "* * * Because of this difficulty this Court has held that the requirement of finality is to be given a 'practical rather than a technical construction.'" Gillespie v. United States Steel Corp., 379 U.S. 148, 85 S.Ct. 308, 13 L.Ed.2d 199 (1964).' 7A Moore's Federal Practice § 1291 pp. JC419, 420.

* *See also,* Duration of Temporary Restraining Orders in Federal Court, 42 U.Balt. L.Rev. 276 (1983).

"The *Gillespie* Court found the prime considerations in determining whether a final order had been entered were the following:

> '[I]n deciding the question of finality the most important competing considerations are "the inconvenience and costs of piecemeal review on the one hand and the danger of denying justice by delay on the other." ' Gillespie v. U.S. Steel Corp., *supra* at 152, 153, 85 S.Ct. at 311."

4. In Office of Personnel Management v. American Federation of Government Employees, AFL–CIO, 473 U.S. 1301, 105 S.Ct. 3467, 3470, 87 L.Ed.2d 603 (1985) plaintiffs sought a temporary restraining order to extend the expiration date of a Congressional stay of new personnel regulations for governmental employees. The District Court denied the temporary restraining order. The Court of Appeals for the District of Columbia Circuit stayed the expiration of the Congressional stay. Chief Justice Burger, as Circuit Justice, distinguished Adams v. Vance and Sampson v. Murray, discussed in notes 1 and 2, *supra,* and said, "since the Court of Appeals was without jurisdiction over the appeal from the District Court's order denying the temporary restraining order, the motions panel was necessarily without authority to grant such a stay." For a comprehensive examination of the history and use of the temporary restraining order see Dorr & Traphagen, Federal Ex Parte Temporary Relief, 61 Den.L.J. 767 (1984).

5. In Carroll v. President and Commissioners of Princess Anne, 393 U.S. 175, 89 S.Ct. 347, 21 L.Ed.2d 325 (1968), the Court ruled that the issuance of an *ex parte* temporary restraining order to enjoin a rally and public meeting of the National States Rights Party violated the first amendment:

> "We need not decide the thorny problem of whether, [on the basis of the events of the preceding evening], an injunction against the announced rally could be justified. The 10–day order here must be set aside because of a basic infirmity in the procedure by which it was obtained. It was issued ex parte, without notice to petitioners and without any effort, however informal, to invite or permit their participation in the proceedings. [T]here is no place within the area of basic freedoms guaranteed by the First Amendment for such orders where no showing is made that it is impossible to serve or to notify the opposing parties and to give them an opportunity to participate. * * *
>
> "Ordinarily, the State's constitutionally permissible interests are adequately served by criminal penalties imposed after freedom to speak has been so grossly abused that its immunity is breached. The impact and consequences of subsequent punishment for such abuse are materially different from those of prior restraint. Prior restraint upon speech suppresses the precise freedom which the First Amendment sought to protect against abridgment.
>
> "The Court has emphasized that '[a] system of prior restraints comes to this Court bearing a heavy presumption against its constitutional validity.' * * * And even where this presumption might otherwise be overcome, the Court has insisted upon careful procedural provisions, de-

signed to assure the fullest presentation and consideration of the matter which the circumstances permit.

"Measured against these standards, it is clear that the 10–day restraining order in the present case, issued ex parte, without formal or informal notice to the petitioners or any effort to advise them of the proceeding, cannot be sustained. * * *

"The value of a judicial proceeding, as against self-help by the police, is substantially diluted where the process is ex parte, because the Court does not have available the fundamental instrument for judicial judgment: an adversary proceeding in which both parties may participate. The facts in any case involving a public demonstration are difficult to ascertain and even more difficult to evaluate. Judgment as to whether the facts justify the use of the drastic power of injunction necessarily turns on subtle and controversial considerations and upon a delicate assessment of the particular situation in light of legal standards which are inescapably imprecise. In the absence of evidence and argument offered by both sides and of their participation in the formulation of value judgments, there is insufficient assurance of the balanced analysis and careful conclusions which are essential in the area of First Amendment adjudication.

"The same is true of the fashioning of the order. An order issued in the area of First Amendment rights must be couched in the narrowest terms that will accomplish the pin-pointed objective permitted by constitutional mandate and the essential needs of the public order. * * * The participation of both sides is necessary for this purpose. * * *

* * *

"We need not here decide that it is impossible for circumstances to arise in which the issuance of an ex parte restraining order for a minimum period could be justified because of the unavailability of the adverse parties or their counsel, or perhaps other reasons. In the present case, it is clear that the failure to give notice, formal or informal, and to provide an opportunity for an adversary proceeding before the holding of the rally was restrained, is incompatible with the First Amendment."

6. Do you think it would have been appropriate for a federal court of appeals to accept jurisdiction over an appeal from the temporary restraining order issued in *Clinton, supra* p. 19 or denied in *Norwalk Core, supra* p. 22?

C. PRELIMINARY INJUNCTIONS

1. *Standards for Issuance*

AMERICAN MOTORCYCLIST ASS'N v. WATT

United States Court of Appeals, Ninth Circuit, 1983.
714 F.2d 962.

Before WRIGHT and SCHROEDER, CIRCUIT JUDGES, and REED, DISTRICT JUDGE.

SCHROEDER, CIRCUIT JUDGE.

This is an appeal from the district court's denial of a preliminary injunction to prevent the federal government from implementing the California Desert Conservation Area Plan. Such a plan for land management is called for by section 601 of the Federal Land Policy and Management Act of 1976, 43 U.S.C. § 1781(d) (FLPMA). The district court considered plaintiffs' claims that implementation of this particular plan would violate portions of FLPMA. Plaintiffs on appeal argue that in addition to those claimed violations, the court should have considered alleged violations of the National Environmental Policy Act, 42 U.S.C. §§ 4321 *et seq.* (NEPA).

We hold that under the applicable standards the district court did not abuse its discretion in refusing to issue an injunction. We further hold that the presence of a claim of violation of NEPA in addition to claims of FLPMA violations would not affect the district court's result in this case. We therefore affirm the district court's decision, reported at 534 F.Supp. 923 (C.D.Cal.1981).

I. The District Court Proceedings

Plaintiffs–Appellants are, first, the American Motorcyclist Association and Sports Committee, District 37, A.M.A., Inc. (AMA), a national organization of motorcyclists who participate in competitive and recreational motorcycle events, and, second, the County of Inyo (Inyo), a political subdivision of the state of California. Defendants-appellees are the Secretary of the Interior (Secretary), the Director of the Bureau of Land Management (BLM), and the California State Director of the BLM.

The land management plan in question governs the use, development and protection of federal land in the California desert. * * *

Plaintiffs moved for a preliminary injunction before the Plan took effect, alleging that in adopting it the defendants violated various procedural provisions of NEPA, FLPMA and BLM planning regulations under FLPMA, 43 C.F.R. §§ 1600 *et seq.* Plaintiffs sought to enjoin implementation of the Plan until the defendants remedied the alleged defects.

In support of its motion for injunctive relief pending trial, AMA alleged that the Plan would prevent traditional recreational vehicle use of the California desert and would diminish the number and quality of motorcycle events. It contended that its members would be "irreparably harmed" by having to comply with time-consuming and frustrating permit applications for races. Inyo alleged that the Plan, which affects approximately half of Inyo County, is inconsistent with its own land use plan, that it failed to protect certain environmental features, and that its operation would erode Inyo's tax base.

The district court found there was a strong likelihood the plaintiffs would be able to prove that the BLM failed in several material respects to follow its planning regulations, in violation of subsections 202(c)(9) & (f) of FLPMA, 43 U.S.C. § 1712(c)(9) & (f). 534 F.Supp. at 935. The defects identified by the district court were the defendants' failure to develop a preferred alternative, to make appendices available to the public in a timely manner, to evaluate inconsistencies with local government plans and to make material changes in the Plan and Environmental Impact Statement (EIS) available for public comment. *Id.* at 935–36.

Despite the plaintiffs' probability of success on the merits, the court nevertheless determined that the equities did not warrant issuing a preliminary injunction because plaintiffs had not shown they would suffer irreparable harm, or that the balance of hardships tipped in their favor. It also found that a preliminary injunction would not be in the public interest.

In reaching its decision, the district court specifically refrained from considering plaintiffs' NEPA claims, holding instead that both plaintiffs lacked standing to raise such claims. 534 F.Supp. at 929 n. 6. The substance of plaintiffs' NEPA claims is similar in nature to their FLPMA claims, in that they challenge the defendants' failure properly to consider alternatives, to circulate documents and to respond to public comment. Plaintiffs contend on appeal that the district court erred in holding they lacked standing to raise the NEPA claims, and that existence of such claims requires issuance of a preliminary injunction.

II. EFFECT OF THE NEPA CLAIMS ON THE PRELIMINARY INJUNCTION DECISION

We recognize two sets of standards for evaluating claims to injunctive relief, which we have termed the "traditional" and the "alternative" tests. The traditional equitable criteria for determining whether an injunction should issue are

> (1) Have the movants established a strong likelihood of success on the merits; (2) does the balance of irreparable harm favor the movants; (3) does the public interest favor granting the injunction?

The "alternative" test permits the moving party to meet its burden by demonstrating either a combination of probable success and the possibility of irreparable injury or that serious questions are raised and the balance of hardships tips sharply in its favor. Benda v. Grand Lodge of IAM, 584 F.2d 308, 314–15 (9th Cir.1978), cert. dismissed, 441 U.S. 937, 99 S.Ct. 2065, 60 L.Ed.2d 667 (1979). The district court here expressly applied both tests, and held that plaintiffs were not entitled to an injunction under either. * * *

Assuming NEPA standing exists, * * * it would not affect all of the factors which the district court considered. Because the NEPA claims are essentially similar to the FLPMA claims which the district court recognized plaintiffs had standing to raise, the injury to the plaintiffs is the same under both statutes. In addition, neither side contends that adding NEPA claims would materially affect the district court's analysis of the plaintiffs' likely success on the merits.

The only question then is whether plaintiffs are correct in their position that the existence of a probable NEPA violation affects the district court's assessment of the public interest. Plaintiffs contend that recognizing their NEPA claims would require us to hold that a preliminary injunction must issue in this case. For the purpose of considering this argument we assume * * * that they have made a strong showing on the merits.

The presence of strong NEPA claims gives rise to more liberal standards for granting an injunction. * * * The premise for relaxing the equitable tests in NEPA cases is that irreparable damage may be implied from the failure of responsible authorities to evaluate thoroughly the environmental impact of a proposed federal action. Friends of the Earth,

Inc. v. Coleman, 518 F.2d 323, 330 (9th Cir.1975). In many instances those charging NEPA violations are able to make a compelling showing of imminent and irreversible harm unless the governmental action is stayed. *See, e.g.,* Lathan v. Volpe, 455 F.2d 1111, 1116–17 (9th Cir.1971).

There are nevertheless cases where public concerns other than failure to comply with NEPA must be weighed in determining whether to grant an injunction. In Alpine Lakes Protection Society v. Schlapfer, 518 F.2d 1089 (9th Cir.1975), we held that "unusual circumstances" required the court to determine whether the equities in fact favored an injunction. *Id.* at 1090. The plaintiffs there sought, on NEPA grounds, to enjoin a grant of access which permitted the logging of infested trees. The court held that the balance of equities weighed against the injunction. It looked both to the risk that the timber would be worthless if not promptly removed, and to the risk that the tree infestation would spread to adjacent national forest-lands. In denying the injunction it stated that defendants had shown a more tangible and immediate harm, as well as a stronger public interest. *Id.*

Alpine thus authorizes the court not only to weigh the relative hardship and harms to the parties, but to examine how the greater public interest may be affected in the unusual case where enjoining government action allegedly in violation of NEPA might actually jeopardize natural resources. * * *

As in *Alpine,* it is clear in this case that strong environmental considerations militated against enjoining the Plan. The district court found there was a danger of harm to the fragile desert resources of the CDCA if the Plan's restrictions were lifted and plaintiffs were allowed to pursue increased motor vehicle use. 534 F.Supp. at 937. This danger of harm is the kind of unusual circumstance which we said in *Alpine* calls for the "individual weighing" of the equities. 518 F.2d at 1090.

* * *

The district court in this case did engage in the required weighing, and it concluded that the balance favored the government because enjoining the Plan would leave fragile desert resources vulnerable to permanent damage from increased recreational use, a harm which Congress expressly intended to prevent. 534 F.Supp. at 937. Plaintiffs assert, though not strenuously, that they demonstrated that the Plan would cause "environmental harm." Many of the allegations in the district court primarily concerned reduced recreation and development opportunities, which the district court properly viewed as posing no danger of irreparable injury to the environment or to the public interest.

More serious allegations of injury concerned inconsistencies between the Plan and Inyo's county plan; but we conclude, however, that the district court properly determined that the harm to Inyo's planning processes was not comparable to the harm enjoining the Plan would cause to the CDCA and the public interest. We agree with the district court's observation that while the claimed procedural deficiencies in the Plan's adoption have caused uncertainty in Inyo's planning process, "issuance of a preliminary injunction would do little to redress that injury, since the Plan's validity will remain uncertain until judgment has been entered on the merits in this action." 534 F.Supp. at 937. The district court's analysis is supported by the record and its decision must therefore be affirmed.

One aspect of the district court's analysis deserves some clarification, however. The court stated that it was adopting a special injunction requirement for environmental cases so that, under either of our two preliminary injunction tests, it would consider whether the public interest is advanced by issuance of an injunction. 534 F.Supp. at 929. This was no doubt because the "alternative test" does not expressly recite the public interest as a factor to be considered. A Supreme Court decision issued since the district court decided this case clarifies the matter, however, by holding that the public interest is a factor which courts must consider in any injunctive action in which the public interest is affected. Weinberger v. Romero–Barcelo, 456 U.S. 305, 312, 102 S.Ct. 1798, 1803, 72 L.Ed.2d 91 (1982). This recognition of the obligation to protect the public interest in injunction cases does not detract from the correctness of the district court's analysis; the court was indeed required to consider the public interest. It simply needed no special rule in order to do so.

Plaintiffs have not demonstrated any abuse of discretion in the district court's determination that enjoining the plan would not be in the public interest. Congress expressly found that the CDCA is a "total eco-system that is extremely fragile, easily scarred, and slowly healed." 43 U.S.C. § 1781(a)(2). Congress' overriding concern was to "provide for the immediate and future protection and administration of the public lands in the California desert." 43 U.S.C. § 1781(b). The Plan seeks to accommodate economic, educational, scientific and recreational uses in the "unique setting" created by the fragility of desert lands, and by the stress that human use places upon arid eco-systems. Plan at 5–6. There is ample support for the district court's conclusion that the public interest in protecting and managing the CDCA would be severely disserved by enjoining the Plan.

* * *

Affirmed.

ABBOTT LABORATORIES v. MEAD JOHNSON & CO.

United States Court of Appeals, Seventh Circuit, 1992.
971 F.2d 6.

Flaum, Circuit Judge.

Abbott Laboratories (Abbott) filed this interlocutory appeal, 28 U.S.C. § 1292(a)(1), after the district court denied its motion for a preliminary injunction against Mead Johnson & Company (Mead). Abbott seeks relief under § 43(a) of the Lanham Act (the Act), 15 U.S.C. § 1125(a), to halt Mead's alleged false advertising and trade dress infringement practices in the oral electrolyte maintenance solution (OES) market. We vacate the district court's denial of preliminary relief, and remand with directions to promptly commence a full trial on the merits.

I.

Oral electrolyte maintenance solutions are over-the-counter medical products used to prevent dehydration in infants suffering from acute diarrhea or vomiting. * * * Despite their medical significance, OES products may be purchased without a prescription at food and drug stores.

Abbott and Mead are, for all practical purposes, the only two competitors in the United States OES market. Abbott's product is called "Pedialyte," while Mead's is called "Ricelyte". Competition in this market is of surprisingly recent vintage, as Pedialyte enjoyed a virtual monopoly until Mead introduced Ricelyte in 1990. The two products are virtually identical; only their carbohydrate components differ. This difference is crucial to understanding the dispute in this case, so we briefly provide some background.

* * *

Ricelyte, unlike Pedialyte, is not a glucose-based solution, for it is manufactured with carbohydrates known as "rice syrup solids." * * *

Since Pedialyte is the incumbent and Ricelyte the challenger, Mead launched a promotional campaign designed to convince physicians and nurses to recommend Ricelyte over Pedialyte. The campaign does so by emphasizing that Ricelyte's carbohydrate components (*i.e.,* rice syrup solids) come from rice, while Pedialyte's carbohydrate component is glucose. Mead focuses on rice for a fairly simple reason. Over the past decade, medical researchers worldwide, many sponsored by the World Health Organization (WHO), have studied the effectiveness of OES products made with powdered whole grains of rice, which are known as "rice-based," or whole grain, solutions. * * *

There remain, however, significant differences between Ricelyte and rice-based solutions. * * *

Nonetheless, Mead's promotional campaign plays up Ricelyte's association with rice. First, it forges a direct link between Ricelyte and rice. To take an obvious example, the name "Ricelyte" conveys the message that the product contains or is made from rice. * * *

* * *

Abbott did not take kindly to Mead's promotional and advertising campaign. It filed suit, alleging that the campaign, up to and including the "Ricelyte" name, was false and misleading in violation of § 43(a)(2) of the Act. * * * Abbott asked for a preliminary injunction, seeking a wide variety of relief, ranging in severity from a product recall to modifications in Mead's advertising and promotional materials. The district court approved an expedited discovery schedule submitted by the parties, held a ten-day evidentiary hearing, and heard one day of oral argument. Shortly thereafter it issued an order, accompanied by a lengthy and thorough memorandum opinion, denying Abbott's preliminary injunction motion in full. * * *

The court's analysis followed the venerable four-part preliminary injunction standard, *see, e.g., Lawson Prods., Inc. v. Avnet, Inc.*, 782 F.2d 1429, 1433 (7th Cir.1986), about which we speak at greater length in the following section. With regard to the false advertising claim under § 43(a)(2), the court ruled that Abbott had established a likelihood of success on the merits. It found certain of Mead's advertisements * * * to be literally true but misleading. Nonetheless, the court declined to enjoin Mead's promotional campaign pending a full trial because the other three preliminary injunction factors tipped the equities in Mead's favor: (1) if Abbott were to prevail on the merits, any harm it would suffer prior to final judgment could be adequately compensated with money damages and would not be irreparable; (2) the balance of hardships favored Mead; and (3) the public interest would be disserved by a preliminary injunction. * * * Abbott appealed.

II.

Despite our recent efforts to clarify the law of preliminary injunctions, *see, e.g., Lawson Prods., Inc. v. Avnet, Inc., supra; American Hosp. Supply Corp. v. Hospital Prods. Ltd.*, 780 F.2d 589 (7th Cir.1986); *Roland Mach. Co. v. Dresser Indus., Inc.*, 749 F.2d 380 (7th Cir.1984), confusion persists, as demonstrated by the contrasting spins both parties place upon the four-part preliminary injunction standard. To guide our analysis, as well as assist litigants in future cases, we briefly outline the following precepts, and note the parties' deviation therefrom in the margin.

As a threshold matter, a party seeking a preliminary injunction must demonstrate (1) some likelihood of succeeding on the merits, and (2) that it has "no adequate remedy at law" and will suffer "irreparable harm" if preliminary relief is denied. *Lawson Prods.*, 782 F.2d at 1433; *Roland Mach.*, 749 F.2d at 386–87. If the moving party cannot establish either of these prerequisites, a court's inquiry is over and the injunction must be denied. If, however, the moving party clears both thresholds, the court must then consider: (3) the irreparable harm the non-moving party will suffer if preliminary relief is granted, balancing that harm against the irreparable harm to the moving party if relief is denied; and (4) the public interest, meaning the consequences of granting or denying the injunction to non-parties. *Lawson Prods.*, 782 F.2d at 1433; *Roland Mach.*, 749 F.2d at 387–88.

The court, sitting as would a chancellor in equity, then "weighs" all four factors in deciding whether to grant the injunction, seeking at all times to "minimize the costs of being mistaken." *American Hosp. Supply*, 780 F.2d at 593. We call this process the "sliding scale" approach: the more likely it is the plaintiff will succeed on the merits, the less the balance of irreparable harms need weigh towards its side; the less likely it is the plaintiff will succeed, the more the balance need weigh towards its side. *Diginet, Inc. v. Western Union ATS, Inc.*, 958 F.2d 1388, 1393 (7th Cir.1992); *Roland Mach.*, 749 F.2d at 387.[2] This weighing process, as

2. Mead, pointing to an isolated dictum in *Maxim's Ltd. v. Badonsky*, 772 F.2d 388, 391 (7th Cir.1985), states that if the balance of irreparable harms (factor number 3 in the text) tips toward the defendant, the preliminary injunction must be denied regardless of

noted, also takes into consideration the consequences to the public interest of granting or denying preliminary relief. *Ping v. National Educ. Ass'n,* 870 F.2d 1369, 1371–72 (7th Cir.1989); *American Hosp. Supply,* 780 F.2d at 594, 601.[3] While we have at times framed the sliding scale approach in mathematical terms, *see American Hosp. Supply,* 780 F.2d at 593–94, it is more properly characterized as subjective and intuitive, one which permits district courts to "weigh the competing considerations and mold appropriate relief." *Lawson Prods.,* 782 F.2d at 1436.

We review a district court's decision to grant or deny a preliminary injunction under the abuse of discretion standard. *Id.* at 1436–37. With regard to analysis of each of the four factors, a court abuses its discretion when it commits a clear error of fact or an error of law. *Lawson Prods.,* 782 F.2d at 1437; *Roland Mach.,* 749 F.2d at 892. Absent any such error, the district court's ultimate weighing of all four factors is entitled to great deference; while our review is more searching than an examination of whether the district court weighed those factors "irrationally or fancifully," we may not "substitute our judgment" for that of the district court. *Roland Mach.,* 749 F.2d at 390; *see also Lawson Prods.,* 782 F.2d at 1437. With this standard in mind, we proceed to the case at hand.

III.

The district court, as noted, denied Abbott's request to enter a preliminary injunction under § 43(a)(2) of the Act to halt Ricelyte's allegedly false and misleading promotional campaign. The court found that Abbott had

the strength of plaintiff's case on the merits. This statement is erroneous. It is the balance of harms *discounted* by the parties' relative chances of succeeding on the merits (and taking account of the public interest), not the *undiscounted* balance of harms, that must weigh in plaintiff's favor for a preliminary injunction to issue. *Id.* at 392; *see also Diginet,* 958 F.2d at 1393; *Ping v. National Educ. Ass'n,* 870 F.2d 1369, 1371–72 (7th Cir.1989); *American Hosp. Supply,* 780 F.2d at 598; *Roland Mach.,* 749 F.2d at 392 ("when there is no clear balance of hardships in favor of the injunction, [plaintiff] must show that it is more likely than not to win" on the merits).

* * *

To illustrate our point, consider the following. Plaintiff X seeks a preliminary injunction against defendant Y. Suppose that the (undiscounted) balance of irreparable harms tips slightly toward Y—in other words, that X will be irreparably harmed $9x$ if the court denies preliminary relief, while Y will be harmed $10x$ if the court grants it. Suppose further that X has a 99 percent chance of succeeding on the merits, Y a one percent chance, and that the public interest is not implicated by the case. The proper course in this instance—recognizing, of course, that quantifying the factors to this degree of precision is likely impossible—would be to grant preliminary relief, for that is the course that would minimize the cost of error. Weighing the equities *as a whole* favors X, making preliminary relief appropriate, even though the undiscounted balance of harms favors Y.

3. Both parties state that a plaintiff, to obtain a preliminary injunction, must show that the injunction would not harm the public interest. This, in effect, adds a third threshold to our preliminary injunction standard by making the public interest factor dispositive. Although the statement finds support from a dictum in *Brunswick Corp. v. Jones,* 784 F.2d 271, 274 n. 1 (7th Cir.1986) (as a prerequisite, plaintiff must establish that "an injunction would not harm the public interest"), we question whether it accurately characterizes the law of the circuit. The public interest is one factor courts must consider in weighing the equities; it is not dispositive. *Ping,* 870 F.2d at 1371–72; *American Hosp. Supply,* 780 F.2d at 601–02. Suppose, to take a simple example, that the balance of harms tips significantly in plaintiff's favor, that plaintiff has an overwhelming chance of succeeding on the merits, but that granting the injunction would ever so slightly impair the public interest (*e.g.,* by removing one of ten products from a given product market). In this instance, preliminary relief would be proper even though it might harm the public interest.

demonstrated a likelihood of succeeding on the merits, but determined that the remaining three preliminary injunction factors favored Mead. We find that the court misconstrued the legal principles underlying each of those three factors, and hence that it abused its discretion in completely denying preliminary relief.

A.

Section 43(a)(2) of the Act prohibits the use of false or misleading statements or representations of fact in commercial advertising, and establishes a private remedy for any violation thereof. * * * The district court determined that Abbott had established a likelihood of prevailing at trial on the merits. Mead, advancing an alternative ground for affirmance, contends otherwise. We consider separate aspects of Mead's promotional campaign in turn, keeping in mind throughout that to pass this threshold Abbott need only demonstrate some likelihood of prevailing on the merits, *Lawson Prods.,* 782 F.2d at 1433, not that it will definitely prevail.

* * *

In sum, we agree with the district court's determination that Abbott has established a likelihood of succeeding on the merits of its § 43(a)(2) cause of action.

B.

The second preliminary injunction threshold requires Abbott to establish that it will be irreparably harmed if it does not receive preliminary relief, and that money damages and/or an injunction ordered at final judgment would not rectify that harm. The district court determined that Abbott did not clear this threshold. In so holding, the court acknowledged the well-established presumption that injuries arising from Lanham Act violations are irreparable, even absent a showing of business loss. * * * This presumption, it appears, is based upon the judgment that it is virtually impossible to ascertain the precise economic consequences of intangible harms, such as damage to reputation and loss of goodwill, caused by such violations. *See Roland Mach.,* 749 F.2d at 386.

There can be no doubt that Mead's Ricelyte campaign, which attempts to convince consumers that Pedialyte is an inferior OES product, has dented Abbott's reputation. * * * The district court nonetheless found the presumption of irreparable harm rebutted owing to the unusual structure of the OES market. It reasoned as follows: Pedialyte enjoyed a virtual monopoly prior to Ricelyte's entry into the market. Any injunction, entered after a full trial, would remove Ricelyte from the market, thereby restoring Pedialyte's monopoly and lost market share. Under these circumstances, one could easily measure the sales Abbott lost while waiting for final judgment. As far as the future is concerned, Abbott's reputational damage will have no tangible economic impact because Pedialyte will have regained its monopoly, leaving those who need OES products with no other choice. It appears, then, that we are faced with a rare situation—any harm to Abbott's reputation and goodwill wreaked by Mead's promotional campaign between now and final judgment will be fully compensable in money damages, and therefore cannot be considered irreparable. Put another way, the fact that injunctive relief in Abbott's favor at final judgment would boot Ricelyte from the market renders compensable any injuries Abbott will have suffered in the interim.

The district court's conclusion rests upon two assumptions. First, the court assumed that if final judgment forced Mead to withdraw Ricelyte, Abbott's losses would be limited to past lost sales in the OES market. In our view, this assumption overlooks the fact that Mead's promotional campaign will probably have lingering, incalculable economic consequences even if final relief on the merits drives Ricelyte from the market. Any monopoly Abbott regains is unlikely to last very long. (We of course do not mean to imply that Abbott deserves a monopoly, or that a monopoly would benefit the OES market, but only that Abbott's damages would be difficult to calculate in the event it could not sustain a monopoly.) It is almost certain that Mead will re-enter, or some other company will enter, the OES market shortly after Ricelyte departs; the market has a proven potential for growth, see Dist.Op. at 80, and the dominant player has proven potentially vulnerable. Pedialyte's loss of goodwill will have tangible economic consequences once competition reemerges, because doubts planted by the Ricelyte campaign will linger in the minds of consumers and physicians, who may avail themselves of an alternative to Pedialyte if given the choice. Moreover, any shifts in the OES market between now and final judgment will affect the closely related competition between Abbott and Mead in the immense infant formula market, which accounts for more than $1.5 billion in annual sales. Mead acknowledged as much in its 1991 Marketing Plan, which opined that "[t]he more market share Ricelyte takes from Pedialyte, the more opportunities Ricelyte creates to" shift infant formula sales from Abbott to Mead. Any suggestion that forcing Ricelyte from the market after a full trial would completely reverse this shift is simply implausible.

The loss of market share Abbott will likely suffer in both the OES market (once competition reemerges) and the infant formula market was not considered by the district court. As an original matter, one could have concluded that Abbott would suffer these harms were preliminary relief denied, and that the difficulty, indeed practical impossibility, of quantifying them would render monetary relief inadequate, and hence Abbott's injuries irreparable. *American Hosp. Supply,* 780 F.2d at 597. It is more difficult, however, to determine whether the court's decision not to consider these harms constitutes an abuse of discretion.

We need not resolve that issue here, for the district court erred by assuming in the first instance that granting final injunctive relief to Abbott would necessarily mean the end of Ricelyte. Granted, some of the relief sought by Abbott—*e.g.,* an order requiring Mead to recall Ricelyte, change its label, and immediately cease use of the "Ricelyte" name—would eliminate Ricelyte from the market at least temporarily, and perhaps permanently. But other relief—*e.g.,* an order prohibiting Mead from purveying the false "rice claims" and directing it to issue corrective advertisements and brochures—would not have such drastic consequences. These less severe remedies would leave Ricelyte a viable, albeit somewhat discredited, competitor with at least part of its current market share.

The district court did not address the possibility of ordering these intermediate forms of relief after a full trial on the merits. * * * This, we believe, constitutes an error of law. It is axiomatic that injunctions, preliminary as well as permanent, have their basis in equity. *Hecht Co. v. Bowles,* 321 U.S. 321, 329, 88 L.Ed. 754, 64 S.Ct. 587 (1944). When faced with a motion for a preliminary injunction, a district court must remain flexible, and weigh the equities as to each element of preliminary relief sought by the plaintiff. *Lawson Prods.,* 782 F.2d at 1435–36. The same applies to final relief if, as here, the potential parameters of a permanent injunction will influence the equities that govern the propriety of issuing a preliminary injunction. The importance of flexibility is enhanced where those equities depend in great measure upon which preliminary and permanent remedies are ordered. * * * We therefore find that the district court abused its discretion by restricting its focus to those final remedies, to the exclusion of all others, that would eliminate Ricelyte from the market.

* * *

C.

We next consider the public interest. The district court concluded that granting Abbott's request for a preliminary injunction would disserve the public interest. Ricelyte, the court reasoned, is a safe and effective product whose presence in the market has promoted the public welfare by focusing attention upon OES products and increasing their use. The court also believed that forcing Ricelyte from the market would restore Abbott's former virtual monopoly, dousing competitive incentives to invest in additional research and develop more effective OES products.

We agree with the district court that forcing Ricelyte from the market would harm the public interest. It is a rare case where purging a safe and effective product serves broad societal interests. This is particularly so when the purged product is one of only two in a given market; monopolies, as a general rule, carry substantial social costs, including higher prices, lower output, and a reduced incentive to engage in product innovation beneficial to consumers. * * * The costs are even higher when, as here, important health concerns are involved. * * *

But we decline to accept the court's implicit assumption that granting Abbott preliminary relief would necessarily mean the demise of Ricelyte, for the same reasons we just rejected that assumption with regard to final injunctive relief. As noted, some forms of intermediate relief, such as ordering Mead to purge the false aspects of its promotional campaign and issue corrective advertising, would leave Ricelyte a viable competitor. In fact, such relief would serve, rather than disserve, the public interest in truthful advertising, an interest that lies at the heart of the Lanham Act. * * * The court therefore committed an error of law by not addressing less severe remedies that would have addressed the allegedly false and misleading aspects of Ricelyte's campaign without eliminating it from the market.

D.

The district court also determined that the balance of hardships tilted in Mead's favor—in other words, that the irreparable harm to Mead of granting preliminary relief would outweigh the irreparable harm to Abbott of denying such relief.[6] It based this ruling upon a finding that the relief requested by Abbott, most notably an injunction prohibiting Mead's further use of the name Ricelyte, would drive Ricelyte from the market for some period of time, and hence might be "fatal" to the product's survival. This, the court stated, would work a "significant" irreparable harm to Mead, a harm which would far outweigh the "possible damage" to Abbott of denying preliminary relief. Dist.Op. at 78. We believe that the court's analysis contains two legal errors which led it to understate the harm to Abbott of denying an injunction and to overstate the harm to Mead of granting an injunction.

The first error we have already discussed: the court abused its discretion in concluding that Abbott would not suffer any irreparable harm if preliminary relief were denied. The second we have discussed as well. The district court's assessment that Mead would be significantly harmed by a preliminary injunction purging Ricelyte from the market rests on the supposition that any injunction entered would do just that. * * *

Having found that the district court (1) overstated the irreparable harm to Mead and the public interest of granting a preliminary injunction, and (2) possibly overlooked the irreparable harm to Abbott of denying an injunction, we cannot accept its conclusion that the equities weigh in Mead's favor as to Abbott's false advertising claim under § 43(a)(2).

* * *

In cases such as this, we traditionally have done one of two things: reverse and direct the district court to order the preliminary relief we deem appropriate, or vacate and remand for renewed consideration under the proper legal standards. We decline to do the former because the district court, owing to its superior familiarity with the underlying facts of this case, is in a far better position than we to weigh the equities and fashion a proper remedy. We also decline to do the latter in the interests of expediency and judicial economy; the parties indicated at argument that they are virtually ready for a full trial on the merits and need only limited time for additional discovery. We therefore vacate the district court's denial of Abbott's request for a preliminary injunction, and remand with directions to commence a full trial on the merits within 60 days. If,

6. We emphasize that the relevant harms are only those that accrue between a court's ruling upon the preliminary injunction motion and the entry of final judgment, *Roland Mach.*, 749 F.2d at 391, and even then only those harms that could not be fully rectified by money damages or injunctive relief at final judgment or, as to the defendant, could not be fully covered by a Rule 65(c) injunction bond. *Id.* at 386, 387. Given its finding that Abbott failed to demonstrate any irreparable injury, the court technically did not have to balance the hardships; demonstrating irreparable injury is a threshold matter, the failure of which dooms a plaintiff's case and renders moot any further inquiry. *Lawson Prods.*, 782 F.2d at 1433. Nonetheless, a court under these circumstances is well advised to consider the irreparable harm that would attend a preliminary injunction, for it gives us something to work with if, as here, we rule that the plaintiff has cleared the irreparable harm threshold.

contrary to our assumptions, there is no prospect for a trial within that time, we remand with directions to fashion appropriate preliminary relief, if any, in accordance with this opinion.

One final note. As we have emphasized throughout, the district court's analysis suffered from its near exclusive focus upon the most drastic remedies requested by Abbott (*e.g.*, product recall) to the exclusion of less severe remedies (*e.g.*, corrective advertising). This focus, we learned at argument, resulted from the district court's decision to adopt, nearly verbatim, the proposed findings of fact and conclusions of law submitted by the parties; obviously, the court selected some of Abbott's proposals and some of Mead's. Each party, it appears, tried to hit a home run, Abbott by submitting conclusions of law granting it all the relief it sought, and Mead by submitting conclusions of law granting Abbott nothing. Neither offered alternative conclusions that steered a reasonable middle ground. So, when it came time for the court to assess the impact upon the parties and the public of granting or denying preliminary relief, the court considered only the impact of either granting the most severe relief or shutting Abbott out altogether.

Of course there is nothing wrong and everything right with zealous advocacy. But counsel, when drafting proposed conclusions of law for the district court, should bear in mind a crucial observation to which we alluded above: courts retain a great deal of flexibility when fashioning preliminary relief, and the equities weighed under the four-part preliminary injunction standard can shift as the nature of that relief varies. *Lawson Prods.*, 782 F.2d at 1435–36; *see also Ideal Indus.*, 612 F.2d at 1026–27. Nor do we cast aspersions upon the widespread practice in the busy district courts of adopting many or most of the parties' proposed findings of fact and conclusions of law, particularly if skillfully and wisely drafted. Nonetheless, district judges also should bear in mind our observations regarding the nature of preliminary relief, and, when presented with proposed findings and conclusions that hug the extremes, consider developing alternatives of their own.

Vacated and Remanded, With Directions.

Notes

1. Professor Dobbs has classified the manner in which the courts combine the factors for awarding a preliminary injunction as unstructured or structured.

"§ 2.11(2) Standards for Issuance of Provisional Injunctive Orders

"Standards

"*Main factors.* To obtain a preliminary injunction the plaintiff must show special justifications. Bearing in mind the possibility that preliminary relief will prove to be erroneous when a full trial on the merits is held, courts have mainly been concerned with three factors: (1) irreparable harm the plaintiff may suffer if relief is denied; (2) irreparable harm the defendant or third parties will suffer if relief is granted; (3) the probability that the plaintiff will prevail on the merits.

* * *

"*Unstructured factors.* Courts often provide an unstructured list of several factors bearing on the decision to grant or deny preliminary injunctions.[3] The lists often resemble that already given.[4] However, courts commonly give no explanation how the several factors are to be weighed or how they work together. For example, suppose the plaintiff has only a so-so chance of success on the merits but is threatened with enormous irreparable harm and that the defendant will suffer very little such harm if the preliminary injunction is issued. The unstructured list invites the judge to exercise her conscience but it does not suggest any particular analysis or reasoning. In particular, the unstructured list does not suggest anything about the relative importance of the irreparable harm as compared to the plaintiff's chance of winning on the merits.

"*Structured factors.* Other courts have tried to provide more structure and to recognize that even the plaintiff who is not very likely to prevail on the merits, may be faced with such irreparable loss that the preliminary injunction should go. The Second Circuit has repeatedly said that the plaintiff must show (1) irreparable harm and (2) *either* (a) 'probable success on the merits,' *or* (b) a balance of hardships 'tipping decidedly' in the plaintiff's favor plus serious questions on the merits.[5]

3. E.g., W.T. Grant Co. v. Srogi, 52 N.Y.2d 496, 438 N.Y.S.2d 761, 420 N.E.2d 953 (1981) ("(1) the likelihood of success on the merits; (2) irreparable injury absent granting the preliminary injunction; and (3) a balancing of the equities"); Solow v. Liebman, 175 A.D.2d 120, 572 N.Y.S.2d 19 (1991).

4. One typical list, for example, tells the judge to consider

> "1. Whether the movant has shown a strong or substantial likelihood or probability of success on the merits. 2. Whether the movant has shown irreparable injury. 3. Whether the preliminary injunction could harm third parties. 4. Whether the public interest would be served by issuing the preliminary injunction."

See Planned Parenthood Ass'n of Cincinnati, Inc. v. City of Cincinnati, 822 F.2d 1390 (6th Cir.1987); Friendship Materials, Inc. v. Michigan Brick, Inc., 679 F.2d 100 (6th Cir.1982) (similar); First-Citizens Bank & Trust Co. v. Camp, 432 F.2d 481 (4th Cir.1970) (similar); Adams County Election Com'n By and Through McMillian v. Sanders, 586 So.2d 829 (Miss.1991) (similar).

The list given in the first paragraph of this section is a version of the list just quoted. In the quoted list, the third and fourth factors could be grouped together because both are concerned with harm to third persons. They can also be expressed in terms parallel to those in the second factor, so that "harm" becomes irreparable harm, which is presumably what the courts mean. When put in uniform terminology, this list seems to say that irreparable harm to third persons is considered, but it omits to say that irreparable harm to the defendant himself is considered. Courts probably do not mean to say that, hence the list formulated in the text adds irreparable harm to the defendant.

5. See Triebwasser & Katz v. American Tel. & Tel. Co., 535 F.2d 1356 (2d Cir.1976); Consolidated Gold Fields PLC v. Minorco, 871 F.2d 252 (2d Cir.1989), modified by, 890 F.2d 569 (1989); Securities and Exchange Com'n v. Unifund SAL, 910 F.2d 1028 (2d Cir.1990).

The formula is murky, but fairly translated into common terminology it seems to mean that if the probability of the plaintiff's success on the merits is more-likely-than-not, that fact plus proof of irreparable harm will justify the injunction. If the plaintiff cannot show such a good probability of success but only shows "serious questions on the merits," then the plaintiff will have to show that her irreparable loss of rights will be greater than the defendant's. * * *

Approving a preliminary injunction to prevent a merger, the court in *Consolidated Gold Fields,* supra, emphasized that the irreparable harm was so overwhelming that doubts were to be resolved *in favor* of the preliminary relief. "Were the merger to be consummated, the Minorco group will likely

The 'balance of hardships' seems to be about the equivalent of irreparable loss."

D. Dobbs, The Law of Remedies, § 2.11(2) at 187–88 (2d ed. 1993).* Which method did the courts in *AMA* and *Abbott Laboratories* use?

2. Although the *AMA* opinion and Professor Dobbs identify two sets of standards for evaluating claims to pre-trial injunctive relief, one law review article claims that there are in fact at least nine different tests applied by the federal courts of appeals. Wolf, Preliminary Injunctions: The Varying Standards, 7 W.New Eng.L.Rev. 173, 183–84 (1984). Other than an en banc decision in the Eighth Circuit, no federal appellate court has convened to reconcile these differences. Dataphase Systems, Inc. v. CL Systems, Inc., 640 F.2d 109 (8th Cir.1981) (en banc).

3. How would you compare the standards for issuing a preliminary (or temporary) injunction with the standards for issuing a temporary restraining order (see Chapter 2, Section 1.B.). Furthermore, either heightened standards, or special applications of the usual standards for determining whether a preliminary injunction should issue, apply where the operations of government are involved, especially if administrative remedies are available, or Congress has restricted the jurisdiction of the Federal courts. *See, e.g.,* Sampson v. Murray, 415 U.S. 61, 71, 94 S.Ct. 937, 943, 39 L.Ed.2d 166 (1974) (loss of job, which may be remedied through proceedings for reinstatement and back pay, absent extraordinary circumstances does not constitute irreparable harm, and established principles would deny "equitable intervention in disputes over tenure of governmental employees"); V.N.A. of Greater Tift County, Inc. v. Heckler, 711 F.2d 1020 (11th Cir.1983) (2–1) (although Congress has deprived courts of jurisdiction over merits of Medicare claims until after exhaustion of administrative remedies, courts have power under the All Writs Act, 28 U.S.C.A. § 1651, to entertain a suit for preliminary injunction against withholding of funds pending administrative decision on the merits. However, allegation that provider of services would be put out of business by withholding of funds by government did not suffice to warrant relief).

4. Sometimes courts use a mathematical formula to express the interrelationship among the factors. *See, e.g.,* Lawson Products, Inc. v. Avnet, Inc., 782 F.2d 1429, 1433–34 (7th Cir.1986):

> "*Roland* [Machinery Co. v. Dresser Industries, 749 F.2d 380 (7th Cir.1984)] and *American Hospital* [Supply Corp. v. Hospital Products Ltd., 780 F.2d 589 (7th Cir.1986)] adopted a 'sliding scale' approach where the possibility of mistake would be minimized by weighing the costs of injunctive relief against the benefits. The benefit of injunctive relief can be determined by combining the probability of success on the merits with the magnitude of the harm to the plaintiff. 'The more likely the plaintiff is to win, the less heavily need the balance of harms weigh in his favor; the less likely he is to win, the more need it weigh in his favor.' *Roland,* 749 F.2d at 387. *See also Maxim's Ltd. v. Badonsky,* 772 F.2d 388, 391 (7th

dominate the strategically important world gold market. Gold Fields and its associated entities would cease to be viable competitors in the market. Such a possibility alone suggests that 'doubts as to whether a [preliminary] injunction * * * is necessary to safeguard [the target group] * * * should be resolved in favor of granting the injunction.' "

* Reprinted with permission of West Publishing Co.

Cir.1985). This principle was stated in mathematical terms, *cf.* Judge Learned Hand's opinion in *United States v. Carroll Towing Co.,* 159 F.2d 169, 173 (2d Cir.1947), in *American Hospital,* at 593. 'Grant the preliminary injunction if but only if:

$$P \times H_p > (1 - P) \times H_d$$'

The left hand of the equation is the magnitude of erroneously denying the injunction, arrived at by multiplying the probability that plaintiff will prevail at trial (P) by the harm to the plaintiff caused by the denial of the injunction (H_p). The right hand represents the magnitude of an erroneously granted injunction measured by multiplying the probability that the defendants will prevail at trial (1 − P, the inverse of the plaintiff's probability of success) by the harm to the defendant caused by the granting of the motion (H_d). *Id.* at 593–94."

Do you find the formula useful?

5. In Roland Machinery Co. v. Dresser Industries, Inc., 749 F.2d 380, 386 (7th Cir.1984) Judge Posner emphasized that the absence of an adequate remedy at law is a precondition to any form of equitable relief. He then listed four types of fact situations in which a damages remedy would be inadequate:

"(a) The damage award may come too late to save the plaintiff's business. He may go broke while waiting, or may have to shut down his business but without declaring bankruptcy. Of course, even if the plaintiff declares bankruptcy, his trustee in bankruptcy can get a damage award; but probably it will not cover all the losses incident to the bankruptcy. The award may be inadequate even if the plaintiff leaves the business without becoming insolvent. As Judge Friendly noted in a case involving the termination of an automobile dealer, 'the right to continue a business in which William Semmes had engaged for twenty years and into which his son had recently entered is not measurable entirely in monetary terms; the Semmes want to sell automobiles, not to live on the income from a damages award.' Semmes Motors, Inc. v. Ford Motor Co., *supra,* 429 F.2d at 1205.

"(b) The plaintiff may not be able to finance his lawsuit against the defendant without the revenues from his business that the defendant is threatening to destroy. But in an age of contingent-fee contracts this will rarely be a decisive consideration.

"(c) Damages may be unobtainable from the defendant because he may become insolvent before a final judgment can be entered and collected. See discussion in Signode Corp. v. Weld–Loc Systems, Inc., 700 F.2d 1108, 1111 (7th Cir.1983).

"(d) The nature of the plaintiff's loss may make damages very difficult to calculate. Consider a loss, but not a crippling loss (that would be case (a)), of business profits. In principle, any profits lost by Roland as a result of being terminated for breach of an implied exclusive-dealing contract can be monetized, and awarded as damages; but in practice it may be very difficult to distinguish the effect of the termination from the effect of other things happening at the same time, and to project that effect into the distant future. On the difficulties encountered in trying to calculate damages for lost profits, *see, e.g.,* Taylor v. Meirick, 712 F.2d 1112, 1119–22 (7th Cir.1983); Hayes v. Solomon, 597 F.2d 958, 976–77 (5th Cir.1979);

Note, Private Treble Damage Antitrust Suits: Measure of Damages for Destruction of All or Part of a Business, 80 Harv.L.Rev. 1566, 1577–86 (1967)."

In at least two other situations, money awards would not provide adequate relief:

(a) Cases involving recurring violations of a long-term contract. *E.g.,* Howell Pipeline Co. v. Terra Resources, 454 So.2d 1353 (Ala.1984) (preliminary injunction granted, ordering defendant to comply with contract requiring it to pay for minimum daily volume of gas).

(b) Suits to protect the public interest. *E.g.,* South Central Bell Tel. Co. v. Miller & Sons, Inc., 382 So.2d 264 (La.Ct.App.1980) (preliminary injunction granted, prohibiting defendant from damaging telephone cables; the damage to telephone users would not be measurable in monetary terms).

STANTON v. BRUNSWICK SCHOOL DEP'T

United States District Court, District of Maine, 1984.
577 F.Supp. 1560.

GENE CARTER, DISTRICT JUDGE.

I. PROCEDURAL BACKGROUND AND FACTS

This is a civil action in which the Plaintiff seeks injunctive relief and damages for the Defendants' refusal to publish in the 1984 Brunswick High School Yearbook a quotation which the Plaintiff had previously selected for inclusion in the yearbook. The quotation selected for publication by the Plaintiff from the January 24, 1983, issue of *Time* magazine, reads as follows:

> The executioner will pull this lever four times. Each time 2000 volts will course through your body, making your eyeballs first bulge, then burst, and then broiling your brains. * * *

It is contended by Plaintiff that representatives of the Defendant Brunswick School Board, which is charged under state law (20 M.R.S.A. § 1011) to exercise overall responsibility for the operation of the Brunswick School Department, have, acting pursuant to their legal authority, refused to permit the inclusion of the selected quotation in the 1984 Brunswick High School Yearbook. Plaintiff brings her cause of action pursuant to the First Amendment of the United States Constitution, 42 U.S.C. § 1983, and 28 U.S.C. § 1343(3).

Plaintiff filed a motion with the original complaint seeking entry of a temporary restraining order "requiring defendants to forward to the publisher her yearbook information form; and to otherwise insure that, pending trial on the merits, Plaintiff's quotation will appear in the 1984 school yearbook." The Court having declined to act on said motion *ex parte,* and notice having been given to the Defendants and a hearing held, the Court treats the motion as one for a preliminary injunction pursuant to Fed.R.Civ.P. 65(a).

The allegations in the original complaint set forth the following facts in support of the application for relief. For the last ten years, approximately, the Defendants have published the High School Yearbook at the conclusion of each school year. Complaint, at ¶ 14. The yearbook has contained a section in which pictures of all of the members of the senior class appear together with biographical information about each student and a short quotation selected for inclusion by each student. *Id.* In years prior to 1984, it is alleged, there has existed no articulated policy, either written or oral, regulating the contents of the quotations selected by students for inclusion in the yearbook. *Id.* at ¶ 5. In the last several years student quotations have appeared in the yearbook encouraging the use of unlawful drugs and alcohol, and student quotations also have appeared in the yearbook from various "rock and roll" artists, some of whom speak in negative terms about traditional American values and promulgate statements which glorify sexual activity. *Id.* at ¶ 6. In addition, quotations reflect the views of such diverse individuals as John F. Kennedy and Bertolt Brecht. *Id.* Plaintiff claims that this utilization of the annual high school yearbook constitutes that publication, for First Amendment purposes, "a public forum." *Id.* at ¶ 7.

On or about November 1, 1983, Brunswick High School senior students were required to turn in information forms providing to the yearbook staff the biographical information to be included in the yearbook, as well as the individual student's selected quotation. *Id.* at ¶ 10. The Plaintiff returned such an information form. *Id.* The Plaintiff's designated quotation was indicated on the information form. Plaintiff chose this quotation "because she wanted to draw people's attention to the horror of both murder and what she believed to be, on occasion, an appropriate punishment for it." *Id.* at ¶ 11. * * * The reason for the rejection of the quotation for publication given by the faculty members and the Defendant Millett was "that the quotation was too graphic and was unacceptable for public consumption. * * * [T]he quotation could not be printed because it would be 'disruptive to the community.' " *Id.* at ¶ 13. * * *

* * *

III. Preliminary Injunctive Relief

As previously noted, the Court treats the pending motion for a temporary restraining order as a motion for preliminary injunction in view of the fact that notice and opportunity for hearing have been afforded to the Defendants with respect to the issues raised by the Plaintiff's claim of entitlement to temporary injunctive relief pending further proceedings and a determination of those issues on the merits. *Supra,* at 1561. Plaintiff must satisfy four essential requirements in order to prevail on a claim for temporary injunctive relief. This Court has had occasion in the past to set out succinctly those requirements in UV Industries, Inc. v. Posner, 466 F.Supp. 1251 (D.Me.1979) (per Gignoux, J.):

> It is well settled law that, in the ordinary case, a plaintiff must satisfy four criteria in order to be entitled to a preliminary injunction. The Court must find: (1) that the plaintiff will suffer irreparable injury if the injunction is not granted; (2) that such injury outweighs any harm

which the granting of injunctive relief would inflict on the defendant; (3) that plaintiff has exhibited a likelihood of success on the merits; and (4) that the public interest will not be adversely affected by the granting of the injunction.

Moreover, the Court should only sparingly exercise its authority to issue an interlocutory injunction which requires a defendant to take affirmative action. The purpose of preliminary injunctive relief is to preserve the *status quo* until a final adjudication can be had upon the merits. In framing the terms of a preliminary injunction the Court is to go no further than is necessary to preserve the litigating posture of the moving party and must avoid any unnecessary encroachment upon that of the adverse party.

Indeed, the Court cannot seriously consider equitable relief as drastic as that proposed by Plaintiff which would effectively act as a final determination of the issue. It is clear that "[a]ny denial of plaintiff's rights pending a determination on the merits would work an irretrievable loss of constitutionally-guaranteed liberties for which no adequate remedy exists at law." * * * The injunction proposed by Plaintiff, however, would cause a similarly irretrievable loss to Defendants if they must publish Plaintiff's quotation before the case is decided on the merits and their position ultimately prevails. A temporary injunction which simply prevents the Defendants from authorizing final printing and publication of the yearbook until resolution of this controversy will adequately protect Plaintiff's rights without foreclosing the possibility of relief for Defendants. This narrower remedy accords with the conservative mode described above as appropriate for the consideration of preliminary injunctions. The Court will, therefore, apply the traditional analysis to this more limited remedy.

(1) Irreparable Injury

Plaintiff in this case founds her claims on alleged deprivations of her First and Fourteenth Amendment rights resulting from the Defendants' denial to her of the opportunity to have her selected quotation published in the 1984 yearbook. "It is well established that the loss of First Amendment freedoms constitutes irreparable injury." Maceira v. Pagan, 649 F.2d 8, 18 (1st Cir.1981) (citing *Elrod v. Burns,* 427 U.S. 347, 373, 96 S.Ct. 2673, 2689, 49 L.Ed.2d 547 (1976)). Plaintiff's claim that she stands at risk of being denied the exercise of her right of free expression of her ideas, secured by the First Amendment, constitutes a colorable showing, rising above a "chilling effect," *see Maceira,* at 18, of a denial of her constitutionally-secured prerogatives. Money damages will not suffice to redress such a deprivation of Plaintiff's one-time opportunity to have her ideas published in the yearbook, which opportunity has been made available to her classmates. * * *

(2) Weighing the Competing Harms to Plaintiff and Defendants

In balancing the hardships that might be occasioned by the Court's action (or inaction), it is clear that failure of the Court to enter any injunctive relief would cause Plaintiff irreparable harm. The temporary injunction postponing publication until after final resolution of this case would prevent this harm while causing only minor difficulties for Defendants.

The affidavits of the Defendants establish only that printing and publication schedules have been established. It is not demonstrated that any harm rising above the level of inconvenience and the incurring of modest additional publishing costs, much less any irreparable harm, will result from delay of those printing and publication schedules. While it is asserted that such delay may occasion increased expense in the form of publication costs, it is not shown that these Defendants will bear those costs. Even if it were so shown, those charges would hardly constitute irreparable injury by comparison to the harm that would be done to the Plaintiff's constitutionally-protected First Amendment rights by presently scheduled publication of the yearbook without the inclusion of her designated quotation. * * *

It is clear, on balance, that the protection of the Plaintiff's constitutionally-based interests predominate on the present factual calculus, and that an adequate showing has been made that the Plaintiff's potential injury, in the absence of temporary injunctive relief, will outweigh any harm which the granting of an appropriately-framed injunction would inflict on these Defendants.

(3) Plaintiff's Likelihood of Success on the Merits

Plaintiff here asserts a claim which challenges the right to *initiate* expression. * * *

* * *

Here the Plaintiff asserts that she feels strongly about the issues of murder and capital punishment. She selected her designated quotation to "provoke some of my classmates to think a little more deeply than if I had written a standard butterfly quote." Plaintiff's supplemental affidavit, at ¶ 8. She seeks to convey her message, in part at least, through the "shock effect" of graphic prose. She seeks to utilize the "emotive function" of language. Yet, it is precisely because the chosen language serves that function well that the quotation has been rejected because, it is said, it is "inappropriate."

* * *

The criteria shown by the existing record to have been actually applied here as a basis for the rejection for publication of the Plaintiff's designated quotation failed to address adequately any of the constitutional requirements. They do not, therefore, pass constitutional muster as criteria sufficient in content to limit the Plaintiff's right to free expression of her ideas in a public forum. If these criteria are ultimately shown to be all that was applied to deny Plaintiff her First Amendment right, she will clearly prevail at trial on this aspect of her claim.

(4) The Public Interest

Justice Frankfurter framed lucidly the pertinent calculus when he said that the right of free expression "means not only informed and responsible criticism but the freedom to speak foolishly and without moderation."

Baumgartner v. United States, 322 U.S. 665, 674, 64 S.Ct. 1240, 1245, 88 L.Ed. 1525 (1944). In the legitimate exercise of her right of free speech, this Plaintiff has the option to convey her conviction by the use of the most graphic language, even, if she so chooses, by language so physiologically stark that others may believe her to "be a jerk."

Government has no legitimate nor compelling interest in preserving this lone woman from that fate if her own utterances shall visit it upon her. Rather, the First Amendment declares that the highest interest of the people is best served if government is required to stay its hand and permit her, and millions like her, to take upon their personal risk the ability of their ideas and convictions to survive and propagate in the marketplace of ideas. It is a matter of little moment, in the larger sense, whether she fails in that endeavor; it is of vital moment that she and her idea not be denied, by the instrumentalities of the political establishment, the *opportunity to succeed* in that marketplace. * * *

* * *

In light of the careful limitation of the scope of the Court's preliminary injunction, no countervailing public interest is damaged by the injunction. The Court requires the Defendants to do nothing save to hold their hand with respect to *final* publication until the rights of both parties to this litigation may be finally adjudicated. The Defendants are no more entitled to commit the preclusive act of final publication in advance of that adjudication *without* Plaintiff's designated quotation than is the Plaintiff entitled to have the Court require, in advance thereof, an equally preclusive publication *with* the quotation. * * * The limited interim injunctive relief here granted serves the public interest in all respects.

(5) Conclusion

The Court concludes that the Plaintiff has made a strong showing of entitlement to preliminary injunctive relief preventing final publication of the 1984 Brunswick High School Yearbook until a final adjudication on the merits of this action. A preliminary injunction shall issue forthwith in the form and substance of Appendix "A" attached hereto.

So Ordered.

APPENDIX "A"

PRELIMINARY INJUNCTION

Plaintiff's motion for a Temporary Restraining Order having come on for hearing and argument on January 11, 1984, and notice and hearing thereon having been ordered by the Court, and the motion now being considered by the Court as one for a Preliminary Injunction, and the Court having this date separately made its findings of fact and conclusions of law in its Findings of Fact, Conclusions of Law, Opinion and Order of this date.

It is hereby ordered, that the Defendant Gerald Millett and all others acting in concert with him, be, and are hereby, enjoined from authorizing, allowing, causing or permitting, pursuant to any authorization, permission or order * * * previously given or to be given after this date, any final printing, publication, or distribution of a 1984 Brunswick High School

Yearbook prior to this Court's final adjudication of the merits of the above-entitled matter, the content of which shall exclude therefrom the Plaintiff's designated quotation, viz:

> "The executioner will pull this lever four times. Each time 2000 volts will course through your body, making your eyeballs first bulge, then burst, and then broiling your brains * * *."

from the Senior Section thereof next to the photograph and biographical data previously submitted by Plaintiff and approved for publication therein by the yearbook editorial staff and said Gerald Millett.

Nothing contained in this Preliminary Injunction shall preclude the interim preparation, including printing, of other material to be included in said 1984 Brunswick High School Yearbook in accordance with existing or other schedules of the editorial staff.

Notes

1. The *Stanton* case illustrates the typical judicial reluctance to issue a mandatory preliminary injunction. In *Stanton,* the court was able to protect the plaintiff's constitutional rights by granting a prohibitory preliminary injunction. Sometimes, however, a court must issue a mandatory preliminary injunction in order to provide effective relief for the plaintiff. Consider, for example, Tustin v. Heckler, 591 F.Supp. 1049, 1054–58 (D.N.J.1984), rev'd on other grounds, 749 F.2d 1055 (preliminary injunction vacated because "district court erred as a matter of law when it found that the plaintiff had made a showing of probable success on the merits"), a nationwide class action for a mandatory preliminary injunction to restore terminated Social Security disability benefits:

> "In a declaration dated June 21, 1984, plaintiff Tustin states that she is a resident of subsidized housing in New Brunswick, New Jersey and applied for and was granted disability and SSI benefits effective June 2, 1972. She was notified in 1982 that her entitlement to these benefits would cease in November, 1982. She challenged the termination and continued to receive benefits of $320 per month until April, 1984. Her disability benefits then stopped entirely, but she received $21.40 in SSI benefits in May. She no longer has the medical coverage available to disability recipients and states that she is still unable to work, is without any source of income, and has had to borrow from friends in May and June to meet her rent and grocery expenses. She also asserts that she has no money to meet her daily expenses. Plaintiff Tustin's benefits were terminated as the result of a periodic review and her individual appeal from the Secretary's decision is pending before a court of this District.
>
> * * *
>
> "Here, plaintiffs seek a mandatory preliminary injunction. The Third Circuit has recognized that it is appropriate to issue such an injunction 'in a case in which the status quo "is a condition not of rest, but of action" * * *' United States v. Price, 688 F.2d 204, 212 (3rd Cir.1982) quoting Toledo, A.A. & N.M. Ry. Co. v. Pennsylvania, 54 F. 730, 741 (C.C., N.D.Ohio 1893). * * *

"The same balancing test that is used in considering whether a prohibitory injunction shall issue is used when it is a mandatory injunction that is being considered. *Id.* As one scholarly commentator put it

> 'Emphasis on preserving the status quo is a habit without a reason. To freeze the existing situation may inflict irreparable injury on a plaintiff deprived of his rights or a defendant denied the right to innovate. The status quo shibboleth cannot be justified as a way to limit interlocutory judicial meddling, because a court interferes just as much when it orders the status quo preserved as when it changes it. The test is not even easy to apply, since it eddies off into conundrums about what status is decisive.
>
> 'Aversion to mandatory injunctions, like the solicitude for the status quo from which it grew, has continued to mark judicial opinions. Although judges should consider how seriously an injunction restricts the defendant's lawful freedom of action, the restriction cannot be measured by whether the injunction compels or forbids action. The distinction between requiring action and prohibiting action is mainly a verbal one unrelated to the likelihood of irreparable loss to the defendant.'

Leubsdorf, The Standard for Preliminary Injunctions, 91 Harvard Law Review 525, 546 (footnotes omitted).

"Moreover, the fact that an injunction may require the payment or expenditure of money does not necessarily foreclose the possibility of equitable relief. Accordingly, the court may consider here the four factors traditionally considered by courts of equity in determining whether preliminary injunctive relief should be made available.

"Plaintiffs argue that they will suffer irreparable harm because they have been financially dependent on disability payments for long periods and the termination of these benefits has severely impaired their ability to provide themselves with basic needs such as housing, food and health care. They are, they argue, unable to perform any substantial gainful employment and are without another sufficient source of income. Defendant retorts that it is well-established that 'the temporary loss of income, ultimately to be recovered, does not usually constitute irreparable injury.' Sampson v. Murray, 415 U.S. 61, 90, 94 S.Ct. 937, 952, 39 L.Ed.2d 166 (1974). She quotes from Oburn v. Shapp, 521 F.2d 142, 151 (3rd Cir.1975) for the proposition that:

> 'Mere injuries, however substantial, in terms of money, time and energy necessarily expended in the absence of a stay are not enough. The possibility that adequate compensatory or other corrective relief will be available at a later date, in the ordinary course of litigation, weighs heavily against a claim of irreparable harm.'

"Plaintiffs respond that they are on a very different footing than the plaintiff in *Sampson*, an unlawful discharge case. While the *Sampson* plaintiff had been earning a livelihood up to the time of discharge and continued to be employable, plaintiffs argue that they 'are not only without any income due to the cutoff of benefits, but because of their continued disability, they are without any means of procuring the necessities of life.' Plaintiffs' Reply Brief at 7.

"Professor Leubsdorf's writings are illuminating on the question of whether there can ever be irreparable injury where the party seeking injunctive relief could, at some point, be compensated with money:

> 'The concept of irreparable injury takes on different meanings in different contexts. At trial, it refers to injury for which there is no adequate remedy at law. At the interlocutory hearing, it denotes injury for which there is no adequate remedy—legal or equitable—at final judgment. Even in the first context, the conclusion that an injury is irreparable involves considerations of policy apart from the feasibility of computing damages. Today, factors including the need for a jury trial, the relative burdens of damages and injunctions, and the substantive law's concern with changing conduct or compensating victims help to shape the remedial choice. If necessary, any injury can be stated in money terms. * * *
>
> 'A finding of irreparable injury in the preliminary injunction context is still farther removed from any equation of irreparability with quantifiability. Injury may be ascertainable but still irreparable, as when the law immunizes a state officer against liability for acts committed before they were clearly unconstitutional. On the other hand, injury may be unascertainable but nevertheless reparable when final injunctive relief can remove it. To decide whether a final remedy is good enough to warrant forgoing an immediate injunction calls for thinking, not just counting.'

91 Harvard L.Rev. at 551–552.

"It is readily apparent to this court that plaintiffs face a 'future injury of uncertain date and incalculable magnitude' if their terminated benefits are not restored. Plaintiffs are not seeking the proverbial pot of gold but merely restoration of the minimal disability benefits they received until recently, benefits which made their lives tolerable. To plaintiffs, whose impecuniousness is aggravated by an inability—actual or merely perceived—to return to the job market, the loss of even the relatively small amount of money that they were receiving has further extended their marginality. Not only can one expect that, when plaintiffs no longer have recourse to borrowed funds, they will face the loss of housing and the ability to maintain proper nutritional standards, but they also will be unable to access continuing medical care through the social security system.

"* * * There is a clear likelihood that, without the relief sought, a realistic danger exists that the plaintiffs seeking relief will be without the means to avail themselves of the basic needs of food, shelter, or medical care, much less the means to be self-sustaining. I 'do not think that it is necessary for [plaintiffs] to show that without an injunction "rigor mortis [would] set in forthwith."' Rockwell Intern. Systems, Inc. v. Citibank, N.A., 719 F.2d 583, 586 (2d Cir.1983) (quoting Studebaker Corp. v. Gittlin, 360 F.2d 692, 698 (2d Cir.1966)). Thus, irreparable harm will accrue to plaintiffs if injunctive relief is withheld."

Accord Ellender v. Schweiker, 550 F.Supp. 1348 (S.D.N.Y.1982).

2. In Miller v. Carlson, 768 F.Supp. 1331 (N.D.Cal.1991) plaintiffs were AFDC recipients who had changed from one training program to another and

as a result lost child care benefits. They claimed they were entitled to those benefits. The court ruled that the plaintiffs had a likelihood of succeeding on the merits. It then found and ordered as follows:

> "Plaintiffs demonstrate that without a preliminary injunction, they will suffer extreme hardship. Lack of child care assistance will force them to choose between dropping out of school and foregoing basic necessities in order to pay for child care. If they drop out of school, plaintiffs not only abandon their hopes of financial self-sufficiency, but they will lose the benefit of the loans, the time, and other resources already invested in their training. *See* Plaintiffs' Memorandum in Support, at 17–19; *see also* Rhome Decl., ¶¶ 7, 11; Martin Decl. ¶¶ 8–12. Most importantly, plaintiffs will be relegated to dependency for an indefinite period on an AFDC grant which does not even reach the federal poverty level.
>
> "In contrast, the only harm defendants may suffer is financial if, pending a full hearing on the merits, they are required to continue providing child care to those plaintiffs who have been or will be terminated from GAIN. Where the government only faces a financial harm, the balance of hardships strongly favors plaintiffs who will be deprived of essential benefits. Lopez v. Heckler, 713 F.2d 1432, 1436–37 (9th Cir. 1983);
>
> * * *
>
> "It is Hereby Ordered that:
>
> (1) Pending judgment in this action, the California Department of Social Services ('DSS') is enjoined from failing to provide continued child care assistance to AFDC recipients who have been or will be terminated from GAIN due to program reductions, but who continue to participate satisfactorily in their approved educational or training activities. DSS shall reinstate child care assistance forthwith to AFDC recipients whose child care assistance has been discontinued solely because of their termination from GAIN due to program reductions.
>
> (2) This preliminary injunction is issued without bond."

Id. at 1339–41. Was this a mandatory or prohibitory injunction? *See also* Doe by Doe v. Perales, 782 F.Supp. 201 (W.D.N.Y.1991) (court temporarily enjoined New York from changing its Medicaid resource limits because, inter alia, plaintiffs who live at the subsistence level suffer irreparable injury when they must pay more for their care).

3. If you represented a plaintiff who wanted the court to enter a mandatory preliminary injunction ordering the defendant to remove a fence erected in the middle of a public road in front of your client's house, what arguments would you make? Consider the following passage from Kjellander v. Smith, 652 S.W.2d 595, 598 (Tex.App.1983):

> "Next [the defendant] argues * * * that the trial court abused its discretion in granting the injunction [ordering the defendant to remove a fence] because the effect thereof would be to give [the plaintiff] the relief sought on final hearing, and to change the status quo. In another point appellant argues the trial court erred by impliedly finding that the last actual, peaceful and noncontested status preceding the controversy was one with no fence in place. We discuss these points together.

"The mere fact that the relief granted by the temporary injunction would be the same as that sought on final hearing does not constitute a basis for refusing to grant the injunction. Gunnels v. North Woodland Hills Community Association, 563 S.W.2d 334, 338 (Tex.Civ.App.—Houston [1st Dist.] 1978, no writ). In that case the court stated, at p. 337:

> Generally, the preservation of the status quo can be accomplished by an injunction prohibitory in form, but it sometimes happens that the status quo is a condition not of rest, but of action, and the condition of rest is exactly what will inflict the irreparable injury on complainant. In such a case, courts of equity issue mandatory writs before the case is heard on its merits. This character of cases has been repeatedly held to constitute an exception to the general rule that [a] temporary injunction may not be resorted to to obtain all relief sought in the main action; such [a] temporary injunction may be mandatory in character.

Here the condition of rest, with the fence in place, is exactly what will inflict irreparable injury on the appellees—by obstructing the only public access to their property.

"Furthermore, the status quo to be preserved by [a] temporary injunction is 'the last actual, peaceable, noncontested status which preceded the pending controversy.' (Emphasis added.) Big Three Industries, Inc. v. Railroad Com'n., 618 S.W.2d 543, 548 (Tex.1981). The presence of the fence in the road is the sole cause of the controversy here. Although the evidence is somewhat conflicting because there were several fences put up and torn down over the years, there is testimony from appellant himself that there was no fence in place at the time the Smiths moved onto the property. No abuse of discretion exists where the trial court bases its decisions on conflicting evidence."

4. Injunctions ordering the performance of an affirmative act may be characterized as "prohibitory" if they require the defendant to comply with (1) a preexisting contract between the parties to the dispute, or (2) a statutory or other legal duty. *E.g.,* People v. Mobile Magic Sales, Inc., 96 Cal.App.3d 1, 157 Cal.Rptr. 749 (1979) (although the act of removing defendant's mobile home from a trailer park was an "affirmative act," it was "incidental to the injunction's prohibitive objective" to restrain further violation of a statute); Lakeshore Hills, Inc. v. Adcox, 90 Ill.App.3d 609, 46 Ill.Dec. 108, 413 N.E.2d 548 (1980) (preliminary injunction granted to enforce a restrictive covenant permitting residents of a subdivision to keep on their property only "household pets"; defendant compelled to remove a 12–year–old, 575–pound Canadian black bear).

5. Should there be a tougher standard for issuing preliminary mandatory injunctions? At least some courts think so.

a. In Benten v. Kessler, 799 F.Supp. 281, 287 (E.D.N.Y.1992) the court said, "if granting the preliminary injunction provides the movant with essentially all the relief requested, the standard is higher; the movant must show a substantial likelihood of success on the merits, as opposed to a mere likelihood of success." There the court preliminarily ordered United States officials to return RU486, a drug to induce abortion, to a woman who had only four days left in which to take it. The plaintiff had brought the drug, which is not approved for use in the United States, into the country under a rule permitting importation of unapproved drugs for personal use. That rule had excluded the importation of RU486, but the court held that the plaintiff had a substantial likelihood of proving that the ban had been promulgated without the necessary notice and comment periods. The court refused to issue a further order and enjoin the ban.

b. In Transamerica Rental Finance Corp. v. Rental Experts, 790 F.Supp. 378, 381 (D.Conn.1992) the court said, "Where the requested injunction is mandatory, rather than prohibitive, an injunction should issue only upon a clear showing that the moving party is entitled to the relief requested." There the court issued a preliminary order that the plaintiff creditor be able to take over the defendant's "rent to own" business because that business secured the loan and was becoming less and less profitable under defendant's management.

Are the tests in these two cases the same? Consider also SCFC ILC, Inc. v. Visa USA, Inc., 936 F.2d 1096 (10th Cir.1991), the next case, *supra.* In that case compare how the trial court applied the factors for a preliminary injunction with how the court of appeals applied them.

2. *Appeals, Stays and Modification*

Federal Statutes Regarding Appeal of Interlocutory Orders

Unlike temporary restraining orders, preliminary injunctions are explicitly covered by the federal statutes and rules governing the appeal of interlocutory orders.

28 U.S.C.A. §§ 1291–92.

§ 1291. Final decisions of district courts

The courts of appeal (other than the United States Court of Appeal for the Federal Circuit) shall have jurisdiction of appeals from all final decisions of the district courts of the United States, the United States District Court for the District of the Canal Zone, the District Court of Guam, and the District Court of the Virgin Islands, except where a direct review may be had in the Supreme Court. * * *

§ 1292. Interlocutory decisions

(a) Except as provided in subsections (c) and (d) of this section, the courts of appeals shall have jurisdiction of appeals from:

(1) Interlocutory orders of the district courts of the United States, the United States District Court for the District of the Canal Zone, the District Court of Guam, and the District Court of the Virgin Islands, or of the judges thereof, granting, continuing, modifying, refusing or dissolving injunctions, or refusing to dissolve or modify injunctions, except where a direct review may be had in the Supreme Court. * * *

FEDERAL RULE OF CIVIL PROCEDURE 62(a), (c), (d), (g)

RULE 62. STAY OF PROCEEDINGS TO ENFORCE A JUDGMENT

(a) Automatic Stay; Exceptions—Injunctions, Receiverships, and Patent Accountings. Except as stated herein, no execution shall issue upon a judgment nor shall proceedings be taken for its enforcement until the expiration of 10 days after its entry. Unless otherwise ordered by the court, an interlocutory or final judgment in an action for an injunction or in a receivership action, or a judgment or order directing an accounting in an action for infringement of letters patent, shall not be stayed during the period after its entry and until an appeal is taken or during the pendency of an appeal. The provisions of subdivision (c) of this rule govern the suspending, modifying, restoring, or granting of an injunction during the pendency of an appeal.

* * *

(c) Injunction Pending Appeal. When an appeal is taken from an interlocutory or final judgment granting, dissolving, or denying an injunction, the court in its discretion may suspend, modify, restore, or grant an injunction during the pendency of the appeal upon such terms as to bond or otherwise as it considers proper for the security of the rights of the adverse party. If the judgment appealed from is rendered by a district court of three judges specially constituted pursuant to a statute of the United States, no such order shall be made except (1) by such court sitting in open court or (2) by the assent of all the judges of such court evidenced by their signatures to the order.

(d) Stay Upon Appeal. When an appeal is taken the appellant by giving a supersedeas bond may obtain a stay subject to the exceptions contained in subdivision (a) of this rule. The bond may be given at or after the time of filing of the notice of appeal or of procuring the order allowing the appeal, as the case may be. The stay is effective when the supersedeas bond is approved by the court.

* * *

(g) Power of Appellate Court Not Limited. The provisions in this rule do not limit any power of an appellate court or of a judge or justice thereof to stay proceedings during the pendency of an appeal or to suspend, modify, restore, or grant an injunction during the pendency of an appeal or to make any order appropriate to preserve the status quo or the effectiveness of the judgment subsequently to be entered.

FEDERAL RULE OF APPELLATE PROCEDURE 8(a)

RULE 8. STAY OR INJUNCTION PENDING APPEAL

(a) Stay Must Ordinarily Be Sought in the First Instance in District Court; Motion for Stay in Court of Appeals. Application for a stay of the judgment or order of a district court pending appeal, or for approval of a supersedeas bond, or for an order suspending, modifying, restoring or granting an injunction during the pendency of an appeal must ordinarily be made in the first instance in the district court. A motion for such relief may be made to the court of appeals or to a judge thereof, but the motion shall show that application to the district court for the relief sought is not practicable, or that the district court has denied an application, or has failed to afford the relief which the applicant requested, with the reasons given by the district court for its action. The motion shall also show the reasons for the relief requested and the facts relied upon, and if the facts are subject to dispute the motion shall be supported by affidavits or other sworn statements or copies thereof. With the motion shall be filed such parts of the record as are relevant. Reasonable notice of the motion shall be given to all parties. The motion shall be filed with the clerk and normally will be considered by a panel or division of the court, but in exceptional cases where such procedure would be impracticable due to the requirements of time, the application may be made to and considered by a single judge of the court.

SCFC ILC, INC. v. VISA USA, INC.

United States Court of Appeals, Tenth Circuit, 1991.
936 F.2d 1096.

In mid–1989, Sears, through its wholly-owned subsidiary, Greenwood Trust Corporation (the issuer of the Discover Card), applied to Visa, U.S.A. ("Visa") to become a Visa member. Visa denied Sears' application. Immediately thereafter, the Board of Directors of Visa enacted several amendments to the Visa by-laws and operating regulations specifically precluding Sears or any of its subsidiaries from issuing Visa cards.

On May 25, 1990, SCFC ILC, Inc. ("SCFC"), another wholly-owned subsidiary of Sears, acquired MountainWest Savings & Loan, a small Utah savings & loan, from the Resolution Trust Corporation ("RTC"). As a result of its purchase of MountainWest, Sears acquired a small Visa program which had been operated by the former MountainWest for the benefit of the local depositors.

In June of 1990, following the SCFC takeover, Visa requested MountainWest to reapply for Visa membership pursuant to its interpretation of Visa By-law § 2.08. MountainWest filled out the forms as requested * * * MountainWest did not at that time notify Visa that it was owned by a subsidiary of Sears, SCFC. On January 8, 1991, Visa's suspicions were aroused when it was notified that MountainWest had ordered 1.5 million Visa cards. The size of the order alone was sufficient to trigger an investigation by Visa because MountainWest, prior to being acquired by SCFC, had issued only 5,800 Visa cards to its account holders. MountainWest requested that the cards be printed with a "Prime Option" logo, which is a registered trademark of Dean Witter, a Sears' subsidiary. Once Visa realized that MountainWest was indirectly owned by Sears, and that Sears was attempting to use MountainWest's membership in Visa to launch its very aggressive Prime Option credit card program, Visa refused to approve the card order.

MountainWest filed suit in the United States District Court for the District of Utah raising federal and state antitrust and state unfair trade practice claims. Shortly after filing the lawsuit, MountainWest moved for a preliminary injunction to force Visa to approve the manufacture and delivery of the 1.5 million cards ordered by MountainWest. The district court granted the preliminary injunction. 763 F.Supp. 1094. Visa appealed to this court and requested that we stay the injunction pending our resolution of the issues. We granted Visa's request for a stay.

We must determine whether the district court erred in granting MountainWest's motion for a preliminary injunction. We will not set aside a preliminary injunction "[u]nless the district court abuses its discretion, commits an error of law, or is clearly erroneous in its preliminary factual findings * * *." * * * We will set aside a preliminary injunction if the district court applied the wrong standard when deciding to grant the preliminary injunction motion. * * *.

In order to obtain preliminary injunctive relief, the moving party must establish:

> (1) substantial likelihood that the movant will eventually prevail on the merits; (2) a showing that the movant will suffer irreparable injury unless the injunction issues; (3) proof that the threatened injury to the movant outweighs whatever damage the proposed injunction may cause the opposing party; and (4) a showing that the injunction, if issued, would not be adverse to the public interest.

* * *

In addition, the following types of preliminary injunctions are disfavored and they require that the movant satisfy an even heavier burden of showing that the four factors listed above weigh heavily and compellingly in movant's favor before such an injunction may be issued: (1) a preliminary injunction that disturbs the status quo; (2) a preliminary injunction that is mandatory as opposed to prohibitory; and (3) a preliminary injunction that affords the movant substantially all the relief he may recover at the conclusion of a full trial on the merits.

A preliminary injunction that alters the status quo goes beyond the traditional purpose for preliminary injunctions, which is only to preserve the status quo until a trial on the merits may be had. * * * Mandatory injunctions are more burdensome than prohibitory injunctions because they affirmatively require the nonmovant to act in a particular way, and as a result they place the issuing court in a position where it may have to provide ongoing supervision to assure that the nonmovant is abiding by the injunction. *See* Note, 78 Harv.L.Rev. 994, 1062–63 (1965). Finally, a preliminary injunction that awards the movant substantially all the relief he may be entitled to if he succeeds on the merits is similar to the "Sentence first—Verdict Afterwards" type of procedure parodied in Alice in Wonderland, which is an anathema to our system of jurisprudence. Thus, in order to prevail on a motion for preliminary injunction where the requested injunction falls into one or more of these three categories, the movant must show that on balance, the four factors weigh heavily and compellingly in his favor.

* * *

The preliminary injunction motion granted by the district court required Visa to approve MountainWest's 1.5 million card order bearing the Prime Option logo. Such an order would clearly have altered the status quo.[6] Visa had steadfastly refused to approve the order authorizing the new cards. As a result, MountainWest did not possess the cards for distribution. Thus, the status quo at the time the district court considered MountainWest's motion was that MountainWest was without the new cards, and Visa was continuing to refuse to approve the order.

MountainWest argues that the preliminary injunction motion granted by the district court would have preserved rather than altered the status quo because MountainWest was entitled, as a Visa member, to solicit new Visa customers, and that Visa was obligated under various federal and state laws to approve the manufacture and delivery of the cards requested by MountainWest. * * * MountainWest confuses "what should be" with "what is." While MountainWest may eventually succeed in convincing the district court, on the merits, to order Visa to issue the cards to it, a final decision so holding would unquestionably alter the status quo. The status quo is not defined by the parties existing *legal rights;* it is defined by the *reality* of the existing status and relationships between the parties, regardless of whether the existing status and relationships may ultimately be found to be in accord or not in accord with the parties' legal rights.[8]

Because the district court incorrectly concluded that the preliminary injunction would not alter the status quo, it failed to require MountainWest to carry its heavy burden of showing that under the four-part test in *Otero,* that the four factors, on balance, weigh heavily in MountainWest's favor. Thus, it abused its discretion. Because the record below is well developed, and because both parties claim a need for a resolution of this issue as quickly as possible, we see no reason to remand this case to the district court on the preliminary injunction issue; instead we will review the record to determine whether the preliminary injunctive relief requested by MountainWest is justified.

The first factor we examine is whether, in the absence of the requested injunctive relief, MountainWest will be irreparably harmed. MountainWest claims that if the injunction is not issued, it will miss its "window of opportunity" to launch the Prime Option program, and thus will be irreparably harmed. * * * MountainWest offers only generalities and business speculation to establish its irreparable injury, and its evidence falls far short of the proof that is required to make a clear showing of irreparable injury. Further, we note that in the event MountainWest

6. In addition, the preliminary injunction entered by the district court would have awarded the movant much of the relief to which it may be entitled in the event it prevails on the merits. Further, the preliminary injunction was mandatory in nature in that it required Visa to take the affirmative step of approving issuance of the new cards, even though in this particular case that would not have required a substantial amount of court involvement in assuring that Visa complied with its terms.

8. To the same effect, *see Stemple v. Board of Education of Prince George's County,* 623 F.2d 893 (4th Cir.1980), *cert. denied,* 450 U.S. 911, 101 S.Ct. 1348, 67 L.Ed.2d 334 (1981). There, status quo was defined as "the last uncontested status between the parties which preceded the controversy until the outcome of the final hearing." *Id.* at 898. *See generally Federal Practice & Procedure* § 2948, at 465. Visa persuasively argues that the last uncontested status between the parties was when Sears, through its Greenwood Trust subsidiary, requested membership in the Visa organization and was turned down. From that time forward, Sears never possessed the ability to market 1.5 million Visa cards under its Prime Option logo.

succeeds on the merits of its lawsuit, the potential for treble damages further undercuts its argument that it will be irreparably harmed unless we uphold the preliminary injunction.

The second factor we address is MountainWest's claim that any injury to Visa is outweighed by the harm MountainWest will suffer if the preliminary injunction is not granted. Irreparable injury is frequently presumed where a trademark is wrongfully appropriated by another. * * * If MountainWest loses the case on the merits in the court below, Visa will have been injured because MountainWest will have improperly availed itself of the Visa mark as well as the good will carried with it. * * *

The third factor we address is MountainWest's claim that the public interest would not be harmed if the preliminary injunction were granted. Visa claims that the public interest requires deliberate consideration, not haste, in this important controversy. There is also the underlying concern about the impact on public confidence in the nation's credit card system if 1.5 million Prime Option cards are ultimately held to have been improperly issued. MountainWest counters by arguing that its Prime Option card is so attractive that the public will be injured if its entry into the Visa charge card market is delayed. * * *

If Visa were to prevail on the merits below, it is uncertain from this record whether Visa would cancel the Prime Option cards in circulation or whether the Prime Option program would simply be sold to an acceptable issuer. Thus, the potential harm to the public if the preliminary injunction is granted and later found to have been improper is speculative. Although this prong of the test does not involve a balancing of public harm, we nonetheless note that MountainWest has not established any credible significant harm to the public that would be caused by a delay in introducing the Prime Option program until after a full trial on the merits. We have reviewed the benefits associated with the Prime Option program, and, even if other credit card issuers were not already offering many of these same benefits to their customers, we do not find anything in that program that would establish a compelling public interest in having that program available to the public even before trial can be held to determine whether MountainWest has the right to provide such a program under the Visa card system.[10] * * *

The last factor MountainWest must establish is a *substantial* likelihood that it will succeed on the merits. The issues are complex and will need significant development before this court could posit a meaningful prediction as to the strength of MountainWest's claims and the eventual outcome on the merits. However, this does not mean that this fourth factor itself is in equipoise. It is MountainWest's burden to prove a substantial likelihood

10. Indeed, MountainWest's public interest claim is undermined by the arguments it raised in the irreparable harm section of its brief. MountainWest argued that other competitors may preempt its Prime Option program if it is not allowed to rush it to market. Clearly, if MountainWest's competitors can quickly fill this "void," the public will not be harmed by the Prime Option card's absence from the charge card market until a trial on the merits can be held.

that it will succeed on the merits, and on the record before us MountainWest has not sustained that burden.[11]

After reviewing these four preliminary injunction factors, we hold that MountainWest has not met its heightened burden of showing that on balance the factors weigh heavily and compellingly in its favor. To the extent the injunction alters the status quo by requiring Visa to approve the issuance of Prime Option cards to MountainWest, it is improper. Therefore, we VACATE the preliminary injunction and REMAND to the district court for further proceedings not inconsistent with this opinion.

FEDERAL TRADE COMM'N v. WEYERHAEUSER CO.

United States Court of Appeals, District of Columbia Circuit, 1981.
648 F.2d 739.

Before MACKINNON, MIKVA and EDWARDS, CIRCUIT JUDGES.

ORDER

PER CURIAM.

On consideration of appellant's motion for injunction pending appeal, and of the responses filed with respect thereto, and for the reasons set forth in the attached *per curiam* opinion to be published at a later date, it is

Ordered by the Court that appellant's motion for injunction pending appeal is granted. It is

Further Ordered by the Court, *sua sponte,* that the parties are directed to return to the *status quo* existing at the time when the motion for injunctive relief was denied in the District Court. It is

Further Ordered by the Court that this case will be expedited on the merits.

Opinion PER CURIAM.

* * *

This case is before us on a motion of the Federal Trade Commission for injunctive relief pending appeal. * * *

The FTC asked the District Court to enjoin the proposed acquisition by Weyerhaeuser Company and its wholly-owned subsidiary, Weybuy, Inc. of certain assets of Menasha Corporation. Weyerhaeuser is the seventh largest producer of corrugating medium on the West Coast, and the largest producer of corrugated containers in the United States; Menasha is the

11. We have no finding from the district court on this factor. It erroneously concluded that it did not need to address this factor because it had found the other three factors in favor of MountainWest. Although there may be occasions when this factor may be deemphasized because of a particularly compelling showing on the other three factors, it ordinarily deserves some attention. Particularly in cases where the requested preliminary injunction alters the status quo, is mandatory in nature, or will grant the movant a significant part of the relief it seeks at trial, the movant will ordinarily find it difficult to meet its heavy burden of showing that the four factors, on balance, weigh heavily and compellingly in its favor, without showing a substantial likelihood of success on the merits.

third largest producer of corrugating medium on the West Coast. District Court Findings of Fact and Conclusions of Law, ¶¶ 5, 7. The District Court Judge found that the proposed merger "will significantly increase concentration in the market; it will result in the elimination of a substantial competitor; and it will increase the likelihood of collusion." *Id.,* ¶ 42. Judge Pratt thus concluded that "the Commission has established a likelihood of success on the merits." *Id.,* ¶ 56.

Despite these findings, the District Court determined that private equities favoring defendant Menasha's shareholders militated against the issuance of a preliminary injunction. *Id.,* ¶¶ 57–56. Because Menasha is a privately held, family-owned corporation, its shareholders have few opportunities to realize the value of their stock. *Id.,* ¶ 58. The District Court concluded that the benefits to Menasha and its shareholders were "important equities favoring denial of a preliminary injunction." *Id.,* ¶ 65.

We believe that there are significant reasons to suggest that the District Court misapplied Section 13(b) of the Federal Trade Commission Act, 15 U.S.C. § 53(b), and misinterpreted the recent decision of this court in FTC v. Exxon Corp., 636 F.2d 1336 (D.C.Cir.1980). In essence, the District Court has ruled that if the shareholders of a company to be acquired stand to gain substantial financial benefits from a proposed transaction, that transaction should be allowed to proceed—subject only to a "hold separate" order—*even though found in all likelihood to be unlawful.* We do not so read Section 13(b). While we agree that private equities may be considered in a motion for injunctive relief, we do not believe that those equities may be given *conclusive effect* at the nearly complete expense of the public interest also present. As a result, we find that there is a strong likelihood that the FTC will prevail on the merits of its appeal. * * * The FTC has met the heavy standard set forth in Virginia Petroleum Jobbers Ass'n v. Federal Power Comm'n, 259 F.2d 921, 925 (D.C.Cir.1958), and we accordingly grant the FTC's motion for an injunction pending appeal. We refer this case to a merits panel to determine on an expedited basis whether the District Court abused its discretion in denying the request for a preliminary injunction.

Enjoining the proposed acquisition is made more difficult, however, by the parties' determination to present the merger to this court as a *fait accompli.* On the evening of March 25, 1981, only a few hours after the District Court had denied the preliminary injunction, Weyerhaeuser and Menasha took the formal steps necessary to consummate their transaction before this court could grant a stay. * * *

The defendants acted at their peril in completing the act that the FTC sought to enjoin. *See* Jones v. SEC, 298 U.S. 1, 18, 56 S.Ct. 654, 658, 80 L.Ed. 1015 (1936). It is well established that "where a defendant with notice in an injunction proceeding completes the acts sought to be enjoined the court may by mandatory injunction restore the *status quo.*" Porter v. Lee, 328 U.S. 246, 251, 66 S.Ct. 1096, 1099, 90 L.Ed. 1199 (1956). *See* Industrial Bank of Washington v. Tobriner, 405 F.2d 1321, 1323 (D.C.Cir. 1968); Ramsburg v. American Investment Co., 231 F.2d 333 (7th Cir.1956) (mandatory injunction may issue to dissolve merger completed on same day motion for temporary injunction denied, where parties had notice that denial of injunction would be appealed). * * * Given the circumstances of this case and our disposition of the FTC's motion, we believe it appropriate to order the parties to return to the *status quo* existing at the time when the motion for injunctive relief was denied in the District Court. The necessary parties, appellees Weyerhaeuser, Weybuy, and Menasha, are all present before this court.

We acknowledge that there is some possibility, albeit speculative, that shareholders of appellee Menasha may be harmed if the proposed merger is barred by injunctive relief. In this case, however, such harm results from the strong showing that has been made that the proposed transaction is unlawful, and not from the issuance of an injunction. Furthermore, whatever need Menasha shareholders may have to liquify their assets, that need cannot be satisfied through a potentially illegal merger that is subject to the strictures of Section 13(b). Additionally, our order requires expedition to ensure a prompt resolution of this matter. We believe that the standards of *Virginia Petroleum Jobbers* have been met in this case, and that an injunction pending appeal must issue. The actions of the parties cannot be allowed to frustrate the public interest by completing a transaction of such dubious validity.*

MacKinnon, Circuit Judge (dissenting):

The majority concludes that "[t]he FTC has met the heavy standard set forth in *Virginia Jobbers Ass'n v. Federal Power Comm'n,* 259 F.2d 921, 925 (D.C.Cir.1958) * * *," Op. at 741, but ignores facts essential to a correct application of that standard and in effect erroneously places the burden of persuasion on the defendants.

Under *Virginia Jobbers,* the FTC must justify the extraordinary relief of an injunction pending appeal on the basis of four factors:

> (1) Has the petitioner made a strong showing that it is likely to prevail on the merits of its appeal? * * * (2) Has the petitioner shown that without such relief, it will be irreparably injured? * * * (3) Would the issuance of a stay substantially harm other parties interested in the proceedings? * * * (4) Where lies the public interest? * * * The public interest may, of course, have many facets. * * * We must determine, these many facets considered, how the court's action serves the public best.

In my view the majority errs by (1) exaggerating the strength of the FTC's case by not considering all of the criteria under which it should be judged,

* The appellate court subsequently affirmed the trial court's denial of a preliminary injunction on the merits. Federal Trade Commission v. Weyerhaeuser Co., 665 F.2d 1072 (D.C.Cir.1981). Judge Ruth Ginsburg observed, "[A]lthough the motions panel * * * ordered the merger undone, the parties have not accomplished the dissolution. * * * The appropriate method of undoing the merger has become an academic question in view of our affirmance of the district court's order." *Id.* at 1076. She then approved the action taken by the motions panel and criticized the district court's resistance to issuing a holding order of any kind: "A temporary restraint pending an application to this court would have provided the breathing space warranted under the circumstances without implying that the district judge was insecure about the judgment he had made." *Id.* at 1077.

(2) ignoring the FTC's inability to demonstrate irreparable harm, (3) excessively discounting the substantial harm that granting interim relief may do to the shareholders of Menasha, and (4) being unduly selective in determining which facets of the public interest it will consider.

* * *

LOPEZ v. HECKLER

United States Court of Appeals, Ninth Circuit, 1983.
713 F.2d 1432.

Before PREGERSON, BOOCHEVER and REINHARDT, CIRCUIT JUDGES.

REINHARDT, CIRCUIT JUDGE.

The Secretary of Health and Human Services seeks a partial stay pending appeal of a preliminary injunction issued by the United States District Court for the Central District of California. *See* Fed.R.App.P. 8(a); * Ninth Circuit R.App.P. 6(h). The order requires the restoration of disability benefits to a large number of Social Security recipients. From 28,000 to 78,000 individuals may be eligible. We reject the Secretary's request for a stay and allow the preliminary injunction to stand.

BACKGROUND

The underlying dispute before the district court involves a class action challenge to policies and procedures used by the Secretary in terminating Social Security disability benefits. * * * According to findings made by the district court, since March of 1981 the Social Security Administration has drastically increased the rate at which it reviews the status of persons receiving disability benefits. As a result, the number of people who have had their benefits terminated annually has doubled—from 98,000 removed from the disability rolls in fiscal year 1981 to 195,474 terminated in fiscal year 1982.

Plaintiffs contend that the procedures used by the Secretary of Health and Human Services in terminating the benefits of disabled persons are in direct violation of two decisions of this court. In Patti v. Schweiker, 669 F.2d 582, 587 (9th Cir.1982), and Finnegan v. Matthews, 641 F.2d 1340, 1345 (9th Cir.1981), we held that before Social Security disability benefits can be terminated on the ground that the recipient is no longer disabled, the Secretary must introduce evidence that the recipient's medical condition has improved. The principal rationale underlying these decisions is that the Social Security Administration's initial determination of disability creates a presumption that the person remains disabled. To terminate benefits, then, the Secretary is "required to 'meet or rebut' " the presumption "with evidence that [the recipient's] condition has improved in the interim." *Patti,* 669 F.2d at 587. *See also* Rivas v. Weinberger, 475 F.2d 255, 258 (5th Cir.1973) ("Once evidence has been presented which supports a finding that a given condition exists it is presumed in the absence of proof to the contrary that the condition has remained unchanged.").

* For the text of Federal Rule of Appellate Procedure 8(a), see *supra* p. 58.

The Secretary of Health and Human Services subsequently announced that she "does not acquiesce" in and therefore would not follow this court's holdings in *Patti* and *Finnegan.*[4] *See* Social Security Rulings 82–10c and 82–49c. Instead, the Secretary has ordered that Social Security disability benefits be terminated on the ground of lack of disability regardless of whether the recipient's medical condition has improved since the time of the initial disability determination. *See* Social Security Ruling 81–6.

This policy was challenged by plaintiffs in district court. Plaintiffs' suit is framed in large part as a constitutional challenge to the policy of nonacquiescence. Plaintiffs argue that the policy violates the principles of separation of powers and *stare decisis* as well as their rights to due process and equal protection.

On June 16, 1983, in a thorough, careful, and well-reasoned decision, Senior District Judge William P. Gray granted plaintiffs' motion for a preliminary injunction. 572 F.Supp. 26. The court restrained the Secretary "[f]rom failing to follow, implement or accord precedential effect to" *Finnegan* and *Patti* and from implementing the nonacquiescence policy announced in Social Security Rulings 82–10c, 82–49c, and 81–6.

The Secretary did not seek to stay these aspects of the district court's order. Rather, the government requested that the following portion of the district court's injunction be stayed pending appeal:

> (c)(i) Within sixty (60) days following the date of this order, the defendants will notify (a) each class member who had been receiving Supplemental Security Income Disability benefits under 42 U.S.C. § 1382c(a)(3)(E), and who was terminated from such benefits after August 25, 1980, and (b) all other persons who have been terminated from either Title II social security disability insurance or Title XVI Supplemental Security Income Disability after August 30, 1981, for the purported reason that his or her disability had ceased, whether or not such person has appealed, that:
>
> > Such person may apply for reinstatement of benefits if he or she believes that his or her medical condition has not improved following the granting of disability benefits.
>
> (ii) Upon receiving such application, the defendants will forthwith reinstate and pay benefits in the monthly amounts such person would have been receiving had his or her benefits not been interrupted. * * *

The Secretary's request for a partial stay and for a temporary stay, characterized by the government as an "emergency motion," was filed on Thursday, August 11, 1983—56 days after the district court issued the preliminary injunction and only four days before the Monday on which the Secretary was required to notify terminated recipients of their eligibility for reinstatement. This court received the lengthy papers and record in this case on Friday, August 12, 1983. On Saturday, August 13, we issued a six

4. The Secretary did not seek Supreme Court review of our decisions in either *Patti* or *Finnegan.* The individual litigants in the two cases did, however, receive the relief mandated by this court.

page order rejecting the Secretary's request for a temporary stay and declining to act "on an emergency basis" on the request for a partial stay. Our decision was based in part on the fact that the requirement that terminated recipients be notified by August 15, 1983 of their potential eligibility for benefits was the only immediate obligation imposed upon the government. We reasoned that the bulk of the administrative costs and the cost of reinstating benefits—the source of the injury which the Secretary argues justifies a stay—would not start to accrue until later, when the former recipients begin reapplying for benefits. Thus, we saw no necessity to issue a temporary stay or to grant a partial stay pending appeal on an "emergency" basis—especially given the Secretary's unexplained delay in seeking such relief.

On Monday, August 15, 1983, the Secretary, in compliance with paragraph (c)(i) of the district court's order, notified 28,557 members of the plaintiff class of their eligibility to reapply for disability benefits. The issue remaining before us is whether the Secretary must now comply with the remainder of paragraph (c). In other words, while the appeal from the preliminary injunction order is pending, must the Secretary reinstate benefits to those disabled persons who file applications, and may she then terminate those benefits only in accordance with the procedures required by our decisions in *Patti* and *Finnegan?*

STANDARD OF REVIEW

The standard for evaluating stays pending appeal is similar to that employed by district courts in deciding whether to grant a preliminary injunction. In this circuit there are two interrelated legal tests for the issuance of a preliminary injunction. These tests are "not separate" but rather represent "the outer reaches 'of a single continuum.'" At one end of the continuum, the moving party is required to show both a probability of success on the merits and the possibility of irreparable injury. At the other end of the continuum, the moving party must demonstrate that serious legal questions are raised and that the balance of hardships tips sharply in its favor. "[T]he relative hardship to the parties" is the "critical element" in deciding at which point along the continuum a stay is justified. Benda v. Grand Lodge of International Association of Machinists, etc., 584 F.2d 308, 314–15 (9th Cir.1978), cert. dismissed, 441 U.S. 937, 99 S.Ct. 2065, 60 L.Ed.2d 667 (1979). In addition, in cases such as the one before us, the public interest is a factor to be strongly considered.

* * *

DISCUSSION

I. Irreparable Injury, the Balance of Hardships, and the Public Interest.

The Secretary's contention that the government will suffer substantial hardship in the absence of a stay pending appeal is premised solely on the financial and administrative costs of reinstating disability benefits to former recipients. According to the Secretary, 28,557 terminated recipients were notified on August 15, 1983, of their eligibility to reapply for benefits. The government estimates that if every one of these former recipients reapplies for benefits, the total monthly cost of restoring benefits pending readjudication of claims will be $12,000,000. The government puts the total administrative cost of implementing the district court order at $10,-300,000.

The district court's injunction will undoubtedly impose some burden on the government. Even if we accept the Secretary's estimates at face value, however, the government has not demonstrated that the balance of hardships tips in its favor.[6] On the contrary, we agree with the district court's conclusion that the balance of hardships in this case strongly favors plaintiffs. * * *

Plaintiffs do not attempt to match in dollars and cents the monetary harms that will allegedly be suffered by the government. Yet the physical and emotional suffering shown by plaintiffs in the record before us is far more compelling than the possibility of some administrative inconvenience or monetary loss to the government. We find ample support for Judge Gray's persuasive finding "that some who have unexpectedly lost benefits have already suffered deprivation of life's necessities, further illness, or even death from the very disabilities that the Secretary deemed them not to have." Faced with such a conflict between financial concerns and preventable human suffering, we have little difficulty concluding that the balance of hardships tips decidedly in plaintiffs' favor.

We also consider it crucial that, because the members of plaintiffs' class are largely infirm and disabled, their resources and life spans are by definition extremely limited. Deprivation of benefits pending trial might cause economic hardship, suffering or even death. Retroactive restoration of benefits would be inadequate to remedy these hardships.[7] * * *

Here, the question of the public interest is inseparable from the issues relating to the relative hardship suffered by the litigants. Up to now, we have discussed the government's interest only in the narrowest terms—the administrative and financial impact of the preliminary injunction. For purposes of determining the relative hardship to the parties, it may be appropriate to do so—to judge the government's narrow interest in terms of its role as a litigant. In a broader sense, however, the government's interest is the same as the public interest. The government must be concerned not just with the public fisc but also with the public weal. In assessing this broader interest, we are not bound by the government's

6. There are several reasons to believe that the Secretary's arguments regarding financial harm are somewhat exaggerated. To begin with, most of the increased administrative workload—the holding of hearings—will not occur automatically; rather, hearings will be necessary only in cases in which the Secretary believes that there is evidence that she can introduce to show an improvement in medical condition, and thus a proper basis for terminating benefits.

Second, there is no evidence in the record that the increased expenditures necessitated by the district court's order would imperil the Social Security trust fund. * * *

Third, the government's cost estimates ignore the increased burden placed on state and local taxpayers by the Secretary's actions. * * *

7. We also note, but do not place much emphasis on, the fact that the government will have the opportunity to recover benefits that were paid erroneously. The district court has expressly conditioned the receipt of reinstated benefits under the preliminary injunction on the Secretary's right to recoup such payments if the recipient is subsequently terminated in accordance with *Patti* and *Finnegan*. This may well be more of an illusory than a practical remedy.

litigation posture. Rather, we make an independent judgment as to the public interest.

It is not only the harm to the individuals involved that we must consider in assessing the public interest. Our society as a whole suffers when we neglect the poor, the hungry, the disabled, or when we deprive them of their rights or privileges. Society's interest lies on the side of affording fair procedures to all persons, even though the expenditure of governmental funds is required. It would be tragic, not only from the standpoint of the individuals involved but also from the standpoint of society, were poor, elderly, disabled people to be wrongfully deprived of essential benefits for any period of time. It would be unfortunate, but far less harmful to society, were the government to succeed in overturning the preliminary injunction but be unable to recoup all or a portion of the funds.

In summary, the balance of hardships as between the litigants lies sharply in favor of the plaintiffs. When the public interest is included, that balance is overwhelming.

II. Probability of Success on the Merits and the Existence of Serious Legal Questions.

The Secretary makes two principal arguments regarding the merits of her appeal from the order granting the preliminary injunction. First, the Secretary attempts to defend her policy of "nonacquiescence" with federal court decisions. This defense, presented in a footnote to the government's brief, is far from persuasive. * * *

* * *

The majority of the Secretary's attention is devoted to her second argument: that the district court improperly exercised jurisdiction over some members of plaintiffs' class. * * *

* * *

Although the Secretary may have raised "serious legal questions," she has failed to make a showing of probability of success on the merits. * * *

CONCLUSION

The Secretary has the weaker position on both aspects of the interrelated test governing stays. The balance of hardships tips sharply toward the plaintiffs, even without including the public interest factor, and it is not probable that the Secretary will succeed on the merits of her appeal from the order granting a preliminary injunction. Finally, the public interest strongly supports denial of the stay.

The request for a partial stay is Denied.

Notes

1. In both *FTC* and *Lopez,* the federal court of appeals was asked to issue "pre-appeal" injunctive relief pending the hearing on the merits of the appeal from the district court's denial (*FTC*) or grant (*Lopez*) of the plaintiff's prayer for preliminary injunctive relief. Was there any difference between the standard applied by the *FTC* trial court in determining whether to issue a preliminary injunction and the standard applied by the appellate court in

considering the plaintiff's motion for an injunction pending appeal? Was there any difference between the preliminary injunction standard in *Lopez* and the standard for evaluating a stay pending appeal?

2. Did the courts in *FTC* and *Lopez* apply an "abuse of discretion" standard in determining whether to grant "pre-appeal" relief? Why not? Does this mean that the trial courts' rulings in *FTC* and *Lopez* regarding preliminary injunctive relief might be affirmed on appeal?

3. Federal Rule of Civil Procedure 62(a), *supra* p. 57, provides for no automatic stay of an interlocutory judgment in an injunction proceeding. Other jurisdictions have different rules, however, as discussed in Developments in the Law—Injunctions, 78 Harv.L.Rev. 994, 1072–74 (1965) *:

> "Today, a great variety of rules involving combinations of automatic stays and supersedeas ** have developed in American jurisdictions * * *: (1) automatic stays of all injunctions by filing of appeal; (2) the California rule: automatic stay of mandatory injunctions; stay of prohibitory injunctions on a showing of hardship; (3) automatic stays of mandatory injunctions; no stay or supersedeas available for prohibitory injunctions; (4) the federal rule: no automatic stays; supersedeas in all cases in which a proper showing can be made; (5) supersedeas available on showing of necessity for mandatory but not for prohibitory injunctions.
>
> "Of these rules, only the federal (4) has sufficient flexibility; under all the others, once an injunction is shown to be mandatory or prohibitory, certain consequences—stay or no stay—automatically flow. * * * The mandatory-prohibitory distinction bears no necessary relation to the hardships resulting from an injunction. If *D* has been enjoined from seeding clouds over his ranch because the seeding results in diverting rainfall from *P*'s land, the injunction should be stayed if at the moment *D* has a crop that might die from lack of water while *P*'s land is fallow, notwithstanding the fact that the injunction would likely be considered prohibitory. Conversely, if *D* has been removing large quantities of water from a stream and is ordered to furnish some to *P*, the injunction should not be stayed pending appeal if *D*'s supply is in excess of his needs and *P*'s is insufficient, despite the fact that the injunction would generally be termed mandatory. In actuality, it is frequently impossible to tell whether action or nonaction is required: when a school board is ordered to stop discriminating against Negroes, is an act or nonact called for? Many jurisdictions retaining the mandatory-prohibitory distinction recognize its limitations and provide that a stay may be granted or denied contrary to the rule by the exercise of special power when necessity requires; these courts may, however, be unduly reluctant to exercise a power regarded as extraordinary."

Consider the impact of the California rule. If the plaintiff succeeds in obtaining a preliminary injunction that orders the defendant to remove a fence obstructing access to the plaintiff's property, what will happen when the defendant appeals the issuance of the preliminary injunction? *See* Kettenhofen v. Superior Court, 55 Cal.2d 189, 10 Cal.Rptr. 356, 358 P.2d 684 (1961).

** A writ of supersedeas stays or "supersedes" the judgment of the lower court pending the appeal.

4. Consider the extent to which traditional stay concepts may have been altered in First Amendment cases by the decision of the United States Supreme Court in National Socialist Party v. Skokie, 432 U.S. 43, 97 S.Ct. 2205, 53 L.Ed.2d 96 (1977). The state trial court issued a preliminary injunction prohibiting the Party from carrying out certain activities in Skokie, Illinois, including "parading in the uniform of the Party"; "displaying the swastika"; and disseminating pamphlets that "incite or promote hatred against persons of Jewish faith or ancestry or hatred against any persons of any faith or ancestry, race or religion." Illinois appellate courts denied requests for stays pending appeal. Moreover, the Illinois Supreme Court denied a stay as well as a request for an expedited appeal to that court. The Party then sought a stay from the United States Supreme Court and the Court reversed the Illinois Supreme Court. According to the Court, the Illinois Supreme Court "finally determined the merits of petitioners' claim that the outstanding injunction will deprive them of rights protected by the First Amendment during the period of appellate review which, in the normal course, may take a year or more to complete. If a State seeks to impose a restraint of this kind, it must provide strict procedural safeguards, Freedman v. Maryland, 380 U.S. 51, 85 S.Ct. 734, 13 L.Ed.2d 649 (1965), including immediate appellate review, see Nebraska Press Ass'n v. Stuart, 423 U.S. 1319, 1327, 96 S.Ct. 237, 251, 46 L.Ed.2d 199, 237 (1975) (Blackmun, J., in chambers). Absent such review, the State must instead allow a stay. The order of the Illinois Supreme Court constituted a denial of that right." 432 U.S. at 44, 97 S.Ct. at 2206. *See also* M.I.C. Ltd. v. Bedford Township, 463 U.S. 1341, 104 S.Ct. 17, 77 L.Ed.2d 1442 (1983).

5. Although the federal courts have appellate jurisdiction over rulings regarding preliminary injunctions, some states authorize appellate jurisdiction in such cases only in extraordinary circumstances: *

> "The purpose of a preliminary injunction is ordinarily to preserve the *status quo* pending trial on the merits. Its issuance is a matter of discretion to be exercised by the hearing judge after a careful balancing of the equities. Its impact is temporary and lasts no longer than the pendency of the action. Its decree bears no precedent to guide the final determination of the rights of the parties. In form, purpose, and effect, it is purely interlocutory. Thus, the threshold question presented by a purported appeal from an order granting a preliminary injunction is whether the appellant has been deprived of any substantial right which might be lost should the order escape appellate review before final judgment. If no such right is endangered, the appeal cannot be maintained. G.S. 1-277; Pruitt v. Williams, 288 N.C. 368, 218 S.E.2d 348 (1975).
>
> * * *
>
> "Our refusal to allow defendants' appeal is not a surrender to technical requirements of finality. The statutes and rules governing appellate review are more than procedural niceties. They are designed to streamline the judicial process, to forestall delay rather than engender it. 'There is no more effective way to procrastinate the administration of justice than that of bringing cases to an appellate court piecemeal through the medium of

* By contrast, a few states permit a wider scope of interlocutory review than that authorized by the federal statutes and rules of civil procedure. *See, e.g.,* Christian, Interlocutory Review in California—Practical Justice Unguided by Standards, 47 Law & Contemp.Probs. 111 (1984).

successive appeals from intermediate orders.' Veasey v. Durham, 231 N.C. 357, 363, 57 S.E.2d 377, 382 (1950)."

State v. Fayetteville Street Christian School, 299 N.C. 351, 261 S.E.2d 908, 913 (1980); *accord* Crafts v. Quinn, 482 A.2d 825 (Me.1984).

Would the appellants in *AMA, supra* p. 31, or in *Abbott Laboratories, supra* p. 35, have been entitled to bring an appeal under the rule quoted above? Would an appeal have been allowed in either *Tustin, supra* p. 52, or *Miller, supra* p. 54? What policy considerations might Congress have taken into account when it enacted 28 U.S.C. § 1292(a)(1) (authorizing appeals from interlocutory orders granting or refusing injunctions)? *See* C. Wright, The Law of Federal Courts § 102 (1983).

6. By the time an appellate court considers the issuance of a preliminary injunction on its merits, equitable relief may be unnecessary in whole or in part. In such cases, the appellate court may dissolve or modify the injunction on the grounds that it is no longer equitably justified. *E.g.,* Cross Wood Products, Inc. v. Suter, 97 Ill.App.3d 282, 52 Ill.Dec. 744, 422 N.E.2d 953 (1981) (dissolving preliminary injunction not to compete with plaintiff's business; order had been in effect for two years).*

D. PERMANENT INJUNCTIONS

1. *Standards for Issuance*

WALGREEN CO. v. SARA CREEK PROPERTY CO.

United States Court of Appeals, Seventh Circuit, 1992.
966 F.2d 273.

POSNER, CIRCUIT JUDGE.

This appeal from the grant of a permanent injunction raises fundamental issues concerning the propriety of injunctive relief 775 F.Supp. 1192 (E.D.Wis.1991). The essential facts are simple. Walgreen has operated a pharmacy in the Southgate Mall in Milwaukee since its opening in 1951. Its current lease, signed in 1971 and carrying a 30–year, 6–month term, contains, as had the only previous lease, a clause in which the landlord, Sara Creek, promises not to lease space in the mall to anyone else who wants to operate a pharmacy or a store containing a pharmacy. Such an exclusivity clause, common in shopping-center leases, is occasionally challenged on antitrust grounds, * * * implausibly enough, given the competition among malls; but that is an issue for another day, since in this appeal Sara Creek does not press the objection it made below to the clause on antitrust grounds.

In 1990, fearful that its largest tenant—what in real estate parlance is called the "anchor tenant"—having gone broke was about to close its store, Sara Creek informed Walgreen that it intended to buy out the anchor tenant and install in its place a discount store operated by Phar–Mor Corporation, a "deep discount" chain, rather than, like Walgreen, just a "discount" chain. Phar–Mor's store would occupy 100,000 square feet, of

* For cases discussing the enforcement of covenants not to compete, *see infra* Chapter 5, Section 4.

which 12,000 would be occupied by a pharmacy the same size as Walgreen's. The entrances to the two stores would be within a couple of hundred feet of each other.

Walgreen filed this diversity suit for breach of contract against Sara Creek and Phar–Mor and asked for an injunction against Sara Creek's letting the anchor premises to Phar–Mor. After an evidentiary hearing, the judge found a breach of Walgreen's lease and entered a permanent injunction against Sara Creek's letting the anchor tenant premises to Phar–Mor until the expiration of Walgreen's lease. He did this over the defendants' objection that Walgreen had failed to show that its remedy at law—damages—for the breach of the exclusivity clause was inadequate. Sara Creek had put on an expert witness who testified that Walgreen's damages could be readily estimated, and Walgreen had countered with evidence from its employees that its damages would be very difficult to compute, among other reasons because they included intangibles such as loss of goodwill.

Sara Creek reminds us that damages are the norm in breach of contract as in other cases. Many breaches, it points out, are "efficient" in the sense that they allow resources to be moved into a more valuable use. * * * Perhaps this is one—the value of Phar–Mor's occupancy of the anchor premises may exceed the cost to Walgreen of facing increased competition. If so, society will be better off if Walgreen is paid its damages, equal to that cost, and Phar–Mor is allowed to move in rather than being kept out by an injunction. That is why injunctions are not granted as a matter of course, but only when the plaintiff's damages remedy is inadequate. * * * Walgreen's is not, Sara Creek argues; the projection of business losses due to increased competition is a routine exercise in calculation. Damages representing either the present value of lost future profits or (what should be the equivalent, * * *) the diminution in the value of the leasehold have either been awarded or deemed the proper remedy in a number of reported cases for breach of an exclusivity clause in a shopping-center lease. * * * Why, Sara Creek asks, should they not be adequate here?

Sara Creek makes a beguiling argument that contains much truth, but we do not think it should carry the day. For if, as just noted, damages have been awarded in some cases of breach of an exclusivity clause in a shopping-center lease, injunctions have been issued in others. * * * The choice between remedies requires a balancing of the costs and benefits of the alternatives. *Hecht Co. v. Bowles,* 321 U.S. 321, 329, 64 S.Ct. 587, 591, 88 L.Ed. 754 (1944); *Yakus v. United States,* 321 U.S. 414, 440, 64 S.Ct. 660, 674, 88 L.Ed. 834 (1944). The task of striking the balance is for the trial judge, subject to deferential appellate review in recognition of its particularistic, judgmental, fact-bound character. * * * As we said in an appeal from a grant of a preliminary injunction—but the point is applicable to review of a permanent injunction as well—"The question for us [appellate judges] is whether the [district] judge exceeded the bounds of permissible choice in the circumstances, not what we would have done if we had been in his shoes." *Roland Machinery Co. v. Dresser Industries, Inc.,* 749 F.2d 380, 390 (7th Cir.1984).

The plaintiff who seeks an injunction has the burden of persuasion—damages are the norm, so the plaintiff must show why his case is abnormal. But when, as in this case, the issue is whether to grant a permanent injunction, not whether to grant a temporary one, the burden is to show that damages are inadequate, not that the denial of the injunction will work irreparable harm. "Irreparable" in the injunction context means not rectifiable by the entry of a final judgment. * * * It has nothing to do with whether to grant a permanent injunction, which, in the usual case anyway, *is* the final judgment. The use of "irreparable harm" or "irreparable injury" as synonyms for inadequate remedy at law is a confusing usage. It should be avoided. * * *

The benefits of substituting an injunction for damages are twofold. First, it shifts the burden of determining the cost of the defendant's conduct from the court to the parties. If it is true that Walgreen's damages are smaller than the gain to Sara Creek from allowing a second pharmacy into the shopping mall, then there must be a price for dissolving the injunction that will make both parties better off. Thus, the effect of upholding the injunction would be to substitute for the costly processes of forensic fact determination the less costly processes of private negotiation. Second, a premise of our free-market system, and the lesson of experience here and abroad as well, is that prices and costs are more accurately determined by the market than by government. A battle of experts is a less reliable method of determining the actual cost to Walgreen of facing new competition than negotiations between Walgreen and Sara Creek over the price at which Walgreen would feel adequately compensated for having to face that competition.

That is the benefit side of injunctive relief but there is a cost side as well. Many injunctions require continuing supervision by the court, and that is costly. *Roland Machinery Co. v. Dresser Industries, Inc., supra,* 749 F.2d at 391–92; *Rodriguez v. VIA Metropolitan Transit System,* 802 F.2d 126, 132 (5th Cir.1986); *Bethlehem Engineering Export Co. v. Christie,* 105 F.2d 933, 935 (2d Cir.1939) (L. Hand, J.). A request for specific performance (a form of mandatory injunction) of a franchise agreement was refused on this ground in *North American Financial Group, Ltd. v. S.M.R. Enterprises, Inc.,* 583 F.Supp. 691, 699 (N.D.Ill.1984); see Edward Yorio, *Contract Enforcement: Specific Performance and Injunctions* § 3.3.2 (1989). This ground was also stressed in *Rental Development Corp. v. Lavery,* 304 F.2d 839, 841–42 (9th Cir.1962), a case involving a lease. Some injunctions are problematic because they impose costs on third parties. * * * A more subtle cost of injunctive relief arises from the situation that economists call "bilateral monopoly," in which two parties can deal only with each other: the situation that an injunction creates. * * * The sole seller of widgets selling to the sole buyer of that product would be an example. But so will be the situation confronting Walgreen and Sara Creek if the injunction is upheld. Walgreen can "sell" its injunctive right only to Sara Creek, and Sara Creek can "buy" Walgreen's surrender of its right to enjoin the leasing of the anchor tenant's space to Phar–Mor only from Walgreen. The lack of alternatives in bilateral monopoly creates a bargaining range, and the costs of negotiating to a point within that range may be high. Suppose the cost to Walgreen of facing the competition of Phar–Mor at the Southgate Mall would be $1 million, and the benefit to Sara Creek of leasing to Phar–Mor would be $2 million. Then at any price between those figures for a waiver of Walgreen's injunctive right both parties would be better off, and we expect parties to bargain around a judicial assignment of legal rights if the assignment is inefficient. R.H. Coase, "The Problem of Social Cost," 3 *J. Law & Econ.* 1 (1960). But each of the parties would like to engross as much of the bargaining range as possible—Walgreen to press the price toward $2 million, Sara Creek to depress it toward $1 million. With so much at stake, both parties will have an incentive to devote substantial resources of time and money to the negotiation process. The process may even break down, if one or both parties want to create for future use a reputation as a hard bargainer; and if it does break down, the injunction will have brought about an inefficient result. All these are in one form or another costs of the injunctive process that can be avoided by substituting damages.

The costs and benefits of the damages remedy are the mirror of those of the injunctive remedy. The damages remedy avoids the cost of continuing supervision and third-party effects, and the cost of bilateral monopoly as well. It imposes costs of its own, however, in the form of diminished accuracy in the determination of value, on the one hand, and of the parties' expenditures on preparing and presenting evidence of damages, and the time of the court in evaluating the evidence, on the other.

The weighing up of all these costs and benefits is the analytical procedure that is or at least should be employed by a judge asked to enter a permanent injunction, with the understanding that if the balance is even the injunction should be withheld. The judge is not required to explicate every detail of the analysis and he did not do so here, but as long we are satisfied that his approach is broadly consistent with a proper analysis we shall affirm; and we are satisfied here. The determination of Walgreen's damages would have been costly in forensic resources and inescapably inaccurate. *Roland Machinery Co. v. Dresser Industries, Inc., supra,* 749 F.2d at 386; *Olympia Equipment Leasing Co. v. Western Union Telegraph Co.,* 797 F.2d 370, 382 (7th Cir.1986); *K–Mart Corp. v. Oriental Plaza, Inc., supra,* 875 F.2d at 914–16. The lease had ten years to run. So Walgreen would have had to project its sales revenues and costs over the next ten years, and then project the impact on those figures of Phar–Mor's competition, and then discount that impact to present value. All but the last step would have been fraught with uncertainty.

* * *

Of course one can hire an expert to make such predictions, Glen A. Stankee, "Econometric Forecasting of Lost Profits: Using High Technology to Compute Commercial Damages," 61 *Fla.B.J.* 83 (1987), and if injunctive relief is infeasible the expert's testimony may provide a tolerable basis for an award of damages. We cited cases in which damages have been awarded for the breach of an exclusivity clause in a shopping-center lease. But they are awarded in such circumstances not because anyone thinks them a clairvoyant forecast but because it is better to give a wronged person a crude remedy than none at all. It is the same theory on which damages are awarded for a disfiguring injury. No one thinks such injuries readily monetizable, *City of Panama,* 101 U.S. 453, 464, 25 L.Ed. 1061 (1880); *McCarty v. Pheasant Run, Inc.,* 826 F.2d 1554, 1557 (7th Cir.1987); Marcus L. Plant, "Damages for Pain and Suffering," 19 *Ohio St.L.J.* 200, 205–06 (1958), but a crude estimate is better than letting the wrongdoer get off scot-free (which, not incidentally, would encourage more such injuries). Randall R. Bovbjerg *et al.,* "Valuing Life and Limb in Tort: Scheduling 'Pain and Suffering,'" 83 *Nw.U.L.Rev.* 908 (1989). Sara Creek presented evidence of what happened (very little) to Walgreen when Phar–Mor moved into other shopping malls in which Walgreen has a pharmacy, and it was on the right track in putting in comparative evidence. But there was a serious question whether the other malls were actually comparable to the Southgate Mall, so we cannot conclude, in the face of the district judge's contrary conclusion, that the existence of comparative evidence dissolved the difficulties of computing damages in this case. Sara Creek complains that the judge refused to compel Walgreen to produce all the data that Sara Creek needed to demonstrate the feasibility of forecasting Walgreen's damages. Walgreen resisted, on grounds of the confidentiality of the data and the cost of producing the massive data that Sara Creek sought. Those are legitimate grounds; and the cost (broadly conceived) they expose of pretrial discovery, in turn presaging complexity at trial, is itself a cost of the damages remedy that injunctive relief saves.

Damages are not always costly to compute, or difficult to compute accurately. In the standard case of a seller's breach of a contract for the sale of goods where the buyer covers by purchasing the same product in the market, damages are readily calculable by subtracting the contract price from the market price and multiplying by the quantity specified in the contract. But this is not such a case and here damages would be a costly and inaccurate remedy; and on the other side of the balance some of the costs of an injunction are absent and the cost that is present seems low. The injunction here, like one enforcing a covenant not to compete (standardly enforced by injunction, Yorio, *supra,* 401–08), is a simple negative injunction—Sara Creek is not to lease space in the Southgate Mall to Phar–Mor during the term of Walgreen's lease—and the costs of judicial supervision and enforcement should be negligible. There is no contention that the injunction will harm an *unrepresented* third party. It may harm Phar–Mor but that harm will be reflected in Sara Creek's offer to Walgreen to dissolve the injunction. (Anyway Phar–Mor *is* a party.) The injunction may also, it is true, harm potential customers of Phar–Mor—people who would prefer to shop at a deep-discount store than an ordinary discount store—but their preferences, too, are registered indirectly. The more business Phar–Mor would have, the more rent it will be willing to pay Sara Creek, and therefore the more Sara Creek will be willing to pay Walgreen to dissolve the injunction.

The only substantial cost of the injunction in this case is that it may set off a round of negotiations between the parties. In some cases, illustrated by *Boomer v. Atlantic Cement Co.,* 26 N.Y.2d 219, 309 N.Y.S.2d 312, 257 N.E.2d 870 (1970), this consideration alone would be enough to warrant the denial of injunctive relief. The defendant's factory was emitting cement dust that caused the plaintiffs harm monetized at less than $200,000, and the only way to abate the harm would have been to close down the factory, which had cost $45 million to build. An injunction against the nuisance could therefore have created a huge bargaining range (could, not would, because it is unclear what the current value of the factory was), and the costs of negotiating to a point within it might have been immense. If the market value of the factory was actually $45 million, the plaintiffs would be tempted to hold out for a price to dissolve the injunction in the tens of millions and the factory would be tempted to refuse to pay anything more than a few hundred thousand dollars. Negotiations would be unlikely to break down completely, given such a bargaining range, but they might well be protracted and costly. There is nothing so dramatic here. Sara Creek does not argue that it will have to close the mall if enjoined from leasing to Phar–Mor. Phar–Mor is not the only potential anchor tenant. Liza Danielle, Inc. v. Jamko, Inc., 408 So.2d 735, 740 (Fla.App.1982), on which Sara Creek relies, presented the converse case where the grant of the injunction would have forced an existing tenant to close its store. The size of the bargaining range was also a factor in the denial of injunctive relief in *Gitlitz v. Plankinton Building Properties, Inc.*, 228 Wis. 334, 339–40, 280 N.W. 415, 418 (1938).

To summarize, the judge did not exceed the bounds of reasonable judgment in concluding that the costs (including forgone benefits) of the damages remedy would exceed the costs (including forgone benefits) of an injunction. We need not consider whether, as intimated by Walgreen, exclusivity clauses in shopping-center leases should be considered presumptively enforceable by injunctions. Although we have described the choice between legal and equitable remedies as one for case-by-case determination, the courts have sometimes picked out categories of case in which injunctive relief is made the norm. The best-known example is specific performance of contracts for the sale of real property. * * * The rule that specific performance will be ordered in such cases as a matter of course is a generalization of the considerations discussed above. Because of the absence of a fully liquid market in real property and the frequent presence of subjective values (many a homeowner, for example, would not sell his house for its market value), the calculation of damages is difficult; and since an order of specific performance to convey a piece of property does not create a continuing relation between the parties, the costs of supervision and enforcement if specific performance is ordered are slight. The exclusivity clause in Walgreen's lease relates to real estate, but we hesitate to suggest that every contract involving real estate should be enforceable as a matter of course by injunctions. Suppose Sara Creek had covenanted to keep the entrance to Walgreen's store free of ice and snow, and breached the covenant. An injunction would require continuing supervision, and it would be easy enough if the injunction were denied for Walgreen to hire its own ice and snow remover and charge the cost to Sara Creek. Cf. *City of Michigan City v. Lake Air Corp.*, 459 N.E.2d 760 (Ind.App.1984). On the other hand, injunctions to enforce exclusivity clauses are quite likely to be justifiable by just the considerations present here—damages are difficult to estimate with any accuracy and the injunction is a one-shot remedy requiring no continuing judicial involvement. So there is an argument for making injunctive relief presumptively appropriate in such cases, but we need not decide in this case how strong an argument.

Affirmed.

HARLINGTON WOOD, JR., SENIOR CIRCUIT JUDGE, concurring.

I gladly join in the affirmance reached in Judge Posner's expert analysis.

SMITH v. WESTERN ELECTRIC CO.

Missouri Court of Appeals, 1982.
643 S.W.2d 10.

DOWD, PRESIDING JUDGE.

Plaintiff appeals from an order dismissing his petition on the ground that it fails to state a claim upon which relief can be granted.

The petition seeks an injunction to prevent plaintiff's employer from exposing him to tobacco smoke in the workplace and from affecting his pay or employment conditions because of his medical reaction to tobacco smoke. The petition alleges that by allowing smoking in the work area, defendant permits its employees to be exposed to a health hazard and thereby breaches its duty to provide a safe place in which to work.

Plaintiff contends the trial court erred in dismissing his petition in that it invokes legal principles entitling him to relief and shows that injunctive relief is appropriate. Plaintiff further contends that federal law does not preempt state common law in this case.

* * *

The petition includes the following allegations. Plaintiff has been employed by defendant since 1950 and has worked in defendant's Missouri branch since 1967. He is a nonsmoker sharing an open office area with other employees, many of whom smoke tobacco products as they work. In 1975 plaintiff began to experience serious respiratory tract discomfort as a result of inhaling tobacco smoke in the workplace. A subsequent medical evaluation determined that plaintiff suffers a severe adverse reaction to tobacco smoke. His symptoms include sore throat, nausea, dizziness, headache, blackouts, loss of memory, difficulty in concentration, aches and pains in joints, sensitivity to noise and light, cold sweat, gagging, choking sensations, and lightheadedness. After a sufficient period of non-exposure to smoke, plaintiff's symptoms abate somewhat. The symptoms have become increasingly severe over the years, however. Doctors evaluating and treating plaintiff have advised him to avoid contact with tobacco smoke whenever possible.

The petition further alleges that plaintiff first complained to defendant about the tobacco smoke in the workplace in 1975. Defendant thereafter moved plaintiff to different locations within the plant, but no improvement resulted because each location contained significant amounts of tobacco smoke. In 1978 plaintiff was informed that he should no longer submit complaints about the smoke through defendant's anonymous complaint procedure since defendant would not process them. In response to recommendations of the National Institute for Occupational Safety and Health, defendant adopted a smoking policy in April 1980. The declared policy was to protect the rights of both smokers and nonsmokers by providing accommodations for both groups and by making a reasonable effort to separate the groups in work areas. Because defendant has failed to implement its policy by making such a reasonable effort, improvement of the air in the workplace has not resulted.

* * *

The petition states that plaintiff has exhausted all avenues of relief through defendant; he has no adequate remedy at law; he is suffering and will continue to suffer irreparable physical injuries and financial losses unless defendant improves working conditions. * * *

* * *

The allegations of the instant case, taken as true, show that the tobacco smoke of co-workers smoking in the work area is hazardous to the health of employees in general and plaintiff in particular. The allegations also show that defendant knows the tobacco smoke is harmful to plaintiff's health and that defendant has the authority, ability, and reasonable means to control smoking in areas requiring a smoke-free environment. Therefore, by failing to exercise its control and assume its responsibility to eliminate the hazardous condition caused by tobacco smoke, defendant has breached and is breaching its duty to provide a reasonably safe workplace. See Shimp v. New Jersey Bell Telephone Co., 145 N.J.Super. 516, 368 A.2d 408 (1976). * * *

If plaintiff's petition establishes defendant's failure to provide a safe place for plaintiff to work, we must next consider whether injunctive relief would be an appropriate remedy. An injunction may issue "to prevent the doing of any legal wrong whatever, whenever in the opinion of the court an adequate remedy cannot be afforded by an action for damages." § 526.030 RSMo 1978. Injunctive relief is unavailable unless irreparable harm is otherwise likely to result, *see* City of Grandview v. Moore, 481 S.W.2d 555, 558 (Mo.App.1972), and plaintiff has no adequate remedy at law. *See* State ex rel. Taylor v. Anderson, 242 S.W.2d 66, 72 (Mo.1951).

The petition alleges that plaintiff's continuing exposure to smoke in the workplace is increasingly deleterious to his health and is causing irreparable harm. Assuming the allegations and reasonable inferences therefrom to be true, we think it is fair to characterize deterioration of plaintiff's health as "irreparable" and as a harm for which money damages cannot adequately compensate. This is particularly true where the harm has not yet resulted in full-blown disease or injury. Money damages, even though inadequate, are the best possible remedy once physical damage is done, but they are certainly inadequate to compensate permanent injury which could have been prevented. Plaintiff should not be required to await the harm's fruition before he is entitled to seek an inadequate remedy.

Moreover, the nature of plaintiff's unsafe work environment represents a recurrent risk of harm that would necessitate a multiplicity of lawsuits. Finally, the petition states that plaintiff has no adequate remedy at law and alleges facts indicating that prior to this action plaintiff unsuccessfully pursued relief, both through his employer's in-house channels and through administrative agencies. Viewing the petition favorably, as we must to determine its sufficiency, we find that injunction would be an appropriate remedy.

* * *

The judgment is reversed and the cause remanded.

Notes

1. The federal court standard for the issuance of a permanent injunction is set forth in Southern Packaging & Storage Co. v. United States, 588 F.Supp. 532, 544 (D.S.C.1984):

> "In determining whether or not to grant permanent injunctive relief, the court must consider: (1) whether plaintiff has actually succeeded on the merits, (2) whether plaintiff has an adequate remedy at law, (3) the public interest, (4) the balance of equities. It is not necessary that plaintiff show irreparable injury to obtain a permanent injunction, although the inadequacy of the legal remedy may be established by showing irreparable injury. *See* Lewis v. S.S. Baune, 534 F.2d 1115, 1123–24 (5th Cir.1976), reh. denied, 545 F.2d 1299 (5th Cir.1977); 11 Wright and Miller, Federal Practice and Procedure: Civil § 2944 at 399–401 (1973)."

How does the above-quoted standard for issuing permanent injunctions compare with the federal standards for issuing temporary restraining orders or preliminary injunctions? How does it compare with Justice Shirley Abrahamson's formulation of the common law standard for issuing permanent injunctions quoted below?

> "Permanent injunctions are not to be issued lightly. The cause must be substantial. Because an injunction is enforceable by the contempt power, it is 'an extremely powerful instrument.' Dobbs, *Remedies,* p. 105 (1973).
>
> "The injunction is a preventive order looking to the future conduct of the parties. To obtain an injunction, a plaintiff must show a sufficient probability that future conduct of the defendant will violate a right of and will injure the plaintiff. To invoke the remedy of injunction the plaintiff must moreover establish that the injury is irreparable, *i.e.* not adequately compensable in damages. Finally, injunctive relief is addressed to the sound discretion of the trial court; competing interests must be reconciled and the plaintiff must satisfy the trial court that on balance equity favors issuing the injunction."

Pure Milk Prod. Co–op. v. National Farmers Org., 90 Wis.2d 781, 800, 280 N.W.2d 691, 700 (1979).

2. The process for determining whether to grant a permanent injunction is described as follows in Prohosky v. Prudential Ins. Co. of America, 584 F.Supp. 1337, 1338 (N.D.Ind.1984):

"A district court deciding whether a permanent injunction should issue must undertake a three stage inquiry. First, the court must decide whether plaintiffs have actually succeeded on the merits of their claim. Second, the court must decide whether the 'balance of equities' favors the granting of injunctive relief. Finally, the court needs to decide what form the injunctive remedy should take.

"Particularly when balancing the equities, a district judge should exercise his discretion in determining the propriety of injunctive relief. Among the factors traditionally considered in this balance are: the adequacy of another remedy; the benefit to the plaintiff if injunctive relief is granted and hardship if such relief is denied; the hardship on the defendant if injunctive relief is granted; the hardship on third parties; the convenience and effectiveness of administration; and the public and social consequences of either granting or denying injunctive relief."

3. Consider the origins and function of the "inadequate remedy at law" prerequisite for injunctive relief:

"A. HISTORICAL BACKGROUND

"The traditional rule has been expressed in a variety of ways by a variety of commentators. Dobbs states that equitable relief was traditionally denied unless the matter was one in which the plaintiff's remedy at law was inadequate.[33] Chafee's interpretation of the traditional rule is that the court lacked power to grant equitable relief unless, in addition to its having personal and subject matter jurisdiction, the 'plaintiff had a reason for coming into equity.'[34] According to Pomeroy, the traditional rule is that 'equity jurisdiction extends to and embraces all civil cases * * * in which there is not a full, adequate, and complete remedy at law.'[35] * * *

* * *

"The origins of the rule are believed to lie in the slow division between law and equity which took place in England between the thirteenth and fifteenth centuries. * * *

* * *

"By the 1500's, this conceptual distinction between law and equity had been established. The former dealt with specific, fixed forms of action and awarded money damages, while the latter addressed injustice and hardship, and fashioned remedies to meet the moral demands of good conscience. * * *

"B. 'INADEQUACY' AND EARLY EQUITY JURISDICTION

* * *

"The commentators generally agree that the 'inadequacy of legal remedy' rule did serve a jurisdictional function in the early days after equity and law courts separated. The rule appears to have operated as an early device to help define the reach and power of the equity courts or, as

33. D. Dobbs, Handbook on the Law of Remedies § 2.5 (1973).

34. Z. Chafee, Some Problems of Equity 304 (1950).

35. Pomeroy, Equity Jurisprudence § 132 (5th ed. 1941).

Dobbs phrases it, to protect the separation of jurisdiction between courts of law and equity. Whether the rule was literally jurisdictional in the modern sense is not clear. If it was, then a court of equity had no power to decide a matter if the petitioner had available an adequate legal remedy. Presumably, any decree issued in the face of this adequate legal remedy would be void. Cox asserts that 'if the cause of action was not of a kind that fell within the province of the Chancellor, a court of equity had no power to decide the cause.' The 'inadequacy' rule was, then, one device to help determine whether a particular cause was 'of a kind' that the Chancellor could act upon. If a legal remedy would adequately redress the wrong complained of, then the case was outside the Chancellor's jurisdiction.

"Others suggest, however, that even if the rule did serve a strictly jurisdictional purpose at one time, it shortly developed into a principle of selection and a guide to action. Thus, the defendant in equity could not disobey an order on the ground that the plaintiff had an adequate legal remedy. He could, however, argue that the equity court should refrain from exercising its power because the plaintiff had available an adequate legal remedy, and he could appeal, arguing the availability of the legal remedy made the case improper for equitable intervention.

"Pomeroy expresses this view of the rule's early development. He notes that writers often incorrectly assume that equity jurisdiction is measured by the absence or existence of remedies at law, that equity reaches wherever law does not. The correct view, according to Pomeroy, is that equity actually creates certain unique rights which it will protect through its own exclusive jurisdiction, independent of the adequacy or inadequacy of available legal remedies. Its jurisdiction in these matters derives from the existence of fundamental equitable interests, not from the inadequacies of the common law.

"On this basis, Pomeroy concludes that while the availability of a legal remedy has nothing to do with defining the jurisdiction of equity, it is relevant in determining whether a court of equity *ought* to exercise its powers in a given situation. In this sense, the rule requires the court to consider whether the claimant can secure justice without resort to the special devices of equity, and whether the interest under attack is one that warrants protection by equitable remedies.

"In summary, Pomeroy maintains that equity has inherent and exclusive jurisdiction over certain wholly equitable rights and interests. Presumably, these are matters in which the claim is based squarely on conscience and right rather than upon the fixed requirements of a cause at law. As a result, equity can act in this sphere without regard to the legal remedies available to the plaintiff.

"However, where the claimant seeks to protect an interest *not* exclusively equitable through the special devices of equity, an equity court has jurisdiction, but must assess the adequacy of the legal remedy before acting. The rule, in these instances, serves as a guidepost to decision, and not as a maxim of jurisdiction.

"C. THE RULE'S PURPOSE TODAY

"Today, the general view of the rule is consistent with Pomeroy's analysis. Professor Rendleman argues that the rule may, through improper application, fail to focus the Chancellor's attention on the proper issues. On the other hand, he contends that the rule, if correctly applied as a remedial guidepost, would focus the decision-maker's resources on several important issues.[36] These issues include the acceptability of substituting money damages for the invaded interest, the moral significance of the invaded interest, and the court's own administrative capacities.[37] The moral component forces the court to define those interests which are too basic to permit the violator to, in effect, buy injustice by paying damages.[38] Rendleman argues that the rule is dead as a strictly jurisdictional doctrine. Its remaining value, however, is its potential ability to force the court to weigh and discern the fundamental interest at stake in an action, and to make essentially moral choices about what rights are important enough to merit equity's extraordinary protection. The rule becomes, in this scheme, a remedial consideration.

"Dobbs embraces a similar conception of the rule's modern function. He states that the 'inadequacy of legal remedy' test should be applied when the plaintiff's substantive claim is at law (such as trespass, slander, assault), but the plaintiff seeks equitable relief because of the extraordinary remedies available.[39] In such a case, the adequacy rule should be used as a limitation on the granting of equitable relief.[40] Dobbs criticizes the notion that the rule is strictly jurisdictional, noting that the logical end of such a view is to declare invalid all equitable orders where an adequate legal remedy is available. He sees the rule, again, as a device to focus attention on certain basic policy considerations, particularly whether the need for an equitable remedy outweighs the defendant's right to a jury trial. Dobbs believes that with the merger of law and equity, the rule became simply a rule of decision or a tool for raising the policy issues which a court should consider before granting equitable relief.

"In light of these views, it is not unreasonable to ask whether the rule has any real meaning today. Reflection reveals that equity courts must employ some principle of selection in the exercise of their powers. Otherwise, equity courts would do nothing but supervise a myriad of in personam orders. The views expressed by Chafee, Dobbs, and Rendleman appear to envision use of the 'inadequacy' rule as just this principle of selection. The rule does not determine jurisdiction, in the sense that an equity court is prohibited from acting if an adequate legal remedy is available. Rather, it helps the court decide whether, in the case in dispute, it *should* act with its extraordinary powers.

"One question yet to be examined in this overview is what, traditionally, has constituted 'inadequacy'? A review of the scholarship in this area reveals several different approaches which appear to reach the same conclusion.

"According to Rendleman, the legal remedy was inadequate if it was less efficient than the equitable remedy, less speedy, or less practical, or if the plaintiff's injury could not be measured monetarily. Thus, the plaintiff

36. Rendleman, The Inadequate Remedy at Law Prerequisite for an Injunction, 33 U.Fla.L.Rev. 346, 347 (1981).

37. *Id.* at 348–52.

38. *Id.* at 352.

39. D. Dobbs, *supra* note 30, at 60.

40. *Id.*

had several avenues of argument for equitable relief; words such as 'efficient' and 'speedy' necessitate considerable subjective interpretation.

"Dobbs offers a more narrow definition. He states that the cases in which the legal remedy was seen as inadequate fell into four general patterns. The first was when the plaintiff had been deprived of something to which he was entitled and which money would not replace. In these situations, only specific restitution or a mandatory injunction could make the plaintiff whole. Second was the case in which the plaintiff would have to bring more than one action to protect his legal interest. A continuing trespass, for example, would require the plaintiff to bring numerous suits at law if he could pursue only legal remedies. Equitable relief, in the form of an injunction, could resolve the problem with more economy and efficiency. The third type of case involved a plaintiff who had a claim for money damages against an insolvent defendant. There, a legal judgment was worthless and only specific performance by the defendant could provide an effective remedy. Fourth was the case in which the plaintiff had been injured, but in which damages could not be accurately measured. Rather than denying recovery because of a problem of proof, equity intervened to fashion a remedy.

* * *

"D. SUMMARY OF THE GENERAL RULE

"From the foregoing, one may conclude that with the merger of law and equity, the rule lost its value as a device to protect the jurisdiction of two independent court systems. It remained valuable, however, as a means of focusing the equity court's attention on the question of whether it ought to act in a given situation, forcing the equity court to consider exactly what rights and social interests merited preservation through the extraordinary remedies of equity. Thus, the rule enables modern courts to rank interests, deciding which should be upheld by legal and equitable devices.

"Under this modern view, 'adequate' simply means 'appropriate' in terms of the value society accords the violated interest. A heinous invasion of a highly regarded interest may require a coercive equitable remedy even if money can compensate the plaintiff, while an invasion of a less crucial interest may be appropriately remedied by damages, even if the facts suggest equitable relief. The concept of 'adequacy' should, today, be used to balance the social significance of the right invaded with the type of remedy applied."

Note, The "Inadequacy of Legal Remedy" Requirement for Equitable Relief: The Development of the Rule and its Application in South Carolina, 35 S.C.L.Rev. 677, 678, 682–88 (1984).*

4. Professor Rendleman suggests that the inadequacy prerequisite now serves a different purpose for several related reasons:

"Due to the merger of law and equity into one form of civil action, equity is now simply a set of rules instead of a subordinate, supplementary system of courts. Procedural flexibility tells today's judges to award all litigants the relief or remedy appropriate on the facts, provided that prejudice can be avoided. Judges possess more self-confidence in their ability to solve problems and they are more willing to protect nonpecuniary, impalpable interests. Witness the practical abolition of Lord Chancellor Eldon's prerequisite that 'equity protects property rights, not personal rights.' Finally, constitutional litigation has increased; and, except for the injunction, judges have yet to discover a way to reapportion a legislature, desegregate a school, or restructure a mental hospital."

Rendleman, The Inadequate Remedy at Law Prerequisite for An Injunction, 33 U.Fla.L.Rev. 346 (1981).*

2. *Stay and Modification*

Federal Statutes Regarding Appeal of Permanent Injunctions

The statutes and rules of federal procedure governing appeals from requests for permanent injunctive relief are quoted at pp. 57–59.

MICHIGAN COALITION OF RADIOACTIVE MATERIAL USERS, INC. v. GRIEPENTROG

United States Court of Appeals, Sixth Circuit, 1991.
945 F.2d 150.

BOYCE F. MARTIN, JR., CIRCUIT JUDGE.

The defendants in this action have filed a motion pursuant to Fed. R.App.P. 8(a) seeking a stay of the judgment and a permanent injunction pending their appeal of the district court's grant of summary judgment in favor of the plaintiff. 769 F.Supp. 999. For the reasons outlined below, we hereby grant the stay. This opinion will clarify the standards we apply in reviewing an application for a stay of judgment pursuant to Fed.R.App.P. 8(a).

The defendants are heads of agencies delegated by the states of Nevada, Washington, and South Carolina, to administer the operation of low-level radioactive waste disposal sites located in these states. There are only three such sites in the United States: the Beatty site in Nevada, the Richland site in Washington, and the Barnwell site in South Carolina. These "sited states", as they are called, objected to the handling of low-level nuclear waste generated by other states and attempted to restrict access to their disposal systems. Congress responded by passing the Low–Level Radioactive Waste Policy Act in 1980 in an effort to motivate other states to assume some of the burden for disposal of such waste. Because progress was not as rapid as hoped, Congress amended the Act in 1985, adding specific incentives and penalties to encourage other states to develop disposal capacities by December 31, 1992. 42 U.S.C. § 2021b *et seq.* Pursuant to the scheme established by the amended Act, * * * the sited states are required to make their disposal capacity available for low-level radioactive waste from non-sited states for the period between January 1, 1986, through December 31, 1992.

In 1990, the defendants concluded that Michigan was not in compliance with the Act and effective November 10, 1990, denied waste generators in Michigan access to their disposal facilities. The plaintiff, the Michigan Coalition of Radioactive Material Users, Inc., is an association whose members engage in the use of radioactive materials and who generate low-level radioactive waste. MICHRAD, as the Coalition calls itself, filed suit seeking declaratory and injunctive relief prohibiting the defendants from denying MICHRAD access to the waste disposal facilities located in the defendants' states. * * * The district court granted judgment in favor of MICHRAD, finding that Michigan had complied with the requirements of the Act and that the defendants had no authority to deny waste generators in Michigan access to the sited states' facilities prior to January 1, 1993. The district court permanently enjoined the defendants from denying access to disposal facilities in their respective states for disposal of low-level radioactive waste generated in Michigan prior to January 1, 1993. An appropriate appeal has followed.

Pursuant to Rule 8(a) of the Federal Rules of Appellate Procedure, 28 U.S.C. Rules, the defendants now request us to issue an order staying the district court's judgment and granting them a permanent injunction. Ordinarily, Rule 8(a) requires that such a motion be made in the first instance in the district court. However,

> [a] motion for such relief may be made to the court of appeals or to a judge thereof, but the motion shall show that the application to the district court for the relief sought is not practicable, or that the district court has denied an application, or has failed to afford the relief which the applicant requested.

Fed.R.App.P. 8(a). In this case, the defendants did file a motion for stay of judgment and permanent injunction pending appeal in the district court. The district court denied both of defendants' motions, concluding that the potential harm to defendants in the absence of a stay is outweighed by public safety concerns in the state of Michigan.

In determining whether a stay should be granted under Fed.R.Civ.P. 8(a), we consider the same four factors that are traditionally considered in evaluating the granting of a preliminary injunction. *See Frisch's Restaurant, Inc. v. Shoney's Inc.,* 759 F.2d 1261, 1263 (6th Cir.1985); *In re DeLorean Motor Co.,* 755 F.2d 1223, 1228 (6th Cir.1985). These well-known factors are: (1) the likelihood that the party seeking the stay will prevail on the merits of the appeal; (2) the likelihood that the moving party will be irreparably harmed absent a stay; (3) the prospect that others will be harmed if the court grants the stay; and (4) the public interest in granting the stay. * * * These factors are not prerequisites that must be met, but are interrelated considerations that must be balanced together. *DeLorean,* 755 F.2d at 1229.

Although the factors to be considered are the same for both a preliminary injunction and a stay pending appeal, the balancing process is not identical due to the different procedural posture in which each judicial determination arises. Upon a motion for a preliminary injunction, the court must make a decision based upon "incomplete factual findings and legal research." * * * Even so, that decision is generally accorded a great deal of deference on appellate review and will only be disturbed if the court relied upon clearly erroneous findings of fact, improperly applied the governing law, or used an erroneous legal standard. * * *

Conversely, a motion for a stay pending appeal is generally made after the district court has considered fully the merits of the underlying action and issued judgment, usually following completion of discovery. As a result, a movant seeking a stay pending review on the merits of a district court's judgment will have greater difficulty in demonstrating a likelihood of success on the merits. In essence, a party seeking a stay must ordinarily demonstrate to a reviewing court that there is a likelihood of reversal. Presumably, there is a reduced probability of error, at least with respect to a court's findings of fact, because the district court had the benefit of a complete record that can be reviewed by this court when considering the motion for a stay.

To justify the granting of a stay, however, a movant need not always establish a high probability of success on the merits. * * * The probability of success that must be demonstrated is inversely proportional to the amount of irreparable injury plaintiffs will suffer absent the stay. Simply stated, more of one excuses less of the other. This relationship, however, is not without its limits; the movant is always required to demonstrate more than the mere "possibility" of success on the merits. * * * For example, even if a movant demonstrates irreparable harm that decidedly outweighs any potential harm to the defendant if a stay is granted, he is still required to show, at a minimum, "serious questions going to the merits." *DeLorean,* 755 F.2d at 1229 (quoting *Friendship Materials, Inc. v. Michigan Brick, Inc.,* 679 F.2d 100, 105 (6th Cir.1982)).

In evaluating the harm that will occur depending upon whether or not the stay is granted, we generally look to three factors: (1) the substantiality of the injury alleged; (2) the likelihood of its occurrence; and (3) the adequacy of the proof provided. * * * In evaluating the degree of injury, it is important to remember that

> [t]he key word in this consideration is *irreparable.* Mere injuries, however substantial, in terms of money, time and energy necessarily expended in the absence of a stay, are not enough. The possibility that adequate compensatory or other corrective relief will be available at a later date, in the ordinary course of litigation, weighs heavily against a claim of irreparable harm.

Sampson v. Murray, 415 U.S. 61, 90, 94 S.Ct. 937, 953, 39 L.Ed.2d 166 (1974) (quoting *Virginia Petroleum Jobbers Ass'n v. Federal Power Comm'n,* 259 F.2d 921, 925 (D.C.Cir.1958)). In addition, the harm alleged must be both certain and immediate, rather than speculative or theoretical. * * * In order to substantiate a claim that irreparable injury is likely to occur, a movant must provide some evidence that the harm has occurred in the past and is likely to occur again.

* * *

EVALUATION OF THE FOUR FACTORS

A. Likelihood of Success

Based upon the record before us, we find that the defendants have demonstrated a sufficient probability of success on the merits. Specifically, we believe the defendants present a compelling argument that the district court erred in finding that it had personal jurisdiction over the various sited state representatives. * * * Based upon the record before us, we feel it a close question as to whether the defendants' contacts to Michigan were sufficient "such that [they] should reasonably anticipate being haled into court there." *World–Wide Volkswagen Corp. v. Woodson,* 444 U.S. 286, 297, 100 S.Ct. 559, 567, 62 L.Ed.2d 490 (1980).

B. Irreparable Injury

* * *

The harm identified by the defendants is that the low-level radioactive waste, once received, must be buried in perpetuity and defendants will be burdened therefore with the responsibility of ensuring perpetual care for the waste. The defendants point out that this harm is also certain to occur because the defendants do not possess adequate short-term storage facilities to store the waste generated by Michigan until the final resolution of their appeal. The amount of waste produced by the plaintiff's members makes up a significant percentage of the waste currently being accepted by the sited states. Thus, we find that this factor weighs in favor of the defendants because of the great likelihood that this storage problem will continue to occur.

C. Harm to Others

We find that the harm to the plaintiff if the stay is issued is relatively slight. Currently, the plaintiff's members are storing their low-level radioactive waste in on-site temporary storage facilities. The plaintiff has not alleged that its members cannot provide the required storage capacity, but merely that they find it inconvenient. In fact, plaintiff admits that some of its members have the storage capacity for some years to come. Plaintiff argues strenuously that having its members house the low-level waste in temporary storage facilities is detrimental to public safety concerns. The fact that the plaintiff's members routinely use these facilities in order to store their waste pending shipment belies this argument. To be sure, public safety concerns would be implicated if, by granting the stay, the plaintiff's members would be forced to use these temporary storage facilities as permanent facilities; here the plaintiff's members will only be required to use these facilities on a temporary basis until the state of Michigan complies with the amendments to the Act. 42 U.S.C. § 2021b *et seq.*

D. The Public Interest

In the most general sense, the public interest in this case lies heavily in providing safe and environmentally sound management, storage, and disposal of radioactive waste. Indeed, this was the underlying purpose behind the passage of the Low–Level Radioactive Waste Policy Act. In deciding whether or not the stay should be granted, however, our immediate concern is with the current public safety aspects. * * * The plaintiff argues that the public is put at risk if its members are required to store low-level radiation at temporary facilities until the resolution of defendants' appeal. We find no reason to believe that the storage of waste at the plaintiff's members' temporary storage facilities puts the public at a greater risk than it would otherwise face when the waste is stored at these locations pending transport to the defendants' facilities. Undoubtedly, as we noted, the public safety would be implicated if the plaintiff's members were required to store permanently the waste in these temporary facilities. Such, however, is simply not the case. The public safety is not adversely effected by the granting of the stay and, therefore, we conclude that the public interests in the development of long-term disposal sites is controlling.

CONCLUSION

Thus, applying the above standards to the facts of this case, it is our belief that the defendants have adequately demonstrated the need for a stay. We grant the defendants' motion that the judgment of the district court requiring the sited states to accept low-level radioactive waste be stayed pending a decision on the merits. The panel of this Court hearing the merits of the appeal will consider the defendants' motion for a permanent injunction.

Note

Is there any difference in obtaining a stay of a preliminary injunction or a permanent injunction?

RUFO v. INMATES OF SUFFOLK COUNTY JAIL

Supreme Court of the United States, 1992.
___ U.S. ___, 112 S.Ct. 748, 116 L.Ed.2d 867.

JUSTICE WHITE delivered the opinion of the Court.

In these cases, the District Court denied a motion of the Sheriff of Suffolk County, Massachusetts, to modify a consent decree entered to correct unconstitutional conditions at the Suffolk County Jail. The Court of Appeals affirmed. The issue before us is whether the courts below applied the correct standard in denying the motion. We hold that they did not and remand the case for further proceedings.

I

This litigation began in 1971 when inmates sued the Suffolk County Sheriff, the Commissioner of Correction for the State of Massachusetts, the Mayor of Boston, and nine city councilors, claiming that inmates not yet convicted of the crimes charged against them were being held under unconstitutional conditions at what was then the Suffolk County Jail. * * *

The Court permanently enjoined the government defendants: "(a) from housing at the Charles Street Jail after November 30, 1973 in a cell with another inmate, any inmate who is awaiting trial and (b) from housing at the Charles Street Jail after June 30, 1976 any inmate who is awaiting trial." *Id.,* at 691. The defendants did not appeal.

In 1977, with the problems of the Charles Street Jail still unresolved, the District Court ordered defendants, including the Boston City Council, to take such steps and expend the funds reasonably necessary to renovate another existing facility as a substitute detention center. * * * The Court of Appeals ordered that the Charles Street Jail be closed on October 2, 1978, unless a plan was presented to create a constitutionally adequate facility for pretrial detainees in Suffolk County.

Four days before the deadline, the plan that formed the basis for the consent decree now before this Court was submitted to the District Court. Although plans for the new jail were not complete, the District Court observed that * * * "[t]here are unequivocal commitments to conditions of confinement which will meet constitutional standards." * * * The Court therefore allowed Suffolk County to continue housing its pretrial detainees at the Charles Street Jail.

Seven months later, the Court entered a formal consent decree in which the government defendants expressed their "desire * * * to provide, maintain and operate as applicable a suitable and constitutional jail for Suffolk County pretrial detainees." * * * The decree specifically incorporated the provisions of the Suffolk County Detention Center, Charles Street Facility, Architectural Program, which—in the words of the consent decree—"sets forth a program which is both constitutionally adequate and constitutionally required." * * *

Although the Architectural Program projected that construction of the new jail would be completed by 1983, *ibid.,* work on the new facility had not been started by 1984. During the intervening years, the inmate population outpaced population projections. Litigation in the state courts ensued, and defendants were ordered to build a larger jail. * * * Thereupon, plaintiff prisoners, with the support of the sheriff, moved the District Court to modify the decree to provide a facility with 435 cells. Citing "the unanticipated increase in jail population and the delay in completing the jail," the District Court modified the decree to permit the capacity of the new jail to be increased in any amount, provided that:

> "(a) single-cell occupancy is maintained under the design for the facility; * * *

In July 1989, while the new jail was still under construction, the sheriff moved to modify the consent decree to allow the double bunking of male detainees in 197 cells, thereby raising the capacity of the new jail to 610 male detainees. The sheriff argued that changes in law and in fact required the modification. The asserted change in law was this Court's 1979 decision in *Bell v. Wolfish,* 441 U.S. 520, 99 S.Ct. 1861, 60 L.Ed.2d 447 (1979), handed down one week after the consent decree was approved by the District Court. The asserted change in fact was the increase in the population of pretrial detainees.

The District Court refused to grant the requested modification, holding that the sheriff had failed to meet the standard of *United States v. Swift & Co.,* 286 U.S. 106, 119, 52 S.Ct. 460, 464, 76 L.Ed. 999 (1932):

> "Nothing less than a clear showing of grievous wrong evoked by new and unforeseen conditions should lead us to change what was decreed after years of litigation with the consent of all concerned."

The court rejected the argument that *Bell* required modification of the decree because the decision "did not directly overrule any legal interpretation on which the 1979 consent decree was based, and in these circumstances it is inappropriate to invoke Rule 60(b)(5) to modify a consent decree." * * * The court refused to order modification because of the increased pretrial detainee population, finding that the problem was "neither new nor unforeseen." *Ibid.*

The District Court briefly stated that, even under the flexible modification standard adopted by other Courts of Appeals, the sheriff would not be entitled to relief because "[a] separate cell for each detainee has always been an important element of the relief sought in this litigation—perhaps even the most important element." *Id.,* at 565. Finally, the court rejected the argument that the decree should be modified because the proposal complied with constitutional standards, reasoning that such a rule "would undermine and discourage settlement efforts in institutional cases." *Ibid.* The District Court never decided whether the sheriff's proposal for double celling at the new jail would be constitutionally permissible.

The new Suffolk County Jail opened shortly thereafter.

The Court of Appeals affirmed * * *.

II

In moving for modification of the decree, the sheriff relied on Federal Rule of Civil Procedure 60(b), which in relevant part provides:

> "On motion and upon such terms as are just, the court may relieve a party or a party's legal representative from a final judgment, order, or proceeding for the following reasons: * * * (5) the judgment has been satisfied, released, or discharged, or a prior judgment upon which it is based has been reversed or otherwise vacated, or it is no longer equitable that the judgment should have prospective application; or (6) any other reason justifying relief from the operation of the judgment * * *."

There is no suggestion in these cases that a consent decree is not subject to Rule 60(b). A consent decree no doubt embodies an agreement of the parties and thus in some respects is contractual in nature. But it is an agreement that the parties desire and expect will be reflected in and be enforceable as a judicial decree that is subject to the rules generally applicable to other judgments and decrees. * * * The District Court recognized as much but held that Rule 60(b)(5) codified the "grievous wrong" standard of *United States v. Swift & Co., supra,* that a case for modification under this standard had not been made, and that resort to Rule 60(b)(6) was also unavailing. This construction of Rule 60(b) was error.

Swift was the product of a prolonged antitrust battle between the Government and the meat-packing industry. In 1920, the defendants agreed to a consent decree that enjoined them from manipulating the meat-packing industry and banned them from engaging in the manufacture, sale, or transportation of other foodstuffs. 286 U.S., at 111, 52 S.Ct., at 461. In 1930, several meat-packers petitioned for modification of the decree, arguing that conditions in the meat-packing and grocery industries had changed. *Id.,* at 113, 52 S.Ct., at 461. The Court rejected their claim, finding that the meat-packers were positioned to manipulate transportation costs and fix grocery prices in 1930, just as they had been in 1920. *Id.,* at 115–116, 52 S.Ct., at 462–463. It was in this context that Justice Cardozo, for the Court, set forth the much-quoted *Swift* standard, requiring "[n]othing less than a clear showing of grievous wrong evoked by new and unforeseen conditions" as a predicate to modification of the meat-packers' consent decree. *Id.,* at 119, 52 S.Ct., at 464.

Read out of context, this language suggests a "hardening" of the traditional flexible standard for modification of consent decrees. * * * But that conclusion does not follow when the standard is read in context. * * * The *Swift* opinion pointedly distinguished the facts of that case from one in which genuine changes required modification of a consent decree, stating that:

> "The distinction is between restraints that give protection to rights fully accrued upon facts so nearly permanent as to be substantially impervious to change, and those that involve the supervision of changing conduct or conditions and are thus provisional and tentative * * *. The consent is to be read as directed toward events as they then were. It was not an abandonment of the right to exact revision in the future, if revision should become necessary in adaptation to events to be." 286 U.S., at 114–115, 52 S.Ct., at 462.

Our decisions since *Swift* reinforce the conclusion that the "grievous wrong" language of *Swift* was not intended to take on a talismanic quality, warding off virtually all efforts to modify consent decrees.

* * *

The upsurge in institutional reform litigation since *Brown v. Board of Education,* 347 U.S. 483, 74 S.Ct. 686, 98 L.Ed. 873 (1954), has made the ability of a district court to modify a decree in response to changed circumstances all the more important. Because such decrees often remain in place for extended periods of time, the likelihood of significant changes occurring during the life of the decree is increased.

* * *

The government petitioners urge that these factors are present in the cases before us and support modification of the decree. They assert that modification would actually improve conditions for some pretrial detainees, who now cannot be housed in the Suffolk County Jail and therefore are transferred to other facilities, farther from family members and legal counsel. In these transfer facilities, the petitioners assert that detainees may be double celled under less desirable conditions than those that would exist if double celling were allowed at the new Suffolk County Jail. The government petitioners also contend that the public interest is implicated here because crowding at the new facility has necessitated the release of some pretrial detainees and the transfer of others to halfway houses, from which many escape.

* * *

It is urged that any rule other than the *Swift* "grievous wrong" standard would deter parties to litigation such as this from negotiating settlements and hence destroy the utility of consent decrees. Obviously that would not be the case insofar as the state or local government officials are concerned. As for the plaintiffs in such cases, they know that if they litigate to conclusion and win, the resulting judgment or decree will give them what is constitutionally adequate at that time but perhaps less than they hoped for. They also know that the prospective effect of such a judgment or decree will be open to modification where deemed equitable under Rule 60(b). Whether or not they bargain for more than what they might get after trial, they will be in no worse position if they settle and have the consent decree entered. At least they will avoid further litigation and perhaps will negotiate a decree providing more than what would have been ordered without the local government's consent. And, of course, if they litigate, they may lose.

III

Although we hold that a district court should exercise flexibility in considering requests for modification of an institutional reform consent decree, it does not follow that a modification will be warranted in all circumstances. Rule 60(b)(5) provides that a party may obtain relief from a court order when "it is no longer equitable that the judgment should have prospective application," not when it is no longer convenient to live with the terms of a consent decree. Accordingly, a party seeking modification of a consent decree bears the burden of establishing that a significant change in circumstances warrants revision of the decree. If the moving party meets this standard, the court should consider whether the proposed modification is suitably tailored to the changed circumstance.[7]

A

A party seeking modification of a consent decree may meet its initial burden by showing either a significant change in factual conditions or in law.

7. The standard we set forth applies when a party seeks modification of a term of a consent decree that arguably relates to the vindication of a constitutional right. Such a showing is not necessary to implement minor changes in extraneous details that may have been included in a decree (*e.g.*, paint color or design of a building's facade) but are unrelated to remedying the underlying constitutional violation. Ordinarily, the parties should consent to modifying a decree to allow such changes. If a party refuses to consent and the moving party has a reasonable basis for its request, the court should modify the decree. In this case the entire architectural plan became part of the decree binding on the local authorities. Hence, any change in the plan technically required a change in the decree, absent a provision in the plan exempting certain changes. Such a provision was furnished by the 1985 modification of the decree. Of course, the necessity of changing a decree to allow insignificant changes could be avoided by not entering an overly detailed decree.

1

Modification of a consent decree may be warranted when changed factual conditions make compliance with the decree substantially more onerous. Such a modification was approved by the District Court in this litigation in 1985 when it became apparent that plans for the new jail did not provide sufficient cell space.

* * *

Respondents urge that modification should be allowed only when a change in facts is both "unforeseen and unforeseeable." Brief for Respondents at 35. Such a standard would provide even less flexibility than the exacting *Swift* test; we decline to adopt it. Litigants are not required to anticipate every exigency that could conceivably arise during the life of a consent decree.

Ordinarily, however, modification should not be granted where a party relies upon events that actually were anticipated at the time it entered into a decree. * * * If it is clear that a party anticipated changing conditions that would make performance of the decree more onerous but nevertheless agreed to the decree, that party would have to satisfy a heavy burden to convince a court that it agreed to the decree in good faith, made a reasonable effort to comply with the decree, and should be relieved of the undertaking under Rule 60(b).

Accordingly, on remand the District Court should consider whether the upsurge in the Suffolk County inmate population was foreseen by the petitioners.

* * *

It strikes us as somewhat strange, if a rapidly increasing jail population had been contemplated, that respondents would have settled for a new jail that would not have been adequate to house pretrial detainees. There is no doubt that the original and modified decree called for a facility with single cells. * * * It is apparent, however, that the decree itself nowhere expressly orders or reflects an agreement by petitioners to provide jail facilities having single cells sufficient to accommodate all future pretrial detainees, however large the number of such detainees might be. * * * The District Court was thus in error in holding that even under a more flexible standard than its version of *Swift* required, modification of the single cell requirement was necessarily forbidden.

2

A consent decree must of course be modified if, as it later turns out, one or more of the obligations placed upon the parties has become impermissible under federal law. But modification of a consent decree may be warranted when the statutory or decisional law has changed to make legal what the decree was designed to prevent.

* * *

Petitioner Rapone urges that, without more, our 1979 decision in *Bell v. Wolfish,* 441 U.S. 520, 99 S.Ct. 1861, 60 L.Ed.2d 447 (1979), was a change in law requiring modification of the decree governing construction of the Suffolk County Jail. We disagree. *Bell* made clear what the Court had not before announced: that double celling is not in all cases unconstitutional. But it surely did not cast doubt on the legality of single celling, and petitioners were undoubtedly aware that *Bell* was pending when they signed the decree. Thus, the case must be judged on the basis that it was immaterial to petitioners that double celling might be ruled constitutional, *i.e.* they preferred even in that event to agree to a decree which called for providing only single cells in the jail to be built.

* * *

To hold that a clarification in the law automatically opens the door for relitigation of the merits of every affected consent decree would undermine the finality of such agreements and could serve as a disincentive to negotiation of settlements in institutional reform litigation. * * *

* * *

While a decision that clarifies the law will not, in and of itself, provide a basis for modifying a decree, it could constitute a change in circumstances that would support modification if the parties had based their agreement on a misunderstanding of the governing law.

* * *

Thus, if the Sheriff and Commissioner could establish on remand that the parties to the consent decree believed that single celling of pretrial detainees was mandated by the Constitution, this misunderstanding of the law could form a basis for modification. In this connection, we note again, see *supra,* at 755, that the decree itself recited that it "sets forth a program which is both constitutionally adequate and constitutionally *required.*" (Emphasis added).

B

Once a moving party has met its burden of establishing either a change in fact or in law warranting modification of a consent decree, the District Court should determine whether the proposed modification is suitably tailored to the changed circumstance. In evaluating a proposed modification, three matters should be clear.

Of course, a modification must not create or perpetuate a constitutional violation. Petitioners contend that double celling inmates at the Suffolk County Jail would be constitutional under *Bell.* Respondents counter that *Bell* is factually distinguishable and that double celling at the new jail would violate the constitutional rights of pretrial detainees. If this is the case—the District Court did not decide this issue, 734 F.Supp., at 565–566—modification should not be granted.

A proposed modification should not strive to rewrite a consent decree so that it conforms to the constitutional floor. Once a court has determined that changed circumstances warrant a modification in a consent decree, the focus should be on whether the proposed modification is tailored to resolve the problems created by the change in circumstances. A court should do no more, for a consent decree is a final judgment that may be reopened only to the extent that equity requires. The court should not "turn aside to inquire whether some of [the provisions of the decree] upon separate as distinguished from joint action could have been opposed with success if the defendants had offered opposition." *Swift,* 286 U.S., at 116–117, 52 S.Ct., at 463.

Within these constraints, the public interest and "[c]onsiderations based on the allocation of powers within our federal system," *Dowell,* 498 U.S., at ___, 111 S.Ct., at 632, require that the district court defer to local government administrators, who have the "primary responsibility for elucidating, assessing, and solving" the problems of institutional reform, to resolve the intricacies of implementing a decree modification. *Brown v. Board of Education,* 349 U.S. 294, at 299, 75 S.Ct. 753 at 755–756, 99 L.Ed. 1083 (1955). See also *Missouri v. Jenkins,* 495 U.S. 33, ___, 110 S.Ct. 1651, ___, 109 L.Ed.2d 31 (1990); *Milliken II,* 433 U.S., at 281, 97 S.Ct., at 2757. Although state and local officers in charge of institutional litigation may agree to do more than that which is minimally required by the Constitution to settle a case and avoid further litigation, a court should surely keep the public interest in mind in ruling on a request to modify based on a change in conditions making it substantially more onerous to abide by the decree. To refuse modification of a decree is to bind all future officers of the State, regardless of their view of the necessity of relief from one or more provisions of a decree that might not have been entered had the matter been litigated to its conclusion. The District Court seemed to be of the view that the problems of the fiscal officers of the State were only marginally relevant to the request for modification in this case. 734 F.Supp., at 566. Financial constraints may not be used to justify the creation or perpetuation of constitutional violations, but they are a legitimate concern of government defendants in institutional reform litigation and therefore are appropriately considered in tailoring a consent decree modification.

IV

To conclude, we hold that the *Swift* "grievous wrong" standard does not apply to requests to modify consent decrees stemming from institutional reform litigation. Under the flexible standard we adopt today, a party seeking modification of a consent decree must establish that a significant change in facts or law warrants revision of the decree and that the proposed modification is suitably tailored to the changed circumstance. We vacate the decision below and remand for further proceedings consistent with this opinion.

It is so ordered.

JUSTICE O'CONNOR, concurring in the judgment.

I agree that these cases should be remanded so that the District Court may reconsider whether to modify the decree. I write separately to emphasize the limited nature of our review; to clarify why, despite our limited review, the cases should be returned to the District Court; and to explain my concerns with certain portions of the Court's opinion. [Discussion omitted]

JUSTICE STEVENS, with whom JUSTICE BLACKMUN joins, dissenting.

Today the Court endorses the standard for modification of consent decrees articulated by Judge Friendly in *New York State Association for Retarded Children, Inc. v. Carey,* 706 F.2d 956 (CA2), cert. denied, 464 U.S. 915, 104 S.Ct. 277, 78 L.Ed.2d 257 (1983). I agree with that endorsement, but under that standard I believe the findings of the District Court in this action require affirmance of its order refusing to modify this consent decree.

When a district court determines, after a contested trial, that a state institution is guilty of a serious and persistent violation of the Federal Constitution, it typically fashions a remedy that is more intrusive than a simple order directing the defendants to cease and desist from their illegal conduct. * * * A district court has a duty to command a remedy that is effective, and it enjoys the broad equitable authority necessary to fulfill this obligation. * * *

The motion to modify that ultimately led to our grant of certiorari was filed on July 17, 1989. * * *

Petitioners' reliance on *Bell v. Wolfish,* 441 U.S. 520, 99 S.Ct. 1861, 60 L.Ed.2d 447 (1979), as constituting a relevant change in the law is plainly misplaced. That case was pending in this Court when the consent decree was entered in 1979. It was the authority on which the sheriff relied when he sought permission to double cell in 1984 and, of course, it was well-known to all parties when the decree was modified in 1985. It does not qualify as a changed circumstance.

The increase in the average number of pretrial detainees is, of course, a change of fact. Because the size of that increase had not been anticipated in 1979, it was appropriate to modify the decree in 1985. But in 1985, the steady progression in the detainee population surely made it foreseeable that this growth would continue. The District Court's finding that "the over-crowding problem faced by the Sheriff is neither new nor unforeseen," * * * is amply supported by the record.

Even if the continuing increase in inmate population had not actually been foreseen, it was reasonably foreseeable. Mere foreseeability in the sense that it was an event that "could conceivably arise" during the life of the consent decree, see *ante,* at 760, should not, of course, disqualify an unanticipated development from justifying a modification. But the parties should be charged with notice of those events that reasonably prudent litigants would contemplate when negotiating a settlement. Given the realities of today's society, it is not surprising that the District Court found a continued growth in inmate population to be within petitioners' contemplation.

Other important concerns counsel against modification of this consent decree. Petitioners' history of noncompliance after the 1973 injunction provides an added reason for insisting that they honor their most recent commitments. * * *

The strong public interest in protecting the finality of court decrees always counsels against modifications. * * * In the context of a consent decree, this interest is reinforced by the policy favoring the settlement of protracted litigation. To the extent that litigants are allowed to avoid their solemn commitments, the motivation for particular settlements will be compromised, and the reliability of the entire process will suffer.

It is particularly important to apply a strict standard when considering modification requests that undermine the central purpose of a consent decree. * * *

After a judicial finding of constitutional violation, petitioners were ordered in 1973 to place pretrial detainees in single cells. In return for certain benefits, petitioners committed themselves in 1979 to continued compliance with the single-celling requirement. They reaffirmed this promise in 1985. It was clearly not an abuse of discretion for the District Court to require petitioners to honor this commitment.

I would affirm the judgment of the Court of Appeals.

Notes

1. "The three traditional reasons for ordering the modification or vacation of an injunction are (1) changes in operative facts, (2) changes in the relevant decisional law, and (3) changes in any applicable statutory law." C. Wright & A. Miller, Federal Practice and Procedure § 2961, at 604–05 (1973). Changes in statutory law probably provide the strongest basis for a modification or dissolution of a permanent injunction. *E.g.,* System Federation No. 91, Ry. Employees' Dept., AFL–CIO v. Wright, 364 U.S. 642, 648, 81 S.Ct. 368, 371, 5 L.Ed.2d 349, 353 (1961). It is important to emphasize, however, that a motion to modify or vacate is not a substitute for an appeal from original issuance of the injunction: "The injunction, whether right or wrong, is not subject to impeachment in its application to the conditions that existed at its making. We are not at liberty to reverse under the guise of adjusting." United States v. Swift & Co., 286 U.S. 106, 119, 52 S.Ct. 460, 464, 76 L.Ed. 999, 1008 (1932).

2. In Ladner v. Siegel, 298 Pa. 487, 148 A. 699 (1930) (injunction prohibiting use of a building as a garage was modified to preclude its use as a public, but not as a private, garage), the court discussed the power of an equity court to modify an injunction:

> "But though a decree may be final, as it relates to an appeal and all matters included or embodied in such a step, yet, where the proceedings are of a continuing nature, it is not final. * * *
>
> * * *
>
> "The injunction in this case prevented an anticipated injury to a property right. The chancellor in granting it placed the protecting arm of the court about this right, and prevented Siegel from using his property in such a way as would injure his neighbors. It was to remain as long as the court felt that protection necessary to complainant's rights, or until conditions demanded a modification of that protection or its entire removal.

The power of the chancellor to modify in such cases cannot be controlled by term rules, otherwise equity would cease to be equity and become a hard and fast taskmaster.

* * *

"The modification of a decree in a preventive injunction is inherent in the court which granted it, and may be made, (a) if, in its discretion judicially exercised, it believes the ends of justice would be served by a modification, and (b) where the law, common or statutory, has changed, been modified or extended, and (c) where there is a change in the controlling facts on which the injunction rested.

* * *

"It is urged, however, that the final decree became the settled law between the parties, and, as such, was protected by both the Fourteenth Amendment of the Federal Constitution and by section 11 of article 1 of our Constitution. We have no doubt that, when the Federal Constitution said: 'Nor shall any *State* deprive any person of life, liberty, or property, without due process of law,' it included all functionaries of state government, judicial as well as political * * *, and the courts may not, through judicial decrees or judgments, violate the due process or equal protection clauses. The state cannot, through legislation, take away a vested right secured by a final judgment * * *; neither may a court take away a vested right secured by a valid decree or judgment. * * *

"We need not discuss this interesting question further, for, notwithstanding the apparent hesitancy to disturb judicial decrees based on the common law as infractions of the Fourteenth Amendment, before the amendment can intervene, there must be a right in existence that has become vested. An injunction decree does not create a right; it protects the right of the owner to the enjoyment of his property from injurious interference by the uses of other land. The right protected is an attribute of property existing through the application of common-law principles. A decree preventing its injury does not give to the complaining party a perpetual or vested right either in the remedy, the law governing the order, or the effect of it. He is not entitled to the same measure of protection at all times and under all circumstances. A decree protecting a property right is given subject to the rules governing modification, suspension, or dissolution of an injunction. The decree is an ambulatory one, and marches along with time affected by the nature of the proceeding." *

* * *

3. When a defendant cannot establish the requisite "changed circumstances" referred to above, a possible alternative approach is to seek a modification of a permanent injunction on the theory that its language is unclear or overbroad. The defendant may be able to get substantial relief from the burden of the injunction under the guise of obtaining a "clarification." *See,*

* *See* Note, Are All Permanent Injunctions Temporary? 23 Mich.L.Rev. 382 (1925); Developments in the Law–Injunctions, 78 Harv. L.Rev. 994, 1080–84 (1965). For applications of *Ladner* principles *see* Mann Manufacturing, Inc. v. Hortex Inc., 439 F.2d 403 (5th Cir.1971); Adams v. Vaill, 158 Conn. 478, 262 A.2d 169 (1969).

e.g., Flavor Corp. of America v. Kemin Industries, Inc., 503 F.2d 729 (8th Cir.1974).

4. Normally, the defendant will raise changed circumstances by filing a motion to modify or vacate with the trial court that issued the injunction. In the federal courts and those state courts that have adopted the language of the Federal Rules of Civil Procedure in this regard, the defendant usually files a Rule 60(b) motion in the trial court. Rule 60(b) provides that "on motion and upon such terms as are just, the court may relieve a party * * * from a final judgment, order, or proceeding for the following reasons: * * * (5) * * * it is no longer equitable that the judgment should have prospective application."

To what extent should the *plaintiff* be able to have the injunction made more stringent because of subsequent changed circumstances of the type discussed above? *See* C. Wright & A. Miller, Federal Practice and Procedure § 2961, at 603 (1973).

DRAVOSBURG HOUSING ASS'N v. BOROUGH OF DRAVOSBURG

Commonwealth Court of Pennsylvania, 1983.
71 Pa.Cmwlth. 144, 454 A.2d 1158.

MacPhail, Judge.

Sometime prior to 1964, the Dravosburg Housing Association (Association), a Pennsylvania non-profit corporation, purchased from the United States government, a housing development in the Borough of Dravosburg (Borough) consisting of some 250 housing units, the land on which the buildings were erected, and the streets, utility lines and sewage lines which were connected to the buildings and ran under the streets. Subsequently, the Borough created the Dravosburg Sanitary Authority (Authority) to put in place a sewage system for the Borough and adopted an ordinance requiring all residents of the Borough to become a part of and make use of the sanitation facilities. The Association then brought an action in equity against the Authority and the Borough alleging that it had its own sewage system and, therefore, should not be required to become a part of the Authority's sewage facility system.

That litigation was resolved by a consent decree dated July 16, 1964 which is at the heart of the instant appeal. By its terms, the decree provided that the Association would grant and convey to the Borough the streets it owned and the sewage facilities it owned. * * *

Pursuant to the terms of that decree, the Borough adopted an ordinance (No. 491) fixing a rate schedule which resulted in the Association paying rates in accord with the decree.

* * *

In 1978, the Borough passed amendments to ordinance No. 491 which established a new rate schedule, the effect of which was to require the Association to pay more than it was obligated to pay under the terms of the consent decree. The Association then instituted an action in equity against the Borough and the Authority to enforce the terms of the 1964 consent decree. The defendants answered by averring, *inter alia,* that the provisions of the 1964 decree were discriminatory, unreasonable and illegal in that the Association was paying less than its proportionate share of the cost of operating the sewage system contrary to various federal and state laws and regulations, including the Federal Water Pollution Control Act, § 204(b)(1)(A), 33 U.S.C. § 1284(b)(1)(A) (Supp.1982), and the terms of the lease agreement negotiated between the Borough and the Authority.

After a non-jury trial, the chancellor found that the passage of time had drastically changed the consequences of enforcing the 1964 decree, that that decree did not encompass a fixed set of terms which could be satisfied (thus discharging the obligations of the parties), that the decree should be treated as an injunction subject to modification as the equities might require and that since the decree no longer represented an equitable agreement, it should not be enforced. The Association's suit was dismissed and exceptions to the decree were likewise dismissed. This appeal followed.

It is the Association's contention that the 1964 consent decree cannot be modified or set aside without the consent of the parties unless the decree was entered as the result of fraud, accident or mistake. Since the trial court's decree was entered without a finding that any of those elements were present, the Association would have us reverse. * * *

Our scope of review of equity matters is limited to a determination of whether the chancellor committed an error of law or abused his discretion. * * *

As we analyze this case, it appears to us that if the chancellor was correct that the 1964 decree was subject to modification by the court or had lost its vitality by reason of changing circumstances, then the final decree which is the order appealed from here, must be affirmed; but if the chancellor erred in his conclusion that the 1964 decree was subject to modification by the court, then the final decree must be set aside.

There is strong support in Pennsylvania law for the Association's contention that in the absence of fraud, accident or mistake, a court has neither the power nor the authority to vary or modify the terms of a consent decree. Pennsylvania Human Relations Commission v. A.K. Graybill, Jr., Inc., 482 Pa. 143, 393 A.2d 420 (1978), * * * and Commonwealth v. Rozman, 10 Pa.Commonwealth Ct. 133, 309 A.2d 197 (1973). In *Rozman,* this Court held that a consent decree is an agreement binding upon the parties thereto who cannot be allowed to repudiate that to which they agreed for purposes of their own and for their own benefit. * * *

In support of his decree, the learned chancellor here notes that where the circumstances and status of the parties are shown to have changed so as to make it just and equitable to do so, other courts have modified equitable decrees, especially where the proceedings are executory and continuing as he concludes this one is. The chancellor cites Ladner v. Siegel, 298 Pa. 487, 148 A. 699 (1930). It is true that such language does appear in the *Ladner* case, but the *Ladner* case does *not* involve a consent decree. This Court would certainly concur that in an equity case, where a preventive injunction is entered adversely as in *Ladner,* the court entering the decree may retain jurisdiction over it and modify it where there is a change in the controlling facts. The point is, however, that the 1964 consent decree here in dispute was *not* a preventive injunction and it was *not* entered adversely.

It is also true that the rule in the federal courts is different. Thus, in United States v. Swift & Co., 286 U.S. 106, 52 S.Ct. 460, 76 L.Ed. 999 (1932) the United States Supreme Court specifically rejected the concept that a consent decree was to be treated as a contract rather than as a judicial act and held, as did the chancellor here, that where the circumstances change, an injunction can be modified even if entered by consent and even though its terms do not expressly permit modification. That Court says this can be done because of principles inherent in equity jurisdiction. * * *

Unfortunately for the Borough and the Authority, however, they have been unable to point to a single appellate case in Pennsylvania which has adopted the principle applied by the federal courts. * * *

We hold, therefore, that the rule in Pennsylvania remains firm that where a decree in equity is entered by the consent of the parties, it is binding upon the parties until *they* choose to amend it.

* * *

Since the chancellor has failed to find the consent decree of 1964 to be the result of fraud, accident or mistake, it must be enforced. The final decree from which this appeal has been taken will be set aside and the case will be remanded for the entry of an appropriate decree consistent with this opinion.

Notes

1. In accord with *Dravosburg* are Weeast v. Borough of Wind Gap, 153 Pa.Cmwlth. 330, 621 A.2d 1074 (1993); and Penn Township v. Watts, 152 Pa.Cmwlth. 359, 618 A.2d 1244 (1992).
2. Is *Rufo* limited to constitutional cases?
3. Do you agree with the federal rule or the Pennsylvania rule? Why?

E. BONDS

Rule 65(c) of the Federal Rules of Civil Procedure provides: "No restraining order or preliminary injunction shall issue except upon the giving of security by the applicant, in such sum as the court deems proper, for the payment of such costs and damages as may be incurred or suffered by any party who is found to have been wrongfully enjoined or restrained." For the full text, *see supra* p. 18. Almost all states have a similar statute or rule providing for an injunction bond. The purposes of the bond requirement are discussed in Dobbs, Should Security Be Required as a Pre–Condition to Provisional Injunctive Relief? 52 N.C.L.Rev. 1091, 1093–94 (1974): *

"[O]ne purpose in requiring a security as a condition to provisional relief is the fear that provisional relief, necessarily given after an attenuat-

* Reprinted with permission from the North Carolina Law Review, Volume 52, October 1974, Number 6, Copyright © 1974 by the North Carolina Law Review Association.

ed hearing or none at all, is especially prone to error. It is one thing to say that, in ordinary trials, the winning party must still pay his own attorney's fees and must even absorb the losses he may have had due to an erroneous trial court decision. But it is entirely something else to say that he must risk such losses without so much as a reasonable opportunity to develop the facts or the legal argumentation in the case. Perhaps one purpose of the injunction bond, then, is simply to recompense the defendant who has been subjected to a process of law that does not meet the kind of standards ordinarily adopted.

"A second policy or purpose of the injunction bond may be more direct: it may be required as a means of guaranteeing that the provisional relief is sought only by those in genuine need of such relief and reasonably confident of the outcome. In other words, its purpose may be more or less frankly to discourage too easy an access to the judicial process in those cases where that process does not involve a full trial of the issues. Not only does access to provisional relief risk harm to the defendant, it also risks enormous pressures that often are not generated when a full trial and hearing are held. The defendant enjoined on a few hours' notice to cease a nuisance may be subjected to enormous losses that could readily be avoided if he were merely subjected to the normal suit for injunction with the usual notice and a full opportunity to defend. By the same token, the plaintiff with even color of a complaint is likely to be well aware of the pressure he can generate by a claim for preliminary injunction. He may be tempted by tactics, if not by need, to pursue such a remedy unless he is discouraged. The bond, if required in a substantial sum, may operate to deter frivolous claims for provisional relief."

SYSTEM OPERATIONS, INC. v. SCIENTIFIC GAMES DEVELOPMENT CORP.

United States Court of Appeals, Third Circuit, 1977.
555 F.2d 1131.

ROSENN, CIRCUIT JUDGE.

[Action by lottery consulting firm against competitors for preliminary injunction restraining product disparagement and interference with contractual relations.]

* * *

The district court failed to require that System post a security bond in support of the preliminary injunction awarded to it. In so doing, the district court committed an error of law which constitutes an independent ground for reversal. An award of a preliminary injunction without requiring a bond by the plaintiff violates Rule 65(c) of the Federal Rules of Civil Procedure which provides in pertinent part:

> *Security.* No restraining order or preliminary injunction shall issue except upon the giving of security by the applicant in such sum as the court deems proper, for the payment of such costs and damages as may be incurred or suffered by any party who is found to have been wrongfully enjoined or restrained.

System contends that although the language of Rule 65(c) appears mandatory, the requirement of a security bond is actually within the discretion of the district court. In support of its argument, System cites Continental Oil Co. v. Frontier Refining Co., 338 F.2d 780 (10th Cir.1964) * * *. *Continental Oil* holds that the requirement for a bond may be waived by the district court where the grant of the injunction carries no risk of monetary loss to the defendant. In the case *sub judice,* the injunction restricts the defendants in their efforts to win new instant lottery ticket contracts and the potential for monetary loss is indeed substantial.

We hold that in these circumstances a district court commits reversible error when it fails to require the posting of a security bond by the successful applicant for a preliminary injunction. *See, e.g.,* Telex Corp. v. IBM Corp., 464 F.2d 1025 (8th Cir.1972); Pioche Mines Consol., Inc. v. Dolman, 333 F.2d 257 (9th Cir.1964), cert. denied, 380 U.S. 956, 85 S.Ct. 1081, 13 L.Ed.2d 972 (1965); Chatz v. Freeman, 204 F.2d 764 (7th Cir.1953); *cf.* Hopkins v. Wallin, 179 F.2d 136 (3d Cir.1949). We do not decide whether a court may dispense with the posting of a bond in a case where the injunction raises no risk of monetary harm to the defendant. *See, e.g., Continental Oil, supra;* Int'l Controls Corp. v. Vesco, 490 F.2d 1334 (2d Cir.), cert. denied, 417 U.S. 932, 94 S.Ct. 2644, 41 L.Ed.2d 236 (1974); Brookins v. Bonnell, 362 F.Supp. 379 (E.D.Pa.1973).

Federal courts have experienced considerable difficulty in interpreting Rule 65(c). Like the court in the principal case, some view it as mandatory and hold that "a court is to expressly entertain a defendant's request for a bond and, absent extraordinary circumstances, the court errs in failing to grant such a request." Smith v. Board of Election Commissioners for the City of Chicago, 591 F.Supp. 70, 71 (N.D.Ill.1984). *See also* Reinders Brothers, Inc. v. Rain Bird Eastern Sales Corp., 627 F.2d 44 (7th Cir.1980). Other courts take the position that "whether or not, and in what amount, a security bond is required is a matter addressed to the sound discretion of the district judge." Bartels v. Biernat, 405 F.Supp. 1012, 1015 (E.D.Wis. 1975). *See also* Scherr v. Volpe, 466 F.2d 1027 (7th Cir.1972). Regardless of whether Rule 65(c) is mandatory or discretionary, a bond is frequently waived for indigent plaintiffs, or for plaintiffs asserting constitutional claims. *See, e.g.,* Toussaint v. Rushen, 553 F.Supp. 1365 (N.D.Cal.1983); Bartels v. Biernat, 405 F.Supp. 1012 (E.D.Wis.1975)); Olshock v. Village of Skokie, 401 F.Supp. 1219 (N.D.Ill.1975). Finally, when the defendant is a governmental entity, the courts often require only a nominal bond or waive the bond requirement altogether. This has been the practice, for example, with respect to suits under the National Environmental Policy Act (NEPA). *See, e.g.,* Friends of the Earth, Inc. v. Brinegar, 518 F.2d 322 (9th Cir.1975). Consider in this regard the language of Natural Resources Defense Council, Inc. v. Morton, 337 F.Supp. 167 (D.D.C.1971) ($100 bond):

> "To require the plaintiffs in the case at bar to post security in the amount requested by the Government to cover the alleged losses would

have the effect of denying three nonprofit environmental organizations from obtaining judicial review of the defendant's actions under NEPA. Congress has indicated that private environmental organizations should assist in enforcing NEPA. Section 101(a) of NEPA states:

'Congress * * * declares that it is the continuing policy of the Federal Government, in cooperation with * * * concerned public and private organizations, to use all practicable means and measures * * * to create and maintain conditions under which man and nature can exist in productive harmony. * * *' 42 U.S.C. § 4331(a) (1970).

The requirement of more than a nominal amount as security would in the Court's opinion stifle the intent of the Act, since these three 'concerned private organizations' would be precluded from obtaining judicial review of the defendant's actions.

* * *

"Lastly, the Court has examined other cases involving similar situations, and it notes that only nominal bonds have been required. *See, e.g.,* Environmental Defense Fund v. Corps of Engineers (Tennessee–Tombigbee), 331 F.Supp. 925 (D.D.C.1971) ($1.00); West Virginia Highlands Conservancy v. Island Creek Coal Co., 441 F.2d 232 (4th Cir.1971) ($100.00); Wilderness Society v. Hickel, 325 F.Supp. 422 (D.D.C.1970) ($100.00). The purpose of the security given under Rule 65(c) is to cover the costs and damages suffered by the party wrongfully enjoined. 7 Moore ¶ 65.09, at 1656. It would be a mistake to treat a revenue loss to the Government the same as pecuniary damage to a private party."

For a discussion of these cases, see Comment, Injunction Bond Amounts in Federal NEPA Litigation, 61 Iowa L.Rev. 580 (1975). For an excellent explanation of why public interest plaintiffs should get injunctions based on nominal bonds, see Henson & Gray, Injunction Bonding in Environmental Litigation, 19 Santa Clara L.Rev. 541 (1979).

The state approach to injunction bonds is even more varied. At one extreme, a few states hold that the bond is jurisdictional. In other words, any interlocutory order issued without a bond is void and a person cannot be held in contempt for violating it. *See, e.g.,* Eichelberger v. Hayton, 814 S.W.2d 179 (Tex.App.1991); Lawrence County v. Brenner, 135 Pa.Cmwlth. 619, 582 A.2d 79 (1990); Bruce v. Maurais, 69 Or.App. 267, 684 P.2d 1243 (1984); Comment, Damages Recoverable on Injunction Bonds in Missouri, 44 Mo.L.Rev. 269, 270 (1979). Numerous states, however, have adopted the language of Federal Rule 65(c) and, like the federal judiciary, the courts in these states have experienced significant difficulty construing it. Some, for example, hold that the failure to require a bond is reversible error. *See, e.g.,* Anders v. Fowler, 423 So.2d 838 (Ala.1982). Others, however, hold that "there are some instances when it is proper for no security to be required of a party seeking injunctive relief." Keith v. Day, 60 N.C.App. 559, 299 S.E.2d 296 (1983). The North Carolina Court of Appeals identified those instances as follows:

"[T]he [trial court] has power not only to set the amount of security but to dispense with any security requirement whatsoever where the restraint will do the defendant 'no material damage,' [citations omitted] where there 'has been no proof of likelihood of harm,' [citations omitted] and where the applicant for equitable relief has 'considerable assets and [is] * * * able to respond in damages if [defendant] does suffer damages by reason of [a wrongful] injunction' [citations omitted]."

Id. at 298. Several other states' approaches are described in Dobbs, Should Security be Required as a Pre–Condition to Provisional Relief?, 52 N.C.L.Rev. 1091, 1097–98 (1974): *

"At least twelve states have statutes which seem to leave the matter of security to the trial judge's discretion, with or without statutory guidelines. Massachusetts reaches this result by judicial decision. A good many statutes imply this by simply providing that the judge 'may' require security instead of saying that he 'shall' do so. Still others insert a specific proviso permitting the judge to dispense with security for any good cause shown. Two states relieve the plaintiff of any obligation to post a bond when he is 'unable' to post one or when the bond would impose 'extraordinary hardship.' In addition to these dozen states, a number of statutes make the bond discretionary in special situations rather than mandatory, for example, in divorce actions. On the other hand, within this group of 'discretionary' states, the bond may be mandatory in special situations, for example, under a local version of the Norris–LaGuardia Act for labor injunctions."

Notes

1. It has been suggested that a mandatory bond requirement may violate the due process clause insofar as it restricts an indigent plaintiff's access to the courts. Dobbs, Should Security Be Required as a Pre–Condition to Provisional Injunctive Relief?, 52 N.C.L.Rev. 1092, 1114–17 (1974).

2. Rule 65(c) provides that "no * * * security shall be required of the United States or an officer or agency thereof." In Egge v. Lane County, 276 Or. 889, 556 P.2d 1372, 1373–74 (1976), when construing a comparable state statute, the court suggested that governmental entities and officials are exempted from the injunction bond requirement for much the same reason that they have traditionally been immune from tort liability. *See also* Southeast Arkansas Landfill, Inc. v. State, 313 Ark. 669, 858 S.W.2d 665 (1993).

PARKER TAMPA TWO, INC. v. SOMERSET DEVELOPMENT CORP.

Supreme Court of Florida, 1989.
544 So.2d 1018.

SHAW, JUSTICE.

Somerset Development Corporation (Somerset) filed a complaint against Hillsborough County seeking injunctive relief based upon the county's alleged breach of a sewer connection agreement whereby the county guaranteed that a certain number of sewer connections for Somerset's projects would be held available at the River Oaks Wastewater Treatment Plant. According to the complaint, the county denied Somerset's requests for sewer connections because it had granted service to so many third parties that the treatment plant was "experiencing intermittent capacity problems." After obtaining an answer from the county and conducting an evidentiary hearing, the trial court attempted to restrict additional third-party connections to River Oaks by issuing a temporary injunction which prohibited the county from issuing building permits to any applicant that held an unused sewer permit for the plant. Somerset, which was exempted from the prohibition, posted a $10,000 injunction bond.

Parker Tampa Two, Inc. (Parker), which was in the process of constructing a residential development, held unused sewer permits for River Oaks and was denied building permits under the injunction. Parker filed a motion to intervene in Somerset's suit against the county and a motion to increase the bond, both of which were denied following a hearing. The court subsequently granted Parker's second motion to intervene. At the hearing on the motion, Roger Stewart, director of the county commission that issues the sewer permits, testified that because the River Oaks treatment plant was then operating over capacity, no developer under any circumstances would be issued a sewer permit.

* * *

Parker filed a cross-claim against Somerset alleging wrongful injunction. Several weeks later, the court dissolved the injunction based on Stewart's earlier testimony. The court granted partial summary judgment in favor of Somerset on the cross-claim, limiting the amount Parker could recover to the $10,000 bond. After Somerset stipulated that Parker's damages exceeded $10,000, the court issued final judgment in favor of Parker in the amount of the bond. Parker appealed; Somerset cross-appealed. The DCA affirmed, certifying the above question. Parker sought review before this Court and Somerset cross-petitioned.

Parker contends that its damages should not be limited to the bond amount. It asserts that to do so is to deny it due process since it had no opportunity to contest the amount. It claims that the amount of such bonds is largely guesswork and that it would be unfair to limit recovery to such a speculative amount. This issue has been addressed by numerous courts throughout the country. *See* Annotation, *Recovery of Damages Resulting From Wrongful Issuance of Injunction as Limited to Amount of Bond,* 30 A.L.R.4th 273 (1984). The minority view, which is followed in five states,[1] holds that liability is not limited to the amount of the bond since the amount is often set in an ex parte proceeding and is at best a

1. *See Smith v. Coronado Foothills Estates Homeowners Ass'n,* 117 Ariz. 171, 571 P.2d 668 (1977); *Howard D. Johnson Co. v. Parkside Dev. Corp.,* 169 Ind.App. 379, 348 N.E.2d 656 (1976); *Davis v. Poitevant & Favre Lumber Co.,* 15 La.App. 657, 132 So. 790 (1931); *Miller Surfacing Co. v. Bridgers,* 269 S.W. 838 (Tex.Civ.App.1924); *Houghton v. Grimes,* 103 Vt. 54, 151 A. 642 (1930).

court estimate based upon opinion or ex parte representations. The majority view, on the other hand, limits liability to the bond amount and is followed in the overwhelming majority of states and by the federal courts.[2] Under both the majority and minority views, the bond amount does not serve as a limit where the injunction is obtained maliciously or in bad faith.

In Florida injunction bonds are addressed by Florida Rule of Civil Procedure 1.610 and section 60.07, Florida Statutes (1987). * * *

Though the rule and statute are silent as to whether liability is limited to the bond amount, two state district courts have addressed the issue and both have followed the majority view. *City Nat'l Bank v. Centrust Savings Bank,* 530 So.2d 317 (Fla. 3d DCA 1988); *Parker Tampa Two.* We too adopt the majority view and limit liability to the bond amount where the injunction is obtained in good faith.

When a court initially sets an injunction bond, this constitutes the court's determination of foreseeable damages based on the good faith representations that are before it. Fla.R.Civ.P. 1.610(b). Should this amount prove insufficient or excessive, an affected party is free to move for modification. A court order denying a motion to modify is directly appealable. Fla.R.App.P. 9.130(a)(3)(B) ("Review of nonfinal orders of lower tribunals is limited to those which * * * refuse to modify or dissolve injunctions * * * "). *See, e.g., Minimatic Components, Inc. v. Westinghouse Elec. Corp.,* 494 So.2d 303 (Fla. 4th DCA 1986). Limiting liability to bond amount thus provides an orderly step-by-step procedure whereby all parties can be continually apprised of the consequences of their actions. To hold the obtaining party fully liable would in many cases expose the party to potentially staggering consequential damages difficult or impossible to project. The public policy encouraging fair access to the courts for those who are in good faith pursuit of their equitable rights must be protected from the deterrent certain to be posed by unknown liability for mistake.

* * *

Limiting liability to the bond amount can also be viewed as an equitable way of apportioning liability between the two entities generally at fault in the issuance of a wrongful injunction, i.e., the obtaining party and the court. The obtaining party often is at fault for asking the court to act hastily, requiring it to dispense with normal procedural safeguards. The court, on the other hand, at times simply misreads or misapplies the law independent of any time constraint imposed upon it by the obtaining party. Limiting liability to the bond amount strikes a median between holding the court fully liable (in which case no recovery could be had), and holding the obtaining party fully liable. *Cf. United Motors Serv. Inc. v. Tropic–Aire, Inc.,* 57 F.2d 479 (8th Cir.1932) (wrongfully issued injunction is court error for which no recovery is available).

Parker contends that its recovery should not be limited to the bond amount because it was given no notice of, or opportunity to participate in,

2. *See* Annotation, *Recovery of Damages Resulting From Wrongful Issuance of Injunction as Limited to Amount of Bond,* 30 A.L.R.4th 273 (1984).

the proceeding in which the bond was set. We disagree. The county, as a named party under the injunction, did participate in the proceeding, and later, on behalf of Parker, did move the court to increase the bond. Parker itself, subsequent to the initial bond proceeding, also moved to increase the bond amount and did participate in the injunction action as a party. We find that Parker had ample opportunity to participate in the setting of the bond via its right to move for an increase in the amount.

On cross-petition, Somerset alleges that the injunction was not wrongfully issued, arguing that mere dissolution of an injunction does not mean that it was wrongful and that in the instant case the injunction was dissolved because it had become moot, not because it had been wrongfully issued. We disagree. The standard for determining whether an injunction was wrongfully issued is simply whether the petitioning party was unentitled to injunctive relief. *See National Surety Co. v. Willys–Overland, Inc.,* 103 Fla. 738, 138 So. 24 (1931); *Sewell v. Huffstetler,* 83 Fla. 629, 93 So. 162 (1922); *Braun v. Intercontinental Bank,* 452 So.2d 998 (Fla. 3d DCA 1984), *review denied,* 462 So.2d 1106 (Fla.1985); *Tracy.* In the instant case, sufficient evidence exists to support the trial court's finding that the injunction should not have been issued.

Somerset alleges that Parker was unentitled to recovery under the bond because it was not an expressly enjoined party. We disagree. Liability under an injunction bond generally is set by the terms of the bond, not by the provisions of the injunction. *Sewell,* 83 Fla. at 642, 93 So. at 162 ("The liability of the obligors is determined by the terms of the bond alone and not by the order."); *Rice v. White,* 147 So.2d 204, 208 (Fla. 1st DCA 1962) ("liability of the obligors is determined by the bond and not by the court order."). *See Hall v. Hanford,* 66 So.2d 474 (Fla.1953). Parker was a party to the action, and the bond under which its wrongful injunction cross-claim was brought expressly provided that the surety's obligation under the bond extended to all "defendants." Though Parker, in fact, was a party-plaintiff, not a defendant, this circumstance was entirely fortuitous. Parker had initially sought to intervene as a defendant, but was allowed to intervene as a plaintiff purely for the court's convenience. * * * To prevent recovery based on this technicality, especially when Somerset has noted that it essentially filled in the blanks on a standardized bond form, would be to exalt form over substance.

Based on the foregoing, we answer the certified question in the affirmative and approve the district court decision.

It is so ordered.

EHRLICH, C.J., and OVERTON, MCDONALD, BARKETT and GRIMES, JJ., concur.

KOGAN, J., concurs in part and dissents in part with an opinion. [opinion omitted]

Notes

1. The majority rule limiting the plaintiff's liability to the amount of the injunction bond is often justified by referring to the historical development of the bond, as in Buddy Systems, Inc. v. Exer–Genie, Inc., 545 F.2d 1164 (9th Cir.1976):

"The practice of giving tangible items as security, called 'gage,' in order to acquire credit arose before any consensual theory of contract obligation emerged. The creditor took possession of the gage and retained it until he was repaid. But there was no underlying duty on the part of the debtor—if he failed to pay, the creditor held the security, but had no action on the debt. A surety was referred to as a 'pledge,' and was at first literally 'an animated gage * * * delivered over to slavery but subject to redemption.' 2 F. Pollock & F. Maitland, The History of English Law, 185–86 (2d ed. 1899).

"Although these devices were used for a number of purposes, they also served a role very similar to that of the Rule 65 injunction bond involved in this case. For example, at early common law the plaintiff in a replevin action against a distrainor was required to give 'gage and pledge'—*i.e.,* a surety's bond. *Id.* at 577; *see* Dobbs, Should Security be Required as a Pre–Condition to Provisional Injunctive Relief?, 52 N.Car.L.Rev. 1091, 1093 (1974).

"At later common law, a bond was a sealed and delivered instrument binding the obligor to pay a sum of money. 1A A. Corbin, Contracts, § 258, at 455 (1963). It did not need to be supported by consideration. 12 Halsbury's Laws of England § 1400 (4th ed. 1975). While common law bonds may be used for many purposes, including security for the performance of independent obligations, *see id.* § 1387, the term 'bond' does not refer to the duty whose performance is secured, but only to the security itself. *See id.* § 1385.

"[N]o duty to recompense the victim of wrongful provisional relief independent of the security instrument may be implied. It is a well-settled rule that there can be no recovery for damages sustained by a wrongful issuance of a preliminary injunction in the absence of a bond, Russell v. Farley, 105 U.S. 433, 437, 26 L.Ed. 1060 (1881); Benz v. Compania Naviera Hidalgo, S.A., 205 F.2d 944, 947–48 (9th Cir.) (on petition for rehearing), cert. denied, 346 U.S. 885, 74 S.Ct. 135, 98 L.Ed. 389 (1953), unless the defendant sues for malicious prosecution or on a theory of unjust enrichment, Northern Oil Co. v. Socony Mobil Oil Co., 347 F.2d 81, 83 (2d Cir.1965); 11 C. Wright & A. Miller, Federal Practice and Procedure § 2973, at 652 (1973); see Note, Greenwood County v. Duke Power Co., 7 U.Chi.L.Rev. 382 (1940). If a bond is posted, liability is limited by the terms of the bond or the order of the court that required the posting. *See* 11 Wright & Miller, *supra,* § 2973, at 652; Comment, The Triggering of Liability on Injunction Bonds, 52 N.Car.L.Rev. 1252, 1258 (1974)."

2. In Dickey v. Rosso, 23 Cal.App.3d 493, 100 Cal.Rptr. 358 (1972), the plaintiff challenged the constitutionality of the majority rule:

"The Rossos contend that the limitation of damages for the improper issuance of an injunction to the amount of the undertaking violates due process of law. They argue that the legal procedures for the use of injunctive remedies fail to make them whole for all losses the use of these remedies may have caused them and that no effective means were given them to challenge the trial court's determination of the amount of the undertaking.

"We find no merit in this argument. In creating legal procedures for use of the provisional remedy of injunctive relief the state has two conflicting interests to balance—that of defendants, who should be compensated for damage caused by legal procedures whose use is later shown to have been unjustified; and that of honest plaintiffs, who should not be deterred from using the courts by fear of incurring unlimited liability from their use of the court's process. The state has established an entirely reasonable scheme for the use of injunctive relief, in that plaintiff is told in advance what his maximum summary liability will be for making use of the court's injunctive powers pending a determination of the merits of his cause, and defendant is provided an opportunity to make a showing what the amount of his damages is likely to be as a consequence of plaintiff's use of the remedy of injunctive relief. Thereafter the court fixes the amount of the undertaking in connection with the use of injunctive relief. If at a later time defendant discovers further possibilities of damages arising during the pendency of the litigation and makes a proper showing of the possibility of such damages, the court may require plaintiff to increase the amount of his undertaking as a condition of the continuance of injunctive relief. (Asevado v. Orr, 100 Cal. 293, 298, 34 P. 777.) The possibility that damages might be inestimable, a possibility not apparent here, is outweighed by the need to provide honest plaintiffs with recourse to the courts.

"Twice the Rossos requested the trial court to increase the amount of the undertaking on the preliminary injunction. Twice the trial court in its sound discretion rejected their request. The Rossos did not seek to challenge the trial court's exercise of its discretion by writ or by appeal, and consequently the cause of their present discontent lies not in lack of effective process but in lack of effective use of existing process."

3. Does the majority approach assume that the defendant has had ample opportunity to contest the amount of the bond? Suppose a trial court issues an ex parte restraining order compelling defendant to perform a personal services agreement pending the resolution of the parties' dispute by arbitration. The bond is set at $1500. The trial judge rebuffs at least two attempts by the defendant to have an evidentiary hearing on the bond. Later the restraining order is reversed by an appellate court and the defendant seeks damages based on the wrongful issuance of the restraining order. Should the defendant's recovery be limited to the amount of the bond? In Seaescape, Ltd., Inc. v. Maximum Marketing Exposure, Inc., 568 So.2d 952 (Fla.App.1990), the court stated:

"It is plain that the injunction should not have been entered in the first instance, and the motion to dissolve should have been granted. The contracts at issue here are ordinary contracts for employment or personal services. Such contracts are not enforceable by injunction or specific performance. * * *

"In *Parker,* the petitioner had moved to increase the bond amount and had ample opportunity to participate in the setting of an appropriate amount. * * * Under those circumstances, the court held that Parker was limited to the amount of the bond when seeking damages for the wrongful obtaining of the injunction. Here, by contrast, [defendant] never obtained the evidentiary hearing despite having diligently sought that relief, including expedited consideration here.

> "On these facts [defendant] cannot be bound by the $1500 ex parte bond amount. One possibility would be to remand for the evidentiary hearing [defendant] was denied, so that a new figure would be set which would serve as the damage limitation. In our view that procedure would waste judicial resources and as a practical matter would revolve around [defendant's] actual claim for damages, since the effect of our vacating the injunction is to determine that [defendant] was wrongfully enjoined. * * * We conclude that where there has been no opportunity for a hearing and where the enjoined party has proceeded expeditiously to exhaust available remedies, the damages for wrongful injunction are not limited to the bond amount."

Id. at 954–56.

4. Under the majority view, the plaintiff has no personal liability beyond the bond amount unless the defendant can prove malicious prosecution. Suppose, however, a judge conditions the grant of a preliminary injunction on the willingness of the plaintiff to accept personal liability for any damages wrongfully sustained by the defendant. According to Professor Dobbs, "[w]here the plaintiff clearly has assets or income more than sufficient to pay predicted damages, this solution is favorable to the defendant because it removes the limitation. If the plaintiff has a high probability of success on the merits, it is also favorable to the plaintiff, because it saves the cost of bonding. When very large sums of money are at issue, the savings may be significant." D. Dobbs, Law of Remedies 198 (2d ed. 1993). At least one case supports this approach. *See* The Continuum Company v. Incepts, Inc., 873 F.2d 801 (5th Cir.1989).

MARGOLIES v. ENCOUNTER, INC.

Court of Appeals of New York, 1977.
42 N.Y.2d 475, 398 N.Y.S.2d 877, 368 N.E.2d 1243.

JONES, JUDGE.

We hold that the purpose and function of an undertaking given by a plaintiff pursuant to the provisions of CPLR 6312 (subd. [b]), prior to the granting of a preliminary injunction, is to reimburse the defendant for damages sustained if it is later finally determined that the preliminary injunction was erroneously granted.

Encounter, Inc., defendant-appellant, is an organization chartered by the New York State Drug Abuse Control Commission to provide residential and ambulatory services for drug dependent persons. On March 1, 1974, in accordance with commission approval, Encounter moved its facilities from Brooklyn to a building located on East 68th Street in Manhattan. Plaintiffs-respondents, tenants of the building and a neighborhood association, instituted the present action against Encounter and the owner of the building seeking a permanent injunction restraining Encounter from taking possession of the leased premises.

Supreme Court on May 17, 1974 granted plaintiffs' motion for a preliminary injunction, conditioned on plaintiffs' posting an undertaking in the amount of $10,000 pursuant to the provisions of CPLR 6312 (subd. [b]), and denied defendants' cross motion to dismiss the complaint. The undertaking was posted and Encounter vacated the premises. On appeal, on July 2, 1974 the Appellate Division modified by vacating the preliminary injunction but affirmed the denial of the cross motion to dismiss the complaint. Encounter then moved back into the premises. * * *

[Eight months later, Encounter vacated the premises, agreed to a discontinuance of the action, and moved to recover damages on the bond. A special referee assessed the damages at more than $10,000, but refused to allow recovery because there had been "no final determination that the plaintiffs were not entitled to an injunction."]

The issue presented is the meaning properly to be attached to the clause in CPLR 6312 (subd. [b])—"if it is finally determined that [plaintiff] was not entitled to an injunction". That is the contingency fixed by the statute on which depends a defendant's right to recover damages on a CPLR 6312 (subd. [b]) undertaking. Plaintiffs argue that the contingency referred to is a determination that plaintiffs are not entitled to prevail in the final outcome of the action itself, and contend that, in view of the discontinuance of the underlying action with Encounter's consent, there has been no such predicate final determination. We reject that view; the statute refers to a final determination that the plaintiffs were not entitled to the preliminary injunction, rather than a determination with respect to their right to a permanent injunction or other favorable outcome on the merits of the main action. The proper focus is on the propriety of the issuance of the preliminary injunction when it was granted at the commencement of the action.

A preliminary injunction is an extraordinary provisional remedy to which a plaintiff is entitled only on a special showing. It operates as a substantial limitation on the defendant's interests prior to any adjudication of the respective rights of the parties on the merits of the controversy between them. To afford reasonable protection to the defendant against an erroneous or improper grant of this special provisional remedy, the plaintiff as beneficiary thereof is required to post an undertaking in an amount fixed by the court. If it is later finally determined that the preliminary injunction was improperly granted there will then be a ready source from which the defendant may recover for damages which he may have sustained.

In many, even most, instances the entitlement to the preliminary injunction will parallel the plaintiff's right to a permanent injunction or to other relief he seeks in the main action. Consequently, it has sometimes been suggested that defendant's right to damages turns on the final outcome in the main action. This is not the critical contingency. The defendant's right to damages depends on whether the plaintiff was entitled to the preliminary injunction, not on whether the defendant eventually prevails on the merits.

* * *

For the reasons stated, the order of the Appellate Division should be reversed, with costs, and the case remitted to Supreme Court for entry of an order directing payment of damages, as found by the special referee, confirmed by Special Term and affirmed at the Appellate Division to the full extent of liability on the undertaking.

BREITEL, C.J., and JASEN, GABRIELLI, WACHTLER, FUCHSBERG and COOKE, JJ., concur.

Notes

1. Does *Margolies* require an "explicit pronouncement" that the preliminary injunction was improperly granted before a cause of action on the bond accrues? According to Cross Properties, Inc. v. Brook Realty Co., Inc., 76 A.D.2d 445, 453, 430 N.Y.S.2d 820, 828 (1980), "*Margolies* stands for the propositions (a) that the ultimate denial of a permanent injunction to plaintiff or a determination that a plaintiff is not entitled to prevail in the final outcome, does not constitute a determination that plaintiff was not entitled to a preliminary injunction, and (b) that a finding must appear, either expressly or by implication, in the trial court's decision prior to the granting of damages that plaintiff was not entitled to the preliminary injunction."

Courts continually have difficulty in determining when a cause of action accrues on an injunction bond. Consider, in this regard, the language of Industrial Innovators, Inc. v. Myrick–White, Inc., 99 N.C.App. 42, 392 S.E.2d 425 (1990) that borrows heavily from Professor Dobb's analysis of the problem:

"There exist three possibilities for determining whether a defendant has been wrongfully enjoined:

> One possibility is that liability on the bond is determined solely by the *ultimate* merits. Regardless how circumstances appeared when the provisional order was issued, the plaintiff would be liable if he lost in the ultimate decision on the merits, and he would be relieved of liability if he won. The other basic possibility is that liability is determined solely by preliminary merits. The plaintiff under this view would be liable if the preliminary injunction was erroneous on the basis of evidence adduced at the time, even if a final decision on the merits went in his favor; by the same token he would be relieved of liability if the preliminary order was correct as of the time it was issued, even though he ultimately lost. A combination of these rules is also possible, for instance, a rule that imposes liability if either preliminary error or ultimate error is demonstrated.

Dobbs, *Should Security be Required as a Pre–Condition to Provisional Injunctive Relief?*, 52 N.C.L.Rev. 1091, 1147 (1974) (emphasis in original). * * *

"Any standard for determining whether the defendant was wrongfully enjoined should be consistent with the very purpose of the bond which is to 'require that the plaintiff assume the risks of paying damages he causes as the "price" he must pay to have the extraordinary privilege of provisional relief.' *Dobbs,* at 1149. Consistent with that purpose * * * Professor Dobbs observed:

> The fact that the plaintiff's position seemed sound when it was presented on the *ex parte* or preliminary hearing is no basis for relieving him of liability, since the very risk that requires a bond is the risk of error because such hearings are attenuated and inadequate. To say that proof of the inadequate hearing, against which the bond is

intended to protect, relieves of liability on the bond is merely to subvert the bond's purpose. Thus the few cases that seem to deal with this situation seem correct in assessing liability to the plaintiff who loses on the ultimate merits, even when his proof warranted preliminary relief at the time it was awarded.

Dobbs, at 1149–1150."

Suppose the plaintiff's underlying claim is voluntarily dismissed. Or suppose it is dismissed by stipulation and the parties do not specify what should happen to defendant's potential claim on the injunction bond. Alternatively, suppose the claim is dismissed either for mootness or lack of jurisdiction. Does defendant have a valid cause of action on the bond in any of these situations? *See Myrick–White* and *Parker Tampa Two, supra;* Note, Recovery for Wrongful Interlocutory Injunctions Under Rule 65(c), 99 Harv.L.Rev. 828, 839–40 (1986).

2. Suppose a plaintiff only partially prevails in the injunction litigation. How should that affect her liability on the bond? Consider the language of Laux v. Chopin Land Associates, Inc., 615 N.E.2d 902, 906 (Ind.App.1993), a case in which a preliminary injunction prohibited defendants from raising any hogs on their property, but the permanent injunction allowed them to continue their hog operation subject to certain specific limitations:

"Without delving into a philosophical conversation regarding what it means to 'prevail', we recognize the fact that it is not a black and white issue; rather it is made up of varying shades of gray. While it is true that the [defendants] did not completely prevail in this case, to the extent that they were less constrained by the permanent injunction than they had been by the preliminary injunction, they have in fact prevailed and may be entitled to some compensation. Furthermore, the narrowing of the scope of the permanent injunction implies that the preliminary injunction was, at least in part, wrongful and the [defendants] were entitled to relief from that wrongful enjoinment.

"In the present action the preliminary injunction was absolute and forbade the [defendants] from raising any hogs on their property. The permanent injunction, on the other hand, allowed the [defendants] a limited right to raise hogs on their property. To the extent that the preliminary injunction prevented the [defendants] from this limited right, it was wrongful and the [defendants] are entitled to relief."

CITY AND COUNTY OF DENVER v. AMERITRUST COMPANY NATIONAL ASSOCIATION

Colorado Court of Appeals, 1992.
832 P.2d 1054.

Opinion by JUDGE DAVIDSON.

* * *

In September 1989, Denver and [Denver Urban Renewal Authority] DURA filed a motion for a preliminary injunction seeking to enjoin certain entities not parties to this appeal and Ameritrust from demolishing the Central Bank West Building (building). The demolition was to be accomplished by December 28, 1989, as a condition of a complicated sale-lease back transaction between the defendants. According to the transaction, if the original owner declined to buy the building and met certain conditions, a surety company was obligated to pay $14.5 million to Ameritrust, the lending institution, under a Property Value Indemnity Bond and take title to the property. In 1988, the original owner opted to demolish the building rather than repurchase or renovate the bank building.

Subsequently, Denver and DURA, claiming that the building was protected from demolition under restrictive covenants within the city's Skyline Urban Renewal Plan and certain agreements between the parties, brought an action for declaratory judgment and for injunctive relief to enjoin defendants from demolishing the building until the legal questions could be determined.

On September 20, 1989, the trial court issued a temporary restraining order. On October 26, 1989, after permitting Historic Denver to intervene as a plaintiff, the court granted the plaintiffs' motion for preliminary injunction enjoining defendants from demolishing the building. At that time, the court ordered Historic Denver to post a $500 bond as security, but waived a security bond for Denver and DURA pursuant to C.R.C.P. 65(c).

The trial was held in April 1990. After the close of plaintiffs' case, the trial court ruled that the restrictive covenant relied on by the plaintiffs to prevent demolition was ambiguous and, thus, must be construed strictly against limitation on the use of property and in favor of its free and unrestricted use. Accordingly, it granted defendants' motion to dismiss pursuant to C.R.C.P. 41(b)(1). The court then issued a declaratory judgment in their favor and dissolved the preliminary injunction.

Thereafter, pursuant to C.R.C.P. 65(c) and 65.1, Ameritrust moved for recovery of costs and damages incurred as a result of the wrongful preliminary injunction. Specifically, claiming its damages might reach $14.5 million, the amount of the Property Value Indemnity Bond that the surety company refused to pay, it asked the court to retain jurisdiction pending the outcome of a related federal action between Ameritrust and the surety. The trial court denied this motion.

In its order, the court assumed without deciding "that Ameritrust was 'wrongfully' enjoined and could establish damages" but nevertheless found that it "would be inequitable and oppressive to award Ameritrust costs and damages in this action." The court also denied Ameritrust's motion for reconsideration for the same reasons.

Ameritrust appeals, basing its various contentions of error on the security requirements mandated by C.R.C.P. 65(c). That rule provides:

> No restraining order or preliminary injunction shall issue except upon the giving of security by the applicant, in such sum as the court deems proper, for the payment of such costs and damages as may be incurred or suffered by any party who is found to have been wrongfully enjoined or restrained. No such security shall be required of the state or of any county or municipal corporation of this state or of any officer or agency thereof acting in official capacity.

* * *

Ameritrust contends that under C.R.C.P. 65(c) plaintiffs are liable for damages caused by the wrongful preliminary injunction. * * *

A.

C.R.C.P. 65(c) imposes two conditions on an enjoined defendant seeking to recover damages on a bond: First, the injunction must have been "wrongful," and second, the defendant must have suffered damages as a result of the issuance of the injunction. *See Wick v. Pueblo West Metropolitan District,* 789 P.2d 457 (Colo.App.1989). Here, because the trial court "assumed that Ameritrust was 'wrongfully' enjoined and could establish damages," these conditions are satisfied. At issue, therefore, is what discretion, if any, the trial court has to refuse damages on a bond if both these conditions are met.

* * *

The great majority of courts which have ruled on this issue have adopted a so-called "judicial discretion" standard in which the trial court has discretion in deciding whether to award damages on the bond. *See Alabama ex rel. Siegelman v. United States Environmental Protection Agency,* 925 F.2d 385 (11th Cir.1991). Although there are two other standards—the automatic damages and the malicious prosecution standards, *see Cappaert Enterprises v. Citizens & Southern International Bank,* 564 F.Supp. 214 (E.D.La.1983), relatively few jurisdictions follow these, and we are persuaded that the judicial discretion standard is most consistent with the plain language of the rule.

By its terms, C.R.C.P. 65(c) requires that an applicant give a bond, but it does not expressly order the court to pay that bond to a prevailing defendant. As we read the rule, the security is merely to ensure that an applicant is able to pay damages in the event that a court so requires.

In deciding to adopt this judicial discretion standard, we must also consider what limits are on that discretion. Although some courts view the trial court as having almost unlimited discretion to deny damages, *see H & R Block, Inc. v. McCaslin,* 541 F.2d 1098 (5th Cir.1976); *Page Communications Engineers, Inc. v. Froehlke,* 475 F.2d 994 (D.C.Cir.1973), most others construe the pertinent rule as implying a preference for awarding damages. *See Alabama ex rel. Siegelman v. United States Environmental Protection Agency, supra; Coyne–Delaney Co. v. Capital Development Board,* 717 F.2d 385 (7th Cir.1983).

Under this principle of preference, a trial court presumes that a prevailing defendant is entitled to damages on the injunction bond, unless there is good reason for not requiring such payment in the particular case. *Coyne–Delaney Co. v. Capital Development Board, supra.* This "good reason" standard is the one we now adopt. As the *Coyne–Delaney* court stated: "Not only is it implied by the text of Rule 65(c) but it makes the law more predictable and discourages the seeking of preliminary injunctions on flimsy (though not necessarily frivolous) grounds."

B.

The trial court applied this standard in denying Ameritrust's motion for costs and damages. Although Ameritrust does not argue that this was inappropriate, it contends that the trial court looked at the wrong factors in determining that "good reason" existed. * * *

1.

In its brief to this court, Ameritrust appears to argue that a determination of "good reason" must be based exclusively on three factors set forth by the *Coyne–Delaney* court—resources of the parties, defendant's mitigation of damages, and outcome of the underlying suit—and that the trial court here erred by considering other factors. We do not read that decision so restrictively. In fact the *Coyne–Delaney* court itself specified those factors only as examples of legitimate grounds for a trial court to consider in determining whether "good reason" exists to deny damages.

* * *

2.

The trial court's order, in pertinent part, stated:

> A prevailing defendant is generally entitled to costs and damages incurred as a result of having been wrongfully enjoined unless there is good reason not to require plaintiff to pay in a particular case. [*Coyne–Delaney*] One good reason not to award such damages is where it would be oppressive and inequitable to do so. [*Page Communications*] In this action, the covenant was ambiguous and under Colorado law the Court had no choice but to construe it in favor of the Defendants. This was the sole basis for dissolving the preliminary injunction. The record in this case clearly supports the contention that all other equitable considerations favored the Plaintiffs. In addition, Plaintiff is a municipal corporation and Plaintiff-in-Intervention is a non-profit, public interest corporation. Therefore, assuming that Ameritrust was 'wrongfully' enjoined and could establish damages, the Court, nevertheless, finds that it would be inequitable and oppressive to award Ameritrust costs and damages in this action.

We have little difficulty in concluding from this order that the court considered and balanced appropriate factors in determining that good reason existed to deny damages.

First, the trial court considered the outcome of the underlying suit, finding that the ambiguity of the covenant was "the sole basis for dissolving the preliminary injunction" and that "substantial evidence support[ed] [p]laintiffs' position" at both the preliminary and permanent injunction hearings. Although plaintiffs ultimately were unsuccessful at trial, it is quite apparent that their contentions were hardly frivolous.

Moreover, implicit in this finding is consideration of the fact that the claims were brought in good faith. Although good faith is not enough to defeat the assessment of damages, it is one of the factors which the court may consider. *See Zenith Radio Corp. v. United States,* 823 F.2d 518 (Fed.Civ.1987).

Third, the court considered the financial status of the parties, that is that plaintiffs were, respectively, a municipal corporation and a non-profit public interest group. *See Coyne–Delaney v. Capital Development Board, supra.* Certainly, insofar as Historic Denver is a non-profit public interest corporation, its financial status weighs heavily against an assessment of several million dollars in damages.

Fourth, and what was given primary consideration by the trial court, was the fact that the action was brought solely in the public interest. Confronted with the imminent destruction of an historic building, the plaintiffs had little choice but to seek an injunction until a court could determine the legal effect of the restrictive covenant. To impose a liability of $14.5 million in damages in this action could, if nothing else, significantly deter any further action brought for the public good.

Ameritrust argues that a damages award should be imposed precisely to make a plaintiff "think long and hard" before seeking such injunctive relief. From our review of the record, these plaintiffs did just that. Considering the circumstances, we conclude that they had few alternatives but to act as they did. To require them to bear the staggering consequential damages requested here would have a clear chilling effect on future good faith efforts brought in the public interest. Thus, the trial court's consideration of this factor was appropriate.

Other courts which have addressed the question have considered similar factors to determine whether good reason exists for denying damages. For example, the *Coyne–Delaney* court discussed good faith and change in the law, in addition to resources of the parties, whether the defendant mitigated the damages, and the outcome of the underlying suit. *See also Alabama ex rel. Siegelman v. United States Environmental Protection Agency, supra* (good faith, although insufficient alone, and public interest); *Cappaert Enterprises v. Citizens & Southern International Bank,* 564 F.Supp. 214 (E.D.La.1983) (enjoined party fails to oppose an injunction diligently, applicant fails to prevail solely because of an unanticipated change in circumstances, enjoined party profits in addition to being damaged by injunction); *Sierra Club v. Hodel,* 848 F.2d 1068 (10th Cir.1988) (legitimate environmental concerns having a high public interest litigated in good faith).

Ameritrust contends, however, that even if the trial court considered some appropriate factors in denying damages, it erred by including in its consideration the requirements set forth in *Rathke v. MacFarlane,* 648 P.2d 648 (Colo.1982) for the issuance of a preliminary injunction. Specifically, it argues that those factors are irrelevant. We disagree.

First, some of the *Rathke* factors, such as whether the injunction serves the public interest, are not only relevant but identical to specific "good reason" factors discussed in other cases. *See Alabama ex rel. Siegelman v. United States Environmental Protection Agency, supra.* Moreover, the fact that the trial court found that all of the *Rathke* equitable factors, except success on the merits, were in favor of the plaintiffs, is supportive of the court's finding that plaintiffs' claims were meritorious and made in good faith. * * *

We conclude, therefore, that the trial court considered and evaluated appropriate factors in deciding that good reason existed to deny damages. In so holding, we do not imply that whenever a government or non-profit group acts in good faith and in the public interest to enjoin a property owner's use of its property that it is necessarily relieved of potential damage assessments. We conclude only that, under the facts at issue here, the trial court's determination of good reason was proper, and that, thus, it did not err in denying Ameritrust's motion for damages. *See Zenith Radio Corp. v. United States, supra.*

* * *

Because we conclude that the trial court did not abuse its discretion in denying Ameritrust's motion for costs and damages, we do not reach Ameritrust's contention that a plaintiff's liability for damages may exceed the limit of its bond.

The judgment is affirmed.

STERNBERG, C.J., and PIERCE, J., concur.

Note

The other two standards governing assessment of damages on injunction bonds only briefly referred to in the principal case are described in greater detail in Alabama ex rel. Siegelman v. U.S.E.P.A., 925 F.2d 385, 389 (11th Cir.1991):

> "The first is the 'automatic damages' standard, which requires an award whenever a party that has obtained a preliminary injunction is subsequently denied permanent injunctive relief. * * * At the opposite extreme is the 'malicious prosecution' standard, which 'applies only in cases where the applicant for injunctive relief fails to furnish adequate security.' Cappaert Enterprises v. Citizens & S. Int'l Bank, 564 F.Supp. 214, 218 (E.D.La. 1983). * * * That standard prohibits a damages award unless the applicant for preliminary injunction acted maliciously and without probable cause."

CARR v. CITIZENS BANK AND TRUST COMPANY

Supreme Court of Virginia, 1985.
228 Va. 644, 325 S.E.2d 86.

COCHRAN, JUSTICE.

[Carr, the holder of a junior deed of trust (mortgage) on certain real estate sought temporary and permanent injunctive relief against foreclosure of the Bank's senior deed of trust alleging that the Bank and others fraudulently obtained from her an agreement subordinating her deed of trust to the Bank's. The trial court granted a temporary injunction and required Carr to post a $25,000 cash bond "to stand for any damages which the Bank suffered as a proximate result of the injunction." Several days later, on Carr's motion, the trial court dissolved the temporary injunction and four months thereafter, again on her motion, dismissed her suit. The Bank then promptly foreclosed its deed of trust. Later it filed suit on the bond and obtained a jury verdict for $10,000. The trial court entered judgment on the verdict and Carr and her surety appealed on the ground that there was insufficient evidence of damages attributable to the temporary injunction.]

In an action on an injunction bond, a plaintiff may recover all damages that are the natural and proximate result of the issuance of the injunction. * * * But damages are recoverable only to the extent that they may be ascertained with reasonable certainty. * * * Properly allowable damages include only those damages that directly result from the suing out of the injunction. * * * It is generally held that damages resulting from the underlying suit but not from the injunction itself are not recoverable in an action on an injunction bond. * * *

The proper measure of a decrease in market value of property caused by delay resulting from wrongful issuance of an injunction is the difference in market value at the time it would have been sold absent any restraint and the market value when the injunction no longer prevented the sale. This formulation allows a reasonable time following dissolution of the injunction to take necessary steps to effect the sale. *See* Callaway v. Sparks, 184 Okl. 569, 570, 89 P.2d 275, 277–78 (1939) (court allowed reasonable time to harvest crop for sale after expiration of injunction order). But where an unreasonable time elapses before the sale occurs, the date of the actual sale may not be used in the comparison of values since this measure might reflect a diminution in value attributable to causes other than the injunction. *See id.* at 571, 89 P.2d at 278.

In the present case, the Bank failed to meet these proof requirements. The Bank presented evidence of several causes for its delay in selling the property—the injunction, the underlying suit, and its own hope that interest rates would continue to drop. Bank officials indicated, however, that the principal reasons were the pending suit and the potential change in interest rates. In this suit on the injunction bond, the Bank may not properly recover for any loss in value occasioned by the underlying suit or a self-imposed delay. It can recover only for the decrease in value directly attributable to the issuance of the injunction. The Bank, however, offered no evidence to establish the value of the property immediately following dissolution of the injunction or a period after dissolution during which the sale could have been effected. (There was evidence that a period of two months would be sufficient to readvertise the property and conduct the sale). Nor did the Bank offer any proof of the amount of loss attributable to each cause. The plaintiff has the burden of proving with reasonable certainty the amount of damages and the cause from which they resulted; speculation and conjecture cannot form the basis of the recovery. Hale v. Fawcett, 214 Va. 583, 585, 202 S.E.2d 923, 925 (1974); Barnes v. Quarries, Inc., 204 Va. 414, 418, 132 S.E.2d 395, 397–98 (1963). Where the loss results from several causes, the plaintiff must show within a reasonable degree of certainty the amount chargeable against a particular defendant. *Hale,* 214 Va. at 586, 202 S.E.2d at 925. If the proof is too uncertain to allow a jury to apportion the part for which the defendant is responsible, the issue should not be submitted to the jury. *Id.,* 202 S.E.2d at 925.

In this case, the court instructed the jury that it must determine whether the injunction order was the natural and proximate cause of an alleged decrease in the amount the Bank received upon foreclosure, and, if so, the amount of the decrease. But there was no evidence of the damages solely attributable to Carr's obtaining the injunction. Therefore, the court erred in overruling defendants' motion to strike the evidence and improperly allowed the jury to assess their liability without evidence to justify the award. * * *

In view of this ruling, we find it unnecessary to reach the other issues raised on appeal. We will reverse the judgment of the trial court and enter final judgment for Carr and Cuthbert.

Reversed and final judgment.

Notes

1. The measure of damages on an injunction bond is discussed in Dobbs. Should Security Be Required As a Pre–Condition to Provisional Injunctive Relief?, 52 N.C.L.Rev. 1091, 1125–27, 1131–32, 1133 (1974): *

> "(b) *Damages measures and items of recovery. (i) General damages.* Courts and, in some states, statutes sometimes speak of measuring damages on the injunction bond by an equitable standard. But in practice this does not seem to result in measures of damages different from those used in other cases. Courts usually permit recovery of nominal damages if no others are proven, general damages roughly of the kind permitted in an analogous tort or contract damages case, and special damages. * * *
>
> "In many instances analogies from the law of tort or contract damages furnish obvious guides. If the injunctive order wrongly deprives the defendant of possession of land or chattels, the rental value during the period in which he was deprived of use is an appropriate measure of damages. * * * If the injunction has the effect of permitting physical damage or destruction to the property of the defendant, the measure ordinarily mentioned is the diminished value of the property. No doubt in an appropriate case, the defendant could repair the property and charge reasonable repair costs instead.
>
> "Not all provisional injunctive orders deal directly with tangible property. One kind of order that appears in some of the cases is the order restraining the defendant from working for plaintiff's competitor in alleged violation of a covenant. Either the covenant or the injunction or both is frequently overbroad in such cases and is overturned when a hearing is held. The defendant has in such cases often lost either wages or an opportunity to make a profit. Subject to the rule requiring him to minimize damages, he is entitled to recover lost wages or loss of earning capacity.
>
> * * *
>
> "*(ii) Special damages. (A) Generally.* In most of the bond cases, the significant award is the award for special rather than general damages, most commonly the award for attorneys' fees. Special damages are those not based on a general model of expected loss like diminished property value or loss of bargain under a contract. They are items of particular expense proven particularly in the case before the court. More exacting proof is often demanded when special damages are sought, and actual, realized loss must be established. When special damages are sought, the

claimant must prove the damages with reasonable certainty and must convince the court that they are not too remote or approximate. He must also show that any expenses incurred and claimed as damages were reasonable.

"Among the kinds of special damages that have been successfully claimed when proof is adequate are: loss of profits, increased construction costs where construction was delayed by the injunction, and various costs of the preliminary litigation. All of these costs, if allowable at all, are allowable in addition to the general damages already mentioned.

* * *

"*(C) Attorney's Fees.* The backbone of special damages awards in most instances is the award of the attorney's fee. Most courts have sustained such awards under governing statutes. Some of the courts limit such fee recoveries to fees earned in procuring a dissolution of the TRO or the preliminary injunction since the statute and the bond are intended to protect against improvident provisional relief, not against the main suit. Other courts have taken a more liberal position and have said that, at least when the attorney seeks dissolution of a provisional order but is forced to defend the main action because the dissolution was improperly denied, the additional fees incurred on the main action are attributable to the improvident provisional relief and can be awarded."

2. As the foregoing materials illustrate, numerous significant substantive and policy problems concerning injunction bonds remain largely unresolved and continue to perplex courts. Consider, in this regard, Professor Dobb's thoughtful commentary:

"Injunction bond cases raise many problems, not the least of which is the fact that judges often underestimate the potential harm to a defendant. This comment, however, only addresses two structural problems that suggest the need for a more comprehensive statutory scheme.

"A bond requirement usually adds to the plaintiff's cost of litigating. Usually the plaintiff pays a premium (annually) for a commercial bond. Alternatives may be cheaper. The court may permit some other form of security; the plaintiff might be permitted to file a certificate of deposit with the clerk, so that if the plaintiff wins, all interest payable on the certificate will accrue to the plaintiff. Or the plaintiff might obtain a non-commercial bond, persuading friends to stand as surety.

"Even these cheaper forms of providing security, however, cost something. Time to make such special arrangements may not be available to one who seeks a preliminary injunction. Those who do not have the funds to risk and those who do not have even the premium funds, may be excluded from access to courts by the bond requirement. Even those who have funds may be deterred from resort to court. So the decision to preserve the defendant's fair-trial/due process rights by a bond requirement has at least a degree of cost attached.

"In addition, some of the potential plaintiffs who are short on funds are likely to be sympathetic; even more, they may at times represent important public interests, suing to enforce rights which, if vindicated, will aid many people or protect the environment from irreparable harm.

"When costs threaten to prevent litigation in the public interest, some courts have thought that the bond requirements should be meliorated. But we do not know before trial that the plaintiff will vindicate public interest; the defendant might be innocent and victimized. Even if we think provisionally that the plaintiff is acting in the public interest to resolve an issue by litigation, it does not follow that the private defendant should pay for the public's chance. The public interest should be paid for by the public treasury, until we can determine that the defendant really was rightfully enjoined. So a more just solution to the defendants who prove in the end to be victims rather than wrongdoers is to invest public funds in a bond or other security, then to demand that those funds be repaid by defendants who are proven to be wrongdoers.

"Public interest comes into bonding rules in another way, too. Public entities are often exempted from the bond requirement. Perhaps the exemption resulted because legislatures assumed that the public entity would be solvent and would pay damages it did to an innocent citizen by obtaining unjustified preliminary relief. But this is not the law in the federal system or in most states. Instead, recovery is allowed only against any security that is filed. Public entities, which are forbidden to take property without payment, should not be permitted to take other rights without a trial."

D. Dobbs, Law of Remedies 205 (2d ed.1993).*

SECTION 2. DEFENSES TO REQUESTS FOR EQUITABLE RELIEF

A. LACHES

DAINGERFIELD ISLAND PROTECTIVE SOCIETY v. LUJAN

United States Court of Appeals, District of Columbia Circuit, 1990.
920 F.2d 32.

RUTH BADER GINSBURG, CIRCUIT JUDGE:

The origin of this case is a 1970 agreement ("Exchange Agreement") by which the National Park Service ("NPS," "the Service") completed its acquisition of Dyke Marsh, an environmentally sensitive wetland on the Potomac River between Alexandria and Mount Vernon, Virginia. In exchange for the wetland property it acquired, NPS granted developer Charles Fairchild & Co. an easement to build an interchange on the George Washington Memorial Parkway ("Parkway"). Fairchild hoped that this interchange would one day channel traffic to Potomac Greens, a mammoth office, hotel and residential complex he planned to build on land he leased from intervenor-appellee Richmond, Fredericksburg & Potomac Railroad Co. ("RF & P"). Twenty years later, Fairchild's hopes remain unrealized: no construction has begun on either the interchange or the Potomac Greens complex.

Daingerfield Island Protective Society and its coappellants (collectively, "the Society") commenced this action in 1986 to set aside the 1970 Exchange Agreement and to void the approval of the interchange design granted by NPS in 1981 and the National Capital Planning Commission ("NCPC") in 1983. In response to defendants' motion for summary judgment, the district court dismissed the complaint in its entirety. The court declared moot all claims to void approval of the interchange design; and it rejected the attack on the 1970 Exchange Agreement on the ground of laches.

* * *

The Agreement provided that Fairchild's construction could not commence until NPS, NCPC, and the Fine Arts Commission approved the design of the Parkway interchange; * * *

* * *

In May 1978, the Society sought to enjoin the Department of Interior and NPS from approving any interchange design. In its prayer for relief, the Society did not demand that the Agreement be set aside, nor, except for a hint in Paragraph 22 of its 52 paragraph complaint, did it even allege that the 1970 Exchange Agreement was unlawful. * * * Because NPS had not yet acted on any proposed design, the district court dismissed the Society's challenge, without prejudice, as premature. *Daingerfield Island Protective Soc'y v. Andrus,* 458 F.Supp. 961 (D.D.C.1978).

In April 1981, * * * NPS approved the interchange design, * * * 710 F.Supp. at 371–72. NPS's October 1983 Environmental Assessment concluded that the design was satisfactory, noting that because of the terms of the 1970 Exchange Agreement, the Service could not recommend a "no build" alternative. *Id.* at 372. The Commission of Fine Arts approved the design in April 1983, as did NCPC in November 1983. NPS issued a deed for the easement in August 1984. Prior to these approvals, in early 1982, RF & P had responded to Fairchild's delays by terminating his lease. The deed therefore went to RF & P as successor to Fairchild. *Id.* at 372 & n. 7.

In 1986, RF & P entered a joint venture with developer Savage/Fogarty Companies, Inc.; in late summer, Savage/Fogarty announced the joint venture's plans to build a somewhat smaller Potomac Greens complex. Admin.Rec. at Tabs 169–70. The Society then commenced this action. The Society's complaint, filed in August 1986, alleged that when NPS approved the 1970 land exchange, the Service violated NEPA (Count I), the Land and Water Conservation Fund Act (Count II), the Mount Vernon Highway Act and the Capper–Cramton Act (Count III), the National Park Service Organic Act (Count IV), the National Capital Planning Act (Count V), the Administrative Procedure Act ("APA") (Count VI), and the National Historic Preservation Act (Count IX). The complaint also alleged that NPS's approval of the interchange design violated NEPA (Count I), the Mount Vernon Highway Act and the Capper–Cramton Act (Count III), the National Park Service Organic Act (Count IV), the National Capital Planning Act (Count V), the APA (Count VI), Executive Order 11988 and Floodplain Management Guidelines (Count VIII), and the National Historic

Preservation Act (Count IX). Plaintiffs further charged that NCPC's approval of the interchange design violated the National Capital Planning Act (Count VII).

The federal defendants and supporting private intervenors, raising threshold defenses, moved for dismissal or summary judgment.

* * *

III.

We turn next to the district court's dismissal, for untimeliness, of the attack on the 1970 Exchange Agreement. Laches, an affirmative defense under Rule 8(c) of the Federal Rules of Civil Procedure, requires a showing of inexcusable delay and undue prejudice. *Both* must be shown; a finding of laches cannot rest simply on the length of delay. * * * As the district court acknowledged, 710 F.Supp. at 373, laches is a disfavored defense in environmental suits. * * * "Nearly every circuit * * *, and numerous district courts have recognized the salutary principle that '[l]aches must be invoked sparingly in environmental cases because ordinarily the plaintiff will not be the only victim of alleged environmental damage. A less grudging application of the doctrine might defeat Congress's environmental policy.' " *Park County Resource Council, Inc. v. United States Dep't of Agriculture,* 817 F.2d 609, 617 (10th Cir.1987) (quoting *Preservation Coalition, Inc. v. Pierce,* 667 F.2d 851, 854 (9th Cir.1982), and collecting cases from the First, Second, Fourth, Fifth, Sixth, Eighth, and Ninth Circuits).

Because laches is an equitable doctrine, courts have generally held that it "is primarily addressed to the discretion of the trial court." *National Wildlife Fed'n,* 835 F.2d at 318. However, the district court's discretion is "confined by established standards." *Park County Resource Council,* 817 F.2d at 617; *see also Ecology Center of Louisiana, Inc. v. Coleman,* 515 F.2d 860, 867 n. 8 (5th Cir.1975). A district court's ruling on laches does not qualify for deference if the court applied the wrong legal standard. *See Park County Resource Council,* 817 F.2d at 617. * * *

We have no cause to disturb the district court's finding that the Society's delay in bringing suit was inexcusable.[6] We reverse the court's laches ruling, nevertheless, on the ground that federal appellees and RF & P failed to demonstrate sufficient prejudice from the delay.

The district court expressly refused to rest its prejudice ruling solely on the amount of money that federal appellees, RF & P, and Potomac Greens spent in reliance on the 1970 Exchange Agreement. On this point, we are in accord with the district court. The documented expenditures of the

6. The Society argues that its delay in opposing the exchange agreement should be measured from 1984, when NPS conveyed the easement deed to RF & P, or 1986, when RF & P formed its joint venture with Savage/Fogarty to develop the property. Appellants, particularly appellant Northeast Citizens Association, further argue that their vigor in opposing the Potomac Greens development as early as 1971 demonstrates that they did not sleep on their rights. We find decisive, however, the fact that the Society filed suit in 1978 to challenge the tentative interchange plans without (contrary to its current claim) challenging the Exchange Agreement. If, as the Society claims, the talk during 1976–84 of repurchasing Fairchild's access rights led it to believe that no challenge to the Exchange Agreement was necessary, why did it file suit in 1978 to challenge the interchange design plans, which presupposed the Agreement's validity?

three appellees, so far as we can tell, add up to less than $692,000. This figure is quite modest, compared to other cases in which no dispositive prejudice was found. *See, e.g., Environmental Defense Fund v. Tennessee Valley Auth.*, 468 F.2d 1164 (6th Cir.1972) ($29 million expended in reliance); *Park County Resource Council,* 817 F.2d at 609 ($1 million); *Coalition for Canyon Preservation,* 632 F.2d at 774 ($1 million); *Ecology Center of Louisiana,* 515 F.2d at 860 ($1 million).

Moreover, in environmental suits, the amount of money spent in reliance has not been considered the prime factor in the prejudice inquiry. Two factors have been accorded heavier weight. The first is the percentage of estimated total expenditures disbursed at the time of suit. *See, e.g., Park County Resource Council,* 817 F.2d at 618. Here, the estimated total expenditures are about $500 million, hence the amount disbursed so far is relatively insignificant. Second, courts have examined whether the relief plaintiffs seek is still practicable. This consideration—the crucial one in the prior cases—has turned on the degree to which construction is complete. *See Preservation Coalition,* 667 F.2d at 855 ("Delay may be prejudicial if substantial work has been completed before the suit was brought, but even substantial completion is sometimes insufficient to bar suit.") (emphasis deleted). *Compare, e.g., Coalition for Canyon Preservation,* 632 F.2d at 774 (no significant prejudice where right of way cleared, but road not built) and *Watershed Assocs. Rescue v. Alexander,* 586 F.Supp. 978 (D.Neb.1982) (no significant prejudice; right of way cleared, but construction of levee not begun), with *Citizens & Landowners Against the Miles City/New Underwood Powerline v. Secretary, United States Dep't of Energy,* 683 F.2d 1171 (8th Cir.1982) (prejudice found, since challenged power line nearly complete) and *National Parks & Conservation Ass'n v. Hodel,* 679 F.Supp. 49 (D.D.C.1987) (prejudice found, since challenged restaurant on Daingerfield Island completed before suit filed). Here, not only has construction not begun, but a construction permit has not issued and cannot issue until Congress passes, if only silently, on the EIS that NPS is still preparing.

The district court expressly determined that appellees' expenditures and the extremely limited development so far carried out would not, taken together, "rise to the requisite level of prejudice that would justify application of the laches doctrine." 710 F.Supp. at 375. Rather, the court rested its finding of prejudice on the environmental consequences of undoing the Exchange Agreement. The Dyke Marsh tract exchanged by Fairchild, the court observed, would revert to private hands, and this "would terminate a right the public has enjoyed for almost a decade: the right to continued enjoyment of the wetlands in their pristine state." *Id.* * * *

* * *

We reverse the district court's laches ruling for a different reason. The court remarked that the Society had considered only one side of the environmental harm issue. The district court itself, however, similarly limited its consideration. The court was sensitive to the harm that might occur if the Dyke Marsh tract were to revert to private ownership, but it did not consider the environmental *benefit* that might result if the Exchange Agreement were voided and the Potomac Greens development blocked.

In principle, the court could have evaluated the public or environmental harms and benefits even-handedly if it had considered not just the harm of losing a portion of Dyke Marsh, but also the benefits that successful suit would bring. As a practical matter, however, the court could not have reliably estimated the environmental benefit of voiding the Exchange Agreement and stopping the Potomac Greens development without, in effect, writing its own EIS. We do not impose on the district court the task of rebalancing the environmental harms and benefits on remand. Laches is a doctrine that prevents courts from reaching the merits of a case; here, however, a fair application of the district court's balancing method would have required that court to do more than rule on the merits of plaintiffs' allegations—it would have required the district judge to undertake the very action plaintiffs originally sought from NPS.

We thus return to the consideration precedent marks as crucial. In both of the briefs that the Society filed in this court, it contended that in every environmental case where a court grounded summary judgment on the defense of laches, the harm-generating activity plaintiffs sought to prevent had already begun to occur, typically because construction of the project plaintiffs sought to block was underway. Since appellees had cited no contrary decision, nor had we discovered one in our own research, we asked federal appellees at oral argument whether one existed. They were unable to identify such a case. Here, no construction has begun on the interchange or on the Potomac Greens complex; the damage that plaintiffs sought to prevent thus has not begun to occur. The defense of laches, we hold, must be rejected under the circumstances this case presents.

CONCLUSION

We vacate the district court's mootness dismissal of the Society's challenges to the 1981 and 1983 interchange design approvals, reverse its ruling that the Society's challenges to the 1970 Exchange Agreement were barred by laches, and remand for further proceedings consistent with this opinion.

It is so ordered.

Note

The defense of laches is discussed in Gull Airborne Instruments, Inc. v. Weinberger, 694 F.2d 838, 843–45 (D.C.Cir.1982):

> "The laches doctrine, of course, reflects the principle that 'equity aids the vigilant, not those who slumber on their rights,' and is designed to promote diligence and prevent enforcement of stale claims. Powell v. Zuckert, 366 F.2d 634, 636 (D.C.Cir.1966); 2 J. Pomeroy, Equity Jurisprudence § 418 (5th ed. 1941). To establish a successful laches defense, the defendant must show that the plaintiff was guilty of unreasonable delay prejudicial to the defendant. * * * Whether the doctrine bars an action in a particular case depends upon the circumstances of that case. * * *
>
> "There are, therefore, two factors to be considered in determining whether laches applies: lack of diligence by the plaintiff and injurious

reliance thereon by the defendant. * * * Laches does not depend solely on the time that has elapsed between the alleged wrong and the institution of suit; it is 'principally a question of the inequity of permitting the claim to be enforced—an inequity founded upon some change in the condition or relations of the property or the parties.' Galliher v. Caldwell, 145 U.S. 368, 373, 12 S.Ct. 873, 875, 36 L.Ed. 738 (1892). * * * It closely tracks the question of whether a defendant suffered prejudice from the delay. * * * If only a short period of time elapses between accrual of the claim and suit, the magnitude of prejudice required before suit would be barred is great; if the delay is lengthy, a lesser showing of prejudice is required. * * *

* * *

"Two kinds of prejudice support a laches defense. Plaintiff's delay in filing suit may have resulted in a loss of evidence or witnesses supporting defendant's position or the defendant may have changed its position in a manner that would not have occurred but for plaintiff's delay."

B. ESTOPPEL

If the court in *Daingerfield* had found that the defendants had been prejudiced, could the court also have found that the plaintiff was estopped from seeking an injunction? What is the difference between laches and estoppel? Consider the discussion of estoppel in Bright v. Michel, 242 Miss. 738, 137 So.2d 155 (1962), a case in which the court held that the plaintiff was estopped from obtaining injunctive relief against an encroachment under the following circumstances:

"The chancellor was justified in finding * * * that * * * the septic tank, was so far over the line that there could be no question of it being beyond the Michel property. The Brights were unconcerned whether the Michels were encroaching on the Bright property. Mr. Bright sold all the materials for the construction which encroached, and Mr. and Mrs. Bright observed the encroachments being built. Mrs. Bright loaned the Michels the money for the original construction of the cafe and residence in 1953, and the additional construction in 1958; therefore, the Brights profited from the construction and saw the improvements made, and no objections were made by the Brights until bad feelings developed between the two families.

"The Michels were not as diligent as they should have been in ascertaining the east line of Mrs. Michel's property, but * * * [t]here is nothing to indicate that the Michels were not in good faith in believing their improvements were being constructed on Mrs. Michel's property.

"The chancellor gave this question careful consideration and concluded: 'I cannot in good conscience order a mandatory and prohibitive injunction as prayed for in the original bill herein, under the evidence and the law applicable thereto, and the same will therefore be denied.' It clearly appears that the improvements erected by the Michels are valuable and that the injunctions prayed for would substantially lessen the value of said improvements. The inference is permissible that the failure to issue the injunctions will not damage the Brights to any considerable extent. In other words, the issuance of the injunctions would cause the Michels to sustain losses far greater than the loss the Brights would sustain if they are not issued. This is not the controlling consideration on the question of estoppel, but it is a significant one under the circumstances.

"The authorities agree that every case of equitable estoppel must rest on the particular facts involved. The cases involving equitable estoppel vary as to the facts from case to case. If the owner of land with full knowledge, or with sufficient notice or means of knowledge, of his rights and of all the material facts, knowingly, though passively, looks on while another person expends money on the land under an erroneous opinion of title, it would be an injustice to permit the owner to exercise his legal rights against such other person. The owner is bound by the doctrine of equitable estoppel."

The elements of estoppel are stated in various ways. In Arnold v. Melani, 75 Wash.2d 143, 437 P.2d 908, 911 (1968), the court said that estoppel requires proof of "(1) An admission, statement, or act inconsistent with the claim afterwards asserted; (2) action by the other party on the faith of such admission, statement, or act; and (3) injury to such other party resulting from allowing the first party to contradict or repudiate such admission, statement, or act." In the Ninth Circuit, the elements of estoppel are:

"(1) The party to be estopped must know the facts; (2) he must intend that his conduct shall be acted on or must so act that the party asserting the estoppel has a right to believe it is so intended; (3) the latter must be ignorant of the true facts; and (4) he must rely on the former's conduct to his injury."

United States v. Wharton, 514 F.2d 406, 412 (9th Cir.1975).

Estoppel, although originating in equity, has long been recognized as a defense to historically legal issues. *E.g.,* McLawhorn v. American Central Life Ins. Co., 208 N.C. 709, 182 S.E. 139 (1935) (insurance claim). *See also* D. Dobbs, The Law of Remedies 66 (2d ed. 1993). Dean Stevens, on ethical grounds, urges a similarly enlarged scope for laches. Stevens, A Plea for the Extension of Equitable Principles and Remedies, 41 Cornell L.Q. 351, 354 (1956).

C. UNCLEAN HANDS

MANOWN v. ADAMS

Court of Special Appeals of Maryland, 1991.
89 Md.App. 503, 598 A.2d 821.

HARRELL, JUDGE.

This appeal arises out of an action brought by appellee and cross-appellant, J. Stephen Adams, against appellant and cross-appellee, Patricia J. Manown, individually, and trading as North Star Design & Publishing (North Star), to recover funds that he allegedly transferred to her and to the business. In defense, Manown claimed that Adams was coming into court with "unclean hands" and that his action should therefore be barred. The Circuit Court for Washington County refused to do so and after a jury trial judgment was entered against Manown in the amount of $43,000.

The parties raise a number of issues on appeal. Manown's first argument is that the circuit court erred in refusing to invoke the unclean hands doctrine to bar Adams' action against her. We agree. Accordingly, we reverse the judgment and do not consider the other issues presented.

FACTS

The ill-starred association between Manown and Adams began in April 1986. Adams had recently separated from his wife and was in difficult financial straits, due at least in part to the failure of a film processing laboratory he owned in Garrett County. * * * That summer Manown and Adams vacationed together in Florida, where they devised the idea of starting a business together. * * * The idea eventually came to fruition; the business was licensed in Maryland in June 1987 under the name North Star. Manown alone, however, was licensed as its owner. A month later a bank account was opened for the new business. Only Manown's name appeared on the signature card.

Meanwhile, the relationship between the two grew more involved. They had been living together in Manown's townhouse in Hagerstown since September 1986. * * * In February 1988, the two purchased a house together in Frederick County. The house, like the business, was titled in Manown's name alone, though Adams was in large part responsible for financing the purchase.

While his involvement with Manown was growing, Adams was attempting to extract himself from the personal and financial problems that beset him. After a lengthy series of negotiations, he and his wife agreed to a separation and property settlement on 10 July 1987. They were finally divorced in September of the same year. He filed a petition for personal bankruptcy on 4 November 1988. He received his discharge in bankruptcy on 21 February 1989.

The transfers of funds that formed the basis of Adams' action in the case *sub judice* began in June 1987 and continued until May or July 1989. Some of the transfers were made by Adams directly into North Star's account, ostensibly to finance the business. Others were made to Manown for purposes of financing the purchase of the Frederick County house and paying other expenses related to the house. * * * Adams also made a number of personal loans to Manown. According to Adams' amended complaint, in total he transferred to Manown and North Star no less than \$97,307.29.

The association between Manown and Adams ended in the spring of 1989. * * * On 13 October 1989 Manown sold the house. She kept the proceeds. North Star's assets also remained in the possession of Manown.

On 26 June 1989, Adams filed an action against Manown to recover the transferred funds and interest thereon, or, in the alternative, seeking an accounting, liquidation, and distribution of all assets and liabilities (including the Frederick County house) of the "partnership" between Manown and Adams. In defense, Manown claimed that Adams was coming into court with "unclean hands" and that his action should therefore be barred. Manown contended that the transfers had all been made in an effort to hide Adams' assets from his wife, his creditors, and the bankruptcy court. In support of this contention, she pointed to the fact that both the business and the house had been titled in her name alone, despite the fact that the two ran the business and purchased the house together. In addition, she asserted that none of the assets Adams claimed to have transferred to her and to North Star were declared by Adams in either the divorce proceeding or the bankruptcy proceeding, though each had occurred within roughly the same period and though in each proceeding it had been specifically inquired of him whether he had made any such transfers.

* * *

DISCUSSION

The unclean hands doctrine refuses recognition and relief from the courts to those guilty of unlawful or inequitable conduct pertaining to the matter in which relief is sought. * * * The doctrine is not for the protection of the parties to a lawsuit, but rather, for the protection of the courts—the idea being that judicial integrity is endangered when judicial powers are interposed to aid persons whose very presence before a court is the result of some fraud or inequity. * * * The doctrine also serves another purpose which was stated long ago by the Court of Appeals in a case with facts parallel to this one:

> The suppression of such illegal and fraudulent transactions is far more likely, in general, to be accomplished by leaving the parties without remedy against each other, and thus introducing a preventative check, than by enforcing them at the instance of one of the parties to the fraud[.]

Roman v. Mali, 42 Md. 513, 533–34 (1875). Thus, where there is evidence of willful wrongdoing in relation to the controversy before it, the doctrine allows a court to literally wash its hands of the affair, leaving the guilty party or parties to the consequences of their actions.

Of course, the doctrine is not one of absolutes. "[I]ts limits are ill-defined, and the circumstances under which it may be invoked are necessarily of infinite variety; nor is it possible to lay down an exact rule by which to determine in all cases when the principle is to be acted on." 30 C.J.S. *Equity* § 99 (1965). Accordingly, the question of whether the principle is to be invoked in a particular case rests in the sound discretion of the trial court. * * *

Manown alleged that Adams had defrauded both his wife and his creditors by hiding his assets in North Star and in her name, that he had perjured himself in the process, and that the money which he was seeking to recover was the fruit of this conduct. Her motion for summary judgment clearly set forth facts sufficient to warrant the circuit court's barring of the action on the basis of the unclean hands doctrine. * * *

The circuit court, of course, was not required to invoke the doctrine at Manown's behest, despite the damning evidence against Adams. As we have already stated, the application of the doctrine rests in the sound discretion of the court. * * * But the circuit court in the case *sub judice* failed to exercise its discretion. Initially, this failure was based on the circuit court's erroneous belief that the unclean hands doctrine is inapplicable to an action at law, as distinguished from a suit in equity. It is settled in this State, however, that the doctrine may be invoked to bar suits at law and in equity. *See Messick v. Smith,* 193 Md. 659, 669, 69 A.2d 478 (1949) ("when Plaintiff and Defendant have participated in fraudulent or illegal conduct, contrary to law or public policy or in fraud of the law itself and are in *pari delicto,*[6] plaintiff cannot maintain suit—at law or in equity—directly arising out of the misconduct."). * * * This corresponds with the general trend of merging procedures at law and equity. *See* Md. Rule 2–301 (1991) (eliminating distinctions between law and equity procedures). The circuit court subsequently changed its mind, but determined that the question of the doctrine's application ought to be submitted to the jury. This determination was erroneous as well. While the unclean hands doctrine may involve factual questions, its purpose is to protect institutional interests. *Niner,* 217 Md. at 309, 142 A.2d 798. It is therefore the judge, who is capable of identifying such interests and weighing them against other considerations, who must determine when the doctrine should be invoked to bar a claim. As the circuit court failed to exercise its discretion, we cannot, as we normally would, defer to its decision in such a matter.

* * *

An examination of the record in the case *sub judice* reveals that Adams was under no illusions as to the nature of his conduct. The questions put to him in his bankruptcy and divorce proceedings were unmistakeably explicit. No legal expertise was required for Adams to comprehend the significance of his omission of information specifically called for in those proceedings. His awareness of the nature and potential consequences of his actions is illustrated by * * * his admission upon cross-examination that he "gave * * * a lot of thought" to the possibility that his actions might subject him to future criminal penalties, and that he "took the chance" in spite of this possibility. * * *

The circuit court was faced with indisputable evidence of fraudulent conduct directly relating to the funds at issue in this case. Adams, having transferred his property to Manown in an attempt to defraud his creditors, and possibly his former wife as well, should not have been allowed to invoke the court's aid to retrieve that property—one ought not to take advantage of one's own wrong. * * * We recognize, of course, that barring Adams' claim works to the advantage of Manown, who, having perhaps willingly participated in the commission of Adams' fraud, will now be allowed to pocket all the proceeds of that fraud. Our task, however, is not to inquire into the relative delinquency of these two parties, but rather to protect judicial integrity. To that end, our judgment is that the circuit court in this case should have applied the unclean hands doctrine to bar Adams' claim. We, therefore, hold that the circuit court abused its

6. The term "in *pari delicto*" literally means "equal fault." Contrary to Adams' argument on appeal, in *pari delicto* is merely a cognate principle to the unclean hands doctrine, and not a separate factual element which must be met in order to bar an action. *See Messick,* 193 Md. at 667–671, 69 A.2d 478 (using "in *pari delicto*" and "clean hands" interchangeably). *See also* 30 C.J.S. *Equity* § 94 (1965) ("In *pari delicto* is a corollary of the clean hands doctrine").

discretion in denying Manown's motion for summary judgment, and we reverse.

Judgment Reversed.

Costs to Be Paid by Appellee.

Notes

1. *See also* Lagonegro v. Lagonegro, 187 A.D.2d 490, 589 N.Y.S.2d 571 (2 Dept.1992) (plaintiffs were barred by unclean hands from seeking constructive trust of property that they transferred to defendants to keep the property from the plaintiffs' creditors).

2. The court in *Manown* said that the unclean hands defense applies in both legal and equitable actions. For another case that permits an unclean hands defense to be used in an action at law, but permits that defense to be presented to a jury, *see* Unilogic, Inc. v. Burroughs Corp., 10 Cal.App. 4th 612, 12 Cal.Rptr.2d 741 (1992). For a further discussion of jury trials and the merger of law and equity see Chapter 9, *supra*. The typical unclean hands analysis is that the defense is one at equity only. Professor Dobbs discusses this disparate use of unclean hands:

> "The most orthodox view of the unclean hands doctrine makes it an equitable defense, that is, one that can be raised to defeat an equitable remedy, but not one that defeats other remedies. Courts repeatedly refer to the defense in that light. Some scholars think there is no justification for any separate doctrine of 'unclean hands.' If there is any justification for such a doctrine, however, it is that it may express the chancellor's discretion to deny a purely equitable remedy, while leaving the plaintiff full access to her legal remedies. Courts do not seem to limit themselves invariably to such a usage.
>
> "The unclean hands phrase is too pithy and convenient; sometimes it is tossed on the conference table like a wild card in a poker game, used to mean whatever one needs it to mean. Sometimes it seems to mean only that some legal rule or policy opposes the plaintiff's claim and that both legal and equitable relief should be denied. Used in this way, 'unclean hands' is only one way of expressing a result that would be reached whether or not such a phrase or doctrine ever existed.
>
> "For example, the unclean hands doctrine may be invoked when the plaintiff has engaged in illegal activity and seeks to reap the fruits of his illegal conduct, but that situation is already covered by the pari delicto rules concerning illegality.[6]
>
> * * *
>
> "*Extending judicial discretion to bar rights.* There is room for concern that the phrase is occasionally used in a very different and disturbing manner, as authority for discretion to reject the plaintiff's legal rights. If judges had the power to deny damages and other legal remedies because a plaintiff came into court with unclean hands, citizens would not have rights, only privileges. Discretion to deny legal relief would mean that the

6. The unclean hands defense used in this way may be just another phrase for the illegality rule under the pari delicto doctrine, and courts frequently seem to use the phrases interchangeably. *E.g.,* Dillon v. Dean, 158 A.D.2d 579, 551 N.Y.S.2d 547 (1990). * * *

judge might refuse to permit recovery of personal injury damages to a pedestrian struck down in a crosswalk on the ground that she was on her way to an illicit rendezvous and would not have been injured had she stayed home with her family. The merger of law and equity suggests that substantive defenses, based on identifiable legal rules or policy, should apply in both law and equity, as in fact is the case with estoppel. But the merger does not suggest that a judge has discretion to bar rights as well as to limit remedies."

D. Dobbs, The Law of Remedies, § 2.4(2) (2d ed. 1993).* What is the difference between unclean hands and pari delicto?

3. When a cookie company sued its former franchisee for unauthorized use of its trademark because the franchisee continued to sell cookies under the cookie company's trade name, the franchisee counterclaimed for wrongful termination of the franchise. The Seventh Circuit reversed the preliminary injunction awarded in favor of the franchisee. As an alternative ground for that reversal Judge Posner wrote:

"The preliminary injunction should have been denied for the additional reason that the Sigels had infringed the Cookie Company's trademarks, in violation of the Trademark Act. * * * Unclean hands is a traditional defense to an action for equitable relief. The purpose is to discourage unlawful activity, and is as relevant to preliminary as to final relief. * * * It is true that a modern chancellor unlike his medieval forbears does not have uncabined discretion to punish moral shortcomings by withholding equitable relief. * * * Modern equity is a system of entitlements. But equitable relief is costly to the judicial system, especially in a case such as this where the relief sought would cast the court in a continuing supervisory role. It would make no sense to incur that cost on behalf of someone who was trying to defraud the person against whom he was seeking the court's assistance. 'One who has defrauded his adversary to his injury in the subject matter of the action will not be heard to assert a right in equity.' *Fruhling v. County of Champaign,* 95 Ill.App.3d 409, 417, 51 Ill.Dec. 508, 513, 420 N.E.2d 1066, 1071 (1981), quoted in *Polk Bros., Inc. v. Forest City Enterprises, Inc., supra,* 776 F.2d at 193; see also *id.* at 194.

"The Sigels argue that they had no choice but to infringe the Cookie Company's trademarks surreptitiously, because, had they stopped selling cookies under the company's trademarks after the company stopped shipping batter to them, they would have been forced to default on their promissory note. They are wrong. They had a choice. They could have sued the company for breach of contract and violation of the disclosure law and moved for a preliminary injunction in that action. Instead of following that route, the open and honorable one, they infringed the company's trademarks covertly and did not move for an injunction until they were discovered and sued for infringement. They should not be rewarded with a preliminary injunction for their putting their franchisor to the expense of suing them for trademark infringement."

Original Great American Chocolate Chip Cookie Co. v. River Valley Cookies, Ltd., 970 F.2d 273, 281–282 (7th Cir.1992). Do you agree?

4. Is a plaintiff who lied on her resume barred from bringing a wage discrimination claim? Consider Calloway v. Partners National Health Plans, 986 F.2d 446, 450–51 (11th Cir.1993):

> "When Calloway initially applied for a position at Partners, she represented that she had received a college degree from Birmingham Southern University. At trial, Partners offered evidence that Calloway had lied regarding her college degree. Although the district court gave Calloway the opportunity to refute Partners claim, Calloway was unable to come forth with any evidence proving that she had actually graduated from Birmingham Southern or any other college. In its order denying Calloway relief, the district court found it unnecessary to reach the issue of whether the doctrine of unclean hands prevented her from recovering because it found Calloway's wage discrimination claim to be time barred. On appeal, Partners argues that because Calloway lied regarding her education, she should not be allowed to recover on her Title VII claim.
>
> "For a defendant to successfully avail itself of the doctrine of unclean hands, it must satisfy two requirements. First, the defendant must demonstrate that the plaintiff's wrongdoing is directly related to the claim against which it is asserted. * * * Second, even if directly related, the plaintiff's wrongdoing does not bar relief unless the defendant can show that it was personally injured by her conduct. * * *
>
> "Neither of these two requirements are satisfied in this case. First, Calloway's false claim of having a college degree is irrelevant to her wage discrimination claim because neither her predecessor nor her successor had college degrees. Second, even if Calloway's misrepresentation were directly related to her claim for wage discrimination, Partners has failed to demonstrate that it was injured by the misrepresentation. If anything, the record indicates that Partners would have been injured if it had not hired her. Winokur, Calloway's immediate supervisor, testified that Calloway performed her job satisfactorily and that when Calloway resigned, Partners wanted to retain her."

5. Can an assault on an antiabortion protestor by a doctor in front of his home create an unclean hands defense to prevent the doctor from seeking an injunction to restrict picketing in front of his home to protect his right of privacy? Consider Murray v. Lawson, 264 N.J.Super. 17, 624 A.2d 3, 13–14 (1993):

> "However, the doctrine 'does not repel all sinners from courts of equity, nor does it apply to every unconscientious act or inequitable conduct' of a complainant.
>
> * * *
>
> "Dr. Murray's assault was punished in the appropriate forum, municipal court.
>
> "A judge's discretionary decision not to invoke the unclean hands doctrine is justified where the conduct was 'not the kind of conduct which a court must punish in order to vindicate its authority.' * * * Judge Boyle ruled that Dr. Murray's admitted 'swing' at Lawson reflected the emotionally charged issues involved and that he would focus on balancing the rights of the parties, not on the misguided assault. In our view he did not abuse his discretion or misapply the law in so deciding."

6. When is a court justified in awarding relief even if the plaintiff's hands are unclean? Consider E.E.O.C. v. Recruit U.S.A., Inc., 939 F.2d 746, 753–54 (9th Cir.1991):

"We need not decide whether the EEOC violated one or both of Title VII's confidentiality provisions. Even assuming it did, we nevertheless hold that the district court did not abuse its discretion in granting the preliminary injunction. Under traditional equitable principles, the substantial public interest permeating this case warrants a departure from the 'clean hands' doctrine.

"First, the clean hands doctrine should not be strictly enforced when to do so would frustrate a substantial public interest. In such cases, equity's lodestar that 'justice be done' prevails. The Supreme Court has instructed that the clean hands doctrine

> does not mean that courts must always permit a defendant wrongdoer to retain the profits of his wrongdoing merely because the plaintiff himself is possibly guilty of transgressing the law in the transactions involved. The maxim that he who comes into equity must come with clean hands is not applied by way of punishment for an unclean litigant but 'upon considerations that make for the advancement of right and justice * * *.' It is not a rigid formula which 'trammels the free and just exercise of discretion.'

"*Yellow Cab,* 321 U.S. at 387, 64 S.Ct. at 624 (quoting *Keystone Driller Co. v. General Excavator Co.,* 290 U.S. 240, 245–46, 54 S.Ct. 146, 147–48, 78 L.Ed. 293 (1933)) (citation and footnote omitted); *see also Bangor Punta Operations, Inc. v. Bangor & Aroostook R.R. Co.,* 417 U.S. 703, 717 n. 14, 94 S.Ct. 2578, 2586 n. 14, 41 L.Ed.2d 418 (1974) ('It is not the function of courts of equity to administer punishment * * *. If a wrong-doer deserves to be punished, it does not follow that others are to be enriched at his expense by a court of equity. A [party] must recover on the strength of his own case, not on the weakness of the [opponent's] case.').

"In investigating race, sex, and age discrimination complaints, the EEOC is effectuating a compelling governmental and public interest in eradicating unlawful employment discrimination and in vindicating the rights of victims of such illegal practices. * * *

"Second, equitable relief should be withheld if its exercise would be 'contrary to the public interest.' Morton Salt Co. v. G.S. Suppiger Co., 314 U.S. 488, 492, 62 S.Ct. 402, 405, 86 L.Ed. 363 (1942). * * *

"To reverse the district court's grant of an injunction because of EEOC conduct in violation of Title VII's confidentiality rules would be adverse to the public interest because it would permit the irreparable alteration and destruction of evidence pertaining to substantial race, sex, and age discrimination charges. As a consequence, a thorough investigation into the very serious charges raised by the EEOC and the companies' former employees would be impossible. * * *

"Denying the injunction on the basis of the EEOC's unclean hands would disserve the public interest in eliminating age, sex, and race discrimination in employment and would punish the innocent victims of discrimination for the errors of the EEOC." * * *

SECTION 3. ENFORCEMENT OF EQUITABLE DECREES AND RELATED MATTERS

A. THE NATURE OF CONTEMPT

D. DOBBS, HANDBOOK ON THE LAW OF REMEDIES

93–94 (1973) *

"A person may find himself in contempt of court for one of two basically different reasons. One reason is that he has in some manner interfered with the trial of a case. This includes disruptive conduct in court, or obstruction of the court's process, as by intimidating jurors, for example. Contempt proceedings based on acts that interfere with the court's process or its dignity often raise serious questions of constitutional law and wise judicial management. Contempt in the form of mere insolence or bad language in court, or in the form of out-of-court publications raises difficult problems concerning the nature of the judicial trial and the right to free speech. In cases of contempt like this that affect the trial adversely, there is no difference between law and equity; either kind of court may punish such contempts. The problems of such punishment are serious ones, but they are not necessarily remedial.

"A rather different kind of contempt occurs when one disobeys a court order. The final judgment at law is not an *order* to the defendant; it is an *adjudication* of his rights or liabilities. No one may be held in contempt for failing to pay some debt as adjudicated by the law court. On the other hand, many equity decrees are personal orders, directing the defendant to act or refrain from acting. Disobedience of such a decree, if done knowingly and with the power to obey it, will constitute contempt, for which sanctions such as fine and imprisonment are appropriate. The law court may, of course, also issue personal orders concerning matters affecting trial. For example, he may order a witness to testify. Such orders are personal orders and may be enforced by the contempt powers, just as equity decrees. However, they are not final decrees that affect the rights of the disputing parties in the litigation. So far as remedies are concerned, then, the equity decree in the form of a personal order to the defendant is the remedy ordinarily enforced by contempt power."

FONAR CORP. v. DECCAID SERVICES, INC.

United States Court of Appeals, Second Circuit, 1993.
983 F.2d 427.

VAN GRAAFEILAND, CIRCUIT JUDGE:

Deccaid Services, Inc., Stephen Steckler, Louis Treglia, Peter Kim, Medical Funding of America, Inc. and David Smith appeal from a preliminary injunction, a contempt order and an order sealing certain documents *pendente lite* issued by the United States District Court for the Eastern District of New York (Wexler, J.) in this copyright infringement and trade secret suit. For the reasons that follow, we vacate and remand the injunction and contempt orders and dismiss the appeal from the protective order.

* * *

In findings of fact and conclusions of law dated February 28, 1992 and amended March 9, 1992, the district court held Deccaid, Kim, Treglia, Steckler and Equi Med Leasing, Inc. in contempt of the temporary restraining order and granted Fonar's motion for a preliminary injunction against all of the defendants. *See* 787 F.Supp. 44. Because we unquestionably have jurisdiction to hear the appeal from the preliminary injunction order, *see* 28 U.S.C. § 1292, we will consider the merits of the contempt order without deciding whether it is appealable *per se. See Emery Air Freight Corp. v. Local Union 295,* 449 F.2d 586, 590 (2d Cir.1971), *cert. denied,* 405 U.S. 1066, 92 S.Ct. 1500, 31 L.Ed.2d 796 (1972).

A district court may punish for disobedience of an order only if the order is clear and unambiguous. "The judicial contempt power is a potent weapon. When it is founded upon a decree too vague to be understood, it can be a deadly one." *International Longshoremen's Ass'n, Local 1291 v. Philadelphia Marine Trade Ass'n,* 389 U.S. 64, 76, 88 S.Ct. 201, 208, 19 L.Ed.2d 236 (1967). "An unclear order provides insufficient notice to justify a sanction as harsh as contempt." *United States v. International Bhd. of Teamsters,* 899 F.2d 143, 146 (2d Cir.1990). The contempt order in the instant case was predicated on alleged violations of an unclear restraining order. The order prohibited defendants from "using plaintiff's copyrighted 'Maintenance Software'," but never defined precisely what constituted "Maintenance Software." Indeed, even at this stage in the proceedings, there is nothing in the record to identify the programs that comprise this protected software. Throughout, Fonar has adhered to the most elusive of definitions and has refused repeatedly to provide the documents that would narrow and clarify the issue. For example, in the affidavits supporting Fonar's motion for a TRO, "Maintenance Software" was defined as "all software other than Operational Software * * *, including but not limited to, 'diagnostic and maintenance software', 'field engineering utilities software' and 'editors and utilities software'." Notably, these affidavits do not define "Operational Software." Even the copyright deposit does not contain a table of contents, program menu, or any other complete listing of the protected programs. The significance of the foregoing omissions is highlighted by the following provision in the same order that held the defendants in contempt:

> Fonar shall produce copies of the copyrighted maintenance software for the Court and for each of the named defendants.

Fonar argues that defendants knew precisely what was prohibited, notwithstanding any vagueness in the restraining order. Even if this were true, Fonar's argument would be unpersuasive. Although specificity is designed in part to ensure that a party receives notice of precisely what conduct is outlawed, it also serves to facilitate appellate review. *Schmidt v. Lessard,* 414 U.S. 473, 476–77, 94 S.Ct. 713, 715–16, 38 L.Ed.2d 661 (1974) (per curiam). "Unless the trial court carefully frames its orders of injunctive relief, it is impossible for an appellate tribunal to know precisely what it is reviewing." *Id.* at 477, 94 S.Ct. at 715. That is the situation in the instant case.

Turning next to the preliminary injunction itself, we hold that it too cannot stand. Fed.R.Civ.P. 65(d) requires a district court, in issuing an injunction, to "set forth the reasons for its issuance," "be specific in terms," and "describe in reasonable detail, and not by reference to the complaint or other document, the act or acts sought to be restrained." This requirement is satisfied only if the enjoined party can "ascertain from the four corners of the order precisely what acts are forbidden." *Sanders v. Air Line Pilots Ass'n, Int'l,* 473 F.2d 244, 247 (2d Cir.1972). The order in the instant case does not satisfy this requirement.

* * *

The district court's preliminary injunction and order of contempt are vacated and remanded. The appeal from the district court's protective order is dismissed.*

Note

In situations such as that in *Fonar Corp.* it is wise in the first instance to raise by motion the question of whether the equity court's order, whether in the form of an injunction or otherwise, is sufficiently clear and precise for enforcement purposes. The trial court's ruling on this question may then be considered on appeal when the proceeding is at an appropriate stage for appellate consideration. As will be seen in the discussion which follows, there are defenses with respect to the validity and enforceability of an equity order which can be raised by a motion to modify, or on appeal as was done in *Fonar,* but cannot be successfully interposed at a later stage where the party is before the court for violating the order. Such efforts to "collaterally attack" an equity order or decree at that point, and the attendant risks of resorting to that tactic, are considered later in this section. *See* pp. M3–92 *infra.*

In *Fonar* the Court considered the question of the propriety of the contempt order in conjunction with the appeal from an award of a preliminary injunction. With respect to whether the civil contempt order is appealable, independent of any other appealable action, *see* the discussion in the *Elmas* case at p. 150, *infra.*

B. THE CIVIL–CRIMINAL CONTEMPT DISTINCTION

Contempt proceedings for the enforcement of equitable decrees are commonly regarded as civil or criminal, depending on whether the dominant purpose is to coerce the defendant into affording the plaintiff the relief awarded in the original case, or to punish the defendant for offending against the authority of the court. Occasionally, the contempt is treated as both civil and criminal. This classification, which is sometimes confusing for courts and practitioners alike, can have numerous practical consequences. This is because "civil contempt must conform to civil procedures and criminal contempt is administered within the framework of criminal procedures." Rendleman, Compensatory Contempt: Plaintiff's Remedy

* To same effect, see: Ex parte Blasingaine, 748 S.W.2d 444 (Tex., 1988).

When a Defendant Violates an Injunction, 1980 Ill.L.F. 971 (1980). Thus, this distinction is important in determining parties, pleading and practice, particularity of the charge, burden and quantum of proof, availability of the privilege against self-incrimination, jury trial, terms of the order, and scope of appellate review. See Dudley, Getting Beyond the Civil/Criminal Distinction: A New Approach to Regulations of Indirect Contempts, 79 Va. L.Rev. 1025 (1993); Dobbs, Contempt of Court, 56 Corn.L.Q. 183 (1971); Martineau, Contempt of Court: Eliminating the Confusion Between Civil and Criminal Contempt, 50 U.Cinn.L.Rev. 677 (1981); Note, The Coercive Function of Civil Contempt, 33 U.Chi.L.Rev. 120 (1965); Note, Procedural Rights of the Individual in Contempt Proceedings in the Federal Courts, 1966 U.Ill.L.F. 755 (1966); Goldfarb, The History of the Contempt Power, 1961 Wash.U.L.Q. 1; Note, Civil and Criminal Contempt in the Federal Courts, 57 Yale L.J. 83 (1947).

ALLEN & OTHERS v. SCHOOL COMMITTEE OF BOSTON

Supreme Judicial Court of Massachusetts, 1987.
400 Mass. 193, 508 N.E.2d 605.

Before WILKINS, LIACOS, ABRAMS, NOLAN and O'CONNOR, JJ.

LIACOS, JUSTICE.

This appeal is here pursuant to the applications of both parties for direct appellate review. The defendant school committee of the city of Boston (school committee) seeks reversal of a judgment of civil contempt entered by a judge of the Superior Court on March 5, 1986. It also seeks relief from the judge's order that it compensate the plaintiffs, who are parents and guardians of "special needs" students resident in Boston, for out-of-pocket expenses, legal costs, and lost days of school which resulted from a twelve-day strike by school bus drivers in January, 1986. See *Allen v. School Comm. of Boston,* 396 Mass. 582, 487 N.E.2d 529 (1986) (relating some background of strike by bus drivers). We affirm.

The case comes to us on an agreed record and a summary of proceedings pursuant to Mass.R.A.P. 8(c), as amended, 378 Mass. 932 (1979). There is no transcript. The judge's findings of fact will not be disturbed on appeal unless clearly erroneous. *Manchester v. Department of Envtl. Quality Eng'g,* 381 Mass. 208, 213, 409 N.E.2d 176 (1980).

Civil contempt is found where there is a clear and undoubted disobedience of a clear and unequivocal command. *Manchester, supra* at 212, 409 N.E.2d 176. In 1976, a consent decree and supplemental consent decree defined the obligations of the school committee to provide services to children within the purview of St. 1972, c. 766. Various orders of implementation have been issued since that time. In 1980, the judge, pursuant to a stipulation, commanded the school committee to provide special needs students "reliable, timely, and substantially uninterrupted transportation." Prior to 1986, the school committee had been adjudicated in contempt as to transportation orders on three occasions. Orders in 1980 and 1981 did not dilute the clarity of the 1980 command, and the school committee had no reasonable basis for doubting that the judge had ordered the school committee to prevent the kind of disruption which inevitably would result during a strike by bus drivers. Nor can it be argued that there was substantial compliance where the judge found that 3,737 students missed at least one day, and 1,550 students missed twelve days of school due to the strike. Because no showing of wilfulness was required, *United Factory Outlet, Inc. v. Jay's Stores, Inc.*, 361 Mass. 35, 36–37, 278 N.E.2d 716 (1972), the judge did not err in finding clear and undoubted disobedience.

Nor did the judge err in deciding implicitly that the school committee had not carried its burden of demonstrating that compliance was impossible. See *Fortin v. Commissioner of the Mass. Dep't of Pub. Welfare,* 692 F.2d 790, 796 (1st Cir.1982). The defense of impossibility is unavailing where an alleged contemnor is responsible for its inability to comply. *United States v. Asay,* 614 F.2d 655, 660 (9th Cir.1980). The judge's factual findings warrant a conclusion that any impossibility of compliance was induced substantially by the school committee's abdication, when it signed management contracts with transport vendors rather than hiring drivers directly, of whatever protections the law might provide. See G.L. c. 150E, § 9A(*a*) (1984 ed.); *Allen v. School Comm. of Boston, supra.*

The judge's award of $20 a student for each day of school missed was proper. In these circumstances, compensatory fines are permissible, *Manchester, supra* at 215, 409 N.E.2d 176; such awards are similar to damages in tort, *Lyon v. Bloomfield,* 355 Mass. 738, 744, 247 N.E.2d 555 (1969); and they are measured only "in some degree" by the pecuniary harm caused by the contemptuous act. *Department of Pub. Health v. Cumberland Cattle Co.,* 361 Mass. 817, 832, 282 N.E.2d 895 (1972). Because the judge found that it cost the school committee $20 a day to educate each of these students, he was not clearly erroneous in awarding a like sum to compensate the students for lost days. See *Darmetko v. Boston Hous. Auth.,* 378 Mass. 758, 763 n. 7, 393 N.E.2d 395 (1979).

Judgment affirmed.

Note

The defense of "impossibility" in a civil contempt sanction context is considered in Commodity Futures Trading Commission v. Wellington Precious Metals, Inc., 950 F.2d 1525 (11th Cir.1992) (evidence of "impossibility" inadequate). *See, also,* Morgan v. Foretich, 564 A.2d 1 (D.C.App.1989) (incarceration for 23 months as a civil contempt sanction for refusal to comply with the equity decree awarding visitation rights was "demonstratively ineffective" and "punitive" in nature, and required a different standard of review as to the adequacy of the procedures followed by the trial court). *See,* Rendleman, Disobedience and Coercive Contempt Confinement: The Terminally Stubborn Contemnor, 48 Wash. & Lee L.Rev. 185 (1991).

"Compensatory fines," as a form of civil contempt sanction, is discussed in greater detail at pp. 151–53, *infra*.

BAGWELL v. INTERNATIONAL UNION, UMWA

Supreme Court of Virginia, 1992.
244 Va. 463, 423 S.E.2d 349, cert. granted ___ U.S.
___, 113 S.Ct. 439, 124 L.Ed.2d 657 (1993).

STEPHENSON, JUSTICE.

In these consolidated appeals, the principal issue we address involves the validity and enforceability of certain contempt fines imposed by the trial court against International Union, United Mine Workers of America and International Union, United Mine Workers of America, District 28 (collectively, the Union) for the Union's violation of the court's injunction.

* * *

IV

Having determined the procedural issues, we now consider whether the fines payable to the Commonwealth and to the two counties are valid and enforceable. In Record No. 910634, the Court of Appeals assumed, without deciding, that the subject fines were civil sanctions and determined that the fines were coercive, rather than compensatory. 12 Va.App. at 128–29, 402 S.E.2d at 902–03. The Court of Appeals further held that "civil contempt fines imposed during or as a part of a civil proceeding between private parties are settled when the underlying litigation is settled by the parties and the court is without discretion to refuse to vacate such fines." *Id.* at 133, 402 S.E.2d at 905. Accordingly, the Court of Appeals ruled that the fines involved in this appeal are moot. *Id.* at 134, 402 S.E.2d at 905. Bagwell assigns error to this ruling.

Bagwell contends that the subject fines are prospective, coercive, civil contempt fines that are not rendered moot by the settlement of the underlying labor dispute. The Union contends that the fines are criminal in character and, therefore, are invalid because they were imposed without the mandated constitutional protections. The Union further contends that, even if the fines are civil, the Court of Appeals properly vacated the fines as moot.

A

Contempts are classified as either "criminal" or "civil," although each " 'may partake of the characteristics' " of the other. *Gompers v. Bucks Stove & Range Co.,* 221 U.S. 418, 441, 31 S.Ct. 492, 498, 55 L.Ed. 797 (1911). "It is not the fact of punishment but rather its character and purpose, that often serve to distinguish between the two classes of cases." *Id.*

The punishment, whether fine or imprisonment, is deemed to be criminal if it is determinate and unconditional, and such penalties "may not be imposed on someone who has not been afforded the protections that the Constitution requires of such criminal proceedings." *Hicks v. Feiock,* 485 U.S. 624, 632–33, 108 S.Ct. 1423, 1429–30, 99 L.Ed.2d 721 (1988). The punishment is deemed to be civil if it is conditional, and a defendant can avoid such a penalty by compliance with a court's order. *Id.* at 633, 108

S.Ct. at 1430. Civil contempt sanctions are either compensatory or coercive. Compensatory, civil contempt sanctions compensate a plaintiff for losses sustained because a defendant disobeyed a court's order. Coercive, civil contempt sanctions are imposed to compel a recalcitrant defendant to comply with a court's order. *See, e.g., United States v. United Mine Workers,* 330 U.S. 258, 303–04, 67 S.Ct. 677, 700–01, 91 L.Ed. 884 (1947); *Gompers,* 221 U.S. at 448, 31 S.Ct. at 500; *United States v. Darwin Const. Co., Inc.,* 873 F.2d 750, 753–54 (4th Cir.1989).

To determine whether the fines imposed in the present case are valid and enforceable, we first must determine what type of contempt fines were assessed by the trial court. After its first contempt hearing, the trial court found that the Union had committed numerous injunction violations and imposed fines therefor. These fines were determinate and unconditional. Subsequently, however, the court vacated these fines, concluding that they were criminal in nature and, therefore, violative of the Federal Constitution. Clearly, the trial court ruled correctly in vacating these fines.

Following the second contempt hearing, the court found that the Union had committed numerous additional violations of its injunction. Accordingly, the court imposed fines in accordance with the previously established fine schedule. Again, the judge made clear the reason for the fine schedule, stating, "I don't know how much money these two defendants are willing to pay before they will obey the law. I hope [the fine schedule] will deter any further violations."

It is abundantly clear from the record that the court established the fine schedule and thereafter imposed the subject fines in an effort to coerce the Union into compliance with the court's injunction. The court continued to make clear that the Union had the power to avoid imposition of fines.

> The Court is convinced, as [it has] stated numerous times, that this is a civil contempt proceeding. The only way that any fines or any penalties can be assessed is for the defendants to fail to comply with the Court's injunctive orders and the laws of the Commonwealth of Virginia as [they] are stated or * * * outlined in the order. This is not punitive. It is compulsory. It is designed to compel compliance and therefore it is not criminal in nature but civil.

Notwithstanding the trial court's clear intent and its consistent imposition of fines pursuant to the previously established fine schedule, the Union asserts that the fines are criminal in nature and, therefore, invalid. The Union acknowledges that civil contempt fines are valid when they are imposed to coerce a party to perform an *affirmative act.* The Union contends, however, that where, as here, the injunction *prohibits* the doing of an act, all fines imposed for violating the prohibition are criminal sanctions. We reject this contention because we think it presents a distinction without a difference.

When a court orders a defendant to perform an affirmative act and provides that the defendant shall be fined a fixed amount for each day he refuses to comply, the defendant has control of his destiny. The same is true with respect to the court's orders in the present case. A prospective fine schedule was established solely for the purpose of coercing the Union to refrain from engaging in certain conduct. Consequently, the Union controlled its own fate.

Thus, we hold that the fines in question are valid, coercive, civil fines. It is important to reiterate that the Court of Appeals also concluded that "these fines [are] coercive civil fines, not compensatory civil fines." 12 Va.App. at 129, 402 S.E.2d at 903. Furthermore, other courts share our view respecting the validity of employing a prospective, civil fine schedule to coerce defendants into future compliance with a court's *prohibitory* injunction. *See, e.g., New York State Nat. Organization For Women v. Terry,* 886 F.2d 1339, 1351 (2d Cir.1989), *cert. denied,* 495 U.S. 947, 110 S.Ct. 2206, 109 L.Ed.2d 532 (1990); *Aradia Women's Health Center v. Operation Rescue,* 929 F.2d 530, 532–33 (9th Cir.1991); *Clark v. International Union, UMWA,* 752 F.Supp. 1291, 1297 (W.D.Va.1990).

B

Next, we must determine whether the subject fines are moot. The Union contends that, even if the fines are valid, the Court of Appeals correctly held that they became moot when the underlying litigation between the Company and the Union was settled. We agree with the Court of Appeals that "whether civil contempt sanctions are mooted by subsequent settlements by the private parties to the litigation is a matter of state law" and that we previously have not addressed the issue. 12 Va.App. at 132, 402 S.E.2d at 904. We do not agree with the Court of Appeals, however, in its conclusion that the settlement mooted the fines.

* * *

Courts of the Commonwealth must have the authority to enforce their orders by employing coercive, civil sanctions if the dignity of the law and public respect for the judiciary are to be maintained. If we were to adopt the Union's mootness contention, any organization which faced coercive, contempt fines would know that, in order to completely avoid payment of the fines, it only had to postpone actual collection of the fines until the settlement of the underlying litigation.

Thus, we hold that the fines in question are not moot. While the mootness issue is governed by state law, our resolution of the issue is consistent with federal decisions. *See, e.g., United States v. Criden,* 633 F.2d 346 (3d Cir.), *cert. denied,* 449 U.S. 1113, 101 S.Ct. 924, 66 L.Ed.2d 842 (1980); *United States v. Work Wear Corp.,* 602 F.2d 110 (6th Cir.1979).

In conclusion, we hold that * * * the fines in question are valid, coercive, civil contempt fines imposed pursuant to an established, prospective fine schedule * * *. Nor is our holding inconsistent with *Gompers* [Gompers v. Buck Stove & Range Co., 221 U.S. 418, 31 S.Ct. 492, 55 L.Ed. 797 (1911)]. * * *

* * *

In *Gompers,* unlike in the present case, the only relief sought was compensatory relief to be paid to the complainant company, which had settled its case. *Gompers* did not involve coecive, civil contempt sanctions.*

* * *

Note

The initial step in the equity contempt process is the equity decree when signed and handed down by the judge. The second, brought on by motion or an order to show cause, is to determine whether the party proceeded against, who may or may not have been a party to the original proceeding, has violated the decree and thus is in contempt of court.

At this hearing the party before the court may be charged with "criminal contempt" or "civil contempt." If criminal, the contempt defendant must be afforded all the rights available to a defendant in an ordinary criminal action. The possible exception relates to the right to a trial by jury. If the sanction imposed—fine or incarceration—is a "serious penalty" a jury trial must be made available to the contempt defendant. This is a separate legal proceeding from which there is right of appeal. The court may appoint an attorney to prosecute the criminal contempt action. The contempt defendant is, however, entitled to insist that the person appointed be impartial and have had no connection with the original equity suit. Portland Feminist Women's Health Center v. Advocates for Life, 877 F.2d 787 (9th Cir.1989). If the defendant is found guilty of violating the decree, a fine in a fixed amount or a jail term of a fixed duration, and in some instances both sanctions, will be imposed.

The "civil contempt" proceeding is begun in the same manner but is considered to be a part of the original equity action and ordinarily is set in motion and pressed upon the court by the attorney for the successful party in the original equity action. The usual rules for equity proceedings are followed with the exception that there must be "clear and convincing proof" of violation. "A party can be found in [civil] contempt only if (1) the order alleged to have been violated is 'clear and unambiguous'; (2) the proof of non-compliance is 'clear and convincing'; and (3) the defendant had not been reasonably diligent and energetic in attempting to accomplish what was ordered. [citing cases]" Charles of the Ritz Group Ltd. v. Quality King Distributors, 664 F.Supp. 152 (S.D.N.Y.1987).

If the original equity decree were "mandatory" in nature—that is, ordered the defendant to do certain acts as was true in the *Allen & Others* case—the sanction imposed may undertake to achieve this goal in one or both of two ways: the defendant may be jailed until he/she does what the original decree ordered, or a fine (perhaps in a specified amount for each day of continued non-compliance) may be imposed. These sanctions are, by the court order, made conditional and are intended to be coercive, that is, to obtain the defendant's cooperation and compliance. Their governing characteristic is that the defendant may obtain release from jail, if incarcerated, at any time by complying, and may avoid the fine by complying at any point in the time prior to a third court proceeding in which the court actually undertakes to impose the civil fine upon the defendant in the amount fixed in the earlier contempt proceeding and it thus becomes enforceable like an ordinary money judgment.

* For a consideration of the effect of the settlement of an action in which a contempt sanction has been imposed, *see* D. Dobbs, Law of Remedies, 2d ed., § 2.8(2) (1993).

The situation is somewhat different where the defendant by the terms of the original equity order was ordered not to take certain steps or do certain things and a contempt proceeding is brought on to punish the person in question for contempt as was the case in *Bagwell.* A criminal contempt sanction may, of course, be imposed. It is not possible, however, to use incarceration as a form of conditional civil contempt sanction here, as in the case of an order to take an affirmative step and a failure to have done so. You can punish someone for not acting by jailing them until they comply, but you cannot in that manner conditionally coerce them into exercising their discretion not to do the acts which the original decree forbade.

It is in this situation, where the original decree undertook to restrain the contempt defendant from engaging in specified conduct, that courts are resorting with increasing frequency to the use of a "coercive fine" as a civil contempt enforcement mechanism, a practice which has given rise to some criticism.

At the second stage hearing in such a case, at the point where the defendant has been ordered to show cause why a contempt sanction should not be imposed, the court, in utilizing the "civil coercive fine," informs the contempt defendant as follows: "the court's decree telling you not to engage in certain conduct remains in effect and if you violate it in the future you will be fined in an amount indicated by this fine schedule the terms of which I now disclose to you."

If the contempt defendant allegedly then does what the decree forbade and is brought before the court again the court may proceed to find that there has in fact been a violation by doing what was prohibited, and proceed to impose a fine upon the contempt defendant in the amount previously set. In this situation (and unlike that in the previously described situation where the order in the original decree mandated or ordered the defendant to do the acts specified there) there is no comparable opportunity to avoid the fine and purge oneself of the contemptuous conduct by going ahead and, at some point prior to the moment of actual imposition of the fine, doing what the contempt defendant was ordered to do. Here, the forbidden act occurred when the contempt defendant, at an earlier point, did what the court ordered not be done and there is no longer a "purge option." This characteristic of the "coercive fine" thus takes on something of the color of a criminal contempt fine which also is imposed for past violations and as to which there is no purge option.

At least one court has held that such a "coercive civil contempt fine" is necessarily "criminal" in nature even if there were a conditional aspect when the fine was first imposed because at the time of actual imposition of the fine there was no longer this purge possibility. Crozer–Chester Med. Center v. Moran, 522 Pa. 124, 560 A.2d 133 (1989). Such a ruling means, in effect, that the coercive civil fine may be used only where the original equity decree orders the doing of an act and not where it forbids or restrains conduct.

The coercive fine, as a civil contempt sanction, is often resorted to in situations such as that in *Bagwell* involving large numbers of people who are engaged in protests and demonstrations such as those relating to the activities of medical clinics where abortions are performed or to labor disputes. Because of the persistence of the defendants the coercive fines often are very large. Those who are found to have violated the decree are jointly and severally liable for the fine that is imposed. New York State Nat'l. Org. For Women v. Terry, 697 F.Supp. 1324 (S.D.N.Y.1988); aff'd, 886 F.2d 1339 (2d Cir.1989).

There was a departure from the *Terry* contempt sanction procedure in Roe v. Operation Rescue, 919 F.2d 857 (3d Cir.1990). There the Court at the second stage of the proceedings, rather than announce the amount of a fine that would be imposed if there were future violations, went ahead and imposed the fines for both past and any future violations but "suspended" them on the condition of no future violations of the Court's orders. When future violations occurred the suspensions were lifted and the fines became effective and enforceable.

Because the initial fines were conditional in nature, rendering imposition "purgeable", this too was considered by the Court to be a civil contempt proceeding and sanction. As authority for this conclusion the court relied upon, *inter alia,* the United States Supreme Court opinion in Hicks on Behalf of Feiock v. Feiock, 485 U.S. 624, 108 S.Ct. 1423, 99 L.Ed.2d 721 (1988).

In *Hicks* the Court states, in a case involving an alleged violation of an equity decree relating to child support, that a contempt action sanction in the form of incarceration for a fixed period followed by release of the party on probation, was a "criminal contempt" form of sanction. On the other hand, if there were such incarceration with probation, but subject to a condition (*e.g.,* payment of all support payments due) which, if satisfied, would result in nullification of the sanction and the probation, the contempt proceeding was "civil" in nature. The coercive fine in *Roe* obviously was prospectively conditional.

The *Hicks* case, and cases such as *Roe* which rely upon it, have been criticized. See, Dudley, "Getting Beyond the Civil/Criminal Distinction: A New Approach to the Regulations of Indirect Contempts," 79 Va.L.Rev. 1025 (1993).

If the coercive civil fine was imposed without the fine ever having had a conditional feature it is, in effect, a conventional criminal contempt type sanction and must be set aside if the defendant did not have the benefits which are associated with ordinary criminal actions. This is so even though the non-conditional fine in question was said by the court to be imposed in order to assure respect for the court's orders in the future. United States v. Ayer, 866 F.2d 571 (2d Cir.1989). (*Compare,* Johnson v. Bednar, 573 So.2d 822 (Fla. 1991) ("coercive civil contempt" sanction is appropriate even though there was no conditional aspect at any time)).

In Whittaker Corp. v. Execuair Corp., 953 F.2d 510 (9th Cir.1992) the Court held that the trial court not only had the power to impose the conditional civil contempt fine in question but also to require that the defendants post a $1,000,000 bond to assure payment of the fine if ultimately it is imposed upon the defendant.

In addition to these two civil contempt sanctions—conditional incarceration and the use of the conditional fine—the court may also utilize a third, the "compensatory civil fine". This sanction involves use of a fine to compensate the plaintiff for costs or losses resulting from the conduct by the contempt defendant which have been incurred by the plaintiff since the original decree was entered as a result of the defendant's failure to respect that decree. This form of relief is discussed at pp. 151–54, *infra*.

SECURITIES AND EXCHANGE COMMISSION v. ELMAS TRADING CORP.

United States Court of Appeals, Ninth Circuit, 1987.
824 F.2d 732.

ORDER

This appeal is dismissed for lack of jurisdiction. Appellant is incarcerated for civil contempt. Orders of civil contempt entered against a party during the course of a pending civil action are not appealable until final judgment. *Union of Professional Airmen v. Alaska Aeronautical Industries, Inc.,* 625 F.2d 881, 883 (9th Cir.1980). After limited review to determine whether the contempt is criminal or civil, the court concludes that the district court did not clearly err in finding that appellant is able to comply with its orders of production. "When the petitioners carry 'the keys of their prison in their own pockets,' the action 'is essentially a civil remedy.'" *Shillitani v. United States,* 384 U.S. 364, 368, 86 S.Ct. 1531, 1534, 16 L.Ed.2d 622 (1965) (citations omitted).

The district court ordered Attarian incarcerated for his failure to obey its order to account for funds and to produce records relating to assets. From the court's order, it is clear that its purpose in incarcerating Attarian is to coerce him to produce the demanded documents that are needed in the litigation and investigation or to provide credible evidence as to his inability to comply. As such, the conditional nature of the order makes it one for civil contempt. *Id.* at 368–69, 86 S.Ct. at 1535.

Regardless of the purpose of the order, if, as Attarian asserts, he lacks the ability to comply with it, or it has lost all coercive effect, the contempt becomes criminal and we have jurisdiction to review it. *Carbon Fuel Co. v. United Mine Workers,* 517 F.2d 1348, 1349 (4th Cir.1975). The determination as to whether a civil contempt sanction has lost its coercive effect upon a particular contemnor rests within the sound discretion of the district court. We review the record to ensure that the district judge made an individualized decision that the continued confinement of Attarian would have a coercive effect. *Simkin v. United States,* 715 F.2d 34, 37 (2d Cir.1983). The district court did not find credible Attarian's assertions that he has done everything he can to comply with its order. The record amply supports the district court's view that Attarian has control of the documents and other materials which the court seeks and that Attarian is simply playing games with the court. Its order directing Attarian to produce documents is sufficiently specific to inform Attarian of the actions he must take to purge his contempt. Accordingly, it was not an abuse of discretion for the court to find that Attarian can comply with its order and to continue his incarceration until he does so. *Id.*

CANCER RESEARCH INSTITUTE, INC. v. CANCER RESEARCH SOCIETY, INC.

United States District Court, Southern District of New York, 1990.
744 F.Supp. 526.

BACKGROUND

This action in which plaintiff sought to protect the exclusivity of its tradename was the subject of a prior decision where this Court permanently enjoined defendant from using the name Cancer Research Society or any other name confusingly similar to plaintiff's name. *See Cancer Research Inst. v. Cancer Research Soc'y,* 694 F.Supp. 1051 (S.D.N.Y.1988). The facts underlying the case are fully depicted in that decision, familiarity with which is assumed, and will not be recounted except to the extent necessary to this decision. Plaintiff now seeks an order adjudging defendant in civil contempt for violating the terms of the Judgment and Permanent Injunction of April 29, 1988, which embodied the decree of this Court's decision. Plaintiff also requests attorney's fees because it contends the alleged contumacy was willful. For the reasons discussed below, the Court finds defendant is in contempt and orders discovery on the issue of damages. The Court declines to award attorney's fees and costs.

FACTS

The Judgment and Permanent Injunction entered by this Court on April 29, 1988 permanently enjoined defendant "from listing or advertising itself in any telephone directory in the United States under the name Cancer Research Society." Inj. ¶ 2. * * *

The Purported Violations

Plaintiff claims that defendant's failure to secure the timely deletion of prohibited listings from numerous directories published between late 1988 and late 1989 warrants a finding of contempt. * * *

* * *

Defendant's Compliance Efforts

Defendant concedes, as it must, that listings have appeared which violate the terms of the injunction. Defendant seeks, however, to lay the entire blame at the feet of its advertising agency, American Ad Management ("AAM") or the individual directories it maintains published the prohibited listing despite cancellation orders. Indeed, defendant claims it was unaware that any of its cancellation orders were ineffectual until it received plaintiff's contempt motion papers. * * *

* * *

DISCUSSION

A party may be held in civil contempt "only if there is a clear and unambiguous order, noncompliance is proved clearly and convincingly, and 'the defendant has not been reasonably diligent and energetic in attempting to accomplish what was ordered.'" *Drywall Tapers, Local 1974 v.*

Local 530, 889 F.2d 389, 394 (2d Cir.1989) (citation omitted); *see Charles of the Ritz Group Ltd. v. Quality King Distrib., Inc.,* 664 F.Supp. 152, 154 (S.D.N.Y.), *aff'd,* 832 F.2d 1317 (2d Cir.1987). The sanction imposed on a civil contemnor should be calculated to advance either (or both) of two ends: to coerce future compliance with the court's order or to compensate the complainant for losses stemming from the contemnor's past noncompliance. *See Perfect Fit Indus., Inc. v. Acme Quilting Co.,* 673 F.2d 53, 56–57 (2d Cir.), *cert. denied,* 459 U.S. 832, 103 S.Ct. 73, 74 L.Ed.2d 71 (1982); *Vuitton et Fils, S.A. v. Carousel Handbags,* 592 F.2d 126, 130 (2d Cir.1979); *United States v. International Bhd. of Teamsters,* 726 F.Supp. 943, 949 (S.D.N.Y.1989). Punishment of the contemnor is not a proper purpose of a civil contempt sanction. *See Manhattan Indus. v. Sweater Bee by Banff, Ltd.,* 885 F.2d 1, 5 (2d Cir.1989), *cert. denied,* ___ U.S. ___, 110 S.Ct. 1477, 108 L.Ed.2d 614 (1990).

Sanctions can be imposed "without a finding of wilfullness." *Canterbury Belts, Ltd. v. Lane Walker Rudkin, Ltd.,* 869 F.2d 34, 39 (2d Cir.1989) (citations omitted). The contemnor's intent, however, may be considered in fashioning an appropriate remedy. *See Vuitton,* 592 F.2d at 130–31. Guided by these principles, the Court turns to plaintiff's application.

* * *

Plaintiff identifies no fewer than 66 instances where the prohibited listing appeared in editions of directories which were published at a time when the deletion would have been effected had defendant acted to ensure compliance with the injunction. *See* Morrison Aff. of December 21, 1989; Morrison Letter of February 21, 1990 at p. 13. Paragraph 4 of the injunction required defendant to delete its old telephone listings by sending out notices to directories "on or before June 1, 1988." It cannot be seriously urged that defendant complied with this instruction. AAM, defendant's advertising agency, mailed the majority of the cancellation notices at the end of August 1988, and some as late as September 1989. *See* Wertheim Aff. ¶ 5. Moreover, it appears that AAM's practice was to wait until about five days before the deadline for accomplishing directory changes, creating the risk that the cancellation would not arrive in time to achieve deletion.

The Court cannot accept defendant's assertion in the Leverich affidavit that a directory's due date is of no moment provided a cancellation request is received within seven days after the closing date. That the prohibited listing continued to appear in so many directories which were sent cancellation orders perilously close to the deadline for receiving the orders belies the assertion. The conclusion is inevitable that untimely transmission of cancellation orders resulted in many instances of noncompliance with the injunction.

Defendant thus may be held in contempt if it has not been reasonably diligent and energetic in attempting to accomplish the ordered deletions. Defendant points out that it engaged an advertising agency which it reasonably believed would carry out the requirements of the injunction. It contends that it had no reason to believe anything was amiss because AAM personnel assured Kip Sturgeon that his instructions were being carried out. The record reveals, however, that defendant failed " 'to energetically police compliance' with the" injunction. *Manhattan Indus., supra,* 885 F.2d at 5 (quoting 1 J. Gilson, *Trademark Protection and Practice,* § 8.07[5], at 8–169 (1988)). Indeed, its efforts were lax.

* * *

As discussed *supra* at 529, contempt sanctions may be imposed either to coerce the contemnor into future compliance or to compensate the complainant for loss stemming from the contumacy. The record does not reveal that defendant continues to violate the injunction. Although its compliance was late, its exhibits display current compliance. Coercion is not called for here.

Sanctions must be imposed, however, "once the plaintiff has proved that he has suffered harm because of a violation of the terms of the injunction." *Vuitton et Fils S.A.,* 592 F.2d at 130. Proof of actual damages, of course, is a precise guide in determining the appropriate award for complainant. *See Powell v. Ward,* 643 F.2d 924, 934 (2d Cir.), *cert. denied,* 454 U.S. 832, 102 S.Ct. 131, 70 L.Ed.2d 111 (1981). Plaintiff adduces no evidence of actual damages resulting from defendant's continued use of the prohibited listing after the injunction issued. Defendant asserts that plaintiff's inability to demonstrate actual loss forecloses more than nominal recovery. The Court disagrees.

"[A] civil contempt fine is not always dependent on a demonstration of 'actual pecuniary loss.' " *Manhattan Indus.,* 885 F.2d at 5 (citation omitted). In circumstances where " 'it seems obvious that there must have been some economic injury to [plaintiff]' * * *, under a theory of unjust enrichment, a contempt plaintiff is entitled to defendant's profits without submitting proof of direct injury." *Id.* at 6 (citations omitted). Here, the Court has already found that the prohibited listing caused a substantial diminution in plaintiff's contributions in 1987 and 1988. *See Cancer Research, supra,* 694 F.Supp. at 1054. No principled reason appears in the record to not extend this finding to revenue generated from listings in 1988–1989 directories.

* * *

When actual loss cannot be demonstrated, plaintiff is entitled to compensatory damages under an unjust enrichment theory. There, plaintiff may recover defendant's net profits derived from the continued use of the prohibited listing after the injunction issued. *See Manhattan Indus.,* 885 F.2d at 7. The Court presently is unable to compute what profits defendant derived from the presence of the prohibited listing in directories after the injunction issued. Plaintiff must conduct discovery on this issue. Accordingly, plaintiff shall complete discovery on the question of what portion of defendant's net profits it is entitled to for the period after the injunction's issuance through the last date a then-current directory carried the prohibited listing.

Plaintiff seeks to recover attorney's fees and its costs in prosecuting this motion. A complainant may not be awarded attorney's fees and costs absent a showing the contumacy was willful. *See Manhattan Indus.,* 885

F.2d at 8. The record does not disclose any deliberateness on defendant's part in the continued appearance of the prohibited listing. The Court declines to award attorney's fees.

CONCLUSION

For the reasons developed above, the Court finds defendant in contempt. Plaintiff is to complete discovery on the damages issue within 60 days of this decision. The Court declines to award attorney's fees and costs. The parties are to appear for a conference on October 22, 1990 at 10:30 a.m. in courtroom 228.

So Ordered.

Note

Other recent cases which illustrate the use of the "compensatory civil fine" are: Vermont Women's Health Center v. Operation Rescue, 159 Vt. 141, 617 A.2d 411 (1992); Curlee v. Howle, 277 S.C. 377, 287 S.E.2d 915 (1982) (compensatory fine award reversed in part because it included expenses incurred not only by plaintiff but by other members of her family as a result of violation by defendant of the original equity decree and plaintiff's efforts to obtain compliance). The following cases also illustrate the use of a restitutionary approach to determine the amount of the compensatory award, as was done in the principal case: Howard Johnson Company, Inc. v. Khimani, 892 F.2d 1512 (11th Cir.1990) (coercive contempt fine for violating plaintiff's trademark measured by the defendant's profits derived from the violation); Commodity Futures Trading Commission v. Wellington Precious Metals, Inc., 950 F.2d 1525 (11th Cir.1992) (disgorgement of profits realized during the period of violation of the equity decree; the defendant failed to meet the burden of proving that incarceration made an award of compensatory restitution "impossible".)

UNITED STATES v. TROXLER HOSIERY CO., INC.

United States Court of Appeals, Fourth Circuit, 1982.
681 F.2d 934.

Before WINTER, CHIEF JUDGE, WIDENER, CIRCUIT JUDGE, and WILKINS, DISTRICT JUDGE.

HARRISON L. WINTER, CHIEF JUDGE:

On February 16, 1982 we adjudged Troxler Hosiery Co., Inc., (Troxler) guilty of criminal contempt, in violation of 18 U.S.C. § 401(3), for willfully disobeying an order of this court in a case styled United States v. Troxler Hosiery Co., Inc., 672 F.2d 365 (4 Cir.1982). Briefly stated, the contempt was committed when, despite the knowledge of its attorney and its president, Robert Andrew Troxler, that our order filed February 6, 1978 and continued on March 8, 1978 prohibited Troxler from removing previously seized sleepwear from the Middle District of North Carolina, Troxler removed most, if not all, of the 9,773.66 dozen garments in violation of the order. [The order had been issued in the context of a suit filed by the Consumer Product Safety Commission to have a large quantity of Tris-treated children's sleepwear condemned as hazardous under the Federal Hazardous Substances Act, 15 U.S.C.A. § 1265(a)]. We invited the government to make a recommendation with regard to punishment, giving Troxler the right to respond thereto and to request oral argument. The matter has been heard at Troxler's request, and the papers and arguments, both written and oral, thoroughly considered.

I.

Despite its request for a jury trial, Troxler was tried and found guilty of criminal contempt without the intervention of a jury, and we are met at the outset with the contention that our authority to punish for criminal contempt, unlimited by the terms of 18 U.S.C. § 401, is narrowly circumscribed by the failure to grant a jury trial.

The Sixth Amendment right to a jury trial applies to criminal contempt proceedings to the same extent that it does to any other criminal proceeding; "petty" contempts may be tried without a jury, but contemnors in serious contempt cases in the federal courts have a right to a jury trial. Muniz v. Hoffman, 422 U.S. 454, 475–476, 95 S.Ct. 2178, 2190, 45 L.Ed.2d 319 (1975).

One criterion for determining whether a criminal offense is serious is the intrinsic nature of the crime charged, regardless of the authorized punishment. *See* Callan v. Wilson, 127 U.S. 540, 555–557, 8 S.Ct. 1301, 1306–1307, 32 L.Ed. 223 (1888). But criminal contempt, in and of itself, or without regard to the punishment imposed, is not a serious offense. Muniz v. Hoffman, 422 U.S. at 476, 95 S.Ct. 2190.

A criminal offense may also be characterized in terms of the punishment imposed on the offender, and should be regarded as serious if the maximum authorized penalty for the offense is serious. *See* Baldwin v. New York, 399 U.S. 66, 68, 90 S.Ct. 1886, 1887, 26 L.Ed.2d 437 (1970). In cases in which the defendant is charged with criminal contempt for which no maximum penalty is prescribed by statute, the gravity of the offense and, therefore, the determination of whether the contemnor has a right to a jury trial must be determined according to the actual punishment imposed. Frank v. United States, 395 U.S. 147, 149, 89 S.Ct. 1503, 1505, 23 L.Ed.2d 162 (1969).

The Supreme Court has adopted a "bright line" test for determining whether a term of imprisonment imposed on a contemnor is serious or petty. If less than six months imprisonment is imposed, the contempt is deemed to be petty; if greater than six months, the contempt is serious. *See* Muniz v. Hoffman, 422 U.S. at 476, 95 S.Ct. at 2190. In adopting this rule, the Court relied on 18 U.S.C. § 1, which defines petty offenses as those for which the punishment is less than six months imprisonment or a fine of not more than $500, or both. *Id.* at 476–477, 95 S.Ct. at 2191. However, in *Muniz,* the Court refused to characterize a criminal contempt as serious where only fiscal sanctions were imposed, despite the fact that the fine imposed on a labor union was $10,000, thereby deciding that the provisions of 18 U.S.C. § 1 with respect to the maximum permissible fine for a federal petty offense do not necessarily define petty and serious for Sixth Amendment purposes. In *Muniz,* the government argued that there is no constitutional right to a jury trial in any criminal contempt case when only a fine is imposed on a corporation or labor union. The Court did not reach that issue, but decided only that the fine of $10,000 imposed in the case at bar was not a "deprivation of such magnitude that a jury should have been interposed to guard against bias or mistake." Muniz v. Hoffman, 422 U.S. at 477, 95 S.Ct. at 2191. *See also* Musidor, B.V. v. Great American Screen, 658 F.2d 60, 66 (2 Cir.1981) (authorizing a $10,000 fine against a corporation found guilty of criminal contempt despite the fact that jury trial had not been waived).[23]

We therefore proceed on the premise that, notwithstanding the denial of a jury trial, we are limited in imposing a fine only to the extent that it is of such magnitude as to constitute a serious deprivation on Troxler. For the reasons, largely factual, which follow, we do not think that we stray into the prohibited area.

II.

The government asserts that Troxler could generate the funds to pay a fine of $100,000–$110,000 (the range of punishment that it recommends), without disruption of its ongoing business operations and therefore without serious hardship, by (1) realizing the net cash surrender value on certain life insurance policies on the life of its president in the amount of $8,000, (2) selling certain investment rental property having a value of approximately $90,000 after payment of an outstanding mortgage, and (3) selling the sleepwear, illegally removed from the Middle District of North Carolina and sent to Venezuela, for its cost ($61,085.44) plus the profit ($15,271.36) it has contracted to receive from its Venezuelan agent who is authorized to sell the goods.

Troxler vehemently contests its ability to pay such a fine. It claims that, as per its balance sheet, its liabilities exceed its assets, and it has incurred substantial operating losses, largely as a result of the purchase of the sleepwear, a part of which was seized, and the cost of money to finance the purchase over the last four years. It does not seriously dispute, however, that its investment real property is carried on its books at original cost and that the present market value of the property is substantially in excess of that amount. Its balance sheet shows the cash surrender value of the life insurance in excess of policy loans in the amount of approximately $10,000. It is quite clear, also, that Troxler purchased the sleepwear at a time that it had full knowledge that the government considered it a health hazard, had previously banned it and might take legal action against such goods again.

23. The courts have rejected an interpretation of *Muniz* which would allow a fine over $500 against an individual contemnor, holding instead that no fine can be imposed over $500 against an individual without a jury trial or a waiver of the right. United States v. Hamdan, 552 F.2d 276, 280 (9 Cir.1977); Douglass v. First National Rlty. Corp., 543 F.2d 894 (D.C.Cir.1976). In *Hamdan,* the court explained that its holding was not contrary to *Muniz* because *inter alia,* it is not unreasonable to assume that any individual considers a fine over $500 as a serious matter. 552 F.2d at 279–280. In addition, the court in *Hamdan* extolled the benefits of adopting a "bright line" test for measuring the seriousness of the offense rather than attempting to measure the "seriousness of the deprivation"—uniformity, objectivity, and practical judicial administration. 552 F.2d at 280.

Nonetheless, it appears that, when a corporation is the contemnor, *Muniz* requires that the right to a jury trial be gauged, somehow, according to the ratio of the fine imposed and the defendant's ability to pay.

[Footnote by the court.]

Of the 29,890.75 dozen sleepwear garments purchased by Troxler for a total sum of $200,000, 7,644.75 dozen were sold. Of the remainder (22,246 dozen), 9,773.66 dozen were seized. After seizure and the entry of our orders, Troxler sent the entire 22,246 dozen to Caracas, Venezuela under an agreement with a Venezuelan agent to sell the sleepwear and remit 25 percent of the profit realized from the sale to Troxler. The sleepwear sent to Venezuela which was subject to our orders cost Troxler $61,085.44, and it expected to make a profit of $15,271.36, a total of $76,356.80.

What has happened to the previously seized sleepwear that was sent to Venezuela is far from clear. Troxler, through the affidavits of its officers, claims that it has received nothing from the sale of any sleepwear in Venezuela, and that it considers the merchandise a total loss, although it has not written off its purchase of the sleepwear (carried as a current asset of $144,716) from its books for fear of causing panic to its other creditors. However, in a statement to an agent of the FBI, one of the officers making such an affidavit, in the presence of the other, expressed his belief that some of the sleepwear had been sold in Venezuela, that if some goods are still there, and it has become illegal to sell them in Venezuela, it might be possible to sell them elsewhere, but that he would make no effort to do so if he were required to remit the proceeds to the government.

On the present record, we think it more likely than not that Troxler will realize some part or all of the value (including profit) on the sleepwear that was sent to Venezuela in willful defiance of our orders. In fixing the fine to be imposed, we proceed from that premise. Of course we also consider the nature of the contemptuous conduct—not only that our orders were willfully disobeyed, but that records were falsified to conceal the disobedience and that Troxler in a verified pleading moved the district court for a return of the goods at a time that it knew that it had removed them from the jurisdiction of the court. We are mindful that in fixing the penalty, we must, within Troxler's ability to pay, not only punish Troxler for its conduct but deter others from such willful disobedience.

We think it fair and just that Troxler be deprived of any return on any of the sleepwear which was seized and that it suffer some fiscal punishment in addition. The latter need not be great because Troxler has already been punished in part by the substantial legal fees that it has incurred and by its expenses, including interest on funds it borrowed to finance the acquisition of the sleepwear, as a result of the transaction. With regard to deprivation of any return on the seized sleepwear, should Troxler arrange for its destruction before a responsible representative of the government or should Troxler be able to adduce substantial persuasive proof to demonstrate that it has realized nothing or less than the amounts estimated by the government from the sale or other disposition of the sleepwear, Troxler may move for a reduction of sentence under and in accordance with the time limitations contained in Rule 35, Fed.R.Crim.P.

III.

It is our judgment that Troxler be sentenced to pay a fine of $80,000 and costs, payment in full to be made within twelve months from the date of the judgment order.

Notes

1. With respect to the right to a trial by jury, and other rights ordinarily associated with a criminal action see, D. Dobbs, Law of Remedies, § 2.8(4) (2d ed. 1993).

2. In McNabb v. Osmundson, 315 N.W.2d 9 (Iowa 1982) the Court held that an indigent who has been conditionally incarcerated for civil contempt for non-payment of child support, but who, as a practical matter, was being incarcerated for "almost ten years," is entitled to court appointed counsel to aid in his defense. Under such circumstances the contempt sanction is tantamount to imprisonment for a fixed term, and thus has become in effect the sanction appropriate for a felony violation. That being the case the defendant must be afforded those rights in the contempt proceeding resulting in such a sanction which are ordinarily available to a criminal defendant of which a right to counsel may be one.

3. The administrative agency in *Troxler* brought contempt proceedings for the violation of a judicial order. Special problems attend the use of contempt proceedings to enforce the orders of administrative agencies. As Professor Davis has stated, "Congress has consistently refused to empower any agency to commit for contempt, customarily providing instead that agencies may apply to the appropriate district court for an order enforceable by contempt proceedings." K. Davis, Administrative Law and Government 311 (2d ed. 1965). *See generally* 5 K. Davis, Administrative Law Treatise § 4:6 (1978); Chamberlin, Dowling & Hays, The Judicial Function in Federal Administrative Agencies 183–187 (1942); Parker, Contempt Procedure in the Enforcement of Administrative Orders, 40 Ill.L.Rev. 344 (1946); Note, Disobedience of a Court Order Issued in Aid of the Executive Branch of the Government—Is it Civil or Criminal Contempt?, 39 Geo.L.J. 263 (1951); Note, The Role of Contempt Proceedings in Enforcing Orders of the N.L.R.B., 54 Colum.L.Rev. 603 (1954).

4. Congress has provided for a right to trial by jury in a variety of contempt settings. *See* 9 C. Wright & A. Miller, Federal Practice and Procedure: Civil § 2308 (1971). For example, there is a statutory jury trial right as to criminal contempts which, in addition to being violations of court orders, constitute criminal offenses under the laws of the United States or a state, except where the suit was brought by the United States. *See* 18 U.S.C.A. §§ 402, 3691. A jury trial right also exists in certain circumstances for contempts arising out of violations of federal court orders in labor disputes. *See* 18 U.S.C.A. § 3691. Finally, jury trial is required in certain contempts arising out of enforcement of federal civil rights legislation. *See, e.g.,* 42 U.S.C.A. § 1995 (criminal contempts arising under Civil Rights Act of 1957, for violation of injunctions aimed at protecting voting rights); 42 U.S.C.A. § 2000h (criminal contempts arising under the Civil Rights Act of 1964).

Note: Use of the Contempt Power to Enforce Payment of Money Judgments

"The potential use of contempt power to enforce payment of money raises several problems including the specter of imprisonment for debt. Imprisonment for debt is, of course, forbidden by most state constitutions, either in absolute terms or with limited exceptions. These prohibitions may make contempt imprisonment, whether civil or criminal in nature, constitutionally impermissible if based on 'debt.'

"What constitutes a 'debt' is, however, another matter. A simple contract debt is a 'debt' that cannot be enforced by an order to pay and a contempt imprisonment. This rule is not to be subverted by first imposing a 'fine' upon the recalcitrant debtor and then imprisoning him for failure to pay it. The imprisonment in such a case, though based on failure to pay the fine rather than the debt, is nevertheless grounded in the debt. When the money claim is something other than simple contract debt it may not be a 'debt' at all, even though it is assuredly a legally enforceable claim. It is commonly held that alimony and child support claims arise not from debt but from a status or an obligation imposed by law, and therefore may be enforced by contempt imprisonment provided the requisite ability to pay exists. But not every money order in a divorce decree is 'alimony' or 'child support'; some of the orders represent debt claims that cannot be enforced by imprisonment. A requirement of a divorce decree that the husband pay off certain creditors, for example, may be regarded as a 'debt,' as may a requirement that the wife repay monies wrongfully taken from the husband. In such cases the order to pay money cannot be constitutionally enforced by imprisonment, even though support and alimony orders may be so enforced.

"Other money obligations not contracted for may also be enforced by jail sentences. Where a money claim arises from fraud, many state constitutions specifically permit enforcement of the claim by imprisonment, and quite probably the same result would obtain without any constitutional reference to fraud since it can be argued that claims based on fraud are not 'debts.' A number of cases so hold, thus removing the constitutional protection against imprisonment.

"A breach of fiduciary obligation may likewise result in a money obligation that is not technically a 'debt.' * * *

* * *

"Another problem arises with consent decrees. If a husband in a divorce suit agrees with his wife on certain alimony or child support, and if this agreement is then incorporated in the divorce decree, is it to be regarded as essentially a contract because the parties agreed upon it, or as alimony because the court ordered it? The difference, of course, is crucial to the enforcement of the order by imprisonment. Where the agreement actually becomes a part of the decree, some courts have enforced it by contempt imprisonment as alimony or child support. Other courts treat such a decree as 'nothing more than a contract between the parties' which is not punishable by contempt unless the decree affirmatively states that contempt is a possible remedy for violation."

Dobbs, Contempt of Court: A Survey, 56 Corn.L.Rev. 183, 269–273 (1971).*

C. PERSONS "BOUND" BY AN EQUITY DECREE

The following material deals with the problem of when a person is "bound" by an injunction so that he or she may properly be held in contempt for violating it. In this connection, first consider Rule 65(d) of the Federal Rules of Civil Procedure, which provides that "every order granting an injunction and every restraining order * * * is binding only upon the parties to the action, their officers, agents, servants, employees, and attorneys, and upon those persons in active concert or participation with them who receive actual notice of the order by personal service or otherwise."

NOTE, BINDING NONPARTIES TO INJUNCTION DECREES, 49 Minn.L.Rev. 719, 721–22, 723–24, 727–28, 732–33, 736–37 (1965): ** "Today it is clearly established that the agents of a person bound by an injunction, whether or not they are parties to the original injunction proceeding, may be punished for contempt for doing the things prohibited by the decree. Moreover, it appears that the courts rely on traditional agency principles to determine whether a person is an 'agent' of the person bound. For example, an injunction which is directed at a corporation also runs against the corporation's officers and employees. Similarly, an injunction restraining a party from operating a particular business is binding upon his partner, co-owner, and attorney at law or in fact.

"The inclusion of agents within the scope of persons bound by an injunction seems to be a legitimate extension of the old equity practice. It is not unfair to deny the agent the right to relitigate the issues underlying issuance of the injunction. On these issues, he has already been granted a hearing—not directly, but by representation. Since by definition an agent acts at the behest and for the benefit of his principal, his interest in the merits of the injunction is a function of the interests of his principal, and the principal has already had his day in court. Of course, the agent ought to and will be given a hearing on the one issue as to which he does have an interest distinguishable from that of his master, *i.e.,* whether his acts constituted a violation of the decree.

"Consistent with this analysis, an agent who severs his legal identity with his principal and acts instead for his own benefit, or otherwise acts outside the scope of his agency, is no longer bound by the decree. Since he may now have an interest in the merits of the injunction distinct from that of the party-principal, he ought not to be condemned without a hearing. This was the rationale of Judge Learned Hand in his frequently cited opinion in Alemite Mfg. Corp. v. Staff, [42 F.2d 832 (2d Cir.1930)]. * * *

* * *

"It is clearly established today that persons who aid or abet the party-defendant in violating the injunction are subject to contempt proceedings. But in dealing with aiders and abettors the courts have not preserved the distinction * * * between breach of an injunction and obstruction of the course of justice. The consequence of the distinction was to make the aider or abettor liable for criminal contempt for flouting the authority of the court, but not for civil contempt for breach of the injunction. In 1930, Judge Learned Hand said in the *Alemite* decision: 'We agree that a person who knowingly assists a defendant in violating an injunction subjects

** Reprinted with permission of the Minnesota Law Review Foundation.

himself to civil as well as criminal proceedings for contempt. This is well settled law.' It appears that there was no precedent for that statement, and that the 'well settled law' was in fact to the contrary. Since *Alemite,* however, courts have held aiders and abettors subject to civil as well as criminal contempt proceedings. Such a procedure, although not well founded in precedent, seems sound both analytically and for reasons of policy. Although the aider or abettor may not act on the order of the party-defendant, he resembles an agent to the extent that he acts for the benefit of the party-defendant and therefore lacks an independent interest in the merits of the injunction. Given this legal identity of interests, there is no reason to deny the plaintiff a civil remedy against the aider or abettor as well as the party-defendant.

* * *

"Injunction decrees commonly purport to bind the defendant and his 'successors and assigns.' However, it is well-established that the mere inclusion of this language does not broaden the obligation which would exist in its absence. Whether a person is subject to an injunction as a 'successor or assign' of the defendant will depend on an appraisal of their relationship and not simply upon a construction of the terms of the decree.

"Courts often state that those successors in privity with the defendant will be bound by an injunction decree. However, they do not agree on what constitutes privity. * * * Since the case law contains little or no analysis of the scope of privity in this context, it is a conclusory term at best. It would seem that it ought to be defined to include only relationships arising from transfers that are designed to evade the decree. In effect this would mean that a successor or assign is bound only if he is an agent or aider or abettor of the defendant. Where the successor acts in collusion with the defendant he will be bound, but where the transfer transaction is bona fide, the successor will possess an independent interest in the merits of the injunction and is entitled to have his day in court.

"The rule binding successors has led in recent years to injunctions against a particular office and its present and future occupants. The foregoing analysis seems to require that only the incumbent at the time of suit and those successors acting in concert with him be bound, e.g., situations where a public official is replaced wholly to avoid the impact of an injunction directed against his office. However, the individual interests of successive officeholders, qua officeholders, in the issues underlying an injunction against their office probably would be negligible. Consequently there should be no concern in treating them essentially as a single party.

"* * * The justification for binding the members of a class by an injunction against its representatives may lie in a conception of the privileges and obligations of membership in a group. If an individual joins an organization which is formed for the purpose of representing its members in a particular endeavor, it seems reasonable to conclude that in return for the advancement of the individual's interest by the organization the individual has relinquished his right to act independently in that area, even in his own self-interest, to the extent that activity by the organization to which he belongs has been enjoined.

"A minimal requirement to create a valid class is the existence of a substantial identity of interest between the representatives and the absent members. But this alone is not sufficient. If it were, a court could extend the scope of an injunction at will to encompass persons wholly unconnected with the party-defendants. To be consistent with the justification of class injunctions stated above, there must also exist a ready-made bond of association between the representatives and the other members. The association must have been formed prior to the commencement of the lawsuit and must have an established structure. Thus, all persons belonging to a specified labor union or a local chapter of the Committee on Racial Equality would be members of a valid class of defendants.

"At the other extreme it seems clear that an injunction could not bind, for example, all persons trespassing on plaintiff's property. Similarly, it would seem that a class injunction could not issue in race relations litigation against all of the white citizens of a community or all persons owning places of public accommodation in a given city. But where the persons involved are organized into a 'citizens' council' or a Ku Klux Klan unit, a valid class may exist.

"* * * Judicial fidelity to Rule 65(d) and its counterparts in the states would result in proper limitation upon the scope of persons bound by an injunction in most cases. Agents and abettors are clearly bound, while successors in interest, as such, are by negative implication beyond its scope. The rule does not explicitly speak to the efficacy of class suits, but a defendant class would probably be construed to be a 'party.' Certainly a decree purporting to bind 'all persons whomsoever' or even 'all persons with knowledge' would be a nullity under the rule.

* * *

"In expanding the scope of persons bound by an injunction beyond the parties to the original action, the courts have done much to protect plaintiffs. However, to the extent that injunctions have been applied to persons pursuing their own interests independently of party-defendants, the courts have exceeded their jurisdiction and become legislatures. The extension to include agents and aiders and abettors acting for the benefit of a defendant is proper since the only interest involved in these cases is that of the original defendant, who has had his day in court. However, where an injunction is extended to successors in interest solely on the ground of successorship, or to a group of persons alleged to be a class solely because of a similarity of independent interests, or to 'all persons with knowledge' of the decree, or to all who come in contact with a certain res, the court has exceeded the limits of its power."*

UNITED STATES v. HALL

United States Court of Appeals, Fifth Circuit, 1972.
472 F.2d 261.

WISDOM, CIRCUIT JUDGE:

This case presents the question whether a district court has power to punish for criminal contempt a person who, though neither a party nor

* *See also* Annot., 61 A.L.R.Fed. 482 (1983).

bearing any legal relationship to a party, violates a court order designed to protect the court's judgment in a school desegregation case. We uphold the district court's conclusion that in the circumstances of this case it had this power, and affirm the defendant's conviction for contempt.

On June 23, 1971, the district court entered a "Memorandum Opinion and Final Judgment" in the case of Mims v. Duval County School Board. The court required the Duval County [Jacksonville], Florida school board to complete its desegregation of Duval County schools, in accordance with the Supreme Court's decision in Swann v. Charlotte–Mecklenburg Board of Education, 1971, 402 U.S. 1, 91 S.Ct. 1267, 28 L.Ed.2d 554, by pairing and clustering a number of schools which had theretofore been predominantly one-race schools. This order culminated litigation begun eleven years before, Braxton v. Board of Public Instruction. This Court affirmed the district court's order in Mims v. Duval County School Board, 5 Cir.1971, 447 F.2d 1330. The district court retained jurisdiction to enter such orders as might be necessary in the future to effectuate its judgment.

Among the schools marked for desegregation under the plan approved by the district court was Ribault Senior High School, a predominantly white school. The plan directed pairing of Ribault with William E. Raines Senior High School, a predominantly black school, so that the black enrollment would be 59 percent at Raines and 57 percent at Ribault. After the desegregation order was put into effect racial unrest and violence developed at Ribault, necessitating on one occasion the temporary closing of the school. On March 5, 1972, the superintendent of schools and the sheriff of Jacksonville filed a petition for injunctive relief in the *Mims* case with the district court. This petition alleged that certain black adult "outsiders" had caused or abetted the unrest and violence by their activities both on and off the Ribault campus. The petition identified the appellant Eric Hall, allegedly a member of a militant organization known as the "Black Front", as one of several such outsiders who, in combination with black students and parents, were attempting to prevent the normal operation of Ribault through student boycotts and other activities. As relief the petitioners requested an order "restraining all Ribault Senior High School students and any person acting independently or in concert with them from interfering with the orderly operation of the school and the Duval County School system, and for such other relief as the court may deem just and proper."

At an ex parte session on March 5, 1972, the district court entered an order providing in part:

1. All students of Ribault Senior High School, whether in good standing or under suspension, and other persons acting independently or in concert with them and having notice of this order are hereby enjoined and restrained from

(a) Obstructing or preventing the attendance in classes of students and faculty members;

(b) Harassing, threatening or intimidating any faculty, staff member or employee of Ribault Senior High School or the Duval County School Board;

(c) Harassing, threatening or intimidating any student en route to and from school;

(d) Destroying or attempting to destroy, defacing or attempting to deface any structure, buildings, materials or equipment of Ribault Senior High School or the Duval County School Board;

(e) Committing any other act to disrupt the orderly operation of Ribault Senior High School or any other school of the Duval County School System;

2. Until further order of this Court, no person shall enter any building of the Ribault Senior High School or go upon the school's grounds except the following:

(a) Students of Ribault Senior High School while attending classes or official school functions;

(b) The faculty, staff, and administration of Ribault Senior High School and other employees of the Duval County School Board having assigned duties at the school;

(c) Persons having business obligations which require their presence on the school's premises;

(d) Parents of Ribault Senior High School students or any other person who has the prior permission of the principal or his designee to be present on the school's premises;

(e) Law enforcement officials of the City of Jacksonville, the State of Florida or the United States Government.

The order went on to provide that "[a]nyone having notice of this order who violates any of the terms thereof shall be subject to arrest, prosecution and punishment by imprisonment or fine, or both, for criminal contempt under the laws of the United States of America. * * *" The court ordered the sheriff to serve copies of the order on seven named persons, *including Eric Hall.* Hall was neither a party plaintiff nor a party defendant in the *Mims* litigation, and in issuing this order the court did not join Hall or any of the other persons named in the order as parties.

On March 9, 1972, four days after the court issued its order, Hall violated that portion of the order restricting access to Ribault High School by appearing on the Ribault campus. When questioned by a deputy United States marshal as to the reasons for his presence, Hall replied that he was on the grounds of Ribault for the purpose of violating the March 5 order. The marshal then arrested Hall and took him into custody. After a nonjury trial, the district court found Hall guilty of the charge of criminal contempt and sentenced him to sixty days' imprisonment.

On this appeal Hall raises two related contentions. Both contentions depend on the fact that Hall was not a party to the *Mims* litigation and the fact that, in violating the court's order, he was apparently acting independently of the *Mims* parties. He first points to the common law rule that a nonparty who violates an injunction solely in pursuit of his own interests cannot be held in contempt. Not having been before the court as a party or as the surrogate of a party, he argues that in accordance with this common law rule he was not bound by the court's order. Second, he contends that Rule 65(d) of the Federal Rules of Civil Procedure prevents the court's order from binding him, since Rule 65(d) limits the binding effect of injunctive orders to "parties to the action, their officers, agents, servants, employees, and attorneys, and * * * those persons in active concert or participation with them who receive actual notice of the order by personal service or otherwise." We reject both contentions.

I.

For his first contention, that a court of equity has no power to punish for contempt a nonparty acting solely in pursuit of his own interests, the appellant relies heavily on the two leading cases of Alemite Manufacturing Corp. v. Staff, 2 Cir.1930, 42 F.2d 832, and Chase National Bank v. City of Norwalk, 1934, 291 U.S. 431, 54 S.Ct. 475, 78 L.Ed. 894. In *Alemite* the district court had issued an injunction restraining the defendant and his agents, employees, associates, and confederates from infringing the plaintiff's patent. Subsequently a third person, not a party to the original suit and acting entirely on his own initiative, began infringing the plaintiff's patent and was held in contempt by the district court. The Second Circuit reversed in an opinion by Judge Learned Hand, stating that "it is not the act described which the decree may forbid, but only that act when the defendant does it." 42 F.2d at 833. In *Chase National Bank* the plaintiff brought suit against the City of Norwalk to obtain an injunction forbidding the removal of poles, wires, and other electrical equipment belonging to the plaintiff. The district court issued a decree enjoining the City, its officers, agents, and employees, "and all persons whomsoever to whom notice of this order shall come" from removing the equipment or otherwise interfering with the operation of the plaintiff's power plant. The Supreme Court held that the district court had violated "established principles of equity jurisdiction and procedure" insofar as its order applied to persons who were not parties, associates, or confederates of parties, but who merely had notice of the order. *See also* Regal Knitwear Co. v. NLRB, 1945, 324 U.S. 9, 13, 65 S.Ct. 478, 89 L.Ed. 661; Scott v. Donald, 1896, 165 U.S. 107, 17 S.Ct. 262, 41 L.Ed. 648.

This case is different. In *Alemite* and *Chase National Bank* the activities of third parties, however harmful they might have been to the plaintiffs' interests, would not have disturbed in any way the adjudication of rights and obligations as between the original plaintiffs and defendants. Infringement of the *Alemite* plaintiff's patent by a third party would not have upset the defendant's duty to refrain from infringing or rendered it more difficult for the defendant to perform that duty. Similarly, the defendant's duty in *Chase National Bank* to refrain from removing the plaintiff's equipment would remain undisturbed regardless of the activities of third parties, as would the plaintiff's right not to have its equipment removed by the defendant. The activities of Hall, however, threatened both the plaintiffs' right and the defendant's duty as adjudicated in the *Mims* litigation. In *Mims* the plaintiffs were found to have a constitutional right to attend an integrated school. The defendant school board had a corresponding constitutional obligation to provide them with integrated schools and a right to be free from interference with the performance of that duty. *See* Brewer v. Hoxie School District, 8 Cir.1956, 238 F.2d 91, 95. Disruption of the orderly operation of the school system, in the form of a racial dispute, would thus negate the plaintiffs' constitutional right and the defendant's constitutional duty. In short, the activities of persons contributing to racial disorder at Ribault imperiled the court's fundamental power to make a binding adjudication between the parties properly before it.

Courts of equity have inherent jurisdiction to preserve their ability to render judgment in a case such as this. This was the import of the holding in United States v. United Mine Workers of America, 1947, 330 U.S. 258, 67 S.Ct. 677, 91 L.Ed. 884. There the district court had issued a temporary restraining order forbidding a union from striking, though there was a substantial question of whether the Norris–LaGuardia Act had deprived the district court of jurisdiction to issue such an order. The Supreme Court upheld the defendants' contempt conviction for violation of this order. As an alternative holding the Court stated that the contempt conviction would have been upheld even if the district court had ultimately been found to be without jurisdiction. This holding affirmed the power of a court of equity to issue an order to preserve the status quo in order to protect its ability to render judgment in a case over which it might have jurisdiction. 330 U.S., at 293, 67 S.Ct., at 677. *See* Walker v. Birmingham, 1967, 388 U.S. 307, 343–344, n. 3, 87 S.Ct. 1824, 18 L.Ed.2d 1210 (Brennan, J., dissenting); United States v. Shipp, 1906, 203 U.S. 563, 573, 27 S.Ct. 165, 51 L.Ed. 319; Stewart v. Dunn, 5 Cir.1966, 363 F.2d 591, 598; Carter v. United States, 5 Cir.1943, 135 F.2d 858, 861.

The integrity of a court's power to render a binding judgment in a case over which it has jurisdiction is at stake in the present case. In *Mine Workers* disruptive conduct prior to the court's decision could have destroyed the court's power to settle a controversy at least potentially within its jurisdiction. Here the conduct of Hall and others, if unrestrained, could have upset the court's ability to bind the parties in *Mims,* a case in which it unquestionably had jurisdiction. Moreover, the court retained jurisdiction in *Mims* to enter such further orders as might be necessary to effectuate its judgment. Thus disruptive conduct would not only jeopardize the effect of the court's judgment already entered but would also undercut its power to enter binding desegregation orders in the future.

The principle that courts have jurisdiction to punish for contempt in order to protect their ability to render judgment is also found in the use of in rem injunctions. Federal courts have issued injunctions binding on all persons, regardless of notice, who come into contact with property which is the subject of a judicial decree. *See* United States v. Dean Rubber Manufacturing Co., 1946, W.D.Mo., 71 F.Supp. 96; Converse v. Highway Construction Co., 6 Cir.1939, 107 F.2d 127; Cherry v. Insull Utility Investments, Inc., 1932, N.D.Ill., 58 F.2d 1022, *rev'd on other grounds sub nom.* Guaranty Trust Co. v. Fentress, 7 Cir., 61 F.2d 329. A court entering a decree binding on a particular piece of property is necessarily faced with the danger that its judgment may be disrupted in the future by members of an undefinable class—those, who may come into contact with the property. The in rem injunction protects the court's judgment. The district court here faced an analogous problem. The judgment in a school case, as in other civil rights actions, inures to the benefit of a large class of persons, regardless of whether the original action is cast in the form of a class action. *See* Bailey v. Patterson, 5 Cir.1963, 323 F.2d 201, 206, cert. denied, 1963, 376 U.S. 910, 84 S.Ct. 666, 11 L.Ed.2d 609; Unemployed Workers Union v. Hackett, 1971, D.R.I., 332 F.Supp. 1372, 1379 n. 3; Snyder v. Board of Trustees, 1968, N.D.Ill., 286 F.Supp. 927. At the same time court orders in school cases, affecting as they do large numbers of people, necessarily depend on the cooperation of the entire community for their implementation.

As this Court is well aware, school desegregation orders often strongly excite community passions. School orders are, like in rem orders, particularly vulnerable to disruption by an undefinable class of persons who are neither parties nor acting at the instigation of parties. In such cases, as in voting rights cases, courts must have the power to issue orders similar to that issued in this case, tailored to the exigencies of the situation and directed to protecting the court's judgment. The peculiar problems posed by school cases have required courts to exercise broad and flexible remedial powers. *See* Swann v. Charlotte–Mecklenburg Board of Education, 1971, 402 U.S. 1, 6, 15, 91 S.Ct. 1267, 28 L.Ed.2d 554. Similarly broad applications of the power to punish for contempt may be necessary, as here, if courts are to protect their ability to design appropriate remedies and make their remedial orders effective.

II.

The appellant also asserts that Rule 65(d) of the Federal Rules of Civil Procedure prevents the court's order from binding him. He points out that he was not a party to the original action, nor an officer, agent, servant, employee, or attorney of a party, and denies that he was acting in "active concert or participation" with any party to the original action.[1]

In examining this contention we start with the proposition that Rule 65 was intended to embody "the common-law doctrine that a decree of injunction not only binds the parties defendant but also those identified

1. The government contends that Hall was acting "in active concert and participation" with parties to the action. In 1962, in an unreported order not made part of the record in the present case, the district court held that the *Braxton* suit was a class action pursuant to Rule 23(a)(3) of the Federal Rules of Civil Procedure. Consequently, the government argues, all minor black children were and are parties to the *Braxton–Mims* litigation. Therefore Hall, by engaging in disruptive activities with some black students, was acting in concert and participation with parties under Rule 65(d).

This argument fails because all minor black children were not parties to *Braxton* and *Mims*. Prior to the 1966 amendment of Rule 23, Rule 23(a)(3) provided for what was then known as a "spurious" class action. The spurious class action was essentially a permissive joinder device, in which the court's decision would bind only those persons actually before the court. 3B J. Moore, Moore's Federal Practice ¶ 23.10[1] (1969); Developments in the Law—Multiparty Litigation in the Federal Courts, 71 Harv.L.Rev. 874, 930 (1958). "It was an invitation and not a command performance." 3B J. Moore, *supra*, at § 23.10[1]. Those persons who did not actually join in the litigation in this case, therefore, were not parties and are not parties now. The district court has not, since 1962, made any further determination that the *Braxton–Mims* litigation could be maintained as a class action, as required by present Rule 23(c). There is no evidence or allegation that Hall was acting in active concert or participation with any of the persons who actually were parties to the suit. [Footnote by the Court]

with them in interest, in 'privity' with them, represented by them or subject to their control." Regal Knitwear Co. v. NLRB, 1945, 324 U.S. 9, 14, 65 S.Ct. 478, 481, 89 L.Ed. 661. Literally read, Rule 65(d) would forbid the issuance of in rem injunctions. Note, Binding Nonparties to Injunction Decrees, 49 Minn.L.Rev. 719, 736 (1965). But courts have continued to issue in rem injunctions notwithstanding Rule 65(d), since they possessed the power to do so at common law and since Rule 65(d) was intended to embody rather than to limit their common law powers. *See* United States v. Dean Rubber Manufacturing Co., 1946, W.D.Mo., 71 F.Supp. 96; In re Lustron Corp., 7 Cir.1950, 184 F.2d 798, *cert. denied,* 1951, 340 U.S. 946, 71 S.Ct. 531, 95 L.Ed. 682; Converse v. Highway Construction Co., 6 Cir.1939, 107 F.2d 127; Zeleznik v. Grand Riviera Theater Co., 6 Cir.1942, 128 F.2d 533.

Similarly, we conclude that Rule 65(d), as a codification rather than a limitation of courts' common-law powers, cannot be read to restrict the inherent power of a court to protect its ability to render a binding judgment. *See* In re Williams, 1969, D.C.D.C., 306 F.Supp. 617. We hold that Hall's relationship to the *Mims* case fell within that contemplated by Rule 65(d). By deciding *Mims* and retaining jurisdiction the district court had, in effect, adjudicated the rights of the entire community with respect to the racial controversy surrounding the school system. Moreover, as we have noted, in the circumstances of this case third parties such as Hall were in a position to upset the court's adjudication. This was not a situation which could have been anticipated by the draftsmen of procedural rules. In meeting the situation as it did, the district court did not overstep its powers.

We do not hold that courts are free to issue permanent injunctions against all the world in school cases. Hall had notice of the court's order. Rather than challenge it by the orderly processes of law, he resorted to conscious, willful defiance. *See* Walker v. Birmingham, 1967, 388 U.S. 307, 87 S.Ct. 1824, 18 L.Ed.2d 1210.

It is true that this order was issued without a hearing, and that ordinarily injunctive relief cannot be granted without a hearing. *See* 7 J. Moore, Moore's Federal Practice ¶ 65.04[3] & n. 8a (1972). But we need not hold that this order has the effect of a preliminary or permanent injunction. Rather, the portion of the court's order here complained of may be characterized as a temporary restraining order, which under Rule 65(b) may be issued ex parte. The prohibition directed to restricting access to the school grounds nowhere purported to be an injunction. Moreover, Hall's violation occurred within four days of the issuance of the order, well within the ten-day limitation period for temporary restraining orders. The present case is therefore distinguishable from the situation presented in Harrington v. Colquitt County Board of Education, 5 Cir.1971, 449 F.2d 161, a direct appeal from a permanent injunction, in which this Court struck language purporting to enjoin persons beyond the scope of Rule 65(d).

We hold, then, that the district court had the inherent power to protect its ability to render a binding judgment between the original parties to the

Mims litigation by issuing an interim ex parte order against an undefinable class of persons. We further hold that willful violation of that order by one having notice of it constitutes criminal contempt. The judgment of the district court is affirmed.

Notes

1. As the *Hall* court states, the *Alemite* case (Alemite Manufacturing Corp. v. Staff, 42 F.2d 832 (2d Cir.1930)) is generally recognized as the guiding precedent with respect to the question of who can be held in contempt of an equity decree.

In that case, two brothers, Joseph and John Staff, and others, allegedly carried on a business as partners and were sued as such. The plaintiff alleged that this firm had violated the plaintiff's patent. While the suit was pending the action was dismissed as to Joseph on the basis of testimony that he was not a partner, but an employee, only. The suit resulted in a finding that the plaintiff's patent was valid and had been infringed by the firm and enjoined future violations by John, "his agents, employees, associates and confederates," [or from] "aiding or abetting or in any way contributing to the infringement" of the patent in issue.

Joseph, following his withdrawal from the firm and dismissal from the suit, went into business for himself. The plaintiff in the original suit now brought on a second civil contempt proceeding in the original action to determine whether Joseph was in contempt for having violated the original decree because of his activities since his dismissal from the law suit against the Staff firm.

Justice Learned Hand, writing for the Court, held that Joseph could not be found to be in contempt for violating this decree because he was not a party to the suit, nor was he the agent, servant, employee, etc. of a party enjoined by that decree, nor had he aided or abetted any such party to violate the decree. Judge Hand reasoned that a decree could not "lawfully enjoin the world at large" and thus "no court can make a decree which will bind anyone but a party" or one who knowingly assists a party to violate it. (*Id.*, at 833)

Hall was not a party to the original action which gave rise to the decree in the *Hall* case, nor was he an agent, etc. of a party named in the decree, nor did he aid and abet such a party or person in violating the decree. He was, therefore, in a position in relation to the *Hall* decree that is comparable to that of Joseph in *Alemite*.

Hall was, however, found to be in contempt of the *Hall* decree. The *Hall* Court, in distinguishing *Alemite,* emphasized that a violation of the decree by Joseph in *Alemite* "would not have disturbed in any way the adjudication of rights and obligations as between the original plaintiffs and defendants." Such was not the case with Hall, however. Hall made it clear at the time of his arrest that his purpose in being on the premises was to impede the enforcement of the original decree [as it "related to both the plaintiff's right and the defendant's duty,"] and thus constituted such an impediment.

Also, the Court of Appeals held, the *Hall* court had stated at the time of issuing its decree that it was retaining jurisdiction over the school premises in question to award whatever further relief was necessary to make effective the relief it was awarding and had thus, as it were, "seized" and taken dominion over the school property for that purpose. This action, the Court suggested, was sufficiently analogous to the conduct of those courts which had proceeded on an *in rem* theory to support a finding of contempt by Hall. Hall was in contempt of the Court's order when he came upon that property with the declared intent to impede enforcement of the decree.

2. The in rem theory relied upon in part by the *Hall* Court has been criticized because it seemingly might be used to justify a finding of contempt on the part of one who was without actual notice of the decree in question. The rationale underlying the theory is that the whole world is bound by the court's control of the res or property. Professor Dobbs has pointed out that "even if one could justify the denial of a hearing and an opportunity to present evidence on the merits, it seems difficult to justify contempt sanctions against one who is not even aware that a decree has been issued. Presumably, cases taking this extreme view would raise serious due process issues." Dobbs, Contempt of Court: A Survey, 56 Corn.L.Rev. 183, 258 (1971). Moreover, he has suggested that Rule 65(d) "forbids the use of the in rem theory since that theory would dispense with the requirement of notice specified" in that rule. *Id.* at 259. For further criticism, see Rendleman, Beyond Contempt: Obligors to Injunctions, 53 Tex.L.Rev. 873, 911–16 (1975).

Some support for the *Hall* approach and the in rem theory can be found in Washington v. Washington State Commercial Passenger Fishing Vessel Association, 443 U.S. 658, 99 S.Ct. 3055, 61 L.Ed.2d 823 (1979) (where there was, however, a requirement that there be actual knowledge if a criminal contempt sanction is to be imposed). In that case, a federal district court entered an injunction allocating certain salmon fishing rights among several Indian tribes and other fishers. In affirming the possible power of the district court to bind fishers who were not parties to its injunction, the Supreme Court stated:

> "In our view, the commercial fishing associations and their members are probably subject to injunction under either the rule that nonparties who interfere with the implementation of court orders establishing public rights may be enjoined, *e.g.*, United States v. Hall, 472 F.2d 261 (CA5 1972), cited approvingly in Golden State Bottling Co. v. NLRB, 414 U.S. 168, 180, or the rule that a court possessed of the res in a proceeding *in rem*, such as one to apportion a fishery, may enjoin those who would interfere with that custody. *See* Vendo Co. v. Lektro–Vend Corp., 433 U.S. 623, 641."

Id. at 692, n. 32, 99 S.Ct. at 3078, n. 32, 61 L.Ed. at 850, n. 32. Moreover, the Court emphasized a third theory for binding the non-party fishers: "[I]n any case, these individuals and groups of citizens of the State of Washington, which was a party to the relevant proceedings, and 'they, in their common public rights as citizens of the State, were represented by the State in those proceedings, and like it, were bound by the judgment.' " *Id.* However, several of the nonparties who violated the order ultimately escaped criminal contempt convictions because the United States failed to prove beyond a reasonable doubt that they had actual knowledge of the order and wilfully violated it. *See* United States v. Baker, 641 F.2d 1311 (9th Cir.1981).

3. Whatever the negative implications of the absence of language in Rule 65(d) purporting to bind "successors," the United States Supreme Court has held that a bona fide successor corporation can be held in contempt for violation of an order issued against its predecessor. Consider the following

language in Golden State Bottling Co. v. NLRB, 414 U.S. 168, 177, 179–80, 94 S.Ct. 414, 421, 422–23, 38 L.Ed.2d 388 (1973):

> "Our holding in no way contravenes the policy underlying Rule 65(d), of not having 'order[s] or injunction[s] so broad as to make punishable the conduct of persons who act independently and whose rights have not been adjudged according to law.' *Regal Knitwear,* 324 U.S., at 13; *see* Alemite Mfg. Corp. v. Staff, 42 F.2d 832 (CA2 1930). The tie between the offending employer and the bona fide purchaser of the business, supplied by a Board finding of a continuing business enterprise, establishes the requisite relationship of dependence. * * * There will be no adjudication of liability against a bona fide successor 'without affording [it] a full opportunity at a hearing, after adequate notice, to present evidence on the question of whether it is a successor which is responsible for remedying a predecessor's unfair labor practices. The successor [will] also be entitled, of course, to be heard against the enforcement of any order issued against it.' 164 N.L.R.B., at 969."

For an analysis of the *Golden State* case, *see* Rendleman, Beyond Contempt: Obligors to Injunctions, 53 Tex.L.Rev. 873, 891–92 (1975).

ROE v. OPERATION RESCUE

United States Court of Appeals, Third Circuit, 1990.
919 F.2d 857.

* * *

C. The Civil Contempt of McMonagle and Krail: Was the Evidence Sufficient?

McMonagle and non-defendant Krail both argue that there was insufficient evidence to hold them in contempt for violating the court's TRO. Once again, we disagree. The record amply demonstrates that plaintiffs satisfied their burden of establishing McMonagle's and Krail's civil contempt by clear and convincing evidence. *See Concerned Citizens of Bridesburg v. Philadelphia Water Dep't.,* 843 F.2d 679, 682 (3d Cir.), *cert. denied,* 488 U.S. 853, 109 S.Ct. 139, 102 L.Ed.2d 112 (1988).

As the district court correctly stated, to show civil contempt, a plaintiff must establish the following: "(1) that a valid court order existed; (2) that the defendants had knowledge of the order; and (3) that the defendants disobeyed the order." McMonagle does not contest the validity of the TRO, his knowledge of it, or his presence at the demonstrations. He instead claims that by protesting, he was merely exercising his right to free speech and that, at all events, there was insufficient evidence to establish his alleged trespass. Both claims are unavailing.

To begin with, McMonagle's right to free speech does not immunize him from liability for engaging in proscribed conduct. Insofar as McMonagle asserts that the TRO was an unreasonable time, place and manner restriction on his speech, the validity of the order may not be collaterally challenged in a contempt proceeding for violating the order. *United States v. Stine,* 646 F.2d 839, 845 (3d Cir.1981). In fashioning its TRO, the district court specifically considered defendants' first amendment rights.[14] On appeal, we employ an abuse of discretion standard to review the details of a court's equitable order. *See Evans v. Buchanan,* 555 F.2d 373, 378 (3d Cir.) (in banc), *cert. denied,* 434 U.S. 880, 98 S.Ct. 235, 54 L.Ed.2d 160 (1977). Nothing in the record indicates that the district court abused its discretion in balancing the legitimate and competing interests of plaintiffs and defendants.

Further, we do not think that actual trespass is a necessary precondition for holding McMonagle in civil contempt. The law does not permit the instigator of contemptuous conduct to absolve himself of contempt liability by leaving the physical performance of the forbidden conduct to others. As a result, those who have knowledge of a valid court order and abet others in violating it are subject to the court's contempt powers. *Cf. Quinter v. Volkswagen of America,* 676 F.2d 969, 972 (3d Cir.1982); *Alemite Mfg. Corp. v. Staff,* 42 F.2d 832, 833 (2d Cir.1930).

McMonagle was personally served with a copy of the TRO on June 30, 1988. According to the record, he nonetheless participated in the protests at WSC on July 5 and at NEWC on July 6. McMonagle was indeed identified as one of the leaders of these demonstrations. With respect to the July 5 protest, one witness testified that McMonagle, wearing an Operation Rescue armband, stood across from WSC where he conferred with other protesters and with various police officials. Testimony regarding the July 6 demonstration at NEWC indicated that McMonagle, wearing a headset and standing with two men wearing Operation Rescue armbands, gave instructions to protesters and spoke with police officials. The district court determined that the above facts, which are sufficient to adjudge McMonagle in civil contempt, were established by clear and convincing evidence. This finding is not clearly erroneous, and we therefore affirm the court's contempt order.

The conduct of Krail, although not as egregious as that of McMonagle, was nonetheless a violation of the TRO. Krail points out that she is not a party to the underlying lawsuit and was not named in the district court's TRO. She asserts, further, that there is insufficient evidence of her knowledge of the court's TRO and that the evidence of her alleged violation of the TRO is far too imprecise to justify her being held in contempt.

"A person who is not a party to a proceeding may be held in contempt if he or she has actual knowledge of a court's order and either abets the defendant or is legally identified with him." *Quinter,* 676 F.2d at 972. The evidence shows that Krail actively participated in the demonstrations at WSC on July 5, at NEWC on July 6, and at CHWC on July 9. Witnesses testified that Krail was one of the first protesters to arrive at these clinics and to blockade their doors. The record also indicates that United States Marshals repeatedly read the TRO at these demonstrations using amplification devices. Based on this evidence, which is clearly supported by the

14. The district court stated that it would "design its restraining order so that both plaintiffs' interest in gaining access to the facilities and the defendants' interest in expressing their views are fairly considered." Accordingly, the court's order allowed defendants to engage in limited "sidewalk counseling." *See supra* note 13. [Footnote by the Court]

record, the district court did not err in concluding that Krail had knowledge of the order and violated its provisions.

* * *

D. CONTEMPT PROCEEDINGS: DEFENSES, COLLATERAL ATTACK AND RELATED CONCERNS

WALKER v. CITY OF BIRMINGHAM

Supreme Court of the United States, 1967.
388 U.S. 307, 87 S.Ct. 1824, 18 L.Ed.2d 1210.

MR. JUSTICE STEWART delivered the opinion of the Court.

On Wednesday, April 10, 1963, officials of Birmingham, Alabama, filed a bill of complaint in a state circuit court asking for injunctive relief against 139 individuals and two organizations. The bill and accompanying affidavits stated that during the preceding seven days:

> "[R]espondents [had] sponsored and/or participated in and/or conspired to commit and/or to encourage and/or to participate in certain movements, plans or projects commonly called 'sit-in' demonstrations, 'kneel-in' demonstrations, mass street parades, trespasses on private property after being warned to leave the premises by the owners of said property, congregating in mobs upon the public streets and other public places, unlawfully picketing private places of business in the City of Birmingham, Alabama; violation of numerous ordinances and statutes of the City of Birmingham and State of Alabama. * * *"

It was alleged that this conduct was "calculated to provoke breaches of the peace," "threaten[ed] the safety, peace and tranquility of the City," and placed "an undue burden and strain upon the manpower of the Police Department."

The bill stated that these infractions of the law were expected to continue and would "lead to further imminent danger to the lives, safety, peace, tranquility and general welfare of the people of the City of Birmingham," and that the "remedy by law [was] inadequate." The circuit judge granted a temporary injunction as prayed in the bill, enjoining the petitioners from among other things, participating in or encouraging mass street parades or mass processions without a permit as required by a Birmingham ordinance.

Five of the eight petitioners were served with copies of the writ early the next morning. Several hours later four of them held a press conference. There a statement was distributed, declaring their intention to disobey the injunction because it was "raw tyranny under the guise of maintaining law and order." At this press conference one of the petitioners stated: "That they had respect for the Federal Courts, or Federal Injunctions, but in the past the State Courts had favored local law enforcement, and if the police couldn't handle it, the mob would."

That night a meeting took place at which one of the petitioners announced that "[i]njunction or no injunction we are going to march tomorrow." The next afternoon, Good Friday, a large crowd gathered in the vicinity of Sixteenth Street and Sixth Avenue North in Birmingham. A group of about 50 or 60 proceeded to parade along the sidewalk while a crowd of 1,000 to 1,500 onlookers stood by, "clapping, and hollering, and [w]hooping." Some of the crowd followed the marchers and spilled out into the street. At least three of the petitioners participated in this march.

Meetings sponsored by some of the petitioners were held that night and the following night, where calls for volunteers to "walk" and go to jail were made. On Easter Sunday, April 14, a crowd of between 1,500 and 2,000 people congregated in the midafternoon in the vicinity of Seventh Avenue and Eleventh Street North in Birmingham. One of the petitioners was seen organizing members of the crowd in formation. A group of about 50, headed by three other petitioners, started down the sidewalk two abreast. At least one other petitioner was among the marchers. Some 300 or 400 people from among the onlookers followed in a crowd that occupied the entire width of the street and overflowed onto the sidewalks. Violence occurred. Members of the crowd threw rocks that injured a newspaperman and damaged a police motorcycle.

The next day the city officials who had requested the injunction applied to the state circuit court for an order to show cause why the petitioners should not be held in contempt for violating it. At the ensuing hearing the petitioners sought to attack the constitutionality of the injunction on the ground that it was vague and overbroad and restrained free speech. They also sought to attack the Birmingham parade ordinance upon similar grounds, and upon the further ground that the ordinance had previously been administered in an arbitrary and discriminatory manner.

The circuit judge refused to consider any of these contentions, pointing out that there had been neither a motion to dissolve the injunction, nor an effort to comply with it by applying for a permit from the city commission before engaging in the Good Friday and Easter Sunday parades. Consequently, the court held that the only issues before it were whether it had jurisdiction to issue the temporary injunction, and whether thereafter the petitioners had knowingly violated it. Upon these issues the court found against the petitioners, and imposed upon each of them a sentence of five days in jail and a $50 fine, in accord with an Alabama statute.

The Supreme Court of Alabama affirmed. That court, too, declined to consider the petitioners' constitutional attacks upon the injunction and the underlying Birmingham parade ordinance.

* * *

Howat v. State of Kansas, 258 U.S. 181, 42 S.Ct. 277, 66 L.Ed. 550, was decided by this Court almost 50 years ago. That was a case in which people had been punished by a Kansas trial court for refusing to obey an antistrike injunction issued under the state industrial relations act. They had claimed a right to disobey the court's order upon the ground that the state statute and the injunction based upon it were invalid under the Federal Constitution. The Supreme Court of Kansas had affirmed the judgment, holding that the trial court "had general power to issue injunctions in equity, and that even if its exercise of the power was erroneous, the injunction was not void, and the defendants were precluded from attacking it in this collateral proceeding, * * * that, if the injunction was erroneous, jurisdiction was not thereby forfeited, that the error was subject to correction only by the ordinary method of appeal, and disobedience to the order constituted contempt." 258 U.S., at 189, 42 S.Ct., at 280.

This Court, in dismissing the writ of error, not only unanimously accepted but fully approved the validity of the rule of state law upon which the judgment of the Kansas court was grounded:

> "An injunction duly issuing out of a court of general jurisdiction with equity powers, upon pleadings properly invoking its action, and served upon persons made parties therein and within the jurisdiction, must be obeyed by them, however erroneous the action of the court may be, even if the error be in the assumption of the validity of a seeming, but void law going to the merits of the case. It is for the court of first instance to determine the question of the validity of the law, and until its decision is reversed for error by orderly review, either by itself or by a higher court, its orders based on its decision are to be respected, and disobedience of them is contempt of its lawful authority, to be punished." 258 U.S., at 189–90, 42 S.Ct., at 280.

The rule of state law accepted and approved in Howat v. State of Kansas is consistent with the rule of law followed by the federal courts.

In the present case, however, we are asked to hold that this rule of law, upon which the Alabama courts relied, was constitutionally impermissible. We are asked to say that the Constitution compelled Alabama to allow the petitioners to violate this injunction, to organize and engage in these mass street parades and demonstrations, without any previous effort on their part to have the injunction dissolved or modified, or any attempt to secure a parade permit in accordance with its terms. Whatever the limits of *Howat v. State of Kansas,* we cannot accept the petitioners' contentions in the circumstances of this case.

Without question the state court that issued the injunction had, as a court of equity, jurisdiction over the petitioners and over the subject matter of the controversy. And this is not a case where the injunction was transparently invalid or had only a frivolous pretense to validity. We have consistently recognized the strong interest of state and local governments in regulating the use of their streets and other public places.

* * *

The generality of the language contained in the Birmingham parade ordinance upon which the injunction was based would unquestionably raise substantial constitutional issues concerning some of its provisions. The petitioners, however, did not even attempt to apply to the Alabama courts for an authoritative construction of the ordinance. Had they done so, those courts might have given the licensing authority granted in the ordinance a narrow and precise scope * * *.

The breadth and vagueness of the injunction itself would also unquestionably be subject to substantial constitutional question. But the way to raise that question was to apply to the Alabama courts to have the injunction modified or dissolved. The injunction in all events clearly prohibited mass parading without a permit, and the evidence shows that the petitioners fully understood that prohibition when they violated it.

The petitioners also claim that they were free to disobey the injunction because the parade ordinance on which it was based had been administered in the past in an arbitrary and discriminatory fashion. In support of this claim they sought to introduce evidence that, a few days before the injunction issued, requests for permits to picket had been made to a member of the city commission. One request had been rudely rebuffed, and this same official had later made clear that he was without power to grant the permit alone, since the issuance of such permits was the responsibility of the entire city commission. Assuming the truth of this proffered evidence, it does not follow that the parade ordinance was void on its face. The petitioners, moreover, did not apply for a permit either to the commission itself or to any commissioner after the injunction issued. Had they done so, and had the permit been refused, it is clear that their claim of arbitrary or discriminatory administration of the ordinance would have been considered by the state circuit court upon a motion to dissolve the injunction.

This case would arise in quite a different constitutional posture if the petitioners, before disobeying the injunction, had challenged it in the Alabama courts, and had been met with delay or frustration of their constitutional claims. But there is no showing that such would have been the fate of a timely motion to modify or dissolve the injunction. There was an interim of two days between the issuance of the injunction and the Good Friday march. The petitioners give absolutely no explanation of why they did not make some application to the state court during that period. The injunction had issued *ex parte;* if the court had been presented with the petitioners' contentions, it might well have dissolved or at least modified its order in some respects. If it had not done so, Alabama procedure would have provided for an expedited process of appellate review. It cannot be presumed that the Alabama courts would have ignored the petitioners' constitutional claims. Indeed, these contentions were accepted in another case by an Alabama appellate court that struck down on direct review the conviction under this very ordinance of one of these same petitioners.

The rule of law upon which the Alabama courts relied in this case was one firmly established by previous precedents. We do not deal here, therefore, with a situation where a state court has followed a regular past practice of entertaining claims in a given procedural mode, and without notice has abandoned that practice to the detriment of a litigant who finds his claim foreclosed by a novel procedural bar. Barr v. City of Columbia, 378 U.S. 146, 84 S.Ct. 1734, 12 L.Ed.2d 766. This is not a case where a procedural requirement has been sprung upon an unwary litigant when prior practice did not give him fair notice of its existence. Wright v. State of Georgia, 373 U.S. 284, 291, 83 S.Ct. 1240, 1245, 10 L.Ed.2d 349.

The Alabama Supreme Court has apparently never in any criminal contempt case entertained a claim of nonjurisdictional error. In Fields v.

City of Fairfield, 273 Ala. 588, 143 So.2d 177, decided just three years before the present case, the defendants, members of a "White Supremacy" organization who had disobeyed an injunction, sought to challenge the constitutional validity of a permit ordinance upon which the injunction was based. The Supreme Court of Alabama, finding that the trial court had jurisdiction, applied the same rule of law which was followed here:

> "As a general rule, an unconstitutional statute is an absolute nullity and may not form the basis of any legal right or legal proceedings, yet until its unconstitutionality has been judicially declared in appropriate proceedings, no person charged with its observance under an order or decree may disregard or violate the order or the decree with immunity from a charge of contempt of court; and he may not raise the question of its unconstitutionality in collateral proceedings on appeal from a judgment of conviction for contempt of the order or decree * * *." 273 Ala., at 590, 143 So.2d, at 180.

These precedents clearly put the petitioners on notice that they could not bypass orderly judicial review of the injunction before disobeying it. Any claim that they were entrapped or misled is wholly unfounded, a conclusion confirmed by evidence in the record showing that when the petitioners deliberately violated the injunction they expected to go to jail.

The rule of law that Alabama followed in this case reflects a belief that in the fair administration of justice no man can be judge in his own case, however exalted his station, however righteous his motives, and irrespective of his race, color, politics, or religion. This Court cannot hold that the petitioners were constitutionally free to ignore all the procedures of the law and carry their battle to the streets. One may sympathize with the petitioners' impatient commitment to their cause. But respect for judicial process is a small price to pay for the civilizing hand of law, which alone can give abiding meaning to constitutional freedom.

Affirmed.

MR. CHIEF JUSTICE WARREN, whom MR. JUSTICE BRENNAN and MR. JUSTICE FORTAS join, dissenting.

* * *

I do not believe that giving this Court's seal of approval to such a gross misuse of the judicial process is likely to lead to greater respect for the law any more than it is likely to lead to greater protection for First Amendment freedoms. The *ex parte* temporary injunction has a long and odious history in this country, and its susceptibility to misuse is all too apparent from the facts of the case. As a weapon against strikes, it proved so effective in the hands of judges friendly to employers that Congress was forced to take the drastic step of removing from federal district courts the jurisdiction to issue injunctions in labor disputes. The labor injunction fell into disrepute largely because it was abused in precisely the same way that the injunctive power was abused in this case. Judges who were not sympathetic to the union cause commonly issued, without notice or hearing, broad restraining orders addressed to large numbers of persons and forbidding them to engage in acts that were either legally permissible or, if illegal, that could better have been left to the regular course of criminal prosecution. The injunctions might later be dissolved, but in the meantime strikes would be crippled because the occasion on which concerted activity might have been effective had passed. Such injunctions so long discredited as weapons against concerted labor activities, have now been given new life by this Court as weapons against the exercise of First Amendment freedoms. Respect for the courts and for judicial process was not increased by the history of the labor injunction.

Nothing in our prior decisions, or in the doctrine that a party subject to a temporary injunction issued by a court of competent jurisdiction with power to decide a dispute properly before it must normally challenge the injunction in the courts rather than by violating it requires that we affirm the convictions in this case. The majority opinion in this case rests essentially on a single precedent, and that a case the authority of which has clearly been undermined by subsequent decisions. Howat v. State of Kansas, 258 U.S. 181, 42 S.Ct. 277, 66 L.Ed. 550 (1922), was decided in the days when the labor injunction was in fashion. Kansas had adopted an Industrial Relations Act, the purpose of which in effect was to provide for compulsory arbitration of labor disputes by a neutral administrative tribunal, the "Court of Industrial Relations." Pursuant to its jurisdiction to investigate and perhaps improve labor conditions in the coal mining industry, the "Court" subpoenaed union leaders to appear and testify. In addition, the State obtained an injunction to prevent a strike while the matter was before the "Court." The union leaders disobeyed both the subpoena and the injunction, and sought to challenge the constitutionality of the Industrial Relations Act in the ensuing contempt proceeding. The Kansas Supreme Court held that the constitutionality of the Act could not be challenged in a contempt proceeding, and this Court upheld that determination.

Insofar as *Howat v. State of Kansas* might be interpreted to approve an absolute rule that any violation of a void court order is punishable as contempt, it has been greatly modified by later decisions. In In re Green, 369 U.S. 689, 82 S.Ct. 1114, 8 L.Ed.2d 198 (1962), we reversed a conviction for contempt of a state injunction forbidding labor picketing because the petitioner was not allowed to present evidence that the labor dispute was arguably subject to the jurisdiction of the National Labor Relations Board and hence not subject to state regulation. If an injunction can be challenged on the ground that it deals with a matter arguably subject to the jurisdiction of the National Labor Relations Board, then *a fortiori* it can be challenged on First Amendment grounds.

It is not necessary to question the continuing validity of the holding in *Howat v. State of Kansas,* however, to demonstrate that neither it nor the *Mine Workers* [45] case supports the holding of the majority in this case. In *Howat* the subpoena and injunction were issued to enable the Kansas Court of Industrial Relations to determine an underlying labor dispute. In the

45. United States v. United Mine Workers, 330 U.S. 258, 67 S.Ct. 677, 91 L.Ed. 884 (1947). [Footnote from the dissent.]

Mine Workers case, the District Court issued a temporary antistrike injunction to preserve existing conditions during the time it took to decide whether it had authority to grant the Government relief in a complex and difficult action of enormous importance to the national economy. In both cases the orders were of questionable legality, but in both cases they were reasonably necessary to enable the court or administrative tribunal to decide an underlying controversy of considerable importance before it at the time. This case involves an entirely different situation. The Alabama Circuit Court did not issue this temporary injunction to preserve existing conditions while it proceeded to decide some underlying dispute. There was no underlying dispute before it, and the court in practical effect merely added a judicial signature to a preexisting criminal ordinance. Just as the court had no need to issue the injunction to preserve its ability to decide some underlying dispute, the city had no need of an injunction to impose a criminal penalty for demonstrating on the streets without a permit. The ordinance already accomplished that. In point of fact, there is only one apparent reason why the city sought this injunction and why the court issued it: to make it possible to punish petitioners for contempt rather than for violating the ordinance, and thus to immunize the unconstitutional statute and its unconstitutional application from any attack. I regret that this strategy has been so successful.

It is not necessary in this case to decide precisely what limits should be set to the *Mine Workers* doctrine in cases involving violations of the First Amendment. Whatever the scope of that doctrine, it plainly was not intended to give a State the power to nullify the United States Constitution by the simple process of incorporating its unconstitutional criminal statutes into judicial decrees. I respectfully dissent.

[The dissenting opinion of MR. JUSTICE DOUGLAS, concurred in by MR. JUSTICE WARREN, MR. JUSTICE BRENNAN and MR. JUSTICE FORTAS, is omitted.] *

MATTER OF PROVIDENCE JOURNAL CO.

United States Court of Appeals, First Circuit, 1986.
820 F.2d 1342.

WISDOM, CIRCUIT JUDGE.

This appeal presents an apparent conflict between two fundamental legal principles: the hallowed First Amendment principle that the press shall not be subjected to prior restraints; the other, the sine qua non of orderly government, that, until modified or vacated, a court order must be obeyed. The district court adjudged the defendants/appellants, the Providence Journal Company and its executive editor, Charles M. Hauser, (collectively referred to as the "Journal") guilty of criminal contempt. The Journal admits that it violated the order but argues that the order was a

* The *Walker* case has been extensively analyzed. *See* Blasi, Prior Restraints on Demonstrations, 68 Mich.L.Rev. 1523, 1560–1563 (1970); Edelman, The Absurd Remnant: Walker v. Birmingham Two Years Later, 34 Albany L.Rev. 523 (1970); Note, 56 Calif.L.Rev. 517 (1968); Note, 81 Harv.L.Rev. 141 (1967); Note, 33 Mo.L.Rev. 152 (1967); Note, Constitutional Law–Procedural Limitations on Defenses Available in Contempt Proceedings, 22 Sw.L.J. 334 (1968); Note, 11 Syr.L.Rev. 124 (1967).

prior restraint and that the unconstitutionality of the order is a defense in the contempt proceeding. We agree. A party subject to an order that constitutes a transparently invalid prior restraint on pure speech may challenge the order by violating it.

* * *

DISCUSSION

This appeal propounds a question that admits of no easy answer. Each party stands on what each regards as an unassailable legal principle. The special prosecutor relies on the bedrock principle that court orders, even those that are later ruled unconstitutional, must be complied with until amended or vacated. This principle is often referred to as the "collateral bar" rule. The Journal relies on the bedrock principle that prior restraints against speech are prohibited by the First Amendment. In this opinion we endeavor to avoid deciding which principle should take precedence by reaching a result consistent with both principles.

Of all the constitutional imperatives protecting a free press under the First Amendment, the most significant is the restriction against prior restraint upon publication. "[T]he chief purpose of [the First Amendment's free press] guaranty [is] to prevent previous restraints upon publication." Indeed, "prior restraints upon speech and publication are the most serious and least tolerable infringement on First Amendment rights". * * *

* * *

Court orders are accorded a special status in American jurisprudence. While one may violate a statute and raise as a defense the statute's unconstitutionality, such is not generally the case with a court order. Nonetheless, court orders are not sacrosanct. An order entered by a court clearly without jurisdiction over the contemnors or the subject matter is not protected by the collateral bar rule. Were this not the case, a court could wield power over parties or matters obviously not within its authority—a concept inconsistent with the notion that the judiciary may exercise only those powers entrusted to it by law.

* * *

Although an exception to the collateral bar rule is appropriate for transparently void orders, it is inappropriate for arguably proper orders. This distinction is necessary both to protect the authority of the courts when they address close questions and to create a strong incentive for parties to follow the orderly process of law. No such protection or incentive is needed when the order is transparently invalid because in that instance the court is acting so far in excess of its authority that it has no right to expect compliance and no interest is protected by requiring compliance.

The line between a transparently invalid order and one that is merely invalid is, of course, not always distinct. As a general rule, if the court reviewing the order finds the order to have had any pretense to validity at the time it was issued, the reviewing court should enforce the collateral bar rule. * * *

* * *

In its nearly two centuries of existence, the Supreme Court has never upheld a prior restraint on pure speech. In *New York Times Co. v. United States,* the Pentagon Papers case, the Court held that the New York Times and other newspapers could not be restrained even during wartime from publishing documents that had been classified top secret and obtained without authorization. Notwithstanding that the source who had provided the documents had obtained them possibly as a result of criminal conduct and notwithstanding the government's contention that publication would gravely and irreparably jeopardize national security, the Court refused to uphold the restraint. * * *

* * *

The only interest implicated by the Journal's publication is Patriarca's right to privacy. That publication would prove embarrassing or infringe Patriarca's privacy rights is, however, an insufficient basis for issuing a prior restraint. Rather, Patriarca's sole remedy was a subsequent action for damages, an alternative that he did not pursue.

Although the Supreme Court has never upheld a prior restraint on publication of news, the Court has implied that such a restraint might be appropriate in a very narrow range of cases, when either national security or an individual's right to a fair trial is at stake. An individual's right to protect his privacy from damage by private parties, although meriting great protection, is simply not of the same magnitude. * * *

* * *

Although the Journal arguably had avenues of appellate relief immediately available to it, we decline to invoke the collateral bar rule because of the Journal's failure to avail itself of these opportunities. When, as here, the court order is a transparently invalid prior restraint on pure speech, the delay and expense of an appeal is unnecessary. Indeed, the delay caused by an appellate review requirement could, in the case of a prior restraint involving news concerning an imminent event, cause the restrained information to lose its value. The absence of such a requirement will not, however, lead to wide-spread disregard of court orders. Rarely will a party be subject to a transparently invalid court order. Prior restraints on pure speech represent an unusual class of orders because they are presumptively unconstitutional. And even when a party believes it is subject to a transparently invalid order, seeking review in an appellate court is a far safer means of testing the order. For if the party chooses to violate the order and the order turns out not to be transparently invalid, the party must suffer the consequences of a contempt citation.

* * *

Because the order was transparently invalid, the appellants should have been allowed to challenge its constitutionality at the contempt proceedings. A fortiori, the order cannot serve as the basis for a contempt citation. The order of the district court finding the Providence Journal Company and its executive editor, Charles M. Hauser, in criminal contempt is therefore reversed.

MATTER OF PROVIDENCE JOURNAL CO.

United States Court of Appeals, First Circuit, 1987.
820 F.2d 1354.*

ORDER

We hereby grant petitioner's suggestion for rehearing en banc. We do not, however, vacate the panel's opinion and order dated December 31, 1986, 820 F.2d 1342. Rather, we issue the attached en banc opinion as an addendum to, and modification of, said panel opinion; and as so modified said panel opinion and order may stand as reflecting the opinion of the en banc court.

Judge Selya does not concur in the above order and attached en banc opinion. Rather, he believes the court should hold a hearing and decide the case anew after full briefing and argument.

OPINION ON REHEARING

PER CURIAM.

In reflecting en banc upon the conflicting principles of "collateral bar" and "no prior restraint against pure speech," the court recognizes, with the panel, the difficulties of imposing upon a publisher the requirement of pursuing the normal appeal process. Not only would such entail time and expense, but the right sought to be vindicated could be forfeited or the value of the embargoed information considerably cheapened. Nevertheless, it seems to us that some finer tuning is available to minimize the disharmony between respect for court orders and respect for free speech.

It is not asking much, beyond some additional expense and time, to require a publisher, even when it thinks it is the subject of a transparently unconstitutional order of prior restraint, to make a good faith effort to seek emergency relief from the appellate court. If timely access to the appellate court is not available or if timely decision is not forthcoming, the publisher may then proceed to publish and challenge the constitutionality of the order in the contempt proceedings.[1] In such event whatever added expense and time are involved, such a price does not seem disproportionate to the respect owing court processes; and there is no prolongation of any prior restraint. On the other hand, should the appellate court grant the requested relief, the conflict between principles has been resolved and the expense and time involved have vastly been offset by aborting any contempt proceedings.

* Appeal dismissed, 485 U.S. 693, 108 S.Ct. 1502, 99 L.Ed.2d 785 (1988).

1. *See* Goodale, *The Press Ungagged: The Practical Effect on Gag Order Litigation of Nebraska Press Association v. Stuart,* 29 Stan.L.Rev. 497, 509–10 (1977) (arguing that *Walker v. City of Birmingham* "may require no more than an attempt to appeal a void restraining order up to the time the constitutionally protected action is planned to take place."). [Footnote by the Court]

We realize that our ruling means that a publisher seeking to challenge an order it deems transparently unconstitutional must concern itself with establishing a record of its good faith effort. But that is a price we should pay for the preference of court over party determination of invalidity. In the instant case, assertions have been made that some eight-and-one-half hours elapsed between the issuance of the order by the district court and the deadline for publication. Not only are we left without a clear conviction that timely emergency relief was available within the restraints governing the publisher's decision making, but we would deem it unfair to subject the publisher to the very substantial sanctions imposed by the district court because of its failure to follow the procedure we have just announced. We recognize that our announcement is technically dictum, but are confident that its stature as a deliberate position taken by us in this en banc consideration will serve its purpose.*

Notes

1. The United States Court of Appeals in Latrobe Steel Co. v. United Steelworkers of America, 545 F.2d 1336 (3d Cir.1976), held that the defense of lack of power could be raised, successfully, during the contempt hearing for violating a civil contempt order, where, in the interval between the handing down of the decree and the hearing in question, the U.S. Supreme Court, in a "closely analogous case," had held that a court was without the power to issue an order such as that upon which the contempt order in question had been based.

2. The California Supreme Court, in In re Berry, 68 Cal.2d 137, 65 Cal.Rptr. 273, 436 P.2d 273 (1968) declined to follow *Walker* in an action involving a petition for a writ of habeas corpus because, it was alleged, the petitioners had been wrongfully imprisoned for contempt of a temporary restraining order issued to enjoin certain conduct in connection with a threatened strike by employees of Sacramento, California. The Court held that such a collateral attack upon the injunction in question was not barred where "the order which petitioners are charged with disobeying is unconstitutionally overbroad in that it unnecessarily restricts the exercise of First Amendment rights; that the order is too vague and uncertain to satisfy the requirements of notice and fair trial inherent in the due process clause of the Fourteenth Amendment * * * [and] the order is therefore void in its entirety." [65 Cal.Rptr., at 286, 436 P.2d, at 286]. Accordingly, the writ was granted and release of the petitioners was ordered.

STATE v. LINSKY

Supreme Court of New Hampshire, 1977.
117 N.H. 866, 379 A.2d 813.

LAMPRON, JUSTICE.

On July 29, 1976, Properties, Inc. and Public Service Company of New Hampshire petitioned the Rockingham County Superior Court for an injunction. The plaintiffs who are in the process of constructing a nuclear power plant in Seabrook were thereby attempting to prevent a demonstra-

* See, generally, Labunski, The "Collateral Bar" Rule and the First Amendment: The Constitutionality of Enforcing Unconstitutional Orders," 37 Amer.U.L.Rev. 323 (1988).

tion against the power plant from occurring on the construction site. The superior court denied the petition without prejudice on July 30, 1976.

On August 20, 1976 the above plaintiffs joined by certain labor unions, whose members are employed in the construction of the plant, filed a motion to amend and bring forward the July 29, 1976 petition. In that petition plaintiffs Properties and Public Service had alleged that certain groups were planning to enter and occupy the described nuclear plant site on August 1, 1976, in sufficient numbers to stop its construction. The amended petition of August 20, 1976, additionally alleged in part that since June 1976, numerous Public Service offices and substation sites in the area of the nuclear plant had been victimized and vandalized and no trespassing signs on the plant site had been torn down and destroyed. On August 1, 1976, approximately 50 persons, among whom were the defendants, had approached the site via a B & M Railroad right-of-way and conducted themselves in such a manner "as to hinder and impede the criminal justice system."

The amended petition also alleged that on August 5, 1976, at a ground breaking ceremony on the site, a large group of demonstrators had blocked traffic upon a public way creating a danger to themselves and to persons traveling to and from the site. It was also alleged that the defendants were planning a large rally at about 1:00 p.m. on August 22, 1976, at Hampton Falls Common, and thereafter planned to occupy the site with 200 to 400 people. The goal of all these incidents being to impede the construction of the plant by acts of civil disobedience (*see* RSA 635:2) and to clog the court dockets to render the criminal justice system ineffective.

On August 20, 1976, the Superior Court (Bois, J.) granted plaintiffs' motion to amend and bring forward the prior petition. On the same date the court also granted *ex parte* plaintiffs' prayer for a temporary injunction enjoining and restraining the defendants from entering upon the site of the plant without the express permission of the Public Service; occupying the site; obstructing the entrance or exit of any person to or from the site; destroying or damaging any property of plaintiffs or of any other person lawfully upon the site; and committing any other act that will obstruct the activities on the site. However, on August 22, 1976, about 200 demonstrators entered the site and were arrested.

* * *

* * * The defendants were arrested and pleaded not guilty to the charge of contempt when arraigned on August 23, 1976.

* * *

* * * After a hearing all defendants were found guilty. Each was sentenced to the county house of correction for a period of 6 months, of which 3 months was suspended. All exceptions taken by the defendants before, during, or after the trial were reserved and transferred.

I. Evidence That The Injunction Was Violated

This is a criminal contempt proceeding. State v. Towle, 42 N.H. 540 (1861); Duval v. Duval, 114 N.H. 422, 425, 322 A.2d 1, 3 (1974). Hence the state must prove the elements of its case beyond a reasonable doubt, In re Winship, 397 U.S. 358, 90 S.Ct. 1068, 25 L.Ed.2d 368 (1970); *see* State v. Matthews, 37 N.H. 450, 456 (1859). The state therefore had the burden to prove beyond a reasonable doubt the existence of an injunction whose terms covered the defendants, and that defendants had notice thereof and intentionally committed one or more of the proscribed acts. * * *

The defendants contend that even though they entered the premises, the terms of the injunction were not violated, and therefore the state has not proven its case beyond a reasonable doubt. The terms of the injunction that are relevant here are those which specifically restrained the defendants from entering the described premises "without the express permission of Properties, Inc. and Public Service Company of New Hampshire," or occupying the site. The defendants claim that they were given permission to enter the site, the ban on entry was thus waived, and they did not occupy the site as that term was used in the injunction.

The evidence shows that the defendants were among two hundred demonstrators who approached the construction site by a railroad right of way which passed through the enjoined premises. * * * They entered the enjoined premises, sat down, and were later arrested.

The state's evidence concerning whether permission had been granted came from John Herrin, the construction site manager for Public Service Company of New Hampshire. Herrin was the representative of his company that day and therefore he was the one individual who could grant or deny permission to enter. Herrin testified that he never gave permission to any of the defendants to enter the premises, and told the group of demonstrators over a loudspeaker that they were not allowed on the premises. When the demonstrators entered the premises, the police did not resist, but instead allowed the demonstrators to enter in order to prevent a confrontation, and kept them in a confined area to facilitate the arrests. We hold that on the evidence before the court, viewed in its entirety, it could be found that the defendants entered the premises without permission. State v. Breest, 116 N.H. 734, 741, 367 A.2d 1320, 1326 (1976). By the terms of the injunction, one would be in violation of it by entering the land without more. The affidavit concerning violation of the injunction charges that the violation occurred when the defendants did "go upon" the premises. We also hold that the defendants were "occupying" the premises in its common and approved usage in the context of the injunction. *See* RSA 21:2.

II. NOTICE AND INTENT

In order to find a person guilty of criminal contempt for violating an injunction, that person must have knowledge or notice of the injunction, 43 C.J.S. Injunctions § 261 (1945); F. Wharton, Criminal Law and Procedure, § 1348 (R.A. Anderson ed. 1957), and the violation must have been intentional. These two elements are interrelated since it is inconceivable that a person could intentionally violate an injunction without having knowledge or notice of the injunction. Being necessary elements for criminal contempt, they must be proved beyond a reasonable doubt. In re Winship, 397 U.S. 358, 90 S.Ct. 1068, 25 L.Ed.2d 368 (1970).

The defendants contend that they were not given the type of notice demanded by due process. *See* Mullane v. Central Hanover Bank and Trust Co., 339 U.S. 306, 70 S.Ct. 652, 94 L.Ed. 865 (1950). Their claim is based on the evidence elicited at the trial that only two of the defendants, Linsky and Roth, received inhand service of the injunction. We need not reach the due process argument of the defendants. Even though in hand service may not have been made to eight of the defendants, actual service is not required to find the necessary element of notice. In fact, a party to an injunction may be chargeable with notice of the injunction in certain cases, even though he does not have actual notice. 43 C.J.S. Injunctions *supra;* F. Wharton *supra.* It is not necessary to determine whether this rule is applicable in the present case, for a party who has actual knowledge or notice of the injunction is bound by the injunction and can be punished for contempt, even though he has not been served or the service was defective. Fowler v. Beckman, 66 N.H. 424, 30 A. 1117 (1891).

The evidence presented at trial shows that defendants Linsky and Roth had inhand service, and defendant Robert Cushing, although not inhand, read a copy of the injunction before the demonstration. Whether the other defendants had knowledge of the injunction is a question of fact, proof of which may be circumstantial. Walker v. City of Birmingham, 388 U.S. 307, 87 S.Ct. 1824, 18 L.Ed.2d 1210 (1967). The evidence shows that copies of the injunction were posted at various places where the defendants would have been able to read them. The injunction was read over a loudspeaker system to the defendants at the place where they organized prior to the walk to the enjoined premises, and again after they reached the enjoined premises. Despite defendants' factual argument in their brief, we hold that there is sufficient evidence in the record to support the finding that the defendants had knowledge of the injunction. State v. Gilbert, 115 N.H. 665, 348 A.2d 713 (1975).

The defendants also press a factual argument upon us that they did not intend to violate the injunction. Whether a defendant has the requisite intent for a crime may be established by circumstantial evidence. State v. Nelson, 103 N.H. 478, 486, 175 A.2d 814, 820 (1961). Various defendants testified that they did not intend to violate the injunction. The trier of fact can choose to disbelieve exculpatory testimony given by a defendant. State v. Cote, 108 N.H. 290, 293, 235 A.2d 111, 114 (1967). When the evidence is viewed most favorably to the state, *State v. Gilbert supra,* we hold that a fair-minded and reasonable trier of fact could accept the evidence as proof of intent beyond a reasonable doubt. In re Joyce, 506 F.2d 373, 376 (5th Cir.1975). We are not convinced by defendants' argument that their so-called acts of symbolic trespass did not impair the integrity or process of the court which issued the injunction and did not constitute a contumacious intent. Nor can we hold that there was entrapment as a matter of law. RSA 626:5; State v. Bacon, 114 N.H. 306, 319 A.2d 636 (1974).

III. The Injunction

The defendants attempt to attack the validity of the injunction by claiming that the court below had no power and jurisdiction to issue it because it was not shown that there was imminent danger of great and irreparable injury, furthermore that there was an adequate remedy at law, and that equity does not enjoin criminal acts. It is their conclusion that they cannot be found in contempt of an injunction which should not have been issued due to one of these equitable principles.

It is the rule in this state, as it is in most jurisdictions, *see* 12 A.L.R.2d 1059 (1949), that an injunction rendered by a court having jurisdiction cannot be impeached collaterally in a contempt proceeding, but only by a direct attack on appeal. State v. Kennedy, 65 N.H. 247, 23 A. 431 (1889). The reference in this rule to jurisdiction is that of subject matter, and not to equitable principles which are loosely referred to as equity jurisdiction. 1 Pomeroy, Equity Jurisprudence § 129 (5th ed. 1941); D. Dobbs, Remedies § 2.7 (1973); *see* Moore v. McAllister, 216 Md. 497, 141 A.2d 176 (1958). Defendants' arguments concerning irreparable injury and criminal acts are concerned with the historic principles of equity which determine whether the party seeking relief is entitled to it. They do not involve the power of the court to adjudicate the controversy, so these issues cannot be raised in this contempt proceeding. The issue of whether there is an adequate remedy at law is not to be confused with the equitable principle which determines whether the court will exercise its discretionary and extraordinary powers. "There is a wide distinction between declining to act because the case is not thought to require it, and not doing the same thing because the court is without power." Wason v. Sanborn, 45 N.H. 169, 171 (1862). * * *

Plaintiffs' amended petition states adequate facts for the court's equity jurisdiction to be invoked. The amended petition alleges a prior instance of trespass on the construction site by the defendants and that they intended to trespass in the near future. Repetition of trespasses is a common ground for finding the legal remedy to be inadequate. * * * "Although equity will not interfere in the case of a trespass which is temporary in its nature and effect, and for which the legal remedy of an action at law is adequate, yet if the trespass is a continuous one, or if repeated acts of wrong are done or threatened, although each act by itself may not be destructive or cause irreparable injury, and for which, if it stood alone, an action at law might be an adequate remedy, the entire wrong may be prevented or stopped by injunction, on the ground of preventing a multiplicity of suits and the inadequateness of the legal remedy." Ellis v. Blue Mountain Forest Assoc., 69 N.H. 385, 388, 41 A. 856, 857 (1898). We therefore hold that the court had jurisdiction to issue the injunction. Defendants' other arguments concerning the injunction deal with whether the court erred under equitable principles in granting the injunctive relief and cannot be raised collaterally in this proceeding. The argument that Walker v. City of Birmingham, 388 U.S. 307, 87 S.Ct. 1824, 18 L.Ed.2d 1210 (1967), does not bar attacking the injunction because the defendants had attempted to have the order modified is inapplicable. The record indicates that two of the defendants received in-hand service the day the injunction was issued, yet no attempt was made to modify the injunction until two days later, on Sunday, hours before the planned demonstration. We cannot say that under these circumstances the defendants so diligently pursued modification of the injunction so as to make the instant case an exception to *Walker*.

IV. The First Amendment

The defendants base two issues on the premise that their activity was protected by the first amendment. First, it is their contention that the order in this case was broader than necessary for the protection of interests jeopardized by their trespass. They base this argument on the language in Carroll v. Princess Anne, 393 U.S. 175, 183, 89 S.Ct. 347, 353, 21 L.Ed.2d 325 (1968), that "[a]n order issued in the area of First Amendment rights must be couched in the narrowest terms that will accomplish the pin-pointed objective permitted by constitutional mandate and the essential needs of the public order." Second, the defendants contend that the temporary injunction was void because it was issued *ex parte,* and "there is no place within the area of basic freedoms guaranteed by the First Amendment for such orders where no showing is made that it is impossible to serve or to notify the opposing parties and to give them an opportunity to participate." *Id.* at 180, 89 S.Ct. at 351. We note that Walker v. City of Birmingham, 388 U.S. 307, 87 S.Ct. 1824, 18 L.Ed.2d 1210 (1967), could be read as foreclosing these issues. However, it is not clear whether *Walker* would foreclose an attack under *Carroll* on the *ex parte* issuance of the injunction, and we will therefore consider it here.

The defendants' reliance on the first amendment to find protection for their activity is misplaced. The act involved in this case is a trespass on private property. The Supreme Court of the United States at one time held that the first amendment would protect peaceful picketing, which involves elements of both speech and conduct, on privately owned property that was being used as the functional equivalent of a business district. Amalgamated Food Employees Union Local 590 v. Logan Valley Plaza, Inc., 391 U.S. 308, 88 S.Ct. 1601, 20 L.Ed.2d 603 (1968). The Court retreated from this position in Lloyd Corp. v. Tanner, 407 U.S. 551, 92 S.Ct. 2219, 33 L.Ed.2d 131 (1972), and in its opinion emphasized the fact that it "has never held that a trespasser or an uninvited guest may exercise general rights of free speech on property privately owned and used nondiscriminatorily for private purposes only." *Id.* at 568, 92 S.Ct. at 2228. The most recent case on this issue, Hudgens v. N.L.R.B., 424 U.S. 507, 96 S.Ct. 1029, 47 L.Ed.2d 196 (1976), specifically rejected the holding in *Logan Valley, supra.* Since defendants' activity was not protected by the first amendment, the temporary injunction and its *ex parte* issuance were not violative of *Carroll v. Princess Anne, supra.* The Supreme Court recognizes that outside the first amendment there is a place for the *ex parte* issuance of temporary injunctions for short durations. Carroll v. Princess Anne, 393 U.S. at 180, 89 S.Ct. 347. We hold that the *ex parte* issuance of the temporary injunction in this case was proper.

* * *

VI. Jury Trial

It is defendants' contention that they were entitled to a jury trial. The trial judge made it clear from the beginning of the case that he would not impose a sentence greater than six months if they were found guilty. The defendants were therefore not entitled to a jury trial either under the law of this state, State v. Matthews, 37 N.H. 450, 456 (1859), or the United States Constitution. Codispoti v. Pennsylvania, 418 U.S. 506, 94 S.Ct. 2687, 41 L.Ed.2d 912 (1974); Taylor v. Hayes, 418 U.S. 488, 94 S.Ct. 2697, 41 L.Ed.2d 897 (1974).

* * *

IX. SENTENCES

The trial court in this case sentenced all ten defendants to the Rockingham County House of Correction for a period of six months, three months suspended. The defendants were released pending appeal. * * *

The defendants were all found guilty of the same offense. We held in State v. Streeter, 113 N.H. 402, 405, 308 A.2d 535, 537 (1973) that: "A convicted criminal should generally receive the same punishment as another with a like background who has committed the same crime." We are not prepared to substitute our judgment for that of the trial court and hold as a matter of law that the sentences were inappropriate or excessive. *Id.* 406, 308 A.2d at 538. * * *

Exceptions overruled.

BOIS, J., did not sit.

The others concurred.

Notes

1. The *Linsky* decision recognizes that "equity jurisdiction" and jurisdiction over the subject matter are separate concepts. If a trial court grants equitable relief when it should not have done so, it is normally not a subject matter jurisdiction or "power" problem. However, as Professor Dobbs has aptly pointed out, courts sometimes have fallen into the practice of "using the word jurisdiction loosely, and they have at times said that a plaintiff suing in equity will have his suit dismissed for want of 'equity jurisdiction' if he has an adequate remedy at law. This kind of statement speaks as if the adequacy test were a limit on the power of the equity court, rather than a directive about how that power is to be used. This makes very little sense, because the adequacy test is mostly judge-made and the jurisdiction of courts is granted and limited by constitutions and statutes; courts do not prescribe their own jurisdiction. For this reason it seems very likely that, except where some particular statute or constitution provides otherwise, 'equity jurisdiction' is not jurisdictional at all." D. Dobbs, Handbook on the Law of Remedies 83 (1973). For an example of judicial confusion of the two "jurisdiction" concepts, see Mile High Kennel Club v. Colorado Greyhound Breeders Ass'n, 38 Colo.App. 519, 559 P.2d 1120 (1977) (temporary restraining order "invalid" and contempt conviction reversed because order did not specify irreparable injury). For a discussion of this distinction, *see* Z. Chaffee, Some Problems of Equity—Lack of Power and Mistaken Use of Power 296–304 (1950); 2 J. Moore's Federal Practice § 2.08 (1970).

2. The *Linsky* opinion seems to indicate that it is not always necessary to establish that the defendant had actual notice of the injunction. The majority view, however, seems to be more unyielding. Consider, for example, the

language of Mechanic v. Gruensfelder, 461 S.W.2d 298, 310, 312 (Mo.App.1970), where the court stated: "[T]wo findings beyond reasonable doubt need to be made as to each petitioner—actual knowledge of the restraining order and conduct in violation of the order * * *. [C]ircumstantial evidence may be used to establish this element [knowledge]. But such evidence must lead to the conclusion that in fact these petitioners had actual knowledge of the order. * * * Missouri courts have consistently held that actual knowledge is required to support a contempt conviction."

3. The *Carroll* case (discussed by the *Linsky* court) prohibits the use of ex parte orders in the First Amendment area unless it is impossible to serve or notify the opposing parties and give them an opportunity for a hearing. Should the fact that an order is issued in violation of the *Carroll* rationale be recognized as a defense to a contempt prosecution? The *Carroll* case itself involved a direct appeal from the granting of an ex parte order and thus did not specifically deal with the question. In Board of Educ. of the Kankakee School Dist. No. 111 v. Kankakee Federation of Teachers Local No. 886, 46 Ill.2d 439, 264 N.E.2d 18 (1970), cert. denied, 403 U.S. 904 (1971), an ex parte temporary restraining order was issued against striking teachers who disobeyed it. The Illinois Supreme Court upheld a contempt judgment and stated:

> "Here, the unlawful strike of the teachers was already in progress when the temporary order was sought, and the picketing the Board was seeking to restrain was being carried on for the purpose of fostering and supporting such unlawful strike. Accordingly, the first amendment considerations which controlled in *Carroll* were not present in this case. And there is another factual distinction worthy of note. Those against whom the order was directed in *Carroll* obeyed it and then judicially challenged its validity, the latter issue carrying over into the appeals; in the case at hand defendants deliberately defied the court by ignoring and disobeying its order instead of seeking judicial relief from its consequences, and the single issue on appeal is whether defendants could properly be found in contempt for their disobedience.
>
> "More in keeping with the circumstances of this case are the teachings of Howat v. Kansas, 258 U.S. 181, 42 S.Ct. 277, 66 L.Ed. 550 (1922) and its progeny, one of the latest of which is *Walker v. City of Birmingham* * * *. The simple and logical rationale of these decisions is that where a court of equity issues an injunction, with jurisdiction of the subject matter and the persons and upon pleadings properly invoking its action, the injunction must be obeyed however erroneous the action of the court may be, until it is reversed for error by orderly review, either by the court itself or a higher court. Disobedience of such an injunction is contempt of the lawful authority of the court, and punishable as such. (*See:* 388 U.S., at 314, 87 S.Ct., at 1828, 18 L.Ed.2d, at 1216 (1967). We agree with the trial court that the principle of these cases is controlling here, and while we do not believe the temporary restraining order was erroneous, that issue is not before us."

Compare Commonwealth *ex rel.* Costa v. Boley, 441 Pa. 495, 272 A.2d 905 (1971) (order issued ex parte in violation of the *Carroll* case termed "void on its face" in the context of an appeal.) For a case suggesting indirectly that all ex parte injunctions may be void, *see* Cuttino v. Lenoir, 271 S.C. 447, 247 S.E.2d 815 (1978).

Note on Enforcement of Decrees by Means Other Than Contempt

At an early stage, courts of equity depended upon the use of the contempt power to compel the defendant to cooperate in carrying out their decrees. Today, this is no longer always the case. For example, where the court has *in personam* jurisdiction, it may direct an officer of the court to execute a deed to land in another jurisdiction and the deed will convey a good title to the prevailing party which will be respected in the jurisdiction where the property is located. *See* Chamberlain v. Wakefield, 95 Cal.App.2d 280, 213 P.2d 62 (1949); Rozan v. Rozan, 49 Cal.2d 322, 317 P.2d 11 (1957); McElreath v. McElreath, 162 Tex. 190, 345 S.W.2d 722 (1961); Allis v. Allis, 378 F.2d 721 (5th Cir.1967). For useful articles on the subject, *see* Currie, Full Faith and Credit to Foreign Land Decrees, 21 U.Chi.L.Rev. 520 (1954); Sumner, Equity Decrees and Their Standing in Sister States, 8 S.C.L.Q. 204 (1955); Note, Equity Decrees Affecting Land in Sister States, 23 Tenn.L.Rev. 882 (1955). Where the court's jurisdiction is *in rem* because of the presence of the disputed property within the territorial jurisdiction of the court, it may follow the course of action described above or the decree itself may be recorded. *See* Churchill v. Bigelow, 333 Mass. 196, 129 N.E.2d 903 (1955); Associated Truck Lines, Inc. v. Baer, 346 Mich. 106, 77 N.W.2d 384 (1956); Conn.Gen.Stats.Ann. § 52–22 (1960) (equitable decree once recorded transfers title); N.C.Gen.Stat. § 1A–1, Rule 70 (Michie 1983) (decree transfers title when property is within the state or, in all cases, a representative of the court may execute a deed); Or.Rev.Stats. § 23.030 (1983). Due process requirements, of course, must be satisfied. *See, e.g.*, Bates v. Old Mac Coal Co., 271 P.2d 315 (Okl.1954) (attempted service on defendants by publication and by registered mail addressed to Washington D.C., but without street address, held to violate minimum due process requirements).

The above problems and solutions arise frequently in specific performance actions. However, such relief has been granted in other situations. For example, in Malis v. Zinman, 436 Pa. 592, 261 A.2d 875 (1970), the Pennsylvania Supreme Court affirmed a lower court decree, in an action based upon *in rem* jurisdiction, setting aside the transfer of title to Pennsylvania real estate that was found to have been transferred to nonresidents to defraud the transferor's creditors.

Where there is either (1) *in personam* jurisdiction over the defendant and the defendant is physically present in the jurisdiction when the decree is handed down, or (2) the controversy relates to property physically within the jurisdiction of the equity court, the court generally has it within its power to carry out its decree without the voluntary cooperation of the defendant. Where neither the defendant nor his property is present, the court may nonetheless be able to make its decree effective by the use of a master or receiver. The court fashioned such relief in Madden v. Rosseter, 114 Misc. 416, 187 N.Y.S. 462 (1921), *aff'd without opinion,* 196 App.Div. 891, 187 N.Y.S. 943:

> "Personal service of the summons upon the defendant has been made in this state, and he has duly appeared by his attorneys. Upon the verified complaint and affidavits the plaintiff now asks for a mandatory injunction requiring the defendant to ship Friar Rock to Kentucky as provided in the agreement, and enjoining other disposition of him; also for a receiver of the stallion, with power to proceed to California and to take appropriate steps there or elsewhere, including the invoking of the aid of the courts of

that or any other state, or of the federal courts, to gain possession of the animal and ship him to the plaintiff's stock farm in Kentucky.

"Plaintiff's application for relief is quite novel, but so is the situation in which he finds himself. Already his rights have been prejudiced, and further irreparable damage is threatening him. There must be a remedy, and I do not believe this court is powerless to give it to him. The relief prayed for seems to be the most practicable and appropriate which is available to him. The courts of sister states may be relied upon to aid in serving the ends of justice whenever our own process falls short of effectiveness.

"The motion will be granted, and the amount of the receiver's bond will be fixed upon the settlement of the order."

In later proceedings in the case, the court allowed the receiver a fee of $5,000 and his counsel $500 to be paid by defendant, saying: "[T]he receiver carried out the order with tact and diplomacy, avoiding any litigation or ancillary receivership in California. He delivered the horse to plaintiff on May 23, 1921, in good condition." 117 Misc. 244, 192 N.Y.S. 113 (1922). *See* D. Dobbs, Law of Remedies, 2d ed., § 2.8(1) (1993); H. Goodrich, Conflict of Laws § 78 (4th ed. 1964).

Chapter 3

BASIC PRINCIPLES OF DAMAGES

SECTION 1. LEGAL DAMAGES DEFINED

As the previous chapter discussed, equitable relief is an order to the defendant to do or not do something which gives plaintiff specific relief. Prior to ordering equitable relief, a court typically requires that legal relief be inadequate. Thus, legal relief must be different from equitable relief.

What is legal relief? With the exception of legal replevin and ejectment, legal damages are substitutionary in that the damages give a plaintiff money to substitute for a remedy that would specifically undo the wrong. For example, if the wrong is a tort of taking an original oil painting, the specific remedy would be getting the painting back, while substitutionary relief would be money as a substitute for the painting in order to compensate for the loss of the painting. However, note that this paragraph began with an exception. One cannot simply say that legal relief is substitutionary while equitable relief is specific. Sometimes, by the quirk of historic rules, some legal relief is specific. As will be seen in later chapters, replevin, which is a remedy that enables a plaintiff to get back personal property, can be either legal or equitable. Ejectment, which is a remedy that enables a plaintiff to get possession of real property is legal although in the proper circumstances an order to return real property to the plaintiff can be equitable. But as a general matter, legal relief is substitutionary and involves money damages.

Why do we worry about whether relief is either legal or equitable? Originally the distinction was historic, as described in Chapter 1. Since the Federal Rules of Civil Procedure merged law and equity in 1938, the distinction in federal courts is not jurisdictional. Except in a few states, a plaintiff does not need to choose between bringing an action in a court of equity or a court of law. But a plaintiff needs to know whether relief is legal or equitable for other purposes. For example, as will be described in Chapter 9, if relief is legal, the parties are entitled to a jury trial, but not if the relief is equitable. As was described in Chapter 2, if relief is equitable, the order is enforced by contempt. A legal judgment is enforced by a sheriff attaching defendant's property if possible, selling it and applying the proceeds to the judgment.

SECTION 2. GOALS

"The stated goal of the damages remedy is compensation of the plaintiff for legally recognized losses. This means that the plaintiff should be fully indemnified for his loss, but that he should not recover any windfall. Stated in this way, damages is an instrument of corrective justice, an effort to put the plaintiff in his or her rightful position." D. Dobbs, The Law of Remedies, § 3.1, at 210 (1993). What is plaintiff's rightful position? In tort law the remedial goal is to put the plaintiff in a position that is as if the tort had not occurred. This is done by compensating plaintiff to "make the plaintiff whole". However, the plaintiff is generally not to be overcompensated, so as to get a "windfall".

In contract law, on the other hand, the remedial goal is to put the plaintiff in a position that is as if the contract had been performed, and thus to give the plaintiff the benefit of the bargain. In other words, this goal is to compensate the plaintiff on the basis of the plaintiff's expectancy interest. Where this cannot be done, the court may award the plaintiff damages that seek to compensate the plaintiff for those expenses incurred in seeking to perform the contract, and thus to relate damages to the reliance interests of the plaintiff. Restitutionary relief, which does not focus upon plaintiff's losses, but rather seeks to return to the plaintiff any benefit conferred by the plaintiff upon the defendant that would be unjust for the defendant to retain, will be discussed in Chapter 4.

SECTION 3. TERMINOLOGY AND LIMITATIONS

The law of remedies has its own terms of art, at times misused or confused. Compensatory damages is an overall term meaning all damages that remedy a plaintiff's loss, or loss of benefit of the bargain. Actual damages are contrasted with nominal damages in that actual damages measure an actual loss while nominal damages indicate that plaintiff was wronged, but either had no damages or could not prove them. Sometimes the cause of action requires damages as an element. In that case, if damages are not proven, then plaintiff will not receive even nominal damages; plaintiff's case will be dismissed.

Compensatory and actual damages are both general terms that are the sum of general, special or consequential, and "substitution cost" or incidental damages. These are generally defined as:

"(1) *General or market damages,* meaning market-measured compensation calculated by the value of the very thing to which the plaintiff was entitled. (2) *Special or consequential damages,* meaning compensation for harms or losses resulting in *consequence* of harm to the very thing to which the plaintiff was entitled, often in the form of lost profits. (3) *Substitution cost damages,* meaning the reasonable costs of procuring a substitute for the very thing to which the plaintiff was entitled, rather than the value of the thing itself." D. Dobbs, The Law of Remedies, § 3.3(1), at 220 (1993). Special and general damages have more detailed definitions that differ in tort and contract. Those differences reflect the disparate limits upon contract and tort liability. Consider as you read the following cases how those limits are different and why.

AMERICAN LIST CORP. v. U.S. NEWS AND WORLD REPORT, INC.

Court of Appeals of New York, 1989.
75 N.Y.2d 38, 550 N.Y.S.2d 590, 549 N.E.2d 1161.

ALEXANDER, JUDGE.

* * *

I

Defendant publishes a national weekly news magazine which, in 1983, had the third largest circulation for such magazines in the Nation. In an attempt to expand its circulation by entering the college student market, defendant negotiated an agreement with plaintiff whereby, for a 10–year period, plaintiff would compile and rent to defendant mailing lists of college student names. Plaintiff had previously produced such mailing lists for high school, but not college, students. Consequently defendant agreed to finance plaintiff's start-up costs by paying a larger fee per name in the first five years of the arrangement. A schedule of the estimated number of names to be provided and the fees to be paid by defendant as well as the estimated losses and profits of plaintiff in each of the 10 years contemplated by the agreement was appended to the agreement. In addition, the agreement, which was drafted by defendant, provided that "[U.S. News and World Report has] agreed to take as much as 25% more names than the estimated compilation at the cost pername [*sic*] shown in years one through five." The agreement further provided for an annual review of the estimated figures for the purpose of adjusting the cost per name to be charged to defendant.

The agreement was signed by the parties on January 25 and 26, 1984. Martin Lerner, plaintiff's president, signed on behalf of plaintiff and Joseph Acerno, the vice-president of circulation, signed on behalf of defendant. One year after the contract was signed, defendant was purchased by a new owner and Acerno was replaced by Jacob Weintraub. Weintraub canceled the contract in September 1985 although prior to that cancellation, defendant had accepted and paid for names provided by plaintiff for three mailings conducted over a one and one-half-year period.

Plaintiff commenced this action for breach of contract. After a bench trial, Supreme Court found defendant liable and awarded damages of $1,449,344 for the breach, which sum constituted the balance due plaintiff on the contract for the years 1985 to 1994, as reduced to present value. * * *

Defendant argues that the damages awarded to plaintiff are actually "lost future profits" which are special damages and not compensable absent a showing that they were foreseeable and contemplated by the parties at the time the contract was made (*see, Kenford Co. v. County of Erie,* 67 N.Y.2d 257, 502 N.Y.S.2d 131, 493 N.E.2d 234) (*Kenford I*), a showing plaintiff failed to make because the lost future profits it seeks, like the lost future profits sought in *Kenford I,* are too speculative for calculation. Plaintiff counters that it seeks general rather than special damages and that it has sufficiently proven that its damages are the natural and direct consequence of defendant's breach of their agreement.

* * *

II

We reject at the outset defendant's contention that the courts below improperly awarded plaintiff "lost future profits" which are special damages not sufficiently proven at the trial.

The distinction between general and special contract damages is well defined but its application to specific contracts and controversies is usually more elusive. General damages are those which are the natural and probable consequence of the breach * * * while special damages are extraordinary in that they do not so directly flow from the breach. These extraordinary damages are recoverable only upon a showing that they were foreseeable and within the contemplation of the parties at the time the contract was made (* * * *Hadley v. Baxendale,* 9 Exch. 341, 156 Eng.Rep. 145). Thus in *Kenford I,* 67 N.Y.2d 257, 502 N.Y.S.2d 131, 493 N.E.2d 234, *supra,* the nonbreaching party to a contract for the management of a domed sports stadium claimed special damages in the form of the lost future profits which that party would have received from its operation of the stadium. We concluded that the claimed lost future profits could not be recovered because it could not be demonstrated that such damages were caused by the breach, the alleged loss was not capable of proof with reasonable certainty, and it had not been proven that those damages were within the contemplation of the parties at the time the contract was made (*id.,* at 261–263, 502 N.Y.S.2d 131, 493 N.E.2d 234; *see also, Hadley v. Baxendale,* 9 Exch. 341, 156 Eng.Rep. 145, *supra* [failure to prove foreseeability of claimed damages of lost profits of mill operation resulting from common carrier's breach of contract to timely deliver broken mill shaft for repairs]).

Here, by contrast, it is clear that plaintiff has sought only to recover moneys which defendant undertook to pay under the contract, thereby assuming a definite obligation. By the express terms of the agreement drafted by defendant, its appended schedule reflected the "cost of this joint venture" to defendant and set forth the fees to be paid to plaintiff for a specific number of names to be provided by plaintiff in each of the 10 years contemplated by the arrangement. That schedule also contemplated that plaintiff would suffer losses during the first five years because of its additional start-up costs, and defendant agreed to pay a larger fee per name for names provided during that period. These contemplated losses, however, do not alter the fact that defendant agreed to pay a specific amount over a period of 10 years—a sum explicitly stated in the contract schedule to be $3,027,500 and thus unquestionably within the contemplation of the parties. Moreover, contrary to defendant's contention, the fact that plaintiff did not incur costs as great as anticipated during part of the time in which the parties had contemplated that plaintiff would suffer losses is irrelevant to defendant's obligation under the agreement. Thus, as the trial proof establishes, plaintiff has sufficiently demonstrated that the moneys it seeks—the present value of the balance owed by defendant under the contract less the costs reasonably saved by plaintiff as a result of the breach—are general damages flowing as a natural and probable consequence of the breach.

* * *

Notes

1. What is the difference between general and special damages in contract law? How did the court distinguish them? Why does it matter whether the damages are general or special?

2. Why must special damages (consequential damages) be contemplated by the parties at the time of contracting?

3. Incidental damages are costs incurred in mitigation. The plaintiff did not try to mitigate. Why not? What would damages have been if the plaintiff had mitigated?

SYMON v. BURGER

Court of Appeals of Indiana, Fourth District, 1988.
528 N.E.2d 850.

MILLER, JUDGE.

Deborah K. Symon appeals the grant of additur to the jury verdict won by Constance and Dean Burger against her. Mr. and Mrs. Burger won verdicts in the amounts of $2,100.15 and $1,482.20 respectively in their negligence action against Symon for personal injuries and property damage sustained in an automobile accident. Upon the Burgers' motion to correct errors, the trial judge granted additur raising the respective awards to $8,100.15 and $4,482.00.

Symon contends that the jury's verdict must be reinstated because additur was error as a matter of law. * * * We have determined that the granting of additur was erroneous and reverse and remand with instructions to reinstate the jury verdict.

* * *

The trial court has three options when it determines that damages awarded are inadequate. The court may "enter final judgment on the evidence for the amount of the proper damages, grant a new trial, or grant a new trial subject to additur or remittitur." T.R. 59(J)(5). The trial court cannot properly vary the jury's award and enter judgment for a different amount unless it finds that the damages awarded were excessive or inadequate as a matter of law. * * * The jury's verdict will be upheld unless the damages awarded are so small as to indicate the jury was motivated by "* * * passion, partiality, corruption or considered some improper element." *State v. Tabler* (1978), 178 Ind.App. 31, 381 N.E.2d 502. Additur or remittitur is error if the jury's award is within the range of the evidence. * * *

Indiana does, however, subscribe to the general principle of tort law that all damages directly attributed to the wrong done are compensable. * * * The jury is not required to award a substantial amount as compensation for general damages. Under appropriate circumstances, a nominal award is appropriate. * * * The Burgers contend that the jury's verdict, which corresponds to their claimed *special* damages to the penny (Mrs. Burger's exact claimed specials and Mr. Burger's exact claimed specials if the jury cut the value of his Vega in half), is inadequate as a matter of law because it fails to compensate them even nominally for pain and suffering and loss of consortium.

According to the Burgers, the following tables demonstrate how their awards were computed by the jury:

Mrs. Burger		Mr. Burger	
Medical Bills	$1117.25	'73 Vega $2300/2	= $1150.00
Lost Wages	982.90	Tow	97.00
Pain and Suffering	-0-	Car Rental	235.20
		Consortium	-0-
Total	$2100.15		$1482.20

Had the evidence not been hotly contested we might agree with the Burgers. Upon analysis of the trial record we conclude that the jury may not have taken the Burgers' claim of special damages at face value, but awarded their claimed specials in order to compensate them nominally for their general damages. When a jury awards a personal injury plaintiff the exact amount, or approximately the exact amount, of his or her claimed medical expenses and other special damages but makes no allowance for pain and suffering, the verdict is not necessarily improper or irregular since the jury could have *disallowed* a portion of the claimed special damages, but awarded the amount claimed with the intention of making the difference constitute compensation for the plaintiff's pain and suffering and other general damages.

* * *

Mrs. Burger's claims of special damages were in dispute. Her credibility was challenged. For example, it was discovered at trial that two of the medical bills submitted as attributable to the accident were for totally unrelated reasons and should be disregarded by the jury. One doctor bill was for the treatment of an earlobe infection resulting from the piercing of Mrs. Burger's ears. Another bill was for the treatment of the common cold. Also, the jury was not required to believe that Mrs. Burger's depression and the resulting treatment expenses were attributable to the accident.

The reasonableness of Mrs. Burger's claim for lost wages was also questioned. She allegedly lost 38½ days of work between October 29, 1984, the day of the accident, and January 7, 1985 as a result of the accident. She was employed as a school bus driver and many days during this period were school holidays. Her doctor testified that he had placed no specific restrictions on her activities and many patients with broken ribs do not miss any work at all.

The size of Mr. Burger's award indicates the jury did not believe his testimony concerning the value of his 1973 Chevrolet Vega. He testified the car was worth $2,300.00 at the time of the accident—the amount he paid for it 21 months earlier—and $50.00 as junk afterwards. Even if we were to accept his contention that the jury awarded him 50% or $1150.00 for his Vega and nothing ($0.00) for loss of consortium, the $50.00 salvage value has not been accounted for. Burger's 50% formula indicates the jury awarded him $50.00, sufficient nominal damages, for the loss of consortium. However, we need not accept Burger's 50% formula; we note that the jury could have employed one of many formulae to award a lesser amount for the Vega and nominal damages for the loss of consortium. Our inability to actually look into the minds of jurors and determine how they computed an award is, to a large extent, the reason behind the rule that a verdict will be upheld if the award falls within the bounds of the evidence. *Annee v. State* (1971), 256 Ind. 686, 271 N.E.2d 711.

The Burgers' claims of special damages were hotly contested. We conclude that the jury awards which correspond to the amount of special damages claimed could easily have included awards for pain and suffering and loss of consortium. Because the Burgers were compensated for all their injuries, the jury verdict was within the range of the evidence and the granting of additur was erroneous.

* * *

Note

How do general and special damages in tort law differ from general and special in contract law? Why are there different limitations to damages in tort and contract law? Consider the next case.

HAP'S AERIAL ENTERPRISES, INC. v. GENERAL AVIATION CORPORATION

Court of Appeals of Wisconsin, 1992.
173 Wis.2d 459, 496 N.W.2d 680.

GARTZKE, PRESIDING JUDGE.

Hap's Aerial Enterprises, Inc., appeals from a summary judgment dismissing its complaint against General Aviation Corporation. Hap's claims damages for General's negligent inspection of an aircraft performed for its prior owner, Regal Beloit Corporation. The issue is whether Hap's, as a subsequent buyer of the used aircraft, can recover purely economic damages in a negligence action against General. We conclude that if General's negligence is established, Hap's can recover damages for its economic loss, unless public policy considerations prevent recovery. The facts should be developed to allow the trial court not only to determine if General was negligent but to evaluate the policy considerations. We therefore reverse and remand.

* * *

The complaint alleges that on July 13, 1988, the defendant General Aviation performed a "hot section inspection" on the engines of an aircraft. It is undisputed that General Aviation inspected the aircraft for its then owner, Regal Beloit Corporation, and that as part of its inspection, General had to check each turbine wheel and grind its surface to obtain the required tolerance. Hap's bought the aircraft from Regal soon after General's inspection. In October 1988, Hap's sold the aircraft, subject to a "pre-buy inspection." During that inspection Hap's learned that because General negligently performed its July inspection, Hap's had to repair the engines in order to sell the aircraft. Hap's incurred repair expenses of $22,997 and lost $535 in interest on its sale. It sues General Aviation for those amounts.

Relying primarily on *Sunnyslope Grading, Inc. v. Miller, Bradford & Risberg, Inc.,* 148 Wis.2d 910, 437 N.W.2d 213 (1989), and *Miller v. United States Steel Corp.,* 902 F.2d 573 (7th Cir.1990), the trial court dismissed the complaint on grounds that Hap's cannot recover damages for purely economic losses caused by General's negligence. In the court's view, the case law establishes that commercial disputes must be resolved by commercial rather than tort law, and purely economic or commercial losses can be recovered only in contract actions. The court declined to carve out an exception to what it considered the law by allowing commercial purchasers of used equipment to recover from parties who negligently provided service or parts to the equipment in the past. We disagree with the trial court's view of the law.

It is true that a commercial purchaser of goods or equipment from a seller cannot recover in this state for purely commercial losses which the buyer attributes to the seller's negligence. The *Sunnyslope* court established that law. *Id.* 148 Wis.2d at 921, 437 N.W.2d at 217–18. In *Sunnyslope,* the purchaser of backhoes sued the seller for the cost of repairs not covered by the manufacturer's warranties. The *Sunnyslope* court confined the purchaser to its contract remedies. The court said:

> We agree with the weight of authority which supports the proposition that the legislative protections granted by the Uniform Commercial Code are not to be buttressed by tort principles and recovery. The duty to provide a product which functions to certain specifications is contractual. If a commercial purchaser wants a machine of higher quality, better durability or one with a better warranty, the purchaser is free to negotiate in the marketplace.

Id. at 916, 437 N.W.2d at 215 (citation omitted).[1]

But Hap's bought the aircraft from Regal Beloit Corporation, not from General. No commercial transaction occurred between Hap's and General. Nothing in the complaint discloses any contact whatever between Hap's

1. Sunnyslope bought the backhoes from a dealer for the manufacturer but the manufacturer had extended each purchaser a written warranty which limited manufacturer's liability to replacement of defective parts and provided that the manufacturer was not liable for any other damage, whether direct, incidental or consequential. Sunnyslope sought to recover lost profits and the cost of repairing the equipment when the manufacturer did not breach its warranty.

and General. Hap's simply bought an aircraft which it claims General had negligently inspected, and that negligence caused damages to Hap's.[2]

The United States Court of Appeals for the Seventh Circuit believes that the Wisconsin Supreme Court would extend the economic or commercial loss doctrine recognized in *Sunnyslope* to a commercial purchaser such as Hap's who asserts a claim against a tortfeasor not in privity with the purchaser.[3] The Seventh Circuit held that the owner of an office in Wisconsin could not recover in tort against U.S. Steel for the cost of replacing defective steel U.S. Steel sold to a subcontractor who fabricated it into panels which the general contractor installed on the building. *Miller,* 902 F.2d at 574–75.[4] The *Miller* court relied on its previous decision in *Rardin v. T & D Mach. Handling, Inc.,* 890 F.2d 24 (7th Cir.1989), as a leading case establishing the economic loss doctrine.

In our view, however, when compared with Wisconsin precedent, the analysis in *Rardin* shows why the Wisconsin Supreme Court is unlikely to approve the *Miller* court's application of the "economic loss" doctrine.

In *Rardin* the plaintiff bought a used printing press from Whitacre for use in his business. The contract provided that Whitacre was responsible only for such damage to the press as might be incurred due to the fault or negligence of its own employees, agents, contractors or representatives. Whitacre hired the defendant T & D Machine Handling to dismantle and load the press on a truck. T & D negligently performed its tasks and damaged the press. Rardin incurred repair costs and lost business profits during the repairs and sued T & D for its damages. The *Rardin* court held that T & D had no liability under Illinois law in negligence for Rardin's economic losses.

The *Rardin* court reasoned that to conclude that a person is "negligent is to affirm that the costs of care to him were less than the costs of his carelessness to all who might be hurt by it; that, essentially, is what negligence means, in Illinois and elsewhere." *Id.* at 26. The court said that

> [i]n deciding how much effort to expend on being careful—and therefore how far to reduce the probability of a careless accident—the potential injurer must have at least a rough idea of the extent of liability.

2. In *Tony Spychalla Farms, Inc. v. Hopkins Agric. Chem. Co.,* 151 Wis.2d 431, 438, 444 N.W.2d 743, 747 (Ct.App.1989), we refused to extend the *Sunnyslope* holding to a commercial transaction where a defective product damaged other property.

3. The Seventh Circuit's interpretation of Wisconsin law does not bind us.

4. In *Midwest Knitting Mills, Inc. v. United States,* 950 F.2d 1295 (7th Cir.1991), the Seventh Circuit held that Wisconsin would recognize a tort claim by a third party against an employer arising out of the negligent supervision of an employee but would not permit the recovery of purely economic losses for the tort. The Seventh Circuit said, "As this court noted in *Miller v. United States Steel Corp.,* 902 F.2d 573, 574–75 (7th Cir.1990), there is now substantial evidence that Wisconsin would decline in all circumstances to allow a negligence suit for the recovery of only economic damages, even when there is no contractual relationship between the parties." *Midwest Knitting,* 950 F.2d at 1300 (footnote omitted). The Wisconsin Supreme Court has not yet declared that to be the law of this state, and we think that when presented squarely with the question, it will not.

Id. T & D was not privy to the circumstances of the owners of the presses, did not deal directly with Rardin, and knew nothing about his business, and could not have determined the financial consequences to Rardin if the press was damaged. *Id.* Rardin, the court said, could have protected himself against the financial consequences of unexpected delay. He could have contracted out some of his printing work in advance, bought business interruption insurance, or negotiated for a liquidated damages clause in his contract with his seller to compensate him for the delay. *Id.* at 27.

Perhaps Hap's could have taken measures comparable to those the *Rardin* court recommended to protect itself from economic loss resulting from the defective condition of the aircraft it bought from Regal. However, the present law of Wisconsin does not prevent Hap's from recovering commercial or economic damages caused by the negligence of a third party who dealt with Regal. The Wisconsin Supreme Court has twice held that the defendant who negligently provides services to one person may be liable for economic losses resulting to a third person, unless public policy dictates otherwise.

In *A.E. Inv. Corp. v. Link Builders, Inc.*, 62 Wis.2d 479, 214 N.W.2d 764 (1974), an architect did not contract with the plaintiffs, but the architect knew that the plaintiffs would operate a supermarket in the building the architect was designing for the contractor. The plaintiffs suffered economic losses when the building floor settled because of a design failure. The *A.E.* court held that the plaintiff's complaint against the architect stated a claim in negligence. *Id.* at 486–87, 214 N.W.2d at 768. The court said, "A party is negligent when he commits an act when some harm to someone is foreseeable. Once negligence is established, the defendant is liable for unforeseeable consequences as well as foreseeable ones. In addition, he is liable to unforeseeable plaintiffs." [5] *Id.* at 484, 214 N.W.2d at 766. The court expressly held that damages for "economic loss" may be recovered in a negligence action, unless public policy considerations require otherwise. *Id.* at 490–91, 214 N.W.2d at 770. * * *

In *Citizens State Bank v. Timm, Schmidt & Co.*, 113 Wis.2d 376, 335 N.W.2d 361 (1983), a firm of certified public accountants was alleged to have negligently prepared financial statements for a company to which the plaintiff bank made a loan after reviewing the statements. When the company went into receivership, the bank sued the accounting firm for its loss on the loan caused by the firm's negligence. That loss was necessarily "economic" or "commercial." The *Citizens* court said, "The fundamental principle of Wisconsin negligence law is that a tortfeasor is fully liable for all foreseeable consequences of his act except as those consequences are limited by policy factors," [6] *Id.* at 386, 335 N.W.2d at 366, and remanded

5. Thus, the *Rardin* court's declaration that negligence means that the costs of care to the actor are less than the costs to all who might be harmed, *Rardin*, 890 F.2d at 26, is simply irrelevant to the Wisconsin definition of negligence.

6. The fundamental principle of Wisconsin negligence law does not apply to the liability of attorneys to non-clients. An attorney is not liable to a non-client plaintiff for mere negligence. *Green Spring Farms v. Kersten*, 136 Wis.2d 304, 307, 401 N.W.2d 816, 817 (1987). An exception-to-the-exception exists. The attorney who draws a will is liable to the intended beneficiary who received nothing by reason of the attorney's

the matter for a full factual resolution. *Id.* at 387, 335 N.W.2d at 366.[7]

Distinctions exist between the facts before us and the facts in *A.E.* and *Citizens*. For one thing, in those cases the defendants were professionals.[8] For another, in *A.E.*, the architects knew that the plaintiff supermarket operator was to operate a store in the building the architect had designed, and in *Citizens*, a member of the accounting firm may have known that the statements his firm prepared would be used by the bank. *Citizens*, 113 Wis.2d at 380, 335 N.W.2d at 363. However, those distinctions do not affect the principle applied in both *A.E.* and *Citizens:* the person who commits an act when some harm to someone is foreseeable is negligent, and a negligent person is liable for unforeseeable consequences to unforeseeable plaintiffs. *A.E. Inv. Corp.*, 62 Wis.2d at 484, 214 N.W.2d at 766.

We conclude that the matter must be remanded to the trial court to determine whether General negligently inspected the engines of the aircraft Hap's bought from Regal and whether that negligence caused the economic damages Hap's claims in its complaint. If General contends that public policy reasons should protect it from liability, each side should be allowed to present evidence on that issue.

Judgment reversed and remanded with directions.

Notes

1. Could Hap's Aerial have sued General Aviation for breach of contract? Why or why not? If it had, would the damages it sought be general or consequential? What would Hap's have had to prove if those damages were in contract? Would Hap's have to prove that if the action were in tort?

2. Where the injury that results from negligence is commercial loss, do you agree with the reasoning in *Hap's Aerial* or with that of Judge Posner in

negligence. *Auric v. Continental Casualty Co.*, 111 Wis.2d 507, 509, 331 N.W.2d 325, 327 (1983).

The statement in *Citizens* that liability is limited to *foreseeable* consequences must be read in light of the facts in that case. In his affidavit, the president of the accounting firm acknowledged that he knew that financial statements are commonly supplied to lenders. The *unforeseeable* consequences, if any, of the firm's alleged negligence was not at issue. The cases relied on by the *Citizens* court held, in one way or another, that a tortfeasor is liable for unforeseeable consequences as well as foreseeable ones. The Wisconsin Supreme Court recently confirmed this position. *Paskiet v. Quality State Oil Co.*, 164 Wis.2d 800, 808, 476 N.W.2d 871, 874 (1991). We recently applied the principle and the public policy considerations in *Cormican v. Larrabee*, 171 Wis.2d 309, 491 N.W.2d 130 (Ct.App.1992).

7. The public policy considerations outlined in *Citizens*, 113 Wis.2d at 387, 335 N.W.2d at 366, include the following: (1) The injury is too remote from the negligence; or (2) the injury is wholly out of proportion to the culpability of the negligent tortfeasor; or (3) in retrospect it appears highly extraordinary that the negligence has brought about the harm; or (4) recovery places too unreasonable a burden on the negligent tortfeasor; or (5) recovery is too likely to open the way for fraudulent claims; or (6) recovery will enter a field having no sensible or just stopping point.

8. In *Milwaukee Partners v. Collins Engineers, Inc.*, 169 Wis.2d 355, 363–64 n. 3, 485 N.W.2d 274, 277 n. 3 (Ct.App.1992), we said that although in Wisconsin a tort remedy for economic damages is not available to a purchaser in a commercial setting where an effective warranty exists between the parties, breach of a professional obligation of due care is a tort, and unless public policy considerations against liability intervene, professionals in Wisconsin (in that case, engineers) are liable in tort for economic damages regardless of whether a contractual relationship exists between the parties.

Rardin v. T & D Mach. Handling, Inc., 890 F.2d 24 (7th Cir.1989), which the court in *Hap's Aerial* discussed but declined to follow?

3. On remand, how do you think the public policy factors listed in note 7 of *Hap's Aerial* should be applied? Consider the following cases and notes on economic loss recovery in a tort action.

AIKENS v. BALTIMORE AND OHIO RAILROAD COMPANY

Superior Court of Pennsylvania, 1985.
348 Pa.Super. 17, 501 A.2d 277.

OLSZEWSKI, JUDGE:

This appeal follows an order by the Court of Common Pleas of Allegheny County, Civil Division, which granted judgment on the pleadings to the appellees and dismissed appellants' complaint. Appellants, employees of the Motor Coils Manufacturing Company, Inc., brought suit seeking damages for lost wages, alleging that appellees' negligence caused a train derailment which damaged the Motor Coils plant. As a result of the derailment, production at the plant was curtailed and appellants suffered loss of work and wages. Appellants did not suffer personal injury or property damage from the derailment.

On appeal, the appellants raise two issues. First, appellants argue that Pennsylvania should recognize a cause of action to compensate a party suffering purely economic loss, absent any direct physical injury or property damage, as a result of the negligence of another party. We find this argument to be without merit.

The general rule is stated in the Restatement (Second) of Torts Sec. 766C:

> **Negligent Interference with Contract or Prospective Contractual Relation.** One is not liable to another for pecuniary harm not deriving from physical harm to the other, if that harm results from the actor's negligently
>
> (a) causing a third person not to perform a contract with the other, or
>
> (b) interfering with the other's performance of his contract or making the performance more expensive or burdensome, or
>
> (c) interfering with the other's acquiring a contractual relation with a third person.

Thus, recovery for purely economic loss occasioned by tortious interference with contract or economic advantage is not available under a negligence theory. *Local Joint Executive Board of Las Vegas v. Stern,* 98 Nev. 409, 651 P.2d 637 (1982). A cause of action exists in this situation only if the tortious interference was intentional or involved parties in a special relationship to one another. *See Petition of S.C. Loveland, Inc.,* 170 F.Supp. 786 (E.D.Pa.1959); W. Prosser, Handbook of the Law of Torts Sec. 130 (4th Ed.1971).

The roots of this well-established rule reach back to the United States Supreme Court decision of *Robins Dry Dock and Repair Company v. Flint,*

275 U.S. 303, 48 S.Ct. 134, 72 L.Ed. 290 (1927). Writing for the Court, Mr. Justice Holmes stated:

> (A)s a general rule, at least, a tort to the person or property of one man does not make the tort-feasor liable to another merely because the injured person was under a contract with that other unknown to the doer of the wrong. The law does not spread its protection so far.

275 U.S. at 309, 48 S.Ct. at 135, 72 L.Ed. at 292. Therefore, negligent harm to economic advantage alone is too remote for recovery under a negligence theory. The reason a plaintiff cannot recover stems from the fact that the negligent actor has no knowledge of the contract or prospective relation and thus has no reason to foresee any harm to the plaintiff's interest. * * *

Recently, the Georgia Court of Appeals was faced with a factual setting quite similar to the case at bar. In *Willis v. Georgia Northern Railway Company,* 169 Ga.App. 743, 314 S.E.2d 919 (1984), the appellants were employees of a plant which was damaged when eight loaded railcars owned by the appellee railroad broke free and rolled into the plant. The plant employees sued the railroad for lost wages. The Georgia Court held that the employees' right to wages existed by virtue of their relationship with the plant and not the railroad. Thus, loss of wages was not a probable consequence of the railroad's negligence and the damages claimed were too remote. *Id.* We find this reasoning persuasive.

Finally, we note that allowance of a cause of action for negligent interference with economic advantage would create an undue burden upon industrial freedom of action, and would create a disproportion between the large amount of damages that might be recovered and the extent of the defendant's fault. *See* Restatement (Second) of Torts Sec. 766C, comment a (1979). To allow a cause of action for negligent cause of purely economic loss would be to open the door to every person in the economic chain of the negligent person or business to bring a cause of action. Such an outstanding burden is clearly inappropriate and a danger to our economic system.

Accordingly, we decline appellants' invitation to adopt the reasoning of the California Supreme Court in *J'Aire Corp. v. Gregory,* 24 Cal.3d 799, 157 Cal.Rptr. 407, 598 P.2d 60 (1979), and to extend negligence liability to embrace purely economic loss. Such an extension would clearly lead to problems in consistency and foreseeability, and could be harmful in scope. Instead, we adopt the majority rule of the Restatement (Second) of Torts Sec. 766C, and hold that no cause of action exists for negligence that causes only economic loss.

* * *

Order affirmed.

Notes

1. The reasoning of J'Aire Corp. v. Gregory, 24 Cal.3d 799, 157 Cal.Rptr. 407, 598 P.2d 60 (1979), rejected by the court in *Aikens* is based on foreseeability where a heating contractor hired by the owner of a building knew that its work was for the benefit of the restaurant lessee. Despite a lack of privity, the

court held the heating contractor liable to the restaurant for lost profits when the restaurant was closed due to delay in repair of the heating and cooling system. *But see* Floor Craft Floor Covering, Inc. v. Parma Community General Hospital Assoc., 54 Ohio St.3d 1, 560 N.E.2d 206 (1990) in which an architectural firm which contracted with a hospital was not liable to the hospital's flooring contractor for providing defective installation specifications because "[i]n the absence of privity of contract between two disputing parties the general rule is 'there is no * * * duty to exercise reasonable care to avoid intangible economic loss or losses to others that do not arise from tangible physical harm to persons and tangible things.' Prosser & Keeton, Law of Torts (5 Ed.1984) 657, Section 92." Id. at 208.

2. The typical products liability rule is that when a product causes physical injury only to itself, liability for consequential economic losses arises only in contract, not in tort. *See* PPG Industries, Inc. v. Sundstrand Corp., 681 F.Supp. 287, 289–90 (W.D.Pa.1988) for a summary of the often followed East River Steamship Co. v. Transamerica Delaval, Inc., 476 U.S. 858, 106 S.Ct. 2295, 90 L.Ed.2d 865 (1986) where the United States Supreme Court articulated the economic loss rule in admiralty cases:

> "In *East River,* charterers of supertankers brought suit against turbine manufacturers seeking damages from alleged design and manufacturing defects which caused the supertankers to malfunction while on the high seas. 476 U.S. 858, 106 S.Ct. 2295, 90 L.Ed.2d 865. The suit had originally alleged breach of contract and warranty as well as tort claims for strict liability for design defects and negligent supervision of the installation. Due to statute of limitations defenses, the contract claims were dropped and the suit was brought in tort only. 106 S.Ct. at 2297.
>
> "The Supreme Court in *East River* had to decide whether injury to a product itself may be brought in tort. Noting that product liability law has expanded to afford greater protection from dangerous products than is available under warranty law, the Court commented that '[i]t is clear, however, that if this development were allowed to progress too far, contract law would drown in a sea of tort.' 106 S.Ct. at 2300. Justice Blackmun, writing for a unanimous Court, first examined the prevailing majority and minority views. The majority approach, exemplified by Seely v. White Motor Co., 63 Cal.2d 9, 45 Cal.Rptr. 17, 403 P.2d 145 (1965) (defective truck), held that preserving a proper role for the law of warranty precludes imposing tort liability if a defective product causes purely monetary harm. East River, 106 S.Ct. at 2301 (*also citing* Jones & Laughlin Steel Corp. v. Johns–Manville Sales Corp., 626 F.2d 280, 287 and n. 13 (3d Cir.1980). Justice Blackmun then reviewed the minority approach, whose progenitor, Santor v. A and M Karagheusian, Inc., 44 N.J. 52, 66–67, 207 A.2d 305, 312–313 (1965) (marred carpeting), held that a manufacturer's duty to make nondefective products encompassed injury to the product itself, whether or not the defect created an unreasonable risk of harm. *Id.* The Court rejected the minority view, holding that 'a manufacturer in a commercial relationship has no duty under either a negligence or strict products-liability theory to prevent a product from injuring itself.' *Id.*
>
> "Explaining why the Court had arrived at the public policy judgment that there should be no tort remedy for economic loss, Justice Blackmun wrote that repair costs, decreased value and lost profit are 'essentially the

failure of the purchaser to receive the benefit of its bargain—traditionally the core concern of contract law.' East River, 106 S.Ct. at 2302. After examining the law's policy concern for spreading costs in products liability cases, Justice Blackmun went on to broader contract law concerns:

> Contract law, and the law of warranty in particular, is well suited to commercial controversies of the sort involved in this case because the parties may set the terms of their own agreements. The manufacturer can restrict its liability, within limits, by disclaiming warranties or limiting remedies. *See* UCC §§ 2–316, 2–719. In exchange, the purchaser pays less for the product. Since a commercial situation generally does not involve large disparities in bargaining power, *cf.* Henningsen v. Bloomfield Motors, Inc., 32 N.J. 358, 161 A.2d 69 (1960), we see no reason to intrude into the parties' allocation of risk.

Id., 106 S.Ct. at 2303."

3. The *East River* rationale has been applied when the defect causes a calamitous injury. *See* National Union Fire Insurance Co. v. Pratt and Whitney Canada, Inc., 107 Nev. 535, 815 P.2d 601 (1991) in which a defective engine caused an airplane crash but, surprisingly, not personal injuries. After discussing *East River,* the court held:

> "The original purchaser of the Cheyenne airplane did not purchase an airplane engine and thereafter install the engine on the plane. Rather, as in the typical situation involving commercial products, the buyer acquired a single integrated product consisting of numerous component parts. Moreover, although the aircraft's warranty had expired prior to the time of its destruction, the owner had acquired and paid for insurance protection from National Union to cover the very eventuality that occurred. To allow National Union to recover for the occurrence of the risk for which it had been paid would be tantamount to extending the manufacturer's warranty with predictable results in the initial pricing of the product to the consumer. This we are unwilling to do.
>
> "We also reject National Union's contention that manufacturers should be liable when a product crashes calamitously or exposes plaintiffs to an unreasonable risk of harm, despite the absence of personal injury or damage to property other than the product itself. National Union would have this court distinguish between accidental or calamitous losses having the potential for human injury on the one hand, and purely economic losses on the other, and hold a manufacturer liable for the former. Although a minority of courts have held to the contrary, we decline to make this distinction. When injury to life or other property results from the use of a dangerously defective product, the law of strict products liability applies as a prophylactic and a basis for redress. When a product 'injures itself' protection derived from the interplay of manufacturer's warranties and insurance supplies a generally adequate basis for consumer redress.
>
> "A major reason for denying liability in *Stern* was 'to shield [the] defendant from unlimited liability for all of the economic consequences of a negligent act' and thus keep 'the risk of liability reasonably calculable.' Stern, 98 Nev. at 411, 651 P.2d at 638. Manufacturers will have difficulty calculating potential liability if it is to be determined by 'the arbitrary factor of whether the purchaser noticed the gradual deterioration of a component part that, left unattended, could result in a calamitous occur-

rence.' Continental Ins. v. Page Engineering Co., 783 P.2d 641, 648 (Wyo.1989). Indeed, the United States Supreme Court has aptly stated:

> [This approach], which essentially turn[s] on the degree of risk, [is] too indeterminate to enable manufacturers easily to structure their business behavior. Nor do we find persuasive a distinction that rests on the manner in which the product is injured. We realize that the damage may be qualitative, occurring through gradual deterioration or internal breakage. Or it may be calamitous. [Citations omitted.] *But either way, since by definition no person or other property is damaged, the resulting loss is purely economic. Even when the harm to the product itself occurs through an abrupt, accident-like event, the resulting loss due to repair costs, decreased value, and lost profits is essentially the failure of the purchaser to receive the benefit of its bargain—traditionally the core concern of contract law.*

East River S.S. Corp., 476 U.S. at 870, 106 S.Ct. at 2301–02 (emphasis added). Moreover, the rule we adopted avoids any difficulty associated with distinguishing between an accidental and economic loss. The district court did not err, therefore, when it granted summary judgment."

The dissenters said at 607–08:

"Economic losses include lost profits, lost productivity, lost wages, business expectations and other losses that flow from the loss of the things damaged by the defective product. However, a plaintiff is not precluded from recovering for loss caused to property on theories of negligence and strict liability. The majority ignores this very clear direction in our prior cases and now states that property damages are precluded when the product 'injures itself.' I find that this distinction is contrary to our previous definition of 'economic loss' and that it has little basis in reason. I see no reason to permit recovery on a strict products liability basis for damage to personal property, but to preclude it if the personal property has been incorporated with the defective component.

"This distinction makes no sense because it ignores the possibility of great disparity in size and value between the component part and the whole. It is as arbitrary as the rule proposed by some legal theorists that property damages should be recoverable in products liability actions only when the plaintiff suffers an accompanying personal injury. Such a rule would mean that a plaintiff could recover for the loss of a million dollar airplane so long as the defect which destroyed the plane also caused the plaintiff to stub a toe. The modern trend is that courts have moved away from arbitrarily drawing lines to mark the break in the causation chain. We could have refrained from doing so in this case by following our prior case law, and drawing the line between property damage and economic loss.

"Many courts have recognized that although plaintiffs in products liability actions should not recover for economic losses, they may recover personal property, which includes an entire product into which a defective part was incorporated. * * * In these cases, the courts realized that there is no reason to distinguish between the different physical items that the defective product destroyed, and permit recovery for some but not for others. Therefore, the better rule is to permit recovery for a product destroyed by a defective component.

"The majority opinion also observes that it would be inequitable to allow National Union to recover for the occurrence of a risk for which it had already been paid a premium. I am sure National Union was paid a premium for insuring the airplane. However, I would suspect that the rate structure upon which that premium was based took into account the fact that some losses would be eliminated or reduced by subrogation actions against third-party tortfeasors. Additionally, I think we should promote, rather than prohibit, recovery by people injured and their subrogees against the tortfeasor and its insurance carrier. An insurance company subrogated to the rights of an injured party should have the same rights as its insured and we should encourage its reimbursement from third-party tortfeasors when possible."

See also Oklahoma Gas & Electric Co. v. McGraw–Edison Co., 834 P.2d 980 (Okl.1992) (same, also with dissents).

4. *But see* Lutz Farms v. Asgrow Seed Co., 948 F.2d 638 (10th Cir.1991) in which onion growers were permitted to recover damages from seller of defective seed in negligence and breach of warranty for the failure of their business. The 10th Circuit was unable to find a clear indication that the Colorado Supreme Court would apply *East River* to overturn existing Colorado precedent involving tort liability of seed distributors.

SECTION 4. PRINCIPLES OF MEASUREMENT

A. SPECULATION, CERTAINTY AND DIFFICULTY IN MEASUREMENT

JOHNSON v. BAKER

Court of Appeals of Kansas, 1986.
11 Kan.App.2d 274, 719 P.2d 752.

RICHARD A. MEDLEY, DISTRICT JUDGE, Assigned:

This is a legal malpractice case. Plaintiffs sought the recovery of damages for both a breach of contract and negligence. They appeal the amount of the damages awarded on the negligence claim and the denial of any recovery for breach of contract.

On February 13, 1981, Joyce Johnson retained the defendant, Lyle Baker, a practicing attorney in Wichita, to represent her in a divorce from her husband, Richard Lee Johnson. Joyce Johnson's primary concern was that defendant secure an agreement from her husband to pay the expenses and cost of college for the parties' daughter, plaintiff Kelly Ann Johnson. Defendant negotiated a property settlement agreement between the Johnsons and incorporated it into the decree of divorce and the journal entry of judgment. Defendant made no attempt, nor did he advise Joyce Johnson to attempt, to secure the signature of Richard Johnson on the journal entry. Baker also did not attempt to reduce the parties' agreement to writing in any instrument other than the journal entry of judgment. He stated that he did not think it was necessary for the parties to sign the journal entry and decree of divorce, although he admitted he was familiar with the provisions of K.S.A. 1980 Supp. 60–1610(a) (repealed L.1982, ch. 152, § 30) with respect to agreements for support of children who have reached the age of majority.

Thereafter, defendant Baker learned that Richard Johnson refused to pay college expenses for his daughter. Baker informed Mrs. Johnson that she should retain another lawyer to represent her in enforcing the provisions of the journal entry because he would undoubtedly be needed as a witness on her behalf in any court hearing. Plaintiff Joyce Johnson hired attorney Keith Richey to represent her and Richey filed a motion to compel Mr. Johnson to perform the obligation stated in the journal entry. Judge Beasley of the Sedgwick County District Court denied the motion concluding that the court lacked jurisdiction to enforce the provision in question because there was no prior written agreement pursuant to K.S.A. 1980 Supp. 60–1610(a). Mrs. Johnson did not appeal from this ruling although she was aware that she had the right to do so.

In February 1983, the plaintiffs filed this action against Baker for breach of contract and negligent failure to obtain an enforceable agreement against Richard Johnson for Kelly's college expenses. * * * [T]he court held that defendant was liable for negligence because his failure to obtain a separate signed agreement did not meet the standard of care normally exercised in the community and resulted in the unfavorable ruling by Judge Beasley.

The trial court assessed Joyce Johnson's damages at $559.40 and fixed Kelly's damages as equivalent to the cost of tuition ($5,380) plus room and board ($3,600) for the two years she has attended college, reduced by the $6,042 received in grants and scholarships, for a net recovery of $2,938. Plaintiffs appeal the amount of damages awarded * * *.

Plaintiffs contend that the trial court erred in calculating the damages of Kelly Johnson because it failed to award damages equivalent to the cost of tuition, room and board for her remaining two years of education. Defendant contends that the evidence of future damage was too speculative to justify a greater award.

Damages cannot be awarded when they are too conjectural and speculative to form a sound basis for measurement. * * * It has also been held, however, that absolute certainty is not required in establishing damages * * *

From the record we have before us, it is clear that Kelly Johnson had enrolled at Kansas Newman College for at least twelve hours a semester during her first two years and had made passing grades. All contingencies of the parties' agreement were met during the first two years of Kelly's college education and it does not appear to us to be too speculative or uncertain to conclude that those contingencies would have been met for the next two years. However, the record reveals that Kelly was enrolled in a two-year program at Kansas Newman and her testimony was unclear with respect to the amount of additional time she would need to complete her education. We conclude that the trial court's refusal to assess damages for tuition, room and board for future educational endeavors by Kelly is supported by the evidence.

Plaintiffs also contend that the court should have included in its award the cost of Kelly's books for a four-year education. However, the testimony offered to prove the amount of this expense was vague and indefinite. In addition, the exhibit which plaintiffs assert estimates the cost of books was not included in the record on appeal. The burden is upon the appellant to designate a record sufficient to present its points to the appellate court and to establish the claimed error. * * *

* * *

The judgment of the trial court is affirmed in all respects except insofar as the award of damages was reduced in contradiction of the collateral source rule. * * *

Note

The collateral source rule is discussed at Section 4.C., *infra* at p. 231.

LEWIS RIVER GOLF, INC. v. O.M. SCOTT & SONS

Supreme Court of Washington, En Banc, 1993.
120 Wash.2d 712, 845 P.2d 987.

BRACHTENBACH, JUSTICE.

The main issue is narrow and essentially factual, *i.e.,* should the testimony of plaintiff's damage expert have been stricken because it was speculative or not supported in the record?

* * *

To understand the present posture of these issues, it is necessary to state the history of this case. Plaintiff, Lewis River Golf, Inc., grew sod or turf. It bought seed from defendant, O.M. Scott & Sons, under an express warranty. The sod grown from the seed had weeds. Plaintiff claimed that the express warranty was breached. Plaintiff lost most of its commercial customers and had been sued by two of its buyers dissatisfied with the sod. Defendant's proposed remedies were unsuccessful in resolving the weed problem. Plaintiff cut production from 275 acres to 45 acres and destroyed all of the turf raised from defendant's seed.

Plaintiff sued defendant for losses, including lost profits. In 1985, a jury awarded plaintiff $1,327,000. The verdict was unsegregated as to the elements of the damages found. In an unpublished 1987 opinion the Court of Appeals affirmed the verdict on liability, but held that the testimony of plaintiff's expert included two improper calculations, that is, inclusion of lost profits on unplanted acreage and certain interest costs. It held: "The award of damages is reversed and remanded for trial on that issue alone. In all other respects, the judgment is affirmed." * * *

Thus, in 1989, when the case was again tried to a jury, there was no question of liability. The trial was limited to determination of damages. However, between the first and second trials, the facts about damages had changed. Plaintiff had sold its sod business. Plaintiff contended that, along with specific damages, it suffered a loss on the sale of its sod business because of damage to its reputation or goodwill from the sale of "bad" sod resulting from defendant's defective seed. The trial court submitted five elements of damages to the jury with a segregated verdict form. The jury followed the verdict form and made a separate award for items 1 through 4, as defined in the instructions. A separate awarded of $1,026,800 was made for the loss plaintiff "suffered on the sale of its sod division". Clerk's Papers, at 969.

Defendant again appealed to the Court of Appeals. In an unpublished decision, * * * that court (1) affirmed the award of $664,430 made for items one through four of the damage instruction, but (2) reversed the verdict as to the loss on sale of the business. * * * We reverse the Court of Appeals to the extent that it reversed the verdict; thus, the judgment below is affirmed in its entirety.

* * *

Recovery of consequential damages is expressly authorized by the Uniform Commercial Code, which governs this action. RCW 62A.2–715(2)(a). The question then is whether the damage to plaintiff's reputation or goodwill is the type of consequential damage allowed under the statute. There is no doubt that such a damage claim is recognized. "In Washington, injury to a buyer's business reputation has been recognized as compensable * * * Goldstein v. J.W. Carter Co., 157 Wash. 405, 288 Pac. 1063 (1930)." * * *

There is substantial authority that damages are recoverable for damage to a business reputation or goodwill and resulting loss in the value of the business. "As a general rule, loss in the value of a business as a going concern, or loss in the value of its good will, may be recovered as an element of consequential damages." * * *

> [R]ecognizing methods for calculation of goodwill by economists and accountants, goodwill has become more widely accepted as a recoverable item of consequential loss.
>
> * * * If one removes the Pennsylvania cases from the count, a significant majority of the cases have allowed for the recovery of lost goodwill in proper circumstances.

(Footnotes omitted.) Anderson, *Incidental and Consequential Damages,* 7 J.L. & Com. 327, 420–21 (1987).

Pennsylvania has overruled the cases referred to in the cited article and now holds that a claim for loss of business reputation or goodwill is a jury question if there is a "reasonable basis" for calculating damages. *AM/PM Franchise Assoc. v. Atlantic Richfield Co.,* 526 Pa. 110, 131 n. 20, 584 A.2d 915 (1990). Defendant relies on a case supplying the now-overruled Pennsylvania law. Brief of Appellant, at 21.

It is clear from the foregoing that the law permits recovery for the kind of damage contained in the jury instruction and verdict form, *i.e.,* an award for damage to goodwill or business reputation. In this case, that loss was evidenced by a diminution in the value of the business when it was sold.

It is true that damages must be proved with reasonable certainty. * * * However, this reasonable certainty requirement must be considered in light of several underlying principles.

First, RCW 62A.1–106 provides:

> The remedies provided by this Title shall be liberally administered to the end that the aggrieved party may be put in as good a position as if the other party had fully performed * * *.

Second, the official comment to RCWA 62A.2–715 states:

> The burden of proving the extent of loss incurred by way of consequential damage is on the buyer, but the section of liberal administration of remedies *rejects any doctrine of certainty which requires almost mathematical precision in the proof of loss. Loss may be determined in any manner which is reasonable under the circumstances.*

(Italics ours.) RCWA 62A.2–715, official comment 4.

Third is the established principle that "the doctrine respecting the matter of certainty, properly applied, is concerned more with the *fact of damage than with the extent or amount of damage.*" * * *

* * *

Further, it is well recognized that the type of damages here involved are not subject to proof of mathematical certainty. " 'Compensatory damages are often at best approximate: they have to be proved with whatever definiteness and accuracy the facts permit, but no more.' Official UCC Comment, § 1–106 * * *." *The Cricket Alley Corp. v. Data Terminal Sys., Inc.*, 240 Kan. 661, 669, 732 P.2d 719 (1987).

> With respect to loss of goodwill, proving damages with reasonable certainty should track the generally expansive recent history of lost profits. However, unlike lost profits, *goodwill relates to the future* and, thus, no actual profit base will exist for use at trial. Accordingly, the expert testimony of accountants and economists will prove invaluable to the aggrieved buyer in presenting his claim for loss of goodwill. *Such testimony will generally be accepted by the courts in assessing goodwill claims.*

(Footnote omitted. Italics ours.) Anderson, *Incidental and Consequential Damages,* 7 J.L. & Com. 327, 422 (1987).

It is important to note that defendant *concedes* the *fact* of damage. To quote the defendant: "Lewis River *produced evidence* that [the] sale of the VBB sod [defendant's product] damaged its reputation and caused loss of sales (RP 238, 268, 290, 391, 796, 830). *That evidence was sufficient to go [to] the jury.*" (Italics ours.) Brief of Appellant, at 11 n. 6.

We now turn to defendant's challenge to the expert's testimony. At several points during the trial, defendant made the following motions to strike the testimony of plaintiff's expert:

> [I]t is not supported by credible facts in the record. It is based on opinions or assumptions that are contrary to facts in this record.

Verbatim Report of Proceedings (VRP) vol. 5, at 791.

> My point is it is just so far out that it should be stricken.

VRP, vol. 5, at 793. Later,

> [W]e moved to strike Jolivet's [expert] testimony for the reason he is not supported, and it is outside the total overall perimeter, and the jury would have to speculate.

VRP, vol. 6, at 880.

At the end of the case, defendant moved, in part, as follows:

> I will separately move, Your Honor, then for a directed verdict or to strike out the testimony that's been offered claimed to be in support of a loss business value pursuant to that element of their case, again being far too speculative to submit to a jury and as being unsupported by credible evidence * * *.

VRP, vol. 8, at 1369.

Several of the grounds advanced in support of its motions are without merit. First, defendant asserts that the expert's opinion is not supported by *credible* evidence. If the evidence was properly admitted, credibility is for the jury. Second, the assertion that the evidence is "just so far out" is a meaningless phrase. This leaves the claim that the expert's testimony was too speculative and based on unsupported assumptions.

Whether the testimony was so speculative as to be inadmissible, or whether it should have been stricken after admission depends upon the nature and quantum of proof required for the particular type of damages involved. As noted above, the matter of certainty of damages is concerned more with the *fact* of damage than with the extent or amount of damage. Damage to business reputation and loss of goodwill have to be proved with whatever definiteness and accuracy the facts permit, but no more. * * * Our discussion hereafter of the evidence supporting the expert's opinions will demonstrate that his opinions were not so speculative as to be inadmissible or subject to striking.

* * *

We first note that defendant does not contend that the witness was not qualified as an expert. * * * Defendant does not contend that the methodology used by the expert was invalid. Defendant's expert used the same methodology.

Thus, defendant's challenge is limited to the six factors which it claims went into the opinions of plaintiff's expert. Those factors are first identified specifically in defendant's reply brief. We find all of the challenged assumptions supported. The evidence was properly admitted and not stricken. As the trial court repeatedly ruled, and as shown hereafter, the challenges went to weight, not to admissibility.

Plaintiff's expert was a Harvard educated economist and a former professor of finance at the University of Washington. He examined and relied upon plaintiff's financial records and facts furnished him prior to trial by the owner of plaintiff corporation, as authorized by ER 703.

The ultimate opinion which defendant attacks is the expert's estimate of the loss plaintiff allegedly sustained when it sold its sod business. To calculate that loss, the expert assumed a sod farm of 195 acres, a certain marketable amount of sod per acre, the ability to sell that sod, and a certain profit margin. He then calculated the net earnings, after taxes, and applied a price earnings ratio to arrive at his opinion of the value of the business. From that value he deducted the price realized when the business was sold, resulting in his opinion of the loss sustained upon sale of the business. The jury awarded $181,917 less than his estimate of loss.

Defendant first attacks the size of the farm, assumed by the expert to be 195 acres. The trial court recognized that this was a key assumption * * * To eliminate any doubt on this critical point, the trial court included in the verdict form a question: "Do you find that the seeding rate for VBB seed as actually planted by Stading was the seeding rate Dr. Jolivet [the expert] used in his testimony? ANSWER: Yes." Clerk's Papers, at 977. In addition, the owner testified that the amount of seed purchased would seed between 190 and 210 acres. VRP, vol. 3, at 375. The overall sod farm was 275 acres. VRP, vol. 4, at 540. There is testimony of 198 acres and 200 acres of sod. VRP, vol. 3, at 476, 352. The record supports the expert's use of a farm of 195 acres as a base of production.

Defendant next challenges the expert's assumption that the sod farm would produce 40,000 marketable square feet of sod per acre. Two items of testimony clearly support this fact. First, the owner testified: "If our sod is in good shape, everything is right, we'll get our 40,000 feet." Defendant's witness found an actual yield on plaintiff's farm of either 39,366 or 39,666 square feet per acre, explaining: "The only difference between 39,666 that I arrived at versus the 40,000 is the rounding". VRP, vol. 7, at 1125. There is adequate support to reject this challenge.

Next defendant questions the expert's conclusion that plaintiff would have been able to sell the sod it produced at market price. Plaintiff was selling such quantities that he purchased additional sod from a competitor who testified that plaintiff was probably selling all the sod he could produce. VRP, vol. 5, at 671. That same competitor went out of business, removing a large supplier. VRP, vol. 5, at 668–71. One landscaper who was installing 1 to 1½ million square feet of sod a year testified that he quit buying sod from defendant's seed because of devastating problems with VBB turf. VRP, vol. 2, at 199. The expert calculated plaintiff's expected market share at 5.8 percent of total market, and estimated that plaintiff would maintain that share with acceptable sod. All in all, there was support for that opinion.

Defendant challenges the level of profit which he assumed plaintiff would earn. While defendant questions the validity of the figures used, the expert started with actual profit for one year, analyzed a 6–year period, and then used an average price for a 3–year period. VRP, vol. 5, at 707, 712–14. It was for the jury to determine whether the average profit level would be maintained. There were facts to which the expert applied his expertise. As noted by a leading commentator, goodwill damages relate to the future, unlike lost profits. He notes that the testimony of accountants and economists (plaintiff's expert) will generally be accepted in making such future projections. Anderson, *Incidental and Consequential Damages,* 7 J.L. & Com. 327 (1987).

The expert applied a price earnings ratio of 9.5. He relied upon public data reflecting the price earnings ratio of publicly owned companies, then used his expert judgment in lowering the median for a privately owned company. He testified this is the most used technique in valuation of a business. VRP, vol. 5, at 725. This is the type of data reasonably relied upon by experts within the scope of ER 703. Defendant does not argue otherwise. The proof of the pudding is that defendant's expert used a multiplier of 4, rather than 9.5. VRP, vol. 8, at 1188. Defendant's expert said it was a difference of opinion whether to use a ratio of 4 or 9.5. VRP, vol. 7, at 1197. Such difference of opinion is the essence of conflicting opinions from experts. There was adequate basis for expert opinion using this factor.

Finally, defendant argues that the expert was wrong in excluding ownership of the farming land from his calculations; part of the land was leased. The expert rendered his opinion and explanation why this was not a necessary factor in his opinion. Defendant argues that no buyer would buy a sod business without the land. The expert explained the difference between valuing a going business and its underlying assets. He took into account the amount attributable to fixed assets in calculating the amount realized from the sale. VRP, vol. 5, at 715–16, 764–65, 773. Again, defendant's argument is with the weight of the opinion, not its admissibility.

The trial court properly admitted the expert testimony and properly denied defendant's motions to strike.

Notes

1. Why is loss of goodwill a consequential rather than a general damage?

2. Why were damages awarded in *Lewis River* and not in *Johnson?*

3. What testimony was needed in *Johnson* in order for Kelly Ann Johnson to recover the cost of more than two years of college? If Kelly Ann cannot truthfully testify as to the certainty of her future intentions, could another remedy have been sought to protect Kelly Ann's right to college payments from her father should she choose to finish school?

4. Did the father in the litigation preceding *Johnson* save two years of tuition but lose a daughter?

5. In the next case consider whether the majority of the Texas Supreme Court reversed the lost profit award on the basis of lack of proof of fact of damage or amount of damage. Do you agree with the majority or the dissent? If with the majority, what should plaintiff's attorney have done to prepare the plaintiff for trial? What should the attorney do on remand?

HOLT ATHERTON INDUSTRIES, INC. v. HEINE

Supreme Court of Texas, 1992.
835 S.W.2d 80.

COOK, JUSTICE

[Roy and Kitty Heine left their bulldozer to be repaired with Holt Atherton's predecessor company, Holt Machinery. The bulldozer remained with Holt Machinery for eight months because the Heines did not pay for repairs because the Heines claimed they were covered by an oral warranty. Holt did not recognize the alleged warranty. The Heines then paid for the repairs and sued Holt Atherton to recover, among other things, lost profits. A default judgment was entered against Holt Atherton and was affirmed by the Texas Supreme Court.]

Once a default judgment is taken on an unliquidated claim, all allegations of fact set forth in the petition are deemed admitted, except the amount of damages. * * * A court rendering a default judgment must hear evidence of unliquidated damages. TEX.R.CIV.P. 243; * * * The trial court, in this case, held a hearing and determined that the Heines suffered damages in the amount of $159,665 including $120,000 for lost profits.[1]

Holt Atherton argues that there is no evidence supporting the trial court's award of damages for lost profits. * * * If there is more than a scintilla of evidence to support the finding, the no evidence challenge fails. * * *

Recovery for lost profits does not require that the loss be susceptible of exact calculation. * * * However, the injured party must do more than show that they suffered some lost profits. The amount of the loss must be shown by competent evidence with reasonable certainty. * * * What constitutes reasonably certain evidence of lost profits is a fact intensive determination. As a minimum, opinions or estimates of lost profits must be based on objective facts, figures, or data from which the amount of lost profits can be ascertained. * * * Although supporting documentation may affect the weight of the evidence, it is not necessary to produce in court the documents supporting the opinions or estimates. *See, e.g., Pena,* 766 S.W.2d at 304; *Keller,* 694 S.W.2d at 357.[2]

The Heines' testimony was the only evidence presented concerning their lost profits and can be divided into two segments. First, Mr. Heine

1. The trial court's judgment includes the $120,000 as "Loss of Income Due to Absence of Dozer." Holt Atherton notes that the correct measure of damages is lost net profit, not gross profits. *See Turner v. PV Int'l Corp.,* 765 S.W.2d 455, 465 (Tex.App.—Dallas 1988, *writ denied per curiam,* 778 S.W.2d 865 (Tex.1989)); *Copenhaver v. Berryman,* 602 S.W.2d 540, 544 (Tex.Civ.App.—Corpus Christi 1980, writ ref'd n.r.e.). However, read most favorably to the Heines, the record indicates that the trial court's judgment is based on an amount the court determined remained after the Heines had paid out expenses. Therefore, the court applied the correct measure of damages. To avoid confusion in this opinion, we refer to the $120,000 award as "lost profits."

2. We disapprove *Automark of Texas,* 681 S.W.2d at 830, to the extent that it holds the supporting records must be produced in court.

was examined by his counsel. Then, the trial judge questioned both Heines.

When Mr. Heine was examined by his counsel, only one question was asked which touched on lost profits. The relevant question and answer are:

> Q. Now as a result of the defendant keeping the dozer for eight months, did you lose out on $200,200 in lost income during that time period?
>
> A. Yes, sir, I did.

Even if this testimony were otherwise sufficient, lost income is not the correct measure of damages. *See supra* note 1. Further, this testimony is legally insufficient because it does not provide any indication of how the Heines determined what their lost profits were. *See, e.g., Village Square, Ltd. v. Barton,* 660 S.W.2d 556, 559–60 (Tex.App.—San Antonio 1983, writ ref'd n.r.e.) (testimony stating only total amount of lost profits held legally insufficient); *Frank B. Hall & Co.,* 733 S.W.2d at 259 (same). The court does not have any basis for determining whether the damages were established with reasonable certainty or were based on pure speculation. This question and answer are legally insufficient to prove lost profits.

After the Heines' counsel completed his questions, the trial judge asked additional questions to determine what the Heines' lost profits were and how the Heines concluded that their lost income was $200,200. The judge started out by questioning Mr. Heine. Mr. Heine could not provide answers to the judge's questions but suggested that Mrs. Heine could be more helpful because she kept the books for the Heines. Mrs. Heine testified that she could not say what their lost profits were without looking at their books. When the judge asked what the Heines showed as profits on their income tax returns for 1985 or 1986, the years preceding the year that Holt Atherton kept their bulldozer, Mrs. Heine did not know. However, Mr. Heine responded that their income tax return showed profits of about $120,000.[3] Both Heines testified that in 1985, they had two bulldozers that operated about half of the time because business was slow. Apparently the trial judge determined that one bulldozer working full-time would earn as much in thirteen months as two bulldozers working half-time would earn in twelve months.

There are two problems with this analysis. First, the Heines never offered any evidence showing that there was enough work to keep two bulldozers working full-time over the relevant thirteen month period. This is particularly significant here because the Heines testified that there had not been enough work in the preceding years to keep both bulldozers working full-time.[4] Second, the Heines never showed that they were entitled to recover lost profits for the entire thirteen month period. *See Morgan,* 675 S.W.2d at 731 (must show damages were caused by event sued on). The total down time may have been thirteen months. However,

3. Although Mr. Heine was not on the witness stand when he made this statement, it was transcribed by the court reporter and appears in the statement of facts.

4. Mr. Heine testified " '85 was light; '86 was disastrous."

according to Mr. Heine's testimony, Holt Atherton only kept the bulldozer for eight months before starting repairs.

In response to further questions by the trial judge, Mr. Heine testified that the Heines lost several contracts because they did not have their bulldozer available. Mr. Heine was not able to specify which contracts they lost, how many they lost, how much profit they would have had from the contracts, or who would have awarded them contracts. The Heines could have supported their lost profits with testimony that they had lost out on *specific* contracts because they did not have their bulldozer available. *See Pace Corp. v. Jackson,* 155 Tex. 179, 284 S.W.2d 340, 349 (1955). However, the bare assertion that contracts were lost does not demonstrate a reasonably certain objective determination of lost profits. * * *

The testimony elicited by the trial judge provides pieces of several different methods of calculating lost profits. However, the Heines were not able to provide evidence supporting one complete calculation. Recovery of lost profits must be predicated on one complete calculation. * * * *Village Square, Ltd.,* 660 S.W.2d at 559–60 (statement of total lost profits without supporting analysis held legally insufficient); *Frank B. Hall & Co.,* 733 S.W.2d at 259 (same); *Barbier v. Barry,* 345 S.W.2d 557, 563 (Tex.Civ. App.—Dallas 1961, no writ) (held no evidence of lost profits because no evidence of supporting calculations). We do not sanction any one method for determining lost profits. * * * However, once a party has chosen a particular method for measuring their lost profits, they must provide a complete calculation. The Heines have not done that. Therefore, the evidence is legally insufficient to provide a reasonable basis for determining the Heines' lost profits.

* * *

We remand the cause to the trial court for a new trial on the issue of lost profits.

Concurring and dissenting opinion by JUSTICE DOGGETT joined by JUSTICE MAUZY.

DOGGETT, JUSTICE, concurring and dissenting.

In overturning a judgment for this family business, the majority imposes new obstacles to any commercial enterprise that has wrongfully suffered a loss of profits.[1] Today's opinion abandons our well established rules governing review of legal sufficiency of the evidence and disavows this particular businessperson's sworn testimony as totally worthless. Although I concur in that part of the judgment affirming liability, I dissent from the court's decision ensuring that lost profits stay lost.

1. In burdening small businesses like the one involved here, the majority continues an unfortunate trend of insensitivity to the realities of independent business. *See Caller–Times Publishing Co. v. Triad Communications, Inc.,* 826 S.W.2d 576, 580, n. 4 (Tex. 1992) (Doggett, J., dissenting) (small business made easy prey for anticompetitive, monopolistic practices); *Crim Truck & Tractor Co. v. Navistar Int'l Trans. Corp.,* 823 S.W.2d 591, 597 (Tex.1992) (Mauzy, J., dissenting) (local dealer denied remedy for abuse by a franchisor).

While covered by a Holt Atherton repair warranty, a part broke on one of the two D–8 Caterpillar bulldozers owned and operated by Roy and Kitty Heine. Instead of providing prompt repairs, Holt Atherton allegedly left them without the use of the bulldozer for about a year. Before granting the Heines a default judgment, the trial court appropriately heard evidence on their unliquidated damages including lost profits. * * *

Roy calculated lost income to be $200,200, based on the days the machine was incapacitated and also on "several" lost land clearing contracts, one of which, the O'Connor contract, was open-ended as to the amount of work. He further testified that by charging $80 per hour for bulldozer work, he realized an "immediate profit" of about $30 to $40 per hour. Additionally, he described a job for other of his equipment, which was lost due to customer impatience with the extended delays resulting from breakdown of the bulldozer. His total figure included an adjustment "for the time that there might not have been anything." Referencing the probable familiarity of experienced business people with approximate costs and profit margins, the trial court inquired as to profits shown on their recent income tax returns. The Heines responded that in the year before the breakdown, they reported a profit of about $120,000 by working both dozers full time for six months. As the trier of fact, the trial judge found damages for lost profits in this lesser amount, rather than the larger initial estimate.

On appeal, Holt Atherton urges that this testimony was "too speculative" and constituted no evidence to support a finding of damages for lost profits. * * * Recognizing that where "more than a scintilla of evidence [supports] the trial court's finding, the no evidence challenge fails," at 84, the majority misapplies the standard and implicitly creates new requirements for what constitutes a "scintilla" in the context of lost profits.

To support a default judgment in *Capitol Brick, Inc. v. Fleming Mfg. Co.*, 722 S.W.2d 399 (Tex.1986), a small business gave evidence of its lost profits arising from loss of use of an inadequately repaired brick-making machine. * * * In reversing the judgment of the court of appeals, we addressed a previously unconsidered no evidence challenge, finding that "the record reflects more than a scintilla of competent evidence to support the * * * lost profits." *Id.* at 402. The record there was strikingly similar to that here, as indicated by the writing of the court of appeals on remand, addressing the remaining factual insufficiency challenge:

> Sprott [its president] testified that * * * Capitol Brick's mold press which would have produced this particular ten inch brick was idle for 11½ weeks; that during normal conditions the press would have produced some 1,750,000 bricks; and that these bricks would have sold for $120 per thousand, or some $207,000. Sprott also indicated a 25% net profit figure which translates into lost profits of $51,750. This was the only evidence concerning Capitol Brick's unliquidated damage claim.

Fleming Mfg. Co. v. Capitol Brick, Inc., 734 S.W.2d 405, 406 (Tex.App.—Austin 1987, writ ref'd n.r.e.).[2] Yet today's opinion burdens businesses by disregarding our prior writing, creating a higher evidentiary standard for small service-oriented companies, and presuming to conduct a factual sufficiency review on a no evidence point of error. * * *

To negate the award of lost profits, the majority must take something and call it nothing—it must treat the Heines' sworn testimony, given in response to a series of questions from the trial judge, as devoid of any legal value. * * *

Denial of relief in this case has ramifications that extend to all commercial litigation in which profits are an issue. The majority begins by eroding the distinction we have long recognized between uncertainty as to the occurrence of lost profits and uncertainty merely as to their exact amount. The former, but not the latter, is fatal to recovery. * * *

It then announces new requirements that a party must chose a particular method for measuring lost profits, at 85, and that "[r]ecovery of lost profits must be predicated on one complete calculation." *Id.* at 85. We have previously declined to construct such inflexible rules that could unfairly bar recovery:

> It is impossible to announce with exact certainty any rule measuring the profits the loss for which recovery may be had * * *. A party who breaks his contract cannot escape liability because it is impossible to state or prove a perfect measure of damages.

Southwest Battery Corp., 115 S.W.2d at 1099; *accord* * * * *Davis v. Small Business Inv. Co. of Houston,* 535 S.W.2d 740, 743 (Tex.Civ.App.—Texarkana 1976, writ ref'd n.r.e.) (victim must present evidence from which factfinder can reasonably infer that some profit would have been made and reasonably estimate the amount of loss). * * *

The majority's professed lack of "any basis for determining whether the damages were established with reasonable certainty or were based on pure speculation," at 84, discounts the Heines' response to the trial court's inquiry about how they "calculate[d]" their damages. They referenced hourly charges, lost contracts, cost factors, and down-time adjustments. Estimations, when "given in terms of calculations, [constitute] more than conjecture, speculation or guesswork" and must be evaluated by the finder of fact. * * *

Though criticized by the majority for failing to explain "that they had lost out on *specific* contracts," at 85, the Heines were not necessarily required to identify specific, measurable, lost contracts because they were an existing business with a history of profitability.[4] Such an operation ordinarily encounters lesser evidentiary hurdles to show lost profits already

2. Similarly, in *Texas Gas Explor. v. Broughton Offshore,* 790 S.W.2d 781, 789 (Tex.App.—Houston [14th Dist.] 1990, no writ), a party's uncontroverted testimony, based on his industry experience, regarding estimated profits from disabled equipment was held to constitute legally sufficient evidence.

4. Nor were they required to prove their previous profits "remain[ed] stable or [grew] to support an award for lost profits in subsequent years." *Martin v. Lou Poliquin Enterprises, Inc.,* 696 S.W.2d 180, 187 (Tex.App.—Houston [14th Dist.] 1985, writ ref'd n.r.e.).

sustained than would a business with little record of past earnings that seeks to show future lost profits. * * * Among the methods a party may use to calculate its lost profits is *either* a history of profitability *or* the actual existence of lost contracts. * * *

There is undoubtedly some legal evidence to support the Heines' lost profits damages. Since there is no factual insufficiency point of error requiring further review by the court of appeals, its judgment should be affirmed.

JUSTICE MAUZY joins in this concurring and dissenting opinion.

Notes

1. The dissent in *Holt Atherton* refers to latitude given to existing businesses in proving lost profits. Consider Migerobe, Inc. v. Certina USA, Inc., 924 F.2d 1330, 1338–39 (5th Cir.1991) in which Migerobe had contracted to buy Certina watches to sell at a substantial discount to attract customers to its store to buy other, "corollary" items. When Certina breached, Migerobe sued Certina for lost profits from resale of the watches and corollary sales. The Court affirmed the jury's damage award and held with respect to the corollary sales:

> "Certina next argues that Migerobe's estimate of corollary damages must be rejected as being too speculative and uncertain. Migerobe's estimate of these losses was based on the success of similarly advertised 'doorbuster' sales that it had held in 1982 and 1983. Certina begins by noting that Migerobe had never used Certina watches as a doorbuster item in the past, and, therefore, its potential for increasing corollary profits was unknown. It also claimed that the watches used in doorbuster sales during 1982 (Seiko) and 1983 (Seiko & Pulsar) were better known than Certina and could not provide an accurate comparison. As already noted, it is unnecessary for a plaintiff to prove his losses with mathematical precision, and we do not believe that a sales estimate based on historical data from similar advertising campaigns would have rendered this estimate speculative or uncertain. * * * Certina is not entitled to complain about Migerobe's inability to provide a more precise estimate when such precision has been made all but impossible because of Certina's own breach. *See* Story Parchment Co. v. Paterson Parchment Paper Co., 282 U.S. 555, 563, 51 S.Ct. 248, 250, 75 L.Ed. 544 (1931); *see also Terrell*, 494 F.2d at 24 ('Very often the nature of the wrong makes ascertainment of the damages difficult.'); Autowest, 434 F.2d at 565 ('The wrongdoer should bear the risk of uncertainty that his own conduct has created.')."

2. Can a new business prove lost profits? Consider Kvassay v. Murray, 15 Kan.App.2d 426, 808 P.2d 896, 903–904 (1991) in which Kvassay had contracted to sell 24,000 cases of baklava to Great American Foods, Inc., Kvassay's only customer. When Great American breached its contract, Kvassay sued for lost profits, but the trial court ruled that evidence of lost profits was inadmissible. The court of appeals reversed:

> "Lost profits may be recovered for new businesses if they can be proved with reasonable certainty. Butler, 226 Kan. at 585, 602 P.2d 1276. Strict application of the certainty doctrine would place a new business at substantial disadvantage. To hold recovery is precluded as a matter of law merely because a business is newly established would encourage those

contracting with such a business to breach their contracts. The law is not so deficient. Vickers, 213 Kan. at 620, 518 P.2d 512. When 84–1–106 and 84–2–708(2) are read in light of *Vickers,* it is clear that, when there has been a breach of contract with a new business, such business should be given an opportunity to prove its damages and to collect profits if the damages can be proved.

"In this case, Kvassay attempted to present an ample basis on which to determine profits earned on the baklava produced under the contract. Uncontested evidence offered included:

1. Kvassay did not go into the bakery business until he had a contract with Great American requiring the purchase of 24,000 cases of baklava at $19 per case.

2. After spending about two months setting up his bakery, Kvassay produced baklava full time for about three months, although there were some temporary shut-downs due to cash flow problems.

3. Production was averaging about 100 cases daily, although a peak of 150 cases was reached.

4. 3,000 cases of the 24,000 contracted for were produced, or 12.5 percent of the contract.

5. Production staff was paid on a commission basis based on the number of trays of baklava prepared at a rate of $1.75–$2.00 per tray.

6. The recipe for each 14–inch × 18–inch tray of baklava called for two pounds of phyllo dough, one pound of margarine, one teaspoon of cloves, one teaspoon of cinnamon, one pound of walnuts, and two pounds of honey.

7. Each tray produced ten 8–ounce pieces of baklava while each case delivered held twelve 8–ounce pieces of baklava.

8. There were two full-time hourly employees and additional help was hired on an hourly basis for maintenance when needed.

In addition, before the court ruled that lost profits could not be proved, Kvassay attempted to offer receipts from suppliers to document his costs. The trial court never permitted those exhibits to be admitted. Further, after the court ruled that lost profits would not be allowed, Kvassay proffered the testimony of two accountants as to the profitability of his enterprise and the profit he would have earned under the contract with Great American. Of particular note was the testimony of Tom Dechant, C.P.A., who testified that, from an accounting standpoint, at least five percent of the baklava contract needed to be completed before profits could be determined with 'reasonable certainty.' In this case, 12.5 percent of the contract had been completed.

"Given the quantity of evidence offered to prove the profitability of Kvassay's business, it is clear the trial court was premature in ruling, as a matter of law, that lost profits could not be proved. Kvassay should have been permitted to offer his evidence and meet his burden of proof on damages."

3. The case universally cited is Story Parchment Co. v. Paterson Parchment Paper Co., 282 U.S. 555, 51 S.Ct. 248, 75 L.Ed. 544 (1931) in which

plaintiff sought damages under the Sherman Anti–Trust Act for defendant's monopolization of the vegetable parchment trade. Justice Sutherland said:

"Nor can we accept the view of that court that the verdict of the jury, in so far as it included damages for [the difference between the amounts actually realized by petitioner and what would have been realized by it from sales at reasonable prices except for the unlawful acts of the respondents] cannot stand because it was based upon mere speculation and conjecture. This characterization of the basis for the verdict is unwarranted. It is true that there was uncertainty as to the extent of the damage, but there was none as to the fact of damage; and there is a clear distinction between the measure of proof necessary to establish the fact that petitioner had sustained some damage, and the measure of proof necessary to enable the jury to fix the amount. The rule which precludes the recovery of uncertain damages applies to such as are not the certain result of the wrong, not to those damages which are definitely attributable to the wrong and only uncertain in respect of their amount. Taylor v. Bradley, 4 Abb.Ct.App. (N.Y.) 363, 366–367:

'It is sometimes said that speculative damages cannot be recovered, because the amount is uncertain; but such remarks will generally be found applicable to such damages as it is uncertain whether sustained at all from the breach. Sometimes the claim is rejected as being too remote. This is another mode of saying that it is uncertain whether such damages resulted necessarily and immediately from the breach complained of.

'The general rule is, that all damages resulting necessarily and immediately and directly from the breach are recoverable, and not those that are contingent and uncertain. The latter description embraces, as I think, such only as are not the certain result of the breach, and does not embrace such as are the certain result, but uncertain in amount.'

"Where the tort itself is of such a nature as to preclude the ascertainment of the amount of damages with certainty, it would be a perversion of fundamental principles of justice to deny all relief to the injured person, and thereby relieve the wrongdoer from making any amend for his acts. In such case, while the damages may not be determined by mere speculation or guess, it will be enough if the evidence show the extent of the damages as a matter of just and reasonable inference, although the result be only approximate. The wrongdoer is not entitled to complain that they cannot be measured with the exactness and precision that would be possible if the case, which he alone is responsible for making, were otherwise. * * * As the Supreme Court of Michigan has forcefully declared, the risk of the uncertainty should be thrown upon the wrongdoer instead of upon the injured party. Allison v. Chandler, 11 Mich. 542, 550–556. That was a case sounding in tort, and at page 555 the court, speaking through Christiancy, J., said:

'But shall the injured party in an action of tort, which may happen to furnish no element of certainty, be allowed to recover no damages (or merely nominal), because he can not show the exact amount with certainty, though he is ready to show, to the satisfaction of the jury, that he has suffered large damages by the injury? Certainty, it is true, would thus be attained; but it would be the certainty of injustice.

* * *

'Juries are allowed to act upon probable and inferential, as well as direct and positive proof. And when, from the nature of the case, the amount of the damages can not be estimated with certainty, or only a part of them can be so estimated, we can see no objection to placing before the jury all the facts and circumstances of the case, having any tendency to show damages, or their probable amount; so as to enable them to make the most intelligible and probable estimate which the nature of the case will permit.' "

B. ADJUSTMENTS FOR TIME

1. *Prejudgment Interest*

GEORGE H. SWATEK, INC. v. NORTH STAR GRAPHICS

Superior Court of New Jersey, Appellate Division, 1991.
246 N.J.Super. 281, 587 A.2d 629.

MICHELS, P.J.A.D.

Defendant North Star Graphics, Inc. appeals from a judgment of the Law Division entered on a jury verdict awarding plaintiff George H. Swatek, Inc. $38,586.84 in damages together with $7,041.94 in interest and dismissing its counterclaim.

A brief summary of the facts giving rise to this appeal follows. In February 1986, defendant and plaintiff entered into a contract under which plaintiff was to supply defendant with shipping containers.

* * *

Defendant later learned that the containers did not meet United Parcel Service's strength standards. Eventually, plaintiff developed a protective cushion that enabled the containers to meet the specifications. In mid-April 1986, plaintiff and defendant agreed that plaintiff would supply defendant with approximately 32,000 cushions. Plaintiff testified that the parties did not set a delivery date, however, defendant believed that the cushions were to be shipped by April 28, 1986. Plaintiff started shipping the cushions in mid-May 1986 and continued shipping the cushions until early June 1986. Because the shipments arrived too late for defendant to meet its obligations with its customers, defendant shipped the containers by air using other packaging materials. Defendant refused to pay for the cushions.

Plaintiff instituted this action to recover damages for monies allegedly due under the contract. Defendant counterclaimed for breach of contract, negligent performance of the contract and fraud. Following a lengthy trial, the jury returned a verdict for plaintiff and the court entered judgment accordingly. This appeal followed.

Defendant first contends that the trial court erroneously directed a verdict in favor of plaintiff and therefore, a new trial is warranted. We disagree. We are satisfied from our study of the record and the arguments presented that the trial court properly enforced the parties' stipulation and framed the jury questions in light of that stipulation.

At the commencement of the trial, the parties agreed on the following stipulation as recounted by the trial court:

> THE COURT: Okay. The attorneys have asked me to read a stipulation. They have made a stipulation or agreement. They agree the facts are rather than having you prove the fact, it is stipulated by the parties that the Plaintiffs Swatek delivered to Defendants counterclaimant Northstar Graphics, Inc. and or to Browerman Die Cutting, a warehouse hired by Northstar Graphics, Inc., certain goods under invoices totalling $38,586.84. It is also agreed that said amount has not been paid. So, those are the facts in the case the parties agree on.

At the end of the case, plaintiff moved "for a directed verdict at least for the amount requested in the complaint." The trial court did not formally grant or deny this request but rather, stated:

> The Court: The charge has, it's already been provided. The issue as far as plaintiff's case is concerned, the charge I proposed to make to the jury is not an issue issue, the 38,000 whatever dollars, is not an issue in the case. The only issue in the case is whether there should be a set off for the breach of contract alleged in the counterclaim, or if—or if it exceeds the amount of $38,000 whether there should be judgment in favor of defendant on the counterclaim.

* * *

In the instant case, defendant offered no evidence that the damages were reasonably foreseeable at the time the contract was made. Because the parties were unclear as to when the cushions were due, recovery of these claims is precluded. Plaintiff could only have foreseen that defendant would incur additional expenses, lose profits or jeopardize future business if it knew that defendant needed the cushions by a specific date. For whatever reason, the delivery date was not clear. As such, damages of the type sought here are not recoverable.

We are also satisfied that the trial court properly awarded prejudgment interest to plaintiff. *Rule* 4:42–11, in pertinent part, provides:

> Except where provided by statute with respect to a public entity or employee, and except as otherwise provided by law, the court shall, in tort actions, including products liability actions, include in the judgment simple interest, calculated as hereafter provided, from the date of the institution of the action or from a date 6 months after the date the cause of action arises, whichever is later, provided that in exceptional cases the court may suspend the running of such prejudgment interest. Prejudgment interest shall be calculated in the same amount and manner provided for by paragraph (a) of this rule except that for all periods prior to January 1, 1988 interest shall be calculated at 12% per

> annum. The contingent fee of an attorney shall not be computed on the interest so included in the judgment.

"While this rule addresses only tort judgments, it is clear that prejudgment interest may run on contract claims as well, not as a matter of right but rather in accordance with equitable principles." *Pressler, Current N.J. Court Rules, Comment R.* 4:42–11(b). *See Meshinsky v. Nichols Yacht Sales, Inc.,* 110 *N.J.* 464, 478–79, 541 *A.*2d 1063 (1988).

Traditionally, prejudgment interest was awarded only in contract cases involving liquidated damages.

> Historically, prejudgment interest has been awarded on liquidated damages, * * * but it was not awarded "where the damages [were] unliquidated and not capable of ascertainment by mere computation, or where a serious and substantial controversy exist[ed] as to the amount due under a contract." * * * The rationale was that "the person who is liable for the debt does not know the sum he owes and cannot be in default until the amount he owes is determined by judgment."

The decisions in *Busik v. Levine,* 63 *N.J.* 351, 307 *A.*2d 571, *appeal dismissed,* 414 *U.S.* 1106, 94 *S.Ct.* 831, 38 *L.Ed.*2d 733 (1973)[1] and *Ellmex Constr. Co., Inc. v. Republic Ins. Co.,* 202 *N.J.Super.* 195, 494 *A.*2d 339 (App.Div.1985), *certif. denied,* 103 *N.J.* 453, 511 *A.*2d 639 (1986), however, removed the traditional distinctions between liquidated and unliquidated damage awards and authorized awards of prejudgment interest when unliquidated damages are recovered.

In *Busik,* the Supreme Court faced a challenge to *R.* 4:42–11(b). In holding the rule valid, the Court noted:

> We mentioned earlier the judge-made limitation that interest should not be allowed if the claim was unliquidated. That limitation apparently rested upon the view that a defendant should not be deemed in default when the amount of his liability has not been adjudged. But interest is payable on a liquidated claim when liability itself is denied, even in good faith * * *. The fact remains that in both situations the defendant has had the use, and the plaintiff has not, of moneys which the judgment finds was the damage plaintiff suffered. This is true whether the contested liability is for a liquidated or for an unliquidated sum. For that reason, the concept of a "liquidated" sum has often been strained to find a basis for an award of interest. * * *

In *Ellmex,* the Court went a step further and specifically authorized awards of prejudgment interest when unliquidated contract damages are awarded. The Court explained that the

> equitable purpose of an award of prejudgment interest is compensatory, "to indemnify the claimant for the loss of what the moneys due him would presumably have earned if the payment had not been delayed." *Ibid.* Whether the claim be liquidated or not is, under the *Busik*

1. Following the decision in *Busik, R.* 4:42–11(b) was amended to permit the discretionary suspension of prejudgment interest in exceptional cases.

rationale, of no realistic importance. This is especially true where the question interfering with disposition of the claim is not the inability of the parties to agree upon the value of the claim but is rather an argument as to coverage. "The fact remains that in both situations the defendant has had the use, and the plaintiff has not, of moneys which the judgment finds was the damage plaintiff suffered." *Id.* [63 *N.J.* at 359 [307 *A.*2d 571]. In the circumstances here presented, the equities favor plaintiff and prejudgment interest should be awarded. We are not to be understood as holding that this will be true in every contest between insurer and insured. Where the contest is legitimately one as to the amount of damage sustained and the reasonable cost of repair, the equities indeed may favor the insurer. * * *

The rule emerging from *Ellmex* is that prejudgment interest can be awarded whether either liquidated or unliquidated damages are recovered and the equities are in the injured party's favor. * * *

In challenging the trial court's decision to award prejudgment interest, defendant offers no authority in support of its claim nor does it demonstrate any abuse of discretion on the part of the trial court. Considering the circumstances of this case, particularly that almost two-and-one-half years elapsed between the filing of the complaint and the entry of judgment, the trial court properly exercised its discretion in awarding prejudgment interest to plaintiff. We find no sound reason or justification to interfere with that decision.

Notes

1. *See also* Royal College Shop, Inc. v. Northern Ins. Co. of N.Y., 895 F.2d 670, 673, 675 (10th Cir.1990) (Kansas law allows prejudgment interest on liquidated claims and "under the equitable theory to make plaintiffs whole"); Orduna S.A. v. Zen–Noh Grain Corp., 913 F.2d 1149, 1158 (5th Cir.1990) (genuine dispute and complex issues are not reasons for denying prejudgment interest; "defendants had use of plaintiff's funds for almost five years before judgment."); Hartford Accident & Indemnity Co. v. U.S. Fire Insurance Co., 710 F.Supp. 164, 167 (E.D.N.C.1989) aff'd, 918 F.2d 955 (4th Cir.1990) ("prejudgment interest should be considered an element of damages on the basis that the plaintiff should be made whole from the date of the loss.")

2. When a jurisdiction does not allow interest on an "unliquidated claim", can a plaintiff recover the interest he paid on a loan he took out to repair his truck? Spreader Specialists, Inc. v. Monroc, Inc., 114 Idaho 15, 752 P.2d 617 (App.1987) said yes:

> "But here Spreader does not seek money it could have earned on investment if Monroc had timely paid compensation. Rather, Spreader seeks to recover a sum *actually expended* by it as a result of Monroc's tortious conduct. The interest on the loan for repairs was an expense occasioned by Spreader's effort to mitigate its losses. Accordingly, we hold that interest charges incurred on a loan obtained in good faith, as part of a reasonable course of action to mitigate losses, may be recovered as an item of consequential damages." *Id.* at 623–24 (emphasis in original).

If a plaintiff seeks actual interest paid at a rate greater than the state's statutory prejudgment interest rate for a breach of contract, what hurdle must the plaintiff overcome? *See* Macal v. Stinson, 468 N.W.2d 34, 36 (Iowa 1991) ("There was no showing the Stinsons knew it would be necessary for the Macals to borrow money at a higher rate if they breached the contract.")

3. How is prejudgment interest computed? Plaintiff needs to identify a principal amount, a time period, and an interest rate. Do you recognize P × t × r from your high school mathematics? What rate (r) should be used? *See e.g.* Ohio River Co. v. Peavey Co., 556 F.Supp. 87, 93 (E.D.Mo.1982) (In admiralty cases "prejudgment interest is not tied to the forum state's statutory limit. Instead, the rate of interest should be fixed at a rate in keeping with interest rates prevailing at the time repairs were completed") *rev'd in part and remanded* for trial court to increase rate since only evidence was that average borrowing rate from time of accident to trial was 15.45% and district court had awarded 10%. 731 F.2d 542 (1984). What incentives or disincentives are created when states have statutes fixing the prejudgment interest rate at a fixed amount?

4. Note that post judgment interest is payable on the award from the date of judgment until payment. This rate is usually statutory.

5. "Tort reform" packages sometimes include provisions restricting prejudgment interest. A Missouri statute, § 538.300 RSMo.Supp.1991, for example, exempts medical malpractice cases from prejudgment interest provisions. *See* Vincent v. Johnson, 833 S.W.2d 859, 866 (Mo.1992) (*en banc*) for a discussion of the Missouri interest statutes.

6. The general rule regarding the recovery of prejudgment interest in breach of contract actions is set forth in Restatement (Second) of Contracts § 354 (1981): *

"§ 354. Interest as Damages

"(1) If the breach consists of a failure to pay a definite sum in money or to render a performance with fixed or ascertainable monetary value, interest is recoverable from the time for performance on the amount due less all deductions to which the party in breach is entitled.

"(2) In any other case, such interest may be allowed as justice requires on the amount that would have been just compensation had it been paid when performance was due."

2. *Present Value and Inflation*

STRINGHAM v. UNITED PARCEL SERVICE, INC.

Appellate Court of Illinois, Second District, 1989.
181 Ill.App.3d 312, 130 Ill.Dec. 81, 536 N.E.2d 1292 *appeal dismissed* 127 Ill.2d 642, 133 Ill.Dec. 677, 541 N.E.2d 1115.

JUSTICE REINHARD delivered the opinion of the court:

Defendant, United Parcel Service, Inc. (UPS), appeals from a judgment of the circuit court of Winnebago County entered on a jury verdict for $252,631.08 ($505,262.16 reduced 50% by the negligence of plaintiff's decedent) in favor of plaintiff, Valerie R. Stringham, as administrator of the estate of David E. Stringham, deceased, and for the use and benefit of her two children, Tracy and Tina Stringham, in this wrongful death action [from an automobile accident].

* * *

Defendant next argues that the circuit court erred in allowing the testimony of plaintiff's witness, Jack Skeels, an economist, as to the value of decedent's projected future earnings because Skeels, in calculating the present value of future earnings, had incorporated a factor accounting for inflation. Defendant maintains that, under Illinois law, the effects of inflation are not to be considered in determining the present value of future earnings. Defendant contends that Skeels' testimony resulted in an excessive verdict unsupported by any proper evidence.

While Skeels' testimony describing the method he followed in computing decedent's future earnings is somewhat lacking in clarity, from examination of this testimony and the written income loss analysis prepared by Skeels and entered into evidence, we understand the method employed by Skeels to be as follows. Skeels first projected how long decedent would have been expected to work, had he lived, based upon actuarial data. Skeels then determined the amount decedent would be expected to earn during his working life based upon decedent's income and certain personal characteristics. In doing so, rather than assuming decedent's income level would remain constant, Skeels generated an age income profile predicting, based upon statistical data, how decedent's income would change over time due to factors such as increased experience. The income age profile data does not account for the effect of inflation on wage levels, as it is apparently based upon data comparing income levels of workers of different ages at the same point in time.

Skeels next discounted decedent's future earnings to present value. In doing so, Skeels used a base discount rate of 7.3% from which he subtracted 6%, representing "growth of earnings," giving a net discount rate of 1.3% used in the present value calculation. Skeels stated during cross-examination that growth of earnings is essentially inflation and that subtracting it from the discount rate "squeezed out" the effect of inflation from the calculation.

Defendant argues that the use of inflation or growth of earnings factors in calculating present value is improper. Defendant cites *American National Bank & Trust Co. v. Thompson* (1987), 158 Ill.App.3d 478, 110 Ill.Dec. 886, 511 N.E.2d 1206, wherein it was held that the plaintiff's expert's method of calculating present cash value which considered growth of earnings and inflation was "not in accordance with the legal definition of present cash value as set forth in IPI Civil 2d No. 34.05 and the relevant case law." 158 Ill.App.3d at 483–84, 110 Ill.Dec. at 889, 511 N.E.2d at 1209.

It is well established that, in weighing the amount of damages to be assessed against a tort-feasor, the jury must discount the amount of future damages to their present value. * * * There is, however, little authority in

Illinois governing whether inflation may be taken into account in computing future awards, and if so, how it is to be taken into account.

In *Jones & Laughlin Steel Corp. v. Pfeifer* (1983), 462 U.S. 523, 103 S.Ct. 2541, 76 L.Ed.2d 768, the United States Supreme Court noted that at one time, many American courts did not allow consideration of the effects of inflation in computing awards of lost earnings. (*Pfeifer,* 462 U.S. at 539–40, 103 S.Ct. at 2552, 76 L.Ed.2d at 785; see also Comment, *Inflation, Productivity, and the Total Offset Method of Calculating Damages for Lost Future Earnings,* 49 U.Chi.L.Rev. 1003, 1011 (1982) (hereinafter Damages for Lost Future Earnings).) These courts accepted evidence of both individual and societal factors that would lead to wage increases even in an inflation-free economy but required proof that those factors were not influenced by predictions of future price inflation, reasoning that such estimates were unreliably speculative. (*Pfeifer,* 462 U.S. at 540, 103 S.Ct. at 2552, 76 L.Ed.2d at 785.) However, in discounting to present value, these courts applied a market interest rate. As market interest rates increase in response to inflation, the Court stated:

> "The effect of [this method] was to deny the plaintiff the benefit of the impact of inflation on his future earnings, while giving the defendant the benefit of inflation's impact on the interest rate that is used to discount those earnings to present value. Although the plaintiff in such a situation could invest the proceeds of the litigation at an 'inflated' rate of interest, the stream of income that he received provided him with only enough dollars to maintain his existing *nominal* income; it did not provide him with a stream comparable to what his lost wages would have been in an inflationary economy." (Emphasis in original.) (462 U.S. at 540, 103 S.Ct. at 2552, 76 L.Ed.2d at 785.)

In other words, predicting future earnings without considering the effects of inflation on wage levels produces an unrealistically low estimate of the plaintiff's total future earnings. When this estimate is discounted by the market interest rate, the plaintiff will receive an award which, even if invested at that rate, would yield fewer dollars than if the plaintiff had continued earnings which kept pace with inflation. See *O'Shea v. Riverway Towing Co.* (7th Cir.1982), 677 F.2d 1194, 1199.

Because of this problem, today, in a majority of jurisdictions, courts attempt to account for the effects of inflation in some way. (See *Pfeifer,* 462 U.S. at 540–41, 103 S.Ct. at 2552, 76 L.Ed.2d at 785; *American National Bank & Trust Co. v. Thompson* (1987), 158 Ill.App.3d 478, 490, 110 Ill.Dec. 886, 511 N.E.2d 1206 (Buckley, J., dissenting).) Courts have developed several approaches. One approach incorporates inflation into the computation of future earnings and then discounts that amount using the market interest rate as the discount rate. Another approach does not consider inflation in estimating total earnings but uses a discount rate equal to the market interest rate minus the inflation rate. (See *O'Shea,* 677 F.2d at 1199; see also *Damages for Lost Future Earnings,* 49 U.Chi. L.Rev. at 1014–15.) Both these approaches yield identical results. *O'Shea,* 677 F.2d at 1199.

Still other courts employ two other methods. One, the "partial offset" or "real interest" method, assumes that market interest rates exceed inflation by an essentially constant amount over time. This amount, generally believed to be 1.5% to 2%, is known as the "real" interest rate. (See 22 Am.Jur.2d *Damages* § 146 (1988); *Damages for Lost Future Earnings,* 49 U.Chi.L.Rev. at 1016–18; *Pfeifer,* 462 U.S. at 541–42, 103 S.Ct. at 2553, 76 L.Ed.2d at 786.) A court employing the partial offset method does not allow consideration of inflation in estimating total future earnings, but, in discounting to present value, uses the real interest rate rather than the market rate.

The final method, the "total offset" method, assumes that inflation and other factors affecting growth of wages will equal the ideal discount rate. Hence, in predicting total future earnings inflation is not considered, nor is any discounting to present value performed as the two steps would cancel each other out. See 22 Am.Jur.2d *Damages* § 145 (1988); *Damages for Lost Future Earnings,* 49 U.Chi.L.Rev. at 1018–1022; *Pfeifer,* 462 U.S. at 544–46, 103 S.Ct. at 2554–55, 76 L.Ed.2d at 787–89.

In the instant case, plaintiff's economist appears to have employed a method accounting for inflation by subtracting the inflation rate from the appropriate market interest rate in discounting to present value, which is equivalent to first increasing future earnings by the inflation rate and then discounting by the market interest rate. Defendant notes that such a method is improper in view of the holding of the Appellate Court for the First District in *American National Bank & Trust Co. v. Thompson* (1987), 158 Ill.App.3d 478, 110 Ill.Dec. 886, 511 N.E.2d 1206. In that case, the court stated that "[w]hile in some jurisdictions the testimony of plaintiff's expert might, with proper explanation, be admissible to demonstrate to the jury the total amount of future damages, *i.e.,* to demonstrate the effect the inflation rate and growth of real earnings would have on future earnings, it has not been the rule in Illinois." 158 Ill.App.3d at 484, 110 Ill.Dec. at 890, 511 N.E.2d at 1210.

We find, however, little support in Illinois case law for the proposition in *Thompson* that evidence of the effects of inflation on future earnings is inadmissible in Illinois. We observe that in *Raines v. New York Central R.R. Co.* (1970), 129 Ill.App.2d 294, 263 N.E.2d 895, *rev'd on other grounds* (1972), 51 Ill.2d 428, 283 N.E.2d 230, the appellate court held that evidence concerning future inflationary trends was speculative and therefore inadmissible. (129 Ill.App.2d at 305–06, 263 N.E.2d at 900.) However, in reversing the decision of the appellate court, on the basis that the award was supported by other proper evidence, our supreme court expressly declined to "examine the validity of the defendant's contention that the admission of evidence regarding future inflation resulted in an excessive verdict." (*Raines v. New York Central R.R. Co.* (1972), 51 Ill.2d 428, 437, 283 N.E.2d 230, 235; see also * * * *Prendergast v. Cox* (1984), 128 Ill.App.3d 84, 83 Ill.Dec. 279, 470 N.E.2d 34, cited in *Thompson,* notes the lack of any authoritative decision as to the propriety of evidence or argument concerning the effects of future inflation. In *Prendergast,* the court merely held that where no evidence as to future inflation was present, it was proper to sustain an objection to argument of counsel urging jurors to consider inflation. 128 Ill.App.3d at 92, 83 Ill.Dec. at 284, 470 N.E.2d at 39.

Illinois Pattern Jury Instructions, Civil, No. 34.05 (2d ed. 1971) (IPI Civil 2d) defines present value as follows:

> " 'Present cash value' means the sum of money needed now, which, together with what that sum will earn in the future, will equal the amounts of the pecuniary benefits at the times in the future when they would have been received."

Defendant notes that the *Thompson* court found that consideration of inflation or growth of earnings is inconsistent with this definition. Both defendant and the court in *Thompson* fail to recognize that two steps are involved in determining a proper award based on loss of future earnings, and that IPI Civil 2d No. 34.05 only pertains to the second step in the process. Before the amount of future earnings can be discounted to present value, it must be determined what that amount is. We agree that once the amount of future earnings to be discounted is known, the inflation rate plays no role in the discount process. However, inflation is relevant to the initial step of determining the total amount of future earnings. In the instant case, plaintiff's economist subtracted inflation from the interest rate during the discount stage. However, as previously noted, this method is mathematically equivalent to inflating earnings and discounting by an unadjusted market interest rate. Thus, we do not find the result of this method inconsistent with the definition of present value in IPI Civil 2d, No. 34.05.

We, therefore, decline to follow *Thompson* as we believe it is illogical and indefensible to build inflation into the discount rate and yet ignore it in calculating the lost future wages that are to be discounted. * * * We further find that the method employed by plaintiff's economist is an appropriate method of accounting for the impact of inflation. We do not hold that it is the only proper method. * * *

* * *

Affirmed.

C. COLLATERAL SOURCE RULE

PHILLIPS v. WESTERN CO. OF NORTH AMERICA

United States Court of Appeals, Fifth Circuit, 1992.
953 F.2d 923.

KING, CIRCUIT JUDGE:

Plaintiff Earl Phillips reinjured his back while he and a co-employee connected a flow line to the bell nipple on the blow-out preventer (BOP) stack of the TRITON III, a jack-up drilling rig off the coast of Louisiana owned by defendant The Western Company of North America (Western). * * * After the close of the plaintiff's case, the district court granted Western's motion for a directed verdict on the unseaworthiness claim, but denied the motion on the Jones Act claim. The jury returned a verdict in favor of Western.

On appeal, Phillips argues that the district court erred (1) in keeping the unseaworthiness claim from the jury, * * * (2) in overruling his objection to Western's introduction of evidence concerning the post-accident benefits it paid him; and (3) in refusing to grant his motion for a new trial. We agree with Western that reasonable minds could not differ on the issue of the TRITON III's unseaworthiness, and therefore affirm the directed verdict on the unseaworthiness claim. However, we find that the district court erred in allowing Western to introduce evidence of the post-accident benefits without first determining whether they fell outside the bounds of the collateral source rule. Although we disagree with Phillips's position that he has shown conclusively that the benefits derived from a collateral source, there is substantial uncertainty about the character of the benefits. If they were indeed collateral and subject to exclusion, their inclusion as part of the defendant's case—and the lack of a limiting instruction—raises the possibility that the jury improperly factored the evidence into its determination of liability. Phillips is therefore entitled to a new trial on the Jones Act claim.

* * *

After the accident, Western began paying Phillips long-term disability benefits equal to two-thirds of his salary, as well as medical benefits and maintenance payments. Without objection by Phillips, Western introduced evidence of the medical benefits. Phillips objected, however, to introduction of evidence of the maintenance pay and the long-term disability benefits. Phillips lodged a written objection, arguing that maintenance pay may not be deducted from an award of past lost wages and that the disability benefits were immune from setoff under the collateral source rule. He renewed his objection to the maintenance pay and the disability benefits at trial. * * * The judge overruled the objection, stating that "the income that the man received is in fact income, and that should be reflected so that he doesn't get a double recovery."

* * *

III. The Jones Act Claim

Phillip's next point of error involves the Jones Act negligence claim, which was submitted to the jury and resolved in favor of Western. Phillips argues that the district court should not have allowed Western to introduce evidence of disability and other payments that Phillips received following the accident. He invokes the collateral source rule, which generally denies to a tortfeasor a reduction in its liability by any amounts the plaintiff receives from a source collateral to, or independent of, the tortfeasor. * * * The substantive rule of no reduction carries with it an evidentiary rule requiring the exclusion of evidence of any collateral benefits. Phillips argues that Western's eliciting of evidence of the benefits during his cross-examination, as well as Western's repeated references to the benefits in its closing argument, did exactly what the evidentiary component of the collateral source rule is supposed to prevent—it prejudiced the jury against finding Western negligent by making the jury think Phillips had already been adequately compensated for his loss.

* * *

The evidence of disability benefits presents a considerably more difficult problem. The concern that juries will factor in evidence of collateral benefits when determining liability has historically been the leading reason for excluding such evidence. * * * *Simmons v. Hoegh Lines,* 784 F.2d 1234, 1237 (5th Cir.1986) ("juries will be more likely to find no liability when they are aware that the plaintiff has already received compensation"). * * *

It is undoubtedly true that knowledge that an injured plaintiff has resources available to compensate him for his loss, separate from the defendant, may divert the jury's attention from its narrow task of determining whether the defendant was negligent. The jury may feel that awarding damages would overcompensate the plaintiff for his injury (even though the defendant would only pay once), and may factor this into the liability calculus. This concern compels us to reject Western's suggestion that, even if introduction of evidence of post-accident benefits was error, it had no effect on the jury's finding of no negligence and therefore constituted a form of harmless error. Although the evidence of negligence was slim, our cases have deemed it to have so prejudicial an effect that we cannot be sure it did not play a role in the jury's deliberations on negligence. *See Simmons,* 784 F.2d at 1237. Moreover, the trial judge gave no curative instruction that would indicate to the jury the use they could make of the evidence, *see id.* (erroneous admission of evidence of collateral benefits requires reversal unless curative instruction given), and Western's attorney repeatedly alluded to the benefits in his closing statement in an effort to bring the possibility of double recovery to the jury's attention. Under these circumstances, we cannot say that any potential error was harmless.

In addition to the possibility of jury prejudice, there is another reason for excluding evidence of collateral benefits, one which perhaps is more consistent with the authority for exclusion found within the Federal Rules of Evidence: if the substantive law disallows a setoff from the tortfeasor's damages for the plaintiff's collateral benefits, evidence of collateral benefits simply has no relevance in the lawsuit. Evidence that is not relevant, of course, is not admissible. Fed.R.Evid. 402. Several justifications have been advanced to support the substantive rule that a tortfeasor may not obtain a setoff: the plaintiff should not be penalized for having had the foresight to obtain insurance, particularly where, but for the tortfeasor's actions, that insurance would have continued to be available for other purposes; allowing the tortfeasor a credit for the plaintiff's insurance detracts from the function of deterrence in tort law; and the defendant deserves to pay for his fault. *See generally* Harper, James & Gray, *The Law of Torts* § 25.22 (2d ed. 1986). While this court has not explored the justifications for the collateral source rule in detail, it is plainly applicable in Jones Act negligence cases. * * *

In most cases, identifying income subject to the collateral source rule is not a difficult task. The rule's formulation—that the plaintiff's recovery is not subject to a setoff for benefits independent of the tortfeasor—leads to the straightforward conclusion that medical insurance,[7] disability insurance and other forms of protection purchased by the plaintiff, as well as gifts the plaintiff receives,[8] cannot reduce recovery. Moreover, workers' compensation, which is paid by an employer, may not diminish recovery when an injured worker sues the tortfeasor. *See Fruge,* 918 F.2d at 1168; *Bourque,* 623 F.2d at 354.[9] Because the tortfeasor has no connection with these types of benefits, they are easily identifiable "independent" sources of income.

In cases where the tortfeasor contributes toward the benefit, however, the justifications for denying a setoff become less compelling. The rule is intended to ensure that the availability of outside sources of income does not diminish the plaintiff's recovery, not make the tortfeasor pay twice. * * * If one goal of the rule is to promote accident avoidance by ensuring that the tortfeasor pays for his faulty conduct, that goal is not marginally advanced if the tortfeasor both pays in advance for the plaintiff's benefit and pays now for the full measure of damages. Thus, we have recognized that it would be unfair to allow the plaintiff a double recovery when both the liability judgment and the collateral benefits are paid for by the defendant. * * * Because (to oversimplify) application of the rule of no setoff turns on whether the tortfeasor also paid for the plaintiff's "collateral" benefit, the "essence" of the rule has been described as the independence of the transaction giving rise to the collateral source. * * *

* * *

In *Haughton* [*v. Blackships Inc.* 462 F.2d 788 (5th Cir.1972)], we recognized that the inquiry into the collateral nature of benefits frequently is more subtle. We stated that "[a]pplication of the collateral source rule depends less upon the source of funds than upon the character of the benefits received." 462 F.2d at 790 (footnote omitted); * * * In *Haughton,* we determined that the fact that an employer-tortfeasor contributed to a fund from which the benefits derived did not preclude a conclusion that the funds were to be treated as collateral. 462 F.2d at 790. We contrasted the payments made by the employer in *Haughton* with payments "characterized as a voluntary undertaking by the employer to indemnify itself

7. *E.g., Helfend v. Southern California Rapid Transit Dist.,* 2 Cal.3d 1, 84 Cal.Rptr. 173, 465 P.2d 61 (1970).

8. *E.g., Varlack v. SWC Carribean, Inc.,* 550 F.2d 171 (3d Cir.1977).

9. Because the injured worker normally cannot sue his employer in tort, workers' compensation benefits usually derive from a source collateral to the tortfeasor. *See, e.g.,* 33 U.S.C. § 905(a) (payment of compensation according to predetermined schedule is employer's sole liability to injured worker under Longshore and Harbor Workers Compensation Act). Although many workers' compensation statutes enable the employer to recover the amounts they pay by subrogating the employer to the worker's claim, *see* Harper, James & Gray, *The Law of Torts* § 25.22 at 653 n. 9 (2d ed. 1986), this does not reduce the total amount of damages paid by the tortfeasor. *See* 33 U.S.C. § 933 (LHWCA subrogation section). This scheme was explained in *Stifle v. Marathon Petroleum Co.,* 876 F.2d 552 (7th Cir.1989), as follows:

> The employer is compelled to pay the benefits regardless of whether it was negligent or not. In return, the employer takes a lien for the total amount of benefits paid on any judgment or settlement the employee may later obtain. Accordingly, the injured employee is fully—but not doubly—compensated; the tortfeasor pays for the injuries for which it is responsible and the employer recovers so much of its workers' compensation payments as is attributable to the tortfeasor's negligence.

Id. at 560 (footnote omitted).

against its possible legal liabilities for payment of maintenance and cure." *Id.* at 791. Finding that the employer's payments into a maritime retirement pension fund were *not* made for the purpose of responding to legal liability, we held that the pension benefits could not be set off against the plaintiff's damages. We indicated that payment by an employer into a fund for the purpose of providing a fringe benefit or deferred compensation would make the benefit subject to the collateral source rule, although we did not explicitly characterize the pension benefit in *Haughton* as such. *Id.*

* * *

In *Allen v. Exxon Shipping Co.,* 639 F.Supp. 1545 (D.Me.1986), the court listed five factors that may assist in distinguishing fringe benefits from benefits intended to respond to legal liability. These include

> (1) whether the employee makes any contribution to funding of the disability payment; (2) whether the benefit plan arises as the result of a collective bargaining agreement; (3) whether the plan and payments thereunder cover both work-related and nonwork-related injuries; (4) whether payments from the plan are contingent upon length of service of the employee; and (5) whether the plan contains any specific language contemplating a set-off of benefits received under the plan against a judgment received in a tort action.

639 F.Supp. at 1548. The disability plan at issue in *Allen* required no contribution of the employee, was not funded pursuant to a collective bargaining agreement, and specifically provided for a setoff in the event the employer was required to pay a judgment to the employee, three features that cut in favor of setoff. But other features cut in favor of disallowing setoff. The plan covered injuries arising from both work-related and nonwork-related injuries, and was to some extent dependent on the length of the employee's service with the company. *Id.* at 1548–49. The court found dispositive the fact that the plan was not established pursuant to a collective bargaining agreement and that the employer had specifically provided for setoff. The latter was evidence that the "payments made to this Plaintiff were made pursuant to a plan intended by the employer, as its dominant purpose, to provide for the employer's indemnification against liability." *Id.* at 1549.

* * *

We agree that the factors enumerated in *Allen* are relevant to the distinction between fringe benefits and benefits intended to respond to legal liability. In the case before us, however, no evidence as to any of these factors was presented to the district judge prior to his ruling on Phillips's objection to introduction of the evidence. The record before us is insufficient to enable us to determine whether the benefits were intended to respond to Western's legal liability under the Jones Act. We do not know any better than the district judge whether the benefits were available for both work-related and nonwork-related injuries, whether Western had made clear any intention to set off payments against Jones Act liability, or the like. Phillips is entitled to a new trial in which these questions are considered before introduction of evidence of Western's benefit plan is introduced.

We note that evidence of the structure of the Western plan should have been presented to the district judge before he ruled on whether the benefits fell within the collateral source rule. Phillips gave contradictory testimony at trial about the funding of the plan, but this question should not have been litigated before the jury. It is elemental that the judge, not the jury, is charged with determining in the first instance whether evidence is admissible; this responsibility applies to ascertaining whether particular benefits are subject to the collateral source rule. As we have already discussed, one of the purposes of the exclusionary rule that accompanies the rule of no setoff is to shield the jury from potentially prejudicial information about the plaintiff's outside sources of income. The judge must examine the plan and decide whether it is admissible.

* * *

Finally, we note that it is quite unnecessary in cases where the defendant is entitled to a setoff to introduce evidence of benefits that already have been paid. At issue in *Allen* was whether the defendant was entitled to a setoff, or whether the plaintiff could avoid introduction of evidence of the defendant's short-term and long-term disability payments. The court first found that the defendant was entitled to a setoff for the amounts paid under both benefit plans because they represented an intent to indemnify against future liabilities. 639 F.Supp. at 1549. But having found this, the court did not automatically allow the defendant to introduce evidence of the benefits: because the short-term benefits had already been paid in full, the court stated that it would perform the setoff itself by subtracting from the jury's verdict. *Id.* There simply was no need to place this information before the jury, and the defendant's right to setoff could be realized without injecting potentially prejudicial information into the trial. The court did, however, allow the evidence of the long-term benefits to go to the jury, reasoning that

> Plaintiff's ultimate recovery by way of verdict is subject to reduction for *the value of the right* to receive such benefits in the future. Because the value of that right is dependent in part upon a factual determination as to how long plaintiff is likely to receive them, the Court is not in a position to make such a deduction in a manner consistent with the factual determinations that will be made by the jury in arriving at a verdict in favor of the Plaintiff * * *.

Id. at 1550 (emphasis in original).

This strikes us as an eminently sensible way of handling evidence of benefits that do not fall within the prohibition of the collateral source rule. Because at bottom we are dealing with substantive rights concerning setoff, there is no reason to risk jury prejudice when it is unnecessary for the jury to perform the setoff calculation. The court in *Allen* identified a purpose for jury consideration of evidence of future benefits, but we agree that evidence of past payments should be excluded and set off after the verdict. The district judge did not consider proceeding in this fashion with respect to the past and future benefits paid by Western to Phillips, but such a procedure would place before the jury only that evidence that is relevant to their task. * * *

* * *

Phillips is entitled to a new trial on the Jones Act claim with evidentiary rulings in accordance with this opinion.

Affirmed in part, Reversed in part and Remanded for a new trial.

Notes

1. When the federal government is the tortfeasor, are payments to the plaintiff from the Social Security system from a collateral source? *See* Berg v. United States, 806 F.2d 978 (10th Cir.1986). There the trial court found that a United States Army hospital's negligence caused plaintiff Berg's injuries. Many of his expenses had been paid by Medicare. The court held that Medicare expenses are a collateral source, reasoning:

> "Berg's medical expenses were paid in large part by Medicare. The government claims that the amount of Medicare assistance that Berg received should be deducted from his FTCA award. Berg argues that Medicare is a collateral source and that no deduction is permitted.
>
> "Colorado law provides that 'compensation or indemnity received by an injured party from a collateral source, wholly independent of the wrongdoer and to which he has not contributed, will not diminish the damages otherwise recoverable from the wrongdoer.' Kistler v. Halsey, 173 Colo. 540, 545, 481 P.2d 722, 724 (1971) quoted in Steckler v. United States, 549 F.2d 1372, 1379 (10th Cir.1977). A collateral source, then, is one which is distinct from the funds of the defendant. In the context of a FTCA suit, an injured party who has already been compensated for his or her injuries can also recover damages from the United States unless the source of the original compensation was funds provided by the United States.
>
> "We considered the collateral source rule as applied to a FTCA action most recently in *Steckler*. 549 F.2d at 1378–79. The injured party in *Steckler* had been compensated by veterans benefits and Social Security disability benefits. The government argued that those payments should be subtracted from any FTCA award. We held that the veterans benefits were not a collateral source and could therefore be deducted from the FTCA award. The court then said that the Social Security disability benefits were logically collateral. Steckler, 549 F.2d at 1379. The test that we applied to determine whether a particular payment was collateral or not focused on whether the injured party had contributed to the fund from which he or she was now collecting. *Id.* *See also* Siverson v. United States, 710 F.2d 557, 560 (9th Cir.1983) ('Courts distinguish between those benefits that come from unfunded general revenues of the United States (deductible) and those that come from "a special fund supplied *in part* by the beneficiary or a relative upon whom the beneficiary is dependent" (nondeductible).') (emphasis in original) (quoting United States v. Harue Hayashi, 282 F.2d 599, 603 (9th Cir.1960). In *Steckler,* however, we hoped to gain more detailed information concerning the 'part or percentage' of the Social Security fund attributable to the government and the 'part or

percentage' attributable to the injured party. 549 F.2d at 1379. We remanded to the district court to obtain this information, but we recognized that '[i]t may be impossible to ascertain the part or percentage of funds attributable to the government which would be deductible since the monies are commingled.' *Id.* We are now convinced that it is in fact impossible to distinguish accurately which part of a fund that has been produced by millions of contributors is attributable to the government and which part is attributable to a particular injured party. Therefore, we require that the plaintiff bear the burden of showing only that he or she contributed to a special fund that is separate and distinct from general government revenues. *See* Siverson, 710 F.2d at 560. * * * Berg testified at trial that he had contributed to the Social Security fund since its creation and was therefore eligible for Medicare benefits. The government does not challenge this assertion.

"We must now decide whether Medicare benefits are paid from a special fund that is separate and distinct from general government revenues. The Social Security Act provides Medicare hospital insurance benefits to, *inter alia,* those who are age 65 or over and are eligible for Social Security retirement benefits. 42 U.S.C. § 1395c. Medicare hospital insurance benefits are paid from the Federal Hospital Insurance Trust Fund. 42 U.S.C. § 1395i. This fund is supplied in great part by the taxes imposed on employees and employers by the Federal Insurance Contributions Act (FICA), 26 U.S.C. § 3101(b), taxes more commonly known as Social Security taxes.

"In *Steckler,* we said that Social Security disability benefits are logically collateral. 549 F.2d at 1379. The Medicare benefits received by Berg in this case were funded by the same employment tax scheme that funded the Social Security disability benefits in *Steckler.* *Compare* 26 U.S.C. § 3101(a) (rate of tax for disability insurance) *with* 26 U.S.C. § 3101(b) (rate of tax for hospital insurance). The nature of an employee's tax contribution is the same in both instances."

2. Are payments from a collateral source inadmissible if the plaintiff did not contribute to them? *See* Johnson v. Baker, 11 Kan.App.2d 274, 719 P.2d 752, 756 (1986). There an attorney was found liable for malpractice because of the unenforceability of the provision of a divorce settlement that he negotiated requiring the husband to pay the college tuition of his daughter. The attorney was liable for the college tuition but contended

"that because the receipt of the grants and scholarships was wholly gratuitous, the collateral source rule should not apply. This appears to be a minority view. See, *e.g.,* Fla. Physician's Ins. Reciprocal v. Stanley, 452 So.2d 514, 515–16 (Fla.1984), and cases cited therein. The majority rule is that gratuitous payments received by injured parties cannot be used to mitigate damages. See, *e.g.,* Werner v. Lane, 393 A.2d 1329, 1335–36 (Me.1978). In a diversity action brought in the federal district court of this state, Judge Frank Theis stated that '[t]he general rule in Kansas is to exclude evidence which would show damages claimed by a party were in fact paid by someone else, or that services had been provided gratuitously.' Doran v. Priddy, 534 F.Supp. 30, 35 (D.Kan.1981). Subsequently, our own Supreme Court adopted much of the reasoning and holding of *Doran* when it held that a statute which sought to abrogate the common-law collateral source rule in medical malpractice actions, K.S.A. 60–471 (repealed, L.1985, ch. 197 § 5), was unconstitutional. Wentling, 237 Kan. at 516–18, 701 P.2d 939. Although the application of the collateral source rule to gratuitous payments was not at issue in *Wentling,* the Court gave tacit approval to *Doran* 's characterization of the Kansas common law as consistent with the majority rule.

"In light of *Wentling* and *Doran,* we conclude that the collateral source doctrine applies to payments or services received gratuitously as well as those received as the result of some obligation. Therefore, the trial court erred in deducting the value of the scholarships and grants received by Kelly Johnson from the damages awarded."

3. Note how some states have limited the collateral source rule by statute. *See, e.g.,* Mitchel v. Borton, 70 Ohio App.3d 141, 590 N.E.2d 832 (1990) in which plaintiff sued the city of Toledo for automobile injuries received from an accident with a driver employed by the city. The court applied a state statute as follows:

"It is well settled that the measure of damages in a tort action is that which will compensate and make the plaintiff whole. Pryor v. Webber (1970), 23 Ohio St.2d 104, 52 O.O.2d 395, 263 N.E.2d 235. Under the collateral source rule, a plaintiff's receipt of collateral benefits is deemed irrelevant and immaterial on the issue of damages. *Id.* at 109, 52 O.O.2d at 397–398, 263 N.E.2d at 238. The receipt of such benefits is not to be admitted into evidence. *Id.* Nor is the amount of such benefits to be deducted from a plaintiff's damage award. *Id.* Sick pay benefits received from a non-tortfeasor employer fall under the scope of the collateral source rule and therefore a plaintiff's sick pay benefits may not be deducted from a plaintiff's damage award. * * *

"However, the purpose behind R.C. 2744.05 is to protect political subdivisions from excessive damage awards which are ultimately paid by the taxpayer. * * * To this end, R.C. 2744.05(B) essentially makes an exception for political subdivisions and abolishes the collateral source rule as it pertains to governmental tort liability. *Id.* at 53, 550 N.E.2d at 527."

Id. at 835–36. *But see* Wentling v. Medical Anesthesia Services, P.A., 237 Kan. 503, 701 P.2d 939 (1985) (statute abolishing collateral source rule for medical malpractice suits violates equal protection and is thus unconstitutional).

4. Does the collateral source rule apply to settlements or to contract disputes? *See* Judge Montgomery's concurring opinion in McConal Aviation, Inc. v. Commercial Aviation Insurance Co., 110 N.M. 697, 799 P.2d 133, 138–40 (1990):

"Had the case gone to the jury against both defendants, the jury would have returned a verdict against one and exonerated the other. McConal concedes that the claims asserted against Commercial and Aviation—a claim for breach of a contract of insurance and a claim for negligent failure to procure insurance, respectively—were mutually exclusive. Since the case proceeded against only one defendant [because Aviation settled by paying $40,000 to McConal before trial] what is the justification for allowing the plaintiff to retain more than the amount of its damages?

"The policy against duplicate recovery, while no doubt strong and longstanding, does admit of exceptions. One of those exceptions—perhaps the most pervasive—is provided by the collateral source rule.[1]

"Still another policy in the mix is that which underlies the collateral source rule: the policy that a wrongdoer should not benefit from a fund provided by a collateral source and that, as between an innocent plaintiff and a culpable defendant, if one party is to benefit from a fund received from another source, it is preferable to allocate the benefit to the innocent party. In this case, it is clear that McConal's loss will be compensated in full. The only question is whether the $40,000 [settlement to McConal] paid by Aviation will augment McConal's recovery or will reduce Commercial's liability.

"I answer this question by resorting to the policy of expecting (and therefore, in the context of this case, requiring) the insurance company and the agent-broker to get their act together. McConal bought and paid for property damage insurance. The insurance company denied liability, pointing the finger at the agent; the agent claimed that it was not responsible and that, at least by implication, it had not failed in its duty to procure insurance from the insurer. Meanwhile, the insured was not compensated for its loss and had to commence litigation. It had done everything required of it to see that its property was insured; the insurer and the agent between them evaded responsibility and placed the onus of going forward on the insured. The insured had to undergo the delays, inconvenience, uncertainties and expense of litigation; the insurer and the agent between them could keep the insured's money until they either voluntarily settled or the court told one of them to pay.

"Under these circumstances it does not seem unreasonable to require the insurer, Commercial, to pay what it contracted to pay and to allow the insured, McConal, to keep what the agent, Aviation, voluntarily contributed in order to settle its alleged liability.

> If there must be a windfall certainly it is more just that the injured person shall profit therefrom, rather than the wrongdoer shall be relieved of his full responsibility for his wrongdoing. We think we may judicially note that notwithstanding that the law contemplates full compensation, incidental losses and handicaps are suffered in a great number of * * * cases which are not, and cannot be, fully compensated.

Grayson v. Williams, 256 F.2d 61, 65 (10th Cir.1958). *See also* Helfend v. Southern Cal. Rapid Transit Dist., 2 Cal.3d 1, 12, 84 Cal.Rptr. 173, 180, 465 P.2d 61, 68 (1970):

> [T]he plaintiff rarely actually receives full compensation for his injuries as computed by the jury. The collateral source rule partially serves to compensate for the attorney's share and does not actually render 'double recovery' for the plaintiff.

1. It is widely believed that the collateral source rule has little or no application to contract claims. *See, e.g., Restatement (Second) of Contracts* § 347, comment e (1979); D. Dobbs, *Handbook on the Law of Remedies* § 8.10, at 587 (1973). For an exhaustive demonstration that this is not correct, *see generally* J.G. Fleming, The Collateral Source Rule and Contract Damages, 71 Calif.L.Rev. 56 (1983).

"The insurance company in this case, seeking a judicial determination as to the existence of coverage under its policy, might not fit the classical picture of the 'wrongdoer' who is denied an offset of the benefit under the collateral source rule. However, Commercial and Aviation between them did force McConal to endure the 'losses and handicaps' entailed by the delay in payment and the necessity for litigation. One of these losses—not insignificant in amount, I have no doubt—was the attorney's fees. Under the policy of the collateral source rule—that the 'windfall' is to be allocated to the innocent claimant rather than the arguably culpable defendant who a jury has determined breached its contract—I concur in giving the plaintiff the 'duplicate recovery' realized in this case."

D. DEFENSES

1. *Offset the Benefits Rule*

MINPECO, S.A. v. CONTICOMMODITY SERVICES, INC.

United States District Court, Southern District of New York, 1987.
676 F.Supp. 486.

LASKER, DISTRICT JUDGE.

Various defendants move for summary judgment on all of plaintiff Minpeco's damage claims on the ground that Minpeco has failed to prove actual damages because its damage calculations do not take into account the extent to which Minpeco benefitted from defendants' allegedly manipulative behavior. The motion is granted in part and otherwise denied.[2]

* * *

Defendants take the position that as a matter of law any damages which Minpeco suffered on the silver futures market as a result of the alleged manipulation were completely offset by profits gained on Minpeco's physical silver positions. At the core of this argument are two important undisputed facts. First, Minpeco has admitted that all of its silver futures trades from October to December 1979 were "hedges" [8] backed by physical silver. Second, it is undisputed that Minpeco's damage calculations do not take into account any profit that Minpeco may have made as a result of its physical silver.

Based on these facts, defendants contend that Minpeco's damage calculations do not represent Minpeco's net economic loss because whatever

2. Defendants' motion is based, *arguendo,* on the assumption that "the defendants did manipulate the silver market and that, but for such conduct, the price of silver would not have risen above $8–$10 per ounce, the highest price that would have prevailed in the absence of a manipulation, according to Minpeco's economics expert." Memorandum in Support of Defendants' Motion for Summary Judgment Dismissing Minpeco's Damage Claims at 3 n. 3 (August 3, 1987). This decision adopts this assumption for the purposes of this motion alone.

8. In a "hedge" transaction, as the term itself implies, a trader with an interest in the cash market for a commodity deals in futures contracts as a means of transferring risks he faces in the cash market. *See Leist v. Simplot,* 638 F.2d 283, 287 (2d Cir.1980), *aff'd sub nom. Merrill Lynch, Pierce, Fenner & Smith, Inc. v. Curran,* 456 U.S. 353, 102 S.Ct. 1825, 72 L.Ed.2d 185 (1982). There is, however, "no bright line difference between hedgers and speculators," whose interests and activities frequently overlap. *Id.* at 288.

losses Minpeco incurred on its futures positions when the price of silver increased were offset by the simultaneous increase in value of Minpeco's physical silver. * * *

A) LEGAL ISSUES

Defendants' "offset" argument has considerable force. Under most circumstances, it is clear that a plaintiff both injured and enriched by illegal activity cannot choose to recover for his injuries yet retain his windfall. This principle has been applied both in securities actions, *see, e.g., Abrahamson v. Fleschner,* 568 F.2d 862, 878 (2d Cir.1977), *cert. denied,* 436 U.S. 913, 98 S.Ct. 2253, 56 L.Ed.2d 414 (1978) (securities fraud plaintiff may not recover for losses, while ignoring his profits, "where both result from a *single* wrong") (emphasis in original); *Byrnes v. Faulkner, Dawkins & Sullivan,* 550 F.2d 1303, 1313–14 (2d Cir.1977) (securities fraud losses must be offset by corresponding gains since "the transaction cannot be fractionated"), and antitrust actions, *see Los Angeles Memorial Coliseum Commission v. NFL,* 791 F.2d 1356, 1366–67 (9th Cir.1986), *cert. denied,* ___ U.S. ___, 108 S.Ct. 92, 98 L.Ed.2d 53 (1987); *Kypta v. McDonald's Corp.,* 671 F.2d 1282, 1285–86 (11th Cir.), *cert. denied,* 459 U.S. 857, 103 S.Ct. 127, 74 L.Ed.2d 109 (1982); *cf. Merit Motors, Inc. v. Chrysler Corp.,* 569 F.2d 666, 671–72 n. 25 (D.C.Cir.1977).

The rationale of these cases is perhaps best articulated in *Los Angeles Memorial Coliseum,* an antitrust action involving the Raiders football team's move from Oakland to Los Angeles. There, the Ninth Circuit held that the district court erred in limiting the National Football League's damage offset defense by excluding from the jury's consideration in calculating damages the benefits which the Raiders incurred as a result of the NFL's anticompetitive behavior. The court based its decision in part on what it described as a

> non-fault based offset theory [which] is simply a corollary of the general principle, applicable outside the antitrust context, that an award of damages should put a plaintiff forward into the position it would have been "but for" the defendant's violation of the law * * *. Under this theory, the ultimate relief awarded must take into account any benefits which would not have been received by plaintiff "but for" the defendant's anticompetitive conduct, or amounts a plaintiff would have expended in the absence of the violation. An antitrust plaintiff may recover only to the "net" extent of its injury; if benefits accrued to it because of an antitrust violation, those benefits must be deducted from the gross damages caused by the illegal conduct.

Los Angeles Memorial, 791 F.2d at 1367. Under this offset theory, Minpeco would be entitled only to its "net" economic injury and would be required to subtract from its gross damages on the futures market any benefits which accrued to it on its physical silver holdings.

Minpeco responds that its damages should not be subject to an offset under the rationale of the Supreme Court's decision in *Randall v. Loftsgaarden,* 478 U.S. 647, 106 S.Ct. 3143, 92 L.Ed.2d 525 (1986). In *Loftsgaarden* a group of investors in a tax shelter real estate scheme brought a securities fraud action seeking rescissionary damages from the general partner. The Court of Appeals for the Eighth Circuit held that under an "actual damages principle," an award of rescissionary damages must be " 'reduced by any value received as a result of the fraudulent transaction,' " *Austin v. Loftsgaarden,* 675 F.2d 168, 181 (8th Cir.1982) (quoting *Garnatz v. Stifel, Nicolaus & Co.,* 559 F.2d 1357, 1360 (8th Cir.1977), *cert. denied,* 435 U.S. 951, 98 S.Ct. 1578, 55 L.Ed.2d 801 (1978)), *rev'd, Randall v. Loftsgaarden,* 478 U.S. 647, 106 S.Ct. 3143, 92 L.Ed.2d 525 (1986), and held that the district court had erred in refusing to reduce plaintiff's damage award by an amount equal to any tax benefits they received as a result of the investment.

The Supreme Court reversed. Stating that "this Court has never interpreted [the 'actual damages' limitation of § 28(a) of the 1934 Act] as imposing a rigid requirement that every recovery * * * under the 1934 Act must be limited to the net economic harm suffered by the plaintiff," 106 S.Ct. at 3153, the Court explained that where appropriate to avoid unjust enrichment, § 28(a) has been interpreted to allow a plaintiff to recover the measure of the defendant's profits rather [sic] the plaintiff's loss:

> Thus, the mere fact that the receipt of tax benefits, plus a full recovery under a rescissionary measure of damages, may place a § 10(b) plaintiff in a better position than he would have been in absent the fraud, does not establish that the flexible limits of § 28(a) have been exceeded.

Id. The Court also justified its holding by explaining that:

> Congress' aim in enacting the 1934 Act was not confined solely to compensating defrauded investors. Congress intended to deter fraud and manipulative practices in the securities markets, and to ensure full disclosure of information material to investment decisions. This deterrent purpose is ill-served by a too rigid insistence on limiting plaintiffs to recovery of their "net economic loss." The effect of allowing a tax benefit offset would often be substantially to insulate those who commit securities frauds from any appreciable liability to defrauded investors. The resulting diminution in the incentives for tax shelter promoters to comply with the federal securities laws would seriously impair the deterrent value of private rights of action, which, we have emphasized, "provide 'a most effective weapon in the enforcement' of the securities laws and are a 'necessary supplement to Commission action.' "

Id. at 3154 (citations omitted).

Although defendants argue that *Loftsgaarden* "is a narrow holding limited to whether *tax* benefits—as distinguished from the receipt of income—should be offset against losses in a suit for rescissionary damages under the securities laws," [11] the extensive language quoted above does not appear to be so limited. *Loftsgaarden* may be fairly read as supporting the proposition that there is no rigid requirement that a plaintiff must always be limited to its net economic injury where such a limitation would be

11. Reply Memorandum in Support of Defendants' Motion for Summary Judgment Dismissing Minpeco's Damage Claims at 2 (Sept. 30, 1987).

inequitable or contrary to deterrent goals. However, Minpeco has made no showing that if an offset is imposed here defendants will be either unjustly enriched or sheltered from any "appreciable liability" as in *Loftsgaarden.* Indeed, as discussed below, Minpeco itself argues that its damages—even if limited to net economic injury—will still be significant if it proves its case at trial. In addition, any damages awarded to Minpeco may, of course, be subject to trebling.

I conclude that Minpeco's claimed damages on its silver futures positions must be offset by the measure of the increase in value which accrued to its own physical silver holdings—but not, as discussed below, those of its clients—as a result of defendants' allegedly manipulative behavior. It is Minpeco's burden to establish the size of the appropriate offset. Although the *Los Angeles Memorial Coliseum* court refers to a "damage offset defense," 791 F.2d at 1366, the accepted rule is that the plaintiff, because it bears the burden of proving its claim for damages, also bears the burden of proof with regard to the offset. * * *

As discussed below, however, the conclusion that Minpeco's damage calculations must take into account the appropriate offset does not allow summary judgment on Minpeco's "out-of-pocket" damage claims, because there remain numerous factual questions relating to such damage claims which must be resolved at trial.

b) Factual Issues for Trial [discussion omitted]

Notes and Questions

1. In King Grain Co. v. Caldwell Manufacturing Co., 820 F.Supp. 569 (D.Kan.1993) King Grain sued for injury to grain under both negligence and breach of warranty claims. It had received $150,000 in insurance proceeds for the damaged grain. The court said that the collateral source rule does not apply to contract actions and ruled:

> "Therefore it is unclear at this time whether the collateral source rule will apply in this case.
>
> "The benefits rule applies where the collateral source rule does not apply. Thus, the benefits rule applies in contract actions and in tort actions if the defendant conferred a benefit on the plaintiff that offsets the plaintiff's loss. The court disagrees, in part, with the plaintiff's argument that the benefits rule applies only if the defendant is the source of the benefit. Plaintiff's argument is correct with respect to tort actions. However, the amount of damages in a contract action is to be reduced by the amount of a benefit the plaintiff has received from a third party. * * *
>
> "When the benefits rule applies, the defendant is permitted to introduce evidence that plaintiff's claimed injury was also a benefit to the plaintiff, and the plaintiff's damages will be reduced by the amount of that benefit. In this case it is clear that plaintiff received a $150,000 benefit as a result of the damage to the grain and that a third party, namely Old Republic, was the source of that benefit. However, because it is not yet clear whether the case will be submitted to the trier of fact on a tort theory or on a contract theory, the court cannot hold that the benefits rule applies in this case. Therefore, the defendant is not entitled to summary judgment on the damages issue."

Id. at 573–74.

Should the $150,000 be treated differently depending upon whether the action in *King Grain* is brought in negligence or breach of warranty? Is the court in *McConal Aviation, supra* n. 4 at p. 241, correct that the collateral source rule applies to both contract and tort actions?

2. Section 920 of the Restatement (Second) of Torts * provides:

§ 920. Benefit to Plaintiff Resulting from Defendant's Tort

> When the defendant's tortious conduct has caused harm to the plaintiff or to his property and in so doing has conferred a special benefit to the interest of the plaintiff that was harmed, the value of the benefit conferred is considered in mitigation of damages, to the extent that this is equitable.

2. *Avoidable Consequences or Mitigation*

SNEAD v. HOLLOMAN

Court of Appeals of North Carolina, 1991.
101 N.C.App. 462, 400 S.E.2d 91.

On 19 February 1988, plaintiff was injured when the car he was driving collided with a 26–foot delivery van being driven by defendant, Jimmy Junior Holloman.

* * *

WYNN, JUDGE.

* * *

The defendants next assign as error the trial judge's failure to instruct the jury on the plaintiff's duty to mitigate personal injury damages. The defendants contend that the plaintiff failed to keep up the exercise regimen prescribed by his orthopedic surgeon, and that such failure justified a jury instruction on the duty to mitigate personal injury damages.

To support their contention, the defendants rely upon the doctrine of unavoidable consequences which was defined by the North Carolina Supreme Court as follows:

> The rule in North Carolina is that an injured plaintiff, whether his case be in tort or contract, must exercise reasonable care and diligence to avoid or lessen the consequences of the defendant's wrong. If he fails to do so, for any part of the loss incident to such failure, no recovery can be had. This rule is known as the doctrine of unavoidable consequences or the duty to minimize damages. Failure to minimize damages does not bar the remedy; it goes only to the amount of damages recoverable.

Miller v. Miller, 273 N.C. 228, 239, 160 S.E.2d 65, 73–4 (1968) (citations omitted).

This court has also addressed this issue by stating that "[d]amages will not be reduced merely because the injured party fails to follow the medical advice given. All he must do is to act reasonably concerning the advice which he receives. Since the test is one of reasonableness, * * * it is a jury question except in the clearest of cases." *Radford v. Norris,* 63 N.C.App. 501, 502–3, 305 S.E.2d 64, 65 (1983), *disc. review denied,* 314 N.C. 117, 332 S.E.2d 483 (1985) (citations omitted).

In *Radford,* the issue was whether the trial judge erred in failing to instruct the jury on the plaintiff's duty to minimize damages. There, the plaintiff, who was injured in a collision with the defendant, consulted an orthopedic surgeon who prescribed a program of back exercises as part of the treatment for plaintiff's back injury. The plaintiff testified that he attempted to do the exercises in the beginning, but stopped doing them because they were too painful. The orthopedic surgeon testified that the back exercises were routine and were designed to work out stiffness and pain in the plaintiff's back. When the plaintiff advised the doctor that he had discontinued the exercises, the doctor repeatedly advised the plaintiff to resume the exercises. The doctor further testified that although he could not say with a reasonable degree of medical certainty that the exercises would have cured the plaintiff's back pain had they been performed regularly, he knew the exercises would make the pain better. Nonetheless, the plaintiff did not resume the regimen.

The *Radford* court held that the above evidence tended to show that the plaintiff's regular and continued performance of the exercises would have alleviated the pain and, thus, the pain was a consequence that may have been avoided. *Id.* at 503, 305 S.E.2d at 65. Since the defendant in *Radford* properly requested an instruction on avoidable consequences which was improperly denied, the *Radford* court remanded the case for a jury determination of the reasonableness of plaintiff's failure to follow his doctor's advice.

We are unable to make a meaningful distinction between the facts in *Radford* and those present here. In the instant case, the plaintiff's orthopedic surgeon, Dr. Tejpal Singh Dhillon, prescribed a certain exercise regimen which the plaintiff, for some unexplained reason, discontinued performing after one month. In his deposition, which was read into evidence at trial, Dr. Dhillon testified that the exercises were designed to "relieve the [plaintiff's back] spasm and [to] make some more room for the nerves to get through to ease the irritation of the nerves." He further testified that he continued to prescribe the exercises for the plaintiff on at least two occasions after the plaintiff ceased performing them.

* * * Since the defendants properly requested that the jury be instructed on the plaintiff's duty to minimize damages, we conclude that the trial judge's failure to so instruct the jury was reversible error under the holding in *Radford.* Accordingly, we remand this case for a new trial on the issue of damages.

Notes and Questions

1. Must a plaintiff endure short term pain to possibly alleviate future pain?

2. Is the refusal to lose weight a failure to avoid the consequences of defendant's action? Consider Aisole v. Dean, 574 So.2d 1248, 1253–54 (La. 1991):

> "In their reply brief, the defendants request a reduction in damages based on the plaintiff's failure to mitigate. Specifically, the defendants contend that because Mrs. Aisole is overweight [9] and did not attempt to lose weight at the suggestion of her doctors, she breached her duty to mitigate damages. The defendants maintain the plaintiff's pre-existing condition did not exacerbate her injuries but rather prevented her prompt recovery.
>
> "It is a well-established principle of law that a tortfeasor takes his victim as he finds him and although the damages caused are greater because of the victims' prior condition which is aggravated by the tort, the tortfeasor is nevertheless responsible for the consequences of his tort. Thames v. Zerangue, 411 So.2d 17, 19 (La.1982); Walton v. William Wolf Baking Co., Inc., 406 So.2d 168, 175 (La.1981). Our jurisprudence has also recognized that an injured plaintiff has a duty to take reasonable steps to mitigate damages. Pisciotta v. Allstate Ins. Co., 385 So.2d 1176, 1182 (La.1979); Dunaway v. Rester Refrigeration Service, Inc., 428 So.2d 1064, 1071 (La.App. 1st Cir.1983), writ denied, 433 So.2d 1056 (La.1983); Reeves v. Louisiana and Arkansas Railway Co., 304 So.2d 370, 375 (La.App. 1st Cir.1974), writ denied, 305 So.2d 123 (La.1974). Reading these two doctrines together, we conclude that although a tortfeasor takes his victim as he finds him at the time of the injury, after that time, the victim has an affirmative responsibility to make every reasonable effort to mitigate damages.
>
> "Our decision regarding this issue of first impression is consistent with the court's holding in Muller v. Lykes Bros. Steamship Co., 337 F.Supp. 700 (E.D.La.1972), aff'd, 468 F.2d 951 (5th Cir.1972), in which an obese plaintiff's recovery was diminished because he neglected his duty to mitigate damages by failing to follow medical advice that he reduce his weight.[10]"

See also Tanberg v. Ackerman Investment Co., 473 N.W.2d 193, 196 (Iowa 1991) (plaintiff does not need to actually lose weight but must reasonably attempt to do so to mitigate damages).

3. If a plaintiff must try to lose weight to mitigate damages, must the plaintiff also retrain? Hale v. Aetna Life and Casualty Insurance Co., 580 So.2d 1053, 1056 (La.App. 3d Cir.1991) said:

> "The trial judge obviously believed that the plaintiff's failure to regain his pre-accident earning capacity during the four years preceding trial was a failure to mitigate his damages. We have been cited no case and have been unable to find one, that says that an individual fails to mitigate his damages if he does not go to college or otherwise retrain himself, and

9. At the time of the accident, the plaintiff was 5′1″ tall and weighed 245 pounds. At trial, the plaintiff weighed 250 pounds.

10. *See also,* Marshbank v. Austin Bridge Co., 669 S.W.2d 129 (Tex.Ct.App.1984) (jury award not inadequate because jury could have concluded that appellant had not mitigated damages by losing weight as advised); Butler v. Anderson, 163 Ga.App. 547, 295 S.E.2d 216 (1982) (no error in jury charge that an injured plaintiff is under a duty to lessen damages by following physician's advise to lose weight).

thereby acquire the capability of earning the same income he enjoyed before suffering an accident which rendered him incapable of returning to his former employment"

Are training and losing weight different? Which is easier?

4. What policies are served by the avoidable consequences rule?

SECTION 5. PUNITIVE AND LIQUIDATED DAMAGES

A. TORT

TXO PRODUCTION CORPORATION v. ALLIANCE RESOURCES CORPORATION

Supreme Court of the United States, 1993.
___ U.S. ___, 113 S.Ct. 2711, 125 L.Ed.2d 366.

JUSTICE STEVENS announced the judgment of the Court and delivered an opinion in which THE CHIEF JUSTICE and JUSTICE BLACKMUN join, and in which JUSTICE KENNEDY joins as to Parts I and IV.

In a common-law action for slander of title, respondents obtained a judgment against petitioner for $19,000 in actual damages and $10 million in punitive damages. The question we granted certiorari to decide is whether that punitive damages award violates the Due Process Clause of the Fourteenth Amendment, either because its amount is excessive or because it is the product of an unfair procedure.

[TXO, a large company engaged in oil and gas production in 25 States, purchased a 1,002 acre tract from Alliance in 1985. TXO's geologists had concluded that the tract would be extremely profitable. TXO agreed to pay Alliance $20 per acre in cash, plus 22 per cent of oil and gas revenues as a royalty.

Soon thereafter, TXO discovered a 1958 deed in which a predecessor in interest of Alliance had conveyed certain mineral rights in the tract. That deed made clear on its face that oil and gas were not conveyed, and TXO through interviews of persons concerned in the 1958 transaction confirmed that none claimed an interest in the oil or gas. Nonetheless, TXO unsuccessfully tried to induce a firm in the chain of title to claim that it had an interest in the oil and gas, and asked the predecessor to sign a false affidavit claiming that the 1958 deed covered oil and gas. TXO paid the predecessor $6,000 for a quitclaim deed, which it used to try to get Alliance to renegotiate downward its royalty, implying that it obtained title from the predecessor rather than from Alliance. When Alliance would not agree, TXO, with the same objective, brought a declaratory judgment action it knew was frivolous.]

I

On August 23, 1985, TXO Production Corp. (TXO) commenced this litigation by filing a complaint in the Circuit Court of McDowell County, West Virginia, for a declaratory judgment removing a cloud on title to an interest in oil and gas development rights. Respondents, including Alliance Resources Corp. (Alliance), filed a counterclaim for slander of title that went to trial before a jury in June 1990. The jury verdict in respondents' favor, which has been affirmed by the Supreme Court of Appeals of West Virginia, makes it appropriate to accept respondents' version of disputed issues of fact.

* * *

TXO's declaratory judgment action was decided on the basis of the parties' written submissions. * * * [T]he court found that TXO had asserted a claim to title to the oil and gas under the Blevins Tract by virtue of the quitclaim deed * * * but that the deed was a "nullity."

The counterclaim for slander of title was subsequently tried to a jury. In addition to the evidence that TXO knew that Alliance had good title to the oil and gas and that TXO had acted in bad faith when it advanced a claim on the basis of the worthless quitclaim deed in an effort to renegotiate its royalty arrangement, Alliance introduced evidence showing that TXO was a large company in its own right and a wholly owned subsidiary of an even larger company; that the anticipated gross revenues from oil and gas development—and therefore the amount of royalties that TXO sought to renegotiate—were substantial; and that TXO had engaged in similar nefarious activities in its business dealings in other parts of the country. * * *

The jury's verdict of $19,000 in actual damages was based on Alliance's cost of defending the declaratory judgment action. It is fair to infer that the punitive damages award of $10 million was based on other evidence.

* * *

The State Supreme Court of Appeals affirmed.

The Court first disposed of the state law issues.[14] It introduced its discussion of the federal issue by describing the kinds of defendants against whom punitive damages had been awarded after our decision in *Haslip*.[15] Turning to the facts of this case, the Court stated that the application of its

14. "Slander of title," the Court noted, "long has been recognized as a common law cause of action." 187 W.Va., at 465, 419 S.E.2d, at 878. The Court found that respondents had demonstrated all the elements of the tort: That TXO, by recording the frivolous quitclaim deed, had published a false statement derogatory to respondents' title, had done so with "malice," and had caused special damages, here the attorneys fees, as a result of its attack on respondents' interest in the oil and gas development rights.

15. "We have examined all of the punitive damages opinions issued since *Haslip* was decided in an attempt to find some pattern in what courts find reasonable. Generally, the cases fall into three categories: (1) really stupid defendants; (2) really mean defendants; and, (3) really stupid defendants who could have caused a great deal of harm by their actions but who actually caused minimal harm." *Id.*, at 474–475, 419 S.E.2d, at 887–886. In a concurring opinion two Justices criticized that categorization and stated that West Virginia's traditional rule summarizing the type of conduct that would give rise to punitive damages was better stated in the following syllabus:

> " 'In actions of tort, where gross fraud, malice, oppression, or wanton, willful, or reckless conduct or criminal indifference to civil obligations affecting the rights of others appear, or where legislative enactment authorizes, it, the jury may assess exemplary, punitive, or vindictive damages * * *.' " *Id.*, at 484, 419 S.E.2d, at 895.

"reasonable relationship" [between actual and potential damages] test required it to consider these three factors:

> "(1) the potential harm that TXO's actions could have caused; (2) the maliciousness of TXO's actions; and (3) the penalty necessary to discourage TXO from undertaking such endeavors in the future." 187 W.Va., at 476, 419 S.E.2d, at 889.

It held that each of those factors supported the award in this case, stating:

> "The type of *fraudulent* action *intentionally* undertaken by TXO in this case could potentially cause millions of dollars in damages to other victims. As for the reprehensibility of TXO's conduct, we can say no more than we have already said, and we believe the jury's verdict says more than we could say in an opinion twice this length. Just as important, an award of this magnitude is necessary to discourage TXO from continuing its pattern and practice of fraud, trickery and deceit." *Ibid.* (emphasis in original).

We granted certiorari, 506 U.S. ___, 113 S.Ct. 594, 121 L.Ed.2d 532 (1992), and now affirm.

II

TXO first argues that a $10 million punitive damages award—an award 526 times greater than the actual damages awarded by the jury—is so excessive that it must be deemed an arbitrary deprivation of property without due process of law.

* * *

Relying heavily on the plurality opinion in *Schad v. Arizona,* 501 U.S. ___, 111 S.Ct. 2491, 115 L.Ed.2d 555 (1991), petitioner argues that " 'history and widely shared practice [are] concrete indicators of what fundamental fairness and rationality require,' " * * * and that therefore we should examine, as "objective" criteria of fairness, (1) awards of punitive damages upheld against other defendants in the same jurisdiction, (2) awards upheld for similar conduct in other jurisdictions, (3) legislative penalty decisions with respect to similar conduct, and (4) the relationship of prior punitive awards to the associated compensatory awards. Brief for Petitioner 16. Under petitioner's proposed framework, when this inquiry demonstrates that an award "exceeds the bounds of contemporary and historical practice by *orders of magnitude,*" *id.,* at 21 (emphasis in original), that award must be struck down as arbitrary and excessive unless there is a "compelling and particularized justification" for an award of such size.

The parties' desire to formulate a "test" for determining whether a particular punitive award is "grossly excessive" is understandable. Nonetheless, we find neither formulation satisfactory. Under respondents' rational basis standard, apparently *any* award that would serve the legitimate state interest in deterring or punishing wrongful conduct, no matter how large, would be acceptable. On the other hand, we reject the premise underlying TXO's invocation of heightened scrutiny. The review of a jury's award for arbitrariness and the review of legislation surely are significantly different. Still, it is not correct to assume that the safeguards in the legislative process have no counterpart in the judicial process. The members of the jury were determined to be impartial before they were allowed to sit, their assessment of damages was the product of collective deliberation based on evidence and the arguments of adversaries, their award was reviewed and upheld by the trial judge who also heard the testimony, and it was affirmed by a unanimous decision of the State Supreme Court of Appeals. Assuming that fair procedures were followed, a judgment that is a product of that process is entitled to a strong presumption of validity. * * *

* * *

In the end, then, in determining whether a particular award is so "grossly excessive" as to violate the Due Process Clause of the Fourteenth Amendment, *Waters–Pierce Oil Co.,* 212 U.S., at 111, 29 S.Ct., at 227, we return to what we said two Terms ago in *Haslip:* "We need not, and indeed we cannot, draw a mathematical bright line between the constitutionally acceptable and the constitutionally unacceptable that would fit every case. We can say, however, that [a] general concer[n] of reasonableness * * * properly enter[s] into the constitutional calculus." 499 U.S., at 18, 111 S.Ct., at 1043.

* * *

III

In support of its submission that this award is "grossly excessive," TXO places its primary emphasis on the fact that it is over 526 times as large as the actual damages award. * * *

That relationship, however, was only one of several factors that the State Court mentioned in its *Garnes* [v. Fleming Landfill, Inc. 186 W.Va. 656 413 S.E.2d 89 (1991)] opinion. Earlier in its opinion it gave this example:

> "For instance, a man wildly fires a gun into a crowd. By sheer chance, no one is injured and the only damage is to a $10 pair of glasses. A jury reasonably could find only $10 in compensatory damages, but thousands of dollars in punitive damages to teach a duty of care. We would allow a jury to impose substantial punitive damages in order to discourage future bad acts." *Id.,* at 661, 413 S.E.2d, at 902 (citing C. Morris, Punitive Damages in Tort Cases, 44 Harv.L.Rev. 1173, 1181 (1931)).

When the Court identified the several factors that should be mentioned in instructions to the jury, the first one that it mentioned reflected that example. It said:

> "Punitive damages should bear a reasonable relationship to the harm *that is likely to occur from the defendant's conduct* as well as to the harm that actually has occurred. If the defendant's actions caused *or would likely cause* in a similar situation only slight harm, the damages should be relatively small. If the harm is grievous, the damages should be much greater." 186 W.Va., at 668, 413 S.E.2d, at 909 (emphasis added).

* * *

Thus, both State Supreme Courts and this Court have eschewed an approach that concentrates entirely on the relationship between actual and punitive damages. It is appropriate to consider the magnitude of the *potential harm* that the defendant's conduct would have caused to its intended victim if the wrongful plan had succeeded, as well as the possible harm to other victims that might have resulted if similar future behavior were not deterred.

* * *

While petitioner stresses the shocking disparity between the punitive award and the compensatory award, that shock dissipates when one considers the potential loss to respondents, in terms of reduced or eliminated royalties payments, had petitioner succeeded in its illicit scheme. Thus, even if the actual value of the "potential harm" to respondents is not between $5.0 million and $8.3 million, but is closer to $4 million, or $2 million, or even $1 million, the disparity between the punitive award and the potential harm does not, in our view, "jar one's constitutional sensibilities." *Haslip,* 499 U.S., at 18, 111 S.Ct., at 1043.

* * *

The punitive damages award in this case is certainly large, but in light of the amount of money potentially at stake, the bad faith of petitioner, the fact that the scheme employed in this case was part of a larger pattern of fraud, trickery and deceit, and petitioner's wealth, we are not persuaded that the award was so "grossly excessive" as to be beyond the power of the State to allow.

IV

* * *

We agree with TXO that the emphasis on the wealth of the wrongdoer increased the risk that the award may have been influenced by prejudice against large corporations, a risk that is of special concern when the defendant is a nonresident.

* * * We note, however, that in *Haslip* we referred to the "financial position" of the defendant as one factor that could be taken into account in assessing punitive damages, * * * Because TXO's constitutional attack on the jury instructions was not properly presented to the highest court of the State, * * * we do not pass on it.

* * *

Petitioner's criticism of the West Virginia Supreme Court of Appeals' opinion is based largely on the Court's colorful reference to classes of "really mean" and "really stupid" defendants. That those terms played little, if any, part in its actual evaluation of the propriety of the damages award is evident from the reasoning in its thorough opinion, succinctly summarized in passages we have already quoted.

* * *

The judgment of the West Virginia Supreme Court of Appeals is affirmed.

It is so ordered.

JUSTICE KENNEDY, concurring in part and concurring in the judgment.

* * *

I agree that the approaches proposed by the parties to this case are unsatisfactory, * * * but I do not believe that the plurality's replacement, a general focus on the "reasonableness" of the award, * * * quoting *Pacific Mutual Life Ins. Co. v. Haslip,* 499 U.S. 1, 18, 111 S.Ct. 1032, 1043, 113 L.Ed.2d 1 (1991), is a significant improvement. To ask whether a particular award of punitive damages is grossly excessive begs the question: excessive in relation to what? The answer excessive in relation to the conduct of the tortfeasor may be correct, but it is unhelpful, for we are still bereft of any standard by which to compare the punishment to the malefaction that gave rise to it. A reviewing court employing this formulation comes close to relying upon nothing more than its own subjective reaction to a particular punitive damages award in deciding whether the award violates the Constitution. This type of review, far from imposing meaningful, law-like restraints on jury excess, could become as fickle as the process it is designed to superintend. Furthermore, it might give the illusion of judicial certainty where none in fact exists, and, in so doing, discourage legislative intervention that might prevent unjust punitive awards.

As I have suggested before, see *id.,* at 41, 111 S.Ct., at 1054 (KENNEDY, J., concurring in judgment), a more manageable constitutional inquiry focuses not on the amount of money a jury awards in a particular case but on its reasons for doing so. The Constitution identifies no particular multiple of compensatory damages as an acceptable limit for punitive awards; it does not concern itself with dollar amounts, ratios, or the quirks of juries in specific jurisdictions. Rather, its fundamental guarantee is that the individual citizen may rest secure against arbitrary or irrational deprivations of property. When a punitive damages award reflects bias, passion, or prejudice on the part of the jury, rather than a rational concern for deterrence and retribution, the Constitution has been violated, no matter what the absolute or relative size of the award. Justice O'Connor is correct in observing that in implementing this principle, courts have often looked to the size of the award as one indication that it resulted from bias, passion, or prejudice, see *post,* at 2729–2731, but that is not the sole, or even necessarily the most important, sign. Other objective indicia of the type discussed by the plurality, * * * as well as direct evidence from the trial record, are also helpful in ascertaining whether a jury stripped a party of its property in an arbitrary way and not in accordance with the standards of rationality and fairness the Constitution requires.

* * *

On its facts, this case is close and difficult; Justice O'Connor makes a plausible argument, based on the record and the trial court's instructions, that the size of the punitive award is explained by the jury's raw, redistributionist impulses stemming from antipathy to a wealthy, out-of-state, corporate defendant. * * * There is, however, another explanation for the jury verdict, one supported by the record and relied upon by the state courts, that persuades me that I cannot say with sufficient confidence that the award was unjustified or improper on this record: TXO acted with malice.

* * *

JUSTICE SCALIA, with whom JUSTICE THOMAS joins, concurring in the judgment.

The jury in this case was instructed on the purposes of punitive damages under West Virginia law, and its award was reviewed for reasonableness by the trial court and the West Virginia Supreme Court of Appeals. Traditional American practice governing the imposition of punitive damages requires no more. * * * It follows, in my view, that petitioner's claims under the Due Process Clause of the Fourteenth Amendment must fail. I therefore have no difficulty joining the Court's judgment.

I do not, however, join the plurality opinion, since it makes explicit what was implicit in *Haslip:* the existence of a so-called "substantive due process" right that punitive damages be reasonable.

* * *

* * * The Court's continued assertion that federal judges have *some,* almost-never-usable, power to impose a standard of "reasonable punitive damages" through the clumsy medium of the Due Process Clause serves only to spawn wasteful litigation, and to reduce the incentives for the proper institutions of our society to undertake that task.

JUSTICE O'CONNOR, with whom JUSTICE WHITE joins, and with whom JUSTICE SOUTER joins as to Parts II–B–2, II–C, III, and IV, dissenting.

In *Pacific Mutual Life Ins. Co. v. Haslip,* 499 U.S. 1, 111 S.Ct. 1032, 113 L.Ed.2d 1 (1991), this Court held out the promise that punitive damages awards would receive sufficient constitutional scrutiny to restore fairness in what is rapidly becoming an arbitrary and oppressive system. Today the Court's judgment renders *Haslip*'s promise a false one. The procedures that converted this commercial dispute into a $10 million punitive verdict were wholly inadequate. Rather than producing a judgment founded on verifiable criteria, they produced a monstrous award—526 times actual damages and over 20 times greater than any punitive award in West Virginia history. Worse, the State Supreme Court of Appeals rejected petitioner's challenge with only cursory analysis, observing that petitioner, rather than being "really stupid," had been "really mean." 187 W.Va. 457, 474–475, 419 S.E.2d 870, 887–889 (1992). The court similarly refused to consider the possibility of remittitur because petitioner "and its agents and servants failed to conduct themselves as gentlemen." *Id.,* at 462, 419 S.E.2d, at 875. In my view, due process does not tolerate such cavalier standards when so much is at stake. Because I believe that neither this award's size nor the procedures that produced it are consistent with the principles this Court articulated in *Haslip,* I respectfully dissent.

I

Our system of justice entrusts jurors—ordinary citizens who need not have any training in the law—with profoundly important determinations. Jurors decide not only civil matters, where the financial consequences may be great, but also criminal cases, where the liberty or perhaps life of the defendant hangs in the balance.

* * *

But jurors are not infallible guardians of the public good. They are ordinary citizens whose decisions can be shaped by influences impermissible in our system of justice. In fact, they are more susceptible to such influences than judges.

* * *

* * * But fundamental fairness requires that impermissible influences such as bias and prejudice be discovered nonetheless, by inference if not by direct proof. As a result, courts at common law in England traditionally would strike any award that appeared so grossly disproportionate as to evidence caprice, passion, or bias.

* * *

* * * This Court similarly has recognized that the requirement of proportionality is implicit in the notion of due process.

* * *

A

In my view, due process at least requires judges to engage in searching review where the verdict discloses such great disproportions as to suggest the possibility of bias, caprice, or passion.

* * *

B

* * *

But even if we assume that the plurality's estimates of potential harm are plausible or supported by the evidence, they are, on this record, entirely irrelevant.

* * *

C

There is another explanation for the verdict, but it is not one that permits affirmance. As I read the record in this case, it seems quite likely that the jury in fact was unduly influenced by the fact that TXO is a very large, out-of-state corporation.

* * *

That a jury might have such inclinations should come as no surprise. Courts long have recognized that jurors may view large corporations with great disfavor. * * * Corporations are mere abstractions and, as such, are unlikely to be viewed with much sympathy. Moreover, they often represent a large accumulation of productive resources; jurors naturally think little of taking an otherwise large sum of money out of what appears to be an enormously larger pool of wealth. Finally, juries may feel privileged to correct perceived social ills stemming from unequal wealth distribution by transferring money from "wealthy" corporations to comparatively needier plaintiffs.

* * *

This is not to say that consideration of a defendant's wealth is unconstitutional. To be sure, there are strong economic arguments that permitting juries to consider wealth is unwise if not irrational * * *. But, "[j]ust as the Fourteenth Amendment does not enact Herbert Spencer's Social Statics, see *Lochner v. New York,* 198 U.S. 45, 75, 25 S.Ct. 539, 546, 49 L.Ed. 937 (1905) (Holmes, J., dissenting)," it does not require us to adopt the views of the Law and Economics school either. As a historical matter, the wealth of the perpetrator long has been thought relevant. See *Browning–Ferris,* 492 U.S., at 300, 109 S.Ct. at 2933 (O'Connor, J., concurring in part and dissenting in part) (citing the Magna Carta and Blackstone's Commentaries).

* * *

Nonetheless, courts must have authority to recognize the special danger of bias that such considerations create.

* * *

The risk of prejudice was especially grave here. The jury repeatedly was told of TXO's extraordinary resources, which respondents estimated at $2 billion. To make matters worse, unlike the jurors or the primary plaintiffs, TXO was not from West Virginia. It was an interloper, from the large State of Texas. * * *

Counsels' arguments, however, converted that grave risk of prejudice into a near certainty. Repeatedly they reminded the jury that TXO was from another State. Repeatedly they told the jury about TXO's massive wealth. And repeatedly they told the jury that it could do anything it thought "fair." The opening line from rebuttal set the tone. "Ladies and gentleman of the jury," one attorney began, "this greedy bunch from down in Texas still doesn't understand this case." * * * Playing on images of Texans as overrich gamblers who profit by chance rather than work, he referred to TXO shortly thereafter as a bunch of "Texas high rollers, wildcatters."

* * *

"Well, what is fair? * * * If someone *comes to town* and intentionally doesn't put a quarter in the meter, stays here all day, [in this] *town that needs it to pay for the police force and the fire department,* they give [him] a fine. And at the end of the day [he] may have to pay a dollar. That person reaches in his billfold at the end of the day and maybe *he's got a hundred bucks in there.* He doesn't want to have to pay that dollar, but he does, because he knows if he doesn't [he'll have legal problems] * * *. The town didn't take everything from the individual, didn't ruin [him], just took one percent of what that person had in cash. One percent. *You can fine TXO one percent if you want, you can fine them one dollar if you want.* But I submit to you a one percent fine, the same as John Doe on this street, would be fair. *That's twelve and a half million dollars, based on what they had left over. And their earnings w[ere] $225,000,000.00 [per year].* I mean, yeah, their cash flow. Their surplus. So anything between twelve and a half million and twenty-two million is only one percent—the same as this poor guy who just tried to cheat a little bit. Now that's a lot of money. I hope, like I said, you *don't analyze this on a lot or a little, but fair.*" *Id.*, at 781–782 (emphases added).

* * *

Given the absence of another plausible explanation for this monumentally large punitive damages award, I believe it likely, if not inescapable, that the jury was influenced unduly by TXO's out-of-state status and its large resources.

* * *

III

[Here Justice O'Connor urged that the West Virginia courts failed either to check excessive awards "by conducting comparative analysis and applying detailed substantive standards", or to provide meaningful post-trial judicial review of such awards.]

IV

As little as 30 years ago, punitive damages awards were "rarely assessed" and usually "small in amount." Ellis, 56 S.Cal.L.Rev., at 2. Recently, however, the frequency and size of such awards have been skyrocketing. One commentator has observed that "hardly a month goes by without a multimillion-dollar punitive damages verdict in a product liability case." * * * The increased frequency and size of punitive awards, however, has not been matched by a corresponding expansion of procedural protections or predictability. On the contrary, although some courts have made genuine efforts at reform, many courts continue to provide jurors with skeletal guidance that permits the traditional guarantor of fairness—the jury itself—to be converted into a source of caprice and bias. This Court's decision in *Haslip* promised that, even if juries occasionally failed to fulfill their function faithfully, trial and appellate courts would provide meaningful review sufficient to discern impermissible influences and guarantee constitutional results. In my view, today's decision fails to make good on that promise. I therefore respectfully dissent.

Notes and Questions

1. Can you think of a concrete situation in which the difference in approach in *TXO* between Justice Kennedy and the other members of the plurality would bring differing results?

2. What problems are created by large punitive damages awards? What benefits do they have? If you were a state legislator, what punitive damages scheme would you recommend for your state? *See, e.g.,* Beverly Enterprises of Texas, Inc. v. Leath, 829 S.W.2d 382 (Tex.App.1992) (interpreting "actual damages" in statute that limits punitive damages to four times actuals).

3. In Dunn v. Hovic, 1 F.3d 1371 (3d Cir.) (*en banc*), *cert. denied sub nom.* Owens-Corning Fiberglas Corp. v. Dunn, ___ U.S. ___, 114 S.Ct. 650, 126 L.Ed.2d 608 (1993), a jury awarded a pipe installer exposed to asbestos $1.3 million in compensatory damages and $25 million in punitive damages. The district judge remitted the damages to $500,000 and $2 million, respectively. In an en banc opinion an 8–5 majority of the Third Circuit held that this defendant had not proved that the multiple punitive damage awards by successive juries in separate cases arising from the same conduct had violated due process but remitted the punitive damages further to $1 million.

The court applied Section 908(2) of the Restatement (Second) of Torts that provides that "[p]unitive damages may be awarded for conduct that is outrageous, because of the defendant's evil motive or his reckless indifference to the rights of others." The majority held that the defendant had failed to prove the aggregate of all of its punitive damage awards and thus had failed to show that that amount had exceeded the amount necessary to punish and deter. The majority also held that the defendant had not proven that it would be unable to pay future awards of compensatory or punitive damages. *Id.* However, in remitting the punitive damages award further the court said, "we take into consideration all the factors listed in comment e to Restatement of Torts (Second) § 908: the defendant's wealth, its act, the extent of harm, the multiplicity of claims, and, as approved in *Haslip*, the awards of punitive damages in similar cases." *Id.* at 1391.

With respect to the due process validity of multiple awards in general the majority said:

> "In concluding that multiple punitive damages awards are not inconsistent with the due process clause or substantive tort law principles, both state and federal courts have recognized that no single court can fashion an effective response to the national problem flowing from mass exposure to asbestos products. Indeed, these courts have noted the arbitrariness of imposing a cap on punitive damages awards in only a single jurisdiction.
>
> * * *
>
> "We refrain from adopting such an activist role on what is essentially a policy matter, and believe that insofar as OCF would have us enunciate a prohibition of successive claims of punitive damages in mass tort litigation as a matter of Virgin Islands law, that decision is best left to the United States Congress or the legislature of the Virgin Islands.
>
> "To the extent that OCF claims that punitive damages in asbestos cases are as a general matter unconstitutional, we are not persuaded by its arguments. Although we recognize that some courts and commentators have called for the abolition of punitive damages altogether, *see, e.g.,* John Dwight Ingram, Punitive Damages Should Be Abolished, 17 Cap.U.L.Rev. 205 (1988); James B. Sales & Kenneth B. Cole, Jr., Punitive Damages: A Relic That Has Outlived Its Origins, 37 Land.L.Rev. 1117 (1984), that position is not without its critics. In fact, the prevalent notion that we are

facing skyrocketing or runaway punitive awards, E. Barrett Prettyman, Jr., Punitive Damages, in A Plan to Improve America's System of Civil Justice From the President's Council on Competitiveness 75, 83 (1992), has been challenged by several commentators. *See* Michael Rustad, Demystifying Punitive Damages in Products Liability Cases: A Survey of a Quarter Century of Trial Verdicts 28 (Papers of the Roscoe Pound Found.1991) [hereinafter Demystifying Punitive Damages]; cf. Stephen Daniels & Joanne Martin, Myth and Reality in Punitive Damages, 75 Minn.L.Rev. 1, 13 (1990) [hereinafter Myth and Reality]; Michael J. Saks, Do We Really Know Anything About the Behavior of the Tort Litigation System—And Why Not?, 140 U.Pa.L.Rev. 1147, 1256 (1992) [hereinafter Behavior of the Tort System].

"One study reported that in those relatively rare cases in which punitive damages are awarded at all, these awards are frequently reduced on appellate review. Demystifying Punitive Damages at 30–32; Behavior of the Tort System, 140 U.Pa.L.Rev. at 1258–62. Another study concluded that '[t]he difference between punitive damages awarded and punitive damages paid is often dramatic.' Demystifying Punitive Damages at 32. Finally, OCF itself candidly admits that in the vast majority of the asbestos cases against it which go to trial, plaintiffs come up empty. See Appellant's Supplemental Brief at 11 (citing App. at 1943); see also App. at 1842–939. We, of course, take no position on the debate regarding the issue of punitive damages in mass tort cases, but merely observe that the underlying facts appear to be far from clear, despite high-profile commentary in that connection.

"In his powerful dissent, Judge Weis has set forth numerous arguments against punitive damages in mass tort cases in general and in asbestos cases in particular. We decline to respond in kind because we do not believe that a judicial opinion of an intermediate appellate court is the appropriate forum for a debate on the policies for and against punitive damages. Indeed, those members of the in banc court supporting the judgment of the court may themselves have differing views on whether and when punitive damages should be awarded."

Id. at 1386–88.

Judge Weis, dissenting, believed that the defendant had proved approximately $20 million in punitive damages to date in other cases and believed that the punitive damages in this case were not needed to deter or punish. He said:

"Asbestos litigation is unique. The large number of persons exposed to asbestos has caused a proliferation of claims, the likes of which courts have never seen, causing serious concern that the traditional tort system cannot adequately process the litigation. As this Court said in In re School Asbestos Litigation, 789 F.2d 996, 1000 (3d Cir.1986), asbestos litigation presents 'an unparalleled situation in American tort law.'

"In 1986, an estimated 30,000 personal injury suits had been filed against asbestos manufacturers and producers. Id. That figure has since increased substantially. By 1990, 30,401 asbestos cases were pending in the federal courts alone, with about double that amount in the state courts, for a total of approximately 90,000 cases. Judicial Conference Ad Hoc Comm. on Asbestos Litig., Report to the Chief Justice of the United States and Members of the Judicial Conference of the United States (Mar. 1991), reprinted in Asbestos Litig. Rep., Mar. 14, 1991, at 22,698, 22,702–03.

* * *

"As might be expected, the flood of asbestos cases has taken its toll on the defendant asbestos manufacturers. The Ad Hoc Committee reported that of the twenty-five major asbestos companies, eleven had filed petitions in bankruptcy.

* * *

"The first of the major asbestos manufacturers to enter bankruptcy was Johns-Manville, which sought to use Chapter 11 essentially as a giant interpleader action. As part of the Manville reorganization, a trust was created to settle pending and future asbestos claims. Although the trust concept had the potential for equitably distributing assets to present and future claimants, the bankruptcy proceeding was itself very expensive and the results ultimately proved to be unsatisfactory.

"Even though punitive damages were not allowed, the trust was essentially insolvent after operating for only a year and a half.

* * *

"Subsequent claims and bankruptcy filings have increased the likelihood that future claimants will not be able to recover for their injuries.

* * *

"When considering punitive awards, several basic principles must be emphasized. First, punitive damages are designed for retribution and deterrence. 'They are not compensation for injury. Instead, they are private fines levied by civil juries to punish reprehensible conduct and to deter its future occurrence.' Gertz v. Robert Welch, Inc., 418 U.S. 323, 350 (1974). The fairness inherent in due process requires that punitive assessments not exceed those amounts necessary to inflict retribution and prevent reoccurrence. *See, e.g.,* Vasbinder v. Scott, 976 F.2d 118, 121 (2d Cir.1992). When retribution and deterrence are accomplished without the imposition of punitive damages, use of that weapon is no longer justified.

"Second, punitive damages are a windfall. They do not reimburse losses that plaintiffs have suffered, but provide an amount over and above that necessary for fair compensation. *See, e.g.,* City of Newport v. Fact Concerts, Inc., 453 U.S. 247, 267 (1981).

"Third, there is no compelling reason why injured but fully compensated plaintiffs should receive punitive awards. The aims of retribution and deterrence can be accomplished by making punitive damages payable to the state. Indeed, nine states have enacted statutes that designate that a portion of any punitive award goes to the state, ranging from 20% in New York to 75% in Iowa and Georgia. * * *

"In the asbestos context, punitive awards are not needed for retribution and deterrence. Actually, there is little conduct to deter because few asbestos-containing products are still manufactured in the United States. * * *

"Moreover, the avalanche of compensatory claims against asbestos manufacturers has surely served as more of a punishment and deterrent than individual punitive assessments in isolated cases against manufacturers of other types of products. As one judge has explained: No manufacturer could engage consciously in wrongdoing that would expose it to such overwhelming strict liability with any reasonable expectation of doing so profitably. On the contrary, the prospect of exposure to massive litigation in strict liability provides the impetus for manufacturers to take affirmative steps to ensure the safety of their products, since mere non-negligent behavior is no guarantee against strict liability. The significance of punitive damages as a deterrent depends upon the size of the penalty increase relative to the 'base penalty' exacted by strict liability compensatory awards."

Id. at 1393–97.

Is the Third Circuit's decision a logical application of the holding of *TXO* that no single bright-line test is appropriate in determining the excessiveness of punitive damage awards?

Note that the court relied on the very factors held insufficient to impose due process clause limitations on punitive damage awards to justify a remittitur of most of the award. Is this adequately explained by the differing role of courts in conducting post-trial review of punitive damage awards under state (or in *Hovic,* territorial) law, and in imposing constitutional limitations on such awards?

Should the reasoning of *TXO* be applied to mass torts at all?

4. If the defendant in *Hovic* had presented evidence that it would be unable to pay any more punitive damages awards, what should the court do? Is the first plaintiff to file suit more likely to recover punitive (and compensatory) damages than the last? Consider footnote 17 in *Hovic:*

"The Reporters' Study noted that two states have taken legislative action in this area. A Georgia statute, applicable to product liability claims in Georgia courts, allows only a single punitive award (the first to be obtained) for all claims arising out of the same conduct. *See* Ga.Code Ann. § 51–125.1(e) (Michie 1990). A Missouri statute, which applies to most tort claims in the state, allows the defendant in a post-trial hearing to request credit for prior punitive damages awards arising from the same conduct. *See* Mo.Ann.Stat. § 510.263(4) (Vernon 1952 & Supp.1992)."

5. Are the punishments and/or procedures imposed by the criminal law relevant in determining whether, or how much, to award punitive damages?

B. CONTRACT

Punitive damages are generally unavailable for a breach of contract unless the breach is accompanied by a tort. *See, e.g.* Pioneer Fuels, Inc. v. Montana–Dakota Utilities Co., Inc., 474 N.W.2d 706, 709–10 (N.D.1991). *See also* D. Dobbs, The Law of Remedies § 12.5(2) (2d ed. 1993). Consider how this rule is applied when parties attempt to agree on damages in the event of breach.

TRUCK RENT–A–CENTER, INC. v. PURITAN FARMS 2nd, INC.

Court of Appeals of New York, 1977.
41 N.Y.2d 420, 393 N.Y.S.2d 365, 361 N.E.2d 1015.

JASEN, JUDGE.

The principal issue on this appeal is whether a provision in a truck lease agreement which requires the payment of a specified amount of money to the lessor in the event of the lessee's breach is an enforceable liquidated damages clause, or, instead, provides for an unenforceable penalty.

Defendant Puritan Farms 2nd, Inc. (Puritan), was in the business of furnishing milk and milk products to customers through home delivery. In January, 1969, Puritan leased a fleet of 25 new milk delivery trucks from plaintiff Truck Rent–A–Center for a term of seven years commencing January 15, 1970. Under the provisions of a truck lease and service agreement entered into by the parties, the plaintiff was to supply the trucks and make all necessary repairs. Puritan was to pay an agreed upon weekly rental fee. It was understood that the lessor would finance the purchase of the trucks through a bank, paying the prime rate of interest on the date of the loan plus 2%. The rental charges on the trucks were to be adjusted in the event of a fluctuation in the interest rate above or below specified levels. The lessee was granted the right to purchase the trucks, at any time after 12 months following commencement of the lease, by paying to the lessor the amount then due and owing on the bank loan, plus an additional $100 per truck purchased.

Article 16 of the lease agreement provided that if the agreement should terminate prior to expiration of the term of the lease as a result of the lessee's breach, the lessor would be entitled to damages, "liquidated for all purposes", in the amount of all rentals that would have come due from the date of termination to the date of normal expiration of the term less the "re-rental value" of the vehicles, which was set at 50% of the rentals that would have become due. In effect, the lessee would be obligated to pay the lessor, as a consequence of breach, one half of all rentals that would have become due had the agreement run its full course. The agreement recited that, in arriving at the settled amount of damage, "the parties hereto have considered, among other factors, Lessor's substantial initial investment in purchasing or reconditioning for Lessee's service the demised motor vehicles, the uncertainty of Lessor's ability to re-enter the said vehicles, the costs to Lessor during any period the vehicles may remain idle until re-rented, or if sold, the uncertainty of the sales price and its possible attendant loss. The parties have also considered, among other factors, in so liquidating the said damages, Lessor's saving in expenditures for gasoline, oil and other service items."

* * *

Puritan tendered plaintiff a security deposit, consisting of four weeks' rent and the lease went into effect. After nearly three years, the lessee sought to terminate the lease agreement. On December 7, 1973, Puritan wrote to the lessor complaining that the lessor had not repaired and maintained the trucks as provided in the lease agreement. Puritan stated that it had "repeatedly notified" plaintiff of these defaults, but plaintiff had not cured them. Puritan, therefore, exercised its right to terminate the agreement "without any penalty and *without purchasing the trucks*". (Emphasis added.) On the date set for termination, December 14, 1973, plaintiff's attorneys replied to Puritan by letter to advise it that plaintiff believed it had fully performed its obligations under the lease and, in the event Puritan adhered to the announced breach, would commence proceedings to obtain the liquidated damages provided for in article 16 of the agreement. Nevertheless, Puritan had its drivers return the trucks to plaintiff's premises, where the bulk of them have remained ever since. At the time of termination, plaintiff owed $45,134.17 on the outstanding bank loan.

Plaintiff followed through on its promise to commence an action for the payment of the liquidated damages. Defendant counterclaimed for the return of its security deposit. At the nonjury trial, plaintiff contended that it had fully performed its obligations to maintain and repair the trucks. Moreover, it was submitted, Puritan sought to cancel the lease because corporations allied with Puritan had acquired the assets, including delivery trucks, of other dairies and Puritan believed it cheaper to utilize this "shadow fleet". The home milk delivery business was on the decline and plaintiff's president testified that efforts to either re-rent or sell the truck fleet to other dairies had not been successful. Even with modifications in the trucks, such as the removal of the milk racks and a change in the floor of the trucks, it was not possible to lease the trucks to other industries, although a few trucks were subsequently sold. The proceeds of the sales were applied to the reduction of the bank balance. The other trucks remained at plaintiff's premises, partially protected by a fence plaintiff erected to discourage vandals. The defendant countered with proof that plaintiff had not repaired the trucks promptly and satisfactorily.

At the close of the trial, the court found, based on the evidence it found to be credible, that plaintiff had substantially performed its obligations under the lease and that defendant was not justified in terminating the agreement. Further, the court held that the provision for liquidated damages was reasonable and represented a fair estimate of actual damages which would be difficult to ascertain precisely. "The parties, at the time the agreement was entered into, considered many factors affecting damages, namely: the uncertainty of the plaintiff's ability to re-rent the said vehicles; the plaintiff's investment in purchasing and reconditioning the vehicles to suit the defendant's particular purpose; the number of man hours not utilized in the non-service of the vehicles in the event of a breach; the uncertainty of reselling the vehicles in question; the uncertainty of the plaintiff's savings or expenditures for gasoline, oil or other service items, and the amount of fluctuating interest on the bank loan." The court calculated that plaintiff would have been entitled to $177,355.20 in rent for the period remaining in the lease and, in accordance with the liquidated damages provision, awarded plaintiff half that amount, $88,-

677.60. The resulting judgment was affirmed by the Appellate Division, with two Justices dissenting. (51 A.D.2d 786, 380 N.Y.S.2d 37.)

The primary issue before us is whether the "liquidated damages" provision is enforceable. Liquidated damages constitute the compensation which, the parties have agreed, should be paid in order to satisfy any loss or injury flowing from a breach of their contract. In effect, a liquidated damage provision is an estimate, made by the parties at the time they enter into their agreement, of the extent of the injury that would be sustained as a result of breach of the agreement. (5 Williston, Contracts [3d ed.], § 776, p. 668.) Parties to a contract have the right to agree to such clauses, provided that the clause is neither unconscionable nor contrary to public policy. Provisions for liquidated damage have value in those situations where it would be difficult, if not actually impossible, to calculate the amount of actual damage. In such cases, the contracting parties may agree between themselves as to the amount of damages to be paid upon breach rather than leaving that amount to the calculation of a court or jury.

On the other hand, liquidated damage provisions will not be enforced if it is against public policy to do so and public policy is firmly set against the imposition of penalties or forfeitures for which there is no statutory authority. * * * It is plain that a provision which requires, in the event of contractual breach, the payment of a sum of money grossly disproportionate to the amount of actual damages provides for penalty and is unenforceable. * * * A liquidated damage provision has its basis in the principle of just compensation for loss. A clause which provides for an amount plainly disproportionate to real damage is not intended to provide fair compensation but to secure performance by the compulsion of the very disproportion. A promisor would be compelled, out of fear of economic devastation, to continue performance and his promisee, in the event of default, would reap a windfall well above actual harm sustained. As was stated eloquently long ago, to permit parties, in their unbridled discretion, to utilize penalties as damages, "would lead to the most terrible oppression in pecuniary dealings". (Hoag v. McGinnis, 22 Wend. 163, 166 * * *.)

The rule is now well established. A contractual provision fixing damages in the event of breach will be sustained if the amount liquidated bears a reasonable proportion to the probable loss and the amount of actual loss is incapable or difficult of precise estimation. * * * If, however, the amount fixed is plainly or grossly disproportionate to the probable loss, the provision calls for a penalty and will not be enforced. * * * In interpreting a provision fixing damages, it is not material whether the parties themselves have chosen to call the provision one for "liquidated damages", as in this case, or have styled it as a penalty. * * * Such an approach would put too much faith in form and too little in substance. Similarly, the agreement should be interpreted as of the date of its making and not as of the date of its breach. * * *

In applying these principles to the case before us, we conclude that the amount stipulated by the parties as damages bears a reasonable relation to the amount of probable actual harm and is not a penalty. Hence, the provision is enforceable and the order of the Appellate Division should be affirmed.

Looking forward from the date of the lease, the parties could reasonably conclude, as they did, that there might not be an actual market for the sale or re-rental of these specialized vehicles in the event of the lessee's breach. To be sure, plaintiff's lost profit could readily be measured by the amount of the weekly rental fee. However, it was permissible for the parties, in advance, to agree that the re-rental or sale value of the vehicles would be 50% of the weekly rental. Since there was uncertainty as to whether the trucks could be re-rented or sold, the parties could reasonably set, as they did, the value of such mitigation at 50% of the amount the lessee was obligated to pay for rental of the trucks. This would take into consideration the fact that, after being used by the lessee, the vehicles would no longer be "shiny, new trucks", but would be used, possibly battered, trucks, whose value would have declined appreciably. The parties also considered the fact that, although plaintiff, in the event of Puritan's breach, might be spared repair and maintenance costs necessitated by Puritan's use of the trucks, plaintiff would have to assume the cost of storing and maintaining trucks idled by Puritan's refusal to use them. Further, it was by no means certain, at the time of the contract, that lessee would peacefully return the trucks to the lessor after lessee had breached the contract.

[T]he existence of the option clause has absolutely no bearing on the validity of the discrete, liquidated damages provision. The lessee could have elected to purchase the trucks but elected not to do so. In fact, the lessee's letter of termination made a point of the fact that the lessee did not want to purchase the trucks. The reality is that the lessee sought, by its wrongful termination of the lease, to evade all obligations to the plaintiff, whether for rent or for the agreed upon purchase price. Its effort to do so failed. That lessee could have made a better bargain for itself by purchasing the trucks for $48,134.17 [3] pursuant to the option, instead of paying $92,341.79 in damages for wrongful breach of the lease is not availing to it now. Although the lessee might now wish, with the benefit of hindsight, that it had purchased the trucks rather than default on its lease obligations, the simple fact is that it did not do so.

We attach no significance to the fact that the liquidated damages clause appears on the preprinted form portion of the agreement. The agreement was fully negotiated and the provisions of the form, in many other respects, were amended. There is no indication of any disparity of bargaining power or of unconscionability. The provision for liquidated damages related reasonably to potential harm that was difficult to estimate and did not constitute a disguised penalty. We also find no merit in the claim of trial error advanced by Puritan.

Accordingly, the order of the Appellate Division should be affirmed, with costs.

3. This sum represents the $45,634.17 still owed by plaintiff on the bank loan, plus $2,500 ($100 for each of the 25 trucks).

Notes

1. The transaction in *Truck Rent-A-Center* was a lease of personal property. Had it been a sale of goods, section 2-718(1) of the Uniform Commercial Code would have been controlling:

> "(1) Damages for breach by either party may be liquidated in the agreement but only at an amount which is reasonable in the light of the anticipated or actual harm caused by the breach, the difficulties of proof of loss, and the inconvenience or nonfeasibility of otherwise obtaining an adequate remedy. A term fixing unreasonably large liquidated damages is void as a penalty." *

2. Section 356(1) of the Restatement (Second) of Contracts (1981) ** authorizes liquidated damages in language that closely parallels that of the Uniform Commercial Code:

> **"§ 356. Liquidated Damages and Penalties**
>
> "(1) Damages for breach by either party may be liquidated in the agreement but only at an amount that is reasonable in the light of the anticipated or actual loss caused by the breach and the difficulties of proof of loss. A term fixing unreasonably large liquidated damages is unenforceable on grounds of public policy as a penalty."

The history of liquidated damages clauses and the correlation between section 2-718(1) and section 356(1) are discussed in Note, Liquidated Damages Recovery Under the Restatement (Second) of Contracts, 67 Cornell L.Rev. 862 (1982). *See also* Rea, Jr., Efficiency Implications of Penalties and Liquidated Damages, 13 J.Legal Stud. 147 (1984).

3. Economic analysis has prompted a reevaluation of the common law's reluctance to enforce liquidated damages clauses that "overcompensate" the nonbreaching party:

> "There has been a great deal of reconsideration by economists and lawyers of these limitations on the ability of contracting parties to stipulate their own remedies.[30] There are good reasons for believing that liquidated damages—and other forms of stipulated remedy—should be routinely enforced by the court, even if they appear to contain a punitive element.[31] The reason is that a stipulation in excess of what appears to be reasonably anticipated compensatory damages may well serve two important functions and serve them more efficiently than would any alternative.

* The New York Court of Appeals discussed its interpretation of U.C.C. section 2-718(1) in Equitable Lumber Corp. v. IPA Land Dev. Corp., 38 N.Y.2d 516, 381 N.Y.S.2d 459, 344 N.E.2d 391 (1976). *See generally* Annot., 98 A.L.R.3d 586 (1980) (contractual liquidated damages provisions under U.C.C. Article 2).

30. *See, e.g.,* Clarkson, Miller & Muris, Liquidated Damages v. Penalties: Sense or Nonsense?, 1978 Wis.L.Rev. 351; Fenton, Liquidated Damages as Prima Facie Evidence, 51 Ind.L.J. 189 (1975); Kaplan, A Critique of the Penalty Limitation on Liquidated Damages, 50 S.Cal.L.Rev. 1055 (1977); Note, Liquidated Damages and Penalties Under the Uniform Commercial Code and the Common Law: An Economic Analysis of Contract Damages, 72 Nw.U.L.Rev. 1055 (1978).

31. In a recent article Professor Polinsky has examined the abilities of various remedies for breach of contract to allocate the risk of certain contingencies between the promisor and promisee. Polinsky, Risk Sharing Through Breach of Contract Remedies, 12 J.Legal Stud. 427 (1983). He concludes that liquidated damages will come closer than will any other remedy to an optimal allocation of risk of loss from breach. *Id.* at 444. * * *

"First, the punitive element may be considered as the payment on an insurance contract written in favor of the innocent party by the breaching party. This situation arises where one party to the contract places a high subjective valuation on performance of the contract and the other party is the best possible insurer of that subjective valuation.[32] If the parties are convinced that the clause will be enforced, the contract will be breached only when it is more efficient to breach than to perform. Since this is precisely the result that one wants from a rule of contract law, this is a strong case for the routine enforcement of liquidated damage clauses.[33]

"A second reason for allowing punitive stipulated damages is that these may be the most efficient means for one party to convey information about his reliability, his ability to perform, and the like. Consider a construction contract in which the buyer is especially eager to have the project completed by a specified date. Suppose that he is extremely doubtful of the contractor's ability to meet that deadline, but that the contractor is certain of his ability to complete performance by the specified date. It may be that the least expensive way for the contractor to convey to the seller his conviction about his ability to perform is for him to stipulate his willingness to pay seemingly punitive damages for each day beyond the deadline that the project remains uncompleted. In those circumstances, if courts are unwilling to allow parties voluntarily to agree to punitive liquidated damages, they force the parties to find a more expensive and, therefore, less efficient way in which to exchange promises.

* * *

"There is another criticism sometimes made of liquidated damages that contain a punitive element: they may induce performance when the more efficient course is breach. Consider the case in which *A* has contracted to sell *B* 1000 widgets at $10 per widget. For simplicity's sake, let us assume that *B* advances the entire sum of $10,000 to *A* at the time that the contract is formed. The widget industry is very highly competitive and *A* is a recent entrant. To get *B* to purchase from him *A* offered the following liquidated damages clause, to which *B* agreed: if he breached the contract, *A* would return *B*'s $10,000 plus another $10,000. Under the circumstances, the second $10,000 constitutes a punitive element of the stipulated damages in that, because of the competitiveness of the industry, *B* can adequately cover the breach for $10,000. Now suppose that after the contract is formed, *A* 's costs suddenly and unexpectedly increase such that

32. Goetz & Scott, Liquidated Damages, Penalties, and the Just Compensation Principle: Some Notes on an Enforcement Model and a Theory of Efficient Breach, 77 Colum.L.Rev. 554, 579–83 (1977). Professors Goetz and Scott give a delightful example of such a case. In their example an alumnus of a college wishes to charter a bus to follow his school basketball team to a tournament. He places a very high value on being at the game, far more than the bus company's hire price. If the bus company breaches, however, the most he can hope to recover in an action for breach of contract is the bus hire price, which will undercompensate him for his loss. The bus company might be willing, however, to pay the alumnus his subjective valuation of performance in the event of a breach in exchange for a payment in excess of their usual hire price. This excess in price could then be considered as the premium on an insurance policy against breach. *Id.* at 578–79.

33. Of course the usual contract defenses would be retained so that if the self-help clause were truly inequitable it would not be enforced.

the costs of completing the contract rise to $15,000. To heighten the point being made, let us assume that none of *A*'s competitors' costs rise.

"Given all of this, one might argue that it would be inefficient for *A* to perform: he will lose $5,000 and *B* will be no better off than if *A* had breached, had had his $10,000 restored, and had then bought his widgets elsewhere for $10,000. That is, if *A* performs, society loses $5,000 that it would not lose if *A* breached and paid *B* only compensatory damages. But *A* will not breach. If he breaches, he will be obliged to return *B*'s $10,000 plus the $10,000 penalty to which he agreed. His losses would then be $10,000. This is double what he would lose if he performs the contract. The conclusion is that when stipulated damages exceed compensatory damages, there is an inducement to perform a contractual promise when it would be more efficient to breach.

"The argument is incorrect. *A* will not necessarily perform on the contract even in the circumstances given above. The reason is that it is possible for post-breach negotiations to make both parties better off without *A*'s having to produce the widgets. *A* stands to lose $5,000 if he performs. He would prefer to lose any sum less than that and not to perform. *B* would like to have 1000 widgets from *A* or his $10,000 to buy them from anyone else. Anything more than this will be preferred by *B*. Clearly, *B* should be willing to take any sum between $1 and $4,999 to release *A* from his duty to perform. And, importantly, he will be willing to take this sum rather than the stipulated damages of $10,000. The reason is that *A* can prevent *B*'s getting anything at all, over his 1000 widgets, by simply losing $5,000 and performing on the contract. Thus, *A* will not inefficiently perform but will pay *B* some sum to release him from the contract.

"It might still be objected, however, that any sum that *A* pays to *B* over $10,000 is a social loss that could have been avoided if only compensatory damages had been stipulated. This is, to an extent, true, but there is a good reason for believing that the sum will be much closer to $1 than to $4,999. *A* can always perform on the contract by simply taking *B*'s $10,000 and buying 1000 widgets from one of his competitors, whose costs, by assumption, did not rise. Thus, the amount over $1 that *A* agrees to pay *B* to release him from the contract can only be equal to the amount of inconvenience that *A* saves by having *B*, rather than himself, purchase the widgets elsewhere.

"A last efficiency concern that should be raised against the routine enforcement of liquidated damage clauses that contain a punitive element is that they create an incentive for one party to induce the other to breach the contract because that party will be better off if the contract is not fulfilled. This possibility arises as a companion to the sort of problem discussed above in the widget example. Suppose that the reason for the insertion of the punitive damage clause in the contract is that there is some special value attached to performance by one of the parties. Suppose, further, that before completion that subjective valuation falls because of changed circumstances.[42] The party who placed the initially high

42. In the alumnus example in note 32 *supra,* the alumnus may discover only after the bus is hired that the starting five of his *alma mater* cannot play. He no longer has an interest in attending the tournament, and he thus has an incentive to induce breach.

subjective value on the contract has an incentive to induce breach of the contract because he will receive a sum that now far exceeds his (subjective) losses from nonperformance.

"It is not at all certain, however, that this sort of problem is weighty enough to argue against the routine enforcement of punitive liquidated damages. First, this problem of so-called moral hazard is not likely to arise frequently. Even if it does, the contractual party who is providing the insurance can protect himself against moral hazard in the same way that commercial insurance companies do: *e.g.*, by requiring co-insurance, a deductible, or a higher premium. Second, since there is the incentive for the breachee to induce breach when circumstances change, the defendant should be allowed to raise the induced breach in mitigation.

"One last point deserves notice here. The literature stresses liquidated damages to the exclusion of any other form of stipulated remedy for breach. In theory, however, there is no reason for contracting parties not to consider binding themselves to perform specifically. Naturally, there are substantial costs to inserting such a clause in a contract: for example, consider the costs of agreeing not to contest an action for specific performance or of agreeing to some burdensome financial alternative unless one specifically performs. There has been only one discussion of this possibility in the literature, and there the principal point was that courts will hesitate to enforce a stipulated specific performance clause. In principle, there is no more reason not to enforce such a clause than there is to enforce any liquidated damages clause not tainted by a valid formation defense. In the absence of legal impediments, parties would insert a stipulated performance clause when the net costs of that clause would be less than those of a stipulated damages clause."

Ulen, The Efficiency of Specific Performance: Toward A Unified Theory of Contract Remedies, 83 Mich.L.Rev. 341, 350–55 (1984).* *See also* D. Dobbs, 3 The Law of Remedies § 12.9(3) (2d ed. 1993); Cooter, Unity in Tort, Contract, and Property: The Model of Precaution, 73 Calif.L.Rev. 1, 29–31 (1985); Craswell, Contract Remedies, Renegotiation, and the Efficient Breach Theory, 61 S.Cal.L.Rev. 629 (1988); Goetz & Scott, The Mitigation Principle: Toward a General Theory of Contractual Obligation, 69 Va.L.Rev. 967, 1000–01 (1983); Rea, Jr., Efficiency Implications of Penalties and Liquidated Damages, 13 J.Legal Stud. 147 (1984).

4. If a liquidated damages clause is unreasonably low it may be unenforceable if it is unconscionable. *See* Varner v. B.L. Lanier Fruit Co., 370 So.2d 61 (Fla.App.1979). *See also* U.C.C. § 2–718, comment 1.

5. Why are there different rules for punitive damages in contract and tort law?

SECTION 6. ATTORNEY'S FEES

BELL v. THE BIRMINGHAM NEWS CO.

Court of Civil Appeals of Alabama, 1991.
576 So.2d 669.

THIGPEN, JUDGE.

This case concerns an award of an attorney's fee by the trial court.

* Reprinted with permission of the Michigan Law Review and the author.

Appellants are members of the City Council of the City of Birmingham. The appellants scheduled a regular formal meeting for December 5, 1989. It was made known prior to the meeting that a president and president pro tempore of the council would be elected at the meeting and that the meeting would be closed. The Birmingham News Company (appellee) objected to the closed session and the appellants responded by announcing that the election would be held in open session. Ultimately, the elections were by secret ballot. The appellee's request that each council member disclose how he or she voted was denied. The appellee filed a complaint in the circuit court seeking to enjoin the appellants and their successors from conducting elections in closed sessions or by secret ballot, and requesting attorney's fees against the appellants. After receiving a joint stipulation of facts from the parties and hearing oral argument from counsel, the trial court entered an order finding the manner in which the appellants conducted the election was an attempt to evade the provisions of §§ 13A–14–2, 11–43–45, and 11–43–49, Ala.Code 1975, and that the appellee was entitled to the injunctive relief prayed for in its complaint. The trial court then ordered the disclosure, retained jurisdiction for the purpose of awarding reasonable attorney's fees, and ordered the appellee to submit an affidavit indicating the time and expenses incurred in the prosecution of this action. * * * The appellants do not challenge the merits of the trial court's decision and appeal only the award of the attorney's fee.

The single issue for review is whether the trial court erred in granting an attorney fee award to the counsel for The Birmingham News in this action.

In its order, the trial court noted its finding that the citizens of the City of Birmingham derive a common benefit "by an action which enforces the requirements of the statute that the business of the City Council be conducted in open and public meetings and, specifically, that the election of Council officers be conducted openly and not in secret." The trial court concluded that it was appropriate under these circumstances to make an award for attorney's fees and expenses.

The appellants contend that the award of attorney's fees in this case is improper and unwarranted. They argue that the appellee failed to show that attorney's fees are authorized by statute or by contract as required, and that they do not fall within any recognized exception to the established rule of law regarding attorney's fees. It is the appellants' position that the trial court erred in awarding attorney's fees under the common benefit exception because there was no common fund, and no finding of fraud or bad faith.

The appellee contends that the award of attorney's fees is appropriate under the common benefit exception and that the trial court clearly stated this in its order. Further, the appellee relies on *Brown v. State,* 565 So.2d 585 (Ala.1990), to support its position that the fact that this litigation has not produced a monetary recovery does not preclude an award of attorney's fees.

It is well established that Alabama follows the "American Rule" in regard to an award for attorney's fees. That rule is that fees may be recovered only where authorized by statute, when provided in a contract, or by special equity, such as in a proceeding where the efforts of an attorney create a fund out of which fees may be paid. *Reynolds v. First Alabama Bank of Montgomery, N.A.,* 471 So.2d 1238 (Ala.1985). In *Reynolds,* the court addressed extensively the issue of attorney's fees and determined that certain exceptions to the rule exist to make the award of attorney's fees appropriate. In addition to the exception concerning a benefit, the court discussed the equitable exception. Our supreme court quoted the opinion in *Hall v. Cole,* 412 U.S. 1, 93 S.Ct. 1943, 36 L.Ed.2d 702 (1973), stating that although the traditional rule ordinarily disfavors the allowance of attorney's fees in the absence of statutory or contractual authorization, such fees may be awarded when the interests of justice so require. *See, Reynolds,* 471 So.2d at 1242.

In support of its decision to award attorney's fees, the trial court stated again, in its order awarding attorney's fees, that the citizens of the City of Birmingham benefit from this action and there is ample evidence in the record supporting that conclusion. The trial court also noted that in *Barton v. Drummond Co.,* 636 F.2d 978 (5th Cir.1981), the U.S. Court of Appeals for the Fifth Circuit, citing *Miles v. Bank of Heflin,* 349 So.2d 1072 (Ala.1977), recognized our supreme court decision that nonpecuniary benefits are within the scope of the equitable exception of the "American Rule."

Our reading of the cases utilized by the trial court in ordering this award, along with the recent supreme court case of *Brown, supra,* leads us to agree with the judgment rendered by the trial court that the circumstances of this case make an award for attorney's fees appropriate. The instant case, like *Brown, supra,* resulted in a benefit to the general public. "It is unquestionable that [the appellee's] attorneys rendered a public service by bringing an end to an improper practice. The public nature of the services rendered by these lawyers justifies an award of attorney fees." *Brown,* 565 So.2d at 592 (see also Justice Adams's comments at 593).

In light of the above, we find no abuse of discretion by the trial court in its decision to award attorney's fees. As a result, this case is due to be affirmed.

Affirmed.

Notes and Questions

1. *Bell* represents the minority rule on attorney's fees for private attorney general actions. Alyeska Pipeline Service Co. v. The Wilderness Society, 421 U.S. 240, 95 S.Ct. 1612, 44 L.Ed.2d 141 (1975) represents the federal rule and majority rule for the states. There the plaintiffs successfully sued the Secretary of the Interior for intending to issue permits for the construction of a trans-Alaskan pipeline in violation of federal statutes and sought attorney's fees under a "private attorney general" exception to the American Rule. The court stated:

"Congress itself presumably has the power and judgment to pick and choose among its statutes and to allow attorneys' fees under some, but not others. But it would be difficult, indeed, for the courts, without legislative guidance, to consider some statutes important and others unimportant and to allow attorneys' fees only in connection with the former. If the statutory limitation of right-of-way widths involved in this case is a matter of the gravest importance, it would appear that a wide range of statutes would arguably satisfy the criterion of public importance and justify an award of attorneys' fees to the private litigant. And, if *any* statutory policy is deemed so important that its enforcement must be encouraged by awards of attorneys' fees, how could a court deny attorneys' fees to private litigants in actions under 42 U.S.C. § 1983 seeking to vindicate *constitutional* rights? Moreover, should courts, if they were to embark on the course urged by respondents, opt for awards to the prevailing party, whether plaintiff or defendant, or only to the prevailing plaintiff? Should awards be discretionary or mandatory? Would there be a presumption operating for or against them in the ordinary case? *See Newman, supra.*

"We do not purport to assess the merits or demerits of the 'American Rule' with respect to the allowance of attorneys' fees. It has been criticized in recent years, and courts have been urged to find exceptions to it. It is also apparent from our national experience that the encouragement of private action to implement public policy has been viewed as desireable in a variety of circumstances. But the rule followed in our courts with respect to attorneys' fees has survived. It is deeply rooted in our history and in congressional policy; and it is not for us to invade the legislature's province by redistributing litigation costs in the manner suggested by respondents and followed by the Court of Appeals.

421 U.S. at 264, 270, 95 S.Ct. at 1625, 1628. The dissent pointed to, *inter alia*, the power to create exceptions:

"In more recent cases, we have reiterated the same theme: while as a general rule attorneys' fees are not to be awarded to the successful litigant, the courts as well as the Legislature may create exceptions to that rule. *See* Mills v. Electric Auto–Lite Co., 396 U.S., at 391–392, 90 S.Ct., at 625; Hall v. Cole, 412 U.S., at 5, 93 S.Ct., at 1946. Under the judge-made exceptions, attorneys' fees have been assessed, without statutory authorization, for willful violation of a court order, Toledo Scale Co. v. Computing Scale Co., 261 U.S. 399, 426–428, 43 S.Ct. 458, 465–466, 67 L.Ed. 719 (1923); for bad faith or oppressive litigation practices, Vaughan v. Atkinson, 369 U.S. 527, 530–531, 82 S.Ct. 997, 999, 8 L.Ed.2d 88 (1962); and where the successful litigants have created a common fund for recovery or extended a substantial benefit to a class, Central Railroad & Banking Co. v. Pettus, 113 U.S. 116, 5 S.Ct. 387, 28 L.Ed. 915 (1885); Mills v. Electric Auto–Lite Co., *supra*. While the Court today acknowledges the continued vitality of these exceptions, it turns its back on the theory underlying them, and on the generous construction given to the common-benefit exception in our recent cases."

Id. at 274, 95 S.Ct. at 1630. Which rule do you favor?

2. *Alyeska* noted the criticism of the "American Rule", but held that Congress has reserved for itself the right to make appropriate changes or exceptions. In Fleischmann Distilling Corp. v. Maier Brewing Co., 386 U.S.

714, 718, 87 S.Ct. 1404, 1407, 18 L.Ed.2d 475 (1967), however, the Court had catalogued justifications of the rule; *e.g.,* "since litigation is at best uncertain, one should not be penalized for merely defending or prosecuting a lawsuit * * *"; and, if the Rule was applied to losing plaintiffs as well as losing defendants, "the poor might be unjustly discouraged from instituting actions to vindicate their rights if the penalty for losing included the fees of their opponents' counsel".

3. Is there a justification for shifting fees only to losing defendants, but not to losing plaintiffs? Is the justification any less persuasive in cases solely between private parties, to which the government is not a party?

4. Is the justification related to the presumed resources of the parties? In this regard, the Equal Access to Justice Act generally allows fee awards against the United States, or its agencies or officials, only to individuals whose net worth does not exceed $2,000,000, and to businesses or other entities with a net worth not exceeding $7,000,000, which do not employ more than 500 employees. 28 U.S.C.A. § 2412(d)(1)(B).

(a) Would it be feasible, and fair, to turn the statute on its head, and allow the Government to recover fees against losing plaintiffs whose resources exceed those limits?

(b) Would it be desirable to provide for fee-shifting in cases solely among private parties, to allow recovery against any party with resources over a pre-established amount?

5. For a discussion of computing fee awards under the Equal Access to Justice Act, *see* Lyden v. Howerton, 731 F.Supp.1545, 1554–56 (S.D.Fla.1990):

> "Having concluded that plaintiffs are entitled to an EAJA award, the amount of such an award remains for determination. Under 28 U.S.C. § 2412(b), the court has the discretion to award whatever fee is reasonable and appropriate that the court determines to be proper. On the other hand, under 28 U.S.C. § 2412(d), the court must explain any deviation it makes from the $75 per hour award specified therein. Under § 2412(d), 'attorney's fees shall not be awarded in excess of $75 unless the court determines that an increase in the cost of living, or some special factor, such as the limited availability of qualified attorneys for the proceedings involved, justifies a higher fee.' * * *
>
> "In recent years, the Supreme Court has five times considered the myriad of issues which necessarily flow from attempts to determine the amount of attorney's fees to be awarded to a prevailing plaintiff.[4] The Eleventh Circuit has mirrored the evolving standards of the Supreme Court and has recently refined their framework for calculating attorney's fees in light of the various Supreme Court rulings. Norman v. Housing Authority of City of Montgomery, 836 F.2d 1292 (11th Cir.1988) (hereafter 'Norman').
>
> "The starting point for determining the amount of a reasonable fee is the number of hours reasonably expended during the litigation multiplied

4. Pennsylvania v. Delaware Valley Citizens Council, 483 U.S. 711, 107 S.Ct. 3078, 97 L.Ed.2d 585 (1987); Pennsylvania v. Delaware Valley Citizens Council, 478 U.S. 546, 106 S.Ct. 3088, 92 L.Ed.2d 439 (1986); Riverside v. Rivera, 477 U.S. 561, 106 S.Ct. 2686, 91 L.Ed.2d 466 (1986); Blum v. Stenson, 465 U.S. 886, 104 S.Ct. 1541, 79 L.Ed.2d 891 (1984); and Hensley v. Eberhart, 461 U.S. 424, 103 S.Ct. 1933, 76 L.Ed.2d 40 (1983).

by a reasonable hourly rate. Norman, 836 F.2d at 1299 (citing Hensley v. Eberhart, 461 U.S. 424, 433, 103 S.Ct. 1933, 1939, 76 L.Ed.2d 40 (1983)). The figure derived from this calculation is commonly referred to as the 'lodestar.' [5]

"A. REASONABLE HOURLY RATE

"Reasonable fees are to be calculated according to the prevailing market rates in the relevant legal community for similar services by lawyers of reasonably comparable skills, experience and reputation. *Norman,* 836 F.2d at 1299 (citations omitted). The applicant bears the burden of producing satisfactory evidence that the requested rate is in line with prevailing market rates by providing evidence, the least of which must be more than the affidavit of the attorney performing the work. *Id.* Invariably, and as a predictable result of our adversarial process, the court will be faced with a high-end range (supplied by the prevailing plaintiff) and a low-end range (supplied by the opposing defendant). *Id.* The court must then determine the appropriate amount of the case at hand.

"Plaintiffs' attorney, Mr. Alfred Frigola, has presented sufficient evidence to meet the requirement of *Norman* to initiate the court's inquiry into a reasonable hourly rate. * * * Plaintiffs' witnesses at the hearing in this matter were plaintiffs' attorney and Ms. Diane Tolbert Covan, who was qualified as an expert in this case in this type of matter. In fact, plaintiffs' attorney, himself, has been acknowledged to be an expert in immigration law by the government. * * * Plaintiffs' attorney testified that $250 to $300 per hour is a reasonable amount for him to be paid in this case.

"Ms. Covan testified that $200 to $250 per hour is, in her opinion, the range of reasonable hourly rates in the South Florida community for similar services by lawyers of reasonably comparable skills, experience, and reputation in 1989. * * * During their testimony, plaintiffs' attorney and Ms. Covan testified that all twelve factors, found to be crucial considerations regarding hourly rates in Johnson, 488 F.2d 714 (5th Cir.1974), were taken into consideration in arriving at their opinion.

"The defendants did not present testimony regarding a reasonable hourly rate under the § 2412(b) claim for attorney's fees, thus depriving the court of the usual 'floor' figure upon which to measure the variance. Accordingly, for the purpose of the 28 U.S.C. § 2412(b) claim, the court finds Mr. Frigola entitled to an hourly rate of $200 per hour.

5. In arriving at the "lodestar," this court may consider a variety of factors. Johnson v. Georgia Highway Express, 488 F.2d 714 (5th Cir.1974), suggests twelve: (1) time and labor required; (2) novelty and difficulty of the questions; (3) skills required to perform the legal work properly; (4) preclusion of employment by the attorney due to acceptance of the case; (5) customary fee; (6) whether the fee is fixed or contingent; (7) time limitations imposed by the client or circumstances; (8) amount involved in results obtained; (9) experience, reputation, and ability of the attorneys; (10) "undesirability" of the case; (11) nature and length of the professional relationship with the client; and (12) awards in similar cases. Johnson, 488 F.2d at 717–19.

Many of these factors, however, "are subsumed within the initial calculation of hours reasonably expended at a reasonable hourly rate." Hensley v. Eberhart, 461 U.S. at 434, n. 9, 103 S.Ct. at 1940, n. 9 (citation omitted). Notwithstanding this observation, some of these factors may be utilized in the court's determination. Norman, 836 F.2d at 1299–1300.

"With respect to the § 2412(d) claim, the defendants' pleadings make a pure statutory argument wherein they oppose an award of attorney's fees in excess of $75 per hour, the statutorily defined rate. The EAJA statute provides in relevant part:

> Attorney's fees shall not be awarded in excess of $75 unless the court determines that an increase in the cost of living or some special factor, such as the limited availability of qualified attorneys for the proceedings involved, justifies a higher fee.

28 U.S.C. § 2412(d)(2)(A). The defendants argue that plaintiffs have identified no 'special factors' or other justification entitling them to recover in excess of $75 per hour. Nothing could be further from the truth.

"The court is somewhat constrained by the Supreme Court's directive in Pierce v. Underwood, 487 U.S. 552, 108 S.Ct. 2541, 101 L.Ed.2d 490 (1988), that 'broad and general' factors including the novelty and difficulty of the issues, the case's undesirability, the expertise of counsel, and the results obtained are not to be considered 'special factors' within the meaning of the statute. *Id.* 108 S.Ct. at 2554. Notwithstanding the Supreme Court's limitation, and being fully respective thereof, the court finds a number of 'special factors' which warrant exceeding the statutory base of $75. In addition to the 'special factors' found in the EAJA statute itself, § 2412(d)(2)(A), an unusual delay in the award of fees has also been considered a 'special factor.' * * * The initial lawsuit, Lyden v. Howerton, 731 F.Supp. 1545 (S.D.Fla.1983), was filed over six years ago. It is clear that there has been an increase in the cost of living since this time. There was direct testimonial evidence stating that there was a shortage of lawyers possessing the specialized skill of immigration law needed for this litigation at the time this suit was filed. The court in Jean v. Nelson, 863 F.2d 759, 774 (11th Cir.1989), suggests that a special expertise in immigration law might qualify as a 'special factor' under the EAJA. In addition, the benefit derived not only for the plaintiffs herein, but a class of people, including over 1,000 vessel owners and captains, warrants this increase. Moreover, evaluating this issue on a case-by-case basis, the exceptional and unusual circumstances present here fit clearly within the flexibility allowed by the statute and espoused in *Pierce* to exceed the statutory base. Accordingly, the court finds Mr. Frigola, under the 28 U.S.C. § 2412(d) claim, entitled to an hourly rate of $200 per hour.

* * *

"B. HOURS REASONABLY EXPENDED

"The next step in the computation of the lodestar is the ascertainment of reasonable hours. Plaintiffs presented well-documented time sheets and other relevant evidence claiming 1,082.3 hours expended over the course of the litigation. * * * The record, expert testimony, and Mr. Frigola's time sheets are clear that he expended far more hours but that due to the exercise of billing judgment and other factors, he has not sought reimbursement for all hours expended. In addition, the court does not find any of the documented hours submitted to qualify as redundant or unnecessary time.

"The defendants did not present any evidence at the hearing to contradict or oppose the number of hours claimed. * * *

"Accordingly, the court finds 1,082.3 hours reasonable and appropriate.

"C. THE LODESTAR CALCULATION AND ADJUSTMENTS THERETO

"The lodestar figure consists of the product of the attorney's prevailing market fee times his compensable hours. Here, $200 times 1,082.3 hours is equal to $216,460.00. The court finds no circumstances present warranting an adjustment of the lodestar figure as permitted in *Norman.*"

6. Five months after *Lyden* a different judge of the Southern District of Florida did not increase the $75 per hour fee for Mr. Frigola in a similar case. Bruland v. Howerton, 742 F.Supp. 629 (S.D.Fla.1990). The court stated:

> "The Equal Access to Justice Act ('EAJA') provides that 'a court shall award to a prevailing party other than the United States fees and other expenses * * * incurred by that party in any civil action (other than cases sounding in tort) including proceedings for judicial review of agency action * * * unless the Court finds that the position of the United States was substantially justified or that special circumstances make an award unjust.' 28 U.S.C. § 2412(d)(1)(A) (1990 Supp.). A different section of the act gives a court discretion to award fees to the extent that a private party would be liable under common law or statute. 28 U.S.C. § 2412(b) (1990 Supp.). The Court finds that Plaintiffs are entitled to fees under § 2412(d), the mandatory fee provision of the EAJA."

Id. at 632.

7. For a discussion of computing a contingent fee award in a class action that resulted in a common fund, *see* Swedish Hospital Corp. v. Shalala, 1 F.3d 1261 (D.C.Cir.1993):

"A. LODESTAR VERSUS PERCENTAGE OF THE FUND

"1. General Principles Governing Fee Awards

"In general, each party to litigation in the United States bears its own attorneys' fees absent a specific fee-shifting statute. Over time, courts have fashioned several equitable exceptions to this 'American rule.' One of the earliest, and still most common, exceptions is the 'common fund' doctrine typically applied in class actions like the present one. *See* Sprague v. Ticonic Nat'l Bank, 307 U.S. 161, 164 (1939) (fee award from fund generated is within 'the historic equity jurisdiction of the federal courts'). That doctrine allows a party who creates, preserves, or increases the value of a fund in which others have an ownership interest to be reimbursed from that fund for litigation expenses incurred, including counsel fees. It is by now well established that 'a litigant or lawyer who recovers a common fund for the benefit of persons other than himself or his client is entitled to a reasonable attorney's fee from the fund as a whole.' *Boeing Co. v. Van Gemert,* 444 U.S. 472, 478 (1980). The underlying justification for attorney reimbursement from a common fund, as explained by the Supreme Court in three early cases, is that unless the costs of litigation were spread to the beneficiary of the fund they would be unjustly enriched by the attorney's efforts. *See* Sprague, 307 U.S. at 166–67; Central R.R. & Banking Co. of Georgia v. Pettus, 113 U.S. 116, 126–27 (1885); Trustees v. Greenough, 105 U.S. 527, 532 (1882).

"When awarding attorneys' fees, federal courts have a duty to ensure that claims for attorneys' fees are reasonable. *See* Hensley v. Eckerhart,

461 U.S. 424, 433 (1983); Pettus, 113 U.S. at 127. Special problems exist in assessing the reasonableness of fees in a class action suit since class members with low individual stakes in the outcome often do not file objections, and the defendant who contributed the fund will usually have no interest in how the fund is divided between the plaintiffs and class counsel.

"2. *The Percentage-of-the-Fund Method for Calculating Fees*

"Historically, courts have exercised considerable discretion and applied a reasonableness standard, focusing upon the particular circumstances of a case, in determining the amount of a common fund fee award. The percentage-of-the-fund method of calculating attorneys' fees in common fund cases was most common. *See Pettus,* 113 U.S. at 128 (paying successful attorneys a percentage of the fund recovered for the class). *See also Court Awarded Attorney Fees, Report of the Third Circuit Task Force,* 108 F.R.D. 237, 242 (1986) ('*Third Circuit Task Force Report*').

"3. *The Lodestar and Twelve–Factor Tests*

"The application of a percentage-of-the-fund approach sometimes resulted in large fee awards, and in the 1970s several courts began a movement to alternative methods of calculating attorneys' fees. In 1973, the Third Circuit led the way in Lindy Bros. Builders, Inc. of Philadelphia v. American Radiator & Standard Sanitary Corp., 487 F.2d 161 (3d Cir. 1973), instructing judges in that circuit to first compute the product of the reasonable hours expended and the reasonable hourly rate to arrive at the 'lodestar.' That amount could then be adjusted upward or downward, based upon additional factors such as the contingent nature of the case and the quality of the attorneys' work. This so-called 'lodestar/multiplier' approach thus shifted the emphasis from a fair percentage of recovery to the value of the time expended by counsel.

"A year later in a case involving a fee-shifting statute rather than a common fund, the Fifth Circuit identified twelve factors as relevant to determining a reasonable fee award: 1) the time and labor required; 2) the novelty and difficulty of the questions involved; 3) the skill requisite to perform the legal services properly; 4) the preclusion of other employment by the attorney due to acceptance of the case; 5) the customary fee; 6) whether the fee is fixed or contingent; 7) time limitations imposed by the client or other circumstances; 8) the amount involved and the results obtained; 9) the experience, reputation, and ability of the attorneys; 10) the 'undesirability' of the case; 11) the nature and length of the professional relationship with the client; and 12) awards in similar cases. Johnson v. Georgia Highway Express, Inc., 488 F.2d 714 (5th Cir.1974), *abrogated in part on other grounds,* Blanchard v. Bergeron, 489 U.S. 87 (1989).

"After the emergence of *Lindy* and *Johnson,* the federal courts experimented with combinations of the *Lindy* lodestar and *Johnson* twelve-factor approaches in both common fund and fee-shifting contexts. In the context of the fee-shifting statutes, the lodestar approach but without enhancement for the *Johnson* factors has emerged as the prevailing method of fee calculation. *See, e.g.,* City of Burlington v. Dague, 112 S.Ct. 2638 (1992); King v. Palmer, 950 F.2d 771 (D.C.Cir.1991) (en banc), *cert. denied,* 112 S.Ct. 3054 (1992). However, at the same time, many courts and commentators have noted differences between the fee-shifting and common fund cases, raising questions as to whether the same methodology should apply. A Third Circuit task force appointed to compare the respective merits of the lodestar and percentage-of-the-fund approaches concluded that the lodestar technique, at least as encumbered with the *Johnson* factors, is a 'cumbersome, enervating, and often surrealistic process of preparing and evaluating fee petitions that now plagues the Bench and Bar.' *Third Circuit Task Force Report,* 108 F.R.D. at 255.

"The task force enumerated nine deficiencies in the lodestar process: 1) it 'increases the workload of an already overtaxed judicial system'; 2) the elements of the process 'are insufficiently objective and produce results that are far from homogeneous'; 3) the process 'creates a sense of mathematical precision that is unwarranted in terms of the realities of the practice of law'; 4) the process 'is subject to manipulation by judges who prefer to calibrate fees in terms of percentages of the settlement fund or the amounts recovered by the plaintiffs or of an overall dollar amount'; 5) the process, although designed to curb abuses, has led to other abuses, such as encouraging lawyers to expend excessive hours engag[ing] in duplicative and unjustified work, inflat[ing] their 'normal billing rate[s], and includ[ing] fictitious hours'; 6) it 'creates a disincentive for the early settlement of cases'; 7) it 'does not provide the district court with enough flexibility to reward or deter lawyers so that desirable objectives, such as early settlement, will be fostered'; 8) the process 'works to the particular disadvantage of the public interest bar' because, for example, the 'lodestar' is set lower in civil rights cases than in securities and antitrust cases; and 9) despite the apparent simplicity of the lodestar approach, 'considerable confusion and lack of predictability remain in its administration.' *Id.* at 246–49.

"The task force, though recommending the retention of a lodestar approach in statutory fee cases, concluded that in common fund cases the best determinant of the reasonable value of services rendered to the class by counsel is a percentage of the fund. *Id.* at 255.

* * *

"2. *The Twenty Percent Figure*

"We are of the opinion that the District Court acted within its discretion in setting the percentage of the fund at twenty percent. The twenty percent figure is well within the range of reasonable fees in common fund cases. As suggested in our discussion above, a review of similar cases reveals that a majority of common fund class action fee awards fall between twenty and thirty percent. Also, the already noted supportive response of the class members to the attorneys' fee notice, though not decisive, is relevant to the District Court's reasonableness determination.

"We also hold that the court was within its discretion in basing its fee calculation only on that part of the fund for which counsel was responsible. The District Court's conclusion that, to a considerable extent, this case rode 'piggyback' on the *Beverly* case is entitled to deference, especially as Judge Oberdorfer was the district court judge in both cases."

See also Camden I Condominium Assn., Inc. v. Dunkle, 946 F.2d 768, 773–74 (11th Cir.1991).

8. In City of Burlington v. Dague, ___ U.S. ___, 112 S.Ct. 2638, 120 L.Ed.2d 449 (1992), the Court held, in a case arising under a fee-shifting provision of the Solid Waste Disposal Act and the Clean Air Act, that no enhancement of the "lodestar" amount should be made to reflect the contingency of the recovery. *See also* King v. Palmer, 950 F.2d 771 (D.C.Cir.1991) (*en banc*) (no enhancement for contingency in employment discrimination fee shifting statute).

9. To recover under typical fee shifting statutes, a plaintiff must be the "prevailing party", *e.g.,* Equal Access to Justice Act, 28 U.S.C.A. § 2412(d); and Civil Rights Attorneys' Fees Awards Act, 42 U.S.C.A. § 1988. Although this standard may sometimes be met without the party having obtained a "favorable 'final judgment following a full trial on the merits' ", the party "must have established his entitlement to some relief on the merits of his claims", Hanrahan v. Hampton, 446 U.S. 754, 100 S.Ct. 1987, 64 L.Ed.2d 670 (1980) and "be able to point to a resolution of the dispute which changes the legal relationship between itself and the defendant," Texas State Teachers Assn. v. Garland Independent School Dist., 489 U.S. 782, 792, 109 S.Ct. 1486, 103 L.Ed.2d 866 (1989). This test is not met by the plaintiff merely being able to obtain a ruling that the complaint should not be dismissed for failure to state a claim on which relief can be granted. Hewitt v. Helms, 482 U.S. 755, 760, 107 U.S. 2672, 2676, 96 L.Ed.2d 654 (1987). Nor can a plaintiff recover attorney's fees, although the prevailing party, when the recovery is nominal damages on a 17 million dollar compensatory claim. Farrar v. Hobby, ___ U.S. ___, 113 S.Ct. 566, 121 L.Ed.2d 494 (1992).

10. When a plaintiff's counsel, in a civil rights case with a fee-shifting statute, feels ethically bound to recommend that the plaintiffs accept a settlement because it affords full injunctive relief even though it excludes attorney's fees, should a court disapprove it? *See* Evans v. Jeff D., 475 U.S. 717, 741, 106 S.Ct. 1531, 1538, 1540, 1543–1545, 89 L.Ed.2d 747 (1986):

* * *

> "The text of the Fees Act provides no support for the proposition that Congress intended to ban all fee waivers offered in connection with substantial relief on the merits.

* * *

> "In fact, we believe that a general proscription against negotiated waiver of attorney's fees in exchange for a settlement on the merits would itself impede vindication of civil rights, at least in some cases, by reducing the attractiveness of settlement.

* * *

> "The question remains whether the District Court abused its discretion in this case by approving a settlement which included a complete fee waiver.

* * *

> "The Court of Appeals, respondents, and various *amici* supporting their position, however, suggest that the court's authority to pass on

settlements, typically invoked to ensure fair treatment of class members, must be exercised in accordance with the Fees Act to promote the availability of attorneys in civil rights cases. Specifically, respondents assert that the State of Idaho could not pass a valid statute precluding the payment of attorney's fees in settlements of civil rights cases to which the Fees Act applies. * * * From this they reason that the Fees Act must equally preclude the adoption of a uniform state-wide policy that serves the same end, and accordingly contend that a consistent practice of insisting on a fee waiver as a condition of settlement in civil rights litigation is in conflict with the federal statute authorizing fees for prevailing parties, including those who prevail by way of settlement. Remarkably, there seems little disagreement on these points. Petitioners and the *amici* who support them never suggest that the district court is obligated to place its stamp of approval on every settlement in which the plaintiffs' attorneys have agreed to a fee waiver. The Solicitor General, for example, has suggested that a fee waiver need not be approved when the defendant had 'no realistic defense on the merits,' or if the waiver was part of a 'vindictive effort * * * to teach counsel that they had better not bring such cases'.

"We find it unnecessary to evaluate this argument, however, because the record in this case does not indicate that Idaho has adopted such a statute, policy, or practice. Nor does the record support the narrower proposition that petitioners' request to waive fees was a vindictive effort to deter attorneys from representing plaintiffs in civil rights suits against Idaho.

"What the outcome of this settlement illustrates is that the Fees Act has given the victims of civil rights violations a powerful weapon that improves their ability to employ counsel, to obtain access to the courts, and thereafter to vindicate their rights by means of settlement or trial. For aught that appears, it was the 'coercive' effect of respondents' statutory right to seek a fee award that motivated petitioners' exceptionally generous offer. Whether this weapon might be even more powerful if fee waivers were prohibited in cases like this is another question, but it is in any event a question that Congress is best equipped to answer. Thus far, the Legislature has not commanded that fees be paid whenever a case is settled. Unless it issues such a command, we shall rely primarily on the sound discretion of the district courts to appraise the reasonableness of particular class-action settlements on a case-by-case basis, in the light of all the relevant circumstances. In this case, the District Court did not abuse its discretion in upholding a fee waiver which secured broad injunctive relief, relief greater than that which plaintiffs could reasonably have expected to achieve at trial."

The dissenters said:

"In May of 1975, this Court in *Alyeska Pipeline Service Co. v. Wilderness Society,* 421 U.S. 240, 95 S.Ct. 1612, 44 L.Ed.2d 141 (1975), ruled that the equitable powers of the federal courts did not authorize fee awards on the ground that a case served the public interest.

* * *

"In the wake of *Alyeska,* Congress acted to correct 'anomalous gaps' in the availability of attorney's fees to enforce civil rights laws, S.Rep. No. 94–

1011, p. 1 (1976) (hereafter S.Rep.). See H.R.Rep. No. 94–1558, p. 2 (1976) (hereafter H.R.Rep.); 122 Cong.Rec. 31472 (1976) (remarks of Sen. Kennedy). Testimony at hearings on the proposed legislation disclosed that civil rights plaintiffs, 'a vast majority of [whom] cannot afford legal counsel,' *Id.* at 1, were suffering 'very severe hardships because of the *Alyeska* decision,' *id.,* at 2. The unavailability of fee-shifting made it impossible for legal aid services, 'already short of resources,' to bring many lawsuits, and, without much possibility of compensation, private attorneys were refusing to take civil rights cases. *Id.,* at 3. * * * Congress found that *Alyeska* had a 'devastating' impact on civil rights litigation, and it concluded that the need for corrective legislation was 'compelling.' H.R.Rep. 3; see also, 122 Cong.Rec. 31471, *supra* (remarks of Sen. Scott), 31472 (remarks of Sen. Kennedy).

"Accepting this Court's invitation, see *Alyeska, supra,* 421 U.S., at 269–271, 95 S.Ct., at 1627–1629, Congress passed the Fees Act in order to reestablish the *Newman* regime under which attorney's fees were awarded as a means of securing enforcement of civil rights laws by ensuring that lawyers would be willing to take civil rights cases.

* * *

"I have gone to great lengths to show how the Court mischaracterizes the purpose of the Fees Act because the Court's error leads it to ask the wrong question. Having concluded that the Fees Act merely creates another remedy to vindicate the rights of individual plaintiffs, the Court asks whether negotiated waivers of statutory attorney's fees are 'invariably inconsistent' with the availability of such fees as a remedy for individual plaintiffs. *Ante,* at 1540. Not surprisingly, the Court has little difficulty knocking down this frail straw man. But the *proper* question is whether permitting negotiated fee waivers is consistent with Congress' goal of attracting competent counsel. It is therefore necessary to consider the effect on *this* goal of allowing individual plaintiffs to negotiate fee waivers.

* * *

IV

"Although today's decision will undoubtedly impair the effectiveness of the private enforcement scheme Congress established for civil rights legislation, I do not believe that it will bring about the total disappearance of 'private attorneys general.' It is to be hoped that Congress will repair this Court's mistake. In the meantime, other avenues of relief are available. The Court's decision in no way limits the power of state and local bar associations to regulate the ethical conduct of lawyers. Indeed, several Bar Associations have already declared it unethical for defense counsel to seek fee waivers. See Committee on Professional Ethics of the Association of the Bar of the City of New York Op. No. 82–80 (1985); District of Columbia Legal Ethics Committee Op. No. 147, *supra* n. 8, 113 Daily Washington Law Reporter, at 389. Such efforts are to be commended and, it is to be hoped, will be followed by other state and local organizations concerned with respecting the intent of Congress and with protecting civil rights.

"In addition, it may be that civil rights attorneys can obtain agreements from their clients not to waive attorney's fees. Such agreements simply replicate the private market for legal services (in which attorneys are not ordinarily required to contribute to their client's recovery), and thus will enable civil rights practitioners to make it economically feasible—as Congress hoped—to expend time and effort litigating civil rights claims."

Id. at 1548, 1550, 1557. With whom do you agree?

11. Could a state bar enforce ethical rules or opinions precluding defendants from requesting fee waivers, in light of the Supreme Court's decision in Evans v. Jeff D.? Or does that decision in effect establish a nationwide ethical rule permitting such requests, at least where federal fee-shifting statutes are involved? In this regard, the majority stated that the issue before it was not an "ethical" one, but one of applying the applicable fee statute, and that imposition of a bar on fee waiver requests "would impede vindication of civil rights, at least in some cases * * * ". Would the majority's decision have been different had Idaho ethical standards, like those of some jurisdictions, unequivocally precluded such requests, and therefore the District Court in granting the motion to approve the settlement in effect would have had to approve the results of attorney conduct that violated those standards? Or, under the majority's reasoning, does the Supremacy Clause of the Constitution (Article 6, cl. 2) render such state ethical rules unenforceable? It would seem at least incongruous that the ability to settle, and dynamics of settlement discussions, in civil rights or other federal statutory cases, should vary from state to state.

12. Is the dissent correct in suggesting that counsel could include in retainer agreements provisions not to waive attorneys fees? Could counsel enforce such a provision and deny his or her client the benefits of a settlement which clearly was otherwise in the client's interest to accept, consistently with the attorney's duty of undivided loyalty to the client?

13. The dissent relied heavily on the purposes of civil rights legislation. If persuaded by its analysis with respect to such cases, would you apply it to other fee-shifting statutes?

Chapter 4

INTRODUCTION TO RESTITUTION

SECTION 1. BACKGROUND

KOVACIC–FLEISCHER, APPLYING RESTITUTION TO REMEDY A DISCRIMINATORY DENIAL OF PARTNERSHIP

34 Syr.L.Rev. 743 (1983) *

Restitution or "liability based in unjust enrichment" is a "generally accepted and widely applied" source of liability * * *. Restitution prevents a defendant's unjust enrichment by enabling a plaintiff to seek recovery, in law or equity, of a benefit that the defendant unjustly gained or retained at the plaintiff's expense. If the benefit to be recovered is money, the action is at law and is often referred to as quasi-contract. If the benefit to be recovered is specific property or money that has been traced, the action is in equity and is often referred to as a constructive trust.

A. Definition of Restitution

In 1937, the *Restatement of Restitution* defined liability based on unjust enrichment by saying: "A person who has been unjustly enriched at the expense of another is required to make restitution to the other." In 1983, the Tentative Draft No. 1 of the *Restatement (Second) of Restitution* elaborated that definition. The *Second Restatement* provided that "[a] person who receives a benefit by reason of an infringement of another person's interest, or of loss suffered by the other, owes restitution to him in the manner and amount necessary to prevent unjust enrichment."

Professor Palmer, in his recent four volume treatise, *The Law of Restitution,* avoided one overriding definition. He said:

> Unjust enrichment is an indefinable idea in the same way that justice is indefinable. But many of the meanings of justice are derived from a sense of injustice, and this is true of restitution since attention is centered on the prevention of injustice. Not all injustice but rather one special variety: the unjust enrichment of one person at the expense of another. This wide and imprecise idea has played a

creative role in the development of an important branch of modern law.

Despite "imprecision," the many definitions of restitution articulated throughout the years consistently contain the following three elements: "(1) the defendant has been enriched by the receipt of a benefit; (2) the defendant's enrichment is at the plaintiff's expense; and (3) it would be unjust to allow the defendant to retain the benefit." Because it is unjust for the defendant to retain the gain, plaintiff's recovery is generally measured by the amount of the defendant's gain, not by the amount of the plaintiff's loss.

* * *

C. Restitution is Unnecessarily Underutilized

* * *

[R]estitution "has been slow to emerge as a general theory" [89] and is not well understood. As Professor Dawson said in 1951, "it is doubtful even now whether most lawyers have an adequate conception of the range and resources of the remedy." It is doubtful whether the situation has much improved in the last thirty years.[90]

One reason restitution is not well understood may be that there is a great deal of confusion in terminology. The word "restitution" is used to refer both to a cause of action and a remedy. At times restitution is used synonymously with "unjust enrichment" and "quasi-contract." Quasi-contract, in turn, is used synonymously with contract-implied-in-law and both are at times confused with contract-implied-in-fact. In addition, restitution "sometimes refer[s] to the disgorging of something which has been taken and other times refer[s] to compensation for injury done."

The confusion has a historic base. Much of the common law developed and evolved through the expansion of forms of action or the substitution of a procedurally preferable form for an older form. Fictions were frequently used to facilitate the expansion or substitution. In order to prevent a defendant's unjust enrichment by applying the well utilized form of action

89. J. Dawson, Unjust Enrichment 22 (1951). Professor Dawson also said: "[M]any lawyers still approach the restitution remedies with uncertainty and wonder." Dawson, *Restitution or Damages!,* 20 OHIO ST.L.J. 175 (1959); *see also* Seavey & Scott, *supra* note 69, at 32. "[Restitution's] outlines have been dimly perceived and little discussed." *Id.*

90. For example, Professor Douthwaite stated:

> When considering the measure of compensation for a wrong, the practitioner typically thinks in terms of proven damages * * *. But if he so restricts his thinking he may be depriving his client of a considerable sum of money.
>
> * * *
>
> * * * [A] wrongdoer's profits as an alternative to his victim's proven damages can, more often than not, be recovered on the theory of a constructive trust * * * [or] in quasi contract.

Douthwaite, *The Tortfeasor's Profits—A Brief Survey,* 19 Hastings L.J. 1071, 1071 (1968). Professor Douthwaite said, over ten years later, that "[i]t simply isn't true to say that restitutionary problems don't often come up on the practitioner's desk. The trouble is that usually he hasn't thought about the restitutionary implications or potential of the problem before him." G. Douthwaite [Attorney's Guide to Restitution] § 1.1, at 2 [1977]. [Footnotes from the original text.]

of assumpsit, for example, the law courts used the fiction of an "implied promise." The law courts held that the law implied a promise to pay in situations in which no intent on the part of the defendant to pay the plaintiff could be inferred from the defendant's words or deeds. This came to be known as a contract-implied-in-law or quasi-contract. As Professor Palmer stated: "The fiction of a contract was being used to allow recovery in a contract form of action, and in retrospect the reason for doing so was to deprive the defendant of an unjust enrichment." Similarly, the equity courts used the fiction of a constructive trust, implying that the defendant, as a constructive trustee, was holding property for the plaintiff, although, again, the defendant had evidenced no intent to act as a trustee and did not have a fiduciary relationship with the plaintiff.

When the old forms of action were abolished, however, the "fictitious promise seemed immortal," and that fiction now creates confusion. For example, sometimes a court will deny liability in quasi-contract because no agreement between the parties was proven or will deny liability in contract-implied-in-fact because the defendant was not enriched. Quasi-contract, or contract-implied-in-law, is, however, an action to prevent unjust enrichment and does not necessarily require proof of consensual elements of contract law, although the action may involve "unwinding" unenforceable or frustrated agreements or remedying a material breach of contract. A contract-implied-in-fact is, in contrast, an actual contract. A similar confusion exists with respect to constructive trusts and actual trusts.

The continued use of the old terms that evolved from the old fictions has not only made application of the terms difficult, but has also obscured the fact that restitution, or liability in unjust enrichment, is an important source of liability. Restitution can provide a plaintiff with a remedy that is measured by the amount of the defendant's gain in situations that could alternatively be remedied with typical tort damages, which compensate for a plaintiff's loss, or with contract damages, which put a plaintiff in the position she would have been in if the contract had been performed. Restitution can also provide that the defendant disgorge his benefit in situations in which neither contract nor tort actions will provide relief.

SECTION 2. QUASI-CONTRACT

MOSES v. MACFERLAN

King's Bench, 1760.
2 Burr. 1005.

Lord Mansfield delivered the resolution of the Court in this case: which stood for their opinion, "whether the plaintiff could recover against the defendant, in the present form of action, (an action upon the case for money had and received to the plaintiff's use;) or whether he should be obliged to bring a special action upon the contract and agreement between them."

It was an action upon the case, brought in this Court by the now plaintiff, Moses, against the now defendant, Macferlan, (heretofore plaintiff in the Court of Conscience, against the same Moses now plaintiff here,) for money had and received to the use of Moses the now plaintiff in this Court.

The case, as it came out upon evidence and without dispute, at Nisi Prius before Ld. Mansfield at Guildhall, was as follows.

It was clearly proved, that the now plaintiff, Moses, had indorsed to the now defendant Macferlan, four several promissory notes, made to Moses himself by one Chapman Jacob, for 30s. each, for value received, bearing date 7th November 1758; and that this was done, in order to enable the now defendant Macferlan to recover the money in his own name, against Chapman Jacob. But previous to the now plaintiff's indorsing these notes, Macferlan assured him "that such his indorsement should be of no prejudice to him:" and there was an agreement signed by Macferlan, whereby he (amongst other things) expressly agreed "that Moses should not be liable to the payment of the money or any part of it; and that he should not be prejudiced, or be put to any costs, or any way suffer, by reason of such his indorsement." Notwithstanding which express condition and agreement, and contrary thereto, the present defendant Macferlan summoned the present plaintiff Moses into the Court of Conscience, upon each of these four notes, as the indorser thereof respectively, by four separate summonses. Whereupon Moses, (by one Smith who attended the Court of Conscience at their second Court, as solicitor for him and on his behalf,) tendered the said indemnity to the Court of Conscience, upon the first of the said four causes; and offered to give evidence of it, and of the said agreement, by way of defence for Moses in that Court. But the Court of Conscience rejected this defence, and refused to receive any evidence in proof of this agreement of indemnity, thinking that they had no power to judge of it; and gave judgment against Moses, upon the mere foot of his indorsement, (which he himself did not at all dispute,) without hearing his witnesses about the agreement "that he should not be liable:" for the commissioners held this agreement to be no sufficient bar to the suit in their Court; and consequently decreed for the plaintiff in that Court, upon the undisputed indorsement made by Moses. This decree was actually pronounced, in only one of the four causes there depending: but Moses's agent, (finding the opinion of the commissioners to be as above-mentioned,) paid the money into that Court, upon all the four notes; and it was taken out of Court by the now defendant Macferlan, (the then plaintiff, in that Court,) by order of the commissioners.

All this matter appearing upon evidence before Lord Mansfield at Nisi Prius at Guildhall, there was no doubt but that, upon the merits, the plaintiff was entitled to the money; and accordingly, a verdict was there found for Moses, the plaintiff in this Court, for 6*l*. (the whole sum paid into the Court of Conscience;) but subject to the opinion of the Court, upon this question, "whether the money could be recovered in the present form of action, or whether it must be recovered by an action brought upon the special agreement only."

* * *

The Court, having heard the counsel on both sides, took time to advise.

Lord Mansfield now delivered their unanimous opinion, in favour of the present action.

There was no doubt at the trial, but that upon the merits the plaintiff was entitled to the money; and the jury accordingly found a verdict for the 6*l*. subject to the opinion of the Court upon this question, "whether the money might be recovered by this form of action," or "must be by an action upon the special agreement only."

Many other objections, besides that which arose at the trial, have since been made to the propriety of this action in the present case.

The 1st objection is, "that an action of debt would not lie here; and no assumpsit will lie, where an action of debt may not be brought:" some sayings at Nisi Prius, reported by note takers who did not understand the force of what was said, are quoted in support of that proposition. But there is no foundation for it.

It is much more plausible to say, "that where debt lies, an action upon the case ought not to be brought." And that was the point relied upon in *Slade's case:* but the rule then settled and followed ever since is, "that an action of assumpsit will lie in many cases where debt lies, and in many where it does not lie."

A main inducement, originally, for encouraging actions of assumpsit was, "to take away the wager of law:" and that might give rise to loose expressions, as if the action was confined to cases only where that reason held.

2d objection.—"That no assumpsit lies, except upon an express or implied contract: but here it is impossible to presume any contract to refund money, which the defendant recovered by an adverse suit."

Answer. If the defendant be under an obligation, from the ties of natural justice, to refund; the law implies a debt, and gives this action, founded in the equity of the plaintiff's case, as it were upon a contract ("quasi ex contractu," as the Roman law expresses it).

This species of assumpsit, ("for money had and received to the plaintiff's use,") lies in numberless instances, for money the defendant has received from a third person; which he claims title to, in opposition to the plaintiff's right; and which he had, by law, authority to receive from such third person.

3d objection. Where money has been recovered by the judgment of a Court having competent jurisdiction, the matter can never be brought over again by a new action.

Answer. It is most clear, "that the merits of a judgment can never be overhaled by an original suit, either at law or in equity." Till the judgment is set aside, or reversed, it is conclusive, as to the subject matter of it, to all intents and purposes.

But the ground of this action is consistent with the judgment of the Court of Conscience: it admits the commissioners did right. They decreed upon the indorsement of the notes by the plaintiff: which indorsement is not now disputed. The ground upon which this action proceeds, was no defence against that sentence.

It is enough for us, that the commissioners adjudged "they had no cognizance of such collateral matter." We can not correct an error in their proceedings; and ought to suppose what is done by a final jurisdiction, to be right. But we think, "the commissioners did right, in refusing to go into such collateral matter." Otherwise, by way of defence against a promissory note for 30s. they might go into agreements and transactions of a great value: and if they decreed payment of the note, their judgment might indirectly conclude the balance of a large account.

The ground of this action is not, "that the judgment was wrong:" but, "that, (for a reason which the now plaintiff could not avail himself of against that judgment,) the defendant ought not in justice to keep the money." And at Guildhall, I declared very particularly, "that the merits of a question, determined by the commissioners, where they had jurisdiction, never could be brought over again, in any shape whatsoever."

Money may be recovered by a right and legal judgment; and yet the iniquity of keeping that money may be manifest, upon grounds which could not be used by way of defence against the judgment.

* * *

This brings the whole to the question saved at Nisi Prius, "viz. whether the plaintiff may elect to sue by this form of action, for the money only; or must be turned round, to bring an action upon the agreement."

One great benefit, which arises to suitors from the nature of this action, is, that the plaintiff needs not state the special circumstances from which he concludes "that, ex aequo & bono, the money received by the defendant, ought to be deemed as belonging to him:" he may declare generally, "that the money was received to his use;" and make out his case, at the trial.

This is equally beneficial to the defendant. It is the most favourable way in which he can be sued: he can be liable no further than the money he has received; and against that, may go into every equitable defence, upon the general issue; he may claim every equitable allowance; he may prove a release without pleading it; in short, he may defend himself by every thing which shows that the plaintiff, ex aequo & bono, is not entitled to the whole of his demand, or to any part of it.

If the plaintiff elects to proceed in this favourable way, it is a bar to his bringing another action upon the agreement; though he might recover more upon the agreement, than he can by this form of action. And therefore, if the question was open to be argued upon principles at large, there seems to be no reason or utility in confining the plaintiff to an action upon the special agreement only.

* * *

This kind of equitable action, to recover back money, which ought not in justice to be kept, is very beneficial, and therefore much encouraged. It lies only for money which, ex aequo et bono, the defendant ought to refund:

it does not lie for money paid by the plaintiff, which is claimed of him as payable in point of honor and honesty, although it could not have been recovered from him by any course of law; as in payment of a debt barred by the Statute of Limitations, or contracted during his infancy, or to the extent of principal and legal interest upon an usurious contract, or, for money fairly lost at play: because in all these cases, the defendant may retain it with a safe conscience, though by positive law he was barred from recovering. But it lies for money paid by mistake; or upon a consideration which happens to fail; or for money got through imposition, (express or implied;) or extortion; or oppression; or an undue advantage taken of the plaintiff's situation, contrary to laws made for the protection of persons under those circumstances.

In one word, the gist of this kind of action is, that the defendant, upon the circumstances of the case, is obliged by the ties of natural justice and equity to refund the money.

Therefore we are all of us of opinion that the plaintiff might elect to waive any demand upon the foot of the indemnity, for the costs he had been put to; and bring this action, to recover the 6*l.* which the defendant got and kept from him iniquitously.

Rule—That the postea be delivered to the plaintiff.

The end of Easter term 1760.

Notes

1. DAWSON, UNJUST ENRICHMENT 22–23 (1951): * "It is broadly true of the modern [quasi-contract] remedy in the United States that there are no distinctions based on the form or nature of the gain received. Lord Mansfield [in Moses v. Macferlan] applied his remarks to the 'common count' for money had and received, which presupposed a transfer or at least a receipt of money. But we have other counts that are almost as common and the same tests apply to them. The benefit may consist of the acquisition or use of chattels, services rendered or acts performed, the use of ideas, or the discharge of an obligation. The list is not yet closed. It is true that two limitations have survived in cases of simple misappropriation—the refusal of quasi-contract relief for use and occupation of land and the requirement that a taking of chattels be followed by a sale. But both limitations have been greatly restricted, even in the tort cases to which they apply. In many states they have been entirely rejected. Where they do survive they are recognized as anomalous and they may in due course disappear. Indeed, there seems to be no rational ground for such distinctions. If restrictions are to be imposed on the remedy they should rest in the grounds for awarding relief, not on the form the gains assume.

"As to grounds, there has been a similar expansion. The main work of quasi-contract is done in the field of express contract, awarding value restitution of performances rendered in actual or supposed conformity with contractual obligations. The modern expansion of grounds for rescission of contract has provided more work to do. As to torts, quasi-contract restitution as an alternative remedy has made steady progress. We can probably say now that damage remedies can be ignored and quasi-contract used as to any kind of legal wrong from which gains are realized. But the tort cases have provided the model for extension into related areas that are not quite tort and not quite contract, where the gain is clear enough. Beside these we should place a large group of equitable wrongs, the breach of various kinds of obligations traditionally enforced in equity for which a simple money judgment seems convenient and suitable."

2. The result in *Moses* was achieved, as a matter of pleading, by allowing the plaintiff to use as a pleading device one of the "common counts" available at common law which had theretofore been appropriate in those contract cases where the plaintiff could prove only an "implied in fact," rather than an express, promise. There were a variety of common counts in use at the time, each of which was an abbreviated and simple form of pleading. Each bore a different title and was an appropriate pleading form depending upon the factual context in which the implied in fact promise in question had occurred. For example, there was "goods sold and delivered" for a sale of goods, "money lent" where there was a loan, "quantum meruit" where services were rendered, and so on.

Lord Mansfield suggested, in effect, that a party seeking restitution at law simply select and use for his pleading form the factually most analogous common count and, at the appropriate time, show an unjust enrichment of the defendant at the plaintiff's expense had resulted. Proof of an "implied in fact" promise is excused, and a "promise" to return the benefit might then be "implied in law" (that is, imposed upon the party defendant by the judgment of the court irrespective of any notion of a consensual obligation). It was only necessary that restitution be possible in the form of a money judgment. It was the unjustly retained benefit which was important, not how it arose. That "money had and received" was the common count which was most suited to the facts in *Moses* was purely happenstance.

It is from this case that we derive our theory of an "implied in law" promise as a basis for restitution relief "at law" and the terminology which has been associated with this remedy over the years. This form of restitution relief at law, which is limited to a money judgment based upon a jury verdict, is to be distinguished from the quite different form which was being made available in the parallel restitution development going on in the courts of equity.

KOSSIAN v. AMERICAN NATIONAL INSURANCE CO.

Court of Appeal of California, Fifth District, 1967.
254 Cal.App.2d 647, 62 Cal.Rptr. 225.

STONE, ASSOCIATE JUSTICE.

On February 19, 1964, fire destroyed a portion of the Bakersfield Inn, owned by one Reichert. At the time, the property was subject to a first deed of trust in which defendant was the beneficiary. Pursuant to the requirements of the deed of trust, defendant's interest in the property was protected by policies of fire insurance. On March 16, 1964, Reichert, as owner in possession, entered into a written contract with plaintiff whereby plaintiff agreed to clean up and remove the debris from the fire damaged portion of the Inn for the sum of $18,900. Defendant had no knowledge of the execution of the agreement between plaintiff and Reichert.

Plaintiff commenced work in the middle of March 1964, and completed it in early April. During the entire time work was in progress Reichert was in possession of the premises as owner, although defendant caused a notice of Reichert's default under the deed of trust to be filed four days after the contract for demolition was entered into between plaintiff and Reichert. The record does not reflect that plaintiff had actual knowledge of the notice of default until after the work was completed.

Some time after plaintiff had fully performed the contract, Reichert filed a petition in bankruptcy. The trustee in bankruptcy abandoned the premises comprising the Bakersfield Inn, together with any interest in the four fire insurance policies up to the amount of $424,000. Each policy contained a provision insuring against the cost of cleaning up and removing debris caused by fire damage.

Following abandonment of the policies by the trustee in bankruptcy, Reichert and his wife assigned their interest in them to defendant in accordance with the terms of the deed of trust. Defendant submitted proofs of loss, claiming a total of $160,000, including the sum of $18,000 as the estimated cost for removing and cleaning up debris. These claims were rejected by the carriers; negotiations followed; the compromise figure of $135,620 was agreed upon and this amount paid to defendant. We do not have an itemization of the adjusted claims of loss upon which the compromised loss settlement was made, so that the record is not clear as to what part of the $18,900 cost of debris removal defendant received. It is clear, however, that the insurance payment included at least a part of the cost of debris removal and demolition.

Defendant demonstrates, by a careful analysis of the facts, that there was no direct relationship between plaintiff and defendant in regard to either the work performed on the property after the fire or in relation to the fire insurance policies. The contract for debris removal was between plaintiff and Reichert, and defendant did not induce plaintiff, directly or indirectly, to enter into that contract. Plaintiff had no lien against the property resulting from his work, and if he had such a lien it would have been wiped out by defendant's foreclosure of its first deed of trust.

Had the circumstances been simply that defendant, by foreclosure, took the property improved by plaintiff's debris removal, there would be a benefit conferred upon defendant by plaintiff, but no unjust enrichment. (See Griffith Co. v. Hofues, 201 Cal.App.2d 502, 19 Cal.Rptr. 900.) It is the additional fact that defendant made a claim to the insurance carriers for the value of work done by plaintiff that is the nub of the case.

Defendant argues that plaintiff was not a party to the insurance contracts, while defendant had a contract right to collect indemnity for losses resulting from the fire, including the debris removal cost. This contract right was embodied in the insurance policies. * * *

* * *

Defendant says it made no agreement, express or implied, with plaintiff that it would pay for the debris removal or that any part of the insurance proceeds would be applied for that purpose. Therefore, concludes defendant, there being no privity of relationship between it and plaintiff, and no fraud or deceit alleged or proved, defendant has the right to the property benefited by plaintiff's work and labor expended in removing the debris and to the insurance payments as well.

Plaintiff makes no claim to the insurance "fund" upon the ground he relied thereon similar to the reliance of a mechanic or materialman that forms the basis of an equitable claim to a building fund. (Smith v. Anglo–California Trust Co., 205 Cal. 496, 271 P. 898; Pacific Ready Cut Homes, Inc. v. Title Insurance & Trust Co., 216 Cal. 447, 14 P.2d 510.) He relies upon the basic premise that defendant should not be allowed to have the fruits of plaintiff's labor and also the money value of that labor. This, of course, is a simplified pronouncement of the doctrine of unjust enrichment, a theory which can, in some instances, have validity without privity of relationship. The most prevalent implied-in-fact contract recognized under the doctrine of unjust enrichment is predicated upon a relationship between the parties from which the court infers an intent. However, the doctrine also recognizes an obligation *imposed* by law regardless of the intent of the parties. In these instances there need be no relationship that gives substance to an implied intent basic to the "contract" concept, rather the obligation is imposed because good conscience dictates that under the circumstances the person benefited should make reimbursement. * * *

Plaintiff's claim does not rest upon a quasi contract implied in fact, but upon an equitable obligation imposed by law. It is true that defendant's right to the insurance payment was a contract right embodied in the policies of insurance, nevertheless the indemnity payment was based in part upon a claim of loss that did not exist because plaintiff had already remedied the loss by his work for which he was not paid.

We are cited no California cases that are close aboard, and independent research reveals none. Lack of precedent applicable to the facts peculiar to this case is not surprising, however, as the authors of the Restatement recognize that the essential nature of equity cases concerned with problems of restitution makes definitive precedent unlikely. We are guided by the "Underlying Principles" delineated in the Restatement on Restitution:

> "The rules stated in the Restatement of this Subject depend for their validity upon certain basic assumptions in regard to what is required by justice in the various situations. In this Topic, these are stated in the form of principles. They cannot be stated as rules since either they are too indefinite to be of value in a specific case or, for historical or other reasons, they are not universally applied. They are distinguished from rules in that they are intended only as general guides for the conduct of the courts * * *." (P. 11.)

The governing principle is expressed in the opening sentence of the Restatement on Restitution, as follows:

> "The Restatement of this Subject deals with situations in which one person is accountable to another on the ground that otherwise he would unjustly benefit or the other would unjustly suffer loss." (P. 1.)

The question, simply stated, is whether in a jurisdiction that recognizes the equitable doctrine of unjust enrichment one party should be indemnified twice for the same loss, once in labor and materials and again in money, to the detriment (forfeiture) of the party who furnished the labor and materials. We conclude that the doctrine of unjust enrichment is applicable to the facts of this case, and that plaintiff is entitled to reimbursement out of the insurance proceeds paid defendant for work done by plaintiff.

The facts concerning the amount of insurance recovered by defendant and the percentage of the total proof of loss attributable to plaintiff's work are not altogether clear, probably because this is a proceeding for summary judgment before trial of the action. In any event, it is clear that defendant, in addition to taking over the property which plaintiff cleared of debris, also received indemnity insurance payments covering at least part of the cost for clearing that property of debris. The amount can be made certain by a trial on the merits, and if it develops that defendant recovered only a part of the cost for debris removal, this fact does not preclude a partial recovery by plaintiff. We learn from the Restatement, page 611:

> "Where a person is entitled to restitution from another because the other, without tortious conduct, has received a benefit, the measure of recovery for the benefit thus received is the value of what was received * * *."

Thus, to the extent defendant received insurance for debris removal performed by plaintiff, plaintiff should recover. If defendant received less than the value of plaintiff's work, as defendant seems to contend, then plaintiff should recover *pro tanto*.

The judgment is reversed.

BASTIAN v. GAFFORD

Supreme Court of Idaho, 1977.
98 Idaho 324, 563 P.2d 48.

DONALDSON, JUSTICE.

On appeal, plaintiff-appellant contends that because the trial court in its decision failed to distinguish between contracts implied in fact and quasi-contracts, the court did not decide this case on the theory alleged in appellant's complaint. We agree and therefore reverse the judgment and remand this case for a new trial.

During March, 1972, the defendant-respondent V.H. Gafford asked plaintiff-appellant Leo Bastian if he would be interested in constructing an office building upon a parcel of respondent's real property located in Twin Falls, Idaho. After several discussions between the parties, appellant orally agreed to construct the building and began drafting the plans therefor. After the plans were substantially completed, respondent contacted First Federal Savings and Loan Association of Twin Falls to seek financing for the building. He was informed that First Federal required a firm bid by a contractor and would not finance the project on a cost-plus basis. Respondent told appellant of the need for a firm bid, but appellant refused to submit one stating that he would only construct the building on a cost-plus basis. Respondent thereafter hired an architect to prepare a second set of plans, and employed another contractor to construct the building using those plans. On June 29, 1972, appellant filed a materialmen's lien upon respondent's real property in the amount of $3,250 for goods and services rendered in preparing the plans. He then commenced this action to foreclose that lien, alleging an implied-in-fact contract to compensate him for his services. After a trial on the merits, however, the court entered judgment for respondent on the ground that respondent had not been unjustly enriched. Since he did not use appellant's plans in constructing the office building, respondent received no benefit from them and was therefore not required to compensate appellant for drafting them.

In basing its decision on unjust enrichment, the trial court failed to distinguish between a quasi-contract and a contract implied in fact. Although unjust enrichment is necessary for recovery based upon quasi-contract, it is irrelevant to a contract implied in fact. *Continental Forest Products, Inc. v. Chandler Supply Co.,* 95 Idaho 739, 518 P.2d 1201 (1974). For appellant to recover under the latter theory, it is not necessary that respondent either use the plans or derive any benefit from them. *Clements v. Jungert,* 90 Idaho 143, 408 P.2d 810 (1965). It is enough that he requested and received them under circumstances which imply an agreement that he pay for appellant's services.

It is apparent from the record that the requested performance may not have been limited to the drafting of the building plans. We express no opinion on what performance was requested, on whether the requested performance was tendered, and on whether the circumstances imply an agreement to compensate appellant.

The judgment is reversed and the cause is remanded for a new trial. Costs to appellants.

MIDCOAST AVIATION, INC. v. GENERAL ELECTRIC CREDIT CORP.

United States Court of Appeal, Seventh Circuit, 1990.
907 F.2d 732.

[The plaintiff, Midcoast Aviation, Inc., as sub-contractor, converted several old "Jetstar" planes into modern "Fanstar" planes. The owner of the planes was defendant General Electric Credit Corp. ("GECC"). The contractor for the work was American Aviation Industries, Inc. ("AAI"). When the latter failed to pay for the work in question the plaintiff, Midcoast, sued the owner, defendant GECC, to recover the value of the work done.]

* * *

Before working on the 1986 deal Midcoast wanted assurances that it would get paid. In late July, 1986, it went to GECC looking for those assurances. A meeting was held at GECC's headquarters. Midcoast made it clear to GECC that it knew AAI's role in the project was only that of marketing. It also made it clear that it knew where the money for the project came from—GECC. Midcoast indicated that before it did any work, including the proposed interior work, it needed assurances from GECC that GECC would finance the Fanstar project to certification. The assurances were given.

Midcoast then went to work. * * *

II.

* * *

Under Illinois law, one may become obligated to another by quasi-contract. Derived from civil law, quasi-contract is " 'an obligation similar in character to that of a contract, but which arises not from an agreement of parties but from some relation between them.' " *Board of Highway Comm'rs v. City of Bloomington,* 253 Ill. 164, 97 N.E. 280, 284 (1911) (quoting texts on Roman and civil law). "[T]he obligation arises not from consent * * * but from the law or natural equity"; id.; it "exists from an implication of law that arises from the facts and circumstances independent of agreement or presumed intention." *Id. See also Century 21 Castles by King, Ltd. v. First Nat'l Bank of Western Springs,* 170 Ill.App.3d 544, 121 Ill.Dec. 174, 177, 524 N.E.2d 1222, 1225 (1988); *Arthur Rubloff & Co. v. Drovers Nat'l Bank of Chicago,* 80 Ill.App.3d 867, 36 Ill.Dec. 194, 200, 400 N.E.2d 614, 620 (1980). Because it exists by implication of law, and because the obligation imposed by it superficially resembles the obligation imposed by contract, the concept of quasi-contract has often been denoted as "contract implied in law." *See, e.g., Board of Highway Comm'rs,* 253 Ill. 164, 97 N.E. at 284. Nevertheless, the concept has nothing to do with "contract" as such. *Mueller v. City of Highland Park,* 166 Ill.App.3d 114, 116 Ill.Dec. 644, 647, 519 N.E.2d 712, 715 *appeal denied,* 122 Ill.2d 578, 125 Ill.Dec. 221, 530 N.E.2d 249 (1988). *See also* H.S. Maine, Ancient Law 286 (Dorsett ed. 1986) (1st ed. 1861).

A claim in quasi-contract is established when "the defendant has unjustly retained a benefit to the plaintiff's detriment, and * * * defendant's retention of the benefit violates the fundamental principles of justice, equity, and good conscience." *HPI Health Care Serv., Inc. v. Mt. Vernon Hosp.,* 131 Ill.2d 145, 137 Ill.Dec. 19, 26, 545 N.E.2d 672, 678 (1989). *Accord Overseas Dev. DISC Corp. v. Sangamo Const. Co.,* 840 F.2d 1319, 1325 (7th Cir.1988); *Lirtzman v. Fuqua Indus., Inc.,* 677 F.2d 548, 553 (7th Cir.1982); *Bloomgarden v. Coyer,* 479 F.2d 201, 211 (D.C.Cir. 1973). *See also* Restatement of Restitution § 1 (1937) ("A person who has been unjustly enriched at the expense of another is required to make restitution to the other."). Obviously, equitable principles play a major role in quasi-contract (although the action is one at law). *See Board of Highway Comm'rs,* 253 Ill. 164, 97 N.E. at 285; *Partipilo v. Hallman,* 156 Ill.App.3d 806, 109 Ill.Dec. 387, 390, 510 N.E.2d 8, 11 (1987); *Arthur Rubloff & Co.,* 80 Ill.App.3d 867, 36 Ill.Dec. at 200, 400 N.E.2d at 620. The key principle is that of unjust enrichment. *City of Marshall v. City of Casey,* 177 Ill.App.3d 1065, 127 Ill.Dec. 292, 294, 532 N.E.2d 1121, 1123 (1989); *Arthur Rubloff & Co.,* 80 Ill.App.3d. 867, 36 Ill.Dec. at 200, 400 N.E.2d at 620. *See also HPI Health Care Serv.,* 131 Ill.2d 145, 137 Ill.Dec. at 25, 545 N.E.2d at 678; *Partipilo,* 156 Ill.App.3d 806, 109 Ill.Dec. at 390,

510 N.E.2d at 11. Quasi-contractual duties arise only in situations of unjust enrichment, situations where "one person has received money or its equivalent under such circumstances that in equity and good conscience he ought not to retain it and which *ex cequo et bono* belongs to another." *Board of Highway Comm'rs,* 253 Ill. 164, 97 N.E. at 285. *See also Rutledge v. Housing Authority of East St. Louis,* 88 Ill.App.3d 1064, 44 Ill.Dec. 176, 179, 411 N.E.2d 82, 85 (1980). If that situation exists, quasi-contract mandates the imposition of an obligation upon the benefit receiver to avoid the unjust enrichment. *See Lirtzman,* 677 F.2d at 553. The obligation imposed is an obligation to pay money to the benefit provider, an obligation "closely akin to a duty to make restitution." *Bloomgarden,* 479 F.2d at 210. *See also Lirtzman,* 677 F.2d at 553.

A niche of quasi-contract law is the law of *quantum meruit.* The concern of *quantum meruit* is situations in which services are rendered, but no payment forthcoming. As would be expected, the doctrine for these situations is in accord with that of quasi-contract generally: The essence of *quantum meruit* liability is " 'the receipt of a benefit by one party which would be inequitable for that party to retain.' " *Telander v. Posejpal,* 94 Ill.App.3d 616, 49 Ill.Dec. 590, 594, 418 N.E.2d 444, 448 (1981) (quoting *First Nat'l Bank of Lincolnwood v. Glenn,* 132 Ill.App.2d 322, 324, 270 N.E.2d 493, 495 (1971)). *See also Partipilo,* 156 Ill.App.3d 806, 109 Ill.Dec. at 389, 390, 510 N.E.2d at 10, 11. The elements of *quantum meruit* liability distilled from this essence are the performance of services by the plaintiff, the receipt of the benefit of those services by the defendant, and the unjustness of the defendant's retention of that benefit without compensating the plaintiff. *See City of Marshall,* 177 Ill.App.3d 1065, 127 Ill.Dec. at 294, 532 N.E.2d at 1123; *Romanek–Golub & Co. v. Anvan Hotel Corp.,* 168 Ill.App.3d 1031, 119 Ill.Dec. 482, 489, 522 N.E.2d 1341, 1348 (1988); *Edens View Realty & Inv., Inc. v. Heritage Enter., Inc.,* 87 Ill.App.3d 480, 42 Ill.Dec. 360, 366, 408 N.E.2d 1069, 1075 (1980). *See also O'Neil & Santa Claus, Ltd. v. Xtra Value Imports, Inc.,* 51 Ill.App.3d 11, 8 Ill.Dec. 78, 81, 365 N.E.2d 316, 319 (1977) (elements of recovery, not elements of liability); *Nardi & Co. v. Allabastro,* 20 Ill.App.3d 323, 314 N.E.2d 367, 370 (1974). *See also* Kovacic, *A Proposal to Simplify* Quantum Meruit *Litigation,* 35 Am.U.L.Rev. 547, 554 (1986).

As is evident from the citations, *quantum meruit* doctrine is well established in Illinois. Yet, like quasi-contract doctrine in general, *quantum meruit* doctrine is somewhat hard to grasp. It is easier to talk about "fundamental principles of justice, equity, and good conscience" than to reduce those principles to a definite calculus. Fortunately for us, we need not make such a reduction. GECC's complaint lies with the district court's denial of its motions for directed verdict and j.n.o.v. Thus, we need only determine whether the evidence and its reasonable implications can support the jury's finding that the "fundamental principles" mentioned above were violated by GECC's retention of a Midcoast-furnished benefit. *See David Copperfield's Disappearing, Inc. v. Haddon Advertising Agency, Inc.,* 897 F.2d 288, 291 (7th Cir.1990) (standard of review for denial of a motion for directed verdict or j.n.o.v.). *See also Adams v. Fred Weber, Inc.,* 849

F.2d 1018, 1020 (7th Cir.1988) (quoting Illinois directed verdict and j.n.o.v. requirement).

GECC argues that the facts and circumstances cannot possibly support a case against it based on the principles of *quantum meruit.* But a review of the facts and circumstances, and a comparison of them with the law stated above, leads us to the opposite conclusion. It is clear to us that Midcoast performed services in 1986 when it improved the interior of GECC's plane, that this work made the plane better than it otherwise would have been, and that this improvement of the plane conferred an enriching benefit on the plane's owner, GECC. The only real question is whether it is unjust for GECC not to compensate Midcoast for the enrichment. We cannot say as a matter of law that it is, nor can we say the opposite. But we can say that a reasonable jury pondering the law of quasi-contract could find the facts indicative of what the words "unjust" and "inequitable" stand for. And that is all we need say to uphold the district court. * * *

[The judgment was reversed on other grounds.]

Notes

1. "The reason there are two definitions for quantum meruit may be because quantum meruit is one of the 'common counts' within the old writ of assumpsit. That writ was initially used to enforce express and implied in fact contracts and was later expanded to enforce contracts implied in law, or quasi-contracts. As the writ system disappeared, the courts continued to use quantum meruit in these two different types of cases.

"A contract implied in law, also known as quasi-contract, is one of the definitions for quantum meruit. It is not a contract at all, but rather is a legal action in restitution. Restitution, in turn, also is referred to as an action in unjust enrichment. The classic elements of restitution, and thus contract implied in law, are: (1) the defendant received a benefit, (2) at the plaintiff's expense, (3) under circumstances that would make it unjust for the defendant to retain the benefit without paying for it. The plaintiff, however, must not confer the benefit gratuitously.

"A contract implied in fact, on the other hand, is an actual contract. The classic elements of contract implied in fact are: (1) the defendant requested the plaintiff to perform work, (2) the plaintiff expected the defendant to compensate him or her for those services, and (3) the defendant knew or should have known that the plaintiff expected compensation. A request made with an expectation of making payment is a contractual offer accepted by performance in the expectation of payment. An implied in fact contract differs from an express contract in that the terms of the latter are expressed orally or in writing while those of the former are inferred from the parties' conduct.

"* * * The distinction between these two types of quantum meruit is important because the two claims provide different recoveries. Technically, recovery in contract implied in fact is the amount the parties intended as the contract price. If that amount is unexpressed, courts will infer that the parties intended the amount to be the reasonable market value of the plaintiff's services. Recovery in quasi-contract, or contract implied in law, however, is in restitution and thus is the amount of the defendant's gain. The courts are often aware of the duality of remedy in quantum meruit, but do not appear to know when one or the other is appropriate, primarily because of a lack of authoritative guidance. Some of the courts applying quantum meruit award the plaintiff the amount of the defendant's gain. More courts, however, award the reasonable market value of the plaintiff's services, even when characterizing the quantum meruit claim as one in quasi-contract. Some courts award the plaintiff's costs.

"In fact, the reasonable market value of plaintiff's services can be viewed as the correct remedy in most quantum meruit cases, even in many cases in unjust enrichment because reasonable value can be viewed as the defendant's gain in certain situations. The value of the plaintiff's services measures the defendant's gain when the defendant requests the work: the defendant's benefit is receiving what he or she requested, those requested services have a market value."

Kovacic–Fleischer, "A Proposal to Simplify Quantum Meruit Litigation," 35 Am.U.L.Rev. 547, 554–57 (1986).*

2. These comments by Professor Kovacic–Fleischer about the role of the "quantum meruit" concept also apply to the discussions of the "implied in fact" and "implied in law" contracts described in the *Kossian* and *Bastian* cases. Those cases differ only in that they do not use the term "quantum meruit." They illustrate a tendency on the part of some courts to avoid using the "common count" terminology ("quantum meruit", "money had and received," "goods sold and delivered", *et al.*) in awarding implied in law (or "quasi-contract") restitution relief. Thus while they apply the basic principles derived from Moses v. MacFerland by implying a non-consensual promise in order to avoid an unjust enrichment of the defendant at the plaintiff's expense, they use language suggested by the Restatement of Restitution.

The Restatement brings together both the case law development that is the heritage of Moses v. MacFerland, that is, our law of "quasi-contract," and the remedies which have developed in equity to serve a similar restitution purpose. The tendency to continue to use the common count terminology is most persistent, today, where the benefit conferred by the plaintiff is in the form of services of some type and the "quantum meruit" terminology persists whether, as Professor Kovacic–Fleischer suggests, the claim be based upon an "implied in fact" or an "implied in law" theory.

JOHN A. ARTUKOVICH & SONS, INC. v. RELIANCE TRUCK CO.

Supreme Court of Arizona, 1980.
126 Ariz. 246, 614 P.2d 327.

HOLOHAN, VICE CHIEF JUSTICE.

After trial to the court plaintiff, John A. Artukovich & Sons, Inc., was granted judgment for compensatory damages of $6,956.59 and punitive damages of $6,000.00 against defendant, Reliance Truck Company, for conversion of plaintiff's crane. The Court of Appeals set aside the trial court's judgment for conversion, and ordered plaintiff's recovery to be reduced to compensatory damages of $1,456.59, which represented the out-of-pocket expenses actually incurred by plaintiff as a result of defendant's unauthorized use of the crane. We granted plaintiff's petition for review. The opinion of the Court of Appeals is vacated.

The facts necessary for determination of this matter are as follows: Plaintiff in an agreement dated July 1, 1975, leased its crane to the Ashton Company for use in Tucson, Arizona, in the construction of the addition to the University Stadium. The lease was for a nine-month term commencing on September 1, 1975, or the first day the crane was actually used, whichever came first, for a stated rental and provided for delivery to Ashton "F.O.B., Tempe, Arizona" on or about July 26, 1975.

Ashton hired the defendant to transport the crane from Tempe to Tucson by August 1, 1975. On Wednesday, July 23, 1975, Reliance dismantled and loaded the crane on its trucks in Tempe for the trip to Tucson. Meantime, Reliance was notified of the arrival in West Phoenix of a 246,000 lb. transformer that Reliance had previously contracted to put into place at a West Phoenix Arizona Public Service sub-station. Reliance's operation manager, Sam Curl, called Ashton's equipment manager to request permission to use the crane to unload the transformer prior to the trip to Tucson. The Ashton employee told Curl that he would have to talk to Harold Ashton but he would get back to Curl. The crane was moved to the West Phoenix jobsite on Thursday and reassembled on Friday before Curl called Ashton Company again and was told, "That the deal would have to be made with John Artukovich." Reliance already owed another Artukovich Company some money.

Curl testified he tried unsuccessfully to obtain permission from Artukovich by telephoning on Friday afternoon and left a message. Nevertheless, on Saturday Reliance used the crane without ever having received permission from Artukovich. The crane was then delivered to Tucson where after replacement of the cable and a safety inspection it was used by Ashton pursuant to the lease.

There was no evidence that Reliance made any further efforts to seek out Artukovich and pay a rental fee for the use of the crane. Artukovich found out about the unauthorized use from Ashton and sued Reliance on three counts: Counts I and III sounding in tort for the act of conversion and Count II on an implied contract theory. The trial judge's minute entry, dated November 3, 1978, awarded plaintiff judgment as follows:

"1. For use of the crane (one month minimum rental) $5,500.00.

2. Crane inspection fee, $493.05.

3. Replaced cable, $963.54.

4. Attorney's fees in the amount of $3,500.00.

5. Punitive damages in the amount of $2,500.00.

6. Plaintiff's costs."

After defendant's motion for a new trial questioned the correctness of awarding attorney's fees and punitive damages in the same action, plaintiff's judgment for the lump sum of $12,956.59 was vacated and plaintiff was given judgment in the amount of $6,956.59 for actual damages and

$6,000.00 punitive damages plus costs. Defendant filed a timely appeal which resulted in the above described action by the Court of Appeals.

The issues presented are (1) can plaintiff, Artukovich, recover on a theory of conversion from the defendant, Reliance, and (2) if not, is plaintiff entitled to judgment based on an implied contract theory.

Before plaintiff can recover in an action for the wrongful detention of its property it must show that it had a legal right to use the property and was in a position to use it and was prevented from such use only by the defendant's wrongful detention. * * *

Plaintiff's lease to Ashton, provided for delivery of a crane F.O.B. Tempe. Since Ashton had taken possession of the crane by authorizing its agent, Reliance, to transport the crane to Tucson, plaintiff, Artukovich, no longer had any right to use nor was it in a position to use the crane at the time of Reliance's unauthorized use. Plaintiff, therefore, cannot recover damages for its loss of use of the crane on a theory of conversion.

Although plaintiff may not recover on its tort theory, Count II of the complaint set forth a claim based on implied contract. It is clear from the trial court's minute entry of November 3, 1978, that the trial judge found sufficient evidence to support plaintiff's claim based on an implied contract. Our review of the evidence leads us to the same conclusion.

Contracts implied-in-law or quasi-contracts, also called constructive contracts, are inferred by the law as a matter of reason and justice from the acts and conduct of the parties and circumstances surrounding the transactions, * * * and are imposed for the purpose of bringing about justice without reference to the intentions of the parties. * * *

Restatement of Restitution, § 1 provides, "A person who has been unjustly enriched at the expense of another is required to make restitution to the other." Comment (a) to that section notes that a person is enriched if he received a benefit and is unjustly enriched if retention of that benefit would be unjust. Comment (b) defines a benefit as being any form of advantage. The facts in this case show that the defendant did receive a benefit or advantage through the use of plaintiff's crane. Defendant received $6,000.00 for putting the transformer in place pursuant to a contract with Arizona Public Service. The defendant has acknowledged throughout the litigation that it recognized and intended to pay someone a reasonable rental value for the crane's use.

Thus, the only issue remaining is what should plaintiff recover for the defendant's unauthorized use of its crane.

Unjust enrichment does not depend upon the existence of a valid contract * * * nor is it necessary that plaintiff suffer a loss corresponding to the defendant's gain for there to be a valid claim for an unjust enrichment. * * * Thus, even though plaintiff had no right to use the crane at the time of defendant's unauthorized use, the defendant is liable to plaintiff because the defendant received a benefit by using plaintiff's crane to perform the contract with Arizona Public Service. To allow the defendant to use plaintiff's crane without compensating plaintiff for its use would unjustly enrich the defendant and would be inequitable. Hertz v.

Fiscus, *supra:* Fleming v. Wineberg, 253 Or. 472, 455 P.2d 600 (1969). *See also* Restatement of Restitution, § 1, Comment (e) and Automotive Tire Service, Inc. v. First National Bank of Arizona, Phoenix, 102 Ariz. 512, 433 P.2d 804 (1967).

The judgment of the trial court is reversed, and the cause is remanded to Superior Court with direction to enter judgment for the plaintiff on Count II of the Complaint, and proceed to re-try only the issue of damages. Each party is to bear their own costs for this appeal.

STRUCKMEYER, C.J., and HAYS, CAMERON and GORDON, JJ., concur.

OLWELL v. NYE & NISSEN CO.

Supreme Court of Washington, 1946.
26 Wash.2d 282, 173 P.2d 652.

MALLERY, JUSTICE. On May 6, 1940, plaintiff, E.L. Olwell, sold and transferred to the defendant corporation his one-half interest in Puget Sound Egg Packers, a Washington corporation having its principal place of business in Tacoma. By the terms of the agreement, the plaintiff was to retain full ownership in an "Eggsact" egg-washing machine, formerly used by Puget Sound Egg Packers. The defendant promised to make it available for delivery to the plaintiff on or before June 15, 1940. It appears that the plaintiff arranged for and had the machine stored in a space adjacent to the premises occupied by the defendant but not covered by its lease. Due to the scarcity of labor immediately after the outbreak of the war, defendant's treasurer, without the knowledge or consent of the plaintiff, ordered the egg washer taken out of storage. The machine was put into operation by defendant on May 31, 1941, and thereafter for a period of three years was used approximately one day a week in the regular course of the defendant's business. Plaintiff first discovered this use in January or February of 1945 when he happened to be at the plant on business and heard the machine operating. Thereupon plaintiff offered to sell the machine to defendant for $600 or half of its original cost in 1929. A counter offer of $50 was refused and approximately one month later this action was commenced to recover the reasonable value of defendant's use of the machine, and praying for $25 per month from the commencement of the unauthorized use until the time of trial. A second cause of action was alleged but was not pressed and hence is not here involved. The court entered judgment for plaintiff in the amount of $10 per week for the period of 156 weeks covered by the statute of limitations, or $1,560, and gave the plaintiff his costs.

Defendant has appealed to this court assigning error upon the judgment, upon the trial of the cause on the theory of unjust enrichment, upon the amount of damages, and upon the court's refusal to make a finding as to the value of the machine and in refusing to consider such value in measuring damages.

The theory of the respondent was that the tort of conversion could be "waived" and suit brought in quasi-contract, upon a contract implied in law, to recover, as restitution, the profits which inured to appellant as a result of its wrongful use of the machine. With this the trial court agreed and in its findings of facts found that the use of the machine "resulted in a benefit to the users, in that said use saves the users approximately $1.43 per hour of use as against the expense which would be incurred were eggs to be washed by hand; that said machine was used by Puget Sound Egg Packers and defendant, on an average of one day per week from May of 1941, until February of 1945 at an average saving of $10.00 per each day of use."

In substance, the argument presented by the assignments of error is that the principle of unjust enrichment, or quasi-contract, is not of universal application, but is imposed only in exceptional cases because of special facts and circumstances and in favor of particular persons; that respondent had an adequate remedy in an action at law for replevin or claim and delivery; that any damages awarded to the plaintiff should be based upon the use or rental value of the machine and should bear some reasonable relation to its market value. Appellant therefore contends that the amount of the judgment is excessive.

It is uniformly held that in cases where the defendant *tort feasor* has benefited by his wrong, the plaintiff may elect to "waive the tort" and bring an action in assumpsit for restitution. Such an action arises out of a duty imposed by law devolving upon the defendant to repay an unjust and unmerited enrichment. Woodward, The Law of Quasi–Contracts, § 272(2), p. 439; Keener on Quasi–Contracts, p. 160. *See also* Professor Corbin's articles, "Waiver of Tort and Suit in Assumpsit," 19 Yale Law Journal, p. 221, and "Quasi–Contractual Obligations," 21 Yale Law Journal, p. 533.

It is clear that the saving in labor cost which appellant derived from its use of respondent's machine constituted a benefit.

According to the Restatement of Restitution, § 1(b), p. 12,

> "A person confers a benefit upon another if he gives to the other possession of or some other interest in money, land, chattels, or choses in action, performs services beneficial to or at the request of the other, satisfies a debt or a duty of the other, or in any way adds to the other's security or advantage. *He confers a benefit not only where he adds to the property of another, but also where he* saves the other from expense or loss. The word 'benefit', therefore denotes any form of advantage." (Italics ours)

It is also necessary to show that while appellant benefited from its use of the egg-washing machine, respondent thereby incurred a loss. It is argued by appellant that since the machine was put into storage by respondent, who had no present use for it, and for a period of almost three years did not know that appellant was operating it and since it was not injured by its operation and the appellant never adversely claimed any title to it, nor contested respondent's right of repossession upon the latter's discovery of the wrongful operation, that the respondent was not damaged because he is as well off as if the machine had not been used by appellant.

The very essence of the nature of property is the right to its exclusive use. Without it, no beneficial right remains. However plausible, the appellant cannot be heard to say that his wrongful invasion of the respondent's property right to exclusive use is not a loss compensable in law. To hold otherwise would be subversive of all property rights since his use was admittedly wrongful and without claim of right. The theory of unjust enrichment is applicable in such a case.

We agree with appellant that respondent could have elected a "common garden variety of action," as he calls it, for the recovery of damages. It is also true that except where provided for by statute, punitive damages are not allowed, the basic measure for the recovery of damages in this state being compensation. If, then, respondent has been *limited* to redress *in tort* for damages, as appellant contends, the court below would be in error in refusing to make a finding as to the value of the machine. In such case the award of damages must bear a reasonable relation to the value of the property. Hoff v. Lester, Wash., 168 P.2d 409.

But respondent here had an election. He chose rather to waive his right of action *in tort* and to sue *in assumpsit* on the implied contract. Having so elected, he is entitled to the measure of restoration which accompanies the remedy.

> "Actions for restitution have for their primary purpose taking from the defendant and restoring to the plaintiff something to which the plaintiff is entitled, or if this is not done, causing the defendant to pay the plaintiff an amount which will restore the plaintiff to the position in which he was before the defendant received the benefit. If the value of what was received and what was lost were always equal, there would be no substantial problem as to the amount of recovery, since actions of restitution are not punitive. In fact, however, the plaintiff frequently has lost more than the defendant has gained, and sometimes the defendant has gained more than the plaintiff has lost.
>
> "In such cases the measure of restitution is determined with reference to the tortiousness of the defendant's conduct or the negligence or other fault of one or both of the parties in creating the situation giving rise to the right to restitution. If the defendant was tortious in his acquisition of the benefit he is required to pay for what the other has lost although that is more, than the recipient benefited. *If he was consciously tortious in acquiring the benefit, he is also deprived of any profit derived from his subsequent dealing with it.* If he was no more at fault than the claimant, he is not required to pay for losses in excess of benefit received by him and he is permitted to retain gains which result from his dealing with the property." (Italics ours) Restatement of Restitution, pp. 595, 596.

Respondent may recover the profit derived by the appellant from the use of the machine.

Respondent has prayed "on his first cause of action for the sum of $25.00 per month from the time defendant first commenced to use said machine subsequent to May 1940 (1941) until present time."

In computing judgment, the court below computed recovery on the basis of $10 per week. This makes the judgment excessive since it cannot exceed the amount prayed for.

* * *

We therefore direct the trial court to reduce the judgment, based upon the prayer of the complaint, to $25 per month for thirty-six months, or $900.

The judgment as modified is affirmed. Appellant will recover its costs.*

Notes

1. When there is a wrongful taking of the plaintiff's personal property followed by a sale, the plaintiff may sue in tort for conversion, and claim the market value at the time of taking. Or, the plaintiff may "waive the tort" and sue in quasi-contract for the amount of the proceeds of the sale.** *See* P. Keeton, D. Dobbs, R. Keeton & D. Owen, Prosser and Keeton on the Law of Torts § 94 (5th ed. 1984). Where there has been no sale by the wrongdoer, the plaintiff can elect to sue in tort for conversion, thus effectuating a "forced sale"

* This case is discussed in Note, 20 Rocky Mt.L.Rev. 300 (1948).

Even in the case of innocent conversion the wronged party ordinarily may choose between quasi-contract recovery of the value when taken, or the proceeds upon sale, or tort damages measured by market value as of the time of taking, or, in the case of property which fluctuates in value, within a limited period before or after the taking. *See* I G. Palmer. The Law of Restitution § 2.12, at 158 (1978). Where there was a sale following the taking at a price in excess of market value at the time of taking, the Restatement of Restitution § 154 limits recovery to that market value.

** This option, and its implications, are considered in Davis v. Tyee Industries, Inc., 295 Or. 467, 668 P.2d 1186, 1188 n. 2 (1983) which, in turn, relies on Professor Dobbs:

"Professor Dobbs described the doctrine as follows:

'If the defendant converts chattels of the plaintiff and sells them, he is enriched by the sum he receives from the sale. It has usually seemed intolerable to allow a tortfeasor to profit from his tort, at least where it was a bad faith one, and for this reason the plaintiff has an appealing claim against the converter for the proceeds of the sale. In the great majority of cases the action of conversion, measuring damages by market value or special value to the plaintiff, will provide a recovery for the plaintiff that is equal to, or perhaps even greater than, the benefits gained by the defendant from the conversion and sale of the plaintiff's goods. But this is not always so. The converter may sell the chattel as an advance over market price, or he may be selling in a market that has risen since the time of conversion. In these circumstances a recovery that gives the plaintiff only the value of the chattel at the time of conversion still leaves the converter with a profit. This has seemed to the law to involve "unjust enrichment" of the converter, and to prevent it, the law allows the plaintiff to recover not merely compensation for his loss, but all of the defendant's gain as well. For example, if the defendant converts a gold watch worth $100 and sells it for $200, the plaintiff has only lost $100; but to prevent unjust enrichment he is allowed to recover the entire $200. The plaintiff's recovery is usually called restitutionary here and the principle is obviously quite different from the principle of compensation for a loss.

'The principle of preventing unjust enrichment in this manner did not spring full blown into the legal world. It developed instead from the use of fictions, which in turn left a certain amount of troublesome intellectual debris in their path. The central fiction was that the plaintiff whose property had been converted could "dispense with the wrong, and suppose the sale made by his consent." This fiction looks at the conversion of plaintiff's chattel and its subsequent sale as if the whole thing were done by agreement of the plaintiff and defendant. If such a sale of the plaintiff's chattel *had* in fact been agreed upon, it would have been tacitly understood by the parties that defendant would give the proceeds of the sale to the plaintiff. By going through this sort of fantasy the common law courts were able to think of a tortious conversion of a chattel as if it were all a matter of contract, at least if the plaintiff preferred to look at it this way. This is the famous waiver of tort and suit in assumpsit. Because it was in theory based upon an implied promise, this kind of claim is also called a quasi-contract claim.' D. Dobbs, Remedies, § 5.15, at 414 (1973). (Emphasis in original; footnotes omitted.)"

to the defendant. In the alternative, the plaintiff may bring a quasi-contract action for the value of the enrichment in most jurisdictions, today.

If the property in question has been returned, the plaintiff may bring a trespass to chattels action for any harm to it, plus damages for loss of use. Alternatively, as the *Artukovich* and *Olwell* cases hold, the plaintiff may sue in quasi-contract for the enrichment resulting from the defendant's use.

Especially where the taking was by a conscious wrongdoer, equitable jurisdiction may be invoked and the plaintiff may seek the remedies of constructive trust or equitable lien. These would be attractive alternatives where the proceeds of disposition can be traced into property with a greater value than that of the property at the time of taking, or the amount of the proceeds upon sale.

Where the defendant has received property from a thief, thus taking no title, or is a purchaser for value of a negotiable instrument but claims through a forged endorsement, he or she is liable for the market value in conversion, or the proceeds in quasi-contract, even though value was given when purchasing the property. I G. Palmer, The Law of Restitution § 2.2 (1978).

Factors which may influence the choice of remedy, apart from the dollar amount of the damages which may be claimed under each theory, are the availability of punitive damages (they may not be available in quasi-contract), survival of the cause of action upon death of the tort-feasor (tort claims may be lost, while quasi-contract claims are not) and right to jury trial. *See generally* I G. Palmer, The Law of Restitution § 2.3 (1978).

2. "*Election of remedies.*" In many cases the plaintiff may be entitled to the benefit of more than one remedy but, of course, is allowed to pursue only one to judgment if double recovery would otherwise result as often would be the case. In such a situation the defendant may endeavor to force the plaintiff to make that choice at an earlier stage in the action. If only one remedy is sought in the pleadings in their initial form the argument may be made that no other may now be sought by amending the pleadings. On the other hand the plaintiff may ask for several remedies, in which event the defendant may argue that there should be an obligation to defend against only one, and ask the court to require the defendant to choose. Both of these arguments have been used with varying degrees of success over the years, and have spawned what is known as the "election of remedies" doctrine.

The doctrine continues to be a cause for caution even though its rigors have been moderated in most jurisdictions.

In all jurisdictions, "election" still has vitality as a defense in the situation where the defendant can show that to allow the plaintiff to abandon one remedy in order to pursue another would prejudice the position of the defendant because he or she is now less well positioned to defend than would have been the case if the remedy now claimed had been asserted at an earlier point.

The adverse implications of the "election" doctrine are avoided only where the plaintiff is aware from the outset what the remedy options are, asserts a claim to all in the pleadings as filed or amended, offers proof of all, and is allowed to send all to the jury (or court) without having to elect until the finders of the facts have determined which among them the plaintiff is entitled to have. This procedure is followed in some jurisdictions.

The fact situation in *Olwell* offers an excellent example of a situation where an election must be made. Among the many considerations which may determine what choice should, or can, be made are the following: the measure of damages, right to punitive damages, applicable statute of limitations, possibility of "laches" as a defense, burden of proof, whether the remedy is available despite the death of the tortfeasor, right to a jury, preferential treatment over other creditors of the defendant, joinder of parties, attachment, suits against governmental bodies, and importantly, the possible right to recover the "fruits" of the wrongful conduct even though present value is greatly in excess of the value of the original benefit received by the defendant.

The pattern the cases follow in the various jurisdictions with respect to the "election" doctrine is summarized in D. Dobbs, Handbook on the Law of Remedies 13–23 (1973); I G. Palmer, The Law of Restitution §§ 2.4, 3.10 & 413 (1978).

VORTT EXPLORATION v. CHEVRON U.S.A.

Supreme Court of Texas, 1990.
787 S.W.2d 942.

OPINION

HIGHTOWER, JUSTICE.

The issue presented by this case is whether the trial court's findings of fact were sufficient to allow Vortt Exploration Company, Inc. (Vortt) to recover under quantum meruit for seismic information provided by Vortt to Chevron U.S.A., Inc. (Chevron). The trial court rendered judgment in favor of Vortt. The court of appeals reversed. We reverse the judgment of the court of appeals and remand the cause to that court for the consideration of points which it did not reach.

The subject of this dispute is a 160 acre tract of land located in Young County. Both Chevron and Vortt acquired mineral rights to various portions of the tract. In 1978 Vortt contacted Chevron requesting that they enter a farm-out agreement concerning a particular portion of the tract owned by Chevron. Chevron rejected the request to enter a farm-out agreement. Soon thereafter Vortt proposed that the two companies enter a joint operating agreement. Chevron informed Vortt that it might be interested in such an arrangement and requested that Vortt submit a proposal. Chevron and Vortt negotiated the specifics of the arrangement until 1983 without reaching an agreement. During this time, they corresponded frequently in an attempt to come to an agreement.

During the negotiations, Vortt provided Chevron with confidential seismic services, graphics, and maps in an attempt to reach a joint operating agreement. After receiving the information, Chevron drilled a producing well at the location identified in the information. Chevron then brought suit to invalidate certain leases held by Vortt. Vortt counterclaimed asserting the validity of the leases, or alternatively to recover under quantum meruit for the seismic services which were provided to Chevron. The trial court rendered judgment in favor of Vortt on its quantum meruit claim. The court of appeals reversed the trial court's judgment and rendered judgment in favor of Chevron. In rendering judgment, the court of appeals held that there was not a factual finding that Vortt furnished this information under such circumstances as to "reasonably notify Chevron that Vortt expected to be paid for the services and assistance" which were provided. Also, the court of appeals held that there was no evidence to support an implied finding of the omitted fact pursuant to Rule 299 of the Texas Rules of Civil Procedure.

Quantum meruit is an equitable remedy which does not arise out of a contract, but is independent of it. *Colbert v. Dallas Joint Stock Land Bank,* 129 Tex. 235, 102 S.W.2d 1031, 1034 (1937). Generally, a party may recover under quantum meruit only when there is no express contract covering the services or materials furnished. *Truly v. Austin,* 744 S.W.2d 934, 936 (Tex.1988). This remedy "is based upon the promise implied by law to pay for beneficial services rendered and knowingly accepted." *Id. See Campbell v. Northwestern National Life Insurance Co.,* 573 S.W.2d 496, 498 (Tex.1978). Recovery in quantum meruit will be had when non payment for the services rendered would "result in an unjust enrichment to the party benefited by the work." *City of Ingleside v. Stewart,* 554 S.W.2d 939, 943 (Tex.Civ.App.—Corpus Christi 1977, writ ref'd n.r.e.). Recognizing that quantum meruit is founded on unjust enrichment, this court set out the elements of a quantum meruit claim in *Bashara v. Baptist Memorial Hospital System,* 685 S.W.2d 307, 310 (Tex.1985). To recover under quantum meruit a claimant must prove that:

1) valuable services were rendered or materials furnished;
2) for the person sought to be charged;
3) which services and materials were accepted by the person sought to be charged, used and enjoyed by him;
4) under such circumstances as reasonably notified the person sought to be charged that the plaintiff in performing such services was expecting to be paid by the person sought to be charged.

Id. (quoting *City of Ingleside,* 554 S.W.2d at 943).

Vortt argues that the findings of fact made by the trial court were sufficient to satisfy *Bashara.* We agree. The trial court made several findings of fact. Those pertinent to the court of appeals' holding are as follows:

9) Vortt provided the aforesaid services and assistance to Chevron in the belief that Chevron and Vortt would jointly develop the subject 160 acres for the production of oil and gas, and but for such belief would not have provided such services and assistance to Chevron, which were undertaken for both Chevron and Vortt.

13) Chevron was reasonably notified that Vortt in performing such services and assistance for Chevron, expected to join with Chevron in a mutually satisfactory agreement for their joint production of oil and gas from the subject 160 acres.

Findings nine and thirteen reflect, as stated by the court of appeals, that "Chevron was on notice that Vortt, in performing the services and assistance, expected to join with Chevron in a mutually satisfactory agreement for production of the well and would not have provided such services and assistance except for such belief." The court of appeals stated that this notification did not rise to the level of notification required by the fourth element in *Bashara,* i.e., that such services were rendered under circumstances that would reasonably notify Chevron that Vortt expected to be *paid* for the seismic information. *Bashara* at 310 (emphasis added).

The expected payment does not have to be monetary; it may be any form of compensation. In *Campbell* the payment which was bargained for was an option to purchase an apartment complex. 573 S.W.2d at 497. When the contract was breached, this court upheld the quantum meruit claim and awarded damages for the reasonable value of services rendered. *Id.* Accordingly, quantum meruit recovery has been allowed when the original payment sought was an interest in land, *Miller v. Graves,* 185 S.W.2d 745 (Tex.Civ.App.—Fort Worth 1945, writ ref'd), and the devise of a residence. *Scott v. Walker,* 141 Tex. 181, 170 S.W.2d 718 (Tex.Comm'n App.1943).

Chevron knew that Vortt furnished the information with the expectation that a joint operating agreement would be reached. The parties had negotiated for over four years trying to achieve this end. At trial, Vortt's president testified that he shared the confidential seismic services, graphics, maps and other seismic information in the spirit of cooperation and that he would not have done so if he had not believed that a joint operating agreement would be reached. We hold that the trial court's findings of fact reflect that Chevron was reasonably notified that Vortt expected to be paid for the services and assistance which were rendered.

Chevron advanced several other points of error in the court of appeals. We have the option of either examining the points of error not considered by the court of appeals to determine if any of those points will support the court of appeal's judgment or, we may remand the cause to that court. *Roark v. Allen,* 633 S.W.2d 804 (Tex.1982). Because the points which were not reached include insufficient evidence points, we remand the cause to the court of appeals to consider the unaddressed points.

For the reasons stated, we reverse the judgment of the court of appeals and remand the cause to that court to consider the points of error which it did not reach.

HECHT, J., files a dissenting opinion in which PHILLIPS, C.J., and GONZALEZ, J., join.

HECHT, JUSTICE, dissenting.

I dissent. I agree with the Court that the only issue presented to us in this quantum meruit case is whether there is any evidence that Vortt Exploration Company, Inc. gave Chevron U.S.A., Inc. seismic information under circumstances as reasonably notified Chevron that Vortt expected to be paid for the information. * * *

* * *

Was ever fainter hope more richly rewarded? For not refusing to look at Vortt's information, Chevron must pay ten times its cost. The Court's ruling today should be a tremendous encouragement to benefaction. A frustrated negotiator should never overlook this tactic in attempting to induce agreement. The recipient of such charity, however, should beware.

I would hold that Chevron could not reasonably have expected to pay when Vortt did not expect to be paid. Accordingly, I would affirm the judgment of the court of appeals.

PHILLIPS, C.J., and GONZALEZ, J., join in this dissenting opinion.

Note

There are many cases involving fact situations which are quite similar to that in *Vortt Exploration.* The factual issue upon which the right to quasi-contract relief turns is whether the services rendered the defendant were undertaken "with an expectation of compensation." The other elements of the quasi-contract cause (measurable benefit to the defendant and its receipt under circumstances which require compensation if there is to be fairness to the plaintiff) are usually apparent.

Typical of the cases where there is a finding that the service in issue was rendered "without expectation" of compensation is Bloomgarden v. Coyer, 479 F.2d 201 (D.C.Cir.1973) ("There simply was no basis on which a jury could rationally find that when he brought the parties together he entertained any thought of a finder's fee for himself, or that those with whom he dealt held the payment of such a fee in prospect. These circumstances defeat Bloomgarden's quasi-contract claim * * *.") Accord, Cherokee Oil Co., Ltd. v. Union Oil of California, 706 F.Supp. 826 (M.D.Fla.1989), aff'd, 901 F.2d 1114 (11th Cir. 1990). *Compare,* Professional Recruiters, Inc. v. Oliver, 235 Neb. 508, 456 N.W.2d 103 (1990) ("Both parties knew or should have known that Professional Recruiters expected a fee if McMaster was hired." (456 N.W.2d at 109)).

DUSENKA v. DUSENKA

Supreme Court of Minnesota, 1946.
221 Minn. 234, 21 N.W.2d 528.

MATSON, JUSTICE. Appeal from an order denying plaintiff's motion for a new trial.

* * *

For several years prior to 1937, the defendant, Frank Dusenka, Jr., in partnership with his father, Frank Dusenka, Sr., operated an on-sale liquor tavern in Minneapolis. In 1937, the elder Dusenka transferred his one-half interest in the business to his son, the defendant, in consideration of the son's promise to support and maintain his father during his lifetime, subject, however, to the understanding that the father would continue to assist in the operation of the business. Plaintiff, wife of the senior Dusenka and stepmother of defendant, was not informed of the transfer and did not learn thereof until after the death of her husband. Practically every day, before and after 1937, inclusive of the period covered by this suit, namely, from September 1, 1938, to February 3, 1943, plaintiff accompanied her husband to the place of business around eight or nine in the morning, remained there until about one in the afternoon, and returned later in the evening. Plaintiff prepared breakfast for her husband after arriving at the tavern and also prepared certain other meals at the tavern for him and defendant as well. She at times also performed such services as cleaning up and scrubbing, tending bar, and furnishing some meals for guests or patrons that might come to the place. Plaintiff testified that her husband first became ill in 1938; that in 1939 he required hospitalization; and that thereafter "he feel badly and I help him." About February 3, 1943, her husband became seriously ill and died about February 9. Plaintiff received no pay from defendant for services performed between September 1938 and February 3, 1943, but for services performed subsequently to the death of her husband, at defendant's request, she was paid by defendant.

Plaintiff's suit is for remuneration for services rendered to defendant between September 1, 1938, and February 3, 1943. There was no contract, either express or implied, between plaintiff and defendant, for the performance of these services. We have no evidence that defendant ever expected to be required to pay for them. Plaintiff, by her brief, concedes that at no time before or during the performance of these services was there any intention or expectation of payment on her part, and she alleges that she rendered these services in the belief that "the place she was helping to run belonged to her 'mister' instead of the defendant." Furthermore, there is no evidence that plaintiff, either before or during the period when she rendered the services, ever requested, or intended, that defendant should pay for even a part of the services to correspond to what she thought was his share in the business as distinguished from that of her husband. Plaintiff does contend, however, that she always believed she was rendering these services for her husband and not for her stepson, the defendant. Clearly, plaintiff assumed at all times prior to her husband's death that he and defendant operated the business as partners. In fact, not until after her husband's death, when she discovered that he had in 1937 transferred his entire interest in the business to defendant, did she conceive a desire to be paid.

From the time the elder Dusenka in 1937 transferred his interest to his son until the time of his death, he received no regular wages or pay for his services, but at all times he enjoyed, and exercised, the unrestricted right or privilege of taking from the cash register whatever money he needed for living expenses, for the maintenance of his home and family, and for the payment of medical and hospital bills.

At the close of plaintiff's case, defendant rested provisionally and moved for a directed verdict on the ground that plaintiff had failed to show an employment or agreement for hire.

1. In determining the principles to be applied, significant is the admitted fact that neither plaintiff nor defendant had, prior to or during the performance of plaintiff's services, any intention or expectation that plaintiff should be paid. Plaintiff's intention or desire to be paid was not conceived until after the services had been fully performed. Obviously, there was no actual contract to pay, either express or implied in fact. A contract may be implied in fact, but not contrary to the common and

undisputed intention of both parties. 1 Williston, Contracts, Rev.Ed., § 21, note 1. * * *

* * *

2. Where services are admittedly rendered or benefits conferred voluntarily, without intention of receiving compensation on the part of the one rendering the services, and the person for whom they were rendered accepted them in reliance upon such intention, no actual contract to pay is *implied in fact.*

* * *

3. If plaintiff is to recover at all, it must be on the theory of a quasi contract, which is sometimes called a contract implied in law. Unfortunately, much confusion has resulted from a careless use of terminology and failure to observe a clear distinction between actual contracts and quasi contracts. * * * The quasi-contractual obligation is raised or imposed by law and is independent of any real or expressed intent of the parties. The obligation is called quasi-contractual because as a matter of legal history the remedy took the contract form just as if based on an actual contract or agreement. Carr v. Anderson, 154 Minn. 162, 191 N.W. 407, 26 A.L.R. 557. Under the theory of a quasi contract, the obligation is defined in equity and good conscience and is imposed by law to prevent unjust enrichment at the expense of another. *See,* Restatement, Restitution, § 1.

In applying the principles of quasi contract to the instant case, the question is whether defendant wrongfully and knowingly permitted plaintiff, through her mistake as to the ownership of the business, to confer upon him, without compensation, the benefit of her services to his unjust enrichment. Restatement, Restitution, § 40, comment c. Neither her husband, the elder Dusenka, nor defendant informed plaintiff of the sale and transfer by her husband of his one-half share in the business to defendant. If there was a duty by the stepson to tell his stepmother that which her husband, for some unknown reason, had not told her, does it reasonably follow that, if she had been so informed, she would have ceased to perform the services without compensation? The evidence indicates that plaintiff's services were rendered for the primary purpose of easing the daily tasks of her sick and ailing husband, whose health she wished to protect. She accompanied him in the morning and at the tavern prepared his and her own breakfast, as well as the other meals of the day. It is apparent that the other tasks she performed were comparatively light and, for the most part, designed to relieve her husband. She came voluntarily and apparently enjoyed the atmosphere. Plaintiff's motive is apparent from the fact that, although she always assumed that defendant owned a half interest in the business, she never at any time asked or expected to be paid by defendant in proportion to such interest. She also knew that her husband had children by his first marriage and that, in case of his death, these children would normally inherit a two-thirds interest in the half share that she supposed he still owned. If plaintiff had been informed of the transfer of her husband's interest, there is no reason to suppose, under all the circumstances of this case, that she would have altered her course of conduct or her expectations, in the slightest degree, and for this reason we can attach no significance to, nor imply any breach of good faith in, defendant's failure to disclose his purchase of the father's interest. Defendant was in a difficult position. If he had asked plaintiff to stay away from the tavern, he would have offended and embarrassed his own father, who was in need of assistance. We find no unjust enrichment for defendant. He had obligated himself to maintain his father for life, and, in fulfillment of that obligation, he permitted his father, plaintiff's husband, to have unrestricted access to the cash register to take whatever money he desired or needed for the payment of his personal and family expenses, inclusive of clothes, groceries, and all medical and hospital bills. We find no evidence of fraud, such as in the case of Boardman v. Ward, 40 Minn. 399, 42 N.W. 202, 12 Am.St.Rep. 749. Construing the evidence in the light most favorable to plaintiff, we hold that the court properly directed a verdict for defendant.*

Affirmed.

Note

The explanation the court offers for its holding in *Dusenka* is that it is likely that the plaintiff would have rendered the services in question gratuitously even had she not been deceived as she apparently was. Factual contexts other than the domestic have prompted a different result, presumably because it is more likely that the services in question would not have been rendered gratuitously, even though the conduct is less egregious because it less clearly involves deception. An illustration is Glazer v. Klughaupt, 116 N.J.L. 507, 185 A. 8 (1936) where the secretary who was working under an employment contract for an attorney continued to work for the attorney without salary following a promise by the attorney to marry her. In approving recovery in this situation, the court emphasized the presence of the contract with respect to prior services. In effect, the transaction was viewed as if a misrepresentation (not necessarily present since, presumably, the mutual promises of future conduct were in good faith) were made to induce rescission by agreement. This formed a basis for reinstating the employment relationship for the purpose of treating the services as though they had not been "volunteered."

WATTS v. WATTS

Court of Appeals of Wisconsin, 1989.
152 Wis.2d 370, 448 N.W.2d 292.

[Plaintiff Sue Ann Bischoff and defendant James E. Watts lived together from May, 1969 to December, 1981. They were not married. Bischoff sued Watts seeking a share of the wealth accumulated by Watts during this period.]

1.

A jury verdict will be upheld unless, "considering all credible evidence and reasonable inferences therefrom in the light most favorable" to the

* See, Thurston, Recent Developments in Restitution, 45 Mich.L.Rev. 935, 941–44 (1947); Wade, Restitution for Benefits Conferred Without Request, 19 Vand.L.Rev. 1183, 1190–1194 (1966); Annot., 7 A.L.R.2d 8 (1949).

verdict, "there is no credible evidence to sustain" it. Rule 805.14(1), Stats.; *Sumnicht v. Toyota Motor Sales,* 121 Wis.2d 338, 360, 360 N.W.2d 2, 12 (1984). Moreover, appellate courts must give weight to a trial court's approval of a verdict challenged on insufficiency-of-evidence grounds. *See Upton v. Tatro,* 68 Wis.2d 562, 570, 229 N.W.2d 691, 695 (1975).

The basis for an unjust enrichment claim in a cohabitation case was framed by the Supreme Court in *Watts I:*

> Many courts have held, and we now so hold, that unmarried cohabitants may raise claims based upon unjust enrichment following the termination of their relationships where one of the parties attempts to retain an unreasonable amount of the property acquired through the efforts of both.

Id., 137 Wis.2d at 532–533, 405 N.W.2d at 314. There was extensive evidence concerning the services that Bischoff performed for Watts, in the upkeep of their home as well as in the service of his business, from which the jury could have determined that Bischoff's efforts fertilized the increased value of Watts' property, not only by helping him in the business but also by freeing him from many nonbusiness tasks. The jury also had ample information from which it could determine the increased value of that property during the time Watts and Bischoff lived and worked together as husband and wife. Financial statements for both Watts and his business for every year from 1970 through 1981 were in evidence, and Bischoff's expert indicated that Watts' net worth had increased by $1,113,900.88, from $382,756.12 in May of 1970 to $1,496,657 in 1981. The jury also knew that in 1972 Watts executed a will that would have given Bischoff ten per cent of his property, excluding personal property "directly used in connection with the operation" of his business, and excluding a parcel of real estate used in the business. The jury could have inferred that this was the value Watts placed on Bischoff's services in 1972, and, although the will excluded much business-related property, it was not unreasonable for the jury to use the ten per cent figure as a guide to determine an appropriate award to Bischoff for unjust enrichment for the 12 year relationship.[7]

Although neither party presented expert testimony on the value of the specific services performed by Bischoff for Watts, such expert testimony was not necessary. *See Redepenning v. Dore,* 56 Wis.2d 129, 135–136, 201 N.W.2d 580, 584 (1972). *Cf. Kujawski v. Arbor View Health Care Center,* 139 Wis.2d 455, 463, 407 N.W.2d 249, 252–253 (1987) (expert testimony not required when "determination involves matters within the common knowledge" or "within the realm of the ordinary experience of mankind.").

We agree with the trial court that there was sufficient evidence to support the jury's finding that Watts was unjustly enriched by Bischoff's efforts by $113,090.08, which is a little less than $12,000 a year.

7. Ten per cent of the increase in Watts' net worth given by Bischoff's expert ($1,113,900.88) is $111,390.08. The jury awarded Bischoff $113,090.08. [Footnote by the Court.]

2.

Watts' second point in connection with the unjust-enrichment award is that all but the last two years of Bischoff's claim is barred by the statute of limitations applicable to personal-service compensation, sec. 893.44(1), Stats. * * *

The *Watts I*-type claim for unjust enrichment that Bischoff asserts accrues when the relationship has terminated, *see Watts,* 137 Wis.2d at 532–533, 405 N.W.2d at 314 ("unmarried cohabitants may *raise claims* based upon unjust enrichment *following the termination of their relationships.*" [emphasis added]), and not before, because termination of the relationship without disgorgement of the benefit conferred and improperly retained *is* the injury for which *Watts I* permits recovery. *Id.* at 531–533, 405 N.W.2d at 313–314. *See also Osborn Plumbing,* 66 Wis.2d at 462, 225 N.W.2d at 632 (a "cause of action accrues and the statute of limitations begins to run when an injury occurs."). Thus, Bischoff had no unjust-enrichment " 'claim capable of present enforcement,' " *Meracle v. Children's Serv. Soc'y,* 149 Wis.2d 19, 26, 437 N.W.2d 532, 534 (1989) (quoting *Barry v. Minahan,* 127 Wis. 570, 573, 107 N.W. 488, 490 [1906]), under *Watts I* until the relationship ended in December, 1981. Since this action was commenced in March, 1982, it is within the shortest possible period of applicable limitations, and is timely. The trial court's September 8, 1988, judgment on the unjust enrichment verdict is affirmed.

Judgment affirmed in part, reversed in part, order vacated, and cause remanded.

Notes

1. A similar result was reached in Burns v. Koellmer, 11 Conn.App. 375, 527 A.2d 1210 (Conn.App.1987) in which the plaintiff, who had begun to live with the defendant, helped to manage a tennis facility. The Court summarized the facts "which could reasonably have been found by the jury" as follows: "The plaintiff then began, at the request of the defendant, to perform all of the managerial functions at the club. * * * The plaintiff expected to be remunerated in excess of those payments [given her by defendant], the defendant benefitted from the plaintiff's service, the defendant had assured the plaintiff that she would receive additional compensation * * *." Accord: Estate of Steffer v. Steffer, 95 Wis.2d 490, 290 N.W.2d 697 (1980).

In the cases in which the plaintiff apparently has "sacrificed" an opportunity to work outside the home while rendering "housewifely services" for the defendant (who has accumulated an estate during the period in question) usually have resulted in a refusal of restitution relief. The reason given is that found in *Dusenka,*—an absence of proof of "expectation of compensation." Perhaps the most publicized case is Marvin v. Marvin, 18 Cal.3d 660, 134 Cal.Rptr. 815, 557 P.2d 106 (1976). In that case the Supreme Court of California considered a claim by the female plaintiff who had given up her professional career and co-habitated, for six years, with the defendant, a successful film actor. At the end of this period, the defendant asked the plaintiff to leave his premises.

The plaintiff alleged that she had given up a lucrative career as an entertainer and singer in order to "devote her full time to the defendant * * * as a companion, homemaker, housekeeper and cook" after the defendant agreed that they would share, equally, the property accumulated "as a result of their efforts whether individual or combined" and would hold themselves out to the public as husband and wife. She sought a declaratory judgment as to her contract and property rights, and a constructive trust of one-half of the property acquired during the course of the relationship. In the course of its opinion the Court stated:

> "The courts may inquire into the conduct of the parties to determine whether that conduct demonstrates an implied contract or implied agreement of partnership or joint venture (*see* Estate of Thornton, 81 Wash.2d 72, 499 P.2d 864 (1972)), or some other tacit understanding between the parties. The courts may, when appropriate, employ principles of constructive trust (*see* Omer v. Omer, 11 Wash.App. 386, 523 P.2d 957 (1974)) or resulting trust (*see* Hyman v. Hyman, 275 S.W.2d 149 (Tex.Civ.App.1954)). Finally, a nonmarital partner may recover in quantum meruit for the reasonable value of household services rendered less the reasonable value of support received if he can show that he rendered services with the expectation of monetary reward. (*See* Hill v. Estate of Westbrook, *supra,* 39 Cal.2d 458, 462, 247 P.2d 19.)
>
> "Since we have determined that plaintiff's complaint * * * can be amended to state a cause of action independent of allegations of express contract, we must conclude that the trial court erred in granting defendant a judgment on the pleadings." *Id.* at 684–85, 557 P.2d at 122–23, 134 Cal.Rptr. at 831–32.

On remand the trial court, without a jury, found that the defendant had made no agreement with the plaintiff for sharing income or to provide for her financial needs, that she had benefitted "economically and socially" from the cohabitation, and that there was no "fiduciary relationship" and no unjust enrichment as a result of the relationship. However, the Court awarded the plaintiff $104,000 to be used for her "economic rehabilitation," because it was doubtful that she could return to the career she enjoyed before the relationship in question began and she, therefore, "was in need of rehabilitation—*i.e.,* to learn new employable skills." The defendant appealed.

The Court of Appeals set the award aside. While the record showed the plaintiff's need and defendant's ability to respond to the need, the Court stated: "The award, being nonconsensual in nature, must be supported by some recognized underlying obligation in law or in equity. A court of equity admittedly has broad powers, but it may not create totally new substantive rights under the guise of doing equity." Marvin v. Marvin, 122 Cal.App.3d 871, 876, 176 Cal.Rptr. 555, 559 (1981). Accord: Tapley v. Tapley, 122 N.H. 727, 449 A.2d 1218 (1982); (no quasi-contract recovery where the plaintiff rendered "housewifely services" to her co-habitant); Johnston v. Estate of Phillips, 706 S.W.2d 554 (Mo.App.1986) (the "mere rendition of the [housewifely] services, admittedly valuable, did not justify allowance of the claim"; there must be evidence of an "understanding that she was to be paid for the services rendered".) (p. 558); Matos v. Gadman, 173 A.D.2d 442, 570 N.Y.S.2d 68 (1991) (a cause of action for constructive trust relief was alleged based upon "representations" that plaintiff, who co-habitated with defendant, would share in the property acquired, but there could be no implied contract cause "for personal services between unmarried persons who live together.") (570 N.Y.S.2d 70, at 71).

A significant difference between the *Watts* case and those just described is that in *Watts* the reasoning of the Supreme Court in Wisconsin, in allowing restitution, emphasized an increase in the value of the property of one party traceable to the efforts (other than "housewifely") of both, rather than engaging upon a search for evidence of a "common understanding" that compensation was expected.

2. Since the often elusive proof of "expectation of compensation" presumably consists of evidence of a statement, somewhere along the way (and not in "jest"), to the effect "I'm not doing all of this for nothing," and corroborating evidence of such a statement ordinarily present problems of proof, the burden of proof can be of great significance. In Shold v. Goro, 480 N.W.2d 892 (Iowa 1992), where one co-habitant, after the relationship ended, sought to recover the sums supplied to the other during the period in question, the Court ruled that the burden of proof to show that the defendant received a benefit from the plaintiff was on the plaintiff, after which the burden was on the defendant to show that it was a gift and not a loan.

In this connection consider Boland v. Catalona, 202 Conn. 333, 521 A.2d 142 (1987) in which the defendant claimed that any agreement between the parties was to "share their earnings and [share equally] the fruits of their joint labor" [plaintiff had turned her earnings over to the defendant who, in turn, provided her with an allowance for household and personal expenses] but only for the duration of the period of co-habitation. The Connecticut Supreme Court ruled that there was inadequate evidence of an express contract. However, the action was remanded for a new trial to consider recovery on an "implied contract theory" which may have been justified because the referee had found as an "ultimate fact" an "agreement" to share for some period of time, and had found as "subordinate facts" that "[t]he defendant referred to the New Milford house as being 'our house' to the plaintiff," and the "referee [also] found additional facts relating to the substantial amount of time and labor the plaintiff had devoted to building and maintaining the home." (521 A.2d at 145.)

3. While the approach of the Supreme Court of Wisconsin in the *Watts* case may be highly advantageous from the plaintiff's point of view (*see* Note 1, *supra*) it may nonetheless leave the plaintiff with the difficult task of offering a justifiable basis for measuring the value of the benefit conferred. A possibility (found to be unnecessary by the *Watts* court) would be the use of expert testimony to show the market value of comparable services much in the manner of a conventional *quantum meruit* claim. Another is that approved by the *Watts* court. The Court stated that "it was not unreasonable for the jury to use the ten percent figure as a guide", *i.e.,* a ten percent increase in the defendant's net worth during the period. From all of the evidence of the labor and skill contributed by both, the jury is thus allowed to determine what proportion of the increase in net worth can "reasonably" be attributed to the plaintiff's services.

See, also, Lawlis v. Thompson, 137 Wis.2d 490, 405 N.W.2d 317 (1987) ("An accountant stated the amount by which Thompson's [the defendant's] expenditures exceeded his wages * * * [and there was testimony as to] the change in Lawliss's [the plaintiff's] net worth during the period of the relationship.") (405 N.W.2d at 322).

4. Where there is no intimate or family relationship between the parties and the services of the co-habitant include more than ordinary housekeeping activities, the "presumption" that services are gratuitous, which arises in some jurisdictions where the plaintiff is a family member, may be inapplicable and recovery in quantum meruit may be more likely. Schanz v. Estate of Terry, 504 S.W.2d 653, 92 ALR3d 719 (Mo.App.1974) (housekeeping and farm help); Morris v. Retz, 413 S.W.2d 544 (Mo.App.1967) (housekeeping, as well as helping as a nurse, with patients treated on the premises). The presumption was applicable, but overcome by the evidence, where two sisters gave up employment and came to live with the decedent in order to take care of both the premises and the decedent during decedent's illness. Estate of Raketti v. Leino, 340 N.W.2d 894 (N.D.1983).

Where the plaintiff does not reside on the premises, but renders services related to household affairs, the same problem of proof of expectation of compensation is present. Burton v. McLaughlin, 117 Utah 483, 217 P.2d 566 (1950) (female plaintiff took care of older homeowner; the services were "not the kind of services that strangers usually give without expecting compensation" and the record showed decedent was aware of this, making relief appropriate); accord, Sparks v. Gustafson, 750 P.2d 338 (Alaska 1988) ("the services * * * were not the sort which one would ordinarily expect to receive from a friend as a mere gratuity." (at p. 343)). *Compare*, Kershaw v. Tracy Collins Bank & Trust Co., 561 P.2d 683 (Utah 1977) (plaintiff was decedent's husband's "lodge brother," and took over supervision of her personal life after his death; the evidence showed decedent viewed the services as those normally expected of a friend and, consequently, quantum meruit relief was not appropriate).

Most of these cases appear to involve alleged "implied in fact," rather than "implied in law," claims.

PYEATTE v. PYEATTE

Court of Appeals of Arizona, 1982.
135 Ariz. 346, 661 P.2d 196.

Opinion

Corcoran, Judge.

This is an appeal by the husband from an award of $23,000 in favor of the wife as ordered in a decree of dissolution. Two issues are before us: (1) The validity of an oral agreement entered into by the husband and wife during the marriage, whereby each spouse agreed to provide in turn the sole support for the marriage while the other spouse was obtaining further education; and, (2) whether the wife is entitled to restitution for benefits she provided for her husband's educational support in a dissolution action which follows closely upon the husband's graduation and admission to the Bar. The word "agreement" is used as a term of reference for the stated understanding between the husband and wife and not as a legal conclusion that the agreement is enforceable at law as a contract.

The husband, H. Charles Pyeatte (appellant), and the wife, Margrethe May Pyeatte (appellee), were married in Tucson on December 27, 1972. At the time of the marriage both had received bachelors degrees. Appellee was coordinator of the surgical technical program at Pima College. Appellant was one of her students. In early 1974, the parties had discussions and reached an agreement concerning postgraduate education for both of them.

Appellee testified that they agreed she "would put him through three years of law school without his having to work, and when he finished, he would put [her] through for [her] masters degree without [her] having to work."

Appellant concedes the existence of an agreement. * * *

* * *

Appellant attended law school in Tucson, Arizona, from 1974 until his graduation. He was admitted to the State Bar shortly thereafter.

During appellant's first two years of law school appellee supported herself and appellant on the salary she earned at Pima College. During the last year, appellee lost her job, whereupon savings were used to support the couple. Although each spouse contributed to the savings, a significant amount was furnished by appellee.

After appellant's admission to the Bar, the couple moved to Prescott, Arizona, where appellant was employed by a law firm. Both parties realized that appellant's salary would not be sufficient to support the marriage and pay for appellee's education for a masters degree simultaneously. Appellee then agreed to defer her plans for a year or two until her husband got started in his legal career. In the meantime, she obtained part-time employment as a teacher.

In April, 1978, appellant told appellee that he no longer wanted to be married to her, and in June of 1978, she filed a petition for dissolution. Trial was had in March of 1979, and a decree of dissolution was granted. At the time of the trial, there was little community property and no dispute as to division of any community or separate property. Spousal maintenance was neither sought by nor granted to appellee.

The trial court determined that there was an agreement between the parties, that appellee fully performed her part of that agreement, that appellant had not performed his part of the agreement, and that appellee had been damaged thereby.

Based on appellee's expert testimony on the cost of furthering *her* education, in accordance with the agreement, the trial court awarded judgment of $23,000 against appellant as damages for breach of contract, with additional directions that the judgment be payable through the court clerk on a quarterly basis in a sum of not less than ten percent of appellant's net quarterly income.

The trial court directed appellant to use his best efforts to produce income and to keep accurate records of his income-producing activities, which records would be available to appellee upon request but not more frequently than on a quarterly basis. The court also retained jurisdiction of the case for the purpose of supervising the administration of the payment of the judgment and the keeping of records by the appellant. * * *

On appeal, appellant argues that the agreement did not rise to the level of a binding contract because, among other things, the terms thereof were not definite and could not be legally enforced.

Appellee advances three theories as grounds upon which the trial court's award should be upheld:

1. The agreement between the parties was a binding contract. Appellant's failure to perform after appellee had fully performed her obligations renders appellant liable in damages.

* * *

3. If the agreement is not enforceable as a binding contract, appellee is nevertheless entitled to restitution in quantum meruit to prevent appellant's unjust enrichment because he received his education at appellee's expense.

We will address each argument in turn.

THE CONTRACT CLAIM

Although the terms and requirements of an enforceable contract need not be stated in minute detail, it is fundamental that, in order to be binding, an agreement must be definite and certain so that the liability of the parties may be exactly fixed. Terms necessary for the required definiteness frequently include time of performance, place of performance, price or compensation, penalty provisions, and other material requirements of the agreement. * * *

Upon examining the parties' agreement in this instance, it is readily apparent that a sufficient mutual understanding regarding critical provisions of their agreement did not exist. * * *

* * *

THE RESTITUTION CLAIM

Appellee's last contention is that the trial court's award should be affirmed as an equitable award of restitution on the basis of unjust enrichment. She argues that appellant's education, which she subsidized and which he obtained through the exhaustion of community assets constitutes a benefit for which he must, in equity, make restitution. This narrow equitable issue is one of first impression in this court. We first addressed the broad outlines of the problem in *Wisner,* but in the context of significantly different facts and legal theories. Our recognition of the disparate considerations involved in a case such as the one before us led us to limit our holding in *Wisner* to its facts. 129 Ariz. at 341, 631 P.2d at 123.

Restitution is available to a party to an agreement where he performs services for the other believing that there is a binding contract.

When Restitution for Services is Granted.

> A person who has rendered services to another or services which have inured to the benefit of another * * * is entitled to restitution therefor if the services were rendered.
>
> * * *
>
> (b) To obtain the performance of an agreement with the other therefor, not operative as a contract, or voidable as a contract and avoided by the other party after the services were rendered, the one performing the services erroneously believing because of a mistake of fact that the agreement was binding upon the other. * * *

Restatement of Restitution § 40(b) at 155 (1937).

In order to be granted restitution, appellee must demonstrate that appellant received a benefit, that by receipt of that benefit he was unjustly enriched at her expense, and that the circumstances were such that in good conscience appellant should make compensation. John A. Artukovich & Sons v. Reliance Truck Co., 126 Ariz. 246, 614 P.2d 327 (1980); Restatement of Restitution § 1 at 13 (1937).

* * *

A benefit may be any type of advantage, including that which saves the recipient from any loss or expense. Appellee's support of appellant during his period of schooling clearly constituted a benefit to appellant. Absent appellee's support, appellant may not have attended law school, may have been forced to prolong his education because of intermittent periods of gainful employment, or may have gone deeply into debt. Relieved of the necessity of supporting himself, he was able to devote full time and attention to his education.

The mere fact that one party confers a benefit on another, however, is not of itself sufficient to require the other to make restitution. Retention of the benefit must be unjust.

Historically, restitution for the value of services rendered has been available upon either an "implied-in-fact" contract or upon quasi-contractual grounds. D. Dobbs, Remedies § 4.2 at 237 (1973); 1 Williston, Contracts §§ 3 and 3A at .10–15 (3d ed., 1957). An implied-in-fact contract is a true contract, differing from an express contract only insofar as it is proved by circumstantial evidence rather than by express written or oral terms. United States v. O. Frank Heinz Construction Co., 300 F.Supp. 396 (D.C.Ill.1969); Plumbing Shop, Inc. v. Pitts, 67 Wash.2d 514, 408 P.2d 382, 383 (1965). In contrast, a quasi-contract is not a contract at all, but a duty imposed in equity upon a party to repay another to prevent his own unjust enrichment. The intention of the parties to bind themselves contractually in such a case is irrelevant. 1 Williston, Contracts § 3A at 12–15 (3d ed. 1957). To support her claim for restitution on the basis of an implied-in-fact contract, appellee must demonstrate the elements of a binding contract. For the reasons we have previously discussed, we cannot find the necessary mutual assent or certainty as to the critical terms of the agreement sufficient to establish such a contract. *See also* Osborn v. Boeing Airplane Co., 309 F.2d 99 (9th Cir.1962).

Restitution is nevertheless available in quasi-contract absent any showing of mutual assent. While a quasi-contractual obligation may be imposed without regard to the intent of the parties, such an obligation will be imposed only if the circumstances are such that it would be unjust to allow retention of the benefit without compensating the one who conferred it. *See* Williston, *supra.* One circumstance under which a duty to compensate will be imposed is when there was an expectation of payment or compensation for services at the time they were rendered.

> [A]n obligation to pay, ordinarily, will not be implied in fact or by law if it is clear that there was indeed no expectation of payment, that a gratuity was intended to be conferred, that the benefit was conferred officiously, or that the question of payment was left to the unfettered discretion of the recipient.

Osborn v. Boeing Airplane Co., 309 F.2d at 102.

Although we found that the spousal agreement failed to meet the requirements of an enforceable contract, the agreement still has importance in considering appellee's claim for unjust enrichment because it both evidences appellee's expectation of compensation and the circumstances which make it unjust to allow appellant to retain the benefits of her extraordinary efforts.

We next address the question of whether restitution on the basis of unjust enrichment is appropriate in the context of the marital relationship. No authority is cited to the court in support of the proposition that restitution as a matter of law is inappropriate in a dissolution proceeding. * * *

* * *

Where both spouses perform the usual and incidental activities of the marital relationship, upon dissolution there can be no restitution for performance of these activities. *Ibid.* Where, however, the facts demonstrate an agreement [that is, "expectation of compensation" in the form of reciprocal help with education costs] between the spouses and an extraordinary or unilateral effort by one spouse which inures solely to the benefit of the other by the time of dissolution, the remedy of restitution is appropriate.

Arizona courts have traditionally utilized the equitable restitutionary device of the constructive trust to prevent unjust enrichment between spouses upon dissolution when there is property to which such a trust may attach. *See, e.g.,* Dawson v. McNaney, 71 Ariz. 79, 223 P.2d 907 (1950); Harmon v. Harmon, 126 Ariz. 242, 613 P.2d 1298 (App.1980); Chirekos v. Chirekos, 24 Ariz.App. 223, 537 P.2d 608 (1975). We see no reason in law or equity why restitution should not be available in an appropriate circumstance to prevent the unjust enrichment of a spouse when a constructive trust is not available, as here, when no property exists. We analogize the two restitutionary devices solely to the extent of illustrating their common essence—prevention of the unjust enrichment of one spouse at the expense of the other.

A number of jurisdictions have addressed the issue of restitution in the context of the marital relationship. The cases which have dealt with the issue involve two factual patterns: (1) The first group consists of those cases in which the couples had accumulated substantial marital assets over a period of time from which assets the wife received large awards of property, maintenance and child support. The courts have refused to apply the theory of restitution on the basis of unjust enrichment in each of these cases. (2) The second group consists of those cases in which the parties are divorced soon after the student spouse receives his degree or license and there is little or no marital property from which to order any award to the working spouse.

* * *

The record shows that the appellee conferred benefits on appellant—financial subsidization of appellant's legal education—with the agreement and expectation that she would be compensated therefor by his reciprocal efforts after his graduation and admission to the Bar. Appellant has left the marriage with the only valuable asset acquired during the marriage—his legal education and qualification to practice law. It would be inequitable to allow appellant to retain this benefit without making restitution to appellee. However, we need not decide what limits or standards would apply in the absence of an agreement. Commentators have discerned in various statutory enactments and the developing case law a renewed and expanded recognition of marriage's economic underpinnings. *See* Comment, The Interest of the Community in a Professional Education, 10 Calif.W.L.Rev. 590 (1974); Erickson, Spousal Support Toward the Realization of Educational Goals: How the Law Can Ensure Reciprocity, 1978 Wis.L.Rev. 947. By our decision herein, we reject the view that the economic element necessarily inherent in the marital institution (and particularly apparent in its dissolution) requires us to treat marriage as a strictly financial undertaking upon the dissolution of which each party will be fully compensated for the investment of his various contributions. When the parties have been married for a number of years, the courts cannot and will not strike a balance regarding the contributions of each to the marriage and then translate that into a monetary award. To do so would diminish the individual personalities of the husband and wife to economic entities and reduce the institution of marriage to that of a closely held corporation.

THE MEASURE OF RECOVERY

Generally, where claims are made by the working spouse against the student spouse, the trial court in each case must make specific findings as to whether the education, degree or license acquired by the student spouse during marriage involved an unjust enrichment of that spouse, the value of the benefit, and the amount that should be paid to the working spouse. A variety of methods of computing the unjust enrichment may be employed in ascertaining the working spouse's compensable interest in the attainment of the student spouse's education, degree or license.

The award to appellee should be limited to the financial contribution by appellee for appellant's living expenses and direct educational expenses. *See DeLa Rosa v. DeLa Rosa,* 309 N.W.2d 755.

Under the agreement between the parties, the anticipated benefit to appellee may involve a monetary benefit in a lesser amount than the benefit conferred by appellee on appellant. In that event, the award to appellee should be limited to the amount of the anticipated benefit to appellee. Appellee should not recover more than the benefit of her bargain. Restatement of Restitution, § 107, Comment b, at 449 (1937).

Appellant further objects to the judgment of $23,000 against him on the ground that it directs the payment on terms over a period of time. The terms of payment were of benefit only to appellant. If he wanted to pay the judgment in a lump sum, he certainly could do so. In any event, the trial court, in entering an equitable judgment for money, has the authority to order that it be paid in periodic payments plus interest through the clerk of the court in a certain percentage of appellant's net income, and that appellee have the right to review his records to determine the accuracy of the net income calculations.

The relief granted, to appellee is equitable in nature. The rule regarding equitable awards is set forth in *Mason v. Ellison,* 63 Ariz. 196, 160 P.2d 326 (1945) in which the Arizona supreme court stated:

> In an equity case the court "* * * adapts its relief and molds its decrees to satisfy the requirements of the case and to conserve the equities of the parties litigant. The court has such plenary power since its purpose is the accomplishment of justice amid all of the vicissitudes and intricacies of life * * *."

63 Ariz. at 203, 160 P.2d at 329 (quoting 19 Am.Jur. Equity § 123 at 123–24 (1939)).

The fact that this case presents a novel resolution of a difficult issue, without precedent, will not prevent this court from ordering relief in an amount and manner appropriate to the circumstances.

> It is the distinguishing feature of equity jurisdiction that it will apply settled rules to unusual conditions and mold its decrees so as to do equity between the parties.

30 C.J.S. Equity § 12 at 798–99 (1965). * * *

* * *

The nature of equity is individual justice. Since the benefit bestowed upon appellant by appellee was periodic in nature and dependent on her income, we find no abuse of the equity power of the court in awarding appellee periodic payments, especially where she can use them periodically to pursue her own education. By our affirmance of an instalment method of payment in this case, we do not mean to promulgate a rule that will uniformly govern all awards in subsequent cases of that nature. Each will, by virtue of the equitable nature of the claim, require relief tailored to the facts and circumstances of the individuals. *DeLa Rosa v. DeLa Rosa,* 309 N.W.2d at 759, n. 11.

The portion of the judgment in the amount of $23,000 is reversed and remanded for proceedings in accordance with this opinion.

FROEB, ACTING P.J., and HATHAWAY, J., concur.

Notes

1. The *Pyeatte* court makes clear that restitution relief based upon a claim of unjust enrichment of one spouse at the expense of the other resulting from conduct during the period of the marriage may be available only where it is the case that the couple had not "accumulated substantial marital assets over a period of time" and as a consequence there was no "marital property from which to order * * * [an] award to the working spouse."

2. Several cases have considered the value of a degree and related "good will" upon divorce. Consider the following: Postema v. Postema, 189 Mich. App. 89, 105, 471 N.W.2d 912, 919 (1991) (The court said "Where a degree is the end product of a concerted family effort, fairness and equity will not permit the degree holder to reap the benefits of the degree without compensating the other spouse for unrewarded sacrifices, efforts and contributions toward attainment of the degree." (471 N.W.2d at 917). The trial court may consider whether a spouse has been compensated during the marriage and whether the spouse was to have had reciprocal efforts devoted to earning a degree); Dugan v. Dugan, 92 N.J. 423, 434, 457 A.2d 1, 6 (1983) ("Much of the economic value produced during an attorney's marriage will inhere in the goodwill of the law practice. It would be inequitable to ignore the contribution of the non-attorney spouse to the development of that economic resource."); Prahinski v. Prahinski, 321 Md. 227, 234, 582 A.2d 784, 787 (1990). (Attorney goodwill was not marital property but noted that "The view most often followed treats goodwill as marital property in all cases. The next largest group considers goodwill to be personal to the practitioner, and therefore not marital property. Finally, a small group of states requires a case-by-case examination to determine how goodwill should be treated." Therefore, the value of the wife's "time and effort which made the practice successful" was not marital property).

SECTION 3. CONSTRUCTIVE TRUST

SSI MEDICAL SERVICES, INC. v. COX

Supreme Court of South Carolina, 1990.
301 S.C. 493, 392 S.E.2d 789.

I. FACTS

Respondent SSI Medical Services, Inc. (SSI) is a corporation headquartered in Charleston engaged in the manufacture and distribution of medical equipment. Its principle product is hospital beds. At one time, SSI provided automobiles and trucks for the business use of some of its employees. These vehicles were leased and the total fleet was comprised of approximately 850 vehicles. During appellant Donald L. Cox's (Cox) tenure with SSI, he was employed as the manager of the automobile and truck fleet. This action stems primarily from Cox's handling of the automobile fleet.

The normal lease term for automobiles was the first of either two years or 50,000 miles. When an automobile lease expired, the automobile was returned to the leasing company for disposal. SSI and the individual leasing company would then agree on the residual value of the automobile. If the leasing company was able to sell the automobile at either the residual value or more, SSI would pay nothing extra or receive the excess. If the leasing company received less than the residual value of the automobile, SSI would pay the leasing company the difference.

This situation provided no incentive to the leasing companies to obtain a sale of the automobiles at a price at or above the residual values as SSI more often had to pay the leasing company an additional amount. Cox believed that he could save SSI money by disposing of the automobiles himself thereby eliminating the leasing companies' participation. SSI agreed and Cox began selling the leased automobiles through wholesalers and occasionally made retail sales. When Cox sold an automobile, he would obtain the purchaser's personal check in the amount of the purchase price which was payable to either him or cash. More often than not, he would obtain a purchase price in excess of the residual value. Cox would then deposit the check into his personal checking account at North Carolina National Bank. Once the check cleared, Cox would obtain a cashier's check payable to the leasing company for the residual value or an amount slightly higher.

Cox was able to process a substantial number of automobiles through his personal disposal system. It is undisputed that Cox kept funds placed in his personal NCNB account for his personal use which constituted the difference between the residual value or slightly higher and the actual price he received from the sales. SSI was not aware that Cox was retaining funds from the automobile sales. Cox did not report or provide a reconciliation statement to SSI detailing the automobile sales, funds obtained, or funds he retained. * * *

B. Whether the Trial Judge Erred in Granting SSI Summary Judgment as to Cox's Liability on SSI's Constructive Trust Claim

SSI asserted a cause of action against Cox for constructive trust. Cox contends that the trial judge erred in granting SSI summary judgment as to his liability on this issue because SSI failed to show any inequity to SSI by his retention of funds received in excess of the residual value of the vehicles. He argues that even though he kept the surplus amounts received, his actions actually benefitted SSI in that he successfully stopped SSI's losses. We disagree.

A constructive trust arises entirely by operation of law without reference to any actual or supposed intentions of creating a trust. *Whitmire v. Adams,* 273 S.C. 453, 257 S.E.2d 160 (1979). A constructive trust arises whenever a party has obtained money which does not equitably belong to him and which he cannot in good conscience retain or withhold from another who is beneficially entitled to it as where money has been paid by accident, mistake of fact, or fraud, or has been acquired through a breach of trust or the violation of a fiduciary duty. *Wolfe v. Wolfe,* 215 S.C. 530, 56 S.E.2d 343 (1949). In order to establish a constructive trust, the evidence must be clear and convincing. *Briggs v. Richardson,* 288 S.C. 537, 343 S.E.2d 653 (Ct.App.1986). A confidential or fiduciary relationship exists when one reposes special confidence in another so that the latter, in equity and good conscience, is bound to act in good faith and with due regard to the interests of the one reposing the confidence. *Island Car Wash, Inc. v. Norris,* 292 S.C. 595, 358 S.E.2d 150 (Ct.App.1987).

We find that a constructive trust is appropriate in this case and SSI is entitled to summary judgment in its favor as to Cox's liability under this cause of action. Cox was an employee of SSI at the time he began the disposal of SSI's leased vehicles. Cox was employed as SSI's fleet manager from 1983 through 1987 and as SSI's director of transportation from October of 1987 through April of 1988. He was in a position of trust and responsibility with SSI.

Cox admitted that when he sold the leased vehicles, he retained part of the funds that he received from the sale of the individual vehicles. Cox never told the management of SSI that while handling the sale of the leased vehicles, he would make a personal profit on each transaction. No one at SSI was aware that Cox was retaining profits from the vehicles sold. The profits Cox retained from the sale of the vehicles were acquired through a breach of trust and fiduciary duty. Although Cox argues in his brief that he had an arrangement with SSI which permitted him to retain these funds, there is nothing in the record to support this assertion. Cox retained funds which did not equitably belong to him and which in good conscience, he should not have retained.

* * *

Affirmed.

HUNTER v. SHELL OIL CO.

United States Court of Appeals, Fifth Circuit, 1952.
198 F.2d 485.

STRUM, CIRCUIT JUDGE. This appeal presents for review a judgment for the plaintiff in two consolidated suits instituted by Shell Oil Company against Paul B. Hunter, and others, to impress constructive trusts upon certain royalty interests, mineral interests and leasehold estates in oil, gas and other minerals, acquired by them in the circumstances hereinafter mentioned.

From 1930 to 1941, when he was discharged, the defendant-Hunter was employed by Shell Oil Company as senior geologist in its Houston office, where he was in direct charge of Shell's extensive exploration activities in a large area along the Gulf coast of Texas and Louisiana. Hunter's principal duties were to collect geological and geophysical information for use by Shell and to advise the company where to purchase oil and gas interests, where to drill test wells, and the like, for which purpose he was employed and paid full time. This information was highly confidential. Hunter's relationship with Shell was of a fiduciary nature, in which the utmost good faith is mandatory. At all times during Hunter's employment, Shell had a rule prohibiting its employees from acquiring royalty and other mineral interests. This rule applied to Hunter, and he was aware of it.

Early in 1941, Shell discovered that Hunter had been unauthorizedly divulging confidential information to one A.M. Joncas, one R.J. St. Germain, and to Southland Royalty Company, based upon which, and acting in numerous instances through the hereinafter mentioned corporations for concealment, they bought up royalty and other interests in oil lands discovered by Hunter in Texas, Louisiana and Arkansas, for which Hunter received, as his compensation for furnishing said information, fractional participations in their purchases. Sometimes these participation interests were taken by Hunter directly in his own name, sometimes under an alias, and in some instances through interests in some of the corporations involved. The company immediately discharged Hunter, and soon thereafter instituted these suits against him and some of those acting in concert with him in buying up mineral interests based upon Hunter's information. In its complaint, Shell prayed that each defendant be required to account for each of the interests so acquired by him, and that they be required to convey to Shell such of said interests as Shell should elect to recover, such conveyance to be conditioned upon Shell reimbursing defendants for the costs to them of such mineral interests.

Shell asserts that by disclosing such confidential information, which was its exclusive property, and in aiding his associates to acquire the above mentioned mineral interests, Hunter breached his fiduciary duty to his employer; placed himself in a position where his personal interests conflicted with those of his employer; and that in consequence Hunter and the persons and corporations who acquired mineral interests through his unauthorized disclosures, hold such interests as constructive trustees for Shell.

After a trial with an advisory jury, extending over a period of five months, the trial court found for the plaintiff as to 59 of the areas involved, and for the defendants as to 15 other areas, holding that mineral interests in the 59 areas had been purchased by Hunter's associates through unauthorized information furnished by Hunter in breach of his fiduciary duty to his employer, Shell Oil Company. The trial court also found that the individual defendants knowingly accepted the benefits of these unauthorized disclosures, and aided Hunter in concealing them from his employer.

Judgment was thereafter entered impressing trusts upon the interests acquired by the defendants in the 59 areas, as well as upon Hunter's ¼ stock ownership in Rotex Company. The defendants were also required to convey to Shell all such interests as were still held by them, and which Shell elects to recover in kind, conditioned upon Shell reimbursing defendants for the original cost of such interests. The judgment further authorized the pursuit and recapture by Shell, on the same terms, of such interests as may have been conveyed by defendants to *non* bona fide purchasers, or at its election to have a judgment against the seller-defendant for the sale price, or for the reasonable market value thereof, and to recover the purchase price or market value of interests sold to bona fide purchasers.

Following a lengthy period of accounting, money judgments were also entered against certain of the defendants in the aggregate sum of $130,-

378.92, representing income and other money accruals from their ostensible ownership of the interests upon which trusts were impressed, some of which had been sold by defendants to bona fide purchasers.

* * *

An agent may trade for his own benefit outside the scope of his principal's business without being accountable for the profits realized. But he is forbidden to deal with a subject matter of the agency, or to use for his own advantage information acquired while acting within the scope of the agency. Nor may an agent put himself in a position in which his personal interests may come into conflict with his duty to his principal, or which may afford him an opportunity to subordinate the interests of his employer to his own individual benefit while discharging his duties. Such conduct is not only morally wrong, it is contrary to public policy. When property has thus been wrongfully acquired, equity converts the holder into a trustee, and compels him to account for all gains from such conduct. * * *

Appellants contend that Shell deals only in leasehold interests, not in royalty or mineral interests, and that it was error to impress trusts upon royalty and mineral interests purchased by Joncas on Hunter's advice, because, as to these, neither Hunter nor Joncas were in competition with Shell. But the evidence is to the contrary. It appears that from 1922 to 1941, Shell purchased royalty or mineral interests in 80 areas along the Gulf coast, for which it paid $510,000. Of this, $350,000 was spent during the period of Hunter's employment. Appellants dispose of this with the observation that since Shell invested millions of dollars every year in leases, this sum of $350,000 "was insignificant, * * * a mere drop in the bucket." But even in these days of astronomical figures, such a sum can not be so casually brushed aside. It is a substantial sum, and Hunter's relationship with Shell was one in which the most perfect good faith was required,—a relationship *uberrima fides.*

We are in accord with the trial court's findings and judgment. Generally speaking, the breach by Hunter of his fiduciary duty to Shell, and the advantage he and his associates knowingly reaped therefrom is abundantly established. Appellants contend, however, that as to certain of the areas upon which trusts were impressed, e.g. areas not under Hunter's supervision as a geologist for Shell; areas which were proven or otherwise generally known to be favorable areas when Joncas purchased; areas in which Joncas could have secured the necessary geological data from others and was not beholden to Hunter for it; areas in which it had been previously announced that a test drill would be made; and areas in which Shell's information was only of the type known as "reconnaissance shooting" and therefore without substantial value, the proof is insufficient to establish a trust in favor of Shell.

The trial judge found the evidence "clear, convincing and trustworthy" as to the 59 areas upon which he imposed a trust in favor of plaintiff. We agree that as to these the evidence fully supports the finding that Hunter was an unfaithful fiduciary, that Joncas was a willing, knowing and active participant in Hunter's breach of duty, and that these two, as well as the other defendants who wrongfully profited thereby to the detriment of Shell, should disgorge their ill gotten gains. While some of these acquisitions, if found in circumstances more immaculate, might seem inherently innocuous, the sordid picture painted by this evidence as a whole imparts to them quite a different character.

The trial judge also found that the conveyance to Hunter by his associates of mineral interests in areas where plaintiff had no confidential information, was a consideration and an incentive to Hunter to disclose confidential information belonging to plaintiff as to other areas in which plaintiff, through Hunter, was possessed of such information. The evidence fully supports this conclusion.

The same may also be said as to the acquisition by Hunter from his associates of mineral interests in areas which were not under Hunter's supervision. These also would constitute an incentive, and would tend to induce Hunter to disclose information as to areas over which he did have supervision. Hunter had frequent and complete reports as to what was going on in other areas. All these circumstances blend into an impressive mosaic, which clearly reveals a studied, comprehensive and systematic scheme by Hunter and Joncas, and others, to clandestinely purloin Shell's confidential information and divert it to their own gain, to Shell's consequent detriment.

* * *

Viewing the evidence as a whole, the trial judge is well supported in his findings and judgment.

Affirmed.*

Notes

1. Violation of the fiduciary obligation of loyalty by an employee-agent, partner, corporate officer, director, or public official,** undue influence, abuse of the relationship of "trust and confidence," misrepresentation, and benefit gained by virtue of position, are species of "equitable fraud." V A. Scott, The Law of Trusts §§ 462, 508.1 (3d ed. 1967). Fraud and mistake are ancient heads of equity jurisdiction. H. McClintock, Handbook on the Principles of Equity § 2 (2d ed. 1948); II G. Palmer, The Law of Restitution § 11.5 (1978). While there is a tendency to apply the "adequacy" test in the mistake and fraudulent misrepresentation areas (V A. Scott, The Law of Trusts § 462.3 (3d ed. 1967); II G. Palmer, The Law of Restitution § 11.5 (1978); I G. Palmer § 3.7), this has not been equally true in the case of "fiduciary fraud." Restatement of Restitution § 163 comment d (1937).

2. Complaints involving fiduciary fraud, "trust and confidence" and "undue influence" are often accompanied by a prayer for equitable accounting. G. Bogert, Trusts & Trustees § 970 (2d ed. 1962); I G. Palmer, The Law of Restitution § 1.5(c) (1978). There are indications in the federal courts of an insistence upon an "accounting" at law where, if necessary, a master may be

* This case is discussed in Notes, 31 N.C.L.Rev. 335 (1953) and 32 Tex.L.Rev. 135 (1953). *Compare* Seavey, Problems in Restitution, 7 Okla.L.Rev. 257, 260–61, Problem III (1954).

** *See* Jersey City v. Hague, 18 N.J. 584, 115 A.2d 8 (1955), discussed in Notes, 55 Colum.L.Rev. 1085 (1955) and 104 U.Pa. L.Rev. 121 (1955) and 69 Harv.L.Rev. 572 (1956).

appointed to aid the jury. In other jurisdictions equitable accounting continues to be an important remedy.

The plaintiff has the burden of proving the existence of the constructive trust. V A. Scott, The Law of Trusts § 462.6 (3d ed. 1967). Should the court by its decree declare such a relationship to exist, it may then order the trustee to account by stating the appropriate debits and credits to the account—that is, those items for which the trustee is liable and off-setting claims for which he or she is entitled to credit. G. Bogert, Trusts & Trustees §§ 970, 972 (2d ed. 1962). It is customary to refer the account to a master, referee or other assistant to the court to examine it, take testimony, and report his recommendations and findings to the court. *Id.* Usually the trustee has the burden of justifying the credit claims. G. Bogert, Trusts & Trustees § 972, at 243 (2d ed. 1962). The plaintiff sought such relief in the *Hunter* case.

3. The burden of proof with respect to identifying particular property to be held subject to a constructive trust, and related problems of tracing, are discussed by the court in Sheldon Petroleum Co. v. Peirce, 546 S.W.2d 954, 958 (Tex.Civ.App.1977) (reversing the trial court and giving instructions to be followed upon remand):

"B. CONSTRUCTIVE TRUST

"Alternatively, Mrs. Peirce contends that Sheldon of Delaware holds property as a constructive trustee for her benefit. A constructive trust will be imposed where it would constitute unjust enrichment if the party in possession of property is allowed to retain it. Fitz–Gerald v. Hull, 150 Tex. 39, 237 S.W.2d 256, 262, 264–65 (1951). Ordinarily, this requires a showing that retention of specific property would constitute unjust enrichment; that is, that the party asserting the constructive trust must be able to show what property he is entitled to have. *See* Meadows v. Bierschwale, 516 S.W.2d 125, 129 (Tex.1974). As noted above, Mrs. Peirce is unable to do so. The courts have recognized, however, that it would be inequitable to place the burden of tracing on the party asserting the trust where the constructive trustee has wrongfully commingled his own funds or property with funds or property against which a trust is asserted, especially where the proof necessary to separate the funds is peculiarly within the knowledge and possession of the trustee. Logan v. Logan, 138 Tex. 40, 156 S.W.2d 507, 510–11 (1941). *Cf.* Humble Oil & Refining Co. v. West, 508 S.W.2d 812, 818 (Tex.1974) (applying the rule in a 'confusion of goods' case). If the property is commingled and the trustee does not establish which is his, the entire fund is considered to be subject to the trust. Eaton v. Husted, 141 Tex. 349, 172 S.W.2d 493, 498–99 (1943). Before this burden will be imposed, however, it is incumbent upon the party asserting the trust to show that the funds were in fact commingled and that commingled funds were used to purchase the property against which the trust is asserted. Landry v. Williamson, 335 S.W.2d 400, 405 (Tex.Civ.App.—Houston 1960, writ ref'd n.r.e.)." *See also* Note, 1964 Wis.L.Rev. 733 (1964).

4. For property to be decreed to be subject to a constructive trust, it is often said that the defendant must have legal title to property acquired in violation of the trust or with its proceeds. *See* V A. Scott, The Law of Trusts § 462 (3rd ed. 1967); I G. Palmer, The Law of Restitution § 1.3 fn. 15 (1978); II G. Palmer § 11.5(c); Restatement of Restitution § 160, at 649 (1937). Such statements may indicate an undesirable preoccupation with the presence of the

characteristics of an express trust. This approach has been criticized because it fails to take account of the function of the constructive trust as a remedy to prevent unjust enrichment. I G. Palmer, The Law of Restitution § 1.3 (1978). Despite a disposition to use the express trust analogy, courts nonetheless have awarded constructive trust relief where the defendant does not have such legal title. This has been done in the case of fungibles where the defendant now has legal title to other such fungibles. Sher v. Sandler, 325 Mass. 348, 90 N.E.2d 536 (1950), discussed in Notes, 63 Harv.L.Rev. 1463 (1950) and 45 Ill.L.Rev. 510 (1950) (defendant ordered to transfer to the plaintiff shares of stock identical to other shares taken by defendant in violation of fiduciary obligation to the plaintiff). Although neither the thief nor one taking through him acquires legal title, the constructive trust remedy has been awarded in the case of such a taking. *See* I G. Palmer, The Law of Restitution § 1.3 fn. 15 (1978). The general nature of a claim to property held subject to constructive trust is discussed in V A. Scott, The Law of Trusts § 462.6 (3d ed. 1967). See also (*Id.,* at 702); Lines v. Bank of America Nat. Trust & Sav. Ass'n., 743 F.Supp. 176 (S.D.N.Y.1990) ("This case [involving a liquidator marshalling the assets of an insurance company in the course of winding up its affairs], despite the absence of a fiduciary relationship or a promise by Occidental not to draw upon both sets of letters of credit [a second was issued by mistake], presents unique circumstances sufficient to warrant imposition of a constructive trust, which is 'the formula through which equity finds expression' * * *.") (*Id.,* at 180).

Interests of bona fide purchasers for value will prevail over those seeking constructive trust relief. G. Bogert, Trusts & Trustees § 471, at 6, and § 472, at 32 (2d ed. 1978); Note, 49 Mich.L.Rev. 150 (1950). Such is also the case in some jurisdictions with respect to competing lienors, usually creditors of the wrongdoer, who obtain legally enforceable liens upon the property otherwise subject to the constructive trust after the date of the wrong which creates the right to equitable relief but before a lien is decreed in the equity action. *See,* G. Bogert, Trusts & Trustees, §§ 471–72 (2d ed. 1978); V A. Scott, The Law of Trusts § 462.1 (3d ed. 1967); International Refugee Organization v. Maryland Drydock Co., 179 F.2d 284 (4th Cir.1950), discussed in Note, 49 Mich.L.Rev. 150 (1950). There is, however, authority for a contrary conclusion on the theory that the right of the party to subject the property to the constructive trust, and to claim at least an equitable lien upon the property in competition with subsequent lienors, arises when the facts justify such a conclusion rather than when the Chancellor, in a final judgment, decrees that the property is subject to the constructive trust. In re General Coffee Corp., 828 F.2d 699 (11th Cir.1987), *cert. denied* 485 U.S. 1007 (1988) ("We are convinced that, if presented with this issue, the Florida Supreme Court would reaffirm the majority approach that a constructive trust arises when the facts giving rise to the fraud occur.")

5. The *Hunter* court states that the plaintiff may consider, separately, each transaction in violation of the defendant's fiduciary duty of loyalty and choose the remedy considered to be most advantageous,—constructive trust, equitable lien, quasi-contract or tort damages at law. This can, of course, have an enormous impact upon the nature and the amount of the recovery.

ST. PAUL FIRE AND MARINE INS. CO. v. SEAFARE CORP.

United States Court of Appeals, Fourth Circuit, 1987.
831 F.2d 57.

WIDENER, CIRCUIT JUDGE:

Seafare Corporation (Seafare) appeals the granting of summary judgment against it and in favor of plaintiff St. Paul Fire and Marine Insurance Company (St. Paul) by the United States District Court for the Eastern District of North Carolina. We vacate the judgment of the district court and remand for that court to hold this proceeding in abeyance until the constructive trust claims pending in the state court are resolved.

At issue in both this proceeding and the one pending in the state court of North Carolina is the claim to certain insurance proceeds to be paid on a policy covering the Seafare Restaurant (restaurant) in Nags Head, North Carolina. The Seafare Restaurant burned on August 23, 1984. Prior to 1983, the restaurant was owned by Seafare. In that year, Seafare conveyed the restaurant to William A. Stafford, who in turn conveyed the property to Trenor Corporation. Trenor took possession of the restaurant in March 1988 and continued in possession until the restaurant was destroyed by fire. St. Paul insured the restaurant against loss including loss by fire. While Central Fidelity Bank held a mortgage on the property, it was not listed as a loss payee on the insurance policy. Trenor was the only one listed on that policy as the named insured.

On or about September 1984, Seafare filed a state civil action in the Dare County, North Carolina Superior Court against Trenor, St. Paul and others.[1] Seafare claimed that the transfer of the restaurant from Stafford to Trenor was fraudulent because Stafford had taken title of the restaurant only as a fiduciary for Seafare's benefit in order to aid the financially distressed Seafare. Seafare sought to have the transaction set aside. Seafare alleged that it was entitled to a constructive trust on Trenor's insurance proceeds to be paid by St. Paul.

In March 1985, St. Paul filed the instant declaratory judgment action seeking to adjudicate all of the claims to the insurance proceeds payable on account of the restaurant fire. In its complaint, St. Paul alleged that it was not obligated to pay the proceeds to Trenor because Trenor intentionally set the fire that destroyed the restaurant. St. Paul claimed that it was under no obligation to pay the proceeds to either Central Fidelity Bank or Seafare because neither was a named insured or loss payee on the policy and that both were subject to St. Paul's claimed arson defense as to Trenor.

Seafare answered that it was entitled to the insurance proceeds because of Trenor's fraud. Additionally, Seafare referred to the suit it had initiated in state court that was still pending at that time.

1. Central Fidelity Bank also filed a suit in the Dare County, North Carolina Superior Court seeking reformation of the insurance policy so that it could be named as a loss payee beneficiary and that it thereby recover from St. Paul enough of the insurance proceeds to cover payment of the outstanding mortgage it held on the property.

Prior to trial, St. Paul moved, pursuant to Fed.Civ.Proc. 56, for summary judgment against Seafare and Central Fidelity Bank. In opposing the motion, Seafare argued that it was entitled to recovery based upon a constructive trust theory and the doctrine of trust pursuit. Under the doctrine of trust pursuit, the beneficiary of a constructive trust may assert his rights in the proceeds from the disposition of trust property. These proceeds must be capable of being traced through any intermediate transfers, but even property which has been converted from one form to another (e.g. from a restaurant, to the charred remains of the restaurant, to the insurance proceeds, as here) may be so pursued. See *Edgecombe Bank & Trust Co. v. Barrett,* 238 N.C. 579, 78 S.E.2d 730 (1953); see generally 5 Scott, *The Law of Trusts* § 521 (3rd ed. 1967). The district court rejected Seafare's contentions and granted summary judgment in favor of St. Paul, concluding that "There is nothing in either St. Paul's complaint or Seafare's answer that gives rise to such a claim [constructive trust and trust pursuit claims] in the action. Further, Seafare has not filed any counterclaim or cross-claim."

We conclude that the district court erred in granting summary judgment against Seafare. Seafare was not required to counterclaim and thereby litigate its fraud, constructive trust, and trust pursuit claims in this action because it already had a pending state court action raising these very issues. Seafare had referred to its pending state court action in its answer to St. Paul's complaint, and a copy of that state court complaint was submitted to the district court for consideration.

FRCP 13(a) provides, with respect to a compulsory counterclaim, that "* * * the pleader need not state the claim if (1) at the time the action was commenced the claim was the subject of another pending action * * *." Since Seafare's claim was "the subject of another pending action" in the state court, the district court erred in granting summary judgment against Seafare while its claims were pending in the state court. Accord, *United States v. Sarman,* 699 F.2d 469 (9th Cir.1983) (a claim in a state court is "another pending action" under Rule 13(a)).

The policy defense St. Paul asserted in this declaratory judgment action was arson on the part of Trenor. Yet that matter has never been adjudicated, and St. Paul's settlement with Trenor and Central Fidelity with full knowledge of Seafare's constructive trust and trust pursuit claims as to the insurance proceeds, coupled with summary judgment against Seafare, would effectively bar Seafare from ever litigating the merits of its claim against St. Paul although it complied with every rule of federal procedure.

We are of opinion that, on remand, the district court should hold this case in abeyance pending the outcome of Seafare's constructive trust and trust pursuit claims in the state court. If Seafare prevails in the action in the state court, then the district court should try the arson policy defense.

Vacated and Remanded With Instructions.

IN RE MAHAN & ROWSEY, INC.

United States Court of Appeals, Tenth Circuit, 1987.
817 F.2d 682.

* * *

This is an appeal from a judgment of a district court sitting as an appellate court in bankruptcy. Two issues are before us. The first is whether funds paid by the plaintiff to the defendant (Debtor) were impressed with a trust so that they did not become an asset of the Debtor's estate. The second issue is whether recovery of those funds is limited by application of the lowest intervening balance rule. The district court answered both questions in the affirmative. We agree.

The facts are not in dispute. Plaintiff Turley and Debtor entered into an oil well operating agreement in which Debtor, as operator, was to bill Mr. Turley for his proportionate share of the drilling and completion costs of the well. Over a period of months, through Debtor's negligence, Mr. Turley was billed for and paid $42,082.65 in excess of his proper share of those costs. Debtor deposited the overpayments into two separate bank accounts from which it made withdrawals until the advent of bankruptcy.

When Debtor filed its petition under Chapter 11 of the Bankruptcy Code, the two accounts had a remaining balance of $11,126.71. Subsequent to the filing of the bankruptcy petition, the two accounts were closed, and the funds were transferred to a general operating account for the benefit of Debtor's bankruptcy estate. Debtor subsequently made deposits to that account.

Plaintiff Turley then filed an action in the bankruptcy court to recover the full amount of his overpayment from the sums on deposit in the operating account. The bankruptcy court, relying upon *Reserve Oil, Inc. v. Dixon,* 711 F.2d 951 (10th Cir.1983), held the operating agreement between the parties was a "trustee type relationship" and therefore the overpayments were held by Debtor in trust for Mr. Turley. The court entered judgment for Mr. Turley in the full amount of the overpayment. *In re Mahan & Rowsey, Inc.,* 35 B.R. 898 (Bankr.W.D.Okla.1983). On appeal the district court affirmed the bankruptcy court's determination that a trust was imposed upon the overpayment, but reversed the judgment on the full amount.[1] The court held that when the overpayments were commingled in accounts that were drawn upon, the trust beneficiary's recovery was limited to the lowest balance between the time of the deposit of the overpayments and the filing of the Chapter 11 petition, *In re Mahan & Rowsey, Inc.,* 62 B.R. 46 (W.D.Okla.1985).

I.

The principal issue is whether the district court correctly held that a trust arose out of the conduct of the parties. We conclude the district court was right. We noted in *Reserve Oil* that an operating agreement of

1. We, too, agree with the bankruptcy court's analysis of the constructive trust issue.

the type present in this case created a "trustee type relationship imposing a duty of fair dealing between the operator and the non-operator owners in the matter of distribution of the shares among the owners." [2] What results from the fiduciary relationship thereby created is a constructive trust imposed on the operator. Because money was given to the operator for a particular purpose (for example, the payment of a debt), the operator received the money in trust to apply it to the intended purpose. 76 Am.Jur. *Trusts* § 233 (1975). Contrary to the arguments of the Debtor in this case, the operator and nonoperator did not enter into an express trust. A constructive trust was imposed involuntarily upon the Debtor by operation of equity.[3]

A constructive trust is frequently imposed when, as a result of an abuse of a confidence, one either obtains or holds the legal right to property which in equity he should not. *Tenneco Oil Company v. Joiner,* 696 F.2d 768, 776 (10th Cir.1982); *Guarantee Reserve Life Ins. Co. v. Hardin,* 404 F.Supp. 961, 963 (W.D.Okla.1974); 76 Am.Jur.2d *Trusts* § 221 (1975). Thus, because of the fiduciary relationship imposed upon Debtor in the operating agreement and the demands of equity, Debtor was bound to properly bill the nonoperator, Mr. Turley, and to pay the sums received only for Mr. Turley's share of the completion and operating expenses.

The sums subject to the constructive trust never became a part of the bankruptcy estate. Because the money was held by the Debtor prior to bankruptcy only for the benefit of Mr. Turley under a trust arising from nonbankruptcy law, that money was not property of the estate by definition. 11 U.S.C. § 541(a)(1) and (c)(2); 4 *Collier on Bankruptcy* § 541.13 (15th ed. 1987). The district court correctly affirmed the bankruptcy court's holding on this issue.

II.

Mr. Turley has cross appealed the district court's reversal of the bankruptcy court's judgment allowing him recovery of the full amount of his overpayment. He argues that failure to allow him such recovery would result in unjust enrichment of the Debtor. While the argument has facial appeal, it is not in keeping with long-standing principles applied to bankruptcy.

Generally, when assets of a trust are improperly transferred by the trustee, the beneficiary may trace those assets and recover them from anyone but a bona fide purchaser for value. 72 Am.Jur.2d *Trusts* § 259 (1975). This trust pursuit will even allow tracing of trust funds into a commingled mass, such as the two accounts of the Debtor, 76 Am.Jur.2d *Trusts* § 261 (1975). Yet, it is only the lowest balance in a commingled account that is subject to trust pursuit. 76 Am.Jur.2d *Trusts* § 265 (1975). When the trustee deposits other funds into a commingled bank account, it is generally held the trustee is not replenishing trust funds. *Id.* This rule

2. *Reserve Oil,* 711 F.2d at 953.

3. Debtor proffers an argument that because the trust was an express trust, it is an executory contract that could be rejected by the Debtor in Possession pursuant to 11 U.S.C. § 365(a). The argument is specious because the trust in this case is a creature of equity involuntarily imposed upon the funds paid to the trustee. A constructive trust is neither executory nor a contract.

has long been followed in bankruptcy, as the district court correctly observed. *Schuyler v. Littlefield,* 232 U.S. 707, 34 S.Ct. 466, 58 L.Ed. 806 (1914); *Cunningham v. Brown,* 265 U.S. 1, 44 S.Ct. 424, 68 L.Ed. 873 (1924); *Sonnenschein v. Reliance Ins. Co.,* 353 F.2d 935 (2d Cir.1965); 4 *Collier on Bankruptcy* § 541.13 (15th ed. 1987). Therefore, the lowest balance rule was properly applied to the commingled accounts in Debtor's possession prior to the date of bankruptcy. Those were the only funds subject to trust pursuit.

This conclusion does not permit the unjust enrichment of the Debtor because Mr. Turley still has a claim against the estate for the difference between the funds subject to trust pursuit and the amount of the total overpayment. Allowing Mr. Turley recovery of the trust amounts does not extinguish that debt; it merely requires Mr. Turley to take his place among the general unsecured creditors of the Debtor. Such treatment of his claim is in accord with the reality of his status.

Affirmed.

Note

Tracing and the priority in insolvency which may result are discussed by Professor Palmer in I G. Palmer, Law of Restitution (1978), § 2.14(c). He quotes Judge Swan's often cited justification for this result: " 'the fiduciary's creditors have accepted the risk of his solvency, while his cestuis have accepted only the risk of his honesty.' " (*Id.,* at 185).

This, of course, is one of the marked advantages which may come from use of the "tracing," or "asset pursuit" technique together with the constructive trust remedy.

SECTION 4. EQUITABLE LIEN

MIDDLEBROOKS v. LONAS

Supreme Court of Georgia, 1980.
246 Ga. 720, 272 S.E.2d 687.

JORDAN, PRESIDING JUSTICE.

Mary Middlebrooks filed a complaint against W.L. Lonas and Elvira Lonas, her parents, alleging that, in reliance on their promise to repay, she had loaned them $25,000 which they had since used to build a home on land which they owned, that they now refused to repay said loan and that, "The above and foregoing transactions, promises, and delays constitute fraud and as such the defendants herein hold the said $25,000 through and by constructive and implied trust in favor of the plaintiff." The plaintiff further alleged that, "The defendants herein have pledged, mortgaged and borrowed money upon the land * * * as well as all improvements thereon."

The defendants moved for summary judgment on the ground that the plaintiff's complaint failed to state a claim upon which equitable relief could be granted and on the ground that they had factually pierced the plaintiff's allegation that they had promised to repay the $25,000 without a present intent to do so. The trial court granted said motion and the plaintiff appeals. We reverse.

1. Appellee's motion to dismiss the appeal as premature is denied. We decline to overrule the holding in Gillen v. Bostick, 234 Ga. 308, 215 S.E.2d 676 (1975). *See* Elwell v. Nesmith, 246 Ga. 430, 271 S.E.2d 827 (1980).

2. Code Ann. § 108–106 states that "Trusts are implied * * * where, from any *fraud,* one person obtains the title to property which rightly belongs to another." (Emphasis supplied.)

A promise made without a present intent to perform is a misrepresentation of a material fact and is sufficient to support a cause of action for fraud. Hayes v. Hallmark Apts., 232 Ga. 307, 309, 207 S.E.2d 197 (1974).

Thus, assuming that the remedies at law are inadequate, if a plaintiff proves that a defendant promised to repay a loan and did so without a present intent to perform, the plaintiff can "enforce either a constructive trust or an equitable lien on the fund," Dobbs, Remedies, Ch. 5, § 5.16, p. 423 (1973), and, further, if a plaintiff proves that the fraudulently procured funds were used by the defendant to purchase other property, the plaintiff can reach the other property "by a proceeding in equity, and * * * can enforce a constructive trust or an equitable lien." Pittman v. Pittman, 196 Ga. 397, 409, 26 S.E.2d 764 (1943); *accord,* U.S. Fidelity & Guaranty Co. v. Richmond County, 174 Ga. 599, 600, 163 S.E. 482 (1931).

In the present case, it is undisputed that the defendants used the $25,000 to build a home on land which they already owned. Accordingly, assuming that the plaintiff's remedies at law are inadequate, if the plaintiff proves that the defendants promised to repay the $25,000 and did so without a present intent to perform, the plaintiff would be entitled to an equitable lien on the home and land. *See, Dobbs, supra,* at pp. 11–12, 249–50, 424; Restatement of Restitution, § 206, p. 837 (1937).

> "A remedy at law, to exclude appropriate relief in equity, must be * * * the substantial equivalent of the equitable relief. It is not enough that there is a remedy at law. It must be plain and adequate, or, in other words, as practical and as efficient to the ends of justice and its prompt administration as the remedy in equity." Atlantic C. & R. Co. v. Gunn, 185 Ga. 108, 110, 194 S.E. 365 (1937).

Regarding the inadequacy of her remedies at law, the plaintiff alleged that the defendants had mortgaged the home and lot. "A creditor of a mortgagor who obtains his judgment [at law] subsequently to the execution of a mortgage which has been duly registered takes it subject to the rights of the mortgagee * * *." Mutual Loan etc. Co. v. Haas, 100 Ga. 111, 115, 27 S.E. 980 (1896). In contrast, a plaintiff who similarly establishes entitlement to an equitable lien takes subject to the rights of a mortgagee only if the mortgagee is a bona fide purchaser. U.S. Fidelity & Guaranty Co. v. Richmond County, *supra,* 174 Ga. at p. 600, 163 S.E. 482; *Dobbs, supra,* at pp. 644–49; Restatement of Restitution, §§ 161(d), 172.

Accordingly, we hold that the plaintiff's complaint did not fail to state a claim upon which equitable relief could be granted.

3. The defendants argue that the plaintiff's deposition testimony factually pierced the plaintiff's allegation that they had promised to repay the $25,000 without a present intent to do so.

We note, however, that the relevant deposition testimony by the plaintiff reads as follows: "Q. Do you think they ever really intended to pay you back?" The plaintiff: "At [the time I made the loan] I did."

This statement by the plaintiff does not constitute an admission that the defendants intended to repay the loan at the time allegedly promised to do so.

Further, we note that the plaintiff filed an affidavit wherein she stated that "they [her parents] never intended to pay that money back from the very start * * *."

Accordingly, we hold that the defendants failed to factually pierce the plaintiff's allegation that they had promised to repay the $25,000 without a present intent to do so.

Judgment reversed.

All the Justices concur, except UNDERCOFLER, C.J., and BOWLES and MARSHALL, JJ., who dissent.

G & M MOTOR CO. v. THOMPSON

Supreme Court of Oklahoma, 1977.
567 P.2d 80.

BERRY, JUSTICE.

The question to be decided has not heretofore been decided in Oklahoma. Specifically, may a trial court impress a constructive trust upon proceeds of life insurance policies where a portion of the premiums were paid with wrongfully obtained funds? We hold sound reason and interest of justice require an affirmative answer.

The facts, for the purpose of deciding this question, are simple. A. Wayne Thompson was an accountant for G & M Motor Company [motor company] from January 1, 1968, until his death on August 2, 1970. During this period decedent embezzled $78,856.45 from motor company; a portion of which was used to pay premiums on various insurance policies insuring the life of decedent. The trial court impressed a constructive trust upon various items of real and personal property and a portion of the insurance proceeds in possession of decedent's surviving wife, Shirley Thompson, and child.

Court of Appeals, Division 1, upon wife's appeal, affirmed trial court's impressment of a constructive trust on the real and personal property, but modified the trust on insurance proceeds. The court, relying on American National Bank of Okmulgee v. King, 158 Okl. 278, 13 P.2d 164, said "only that part of the funds that the trial court found was used to pay for the payments of the policies while deceased was employed for appellee * * * together with interest at the rate of 10% per annum from date of judgment * * * until paid" are subject to a constructive trust in favor of motor company.

Motor company, after motion for rehearing was denied, sought certiorari.

* * *

The proper basis for impressing a constructive trust is to prevent unjust enrichment. Restatement of Restitution § 160, Comment c [1937]. The Restatement of Restitution foresaw that a wrongdoer may exchange misappropriated property for other property; thus, § 202 provides:

> "Where a person wrongfully disposes of property of another knowing that the disposition is wrongful and acquires in exchange other property, the other is entitled * * * to enforce * * * a constructive trust of the property so acquired."

The drafters explained § 202 as follows:

> "Where a person by the consciously wrongful disposition of the property of another acquires other property, the person whose property is so used is * * * entitled * * * to the property so acquired. If the property so acquired is or becomes more valuable than the property used in acquiring it, the profit thus made by the wrongdoer cannot be retained by him; the person whose property was used in making the profit is entitled to it. The result, it is true, is that the claimant obtains more than the amount of which he was deprived, more than restitution for his loss; he is put in a better position than that in which he would have been if no wrong had been done to him. Nevertheless, since the profit is made from his property, it is just that he should have the profit rather than that the wrongdoer should keep it. It is true that if there had been a loss instead of a profit, the wrongdoer would have had to bear the loss, since the wrongdoer would be personally liable to the claimant for the value of the claimant's property wrongfully used by the wrongdoer. If, however, the wrongdoer were permitted to keep the profit, there would be an incentive to wrongdoing, which is removed if he is compelled to surrender the profit. The rule which compels the wrongdoer to bear any losses and to surrender any profits operates as a deterrent upon the wrongful disposition of the property of others. Accordingly, the person whose property is wrongfully used in acquiring other property can by a proceeding in equity reach the other property and compel the wrongdoer to convey it to him. The wrongdoer holds the property so acquired upon a constructive trust for the claimant."

Thus, it is not necessary for a plaintiff to have suffered any loss or suffer a loss as great as the benefit of defendant. *See Id.* § 160, Comment d.

Where the wrongdoer mingles wrongfully and rightfully acquired funds, owner of wrongfully acquired funds is entitled to share proportionately in acquired property to the extent of his involuntary contribution. *Id.* § 210(2). This principle is specifically applicable to life insurance proceeds where a portion of the premiums were paid with wrongfully acquired money. *Id.* § 210, Comment a. The drafters said:

> "* * * Just as the claimant is entitled to enforce a constructive trust upon property which is wholly the product of his property, so he

> is entitled to enforce a constructive trust upon property which is the product in part of his own property and in part of the property of the wrongdoer. The difference is that where the property is the product of his property only in part, he is not entitled by enforcing a constructive trust to recover the whole of the property, but only a share in such proportion as the value of his property bore to the value of the mingled fund."

More particularly, § 210, Comment d, Illustration 5 addressed the instant matter. Illustration 5 provides:

> "A insures his life for $10,000 and pays the premiums half with money wrongfully taken from B and half with money of his own. A dies. B is entitled to half of the proceeds of the policy * * *."

The record indicates trial court determined extent of premiums paid with wrongfully acquired funds and impressed a constructive trust upon proceeds consistent with Illustration 5.

Having carefully considered the matter, we adopt the Restatement view. However, Motor Company has sought no more than the embezzled monies, interest and costs. Further, the surviving wife is an innocent beneficiary. Therefore, we cannot say trial court's judgment is against the clear weight of evidence. We hold Motor Company is entitled to a pro rata share of insurance proceeds, but not to exceed the total amount of embezzled monies, interest and costs.

Appellee granted certiorari. Appellant denied certiorari. Court of Appeals opinion vacated in part. Judgment of trial court affirmed.

LAVENDER, V.C.J., and DAVISON, IRWIN and BARNES, JJ., concur.

HODGES, C.J., and WILLIAMS, SIMMS and DOOLIN, JJ., concur in result.

Note

"Tracing" is a relatively simple concept except where "trust" funds or proceeds are changed into a form of property which was acquired partly with non-trust assets. In this situation, equity will decree an "equitable lien" on the property in question to the extent of the proceeds traced into it. I G. Palmer, The Law of Restitution § 1.5 (1978). A decree creating such a lien may serve to give the plaintiff preference or priority over competing creditors. II G. Palmer § 11.5. Furthermore, as the *G & M Motor Co.* case holds, the lienor's recoverable restitution damages may exceed the dollar value of the proceeds originally invested in the property by the wrongdoer and thus, like the constructive trust, give the plaintiff a proportionate benefit from any enhancement in the value of the property since the time that the trust proceeds were originally invested in it. However, the lienor's claim may be limited to the amount of the funds traced into the asset in question where mistake rather than fraud gave rise to the relief in question. II G. Palmer § 11.5.

The special complexities of "tracing" begin when the trust funds are "mingled" with other funds in a common fund such as a bank account. The leading cases, which give the plaintiff the benefit of several valuable presumptions to enable the plaintiff to claim either what remains in the account or to trace into other property the funds first removed, are discussed by Professor Palmer. *Id.* at §§ 2.16–2.18. When the res was deposited in an account and there mingled with other funds unrelated to the wrong of which complaint is being made, the plaintiff often has the benefit of two, seemingly inconsistent, "presumptions", one or both of which may be resorted to as the circumstances dictate. One is that the first funds removed from the mingled account were the funds constituting the fruits of the wrong to the plaintiff; the other, that the trust funds are removed last, as a consequence of which they remain in the account until diminished in whole or in part when the lowest intermediate balance in the account falls below the total of the trust funds in question. *See* In re Seneca Oil Co., 906 F.2d 1445 (10th Cir.1990). Other "presumptions" come into play when there are several debits and credits to the account on the same date, and there are delays or other reasons to cause the items not to be posted to the account in chronological order, as well as in those situations where the funds of several beneficiaries have been commingled in the same fund. *See generally* V A. Scott, The Law of Trusts §§ 515–519 (3d ed. 1967); G. Bogert, Trusts & Trustees §§ 921–930 (2d ed. 1962); Restatement of Restitution §§ 211–213 (1937); I G. Palmer §§ 2.14–2.16 (discussing these presumptions and the amount of the lien which may be claimed against the product).

A "swollen assets" theory, as a substitute for "tracing" ("using trust funds to pay personal debts had 'swelled' the assets on hand at the time of determining the rights of creditors and other claimants") is considered in TMG II v. United States, 778 F.Supp. 37 (D.D.C.1991) at 53. Professor Palmer, in I G. Palmer, Law of Restitution (1978), § 2.14, has pointed out that, today, "most courts have rejected the swelling of assets theory, and have required tracing into some specific asset in the insolvent estate as a basis for preference." (*Id.*, at 183). *Accord,* In re Seneca Oil Co., 906 F.2d 1445 (10th Cir.1990).

For a detailed discussion of "tracing," with illustrations, see D. Laycock, Modern American Remedies 542–42 (1985).

SECTION 5. SUBROGATION

Where there are two parties who are obligated to pay the same obligation and it can be said that, because of the circumstances, such as acting as an endorser for another as a favor and accommodation, one rather than the other, as a matter of fairness, should pay when payment is required, the law treats the party who should not have to pay as a "surety." The party who should pay is referred to in the cases as the "principal obligor."

The equity court's ability to prevent unjust enrichment in compelling situations is illustrated by the dilemma of a surety who is forced to pay the obligation under these circumstances. Ordinarily, payment by a surety to the creditor would extinguish the debt in question and leave the surety without the benefit of whatever other advantages the creditor might have had to obtain payment from the principal obligor. Equity's remedy of "subrogation" could prevent that result. Where, for instance, the creditor who has been paid by the surety held property of the principal obligor as security, the surety, rather than, for example, the principal obligor, or his other creditors, would obtain, through subrogation, the benefit of that security position. By thus enabling the petitioner to be substituted for the position of another the possible unjust enrichment of others is avoided in this and in a variety of other analogous situations. Those include circumstances where: funds are loaned to purchase property but instead are used by the borrower to pay off a secured debt and the lender is subrogated to the position of the creditor with respect to the security interest; funds are loaned to pay off an obligation on land, with the lender to have a first lien on the property in question, and the obligation is discharged but there is an unknown second lien on the property, and the lender is subrogated to the position of the creditor who has been paid with respect to the first lien; an insurance company who has paid the insured for property damage is subrogated to the insured's cause of action against the tortfeasor who caused the damage. *See generally,* IV G. Palmer, Law of Restitution (1978), §§ 23.15–23.18.

SECTION 6. DEFENSES TO RESTITUTION

NORTON v. HAGGETT

Supreme Court of Vermont, 1952.
117 Vt. 130, 85 A.2d 571.

BLACKMER, JUSTICE.

The plaintiff, K.E. Norton, seeks equitable relief because he paid and discharged a note and the mortgage securing it. The bill alleges that the payment was made under a mutual mistake, and that the defendants, Roy M. and Hazel C. Haggett and the Northfield Savings Bank are guilty of fraud and conspiracy. The case was heard by the chancellor, facts found, and a decree entered dismissing the bill; it is here on the plaintiff's exceptions.

So far as it is necessary to state them, the chancellor found these facts. The bank held a note and mortgage given to it by the Haggetts. On November 30, 1948, the plaintiff went to the bank for the purpose of securing possession of this note and mortgage. He told the clerk on duty that he wanted to "take up" the Haggett note and mortgage. Whereupon the clerk asked the plaintiff if he wanted to pay off the note, and the plaintiff replied "yes". The amount due was computed, and the plaintiff gave the bank his check for that amount. The clerk made the proper entries to cover the transaction; he stamped the note "Paid" with a large stamp with red ink, and prepared a discharge for the signature of the bank's president. As the president executed the discharge he said to the plaintiff "You junk men must be making plenty of money in order to be paying someone elses' mortgage;" the plaintiff made no reply. The cancelled note and discharged mortgage were handed to the plaintiff * * * Both the clerk and the president understood that the plaintiff desired to pay the debt. On the same day the plaintiff wrote Roy M. Haggett that he had purchased the note and mortgage. This was the first dealing about the note and mortgage between the plaintiff and the Haggetts. Roy M. Haggett was much disturbed, because the plaintiff had had recent arguments with him on two occasions, and was apparently desirous of harming him. On December 1, Roy M. Haggett communicated with the bank, which told him the note had been paid, not sold. * * * The plaintiff interfered in the business relation between the bank and the Haggetts without any occasion, reason or inducement on the part of the Haggetts. * * *

On these findings we are dealing with a unilateral mistake, not a mutual mistake as claimed in the bill. It is quite safe to infer from the findings that the plaintiff intended to purchase the note and mortgage, and not to pay the note and discharge the mortgage. But the bank did not share in the plaintiff's mistake. It understood and acted in accordance with the plaintiff's expressed wish, which was to pay. The bank cannot be charged with a mistake simply because it did not know that the plaintiff entertained an unexpressed intent which was the opposite of his mistakenly expressed desire.

Insofar as the plaintiff's mistake is involved, the bank can be removed immediately from the picture. A person who confers a benefit upon another, manifesting that he does so as an offer of a bargain which the other accepts, is not entitled to restitution because of a mistake which the other does not share and the existence of which the other does not suspect. Restatement, Restitution, § 12. The equitable principle by which a person is entitled to restitution for what he has transferred to another by mistake is modified by the principle that a person is entitled to the benefit of a bargain made by him without fraud or duress. * * *

The situation as to the Haggetts stands differently. They were not a party to the bargain; they have not changed their position, they parted with no consideration; they will gain an unearned benefit if the plaintiff is refused relief. However, whether a mistake is to be corrected depends always upon the circumstances of the case. * * * On the other side of it there is a compelling combination of circumstances. (1) The plaintiff has no one and nothing to blame except his own negligence and inattention. * * * (2) He was an intermeddler, and officiousness is not to be encouraged. (3) His good faith was apparently questionable. (4) He had no motive of self-interest; he was not protecting any interest which he had or thought he had; nor was he discharging any duty which he owed or thought he owed. (5) He was not related to, nor even friendly with the Haggetts, nor was he protecting any interest of theirs. (6) To give the plaintiff restitution from the Haggetts would be to substitute him for the bank as creditor of the Haggetts without the consent of either the bank or the Haggetts. No protection is deserved by one who intermeddles by paying another's debt either without reason or to secure rights against the debtor without the consent of the creditor. Restatement, Restitution, Comment on § 43, p. 173. These latter considerations weigh more than the former, and dictate that the loss remain where it has fallen.

* * *

[The court found that the plaintiff had failed to prove fraud and conspiracy.]

* * *

No error has been made to appear.

Decree affirmed.*

Note

In TMG II v. United States, 778 F.Supp. 37 (D.D.C.1991), the Court emphasized that the ordinary rules of equity require that one claiming a constructive trust come into court "with clean hands" and [with respect to the facts before the Court] "[i]t is hard to imagine a plaintiff approaching the Court with more soiled hands because "the only way that plaintiffs can claim title over the * * * commissions is to admit that they are actively engaged in a bogus transaction designed to generate fraudulent tax losses." (*Id.,* at 52).

TRAVELERS INSURANCE COMPANY v. WILLIAMS

Supreme Court of Tennessee, 1976.
541 S.W.2d 587.

OPINION

BROCK, JUSTICE.

This is a dispute between an insurance company and its insured over which of them should pay the attorney's fee incurred in collecting a subrogation claim.

On March 18, 1972, the minor son of the appellee, Williams, was injured in an automobile accident caused by a third party. The appellant, Travelers, paid the sum of $1,000.00 under the Medical Pay provision of an insurance contract issued to the appellee. The policy provides that "[in] the event of payment * * * the Company shall be subrogated to all the insured's rights of recovery against any person or organization. * * *"

On June 16, 1972, Travelers advised the tortfeasor's insurer, State Farm Mutual Insurance Agency, of its right to be subrogated to a portion of Williams' claim and requested that State Farm protect this subrogation interest in the event settlement should be made. At the same time, Williams was notified that the Travelers Company would "handle [its] own subrogation." Some months later, State Farm acknowledged the correspondence, agreeing to honor the subrogation claim.

Williams filed his suit against the tortfeasor on March 5, 1973, which was concluded by a settlement executed on August 23, 1973. A State Farm draft, payable to Williams and the Travelers Company, is in the Registry of the Court.

Travelers has asserted its right to subrogation under the policy, a right which is not disputed by the appellee. The only controversy is whether the insurer's recovery is to be measured by the entire amount paid by it, $1,000.00, or whether it should be reduced by one-third, the fraction claimed by the appellee's attorney as his fee.

In Tennessee Farmers Mutual Ins. Co. v. Pritchett, 54 Tenn.App. 410, 391 S.W.2d 671 (1969) (certiorari denied), the Court of Appeals held that

* This case is discussed in 3 A. Corbin, Contracts § 617 (1960). *See also* Gruenwald v. Mason, 139 Colo. 1, 335 P.2d 879 (1959) (divorced wife, without agreement or encouragement from her ex-husband, executed, recorded and sent him a deed to her interest in jointly owned real estate; held, no relief in equity).

an insurer subrogated to the rights of its insured against a tortfeasor must bear its pro rata portion of the insured's expenses in securing the recovery if it sits idly by and acquiesces in the action of the insured's attorney in its behalf. The decision was based upon an implied contract between the insurer and the attorney although some language in the opinion speaks in terms of a quasi contractual duty. In the words of the Chancellor, the case was:

> "Another glaring example of an insurance company sitting back on its haunches, doing nothing and waiting to get its share of a claim procured by attorneys, but not wanting to pay its share of an attorney's fee." *Id.* at 414, 391 S.W.2d at 674.

The appellant seeks to avoid the rule applied in *Pritchett* by contending that it did not sit idly by while the insured's attorney performed services for it; that, instead, it gave proper notice to the insured that it did not desire the participation of his attorney in its behalf.

The decisions in other jurisdictions are interesting, if not conclusive. Attorneys' fees have been awarded in at least one state even though the insurer expressly advised the insured's attorney not to represent it; the reason being that it claimed an interest in the judgment or settlement which he recovered. * * * Both opinions explain this result as a consequence of the rule against splitting a cause of action. However, as the dissent in *Hills* points out, the rule does not prevent a plaintiff from suing for only a portion of his damages; he is merely precluded, if he does, from maintaining a later action for the omitted elements of damage.

Wisconsin has announced a rule, of prospective application, that the attorney must notify the subrogated insurer that it will be liable, pro rata, to him for his fee unless it elects to become a party to the action and is represented by counsel of its own choosing. State Farm Mutual Automobile Ins. Co. v. Geline, 48 Wis.2d 290, 179 N.W.2d 815 (1970).

Elsewhere, it appears that, when fees have been denied to the insured's attorney, the subrogee either realized no actual benefit from the attorney's services or took action of its own to protect its interest. * * *

There are, of course, many situations in which the work of an attorney proves useful to persons other than his own client. The normal rule in such cases is that he must look only to his client, with whom he has contracted, for his compensation, notwithstanding the acceptance of benefits by others. * * * But, an exception to this rule is made whenever one person, having assumed the risks and expense of litigation, has succeeded in securing, augmenting, or preserving property or a fund of money in which other people are entitled to share in common. In that event, the expenses of the action are borne by each participant according to his interest. * * * The fairest and most efficient means of distributing these costs is thought to be to make them a charge upon the fund itself. This device, known as the "fund doctrine," was invented by courts of equity to prevent passive beneficiaries of the fund from being unjustly enriched. It is, therefore, never applied against persons who have employed counsel on their own account to represent their interests. * * * Thus, the right to employ counsel of one's own choosing is preserved.

* * * Travelers contends that the appellee was put on notice not to protect its subrogation right; and, therefore, any services rendered by Attorney Winfrey under his contract with appellee, Williams, whereby Travelers was benefited were performed as a volunteer and Travelers should not be held liable for them.

Varied fact situations are disclosed by the reported cases dealing with this problem. We doubt the advisability of attempting to devise a single "rule" to govern all such cases, whatever the facts might be. Instead, each case, with its peculiar facts must be decided by applying general, fundamental principles of contract law.

Upon payment by the insurer of a loss, it becomes the real party in interest with respect to the subrogation claim, and has the right to bring suit in the name of the insured, Emmco Ins. Co. v. Beacon Mut. Indemnity Co., 204 Tenn. 540, 322 S.W.2d 226 (1959), or in its own name. Rule 17.01, Tennessee Rules of Civil Procedure. The insurer may intervene in an action brought by the insured against a wrongdoer and assert its subrogation claim therein. Globe & Rutgers Fire Ins. Co. v. Cleveland, 162 Tenn. 83, 34 S.W.2d 1059 (1931); but, it cannot bring suit against the wrongdoer after judgment has been rendered in the insured's action. *Ibid.* * * * In short, the subrogation claim is the property of the insurer to deal with as it pleases so long as the rights of others, e.g., the insured or the wrongdoer, are not prejudiced.

It follows that whether or not an attorney is entitled to collect from the insurer a fee with respect to a subrogation claim depends upon whether an express or implied contract or a quasi contractual relation exists between them.

In the instant case, we find no evidence that an express or implied contract existed between the insurer and the insured's attorney. On the contrary, unlike the subrogee in the *Pritchett* case, the insurer here expressly stated to the insured that it would handle its own subrogation claim and that the insured was not to protect the same. A promise cannot be implied in fact in the face of a declaration to the contrary by the party to be charged. Any authority which the insured might otherwise have had to direct his attorney to prosecute the subrogation claim was expressly revoked.

Neither do we find evidence of unjust enrichment of the insurer from the services of the insured's attorney upon which a quasi or constructive contractual duty could be based. In our view, one is not unjustly enriched by a benefit "forced upon" him as the result of services voluntarily and officiously performed by another who has been expressly informed by the alleged promisor that his services are not desired.

We conclude that the facts of this case do not entitle the insured's attorney to receive any fee from the insurer with respect to the subrogation claim; he acted as a volunteer.

The judgment of the trial court is reversed, the appellant is awarded judgment against appellee for the sum of $1,000.00, with interest and costs;

the original complaint filed by the appellee against the appellant is dismissed and costs taxed against appellee.

Cooper, C.J., and Fones, J., Henry and Harbison, JJ., concur.

Notes

1. In Saltz Brothers Inc. v. Saltz, 122 F.2d 79 (D.C.Cir.1941), the plaintiff corporation, through its officials, "fired" two senior corporate officials. The latter, however, refused to be fired and to give up their offices and roles. They continued to undertake to fill the positions in question for some months and to receive compensation. The corporation brought the present action for injunctive relief and an accounting of, among other things, the compensation received during the period in question. The court set aside the trial court's allowance of salary for the period: "The rule in such circumstances is that, however valuable the services, the person in whose behalf they are rendered cannot be required to pay for them where they are rendered against his will and without his consent."

Id., at 81.

2. In the principal cases the party seeking relief is said to be a mere "volunteer", intruding himself upon the scene and into the defendant's affairs. In a variety of situations services may be rendered voluntarily under *emergency* conditions to protect the well-being of the person or property of another. In the cases involving preservation of another's property (outside the area of maritime law) there generally can be no restitution relief unless the plaintiff has some relationship to the property or its owner. II G. Palmer, The Law of Restitution § 10.3 (1978). Where the plaintiff's intervention protected another from serious bodily harm or pain (such as intervention by a physician in an attempt to preserve the life or health of the defendant), quasi-contract relief has been granted. Restatement of Restitution § 116 (1937); II G. Palmer § 10.4. Quasi-contractual recovery for conferring non-emergency benefits, such as hospital treatment and care, funeral expenses and "necessaries" supplied to a spouse, child or other relative are discussed by Professor Palmer. *Id.*

These cases should be considered along with those discussed in Section 2, above, involving receipt of a benefit as a consequence of a tortious interference with the defendant's property rights.

3. Somewhat different are those cases where the plaintiff "voluntarily" sustains a physical injury in order to prevent what he reasonably, and spontaneously, concludes is a risk of more serious injury to the defendant. Here, "enrichment" in the usual sense is not present, but rather the physical well-being of the party whose hurt was prevented, and who, as a consequence, will enjoy greater ability to increase his or her estate. In these cases, the courts deny recovery from the benefitted party in the absence of a subsequent promise to compensate the injured plaintiff. Webb v. McGowin, 232 Ala. 374, 168 So. 199 (1936), discussed in 1A A. Corbin, Contracts § 231 (1963); Note, 31 Ill.L.Rev. 390 (1936). *Contra* Harrington v. Taylor, 225 N.C. 690, 36 S.E.2d 227 (1945). *See also* Dawson, Rewards for the Rescue of Human Life?, in 20th Century Comparative and Conflicts Law—Legal Essays in Honor of Hessell E. Yntema 142 (1961); Note, 7 U.Chi.L.Rev. 124 (1939).

ASSOCIATION LIFE INS. CO. v. JENKINS

United States District Court, Middle District of Tennessee, 1992.
793 F.Supp. 161.

* * *

II. Analysis

Very few recent cases exist in Tennessee on the issues before the Court today. Nevertheless, it is well established that in Tennessee, as elsewhere, insurance companies may sue to recover benefit payments made due to mistake or fraud. *See Aetna Casualty and Surety Co. v. Parton,* 609 S.W.2d 518, 518 (Tenn.Ct.App.1980) (arson); *Tennessee Hospital Service Association v. Strang,* 49 Tenn.App. 263, 354 S.W.2d 488, 491 (1962) (physician fraud); *see also* 18 George J. Couch, Couch Cyclopedia of Insurance Law § 74:156 (2d ed. rev. vol. 1983). Absent fraud, suits for recovery of insurance benefit payments are suits under implied contracts. *Strader v. Aetna Life Insurance Co.,* 181 Tenn. 444, 181 S.W.2d 622, 625 (1944).

Implied contracts differ from express contracts in that the former are inferred by a court from conduct, while the latter are expressed by the parties in words. *V.L. Nicholson Co. v. Transcon Investment and Financial Ltd.,* 595 S.W.2d 474, 482 (Tenn.1980). The Tennessee Supreme Court has observed that courts employ the terms "contracts implied in law," "unjust enrichment," "quasi-contract," and "quantum meruit" interchangeably. *Paschall's, Inc. v. Dozier,* 219 Tenn. 45, 407 S.W.2d 150, 154 (1966). In the past, such actions were also known as actions in assumpsit for money had and received. *United States Fidelity & Guaranty Insurance Co. v. Hartsook,* 487 S.W.2d 649, 651 (Tenn.1972).

Contracts implied in law, or quasi-contracts, are obligations imposed by law without assent of the parties bound, on the ground that they are dictated by reason and justice and are allowed to be enforced by actions ex contractu. *Weatherly v. American Agricultural Chemical Co.,* 16 Tenn.App. 613, 65 S.W.2d 592, 598 (1934). Thus, courts apply equitable principles in deciding cases under these theories. *See Lawler v. Zapletal,* 679 S.W.2d 950, 955 (Tenn.Ct.App.1984).

In the instant case, Association Life's complaint alleges fraud and negligent misrepresentation as bases for recovery. Although not exactly textually congruent with the applicable law in Tennessee, the plaintiff's assertions, if proved, could allow recovery, because, as discussed above, insurance benefits paid because of fraud, or mistake in certain circumstances, are recoverable. However, after reviewing the evidence, the Court holds, under equitable principles of contracts implied in law, that the plaintiff is not entitled to recover the insurance benefits paid.

To begin with, the plaintiff failed to prove that the defendants acted fraudulently. In Tennessee, to succeed on an action for fraudulent misrepresentation, a plaintiff must prove that the defendant made a false representation about an existing or past material fact, that it was made knowingly without belief in its truth, or recklessly, and that the plaintiff suffered injury as a result of relying on the misrepresentation. *Graham v. First American National Bank,* 594 S.W.2d 723, 725–26 (Tenn.Ct.App.1980).

Further, no evidence presented at trial even indicates that these boxes were checked by Startup or Jenkins. On a few claim forms on which the boxes were checked, Startup's signature appears in a box that states "I authorize the release of any medical information necessary to process this claim. I also request payment of government benefits either to myself or to the party who accepts assignment below." On some of the claim forms that have checked employment boxes, Startup's signature does not appear. Instead, only the typed phrase "patient's request for payment on file" appears. Although no evidence was presented at trial regarding this fact, most likely, whoever gave Startup the document to sign, when it was given, checked the box. Startup's signature in the other space only authorizes the release of medical information and requests payment. It does not purport to represent his confirmation of the truth of any other information on the document. Therefore, Association Life has not shown that Startup or Jenkins knowingly made any misrepresentation.

The other theory upon which Association Life could succeed in this action is that it mistakenly paid out benefits and is entitled to recovery under unjust enrichment. This seems to be closer to the theory on which the plaintiff focused at trial. Association Life attempted to prove that no employee of Murfreesboro Truck Sales worked the requisite number of hours under the insurance contract after April, 1987, and therefore Murfreesboro Truck Sales was not eligible for group insurance coverage under the insurance contract as an employer because it had no employees. Although the Court is persuaded by the evidence that Association Life probably paid the benefits out by mistake, the equitable principles that control this action still prevent Association Life's recovery.

The Tennessee cases closest to the one at bar happen to be very old. Nonetheless, their law remains valid under stare decisis and as it is consistent with that of other jurisdictions. In 1852, the Tennessee Supreme Court held, in a case for recovery of insurance payments made under mistake of fact, that an insurance company could recover such payments. *Guild v. Baldridge,* 2 Swan 295, 32 Tenn. 210, 216 (1852). The court qualified its holding, however, aptly stating: "We do not, of course, mean to say that the plaintiff, in a case of payment without knowledge of all the material facts, may not be repelled upon other grounds, involving different principles; we think he may—as for instance, upon the ground of injury or injustice to the defendant in a particular case." *Id.* Similarly, fifty-nine years later, the Tennessee Supreme Court again applied equitable principles in holding that money had and received under a mistake of law, as opposed to mistake of fact, cannot be recovered unless such circumstances exist that

> it would be unconscionable for the party who obtained the advantage in such transaction or settlement to retain that advantage, and *e converso,* although there was a clear mistake of law, *yet if the party benefiting by the transaction may retain the advantage in good con-*

> *science, neither a court of law nor equity will give relief to the complaining party.*

Leach v. Cowan, 125 Tenn. 182, 207, 140 S.W. 1070 (1911) (emphasis added).

This result is consistent with the law in other jurisdictions. A federal district court in Arkansas, for instance, held, under Arkansas law, that an insurance company could not recover benefits paid under a mistake of fact when the defendant's had changed their position in reliance on the paid benefits. *Woolsey v. Nationwide Insurance Co.,* 697 F.Supp. 1053, 1056–57 (W.D.Ark.1988). Other federal courts have made similar holdings that applied equitable principles in other jurisdictions. *See Glover v. Metropolitan Life Insurance Co.,* 664 F.2d 1101 (8th Cir.1981) ("The Missouri courts, when weighing the equities of a case, lay great emphasis on whether or not the payee has relied on retention of the payment received."); *Myers v. Fidelity & Casualty Co. of New York,* 759 F.2d 1542, 1548 (11th Cir.1985) (citing 13 S. Williston & W. Jaeger, A Treatise on the Law of Contracts § 1595 at 584 and 586 (1970)); *Terra Nova Insurance Co v. Associates Commercial Corp.,* 697 F.Supp. 1048, 1052 (E.D.Wisc.1988) ("In reliance on the insurance settlement, [the defendant] changed its position to its detriment, and restitution is therefore inappropriate.").

Here, the defendants would suffer great injury or injustice if the Court allowed Association Life to recover the money it paid under mistake of fact. The defendants relied on the benefit payments in undergoing the medical treatment. Startup changed his position by undergoing medical treatment that he may not have if he could not have relied on the benefits. Also, since those payments have been paid to the physicians and medical suppliers and are not in the hands of the defendants, the nature of the benefits received by the defendants is not a windfall. Under the above principles, the Court holds that the defendants "may retain the advantage in good conscience." Therefore, the Court declines to allow the plaintiff, Association Life, to recover its payments made for the benefit of Startup.

III. CONCLUSION

For the reasons stated above, the Court enters judgment in favor of the defendants. An order consistent with the above reasoning and result will be entered simultaneously.

Notes

1. In situations such as that in Association Life Ins. Co. v. Jenkins the fact that the benefit received has undergone a change of form after coming into the hands of the defendant is not sufficient to constitute a "detrimental change of position" making quasi-contract relief inequitable. Messersmith v. G.T. Murray & Co., 667 P.2d 655 (Wyo.1983) (payments by mistake for a greater number of shares than were owned by the defendant; proceeds applied to bills and down payment on a house inadequate to prevent restitution); *accord:* United States v. Reagan, 651 F.Supp. 387 (D.Mass.1987) (erroneous tax refund); Gulf Life Ins. Co. v. Folsom, 256 Ga. 400, 349 S.E.2d 368 (1986) (mistaken payment of insurance benefits); Monroe Financial Corp. v. DiSilves-

tro, 529 N.E.2d 379 (Ind.App.1988) (payment by mistake for stock not owned by defendant).

2. While the fact that a contract is "illegal," may prevent an action for damages for breach it will not prevent quasi-contractual relief where the record shows the plaintiff, suing in quantum meruit, rendered the services in good faith without knowledge of the illegality. McDaniel v. State of Arkansas, 291 Ark. 596, 726 S.W.2d 679 (1987); *accord,* Armijo v. Cebolleta Land Grant, 105 N.M. 324, 732 P.2d 426 (1987). Such a party is not "in pari delicto", that is, of equal guilt with the defendant. See, also, William J. Davis, Inc. v. Slade, 271 A.2d 412 (D.C.App.1970). A variety of defenses have been relied upon to overcome the "in pari delicto" defense (such as undue influence, duress, mistake and misrepresentation) to justify the conclusion that the "guilt" is not "equal" and therefore restitution is justified. These are described in II G. Palmer, Law of Restitution § 8.6 (1978). An interesting variation is that of "*in locus poenitentiae* " ("I was involved in an illegal activity but when I realized it I stopped and tried to undo it"). *Id.,* at § 8.7. See, also, Ryan v. KVL, Inc., 198 Wash. 459, 88 P.2d 836 (1939), discussed in Notes, 27 Calif.L.Rev. 601 (1934) and 40 Va.L.Rev. 1063 (1954).

The problem of determining legislative intent to deny restitution in situations where a statute makes the conduct unlawful is discussed in II G. Palmer § 8.3. See, in this regard, Rosasco Creameries, Inc. v. Cohen, 276 N.Y. 274, 11 N.E.2d 908, 242 N.Y.S.2d 1 (1937), discussed in Notes, 32 Ill.L.Rev. 102 (1937); 37 Mich.L.Rev. 136 (1938), and 22 Minn.L.Rev. 1058 (1938).

In the case of transfer of property intended by the transferor to place it beyond the reach of creditors, some courts have allowed restitution where there were, in fact, no creditors with valid claims against the transferor at the time of the transfer in question. Compare, Palumbo v. Palumbo, 55 Misc.2d 264, 284 N.Y.S.2d 884 (1967) (restitution allowed) and MacRae v. MacRae, 37 Ariz. 307, 294 P. 280 (1930) (restitution denied), discussed in Note, 44 Harv.L.Rev. 1143 (1931).

GENERAL NOTE

Governmental Use of Disgorgement of Wrongfully Acquired Benefits to Effectuate the Policy Underlying Statutes Prohibiting the Conduct in Question

In a number of recent opinions the courts have held that a court has broad remedial power to effectuate the policy of statutes ("to make effective" the legislative purpose) which make certain types of conduct unlawful by, *inter alia,* ordering disgorgement of the profits obtained in the course of the unlawful conduct. Illustrative is Securities Exchange Commission v. Bilzerian, 814 F.Supp. 116 (D.D.C.1993) where the Court stated that "disgorgement for violations of the Exchange Act is appropriate and within the authority of this Court * * *. 'Disgorgement is an equitable remedy designed to deprive a wrongdoer of his unjust enrichment and to deter others * * *'. This is accomplished by compelling defendants to 'give up the amount by which [they] were unjustly enriched' " which total, in this instance, $33,140,787.07. (*Id.,* at 121).

Accord, United States v. Bonanno Organized Crime Family, 683 F.Supp. 1411 (E.D.N.Y.1988), *aff'd,* 879 F.2d 20 (2d Cir.1989) (the power to order disgorgement of profits by, *inter alia,* organized crime "derives from the broad equitable powers given the courts" under applicable statutes " 'to provide such remedies as are necessary to make effective the congressional purpose.' " (683 F.Supp., at 1448); United States v. Nagelberg, 772 F.Supp. 120 (E.D.N.Y.1991) (unjust enrichment cause alleged for conduct of the defendants in obtaining funds belonging to a credit union to which they were not entitled); United States v. Rivieccio, 661 F.Supp. 281 (E.D.N.Y. 1987) (cause of action stated for fraudulent transfer of credit union funds justifying constructive trust, unjust enrichment and accounting remedies).

Chapter 5

DECLARATORY JUDGMENTS

The declaratory judgment action is one of the traditional Civil Law remedies, but was not recognized in England until the late 1800's. In the United States, the Uniform Declaratory Judgments Act was approved by the Commissioners on Uniform Laws in 1921 and the Federal Declaratory Judgment Act was enacted by Congress in 1934. Today almost every state has enacted legislation or rules of court recognizing the remedy.*

UNIFORM DECLARATORY JUDGMENTS ACT (1922) **

§ 1. *Scope.* Courts of record within their respective jurisdictions shall have power to declare rights, status, and other legal relations whether or not further relief is or could be claimed. No action or proceeding shall be open to objection on the ground that a declaratory judgment or decree is prayed for. The declaration may be either affirmative or negative in form and effect; and such declarations shall have the force and effect of a final judgment or decree.

* The pioneer discussions of the declaratory judgment remedy in this country are Sunderland, A Modern Evolution in Remedial Rights—The Declaratory Judgment, 16 Mich. L.Rev. 69 (1917), and Borchard, The Declaratory Judgment—A Needed Procedural Reform, 28 Yale L.J. 1 (1918).

The principal treatises are E. Borchard, Declaratory Judgments (2d ed. 1941) and W. Anderson, Actions for Declaratory Judgments (2d ed. 1951).

For appraisals of the current scene, *see* Dickson, Declaratory Remedies and Constitutional Change, 24 Vand.L.Rev. 257 (1971); Fraser, A Survey of Declaratory Judgment Actions in the United States, 39 Ia.L.Rev. 639 (1954); Vanneman & Kutner, Declaratory Judgments in the Federal Courts, 9 Ohio St.L.J. 209 (1948); Developments in the Law: Declaratory Judgments, 1941–1949, 62 Harv. L.Rev. 787 (separate Index at 883) (1949).

** The Uniform Act, substantially or with modifications, has been adopted in Alabama, Arizona, Arkansas, Colorado, District of Columbia, Florida, Georgia, Idaho, Illinois, Indiana, Iowa, Louisiana, Maine, Maryland, Massachusetts, Minnesota, Missouri, Montana, Nebraska, Nevada, New Jersey, North Carolina, North Dakota, Ohio, Oklahoma, Oregon, Pennsylvania, Puerto Rico, Rhode Island, South Carolina, South Dakota, Tennessee, Texas, Utah, Vermont, Washington, Virginia, West Virginia, Wisconsin, Wyoming and the Virgin Islands. *See* Handbook of the National Conference of Commissioners on Uniform State Laws 391 (1985).

Alaska, California, Connecticut, Delaware, Hawaii, Kansas, Kentucky, Michigan, New Hampshire, New Mexico, and New York have various types of statutes and rules of court, other than the Uniform Act, though similar thereto in some instances, authorizing declaratory judgments. Some statutes, such as Alaska's, are patterned on the federal statute.

§ 2. *Power to Construe, etc.* Any person interested under a deed, will, written contract or other writings constituting a contract, or whose rights, status or other legal relations are affected by a statute, municipal ordinance, contract or franchise, may have determined any question of construction or validity arising under the instrument, statute, ordinance, contract, or franchise and obtain a declaration of rights, status or other legal relations thereunder.

§ 3. *Before Breach.* A contract may be construed either before or after there has been a breach thereof.

§ 4. *Executor, etc.* Any person interested as or through an executor, administrator, trustee, guardian or other fiduciary, creditor, devisee, legatee, heir, next of kin, or cestui que trust, in the administration of a trust, or of the estate of a decedent, an infant, lunatic, or insolvent, may have a declaration of rights or legal relations in respect thereto: (a) To ascertain any class of creditors, devisees, legatees, heirs, next of kin or others; or (b) To direct the executors, administrators, or trustees to do or abstain from doing any particular act in their fiduciary capacity; or (c) To determine any question arising in the administration of the estate or trust, including questions of construction of wills and other writings.

§ 5. *Enumeration Not Exclusive.* The enumeration in sections 2, 3, and 4 does not limit or restrict the exercise of the general powers conferred in section 1, in any proceeding where declaratory relief is sought, in which a judgment or decree will terminate the controversy or remove an uncertainty.

§ 6. *Discretionary.* The court may refuse to render or enter a declaratory judgment or decree where such judgment or decree, if rendered or entered, would not terminate the uncertainty or controversy giving rise to the proceeding.

§ 7. *Review.* All orders, judgments and decrees under this Act may be reviewed as other orders, judgments and decrees.

§ 8. *Supplemental Relief.* Further relief based on a declaratory judgment or decree may be granted whenever necessary or proper. The application therefor shall be by petition to a court having jurisdiction to grant the relief. [Notice to adverse parties required.]

§ 9. *Jury Trial.* When a proceeding under this Act involves the determination of an issue of fact, such issue may be tried and determined in the same manner as issues of fact are tried and determined in other civil actions in the court in which the proceeding is pending.

§ 11. *Parties.* When declaratory relief is sought, all persons shall be made parties who have or claim any interest which would be affected by the declaration, and no declaration shall prejudice the rights of persons not parties to the proceeding. [Parties required if validity of municipal ordinance or franchise is involved.]

§ 12. *Construction.* This act is declared to be remedial; its purpose is to settle and to afford relief from uncertainty and insecurity with respect to rights, status and other legal relations; and is to be liberally construed and administered.

[Sections 10, 13–17 have been omitted.]

FEDERAL DECLARATORY JUDGMENT ACT AND FEDERAL RULES OF CIVIL PROCEDURE *

28 U.S.C.A. sec. 2201 (as amended 1988).

(a) In a case of actual controversy within its jurisdiction, except with respect to Federal taxes other than actions brought under section 7428 of the Internal Revenue Code of 1986 or a proceeding under section 505 or 1146 of title 11, or in any civil action involving an antidumping or countervailing duty proceeding regarding a class or kind of Canadian merchandise, as determined by the administering authority, any court of the United States, upon the filing of an appropriate pleading, may declare the rights and other legal relations of any interested party seeking such declaration, whether or not further relief is or could be sought. Any such declaration shall have the force and effect of a final judgment or decree and shall be reviewable as such.

(b) For limitations on actions brought with respect to drug patents, see section 505 or 512 of the Federal Food, Drug, and Cosmetic Act.

F.R.C.P. Rule 57 (as amended 1949).

The procedure for obtaining a declaratory judgment pursuant to Title 28 U.S.C. § 2201, shall be in accordance with these rules, and the right to trial by jury may be demanded under the circumstances and in the manner provided in Rules 38 and 39. The existence of another adequate remedy does not preclude a judgment for declaratory relief in cases where it is appropriate. The court may order a speedy hearing of an action for a declaratory judgment and may advance it on the calendar.

SENATE REPORT NO. 1005, 73rd Cong.2d Sess. 2–3, 5 (1934) [excerpts from the Senate Report recommending enactment of what is now the Federal Declaratory Judgment Act]: "The declaratory judgment differs in no respect from any other judgment except that it is not followed by a decree for damages, injunction, specific performance, or other immediately coercive decree. It declares conclusively and finally the rights of parties in litigation over a contested issue, a form of relief which often suffices to settle controversies and fully administer justice. It enables parties in disputes over their rights over a contract, deed, lease, will or any other written instrument to sue for a declaration of rights, without breach of the contract, etc., citing as defendants those who oppose their claims of right. It has been employed in State courts mainly for the construction of instruments of all kinds, for the determination of status in marital or domestic relations, for the determination of the rights contested under a

* *See* Borchard, The Federal Declaratory Judgment Act, 21 Va.L.Rev. 35 (1934).

For an excellent brief discussion of the declaratory judgment in federal courts, see C. Wright, Law of Federal Courts § 100 (4th ed. 1983).

statute or municipal ordinance, where it was not possible or necessary to obtain an injunction.

"The procedure has been especially useful in avoiding the necessity, now so often present, of having to act at one's peril or to act on one's own interpretation of his rights, or abandon one's rights because of a fear of incurring damages. * * * In jurisdictions having the declaratory judgment procedure, it is not necessary to bring about such social and economic waste and destruction in order to obtain a determination of one's rights.

* * *

"The fact is that the declaratory judgment has often proved so necessary that it has been employed under other names for years, and that in many cases the injunction procedure is abused in order to render what is in effect a declaratory judgment. For example, in the case of Pierce v. Society of Sisters (268 U.S. 510, 525, 45 S.Ct. 571, 1925), the court issued an injunction against the enforcement of an Oregon statute which was not to come into force until 2 years later; in rendering a judgment declaring the statute void, the court in effect issued a declaratory judgment by what was, in effect, apparently, an abuse of the injunction. *See also* Village of Euclid v. Ambler Realty Co. (272 U.S. 365, 47 S.Ct. 114, 1926). Much of the hostility to the extensive use of the injunction power by the Federal courts will be obviated by enabling the courts to render declaratory judgments.

"An important practical advantage of the declaratory judgment lies in the fact that it enables litigants to narrow the issue, speed the decision, and settle the controversy before an accumulation of differences and hostility has engendered a wide and general conflict, involving numerous collateral issues. * * *"

PUBLIC SERVICE COMM'N v. WYCOFF CO.

United States Supreme Court, 1952.
344 U.S. 237, 73 S.Ct. 236, 97 L.Ed. 291.

MR. JUSTICE JACKSON delivered the opinion of the Court.

As this suit in equity was commenced in United States District Court it sought two kinds of specific relief: (1) a declaratory judgment that complainant's carriage of motion picture film and newsreels between points in Utah constitutes interstate commerce; (2) that the Public Service Commission of Utah and its members be forever enjoined from interfering with such transportation over routes authorized by the Interstate Commerce Commission.

The complaint alleged a course of importing, processing and transporting picture film and newsreels to support the contention that carriage between points in Utah was so integrated with their interstate movement that the whole constituted interstate commerce. It averred that the Commission and its members "threatened to and are attempting to stop and prevent plaintiff from transporting motion picture film and newsreels between points and places within the State of Utah, and they are thereby interfering with the conduct of interstate commerce by the plaintiff and imposing an undue burden upon interstate commerce," and that unless the defendants are enjoined they will "block, harass and prevent plaintiff in the transportation of said motion picture film and newsreels in Utah."

The Commission and its members answered that respondent's transportation between points in Utah was nothing more than intrastate commerce. They specifically denied attempting, threatening, or intending to interfere with or burden interstate commerce.

The District Court, after trial, sustained the contention of the Commission and dismissed the complaint. The Court of Appeals considered only "whether the intrastate transportations are nonetheless integral parts of interstate transportations." It held the evidence to warrant an affirmative answer, reversed the judgment of the District Court and ordered further proceedings in conformity with that view. We granted certiorari. * * *

* * *

For more reasons than one it is clear that this proceeding cannot result in an injunction on constitutional grounds. In addition to defects that will appear in our discussion of declaratory relief, it is wanting in equity because there is no proof of any threatened or probable act of the defendants which might cause the irreparable injury essential to equitable relief by injunction. The respondent appears to have abandoned the suit as one for injunction but seeks to support it as one for declaratory judgment, hoping thereby to avoid both the three-judge court requirement and the necessity for proof of threatened injury. Whether declaratory relief is appropriate under the circumstances of this case apparently was not considered by either of the courts below. But that inquiry is one which every grant of this remedy must survive.

The Declaratory Judgment Act of 1934, now 28 U.S.C.A. § 2201, styled "creation of a remedy," provides that in a case of actual controversy a competent court may "declare the rights and other legal relations" of a party "whether or not further relief is or could be sought." This is an enabling Act, which confers a discretion on the courts rather than an absolute right upon the litigant.

Previous to its enactment there were responsible expressions of doubt that constitutional limitations on federal judicial power would permit any federal declaratory judgment procedure. *Cf.* Liberty Warehouse Co. v. Grannis, 273 U.S. 70, 47 S.Ct. 282, 71 L.Ed. 541. Finally, as the practice extended in the states, we reviewed a declaratory judgment rendered by a state court and held that a controversy which would be justiciable in this Court if presented in a suit for injunction is not the less because the relief was declaratory. Nashville, C. & St. L.R. Co. v. Wallace, 288 U.S. 249, 53 S.Ct. 345, 77 L.Ed. 730. Encouraged by this and guided by the experience of the thirty-four states that had enacted such laws, the Senate Judiciary Committee recommended an adaptation of the principle to federal practice. Its enabling clause was narrower than that of the Uniform Act adopted in 1921 by the Commissioners on Uniform State Laws, which gave comprehensive power to declare rights, status and other legal relations. The

Federal Act omits status * and limits the declaration to cases of actual controversy.

This Act was adjudged constitutional only by interpreting it to confine the declaratory remedy within conventional "case or controversy" limits. * * *

In Aetna Life Insurance Co. v. Haworth, 300 U.S. 227, 57 S.Ct. 461, 463, 81 L.Ed. 617, Mr. Chief Justice Hughes used the whole catalogue of familiar phrases to define and delimit the measure of this new remedy. If its metes and bounds are not clearly marked, it is because his available verbal markers are themselves elastic, inconstant and imprecise. It applies, he points out, only to "cases and controversies in the constitutional sense" of a nature "consonant with the exercise of the judicial function" and "appropriate for judicial determination." Each must present a "justiciable controversy" as distinguished from "a difference or dispute of a hypothetical or abstract character * * *. The controversy must be definite and concrete, touching the legal relations of parties having adverse legal interests. * * * It must be a real and substantial controversy admitting of specific relief through a decree of a conclusive character, as distinguished from an opinion advising what the law would be upon a hypothetical state of facts." The relief is available only for a "concrete case admitting of an immediate and definite determination of the legal rights of the parties."

Other sources have stated relevant limitations. The Senate Judiciary Committee report regarded the 1,200 American decisions theretofore rendered on the subject as establishing that "the issue must be real, the question practical and not academic and the decision must finally settle and determine the controversy." Indeed the Uniform Act, unlike the Federal Act, expressly declares the discretion of the Court to refuse a decree that would not "terminate the uncertainty or controversy giving rise to the proceeding." * * *

But when all of the axioms have been exhausted and all words of definition have been spent, the propriety of declaratory relief in a particular case will depend upon a circumspect sense of its fitness informed by the teachings and experience concerning the functions and extent of federal judicial power. While the courts should not be reluctant or niggardly in granting this relief in the cases for which it was designed, they must be alert to avoid imposition upon their jurisdiction through obtaining futile or premature interventions, especially in the field of public law. A maximum of caution is necessary in the type of litigation that we have here, where a ruling is sought that would reach far beyond the particular case. Such

* Professor Borchard has explained that the term "rights and other legal relations" in the Federal Act "was designed to insure technical accuracy, by indicating that 'rights' have a limited connotation, and are different from duties, privileges, immunities, powers, disabilities and liabilities." Borchard, The Federal Declaratory Judgments Act, 21 Va. L.Rev. 35, 45 (1934). In his opinion, "[t]he Hohfeldian analysis of jural relations has helped greatly to clarify legal thinking, and has been especially useful in the application of the declaratory judgment * * *." *Id.* Therefore he is critical of the Commissioners on Uniform State Laws for including the term "status" in the Uniform Act, and praises Congress for maintaining "scientific unity" in the Federal Act. *Id.* Nevertheless, he acknowledges that there is no difference between the two acts at the level of "practical administration." *Id.*

differences of opinion or conflicts of interest must be "ripe for determination" as controversies over legal rights. The disagreement must not be nebulous or contingent but must have taken on fixed and final shape so that a court can see what legal issues it is deciding, what effect its decision will have on the adversaries, and some useful purpose to be achieved in deciding them.

The complainant in this case does not request an adjudication that it has a right to do, or to have, anything in particular. It does not ask a judgment that the Commission is without power to enter any specific order or take any concrete regulatory step. It seeks simply to establish that, as presently conducted, respondent's carriage of goods between points within as well as without Utah is all interstate commerce. One naturally asks, so what? To that ultimate question no answer is sought.

A multitude of rights and immunities may be predicated upon the premise that a business consists of interstate commerce. What are the specific ones in controversy? The record is silent and counsel little more articulate. * * *

* * * We are told that the Commission filed a petition in a Utah state court to enjoin respondent from operating between a few specified locations within the State, but that process was never served and nothing in the record tells us what has happened to this action. We may conjecture that respondent fears some form of administrative or judicial action to prohibit its service on routes wholly within the State without the Commission's leave. What respondent asks is that it win any such case before it is commenced. Even if respondent is engaged solely in interstate commerce, we cannot say that there is nothing whatever that the State may require.

A declaratory judgment may be the basis of further relief necessary or proper against the adverse party, 28 U.S.C.A. § 2202. The carrier's idea seems to be that it can now establish the major premise of an exemption, not as an incident of any present declaration of any specific right or immunity, but to hold in readiness for use should the Commission at any future time attempt to apply any part of a complicated regulatory statute to it. If there is any more definite or contemporaneous purpose to this case, neither this record nor the briefs make it clear to us. We think this for several reasons exceeds any permissible discretionary use of the Federal Declaratory Judgment Act.

In the first place, this dispute has not matured to a point where we can see what, if any, concrete controversy will develop. It is much like asking a declaration that the State has no power to enact legislation that may be under consideration but has not yet shaped up into an enactment. If there is any risk of suffering penalty, liability or prosecution, which a declaration would avoid, it is not pointed out to us. If and when the State Commission takes some action that raises an issue of its power, some further declaration would be necessary to any complete relief. The proposed decree cannot end the controversy.

Nor is it apparent that the present proceeding would serve a useful purpose if at some future date the State undertakes regulation of respondent. After a sifting of evidence and a finding of facts as they are today, there is no assurance that changes of significance may not take place before the State decides to move. * * *

Even when there is no incipient federal-state conflict, the declaratory judgment procedure will not be used to preempt and prejudge issues that are committed for initial decision to an administrative body or special tribunal any more than it will be used as a substitute for statutory methods of review. It would not be tolerable, for example, that declaratory judgments establish that an enterprise is not in interstate commerce in order to forestall proceedings by the National Labor Relations Board, the Interstate Commerce Commission or many agencies that are authorized to try and decide such an issue in the first instance. * * *

But, as the declaratory proceeding is here invoked, it is even less appropriate because, in addition to foreclosing an administrative body, it is incompatible with a proper federal-state relationship. * * *

* * *

The procedures of review usually afford ample protection to a carrier whose federal rights are actually invaded, and there are remedies for threatened irreparable injuries. State courts are bound equally with the federal courts by the Federal Constitution and laws. Ultimate recourse may be had to this Court by certiorari if a state court has allegedly denied a federal right.

* * *

We conclude that this suit cannot be entertained as one for injunction and should not be continued as one for a declaratory judgment. The judgment below should be reversed and modified to direct that the action be dismissed.

Reversed and so ordered.

Note

Neither the Federal Act nor the Uniform Act expressly provides for obtaining a declaratory judgment to determine questions of administrative law. Nevertheless, the action often is used to ascertain the validity and construction of administrative decisions and regulations. K. Davis, Administrative Law 444–45 (3d ed. 1972). If the remedy is refused, it is usually for one of the following reasons: "lack of a justiciable controversy, availability of other remedies or the existence of an exclusive statutory remedy, and the failure to exhaust administrative remedies." Developments in the Law: Declaratory Judgments—1941–1949, 62 Harv.L.Rev. 787, 878 (1949).

At least three distinct grounds are discernable in the decision in *Wycoff:* vagueness of the controversy, and hence lack of a constitutional case or controversy; prematurity or lack of ripeness; and need to avoid improper interference with administrative tribunals. The following cases also illustrate the interplay of those considerations:

a. In International Longshoremen's & Warehousemen's Union v. Boyd, 347 U.S. 222 (1954), the plaintiffs, lawful resident aliens of Washington, brought an action for declaratory and injunctive relief against the District Director of Immigration and Naturalization at Seattle. Their purpose was to obtain a declaration that section 212(d)(7) of the Immigration and Nationality Act of 1952 would not be applied to them when they went to work in the territory of Alaska during the 1953 canning season. Section 212(d)(7) contained language which, given one construction, provided that all aliens seeking admission from Alaska to the continental United States had to be examined as if entering from a foreign country, even though they had previously been accepted as permanent United States residents. The new law created an acute problem for the plaintiffs because aliens could be excluded for reasons that did not justify deportation of lawful resident aliens. The plaintiffs contended that the Act was not intended to apply to resident alien workers engaged in work under a legally authorized collective-bargaining contract. The Supreme Court never reached the merits of the case because it held that there was no case or controversy:

> "Appellants in effect asked the District Court to rule that a statute the sanctions of which had not been set in motion against individuals on whose behalf relief was sought, because an occasion for doing so had not arisen, would not be applied to them if in the future such a contingency should arise. That is not a lawsuit to enforce a right; it is an endeavor to obtain a court's assurance that a statute does not govern hypothetical situations that may or may not make the challenged statute applicable. Determination of the scope and constitutionality of legislation in advance of its immediate adverse effect in the context of a concrete case involves too remote and abstract an inquiry for the proper exercise of the judicial function. United Public Workers v. Mitchell, 330 U.S. 75, 67 S.Ct. 556, 91 L.Ed. 754 * * *."

JUSTICE BLACK spoke for the two dissenting judges:

"This looks to me like the very kind of 'case or controversy' courts should decide. With the abstract principles of law relied on by the majority for dismissing the case, I am not in disagreement. * * * But as I read the record it shows that judicial action is absolutely essential to save a large group of wage earners on whose behalf this action is brought from irreparable harm due to alleged lawless enforcement of a federal statute. * * *

"* * * True, the action was begun before the union members went to Alaska for the 1953 canning season. But it is not only admitted that the Immigration official intended to enforce § 212(d)(7) as the union and these workers feared. It is admitted here that he has since done precisely that. * * *

"Thus the threatened injury which the Court dismisses as 'remote' and 'hypothetical' has come about."

b. In Renne v. Geary, ___ U.S. ___, 111 S.Ct. 2331, 115 L.Ed.2d 288 (1991), the Court held non-justiciable a suit brought by various voters, including committee members of the Democratic and Republican parties, who challenged a provision of the California Constitution that "No political party or party central committee may endorse, support, or oppose a candidate for nonpartisan office". That term included "all judicial, school, county, and city offices". Plaintiffs sought a declaration that the provision violated the First and Fourteenth Amendments, and an injunction preventing the City and County of San Francisco, its Board of Supervisors, and certain local officials from continuing to delete references to partisan endorsements from pamphlets sent to voters by the city and county officials.

The Court of Appeals ruled for the plaintiffs on the merits. 911 F.2d 280 (9th Cir.1990) (*en banc*). In vacating that ruling, the Supreme Court cited several factors: (1) it was unclear that plaintiffs had standing to litigate for the political committees of which they were members; (2) plaintiffs "have failed to demonstrate a live dispute involving the actual or threatened application of" the provision, as the claims did not relate to any pending election, and there was no allegation as to what specific candidates, for what offices, they wished to endorse in the future; (3) it was doubtful that, apart from the deletions in officially distributed pamphlets, any specific civil or criminal enforcement action would occur in the future; the Republican plaintiffs had made endorsements for such offices yet the record did not reflect that any adverse consequences followed, and although the Democratic plaintiffs had refrained from endorsements due to fear of enforcement they did not specify any specific criminal provision that might be applied, and the defendants had advised the Court that the California constitutional provision could be enforced only by injunction; (4) deferring adjudication as to deletions of reference to endorsements would impose no substantial hardship on plaintiffs, who "[i]n all probability * * * can learn which candidates have been endorsed by particular parties or committee members through other means"; and (5) the State courts might interpret the provision so as to narrow the issue, for example, by holding that it did not apply to individual members of county committees.

In dissent, Justice White argued that the redaction issue was ripe for review. Justices Marshall, joined in dissent by Justice Blackmun, argued that all the issues were justiciable, stating that the record "clearly demonstrates the likelihood of both future disobedience of [the provision] and future enforcement of that provision by way of petitioners' redaction policy". They urged that the identity of future candidates, the nature of the proposed endorsements, and the precise language that might be deleted from future pamphlets were irrelevant to the constitutional issues.

c. In Government Suppliers Consolidating Services, Inc. v. Bayh, 975 F.2d 1267 (7th Cir.1992), the court entertained a suit for a pre-enforcement declaration that an Indiana statute restricting the vehicles used for transport of municipal solid waste, and placing certain administrative burdens, such as surety bond requirements and disposal fees, on haulers of waste, violated the Commerce Clause. As the brokers who were the plaintiffs arranged for such transport by others, "their business would suffer severe adverse effects" from enforcement of the restrictions on the kinds of trucks that could be used, and from other challenged portions of the statute. The Seventh Circuit viewed the case as one in which present harm would flow from the threatened enforcement of the statute's prohibitions, as advance planning necessary for the conduct of plaintiffs' business was impaired by the fear of increased future costs. 975 F.2d at 1274–1275. It held that the surety bond and disposal fee provisions could be challenged, though Indiana had not yet promulgated enabling rules which had to precede their enforcement, for "only procedures and amounts are uncertain." *id.*

Was the prospective injury actually more certain in this case than in *Boyd* and *Renne*? Do the cases, taken together, suggest that prospective economic injury is a better candidate for declaratory relief than less tangible injury to constitutional rights?

STEFFEL v. THOMPSON

United States Supreme Court, 1974.
415 U.S. 452, 94 S.Ct. 1209, 39 L.Ed.2d 505.

MR. JUSTICE BRENNAN delivered the opinion of the Court.

When a state criminal proceeding under a disputed state criminal statute is pending against a federal plaintiff at the time his federal complaint is filed, Younger v. Harris, 401 U.S. 37, 91 S.Ct. 746, 27 L.Ed.2d 669 (1971), and Samuels v. Mackell, 401 U.S. 66, 91 S.Ct. 764, 27 L.Ed.2d 688 (1971), held, respectively, that, unless bad-faith enforcement or other special circumstances are demonstrated, principles of equity, comity, and federalism preclude issuance of a federal injunction restraining enforcement of the criminal statute and, in all but unusual circumstances, a declaratory judgment upon the constitutionality of the statute. This case presents the important question reserved in *Samuels v. Mackell, id.*, at 73–74, 91 S.Ct., at 768–769, whether declaratory relief is precluded when a state prosecution has been threatened, but is not pending, and a showing of bad-faith enforcement or other special circumstances has not been made.

Petitioner, and others, filed a complaint in the District Court for the Northern District of Georgia, invoking the Civil Rights Act of 1871, 42 U.S.C.A. § 1983, and its jurisdictional implementation, 28 U.S.C.A. § 1343. The complaint requested a declaratory judgment pursuant to 28 U.S.C.A. §§ 2201–2202, that Ga.Code Ann. § 26–1503 (1972) [1] was being applied in violation of petitioner's First and Fourteenth Amendment rights, and an injunction restraining respondents—the Solicitor of the Civil and Criminal Court of DeKalb County, the chief of the DeKalb County Police, the owner of the North DeKalb Shopping Center, and the manager of that shopping center—from enforcing the statute so as to interfere with petitioner's constitutionally protected activities.

The parties stipulated to the relevant facts: On October 8, 1970, while petitioner and other individuals were distributing handbills protesting American involvement in Vietnam on an exterior sidewalk of the North DeKalb Shopping Center, shopping center employees asked them to stop handbilling and leave. They declined to do so, and police officers were

1. This statute provides:

"(a) A person commits criminal trespass when he intentionally damages any property of another without his consent and the damage thereto is $100 or less, or knowingly and maliciously interferes with the possession or use of the property of another person without his consent.

"(b) A person commits criminal trespass when he knowingly and without authority:

* * *

"Remains upon the land or premises of another person * * * after receiving notice from the owner or rightful occupant to depart.

"(c) A person convicted of criminal trespass shall be punished as for a misdemeanor."

summoned. The officers told them that they would be arrested if they did not stop handbilling. The group then left to avoid arrest. Two days later petitioner and a companion returned to the shopping center and again began handbilling. The manager of the center called the police, and petitioner and his companion were once again told that failure to stop their handbilling would result in their arrests. Petitioner left to avoid arrest. His companion stayed, however, continued handbilling, and was arrested and subsequently arraigned on a charge of criminal trespass in violation of § 26–1503. Petitioner alleged in his complaint that, although he desired to return to the shopping center to distribute handbills, he had not done so because of his concern that he, too, would be arrested for violation of § 26–1503; the parties stipulated that, if petitioner returned and refused upon request to stop handbilling, a warrant would be sworn out and he might be arrested and charged with a violation of the Georgia statute.

After hearing, the District Court denied all relief and dismissed the action * * *.

We granted certiorari, 410 U.S. 953, 93 S.Ct. 1424, 35 L.Ed.2d 686 (1973), and now reverse.

* * * At the threshold we must consider whether petitioner presents an "actual controversy," a requirement imposed by Art. III of the Constitution and the express terms of the Federal Declaratory Judgment Act, 28 U.S.C.A. § 2201.

* * * [P]etitioner has alleged threats of prosecution that cannot be characterized as "imaginary or speculative," [Younger v. Harris, 401 U.S.] at 42, 91 S.Ct., at 749. He has been twice warned to stop handbilling that he claims is constitutionally protected and has been told by the police that if he again handbills at the shopping center and disobeys a warning to stop he will likely be prosecuted. The prosecution of petitioner's handbilling companion is ample demonstration that petitioner's concern with arrest has not been "chimerical." In these circumstances, it is not necessary that petitioner first expose himself to actual arrest or prosecution to be entitled to challenge a statute that he claims deters the exercise of his constitutional rights. * * *

Nonetheless, there remains a question as to the *continuing* existence of a live and acute controversy that must be resolved on the remand we order today. In Golden v. Zwickler, 394 U.S. 103, 89 S.Ct. 956, 22 L.Ed.2d 113 (1969), the appellee sought a declaratory judgment that a state criminal statute prohibiting the distribution of anonymous election-campaign literature was unconstitutional. The appellee's complaint had expressed a desire to distribute handbills during the forthcoming reelection campaign of a Congressman, but it was later learned that the Congressman had retired from the House of Representatives to become a New York Supreme Court Justice. In that circumstance, we found no extant controversy, since the record revealed that appellee's sole target of distribution had been the Congressman and there was no immediate prospect of the Congressman's again becoming a candidate for public office. Here, petitioner's complaint indicates that his handbilling activities were directed "against the war in Vietnam and the United States' foreign policy in Southeast Asia." Since we cannot ignore the recent developments reducing the Nation's involvement in that part of the world, it will be for the District Court on remand to determine if subsequent events have so altered petitioner's desire to engage in handbilling at the shopping center that it can no longer be said that this case presents "a substantial controversy, between parties having adverse legal interests, of sufficient immediacy and reality to warrant the issuance of a declaratory judgment." Maryland Casualty Co. v. Pacific Coal & Oil Co., 312 U.S. 270, 273, 61 S.Ct. 510, 512, 85 L.Ed. 826 (1941) *. * * *

We now turn to the question of whether the District Court and the Court of Appeals correctly found petitioner's request for declaratory relief inappropriate.

* * *

* * * When no state criminal proceeding is pending at the time the federal complaint is filed, federal intervention does not result in duplicative legal proceedings or disruption of the state criminal justice system; nor can federal intervention, in that circumstance, be interpreted as reflecting negatively upon the state court's ability to enforce constitutional principles. In addition, while a pending state prosecution provides the federal plaintiff with a concrete opportunity to vindicate his constitutional rights, a refusal on the part of the federal courts to intervene when no state proceeding is pending may place the hapless plaintiff between the Scylla of intentionally flouting state law and the Charybdis of forgoing what he believes to be constitutionally protected activity in order to avoid becoming enmeshed in a criminal proceeding. *Cf.* Dombrowski v. Pfister, 380 U.S. 479, 490, 85 S.Ct. 1116, 1123, 14 L.Ed.2d 22 (1965).

When no state proceeding is pending and thus considerations of equity, comity, and federalism have little vitality, the propriety of granting federal declaratory relief may properly be considered independently of a request for injunctive relief. Here, the Court of Appeals held that, because injunctive relief would not be appropriate since petitioner failed to demonstrate irreparable injury—a traditional prerequisite to injunctive relief, *e.g., Dombrowski v. Pfister, supra*—it followed that declaratory relief was also inappropriate. Even if the Court of Appeals correctly viewed injunctive relief as inappropriate—a question we need not reach today since petitioner has abandoned his request for that remedy, * * * the court erred in treating the requests for injunctive and declaratory relief as a single issue. "[W]hen no state prosecution is pending and the only question is whether declaratory relief is appropriate[,] * * * the congressional scheme that makes the federal courts the primary guardians of constitutional rights,

* For other cases discussing the issue of mootness in the context of an action for declaratory relief, see Familias Unidas v. Briscoe, 544 F.2d 182 (5th Cir.1976) (judge withdrew request for information pursuant to allegedly unconstitutional statute; declaratory judgment action not moot); Flynt v. Weinberger, 762 F.2d 134 (D.C.Cir.1985) (ban on press coverage of the initial stages of the United States' military intervention in Grenada lifted; action for declaratory judgment moot); State ex rel. Watts v. Combined Community Serv. Bd., 122 Wis.2d 65, 362 N.W.2d 104 (1985) (plaintiffs no longer detained in mental health center pursuant to allegedly unconstitutional statute; declaratory judgment action not moot).

and the express congressional authorization of declaratory relief, afforded because it is a less harsh and abrasive remedy than the injunction, become the factors of primary significance." Perez v. Ledesma, 401 U.S. 82, 104, 91 S.Ct. 674, 686, 27 L.Ed.2d 701 (1971) (separate opinion of Brennan, J.).

The subject matter jurisdiction of the lower federal courts was greatly expanded in the wake of the Civil War. A pervasive sense of nationalism led to enactment of the Civil Rights Act of 1871, 17 Stat. 13, empowering the lower federal courts to determine the constitutionality of actions, taken by persons under color of state law, allegedly depriving other individuals of rights guaranteed by the Constitution and federal law, *see* 42 U.S.C.A. § 1983, 28 U.S.C.A. § 1343(3). Four years later, in the Judiciary Act of March 3, 1875, 18 Stat. 470, Congress conferred upon the lower federal courts, for but the second time in their nearly century-old history, general federal-question jurisdiction subject only to a jurisdictional-amount requirement, *see* 28 U.S.C.A. § 1331. * * * These two statutes, together with the Court's decision in Ex parte Young, 209 U.S. 123, 28 S.Ct. 441, 52 L.Ed. 714 (1908)—holding that state officials who threaten to enforce an unconstitutional state statute may be enjoined by a federal court of equity and that a federal court may, in appropriate circumstances, enjoin future state criminal prosecutions under the unconstitutional Act—have "established the modern framework for federal protection of constitutional rights from state interference." Perez v. Ledesma, *supra,* 401 U.S., at 107, 91 S.Ct., at 688 (separate opinion of Brennan, J.).

A "storm of controversy" raged in the wake of *Ex parte Young,* focusing principally on the power of a single federal judge to grant *ex parte* interlocutory injunctions against the enforcement of state statutes * * *. This uproar was only partially quelled by Congress' passage of legislation, 36 Stat. 557, requiring the convening of a three-judge district court * * *. Furthermore, plaintiffs were dissatisfied with this method of testing the constitutionality of state statutes, since it placed upon them the burden of demonstrating the traditional prerequisites to equitable relief—most importantly, irreparable injury. * * *

To dispel these difficulties, Congress in 1934 enacted the Declaratory Judgment Act, 28 U.S.C.A. §§ 2201–2202. That Congress plainly intended declaratory relief to act as an alternative to the strong medicine of the injunction and to be utilized to test the constitutionality of state criminal statutes in cases where injunctive relief would be unavailable is amply evidenced by the legislative history of the Act, traced in full detail in Perez v. Ledesma, *supra,* 401 U.S., at 111–115, 91 S.Ct., at 690–692 (separate opinion of Brennan, J.). The highlights of that history, particularly pertinent to our inquiry today, emphasize that: * * *

> "The express purpose of the Federal Declaratory Judgment Act was to provide a milder alternative to the injunction remedy. * * *
>
> "Much of the hostility to federal injunctions referred to in the Senate report was hostility to their use against state officials seeking to enforce state regulatory statutes carrying criminal sanctions; this was the strong feeling that produced the Three–Judge Court Act in 1910, the Johnson Act of 1934, 28 U.S.C.A. § 1342, and the Tax Injunction

Act of 1937, 28 U.S.C.A. § 1341. The Federal Declaratory Judgment Act was intended to provide an alternative to injunctions against state officials, except where there was a federal policy against federal adjudication of the class of litigation altogether. * * *"

It was this history that formed the backdrop to our decision in Zwickler v. Koota, 389 U.S. 241, 88 S.Ct. 391, 19 L.Ed.2d 444 (1967), where a state criminal statute was attacked on grounds of unconstitutional overbreadth and no state prosecution was pending against the federal plaintiff. There, we found error in a three-judge district court's considering, as a single question, the propriety of granting injunctive and declaratory relief. * * *

* * *

The "different considerations" entering into a decision whether to grant declaratory relief have their origins in the preceding historical summary. First, as Congress recognized in 1934, a declaratory judgment will have a less intrusive effect on the administration of state criminal laws. As was observed in Perez v. Ledesma, 401 U.S., at 124–126, 91 S.Ct., at 696–697 (separate opinion of Brennan, J.):

> "Of course, a favorable declaratory judgment may nevertheless be valuable to the plaintiff though it cannot make even an unconstitutional statute disappear. A state statute may be declared unconstitutional *in toto*—that is, incapable of having constitutional applications; or it may be declared unconstitutionally vague or overbroad—that is, incapable of being constitutionally applied to the full extent of its purport. In either case, a federal declaration of unconstitutionality reflects the opinion of the federal court that the statute cannot be fully enforced. If a declaration of total unconstitutionality is affirmed by this Court, it follows that this Court stands ready to reverse any conviction under the statute. If a declaration of partial unconstitutionality is affirmed by this Court, the implication is that this Court will overturn particular applications of the statute, but that if the statute is narrowly construed by the state courts it will not be incapable of constitutional applications. Accordingly, the declaration does not necessarily bar prosecutions under the statute, as a broad injunction would. Thus, where the highest court of a State has had an opportunity to give a statute regulating expression a narrowing or clarifying construction but has failed to do so, and later a federal court declares the statute unconstitutionally vague or overbroad, it may well be open to a state prosecutor, after the federal court decision, to bring a prosecution under the statute if he reasonably believes that the defendant's conduct is not constitutionally protected and that the state courts may give the statute a construction so as to yield a constitutionally valid conviction. Even where a declaration of unconstitutionality is not reviewed by this Court, the declaration may still be able to cut down the deterrent effect of an unconstitutional state statute. The persuasive force of the court's opinion and judgment may lead state prosecutors, courts, and legislators to reconsider their respective responsibilities toward the statute. Enforcement policies or judicial construction

may be changed, or the legislature may repeal the statute and start anew. Finally, the federal court judgment may have some *res judicata* effect, though this point is not free from difficulty and the governing rules remain to be developed with a view to the proper workings of a federal system. What is clear, however, is that even though a declaratory judgment has 'the force and effect of a final judgment,' 28 U.S.C.A. § 2201, it is a much milder form of relief than an injunction. Though it may be persuasive, it is not ultimately coercive; noncompliance with it may be inappropriate, but is not contempt."

Second, engrafting upon the Declaratory Judgment Act a requirement that all of the traditional equitable prerequisites to the issuance of an injunction be satisfied before the issuance of a declaratory judgment is considered would defy Congress' intent to make declaratory relief available in cases where an injunction would be inappropriate. * * *

The only occasions where this Court has disregarded these "different considerations" and found that a preclusion of injunctive relief inevitably led to a denial of declaratory relief have been cases in which principles of federalism militated altogether against federal intervention in a class of adjudications. *See* Great Lakes Dredge & Dock Co. v. Huffman, 319 U.S. 293, 63 S.Ct. 1070, 87 L.Ed. 1407 (1943) (federal policy against interfering with the enforcement of state tax laws). In the instant case, principles of federalism not only do not preclude federal intervention, they compel it. Requiring the federal courts totally to step aside when no state criminal prosecution is pending against the federal plaintiff would turn federalism on its head. * * *

Respondents, however, relying principally upon our decision in Cameron v. Johnson, 390 U.S. 611, 88 S.Ct. 1335, 20 L.Ed.2d 182 (1968), argue that, although it may be appropriate to issue a declaratory judgment when no state criminal proceeding is pending and the attack is upon the *facial validity* of a state criminal statute, such a step would be improper where, as here, the attack is merely upon the constitutionality of the statute as applied, since the State's interest in unencumbered enforcement of its laws outweighs the minimal federal interest in protecting the constitutional rights of only a single individual. We reject the argument.

* * *

Indeed, the State's concern with potential interference in the administration of its criminal laws is of lesser dimension when an attack is made upon the constitutionality of a state statute as applied. A declaratory judgment of a lower federal court that a state statute is invalid *in toto*—and therefore incapable of any valid application—or is overbroad or vague—and therefore no person can properly be convicted under the statute until it is given a narrowing or clarifying construction—will likely have a more significant potential for disruption of state enforcement policies than a declaration specifying a limited number of impermissible applications of the statute. * * *

We therefore hold that, regardless of whether injunctive relief may be appropriate, federal declaratory relief is not precluded when no state prosecution is pending and a federal plaintiff demonstrates a genuine threat of enforcement of a disputed state criminal statute, whether an attack is made on the constitutionality of the statute on its face or as applied. The judgment of the Court of Appeals is reversed, and the case is remanded for further proceedings consistent with this opinion.

* * *

MR. JUSTICE STEWART, with whom THE CHIEF JUSTICE joins, concurring.

While joining the opinion of the Court, I add a word by way of emphasis.

Our decision today must not be understood as authorizing the invocation of federal declaratory judgment jurisdiction by a person who thinks a state criminal law is unconstitutional, even if he genuinely feels "chilled" in his freedom of action by the law's existence, and even if he honestly entertains the subjective belief that he may now or in the future be prosecuted under it.

* * *

The petitioner in this case has succeeded in objectively showing that the threat of imminent arrest, corroborated by the actual arrest of his companion, has created an actual concrete controversy between himself and the agents of the State. He has, therefore, demonstrated "a genuine threat of enforcement of a disputed state criminal statute * * *." Cases where such a "genuine threat" can be demonstrated will, I think, be exceedingly rare.

Notes

1. As the *Steffel* case illustrates, the declaratory judgment action is often the best remedy for obtaining protection against threatened criminal prosecutions.* The remedy is clearly appropriate when the plaintiff is challenging the validity of a statute or administrative regulation. *E.g.,* Chas L. Harney, Inc. v. Contractors' State License Bd., 39 Cal.2d 561, 247 P.2d 913 (1952) (declaratory judgment approved to challenge validity of licensing regulation); Gaffey v. Babb, 50 Or.App. 617, 624 P.2d 616 (1981) (declaratory judgment was proper to challenge unconstitutionally vague ordinance that prohibited dealing in drug paraphernalia). If the plaintiff seeks to challenge the applicability of a statute or administrative regulation to a particular set of facts, the courts may be reluctant to grant declaratory relief when the facts are either in dispute or subject to varying interpretations. *Compare* Reed v. Littleton, 275 N.Y. 150, 9 N.E.2d 814 (1937) (disapproving declaratory relief when the plaintiff sought to establish that its method of purchase and sale of racing greyhounds and the sale of options thereon did not violate the state's gambling statutes) *with* New York Foreign Trade Zone Operators, Inc. v. State Liquor Authority, 285 N.Y. 272, 34 N.E.2d 316 (1941) (granting declaratory judgment to determine wheth-

* *See generally* D. Dobbs, Handbook on the Law of Remedies 114 (1973); Blanchard, Challenging Penal Statutes By Declaratory Judgment, 52 Yale L.J. 445 (1943); Laycock, Federal Interference with State Prosecutions: The Need for Prospective Relief, 1977 Sup.Ct. Rev. 193; Rendleman, Prospective Remedies in Constitutional Adjudication, 78 W.Va. L.Rev. 155 (1976); Wilkinson, Anticipatory Vindication of Federal Constitutional Rights, 41 Alb.L.Rev. 459 (1977); Developments in the Law—Declaratory Judgments—Penal Legislation, 62 Harv.L.Rev. 787, 870–72 (1949).

er the addition of pure water to foreign distilled spirits constituted "rectification").

2. When a criminal prosecution is pending, both state and federal courts have expressed an unwillingness to grant declaratory relief for purposes of testing the validity of the criminal statute. As stated in Norcisa v. Board of Selectmen of Provincetown, 368 Mass. 161, 330 N.E.2d 830 (1975):

> "The fundamental jurisprudential considerations underlying the general prohibition against enjoining a pending criminal prosecution apply with full force to support a prohibition against issuing declaratory decrees concerning a pending criminal prosecution. To conclude otherwise would encourage fragmentation and proliferation of litigation and disrupt the orderly administration of the criminal law.
>
> "The rule we adopt today in regard to the issuance of declaratory judgments when criminal litigation is pending is merely a logical extension of our rules which generally proscribe the issuance of such a judgment when an appropriate administrative proceeding is in progress, or when a civil proceeding in which the same issue is or can be raised is already pending between the parties. In applying these principles in the criminal prosecution context, we follow the Federal rule, Samuels v. Mackell, 401 U.S. 66, 69–73, 91 S.Ct. 764, 27 L.Ed.2d 688 (1971); Kugler v. Helfant, 421 U.S. 117, 95 S.Ct. 1524, 44 L.Ed.2d 15 and the rule adopted in most States which have considered the issue."

3. The *Younger* doctrine prevents declaratory relief against some civil, as well as criminal, proceedings in a state court. The Supreme Court initially held within that doctrine civil proceedings brought by a state to enforce laws "in aid of and closely related to criminal statutes * * *" Huffman v. Pursue, Ltd., 420 U.S. 592, 95 S.Ct. 1200, 43 L.Ed.2d 482 (1975). The class of civil cases subject to the *Younger* doctrine has been expanded by the Court's broadened view as to what state laws were related to state criminal laws, *see* Trainor v. Hernandez, 431 U.S. 434, 97 S.Ct. 1911, 52 L.Ed.2d 486 (1977) (suit by state agency to recover welfare benefits fraudulently obtained pursued in lieu of bringing criminal proceedings subject to *Younger* doctrine), and by the Court's inclusion of civil cases in which it deemed the state's interest to be of an importance comparable to its enforcement of criminal laws, *see* Juidice v. Vail, 430 U.S. 327, 97 S.Ct. 1211, 51 L.Ed.2d 376 (1977) (civil contempt proceeding subject to *Younger,* in view of states' interest in enforceability of court orders).

Doubts in the lower courts as to whether *Younger* ever applied in a civil action solely between private parties, *see* Diaz v. Stathis, 576 F.2d 9 (1st Cir.1978), were settled by Pennzoil Co. v. Texaco, Inc., 481 U.S. 1, 107 S.Ct. 1519, 95 L.Ed.2d 1 (1987), which held that the federal courts should not have entertained an injunctive suit challenging the constitutionality of a Texas appeal bond statute in an on-going case between private litigants in the Texas courts. The Supreme Court reasoned that the state's interest in the enforceability of judgments of its courts was comparable to its interest in the enforceability of orders by its courts held in Juidice, *supra,* to justify invocation of *Younger.* The majority opinion, however, disclaimed any rule that "*Younger* abstention is always appropriate whenever a civil proceeding is pending in a state court." 481 U.S. at 14 n. 12, 107 S.Ct. at 1527 n. 12. In concurring in the judgment, Justice Brennan stated that the merits should have been decided, and the validity of the statute upheld on the merits. He adhered to his view "that Younger is, in general, inapplicable to civil proceedings, especially when the plaintiff brings a § 1983 action alleging violation of federal constitutional rights." He argued that "The State's interest in this case is negligible." 481 U.S. at 19, 107 S.Ct. at 1530.

In New Orleans Public Service, Inc. v. Council of the City of New Orleans, 491 U.S. 350, 109 S.Ct. 2506, 105 L.Ed.2d 298 (1989), the Court reaffirmed that not all civil proceedings are subject to the Younger doctrine. It held that a state rate-making proceeding was not, even though its product was a ruling that was reviewable in the state courts, and that the federal courts therefore should have entertained a suit seeking, *inter alia,* a declaration that the rate-makers' action was preempted by federal law. 491 U.S. at 367–372, 109 S.Ct. at 2517–2520.

Under the majority's ruling in *Pennzoil,* could the federal constitutional question raised ever have been litigated as a practical matter in a federal court, by means of a declaratory judgment action? Should the lack of a realistic prospect that some plaintiff could obtain declaratory or other relief from a federal court, and hence that the federal constitutional question could in some manner be decided by a lower federal court, be a relevant factor in determining the applicability of the *Younger* doctrine? *See* Ohio Civil Rights Commission v. Dayton Christian Schools, Inc., 477 U.S. 619, 106 S.Ct. 2718, 91 L.Ed.2d 512 (1986) (federal courts should have abstained from considering First Amendment challenge to administrative employment discrimination proceedings; availability of state court forum to challenge any violation of First Amendment rights counsels abstention).

4. The Supreme Court has not yet ruled on the res judicata or collateral estoppel effect of a federal declaratory judgment in subsequent state proceedings.* The issue was mentioned in two concurring opinions in *Steffel:*

MR. JUSTICE REHNQUIST, with whom THE CHIEF JUSTICE joins, concurring.

* * *

> "A declaratory judgment is simply a statement of rights, not a binding order supplemented by continuing sanctions. State authorities may choose to be guided by the judgment of a lower federal court, but they are not compelled to follow the decision by threat of contempt or other penalties. If the federal plaintiff pursues the conduct for which he was previously threatened with arrest and is in fact arrested, he may not return the controversy to federal court, although he may, of course, raise the federal declaratory judgment in the state court for whatever value it may prove to have.[3] In any event, the defendant at that point is able to present his case

* *See* Shapiro, State Courts and Federal Declaratory Judgments, 74 Nw.U.L.Rev. 759 (1979); Note, Federal Declaratory Relief from Unconstitutional State Statutes: The Implications of *Steffel v. Thompson,* 9 Harv. C.R.—C.L.L.Rev. 520 (1974); Note, The Res Judicata Effect of Declaratory Relief in the Federal Courts, 46 S.Calif.L.Rev. 803 (1973); Comment, the Binding Effect of Federal Declaratory Judgments on State Courts, 51 Tex. L.Rev. 743 (1973).

3. The Court's opinion notes that the possible res judicata effect of a federal declaratory judgment in a subsequent state court prosecution is a question " 'not free from difficulty.' " *Ante,* at [468]. I express no opinion on that issue here. However, I do note that the federal decision would not be accorded the *stare decisis* effect in state court that it would have in a subsequent proceeding within the same federal jurisdiction. Although the state court would not be compelled to follow the federal holding, the opinion might,

for full consideration by a state court charged, as are the federal courts, to preserve the defendant's constitutional rights. Federal interference with this process would involve precisely the same concerns discussed in *Younger* and recited in the Court's opinion in this case."

* * *

MR. JUSTICE WHITE, concurring.

"I offer the following few words in light of MR. JUSTICE REHNQUIST'S concurrence in which he discusses the impact on a pending federal action of a later filed criminal prosecution against the federal plaintiff, whether a federal court may enjoin a state criminal prosecution under a statute the federal court has earlier declared unconstitutional at the suit of the defendant now being prosecuted, and the question whether that declaratory judgment is res judicata in such a later filed state criminal action.

"It should be noted, first, that his views on these issues are neither expressly nor impliedly embraced by the Court's opinion filed today. Second, my own tentative views on these questions are somewhat contrary to my Brother's.

"At this writing at least, I would anticipate that a final declaratory judgment entered by a federal court holding particular conduct of the federal plaintiff to be immune on federal constitutional grounds from prosecution under state law should be accorded res judicata effect in any later prosecution of that very conduct. There would also, I think, be additional circumstances in which the federal judgment should be considered as more than a mere precedent bearing on the issue before the state court.

"Neither can I at this stage agree that the federal court, having rendered a declaratory judgment in favor of the plaintiff, could not enjoin a later state prosecution for conduct that the federal court has declared immune. The Declaratory Judgment Act itself provides that a 'declaration shall have the force and effect of a final judgment or decree,' 28 U.S.C.A. § 2201; eminent authority anticipated that declaratory judgments would be res judicata. E. Borchard, Declaratory Judgments 10–11 (2d ed. 1941); and there is every reason for not reducing declaratory judgments to mere advisory opinions. * * * The statute provides for '[f]urther necessary or proper relief * * * against any adverse party whose rights have been determined by such judgment,' 28 U.S.C.A. § 2202, and it would not seem improper to enjoin local prosecutors who refuse to observe adverse federal judgments."

Also *cf.* Green v. Mansour, 474 U.S. 64, 106 S.Ct. 423, 88 L.Ed.2d 371 (1985) (where the Eleventh Amendment barred a damage claim to recover benefits under the Aid to Families with Dependent Children program, which a state had withheld in violation of federal law, and a claim for injunctive relief was mooted by changes in the federal law, a federal court could not proceed to render a declaratory judgment). Justice Rehnquist reasoned that the only remaining purpose of such a declaration would be to serve as *res judicata* on the merits of a later damage claim in state tribunals; that if such a declaratory judgment were not asserted as *res judicata* it would serve no purpose, but if it

of course, be viewed as highly persuasive.
[Footnote by Mr. Justice Rehnquist.]

were, it would constitute an impermissible end run around the Eleventh Amendment. *Id.,* 474 U.S. at 73 and n. 2, 106 S.Ct. at 428 and n. 2.

Does this holding tacitly assume, in accordance with Justice White's concurrence in *Steffel,* that if the federal court were to proceed to issue a declaratory judgment in the circumstances of *Green,* it would have preclusive effect?

The Supreme Court has stated that in the converse situation a federal court would be bound to honor, as *res judicata,* a State Court's declaratory judgment as to whether or not a controversy was arbitrable. Moses H. Cone Memorial Hosp. v. Mercury Construction Corp., 460 U.S. 1, 10–11, 103 S.Ct. 927, 933–35, 74 L.Ed.2d 765 (1983).

5. The Restatement (Second) of Judgments § 76 (1980) provides:

> "A judgment in an action brought to declare rights or other legal relations of the parties is conclusive in a subsequent action between them as to the matters declared, and, in accordance with the rules of issue preclusion, as to any issues actually litigated by them and determined in the action."

The comments to section 76 explain that a declaratory judgment is preclusive as to matters actually declared, but does not bar claims that were not adjudicated, even though they could have been asserted in the complaint. *Id.* comments b, c, e.

6. Because the declaratory judgment remedy is statutory, it is sometimes characterized as "legal" and sometimes as "equitable," *see* C. Wright, Law of Federal Courts § 100 (4th ed. 1983) or as "neither legal nor equitable * * *," Gulfstream Aerospace Corp. v. Mayacamas Corp., 485 U.S. 271, 284, 108 S.Ct. 1133, 1141, 99 L.Ed.2d 296 (1988).

Although the issue arises most often in determining whether there is a right to jury trial (*see* Chapter 9 *infra*), it is also a necessary consideration when applying the statute of limitations and laches defenses to declaratory judgment actions:

> "*Limitations.* In dealing with the application of statutes of limitations to the declaratory judgment, the courts have generally taken one of two approaches: either they have recognized the purpose of noncoercive relief and adapted existing rules accordingly, or they have applied those rules mechanically to the new remedy. Thus, the courts have differed both as to the appropriate period of limitations to be applied and as to the moment from which the statute begins to run. Perhaps the sole point of agreement is that if coercive relief for the violation of a right has been barred, a claimant may not circumvent the statute by obtaining a declaratory judgment. The cases are less settled where the right to coercive relief has not been extinguished or has not even accrued. Some courts have argued that the statute always runs from the time a justiciable controversy arises. Such a view might have the unfortunate result of eliminating the preventive remedy when it may be most usefully employed, since declaratory relief may be barred before a coercive cause of action arises. If the period should happen to expire after the accrual but before the barring of the cause of action for a coercive remedy, it would mean that the milder remedy had been arbitrarily disallowed. Equally undesirable results might be reached in those jurisdictions which apply to all declaratory actions a

special period of limitations rather than the different periods fixed for the corresponding coercive actions. The better rule, toward which the cases seem to be moving, is that the right to declaratory relief continues until the right to coercive relief, as between the parties, has itself been extinguished.

* * *

"The possibility of declaratory relief cannot be said to subject the party to undue uncertainty so long as coercive relief is or will be available; the evidence of a right cannot be deemed stale so long as that right may yet be transgressed in such a way as to entitle either party to coercive relief. And indeed if the uncertainty is burdensome, the aggrieved party may himself seek a declaration and eliminate his doubt. Moreover, if the evidence that there was a dispute should grow stale because of the termination of the dispute, the court may properly refuse to hear the dead controversy on the ground that it is 'moot' and no longer 'justiciable.'

"*Laches.* The courts have also differed on the applicability of laches. Some have indicated that the doctrine of laches may be applicable in any declaratory action on the ground that the declaratory judgment has its historical roots in equity. The better rule would seem to be that, in the absence of a prayer for coercive relief, the court must look to the precise issues being litigated to determine whether the action sounds in equity so that the defense of laches may be interposed * * *. Where coercive equitable relief would not itself be barred by laches, defendant cannot be considered prejudiced by being subjected to the milder remedy of a declaration. But the availability of declaratory relief may accelerate the time at which laches could be successfully asserted in the coercive equitable action. Since plaintiff may be in a position to act sooner than otherwise, his delay may be considered negligent at an earlier stage. However, the court must also consider whether plaintiff should have known that the controversy was justiciable, and whether he might reasonably have expected defendant himself to seek declaratory relief before changing position. Plaintiff's failure to act should be considered negligent only if he was involved in a dispute which would have prompted a reasonable man to bring suit or initiate other steps to clarify his position. Although this rule is in accord with general equity principles, case law to date has shown little overt recognition that the availability of declaratory relief may accelerate laches."

Developments in the Law: Declaratory Judgments—1941–49, 62 Harv.L.Rev. 787, 830–33 (1949).*

ASHCROFT v. MATTIS

United States Supreme Court, 1977.
431 U.S. 171, 97 S.Ct. 1739, 52 L.Ed.2d 219.

PER CURIAM.

Appellee's 18–year–old son was shot and killed by police while attempting to escape arrest. Appellee filed suit under 42 U.S.C.A. § 1983 against the police officers in the United States District Court for the Eastern District of Missouri. He sought to recover damages, and also to obtain a declaratory judgment that the Missouri statutes authorizing the police action were unconstitutional.[1] The District Court held that a defense of good faith had been established, and denied both forms of relief. No appeal was taken from the denial of damages, but appellee did seek review of the denial of declaratory relief. The Eighth Circuit held that declaratory relief was available and remanded for consideration of the merits of the constitutional issue. Mattis v. Schnarr, 502 F.2d 588 (1974).

On remand, appellee filed an amended complaint, in which he made no claim for damages. The Missouri Attorney General was allowed to intervene in defense of the statutes, and the case was then submitted on stipulated facts. The District Court upheld the statutes, Mattis v. Schnarr, 404 F.Supp. 643 (1975), but was reversed by a divided Court of Appeals, sitting en banc, 547 F.2d 1007 (1976). The Attorney General brought an appeal under 28 U.S.C.A. § 1254(2) from the holding that the state statutes were unconstitutional.

Although we are urged to consider the merits of the Court of Appeals' holding, we are unable to do so, because this suit does not now present a live "case or controversy." This suit was brought to determine the police officers' liability for the death of appellee's son. That issue has been decided, and there is no longer any possible basis for a damages claim. Nor is there any possible basis for a declaratory judgment. For a declaratory judgment to issue, there must be a dispute which "calls, not for an advisory opinion upon a hypothetical basis, but for an adjudication of present right upon established facts." Aetna Life Ins. Co. v. Haworth, 300 U.S. 227, 242 (1937). Here, the District Court was asked to answer the hypothetical question whether the defendants would have been liable apart from their defense of good faith. No "present right" of appellee was at stake. Indeed, appellee's primary claim of a present interest in the controversy is that he will obtain emotional satisfaction from a ruling that his son's death was wrongful.[2] * * * Emotional involvement in a lawsuit is not enough to meet the case-or-controversy requirement; were the rule otherwise, few cases could ever become moot.

The judgment of the Court of Appeals is vacated, and the case is remanded with instructions to direct the District Court to dismiss the second amended complaint.

Notes

1. The use of the declaratory judgment action in the torts context is described in Fraser, A Survey of Declaratory Judgment Actions in the United

1. These statutes permit police to use deadly force in apprehending a person who has committed a felony, following notice of the intent to arrest. Mo.Rev.Stat. §§ 559.-040 and 544.190 (1969) * * *.

2. The second amended complaint also alleges that appellee has another son who "*if* ever arrested or brought under an attempt at arrest on suspicion of a felony, *might* flee or give the appearance of fleeing, and would therefore be *in danger* of being killed by these defendants or other police officers * * *." * * * Such speculation is insufficient to establish the existence of a present, live controversy.

States, 39 Iowa L.Rev. 639, 649–50 (1954) *:

"Declaratory judgment suits have been granted infrequently in cases where there is a completed tort. The injured party may not seek declaratory relief, because the judgment would not settle the controversy, a second suit to determine damages being necessary. However, such a suit should be permitted if the plaintiff wishes to vindicate a right and is willing to waive damages. Prospective defendants have not fared much better. One court permitted a person to bring an action to determine nonliability for a tort, but another court dismissed a similar action on the ground that the injured plaintiff had a right to pick the place of trial. In spite of these limitations on declaratory judgment suits, it is believed that they could be used effectively to determine the question of liability in cases where there are many claimants and several possible tortfeasors. Where there is a continuing injury to or invasion of realty, thus involving future rights, declaratory relief may be granted. A court also may determine whether a person's proposed course of action would constitute a trespass or nuisance, before he acts."

2. The question of whether declaratory relief is appropriate when damages are available as an alternative remedy is discussed in Warren v. Kaiser Foundation Health Plan, Inc., 47 Cal.App.3d 678, 121 Cal.Rptr. 19 (1975). The plaintiff sought a declaration that the expenses of hospitalizing his severely burned wife in a non-Kaiser facility were covered under the emergency clause of his Kaiser health insurance coverage. Kaiser demurred to the complaint on the grounds that the claim was not covered by the Kaiser plan and that declaratory relief was an inappropriate remedy because the plaintiff could sue for breach of contract:

"Any doubt should be resolved in favor of granting declaratory relief. * * * While the court may refuse to entertain the action where 'the rights of the complaining party have crystallized into a cause of action for past wrongs, [and] all relationship between the parties has ceased to exist * * *' (Travelers v. Louden, 254 Cal.App.2d 926, 929, 62 Cal.Rptr. 654, 656), it may not exclude the action where the alternative remedy of suing upon the matured breach is not as 'speedy and adequate or as well suited to the plaintiff's needs as declaratory relief.' (Maguire v. Hibernia S. & L. Soc., 23 Cal.2d 719, 732, 146 P.2d 673, 680; 3 Witkin, Cal.Procedure (2d ed.), Pleading, § 724.) A lawsuit for breach of contract is neither as speedy and adequate nor as well suited as declaratory relief to the plaintiff's needs where, despite the breach, a relationship between the parties continues so that a declaration may guide their future conduct (Columbia Pictures Corp. v. DeToth, *supra,* 26 Cal.2d 753, 161 P.2d 217; Ermolieff v. R.K.O. Radio Pictures, 19 Cal.2d 543, 549, 122 P.2d 3), or where the use of declaratory relief will avoid a multiplicity of suits that may ensue if a different remedy is pursued (California Bank v. Diamond, 144 Cal.App.2d 387, 301 P.2d 60 * * *.)

"Here, although the complaint claims that Kaiser breached its contract, it also shows on its face that the relationship between appellant and Kaiser is a continuing one since appellant continued to be a member of the plan after the claimed breach. A declaration of the right of a member of the plan for reimbursement of medical expense incurred in an emergency so grave as to preclude access to Kaiser contract hospitals and physicians will guide the future conduct of the parties. If nothing else, a declaration in Kaiser's favor will be the warning that the plan may not be adequate to the needs of its members, including appellant. Here, also, the remedy of declaratory relief will avoid multiplicity of litigation. Appellant has incurred substantial obligations for the care of his late wife. If those obligations must be reimbursed by Kaiser, threatened lawsuits by those who provided the medical and hospital care will be avoided."

a. In Loyd v. City of Irwinton, 142 Ga.App. 626, 236 S.E.2d 889 (1977), the plaintiff-appellee and defendant-appellant owned adjacent parcels of land. The plaintiff-appellee petitioned for a declaratory judgment as to the proper location of the common boundary line. The appellate court affirmed the denial of declaratory relief:

"The pleadings and evidence indicate that the appellant had structures encroaching upon the contested strip of land and that the appellee was in the process of building a city hall complex on its tract. In its petition, the appellee alleged the existence of an 'actual controversy' and the need for relief from uncertainty and insecurity. However, there was no allegation of danger to the appellee. Nor was there any evidence that the appellee was in danger of repudiating any of its obligations or suffering a violation of its rights in the absence of a declaratory judgment.

" 'Although the realm wherein there is uncertainty in leases and real estate grants is one which lends itself to the jurisdiction of the court in its declaratory judgment powers, yet the basis for a declaratory judgment is not established by a simple showing of uncertainty or ambiguity in a grant involving real estate.' Moore v. Young, 101 Ga.App. 553, 554, 114 S.E.2d 446, 447 (1960).

"A declaratory judgment may not be granted in the absence of a justiciable controversy. 'The object of the declaratory judgment is to permit determination of a controversy before obligations are repudiated or rights are violated. As many times pointed out by this court, its purpose is to permit one who is walking in the dark to ascertain where he is and where he is going, to turn on the light before he steps rather than after he has stepped in a hole. 7 Ga.Bar Journal, p. 132; Venable v. Dallas, 212 Ga. 595, 94 S.E.2d 416.' Rowan v. Herring, 214 Ga. 370, 374, 105 S.E.2d 29, 32 (1958).

"State Hwy. Dept. v. Williams Lmbr. Co., 222 Ga. 23, 148 S.E.2d 426 (1966), which the appellee cites in support of its position, is distinguished from the case at bar. In *Williams,* the petitioner desired to build improvements on the contested property, thus showing a clear need to have 'the lights turned on' before it acted."

What result would have been reached if the same suit had been cast as one to quiet title, or for trespass, rather than one for a declaratory judgment?

b. In Stop 'N Go Markets of Texas, Inc. v. Executive Security Systems, Inc., 556 S.W.2d 836 (Tex.Civ.App.1977), Executive sought a declaration that Stop 'N Go was obligated to indemnify Executive for any liability incurred in a lawsuit then pending against both of them. The appellate court vacated the trial court's "advisory opinion":

"A justiciable controversy does not exist and an advisory opinion is being sought if a party requests a court to render a declaratory judgment premised upon the happening of a future, hypothetical event. The possibility that liability triggering indemnity will be incurred in a pending action is a future hypothetical event within the meaning of this rule. *See* Firemen's Ins. Co. of Newark, New Jersey v. Burch, 442 S.W.2d 331 (Tex.1968) * * *.

* * *

"The fact that the indemnity issue may eventually have to be litigated is immaterial. The proper vehicle for determining that matter is a cross-claim by Executive against Stop 'N Go in the Fields case under Tex. R.Civ.P. 97(e), or if Fields is successful against Executive in that suit, then by a separate suit by Executive against Stop 'N Go. Such an approach upholds the principle that the Declaratory Judgment Act was not intended to provide for the 'piecemeal' trial of lawsuits, and the rule that a declaratory judgment is not proper if there is pending, at the time it is filed, another action or proceeding between the same parties and in which may be adjudicated the issues involved in the declaratory action." *

* * *

c. In Proler Steel Corp. v. Luria Brothers & Co., 223 F.Supp. 87 (S.D.Tex. 1963), the plaintiff filed a suit for a declaratory judgment that the defendant had begun the construction of a plant in California with the intent to produce a product that would infringe the plaintiff's patent. The defendant moved to dismiss the complaint:

"Defendant first contends that this action is in reality a suit for patent infringement, and as such, is based solely on Title 35 U.S.C.A. § 281, which provides: 'A patentee shall have remedy by civil action for *infringement* of his patent.' (emphasis added) It is urged that since there is no allegation of infringement made in the complaint, the case should not be heard. * * *

"However, this particular suit clearly was instituted in order to prevent the defendant from pursuing a course of action allegedly designed to result in *future* infringement. The plaintiff freely admits that there has been no past infringement by this defendant. And on that basis this suit for declaratory judgment was instituted in accordance with Title 28 U.S.C.A. § 2201. * * *

* * *

"Putting aside, for the moment, considerations of the question of justiciable controversy, there would seem to be no good reason for denying declaratory relief to a patentee. The very fact that the declaratory judgment provision is remedial calls for a liberal interpretation of the section. A patentee should not be denied the use of this remedy simply because he has another remedy available after there has been actual infringement.

* * *

* *See generally* Kirkland & Berkeley, Declaratory Judgment Suits: Use in Insurance Coverage Litigation, 33 Fed'n Ins. Couns.Q. 243 (1983).

"The second ground on which defendant moves to dismiss the complaint is that it fails to allege the existence of an actual controversy. * * *

"It would best be noted at this point that both parties admit the absence of any cases presenting the exact same questions as those presently before this court. However there are cases in a slightly different posture which are of some significance in analyzing this particular argument. The primary use made of the declaratory judgment provision in patent suits has been in situations where the patentee has charged his adversary with patent infringement, but has failed to formally file suit. Prior to the enactment of Sec. 2201, the party so charged was helpless to determine his legal rights until the patentee brought suit. He was subject to harassment and the accrual of damages which otherwise might have been avoidable. With the enactment of the declaratory judgment provision, the alleged infringer was given an entry into court to obtain a judicial determination of the rights and relations of the parties. However, the courts required that the defendant patentee in these suits have made some charge of infringement.

"It has also been repeatedly held that *actual* manufacture, use or sale is not essential, and that it is sufficient if the party charged is *about to infringe* or take some action which is prejudicial to the interests of the patentee. The courts clearly feel that there is an immediate controversy in these cases even though actual infringement has not taken place. There should not be a different disposition of the question depending on which party initiates the suit for declaratory judgment. Such would be the result, however, if the court were to rule that no controversy existed in the instant case. This court is no more being asked for an advisory opinion than were the courts in the cases cited above. There is a sufficient justiciable controversy existing under the facts of the instant case." *

* *See generally* Comment, Patent Licensee Standing and the Declaratory Judgment Act, 83 Colum.L.Rev. 186 (1982).

Chapter 6

REMEDIES FOR SELECTED TORTIOUS WRONGS

SECTION 1. INTERFERENCE WITH INTERESTS IN PERSONAL PROPERTY

Introductory Note

Personal property can be interfered with in a variety of ways. It can be destroyed, taken or damaged. When it is destroyed or damaged, plaintiff can sue for substitutionary relief to compensate the loss. Many issues arise concerning how to measure the loss.

If the property has been taken but not destroyed, plaintiff has a number of options. Plaintiff can sue to be compensated for the loss, can sue for specific relief to get it back or can sue to recover defendant's gain from having taken the chattel. While damages to compensate loss are legal, specific relief to get the chattel back can be either legal or equitable. Specific relief involving chattels is called replevin. The fact that it can be legal as well as equitable is an exception to the general understanding that the only legal relief is money damages.

When the plaintiff sues to recover defendant's gain from having taken the chattel, the plaintiff is suing in restitution for unjust enrichment. Frequently in the case of wrongfully taken chattels, that gain will be the same amount as the value of what the plaintiff lost.

A. LEGAL SUBSTITUTIONARY RELIEF—COMPENSATORY DAMAGES

1. Destroyed or Converted Goods

BLACKMON v. MIXSON

Court of Appeals of Texas, Dallas, 1988.
755 S.W.2d 179.

WHITHAM, JUSTICE.

Appellants, James C. Blackmon and Mary E. Blackmon, brought this action to recover damages from the appellees, Raymond Mixson and William B. Mixson, asserting that Raymond, a juvenile, set fire to the Blackmons' trailer house and that, as Raymond's father, William was also liable under section 33.01 of the Texas Family Code. We find no merit in the Blackmons' challenge to jury findings or assertions of jury misconduct. Accordingly, we affirm.

In their first point of error, the Blackmons contend that the jury's findings to questions three and four were contrary to the great weight and preponderance of the evidence. The question in the Blackmons' first point of error requires this court to consider and weigh all of the evidence in the case and to set aside the verdict and remand the cause for a new trial, if it thus concludes that the verdict is so against the great weight and preponderance of the evidence as to be manifestly unjust—this, regardless of whether the record contains some "evidence of probative force" in support of the verdict. *In re King's Estate,* 150 Tex. 662, 664–65, 244 S.W.2d 660, 661 (1951). Questions three and four and the jury's answers are as follows:

> Find from a preponderance of the evidence the market value of the Blackmon's trailer house on March 21, 1983.
>
> Market value means the amount that would be paid in cash by a willing buyer who desires to buy, but is not required to buy, to a willing seller who desires to sell, but is under no necessity of selling.
>
> Answer in dollars and cents, if any.
>
> Answer: $0

* * *

> Find from a preponderance of the evidence the market value of the Blackmon's personal effects and/or personal property that was in the trailer house on March 21, 1983.
>
> Market value means the amount that would be paid in cash by a willing buyer who desires to buy, but is not required to buy, to a willing seller who desires to sell, but is under no necessity of selling.
>
> Answer in dollars and cents, if any.
>
> Answer: $0

Market value of the Blackmons' property is the issue. The Blackmons assert that the testimony on market value of the destroyed property establishes market value in accordance with the instructions provided in questions three and four. The following constitutes *all* of the evidence that the Blackmons identify as establishing that the findings on market value are contrary to the great weight and preponderance of the evidence. The only evidence on damages is the testimony of owner James Blackmon. We recognize that the owner of the property can testify to its market value, even if he could not qualify to testify about the value of like property belonging to someone else. *Porras v. Craig,* 675 S.W.2d 503, 504 (Tex. 1984). First we note Blackmon's testimony as to the trailer on direct examination.

[BLACKMONS' ATTORNEY]: All right. Now, have you, Mr. Blackmon, made a statement as to the damages or the market value of that trailer house that burned down out there?

[BLACKMON]: Yes, sir.

[BLACKMONS' ATTORNEY]: Did you check the market out for the purpose of replacing it?

[BLACKMON]: Yes, sir.

[BLACKMONS' ATTORNEY]: And, can you tell the jury what it cost? Did you replace it with something you thought was reasonably comparable?

[BLACKMON]: I thought it was comparable, yes, sir.

[BLACKMONS' ATTORNEY]: What did that replacement cost?

[MIXSONS' ATTORNEY]: Objection. Replacement cost has no bearing on the market value of this particular trailer at the time of the incident.

THE COURT: Sustained.

[BLACKMONS' ATTORNEY]: Do you feel like you are aware, Mr. Mixson, excuse me, Mr. Blackmon, of the market value of the trailer that burned at the time, based on your survey of trailers at about that time?

[BLACKMON]: *Oh I would think it was probably compared with what we got the replacement for.*

[BLACKMONS' ATTORNEY]: All right. And what was that value then, or the market value of that one?

[BLACKMON]: We paid around sixteen thousand for the replacement trailer.

[BLACKMONS' ATTORNEY]: And that was a similar trailer to the one that burned?

[BLACKMON]: Similar, yes.

(emphasis added). Next, we note Blackmon's testimony as to the personal property on direct examination.

[BLACKMONS' ATTORNEY]: And what kind of contents, what contents were burned? Do you have a list of those contents? You don't have the list up there with you now, do you?

[BLACKMON]: No, sir.

[BLACKMONS' ATTORNEY]: Did you make a list of stuff that was in there?

[BLACKMON]: Yes, sir.

[BLACKMONS' ATTORNEY]: Did you make your estimates as to the value to the best of your knowledge at that time of the contents of that trailer house?

[BLACKMON]: Yes, sir.

[BLACKMONS' ATTORNEY]: And what was that estimate?

[BLACKMON]: Almost ten thousand dollars.

Blackmon was then given Plaintiffs' Exhibit four, a list of the Blackmons' personal property in the trailer house. The exhibit was not admitted into evidence.

[BLACKMONS' ATTORNEY]: If you look at what they call the bottom line, the very end of it, the total of the value of those—

[BLACKMON]: Yes, sir.

[BLACKMONS' ATTORNEY]: —does that refresh your memory as to the estimate at the time of the exact total value?

[BLACKMON]: Yes, sir.

[BLACKMONS' ATTORNEY]: What was that figure?

[BLACKMON]: Nine thousand, six hundred sixty-three dollars, seventy-three cents.

[BLACKMONS' ATTORNEY]: Nine thousand, six sixty-two—

[BLACKMON]: —six sixty-three, seventy-three.

[BLACKMONS' ATTORNEY]: That was what you felt in your opinion at the time was the market value of those items that had been destroyed?

[BLACKMON]: Yes, sir.

The Mixsons' attorney then cross-examined Blackmon as to the trailer house.

[MIXSONS' ATTORNEY]: Now you know it wasn't as valuable as a new one, or are you going to tell us—

[BLACKMON]: No, sir, I'm not going to say it wasn't as valuable as a new one. An old Cadillac is more valuable than perhaps a new Chevrolet.

[MIXSONS' ATTORNEY]: You're not telling me this is a valuable antique or something.

[BLACKMON]: No, sir.

[MIXSONS' ATTORNEY]: It was a used trailer house.

[BLACKMON]: That is correct.

[MIXSONS' ATTORNEY]: And it's not as valuable as a new trailer house.

[BLACKMON]: I'm not going to say that.

[MIXSONS' ATTORNEY]: But you never tried to sell it to find out.

[BLACKMON]: No, sir.

The Mixsons' attorney then cross-examined Blackmon as to the personal contents in the trailer house.

[MIXSONS' ATTORNEY]: Again, Mr. Blackmon, when you were asked what the market value of all these items in the house was, you

> gave us a total of about ninety-six hundred dollars and some change, and up over each column is listing a value and, again, *it shows replacement value; correct*?
>
> [BLACKMON]: *That's what it shows, yes, sir.*
>
> [MIXSONS' ATTORNEY]: And, this was if you wanted [sic] for example the first item is a chest of drawers, and that's what it would have cost you to go buy a new one; right?
>
> [BLACKMON]: Not necessarily. That's what we thought we had to get [sic] something comparable to that.

(emphasis added). The Mixsons' attorney then mentioned various items that were on the list—golf clubs, record player, hunting vest, television, popcorn popper, coffee maker, clothes, bed spreads, electric blanket, quilt, floor fan. This is the sum total of the evidence asserted to be contrary to the jury's findings.

Even an owner's testimony is subject to some restrictions. In order for a property owner to qualify as a witness to the damages to his property, his testimony must show that it refers to market, rather than intrinsic or some other value of the property. This requirement is usually met by asking the witness if he is familiar with the market value of his property. *Porras,* 675 S.W.2d at 504–05. We conclude that Blackmon's testimony is no evidence of market value. Along with the Supreme Court, we should not be understood as retreating from the general rule that an owner is qualified to testify about the market value of his property. *See Porras,* 675 S.W.2d at 505. However, this is not just a case in which the lawyer failed to ask his client if he was familiar with the market value of the property. Instead, in this case the owner's testimony affirmatively showed that he referred to replacement costs rather than market value. *See Porras,* 675 S.W.2d at 505. While Blackmon was qualified to give an opinion of the market value of his property, he simply failed to do so. *See Porras,* 675 S.W.2d at 505. Because we have held that there is no evidence in the record of market value, it follows that the jury's findings of zero market value cannot be against the great weight and preponderance of the evidence. Indeed, the jury's two "$0" findings simply reflect what the jury heard about market value—nothing. We overrule the Blackmons' first point of error.

Although we agree with the Mixsons that the Blackmons did not prove market value for the personalty at the time of the loss and, therefore, overrule the Blackmons' first point of error, we make one further observation concerning replacement value. We begin our observation by pointing out that the jury, without objection from the Blackmons, was charged to find the market value of the Blackmons' personal effects and/or personal property. Hence, the actual value to the owner of property such as household goods and wearing apparel was not at issue. Where property, such as household goods and wearing apparel, has no recognized market value, the actual value to the owner must be determined without resort to market value. * * * Thus, the rule that where household goods have no recognized market value, the trier of fact may consider, in determining the *actual value to the owner at time of loss,* the original cost, cost of replacement, opinions of qualified witnesses, including the owner, the use to which the property was put, as well as any other reasonably relevant facts. *Allstate Insurance Co.,* 590 S.W.2d at 704 (emphasis added). Consequently, the jury could consider replacement value of the personalty in determining the *actual value to the owner at the time of loss.* Nevertheless, the Blackmons made no objection to the charge directing the jury to find *market value* of the Blackmons' personal property, market value meaning the amount a willing buyer would pay to a willing seller. The record does not reflect that the Blackmons requested that the jury find the *actual value* of the personalty to the Blackmons at the time of the fire. Again, the only evidence presented by the Blackmons to establish damages to their personalty was in the form of replacement cost of the property. Thus, there was no evidence of the amount a willing buyer would pay to a willing seller. There being no evidence of market value of the personalty, we again conclude that the jury's findings of zero market value cannot be against the great weight and preponderance of the evidence.

In their second point of error, the Blackmons contend that the trial court erred in refusing to grant them a hearing on their motion for new trial in connection with asserted jury misconduct; to wit: discussion of liability insurance among jurors during jury deliberations. The Blackmons sought to establish the misconduct by a juror's testimony. A juror may not testify as to any matter or statement occurring during the course of the jury's deliberations or to the effect of anything upon his or any other juror's mind or emotions as influencing him to assent to or dissent from the verdict concerning his mental processes in connection therewith, except that a juror may testify whether any *outside influence* was improperly brought to bear upon any juror. * * * [W]e conclude further that a discussion of liability insurance among jurors during jury deliberations is not an "outside influence." An "outside influence" on the jury must emanate from outside the jury and its deliberations. * * * It follows that the juror could not testify. Therefore, we conclude that the trial court did not err in refusing to grant the Blackmons a hearing on the motion for new trial. We overrule the Blackmons' second point of error.

Affirmed.

Notes

1. What was the plaintiff's lawyer's problem: the plaintiff's testimony, the form of the question to the jury, or both? What should the lawyer have done at trial?

2. Why do you suppose the jury awarded nothing? Should juries be instructed on the policies underlying the collateral source rule to head off the possibility of jury speculation not suggested by anything that happened at trial? Would such an instruction be effective? *See* p. 233 *supra,* for a discussion of that rule.

3. The court indicates that replacement value might have been an appropriate measure of damage. Do you agree? Consider Strzelecki v. Blaser's Lakeside Indus. of Rice Lake, Inc., 133 Mich.App. 191, 348 N.W.2d 311 (1984):

> "[T]he [trial] court concluded that plaintiffs' proof of damages for loss of the home and contents, based on a replacement cost less depreciation method of valuation, was inadequate to establish the requisite market

value of the real and personal property at the time of the fire. Plaintiffs' proofs consisted of evidence establishing the cost of replacing the home, less depreciation based on the age of the home and improvements thereto, and the cost of replacing the personal property destroyed with the home, less depreciation based on the age of each specific item of personalty.

"The rule of damages for property loss is as follows:

> 'It is the settled law of this state that the measure of damages to real property, if permanently irreparable, is the difference between its market value before and after the damage. However, if the injury is reparable, and the expense of repairs is less than the market value, the measure of damage is the cost of the repairs.'

Bayley Products, Inc. v. American Plastic Products Co., 30 Mich.App. 590, 598; 186 N.W.2d 813 (1971), *lv. den.* 385 Mich. 754 (1971). * * * It is undisputed in the present case that the real and personal property was permanently and irreparably injured, and that the property had no value after the fire. Thus, under the above-stated rule, the measure of damages is the market value of the real and personal property at the time the fire occurred.

"Whether the replacement cost less depreciation method of valuation may suffice as prima facie proof of market value at the time of the loss is an issue not definitively decided by prior case law in our jurisdiction. Clearly, replacement cost alone, without any deduction for depreciation, is not sufficient evidence of market value at the time of the loss. If replacement cost without depreciation was allowed, the plaintiff would recover an amount as if the property were new at the time it was destroyed. However, in the instant case, plaintiffs' evidence of damages did include deductions for depreciation.

* * *

"It is true, as defendants point out, that * * * there was no evidence presented in the instant case establishing the absence of a market for the home or the personalty. Thus, defendants argue, plaintiffs were required to submit proof of the property's market value, *i.e.,* the price which could have been obtained at a private sale, through some method other than replacement cost less depreciation, such as an appraisal of the property, the valuation of the home for property tax purposes, or the selling price of similar homes in the area. We agree that market value is the applicable measure of plaintiffs' damages, but do not agree that plaintiffs' evidence based on replacement cost less depreciation was inadequate to present prima facie proof of the amount of damages.

"In another case involving the measure of damages for injury to property, this Court stated 'there is and should be no fixed rule for measuring compensation in cases such as this'. Baranowski v. Strating, 72 Mich.App. 548, 562, 250 N.W.2d 744 (1976), *lv. den.* 399 Mich. 881 (1977). (Footnote omitted.) The general principle is that proof of the amount of damages may not be founded on mere conjecture or speculation, but mathematical certainty is not required.

"It is important to recognize that the property destroyed in this case was a home, being unique real property, and its contents, for which only a second-hand market existed. This is not a case, for example, involving a

> business's loss of its merchandise, items which are not unique and for which a ready retail market exists, thus facilitating establishment of the price at which the items could be sold. Also, it must be borne in mind that the property injured in the present case was totally destroyed, thus making a post-injury appraisal of the property impossible. The replacement cost less depreciation method of valuation has been recognized as indicative of market value. We do not believe that it can be said, under the circumstances of this case, that this method of valuation is so inferior to the other methods by which the market value of plaintiffs' property could be established that plaintiffs' proofs submitted under this method should be deemed inadequate as prima facie evidence of the amount of damages. Measure of market value through pre-injury appraisals (if any), the original purchase price of the property, the valuation of the home for tax assessment purposes, or the selling price of similar homes, are not necessarily more accurate methods than replacement cost less depreciation. To the extent methods other than replacement cost less depreciation might be more reliable based on the particular facts of the case, defendants are free to introduce other proofs and so argue; the weight to be given the evidence is a matter for the fact finder."

4. Is full replacement cost ever appropriate? Consider Puget Sound Power & Light Co. v. Strong, 117 Wash.2d 400, 816 P.2d 716, 716–17, (1991) (en banc):

> "Generally, the measure of damages in tort actions is the amount that will adequately compensate for the loss suffered as the direct and proximate result of the wrongful act. * * * As recognized by the court below, if the damaged property has no market value, the measure of damages is the cost of replacement. * * * It is undisputed that there is no market for used utility poles. However, in denying Puget Power the full replacement cost of the pole, the court stated: 'Puget would gain an estimated additional 14 years of service life if it were permitted to recover the cost of a new pole. Such compensation exceeds the loss incurred by Puget and, thus, would result in a windfall to Puget.' Strong, 59 Wash.App. at 434, 798 P.2d 1162.
>
> "We would agree with that reasoning if the actual life expectancy of a specific pole could be determined. It cannot. As acknowledged by both *Miller* and the court below, the unpredictable forces affecting the life span of a pole render such a determination impossible."

See also Kansas Power and Light Co. v. Thatcher, 14 Kan.App.2d 613, 797 P.2d 162 (1990) (holding that full replacement cost without a deduction for depreciation measures loss of utility pole, a depreciable item, and listing 12 states that adopt that view and 5 that do not).

Compare Minerva Enterprises, Inc. v. Howlett, 308 Ark. 291, 824 S.W.2d 377, 381–82 (1992) which involved a sewage overflow into a mobile home, destroying it and its contents:

> "With respect to Howlett's personal effects inside the mobile home, she testified she made a list of this property two or three days after the accident. She valued some of the items on the list according to replacement cost; however, the items she purchased most recently were valued according to purchase price. Howlett testified these items were worthless to her after the accident because of their bacterial contamination. Again,

we note that she advertised the items for sale along with the mobile home, but received no offers to buy anything.

* * *

"There is no question that Howlett was the owner and could testify to the value of the contents. * * * The before-injury value she stated on the itemized list was $5,124.00. Her statements that the items were worthless to her because of the bacteria along with her unsuccessful attempts to sell the items established the after-injury value at $0.00.

* * *

"Accordingly, we hold Howlett and Carter presented sufficient proof of damages to their respective properties."

Was this valuation incorrect? *See also* D. Dobbs, The Law of Remedies 577–78 (2d ed. 1993):

"When clothing or household goods are destroyed the courts have departed from the market value formula in favor of one that gives the plaintiff the 'value to owner' or 'real value,' frequently adding that this does not include 'sentimental value.' Such statements provide a goal but not a measure of damages. 'Value to the owner' cannot yield any dollar figure by computation, by analysis or by empirical investigation. The point seems to be to give the plaintiff something more than the market value, but something less than the full replacement cost of a new item."

CAMPINS v. CAPELS

Court of Appeals of Indiana, 1984.
461 N.E.2d 712.

MILLER, JUDGE.

Julio Campins, Jr. brings his appeal to this court after John Capels and his wife, Dana, recovered $11,100* in their suit against him, individually, and as his two business entities, Hollywood Gold and Silver and Zeboné Gallery, Jewelry & Coin. The Capelses sued under IND.CODE 34–4–30–1, which authorized them to sue for treble damages because they were victims of a criminal offense against property—they suffered a burglary and consequent theft of their jewelry. The trial court ruled Campins liable for the value of some of their jewelry because he had purchased and had then destroyed some pieces when he knew or should have known they were stolen. This being the offense of criminal mischief, the trial court awarded the Capelses treble damages. * * *

ISSUES

Campins's issues, trimmed to their essential elements, are:

1. Whether the trial court erred in determining Campins liable to the Capelses under IC 34–4–30–1, *i.e.* did the preponderance of the evidence show him liable for criminal mischief?

* The trial court computed damages as follows:

3 USAC award rings at $1,000 each	=	$3,000
1 Free design wedding band at $700 each	=	700
TOTAL		$3,700
Application of Treble Damages		× 3
TOTAL		$11,100.

2. Whether, if Campins is indeed liable, the trial court granted excessive damages.

FACTS

Sometime between January 11 and January 13, 1981, one Earl Hall, eighteen years old, stole various items of jewelry from the Capelses' home (for which he was later convicted). * * * On January 15 or 16, in the course of the search, Mrs. Capels spoke with Campins, sole proprietor of two such dealerships. She claims he admitted purchasing some of the Capelses' jewelry but told her he had already melted it down with the exception of a sterling silver ring which he returned to her. Upon Campins's refusal to make restitution for the destruction of the jewelry, the Capelses brought suit against him. * * *

At trial, the nucleus of the action revolved around the jewelry allegedly melted down at Zeboné Gallery, particularly three national racing championship rings awarded by United States Auto Club (USAC) and a free-form wedding band with twelve diamonds. * * *

* * *

After presenting evidence of Campins's liability, the Capelses presented evidence of the value of their rings. Mrs. Capels's wedding band, having been recently appraised at $700, was easily valuated. The USAC rings, for which the Capelses had requested $350 apiece in their complaint, proved a different matter.

The three USAC rings at issue here had been awarded to Capels in 1972, 1977, and 1978. (He had won five in all.) Each ring signified a national championship earned in a particular automobile category and given to the car's owner and the driver. In 1972, Parnelli Jones gave Capels his owner's ring in appreciation for his work as chief mechanic of Jones's Indy car. Capels later won his 1977 and 1978 rings as the actual owner of championship dirt division cars, driven by Bill Vukovich and Pancho Carter. The 1972 ring signified Capels's work as supervisor of what the media labelled a "super team" after having been instrumental in winning three straight Indy car championships (1970, 1971, 1972). As for his own owner's rings, they represented the large financial investment as well as time required to excel in any division of USAC competition. Sentimentally, Capels described these rings as being enduring symbols of his accomplishments and USAC's recognition thereof. * * *

Each heavy, gold ring bore a synthetic stone and had been molded to display the USAC emblem, the name of the recipient, the specific achievement being rewarded, and the year of that achievement. They were custom-made annually by Josten's with a different design each year. Capels specifically testified there was no market for these rings: "You can't buy these rings from any gift shop or jewelry store or anything." Record, p. 26. Capels admitted that in 1977, he purchased a duplicate of his 1977 ring for a business associate for $349, and Campins himself testified the price of gold at the time of the theft was double that of at least 1979, from $300 to $580–$600. Capels went on to testify he would not have sold the rings, even for $1,500 or $2,000 apiece. He then estimated their worth as between $700 and $1000, finally settling on $750 when asked to be specific.

* * *

[T]he distinctive anomaly of the eighteen-year-old Hall selling three USAC championship rings embossed with "P. Jones" and "J. Capels" as well as an expensive wedding ring, is sufficient to constitute reckless conduct under a preponderance of the evidence standard. Campins realized or should have realized he was destroying property to which he had no rightful claim. The trial court did not err in establishing Campins's liability for criminal mischief. * * *

DAMAGES

The remaining issue, now that liability has been established, is the size of the actual damages which Campins asserts are excessive. * * *

When personal property is the subject of an award, damages are measured by its fair market value at the time of the loss, fair market value being the price a willing seller will accept from a willing buyer. Such appears to be the measure of worth for the twelve-diamond wedding band, appraised at $700. This assessment has never really been contested by Campins; he mainly questions the value placed on the USAC rings. And to our knowledge, the problems raised in valuating them have never been addressed in Indiana.

Both parties have argued this issue in terms of the methods of valuating used household goods and wearing apparel. Such system would appear appropriate because used household goods and clothing have a greater actual value to their owners than they do on the secondhand market, similar to the problem here, where Capels's feelings about the rings as mementos outstrips his feelings for them as jewelry. Instead of allowing only the fair market value of secondhand goods, the court determines "the owner may recover the value of the goods to him, based on his actual money loss resulting from his being deprived of the property, or the difference in actual value caused by the injury *excluding any fanciful or sentimental values which he might place on them.*" Anchor Stove & Furniture Co. v. Blackwood, (1941) 109 Ind.App. 357, 363, 35 N.E.2d 117, 119 (emphasis added) * * *. We believe that standard is useful but not altogether appropriate to the problem here.

First of all, jewelry is neither a household good nor wearing apparel. Thus, ordinarily, jewelry is valuated at its fair market value. However, these USAC rings were not ordinary jewelry and could not be bought and sold in a readily available market. Rather, they were coveted awards and symbols of certain achievements accomplished by very few, such awards not having many willing sellers and therefore no real market. These rings should be valued differently than other jewelry. * * * This, therefore, is our starting point—how do we find jewelry's actual value to its owner when it has a high value for its extrinsic content but also has a primary function and a consequently raised value based on pure sentimentality?

We find a basis for proceeding in the fundamental reasoning behind awarding higher actual values to owners of used household goods and wearing apparel:

> "The underlying principle of universal application is that of fair and just compensation for the loss or damage sustained. * * * Where subordinate rules for the measure of damages [fair market value for personal property] run counter to the paramount rule of fair and just compensation, the former must yield to the principle underlying all such rules."

Aufderheide v. Fulk, 112 N.E. at 400. * * *

* * *

The emphasis in the cases where the actual value of the goods exceeded the market value or where there was no market value at all is upon looking at all the circumstances and the available elements of loss in a rational, reasonable fashion. * * * We believe the best method to ensure fairness to both parties is to receive a wide range of elements for consideration in the actual value. * * * Such elements that have been introduced and relied upon are often such typical factors as cost of replacement, original cost, and cost to reproduce. * * * But our courts and juries have also examined elements of a less prosaic nature, such as the proposed use of woodland for a forestry course (Alfred Atmore Pope Foundation Inc. v. New York, New Haven & Hartford Railroad Co., supra), uniqueness (Lack v. Anderson, (1946) La.App., 27 So.2d 653), the feelings of the owner (Harvey v. Wheeler Transfer & Storage Co., (1938) 227 Wis. 36, 277 N.W. 627), and the cost to build and decorate a room to match a single painting (Cherry v. McCutchen, (1942) 68 Ga.App. 682, 23 S.E.2d 587). We believe that sentimental value, in limited circumstances, is also such a consideration.

When we refer to sentimental value, we do not mean mawkishly emotional or unreasonable attachments to personal property. *See* Mieske v. Bartell Drug Co., (1979) 92 Wash.2d 40, 593 P.2d 1308.* Rather, we are referring to the feelings generated by items of almost purely sentimental value, such as heirlooms (Brown v. Frontier Theatres, Inc., (1963) Tex. 369 S.W.2d 299), family papers and photographs (Bond v. A.H. Belo Corp., (1980) Tex.Civ.App., 602 S.W.2d 105), handicrafts (Monahan v. Scott Cleaning Co., (1922) Mo.App., 241 S.W. 956), and trophies (Shaffer v. Honeywell, Inc., (1976) S.D., 249 N.W.2d 251). What we are referring to basically are those items *generally* capable of generating sentimental feelings, not just emotions peculiar to the owner. In other words, any owner of these USAC rings would have similar feelings. The most apt analogy to our situation is

* In *Mieske,* the court discussed the general rule "that compensation for sentimental or fanciful values will not be allowed":

> "What is sentimental value? The broad dictionary definition is that sentimental refers to being 'governed by feeling, sensibility or emotional idealism. * * *' Webster's Third New International Dictionary (1963). Obviously that is not the exclusion contemplated by the statement that sentimental value is not to be compensated. If it were, no one would recover for the wrongful death of a spouse or a child. Rather, the type of sentiment which is not compensable is that which relates to 'indulging in feeling to an unwarranted extent' or being 'affectedly or mawkishly emotional * * *.' Webster's Third New International Dictionary (1963)."

Id. at 45, 593 P.2d at 1311.

that of the trophies. In two cases, courts have awarded damages based on the consideration of the "blood, sweat and tears" expended to win these objects. Mosely v. Sears, Roebuck & Co., (1964) La.App., 167 So.2d 408 (tennis trophies); *Shaffer v. Honeywell, Inc., supra* (horse trophies); *see also Monahan v. Scott Cleaning Co., supra* (hand-crocheted bedspread valued by work, labor and time spent). We see no difference in giving special consideration to items such as these and to the three USAC rings, awarded for three years of "blood, sweat and tears" and thus having special sentimental meaning for Capels. The question remains whether Capels's evidence supported the $3000 award.

Capels testified not only to the actual worth of the rings as mere pieces of custom-embossed gold but also to his emotional attachment to each. He described the pride and gratification he felt upon their ownership and elaborated on the effort required to win them. Actual estimates of their worth—to *him*—ranged from $700 to $1000 each; however, he himself settled upon the $750 figure. Campins alternatively argues each ring was worth $67 (wholesale gold), $135–200 (retail gold), or $349 (replacement in 1977). We believe the evidence justified an award of $750.

In light of the substantial evidence of the replacement value of the rings, the increase in the price of gold, and Capels's justifiable sentimental feelings, we would see no error in finding damages in the amount of $750 apiece. *See also Bond v. A.H. Belo Corp., supra* (sentimental value of family papers and photographs stipulated as greater than $2,500); *Brown v. Frontier Theatres, Inc., supra* (heirlooms valued in 1963, as high as $666.66 for wedding veil, shoes, point lace collar, $666.66 for key-wound watch, $333.33 for cameo pins, etc.)

However, while we ultimately conclude the court did not act erroneously in allowing an award in excess of the replacement value of the rings (based on the unique circumstances here and special attachment to this property), we can hardly deem it appropriate to fix a value higher than that asserted by the owner. Capels finally settled upon a figure of $750 per ring; the court's award of $1000 apiece could only have been improperly based on speculation. * * * By our decision here, we simply conclude that certain property, by its very nature, has an element of sentiment essential to its existence. In this case, we refer to symbols for achievements of national stature and recognition and the calculation of their actual value. But we must also add the proviso that even for significant awards or mementos we do not intend to permit fanciful speculation as to their worth. We must fashion our remedy within the realm of sensibility, as here, where $750 is only slightly above the established range of replacement values. Such would naturally also be our standard in valuating similar significant awards, such as an Oscar, the Heisman Trophy, or an Olympic medal, where the recipient retains the honor despite the loss of the trophy, such trophy being merely the symbol of the achievement and perhaps replaceable by a surrogate. A certain amount of sentiment is inherent in the value of these objects to the owner, and each case must be based on its own facts. * * * We believe in this case, Capels's $750 figure was just such a reasonable value of each ring with the sentiment included therein.

* * *

Affirmed, modified, and remanded for hearing on fees.

RIDENOUR v. FURNESS

Court of Appeals of Indiana, First District, 1989.
546 N.E.2d 322.

BAKER, JUDGE.

* * *

For over two decades, the DNR [Department of Natural Resources] has been actively involved in enhancing and protecting the ecology of Lake Michigan.

* * *

[T]he DNR promulgated an emergency order on August 22, 1986, temporarily banning the use of gill fishing nets by commercial fishermen for a 47-day period from September 15 to October 31, 1986. The stated purpose of the ban was to prevent the incidental catch of salmon and trout by commercial fishermen using gill nets.

In response, the fishermen filed suit in Marion Circuit Court seeking to enjoin the DNR from enforcing the emergency order. The fishermen also moved for a temporary restraining order. Following a hearing on the motion for a temporary restraining order, the Marion Circuit Court, on September 12, 1986, enjoined the DNR's enforcement of the gill net ban. Upon stipulation by the parties, the cause was venued to the Boone Circuit Court which subsequently denied the DNR's motion to dissolve the preliminary injunction. On appeal, the Indiana Court of Appeals reversed the preliminary injunction entered against the DNR. * * * That decision was subsequently approved by the Supreme Court of Indiana on transfer. * * *

* * *

The cause then proceeded to trial on the issue of the damages sustained from the incidental catch of the protected sport fish. DNR fisheries biologist, Dan Brazo (Brazo), testified on behalf of the DNR.

* * *

The DNR determined to assign a value for the various species of sport fish incidentally caught according to the individual size or weight of the fish as set forth in the American Fisheries Society (AFS), Pub. No. 13. Upon this basis, Brazo testified that the total value for the 6,044 salmon and trout incidentally caught to be $21,383.58. On the other hand, the fishermen argued during their case-in-chief that the DNR's actual hatchery production cost of producing a 3½ inch fingerling fish was the appropriate method for assessing the damages incurred by the DNR. The fishermen produced evidence establishing that the DNR's hatchery production costs for the fish varied between $.09 and $.57 per fish depending upon the species of fish raised. As an alternative method of assessing damages, fishermen, Mayoch and Bucy, offered into evidence a contract between the state of Michigan and a private contractor accompanied by a cover letter from an official with the Michigan Department of Natural Resources. That letter explained that Michigan valued maturing salmon at $1 to $3 per pound and permitted a liquidated damage value of the greater of $10 per fish or $10 per pound. In its findings of fact and conclusions of law, the trial court accepted the actual hatchery production cost theory of damages, but permitted allowance for a 50% mortality rate between the time of stocking and the time of the incidental catch. On this basis the trial court assessed damages in favor of the DNR in the amount of $1,906.16. The DNR subsequently instituted this appeal.

* * *

ISSUE I: DESTRUCTION OF SPORT FISH

The DNR contends that the trial court's award of damages for the protected sport fish incidentally caught in gill nets utilized by the fishermen during the period of the erroneous injunction was inadequate. * * *

Generally speaking, damages for total destruction to personal property are measured by the fair market value of the property at the time of loss. *Campins v. Capels* (1984), Ind.App., 461 N.E.2d 712; *Bottoms v. B & M Coal* (1980), Ind.App., 405 N.E.2d 82; *Ross v. Felter* (1919), 71 Ind.App. 58, 123 N.E. 20. This rule is the same when determining the measure of damages for the loss or destruction of animals. * * * A problem arises, however, where, as here, there exists no market value for the property destroyed.[1]

* * *

Recognizing that the 10 to 14 inch fish had a value beyond that contemplated by the replacement costs of 3½ inch fingerlings is wholly consistent with prior decisions regarding the proper measure of damages for the destruction of personal property. * * *

Assigning a value for the 10 to 14 inch sport fish still remains a difficult proposition, however. Of course there existed a readily ascertainable market for wheat where, as mentioned earlier, no such commercial market existed for the sport fish destroyed here. Nevertheless, we believe AFS Publication No. 13 and the values assigned to the sport fish pursuant to the Michigan contract submitted by fishermen Bucy and Mayoch provide relevant evidence upon which the trial court could establish a value for the destroyed sport fish. The fishermen argue, however, that the values for the fish set forth in AFS Publication No. 13 are based in part on feeding costs in raising the fish entirely in a hatchery until the 10 to 14 inch size is realized. They contend the State does not incur such feeding costs beyond the time the fish are released for stocking at 3½ inches long. Although the State does not per se feed the fish after they are released for stocking, it does invest a considerable amount of time, money, and effort protecting the integrity of the environment in and around the Indiana waters of Lake

1. There exists no fair market value upon which to base a computation of damages because it is illegal in Indiana to sell the various species of sport fish destroyed here.

Michigan. It is in these waters that the fish feed, live, and reproduce. Thus, in at least an indirect manner, the State incurs significant costs to feed the fish. This is not dissimilar to the farmer who rotates his crops and takes other protective measures to insure fertile ground in which to raise a healthy crop. Thus, the lack of direct feeding costs is not a relevant ground upon which to distinguish AFS Publication No. 13 and preclude its consideration in calculating the value of the sport fish caught and destroyed during the period of the erroneous injunction.[3]

ISSUE II: PERCH

We must next determine whether the trial court erred in granting summary judgment on the perch profit element of damages sought by the DNR. In granting the fishermen's motion for partial summary judgment, the trial court stated that profits earned from the catch of perch were not an element of damages recoverable by the DNR for having been wrongfully enjoined. We disagree.

In support of their position, the fishermen argue that they utilized gill nets under the authority of a valid injunction which was issued after notice and a hearing by a court of competent jurisdiction, and thus the perch caught during the injunction period cannot constitute a basis for damages. This contention is without merit. It has long been established that a party wrongfully enjoined is entitled to all damages he suffers under the injunction regardless of whether the injunction was legally instituted. * * * Recognizing this right, our supreme court requires the posting of sufficient surety to insure the recovery of damages sustained by a party subsequently determined to have been wrongfully enjoined. Ind. Rules of Procedure, Trial Rule 65(C). * * * The fishermen accepted the risk that the preliminary injunction would be reversed, subjecting them to liability, when they proceeded to fish with gill nets during the prohibited period.

The fishermen argue further their exposure under T.R. 65(C) is limited to damages which flow directly and as an immediate consequence of the injunction. They point out that the DNR's emergency rule only banned the use of gill nets, not all commercial fishing. Thus, they assert the imposition of damages for perch go[es] beyond the loss suffered by the DNR.

* * * There is indication that the commercial fishermen could have caught some perch through the use of alternative fishing methods. Thus, the damages recoverable by the DNR would be the difference in profits the fishermen received for the perch harvested with the use of gill nets and the profits the fishermen would receive for the perch harvested using alternative fishing methods and technology. The fishermen would be entitled to diminish the amount of damages recoverable by the DNR, however, only if they come forward with information that they would have legitimately captured some perch through the use of equipment other than the gill nets and of the profits they would have derived therefrom. Absent such evidence, it would not be unreasonable to allow the DNR to recover all the

3. This is not to suggest, however, that the cost of the ecological protection of the fish habitat is a measurable element of damage or that such may be computed as a portion of the DNR's recoverable damages.

profits the fishermen obtained from the sale of perch harvested while under the protection of the erroneous injunction. * * *

Accordingly, this cause is reversed and remanded to the trial court for proceedings consistent with this opinion.

Notes

1. Note that *Ridenour* arises in the context of measuring damages for a wrongfully issued temporary restraining order and preliminary injunction. If no bond had been required upon the issuance of the injunction, would an award of damages have been proper? *See* pp. 103–125, *supra.*

2. How did *Ridenour* and *Campins* find values when there was no market? Would their approach have helped *Blackmon?*

3. In Gill v. Brown, 107 Idaho 1137, 1138–39, 695 P.2d 1276, 1277–78 (1985), the plaintiffs sought recovery both for property damage and for mental anguish caused by the defendant's killing of their pet donkey:

> "The sole issue is whether the Gills' complaint alleges facts that, if proven, would permit them to recover damages for mental anguish. * * *
>
> "The measure of damages when personal property is destroyed by the tortious conduct of another is the fair market value of the property at the time of its destruction. * * * In the case of destroyed animals, the majority of jurisdictions use this measure and specifically deny recovery for mental anguish suffered by the property owner. Annot., 1 A.L.R.3d 997, 1010 (1965). We are not persuaded to depart from this general rule.
>
> "However, a claim for damages for emotional distress and mental anguish may be asserted in connection with the independent torts of negligent or intentional infliction of emotional distress. Hatfield v. Max Rouse & Sons Northwest, 100 Idaho 840, 606 P.2d 944 (1980). * * * [The plaintiffs failed to state a cause of action for negligent infliction of emotional distress.]
>
> "In respect to the tort of intentional infliction of emotional distress, our Supreme Court in *Hatfield* adopted the view expressed in RESTATEMENT (SECOND) TORTS § 46 (1948). That rule provides:
>
>> One who by extreme and outrageous conduct intentionally or recklessly causes severe emotional distress to another is subject to liability for such emotional distress, and if bodily harm to the other results from it, for such bodily harm.
>
> Under this view, a plaintiff may recover for mental anguish if the defendant's conduct was 'outrageous' and if the mental anguish suffered was 'severe'. * * * In their complaint, the Gills allege that Brown 'negligently and recklessly' shot and killed the donkey, that the donkey was both a pet and a pack animal, and that the loss of the donkey has caused the Gills to suffer 'extreme mental anguish and trauma.' By alleging that Brown's conduct was reckless and that they thereby suffered extreme mental anguish and trauma, the Gills have alleged facts that, if proven, could permit recovery under an intentional infliction of emotional distress cause of action. Accordingly, we hold the district court erred by striking the Gills' claim for damages caused by mental anguish." *

* For a discussion of negligent and intentional infliction of emotional distress, see W. Keeton, D. Dobbs, R. Keeton, D. Owen, Prosser & Keeton on the Law of Torts §§ 12, 54 (5th ed. 1984).

ASHARE v. MIRKIN, BARRE, SALTZSTEIN & GORDON, P.C.

Supreme Court of Suffolk County, New York, 1980.
106 Misc.2d 866, 435 N.Y.S.2d 438.

JOHN V. VAUGHN, JUSTICE.

In this action for compensatory and punitive damages, flowing from the conversion of the plaintiff's property, this court, on February 14, 1980, granted plaintiff summary judgment on the issue of conversion, severed the counterclaims and directed an assessment of damages. Pursuant to that order, a trial on the issue of damages was held in this court.

The function of an award of damages in an action for conversion is to indemnify the injured party by awarding him the value of the converted property. Where the nature of the goods involved is such that they are readily exchanged in the market place, the measure of damages is the fair market value of the goods at the time of conversion which is generally the price at which the goods can be replaced in the market. In this case, the evidence established the price at which the converted law books would be purchased and sold in the secondary market by a used book dealer. The significant difference in value between the price the company would pay and the price [at which] it would sell these books was attributed to the cost of maintenance, upkeep, storage and profit. The court finds that the market value of the converted books in this case is the cost of replacement by the plaintiff in the used book market and not the lower market at which the used book dealer would purchase the volumes. Plaintiff is not in the used book business and would have to pay the higher cost in order to replace his library. The value of these books is found to be $6989.00. * * *

* * *

In addition, the plaintiff seeks punitive or exemplary damages against these defendants. Such damages may be recovered for an act of conversion where the circumstances establish that the conversion was accomplished by malice or reckless or willful disregard of the plaintiff's right. An act is done maliciously when it is done deliberately with knowledge of the plaintiff's rights and with the intent to interfere therewith. Exemplary damages are awarded in addition to compensatory damages in order to deter the defendants from a repetition of a wrongful act and to serve as a warning to others. There is no set formula by which to determine the exact amount of punitive damages although they should bear some relation to the injury inflicted and the cause thereof (I.H.P. Corp. v. 210 Central Park South Corp., 16 A.D.2d 461, 228 N.Y.S.2d 883, aff'd 12 N.Y.2d 329, 239 N.Y.S.2d 547, 189 N.E.2d 812).

The court finds that exemplary damages should be awarded in this case. The court further finds that at the time of the plaintiff's employment with the defendant firm, the defendants had incurred significant expenses in the establishment of their new Hauppauge office. At that time the parties agreed that the plaintiff would bring in his law library and office equipment for plaintiff and other members of the firm to use in that office and thus, save the defendant firm any additional expense. Defendants, in turn, agreed to maintain the library during the period of plaintiff's employment, but the books, furniture and equipment were to remain the plaintiff's. * * * [T]he court finds that, contrary to the original agreement, the defendants willfully and maliciously refused to return the plaintiff's property to him after categorizing him as an "ingrate" for his desire to leave the firm.

Although the plaintiff analogizes the conversion of his law books to a conversion of a worker's tools, thereby depriving him of a livelihood, the analogy is not entirely correct. It is apparent that the law books were readily available in a local law library.

Accordingly, in considering the nature of the defendants' willful and malicious conduct, the participation by each of the six defendants in the decision to convert the property, and the harm inflicted to the plaintiff, the court awards the plaintiff exemplary damages in the amount of $6000.00.

Notes

1. The Appellate Division of the Supreme Court modified Ashare as follows in full:

> "In an action, inter alia, to recover damages for conversion, defendants appeal from (1) an order * * * which, inter alia, (a) granted plaintiff's motion for summary judgment as to liability, (b) dismissed stated counterclaims, and (c) ordered an assessment of damages, and (2) a judgment of the same court, entered October 14, 1980, which, after a nonjury trial, awarded plaintiff compensatory damages of $12,000 and punitive damages of $6,000. * * * We have reviewed the order upon the appeal from the judgment. Judgment modified, on the law, by deleting the provision which awarded punitive damages and substituting a provision dismissing the claim for such damages. As so modified, judgment affirmed, without costs or disbursements. Under the circumstances, there was no basis for the award of punitive damages."

Ashare v. Mirkin, 81 A.D.2d 650, 441 N.Y.S.2d 408 (1981).

Why did the court say there was no basis for awarding punitive damages?

2. In *Ashare* the cause of action was conversion, not destruction of chattels. The measurement of damages is the same. Note that since a thief cannot pass title, a plaintiff can recover damages for conversion from a good faith purchaser of plaintiff's stolen goods. *See, e.g.,* Kahn v. Quintana, 811 P.2d 458 (Colo.App.1991) (buyer who purchased in good faith stolen flatware liable to owners); Hossner v. Idaho Forest Industries, Inc., 122 Idaho 413, 835 P.2d 648 (1992) (defendant had purchased timber from a local logger who had purchased it from someone falsely claiming to own the land on which the timber was logged; defendant was liable to owner of timber).

3. If a plaintiff is a merchant whose stock is destroyed, the measurement of damages is the wholesale value since that is the plaintiff's replacement cost.

See Felice Fedder Oriental Art, Inc. v. Scanlon, 708 F.Supp. 551 (S.D.N.Y.1989) (inventory of art gallery destroyed when car crashed into the gallery was measured at wholesale, not retail cost).

4. At common law, loss of use damages were allowed only when personal property was damaged, but not when it was totally destroyed or converted. D. Dobbs, Handbook on the Law of Remedies § 5.11, at 384 (1973). The common law rule apparently was based on a legal fiction that a plaintiff who sued for the value of the converted or destroyed chattel was forcing the defendant to buy it, and that a plaintiff who so "chose" to "sell" the chattel rather than further use it had no loss of use. *Id.* The modern rule, which makes no distinction between destroyed, damaged or converted goods, is discussed in DTS Tank Service, Inc. v. Vanderveen, 683 P.2d 1345, 1346 (Okl.1984), *citing* Reynolds v. Bank of America National Trust and Savings Assoc., 53 Cal.2d 49, 345 P.2d 926 (1959):

> "There appears to be no logical or practical reason why a distinction should be drawn between cases in which the property is totally destroyed and those in which it has been injured but is repairable, and we have concluded that when the owner of a negligently destroyed commercial vehicle has suffered injury by being deprived of the use of the vehicle during the period required for replacement, he is entitled, upon proper pleading and proof, to recover the loss of use in order to 'compensate for all the detriment proximately caused' by the wrongful destruction."

Professor Dobbs in his updated hornbook has eliminated all mention of the old common law rule. He says "The owner who uses a chattel in the production of income is always entitled to claim profits lost when the chattel is unavailable during a reasonable period for repair or replacement as a result of tortious destruction, damage, or conversion." D. Dobbs, The Law of Remedies 561 (2d ed. 1993) (footnotes omitted). Not all courts follow that modern rule. *See, e.g.,* Pillsbury Co. v. Midland Enterprises, Inc., 715 F.Supp. 738, 763 (E.D.La. 1989) (in admiralty cases "the measure of damages is generally the market value of the property just before the loss (less the [salvage value]) and does not include loss of use or other consequential damages", *citing* Albany Insurance Co. v. Bengal Marine, Inc., 857 F.2d 250, 253 (5th Cir.1988); Boral Bricks, Inc. v. Old South Transportation Management, Inc., 198 Ga.App. 678, 402 S.E.2d 777, 777 (1991) ("Since appellant's truck was destroyed, it follows that the measure of recoverable damages is the full fair market value of the truck and not the 'loss of use' thereof."); Winkle Chevy–Olds–Pontiac v. Condon, 830 S.W.2d 740, 746 (Tex.App.1992) (loss of use awarded in conversion if sue for return of property, not if sue for value of property); First Nat. Bank v. Gittelman, 788 S.W.2d 165, 169 (Tex.App.1990) (same). For a discussion of how to measure loss of use *see* notes 5–8 in the damaged goods section which follows.

2. *Damaged Goods*

Unlike destroyed or taken goods, damaged goods generally are still in plaintiff's possession and retain some value. Typically plaintiffs do not seek specific relief to have the defendant repair the property. Why not? Rather, plaintiffs seek compensatory damages. The cases below illustrate some issues with respect to the measurement of the compensation.

FARMERS INS. CO. OF ARIZ. v. R.B.L. INV. CO.

Court of Appeals of Arizona, 1983.
138 Ariz. 562, 675 P.2d 1381.

OPINION

HATHAWAY, JUDGE.

Whether the owner of a negligently damaged motor vehicle may be compensated for damages for loss in the fair market value above and beyond the cost of repair, and whether he may be compensated for loss of use of the motor vehicle during the period in which it is being repaired, are questions raised on this appeal. * * * We disagree with the trial court's conclusions limiting damages to the cost of repair and disallowing the cost of "flooring" during the period of repair.

On October 30, 1980, a new, unsold, 1980 Audi, available for sale from appellant's new car dealership, while being taken for a test drive, was involved in a collision with a vehicle insured by Farmers. Farmers admitted that the accident was the fault of its insured.

Repairs to the new Audi at the retail cost of $3,495.70, were required. Farmers offered to pay the repair costs, but appellant refused the offer on the basis that it would not fully compensate the loss. Farmers thereafter erroneously issued its draft to appellant for the sum of $9,460, which appellant accepted and cashed. Farmers asked for a refund of all funds in excess of its original $3,495.70 offer, and appellant counteroffered to return the amount in excess of the loss it claimed. Farmers refused and this suit ensued for return of the funds. This accounts for the unusual posture wherein Farmers, in seeking recovery of the overpayment, is litigating the damage and losses of the "defendant"/appellant.

The issue of the proper measure of appellant's damages was tried to the trial court on stipulated facts. The trial court's findings of facts include:

> "* * * 9. That the dealer's wholesale factory cost of the car is $15,526.00.
>
> 10. That the amount of $3,122.63 was spent to fix the car after it was damaged in the accident.
>
> 11. That the dealership spent $1,971.91 in interest to the Valley National Bank paid on this particular car during the time it was in the shop being repaired.
>
> 12. That also, added to these numbers are normal, average gross profit in the sum of $889.00, and from that total they are deducting the amount of money for which the car was sold, $13,500.00, leaving a difference of $8,009.54 due from plaintiff."

The trial court held that the compensable damages were limited to the cost of repair. * * *

Appellant begins its loss-to-fair-market-value argument with a submission that an automobile that has been in a major accident is worth less than an identical automobile that has not been in an accident, suggesting that one need only examine their own biases as a consumer to acknowledge a disparity in the price they would be willing to pay for either vehicle. They further argue that where the choice is between an automobile that is "new" versus one that was new but was in an accident and is now repaired, the disparity is magnified.

* * *

We believe that the rule is clearly enunciated in the Restatement (Second) of Torts, § 928 (1977):

> "§ 928. Harm to Chattels. When one is entitled to a judgment for harm to chattels not amounting to a total destruction in value, the damages include compensation for
>
> (a) the difference between the value of the chattel before the harm and the value after the harm or, at his election in an appropriate case, the reasonable cost of repair or restoration, *with due allowance for any difference between the original value and the value after repairs,* and
>
> (b) the loss of use." (Emphasis added).

Other authority supporting damages for depreciation beyond the cost of repair includes Professor Dobbs, who writes:

> "There seems no warrant at all for insisting that the owner content himself with the repair costs if they are less than the depreciation, provided depreciation can be and is adequately proven. However satisfactory the repairs may be in, say, the operation of a car, the owner may quite possibly find that the trade-in value of his car is less when he seeks to purchase a new automobile, or that its cash sale value is less throughout the immediate life of the car. If this sort of depreciation is real, and can be established, there seems no reason at all to deny full compensation by limiting recovery to cost of repairs." D. Dobbs, Remedies, § 5.10, at 380 (1973).

Jurisdictions that have addressed the issue seem to have generally held that the measure of compensation to the owner of a negligently damaged motor vehicle may include the cost of repair and proven residual diminution in fair market value. *See, e.g.,* Perma Ad Ideas of America, Inc. v. Mayville, 158 Ga.App. 707, 282 S.E.2d 128, 130 (1981); Trailmobile Division of Pullman, Inc. v. Higgs, 12 Ill.App.3d 323, 297 N.E.2d 598 (1973); Gary v. Allstate Insurance Company, 250 So.2d 168 (La.App.1971). We believe this is the appropriate standard.

Appellant contends that the trial court erred by denying as a matter of law the claim for interest paid during the period of repair on the loan it had taken out to purchase and "floor" the damaged vehicle. It is argued that having the vehicle available for show and sale is the "use" to which the vehicle would have been put but for the negligence of Farmers' insured. The interest expense paid during the period of time between the accident and the vehicle's repair is stipulated to be $1,971.91, and is the interest paid by appellant to the Valley National Bank for the car while being repaired only. The repairs took many months due to parts shipping. Loss of use is an appropriate item of damages. Restatement (Second) of Torts, § 928(b). * * * Professor Dobbs, in his treatise on remedies, states, at p. 168–9:

> "*Where plaintiff has a claim for rental value or other loss of use.* In cases where the plaintiff's claim is one for the loss of use of his property, the rental value of the property during the period in which the plaintiff was deprived of it is often one element of damages he is allowed to recover. If his automobile is damaged and he loses the use of it for a month, he may be entitled to its rental value or the rental value of some substitute transportation, as well as to some recovery for the physical damage itself. *But it would be possible, if the occasion arose, to mentally convert the car into cash. Instead of talking of renting the car, it would then be possible to talk of 'renting' the cash—that is, to talk of paying interest for the use of money in a sum equal to the value of the car.* The amount of interest on the cash value of the car is not necessarily the same as the amount of rental value of the car itself. Nevertheless, rental value of the car and interest on the cash value of the car can be seen as two measurements of the same underlying value, since it is almost always acceptable to express the value of property in terms of money. * * * " [footnotes omitted] (Emphasis added).

We deem the out-of-pocket interest expense paid by appellant to be includable as a fair measure of compensation for the loss of use of the vehicle during the period of repairs. The time in the shop for repairs was occasioned through negligent conduct and the interest expense incurred when the vehicle was not available for sale by appellant would not have been incurred but for the negligence of the plaintiff's insured. It is a direct and proximate result of the plaintiff's insured's negligence and should be compensable. It is the policy of the law to award those damages which will fairly and adequately compensate the injured party.

The parties stipulated that the vehicle cost the dealership $15,526 wholesale and the average gross profit on such a car is $889, making its pre-collision value total $16,415. After the repairs were performed, the automobile sold for $13,500, leaving appellant out of pocket $2,915 after repairs. The judgment is modified to include this amount plus $1,971.91 for loss of use.

As modified, the judgment is affirmed.

Notes

1. Will all automobile accidents result in an award for diminished value in addition to the cost of repair? *See* Ellis v. King, 184 W.Va. 227, 400 S.E.2d 235, 238–39 (1990) (damage to automobile must be structural for court to award diminution in value in addition to cost of repairs).

2. When is it appropriate for an owner of damaged personal property to elect compensatory damages measured by the reasonable cost of repair or restoration? What if the cost of repair will exceed the fair market value of the property at the time of the injury? These issues are considered in Stettner v. Graubard, 82 Misc.2d 132, 368 N.Y.S.2d 683 (Town Ct.1975):

"This is an action to recover the $220 cost of veterinary services required for plaintiff's dog as a result of injuries the dog suffered through defendant's negligence. * * *

"Defendant's arguments, at the hearing, and in his brief, may be summarized as follows:

"1. That plaintiff's damages cannot exceed the dog's 'market value' regardless of how much higher than market value the actual veterinary bills may have been; and

"2. That a dog's 'market value' is no more or less than the purchase price originally paid for it minus depreciation.

In short, that the measure of damages for the death or injury of a dog is the same as might be applied in the case of an automobile or any other item of personal property.

"It is the law of this State as urged by defendant that market value is the correct measure of damages for the destruction of a dog (Melton v. South–Shore U–Drive, Inc., 32 A.D.2d 950, 303 N.Y.S.2d 751 (2d Dept. 1969)); however, a dog's purchase price is but one—and not necessarily the most important—factor in determining that market value (Blauvelt v. Cleveland, 198 App.Div. 229, 190 N.Y.S. 881 (4th Dept.1921); * * * 1 A.L.R.3d 997 *et seq.*).

"Other relevant factors to be considered, in addition to purchase price, include the dog's age, health, breed, training, usefulness and any special traits or characteristics of value. Sentiment, however, may not be considered since that often is as much a measure of the owner's heart as it is of the dog's worth. Similarly, depreciation is no factor at all; manifestly, a good dog's value increases rather than falls with age and training.

"Accordingly, upon plaintiff's testimony as to this six year old pedigreed dog's $125–$150 purchase price (as to which the parties stipulated), the relatively long life of this breed, the animal's training, usefulness and desirable character traits, the Court finds the dog to have a market value of $200.

"Judgment will be entered, therefore, in favor of plaintiff in the amount of $200, together with costs of this action, and the motion."

3. What if the cost of repair will exceed the diminution in value caused by the injury? *See* Spreader Specialists, Inc. v. Monro, Inc., 114 Idaho 15, 752 P.2d 617, 623 (App.1987):

"[W]e hold that where a plaintiff reasonably undertakes to repair a damaged commercial vehicle, and he does so with the genuine aim of mitigating business losses, he may recover the actual cost of repairs plus the diminution in value of the vehicle as repaired. Such recovery is not defeated by the bare fact that this sum exceeds the difference between the market value of the vehicle before and immediately after the injury. * * * However, in determining the reasonableness of the plaintiff's course of action, the court may consider whether damages actually have been mitigated in light of all the expenses incurred."

See also Hewlett v. Barge Bertie, 418 F.2d 654 (4th Cir.1969), cert. denied sub nom., C.G. Willis, Inc. v. Hewlett, 397 U.S. 1021, 90 S.Ct. 126, 25 L.Ed.2d 531 (1970) (cost of repair to barge awarded even though barge was old and the new dent did not diminish its market value; dissent said the plaintiff was gaining a windfall). *See also* Myers v. Arnold, 83 Ill.App.3d 1, 38 Ill.Dec. 228, 403 N.E.2d 316 (1980) at p. 450, *supra*.

Is it a just result to limit the recovery to the "market value" of an injured pet, so that its owner must absorb part of the costs of treatment? If not, is there a limit on the recoverable costs of treatment? Should there be? Should a recovery exceeding the loss in market value for a damaged commercial truck, but not for a damaged pet, be allowed?

4. Should an award for cost of repairs be reduced to take account of the fact that repairs are made with new materials? *See* Phillips Petroleum Co. v. Stokes Oil Co., Inc., 863 F.2d 1250, 1257–58 (6th Cir.1988) (court awards cost of repairs which are less than fair market value of the terminal even though the repairs are made with new materials; defendant "does not suggest another available option" and did not show that less expensive repairs were possible.) *But see* D. Dobbs, The Law of Remedies 556 (2d ed. 1993) ("When the repairs enhance the value of the damaged property and the measure of damages is the cost of repairs, the general rule is that the defendant's liability for repair costs must be reduced by any enhancement or appreciation in value resulting from the repair.")

5. The traditional measure of recovery for loss of use of a damaged vehicle is defined in Roberts v. Pilot Freight Carriers, Inc., 273 N.C. 600, 609, 160 S.E.2d 712, 718 (1968):

> "Ordinarily the measure of damages for loss of use of a business vehicle is not the profits which the owner would have earned from its use during the time he was deprived of it; it is the cost of renting a similar vehicle during a reasonable period for repairs. Drewes v. Miller, 25 So.2d 820 (La.App.); Annots., Damages to Commercial Vehicle, 169 A.L.R. 1074, 1087–1098 (1947), 4 A.L.R. 1350, 1351–1363 (1919). This limitation is an application of the rule that one who seeks to hold another liable for damages must use reasonable diligence to avoid or mitigate them. * * * Thus, before a plaintiff may recover lost profits resulting from the deprivation of his vehicle, he must show (1) that he made a reasonable effort to obtain a substitute vehicle for the time required to repair or replace the damaged one, and (2) that he was unable to obtain one in the area reasonably related to his business. In the absence of such a showing, he may not recover lost profits. * * * When, however, he has carried the burden of proving that no substitute vehicle could be rented, a plaintiff may recover lost profits if he can establish the amount of the loss with reasonable certainty. * * * If a plaintiff could have rented a substitute vehicle, the cost of hiring it during the time reasonably necessary to acquire a new one or to repair the old one is the measure of his damage even though no other vehicle was rented. The burden is on the plaintiff to establish the cost of such hire. 8 Am.Jur.2d Automobiles and Highway Traffic § 1047 (1963)."

Professor Dobbs has identified four different measures of loss of use damages: "(1) lost profit, (2) cost of renting a substitute chattel, (3) rental value of the plaintiff's own chattel, or (4) interest." 1 D. Dobbs, The Law of Remedies 875 (2d ed. 1993). Which measure was used by the court in *Farmers?* For an excellent discussion of the traditional measures of loss of use, see Brownstein, What's The Use? A Doctrinal and Policy Critique of the Measurement of Loss of Use Damages, 37 Rutgers L.Rev. 433, 436–75 (1985).

6. If personal property is damaged, should the plaintiff be allowed to recover repair costs (not to exceed the diminution in value) plus loss of use? Or should " 'the maximum recovery for a repairable automobile including loss of use * * * not exceed [the fair market] value before the [damage].' " Boral Bricks, Inc. v. Old South Transportation Management, Inc., 198 Ga.App. 678, 402 S.E.2d 777, 778 (1991), *quoting* Firestone Tire Co. v. Jackson Transp. Co., 126 Ga.App. 471, 478, 191 S.E.2d 110, 116 (1972) (emphasis omitted, brackets in original).

Consider the court's holding in Gamble v. Smith, 386 A.2d 692, 695 (D.C.App.1978) (repairable damage to automobile):

> "We also think the trial court is correct in not aggregating the amount of the award for loss of use with the cost of repairs in making its comparison with the diminution in value to decide on which measure of damages to use. No matter which award is proper for the damages actually done to appellee's car, he would not be made whole without recovery for the damages he suffered as a result of being without any vehicle for a period of time reasonably necessary to replace or repair his damaged auto." *See generally* D. Dobbs, Handbook on the Law of Remedies § 5.11, at 383 (1973) (favoring rule in *Gamble*).

7. In noting a split of authority on the issue whether actual pecuniary loss is necessary for recovery of loss of use damages, Judge Dearie of the Eastern District of New York held that such loss was not necessary, but denied plaintiff's motion for partial summary judgment that it was entitled to a reasonable rental value of a Boeing 747 that was damaged in a "fender bender" accident with a truck because there was no actual rental market. He ordered a trial on the issue of how to value the loss of opportunity during the time when the 747 was being repaired, saying:

> "Defendant submits evidence that, because no flights were cancelled and the Airbus had sufficient capacity to seat all passengers who would have flown on the grounded 747, plaintiff suffered no lost profits—and may indeed have benefitted financially—as a result of the 747's grounding. Absent an actual pecuniary loss resulting from the accident, defendant contends, there can be no recovery of damages for loss of use of the jumbo jet.
>
> * * *
>
> "To an airline, ownership of a 747 represents a bundle of valuable opportunities. Those opportunities range from the chance to use the plane to entertain the board of directors and important shareholders, through flying the plane on regularly-scheduled routes, through leasing it to another airline, through holding it in reserve for use as a replacement in case another aircraft must be taken out of service. Those opportunities are all temporarily lost when a tortfeasor renders the aircraft unserviceable for a period of time. That opportunity cost *cannot* be valueless; it *must* be worth something. The difficulty sometimes encountered, of course, is choosing the appropriate method by which to measure that value.
>
> "The plaintiff asks for more, however, than a determination that it is entitled to recover loss of use damages. Plaintiff also seeks a ruling 'that

these damages are to be measured by the reasonable rental value of a substitute aircraft.' To this second requested ruling plaintiff is not entitled.

* * *

"Thus while it is at this time for the Court to determine that plaintiff may recover a reasonable measure of loss of use damages, it would be premature for the Court to hold that any particular measure of damages is the one to be applied."

Kuwait Airways Corp. v. Ogden Allied Aviation Services, 726 F.Supp. 1389, 1390, 1396–97, 1398–99 (E.D.N.Y.1989).

If you represented Kuwait Airways, how would you prove the value?

For a thoughtful critique of the *KLM* case, a case discussed by Judge Dearie that allowed loss of use measured by the fair market rental value of an airplane, although none was rented, see Brownstein, What's The Use? A Doctrinal and Policy Critique of the Measurement of Loss of Use Damages, 37 Rutgers L.Rev. 433, 498–507 (1985). Professor Brownstein recommends that loss of use damages be measured by "awarding interest on the fair market value of the chattel where no substitute is hired and [by awarding] the cost of the substitute where a replacement is rented." *Id.* at 541.

See also D. Dobbs, The Law of Remedies § 5.15(2), at 566–69 (2d ed. 1993).

8. A plaintiff who has sustained harm to personal property is under a general obligation to take reasonable action to limit or mitigate special (consequential) damages. In cases involving claims for loss of use, this translates into a general rule that recovery is limited to the time reasonably necessary to repair (or replace) the damaged property. In special circumstances, however, a plaintiff may be entitled to loss of use damages for a longer period of time than that necessary to make repairs. The courts consider such circumstances as the financial situation of the plaintiff * and the role played by the defendant in contributing to the plaintiff's difficulty in mitigating damages.**

The courts differ as to whether settlement delays will extend the period for loss of use. Consider, for example, Urico v. Parnell Oil Co., 708 F.2d 852, 855–56 (1st Cir.1983):

[The defendant's insurer, B & S, initially agreed with the driver of the damaged truck to settle the claim for the cost of repairs, but the driver did not have settlement authority. The Uricos, owners of the truck, refused to waive their loss of use claim, and B & S refused to pay for repairs. The Uricos could not afford the repairs and thus could not retrieve their truck from the repair shop.]

"[T]he jury found that the Uricos were entitled to additional loss of use damages beyond the repair period, because of B & S's unreasonably dilatory settlement tactics.

"The extension of loss of use damages beyond the repair period raises difficult policy questions. Limiting loss of use damages to a reasonable repair period recompenses the plaintiff for a finite period in which the

* McPherson v. Kerr, 195 Mont. 454, 636 P.2d 852 (1981).

** Valencia v. Shell Oil Co., 23 Cal.2d 840, 147 P.2d 558 (1944); Persinger v. Lucas, 512 N.E.2d 865, 869 (Ind.App.1987).

vehicle is simply unavailable for use. An award of loss of use damages after the vehicle has been repaired, however, is potentially boundless. Anticipation of such an award could conceivably reduce any incentive that a plaintiff might have to mitigate losses. The evidence here, however, relieves us of these theoretical concerns. The Uricos, despite their good faith best efforts, could not mitigate their losses without possession of the repaired truck. B & S knew this. Nonetheless, B & S refused to issue payment for the repairs, despite the fact that they had previously done so to an unauthorized party.

"Arbitrary conduct by an insurer, which serves to prolong rather than contain the interval of loss, is an appropriate circumstance for awarding damages beyond the traditional reasonable repair period. In Valencia v. Shell Oil Co., 23 Cal.2d 840, 147 P.2d 558 (1944), defendant initially promised to pay for repairs to a truck damaged in a collision with plaintiff. Repairs were undertaken in reliance on this promise. After the repairs were completed, defendant refused to pay unless plaintiff agreed to waive all other claims. In *Valencia,* the Supreme Court of California held that where plaintiff was financially incapable of paying for the repairs, and defendant's refusal to pay caused additional losses, plaintiff could recover loss of use damages for an extended period. *Id.* 147 P.2d at 561. The application of that theory in no way diminishes the traditional requirement that plaintiffs may not recover for damages which could have been avoided by their reasonable efforts to mitigate." *

Contrast *Urico* with Airborne, Inc. v. Denver Air Center, Inc., 832 P.2d 1086, 1089–90 (Colo.App.1992):

"In a very few limited circumstances, courts have ruled that financial inability to pay, *in combination with other factors,* has been one relevant factor in determining the reasonableness of the length of time necessary for repair. *See* Urico v. Parnell Oil Co., supra (relevant where arbitrary conduct of insurer wrongfully delayed or interfered with repairs which were begun); *see also* Valencia v. Shell Oil Co., 23 Cal.2d 840, 147 P.2d 558 (1944) (defendant promised but failed to pay for repairs and plaintiff was financially unable to do so).

"Other courts have refused to consider financial inability to pay. *See* Prothro v. Dillahunty, 488 So.2d 1163 (La.Ct.App.1986) (the fact that finances are not available to replace destroyed property cannot be used to extend the time for recovery of damages for loss of use).

"Under the circumstances presented here, we conclude as a matter of law that no extension of time was warranted. Although Denver Air refused to pay for repairs on the aircraft and Airborne claimed it lacked funds to make the repairs, Airborne presented no evidence that Denver Air 'wrongfully prolonged' any repair process. Contrary to Airborne's assertion, Denver Air's refusal to admit liability and pay for repairs does not in itself constitute a 'wrongful delay or interference with the repair process.' *Cf.* Urico v. Parnell Oil Co., supra (although liability was uncontested and

* In *Urico,* the court allowed the jury to consider projected lost profits (based on the record of plaintiff's past earnings) in assessing loss of use damages. The evidence established that the fair rental value of a replacement truck would have been substantially less than Urico's lost profits. *Id.* at 856.

insurer had agreed to pay for repairs, insurer then refused to make payments unless plaintiff waived all other claims).

"Thus, we conclude as a matter of law that no extension of time was warranted and that Airborne's damages for loss of use are limited to the three-month period which the trial court found was reasonably necessary to complete repair."

See also Badillo v. Hill, 570 So.2d 1067, 1069 (Fla.App. 5 Dist.1990):

"A breakdown in settlement negotiations with the defendant or his insurer, regardless of who is at fault, is not relevant to expand the time frame. * * * The rationale for this view is that once the courts start to consider subjective peculiar circumstances beyond the fact of injury, it would make the rule of law difficult to apply and could open the door to the possibility of considerable abuse.

"It appears to us that the better view is to adhere to the more 'objective' rather than the 'subjective' approach. If the evidence sustained a finding that the defendant caused or contributed to the delay in making repairs, a greater time could be awarded. But that is not the situation presented in this case."

Which approach do you agree with? What remedial goals are met in each approach?

B. SPECIFIC RELIEF—LEGAL OR EQUITABLE REPLEVIN

The traditional common law remedies for the wrongful detention of chattels included detinue, trover (or conversion), and replevin. In a detinue action, the plaintiff could obtain either the market value of a wrongfully detained chattel or the chattel itself, at the option of the defendant. As discussed in the preceding section, under trover the plaintiff could recover the market value of an unlawfully appropriated chattel, but not the chattel itself. In a traditional common law replevin action, the plaintiff could recapture a wrongfully taken chattel, but only after posting a bond for its value. Typically, however, a defendant could retain possession by also posting a bond. *See* W. Walsh, Equity § 60 (1930). Today, most states have enacted claim and delivery or replevin statutes that incorporate and modify the common law remedies. *E.g.,* Brook v. James A. Cullimore & Co., 436 P.2d 32 (Okl.1967); Note, Reconciliation of Damage Awards for Conversion, Replevin, and Destruction of Personalty, 34 Okla.L.Rev. 653 (1981). *See generally* D. Dobbs, The Law of Remedies § 5.17 (2d ed. 1993).

In order to recover a chattel in a replevin action, the plaintiff must have an immediate right to possession of it and that right must be superior to that of the defendant. *See* Dubied Machinery Co. v. Vermont Knitting Co., Inc., 739 F.Supp. 867, 872 (S.D.N.Y.1990). In the following cases consider the difference between legal and equitable replevin.

MODERN DUST BAG CO., INC. v. COMMERCIAL TRUST CO.

Court of Chancery of Delaware, 1952.
33 Del.Ch. 208, 91 A.2d 469.

BRAMHALL, VICE CHANCELLOR. Upon petition to this court by plaintiff a rule was issued upon the defendant to show cause why this court should not issue an order upon defendant to deliver to plaintiff certain warehouse receipts held by defendant upon payment into court by the plaintiff of such sum as the court might fix as security for the payment of defendant's claim against the plaintiff, in the event that the defendant should prevail in this action.

The warehouse receipts represent certain paper belonging to plaintiff, of a special kind and quality required by the plaintiff in the conduct of its business and is not available for purchase by reason of the fact that the concern from whom plaintiff originally purchased the paper is now in bankruptcy and the particular kind and quality of paper represented by the warehouse receipts cannot be purchased elsewhere. The plaintiff has been using this particular type of paper in the manufacture of certain articles, in which a continuity of product is required. Since it will be necessary for plaintiff shortly to begin to use another kind of paper in the manufacture of its products, plaintiff cannot then use the paper represented by the warehouse receipts, in which event it will be of no value to plaintiff and have little or no market value.

The situation is a novel one, since there is no reported decision in this state in which the precise situation and the relief here sought is involved. However, where the circumstances of a case are such as to require the application of equitable principles, the fact that no precedent can be found in which relief may be granted under a similar state of facts is no reason for refusing relief. * * *

Plaintiff does not have an adequate remedy at law. An action for the value of the paper would not give plaintiff complete relief since plaintiff is not in a position to purchase the paper in question on the market or elsewhere. Plaintiff's damage, therefore, cannot be definitely determined. Under the practice in this state in an action in replevin defendant would be entitled to retain possession of the paper by posting the required bond. I know of no adequate remedy at law under which the plaintiff might proceed. Plaintiff is therefore entitled to equitable relief.

There is an unreported opinion in this state in which similar relief was granted under like circumstances. In the case of Wilmington Provision Company v. Sinskey, in New Castle County, being Civil Action No. 47, the Chancellor granted relief from the lien of a judgment upon the deposit of cash equivalent to the amount of the judgment prior to a trial to determine the validity of the judgment. While the Sinskey case involved the lien of a judgment against real estate, whereas the present case involves the right of the defendant to hold the personal property as security for an indebtedness alleged to be due, the situation is otherwise similar. Both cases involved claims for the recovery of money. Both relate to the validity of a lien. In both cases immediate need for relief was shown.

In the case of Price v. Gordon, 129 Fla. 715, 177 So. 276, 279, complainants after leasing a house and taking possession thereof found it unfit for habitation and notified defendant that they would not be bound by the terms of the lease. Upon subsequently returning to the house for their personal belongings they were refused permission to remove them. In an action for a mandatory preliminary injunction to compel defendants to return the personal property to complainants, the Chancellor directed the delivery of the personal belongings to the complainants forthwith upon posting of a bond by complainants in a sufficient amount to protect defendants. In affirming upon appeal the supreme court of Florida said:

> "Under the facts alleged in the bill of complaint and shown by affidavits in support thereof, the showing was adequate that the complainants could not have full, complete and adequate relief in a court of law and that a more ample and appropriate remedy would be afforded by resort to equity. A sick person's medicines and a person's entire supply of wearing apparel, except that which they may have on their person at the time the other is taken from their possession, are not things that may be taken from one without authority of law and he, or she, be required to await the slow process of replevin or other law procedure, to regain possession of same. The necessity for the use of such articles is immediate and continuing. It is not a sufficient answer that such persons so deprived of the possession of such articles may go into the marts of trade and buy more and resupply themselves with the same class of articles which have been wrongfully taken from their possession. Although by doing so and awaiting process of a court of law, such person might have ultimate and complete remedy, that remedy would not be full and adequate as would be the remedy which he may have by proceeding in equity, as was done in this case."

Defendant does not of course claim title to the paper. It is merely trying to impress thereon its lien for an unpaid balance which may or may not hereafter be determined to be due it by plaintiff. Defendant will suffer no injury by the substitution of cash for the security of the warehouse receipts. In fact, it would seem that defendant's position relative to the security offered for the payment of defendant's claim would be definitely improved. In view of the fact that the paper will shortly be of no value at all to the plaintiff, to permit the defendant to retain the warehouse receipts as security for the disputed claim of defendant, pending the determination of this dispute, would cause the plaintiff to sustain irreparable injury and would be of little or no benefit to defendant. I conclude that equity has jurisdiction and that the prayer of the petition should be granted.*

GINDIN v. SILVER

Supreme Court of Pennsylvania, 1968.
430 Pa. 409, 243 A.2d 354.

COHEN, JUSTICE. This is an appeal from a decree in equity ordering appellant to return an engagement ring given her by appellee in contemplation of their marriage. At the time of the gift, as well as at the time of the institution of the present action, appellant was a minor.

The first question presented for our determination is whether or not appellee is barred from recovering the engagement ring either in an action at law or in equity because the donee of the ring was a minor at the time of the gift. * * * [H]ad this action been instituted by way of replevin

* This case is discussed in Note, 41 Geo. L.J. 266 (1953).

proceedings, recovery of the ring would have been proper assuming the donee still had possession of the ring. * * * [T]he law in this Commonwealth as well as in most jurisdictions denies recovery only in the event that the donee in good faith had already disposed of the property. *See* 24 A.L.R.2d 599.

On the issue of whether equity has the power to afford the relief requested, i.e., the return of the ring, appellant urges that if any cause of action exists under these facts and circumstances, it is not in equity because appellee has an adequate remedy at law. * * * Appellee seeks to justify resort to equity on three independent grounds: (1) that the diamond engagement ring is so unique and unusual it cannot easily or readily be obtained elsewhere; (2) it has a great deal of sentimental value; and (3) if replevin proceedings had not been instituted in the first instance, appellant could have entered a bond, sold or otherwise disposed of the ring and hence have relegated appellee to an action for damages on the bond, which right to recover would be barred because of the defense of infancy.

None of these grounds support appellee's position. The relief requested here is the recovery of the engagement ring which recovery as previously determined may be had in an action at law (replevin). Assuming arguendo that the ring has unusual characteristics and a certain degree of sentimentality, this does not justify the intrusion of equity when the identical relief prayed for can be obtained by way of an action of replevin. If appellant still possessed the ring, recovery would be permitted in replevin only, but if the ring had been disposed of no relief could be afforded either in assumpsit or replevin, since infancy would be a good defense in any action seeking a money judgment for the value of the ring. However, in no event would equity be proper since an adequate remedy at law exists to obtain the return of the ring. It is obvious that appellee would not have suffered any harm had he instituted an action of replevin initially.

The third ground asserted in support of equity likewise is spurious. It cannot be said that the law would ignore substance in favor of form in a situation where the minor by the simple expedient of posting a bond and disposing of the ring after the institution of replevin proceedings, would avoid the obligation of returning the ring. Since we are certain that the law would not sanction such conduct and would undoubtedly view this as nothing less than a fraud perpetrated on the court, such possible actions on the part of appellant should not and will not serve to form the basis for the intrusion of equity where an adequate remedy at law otherwise exists.

Moreover, our rules of civil procedure with respect to actions of replevin provide adequate protections and safeguards to eliminate the possibility of this type of conduct on the part of any defendant in a replevin proceeding. *See* Pa.R.C.P. 1073, and 1076, 12 P.S.Appendix, and in particular Rule 1079 wherein the court shall under appropriate circumstances order the property involved to be impounded pending a determination as to the right of possession.

Decree reversed and case dismissed for want of equity. Each party to bear own costs.

ROBERTS, J., concurs in the result.

BELL, C.J., and MUSMANNO and JONES, JJ., dissent.

BOARD OF COMMISSIONERS OF RANDOLPH COUNTY v. FAIRCLOTH

Supreme Court of Georgia, 1976.
237 Ga. 136, 227 S.E.2d 35.

NICHOLS, CHIEF JUSTICE.

Randolph County, by and through its Board of Commissioners, brought a suit in equity asking for the return of a county automobile being held by T.E. Faircloth, Randolph County Sheriff. The automobile was purchased by the county through a jointly funded program with the Law Enforcement Assistance Administration. * * * The county was permitted to expend funds received under the grant for equipment designed to improve and strengthen law enforcement and criminal justice, including activities pertaining to crime prevention.

The automobile in question was part of the equipment purchased by the appellant with such funds and was titled solely in the name of the county. The automobile was placed in the sheriff's possession to be used as a special investigator's car. In August, 1975 the County Commission voted unanimously to discontinue the special investigator's position in Randolph County, which position was also jointly funded with Law Enforcement Assistance Administration funds. Upon termination of the program, the County Commissioners made demand upon the sheriff for return of the county-owned automobile. The demand was not complied with and thereafter, the present complaint seeking a mandatory order directing the sheriff to turn over the automobile and for a restraining order forbidding the sheriff to use the said automobile was filed. The case was heard and the court entered an order that the county had an adequate remedy at law and therefore could not seek equitable relief. The court dissolved a temporary restraining order prohibiting the sheriff from using the automobile.

The trial court has made no adjudication upon the merits of the county's claim to the automobile and such question will not be passed upon in this court. The sole issues presented relate to whether or not an action in equity would lie and whether or not the trial court erred in dissolving the temporary restraining order and in failing to grant the temporary injunction.

> " 'A remedy at law, to exclude appropriate relief in equity, must be complete and the substantial equivalent of the equitable relief. It is not enough that there is a remedy at law. It must be plain and adequate, or, in other words, as practical and as efficient to the ends of justice and its prompt administration as the remedy in equity.' Atlantic C.L.R. Co. v. Gunn, 185 Ga. 108, 110, 194 S.E. 365, 367; Davis v. Logan, 206 Ga. 524, 526(4), 57 S.E.2d 568, and cases cited." Ward v. Walker, 222 Ga. 451, 453, 151 S.E.2d 228, 230 (1966).

The complaint in this case was not merely to obtain the alleged county-owned vehicle but to prevent its further use and depreciation by the defendant, as well as to obtain its use for other county purposes to which it could legally be put. The judgment of the trial court dissolving the temporary restraining order and refusing to enter a temporary injunction upon the ground that the appellant could not seek the aid of equity to recover such property must be reversed.

Judgment reversed.

Notes

1. Why was the legal remedy inadequate in *Faircloth?* Compare Charles Simkin & Sons, Inc. v. Massiah, 289 F.2d 26 (3d Cir.1961), in which a subcontractor sought to enjoin a contractor's use of the subcontractor's tools and equipment to complete cement work that the subcontractor had agreed to do, but had refused to complete following a dispute regarding the terms of the contract:

> "The district court denied defendant's petition for an injunction against plaintiff's continued possession and use of defendant's equipment and tools. We agree with the district court's conclusion.
>
> "The relief sought by the defendant is in the nature of equitable replevin. The basis for invoking this type of relief is well-settled:
>
>> '* * * A court of equity may compel the delivery of a specific chattel wrongfully withheld, notwithstanding replevin or trover may lie therefor, but only in cases where damages would be an inadequate redress for the injury, for instance, as in the case of heirlooms, and other articles incapable of being replaced, which are prized for their associations rather than for intrinsic value.'
>
> "To support the assertion that the tools and equipment are a proper subject for equitable relief, the defendant has cited several cases. In no way do they support his position. In all of them the chattels involved were 'unique' and could not be replaced by purchase on the open market. *E.g.*, Coven v. First Savings and Loan Ass'n, Ch. 1947, 141 N.J.Eq. 1, 55 A.2d 244 (an attorney's title plant); Redmond v. New Jersey Historical Society, E. & A.1942, 132 N.J.Eq. 464, 28 A.2d 189 (Stuart's portrait of Captain Lawrence); Burr v. Bloomsburg, Ch. 1927, 101 N.J.Eq. 615, 138 A. 876 (a family heirloom). * * *
>
> "In this appeal, the tools and equipment are not 'unique' but are standard-made and readily available on the open market. Items such as electric fans, electric drills, shovels, boots, wheelbarrows, rakes, scrapers, wire cutters, etc., are not within the category of personalty which affords a proper basis to invoke the remedy of equitable replevin." [1]

1. In his brief the defendant argues: "But * * * [defendant's] remedy may not be measured by the loss of wheelbarrows and concrete mixers. It is the sum total of what was taken, embracing as it did the defendant's entire working tools and equipment, that lends significance and invokes the remedy."

This misconceives the theory that invokes equitable remedies in the case of chattels. *It is not a quantitative evaluation.* The reason for the granting of equitable relief is the inadequacy of the remedy at law. "Such a case is established, where a chattel * * * is unique, or not purchasable in the market." Williston on Contracts § 1419, p. 3954 (Rev. ed. 1937). "The equitable jurisdiction in these cases really rests upon the fact that the only relief which the plaintiff can have is possession of the *identical* thing, and this remedy cannot *with certainty* be obtained by any common-law action." Pomeroy, Equity Jurisprudence § 185, at 265–66 (5th ed. 1941).

2. As we saw in the previous section on destroyed, converted or damaged goods, the modern view is to award loss of use damages in all situations although not all courts follow the modern view. It has always been held that loss of use damages are appropriate in replevin actions, even if such damages would not be awarded in a conversion action for the same wrongful taking, because in a replevin suit the plaintiff seeks the return of the property and continues to want its use rather than its value. *See, e.g.,* Foresight Enterprises, Inc. v. Leisure Time Properties, Inc., 466 So.2d 283, 286 (Fla.App.1985) ("It is well established in Florida that in a statutory replevin suit, a party may recover not only the object sought to be replevied, but also damages for the loss of its use. This is in contrast to a suit for conversion where recovery is limited to the value of the object at the time of taking or destruction, plus interest at the legal rate.")

3. Punitive damages are recoverable in legal replevin.* Are they also recoverable in an action for equitable replevin? *See infra* Chapter 9, Section 2.

4. The essence of the remedy of equitable replevin is "compulsion upon the defendant to deliver the chattel in specie when it has been demonstrated that the plaintiff has a special need therefor." Van Hecke, Equitable Replevin, 33 N.C.L.Rev. 57, 79 (1954). At the pre-trial stage an equity court has at least two alternatives. First, upon plaintiff's posting a suitable injunction bond, the court may utilize an interlocutory, mandatory injunction to compel the delivery of the chattel to plaintiff pending a trial on the merits. On the other hand, it could simply issue a temporary prohibitive injunction prohibiting defendant from alienating, selling, harming or in any other way disposing of the chattel pending the trial on the merits. These temporary injunctions normally will entail some type of an abbreviated adversary hearing. Ultimately there will be a final hearing on the merits. If the court finds for the defendant, the chattel will be returned to defendant, or the temporary prohibitive injunction will be dissolved. If the decision is in plaintiff's favor, a final order will be entered ordering the defendant to deliver the chattel to plaintiff. In any event, it is important to note that at all stages of the proceedings, equitable replevin is in personam and entails the use of the contempt power to insure the ultimate delivery and safety of the chattel.

On the surface, modern replevin statutes would seem to constitute a completely adequate legal remedy to plaintiffs even in situations involving unique chattels. Since the defendant loses possession pending trial, the plaintiff, in theory, is assured of obtaining the chattel in specie. However, there are two complicating factors. First, as previously mentioned, most statutes permit the defendant to regain possession of the chattel pending trial by rebonding. Secondly, it is not clear under many state statutes that court orders for delivery of the chattel, either pretrial or after final judgment, are enforceable under the contempt power.** Thus it would appear to be possible in some states for a defendant in such a situation to secrete, alienate, or destroy a chattel and ultimately be answerable only in money damages. As a consequence, resort to equity may still be a necessity. Other states, however, including California, Oklahoma, Kansas, Arkansas, and Texas, may have rendered resort to equity unnecessary because they have incorporated into their statutory procedures the use of the contempt power to compel the defendant to deliver the chattels in

* Harris v. Dixon Cadillac Co., 132 Cal. App.3d 485, 183 Cal.Rptr. 299 (1982).

** *E.g.,* Missouri Rules of Civil Procedure, Rule 99 (1986).

specie. *See* Van Hecke, Equitable Replevin, 33 N.C.L.Rev. 57, 79 (1954). For a discussion of the California statute, *see* pp. 426–429, *infra* of this section.

5. Professor Margaret Radin provides a philosophical justification for equitable replevin:

> "The Calabresi–Melamed distinction between protecting entitlements with 'property rules' or 'liability rules' is now a widely recognized tool of economic analysis.[93] An entitlement is protected by a property rule if *B* can obtain it from *A* only by paying whatever price *A* sets as a willing seller, or if *A* can obtain an injunction to prevent *B* 's interference. An entitlement is protected by a liability rule if *B* can obtain it from *A* by paying some extrinsically determined price (such as the "market" price), even if *A* is not a willing seller, or if *A* can obtain only damages on account of *B* 's interference. * * *
>
> * * *
>
> "I am interested in developing a non-utilitarian, moral theory which would provide an alternative explanation for the observed hierarchy of protection, as well as help us to critique it where it goes wrong. It should be possible to give moral reasons why some claims are or should be subject to greater protection (either inalienability or property rules) than others (either liability rules or no entitlement), either as between individuals or between individuals and the government. * * *
>
> "C. The Personhood Dichotomy
>
> "The personhood dichotomy comes about in the following way: A general justification of property entitlements in terms of their relationship to personhood could hold that the rights that come within the general justification form a continuum from fungible to personal. It then might hold that those rights near one end of the continuum—fungible property rights—can be overridden in some cases in which those near the other—personal property rights—cannot be. This is to argue not that fungible property rights are unrelated to personhood, but simply that distinctions are sometimes warranted depending upon the character or strength of the connection. Thus, the personhood perspective generates a hierarchy of entitlements: The more closely connected with personhood, the stronger the entitlement. * * *
>
> "Since the personhood perspective depends partly on the subjective nature of the relationships between person and thing, it makes more sense to think of a continuum that ranges from a thing indispensable to someone's being to a thing wholly interchangeable with money. Many relationships between persons and things will fall somewhere in the middle of this continuum. Perhaps the entrepreneur factory owner has ownership of a particular factory and its machines bound up with her being to some degree. If a dichotomy telescoping this continuum to two end points is to be useful, it must be because within a given social context certain types of person-thing relationships are understood to fall close to one end or the other of the continuum, so that decisionmakers within that social context can use the dichotomy as a guide to determine which property is worthier of protection. For example, in our social context a house that is owned by

93. Calabresi & Melamed, Property Rules, Liability Rules, and Inalienability: One View of the Cathedral, 85 Harv.L.Rev. 1089 (1972).

someone who resides there is generally understood to be toward the personal end of the continuum. * * *

"The same claim can change from fungible to personal depending on who holds it. The wedding ring is fungible to the artisan who made it and now holds it for exchange even though it is property resting on the artisan's own labor. Conversely, the same item can change from fungible to personal over time without changing hands. People and things become intertwined gradually.

"The Calabresi–Melamed distinction between property rules and liability rules is initially positivist; it merely recognizes that some entitlements are harder to extinguish than others. In order to make it take on a moral function, there would be a nice simplicity in hypothesizing that personal property should be protected by property rules and that fungible property should be protected by liability rules. If that were true, much that is now protected by a property rule—for example, property held only for investment—is overprotected. In that respect, the claim would be truly revolutionary. Yet it would not be revolutionary enough for those who think fungible property should not always be protected even by liability rules—for example, when fungible claims of the rich deprive the poor of meaningful opportunities for personhood. But although the problem does not reduce to such nice simplicity, one might claim that *at least* personal property should be protected by property rules."

Radin, Property and Personhood, 34 Stan.L.Rev. 957, 984–88 (1982).*

HOCK IT TO ME PAUN, INC. v. PARKER

District Court of Appeal of Florida, Fifth District, 1992.
591 So.2d 1145.

HARRIS, JUDGE.

Dennis and Georgia Parker were in the process of purchasing 45% of the stock of Hock It To Me Paun, Inc. from Judy and Armand Savoie when a dispute arose. To protect their interest under the stock purchase agreement, the Parkers confiscated jewelry belonging to the corporation.

In the replevin action that followed, the court found that the jewelry did in fact belong to the corporation and required its return upon the posting of a $50,000 replevin bond.

The court, in the order establishing the bond, also required that the corporation "control the sale of the jewelry by maintaining records which show which item of jewelry was sold, when it was sold and for what amount it was sold and the form of payment received."

The bond was posted [1] and the corporation regained possession of its property. Ultimately the corporation went out of business and it was

1. The bond was titled "replevin bond" and provided:

The condition of this bond is that an affidavit has been duly made in this action that the said defendant wrongfully detains from said plaintiff certain personal property as contained in the complaint filed with the court and from which the value of this bond is set, said plaintiff claims the imme-

determined that the records required by the court had not been properly maintained. As punishment for noncompliance with its previous order, the court forfeited the replevin bond to the Parkers. We reverse.

The Parkers concede that the property redelivered under the replevin bond did in fact belong to the corporation. Thus we do not have a wrongful replevin claim. Although the court has various methods to enforce its orders, including contempt, improperly forfeiting a replevin bond is not one. In addition, since the Parkers had made only a small portion of the substantial purchase price for their stock, there is nothing in the record which indicates that their damages even approach the bond forfeiture amount.

Reversed and Remanded for further proceedings consistent herewith.

Note

What did Hock It To Me have to do to replevy the jewelry? Was the requirement of record keeping part of the replevin action? What was the purpose of the replevin bond? Why was its forfeiture inappropriate? What was the appropriate remedy? Why?

SEARLES v. FIRST NAT'L BANK OF ARIZONA

Court of Appeals of Arizona, 1980.
127 Ariz. 240, 619 P.2d 749.

OGG, CHIEF JUDGE.

In this appeal we must determine if A.R.S. § 12–2402(A)(2) [ex parte prejudgment seizure statute] is constitutional as drafted and as applied to the facts of this case.

In October of 1976, the First National Bank of Arizona filed a Complaint and Application for Issuance of Provisional Remedy in the Maricopa County Superior Court. The Bank sought recovery of the amounts due and owing under the terms of a security agreement executed by appellants and assigned to the Bank at the time appellants purchased a mobile home. The Bank also sought immediate possession of the mobile home under the terms of the Security Agreement and pursuant to the provisions of A.R.S. § 12–2402.

The trial judge issued an Order for Provisional Remedy Without Notice in the nature of replevin on October 8, 1976. According to the Searles affidavit, the Searles were served with the complaint, summons and other pleadings on October 26, 1976. The deputy sheriff who served the papers advised the Searles that they had no right to a hearing or notice. However, he indicated that while he was supposed to take immediate possession of the mobile home, he would give the Searles two days to vacate the premises. On October 28, 1976, the Searles were informed that the repossession would be delayed until 10:00 a.m. on November 1, 1976.

diate delivery of such property to him as authorized by the statutes. Said property shall be returned to defendant if a return shall be adjudged and payment shall be made to said defendant of such sum as for any cause may be adjudged in his favor then the obligation shall be void; otherwise to remain in full force.

A hearing was held on October 29, 1976 to consider a request by the Searles for a temporary restraining order to prevent eviction and repossession. The trial judge denied the request on November 1, 1976, and the sheriff took possession of the mobile home on November 3, 1976. The Searles then filed an answer which denied liability and counterclaimed for damages suffered as a result of the repossession of the mobile home. On May 13, 1977, the Searles filed a motion for partial summary judgment on their first counterclaim. The Bank filed a cross motion for summary judgment on all issues, which was granted. Judgment against the Searles was entered on September 23, 1977. The Searles appealed the part of the judgment relating to their first counterclaim. The counterclaim challenged the constitutionality of Arizona's Provisional Remedies Statutes and sought damages under 42 U.S.C. § 1983 for deprivation of their due process rights. They characterize the question presented as follows:

> Whether A.R.S. § 12–2402(A)(2), which permits ex parte prejudgment seizures of property upon a showing that the debtor has defaulted on an obligation secured by a purchase money security interest, violates the due process clauses of the Arizona and United States Constitutions on the facts of this case and as a matter of law.

Appellee contends that the Searles lack standing to challenge A.R.S. § 12–2402(A)(2), since they were afforded notice and hearing prior to the seizure of the mobile home. However, the initial order issued was for a provisional remedy *without notice,* and in any event, we note that the hearing before the court on the issue of the constitutionality of the Arizona prejudgment replevin statute did not offer the Searles a "meaningful" opportunity to be heard on the issue of *their liability.* Bell v. Burson, 402 U.S. 535, 91 S.Ct. 1586, 29 L.Ed.2d 90 (1971). We therefore conclude that the appellants do have standing to challenge A.R.S. § 12–2402(A)(2).

Appellants argue that A.R.S. § 12–2402(A)(2), as written, violates the due process clause of the 14th Amendment to the Constitution of the United States and Art. II, § 4 of the Arizona Constitution. Article II, § 4 of the Arizona Constitution provides:

> No person shall be deprived of life, liberty, or property without due process of law.

This section is the corollary to the first clause of the 14th Amendment of the United States Constitution.

Appellants rely upon Mitchell v. W.T. Grant Co., 416 U.S. 600, 94 S.Ct. 1895, 40 L.Ed.2d 406 (1974). Appellants contend that *Mitchell* requires extraordinary circumstances as a precondition to a prejudgment seizure. Appellants further contend that the bank has failed to establish the existence of such extraordinary circumstances. However, a review of the relevant United States Supreme Court opinions indicates that an extraordinary situation is not a prerequisite for prejudgment seizure of collateral in which a secured creditor has a purchase money security interest. The salient factors discussed in the Supreme Court opinions also indicate that the pertinent Arizona statutes are constitutional as drafted and as applied in the instant case.

The procedural due process standards governing prejudgment remedies have been in flux since the decision in Sniadach v. Family Finance Corp., 395 U.S. 337, 89 S.Ct. 1820, 23 L.Ed.2d 349 (1969). *Sniadach* was followed by Fuentes v. Shevin, 407 U.S. 67, 92 S.Ct. 1983, 32 L.Ed.2d 556 (1972), *Mitchell v. W.T. Grant Co.,* and North Georgia Finishing v. Di–Chem, 419 U.S. 601, 95 S.Ct. 719, 42 L.Ed.2d 751 (1975). While the four decisions are the controlling authority in any analysis of the constitutional validity of provisional remedies, commentators in various jurisdictions have noted that the cases appear unclear and contradictory.[1] Since "[t]he Supreme Court opinions have produced not only varying results, but differing analytical approaches to due process problems", the resulting confusion is understandable. Jonnet v. Dollar Savings Bank of City of New York, 530 F.2d 1123, 1126 (3d Cir.1976).

In *Sniadach,* the Supreme Court held that a Wisconsin prejudgment garnishment procedure which resulted in garnishment of a debtor's wages without notice and without a prior hearing violated due process. The Court characterized wages as "a specialized type of property presenting distinct problems in our economic system." 395 U.S. at 340, 89 S.Ct. at 1822, 23 L.Ed.2d at 353. *Sniadach* led to two divergent lines of cases—"one limiting *Sniadach's* predeprivation notice and hearing rule to wages or property of similar importance to the individual, the other invalidating prejudgment procedures generally." 530 F.2d at 1126. * * *

The Supreme Court subsequently approved the latter line of cases in *Fuentes.* * * *

1. *See* Clarkson, Creditors' Prejudgment Remedies and Due Process of Law—Connecticut's Summary Procedure Summarily Upheld; Fermont Division, Dynamics Corp. of America v. Smith, 12 Conn.L.Rev. 174, 175 n. 5 (1975) which notes that the problems presented by the Supreme Court cases are discussed in numerous articles analyzing legislative changes in other states:

See, e.g., Alabama, Comment, Garnishment in Alabama, 29 Ala.L.Rev. 649 (1978); Arkansas, Nickles, Creditors' Provisional Remedies and Debtors' Due Process Rights: Attachment and Garnishment in Arkansas, 31 Ark.L.Rev. 607 (1978); California, Comment, Attachment in California: Another Round of Creditors' Rights and Debtor Protection, 20 U.C.L.A.L.Rev. 1015 (1973); Connecticut, Levine, Due Process of Law in Pre–Judgment Attachment and the Filing of Mechanics' Liens, 50 Conn.B.J. 335 (1976); Georgia, Comment, Can Georgia Bank on Its Garnishment Laws? 28 Mercer L.Rev. 341 (1976); Iowa, Comment, Prejudgment Seizure and Due Process: A Proposal for an Iowa Provisional Remedies Statute, 63 Iowa L.Rev. 151 (1977); Kansas, Comment, Civil Procedure: Kansas Prejudgment Attachment and the Due Process Clause, 17 Washburn L.J. 163 (1977); New York, Kheel, New York's Amended Attachment Statute: A Prejudgment Remedy in Need of Further Revision, 44 Brooklyn L.Rev. 199 (1978); Oklahoma, TeSelle & Love, Attachment, Garnishment, Replevin, and Self–Help Repossession in Oklahoma, 30 Okla.L.Rev. 253 (1977); Texas, Note, Texas Rules of Civil Procedure 592, 598a, 599, 608: The Constitutionality of the Amended Attachment Rules in Light of Recent Supreme Court Decisions, 19 S.Tex.L.J. 342 (1978); Virginia, Brabham, Sniadach Through Di Chem and Backwards: An Analysis of Virginia's Attachment and Detinue Statutes, 12 U.Rich.L.Rev. 157 (1977).

[end of court's footnote]

See also Note, H.B. 254: Changes in Ohio's Attachment, Replevin and Garnishment Statutes, 8 U.Dayton L.Rev. 407 (1983).

See generally Leubsdorf, Constitutional Civil Procedure, 63 Tex.L.Rev. 579 (1984); Rendleman, Analyzing the Debtor's Due Process Interest, 17 Wm. & Mary L.Rev. 35 (1975).

Fuentes was followed by the *Mitchell* decision, which in the words of Justice Powell's concurring opinion "withdraws significantly from the full reach of [the principle of preseizure hearings]" as enunciated in *Fuentes.* 416 U.S. at 623, 94 S.Ct. at 1908, 40 L.Ed.2d at 423. Numerous commentators also interpreted the decision as a "retreat" or "repossession" of *Fuentes* even though the *Mitchell* opinion stated that "we are convinced that *Fuentes* was decided against a factual and legal background sufficiently different from that now before us and that it does not require the invalidation of the Louisiana sequestration statute, either on its face or as applied in this case." 416 U.S. at 615, 94 S.Ct. at 1904, 40 L.Ed.2d at 418. *See* 31 Ark.L.Rev. 607, 616 n. 36; 12 Conn.L.Rev. 174, 180 n. 50.

* * *

The *Mitchell* decision was followed by *North Georgia Finishing v. Di–Chem,* in which the creditor, Di–Chem, had filed suit against North Georgia Finishing and had garnished the debtor's bank account without providing notice or a hearing. The Court found that Georgia's garnishment statute was unconstitutional and "vulnerable for the same reasons" as those used to invalidate the Pennsylvania and Florida statutes in *Fuentes.* 419 U.S. at 606, 95 S.Ct. at 722, 42 L.Ed.2d at 757. While the *North Georgia* opinion apparently revitalized *Fuentes,* it also indicated that the statute in question had "none of the saving characteristics of the Louisiana statute" considered in *Mitchell.* 419 U.S. at 607, 95 S.Ct. at 722, 42 L.Ed.2d at 757.

The bifurcated reasoning in *North Georgia* has resulted in various attempts at harmonizing the Supreme Court's opinions.[2] However, we conclude that in the instant case, the correct interpretation of *Mitchell*—and for that matter, an application of any of the previously noted theories attempting to harmonize *Sniadach, Fuentes, Mitchell* and *North Georgia*—requires a decision upholding the Arizona Statutes.

For instance, since we are concerned with a purchase money security interest in the instant case, even the least expansive interpretation of *Mitchell*—limiting it to situations involving security interests—indicates that *Mitchell's* reasoning should control in this case. Once it is determined that *Mitchell* is the controlling authority, it is necessary to consider the specific procedural safeguards emphasized in that opinion. The safeguards may be summarized as follows:

2. *See, e.g.,* 17 Washburn L.J. 163, 168 (suggests limiting *Mitchell* to situations in which the creditor has an existing security interest in the property); 31 Ark.L.Rev. 607, 621–23 (suggests *North Georgia* expands *Mitchell's* applicability to some unsecured transactions); 12 Conn.L.Rev. 174, 187–190 (suggests checklist of procedural safeguards or an ad hoc balancing test).

(1) The creditor must furnish "a sufficient bond to protect the vendee against all damages in the event the sequestration is shown to have been improvident."

(2) The creditor's claims of entitlement to possession "must be made to a judge, and the writ will issue only upon his authorization."

(3) The writ "will not issue on the conclusory allegation of ownership or possessory rights."

(4) The debtor is entitled to immediately "seek dissolution of the writ, which must be ordered unless the creditor 'proves the grounds upon which the writ was issued', * * * the existence of the debt, lien, and delinquency, failing which the court may order return of the property and assess damages in favor of the debtor including attorney's fees."

(5) The debtor, with or without moving to dissolve the sequestration, may also regain possession by filing his own bond to protect the creditor against interim damage to him should he ultimately win his case and have judgment against the debtor for the unpaid balance of the purchase price which was the object of the suit and of the sequestration.

416 U.S. at 605–07, 94 S.Ct. at 1899–1900, 40 L.Ed.2d at 412–13.

A review of Arizona's statutes indicates that they incorporate all of the preceding safeguards. For instance, the bond requirement specified in *Mitchell* is met in A.R.S. § 12–1303, which requires delivery of "a bond payable to the defendant, in an amount not less than double the value of the property as stated in the affidavit." Judicial supervision is provided by A.R.S. § 12–2402(A), which requires that "[a]ny provisional remedy may be issued by a judge of any superior or justice court." The party seeking the remedy must also satisfy the third safeguard by "establish[ing] with particularity by affidavit to the court's satisfaction sufficient facts supporting the party's claim." A.R.S. § 12–2402(B). The fourth safeguard is incorporated in A.R.S. § 12–2402(C), which allows the party against whom the provisional remedy will operate to "immediately move to quash such order." The hearing must be held in five days and the creditor must show the "probable validity" of his claim and the "existence of any statutory requirement for the issuance of any provisional remedy sought." The debtor has the opportunity to present any defense to the claim as well as claims of personal property exemptions. If the provisional remedy issued is quashed, A.R.S. § 12–2411 allows the court to "award reasonable attorney's fees to the party against whom the provisional remedy was issued or was sought to be issued." Finally, the fifth safeguard is provided by A.R.S. § 12–1304, which allows the debtor to regain possession by filing "a bond payable to the plaintiff in an amount not less than double the value of the property."

Other jurisdictions have also accepted the *Mitchell* safeguards as the appropriate criteria for determining the validity of statutes similar to Arizona's:

> Since *Mitchell* the lower federal courts, faced with the constitutional issue, have relied generally on the *Mitchell* safeguards for determining the validity of state statutory attachment procedures. In

> Guzman v. Western State Bank of Devils Lake, No. Dak. (8th Cir.1975) 516 F.2d 125, the court found the North Dakota attachment statute unconstitutional for failure to meet *Mitchell* requirements due to the allowance of conclusory affidavits, lack of judicial supervision, and the requirement that the debtor post a bond when challenging the attachment. The court termed the posting of a bond an extreme hardship on the debtor. The Illinois statute was found to lack the *Mitchell* safeguards and declared unconstitutional in Hernandez v. Danaher (N.D.Ill.1975) 405 F.Supp. 757. A similar result was reached in Terranova v. Avco Financial Services of Barre, Inc. (D.C.Vt.1975) 396 F.Supp. 1402, which held unconstitutional the Vermont attachment procedures. The prejudgment attachment statutes of two other states have withstood constitutional attack. The court in each case applied the *Mitchell* standards and found them satisfied. (Matter of Northwest Homes of Chehalis, Inc. [9th Cir.1975] 526 F.2d 505 [Washington attachment statute]; Hutchison v. Bank of North Carolina [M.D.N.C. 1975] 392 F.Supp. 888 [North Carolina attachment statute].)

Hillhouse v. City of Kansas City, 221 Kan. 369, 559 P.2d 1148, 1153 (1977).
* * *

Appellants also contend that the nature of the property involved should be considered. However, following the reasoning in *Mitchell,* we conclude that while the taking of the mobile home might cause a "real impact" on the debtor, "his basic source of income is unimpaired." 416 U.S. at 610, 94 S.Ct. at 1901, 40 L.Ed.2d at 415. We further note that in *North Georgia* the Court stated:

> We are no more inclined now than we have been in the past to distinguish among different kinds of property in applying the Due Process Clause.

419 U.S. at 608, 95 S.Ct. at 723, 42 L.Ed.2d at 758. We therefore conclude that the nature of the property involved is not determinative in the instant case.

Since Arizona's statutory protections correspond with those noted in *Mitchell,* the court's concluding comments are applicable to this case:

> To summarize, the Louisiana system seeks to minimize the risk of error of a wrongful interim possession by the creditor. The system protects the debtor's interest in every conceivable way, except allowing him to have the property to start with, and *this is done in pursuit of what we deem an acceptable arrangement pendente lite* to put the property in the possession of the party who furnishes protection against loss or damage to the other pending trial on the merits.

416 U.S. at 618, 94 S.Ct. at 1905, 40 L.Ed.2d at 420 (emphasis added). Similarly, Justice Powell's concurring remarks in *Mitchell* that "[t]he governmental function in the instant case is to provide a *reasonable* and *fair* framework of rules which facilitate commercial transactions on a credit basis" describes well the Arizona statutes. 416 U.S. at 624–25, 94 S.Ct. at 1908, 40 L.Ed.2d at 423–4 (emphasis added).

We therefore hold that A.R.S. § 12–2402(A)(2) [ex parte prejudgment seizures] does not violate the due process clauses of the United States and the Arizona Constitutions as drafted and as applied.

Notes

1. A later Arizona case, Wallace v. Shields, 175 Ariz. 166, 854 P.2d 1152, 1161–62 (1992), did declare the seizure provisions of the Arizona Native Plants Act unconstitutional. There the Arizona Agriculture and Horticulture Commission sought to seize eight crested saguaro cacti on the ground that they had been stolen although the people possessing the cacti claimed to have purchased them with valid state tags. The Court of Appeals said:

> "We must also disagree with the Commission's view that the procedures provided by the statutes applicable in this case comported with due process. The requirements of procedural due process in this context are reasonably well settled:
>
>> [F]or the requirements of due process to be met, it is necessary that the statute authorizing preliminary relief provide that the relief issue only after there has been an application made under oath alleging personal knowledge of facts which form the basis for prejudgment seizure, and after the application has been approved by a competent officer acting judicially who has found that the requisite showing has been made.
>>
>> Additionally, due process requires that the statute authorizing relief afford the debtor an opportunity for an immediate, or at least a prompt, hearing after seizure....
>
> 16D C.J.S. Constitutional Law § 1145, at 23–24. *See* generally Thornton v. Carson, 111 Ariz. 490, 533 P.2d 657 (1975); Bennett v. Arizona State Bd. of Public Welfare. Due process also requires that, at the post-seizure hearing, the party at whose instance the seizure was made demonstrate at least the probable validity of the claim on which the seizure was founded. *See* Mitchell v. W.T. Grant Co., 416 U.S. 600, 94 S.Ct. 1895, 40 L.Ed.2d 406 (1974); North Georgia Finishing Co. v. Di–Chem, 419 U.S. 601, 95 S.Ct. 719, 42 L.Ed.2d 751 (1975); Jonnet v. Dollar Savings Bank, 530 F.2d 1123 (3d Cir.1976); Searles v. First Nat'l Bank of Arizona, 127 Ariz. 240, 619 P.2d 749 (App.1980). Cf. Connecticut v. Doehr, 501 U.S. 1, ___, 111 S.Ct. 2105, 115 L.Ed.2d 1 (1991) (tacitly reaffirming Mitchell and North Georgia Finishing Co.)
>
> "A.R.S. section 3–931(C) falls short of meeting these requirements. The statute provides no opportunity for a prompt post-seizure hearing at which the Commission is required to demonstrate the probable existence of grounds for the seizure. Moreover, contrary to the Commission's argument, the hearing procedure available under A.R.S. section 13–3922 does not cure the deficiency. Our supreme court has held that, when items have been seized under a search warrant, the individual who challenges the seizure, not the state, has the burden of proof at a hearing under section 13–3922. Greehling v. State, 136 Ariz. 175, 665 P.2d 57 (1983). The seizure and threatened confiscation to which the Wallaces were subjected accordingly violated their due process rights and were therefore illegal and subject to being enjoined. *See* State ex rel. Berger v. Myers, 108 Ariz. at 250, 495 P.2d at 846 (A.R.S. section 12–1802 does not prevent injunction against state official who acts illegally). The trial court erred in dissolving

the temporary restraining order [sought by the Wallaces to enjoin enforcement of the seizure] and dismissing the Wallaces' amended complaint."

2. In Connecticut v. Doehr, 501 U.S. 1, 111 S.Ct. 2105, 115 L.Ed.2d 1 (1991), the Court held that due process had been violated by a statute that permitted an ex parte prejudgment attachment of real estate merely to ensure the availability of assets to satisfy a potential judgment where there was no showing that the property was going to be transferred or encumbered. *See also* United States v. James Daniel Good Real Property, ___ U.S. ___, 114 S.Ct. 492, 126 L.Ed.2d 490 (1993) (due process requires notice and opportunity to be heard, absent exigent circumstances, prior to seizure of real property subject to forfeiture because of use in commission of drug offense).

3. After *Fuentes,* California (like many other jurisdictions) amended its replevin statute to provide for a pre-seizure notice and hearing. As you read the statute, consider its application to the facts in *Searles.*

California Code of Civil Procedure

§ 512.010. Application for Writ—Contents

(a) Upon the filing of the complaint or at any time thereafter, the plaintiff may apply pursuant to this chapter for a writ of possession by filing a written application for the writ with the court in which the action is brought.

(b) The application shall be executed under oath and shall include all of the following:

(1) A showing of the basis of the plaintiff's claim and that the plaintiff is entitled to possession of the property claimed. If the basis of the plaintiff's claim is a written instrument, a copy of the instrument shall be attached.

(2) A showing that the property is wrongfully detained by the defendant, of the manner in which the defendant came into possession of the property, and, according to the best knowledge, information, and belief of the plaintiff, of the reason for the detention.

(3) A particular description of the property and a statement of its value.

§ 512.020. Necessity for Hearing on Noticed Motion for Issuance of Writ—Ex Parte Issuance of Writ

(a) Except as otherwise provided in this section, no writ shall be issued under this chapter except after a hearing on a noticed motion.

(b) A writ of possession may be issued ex parte pursuant to this subdivision if probable cause appears that any of the following conditions exists:

(1) The defendant gained possession of the property by feloniously taking the property from the plaintiff. This subdivision shall not apply where the defendant has fraudulently appropriated property entrusted to him or obtained possession by false or fraudulent representation or pretense or by embezzlement.

(2) The property is a credit card.

(3) The defendant acquired possession of the property in the ordinary course of his trade or business for commercial purposes and:

(i) The property is not necessary for the support of the defendant or his family; and

(ii) There is an immediate danger that the property will become unavailable to levy by reason of being transferred, concealed, or removed from the state or will become substantially impaired in value by acts of destruction or by failure to take care of the property in a reasonable manner; and *

(iii) The ex parte issuance of a writ of possession is necessary to protect the property.

* * * Where a writ of possession has been issued pursuant to this subdivision, a copy of the summons and complaint, a copy of the application and any affidavit in support thereof, and a notice which * * * informs the defendant of his rights under this subdivision shall be served upon the defendant * * *. Any defendant whose property has been taken pursuant to a writ of possession issued under this subdivision may apply for an order that the writ be quashed and any property levied on pursuant to the writ be released. * * * Pending the hearing on the defendant's application, the court may order that delivery pursuant to Section 514.030 of any property previously levied upon be stayed. * * *

§ 512.070. Order for transfer of possession to plaintiff; failure to comply; contempt or arrest

If a writ of possession is issued, the court may also issue an order directing the defendant to transfer possession of the property to the plaintiff. Such order shall contain a notice to the defendant that failure to turn over possession of such property to plaintiff may subject the defendant to being held in contempt of court.

* * *

§ 512.120. Failure of plaintiff to recover judgment; redelivery of property to defendant; liability for damages

If the plaintiff fails to recover judgment in the action, he shall redeliver the property to the defendant and be liable for all damages sustained by the defendant which are proximately caused by operation of the temporary restraining order and preliminary injunction, if any, the levy of the writ of possession, and the loss of possession of the property pursuant to levy of the writ of possession or in compliance with an order issued under Section 512.070.

* * *

§ 513.010. Law governing; application for order; grounds; requirements for ex parte issuance

(a) Except as otherwise provided by this chapter, the provisions * * * of this title relating to the issuance of a temporary restraining order apply. At or after the time he files his application for writ of possession, the plaintiff may

* A defendant who attempts to defeat the court's jurisdiction in a replevin action by transferring the property to a third person before it is seized by the sheriff may be held liable to the plaintiff in damages. Black v. City of Cleveland, 58 Ohio App.2d 29, 387 N.E.2d 1388, 12 Ohio Op.3d 36 (1978).

apply for a temporary restraining order by setting forth in the application a statement of grounds justifying the issuance of such order.

(b) A temporary restraining order may issue ex parte if all of the following are found;

(1) The plaintiff has established the probable validity of his claim to possession of the property.

(2) The plaintiff has provided an undertaking as required by Section 515.010.

(3) The plaintiff has established the probability that there is an immediate danger that the property claimed may become unavailable to levy by reason of being transferred, concealed, or removed or may become substantially impaired in value.

(c) If at the hearing on issuance of the writ of possession the court determines that the plaintiff is not entitled to a writ of possession, the court shall dissolve any temporary restraining order; otherwise, the court may issue a preliminary injunction to remain in effect until the property claimed is seized pursuant to the writ of possession.

§ 513.020. Prohibition of certain acts by defendant

In the discretion of the court, the temporary restraining order may prohibit the defendant from doing any or all of the following:

(a) Transferring any interest in the property by sale, pledge, or grant of security interest, or otherwise disposing of, or encumbering, the property. If the property is farm products held for sale or lease or is inventory, the order may not prohibit the defendant from transferring the property in the ordinary course of business, but the order may impose appropriate restrictions on the disposition of the proceeds from such transfer.

(b) Concealing or otherwise removing the property in such a manner as to make it less available to seizure by the levying officer.

(c) Impairing the value of the property either by acts of destruction or by failure to care for the property in a reasonable manner.

§ 514.030. Custody of seized property; delivery to plaintiff; redelivery to defendant; sale of perishable property

(a) After the levying officer takes possession pursuant to a writ of possession, the levying officer shall keep the property in a secure place. Except as otherwise provided by Section 512.020:

(1) If notice of the filing of an undertaking for redelivery or notice of objection to the plaintiff's undertaking is not received by the levying officer within 10 days after levy of the writ of possession, the levying officer shall deliver the property to plaintiff * * *.

(2) If notice of the filing of an undertaking for redelivery is received by the levying officer within 10 days after levy of the writ of possession and defendant's undertaking is not objected to, the levying officer shall redeliver the property to defendant * * *.

(3) If notice of objection to the plaintiff's undertaking or notice of the filing of an undertaking for redelivery is received within 10 days after levy of the writ of possession and defendant's undertaking is objected to, the

levying officer shall not deliver or redeliver the property until the time provided in Section 515.030.

(b) Notwithstanding subdivision (a), where not otherwise provided by contract and where an undertaking for redelivery has not been filed, upon a showing that the property is perishable or will greatly deteriorate or depreciate in value or for some other reason that the interests of the parties will be best served thereby, the court may order that the property be sold and the proceeds deposited in the court to abide the judgment in the action.

§ 515.010. Plaintiff; necessity prior to issuance of temporary restraining order or writ of possession; requirements

The court shall not issue a temporary restraining order or a writ of possession until the plaintiff has filed with the court an undertaking. The undertaking shall provide that the sureties are bound to the defendant for the return of the property to the defendant, if return of the property is ordered, and for the payment to the defendant of any sum recovered against plaintiff. The undertaking shall be in an amount not less than twice the value of defendant's interest in the property or in a greater amount. The value of the defendant's interest in the property is determined by the market value of the property less the amount due and owing on any conditional sales contract or security agreement and all liens and encumbrances on the property, and such other factors as may be necessary to determine the defendant's interest in the property.

§ 515.020. Defendant; purpose; requirements

(a) The defendant may prevent the plaintiff from taking possession of property pursuant to a writ of possession or regain possession of property so taken by filing with the court in which the action was brought an undertaking in an amount equal to the amount of the plaintiff's undertaking required by Section 515.010. The undertaking shall state that, if the plaintiff recovers judgment on the action, the defendant shall pay all costs awarded to the plaintiff and all damages that the plaintiff may sustain by reason of the loss of possession of the property. The damages recoverable by the plaintiff pursuant to this section shall include all damages proximately caused by the plaintiff's failure to gain or retain possession. * * *

4. Why does a plaintiff need § 513.010 and § 513.020 if plaintiff can get an order for the defendant to restore the property to the plaintiff pursuant to § 512.070? Does the plaintiff have to make any particular showing under § 512.070 to get an order against the defendant enforceable by contempt? Should plaintiff have to make any showing? Has the California replevin statute eliminated the distinction between law and equity? Should it have? *See* D. Laycock, The Death of the Irreparable Injury Rule (1991).

5. Would equitable replevin have been an appropriate remedy for the Capels to have invoked against Hall before he sold their rings to Campins? See *Campins, supra* p. 390. Would the Capels have been entitled to a temporary restraining order under § 513.010 of the California Code of Civil Procedure, quoted in note 1 *supra?* Would *ex parte* legal replevin under California Code of Civil Procedure § 512.020, *supra* p. 426, have been an even more effective remedy against Hall? In answering these questions, consider Sea Rail Truckloads, Inc. v. Pullman, Inc., 131 Cal.App.3d 511, 182 Cal.Rptr. 560 (1982). The plaintiff, a debtor, was attempting to repossess collateral (trailer vans) from its

creditors by means of an ex parte pre-judgment writ of possession under California Code of Civil Procedure § 512.020(b)(3). The court ruled that the trial court had erred in issuing such a writ:

> "The facts do not show *an immediate danger that the property will become unavailable to levy* by reason of being transferred, concealed or removed from the state. At most, the facts show that appellants [the creditors] repossessed the vans and intended at some future time to sell them. The burden was on respondent to show that there was an immediate danger of the vans being transferred, concealed or removed. It failed to meet that burden. Respondent also failed to offer any evidence of an immediate danger that the vans would become substantially impaired in value by acts of destruction or by failure to take care of the property in a reasonable manner. Thus the court could not find that respondent had shown sufficient evidence to comply with subdivision (3)(ii).
>
> "Moreover, respondent offered no evidence that a forced transfer of possession to respondent was necessary to protect the property, as required by subdivision (3)(iii). The less drastic remedy of a temporary restraining order, issued pursuant to Code of Civil Procedure section 513.010, would have sufficed to prevent any sale contemplated by appellants and would have assured that appellants safeguarded the vans. Code of Civil Procedure section 512.020 subdivision (b), permits transfer of possession of property only when less intrusive remedies would be ineffective. Respondent failed to offer any evidence that a temporary restraining order would not have been effective to preserve the status quo and protect the property from harm while the rights of the parties were being adjudicated.
>
> "An ex parte writ of possession is a drastic remedy which is disfavored except in the narrowly drawn, exigent circumstances set forth in this statute. The California Supreme Court stated in Blair v. Pitchess (1971) 5 Cal.3d 258, 96 Cal.Rptr. 42, 486 P.2d 1242, that an ex parte writ of possession can issue only if it is justified by weighty state or creditor interests. The court said that where 'a very real danger may exist that the debtor may abscond with the property or that the property will be destroyed' an ex parte procedure may be constitutional. (At p. 278, 96 Cal.Rptr. 42, 486 P.2d 1242). In the case before us there is no evidence to suggest that appellants would have absconded with the property or that the property would have been destroyed."

Id. at 515–16, 182 Cal.Rptr. at 562–63.

C. RESTITUTION: PERSONAL AND INTANGIBLE PROPERTY INTERESTS

Introductory Comment. The restitution material in Chapter 4 includes a selection of cases which illustrate the use of restitutionary remedies in situations where there has been a tortious interference with one's personal property as a consequence of which the wrongdoer is enriched. Of special interest in this regard are Olewell v. Nye & Nissen Co. (*supra,* p. 303) and Artakovich & Sons, Inc. v. Reliance Trust Co. (*supra,* p. 300). These cases, together with attendant notes, should be re-considered at this point.

The cases which follow focus upon situations where the plaintiff complains of interference with intangible property interests. These claims may be based upon existing contract relationships, the "expectation" of becoming a party to a contract or upon "trade secrets" and similar secret information.

Much of the law of remedies in the intangible property area involves claims to a right in a patent, copyright, trademark or trade name. To a large extent there has been pre-emption of these areas, including the related matter of remedies, by federal law. This is especially true in the areas of patent and copyright protection. The United States Supreme Court has made it clear, however, that state law may still be resorted to for protection based upon the wrongful acquisition and use of "trade secrets", and certain other secret information. These federal statutes in the patent, copyright and trademark areas provide for damages for infringement including the recovery of compensatory damages which may include the plaintiff's lost profits. However, the patent law, unlike that relating to copyright and trademarks, does not provide for restitution damages in the form of recovery of the infringer's profits.

With respect to federal pre-emption in the areas of patent, copyright and trademark law, and related questions concerning protection of trade secrets *see,* I G. Palmer, Law of Restitution, § 2.7 (1978); *see, also,* D. Dobbs, Law of Remedies, § 10.5(3) (2d ed. 1993). Remedies which are available for violating these statutes are discussed in Brown, "Civil Remedies for Intellectual Property Invasions: Themes and Variations," 55 Law & Contem. Prob. 45 (1992). *See,* generally, York, "Extension of Restitutional Remedies in the Tort Field," 4 U.C.A.L.Rev. 499 (1957).

HOFFMAN v. REINKE MANUFACTURING COMPANY, INC.

Supreme Court of Nebraska, 1987.
227 Neb. 66, 416 N.W.2d 216.

* * *

We next observe that although Hoffman originally pled two alternative theories of recovery, express contract or implied contract, during a pretrial conference he relinquished the express contract theory by announcing that "he was basing his theory of recovery upon the general principles of 'quantum meruit.' " We therefore are concerned only with the contract implied in law theory of recovery based on the equitable doctrine that one will not be allowed to profit or enrich oneself unjustly at the expense of another. *Haggard Drilling, Inc. v. Greene,* 195 Neb. 136, 236 N.W.2d 841 (1975). It has been said that where benefits have been received and retained under such circumstances that it would be inequitable and unconscionable to permit the party receiving them to avoid payment therefor, the law requires the party receiving and retaining the benefits to pay their reasonable value. *Haggard Drilling, Inc. v. Greene, supra; Bush v. Kramer,* 185 Neb. 1, 173 N.W.2d 367 (1969).

The facts relevant to the foregoing implied contract theory and the defenses raised by Reinke Manufacturing are that in August of 1968 Hoffman approached Richard Reinke (Reinke), then president of Reinke Manufacturing, about an idea Hoffman had for a corner irrigation system.

As a result, Reinke arranged to meet with Hoffman at the latter's home to discuss the matter.

Prior to this meeting, Hoffman and his brother-in-law had roughly sketched a drawing of the system, the concept of which Hoffman then thought to be original with him, and had the sketch notarized. In essence, the idea involved attaching a swinging arm controlled by a steerable wheel to an irrigation system.

According to Hoffman, Reinke looked the drawings over and said he thought the idea was a good one. Hoffman and Reinke discussed developing the idea and obtaining a patent on it, as well as the employment of Hoffman by Reinke Manufacturing.

As a consequence, Hoffman began working for Reinke Manufacturing that month. Hoffman thought his duties included aiding Reinke in the development of Hoffman's idea. Hoffman worked for Reinke Manufacturing until 1973 or 1974, then worked elsewhere for 9 months and returned to Reinke Manufacturing, where he remained until approximately 1976. However, Reinke never worked with Hoffman to develop the system Hoffman had conceived.

Believing that Reinke Manufacturing was not going to develop his system, Hoffman, unknown to Reinke, took his idea to Valmont Industries sometime during the spring of 1971. Valmont, however, was not interested. Later, Reinke Manufacturing became involved in litigation with Valmont. On March 14, 1981, Reinke asked Hoffman for his cooperation in the Valmont suit and to make copies of Hoffman's original drawings. Hoffman did cooperate with Reinke and gave a deposition in connection with the Valmont suit.

In April 1981 Hoffman became aware through sales literature prepared by Reinke Manufacturing that it was selling a corner irrigation system which utilized a swinging arm and steerable wheels.

This matter comes to us on the sustainment of a motion for summary judgment; thus, we must view the evidence most favorable to Hoffman and give him the benefit of all favorable inferences which may reasonably be drawn from the evidence. *Moseman v. L & P Investment Co.*, 226 Neb. 677, 414 N.W.2d 254 (1987); *Chadd v. Midwest Franchise Corp.*, 226 Neb. 502, 412 N.W.2d 453 (1987).

So viewed, the evidence leads to the conclusion that Reinke Manufacturing developed Hoffman's concept for a corner irrigation system, is selling a system based upon that idea, and is profiting therefrom. Under such circumstances, it would be unjust, inequitable, and unconscionable not to require Reinke Manufacturing to pay Hoffman a reasonable portion of the profits Reinke Manufacturing makes from selling systems conceived by Hoffman. Accordingly, the law implies the existence of a contract requiring Reinke Manufacturing to pay Hoffman a reasonable royalty on each such corner irrigation system it sells.

Reinke Manufacturing asserts, however, that any cause of action Hoffman might have had based upon such an implied contract is time barred. Neb.Rev.Stat. § 25–204 (Reissue 1985) provides that, with an exception not material to this inquiry, civil actions "can only be brought within the following periods, after the cause of action shall have accrued." Neb.Rev.Stat. § 25–206 (Reissue 1985) provides: "An action upon a contract, not in writing, expressed or implied * * * can only be brought within four years." Thus, the cause of action on which Hoffman proceeds must have been instituted within 4 years from the date it accrued. A cause of action "accrues" when the aggrieved party has the right to institute and maintain suit. *Lake v. Piper, Jaffray & Hopwood Inc.,* 219 Neb. 731, 365 N.W.2d 838 (1985). Hoffman acquired the right to institute and maintain this suit when Reinke Manufacturing sold a corner irrigation system, for that is when Reinke Manufacturing began to benefit from Hoffman's idea. So far as the record shows, the sale of the system occurred at the same time Hoffman became aware of the fact, sometime in April of 1981. This suit was first filed on March 9, 1984, and last amended on March 18, 1985. Thus, whether the operative amended petition relates back to March 9, 1984, is immaterial, for the suit was instituted in any event within 4 years from April 1, 1981.

REVERSED [as to the award of summary judgment to the defendant Corporation]. AND REMANDED for Further Proceedings.

* * *

Note

Illustrative of the recent cases in which restitution is found to be an appropriate remedy for misuse of trade secrets and similar interests are: Skinner v. Shirley of Hollywood, 723 F.Supp. 50 (N.D.Ill.1989) (cause alleged in quasi-contract for alleged appropriation of plaintiff's customer list and good will); Ocor Products Corporation v. Walt Disney Productions, Inc., 682 F.Supp. 90 (D.N.H.1988) (quasi-contract cause would lie for misuse of unregistered bag design); G.S. Rasmussen & Associates v. Kalitta Flying Service, Inc., 958 F.2d 896 (9th Cir.1992) (quasi-contract cause will lie for unauthorized use of plaintiff's "Certificate" from the Federal Aviation Authority allowing modification of cargo planes in a designated manner to increase cargo carrying capacity; the procedure and protection in question were not pre-empted by federal copyright or patent law); and Avtec Systems, Inc. v. Peiffer, 805 F.Supp. 1312 (E.D.Va.1992) (constructive trust imposed upon benefits received by former employee and employee's employer for misuse of plaintiff's trade secret).

The Hunter v. Shell Oil case, which is found at p. 328, *supra,* also involves a claim based upon "trade secrets" (in that case information relating to the location of potentially valuable mineral deposits). There, it will be recalled, the court ruled that the plaintiff could treat each transaction involving misuse, separately, for purposes of selecting the most advantageous remedy. This, of course, has very serious implications for a variety of reasons, including, *inter alia,* the amount of damages which may be recovered. See, Note 2, at p. 307, *supra.*

A recent example of the use of the constructive trust remedy in the area of "state secrets" is Snepp v. United States, 444 U.S. 507, 100 S.Ct. 763, 62 L.Ed.2d 704 (1980). There, the Supreme Court held that the Government, as plaintiff, could recover from the defendant what he had received as proceeds of a publication which contained information which the defendant, as an employee of the C.I.A., had agreed not to make public.

DEVELOPERS THREE v. NATIONWIDE INS. CO.

Ohio Court of Appeals, 10 Dist., 1990.
64 Ohio App.3d 794, 582 N.E.2d 1130.

[Plaintiff is a general partnership in which Margulies, Foley and Harris were partners. The partnership owned an option to purchase certain real estate. The defendant, Nationwide Ins. Co., Inc., allegedly wrongfully induced Foley and Harris to sell the option to it in violation of the partnership rights of the firm and the other partner, Margulies. The Trial Court granted a directed verdict to the plaintiffs on the issue of liability, but the jury found that the plaintiffs had failed to prove damage.]

* * *

Before addressing the merits of the parties' arguments, however, we will discuss the cause or causes of action under which plaintiff seeks to recover damages. In the course of directing a verdict in plaintiff's favor on the issue of liability, the trial court stated that "[p]laintiffs', the Developers Three's, cause of action is that Nationwide Development Company wrongfully induced Foley and Harris to breach their fiduciary duties to the Plaintiffs." Plaintiff, in its reply brief, argues that Foley and Harris breached their duty, and that defendants' inducing the breach was "constructively fraudulent," thereby rendering defendants liable as well. Plaintiff cites *Hulett v. Fairbanks* (1883), 40 Ohio St. 233, and *Sterman v. Ziem* (1936), 17 Cal.App.2d 414, 62 P.2d 160, in support. Plaintiff, however, also cites cases in which parties sued for conspiracy or for tortious interference with contract. See *Minarik v. Nagy* (1963), 8 Ohio App.2d 194, 26 O.O.2d 359, 193 N.E.2d 280 (conspiracy); *Reichman v. Drake* (1951), 89 Ohio App. 222, 226, 45 O.O. 444, 446, 100 N.E.2d 533, 536; *Leibovitz v. Central National Bank* (1944), 75 Ohio App. 25, 30 O.O. 288, 60 N.E.2d 727 (tortious interference with contract). Paragraph twenty-two of plaintiff's first amended complaint alleged that defendants "maliciously conspired to interfere with the valuable contractual rights and expectancies of plaintiffs * * *."

Ultimately, we conclude that we can best characterize plaintiff's claim as one for tortious interference, as this court did in the first appeal of this case. See *Developers Three v. Nationwide Ins. Co., supra,* at 5. Section 766 of the Second Restatement of Torts defines "Intentional Interference with Performance of Contract by Third Person" as follows:

"One who intentionally and improperly interferes with the performance of a contract (except a contract to marry) between another and a third person by inducing or otherwise causing the third person not to perform the contract, is subject to liability to the other for the pecuniary loss resulting to the other from the failure of the third person to perform the contract." 4 Restatement of the Law 2d, Torts (1979) 7, Section 766.

See, also, *Donald G. Culp Co. v. Reliable Stores Corp.* (1983), 14 Ohio App.3d 161, 163, 14 OBR 178, 180, 470 N.E.2d 193, 196 (citing Section 766 of the Restatement); *Reichman, supra,* 89 Ohio App. at 226, 45 O.O. at 446, 100 N.E.2d at 536 (citing First Restatement of Torts). A difficulty arising from application of Section 766 to the present case is the fact that the fiduciary duty that partners Foley and Harris allegedly breached did not derive from a specific provision of the partnership agreement but from R.C. 1775.08, which defines an individual partner's scope of authority. Nevertheless, we find that plaintiff's cause of action is sufficiently analogous to the cause of action stated in Section 766 of the Restatement to permit a court to analyze plaintiff's claims under tortious interference with contract principles, since the Restatement's definition of tortious interference substantially encompasses plaintiff's allegations of inducing a breach of a duty.

In regard to the unjust enrichment issue, the Ohio Supreme Court has stated that unjust enrichment occurs when a person "has and retains money and benefits which in justice and equity belong to another." *Hummel v. Hummel* (1938), 133 Ohio St. 520, 528, 11 O.O. 221, 224, 14 N.E.2d 923, 927. However, Ohio courts have apparently not yet addressed the issue of unjust enrichment in tortious interference cases. Similarly, the Restatement of Torts does not mention unjust enrichment in its section on damages for tortious interference. Restatement of Torts, *supra,* at 54, Section 774A. The Restatement of Restitution generally recognizes actions for the recovery of unjust enrichment in cases in which benefits have been tortiously acquired, Restatement of the Law, Restitution (1937) 522, Section 128 *et seq.;* however, the Restatement of Restitution explicitly "takes no position as to a person's duty of restitution to another where the first person has made a profit by tortiously causing a third person to break his contract with the other." Restatement of Restitution, *supra,* at 549, Section 133.

In jurisdictions other than Ohio, several courts have not been as noncommittal as the American Law Institute's Restatements and have permitted an unjust enrichment recovery in a tortious interference action. See, *e.g., Zippertubing Co. v. Teleflex Inc.* (C.A.3, 1985), 757 F.2d 1401, 1411–1412; *Second Natl. Bank v. M. Samuel & Sons, Inc.* (C.A.2, 1926), 12 F.2d 963, 967–968, certiorari denied (1926), 273 U.S. 720, 47 S.Ct. 110, 71 L.Ed. 857; *Colorado Interstate Gas Co. v. Natural Gas Pipeline Co.* (D.Wyo. 1987), 661 F.Supp. 1448, 1478–1479, reversed on other grounds (C.A.10, 1989), 885 F.2d 683, 697; *Federal Sugar Refining Co. v. United States Sugar Equalization Board* (S.D.N.Y.1920), 268 F. 575, 582–583; *National Merchandising Corp. v. Leyden* (1976), 370 Mass. 425, 431–434, 348 N.E.2d 771, 775–776; *Caskie v. Philadelphia Rapid Transit Co.* (1936), 321 Pa. 157, 158–162, 184 A. 17, 18–19. Other courts have not permitted an unjust enrichment recovery. See, *e.g., Marcus, Stowell & Beye Government Securities, Inc. v. Jefferson Investment Corp.* (C.A.5, 1986), 797 F.2d 227, 232; *American Air Filter Co. v. McNichol* (C.A.3, 1975), 527 F.2d 1297, 1300. Cf. *Dorsett Carpet Mills, Inc. v. Whitt Tile & Marble Distributing Co.* (Tenn.1987), 734 S.W.2d 322, 325 ("While we will not rule out the possibility of the use of such a measure in some factual situations, we are of the opinion that generally the lost profit element of damage must be measured by the loss sustained by the plaintiff's business and not by its effect upon defendant's business."). See, generally, Annotation, Recovery Based on Tortfeasor's Profits in Action for Procuring Breach of Contract (1981), 5 A.L.R.4th 1276; Comment, Plaintiff's Measure of Recovery for Tortious Inducement of Breach of Contract—Profits or Losses? (1968), 19 Hastings L.J. 1119, 1120.

The usual justification for awarding a defendant's unjust enrichment to the plaintiff is that "an intending tortfeasor should not be prompted to speculate that his profits might exceed the injured party's losses, thus encouraging commission of the tort." *National Merchandising, supra,* 370 Mass. at 433, 348 N.E.2d at 776. See, also, *Zippertubing, supra,* at 1411. This view is consistent with the Restatement of Restitution's general rules for the measure of recovery in a restitution action:

"Actions for restitution have for their primary purpose taking from the defendant and restoring to the plaintiff something to which the plaintiff is entitled, or if this is not done, causing the defendant to pay the plaintiff an amount which will restore the plaintiff to the position in which he was before the defendant received the benefit. If the value of what was received and what was lost were always equal, there would be no substantial problem as to the amount of recovery, since actions of restitution are not punitive. In fact, however, the plaintiff frequently has lost more than the defendant has gained, and sometimes the defendant has gained more than the plaintiff has lost.

"In such cases the measure of restitution is determined with reference to the tortiousness of the defendant's conduct or the negligence or other fault of one or both of the parties in creating the situation giving rise to the right to restitution. If the defendant was tortious in his acquisition of the benefit he is required to pay for what the other has lost although that is more than the recipient benefited. *If he was consciously tortious in acquiring the benefit, he is also deprived of any profit derived from his subsequent dealing with it.* If he was no more at fault than the claimant, he is not required to pay for losses in excess of benefit received by him and he is permitted to retain gains which result from his dealing with the property." (Emphasis added.) Restatement of the Law, Restitution (1937) 595–596, Introductory Note to Section 150 *et seq.*

See, also, *Olwell v. Nye & Nissen Co.* (1946), 26 Wash.2d 282, 286–287, 173 P.2d 652, 654 (quoting the Restatement). In contrast, the courts opposing a recovery of a defendant's profits emphasize the fact that "[t]o compel defendant to disgorge [its] profits could give plaintiff a windfall and penalize the defendant. * * *" *American Air Filter, supra,* at 1300. See, also, *Marcus, Stowell & Beye Government Securities, supra,* at 232.

Both arguments have merit. We recognize the incongruity of a court labeling a defendant's conduct as wrongful and yet permitting the defendant "to retain some part of his ill gotten gains." *National Merchandising, supra,* 370 Mass. at 433, 348 N.E.2d at 776. On the other hand, there is also something incongruous about putting a plaintiff in a better position than if no tort had been committed, since "the law of torts attempts primarily to put an injured person in a position as nearly as possible equivalent to his position prior to the tort." 4 Restatement of Torts, *supra,* at 452, Section 901, Comment *a.*

On balance, we find the arguments against recovery of a defendant's profits more persuasive than the arguments in favor. * * * In fact, punitive damages may serve to counter balance the unavailability of an unjust enrichment theory in tortious interference cases. * * * Thus, in the appropriate case, punitive damages may serve the same damage role as in unjust enrichment theory.

JUDGMENT AFFIRMED.

Note

"When the Restatement of Restitution was issued in 1937 the question of restitution for inducing breach of contract was left open because of insufficient authority, but indications now are that such relief will be given." I G. Palmer, Law of Restitution 86 (1978). The successful plaintiff also may claim general, special or consequential and punitive damages (where the conduct is sufficiently "wilful") and, in some cases, damages for emotional distress. *See,* D. Dobbs, Law of Remedies § 6.6 (2d ed. 1993).

Probably the most publicized case in this area in recent years—and the case involving the largest damages claims and recovery—is the *Texaco–Pennzoil* litigation. *See,* in this connection, Texaco v. Pennzoil, Co., 729 S.W.2d 768 (Tex.App.1987).

DORSETT CARPET MILLS v. WHITT TILE & MARBLE DISTRIBUTING CO.

Supreme Court of Tennessee, 1987.
734 S.W.2d 322.

[The defendant, Whitt Tile and Marble Distributing Company, Inc. ("Whitt") carried on the business of a wholesaler of carpet products through one of its divisions. During the period referred to Walter O. Hill was the general manager of Whitt's carpet division. The plaintiff, Dorsett Carpet Mills, Inc., ("Dorsett"), was a manufacturer and supplier of carpets. One of Dorsett's customers was Whitt. Dorsett sued Whitt to recover the balance due for carpet sold on open account. Whitt counterclaimed, alleging, *inter alia,* that Dorsett had wrongfully induced Hill to breach and violate his employment contract with Whitt, and for interference with business relations. Whitt asserted a right to compensatory damages and also to restitution based upon plaintiff's profits resulting from inducing the contract breach. Whitt also sought the benefit of a Tennessee statute providing treble damages for "procurement of breach of contract."]

* * *

We granted Dorsett's application for permission to appeal to consider whether the appropriate measure of damages has been applied in the award against that defendant [sic].

* * *

The procurement of a breach of contract was a tort at common law and the legislature's enactment of T.C.A. § 47–50–109 merely codified that cause of action. *See Emmco Ins. Co. v. Beacon Mutual Indem. Co.,* 204 Tenn. 540, 322 S.W.2d 226 (1959). The statute does not address the basic measure of damages for the tort, but mandates the trebling of "the amount of damages resulting from or incident to the breach of the contract." *Dukes v. Brotherhood of Painters,* 191 Tenn. 495, 235 S.W.2d 7 (1950) is the only Tennessee case wherein a measure of damages for the tort of inducing a breach of contract has been articulated. Dukes was a painter and had been a member of the local union for twelve years. He sued the union and several individuals alleging that they conspired to deprive him of his livelihood. In pursuit of that plan they allegedly informed his employer that he had been expelled from the union, which statement was false; and that unless he was discharged there would be a strike on the job. The trial court sustained a demurrer to Dukes' declaration but this Court reversed, holding that the declaration stated a cause of action for inducing the employer to break the contract of employment with Dukes. In remanding for a trial on the merits, the Supreme Court had this to say about damages:

> We think that a fair statement as to the measure of damages under the situation here presented is: "The measure of damages for unlawfully procuring the discharge of an employee is based on the direct and proximate results of the wrongful acts of defendant, and not on the breach of the contract of employment, and ordinarily plaintiff may recover the amount which would have been earned by him except for defendant's interference, less such sums as were actually earned at other employments." 57 C.J.S., Master and Servant, § 632, p. 439.

Id. at 10.

That measure of damages obviously cannot be literally applied where the injured plaintiff is an employer engaged in business. However, the basic principle that the damages awarded to the plaintiff must be based on the direct and proximate result of the wrongful acts of the person procuring the breach of contract, remains viable.

Where the injury involved is interference with a business relationship, the plaintiff's loss of profits that result from the wrongful act are a proper item to be included in the measure of damages. *See McRoberts Protective Agency Inc. v. Lansdell Protective Agency Inc.,* 61 A.D.2d 652, 403 N.Y.Supp.2d 511 (1978); *National Merchandising Corp. v. Leyden,* 370 Mass. 425, 348 N.E.2d 771 (1976); *Coonis v. Rogers,* 429 S.W.2d 709 (Mo.1968) and cases cited in 45 Am.Jur.2d *Interference* § 58. There may be other losses suffered by plaintiffs directly and proximately resulting from the wrongful interference that should be included within the measure of damages and for that reason, it is neither possible nor appropriate to articulate an inflexible measure of damages for interference with business relationships in general or for the more limited factual situation involved in the instant case. The measure of damages for this tort in Restatement (Second) of Torts § 774A is as follows:

> (1) One who is liable to another for interference with a contract or prospective contractual relation is liable for damages for
>
> (a) the pecuniary loss of the benefits of the contract or the prospective relation;

(b) consequential losses for which the interference is a legal cause; and

(c) emotional distress or actual harm to reputation, if they are reasonably to be expected to result from the interference.

(2) In an action for interference with a contract by inducing or causing a third person to break the contract with the other, the fact that the third person is liable for the breach does not affect the amount of damages awardable against the actor; but any damages in fact paid by the third person will reduce the damages actually recoverable on the judgment.

In comment d to § 774A of the Restatement (Second) of Torts the following appears: "The tests for legal causation [of damages] for the tort of interference with contract * * * have not been reduced to precise rules."

Some authorities have allowed business plaintiffs who were victims of interference with their contractual relations a recovery based in part upon profits realized by the defendant procurer of the breach. *See Phillips Chemical Co. v. Morgan,* 440 So.2d 1292 (Fla.App.1983), petition for review denied 450 S.2d 486 (Fla.1984); and *Schechter v. Friedman,* 141 N.J.Eq. 318, 57 A.2d 251 (1948). While we will not rule out the possibility of the use of such a measure in some factual situations, we are of the opinion that generally the lost profit element of damage must be measured by the loss sustained by the plaintiff's business and not by its effect upon defendant's business.

In the present case, the carpet division of the Whitt Tile and Marble Company was a wholesale distributor. As general manager of this division, Hill's duties included purchasing carpet products from various manufacturers, as well as selling those products to retail establishments.

Beginning in May of 1973 and continuing until Hill's resignation from Whitt on 31 March 1975, Dorsett, a manufacturer-supplier of Whitt, paid three forms of secret commissions to Hill. First, Hill received a 2% commission on all purchases of Dorsett carpet by Whitt. Second, a system was established whereby Whitt's salespersons could make "direct sales" of Dorsett carpet straight from the mill without taking the carpet into Whitt's inventory. Whitt received a commission for sales consummated in this manner. Simultaneously with a reduction of Whitt's commission from 6% to 4%, Hill began receiving a 2% commission on all of Whitt's direct sales. Third, Whitt would sell certain styles of Dorsett carpet, which were not kept in Whitt's inventory, only through special order. When Hill sold this style of carpet, however, Dorsett directly paid Hill a 3% commission and nothing was paid to Whitt.

T.C.A. § 47–50–109 renders it "unlawful for any person by inducement, persuasion, misrepresentation or other means to induce or procure the breach or violation, refusal, or failure to perform any lawful contract by any party thereto * * *." The statute declares that "the person so procuring the [breach] shall be liable in treble the amount of damages resulting from or incident to the breach of contract * * *." Thus, only Dorsett, as the procurer of the breach, is liable to Whitt under the statute and only the damages appropriate to be awarded against Dorsett may be trebled.

The trial court and the Court of Appeals based the judgment against Dorsett upon the salary and expenses Whitt paid Hill during the period of his duplicitous conduct. This element of Whitt's loss was the direct and proximate result of Hill's wrongful act and is an appropriate element of damage to compensate plaintiff for the employee's tort, and in our opinion an inappropriate element of damage to charge against the procurer of the breach.

The direct and proximate loss sustained by Whitt as a result of Dorsett's wrongful act was the reduction of Whitt's commission from 6% to 4% and the diversion of 2% to Hill.

Inherent in Hill's fiduciary duty as a purchasing agent and salesman for Whitt was an obligation to ensure that his employer's profit margin was maximized. *See Memphis & Arkansas River Packet Co. v. Agnew,* 132 Tenn. 265, 177 S.W. 949 (1915). Not only did Dorsett's kickbacks cause Hill to breach this duty, but also Whitt suffered damages, by paying more and receiving less (or nothing at all), in the precise amount of the secret commissions. In other words, had Dorsett not paid this money to Hill, it may be presumed that these funds would have inured to the benefit of Whitt in the form of lower prices or greater commissions.

Therefore, the $30,991.20 in secret kickbacks received by Hill were damages sustained by Whitt as a direct and proximate consequence of the wrongful interference by Dorsett. This element of damages is trebled pursuant to T.C.A. § 47–50–109.

In the complaint upon which this case was tried, Whitt also sought damages for "the loss of profits that reasonably could be anticipated had the time expended by Hill and Whitt's salesmen been devoted to the business of Whitt and not to the unlawful devotion to the business of Dorsett and Hill," as well as for the general demise of Whitt's carpet division. There was a reference to a master and a substantial amount of proof adduced upon Whitt's claim of lost profit. The master's report contained no positive findings of lost profits by Whitt nor did the opinion of the trial judge.

Although there is evidence that during the two years of devious conduct Whitt's carpet suppliers dwindled from at least sixteen to two, there is no evidence the prices charged or commissions paid by Dorsett were commercially unreasonable.

However, we find that the evidence clearly supports an additional item of lost profit sustained by Whitt as a direct and proximate result of Dorsett's use of Hill's services.

Plaintiff proved that in 1974 Hill, while still employed by Whitt, sold Dorsett carpet in the total sum of $91,312.04 for which he was paid a 3% commission by Dorsett and Whitt was paid nothing. Whitt did not know anything about those sales until after the litigation was instituted and did not receive the 4% commission that Dorsett remitted to Whitt on all other sales. The $91,312.04 sales of carpet are referred to in the record as the

"Magic Touch and other accounts commission" and a 3% commission on that sum was included in the total secret commission paid Hill of $30,-991.20. However, the lower courts have found and we agree that but for Dorsett and Hill's duplicity, Whitt would have been paid a 6% commission on all sales. It follows therefore that Whitt is entitled to recover an additional 3% of $91,312.04 from Dorsett and to have that sum trebled.

In lieu of the judgment awarded against Dorsett in the Court of Appeals, a judgment will be awarded Whitt against Dorsett in the sum of $102,091.68 for the reasons stated herein. [The Supreme Court also affirmed the ruling by the Court of Appeals that the judgment against Hill should not be trebled "because only the party procuring the breach of contract i.e., Dorsett, could be liable for treble damages under the statute."] * * *

The case is remanded to the trial court for enforcement of the judgment.

ZIPPERTUBING CO. v. TELEFLEX INC.

United States Court of Appeals, Third Circuit, 1985.
757 F.2d 1401.

* * *

II.

TELEFLEX'S CONTENTIONS

Zippertubing filed suit on June 19, 1981. Surf filed its action on August 14, 1981, and the cases were consolidated for trial. Both sought compensatory and punitive damages. The trial resulted in the judgment described above. Teleflex contends that it is entitled to a judgment notwithstanding the verdict on the entire case; that the court's charge misstates New Jersey laws; that the plaintiffs' disgorgement of profits theory of recovery cannot be sustained; that it is at least entitled to a judgment notwithstanding the verdict with respect to punitive damages; that prejudgment interest should not have been awarded; and that trial errors warrant a new trial.

A. Sufficiency of Plaintiffs' Evidence on Interference with a Prospective Advantage

Having made a firm quotation to Surf, which was by its terms to remain open for thirty days and which would have produced a $715,205 profit if accepted, Teleflex was asked by Surf and Zippertubing to permit their customer Nab, until then undisclosed, to inspect its facilities. Teleflex agreed to the inspection. It contends that in these circumstances New Jersey law would not impose any obligation on it to refrain from taking actions which would interfere with the prospective contract between Zippertubing and Nab, even when those actions amount to Teleflex's making false representations to Nab with respect to its relationship with Zippertubing and Surf, and Teleflex's resort to deceit in its dealings with Zippertubing and Surf with regard to its intention to make the extrusions.

The law of New Jersey is otherwise. Tort liability for interference with a prospective advantage has been a settled feature of that state's law for many years. * * *

* * *

Teleflex urges that the tort recognized in *Kamm v. Flink* is confined to the real estate brokerage context. While the tort has received widespread recognition in that context, it has historically been applied, as noted above, in other contexts. New Jersey continues to impose liability for interference with forms of prospective advantage other than brokerage commissions. *E.g. Zelenka v. Benevolent and Protective Order of Elks,* 129 N.J.Super. 379, 324 A.2d 35 (App.Div.1974) (interference with membership in a fraternal order); *Association Group Life, Inc. v. Catholic War Veterans,* 120 N.J.Super. 85, 293 A.2d 408 (App.Div.1971) (Conford, J.) (interference with expectancy of commissions on insurance policy renewals); *Mayflower Industries v. Thor Corp.,* 15 N.J.Super. 139, 83 A.2d 246; 15 N.J.Super. 337, 83 A.2d 366 (Ch.Div.1951) (Francis, J.), *aff'd o.b.,* 9 N.J. 605, 89 A.2d 242 (1952) (interference with proposed distributorship agreement by threats of groundless litigation); *Di Cristofaro v. Laurel Grove Memorial Park,* 43 N.J.Super. 244, 128 A.2d 281 (App.Div.1957) (fee requirements imposed by cemetery constituted interference with business of independent monument sellers); *Newark Hardware & Plumbing Supply Co. v. Stove Mfrs. Corp.,* 136 N.J.L. 401, 56 A.2d 605 (Sup.Ct.), *aff'd* 137 N.J.L. 612, 61 A.2d 240 (1948) (accepting misdelivery of a consignment intended for a competitor an interference with competitor's business). * * *

* * *

B. *The Adequacy of the Court's Charge*

In submitting the case to the jury the trial court gave a lengthy instruction on the elements of the tort of interference with a prospective advantage. Carefully and repeatedly the court instructed that if Teleflex and the plaintiffs were competitors, both seeking to obtain Nab as a customer, absent a contract, "there would be no prohibition against Teleflex getting to Nab first." App. 2625. The court charged:

> Now, in order for the plaintiff to recover damages for unlawful interference with prospective economic advantage, it must be found that the defendant interfered with a reasonable expectancy of economic advantage and benefit on the part of the plaintiff.
>
> Thus, the plaintiff must prove the following elements: First, the existence of a reasonable expectation of economic advantage or benefit belonging to it; Second, that the defendant had knowledge of that expectation of economic advantage; Third, that the defendant wrongfully and without justification interfered with the plaintiff's reasonable expectation of economic advantage or benefits; Fourth, that in the absence of the wrongful act of the defendant, it is reasonably probable that the plaintiff would have realized its economic advantage or benefit; And fifth, that the plaintiff sustained damages as a result of this activity.

App. 2626–27. Teleflex does not contend that the foregoing misstates the elements of the tort under New Jersey law. * * *

* * *

C. Disgorgement of Profits

The plaintiffs presented evidence from which the jury could reasonably have inferred that Zippertubing and Surf lost anticipated profits. They did not attempt, however, to establish the amount of their lost profits. Instead they proved the amount of profits made by Teleflex as a result of its wrongdoing.

Teleflex urges that even assuming a jury question and a proper charge on liability, it is entitled to a judgment notwithstanding the verdict because the plaintiffs' evidence on damages was presented on a theory which New Jersey would not countenance.

It is undoubtedly so that in most instances in which a New Jersey plaintiff has established liability for interference with a prospective advantage the judgment has been for the plaintiff's lost profits. Probably that is because in most instances the amount of plaintiff's loss and defendant's gain is the same. In the one case dealing with the question in New Jersey, however, the Court of Errors and Appeals held that an accounting for profits is an appropriate remedy for interference with a prospective advantage. *Schechter v. Friedman,* 141 N.J.Eq. 318, 57 A.2d 251 (1948). That holding is consistent with the New Jersey law respecting the analogous business tort of misappropriation of a business name, *L. Martin Co. v. L. Martin & Wilckes Co.,* 75 N.J.Eq. 257, 72 A. 294 (1909), and that of misuse of trade secrets. *A. Hollander & Son, Inc. v. Imperial Fur Blending,* 2 N.J. 235, 66 A.2d 319 (1949). Teleflex points out that these accounting for profits cases were suits in equity, and urges that such a remedy is unavailable in an action at law. That simply is not the case. In a diversity suit the distinction between cases at law or in equity is significant only with regard to the respective roles of judge and jury. Fed.R.Civ.P. 1; *Goodman v. Mead Johnson & Co.,* 534 F.2d 566 (3d Cir.1976). The equitable or legal nature of the relief does not relieve the federal forum of the obligation to afford the same relief which a state court would afford with respect to state law claims. *Guaranty Trust Co. v. York,* 326 U.S. 99, 105, 65 S.Ct. 1464, 1467, 89 L.Ed. 2079 (1945). Moreover the plaintiff in *Schechter v. Friedman, supra,* proceeded in equity because he sought injunctive relief as well as money damages. No New Jersey case has been called to our attention suggesting that if the victim of a tort who has suffered actual damages cannot or does not elect to seek injunctive relief he may not seek an accounting for profits. Certainly *Red Devil Tools v. Tip Top Brush Co., Inc.,* 92 N.J.Super. 570, 224 A.2d 336 (App.Div.1966) *modified,* 50 N.J. 563, 236 A.2d 861 (1967), on which Teleflex relies is not such a case. In *Red Devil* the owner of a common law trademark, who neither made nor sold paint brushes, successfully enjoined the use of the trademark for paint brushes. An accounting for profits was denied, not because profits of a tortfeasor cannot be recovered at law, but because the trademark owner, not in the brush business, lost no prospective business advantage of its own. Here, plainly, the plaintiffs lost a prospective advantage.

The remedy applied in *Schechter v. Friedman, supra,* is consistent with constructive trust principles, and "it is possible to think of the accounting for profits in this kind of case as simply a special form of constructive trust." D. Dobbs, *Remedies* 253 (1973). The constructive trust is, of course a familiar remedy in the New Jersey courts. *Clark v. Judge,* 84 N.J.Super. 35, 200 A.2d 801 (Ch.Div.1964), *aff'd o.b.,* 44 N.J. 550, 210 A.2d 415 (1965); *D'Ippolito v. Castoro* 51 N.J. 584, 242 A.2d 617 (1968). The *Schechter v. Friedman* remedy is, moreover consistent with the election of remedies available in New Jersey to the victim of a conversion of personal property. *Kaplan v. Cavicchia,* 107 N.J.Super. 201, 257 A.2d 739 (App.Div. 1969). All of these closely related damage rules are consistent with the policy of discouraging tortious conduct by depriving the tortfeasor of the opportunity to profit from wrongdoing. Consistent with that policy, the trial court properly permitted the plaintiffs to prove as damages the amount of Teleflex's profits. The court charged:

> The law says that when one has unlawfully deprived another of a contract or a business opportunity and has made that opportunity his own, he is not to be permitted to retain any of the profits, any of the benefits of his unlawful conduct.
>
> Therefore, if you were to find that the plaintiff has met its burden of proof as I have defined it to you on each and every one of the elements of the case, it would be your job to award such damages as would deprive the defendant of any unlawful benefit of its unlawful conduct.

App. 2633. This charge was correct, and the jury's verdict, consistent with it, must stand. * * *

* * * The judgment [based upon evidence on the basis of which the jury reasonably could have inferred that the plaintiff lost anticipated profits, and proceeded to award damages to the plaintiff on the basis of "the profits made by Telex as a result of its wrongdoing"] will therefore be affirmed in all respects.

Note

For a discussion of the use of the restitution remedies where the plaintiff complains of tortious interference with his expectancies based upon his contractual relationships and negotiations with others, *see* Note, 19 Hastings L.J. 1119 (1968); Scymanski v. Dufault, 80 Wash.2d 77, 491 P.2d 1050 (1971).

CABLEVISION OF BRECKENRIDGE, INC. v. TANNHAUSER CONDOMINIUM ASS'N

Supreme Court of Colorado, 1982.
649 P.2d 1093.

En Bank.

LOHR, JUSTICE.

We granted certiorari to review the decision of the Colorado Court of Appeals in Cablevision of Breckenridge, Inc. v. Tannhauser Condominium

Association, (Colo.App. No. 79CA0924, announced September 18, 1980) (not selected for official publication), which reversed the judgment of the Summit County District Court awarding the plaintiff, Cablevision of Breckenridge, Inc. (Cablevision), damages for the wrongful conversion of its subscription cable service. We reverse the decision of the court of appeals and remand for reinstatement of the district court judgment.

I.

This case was tried to the district court under a stipulated set of facts which included those that follow. Cablevision is a corporation engaged in providing cable television and FM radio to its subscribers in areas where the television signals are weak or nonexistent. This is a frequently encountered problem in the vicinity of Breckenridge, Colorado, because the topography of the community and its distance from the originating broadcast stations generally result in an inability to receive a useful broadcast signal when using only the traditional antennas normally employed by individual households.

In order to provide its service, Cablevision constructed several antennas on a mountain peak near Breckenridge, by which it receives six television stations as well as FM radio. At the point of reception, the television signals are strong enough to reproduce a black and white picture, but are too weak to allow color reproduction. Consequently, the signals are fed into a "preamp," which magnifies their strength. The signals are then transmitted to a "head-end" building, located near the receiving antennas, where they are passed through a channel processor and mixer for the purpose of improving the clarity of the picture produced by the transmission. From this building, the signals are sent by coaxial cable to the "hub" facility in Breckenridge, and thence through distribution lines to the individual subscribers. Additional amplification of the signals is necessary as they are transmitted through the system, so amplifiers are installed along the distribution lines. Cablevision's capital investment in the transmission system is approximately $450,000.

The stipulated facts further establish that in October 1972 Cablevision entered into an oral agreement for the provision of subscription cable services with Judy Keller, who was acting on behalf of the owners of the condominium units comprising the Tannhauser I development in Breckenridge. The Tannhauser I building consisted of 33 condominium units, and each was to receive the Cablevision service. Pursuant to this agreement Cablevision installed the equipment necessary to provide its service to each of the units. This was accomplished by running a connecting line from the distribution system to an amplifier located inside Tannhauser I. The signals were then transmitted from this amplifier to individual wall plates serving each of the units. From January 1, 1972, through March 1974, Tannhauser I paid for the service to these 33 units at a specified rate per unit.

Effective May 1974, Cablevision ceased billing for service to 33 units and began billing for service to only three units. This was done at the request of Jerry White, whose status is not described in the stipulation but who apparently acted as a representative for the Tannhauser I owners.

The stipulation reflects disagreement over the exact events leading to this change in service, but it is undisputed that the Cablevision amplifier inside Tannhauser I was removed; that White then substituted his own amplifier and connected it to the Cablevision line; and that, following May 1, television and FM radio service was still provided to all 33 units of Tannhauser I despite the payment to Cablevision for service to only three of those units. This state of affairs continued from May 1, 1974, to approximately December 1, 1976.

In the fall of 1974 a second building, known as Tannhauser II and comprised of 25 condominium units, was constructed near Tannhauser I. Cablevision was never requested to supply service to Tannhauser II. However, the new building was wired internally for cable television and FM radio, and in November 1974 White supervised and assisted in the installation of a cable between Tannhauser I and Tannhauser II enabling extension of the Cablevision service to each of the 25 units in Tannhauser II. Tannhauser II began receiving the Cablevision transmission approximately November 30, 1974. Cablevision subsequently discovered the unauthorized use of its transmission by Tannhauser I and II and terminated all service to the condominiums about December 1, 1976.

Thereafter, Cablevision brought the present action, naming the condominium associations for Tannhausers I and II and the owners of the individual condominium units as defendants. Cablevision's amended complaint contained eight claims for relief, including breach of contract, concealment, conversion, various claims of unjust enrichment, and a request for injunctive relief.

However, as part of the pre-trial stipulation of facts summarized above, the parties submitted for judicial resolution the following single stipulated issue:

> Have the Defendants, or any of them, breached any contract with Plaintiff, written or oral, in fact or implied, for which Plaintiff is entitled for damages, actual or punitive?

After a hearing, the trial court entered an oral ruling incorporating the parties' stipulated facts, and holding that the defendants were liable for conversion of Cablevision's service. The parties had originally provided in their stipulation that, in the event of recovery, the damages would be $12,195, plus appropriate interest. However, the defendants advised the court subsequent to entry of the stipulation that they objected to this figure, so a further hearing was held on the question of damages. The court then entered its written judgment. The court again adopted the stipulation of the parties as its findings of fact and concluded:

> [T]he plaintiff's property and services in the furnishing of cable television is a legally protected interest for which it is entitled to charge an appropriate and lawful rate to its subscribers. The defendants, through the actions stated in the Stipulation, have converted those protected interests without fully paying for them.

Based upon the damages hearing, the court entered judgment for actual damages of $11,597.50 plus statutory interest and court costs, and denied the prayer for punitive damages. The defendants then appealed.

The court of appeals reversed. It held that the trial court erred in ruling that the defendants were liable on the basis that they converted Cablevision's property interests because, pursuant to the parties' stipulation, "the only issue before the trial court was whether any defendant breached any contract with [Cablevision]." It further held that, because the stipulation did not establish the essential elements of a contract, Cablevision had not proved its breach of contract claim. Therefore, it directed the trial court to enter judgment for the defendants.

We accepted certiorari to review the court of appeals' decision. Cablevision contends that the propriety of the trial court's departure from the stipulated issue was not properly before the court of appeals because it was not raised in the defendants' motion for a new trial. It further argues that, in any case, the trial court did not err in considering the liability of the defendants under a theory of conversion and that the court was correct on the merits of this issue. However, we do not address these arguments because we conclude that the judgment of the trial court is supported by an alternative basis of liability raised by the stipulated issue submitted by the parties.

II.

As stipulated by the parties, the issue for decision was whether "the Defendants, or any of them, breached any contract with Plaintiff, written or oral, in fact or *implied.*" (Emphasis added.) We read the mention of "implied" contracts as a reference to the doctrine of quasi-contract or unjust enrichment, under which courts imply a contract as a matter of law where necessary to avoid unjust enrichment. This interpretation is based in part upon the apparent intent of parties in distinguishing "implied contracts" and contracts "in fact," and draws further support from the inclusion of unjust enrichment claims in the complaint.

In addressing only the issue of whether the stipulated evidence established a contract in fact, the court of appeals did not consider this alternative basis of liability. We conclude that the facts of this case present an appropriate basis for application of the doctrine of unjust enrichment, and reverse the decision of the court of appeals for that reason.

To recover under a theory of quasi-contract or unjust enrichment, a plaintiff must show (1) that a benefit was conferred on the defendant by the plaintiff, (2) that the benefit was appreciated by the defendant, and (3) that the benefit was accepted by the defendant under such circumstances that it would be inequitable for it to be retained without payment of its value. Dass v. Epplen, 162 Colo. 60, 424 P.2d 779 (1967); Mountain Medical, Inc. v. City of Colorado Springs, 43 Colo.App. 391, 608 P.2d 821 (1979); Jordan v. Lone Pines, Ltd., 41 Colo.App. 152, 580 P.2d 1273 (1978); 66 Am.Jur.2d Restitution and Implied Contracts § 4 at 947 (1973). Application of the doctrine does not depend upon the existence of a contract, express or implied in fact, but on the need to avoid unjust enrichment of the defendant notwithstanding the absence of an actual agreement to pay for the benefit conferred. *E.g.*, Valley Realty & Investment Co. v. McMillan, 160 Colo. 109, 414 P.2d 486 (1966); Wistrand v. Leach Realty Co., 147 Colo. 573, 364 P.2d 396 (1961); *see generally* I G. Palmer, The Law of Restitution § 1.2 (1978). 66 *Am.Jur.2d Restitution and Implied Contracts, supra,* § 2. The scope of this remedy is broad, cutting across both contract and tort law, with its application guided by the underlying principle of avoiding the unjust enrichment of one party at the expense of another. I G. Palmer, The Law of Restitution § 1.1 (1978); 66 *Am.Jur.2d Restitution and Implied Contracts, supra,* § 11.

In the present case, we conclude that a benefit was conferred upon the defendants by Cablevision and that the defendants appreciated this benefit. The defendants' initial payment for this service in connection with the 33 Tannhauser I condominium units and their continued payment for service to three of those units amply demonstrate both the beneficial service provided by Cablevision and the appreciation of that service by the defendants. Instructive in this regard is the broad definition of benefit contained in the Restatement of Restitution § 1, comment b (1937):

> A person confers a benefit upon another if he gives to the other possession of or some other interest in money, land, chattels, or choses in action, performs services beneficial to or at the request of the other, satisfies a debt or a duty of the other, or in any way adds to the other's security or advantage. He confers a benefit not only where he adds to the property of another, but also where he saves the other from expense or loss. The word "benefit," therefore, denotes any form of advantage.

We also conclude that the defendants have retained this service under such circumstances that it would be inequitable to allow its use without payment for its value. The stipulated facts demonstrate that Cablevision never intended to provide its service to all of Tannhausers I and II in exchange for payment in connection with only three units. Indeed, upon discovery of the unauthorized use of its signals, Cablevision terminated all service to the defendants. Further, the defendants were not innocent or unwilling recipients of this benefit, but actively facilitated its provision.

The defendants contend that Cablevision was not harmed by the use made of its signal because it received compensation for the three signals delivered to the three Tannhauser I units pursuant to oral agreement; additional signals were not appropriated by the defendants; and the amplification and use of these signals within Tannhausers I and II did not impair Cablevision's ability to serve its other subscribers. However, this argument ignores the substance and effect of the defendant's conduct and the nature of the harm suffered by Cablevision. The ability of Cablevision to charge for its service is necessary to its economic viability. "Subscription stations rely upon fees paid by viewers rather than upon advertising proceeds for their support. Continued existence of the subscription television industry therefore depends upon the stations' ability to charge fees by limiting reception of their message to subscribers." Note, Decoding Section 605 of The Federal Communications Act: A Cause of Action for Unauthorized Reception of Subscription Television, 50 U.Cin.L.Rev. 362

(1981). By retransmission of the signals purchased in connection with three Tannhauser I units to non-subscribers, the defendants have undercut Cablevision's ability to sell its signal to these other potential customers. These business realities highlight the inequity of permitting the defendants to retain the benefits of Cablevision's service without payment of its value.

For similar reasons we reject the defendants' contention that their conduct is analogous to a subscriber moving his television set from room to room within his house or to a subscriber recording Cablevision's transmission by means of a video tape recorder. Such devices or activities merely increase the utility of the signals to the paying subscriber. In contrast, the defendants' conduct in the present case impairs the ability of Cablevision to sell its service to other potential subscribers.

The defendants also point to the fact that Cablevision acquires its signals free of charge and contends that, because Cablevision merely intercepts broadcast signals originated by others, it has no legally protected interest in those images and transmissions. Again, we find this argument unpersuasive. Although Cablevision does not acquire an exclusive right in the broadcast signals it receives, in the sense that it could prohibit others from independently receiving those signals by use of a home antenna or a competing, properly licensed subscription service, see Intermountain Electronics, Inc. v. Tintic School District, 14 Utah 2d 86, 377 P.2d 783 (1963), Cablevision does have a legally protected interest in the reception, processing and distribution system it has installed and in the service that this system enables Cablevision to provide. It is the unauthorized use of this valuable service that is at issue, and the defendants' focus upon the absence of an exclusive proprietary interest to receive and distribute the programming delivered by that service misses the point.

The defendants have accepted a service from Cablevision that is customarily paid for and, in fact, was initially paid for by these defendants. The defendants were active participants in obtaining this benefit from Cablevision, and, based on the initial agreement to serve Tannhauser I, their representatives must have acted with the knowledge that Cablevision expected compensation for each Tannhauser unit receiving the Cablevision transmission. Under these facts, restitution is appropriate to avoid unjust enrichment to the defendants. *See Dass v. Epplen, supra; Valley Realty & Investment Co. v. McMillan, supra; 66 Am.Jur.2d Restitution and Implied Contracts, supra,* § 24.

The damages awarded were based upon the rate prescribed in Cablevision's franchise from Breckenridge, which correspond to the rate paid for the three Tannhauser I units during the period of unauthorized use of the Cablevision signals. This was an appropriate measure of the benefit conferred upon the defendants and the amount of restitution due. *See 66 Am.Jur.2d Restitution and Implied Contracts, supra,* § 166; *Restatement of Restitution, supra,* § 157.

Although we do not reach the correctness of the grounds relied upon by the trial court in support of its decision, we conclude that the judgment was proper based upon a theory of quasi-contract or unjust enrichment, and that the court of appeals therefore erred in reversing that judgment.

See, e.g., Metropolitan Industrial Bank v. Great Western Products Corp., 158 Colo. 198, 405 P.2d 944 (1965); Consolidated Oil & Gas, Inc. v. Superior Oil Co., 157 Colo. 86, 401 P.2d 89 (1965).

We reverse the decision of the court of appeals and return the case to that court for remand to the trial court with directions to enter judgment in accordance with the views expressed in this opinion.

Lee, J., does not participate.*

SECTION 2. INTERFERENCE WITH REAL PROPERTY AND ENVIRONMENTAL INTERESTS

A. SUBSTITUTIONARY RELIEF

1. Damages For Trespass and Nuisance

MYERS v. ARNOLD

Appellate Court of Illinois, 1980.
83 Ill.App.3d 1, 38 Ill.Dec. 228, 403 N.E.2d 316.

MILLS, PRESIDING JUSTICE:

This case involves 60–80 truckloads of concrete—all dumped on plaintiffs' property.

A jury found such dumping wrongful and gave plaintiffs a verdict of $12,000.

Defendant appeals, claiming: (1) The trial court erred when it allowed plaintiffs to recover the cost of repair rather than the diminution in market value. * * *

We affirm.

FACTS

In 1972 or 1973, the plaintiffs purchased a 20–acre tract of land near Leroy, Illinois. In July of 1974, they began constructing a residence on the western portion of this land and at the time of trial they were residing at this location. The land is divided diagonally by a creek and when the land was originally purchased, the plaintiffs intended to construct their present residence, sell it, and then build another residence on the eastern portion of the property.

The creek which ran through the plaintiffs' property created an erosion problem and it was thought that broken concrete could be used to correct this problem. In the fall of 1974, the plaintiffs discovered that the defendant was engaged in a road repair and construction project on U.S. Route 16 near Leroy. Plaintiff, Mrs. Anna Myers, contacted Howard Arnold, president of the defendant, about getting some concrete fill. * * *

* See, also, Note, Hastings L.J. 1119 (1968); Scymanski v. Dufault, 80 Wash.2d 77, 491 P.2d 1050 (1971); York, Extension of Restitutional Remedies in the Tort Field, 4 U.C.L.A. L.Rev. 469 (1957) (including consideration of "waiver of tort" in the area of intangible property interests).

According to Mrs. Myers' testimony, she told the supervisor that she wanted a couple of loads of concrete and that she preferred that it not include rubble or dirt. * * * [T]he amount of concrete delivered far exceeded the amount desired. The concrete contained reinforcing rods, was stacked 8 feet high in some places, and covered an area approximately 50 × 150 feet. It had been placed where the plaintiffs intended to build the second house. Mrs. Myers immediately contacted Howard Arnold but he would not agree to remove the concrete.

On the issue of damages, the plaintiffs presented the testimony of John Nord who is self-employed in the refuse removal and demolition business. He detailed the various costs for removing the concrete and estimated that the total expense would be $18,200. However, he admitted that if he were able to find area farmers who wanted the material for erosion control, the costs would be decreased because the material would not have to be hauled as far as he had planned when estimating the cost of removal.

* * *

By way of an offer of proof, the defendant presented the testimony of a real estate appraiser who had examined plaintiffs' property four days before trial. The appraiser testified that on the date of trial the fair market value of the plaintiffs' property was $750 per acre. This value, however, was based only on the land and did not include plaintiffs' house. In 1974, plaintiffs' property would have been worth $650 per acre. The appraiser also testified that the fact that one-half acre of plaintiffs' property was covered with concrete would have no great effect on its value for resale purposes.

At the conference on instructions, the court—over the defendant's objection—ruled that it would give the plaintiffs' instruction concerning the measure of damages. This instruction measures damages by the reasonable expense of removing the concrete. The court therefore rejected defendant's tendered instruction which stated that the measure of damages was "the lesser of the reasonable expense of necessary repairs to the property which was damaged or the difference between the fair market value of the property immediately before the occurrence plus [*sic*] its fair market value immediately after the occurrence."

I

The defendant argues that the trial court erred in failing to give its tendered instruction on the issue of damages. Defendant therefore claims that this case must be remanded because the verdict of $12,000 (which represents the cost of repair) far exceeds the diminution in the market value of the plaintiffs' property.

Initially, we note that defendant's tendered instruction did not state the rule on which the defendant relies. The tendered instruction would have informed the jury that the measure of damages was the lesser of the reasonable expense of repair or the difference in the fair market value of the property before the occurrence "plus" its fair market value after the occurrence. The word "plus" should not appear in this instruction. Illinois Pattern Jury Instruction, Civil, Number 30.11, uses the word "and" where defendant submitted the word "plus." We are confident defendant would not have the jury fix damages in the manner provided by the tendered instruction.

* * *

Defendant relies on the rule generally stated that tort damages for an injury to real property are to be measured by the difference between the market value of the property before the injury and its value after the injury. * * *

We believe that the criticisms which have been directed at an automatic application of the diminution rule are well founded. (*See generally* Dobbs, Handbook on the Law of Remedies, § 5.1 (1973).) The law of torts attempts primarily to restore the injured party to as good a position as he held prior to the tort. (Restatement of Torts 2d, § 901 (1979).) In accomplishing that result, courts must be mindful of the fact that rules governing the proper measure of damages in a particular case are guides only and should not be applied in an arbitrary, formulaic, or inflexible manner, particularly where to do so would not do substantial justice. Roark v. Musgrave (1976), 41 Ill.App.3d 1008, 355 N.E.2d 91.

When a land owner has shown that he has suffered a compensable injury, we believe it is necessary to examine the exact interest harmed before answering the question of what amount is necessary to fully compensate for that harm. Allowing a plaintiff to recover the lesser of the cost of repair or the diminution in market value may be appropriate where the interest which has been harmed is purely financial, as where the land was purchased as a business investment with an eye towards speculation or where it is held solely for the production of income. However, the same measure of damages may be painfully inadequate when the land is held for a personal use such as a family residence and the harm may be corrected with a reasonable expenditure even though the expenditure exceeds the amount the land has diminished in value. In the latter case, the full repair cost will come much closer to restoring what was actually lost and will not require the injured party to correct the harm with funds from his own pocket. Automatic application of the rule advocated by the defendant could, in many cases, force plaintiffs to sell their property to a defendant and, in effect, grant a private right of eminent domain. To grant such a right in cases such as the one at bench would inadequately protect plaintiffs' legitimate interest in the use and enjoyment of their property. The courts of this state have recently begun to recognize this fact as they have rejected application of the diminution rule in similar cases.

In Arras v. Columbia Quarry Co. (1977), 52 Ill.App.3d 560, 10 Ill.Dec. 192, 367 N.E.2d 580, the defendant's blasting activities destroyed a well located on land where plaintiffs had lived for almost 30 years. At the trial of that case, the only evidence which was presented on the issue of damages was expert testimony concerning the cost of drilling a new well. On appeal, the defendant strenuously argued that the only relevant measure of damages was the diminution in the fair market value of the property. Our sister court disagreed and felt that the permanent/nonpermanent dichotomy which Indiana applied when ascertaining damages for an injury to realty was a logical and well reasoned approach. The rule which the court adopted requires a determination of whether the injury is permanent or nonpermanent. If permanent, the measure of damages is the market value of the realty before the injury less its market value after the injury. When the injury is nonpermanent, the measure of damages is the cost of restoring the property to its original condition. Similarly, in Zosky v. Couri (1979), 77 Ill.App.3d 1033, 33 Ill.Dec. 837, 397 N.E.2d 170, the permanent/nonpermanent approach was applied where the injury consisted of tire ruts on the plaintiff's lawn.

We agree with the approach adopted in *Arras* and *Zosky* and conclude that the plaintiffs in this case were entitled to recover the cost of repairing the damages. Here, as in those cases, the damage was to realty held for personal rather than a business use, the injury was capable of repair, and this repair could be accomplished without expending amounts wholly disproportionate to the value of the land. The trial court, accordingly, did not err in refusing defendant's tendered instruction.

Notes

1. Compare the approach adopted by the Nebraska Supreme Court in "L" Investments, Ltd. v. Lynch, 212 Neb. 319, 322 N.W.2d 651 (1982) (defendant struck plaintiff's building while operating a motor vehicle):

> "[T]he municipal * * * court entered judgment for 'L' Investments and against Lynch in the sum of $2,640.
>
> "Lynch then appealed to the District Court for Douglas County, Nebraska. * * *
>
> "The [District Court], relying upon what it correctly understood to be the rule in Nebraska, as announced in Hunt v. Chicago, B. & Q.R.R. Co., 180 Neb. 375, 143 N.W.2d 263 (1966), found that the injury sustained by 'L' Investments as a result of Lynch's negligence was temporary in character and that therefore the proper measure of damages for recovery was the cost of restoration, if less than the diminution in value measured by the difference in value of the premises immediately before the accident and immediately after the accident. The District Court further found that the record was wholly lacking as to any evidence concerning the diminution in value to the real estate caused by the accident. Therefore, the court concluded that 'L' Investments had failed to establish the fact that the cost of the repairs was less than the diminution in value to the property, and could not recover. The judgment of the municipal court was reversed and the case was dismissed.
>
> "As we indicated at the outset, this case presents to the court an opportunity to clarify what should be the rule of law regarding the proper measure of damages to be awarded where injury is caused to an improvement located upon the real estate and the injury can be repaired or the improvement restored. One might anticipate that the answer to that question would be relatively simple. However, an examination of the cases both within this jurisdiction and elsewhere, discloses that there is some confusion regarding the proper measure of damages.
>
> "Dobbs, in his Handbook on the Law of Remedies, observes: 'Most courts follow the rule that repair costs, when used as a measure, may not

exceed the diminution in value of the property. Several courts have varied this formula by allowing repair or restoration cost to exceed the diminution in the value of the property but limiting such cost to the total pre-tort value of the property * * *. A few courts have allowed recovery for cost of restoration that exceeds the diminished value of the property, or have at least stated that cost of restoration is the measure without any ceiling.' § 5.1 at 317–18 (1973).

"An examination of just some of the cases reported discloses that there may in fact be as many as four or five different rules. [Citations to cases from 20 jurisdictions omitted.]

* * *

"An examination of our own cases discloses that the confusion which has occurred elsewhere may also be found in Nebraska.

* * *

"We therefore now declare that the proper measure of damages for injury to an improvement upon real estate which can be repaired is as follows: Except as otherwise hereinafter limited, where an improvement upon realty is damaged without damage to the realty itself and where the nature of the thing damaged is such that it is capable of being repaired or restored and the cost of doing so is capable of reasonable ascertainment, the measure of damages for its negligent damage is the reasonable cost of repairing or restoring the property in like kind and quality. This would be in addition to any other consequential damages which the injured party may establish by proper proof.

"While certain of the writers, including Dobbs, and perhaps some courts, argue that right of recovery should be without limitation (*see* Dobbs, Handbook on the Law of Remedies, § 5.1 (1973)), we believe the award for such damage should not exceed the market value of the property immediately preceding the damage to the property. It seems that one ought not to be able to recover a greater amount for partial destruction than one could recover for total destruction. To the extent that our previous decisions on this matter, including Hunt v. Chicago, B. & Q.R.R. Co., 180 Neb. 375, 143 N.W.2d 263 (1966), are to the contrary, they are overruled. If, in fact, the cost of repair or restoration exceeds the market value of the property just before the injury, then the proper measure of damages is the market value of the property just before the damages were incurred, less any salvage.

"The burden of establishing the cost of repair shall be upon the party seeking recovery. If the party against whom recovery is sought believes that the cost of repair exceeds the market value of the property just before damage, then the burden shall be upon such party to introduce evidence to establish that fact, and it will then be up to the trier of fact to determine which of the two measures of damages should be employed. Absent evidence that the cost of repair or restoration exceeds the market value of the property just before damage, it will be presumed that the cost of repair or restoration does not exceed the market value of the property just before damage.

> "Under the rule now adopted by the court, the record in this case discloses that the evidence adduced was sufficient to entitle 'L' Investments to recover for its damages, and the decision of the District Court should be reversed. This is not a reflection on the trial judge who could not have anticipated our action in this case.
>
> * * *
>
> "The judgment of the District Court is reversed and remanded. Appellee is given 20 days in which to request leave to introduce evidence that the cost of the repairs in the amount of $2,640 exceeds the pretort value of the entire improvement. Should appellee desire not to offer such evidence, or upon failing to do so within said 20 days, the District Court is directed to reinstate the judgment of the municipal court."

Does the following standard, advanced by the West Virginia Supreme Court in Jarrett v. E.L. Harper & Son Inc., 160 W.Va. 399, 235 S.E.2d 362 (1977), differ from the foregoing approaches?

> "When realty is injured the owner may recover the cost of repairing it plus his expenses stemming from the injury including loss of use during the repair period. If the injury cannot be repaired or the cost of repair would exceed the property's market value, then the owner may recover the money equivalent of its lost *value* plus his expenses resulting from the injury including loss of use during the time he has been deprived of his property."
>
> "Our cases that differentiate between 'temporary' or 'permanent' bases are overruled on that point."

Id. at 160 W.Va. 403, 235 S.E.2d 365. *See also* Reeser v. Weaver Brothers, Inc., 78 Ohio App.3d 681, 605 N.E.2d 1271 (1992).

2. Should the plaintiff in *"L" Investments Ltd., supra* note 1, be entitled to recover loss of use damages during the period of repair? *See* Nisbet v. Yelnick, 124 Ill.App.3d 466, 79 Ill.Dec. 877, 464 N.E.2d 781 (1984) (plaintiff awarded damages for loss of use of home in addition to cost of repairing defects).

3. In Rovetti v. City & County of San Francisco, 131 Cal.App.3d 973, 183 Cal.Rptr. 1 (1982), the court awarded $58,479 to repair the plaintiff's home; $18,000 of this sum represented compensation for the effects of inflation between the time of the damage and the time of the trial seven years later. The court explained that increasing an award to compensate for the effects of inflation insures that a plaintiff will not receive less than the amount to which the plaintiff is entitled.

4. Is it fair to draw a distinction between commercial and residential property for purposes of when restoration damages are available in trespass cases? Suppose, for example, that a trespasser dumps 60 loads of concrete on land that is used in a sod growing business. If the trespass did not cause the land to decline in value because it is suitable for other commercial uses, should restoration damages be denied? Should the owner have to relocate her business? *See* Wujcik v. Gallagher and Henry Contractors, 232 Ill.App.3d 323, 172 Ill.Dec. 920, 596 N.E.2d 199 (1992) ("[W]e agree with the reasoning that the diminution in value may be an inadequate measure of damages when land is damaged, even with commercial property.").

5. In addition to compensatory damages, other types of damages are available in trespass actions:

a. Nominal damages are awarded to establish the defendant's liability. *E.g.,* Johnson v. Martin, 423 So.2d 868 (Ala.Civ.App.1982).

b. Punitive damages are recoverable upon proof that the defendant acted with "actual malice or ill will." McElwain v. Georgia Pacific Corp., 245 Or. 247, 421 P.2d 957 (1966). Suppose the trespass is intentional, but under a mistaken claim of right?

> "While our courts have previously held that an intentional trespass, under a mistaken claim of right, does not entitle the landowner to punitive damages, it is equally true that when a wrongful act is accompanied by aggravating circumstances such as willfulness, wantonness, malice or oppression, punitive damages are recoverable. * * * Willful and wanton misconduct is that act intentionally done or that act taken, under the circumstances known, in reckless or conscious disregard of probable injurious consequences. * * * Here, plaintiff introduced evidence at trial that defendant not only crossed over plaintiff's property line prior to obtaining the outcome of a survey ordered after being informed the boundary line had not yet been located because of dense vegetation, but also crossed over the property line repeatedly after being advised by plaintiff of his trespass on her land. Such evidence was more than sufficient to submit the issue of punitive damages to a jury."

Rodrian v. Seiber, 194 Ill.App.3d 504, 510, 141 Ill.Dec. 585, 590, 551 N.E.2d 772, 774 (1990).

Although some jurisdictions require compensatory damages as a predicate for the recovery of punitive damages, a substantial number of states have adopted the rule that "proof of nominal damages will support a claim for punitive damages." Rushing v. Hooper–McDonald, Inc., 293 Ala. 56, 300 So.2d 94, 98 (1974).

c. Consequential compensatory damages may be recovered for "physical harm to the possessor of the land at the time of the trespass, * * * or to his [or her] things, or to members of the household or to their things." Baker v. Shymkiv, 6 Ohio St.3d 151, 451 N.E.2d 811, 814 (1983).

d. Although damages for emotional distress are often disallowed in trespass actions, some jurisdictions recognize mental anguish as a compensable harm if it is "the direct and natural result of a specific trespass." Senn v. Bunick, 40 Or.App. 33, 594 P.2d 837, 841 (1979) (plaintiff awarded damages for mental distress caused by destruction of fence and dumping of dirt on his land). *Accord* McGregor v. Barton Sand & Gravel, Inc., 62 Or.App. 24, 660 P.2d 175 (1983). Others allow recovery for emotional distress when the trespass was committed "under circumstances of insult or contumely or wilfully." Rushing v. Hooper–McDonald, 293 Ala. 56, 300 So.2d 94, 98 (1974) (plaintiff stated cause of action for emotional distress where defendant dumped asphalt on plaintiff's land seven times).

HENINGER v. DUNN

California Court of Appeal, 1980.
101 Cal.App.3d 858, 162 Cal.Rptr. 104.

CHRISTIAN, ASSOCIATE JUSTICE.

Appellants David and Eliza Heninger sued respondents Bernard and Elise Dunn for an injunction and damages for trespass. After a nonjury trial the court granted injunctive relief as prayed, but denied any award of damages. The appeal challenges the judgment insofar as it denied damages.

In April 1971 respondents, who owned mountain land adjoining land owned by appellants, bulldozed a rough road, approximately seven-tenths of a mile long, on appellants' land. Respondents acted despite appellants' objections, relying on the advice of an attorney who had erroneously told respondents that they held a valid easement permitting the cutting of the road. The bulldozing killed or damaged 225 trees, and destroyed much vegetative undergrowth, but the road provided additional access to appellants' property, thereby increasing its market value $5,000—from $179,000 just before the trespass to $184,000 immediately following the trespass.

The trial court found that it was technically possible to replace the dead or dying trees, at a cost of $221,647, and that the vegetative undergrowth could be restored at a cost of $19,610. But the court denied damages because there was no depreciation in the value of appellants' property, concluding that "[i]t is the rule in California that if the cost of repair or restoration of damaged property amounts to more than its depreciation in value because of the damage, the plaintiff cannot obtain a greater sum than the amount of the depreciation." Appellants contend that the court's understanding of the rule of damages was incorrect, and that the proper measure of their damages was the lesser of costs of restoration or the pretrespass value of their property, *i.e.*, $179,000.

The measure of damages in California for tortious injury to property is "the amount which will compensate for all the detriment proximately caused thereby * * *." (Civ.Code, § 3333.) Such damages are generally determined as the difference between the value of the property before and after the injury. * * *

One alternative measure of damages is the cost of restoring the property to its condition prior to the injury. * * *

The rule precluding recovery of restoration costs in excess of diminution in value is, however, not of invariable application. Restoration costs may be awarded even though they exceed the decrease in market value if "there is a reason personal to the owner for restoring the original condition" (Rest.2d Torts, § 929, com. b, at pp. 545–546), or "where there is reason to believe that the plaintiff will, in fact, make the repairs" (22 Am.Jur.2d, Damages, § 132, at p. 192). * * *

The "personal reason" exception has been invoked in many jurisdictions in cases involving destruction of shade or ornamental trees that were of personal value to the owner. In recent years, "courts throughout the country have placed a greater emphasis on the rights of a property owner to enjoy the aesthetic value of trees and shrubbery, notwithstanding the fact they may have little commercial value or that their destruction may, indeed, even enhance the market value of the property." (Rector, etc. v. C.S. McCrossan (1975) 306 Minn. 143, 146, 235 N.W.2d 609, 610.) Where such trees or shrubbery are destroyed by a trespasser, "[s]ound principle and persuasive authority support the allowance to an aggrieved landowner of the fair cost of restoring his land to a reasonable approximation of its former condition, without necessary limitation to the diminution in the market value of the land * * *." (Huber v. Serpico (1962) 71 N.J.Super. 329, 345, 176 A.2d 805, 813.) * * * If restoration of the land to a reasonable approximation of its former condition is impossible or impracticable, the landowner may recover the value of the trees or shrubbery, either as timber or for their aesthetic qualities, again without regard to the diminution in the value of the land. * * *

The common law principles guiding the assessment of damages for destruction of trees with personal value to their owner are controlling in the present case. * * *

There was substantial evidence that appellants had personal reasons for restoring the land to its original condition. David Heninger testified, "I think the land is beautiful, the natural forest beautiful, and I would like to see it remain that way." He and his family lived on the land, and, aside from the portion of the property on which they resided, they intended to leave it unimproved. The cost of a substantially identical restoration, however, including the transplanting of a large number of mature trees and the restoration of the vegetative undergrowth is, at $241,257, a manifestly unreasonable expense in relation to the value of the land prior to the trespass.

A plant ecologist estimated the cost to restore the vegetative undergrowth at $19,610. This estimate included the costs of planting 230 sapling trees as well as numerous shrubs and ground cover. The plant ecologist testified that a restoration of small trees and shrubs "would leave a scar, but it would not be unsightly," and that it would prevent erosion. On retrial, the court's determination whether a reasonable restoration is possible should focus on the question whether an award of the cost of restoring the vegetative undergrowth (or some other method of covering the scar on the land and preventing further erosion) would achieve compensation within the overall limits of what the court determines to be just and reasonable.

Appellants contend that they are entitled to recover double damages pursuant to Civil Code section 3346, which provides for recovery of "twice the sum as would compensate for the actual detriment" for wrongful injury to timber, trees, or underwood as a result of a trespass that was "casual or involuntary" or committed by a defendant with "probable cause to believe that the land on which the trespass was committed was his own."[3] * * *

3. Civil Code section 3346:
"(a) For wrongful injuries to timber, trees, or underwood upon the land of another, or removal thereof, the measure of damages is three times such sum as would compen-

Statutes providing for recovery of double or treble damages for injuries to trees are intended to make timber appropriation unprofitable. * * *

Whatever the original policy behind Civil Code section 3346 and the context within which it is normally used, the language of the statute is broad-sweeping, applying to "timber, trees, or underwood." Its application in a case involving damage to fruit trees has been upheld. (Paul A. Mosesian & Sons v. Danielian (1942) 52 Cal.App.2d 387, 388–389, 126 P.2d 363.) The term "underwood" commonly includes seedlings, saplings, shrubs, bushes, and small trees. * * * Neither the language of the statute nor past judicial constructions supports respondents' contention that it is applicable only to injuries to trees that are valuable as timber.

[W]e conclude that the damages to be doubled or trebled pursuant to Civil Code section 3346 are those determined by the trier of fact to constitute just compensation within the overall limits of reasonableness, regardless of what specific measure of damages is used. (See *Roche v. Casissa, supra,* 154 Cal.App.2d 785, 788, 316 P.2d 776 [upholding trebling of damages measured by the diminution in the value of land on which trees stood].)

Notes

1. Courts increasingly allow recovery of replacement costs in excess of diminution value where trespass destroys trees and other vegetation that are ornamental or have other personal value to the owner. *See e.g.,* Wujcik v. Gallagher and Henry Contractors, 232 Ill.App.3d 323, 172 Ill.Dec. 920, 596 N.E.2d 199 (1992); Rodrian v. Seiber, 194 Ill.App.3d 504, 141 Ill.Dec. 585, 551 N.E.2d 772 (1990); Keitges v. VanDermeulen, 240 Neb. 580, 483 N.W.2d 137 (1992). On the other hand, courts continue to limit damages to diminution value where the trees are not ornamental, rare or unique. *See e.g.,* Kebschull v. Nott, 220 Mont. 64, 714 P.2d 993 (1986); Kapcsos v. Hammond, 13 Ohio App.3d 140, 468 N.E.2d 325 (1983).

2. The trial court's decision in *Heninger* illustrates the operation of a general principle of damages known as the "benefits rule." Professor Dobbs describes the rule as follows: "Where the defendant's tortious conduct causes damages, but also operates directly to confer some benefit upon the plaintiff, the plaintiff's claim for damages may be diminished by the amount of the benefit received. In the language of the Restatement of Torts, this is to be done, however, only where it is 'equitable.' " D. Dobbs, Handbook on the Law of Remedies § 3.6, at 181 (1973).

3. When real property has no buildings or trees on it, the courts are reluctant to allow recovery in excess of the diminution in fair market value. For example, in Whitaker Acres, Inc. v. Schrenk, 170 Ga.App. 238, 316 S.E.2d

sate for the actual detriment, except that where the trespass was casual or involuntary, or that the defendant in any action brought under this section had probable cause to believe that the land on which the trespass was committed was his own or the land of the person in whose service or by whose direction the act was done, the measure of damages shall be twice the sum as would compensate for the actual detriment. * * * "

For a discussion of the relationship between such statutory penalties and punitive damages, see D. Dobbs, Handbook on the Law of Remedies 210 (1973).

537 (1984), the plaintiff sought to recover the costs of restoring a lot "uniquely suited" to his house building needs, but the court applied the traditional measure of damages on the ground that the property's uniqueness resulted only from the plaintiff's "subjective evaluation."

WILLIAMS v. MONSANTO COMPANY

Missouri Court of Appeals, Eastern District, 1993.
856 S.W.2d 338.

SMITH, JUDGE.

Plaintiff appeals from the judgment of the trial court based in part on a jury verdict on plaintiff's claim of nuisance and in part from the court's direction of a defendant's verdict on plaintiff's trespass count. We affirm.

Plaintiff owned and operated an automobile repair business on land abutting property owned by Monsanto upon which it operates a chemical plant. Beginning in the spring of 1984 and continuing for several months, particulate from the Monsanto plant fell on occasion on the premises used by plaintiff "dusting" his and his customers' vehicles. Monsanto admitted that particulate did fall on several occasions on the plaintiff's premises although it disputed that the severity of the fall-out was as plaintiff contended. Plaintiff also contended that the particulate, sodium tripolyphosphate (STP), caused pitting of the paint of customers' cars and resulted in loss of business. Monsanto's evidence was that STP is a food additive used in a variety of products such as pasta and canned hams and does not cause pitting of automobile paint. Only plaintiff professed to have found such pitting. Monsanto would provide for having cars dusted by the particulate to be cleaned by a neighborhood car wash.

Monsanto expended approximately $500,000 attempting to identify the source of the particulate leak and to remedy it. Testimony from governmental employees involved with pollution control indicated that Monsanto was extremely cooperative and involved in attempting to correct the problem. Some of the complaints made against Monsanto turned out to involve emissions from a neighboring plant, Carondolet Coke Plant. Two witnesses with business in close proximity to plaintiff testified that they had no problems in operating their businesses in the area and had never observed or had complaints by customers of damage to their automobiles caused by white dust from Monsanto.

Plaintiff contended that the loss of customers caused him to have to close his business with a resulting loss of income. There was considerable evidence that plaintiff's business was a losing proposition before any complained of emissions occurred, that he was seriously overextended before the emissions, and that none of his major customers reduced their business during the period in question, although he had lost the customer providing about 50% of his revenue in the year before the emissions began for reasons unrelated to the emissions.

Plaintiff's amended petition was in fourteen counts including among others trespass, nuisance, negligence, intentional infliction of emotional distress, and consortium claims by plaintiff's wife. The court limited the trial to trespass and nuisance and at the close of the evidence, refused to instruct on the trespass issue thereby effectively directing a verdict on that claim. The jury unanimously found for defendant on the nuisance claim. On appeal plaintiff challenges the court's action in directing a verdict on the trespass claim, in failing to grant a judgment notwithstanding the verdict to plaintiff on the nuisance claim * * *.

The availability and relationship between nuisance actions and trespass actions in suits involving pollutants was discussed thoroughly by Judge Simon in *Maryland Heights Leasing, Inc. v. Mallinckrodt,* 706 S.W.2d 218 (Mo.App.1985). For trespass to lie the pollution must be at a level so as to constitute an actual interference with the possession of the land, not merely interference with its use and enjoyment. *Id.* at [14–15]. Quoting from *Borland v. Sanders Lead Co.,* 369 So.2d 523 (Ala.1979) [8, 11–14] the court stated that "if, as a result of the defendant's operation, the polluting substance is deposited upon the plaintiff's property, thus interfering with his exclusive possessory interest by causing substantial damage to the *res,* then the plaintiff may seek his remedy in trespass, * * *."[1] *Maryland Heights, supra* at [13]. Nuisance, on the other hand, requires an interference with the use and possession of the land. As stated in *Maryland Heights,* again quoting from *Borland,* "For example, if the smoke or polluting substance emitting from a defendant's operation causes discomfort and annoyance to the plaintiff in his use and enjoyment of the property, then the plaintiff's remedy is for nuisance."

The evidence presented here all dealt with the effect of the STP on the operation of the defendant's business. None of the evidence dealt with the damage which the STP did to the property itself. The evidence established that whatever injury plaintiff suffered it was to the use and enjoyment of his property and was not substantial damage to the res itself. The trial court did not err in directing a verdict on the trespass claim.

Plaintiff next contends that the evidence established as a matter of law that he was entitled to a verdict on the nuisance claim. Nuisance requires that one unreasonably use his property such that it substantially impairs the rights of another to peacefully use his property. *Racine v. Glendale Shooting Club, Inc.,* 755 S.W.2d 369 (Mo.App.1988) [1–3]; *Davis v. J.C. Nichols Company,* 714 S.W.2d 679 (Mo.App.1986) [6–9]. Whether a use is unreasonable to the point of a nuisance depends upon factors such as the locality, character of the neighborhood, nature of use, extent of injury, and effect upon enjoyment of life.

Here no other neighbors complained during the period in question. The area was largely industrial, with a coke plant and a cement plant nearby. Monsanto made substantial, expensive efforts to diagnose and correct the problem. It provided car cleaning at its expense when requested for vehicles which were dusted by STP. There was considerable

1. Several cases have indicated that trespass occurs upon unauthorized entry, regardless of the amount of force used or the damage done. *See Vecchiotti v. Tegethoff,* 745 S.W.2d 741 (Mo.App.1987) [10–12]; *Crook v. Sheehan Enterprises, Inc.,* 740 S.W.2d 333 (Mo.App.1987) [1, 2]; *Weldon v. Town Properties, Inc.,* 633 S.W.2d 196 (Mo.App.1982) [7, 8]. Each of those cases involved actual physical entry by a person, not entry by airborne pollutants.

evidence that plaintiff exaggerated his claims and that his business difficulties arose from causes other than Monsanto. The questions of whether a use is "unreasonable" and whether it impairs "substantially" the rights of another to use his property are particularly fact intensive and are particularly suited for jury resolution. *Davis, supra,* at 10, 11. The trial court did not err in denying plaintiff's motion for judgment notwithstanding the verdict and for new trial premised on the absence of evidence to support the verdict.

Judgment affirmed.

GARY M. GAERTNER, P.J., and STEPHAN, J., concur.

Note

Consider the following analysis of the relationship of trespass to nuisance:

"Trespass is defined as an intrusion or invasion of tangible property, either real or personal, which interferes with the possessor's interest in the right of *exclusive possession* of the property. An intrusion can, and often does, constitute both trespass and nuisance because it interferes with both the right of possession and the use and enjoyment of the possessor's property. However, a person who intentionally interferes with another's exclusive right of possession of the res, without privilege to do so, is liable to the other for trespass without proof of actual damages, while intentional nuisance requires proof of actual damages.

"Because trespass protects a possessor's right to exclusive possession of the property, trespass requires proof of an entry on the plaintiff's land, either by the defendant, or by some physical or observable object which the defendant caused to enter onto the property. The modern action for trespass to land evolved from the common-law action which required proof that the intrusion actually interfered with the right of exclusive possession of the property. Nuisance applied in cases in which the injuries were indirect and less substantial. The distinction between injuries which were direct and substantial and those which were considered indirect and less substantial eventually evolved into a fictitious 'dimensional' test: '[I]f the intruding agent could be seen by the naked eye, the intrusion was considered a trespass. If the agent could not be seen, it was considered indirect and less substantial, hence, a nuisance.'

"The traditional rule limiting trespass to invasion of things that can be seen with the naked eye is an arbitrary one that has been discarded in some modern airborne pollution cases. However, the traditional distinction serves a useful function. By limiting actions for trespass to physical intrusion, the law affirms the nature of the interest protected—the right of plaintiff's exclusive possession of the res. By limiting liability for injury to the res that results from intrusion of an observable object onto the property, the rule also limits the scope of a defendant's liability for trespass.

"Historically, a plaintiff could maintain an action for trespass even though a defendant was not at fault in causing the invasion of plaintiff's property. With the development of negligence law, however, the strict liability rule of trespass became difficult to justify. As one writer pointed out, 'There is no great triumph of reason in a rule which makes a street railway, whose car jumps the track, liable only for negligence to a pedestrian on the sidewalk, but absolutely liable to the owner of the plate glass window behind him.'

"Today, the 'strict liability' rule in trespass has been repudiated both in England and in the United States, and under the law of trespass, like nuisance, a defendant is only liable for an intentional, reckless, or negligent intrusion onto the plaintiff's property, unless the defendant is engaged in an 'ultra hazardous' activity for which strict liability is imposed.

"A historical distinction between trespass and trespass on the case has occasionally created a problem for modern courts in cases in which the invasion is 'indirect' rather than 'direct.' Under traditional common law, trespass required proof of direct, rather than indirect invasion by the defendant, and any 'indirect' invasion constituted trespass on the case requiring proof of substantial damages. This distinction has been discarded by most courts today. Under the modern view, the defendant may be liable for trespass even though a substance was not placed directly on plaintiff's land so long as the force causing the deposit, such as natural flow to the land, was direct. Thus, if a defendant places a pile of sand and gravel onto her own property, and rain causes the sand and gravel to flow onto the property of a neighbor, an action for trespass is appropriate. The defendant is liable even though the entry of the 'thing' was indirect, rather than direct, so long as the defendant acted with knowledge that an invasion was 'substantially certain' to follow as a result of defendant's actions.

"Holding a defendant liable in trespass for indirectly as well as directly causing matter to be deposited on the plaintiff's land is consistent with the rule that a defendant is liable for the direct and indirect consequences of her intentional tort. Imposing liability for indirect trespass only in cases in which a defendant has 'knowledge' that such actions are 'substantially certain' to cause a trespass is also consistent with the modern rule requiring proof of defendant's intent, recklessness, or negligence in order to recover damages for trespass unless the defendant is engaged in an ultra hazardous activity.

"Nuisance law protects the plaintiff's right to use and enjoy his property. Unlike trespass, nuisance does not require a physical invasion of the property but occurs if a condition is maintained on the defendant's land that interferes with the plaintiff's use and enjoyment of the plaintiff's property. A nuisance is a state of affairs, and may be merely a right thing in the wrong place, like a pig in the parlor instead of the barnyard.

"In order to recover damages for private nuisance, a plaintiff must prove that the defendant engaged in an 'unreasonable' activity on the defendant's land that 'substantially' interfered with the plaintiff's enjoyment of his property. In order to determine whether a defendant's use of his own land is 'unreasonable' and to determine whether the defendant's interference with plaintiff's use and enjoyment was substantial, nuisance law requires a court to engage in a balancing test and to weigh the particular facts in each case. Because the facts of each case are unique and the outcome of each dispute depends on balancing of equitable factors, the law of nuisance has been called a 'quintessential judgment-entitlement' rule in contrast to the more 'mechanical' rule of trespass. It has also been frequently criticized for its doctrinal confusion, 'ad hocery' and question-begging Latin phrases."

Powell, Trespass, Nuisance, and the Evolution of Common Law in Modern Pollution Cases, 21 Real Estate L.J. 182, 185–89 (1992).* Do odors from a sewage treatment plant constitute a trespass? See Brown v. County Commissioner of Scioto County, 87 Ohio App.3d 704, 622 N.E.2d 1153 (1993).

D. DOBBS, LAW OF REMEDIES

513–17 (2d Ed.1993).**

§ 5.6 Harms to Interests in Use and Enjoyment: Damages for Nuisance

"§ 5.6(1) Substantive Background: Nuisance and Trespass

"The use and enjoyment interest in land might be invaded both by trespass and by nuisance. The balancing of hardships in injunction cases may at times differ according to whether the theory of the plaintiff's claim is trespass or nuisance;—but the measurement of harm to the landowner's enjoyment interest is much the same in either case, once it is established that the owner's legal right has been violated. Even so, the most common way in which use and enjoyment interests are violated is through a private nuisance.

"As a matter of substantive law, a nuisance is in fact defined as an unreasonable interference with the use and enjoyment of land as distinct from an interference with possession, which has traditionally been allocated to the trespass action. Pollution of the air or water, or excessive noise or lights, if extreme enough, can count as nuisances. So may certain invasions, like the backup of waters or sewage, which may be considered too indirect to qualify as trespasses. Even dangerous conditions outside the land, or unpleasant ones, might at times qualify. The distinction between nuisance and trespass may be less significant than it once was, and today it may be possible for a plaintiff to claim a trespass when pollution of the land occurs—a micro-trespass.

"Damages for nuisance vary with the facts. If the effects of the nuisance are more or less permanent, the diminution in land value due to the nuisance will be recoverable; if temporary, the diminished rental value during the period of harm. Cost of repair and personal discomfort or inconvenience may also form bases for recovery. Where the nuisance causes harm besides that claimed by the plaintiff personally, damages awards can be structured to provide incentives to cease pollution.

"§ 5.6(2) Nuisance Damages Generally

"Objective or Market Measures

"*Diminished market value.* Apart from special and punitive damages, the measures most commonly invoked when the plaintiff has lost use and enjoyment of land are the diminished land value, the diminished rental value and the cost of repairing the condition in question. These measures are appropriate when the nuisance or trespass actually involves physical harm to the land. The same measures of damages are invoked when the nuisance does no physical harm at all, but affects use and enjoyment directly. Noise, air pollution and sight nuisances are in this category. Interference with easements is treated in the same way as nuisances. If the nuisance is significant and the effects more or less permanent, the diminished use and enjoyment will be reflected in diminished market value and the plaintiff may recover an award based on that diminution.

"*Diminished rental value.* If the effects of the nuisance are transitory, as in the case of a pollution which has now been stopped at its source and the effects of which will abate with time, then the damages are not measured by depreciation in market value but by depreciation in rental value of the property for the period in which the nuisance has been or will be in existence. This is a market measure, but it is one based on the rental rather than the sales market; it reflects the fact that the harm will last only a limited period of time.

"*Costs of repair or abatement.* In some cases it will be appropriate for the plaintiff to recover costs reasonably incurred in abating the nuisance or in preventing future injury. For example, the plaintiff who has sewer lines relaid after a sewage backup, may avoid future damage and if the expense was reasonably incurred to that end, it is a recoverable element in the nuisance action. In the case of hazardous substances controlled by federal law under CERCLA,[7] liability is for the cost or removal or remedial action, but remedial action is site clean-up, not necessarily full compensation for consequential damages. On the other hand, CERCLA also authorizes recovery by the state or other governmental entity for damage to natural resources themselves. To the extent the nuisance is abated, permanent damages are not to be assessed.

"*Ceilings on recovery of repair or abatement costs.* There are limits to damages recovered to remove the nuisance or minimize future harm. The expense incurred for such purposes must be reasonable. In addition, some cases have said that the recovery of damages based on the cost of repair or the like may not exceed the sum by which the property value has been diminished. There are no doubt cases for which this rule is correct, as suggested by the rules concerning physical harms of land. But if the expenditure is reasonably made to forestall future damages, that expenditure should qualify as an item recoverable under the affirmative version of the avoidable consequence rule; this in turn seems to imply that the plaintiff could recover for the expenditures reasonably made even if hindsight shows that the attempt to minimize damages cost more than it saved.

"Damages Not Based on Property Value or Repair

"*Personal discomfort, illness and anguish.* Plaintiffs often emphasize personal discomfort, illness or mental anguish resulting from the nuisance.

7. The Comprehensive Environmental Response, Compensation and Liability Act (CERCLA), 42 U.S.C.A. § 9601 *et seq.* (also known as the Superfund Act). References here include the amendments known as SARA. *See* § 5.2(5) for further explication of CERCLA.

These are recoverable elements of damages, as is simple inconvenience caused by the nuisance. In contrast, courts usually compensate only for pecuniary losses when the tort physically harms the property or dispossess the plaintiff. In those cases, as distinct from nuisance cases, the plaintiff might recover the diminished value of the property or the cost or repair, or (in dispossession cases) the use value of the property, but no damages for emotional distress. Where serious personal injury results from a nuisance, as in some toxic torts cases, the damages emphasis tends to become an emphasis on personal injury rather than property damage.

"*Combining claims for discomfort and claims for diminished value.* In many cases plaintiffs claim both discomfort damages and diminished value damages. But since the diminished value award is itself a reflection of the discount that potential buyers would require to be willing to live with the discomforts of the nuisance in question, it may be quite inappropriate to award both a sum for diminished value and an additional sum for discomfort the plaintiff will suffer from a continuance of the nuisance in the future. Many writers wish to see the law expand liability for the plaintiff's subjective sense of loss in addition to liability for market diminution, so perhaps plaintiffs should have a choice of either measure but not both.

"Most decisions, however, seem to have gone further by routinely allowing the plaintiff to recover both depreciated value *and* discomfort or illness, with a little authority to the contrary. The recovery of both seems right enough where the sums are trivial or where the plaintiff's illness is idiosyncratic and unlikely to be reflected in diminished value, where the illness is likely to continue even if the plaintiff were to correct the nuisance or leave it, and where the recovery for illness or discomfort is limited to that which occurs before judgment. Otherwise a recovery of both diminished value and future discomfort seems duplicative."

Notes

1. The distinction between damages for loss of use and damages for annoyance and discomfort is discussed in Miller v. Carnation Co., 39 Colo.App. 1, 4–5, 564 P.2d 127, 130 (1977) (trespass and nuisance action brought by husband and wife against adjoining egg ranch for harm caused by flies and rodents):

> "In its special verdict, the jury apportioned the damages, awarding $28,000 for deprivation of use and enjoyment of the property, evenly divided between Mr. and Mrs. Miller, and $72,000 for 'annoyance, discomfort, inconvenience, and loss of ability to enjoy their lives,' attributing $18,000 to Mr. Miller and $54,000 to Mrs. Miller.
>
> "Contrary to Carnation's contention, damages for loss of use and enjoyment of property, on the one hand, and for annoyance and discomfort, on the other hand, are not duplicative. The use and enjoyment of land is a proprietary interest, while annoyance and discomfort are personal, not proprietary, interests. In its remittitur the trial court correctly limited recovery for loss of use and enjoyment to the loss of rental value occasioned by the invasion. This distinction between the elements of damage leads to the rule that the owner of land who is not an occupant may recover only for the impaired value of his property, while an occupant-owner may

recover both his proprietary and personal loss. Restatement of Torts, § 929, Comment g; Restatement, Second, Torts, § 929, Comment e (Tent. Draft No. 19)."

2. Your clients purchased lakeshore property for investment purposes. They have wanted to sell it, but have felt it was not possible to put it on the market because the defendant's sewage treatment plant is discharging effluent into the lake, causing the intense growth of algae. The water would clear itself in about ten years if the discharge were stopped. The treatment plant was constructed 30 years ago, your clients purchased their property 10 years ago, and the algae began to develop 5 years ago. May your clients bring an action for damages for a continuing nuisance and recover for the loss of use of their property? These issues were considered in Sundell v. Town of New London, 119 N.H. 839, 409 A.2d 1315 (1979):

> "In our view, however, the trial court correctly determined that the condition complained of by the plaintiffs constitutes an abatable nuisance for which successive causes of action will lie. The fact that the damage will not stop the instant the town's offending activities cease, but may take ten years before improvement results, does not make the nuisance permanent. By continuing the discharge into the brook and lake, the town is continually causing new damage by prolonging the time before which improvement can begin.
>
> "In determining the nature of a plaintiff's remedy in private nuisance, the general rule is that recovery may be had only for past harm. Restatement, (Second), Torts § 930 comment *a* (1977). Where the injury complained of is temporary or intermittent, depending on uncertain future conditions, the nuisance is characterized as temporary or abatable and the plaintiff may not recover prospective damages. Instead, the injured party must bring successive actions to recover for successive injuries, as they occur. In each successive action, the plaintiff may recover for all injury sustained during the statutory period prior to the commencement of suit.
>
> "On the other hand, a nuisance may be characterized as permanent when it exists under circumstances that give rise to the presumption that it will continue indefinitely or affect the value of the property permanently, 'being at once necessarily productive of all the damage which can ever result from it.' Where the nuisance is so characterized, the plaintiff may recover in one action for all harm sustained, whether past or prospective. In such a case, the measure of damages becomes the total diminution in the value of the property. Prospective relief becomes appropriate because of the inadequacy to the injured party of successive suits at law. Thus, the distinction between abatable and nonabatable nuisances serves to more fully compensate the injured landowner for an interference that is tantamount to a permanent taking, and should not serve to deprive the plaintiffs of any recovery. Restatement, (Second), Torts § 930 comment *a* (1977).*

* * *

* For a discussion of the concept that the plaintiff should have a right to elect between characterizing an ongoing nuisance as temporary or permanent, see Kornoff v. Kingsburg Cotton Oil Co., 45 Cal.2d 265, 288 P.2d 507 (1955); Spaulding v. Cameron, 38 Cal.2d 265, 239 P.2d 625 (1952).

"A final contention of the defendant's is that the court erred in allowing plaintiffs Rolfe and Avery to recover damages. The town argues that because they purchased their property for investment purposes and had not yet sold them, they had not realized any loss. The court allowed these plaintiffs to introduce evidence of the loss in value of their properties due to the condition of the lake and to recover on the basis of applying prevailing rates of interest to this reduction for the period of the statute of limitations. Defendant argues that because the condition is abatable and that there are in fact plans to eliminate the discharge of effluent altogether, it is possible that by the time the property is sold, there will be no damage and plaintiffs will have received a windfall because they would have suffered no damage and yet they will have recovered damages.

"We find no merit in this argument. There was evidence that these plaintiffs have held their property for a much longer time than they would have because of the diminished value. If the condition were permanent and they had sold their property at the reduced value they could have recovered their full loss. They should not be deprived of recovering the cost of holding their property until the temporary nuisance has been abated. The measure of damages allowed by the court was a fair method of compensating these plaintiffs for the loss of use of their property."

L'ENFANT PLAZA EAST, INC. v. JOHN McSHAIN, INC.

District of Columbia Court of Appeals, 1976.
359 A.2d 5.

NEBEKER, ASSOCIATE JUDGE:

Appellant L'Enfant Plaza East, Inc. (L'Enfant) complains of the trial court's order granting summary judgment against it in its suit seeking damages against appellee John McShain, Inc. (McShain) for trespass and delay in a construction project. The judgment was based upon McShain's motion for summary judgment on the ground that the suit was untimely filed under the applicable statute of limitations.[1] We find error and reverse.

In the late 1960's McShain, a general contractor, constructed a building for the Department of Housing and Urban Development (HUD). The western boundary of the HUD building adjoined the property leased to L'Enfant. During construction of the HUD building, a portion of the footings extended beyond HUD's boundary line and into L'Enfant's property. This encroachment, consisting of concrete with steel reinforcing bars, ran along the common boundary line for approximately 240 feet. It extended 1½ to 3½ feet into L'Enfant's property. The encroaching struc-

1. D.C.Code 1973, § 12–301(3) provides in pertinent part:

[A]ctions for the following purposes may not be brought after the expiration of the period specified below from the time the right to maintain the action accrues:

* * *

(3) for the recovery of damages for an injury to real * * * property—3 years[.]

"Our statute of limitations comes from Maryland, and requires [the suit] to be brought within three years ensuing the cause of action." Meloy v. Johnston, 2 MacArthur (9 D.C.) 202, 206 (1875).

ture was approximately 3 feet thick and was buried 23 feet below the surface.

L'Enfant, through a contractor, commenced development of its property on May 11, 1971. On June 11, 1971, during excavation for the construction of its building, the encroachment was discovered. After demand, McShain contracted for the removal of the encroachment during the month of July 1971. Construction resumed following such removal and L'Enfant's building was completed on June 25, 1973. The complaint was filed on June 21, 1974.

Our research, and that of the parties, reveals that this is a case of first impression in this jurisdiction. A cause of action for trespass usually accrues at the time of the original encroachment. *See* Jackson v. Emmons, 19 App.D.C. 250, 255 (1902). We note a similarity to this general rule for permanent structural encroachments. In such cases, the cause of action accrues at the time the trespass occurs (*see* Bertram v. Orlando, 102 Cal.App.2d 506, 227 P.2d 894 (1951)); [3] however, we believe that a continuing unknown encroachment is another matter.

McShain argues, pursuant to the general rule, that the encroachment occurred and was discovered more than three years before L'Enfant filed its complaint for damages and therefore the cause of action is barred. We agree that D.C.Code 1973, § 12–301(3), is the controlling statutory provision. The encroachment, however, was unlike that in most cases regarding permanent structures. First, we are not persuaded that the encroachment was permanent in nature simply because it was an injury to real property. Moreover, it is significant that the encroachment was not vital to or supportive of the HUD building since it was easily removed without affecting the stability of that building. It was not included in the HUD construction plans and was promptly removed at a reasonable expense. Three factors for determining permanency are articulated in D. Dobbs, Remedies § 5.4 at 338 (1973):

> (1) is the source of the invasion physically permanent, i.e., is it likely, in the nature of things, to remain indefinitely? (2) is the source of the invasion the kind of thing an equity court would refuse to abate by injunction because of its value to the community or because of relations between the parties? (3) which party seeks the permanent or prospective measure of damages?

Once this encroachment was discovered, it was removed without undue difficulty. Therefore, "in the nature of things" it was not likely to remain indefinitely. Second, this case reveals a concealed subterranean encroachment buried at least 23 feet below the surface. Such a trespass is unlike that in Sustrik v. Jones & Laughlin Steel Corp., 413 Pa. 324, 197 A.2d 44, 46 (1964). There, a pipe was installed "more than forty years before the * * * action was instituted. While constructed underground, [the pipe] was clearly visible in certain sections of plaintiffs' property". The claim

3. *See also* Annot., 12 A.L.R.3d 1265, 1266 (1967). *But compare* Barberi v. Bochinsky, 43 N.J.Super. 186, 128 A.2d 1, 3 (1956).

for damages based upon what was viewed as a readily apparent trespass was properly barred by the statute of limitations.

After an extensive survey of the case law, we conclude that the instant subterranean encroachment was a continuing trespass.[4] *See* Milton v. Puffer, 207 Mass. 416, 93 N.E. 634 (1911); Curtis Mfg. Co. v. Spencer Wire Co., 203 Mass. 448, 89 N.E. 534, 536 (1909); 509 Sixth Ave. Corp. v. New York City Transit Authority, 15 N.Y.2d 48, 255 N.Y.S.2d 89, 92, 203 N.E.2d 486, 488 (1964). "[A]lthough the nature of the structure may be permanent, the nature of the trespass is continuous." *Id.*, 255 N.Y.S.2d at 92, 203 N.E.2d at 488. L'Enfant's knowledge of the trespass for more than three years prior to filing a complaint does not necessarily bar its cause of action. * * * The cause of action accrued on the date of the trespass and continued until three years after the encroachment had been removed. We further note that L'Enfant's recovery is limited to damages resulting from the trespass during "the [three-year] statutory period preceding the filing of the suit." Underwater Storage, Inc. v. United States Rubber Co., 125 U.S.App.D.C. 297, 300, 371 F.2d 950, 953 (1966).[6] This calculation will allow L'Enfant to recover damages for delay which occurred after June 21, 1971. However, damages experienced prior to June 21, 1971, are barred by the statute of limitations.

We hold that the instant subterranean encroaching structure was a continuing trespass which gave rise to successive causes of action until its removal. * * * Accordingly, the trial court's ruling on the motion for summary judgment is reversed and the case is remanded for further proceedings.

Notes

1. Compare Dolph v. Mangus, 400 N.E.2d 189, 190–92 (Ind.App.1980), in which the defendants had altered the natural flow of surface waters, causing flooding and erosion of plaintiff's crop land since 1948:

> "The [trial] court found that these actions constituted a trespass but that plaintiffs' complaint, which was not filed until July 24, 1974, was barred by the statute of limitations.
>
> "The plaintiffs acknowledge that the six (6) year statute of limitations found in IC 34–1–2–1 applies to the claim before us. It is the plaintiffs' position on appeal, however, that while the statute would bar a 'permanent' injury created in 1948, the injuries complained of were of the type referred to as 'temporary' or 'recurring.' Thus, they argue that recovery should have been permitted for the damages incurred up to six years prior to commencement of the action. The defendants respond that in reality the court found the existence of a prescriptive easement since more than twenty (20) years had elapsed since the origin of the injury.

4. *See* Restatement (Second) of Torts § 161(1) (1965); W. Prosser, Law of Torts § 13 at 74–75 (4th ed. 1971).

6. Since the "trespass is * * * 'continuous', a new cause of action arises day by day * * * with the result that the plaintiff in such a case can always recover for such damages as have accrued within the statutory period immediately prior to suit." D. Dobbs, Remedies, *supra* at 343.

"We do not accept defendants' assertion that the court found a prescriptive easement. The essential difference between prescription and the operation of a statute of limitations is that the former is positive and creates rights while limitation is negative and destroys. To establish an easement by prescription the burden is upon the party asserting the easement to show actual, open, notorious, continuous, uninterrupted, adverse use. Here the court repeatedly stated that it found plaintiffs' claim *barred* by the statute of limitations. Moreover, neither the defendants' answer nor the evidence adduced at trial were directed to prescription. Rather they merely asserted the claims were barred by the statute of limitations.

"As the plaintiffs have pointed out, many jurisdictions dealing with this type of problem have drawn a distinction between injuries termed 'original' or 'permanent' on the one hand and those referred to as 'temporary,' 'transient,' 'continuing' or 'recurring' on the other. In the former category the courts have held that a plaintiff has but one claim for relief in which he may recover for all damages, past, present and prospective. In the latter category each new injury is treated as a new claim for relief and recovery is limited to that specific injury.

"Thus, if the claim is of the permanent variety, the action must be commenced within the statutory period or it is barred. On the other hand, if the injury is of the temporary variety each new injury starts the limitations statute running anew with the effect that at any given time the plaintiff can recover the actual damage incurred for the various temporary injuries which have occurred within the statutory period preceding the filing of the complaint.

"We also agree that Indiana subscribes to this 'dual rule' distinction. * * *

"The problem that arises in any given case, of course, is to determine into which category the injury properly falls. The annotation in 5 A.L.R.2d 302 collects the cases from the various jurisdictions and attempts to identify various factors the courts have deemed significant in particular cases involving waters overflowing the lands of another.[2] What is readily apparent is that no particular factor is controlling and that even within a single jurisdiction the cases are often irreconcilable. * * *

"One additional observation may be made. Apart from its involvement with the statute of limitations, the underlying purpose in these distinctions is an effort to accurately assess the damages the plaintiff has suffered. Is the injury such that he should recover only for the damage experienced from a particular occurrence, or are the consequences sufficiently certain that a broader recovery should be permitted and required? In response to this concern it is reasonable that the courts have recognized that injuries of the 'recurring' variety when continued over a protracted period of time may, through the regularity of their recurrence and the

2. These include (1) whether the structure causing the injury is necessarily injurious; (2) the extent to which the injurious result is certain and predictable; (3) whether the overflows are intermittent and caused only in conjunction with a supervening cause; (4) whether the structure causing the injury is permanent; (5) whether the structure was lawfully erected on property other than the plaintiff's; (6) whether the structure was negligently and improperly constructed, maintained or operated; (7) whether a nuisance created is abatable; (8) which theory the plaintiff used in bringing his action.

nature of the damage caused, become 'permanent.' In such cases, the statute of limitations should commence to run upon the permanent injury when its permanence is discernable. *See* City of Stillwater v. Robertson (1943), 192 Okl. 395, 136 P.2d 923 and cases cited in 5 A.L.R.2d 320 n. 12. *Compare* Hayes v. St. Louis & S.F.R. Co. (1913), 177 Mo.App. 201, 162 S.W. 266.

* * *

"While the flooding of plaintiffs' cropland might be considered a recurring type of injury, the complaint appears to have alleged permanent injury. The evidence favoring the decision supports the determination that in the more than twenty-five years which occurred between the installation of the defendants' tile system and the bringing of the action the damages had become permanent. Plaintiff Robert Dolph described the overflow as continuous. There was evidence concerning the gulleys that had quickly washed into the area in question. In addition much of plaintiffs' damage evidence described permanent damage and depreciated the value of 51 acres of plaintiffs' land by 50% as a result thereof.

"Accordingly, we find that the evidence supports the conclusion that the injuries to plaintiffs' land had become permanent more than six years prior to commencement of the action and the court therefore correctly concluded the claim was barred by the statute of limitations."

2. How do you think the Supreme Court of Appeals of West Virginia would have decided either *L'Enfant Plaza* or *Dolph* after its opinion in *Jarrett, supra* p. 188? The West Virginia court has not yet had the opportunity to address this issue. Should gasoline contamination of the soil be viewed as a permanent or a continuing nuisance? See Wilshire Westwood Associates v. Atlantic Richfield Co., 20 Cal.App.4th 732, 24 Cal.Rptr.2d 562 (1993).

D. DOBBS, HANDBOOK ON THE LAW OF REMEDIES

335, 343–44 (1973).*

"§ 5.4 The Permanent Nuisance and Prospective Damages

"Repeated, Continuing and Permanent Invasions

"In a number of cases courts have drawn a distinction between *damages* that are permanent and those that are temporary, allowing recovery of diminished market value where the injury was permanent and allowing cost of repairs where it was temporary or repairable at reasonable cost. In other situations courts have drawn a confusingly similar, but actually quite different distinction. This is the distinction between permanent *sources* of damages, such as nuisances or trespasses that cannot or will not be abated, and temporary sources of damage, such as nuisances or trespasses that will naturally terminate or those that will be terminated by court order. Courts sometimes overlook the distinction with resulting confusion. * * *

"Permanent Invasions and the Statute of Limitations

"Courts classify invasions as 'permanent' for two purposes: one purpose is related to assessment of damages, and a distinct purpose is applica-

* Reprinted with permission of West Publishing Co.

tion of the statute of limitations. There is not much doubt that the classification as permanent is much influenced by the purpose for which the classification is made, so that what is permanent for damages purposes is not necessarily permanent for statute of limitations purposes. Put more bluntly, the classification as 'permanent' is not a finding of fact nor a logical deduction; it is only a short-hand way of saying that certain policy decisions have been made.

"In theory, if a nuisance is deemed permanent, there is only one unceasing invasion of the plaintiff's interests and only one cause of action. This necessarily arises when the invasion first began or was first manifest. The statute of limitations on the one cause of action must, then, begin running from the time the invasion began, or from the time it became manifest. In contrast, if the nuisance or trespass is 'temporary,' or 'continuous,' a new cause of action arises day by day or injury by injury, with the result that the plaintiff in such a case can always recover for such damages as have accrued within the statutory period immediately prior to suit. There is a hybrid situation in which a permanent nuisance or trespass is created, so that the statute of limitations begins to run from its inception, but in which the defendant later substantially increases the damaging character of the invasion, either by a new permanent nuisance or by a series of new damage-causing acts that are not permanent. In such cases, the statute begins to run from the inception of the original invasion, but a new cause of action or series of actions may be created with their own statutes of limitations when the substantial new damage appears. In deciding statute of limitations questions in these cases, courts are not always influenced by the same considerations involved in deciding the measure of damages, even though the word 'permanent' may be used to explain conclusions in both kinds of cases. For instance, there is an Illinois decision in which a city raised a street grade, blocking access to the plaintiff's alley by vehicles. This could have been remedied by building a ramp, apparently at relatively small cost. Had the plaintiff brought an action within weeks or months after the grade was raised, * * * the nuisance would be called a temporary one and cost of repair rather than diminution in property value would be the measure of damages. However, in the actual case the plaintiff waited over 15 years to bring his action. The question before the court was not the measure of damages, but whether a five year statute of limitation had run, and the court, not surprisingly, held that it had and that the plaintiff was barred. It expressed this conclusion in part by treating the nuisance as 'permanent.' This might not be a very good solution if the issue were damages, but it was a very good solution indeed on the statute of limitations issue."

Note

If anything, the "permanent—temporary" distinction has created more difficulty in applying the statute of limitations in nuisance cases than in the trespass context. Consider, in this regard, how one recent California decision analyses this problem:

> "If a nuisance is *permanent,* then in the ordinary case the plaintiff must 'bring one action for all past, present and future damage within three

years after the permanent nuisance is erected. [Citations.] * * * Damages are not dependent upon any subsequent use of the property but are complete when the nuisance comes into existence. [Citation.]' (Baker v. Burbank–Glendale–Pasadena Airport Authority (1985) 39 Cal.3d 862, 869, 218 Cal.Rptr. 293, 705 P.2d 866.) If, on the other hand, the nuisance is *continuing,* then '[e]very repetition of [the] continuing nuisance is a separate wrong,' subject to a new and separate limitation period, 'for which the person injured may bring successive actions for damages until the nuisance is abated, even though an action based on the original wrong may be barred' (Phillips v. City of Pasadena (1945) 27 Cal.2d 104, 107–108, 162 P.2d 625), but '[r]ecovery is limited * * * to actual injury suffered [within the three years] prior to commencement of each action' (Baker v. Burbank–Glendale–Pasadena Airport Authority, *supra,* 39 Cal.3d at p. 869, 218 Cal.Rptr. 293, 705 P.2d 866; cf. Mangini v. Aerojet–General Corp., *supra,* 230 Cal.App.3d 1125, 1148, 281 Cal.Rptr. 827) and '[p]rospective damages are unavailable.' (Baker v. Burbank–Glendale–Pasadena Airport Authority, *supra,* 39 Cal.3d at p. 869, 218 Cal.Rptr. 293, 705 P.2d 866.)

"Perhaps the clearest explanation of California's rationale for these distinctions, and of how the distinctions are to be drawn in particular cases, was provided by Justice Traynor in Spaulding v. Cameron (1952) 38 Cal.2d 265, 239 P.2d 625; * * *

"In early decisions of this court it was held that it should not be presumed that a nuisance would continue, and damages were not allowed for a decrease in market value caused by the existence of the nuisance but were limited to the actual physical injury suffered before the commencement of the action. [Citations.] The remedy for a continuing nuisance was either a suit for injunctive relief or successive actions for damages as new injuries occurred. Situations arose, however, where injunctive relief was not appropriate or where successive actions were undesirable either to the plaintiff or the defendant or both. Accordingly, it was recognized that some types of nuisances should be considered permanent, and in such cases recovery of past and anticipated future damages were allowed in one action. [Citations.]

"The clearest case of a permanent nuisance or trespass is the one where the offending structure or condition is maintained as a necessary part of the operations of a public utility. Since such conditions are ordinarily of indefinite duration and since the utility by making compensation is entitled to continue them, it is appropriate that only one action should be allowed to recover for all the damages inflicted. It would be unfair to the utility to subject it to successive suits and unfair to the injured party if he were not allowed to recover all of his probable damages at once. [Citation.]

"A more difficult problem is presented, however, if the defendant is not privileged to continue the nuisance or trespass but its abatement is impractical or the plaintiff is willing that it continue if he can secure full compensation for both past and anticipated future injuries. To attempt categorically to classify such a nuisance as either permanent or not may lead to serious injustice to one or the other of the parties. Thus, if the plaintiff assumes it is not permanent and sues only for past damages, he may be met with the plea of res judicata in a later action for additional injury if the court then decides the nuisance was permanent in character from its inception. [Citation.] Similarly, if the initial injury is slight and plaintiff delays suit until he has suffered substantial damage and the court then determines that the nuisance was permanent, the defendant may be able to raise the defense that the statute of limitations ran from the time of the initial injury. [Citation.] On the other hand, if the defendant is willing and able to abate the nuisance, it is unfair to award damages on the theory that it will continue. [Citations.]

"Because of these difficulties it has been recognized that in doubtful cases the plaintiff should have an election to treat the nuisance as either permanent or not. [Citations.] If the defendant is not privileged to continue the nuisance and is able to abate it, he cannot complain if the plaintiff elects to bring successive actions as damages accrue until abatement takes place. [Citations.] On the other hand, if it appears improbable as a practical matter that the nuisance can or will be abated, the plaintiff should not be left to the troublesome remedy of successive actions. [Citations.] 38 Cal.2d at pp. 267–269, 239 P.2d 625. * * *

"The great weight of California authority has articulated the basic distinction between permanent and continuing nuisances in broad terms of whether the nuisance can be discontinued, or abated, 'at any time': '[I]f the nuisance may be discontinued at any time it is considered continuing in character.' (Phillips v. City of Pasadena, *supra,* 27 Cal.2d 104, 107–108, 162 P.2d 625.) * * *

"The relatively recent Court of Appeal opinion in Field–Escandon v. DeMann (1988) 204 Cal.App.3d 228, 234, 251 Cal.Rptr. 49, apparently focusing on the semantics of the term 'continuing nuisance' rather than on the term's jurisprudential background as explained in *Spaulding,* proposed a different rubric: 'The salient feature of a continuing trespass or nuisance is that its impact may vary over time.' Subsequent Court of Appeal opinions have acknowledged *Field–Escandon's* proposal but have explicitly or implicitly recognized that '[m]ost cases * * * analyze the condition to determine whether the nuisance/trespass may be discontinued.' (Spar v. Pacific Bell (1991) 235 Cal.App.3d 1480, 1485, 1 Cal.Rptr.2d 480; cf. also Mangini v. Aerojet–General Corp., *supra,* 230 Cal.App.3d 1125, 1147, 281 Cal.Rptr. 827 [concluding complaint could be amended to meet either rubric].)

"It should be apparent, however, that the discontinued-or-abated rubric cannot be mechanically applied. It may be assumed that if it can reasonably be foreseen that a nuisance *cannot* in any event be abated, the nuisance must be regarded as permanent. But it would be a rare case in which an alleged nuisance could *not* be abated were countervailing considerations (such as expense, time, and legitimate competing interests) disregarded. Thus, for example, in a strictly literal sense even a nuisance represented by an encroaching building or an underlying public utility pipeline might be discontinued or abated, 'at any time,' by tearing down the building or digging up the pipeline. But as *Spaulding* makes clear, it was for just such situations that the concept of permanent nuisance, as an exception to the preexisting rule that all nuisances should be treated as abatable and thus continuing, was developed. Regardless of literal abatability, where as a *practical* matter either abatement or successive lawsuits would be inappropriate or unfair then the nuisance may be regarded as permanent and the plaintiff relegated to a single lawsuit, subject to a single limitation period, for all past and anticipated future harms. This practical qualification of a too-literal abatability rule was implicitly recognized in two recent Court of Appeal decisions, involving public-utility installations, on which the Spences rely. (Spar v. Pacific Bell, *supra,* 235 Cal.App.3d 1480, 1486, 1 Cal.Rptr.2d 480 [25–year–old telephone conduits, wires, and manhole, originally intended to be serviceable for at least 100 years, constituted a permanent nuisance even though the telephone company in fact removed them before trial but apparently after the plaintiffs filed their lawsuit]; Field–Escandon v. DeMann, *supra,* 204 Cal.App.3d 228, 234, 251 Cal.Rptr. 49 [25–year–old sewer pipe, buried eight feet beneath plaintiff's property, constituted a permanent nuisance].) Because a literal answer to the question whether a particular nuisance can be discontinued or abated will not invariably serve the purposes of the rules as discussed in *Spaulding,* the discontinued-or-abated rubric should be regarded as no more than a convenient shorthand for the fundamental considerations *Spaulding* outlined.

"Over the years the courts, presumably mindful of the genesis of permanent nuisance as a practical exception to a preferred rule, have maintained a preference for finding a *continuing* nuisance, both to protect the plaintiff from 'contingencies' such as unforeseen future injury and the statute of limitations itself (Baker v. Burbank–Glendale–Pasadena Airport Authority, *supra,* 39 Cal.3d 862, 870, 218 Cal.Rptr. 293, 705 P.2d 866, citing and quoting from United States v. Dickinson (1947) 331 U.S. 745, 749, 67 S.Ct. 1382, 1385, 91 L.Ed. 1789) and to encourage abatement of nuisances. * * * And the courts have consistently adhered to *Spaulding's* rule that in a case in which the distinction between permanent and continuing nuisance is close or doubtful the plaintiff will be permitted to *elect* which theory to pursue. (Cf., e.g., Mangini v. Aerojet–General Corp., *supra,* 230 Cal.App.3d 1125, 1145, 281 Cal.Rptr. 827; Baker v. Burbank–Glendale–Pasadena Airport Authority, *supra,* 39 Cal.3d 862, 870, 218 Cal.Rptr. 293, 705 P.2d 866.)"

Capogeannis v. Superior Court, 12 Cal.App.4th 668, 15 Cal.Rptr.2d 796 (1993).

2. *Restitution*

RAVEN RED ASH COAL CO. v. BALL

Supreme Court of Appeals of Virginia, 1946.
185 Va. 534, 39 S.E.2d 231.

HUDGINS, JUSTICE.

Plaintiff, Estil Ball, stated, in his notice of motion, that he was entitled to recover $5,000 from the defendant for the use and occupation of an easement across his land. Defendant denied any liability. The trial court entered judgment for plaintiff in the sum of $500 on the verdict returned by the jury. From that judgment, defendant obtained this writ of error.

* * *

Plaintiff did not prove any specific damage to the realty by the illegal use of the easement, and admitted that he suffered "no more damage other than the exclusion of use during that moment and that's the reason we have sued for use and occupancy."

It thus appears that plaintiff bases his sole ground of recovery on the right to maintain assumpsit for use and occupation.

* * *

Since plaintiff failed to prove that he gave express permission for the additional use of the easement or that defendant promised to pay for such use, it became necessary for the plaintiff to establish facts and circumstances from which the law will imply the promise to pay for use and occupancy.

* * *

Where a naked trespass is committed, whether upon the person or property, assumpsit will not lie. If one commits an assault and battery upon another, it is absurd to imply a promise by the defendant to pay the victim a reasonable compensation. There is no basis for an implication of a contract where cattle inadvertently invade a neighbor's premises and trample down and destroy his crops. In each instance, a wrong and nothing more and nothing less has been committed. On the other hand, if a trespasser invades the premises of his neighbor, cuts and removes timber or severs minerals from the land and converts them to his own use, the owner may waive the tort and sue in assumpsit for the value of the materials converted. 1 Cooley on Torts, 4th Ed., sec. 61, p. 181. Such a person has depleted the value of the owner's property and materially enhanced his own possessions.

The same principle is stated in 4 Am.Jur., 503, 504, as follows: "* * * in the absence of a contractual relationship, the general rule is that where one person derives a benefit from the commission of a tort against the property of another, the law will, at the election of the person injured, imply a contract on the part of the tort-feasor to pay to the person injured a just remuneration for the damages sustained as a consequence of the wrong, and on this contract implied by law general assumpsit lies. But a promise will be implied in such a case only because *it will be deemed that it was intended that it should be, or because natural justice requires it on consideration of some benefit received,* and where no benefit accrues, or is intended to accrue to the tort-feasor, the action of assumpsit cannot, as a general rule, be substituted for the proper form of action on the tort." (Italics supplied.) *See* 1 C.J.S., Actions, § 50, p. 1131.

* * *

The facts in Edwards v. Lee's Adm'r, 265 Ky. 418, 96 S.W.2d 1028, were that Edwards discovered a cave on the land belonging to himself and his wife, which he developed and advertised as the "Great Onyx Cave." Later, Lee, the owner of an adjoining tract, filed suit against Edwards and the heirs of his wife, claiming that a portion of the cave was under his land. He asked for an accounting of the profits which resulted from the operation of the cave and for an injunction prohibiting Edwards and his associates from further trespassing or using that part of the cave under his land. It was said that the action was based on repeated trespasses to land and that, although no damage or injury was shown to plaintiff's land, plaintiff was entitled to recover on the ground of an implied promise to pay. The measure of recovery was fixed at one-third of the net profits inasmuch as one-third of the cave was under plaintiff's land. It was contended that the use of the cave by the trespasser did not damage or diminish Lee's property, but the court held that the gist of the action was the unjust enrichment of the wrongdoer, which would support an implied promise to pay.

In the Notes on Restatement of Restitution, *supra,* commenting on this case at p. 194, this is said: "The decision (Edwards v. Lee's Adm'r) is a welcomed departure from the result in Phillips v. Homfray, 24 Ch.D. 439 (1883), where recovery was denied against a person who had used a passage-way under the plaintiff's land for the removal of coal."

The illegal transportation of the coal in question across plaintiff's land was intentional, deliberate and repeated from time to time for a period of years. Defendant had no moral or legal right to enrich itself by this illegal use of plaintiff's property. To limit plaintiff to the recovery of nominal damages for the repeated trespasses will enable defendant, as a trespasser, to obtain a more favorable position than a party contracting for the same right. Natural justice plainly requires the law to imply a promise to pay a fair value of the benefits received. Defendant's estate has been enhanced by just this much. Pomeroy's Remedies and Remedial Rights, 2d Ed., pp. 630–635.

The facts in DeCamp v. Bullard, 159 N.Y. 450, 54 N.E. 26, 28, were that plaintiff owned a tract of land in the Adirondack wilderness through which the north branch of the Moose river flows for 20 to 30 miles. The defendants had cut a large number of logs upstream from plaintiff's land under the belief that they had the right to float the logs down the river through plaintiff's land to a mill. Plaintiff obtained an injunction restraining defendants from entering his land and transporting the logs downstream. This judgment was suspended for a definite period upon condition that defendant execute a bond in the penalty of $5,000 with surety to indemnify plaintiff "against any and all loss or damage * * * sustained by the plaintiff" during the period that the injunction order was suspended. Defendants thereupon floated the logs downstream. Defendants refused to comply with the condition of the bond and an action was instituted thereon. Plaintiff, on the trial, admitted that the floating of the logs through his land did not injure or damage his realty but proved that the prevailing price for the floating of the logs, which measured two million feet when manufactured into lumber, was two cents a mile per thousand feet. The jury were told that plaintiff was entitled to a "fair compensation for the use of the river to float the 2,000,000 feet of logs." A verdict was rendered in favor of plaintiff for $500. In sustaining this verdict, the court said:

> "The defendants insist that the measure of damages is not what the privilege of trespassing was worth to the trespassers, but what the plaintiff actually lost through interference with his business,—loss of

rent and the like. As there was no proof of actual loss of this character, they further insist that the plaintiff is entitled to nominal damages only. This position would place a premium on trespassing, because it makes the position of the trespasser more favorable than that of one lawfully contracting. If a man's house is vacant, with no prospect of a tenant and no intention on his part of occupying it himself, and a trespasser occupies it, he must pay as damages for the trespass the value of the use and occupation; for this would be the duty of a tenant contracting upon a quantum meruit for the use, by consent, of that which the trespasser uses without consent.

"In cases of involuntary trespass the damages are restricted as much as possible, but, when the trespass is deliberate, intentional and continuous, they include at least the value of the use of the premises for the period that the owner is kept out of possession."

Plaintiff proved: (1) Ownership of the 100–acre tract, (2) the grant of an easement across the 100 acres for a limited purpose, and (3) the use of the easement over a period of years for a purpose not specified in the grant. He admitted that the illegal use caused no damage to the realty. Plaintiff, without attempting to prove any damage to the realty or the value of the benefits received by defendant, rested his case. Defendant's motion to strike the evidence was overruled, and it is from the testimony of its witnesses that the proof of the value of the benefit is ascertained.

While plaintiff offered no evidence to establish the value of the illegal use of the easement, we, as reasonable men, know that the transportation of 49,016 tons of coal over the tramroad across the plaintiff's land was a benefit to defendant. However, in the absence of proof of the value of the benefit, the court could enter no judgment for plaintiff. This proof is supplied by the testimony of the general manager on his cross-examination. The substance of his testimony on this point is that the prevailing rate of payment, or purchase of a right of way for transportation of coal across another's land, is one cent per ton, and that this purchase includes the right to construct and maintain a tramway for distances varying up to 2½ miles; but that, where the owner of the easement has already entered upon the land, and has constructed and is maintaining a tramroad for the transportation of coal from certain specified tracts, the purchase price should be much less—a small fraction of a cent per ton. The jury were instructed that they should fix the amount of damages, if any, at such as would fairly compensate plaintiff for the use and occupation of this strip of land in the hauling and transportation of 49,016 tons of coal over the same.

While the evidence on the value of the benefits retained by defendant is not as clear and full as it could be, and perhaps should have been, the jury had all the facts and circumstances before it and evidently concluded that the value of the benefit to the defendant for the illegal use of the easement should be computed at one cent per ton. Viewing the case as a whole, we find no reversible error, and the judgment of the trial court is affirmed.*

* This case is discussed in Notes, 45 Mich. L.Rev. 519 (1947) and 33 Va.L.Rev. 666 (1947).

See P. Keeton, D. Dobbs, R. Keeton & D. Owen, Prosser and Keeton on the Law of Torts § 94 (5th ed. 1984); Thurston, Recent

Affirmed.

Notes

1. Although it might be said, as suggested by Lord Mansfield in Moses v. Macferlan, that an analogous form of "common count" could be found for any form of enrichment, thus providing a conceptual basis for recovery whenever the enrichment could be said to be unfair, the courts at an early stage imposed limitations upon the use of two of these procedural forms. There could be no quasi-contractual recovery for a wrongful taking of chattels when this was not followed by a sale (I G. Palmer, The Law of Restitution § 2.5 (1978)), nor could a landowner recover where there was unprivileged occupation and use of his land. These limitations generally have been rejected in the later cases, a precedent set by *Raven Red Ash.*

2. Where, in the situation involving wrongful trespass to land, there is actual damage to the estate by, for example, cutting and removing timber, the landowner has a wide choice of remedies, including those related to damage to the land (*see supra* p. 450, *et seq.,*) and those related to wrongful interference with chattels (*see supra* p. 306, *et seq.*). *See* I G. Palmer, The Law of Restitution § 2.5 (1978).

MONARCH ACCOUNTING SUPPLIES, INC. v. PREZIOSO

Supreme Court of Connecticut, 1976.
170 Conn. 659, 368 A.2d 6.

LOISELLE, ASSOCIATE JUSTICE.

The plaintiff tenant brought an action against the defendant landlord claiming, inter alia, unjust enrichment. From a judgment awarding money damages, the defendant has appealed.

The plaintiff, Monarch Accounting Supplies, Inc., conducts its mailorder business from a building leased to it by the defendant, William Prezioso. The defendant leased the building to the plaintiff in 1969, and again in 1972. The second lease was for a term of five years beginning on June 1, 1972.

In 1973, the plaintiff's president learned that Murphy, Inc., an outdoor advertising concern, would erect a large sign on the roof of the building. The defendant had agreed to the erection of the sign and purported to lease the roof to Murphy, Inc., but had neither notified the plaintiff of his actions nor sought its consent. * * *

After numerous holes were made in the building's walls and roof, and after much of the supporting structure was in place, the plaintiff brought this action against the defendant landlord, [and] Murphy, Inc. * * * seeking, with other relief, an order enjoining further work on the sign. At a hearing on September 6, 1973, at which the defendant Prezioso did not

Developments in Restitution, 45 Mich.L.Rev. 935, 944–950 (1947); Douthwaite, The Tort-feasor's Profits—A Brief Survey, 19 Hastings L.J. 1071 (1968).

appear either personally or by counsel, the plaintiff and Murphy, Inc., stipulated that the sign could be installed upon the completion of structural changes designed to strengthen the sign's supporting structure, the structure's attachment to the roof, and the walls of the building. Liability for the expense of the changes, which had been recommended by a structural engineer, was to be adjudged at the trial. They further stipulated that the rent to be paid by Murphy, Inc., to the defendant would be held in escrow until the plaintiff's rights to the rent were determined.

On December 10, 1974, just prior to trial, the plaintiff filed an amended complaint against Prezioso alone which asserted: "As a result of the act of defendant in authorizing installation of said sign and the subsequent erection thereof plaintiff (a) suffered a substantial interruption of its business for approximately one month; (b) was obliged to expend large sums of money for the services of an engineer and legal counsel to insure [sic] the safety of the leased building and the safety of plaintiff's employees and property; (c) suffered a diminution of storage space in the leased building; and (d) has been deprived of the benefit of defendant's covenant that plaintiff have the quiet use and enjoyment of the premises leased to it." And in a separate paragraph: "As a further result of the act of defendant in authorizing installation of said sign, defendant will be unjustly enriched at the expense of plaintiff." The plaintiff claimed the following relief: "1. $15,000 damages. 2. A decree determining the respective rights of the parties to rental income from Murphy, Inc., or, in the alternative, 2. [a] mandatory injunction requiring the defendant forthwith to restore the leased building to its condition prior to erection of said sign."

The court disallowed the second claim, originally and in the alternative, and ordered the plaintiff to proceed under the claim for damages. The action was then tried with damages as the sole claim for relief.

On January 23, 1975, the court awarded the plaintiff $245, which is one-half of the expenses it incurred for fees paid to the structural engineer, and $1360, which is one-half of the rent accrued from Murphy, Inc., and it found that the plaintiff would be entitled to one-half of the rent to be paid for the period from February 1, 1975, to, and including, the month of May, 1977. The defendant appealed from the judgment, assigning as error the court's award to the plaintiff of a portion of the rent. * * *

* * *

* * * The court was not in error in concluding that, under the terms of the lease, the defendant did not reserve control of the roof of the premises leased and therefore did not have the right to lease the roof of the premises.

The court found that the plaintiff was entitled to receive, on an equitable basis by way of reimbursement, one-half of the total rent received by the defendant from Murphy, Inc. The court also awarded one-half of the rent to be expected from Murphy, Inc., for the remainder of the plaintiff's term. The plaintiff claims the award can be sustained under the doctrine of unjust enrichment. The inquiry then, is whether the plaintiff is entitled to damages for the unjust enrichment of the defendant. The inquiry goes not only to the type of recovery but also to whether recovery of any type was allowable.

The doctrine of unjust enrichment "is based upon the principle that one should not be permitted unjustly to enrich himself at the expense of another but should be required to make restitution of or for property received, retained or appropriated." * * *

The defendant, under its agreement with Murphy, Inc., receives rental payments. That agreement overlooks the plaintiff's possessory interest in the roof, and, in that regard, it is to the detriment of the plaintiff. Although the plaintiff did not show any material physical damage to the premises it has a right either to sublet or assign the roof with the defendant's permission. The defendant can hardly claim that permission would not be granted to sublet or assign the roof in view of his agreement with Murphy, Inc. Even if the circumstances of this case admitted of a conditional right in the plaintiff to assign or sublet, the defendant, by his actions, removed the plaintiff's ability to negotiate with the defendant for the use of the roof. The facts of the case, therefore, show the defendant's receipt of a benefit, to which he was not entitled, to the detriment of the plaintiff. Furthermore, that showing entitles the plaintiff to an award of money damages. See Restatement, Restitution § 4(f).

The measure of recovery in this case focuses on the benefit to the defendant rather than on the loss to the plaintiff. The damages should be the benefit received. The benefit was the rent that was received by the defendant less his expenses, if any, in dealing with Murphy, Inc. The court, therefore, was in error in awarding only one-half of the accrued rent.

The court also erred by awarding a portion of the rent from the date of judgment until the end of the plaintiff's term. That rent has been neither received nor retained by the defendant even though he has the right, under the agreement with Murphy, Inc., to receive it. A prospective award is not properly includable within the concept of damages in this case since the focus of damages in unjust enrichment is not on the damage proximately caused by an injury, but on the benefit unjustly received and retained by the defendant. *See* 66 Am.Jur.2d, Restitution and Implied Contracts, §§ 166, 170; Restatement, Restitution § 155. Whether the defendant will retain the rent from the sign for the period from February, 1975 to May, 1977, the unexpired term of the plaintiff's lease at the time of judgment, cannot be adjudged.

Further, the other item of damages awarded, one-half of the expense of the structural engineer, appears to have been part of an expenditure that was necessary for the proper support of the sign on the roof and as the defendant is not entitled to retain the benefit of the lease to Murphy, Inc., he would not be liable for such expenditures.

There is error in part, the judgment is affirmed except as to the amount of damages awarded and a new trial is ordered limited to that issue.

In this opinion the other Judges concurred.

BRANCH v. MOBILE OIL CORPORATION

United States District Court, Western District of Oklahoma, 1991.
778 F.Supp. 35.

DAVID L. RUSSELL, DISTRICT JUDGE.

Before the Court is Plaintiffs' motion to reconsider this Court's Order of February 4, 1991, granting Defendant Citation Oil & Gas Corporation's motion to dismiss Plaintiffs' claims of unjust enrichment and public nuisance pursuant to Local Court Rule 14(A). Plaintiffs are correct that because service of Citation's motion was by mail, they had until February 4, 1991, in which to respond to the motion pursuant to Local Court Rule 11 and F.R.Civ.P. 6(e). Accordingly, the Court's Order of February 4, 1991, is vacated and the Court now considers Defendant Citation's motion to dismiss on its merits.

Defendant Citation's motion to dismiss Plaintiffs' claims of unjust enrichment and public nuisance is denied. Unjust enrichment can occur when a defendant uses something belonging to the Plaintiff in such a way as to effectuate some kind of savings which results in or amounts to a business profit. *See* D. Dobbs, *Handbook on the Law of Remedies* § 4.5 (1973) at p. 278. *See also Tilghman v. Proctor,* 125 U.S. 136, 146, 8 S.Ct. 894, 899, 31 L.Ed. 664, 667 (1888); *Olwell v. Nye & Nissen Co.,* 26 Wash.2d 282, 173 P.2d 652 (1946). Oklahoma recognizes a claim for negative unjust enrichment. [That is, by preventing another, who is thus "benefitted," from being able to avoid incurring an expenditure.] *See McBride v. Bridges,* 202 Okla. 508, 215 P.2d 830, 832 (1950). *See also Booker v. Sears Roebuck & Co.,* 785 P.2d 297, 303 (Okla.1989) (Summers, J., dissenting). The Court cannot say that Plaintiffs' Complaint does not state a claim for unjust enrichment on which relief can be granted based on a failure to allege a benefit conferred on Defendants. *See* First Amended Complaint at ¶ 25. It can be inferred from Plaintiffs' Amended Complaint that Defendants used Plaintiffs' property to dispose of pollutants and saved the expenses of otherwise collecting and disposing of same. Upon consideration of Okla.Stat. tit. 82, § 926.4, Okla.Stat. tit. 50, §§ 8 & 10, and Plaintiffs' First Amended Complaint, the Court cannot say that Plaintiffs have failed to state a claim for abatement of a public nuisance* on which relief can be granted.

The motion of Defendant Citation Oil & Gas Corporation to dismiss Plaintiffs' claims of unjust enrichment and public nuisance is Denied.

INDEPENDENT SCHOOL DIST. NO. 197 v. W.R. GRACE & CO.

United States District Court, District of Minnesota, 1990.
752 F.Supp. 286.

* * *

[Plaintiff school district brought an action against defendant, asbestos manufacturer to recover costs of removing asbestos from district's school buildings as required by federal regulations.]

* With respect to nuisance, public and private, in connection with which the wrongdoer may have received a "benefit," see text at p. 450, *et seq.*

* * *

Plaintiff bases Count I of its complaint upon Restatement of Restitution § 115 (1937), otherwise known as the "Emergency Assistance Doctrine." Restatement § 115 provides:

> A person who has performed the duty of another by supplying things or services, although acting without the other's knowledge or consent, is entitled to restitution from the other if:
>
> (a) he acted unofficiously and with intent to charge therefor; and
>
> (b) the things or services supplied were immediately necessary to satisfy the requirements of public decency, health, or safety.

In *State and Regents Building Asbestos Cases,* File Nos. 99081, 99082 (Dakota Cty. Dist.Ct. July 23, 1986), the court held that schools seeking recovery of costs of abating hazards allegedly caused by the presence of asbestos in their buildings stated a claim for restitution pursuant to Restatement § 115. According to the court, the emergency assistance doctrine of section 115 is grounded upon principles of unjust enrichment; such unjust enrichment, according to the court, "occurs when the cost of performing an act is shifted from the one whose duty it was to perform the act to another." Slip op. at 3. In holding that plaintiff had stated a claim for restitution, the court rejected the decision of the United States District Court for the Eastern District of Tennessee in *County of Anderson v. U.S. Gypsum,* No. CIV. 3–83–511 (E.D.Tenn.1984) which held that defendants had no duty to remove the asbestos which would trigger a claim of restitution. In rejecting this conclusion, the Minnesota district court found that the decision

> ignores the reality that the defendants may be under a duty to answer in damages—to pay for the consequences of the harm done unless the harm were removed, avoided or abated by them * * *. If the defendants are unwilling to remove the product (to restore the property to an "uninjured" nonhazardous condition) notwithstanding a duty to refrain from putting abroad in the marketplace a defective product, the plaintiffs may well find themselves confronted with an emergency (the impending exposure of an unaware public of users and occupants of the plaintiffs' facilities) to which the plaintiffs must respond. When, then, defendants have been given the opportunity to restore the properties and have refused to do so, all expenses to which the plaintiffs are put in the restoration confer on the defendants a dollar for dollar benefit for which they may be liable.

State v. Regents, slip op. at 4. With regard to the "emergency" element of section 115, the court held that the "lengthy timetable for pending and future abatement actions" does not indicate "an absence of immediate concern." *Id.* at 5. The court held:

> It is no more than evidence of the realities of limited funding being available to the plaintiffs, limited resources in the form of technically competent personnel to accomplish the abatement, and the ironic circumstance that in some instances abatement with its attendant disturbance of otherwise fixed and stable quantities of asbestos-con-

> taining products may result, at least temporarily, in a greater health hazard than doing little or nothing.

Id. According to the Minnesota district court, the unjust enrichment at issue consists of the "defendants' avoidance and consequent shifting to [plaintiffs] of the cost of performing the duty to prevent exposure of the public to asbestos-containing products that is primarily the obligation of the defendants." *Id.* A number of courts in Minnesota and nationwide have held that section 115 applies in an asbestos removal case. *See, Federal Reserve Bank v. Carey-Canada, Inc., et al.,* CIVIL 3–86–185, 1988 WL 220489 (D.Minn. Aug. 30, 1988) (adopting reasoning of the court in *State and Regents*); *Drayton Public School District 19 v. W.R. Grace & Co.,* 728 F.Supp. 1410 (D.N.D.1989) (asbestos removal action states restitution claim); *Adams–Arapahoe School District No. 28–J v. Celotex Corp.,* 637 F.Supp. 1207, 1209 (D.Colo.1986) (asbestos manufacturer had duty to abate hazard which established restitution claim); *City of New York v. Keene Corp.,* 132 Misc.2d 745, 505 N.Y.S.2d 782, *aff'd,* 129 A.D.2d 1019, 513 N.Y.S.2d 1004 (N.Y.App.1987) (ultimate duty to remove hazardous asbestos lies with manufacturer.) *But see, Independent School District No. 709 v. Air–O–Therm Application Co., et al.,* File No. 155716, slip op. at 9 (St. Louis Cty Dist.Ct. May 20, 1987) (rejecting restitution claim because "district has not identified the source of Grace's duty * * *."); *Board of Education of City of Chicago v. A, C & S, Inc.,* 131 Ill.2d 428, 137 Ill.Dec. 635, 651–52, 546 N.E.2d 580, 596–97 (1989) (no restitution claim for asbestos removal in absence of independent duty on defendant); *Town of Hooksett School District v. W.R. Grace & Co.,* 617 F.Supp. 126, 134 (D.N.H.1984) (same); *Corporation of Mercer University v. National Gypsum Co.,* 1986 WL 12447 (M.D.Ga.1986) (dismissing restitution claim because plaintiff failed to show that removal of asbestos was "immediately necessary").

The Court agrees with the reasoning in the *State and Regents Building* case discussed above. Based on plaintiff's allegations Grace has been unjustly enriched to the extent the plaintiff is required to abate a hazard created by defendant. Further, the Court finds that the hazard posed by the presence of the asbestos constitutes no less of an "emergency" because abatement will require an extended amount of time, and has not yet been completed. Accordingly, the Court finds that plaintiff has stated a valid restitution claim and defendant's motion to dismiss this claim will be denied.*

Note

In recent months much media and other attention has been given to those situations where premises have been left in a condition which are found to be a threat to the health of those in the area. This form of "environmental pollution" presents many problems for those who are anxious, for one reason or another, to restore the property in question to a condition which again permits its use in conventional ways. Identifying and locating those responsible are

* Accord Unified School Dist. No. 500 v. U.S. Gypsum Co., 788 F.Supp. 1173 (D.Kan., 1992). See also Mayor and Council v. Blockmen & Blockmen, 811 F.Supp. 1039 (D.N.J., 1993).

often a problem. Once jurisdiction is obtained the litigation which ensues is likely to be long drawn out and costly and, in many instances, it is not feasible to sue until responsibility has been established by a suit brought by a governmental agency. There is also the fact that there may be a pressing need for early return of the premises to the use for which they were intended.

This situation has prompted a number of local governments to proceed to remedy the situation themselves and then to sue the party allegedly responsible in quasi-contract. The theory on which the suits proceed is that the defendant, having been "enriched" by the amount expended by the plaintiffs in the clean-up process (because the defendants otherwise eventually would have had to make a like expenditure to achieve the result themselves) and this benefit should be returned to the plaintiff.

It is immediately apparent that such plaintiffs, arguably, are "intermeddlers" of a sort because they are going about things in the wrong order, that is, cleaning up first rather than giving the defendants an opportunity to do so themselves, perhaps as a result of an equity decree requiring them to do so.

Where the plaintiffs are government bodies which, for example, own the property in question, they are not, of course, "intermeddlers" who are strangers as has often been the case in conventional situations, and, even were they to be viewed in this way, quasi-contract relief, as a general matter, may be justified. As stated by Professor Palmer: "When a person acts [voluntarily] to protect the interests of another [perhaps, here, members of the public], we have seen that restitution having this consequence is awarded within very narrow limits, usually where there is a strong public interest in encouraging such protection, such as the preservation of another's life or health." See discussion of "volunteers" and restitution at p. 314 *et seq.*, and p. 349 *et seq.*

The *Branch* and *Independent School District No. 197* cases are illustrative of this approach. There are a number of cases which involve the same or similar fact situations, but it is noteworthy that these theories are still to be tested in the appellate courts.

B. SPECIFIC RELIEF AGAINST TRESPASS

1. Ejectment

HEROUX v. KATT

Supreme Court of Rhode Island, 1949.
76 R.I. 122, 68 A.2d 25.

FLYNN, CHIEF JUSTICE.

This action in trespass and ejectment was brought by a lessee for years to obtain possession of a portion of the demised premises alleged to be occupied by the defendants and wrongfully detained by them from the plaintiff. In the superior court, at the conclusion of the evidence for the plaintiff, the defendants rested their case and each party then moved for a directed verdict. The trial justice granted the plaintiff's motion and denied that of the defendants. * * *

The following undisputed facts appear in the evidence. The land described in the writ and declaration is located at the corner of Broad and Babcock streets in the city of Providence and is owned in fee simple by

George A. and Elizabeth Follett. By a lease in writing, said premises were demised by these owners to the plaintiff Joseph F. Heroux for a period of five years from April 27, 1948, the lease also containing a privilege of renewal for an additional period of five years on the same terms and conditions.

At the time this lease was executed the defendants were the owners of land adjoining the demised premises and were the occupants of a building located in part upon their own land and in part upon the land leased by the plaintiff. The portion of the building thus upon the leased land measures approximately 22.50 feet long by 20.05 feet wide.

The defendants were aware that such part of this building was located upon land that did not belong to them. Indeed, they had deliberately erected the building knowing that it encroached upon the land belonging to the Folletts. However, neither of the Folletts nor the plaintiff was aware at any time prior to entering into the lease that such building encroached upon the demised premises. Only after plaintiff had a survey of the premises made did it become known to him and the owners of the land that a portion of the defendants' building approximating 451 square feet in area was wrongfully located and maintained upon a part of the leased premises.

When the defendants refused to deliver possession of the land to the plaintiff the instant action was commenced in the district court by a writ of trespass and ejectment. * * *

[T]he defendants * * * make several contentions which may be briefly summarized as follows. (1) Trespass and ejectment is not a proper action to remove encroachment by a building owned and occupied by defendants on the "locus in quo" because the only proper action was in equity to enjoin the continuing trespass or nuisance and because an execution to the sheriff would be ineffective to deliver possession in an action at law. (2) The plaintiff is not a proper party to bring trespass and ejectment because the ejector at the commencement of the action must possess the fee to the reversionary interest of the locus in quo. * * *

In our opinion the trial justice was correct in directing a verdict for the plaintiff and in denying defendants' motion for a directed verdict. In support of their first contention that the plaintiff was restricted to a suit in equity to enjoin them from a continuing trespass and that only a court of equity had jurisdiction to give relief in the circumstances of record the defendants have cited several cases from other jurisdictions and rely strongly on the case of Rasch v. Noth, 99 Wis. 285, 74 N.W. 820, 40 L.R.A. 577, 67 Am.St.Rep. 858. However, most, if not all, such cases relate generally to suits brought in equity where the respondents sought to defeat equity's jurisdiction by contending that there was an adequate remedy at law. The courts therein rightly held that equity jurisdiction can be justified where the remedy at law is found to be inadequate, as for example in a case of a continuing trespass or nuisance. But in our opinion none of those cases hold that equity is the *exclusive* forum where relief can be had in circumstances like those in the instant case. Undoubtedly equity could have taken and justified its jurisdiction and perhaps might have granted more effective and complete relief. Nevertheless it does not follow from that potentiality that the law court must be ousted of its ordinary jurisdiction if the plaintiff elected to pursue his legal remedy in trespass and ejectment. Such an election is a matter for plaintiff's consideration and not one of defense to the action in trespass and ejectment.

* * *

Even where it appears that the ability of a sheriff to deliver possession upon serving an execution is accepted as a test of whether the action of trespass and ejectment may properly be brought, it has been held that ejectment will lie because there is a disseisin measured by the size of the visible and tangible encroachment; and the sheriff can physically remove the structure and thereby restore the owner to possession. Butler v. Frontier Telephone Co., 186 N.Y. 486, 79 N.E. 716, 11 L.R.A., N.S., 920, 116 Am.St.Rep. 563, 9 Ann.Cas. 858. * * * The defendants' first contention is without merit.

Nor do we agree with his second contention to the effect that only the owner of the fee in reversion may maintain an action of trespass and ejectment against an admitted trespasser who is wrongfully detaining a portion of the premises from the possession of a lessee. * * * As plaintiff points out, a lessee for years in this state has a right to bring trespass and ejectment against such strangers under General Laws 1938, chapter 435, § 10, and G.L.1938, chap. 538, § 12.

* * *

Moreover, this statute seems to carry out the concepts of the old action of ejectment. In Tyler on Ejectment, at page 169, it is stated: "Clearly, a tenant for life, or for years, has the exclusive right of possession of the land, and his title, therefore, enables him to maintain the action of ejectment. * * * Indeed, the very object of the remedy by ejectment in its original conception was to enable one who had a lease for years, to repair the injury done him by dispossession, and enable him to recover his term." To a similar effect, see 2 Taylor's Landlord and Tenant, 9th Ed., 310, § 698; Tiedeman on Real Property, 3d Ed., 165, § 131.[80]

* * * Therefore, whether we consider the instant case under our statute or at common law, we think there is ample authority for a plaintiff lessee for years to bring an action of trespass and ejectment to vindicate his rights of entry and immediate possession against one who wrongfully detains from him possession of a portion of the leased premises.

* * *

The defendants' exceptions are overruled, and the case is remitted to the superior court for entry of judgment for the plaintiff on the verdict as directed.

80. For a fuller discussion of the historical development of ejectment, *see* Soffer v. Beech, 487 Pa. 255, 409 A.2d 337 (1979) (lessee who has not entered into possession may bring ejectment action against lessor and lessees in possession under allegedly expired lease).

Notes

1. At common law, the plaintiff who obtained possession by means of an ejectment action could bring a second suit for "mesne profits." Under modern procedural rules, the two actions often are joined. Wilkerson v. Gibbs, 405 So.2d 1053 (Fla.App.1981). Mesne profits are typically "measured by the [rental] value of the land" during the period held by the defendant. D. Dobbs, Law of Remedies 529 (2d ed. 1993). Although the measure of damages in actions for mesne profits and trespass are usually the same, the statute of limitations for mesne profits may be longer. *E.g.,* Dumas v. Ropp, 98 Idaho 61, 558 P.2d 632 (1977).

2. An unlawful detainer action is another form of specific legal relief that can be used to protect a possessory interest in real property. It is most often invoked by landlords against tenants who refuse to leave upon the termination of the tenancy. The actions for ejectment and unlawful detainer are compared in D. Dobbs, Handbook on the Law of Remedies 370–71 (1973): *

> "[The unlawful detainer] remedy, affording both damages and possession as it does, bears resemblance to ejectment. But there are important differences. Aside from historical differences, the unlawful detainer action differs from ejectment in its summary character—trial, usually in a justice or some other inferior court, is summary at least in the sense that trial and eviction can be had within a few days after service of process. Because the procedure is summary and because the jurisdiction of inferior courts is usually invoked, statutes often provide that the decision in forcible entry or unlawful detainer suits is not binding as to title. Thus if title is in any serious issue, a second and more plenary suit in ejectment or possibly trespass is contemplated. Further than this the forcible entry or unlawful detainer suit is limited to cases in which the plaintiff's right to possession is probably very clear, since summary proceedings would hardly be justified under any other circumstances."

MICELI v. RILEY

New York Supreme Court, Appellate Division, 1981.
79 A.D.2d 165, 436 N.Y.S.2d 72.

MOLLEN, PRESIDING JUDGE.

This appeal presents us with a difficult and troubling issue. Both sides have important interests at stake. Both are entirely blameless and without responsibility for the controversy which has engulfed them and which we are now called upon to resolve. The determination we reach is not a happy one, but we can come to no other in view of the principles of law involved and the virtually unique circumstances surrounding the dispute.

[The plaintiff claimed that she purchased a one-acre parcel of land (Miceli East) as unimproved land in 1951.] * * * The defendants involved in the dispute over Miceli East predicate their claims to the parcel upon a deed from the same DeMares to the Selden Land Corporation. That deed was dated June 7, 1955, and was recorded in the office of the County Clerk on August 8, 1955. In 1969 and 1970, the property purchased by the

* Reprinted with permission of West Publishing Co.

Selden Land Corporation was improved by the construction of houses and was sold to the individual defendant homeowners. Plaintiff's claim is that the land and houses purchased by five of those defendants, and for which two of the defendant mortgagees hold mortgages, encroach upon Miceli East.

After reviewing the entire record, we agree with Trial Term that the plaintiff established her claim. * * *

Although Trial Term found that the plaintiff had established her cause of action, it declined to adhere strictly to section 601 of the Real Property Actions and Proceedings Law and refused to order ejectment and delivery of the property to the plaintiff. Instead, the court chose to invoke its equity powers in order to fashion a remedy which, in its view, would avoid hardship and an unjust result based upon "what can only fairly be called a mistake either of the surveyors or title examiners or both." Accordingly, the court ordered the plaintiff to elect between two options as a method of calculating her damages. She could either sell Miceli East to the defendants at a sum equal to twice the value of any one acre of undeveloped land in the immediate vicinity of the property or she could take possession of Miceli East upon payment to the defendants of the market value of the improvements made thereon together with reimbursement for all realty taxes paid by the defendants on the property for the preceding six years.

Both sides appealed and, following oral argument in this court, decision was withheld as the parties made serious efforts to settle the dispute. * * *

It is clear that Trial Term invoked its equity powers out of concern for the plight of the defendant homeowners. The record shows beyond question that they acted entirely in good faith and under color of title. They invested much in their homes, moved in with their possessions and established a good life for their families as welcome members of the community in which they had chosen to live. The plaintiff, on the other hand, had long shown little interest in the property, allowing it to remain unimproved for over 20 years. Yet it is equally clear that she did everything the law requires of a property owner. She properly recorded her deed in the office of the County Clerk, thereby giving notice to the world that she owned Miceli East, and she consistently paid taxes on the property from the time she acquired it. Moreover, we agree with Trial Term that plaintiff did not lose any right to the property through adverse possession since the land was not cultivated, improved or enclosed by the defendants prior to 1969 (see Real Property Actions and Proceedings Law, § 512, subds. 1, 2).

The crucial factor in the case, however, and the one which, in our view, must resolve the dispute, is the finding of the trial court that the plaintiff did not have knowledge of the encroachment upon her property until sometime *after* the construction of the homes. The record contains sufficient evidence to support the court's conclusion in that regard. However, it is that very conclusion that makes the court's resort to its equity powers inappropriate in the case at bar.

An action to recover real property pursuant to section 601 of the Real Property Actions and Proceedings Law, where plaintiff seeks ejectment of the defendant, is an action at law. Nevertheless, it has long been held that a defendant in such an action may raise equitable defenses. (*See, e.g.,* Crary v. Goodman, 12 N.Y. 266.) It appears, however, that in each case in which the court has chosen to fashion an equitable remedy rather than to award the plaintiff unconditional possession of the property, there has been a finding that the plaintiff himself had engaged in some inequitable conduct or had failed to act appropriately when he knew, or should have known, that something was amiss with respect to his property rights. * * *

Hence, the question upon which this case must finally turn is whether equity will compel * * * a property owner—one who has complied with all notice requirements and who is entirely innocent of any inequitable conduct—to reach an accommodation with a trespasser simply because the trespasser himself has acted in good faith and in ignorance of the owner's rights and would suffer substantial loss if forced to surrender his wrongful possession of the land. We hold that a fee owner may not be so compelled for, plainly, were it otherwise, property rights and rights of title would be rendered uncertain.

Regardless, then, of the hardship that may befall the individual homeowner defendants here through no fault of their own, we are constrained to modify the judgment by granting unconditionally to the plaintiff's executrix the right of possession to the property known as Miceli East.

The final question concerns the plaintiff's claim for damages. Since the defendants acted wholly in good faith under color of title and in ignorance of the plaintiff's rights, they are entitled to offset the value of their improvements up to, but not beyond, the amount by which plaintiff has been damaged by the wrongful withholding of her property. (See Real Property Actions and Proceedings Law, § 601.) The record here supports Trial Term's finding that the defendants' improvements "are so substantial * * * as to render plaintiff's recovery of money damages impossible." Accordingly, although entitled to delivery of the land, plaintiff may not have money damages.

2. *Request for Restitution by Mistaken Improver*

SOMERVILLE v. JACOBS

Supreme Court of Appeals, West Virginia, 1969.
153 W.Va. 613, 170 S.E.2d 805.

HAYMOND, PRESIDENT: The plaintiffs, W.J. Somerville and Hazel M. Somerville, herein sometimes referred to as the plaintiffs, the owners of Lots 44, 45 and 46 in the Homeland Addition to the city of Parkersburg, in Wood County, believing that they were erecting a warehouse building on Lot 46 which they owned, mistakenly constructed the building on Lot 47 owned by the defendants * * *.

* * *

Though there are numerous decisions by this Court relating to improvements to land, the precise question here involved is one of first impression in this jurisdiction. The statute dealing with allowance for improvements to real estate, Article 5, Chapter 55, Code, 1931, provides for allowance for improvements only to a defendant against whom a decree or judgment shall be rendered for land where no assessment of damages has been made and permits such defendant, at any time before the execution of a decree or judgment, to present a petition to the court rendering such decree or judgment praying that he may be allowed the fair and reasonable value of such improvements. That statute has no application to the facts of this case, and this case, for that reason, is not within the statute. Green v. Mullins, 146 W.Va. 958, 124 S.E.2d 244.

Though the precise question here involved has not been considered and determined in any prior decision of this Court, the question has been considered by appellate courts in other jurisdictions and though the cases are conflicting the decisions in some jurisdictions, upon particular facts, recognize and sustain the jurisdiction of a court of equity to award compensation to the improver to prevent unjust enrichment to the owner and in the alternative to require the owner to convey the land to the improver upon his payment to the owner of the fair value of the land less the improvements.

* * *

In Voss v. Forque, Fla., 84 So.2d 563, the court held that where a landowner mistakenly constructed a dwelling on a lot adjacent to one he owned and the two adjoining lots were substantially the same in value and the landowner was innocent of wrongdoing and the adjacent landowner was not shown to have been harmed, equity at the suit of the first landowner compelled both landowners to exchange deeds to their respective lots, upon payment by the first landowner of a certain sum and court costs. * * *

* * *

In Fitzpatrick v. Allied Contracting Company, 24 Ill.2d 448, 182 N.E.2d 183, the court, in discussing the general rule with respect to improvements by a stranger upon the land of another without his consent, said: "While, as a general rule, if a stranger improves the land of another without consent, the improvement becomes the property of the owner (Olin v. Reinecke, 336 Ill. 530, 168 N.E. 676), nevertheless, equity will not hesitate to soften the harshness and rigor of the rule of law, when the circumstances of the case require it to be done to meet the ends of justice. (Cable v. Ellis, 120 Ill. 136, 11 N.E. 188.) We recently stated the equitable rule in Elder v. Clarke, 385 Ill. 335, 339, 52 N.E.2d 778, 780: 'The rule is that where improvements of a permanent character are made in good faith by one in possession, believing himself to be a *bona fide* purchaser, or an owner for full value, and under circumstances justifying such a belief, and the expenditure is reasonable and of benefit to the estate, an allowance may be made in a court of equity, where title is found to be in another.' "

In the recent case of Beacon Homes, Inc. v. Holt, 266 N.C. 467, 146 S.E.2d 434, the court said in the opinion: "It is as contrary to equity and good conscience for one to retain a house which he has received as the result of a bona fide and reasonable mistake of fact as it is for him to retain money so received. We, therefore, hold that where through a reasonable mistake of fact one builds a house upon the land of another, the landowner, electing to retain the house upon his property, must pay therefor the amount by which the value of his property has been so increased."

In Section 625, Chapter 11, Volume 2, Tiffany Real Property, Third Edition, the text contains this language:

> "Since the rule that erections or additions made by one who has no rights to land are fixtures, and therefore not removable by him, even though he made them in the belief that he was the owner of the land, is calculated to cause hardship to an innocent occupant of another's land, by giving the benefit of his labor and expenditures to the landowner, the courts of this country, without either imputing fraud or requiring proof of it, hold it inequitable to allow one to be enriched under such circumstances by the labor and expenditures of another who acted in good faith and in ignorance of any adverse claim or title. Applying this doctrine of 'unjust enrichment,' a court of equity will, on the principle that he who seeks equity must do equity, refuse its assistance to the rightful owner of land as against an occupant thereof unless he makes compensation for permanent and beneficial improvements, made by the latter without notice of the defect in his title.
>
> "According to one line of decisions, the innocent occupant will be allowed compensation for such improvements upon a bill filed by him against the true owner for the purpose.
>
> "Under other decisions relief of this character is accorded only in a proceeding instituted by the true owner, as an incident to the relief given him."

See also 57 A.L.R.2d, Annotation, Compensation for Improvements Made or Placed on Premises of Another by Mistake, Sections 11 and 12, pages 281–294.

From the foregoing authorities it is manifest that equity has jurisdiction to, and will, grant relief to one who, through a reasonable mistake of fact and in good faith, places permanent improvements, upon land of another, with reason to believe that the land so improved is that of the one who makes the improvements, and that the plaintiffs are entitled to the relief which they seek in this proceeding.

The undisputed facts, set forth in the agreed statement of counsel representing all parties, is that the plaintiff W.J. Somerville in placing the warehouse building upon Lot 47 entertained a reasonable belief based on the report of the surveyor that it was Lot 46, which he owned, and that the building was constructed by him because of a reasonable mistake of fact and in the good faith belief that he was constructing a building on his own property and he did not discover his mistake until after the building was completed. It is equally clear that the defendants who spent little if any time in the neighborhood were unaware of the construction of the building until after it was completed and were not at any time or in any way guilty of any fraud or inequitable conduct or of any act that would constitute an estoppel. In short, the narrow issue here is between two innocent parties and the solution of the question requires the application of principles of equity and fair dealing between them.

It is clear that the defendants claim the ownership of the building. Under the common law doctrine of annexation, the improvements passed to them as part of the land. This is conceded by the plaintiffs but they assert that the defendants cannot keep and retain it without compensating them for the value of the improvements, and it is clear from the testimony of the defendant William L. Jacobs in his deposition that the defendants intend to keep and retain the improvements and refuse to compensate the plaintiffs for their value. The record does not disclose any express request by the plaintiffs for permission to remove the building from the premises if that could be done without its destruction, which is extremely doubtful as the building was constructed of solid concrete blocks on a concrete slab, and it is reasonably clear, from the claim of the defendants of their ownership of the building and their insistence that certain fixtures which have been removed from the building be replaced, that the defendants will not consent to the removal of the building even if that could be done.

In that situation if the defendants retain the building and refuse to pay any sum as compensation to the plaintiff W.J. Somerville they will be unjustly enriched in the amount of $17,500.00, the agreed value of the building, which is more than eight and one-half times the agreed $2,000.00 value of the lot of the defendants on which it is located, and by the retention of the building by the defendants the plaintiff W.J. Somerville will suffer a total loss of the amount of the value of the building. If, however, the defendants are unable or unwilling to pay for the building which they intend to keep but, in the alternative, would convey the lot upon which the building is constructed to the plaintiff W.J. Somerville upon payment of the sum of $2,000.00, the agreed value of the lot without the improvements, the plaintiffs would not lose the building and the defendants would suffer no financial loss because they would obtain payment for the agreed full value of the lot and the only hardship imposed upon the defendants, if this were required, would be to order them to do something which they are unwilling to do voluntarily. To compel the performance of such an act by litigants is not uncommon in litigation in which the rights of the parties are involved and are subject to determination by equitable principles. And the right to require the defendants to convey the lot to the plaintiff W.J. Somerville is recognized and sustained by numerous cases cited earlier in this opinion. Under the facts and circumstances of this case, if the defendants refuse and are not required to exercise their option either to pay W.J. Somerville the value of the improvements or to convey to him the lot on which they are located upon his payment of the agreed value, the defendants will be unduly and unjustly enriched at the expense of the plaintiff W.J. Somerville who will suffer the complete loss of the warehouse building which by bona fide mistake of fact he constructed upon the land of the defendants. Here, in that situation, to use the language of the Supreme Court of Michigan in Hardy v. Burroughs, 251 Mich. 578, 232 N.W. 200, "It is not equitable * * * that defendants profit by plaintiffs' innocent mistake, that defendants take all and plaintiffs nothing."

To prevent such unjust enrichment of the defendants, and to do equity between the parties, this Court holds that an improver of land owned by another, who through a reasonable mistake of fact and in good faith erects a building entirely upon the land of the owner, with reasonable belief that such land was owned by the improver, is entitled to recover the value of the improvements from the landowner and to a lien upon such property which may be sold to enforce the payment of such lien, or, in the alternative, to purchase the land so improved upon payment to the landowner of the value of the land less the improvements and such landowner, even though free from any inequitable conduct in connection with the construction of the building upon his land, who, however, retains but refuses to pay for the improvements, must, within a reasonable time either pay the improver the amount by which the value of his land has been improved or convey such land to the improver upon the payment by the improver to the landowner of the value of the land without the improvements.

It is pertinent to observe that, in cases involving the right to recover for improvements placed by mistake upon land owned by one other than the improver, the solution of the questions involved depends largely upon the circumstances and the equities involved in each particular case. Here, under the facts as stipulated by the parties, the equities which control the decision are clearly in favor of the plaintiffs.

To reverse the judgment of the circuit court the defendants cite and rely upon several cases which are clearly distinguishable upon their facts from the case at bar and are not applicable to or controlling of the decision in the instant proceeding.

* * *

The judgment of the Circuit Court of Wood County is affirmed.

Affirmed.

CAPLAN, JUDGE, dissenting:

Respectfully, but firmly, I dissent from the decision of the majority in this case. Although the majority expresses a view which it says would result in equitable treatment for both parties, I am of the opinion that such view is clearly contrary to law and to the principles of equity and that such holding, if carried into effect, will establish a dangerous precedent.

Basically, I believe that the principles expressed in Cautley v. Morgan, 51 W.Va. 304, 41 S.E. 201, reflect my view of this matter and that that case cannot realistically be distinguished from the instant case, as was attempted in the majority opinion. In that opinion it was said that the plaintiff who encroached upon the defendant's property was guilty of "careless or negligent conduct in making the mistake." The opinion reasoned that the plaintiff had the duty to see that the wall was properly located and that she had sufficient data to enable her to avoid the mistake if she had used the data with proper care. Certainly, in the instant case the plaintiff, had he caused to be made a proper survey and had exercised proper care, would have constructed the subject building on his own property rather than on that of the defendant. It occurs to me that the failure to use proper care is more evident in this case than it was in *Cautley*.

* * *

I am aware of the apparent alarmist posture of my statements asserting that the adoption of the majority view will establish a dangerous precedent. Nonetheless, I believe just that and feel that my apprehension is justified. On the basis of unjust enrichment and equity, the majority has decided that the errant party who, without improper design, has encroached upon an innocent owner's property is entitled to equitable treatment. That is, that he should be made whole. How is this accomplished? It is accomplished by requiring the owner of the property to buy the building erroneously constructed on his property or by forcing (by court edict) such owner to sell his property for an amount to be determined by the court.

What of the property owner's right? The solution offered by the majority is designed to favor the plaintiff, the only party who had a duty to determine which lot was the proper one and who made a mistake. The defendants in this case, the owners of the property, had no duty to perform and were not parties to the mistake. Does equity protect only the errant and ignore the faultless? Certainly not.

It is not unusual for a property owner to have long range plans for his property. He should be permitted to feel secure in the ownership of such property by virtue of placing his deed therefor on record. He should be permitted to feel secure in his future plans for such property. However, if the decision expressed in the majority opinion is effectuated then security of ownership in property becomes a fleeting thing. It is very likely that a property owner in the circumstances of the instant case either cannot readily afford the building mistakenly built on his land or that such building does not suit his purpose. Having been entirely without fault, he should not be forced to purchase the building.

In my opinion for the court to permit the plaintiff to force the defendants to sell their property contrary to their wishes is unthinkable and unpardonable. This is nothing less than condemnation of private property by private parties for private use. Condemnation of property (eminent domain) is reserved for government or such entities as may be designated by the legislature. Under no theory of law or equity should an individual be permitted to acquire property by condemnation. The majority would allow just that.

I am aware of the doctrine that equity frowns on unjust enrichment. However, contrary to the view expressed by the majority, I am of the opinion that the circumstances of this case do not warrant the application of such doctrine. It clearly is the accepted law that as between two parties in the circumstances of this case he who made the mistake must suffer the hardship rather than he who was without fault. *Cautley v. Morgan, supra.*

I would reverse the judgment of the Circuit Court of Wood County and remand the case to that court with directions that the trial court give the defendant, Jacobs, the party without fault, the election of purchasing the building, of selling the property, *or* of requiring the plaintiff to remove the building from defendant's property.*

I am authorized to say that Judge Berry concurs in the views expressed in this dissenting opinion.**

Notes

1. The general rule, on the facts involved in the *Somerville* case, denies recovery to the trespasser. *See* Note, 18 Kan.L.Rev. 693 (1970). There are, however, cases like *Somerville* which show a changed attitude by the courts toward restitution by one who, mistakenly and in good faith, improves the property of another, especially where the "mistake" is not the result of reckless lack of concern for possible intrusion upon the property of the other. In no case, however, should the recoverable damages exceed the dollar amount of the increase in market value of the property, and the cases limit damages in this manner. II G. Palmer, The Law of Restitution § 10.9(c), (e) (1978). Even then it may be necessary for the court to frame a conditional decree to protect the defendant against a possible forced sale of his property when he cannot otherwise pay the judgment. *Id.* Relief to the "mistaken improver" seems much easier to justify in the case of marketable property bought for trading purposes. It is not easy to justify if the "improvement" is an unwanted one on property held for a special purpose and for which the owner is unable to pay without a sale of the property.

2. *Compare,* Smith Development, Inc. v. Flood, 198 Ga.App. 817, 403 S.E.2d 249 (1991) (quasi-contract relief denied where the plaintiff builder began construction on behalf of a third party on land belonging to the defendant and "continued construction during the negotiation process [an unsuccessful effort to purchase the building lot in question], and the house was substantially completed * * *." (403 S.E.2d, at 250); Kincaid v. Morgan, 188 W.Va. 452, 425 S.E.2d 128 (1992) (restitution to encroacher denied, distinguishing Somerville v. Jacobs on the ground that here the plaintiffs "have admitted that, even if the boundary between the properties is where they [the plaintiffs] believed it to be, their building still trespasses on the [defendant's] * * * property" as a consequence of which there can be no "good faith * * * reasonable belief" of ownership. (425 S.E.2d, at 133)).

See, also Schweigert v. Fowler, 240 Mont. 424, 784 P.2d 405 (1990) (restitution denied where plaintiffs were the defaulting purchasers and the contract for deed expressly stated that in the event of purchaser's default, "all payments made and any improvements to the property would be retained by seller." (*Id.,* at 411)).

3. A majority of states have enacted what are called "Betterment Statutes" which take a variety of forms to allow quasi-contractual recovery in special situations. II G. Palmer, Law of Restitution, § 10.9(b). See, for

* *Compare* Shick v. Dearmore, 246 Ark. 1209, 442 S.W.2d 198 (1969) (landowner cannot enjoin innocent improver from removing the improvement, in this case a casing in a well; the wrongdoer may remove the improvement and restore the property to its original condition if that can be done without damaging the land).

** This case is discussed in Note, 18 Kan. L.Rev. 693 (1970); Note, 15 N.Y.L.Forum 958 (1969), and Note, 72 W.Va.L.Rev. 182 (1970). *See also* Casad, The Mistaken Improver—A Comparative Study, 19 Hastings L.J. 1039 (1968); Annot., 57 A.L.R.2d 263 (1958).

example, Meyers v. Canutt, 242 Iowa 692, 46 N.W.2d 72 (1951) (husband improves land which he and his wife occupied, which he reasonably assumed belonged to his wife—when in fact she previously had conveyed it to her child by an earlier marriage—and in which he was left no interest upon her death).*

4. Professor Palmer has categorized the cases in which the plaintiff's claim was based upon a "voluntarily imposed benefit" in this manner:

a. "[T]he recipient of the benefit either had an antecedent obligation in a definite amount, or there was an equivalent lien on his property, and restitution does not impose a new obligation or lien." [Quasi-contract relief is usually granted.]

b. "[T]he recipient had an antecedent but unliquidated liability, usually in tort; restitution does not impose a wholly new liability on him, although if allowed in the amount of the payor's settlement, it does permit the payor in effect to liquidate the liability." [Quasi-contract relief is usually granted.]

c. "[T]he recipient had no pre-existing obligation or liability, which means that if restitution is awarded for the value of nonreturnable goods or services transferred, this imposes on the recipient a wholly new obligation to pay for something he did not request and for which he did not bargain to pay. When a person acts to protect the interests of another, we have seen that restitution having this consequence is awarded within very narrow limits, usually where there is a strong public interest in encouraging such protection, such as the preservation of another's life or health."

[1. The plaintiff was aware that he or she was conferring a benefit upon the defendant.]

"[T]he promotion of self-interest will rarely justify restitution which has the effect of imposing a new money obligation on the recipient of the benefit. The significant policy is not directed against intermeddling, since the benefit received by the defendant usually is the unavoidable consequence of action taken by the plaintiff in pursuit of his own interests. It takes nearly all useful meaning out of the term to describe the plaintiff as an intermeddler in the affairs of the defendant. The denial of restitution in these cases is explained instead by a general reluctance to force a person to pay for a benefit which he did not bargain to receive or pay for. Other factors may influence decision, but this fact is always central to the case."

* * *

[2. The plaintiff was not aware that he or she was conferring a benefit upon the defendant.]

"In the typical case the plaintiff has placed an improvement upon the defendant's land in the mistaken belief that it was his own land. When mistake causes a payment of money which benefits another, courts nearly always grant restitution so as to avoid the resulting enrichment. Thus, if a person pays taxes or a mortgage on the land of another in the mistaken belief that he is paying these charges on his own land, most courts will grant restitution, commonly through the technique of subrogation. In contrast, if

* *See* Note, The Rights and Remedies of One Who Improves the Land of Another Under the South Carolina Betterment Statute, 17 S.C.L.Rev. 397 (1965); Note, 6 W.Res. L.Rev. 397 (1955) and Note, 48 Mich.L.Rev. 885 (1950).

such a charge is paid by one who knows that the land is owned by another, restitution will not be granted * * *." [The *Somerville* case, because of reliance upon an erroneous survey, and, perhaps, the *Prezioso* case, illustrate the placing of an improvement by a "good faith" mistake.]

II G. Palmer, The Law of Restitution §§ 10.7, 10.9, at 416–417, 435 (1978).*

5. The equitable remedy of "subrogation," which is referred to in the final sentences of par. 4, *supra,* is of great importance today. An early use of the remedy was to prevent unjust enrichment at the expense of a surety who guaranteed the obligation of another, and paid the creditor of that other, when the creditor had a security interest to which the surety had no contractual right. The effect of the action of the court of equity in recognizing a right of "subrogation" is to give to the surety who has paid the creditor to discharge the obligation of another that same security interest which the creditor enjoyed before payment by the surety. I G. Palmer, The Law of Restitution § 1.5 (1978). With respect to "subrogation", see text at p. 343, *supra.*

3. *Injunction*

D. DOBBS, HANDBOOK ON THE LAW OF REMEDIES 348 (1973) **: "Historically courts have shown some reluctance to enjoin trespasses. At least three separate strands of this reluctance can be identified, though at times they are inseparably woven together. First, there is the adequacy test: a trespass will not be enjoined if there is what is conceived to be an adequate remedy at law. Second, there is, or was, a rule that equity would not try title, and hence if title was in issue, would withhold any injunction until the law courts had decided title. Third, and somewhat less obvious in the decisions, there was a feeling if not a rule that equity should not transfer possession by injunction."

ATTORNEY GENERAL v. DIME SAVINGS BANK OF NEW YORK

Supreme Judicial Court of Massachusetts, 1992.
413 Mass. 284, 596 N.E.2d 1013.

ABRAMS, JUSTICE.

The Attorney General brought this action for declaratory and injunctive relief against The Dime Savings Bank of New York, FSB (Dime). The dispute arises out of mortgage loans made by Dime in Massachusetts which have resulted in foreclosure. After foreclosing, Dime has brought actions in trespass against foreclosed mortgagors and tenants holding over after notice to quit and has sought and obtained injunctions to eject holdover mortgagors and tenants from the mortgaged properties. The Attorney General seeks a declaration that Dime's practice violates G.L. c. 184, § 18 (1990 ed.). The complaint also asks that we enjoin Dime from pursuing such a course in the future. For the reasons stated, we hold that the procedure employed by Dime in these cases violates G.L. c. 184, § 18. We therefore remand the matter to the county court for entry of a declaration that a mortgagee who forecloses on residential property by sale may not bring a trespass action against a holdover tenant or mortgagor in actual possession of the foreclosed premises.

1. *Background.* On April 7, 1992, the Attorney General began this action by filing a complaint in the Supreme Judicial Court for Suffolk County. The complaint invokes the court's equitable and supervisory powers under G.L. c. 214, § 1 (1990 ed.), and G.L. c. 211, § 3 (1990 ed.), respectively, as well as G.L. c. 231A (1990 ed.) (declaratory judgment). The case came before a single justice of the county court on a statement of agreed facts. The stipulations of fact concern a number of individual foreclosures and resulting dispossessions. After oral argument, the single justice reserved and reported the matter to this court.

The following is a summary of the statement of agreed facts. In each of the cases on which this controversy is founded, Dime held a mortgage of real property as security for an obligation. In each instance, the mortgagor defaulted on the obligation. After default, Dime recorded memoranda of entry, conducted foreclosure sales, and acquired perfected title to the properties by purchasing them at the foreclosure sales. Dime has neither sought nor accepted payments of rent from the occupants, and the Commonwealth stipulates that Dime has done nothing to create new, postforeclosure tenancies between itself and the occupants.

In each of the cases in question, the property was occupied at the time of foreclosure either by the mortgagor or a tenant of the mortgagor. All such occupants initially entered the respective properties lawfully. In each of the cases in which the holdover occupants were tenants of the mortgagor, the creation of the tenancy postdated the grant of the mortgage.

After Dime foreclosed its mortgages, it sent notices to the occupants demanding immediate possession of the properties. In each case, the occupants refused to relinquish possession on receiving notice to do so. Dime responded by bringing actions for trespass against the occupants in Superior Court. In each of these actions, Dime sought preliminary and permanent injunctions ordering the occupants to vacate the mortgaged premises. In some cases, the prayer for preliminary relief was heard on a "short order[ ] of notice." In no case, however, have fewer than thirty days passed between the issuance of the demand and the commencement of legal proceedings.

* * *

[The Court then concluded that the Attorney General had statutory authority to bring the action.]

3. *G.L. c. 184, § 18.* General Laws c. 184, § 18, provides, in pertinent part, that "[n]o person shall attempt to recover possession of land or tenements in any manner other than through an action brought pursuant to [G.L. c. 239] or such other proceedings authorized by law." Dime argues that a mortgagee's use of a trespass action to recover possession of mortgaged premises is "authorized by law." G.L. c. 184, § 18. Dime further maintains that a court's common law power to enjoin a continuing

trespass justifies an injunction ordering holdover mortgagors or their tenants to vacate the premises. Because an action for trespass will not lie in the cases as stated, however, we conclude that the "other proceedings authorized by law" include neither a common law action for trespass nor an injunction based thereon.

It is well settled that "[a]n action of trespass, being a possessory action, cannot be maintained, unless the plaintiff had the actual or constructive possession of the property trespassed upon at the time of the trespass." *Emerson v. Thompson,* 2 Pick. 473, 484 (1824). * * * Neither party contends that Dime has actual possession of the properties in question. Indeed, the disputed issue in this case is the means by which Dime may gain such possession.

We have not addressed the question whether an owner out of possession has constructive possession sufficient to maintain an action of trespass where actual possession is in another. Courts that have considered the question, however, have concluded that, for the purposes of a trespass action, there can be no constructive possession by an owner of property actually possessed by another. See *Frost v. Johnson,* 256 Ala. 383, 54 So.2d 897 (1951); *More v. Urbano,* 151 Conn. 381, 198 A.2d 211 (1964); *McCausland v. York,* 133 Me. 115, 174 A. 383 (1934); *Jaycox v. E.M. Harris Bldg. Co.,* 754 S.W.2d 931 (Mo.Ct.App.1988); *Green v. Pettingill,* 47 N.H. 375 (1867); *Daniels v. Coleman,* 253 S.C. 218, 169 S.E.2d 593 (1969). The "fiction of 'constructive possession' has no application when another is in actual possession." W. Prosser & W. Keeton, Torts § 13, at 77 n. 99 (5th ed. 1984).

Dime argues that the label attached to its action is irrelevant. Dime suggests that it might have brought an action for writ of entry under G.L. c. 237, or a common law action in ejectment. The short answer to this argument is that Dime did not bring such actions. The propriety of such other actions therefore is not before us.

Moreover, Dime's argument is self-contradictory. Although it maintains that the trespass label is insignificant, Dime also contends that a court's traditional power to enjoin a continuing trespass justifies the injunctions it has obtained. However, each case cited by Dime for the proposition that a court will enjoin a continuing trespass involves an owner or owners of real property in actual or constructive possession. See, e.g., *Fenton v. Quaboag Country Club, Inc.,* 353 Mass. 534, 233 N.E.2d 216 (1968) (homeowners suffered injuries to person and property from golf balls which were hit from adjacent course); *Anntco Corp. v. Shrewsbury Bank & Trust Co.,* 353 Mass. 250, 230 N.E.2d 795 (1967) (store owner and commercial landlord aggrieved by overburdening of easement for drainage); *Chesarone v. Pinewood Builders, Inc.,* 345 Mass. 236, 186 N.E.2d 712 (1962) (owner of unoccupied land complained of flooding caused by drainage system constructed on neighboring land); *Doody v. Spurr,* 315 Mass. 129, 51 N.E.2d 981 (1943) (homeowner sought decree enjoining defendant from parking automobile on and driving over homeowner's property); *Suburban Land Co. v. Billerica,* 314 Mass. 184, 49 N.E.2d 1012 (1943) (land owner and water company complain of town's construction of water pipes across plaintiffs' property without taking by eminent domain); *Ferrone v. Rossi,* 311 Mass. 591, 42 N.E.2d 564 (1942) (owner of vacant land aggrieved by defendant's construction of wall that encroached on landowner's property); *Franchi v. Boulger,* 12 Mass.App.Ct. 376, 425 N.E.2d 372 (1981) (trustees of condominium trust object to improperly constructed retaining wall built partially on plaintiffs' property). In all but two of these cases, *Chesarone* and *Ferrone,* the plaintiff was in actual possession of the property in question. In both *Chesarone v. Pinewood Builders, Inc., supra,* and *Ferrone v. Rossi, supra,* the land in question was unoccupied. Thus, none of the cases cited by Dime supports its argument that, in these circumstances, it is entitled to an injunction for continuing trespass.

Dime argues that, even if it could not properly invoke the doctrine of continuing trespass, it could have brought actions in ejectment. Dime contends that it could then invoke the court's general equitable jurisdiction to obtain an injunction. Dime, however, could not get equitable relief at common law.[10] Dime next asks the courts to "fashion a remedy to fit [Dime's] right" to immediate possession of the properties on which it has foreclosed. There is no need. The Legislature already has fashioned a remedy; it is the summary process statute. See *Serreze v. YWCA of W. Mass., Inc.,* 30 Mass.App.Ct. 639, 644, 572 N.E.2d 581 (1991) ("[I]t is not a characteristic feature of summary process law that the landlord who seeks possession is without a speedy remedy").[12] See also *Weiss v. Levy,* 166 Mass. 290, 44 N.E. 225 (1896).

We remand this matter to the Supreme Judicial Court for the county of Suffolk for entry of a declaration that a mortgagee who forecloses on residential property by power of sale may not bring a trespass action against a holdover tenant or mortgagor in actual possession of the foreclosed premises.

Note

In a sense, *Dime Savings Bank* is hardly an extraordinary case in that it applies the traditional rule that an injunction ordinarily may not be used to

10. At common law, a bill in equity brought by an owner out of possession to recover possession of his estate would have been dismissed because summary process offers "a plain, adequate, and complete remedy at law." *Weiss v. Levy,* 166 Mass. 290, 293, 44 N.E. 225 (1896). See *Glickman v. Kastel,* 323 Mass. 148, 150, 80 N.E.2d 469 (1948) ("There is not, and has never been, any equity in the bill requesting an injunction to recover possession of land"), and cases cited. Accord *Root v. Woolworth,* 150 U.S. 401, 410, 14 S.Ct. 136, 138, 37 L.Ed. 1123 (1893) ("It is undoubtedly true that a court of equity will not ordinarily entertain a bill solely for the purpose of establishing the title of a party to real estate, or for the recovery of possession thereof, as these objects can generally be accomplished by an action of ejectment at law," citing *Hipp v. Babin,* 60 U.S. (19 How.) 271, 15 L.Ed. 633 [1856]); *Rocky Mountain Fuel Co. v. New Standard Coal Mining Co.,* 89 F.2d 147 (10th Cir.1937); *Perry v. Warnock,* 246 Ala. 470, 20 So.2d 867 (1945); *Welbrot v. Levenberg,* 98 Conn. 217, 118 A. 911 (1922); *Slaughter v. Land,* 190 Ga. 491, 9 S.E.2d 754 (1940); *Kertesz v. Falgiano,* 140 W.Va. 469, 84 S.E.2d 744 (1954). "[P]laintiffs in such cases [were required to] resort to the ordinary remedies for the recovery of the possession of land." *Glickman v. Kastel, supra,* 323 Mass. at 150, 80 N.E.2d 469.

12. At oral argument, counsel for Dime stated:

> "It certainly is true that in 98 percent of the summary process cases that are heard in the District Courts in the Commonwealth of Massachusetts * * *, the demandant wins; there's a judgment for possession; there is no appeal; and [the cases] are over within 27.82 days, or whatever it said in that study [submitted by the amici] * * *."

deliver possession of real estate. Rather, an out of possession plaintiff must rely either on ejectment or a summary proceeding. On the other hand, Dime, the lender, clearly had a right to possession after having validly foreclosed on the real estate. Should it really matter which remedy is used to regain possession so long the defendants receive adequate procedural protection? Does the court's result and reasoning illustrate a rigid adherence to form over substance? Does the intervention by the Massachusetts Attorney General suggest a political dimension to this case?

NEW YORK REAL PROPERTY ACTIONS AND PROCEEDINGS LAW, section 871. Action for the removal of encroaching structures. "1. An action may be maintained by the owner of any legal estate in land for an injunction directing the removal of a structure encroaching on such land. Nothing herein contained shall be construed as limiting the power of the court in such an action to award damages in an appropriate case in lieu of an injunction or to render such other judgment as the facts may justify."

REPORT, 1942, NEW YORK LAW REVISION COMMISSION 73–74: "In most American jurisdictions it is recognized that a mandatory injunction is a proper remedy to compel the removal of encroaching structures. This is an exception to the general rule that equity will not grant possession by injunction, made necessary by the insufficiency of the legal remedy of ejectment. In ejectment actions the sheriff will usually return an execution unsatisfied and refuse to deliver possession by taking down the encroaching structure, because it would subject him to an unreasonable risk to do so. *Cf.* Baron v. Korn, 127 N.Y. 224, 228, 27 N.E. 804, 1891; Blake v. McCarthy, 115 N.Y.S. 1014, Sup.1909. In most states, therefore, the landowner has been held entitled to the remedy of injunction which will place the risk and the cost of the removal of the encroachment on the shoulders of the wrongdoer. * * *

"The long established rule permitting equitable relief was brought into question when the Court of Appeals, in City of Syracuse v. Hogan, 234 N.Y. 457, 138 N.E. 406, 1923, held that an action for an injunction against an encroachment was in essence an action to recover real property and therefore section 425 of the Civil Practice Act, requiring a jury trial, was applicable. In Johnson v. Pupura, 208 App.Div. 505, 203 N.Y.S. 581, 1924, this decision was held to preclude the granting of an injunction for the removal of encroaching structures. Consequently, a landowner is now without any effective remedy in such a case.

"The Commission believes that the equitable remedy by injunction should not be withheld, for the reasons stated by Cardozo, J., in his dissenting opinion in *Syracuse v. Hogan, supra:*

> 'This is not an action of ejectment. It is an action in equity to enjoin the obstruction of a highway. Ejectment furnishes some remedy, but not one complete and adequate. In an action at law, execution must direct the sheriff to deliver the possession of the property to the party thereto entitled. "The sheriff might not regard it as his duty to deliver possession by taking down the wall, which would burden him with the risk of injury to other portions of defendant's buildings" (Baron v. Korn, 127 N.Y. 224, 228, 27 N.E. 804.). Even if he stood ready to assume the risk, he would expect the plaintiff to assume the cost. "In equity, the obligation to remove can be placed directly on the party who caused the wall to be erected" (*Baron*

v. Korn, supra). An owner is entitled to the remedy that will place the risk and the cost upon the shoulders of the wrongdoer.

'Equitable remedies being necessary for the attainment of complete relief, there is no rule that a court of equity must wait until the suitor's title to the land has been first made out at law. Such a rule there may once have been. It may still prevail in other states. In this state it has long been abandoned. * * * We have left far in the distance the wasteful duplication of remedies and trials. We shall set the clock back many years if we return to it today.'

"The Commission further believes that the remedy by injunction should be expressly made available to the owners of any legal estate, so as to afford protection against impairment of the rights of holders of future interests.

"The proposed remedy is designed to be supplemental to the action of ejectment, not to replace it. In its application, the court will still retain all its equitable powers, and in reaching a determination it may consider hardship on one side and a corresponding lack of benefit upon the other. In a proper case, it may even withhold the injunction in whole or in part and compensate the plaintiff in damages."

JONES v. WAGNER

Superior Court of Pennsylvania, 1993.
425 Pa.Super. 102, 624 A.2d 166.

Before OLSZEWSKI, TAMILIA and FORD ELLIOTT, JJ.

OLSZEWSKI, JUDGE:

* * *

The complaint alleges that appellants and appellees are adjoining landowners with a fence separating their properties. Appellants are the owners of a row of tall hemlock trees. While appellants were on vacation, appellees trimmed the branches of the trees to the extent that the branches hung over the boundary line separating the neighbors' property. * * * Appellants seek the replacement value of each of the twenty-six trees which adorn the property line, a combined figure of approximately $31,000.

Appellants' theory for recovery is one that has not been addressed by an appellate court in this Commonwealth. Appellants claim that appellees are liable to them at law since appellees, having suffered no appreciable damage by the overhanging branches, are not entitled to exercise a self-help remedy by trimming the trees. Thus, appellants claim that appellees' action, pursuing a remedy without a right, renders appellees liable for damage to the trees. This theory mischaracterizes the common law of encroachments.

The issue of whether a landowner who suffers a trespass caused by overhanging tree limbs, branches, or roots is entitled to a self-help remedy has been considered at length by other jurisdictions. *Michaelson v. Nutting,* 275 Mass. 232, 175 N.E. 490 (1935); *Smith v. Holt,* 174 Va. 213, 5 S.E.2d 492 (1939); *Gostina v. Ryland,* 116 Wash. 228, 199 P. 298 (1921); *Sterling v. Weinstein,* 75 A.2d 144 (D.C.Ct.App.1950); *Whitesell v. Houlton,* 2 Haw.App. 365, 632 P.2d 1077 (1981); *Cannon v. Dunn,* 145 Ariz. 115, 700

P.2d 502 (1985). *See generally,* Annotation, *Encroachment of Tree, Shrubbery, or Other Vegetation Across Boundary Line,* 65 A.L.R.4th 603. While there does exist some conflict regarding when a landowner may institute an action for injunctive or monetary relief against an adjoining landowner whose trees overhang the property line, one common thread connects all of these cases: the landowner whose land is encroached by the overhanging branches may trim the limbs to the extent of the encroachment.

* * *

Thus, there is no question that a branch overhanging a landowner's property line is a technical trespass which he may alleviate by exercising self-help, as did appellees here. They were entitled to trim the encroaching branches without regard to the degree of physical harm done to their property. The redressable harm caused by the trees is that of the trespass onto appellees' property, not physical damage done to their land.

Although self-help is always available to a landowner whose neighbors' trees protrude onto his property, it is also necessary to address the available judicial remedies. In some jurisdictions, damage caused by encroaching branches and roots are never actionable, self-help being the landowner's only remedy. This is referred to as the "Massachusetts Rule." *Michaelson v. Nutting, supra; Richmond v. General Engineering Enterprises,* 454 So.2d 16 (Fla.Dist.Ct.App., 1984). Others require proof of some "sensible or substantial" damage before an action for damages in trespass are available, *Smith v. Holt, supra,* while some jurisdictions allow both actions at law and at equity upon this showing. *Cannon v. Dunn, supra* (and cases cited therein). Hawaii allows an action upon a showing of actual damage or upon "imminent danger" of damage. *Whitesell v. Houlton, supra; see also, Pierce v. Casady,* 11 Kan.App.2d 23, 711 P.2d 766 (1985). Finally, some jurisdictions hold that proof of damage only determines the amount of damages recoverable, and not whether a cause of action exists. These jurisdictions, however, are ones in which statutes, not common law, recognize the existence of the cause of action. *Rautsaw v. Clark,* 22 Ohio App.3d 20, 488 N.E.2d 243 (1985). We must now decide how Pennsylvania should address the issue.

It is a fundamental maxim of law which states that an owner of realty has a cause of action in trespass against any person who has committed a trespass upon his lands, and it is not necessary for the landowner to allege any actual injury or damage as an element of the cause of action. 37 P.L.E., Trespass § 6 (and collected cases). There is no need to allege harm in an action for trespass, because the harm is not to the physical wellbeing of the land, but to the landowner's right to peaceably enjoy full, exclusive use of his property. *See, Houston v. Texaco, Inc.,* 371 Pa.Super. 399, 538 A.2d 502 (1988), *alloc. den.* 520 Pa. 575, 549 A.2d 136 (1988). Moreover, as Prosser notes:

> Any physical entry upon the surface of the land is a trespass, whether it be by walking upon it, flooding it with water, casting objects upon it, or otherwise. One may commit a trespass upon the vertical surface of another's premises, as well as the horizontal—as where he piles dirt or attaches wires against a boundary wall. But the interest in exclusive

> possession is not limited to the surfaces; it extends above and below. There is a property right in the air space above the land, which may be invaded by overhanging structures, or telephone wires, by thrusting an arm above the boundary line, or by shooting across the land, even though the bullets do not fall upon it.

Prosser, Torts (5th ed., 1984); *See also* Restatement (Second) of Torts, § 159 (trespass may be committed above the surface of the earth).[1] Thus, an aggrieved landowner has a cause of action against an adjoining landowner whose trees overhang the boundary line. Otherwise, his right to enjoy exclusive peaceable use of his property is diminished.

The continuing presence of the branches and trees overhanging property lines indicates that the nature of the relief afforded to the aggrieved landowner is not limited to monetary relief. The Restatement notes that a continuing trespass is committed by the "continued presence of a structure, chattel, or other thing which the actor has tortiously placed there, whether or not the actor has the ability to remove it." Restatement (Second) of Torts § 161(a). An actor places branches "tortiously" on another's property when he is subject to liability in tort, that is, when he is trespassing onto another's property. *Id.*, comment a. As we have noted, a trespass occurs by a mere overhang. Furthermore, given the rather unremarkable observation that trees will tend to grow, the trespass, even if remedied once, is bound to recur just as soon as the trees or shrubbery regenerate. *See, Graybill v. Providence Twp.*, 140 Pa.Commw. 505, 593 A.2d 1314 (1991) (recurring flooding on plaintiff's land caused by defendant's conduct is a continuing trespass). Thus, the trespass is "continuing" and the possessor of land is entitled to pursue a proper remedy.

Our Supreme Court has continually held that equity is available to a landowner who suffers trespasses of a continuing nature:

> It is hornbook law that a Court of Equity possesses jurisdiction to enjoin repeated trespasses on land as well as to enjoin a nuisance. *In Tri Cities Water Co. v. City of Monessen,* 313 Pa. 83, 85, 169 A. 159, it is said: "There is no doubt equity has power to grant a restraining order preventing actual or threatened trespasses of a continuing character. *Gray v. Philadelphia & Reading Coal & Iron Co.,* 286 Pa. 11, 132 A. 820."

Gardner v. County of Allegheny, 382 Pa. 88, 102, 114 A.2d 491 (1955). Furthermore, the recurring nature of the trespass is one that cannot be redressed in one action. Our courts have held that in such a case, the aggrieved landowner may maintain successive actions to cure the harm. Comment b to § 161 of the Restatement (Second) of Torts provides:

> The actor's failure to remove from the land in the possession of another a structure, chattel or other thing which he has tortiously

1. The only exception to the ancient rule that a landowner owns his property "to the heavens" is in aviation, where a landowner cannot claim a trespass if aircraft flies above his land and does not substantially interfere with his use thereof. Restatement (Second) of Torts, § 159(b) (incorporating *United States v. Causby,* 328 U.S. 256, 66 S.Ct. 1062, 90 L.Ed. 1206 (1946)); *accord, Gardner v. County of Allegheny,* 382 Pa. 88, 114 A.2d 491 (1955).

> erected or placed on the land constitutes a continuing trespass for the entire time during which the thing is wrongfully on the land and * * * confers on the possessor of the land an option to maintain a succession of actions based on the theory of continuing trespass or to treat the continuance of the thing on the land as an aggravation of the original trespass.

Id.; see, Sustrik v. Jones and Laughlin Steel Corp., 413 Pa. 324, 197 A.2d 44 (1964). We are convinced that Pennsylvania law, as embodied in the Restatement, entitles a landowner to protect his property interest by maintaining an action to compel a person who has caused a trespass to remove it. It is not suggested anywhere that a showing of harm is a prerequisite to recovering in trespass. A landowner in this Commonwealth may avail himself of every available remedial avenue in an effort to protect the incidents of land ownership. Anything less, in our view, is a travesty.

Therefore, based on the reasoning above, we conclude that Pennsylvania law affords a full panoply of remedies to a landowner whose property is encroached by overhanging branches or tree limbs. First, an aggrieved landowner is entitled to exercise a self-help remedy by either trimming or lopping off the branches to the extent his property is encroached. Second, if the landowner has incurred reasonable expenses in the course of exercising a self-help remedy, he may recoup those expenses from the trespasser. Third, he may, on a trespass theory, seek equitable relief compelling the trespassing neighbor to remove the trees to the extent of the encroachment and seek appropriate incidental and consequential damages. We emphasize that Pennsylvania law requires no showing of physical harm or damage to the land before a possessor of land can enforce his right to freely enjoy unencumbered and exclusive use of property he rightfully possesses.

Since appellees in this case were only exercising their right to trim the branches and limbs of appellants' encroaching trees, they may not be held liable in damages for doing so. *See, Rosa v. Oliviera*, 115 R.I. 277, 342 A.2d 601 (1975) (damages not available for harm to encroaching shrubbery caused by party exercising common law right to self-help).

The order granting appellees' preliminary objections in the form of a demurrer is affirmed.

Note

In Cobai v. Young, 679 P.2d 121 (Colo.App.1984), the court issued a permanent injunction prohibiting the defendants from allowing snow to slide from their roof in such a manner as to strike the plaintiff's house:

> "Defendants next argue that the trial court improperly granted the Cobais an injunction because a suit at law for damages is an adequate remedy. We disagree. Since defendants' trespass is continuous, the Cobais' only remedy at law would involve a multiplicity of suits for each recurrence of the trespass. As such, the remedy at law is inadequate. And, where further trespasses of the same kind are threatened, an injunction will lie.
>
> "Citing Cass Company–Contractors v. Colton, 130 Colo. 593, 279 P.2d 415 (1955), defendants contend that the injunction should not stand

because it is vague and uncertain. There, our Supreme Court reversed the trial court's injunction because it had ordered the parties to negotiate the blasting methods the defendant could use in its quarry operations so as to prevent damage to the plaintiff's homes. In contrast, the injunction here does not order the parties to negotiate how defendants may use their property; rather it provides that defendants:

> 'are enjoined and prohibited from allowing snow and related materials to slide or be propelled from their house in such a manner as to strike or otherwise impact upon the Plaintiffs' house with sufficient force to cause damage to the Plaintiffs' house. The solution devised by the Defendants to comply with this injunction shall not unreasonably interfere with the Plaintiffs' ability to remove snow from the roof of their house.'

We find the order to be clear and unambiguous."

PETERS v. ARCHAMBAULT

Supreme Judicial Court of Massachusetts, 1972.
361 Mass. 91, 278 N.E.2d 729.

Before TAURO, C.J., and CUTTER, REARDON, QUIRICO and HENNESSEY, JJ.

CUTTER, JUSTICE. The plaintiffs by this bill seek to compel the defendants (the Archambaults) to remove a portion of the Archambault house which encroaches on the plaintiffs' land in Marshfield. The plaintiffs and the Archambaults own adjoining ocean-front lots. Both lots are registered (G.L. c. 185). Neither certificate of title shows the Archambault lot to have any rights in the plaintiffs' lot.

The Archambaults' predecessor in title obtained a building permit in 1946 and built a house partly on their own lot and partly on the plaintiffs' lot, of which the total area is about 4,900 square feet. Each lot had a frontage of only fifty feet on the adjacent way. The encroachment contains 465 square feet, and the building extends fifteen feet, three inches, onto the plaintiffs' lot, to a depth of thirty-one feet, four inches. The trial judge found that it will be expensive to remove the encroaching portion of the Archambaults' building. He ruled (correctly, so far as appears from his subsidiary findings and from the small portion of the evidence which has been reported) that there had been established no estoppel of, or laches on the part of, the plaintiffs in seeking to have the encroachment removed. It appears from the evidence that the Archambaults bought their lot from one vendor and the plaintiffs on June 14, 1966, bought their lot from another vendor. The judge found no evidence of any permission by the owners of the plaintiffs' lot for the encroachment. The encroachment was discovered on July 14, 1966, when the plaintiffs had a survey of their land made.

A final decree ordered the removal of the encroachment. The Archambaults appealed. The judge adopted as his report of material facts the findings already summarized.

1. In Massachusetts a landowner is ordinarily entitled to mandatory equitable relief to compel removal of a structure significantly encroaching on his land, even though the encroachment was unintentional or negligent

and the cost of removal is substantial in comparison to any injury suffered by the owner of the lot upon which the encroachment has taken place. In rare cases, referred to in our decisions as "exceptional" (see the *Ottavia* case, *supra,* 338 Mass. at 336, 155 N.E.2d at 436), courts of equity have refused to grant a mandatory injunction and have left the plaintiff to his remedy of damages, "where the unlawful encroachment has been made innocently, and the cost of removal by the defendant would be greatly disproportionate to the injury to the plaintiff from its continuation, or where the substantial rights of the owner may be protected without recourse to an injunction, or where an injunction would be oppressive and inequitable * * *. But these are the exceptions. What is just and equitable in cases of this sort depends very much upon the particular facts and circumstances disclosed."

2. We here are considering the remedies to be applied with respect to registered land.* Such land is protected to a greater extent than other land from unrecorded and unregistered liens, prescriptive rights, encumbrances, and other burdens. * * * Adverse possession (c. 185, § 53) does not run against such land. To recognize the encumbrance created by the Archambaults' encroachment would tend to "defeat the purpose of the land registration act." * * *

3. The present record discloses no circumstances which would justify denial of a mandatory injunction for removal of an encroachment taking away over nine per cent (465/4900) of the plaintiffs' lot. The exceptions * * * to the general Massachusetts rule, hitherto recognized as sufficient to justify denial of mandatory relief, have related to much less significant invasions of a plaintiff's land, or have involved circumstances not here present. The invasion of the plaintiffs' lot is substantial and not de minimis.** Photographs and maps in evidence, portraying the encroachment, show that the intrusion of the Archambaults' building on the plaintiffs' small lot greatly increases the congestion of that lot. The plaintiffs were entitled to receive whatever was shown by the land registration certificate as belonging to their grantor, unencumbered by any unregistered prescriptive easement or encroachment.

4. The Massachusetts rule in cases like this is well established. There is no occasion for resort to cases from other jurisdictions.

Decree affirmed with costs of appeal.

TAURO, CHIEF JUSTICE (dissenting).

* * *

* "Registered land" is land that is part of a Torrens Title System. Torrens systems are in effect on an optional basis in Massachusetts, Illinois, Minnesota, Colorado and a few other states. *See generally,* 2 Patton on Land Titles (1957), ch. 14.

** Our position avoids constitutional doubts (see Opinion of the Justices, 341 Mass. 760, 785, 168 N.E.2d 858) which might arise were we to allow the Archambaults, at their option and as a result of the trespass of their predecessor in title, to expropriate part of the plaintiffs' land by essentially an informal exercise of private eminent domain. *See* Constitution of the Commonwealth, Declaration of Rights, art. 10 (as affected by art. 39 of the Amendments); Riverbank Improvement Co. v. Chadwick, 228 Mass. 242, 248, 117 N.E. 244. *Cf.* Machado v. Board of Pub. Works of Arlington, 321 Mass. 101, 103–104, 71 N.E.2d 886.

To conclude, as does the majority opinion, that this court must grant a mandatory injunction because the facts in the instant case do not precisely fit the factual pattern adjudged to be "exceptional" in prior Massachusetts cases is illogical and untenable. Courts, especially courts of equity, should not be restricted to so fossilized a concept of what the law is or should be. The cause of justice deserves a better fate. The overwhelming weight of authority in other jurisdictions recognizes and applies the doctrine I urge be adopted here. * * *

This court has recognized the existence of exceptional cases even as we laid down the general rule governing the treatment of suits in equity for the removal of encroaching structures. * * *

While it is true that this court in the past has denoted various classes of exceptions,[87] I cannot agree with the view which the plaintiffs urge, and which the majority find persuasive, that these cases bar this court from considering the particular facts of each case independently of recognized categories of exceptions. I believe that equity and justice require different standards. * * *

* * *

While I agree that the pattern of facts in the instant case does not conform to the pattern in any of the decided Massachusetts cases, this factor is not decisive. I have examined the cases where this court has made an exception and I have found no stronger case on the facts than the instant case for the denial of injunctive relief on the basis of established principles of equity and justice. If we are to give any continuing validity to the long established rule that, in exceptional cases, where equity and justice do not require the removal of an encroachment, injunctive relief will not be granted, it would be difficult to envision a set of facts and circumstances which would present a more meritorious case in which to refuse a mandatory injunction.

* * *

The discovery of the encroachment in these circumstances is best characterized as an unexpected windfall rather than an intentional injury. The defendants are innocent of any wrongdoing and are at most guilty of unknowingly continuing a longstanding encroachment. * * *

87. It is thus well established that injunctive relief may be refused where the plaintiff is guilty of estoppel or laches (Malinoski v. D.S. McGrath, Inc., 283 Mass. 1, 11, 186 N.E. 225; Ferrone v. Rossi, 311 Mass. 591, 594–595, 42 N.E.2d 564; *see* Geragosian v. Union Realty Co., 289 Mass. 104, 109, 193 N.E. 726, and Westhampton Reservoir Recreation Corp. v. Hodder, 307 Mass. 288, 290–291, 29 N.E.2d 913), or where the encroachment is small or slight and thus within the de minimis principle (Harrington v. McCarthy, 169 Mass. 492, 494–495, 48 N.E. 278; Tramonte v. Colarusso, 256 Mass. 299, 301, 152 N.E. 90; Triulzi v. Costa, 296 Mass. 24, 28, 4 N.E.2d 617; *see* Lynch v. Union Inst. for Sav., 159 Mass. 306, 308–309, 34 N.E. 364, and Goldstein v. Beal, 317 Mass. 750, 758, 59 N.E.2d 712), or where the plaintiff refuses to consent to acts necessary to removal (Tramonte v. Colarusso, *supra,* 256 Mass. at 301, 152 N.E. 90; *see* Geragosian v. Union Realty Co., *supra,* 289 Mass. at 109, 193 N.E. 726), or where the plaintiff holds a lease which will expire shortly (Brande v. Grace, 154 Mass. 210, 213, 31 N.E. 633); Lynch v. Union Inst. for Sav., *supra,* 159 Mass. at 309–310, 34 N.E. 364.

Moreover, removal would be a severe burden upon the defendant. As the trial judge indicated, it would "cost a lot of money, and [involve] a lot of inconvenience, and * * * reduce * * * [the defendants'] property value to a great extent." The judge does not appear to have considered whether removal might require the razing of a substantial portion of the defendants' house, but from the exhibits, we should not be unaware of this possibility. The judge made no finding of irreparable injury to the plaintiffs. Under the other facts which he did find, however, I conclude to the contrary that the injury to the plaintiffs, if any, is not of great significance compared with the defendants' loss and that money damages should be a sufficient remedy.

In the totality of circumstances, I conclude that equity does not, in the exercise of our sound discretion, require us to grant injunctive relief. Removal imposes upon the defendants substantial cost and inconvenience which are entirely disproportionate to the injury to the plaintiffs. Where, as here, it appears that the plaintiffs were content with the status quo until fortuitous discovery of the encroachment, it would be oppressive and inequitable for this court to grant a mandatory injunction against the defendants who have acted in good faith, albeit their predecessor in title made a mistake which remained undiscovered for some twenty years. Hardship alone is of course not a ground for denial of injunctive relief (Kershishian v. Johnson, 210 Mass. 135, 139, 96 N.E. 56), but this court should take relative hardship into account, if, as in the instant case, the owner of the encroaching structure is not guilty of an intentional trespass. Malinoski v. D.S. McGrath, Inc., 283 Mass. 1, 11, 186 N.E. 225. The view I express is not only in accordance with our own case law but also in accordance with decisions in other jurisdictions. * * *

3. The majority lay much stress on the fact that we are here dealing with registered land. The majority opinion states: "To recognize the encumbrance created by the Archambaults' encroachment would tend to 'defeat the purpose of the land registration act.'" I cannot agree. * * * It does not follow that a decision denying injunctive relief and leaving the plaintiffs to their remedy at law would be the same as enlarging the defendants' title at the plaintiffs' expense by means of prescription or adverse possession. See G.L. c. 185, § 53. It would seem that after an award of damages the plaintiffs and the defendants would be free voluntarily to reform the titles and establish corrected boundaries.

* * *

4. I do not intend that the long established rule in Massachusetts in reference to unlawful encroachments should be extended or varied. On the contrary, I feel that it is incumbent upon this court in the circumstances of the instant case to weigh the relative equities of the parties and determine whether this is an exceptional case under our Massachusetts rule.

Upon reviewing the present record, I conclude that this is an exceptional case which does not require injunctive relief. The defendants neither initiated the encroachment nor had notice of it when they acquired their property in 1954. The plaintiffs purchased the adjoining lot in 1966 with full knowledge of the proximity of the defendants' dwelling to their own, and in concluding the transaction, they necessarily believed that they were purchasing a small house on a congested lot. It seems unlikely that the proximity of the dwellings, apparently satisfactory at the time of purchase, has since become such an unbearable hardship to the plaintiffs that only the removal of the defendants' dwelling will suffice.

If we were to refuse injunctive relief, common sense suggests that, in all probability, this dispute would be settled eventually without the need for the destruction of the defendants' dwelling. This could be accomplished through an agreement by the plaintiffs to voluntarily relocate their boundary line in return for payment by the defendants of an amount negotiated between them. The parties would then have their certificates of title reformed to reflect the agreement. In the alternative, the plaintiffs could bring an action at law and the court would make an impartial assessment of damages. The placing of the potent weapon of injunctive relief in the hands of the plaintiffs is hardly conducive to a fair and just settlement. In circumstances such as those in the instant case, the court in Christensen v. Tucker, 114 Cal.App.2d 554, 563, 250 P.2d 660, 665 said: "[T]he injunction should be denied, otherwise, the court would lend itself to what practically amounts to extortion." *See* Golden Press, Inc. v. Rylands, 124 Colo. 122, 126, 235 P.2d 592. I would dismiss the bill and relegate the plaintiffs to their remedy at law.

Note

When an encroachment is intentional, courts usually will not "balance the hardships" in order to substitute permanent damages for injunctive relief. To do so, would allow the wrongdoer knowingly to exercise the power of eminent domain, a governmental prerogative. On the other hand, in the case of innocent encroachments, courts normally engage in such a balancing process. Consider how the Michigan Supreme Court recently characterized this process:

> "Fashioning an appropriate remedy where a structure encroaches on the land of another poses special problems and has resulted in special solutions. Dobbs, Remedies, § 5.6, p. 355. On such cases the approach is to balance several factors—the relative hardship to the parties and the equities between them—and to grant or deny the injunction as the balance may seem to indicate. *Id.*
>
> "This Court has long recognized that 'it will examine into all the circumstances of the case, and, if it is apparent that the relief sought is disproportioned to the nature and extent of the injury sustained, or likely to be, the court will not interfere but will leave the parties to seek some other remedy.' *Hall v. Rood,* 40 Mich. 46, 49 (1879).
>
> "The process is perhaps best described as 'balancing all of the equities of the situation.' 4 Restatement Torts, 2d, § 941, comment a, p 581. In balancing the hardships and equities regarding encroachment, courts are guided by two central considerations: An interest in avoiding judicial approval of private eminent domain by the encroacher, and an interest in preventing extortion by the encroachee, who may use the injunction to 'compromise' the claim. Dobbs, *supra.*
>
> "Thus, unless the burden to the defendant of removing the encroachment is disproportionate to the hardship to the plaintiff in allowing the

encroachment to remain, an injunction will issue. *Id.* at 356; *Hall, supra* at 49. However, the question is not resolved merely by determining what advantage the plaintiff will gain if an injunction issues; a just resolution of the question requires examining the hardship the plaintiff will suffer in the absence of an injunction. In other words, the inquiry is not merely

> a nice measurment [sic] of relative advantages and a denial of the injunction if the scales tip in the defendant's favor. The law does not grant an injunction merely because of the advantage that the plaintiff might reap from it, and it does not refuse an injunction merely because of the convenience that the refusal might afford the defendant. [4 Restatement Torts, 2d, § 941, comment a, pp 580–581.]

"As the drafters of the Restatement recognized, the inquiry goes further. The court should also examine the 'character of the conduct (including the respective motives) of the defendant and the plaintiff * * *.' *Id.* at 581.

"Thus, the drafters of the Restatement expressly noted that a plaintiff may be partially responsible for the hardship a defendant would suffer from the grant of an injunction and that a factor that would weigh against a plaintiff is the plaintiff's 'knowledge of the existence of * * * adverse affects [sic]' of the plaintiff's decision to move to an adversely affected area. *Id.*, comment b, p 581.

"While a court is not bound to engage in a balancing of the relative hardships and equities if the encroachment resulted from an intentional or wilful act, Dobbs, *supra* at 355, 357, we agree with the defendant's assertion that there is no evidentiary support that the encroachment was wilful or intentional, and that the trial court erred in issuing a mandatory injunction without balancing the relative hardships to the parties."

Kratze v. Independent Order of Oddfellows, 442 Mich. 136, 142–43, 500 N.W.2d 115, 120–21 (1993).

DAVIS v. JOYNER

District Court of Appeal of Florida, 1982.
409 So.2d 1193.

HURLEY, JUDGE.

At issue is whether the trial court abused its discretion by refusing to grant an injunction. We find no abuse of discretion and, accordingly, affirm.

This appeal emanates from a suit brought by Ms. Davis, the owner and landlord of two adjoining lots, against one of her tenants and a subtenant. Ms. Davis, appellant herein, attempted to invoke the trial court's equity jurisdiction to obtain an injunction prohibiting the tenant and the subtenant of one lot, Mr. Joyner and Atlantic Las Olas, from trespassing on the adjoining lot. According to her complaint, the trespass is in the form of an encroachment by a building. Ms. Davis, however, does not want the encroachment removed; she merely wants to prohibit Mr. Joyner and Atlantic Las Olas, the appellees, from using it.

The encroachment consists of the supporting wall and a portion of the interior of a building. The building extends about one foot over the property line and occupies about 30 square feet. Because the appellees' building abuts a building on the adjoining lot, which is leased to another tenant under a long term lease, Ms. Davis would have little or no use for the small strip of encroached upon property. By contrast, the encroaching portion of the building is essential to the subtenant's business because it contains part of the restrooms and a staircase.

The unusual controversy in this case becomes more understandable when put in historical context. Both lots were previously owned by Ms. Davis' parents. In 1941 they executed a 95 year lease of one lot to Mr. Joyner's predecessor in interest. As a result of the lease, Mr. Joyner pays Ms. Davis rent which is minimal by today's standards.

In 1951 Mr. Joyner's predecessor subleased the lot to a subtenant, Mr. Leonard. Mr. Leonard constructed or renovated a building on the lot sometime prior to 1956. This resulted in the west wall of the building encroaching slightly across the boundary line onto the Davises' other lot. Whether Mr. Leonard constructed the encroachment with the consent of Ms. Davis' mother (Ms. Davis' father having died before that time) is uncertain. But in any event, Ms. Davis' mother did sanction the encroachment by executing an unrecorded lease in favor of Mr. Leonard allowing him to use the small strip of land underlying the encroachment. The latter lease expired in 1971, at the same time Mr. Leonard's sublease expired, and was not renewed.

By 1972 the interested parties had changed. Ms. Davis had succeeded to her mother's interests in both lots. Mr. Leonard had died, and Atlantic Las Olas had succeeded to Mr. Leonard's interests as subtenant. When Mr. Leonard's sublease expired, Atlantic Las Olas obtained a new sublease from Mr. Joyner.

In 1972 Ms. Davis notified Mr. Joyner and Atlantic Las Olas that they were trespassing on the lot adjoining theirs by using the encroaching portion of their building and requested that they stop. This was the first time Ms. Davis or her mother informed Mr. Joyner or his predecessors in interest that the building encroached. Previously, Ms. Davis' mother had dealt directly with Mr. Leonard, the subtenant, concerning the encroachment, notwithstanding that the tenant was the one paying her the rent on the primary lot and that the tenant may have had a right to insist that Mr. Leonard keep the building within the boundaries of that lot.

When the appellees continued to use the encroachment, Ms. Davis filed suit. She sought damages and requested that the appellees be enjoined from exercising use and possession of approximately the rear foot and one-half of the building and its rear wall. The trial court refused to enjoin future use of the building but awarded Ms. Davis damages in the amount of the reasonable rental value of the encroached upon property from October 1971 through March 1979. Neither party appealed the damages award, and therefore we are faced only with the question of whether the trial court erred in refusing to issue an injunction.

* * *

In deciding whether to issue an injunction in a particular case, a trial court must consider the totality of the circumstances and determine whether injunctive relief is necessary to achieve justice between the parties. * * * This well-settled maxim of equity jurisprudence is summarized in § 936 of the Restatement (Second) of Torts (1979):

> (1) The appropriateness of the remedy of injunction against a tort depends upon a comparative appraisal of all of the factors in the case, including the following primary factors:
>
> (a) the nature of the interest to be protected,
>
> (b) the relative adequacy to the plaintiff of injunction and of other remedies,
>
> (c) any unreasonable delay by the plaintiff in bringing suit,
>
> (d) any related misconduct on the part of the plaintiff,
>
> (e) the relative hardship likely to result to defendant if an injunction is granted and to plaintiff if it is denied,
>
> (f) the interests of third persons and of the public, and
>
> (g) the practicability of framing and enforcing the order or judgment.

The above passage accurately reflects the law in Florida.

Even this brief survey of the rules governing equitable injunctions reveals that the trial court properly exercised its discretion by denying injunctive relief. The totality of circumstances, especially the factors discussed below, indicates that injunctive relief would have been inappropriate in this case.

The first factor we consider particularly important in this case is the balance of the relative hardships to the parties. The proper measure is the harm the defendants will suffer by the issuance of an injunction balanced against the harm the plaintiff will suffer by a denial. *See* Restatement (Second) of Torts § 941 (1979). Intertwined in this balance are other factors, *viz.*, the nature of the interest the plaintiff seeks to protect and the adequacy of other remedies.

In this case the plaintiff, Ms. Davis, does not want the encroachment removed. She owns all the underlying property and so it is to her advantage to have the building remain intact. Moreover, the appellees readily admit that Ms. Davis owns all the underlying property and thus she is in no danger of losing title by a claim of adverse possession. Furthermore, Ms. Davis does not assert that she should have the right to use the small portion of the interior of the building which encroaches. All she wants is to prevent the appellees from using it. We are at a loss to discover any legally cognizable harm that Ms. Davis will suffer because injunctive relief has been denied. By contrast, the appellees would suffer substantial inconvenience if they were forced to remodel the building.

The second factor, which we consider particularly important, is the lapse of time that has occurred since this encroachment was constructed and the prejudice the landlord and her predecessors have caused to the tenant's rights. The primary tenant and his predecessors were not informed of the encroachment until sixteen years after the building's construction. During that sixteen year period essential witnesses have died and evidence has disappeared. Surely the appellees have been prejudiced. Had the landlord sought to prevent the use of the encroachment in 1956, a court might or might not have granted injunctive relief depending on the totality of the circumstances then existing. The proof of those circumstances has now disappeared. In addition, if the landlord had not chosen to deal directly with the subtenant and had not neglected to inform the tenant of those dealings, then the tenant might have been able to seek recourse against the subtenant that constructed the encroachment. That subtenant is now dead and gone.

To summarize, we hold that considering the totality of the circumstances in this case, and considering the balance of equities between the parties, the inescapable conclusion that follows is that the injunction sought by Ms. Davis would have been both unjust and unfair. Therefore, we affirm the trial court's refusal to grant injunctive relief.

Notes

1. In *Davis,* the court held that the defense of laches barred the plaintiff's request for injunctive relief. Not only had there been a lapse of sixteen years since the construction of the encroachment, but the defendant had also been prejudiced by the delay. Could the court have found that the plaintiff was estopped from seeking an injunction? What is the difference between laches and estoppel? Consider the discussion of estoppel in Bright v. Michel, supra, p. 130.

2. Suppose defendant encroaches on an easement rather than on land owned by the plaintiff in fee simple absolute. Here there are fewer conceptual roadblocks to injunctive relief than there are in the fee simple context. Because an easement is not an estate in land, the holder has no "possessory" rights in it. Rather, she is deemed to have only an "incorporeal" right to "use" land. Thus, the traditional possessory legal remedies of trespass, ejectment and the summary proceeding are unavailable. As a result, such remedies stand as no bar to injunctive relief. Consequently, injunctions are a commonly granted remedy in the easement encroachment setting. *See* D. Dobbs, Law of Remedies § 5.10(3) (2d ed. 1993). Such injunctions "may issue to prevent obstructions or to restore access; injunctions may issue to require removal of substantial structures or to regulate the extent and nature of use." Id. To what extent will courts in easement encroachment cases "balance the equities" and substitute damages for injunctive relief? Consider the language used by a Florida appellate court to reverse a trial court that denied an injunction to compel removal of a masonry retaining wall that encroached on plaintiff's and other subdivision owners' 50 foot right of way easement for ingress and egress:

> "Injunctions may be refused in the court's discretion even if the party's rights are clear and the legal remedy is inadequate because of various factors including delay in asserting one's legal rights, a large discrepancy between the cost to restore the easement to its former unobstructed condition and the benefit to the dominent tenement owner, and other equitable considerations. * * *

"The record in this case is not appropriate for denial of a mandatory injunction because of the 'balancing of the equities' doctrine. In a proper case a mandatory injunction can be refused but some damages or costs must be assessed to compensate the dominant tenement owners for any loss. * * * In this case no delay or laches were proved against [plaintiff]. *Compare, e.g.,* Davis v. Joyner, 409 So.2d 1193 (Fla. 4th DCA 1982). Nor is the encroachment of the subdivision wall *de minimus. Compare Davis.*

"However, the most distinguishing factor in this case is that [defendant] (through its agents) *intentionally* placed the wall in its present location with full knowledge of the exact location of the [easement line]. When necessary to save trees, the wall was jogged always south into the easement area and never north into the subdivision's landscape easement area. In places it jogged at least twenty feet—far more than necessary to preserve the largest of the trees.

"We, as well as authorities writing in this area of the law, acknowledge that the application of the 'balancing the equities' or 'comparative hardships' doctrine under some circumstances amounts to allowing the servient tenement owner to acquire the dominent tenement owner's easement interest by a form of private eminent domain. This raises serious constitutional problems. * * * That is no doubt why courts usually refuse to apply this balancing doctrine where the encroachment is done intentionally or willfully."

Diefenderfer v. Forest Park Springs, 599 So.2d 1309, 1313–14 (Fla.App.1992). In *Diefenderfer,* defendant, prior to building the wall, offered to pay each of the other affected easement owners $2500 for permission to build the wall in the easement. The other owners agreed and only plaintiff refused this offer. Do you think this should have influenced the court?

C. SPECIFIC RELIEF AGAINST VIOLATION OF RESTRICTIVE COVENANT OR ZONING ORDINANCE

GLOVER v. SANTANGELO

Court of Appeals of Oregon, 1984.
70 Or.App. 689, 690 P.2d 1083.

ROSSMAN, JUDGE.

Defendant appeals the issuance of a mandatory injunction which ordered him to tear down his house because it obstructed plaintiffs' view in violation of a restrictive covenant. After *de novo* review we affirm, but we remand for consideration of alternatives to razing the encroaching structure.

Plaintiffs and defendant are the owners of adjacent parcels of real property in Klamath Falls. Both lots are on a hillside overlooking Mt. Shasta, Lake Ewana and the downtown area. Defendant's lot is on the downhill side of plaintiffs' lot and is encumbered by a restrictive covenant which benefits plaintiffs' property.

At the time the covenant was executed, the house in which plaintiffs now live was completed or nearly completed, and defendant's property was bare land. The covenant was executed "so that the value of Lot 9 [plaintiffs' lot] as a 'view Lot' would not be impaired by future erections on Lot 10 [defendant's lot]." It provides, in pertinent part:

> "* * * [N]o second story shall ever be erected on any building on said Lot 10 except in the area which is within 51 feet of the front lot line (bordering on Huron Street) and that any one-story dwelling erected anywhere on said Lot 10 other than in said 51 foot area shall have a roof pitch of not to exceed 2:12.[1] This covenant shall be appurtenant to and forever run with the land as a burden upon said Lot 10 for the benefit of said Lot 9."

In the fall of 1980, defendant began construction of a house on his property, a substantial portion of which lies outside the 51–foot area. The house consists of a main level and a daylight basement. As soon as it became apparent to plaintiffs that the house was going to ruin their view, they attempted to obtain a temporary injunction to halt construction. Although it was denied, the trial judge told defendant that any further construction was at his own peril. It is beyond dispute that defendant's house substantially impairs plaintiffs' western view. However, their southern view of Mt. Shasta and Lake Ewana, across another neighbor's property, remains unaffected.

After completion of defendant's house, plaintiffs' request for a permanent injunction was tried to the bench. The court concluded that defendant's house violated the covenant, because it was a two-story structure which he finished at his own risk with full knowledge of plaintiffs' complaint. The court based its conclusion on a finding that on the uphill side of the house, approximately one-third of the basement is constructed above what would have been the original grade of the property. It was also found that damages would be very difficult, if not impossible, to determine in regard to the loss of view. Accordingly, the court issued a mandatory injunction ordering removal of the encroaching structure.

Defendant raises a number of arguments on appeal, but they can be distilled down to three basic contentions. First, he argues that his house complies with the intent of the covenant. He contends that because the best view from plaintiffs' property is to the south, toward Mt. Shasta and Lake Ewana, the covenant must have been intended to protect the view in that direction. * * * It seems highly unlikely that the original parties to the covenant intended to protect plaintiffs' southern view by imposing height restrictions on a lot which lay directly west of their property. Rather, we conclude, protection of the western view was the object of the covenant.

Next defendant argues that his house complies with the express terms of the covenant. * * *

From the express language prohibiting a second story, it is apparent that the covenant in this case was designed to limit construction on defendant's lot to a one story structure. Defendant asserts that, because

1. A 2:12 pitch roof means that, for every two inches of vertical rise, there is a 12–inch horizontal run. Defendant's compliance with the roof pitch restrictions is not an issue in this appeal.

his house complies with the Uniform Building Code definition of a single story structure, it cannot violate the covenant. Whether it does or not is irrelevant, because the code definition to which he refers did not exist when the covenant was executed, so it could not have been contemplated as the proper standard for judging compliance.

There is other, more compelling evidence that clearly establishes a violation. After examining the evidence and reviewing the testimony, we note that defendant's house was built so that there are basement windows on its uphill side. To accommodate the windows, the main floor had to be raised off the ground several feet, necessitating a split entry design, where one enters at ground level but must climb either up or down a short flight of stairs to reach the main floor or the lower level. Clearly, defendant's house is higher than one story.

For his last argument, defendant asserts that, under the circumstances of this case, an award of damages would be more equitable than demolition of his house. In a proper case, a mandatory injunction can be denied if the damages associated with removal of the encroaching structure are disproportionate to the injury which the encroachment causes. Tauscher v. Andruss, 240 Or. 304, 308–09, 401 P.2d 40 (1965). This is not such a case. A view is a unique asset for which a monetary value is very difficult to determine. Plaintiffs testified that the view was a crucial factor in their decision to buy the house. In fact, the view was one of the main reasons they were willing to negotiate the steep and occasionally icy streets leading to the house. Defendant's position is made weaker by the fact that he purchased with full knowledge of the covenant. He was, therefore, obligated to comply with it. * * * Furthermore, following the preliminary injunction hearing, he made no effort to modify the design of his house, even though he had been advised by the trial judge that he would finish construction at his peril. Accordingly, we hold that plaintiffs are entitled to have the illegally obstructed portion of their view restored.

Nevertheless, we do not believe that defendant should be required to tear down his house if the structure can be modified to comply with the covenant. There is nothing in the record regarding any feasible alternatives. Recognizing the equitable nature of these proceedings and our need to balance the competing interests, we remand this case for further proceedings to determine whether defendant's house can be modified to comply with the deed restrictions. We leave it to the trial court to specify what modification must be made by defendant if the court concludes that modification can bring defendant's house into compliance. We do not intend to preclude the trial court from again ordering that the house be torn down if the court determines that there is no alternative.

Affirmed and remanded for further proceedings.

Notes

1. The nature of restrictive covenants is discussed in United Properties, Inc. v. Walsmith, 312 N.W.2d 66, 70–71 (Iowa App.1981):

> "The law reflects a two-fold nature. Such covenants are promises respecting the use of the land which, on the one hand, create proprietary

interests and, on the other hand, create contractual rights. Compiano v. Kuntz, 226 N.W.2d 245, 248 (Iowa 1975); Thodos v. Shirk, 248 Iowa 172, 179, 79 N.W.2d 733, 737 (Iowa 1956). Historically, there has been no unanimity of opinion among the jurisdictions as to whether equity is enforcing the promise as a contract or as an incorporeal property interest. *Id.* * * *

"Promises respecting the use of land can be made in a variety of ways: a) by a single restricting instrument in which all lot owners join; b) by a landowner's series of deeds containing restrictions on lots in a tract; or c) by a landowner's restricting instrument on lots in a tract followed by deeds to these lots."

2. Modern courts are often willing to presume that the legal remedy for a violation of a restrictive covenant is inadequate:

"Finally, respondents argue appellants are not entitled to an injunction because they have shown no irreparable harm and money damages are an adequate remedy. Generally, restrictive covenants may be enforced irrespective of the amount of damages which will result from a breach. 7 Thompson on Real Property 187 § 3171."

Gladstone v. Gregory, 95 Nev. 474, 480, 596 P.2d 491, 495 (1979); *accord* Tubbs v. Brandon, 374 So.2d 1358 (Ala.1979); Crimmins v. Simonds, 636 P.2d 478, 480 (Utah 1981).

3. What would have been the measure of damages in *Glover?* In Drulard v. LeTourneau, 286 Or. 159, 169, 593 P.2d 1118, 1123 (1979), the court refused to enjoin the alleged violation of building restrictions designed to protect the view from plaintiff's house and authorized damages in the following amount:

"[W]e believe that the proper measure of damages in such a case would be the difference between the value of plaintiffs' property with the nonconforming structure on defendants' lot (defendants' house, as built), and the value of plaintiffs' property with a structure that *conformed* to the restrictions on defendants' lot."

4. In *Glover,* why do you think the trial court denied the plaintiff's request for a "temporary" injunction?

5. The balance of hardships defense is discussed in the context of an action to enjoin the violation of a restrictive covenant in Crimmins v. Simonds, 636 P.2d 478, 480 (Utah 1981):

"[U]nder a 'balance of injury' test * * *, an equity court may exercise its discretion not to grant injunctive relief when the plaintiff is not irreparably harmed by the violation, the violation was innocent, defendants' cost of removal would be disproportionate and oppressive compared to the benefits plaintiffs would derive from it, and plaintiffs can be compensated by damages. Papanikolas Bros. Ent. v. Sugarhouse Shopping Ctr. Ass'n, Utah, 535 P.2d 1256 (1975)."

And in Gladstone v. Gregory, 95 Nev. 474, 481, 596 P.2d 491, 495 (1979), the court said:

"The equitable principle of relative hardship is available only to innocent parties who proceed without knowledge or warning that they are acting contrary to others' vested property rights. * * * Respondents clearly assumed the risk of increased damages when they continued construction after notice of Gladstone's objections. * * * Moreover, respondents had constructive notice of the building limitation. Where one takes land with notice of restrictions, equity and good conscience will not permit that person to act in violation thereof, and one seeking to enjoin such a violation is entitled to relief regardless of relative damage."

Did the *Glover* court apply a "balance of hardships" test?

6. If a court issues an injunction enforcing a restrictive covenant, may the defendant subsequently obtain a modification of the decree on the ground that the restrictive covenant is contrary to legislative policy? *See* Welsch v. Goswick, 130 Cal.App.3d 398, 181 Cal.Rptr. 703 (1982) (modifying a permanent injunction that restrained the defendant from operating a residential rest home or care facility after the legislature provided that "a residential facility which serves six or fewer persons shall be considered a residential use of property and a use of property by a single family * * *.")

TURPIN v. WATTS

Missouri Court of Appeals, 1980.
607 S.W.2d 895.

HOGAN, JUDGE.

This is an action for a mandatory injunction. Plaintiffs and defendants, to whom we shall refer in the singular, own adjoining lakefront lots situated on the Osage arm of the Lake of the Ozarks. Alleging that defendant had violated a restrictive covenant by constructing a residence lakewards of a setback or building line, thereby obstructing his view, plaintiff sought to compel defendant to move the residence to comply with the restrictive covenant. The cause was tried to the court sitting without a jury. No request for findings was made by either party. The trial court entered a general finding for the defendant. Plaintiff appeals.

* * *

Chimney View Estates is divided into 12 lots. Lots 1, 2, 3, 4 and half of Lot 5 abut the lake on the east. We are concerned with Lots 3 and 4. Plaintiff's property is Lot 3; defendant owns Lot 4, upon which the allegedly offending residence was constructed. The shoreline of Lot 4 meanders from southeast to northwest a distance of 90 feet more or less; the lake frontage of Lot 3, which adjoins Lot 4 on the south, is 75 feet more or less. The plat bears the following legend, among others:

> "No building shall be erected between the 20 foot minimum building line and the 660 countour [sic] line of the Lake of the Ozarks."

The "building line" or setback is sketched along the perimeter of the subdivision. By warranty deed dated March 6, 1973, [prior owners] conveyed all of Lots 3 and 4 to defendant and his wife. The parcel conveyed is described as follows:

> "All of Lots 3 and 4 in Chimney View Estates, a subdivision, filed for record in Book 14 at page 82 in the Camden County Recorder's Office, being a resurvey of Lots 51 and 51A in SHAWNEE BEND NO. 3, all as

shown on the plat of said subdivision filed for record in Plat Book 4, page 27, Office of Recorder of Deeds, Camden County, Missouri. Subject to restrictions, reservations, conditions and easements of record * * *."

* * *

Two other factual aspects of the case must be considered. The course of dealing between the plaintiff and the defendant is of considerable importance. Plaintiff testified that he became interested in buying his lakeshore property—Lot 3 in Chimney View subdivision—about the middle of November 1975. Lot 3 had a residence on it; Lot 4 was unimproved. Plaintiff negotiated with defendant and on December 4, the parties entered into a contract for the sale and purchase of Lot 3 and some miscellaneous chattels. For the total sum of $52,000 plaintiff was to receive Lot 3, together with the improvements thereon; defendant was to provide a title insurance policy; the sale included a good deal of furniture, "major" appliances, a boat and a boat dock. At plaintiff's request, "closing" was deferred to April 3, 1976.

In March 1976, plaintiff observed stakes on Lot 4. Plaintiff testified he spoke to the defendant, telling defendant he was "entirely too close" to the setback. Defendant replied that he could not build "further back" because dynamiting would be required, and defendant was unable to obtain a permit to blast. Plaintiff rejoined: " * * * change your style of house."

On cross-examination, plaintiff was asked if, in March, defendant did not offer to rescind the whole transaction. Plaintiff's testimony was that defendant only offered to move plaintiff's furniture back to Kansas City; counsel went over the offer of rescission several times, but plaintiff denied that defendant ever offered to make full restitution. Plaintiff nevertheless signed the contract, watched the construction proceed, and finally commenced this action on July 16, 1976.

Defendant's testimony about his offer to rescind was considerably different. His testimony was that in March 1976, plaintiff was "very objectionable to the constructing on [defendant's] property." Plaintiff became irate, according to the defendant, and defendant "told [plaintiff] [defendant] would be happy to give [plaintiff] his money back and pay for the boat and pay for the shipping of his furniture back to Kansas City." Defendant "even offered to go to the house and make the telephone call to cancel the real estate contract that was made at that point." Defendant's evidence was that his construction was three-fourths complete when this action was commenced.

A final factual aspect of the case to be noted is the gross disproportion between the injury proved and the relief sought. Defendant's surveyor, as noted, produced a number of plats or surveys. Defendant's exhibit D was designed to show the "percent of view" defendant's residence blocked or shut off beyond the setback. The defendant's surveyor then testified as follows concerning his calculations which were incorporated into exhibit D: (our emphasis)

"Q. With respect to the percentage of the loss of view on the side of [plaintiff's] house closest to the common lot lines between 3 and 4, what is that percentage? * * *

"A. *It would be 3.9 percent.*"

By comparison, there was evidence that the cost of razing and reconstructing defendant's residence, assuming salvaged materials were used, would be about $39,000.

* * *

The only conclusion permitted by the pleadings and the proof is that this is an action upon an express restrictive covenant. There is no claim of encroachment; the evidence completely negatives plaintiff's acquisition of a reciprocal negative easement or implied equitable servitude of the order discussed in Campbell v. Stout, 408 S.W.2d 585 (Mo.App.1966). The sole question before the court is whether plaintiff was entitled to a *mandatory* injunction; in all such cases, the chancellor has discretion, and should refuse relief if it would be inequitable to grant relief.

The court is well aware that proof of damages is not essential to an award of mandatory injunctive relief to enforce restrictive covenants. * * * All the same, "In granting, or refusing to grant, a mandatory injunction to enforce a restrictive covenant * * *, the courts apply the general principles of equity with some strictness, and the complainant may often find himself deprived of this remedy by his own conduct * * *." Annot., 57 A.L.R. 336, 337 (1928). Two of the basic maxims of equity are that he who seeks equity must have done equity, and that equity aids the vigilant. Upon the record, the chancellor could have found that the defendant offered to rescind the contract and make full restitution before plaintiff ever became bound to purchase lot 3, and the offer was refused out of hand. Further, the chancellor could have found that the plaintiff, aware that his rights were being infringed, allowed the defendant to proceed, to defendant's injury. No temporary restraining order was sought; no legal redress of any order was sought until defendant's construction was almost complete. In addition, there was evidence that violation of the setback restriction was widespread in the Chimney View subdivision. Given these circumstances, the chancellor might well have found the plaintiff estopped to complain. *See,* as illustrative: Loud v. Pendergast, 206 Mass. 122, 92 N.E. 40 (1910); Meaney v. Stork, 80 N.J.Eq. 60, 83 A. 492 (1912), aff'd 81 N.J.Eq. 210, 86 A. 398 (1913).

More importantly, the relief sought is wholly disproportionate to the injury sustained. Whatever status one accords the testimony of defendant's surveyor, it is clear that the obstruction of plaintiff's "view" is minimal. To compel the defendant to raze and reconstruct his residence at a cost of nearly $39,000 so plaintiff might enjoy an unobstructed view of the lake would be manifestly inequitable. Relief was rightfully refused upon this ground, if no other. Forsee v. Jackson, 192 Mo.App. 408, 411–412, 182 S.W. 783, 785[4, 5] (1916). *See also,* Freed v. Miami Beach Pier Corporation, 93 Fla. 88, 113 So. 841, 52 A.L.R. 1177 (1927). As plaintiff neither prayed for nor proved any money damages, none could have been allowed.

For the reasons noted, the judgment is in all respects affirmed.

Notes

1. The distinction between laches and estoppel is discussed in Tubbs v. Brandon, 374 So.2d 1358, 1360–61 (Ala.1979) (action to enjoin a violation of a "setback" restriction):

> "Laches concerns a prior failure to enforce a restrictive covenant against this defendant rather than a prior failure to enforce a restrictive covenant against other prior violators. Lapse of time alone is insufficient to establish laches. Prejudice to the party arguing laches, sufficient to make it inequitable to disregard the delay and its consequences, must be caused by plaintiff's delay in asserting his rights. 5 R. Powell, *The Law of Real Property* ¶ 683 at pp. 228.4–228.5 (rev. ed. 1979). Whether laches is established will vary from case to case depending on the operative facts therein.
>
> "Estoppel, however, requires activity both by the plaintiff and by the defendant. The plaintiff must have acted so as to evidence an intent not to enforce his rights under the restrictive covenant and the defendant must have acted in reliance upon plaintiff's conduct so as to make it inequitable for the plaintiff to assert his rights. 5 R. Powell, *supra,* at p. 228.7. One will not be estopped from enforcing restrictive covenants just because he has previously allowed others to deviate in minor respects from the covenants. Abbott v. Arthur, 261 S.C. 31, 198 S.E.2d 261 (1973)."

2. In Goodfarb v. Freedman, 76 A.D.2d 565, 431 N.Y.S.2d 573 (1980), the court rejected the defendant's assertion that the plaintiff's claim was barred by "post-summons" laches. The plaintiffs sought to enjoin the construction of a professional photographic studio as a violation of a "residential use" restriction. Prior to construction, the defendants had misrepresented that they were going to build a "small studio" for personal use. The defendants appealed from the trial court's grant of a mandatory injunction:

> "[O]n their appeal the Freedmans have turned much of their focus from their original emphasis on plaintiffs' laches in failing to take action earlier to plaintiffs' omission to make any effort to preserve the *status quo* once the action commenced. The Freedmans argue that plaintiffs' failure to move for a temporary injunction resulted in further expenditures for construction after the lawsuit began thus depriving the plaintiffs of the right to the remedy of demolition. * * *
>
> "The defendants' postulation of post-summons laches as a substitute for their failed contention of pre-action laches suffers from two serious ailments. * * * Successful invocation of the defense of laches requires proof of prejudice as well as lapse of time (Marcus v. Village of Mamaroneck, 283 N.Y. 325, 28 N.E.2d 856; Pomeroy, Equity Jurisprudence [5th ed.], § 419d). Unfortunately for the Freedmans, the record does not reflect how much money they spent on the construction once the lawsuit began. During the trial, both counsel stipulated that the amount expended by the Freedmans up to September 1, 1977, shortly before they were sued, was $26,454. * * * What the defendants have, then, is their statement

that sums were expended on construction after September 1, 1977, but there is no indication as to how much, if any, was spent after October 24, 1977 when the legal action commenced. * * *

"On this record, moreover, defendants' reliance on Finn v. Morgan Is. Estates, 283 App.Div. 1105, 132 N.Y.S.2d 46, modfg., Sup., 124 N.Y.S.2d 645, and Forstmann v. Joray Holding Co., 244 N.Y. 22, 154 N.E. 652, is misplaced. In *Finn,* the laches of which the court spoke occurred before the action was commenced, for the structure was 70% completed by that time. Here, pre-action laches is not available to the defendants because of their own conduct in misleading their neighbors into inaction. * * *

"When the *Forstmann* criteria are applied to the instant facts, affirmance seems well warranted. Thus, the current restrictive covenants run with the land and are not limited by time; the Twenty–One Acres area has special advantages for residential use and constitutes an ideal residential setting; the defendants' property is residential in nature and clearly has significant value for such use; and while it is apparent that demolition will impose a financial loss upon the defendants, the eradication of their offending structure obviously will add to the value of their neighbors' property. Plaintiffs' real estate expert testified that the Goodfarbs' property was reduced in value by 20% and that of the other plaintiffs 10% as a result of the structure."

3. One way to avoid the defense of "pre-action" laches is to file a request for a declaratory judgment determining the application of a restrictive covenant to the defendant's proposed structure, *E.g.,* Ellis v. George Ryan Co., 424 N.E.2d 125 (Ind.App.1981).

4. Why might the plaintiff in *Turpin* have requested a permanent injunction, but not a temporary restraining order or a preliminary injunction? *See* DeVilbiss v. Zoning Board of Adjustment, 690 P.2d 260 (Colo.App.1984) (security is required only for pre-trial injunctive relief).

5. Another way of characterizing the outcome in *Turpin* might be to say that the plaintiff "came to the violation of the restrictive covenant." In Egan v. Catholic Bishop of Lincoln, 219 Neb. 365, 363 N.W.2d 380 (1985), the court recognized this defense. The plaintiff attempted to dissuade the court from recognizing the defense by analogizing the violation of a restrictive covenant to the maintenance of a nuisance:

"We have held that one's right to enjoin a nuisance is not defeated by the fact that he purchased his property after the nuisance came into existence. Seifert v. Dillon, 83 Neb. 322, 119 N.W. 686 (1909). The analogy, however, is inapposite. The law does not tolerate a nuisance, because it is essentially unlawful or wrongful in character. City of Omaha v. Flood, 57 Neb. 124, 77 N.W. 379 (1898). On the other hand, the law disfavors restrictions on the use of land. Knudtson v. Trainor, 216 Neb. 653, 345 N.W.2d 4 (1984). Thus, the law of nuisances bears no relationship to the question of when one has waived the right to enforce a restriction on the use of land."

RADACH v. GUNDERSON

Court of Appeals of Washington, 1985.
39 Wash.App. 392, 695 P.2d 128.

WORSWICK, CHIEF JUDGE.

Ole and Barbara Gunderson decided to build a house on their ocean-front lot in the City of Ocean Shores. They contracted the job to David Bickmore. Bickmore mistakenly placed the house 10 feet closer to the ocean-front property line than permitted by the City's zoning code. Eugene and Adriana Radach, neighbors two lots away, complained to the City from almost the beginning, but the City did nothing and the house was completed. The Radachs brought action against the Gundersons and the City for injunctive relief. The Gundersons cross-claimed for indemnity against the City and Bickmore.

The trial court found a zoning code violation, but also found that the Gundersons were "completely innocent," and that the Radachs had suffered no substantial injury. It also found the City negligent, but concluded that it had no duty to the Radachs.[1] Therefore, having balanced the equities between the Radachs and Gundersons only, it concluded that no injunction or other relief was warranted.

On the Radachs' appeal, we reverse. We hold that the City had a duty to the Gundersons which, in the circumstances of this case, was sufficient to impose ultimate liability on the City, and that a balancing of the equities should have taken the egregious negligence of the City into account. We hold, on the undisputed facts in this record, that an injunction must issue compelling the Gundersons to move the house, and that the City must bear the entire expense. The Radachs have owned their Ocean Shores vacation home since about 1971. The Gundersons owned the second lot to the south, separated by a 60 foot wide vacant lot. The City's zoning code specifies that structures on such lots be no nearer than 50 feet to the property line that parallels and is closest to the waterfront. City Ordinance § 17.50.080. The City building inspector is required to enforce the setback provisions. City Ordinance § 17.62.010.

In 1977, the Gundersons hired Bickmore to build their house and obtain all necessary permits. The Gundersons were not residents of the area; they left all the details to Bickmore. Unfortunately, he thought the setback was 40 feet. When he applied for the building permit, he submitted a plot plan showing the proposed house 40 feet from the ocean-front property line. A secretary for the City Building Department issued the permit without noticing that it violated the zoning code. A few days later, the building inspector checked the foundation forms on the ground and approved them because they were set as shown on the plot plan. He also failed to notice the violation.

The Radachs first saw the construction during the 1977 Thanksgiving vacation. Mr. Radach noticed that the foundation was too close to the

1. The claim against Bickmore fell by the wayside when Gundersons settled Bickmore's claim against them for the balance of the construction cost.

ocean. He reported the violation to the Building Department the following Monday. There were no workmen on the site at the time, and Mr. Radach did not know how to contact the Gundersons. The complaint prompted the building inspector to check the Gundersons' plan against the code. Now realizing that he had approved an illegal building, he visited the site and attempted unsuccessfully to locate Bickmore. He made no attempt to contact the Gundersons. By now, the exterior walls and roof were nearly completed.

During December, the inspector tried, again unsuccessfully, to call Bickmore or to talk with him at the site. He left messages with workmen to have Bickmore call him, but never told them that the building violated the code. He decided not to contact the Gundersons, feeling that his first responsibility was to work something out with Bickmore. Meanwhile, at least two other residents complained to the inspector about the violation. Still, he did nothing more until January, and then only referred the problem to the city attorney's office.

On January 4, the City sent letters to the Gundersons and Bickmore urging them to review the situation with neighbors before continuing the construction. The letter intimated that the house violated restrictive covenants,[2] but said nothing about the zoning code violation. It did not mention that construction could be stopped by the City. This was the first notice of a problem to be received by the Gundersons. They contacted Bickmore who suggested they ask for a zoning variance. They did so.

A hearing was conducted before the Board of Adjustment on February 2. The Radachs and several other property owners appeared and objected. The Board unanimously rejected a variance; the Gundersons thereupon stopped construction.

On February 7, the City notified the Gundersons that the building permit would not be revoked. On March 9, the City notified property owners in the area that it would allow the house to be completed. On March 10, it notified the Gundersons that it had no objections to their continuing construction. The Gundersons then completed the house. This action followed.

The Radachs make two basic assertions here. First, they argue that the City owed them a duty, for violation of which the City should be held liable. Second, they argue that they were absolutely entitled to an injunction, because the court was not permitted to balance the equities in view of a clear violation of the zoning code. We conclude that the Radachs should prevail, but for reasons other than those argued.

As to the City's duty, the questioned acts of the City here were entirely ministerial. It cannot assume the cloak of discretionary immunity. Miotke v. Spokane, 101 Wash.2d 307, 678 P.2d 803 (1984). The only remaining question is whether its acts and omissions violated a duty running not just to the general public, but to any interested individual;

2. The area is also subject to restrictive covenants. However, no issue as to these covenants is before us on this appeal.

liability must be predicated on such a violation of a duty to an individual. * * *

A City owes an actionable duty to an individual where a special relationship exists or has developed between that individual and the city's agents. Chambers–Castanes v. King Cy., 100 Wash.2d 275, 669 P.2d 451 (1983). Such a duty clearly ran from the City to the Gundersons. The Gundersons' liability runs to Radach and the City's duty runs to the Gundersons. The Gundersons have claimed indemnity from the City. For the reasons that follow, we conclude that a sufficient basis exists for imposing ultimate liability on the City regardless of whether the City owed a specific duty to the Radachs.

The posture of the case is this: the City was negligent; because of that negligence, the Gundersons innocently violated the zoning code; the Radachs are entitled to redress. Because the Radachs have been unable to show monetary damages, their remedy must be an injunction. Were this purely an action at law, there is no doubt at all that the Gundersons would be entitled to indemnity from the City for any relief granted against them. * * * We see no reason why the same principles should not apply in equity. We hold that they do.

There remains the question of balancing the equities. The Radachs essentially argue that this is appropriate only where the litigation concerns purely private interests. They are incorrect. The process of balancing the equities involves the recognition that, in certain instances, courts should refuse equitable remedies where legal rights have been violated. The factors to be considered are:

> (a) the character of the interest to be protected, (b) the relative adequacy to the plaintiff of injunction in comparison with other remedies, (c) the delay, if any, in bringing suit, (d) the misconduct of the plaintiff, if any, (e) the relative hardship likely to result to the defendant if an injunction is granted and to the plaintiff if it is denied, (f) the interest of third persons and of the public, and (g) the practicability of framing and enforcing the order or judgment. * * *

The protection afforded by this process is not available to one who proceeds with knowledge that his actions encroach on the property rights of others. * * *

The dispositive question in this case is whether the trial court balanced the conduct of the right parties. We hold it did not. * * *

The trial court balanced the equities between the Radachs and the Gundersons only, and found that the scale tipped in favor of the Gundersons. This was not tenable, as the actions of the City were completely excluded from the equation.

The posture of this case being what it was, the Radachs had the right to have their interest and injury balanced against the interest and actions of the City, which had a duty to—and therefore, as to ultimate liability, stands in the shoes of—the Gundersons. When the City's conduct is included in the balance, it becomes plain that equitable relief must be granted to the Radachs at the expense of the City.

The Radachs sued to protect their view and to prevent the City from allowing encroaching buildings to destroy the legally enforceable setback line. Injunctions have often been used to protect such interests. * * * Although the trial court found that the injury did not devalue the Radachs' property, a demonstrable financial loss is not essential to support an injunctive remedy for a zoning violation. Welton v. 40 East Oak Street Building Corp., 70 F.2d 377 (7th Cir.1934). The improper setback creates a continuing condition which adversely affects the Radachs' enjoyment of their property. A continuing injury is remedied properly by injunction. In our view, the equities must be very compelling indeed to avoid an injunction to correct a clear violation of a zoning ordinance. Therefore, we generally agree that:

> [A]n action for injunctive relief is the appropriate remedy of an aggrieved property owner who seeks to bar the erection of a structure on adjoining or nearby premises in violation of express zoning regulations.

Lesron, Jr., Inc. v. Feinberg, 13 A.D.2d 90, 213 N.Y.S.2d 602, 607 (1961).

Coupled with the injury to Radachs' property interest is the public injury caused by the City's complete failure to enforce the setback ordinance. The public interest is properly considered in determining if a zoning violation should be enjoined. Welton v. 40 East Oak Street Building Corp., 70 F.2d at 383. "The enforcement of a zoning ordinance by injunction is essential if the amenities of the area sought to be protected are to be preserved." Mercer Island v. Steinmann, 9 Wash.App. 479, 486, 513 P.2d 80 (1973). The City's inaction served to defeat rather than preserve the public interest which it was charged with protecting.

The Radachs were not guilty of delay or misconduct, and the injunction can be practicably framed and enforced. The injunction will affect the City financially, but the City ignored its responsibility and allowed the Gundersons to expend a great deal of money constructing a house that was illegally situated. In so doing, it knowingly violated its duty to the Gundersons, apparently taking a calculated risk that the problem would disappear. It was or should have been aware of the serious exposure this created for the Gundersons. The City was egregiously negligent; its financial hardship will not now insulate it. * * * Because it is clear to us that an injunction must issue, we see no need to burden the trial court with unnecessary further proceedings. This is an appropriate case for the application of RAP 12.2. Therefore, we reverse and remand with directions to issue an injunction requiring the Gundersons' house to be brought into compliance with zoning setback requirements and, after appropriate further proceedings, to enter judgment against the City for the expense thereof.

TOWN OF SHERBURNE v. CARPENTER

Supreme Court of Vermont, 1990.
155 Vt. 126, 582 A.2d 145.

Before PECK and DOOLEY, JJ., KATZ, SUPERIOR JUDGE, and CONNARN and SPRINGER, DISTRICT JUDGES (Ret.), Specially Assigned.

DOOLEY, JUSTICE.

* * *

Defendant owned a building on Route 4 in Sherburne and used it to operate his plumbing business. The zoning ordinance required structures in defendant's zone to be set back one hundred feet from Route 4. Defendant's building represented a nonconforming preexisting use that was set back only fifty-five feet from Route 4. In addition, the building had a preexisting porch that further reduced the set-back, although the actual depth of the porch (between eight and ten feet) is in dispute. In 1986, the Town granted defendant a zoning permit to enclose the porch without changing the amount of set-back from Route 4.

Defendant actually tore down the porch and built an enclosed structure in its place. During construction work, the Town zoning administrator viewed the property and determined that the new enclosure would be ten feet deep even though the plan submitted by defendant showed that the porch had been only eight feet deep and the new enclosure would retain this dimension. The zoning administrator sent defendant a letter stating that the new enclosure would be two feet closer to Route 4 than the former porch and, therefore, violated the zoning ordinance. The letter stated that unless defendant reduced the size of the enclosure the Town would sue to have the extra two feet removed from the building. Defendant completed the enclosure without reducing its size, and the Town brought suit for an injunction * * *.

Defendant responded to the Town's action by arguing that the dimensions on the plans he had submitted were erroneous and the enclosed building front was only two inches closer to Route 4 than the edge of the roof on the former porch. He also testified that the zoning administrator, when he issued the permit, had assured him that a couple of feet would not matter. The trial court rejected both of these defenses and found that the porch violated the set-back requirements of the zoning ordinance.

Without findings or reasons addressing the law of injunctive relief, the court determined, however, that it would not require the defendant to tear down the new enclosure. * * *

On appeal, the Town argues that it was entitled to an injunction as a matter of law * * *.

It is clear that 24 V.S.A. § 4445 authorizes the Town to bring an action to abate or correct a violation of the zoning ordinance. See, e.g., *Town of Brighton v. Griffin,* 148 Vt. 264, 267, 532 A.2d 1292, 1293 (1987). The section does not specify the nature or extent of trial court discretion in acting on such a request. It is a command to the zoning administrator to bring an appropriate proceeding. It is silent on the court's power in acting on the administrator's action.

In *Town of Bennington v. Hanson–Walbridge Funeral Home,* 139 Vt. 288, 295–96, 427 A.2d 365, 369–71 (1981), this Court considered whether a trial court had discretion under § 4445 to refuse to enjoin the operation of a funeral home crematory being operated in violation of the town zoning ordinance. The Court discussed the concept of relative injury in deciding whether to issue an injunction but declined to rule whether this concept was consistent with § 4445, finding that on the facts of the case it would not apply in any event. It concluded that the town was entitled to an injunction as a matter of law and enjoined the defendant from using its premises for the cremation of human bodies.

The opinion in *Hanson–Walbridge Funeral Home* distinguished *Thompson v. Smith,* 119 Vt. 488, 509–10, 129 A.2d 638, 652–53 (1957), where the Court held that in an injunction action brought by a neighbor to remove a building constructed in violation of a zoning ordinance, a balancing test applies. The balancing test in *Thompson* requires the trial court to weigh the "relative convenience or inconvenience, the relative injury sought to be cured as compared with the hardship of injunctive relief." *Id.* at 509, 129 A.2d at 652. *Hanson–Walbridge Funeral Home* emphasized that *Thompson* dealt with private landowners where it was possible to compare the "respective hardships" and noted that the "harm upon development of the town as a whole * * * cannot be weighed against the financial loss to the defendant." 139 Vt. at 295–96, 427 A.2d at 370.

The issue left open in *Hanson–Walbridge Funeral Home* is present here since the Town seeks a mandatory injunction to require defendant to tear down his enclosure or that part of the enclosure that reduces the set-back by two feet and the trial court refused to issue the injunction. The question is whether the trial court had such discretion.

There is a split of authority on which of the equitable requirements for injunctive relief must be shown if a governmental entity seeks to enjoin a violation of a statute or ordinance, and especially when a municipality seeks a mandatory injunction to require a property owner to remove a structure erected in violation of an ordinance. Generally, where a statute authorizes a municipality or public agency to seek an injunction in order to enforce compliance with a local ordinance or state statute, and is silent as to the injury caused, the municipality is not required to show irreparable harm or the unavailability of an adequate remedy at law before obtaining an injunction; rather, all that must be shown is a violation of the ordinance. See, e.g., *Johnson v. Murzyn,* 1 Conn.App. 176, 180–81, 469 A.2d 1227, 1230 (1984).* The divergence of views comes on whether the state or municipality must also show that the balance of equities lies on the side of issuance of the injunction.

Some states hold that it is also inappropriate to allow the trial court to balance the equities in a statutory injunction case, reasoning that

> there is no need for judicial accommodation of the defendant's use to that of the plaintiff. For a court to do so would be to usurp the legislative function. Specifically, in the case now before us, if the defendants can continue the unlawful use of the property after comply-

* Accord: Midland Enterprises, Inc. v. City of Elmhurst, ___ Ill.App. ___, 191 Ill.Dec. 725, 624 N.E.2d 913 (1993).

> ing with the relief granted on remand, the trial court's judgment would have worked to rezone the land with conditions notwithstanding the fact that the power to do so is reserved to the town board alone.

Little Joseph Realty, Inc. v. Town of Babylon, 41 N.Y.2d 738, 745, 363 N.E.2d 1163, 1168, 395 N.Y.S.2d 428, 433–34 (1977). See also *Metropolitan Development Comm'n v. Douglas,* 180 Ind.App. 567, ___, 390 N.E.2d 663, 666 (1979). In *Ackerman v. Tri–City Geriatric & Health Care, Inc.,* 55 Ohio St.2d 51, 378 N.E.2d 145, 149 (1978), an action to enjoin the operation of an unlicensed nursing home, the Supreme Court of Ohio held that the Director of Health did not need to show irreparable injury or lack of an adequate legal remedy once he had shown the statutory violation, and that it would be inappropriate to balance the equities because statutory provisions "which authorize a governmental agent to sue to enjoin activities deemed harmful by the [legislature] are not designed primarily to do justice to the *parties* but to prevent harm to the general public." *Id.* at 57, 378 N.E.2d at 149 (emphasis in original); see also Plater, *Statutory Violations and Equitable Discretion,* 70 Calif.L.Rev. 524, 527 (1982) (when there is a continuing violation of statutory law, the court "has no discretion or authority to balance the equities so as to permit that violation to continue"). This reasoning is much the same as our discussion in *Hanson–Walbridge Funeral Home.*

Other states still retain the equitable requirement of balancing the equities. See, e.g., *Town of Shapleigh v. Shikles,* 427 A.2d 460, 464–65 (Me.1981); *City of East Providence v. Rhode Island Hosp. Trust Nat'l Bank,* 505 A.2d 1143, 1145–46 (R.I.1986). In the *Shikles* and *Rhode Island Hospital Trust* cases, the Supreme Courts of Maine and Rhode Island emphasized that injunctive relief remains within the discretion of the trial court to be exercised under basic principles of equity and justice and that the statutory authorization for injunctive relief in zoning cases did not eliminate that discretion.

We are faced with two levels of difficulties with the trial court's action in this case. The trial court was silent on why it declined to grant the injunction. Since it refused to grant the injunction, it is fair to assume that it balanced the equities and found that they tipped in defendant's favor. We are left to speculate, however, on the grounds relied upon by the trial court in denying the injunction request. Even if we accept that it could balance the equities in this case, we cannot fairly review the trial court's action and must reverse and remand for an explicit statement of the balance struck. See, e.g., *McCormick v. McCormick,* 150 Vt. 431, 438, 553 A.2d 1098, 1103 (1988).

The second level of difficulty is with the balancing of the equities in this case. For the guidance of the trial court on remand, we must answer the question left open by *Hanson–Walbridge.* We hold that the trial court has only limited discretion to refuse to issue a mandatory injunction in a case like this. *Hanson–Walbridge Funeral Home* teaches that trial courts cannot weigh the injury to the public of a property use in violation of the zoning ordinance against the cost of compliance to defendant. 139 Vt. at 296, 427 A.2d at 370. Normally, we must assume that the public injury outweighs the private cost.

In considering the issuance of an injunction on remand, the trial court's decision should focus on two areas of inquiry. The first is whether the violation of the zoning ordinance is substantial. While we recognize the difficulty in weighing public injury against private loss in the typical case, there comes a point where the violation is so insubstantial that it would be unjust and inequitable to require the removal of an offending structure through a mandatory injunction. See 4 A. & D. Rathkopf, The Law of Planning and Zoning § 45.07, at 45–78 (1981). We emphasize that once the court finds that a violation is substantial, further balancing of injury and cost is generally inappropriate.

The second area is whether the landowner's violation is innocent or, alternatively, involves conscious wrongdoing. See, e.g., *County of Kauai v. Pacific Standard Life Ins.,* 65 Haw. 318, 339 n. 22, 653 P.2d 766, 781 n. 22 (1982). Courts have generally found that a conscious decision to go forward, in the face of a direction not to from the regulatory body, outweighs factors pointing against the issuance of a mandatory injunction. See, e.g., *Planning & Zoning Comm'n v. Desrosier,* 15 Conn.App. 550, 556, 545 A.2d 597, 601 (1988); *Town of East Hampton v. Buffa,* 157 A.D.2d 714, 716, 549 N.Y.S.2d 813, 815 (1990). An injunction may be an excessive remedy where the nonconforming use was constructed without knowledge that it violated the zoning ordinance. See *Hargreaves v. Skrbina,* 662 P.2d 1078, 1081 (Colo.1983) (no injunction can be issued against construction in violation of set-back requirement where permit allowing construction was given erroneously by city).

The record does not disclose whether the factors that would allow denial of the injunction were present in this case, because the trial court made no findings in those areas. Defendant testified and argued that he went forward with the construction because the enclosure encroached on the set-back only a few inches more than the former porch roof. An additional encroachment of a few inches might well not be substantial enough to warrant a mandatory injunction. Nor do we preclude the possibility that the trial court could find that a two-foot encroachment into the set-back was insubstantial in this case. Even if defendant's measurements were inaccurate, it is possible that defendant believed in good faith that he had not reduced the set-back more than a few inches. The question may, in turn, depend on whether the former porch roof overhang is counted in determining the set-back. We leave the resolution of these questions to the trial court on remand.

* * *

Reversed and remanded.

D. SPECIFIC RELIEF AGAINST INTERFERENCE WITH USE AND ENJOYMENT

1. *Private Nuisance*

PATE v. CITY OF MARTIN

Supreme Court of Tennessee, 1981.
614 S.W.2d 46.

COOPER, JUSTICE.

Appellants filed an action in the Chancery Court of Weakley County seeking the abatement of a nuisance and damages to real property resulting from the nuisance. The chancellor found that a sewage lagoon, owned and maintained by the City of Martin, was a permanent nuisance and awarded appellants $10,000.00 in damages. The chancellor also found that "an injunction would be too harsh a remedy and should be denied." The Court of Appeals concurred in the chancellor's finding that the lagoon, as maintained, is a nuisance; however, the court classed the nuisance as temporary rather than permanent, reversed the award of damages which was based on the before and after value of appellants' property, and dismissed appellants' action for failure to prove damages for impairment of the use and enjoyment of property, which is the basis for damages resulting from a temporary nuisance. We granted an appeal to review the action of the Court of Appeals in dismissing appellants' suit.

In 1969, the City of Martin built a lagoon into which raw sewage is piped from the city's sewer system. Theoretically, in a properly constructed and maintained sewage lagoon, sewage sinks to the bottom of a lagoon, where it is decomposed through bacterial action. Little, if any, odor is attendant to this process.

The evidence establishes that objectionable odors did not emit from the lagoon for the first two or three years of its operation, indicating that the lagoon was properly constructed. However, since that time, more often than not the surface of the lagoon has had a thick scum of raw sewage floating on top of the water. The odor from the scum is so strong that it makes habitation of dwellings in the vicinity almost impossible. The evidence further shows that this condition can be remedied by the adding of additional enzymes to the sewage and by scattering or churning the surface scum so that it will settle to the bottom of the lagoon.

After receiving complaints of the unsightly condition of the lagoon and odors emanating therefrom, the City of Martin purchased a motor boat and used it in the lagoon to churn the scum. However, the city ceased this activity after a few months, and at a time the city should have known the odors would be magnified by seasonal heat and lack of wind and rain. There is no indication in the record that the City of Martin ever added more than a minimal amount of enzymes to the sewage.

A nuisance has been defined as anything which annoys or disturbs the free use of one's property, or which renders its ordinary use or physical occupation uncomfortable. In City of Nashville v. Nevin, 12 Tenn.App. 336, it was said that a nuisance extends to everything that endangers life or health, gives offense to the senses, violates the laws of decency, or obstructs the reasonable and comfortable use of property.

* * *

In this case, the description of the odors emanating from the sewage lagoon convinces us, as it did the chancellor and the Court of Appeals, that the lagoon as maintained is a nuisance in fact. We also are of the opinion, as was the Court of Appeals, that the nuisance can be corrected by the expenditure of labor and money on the part of the City of Martin.

A nuisance which can be corrected by the expenditure of labor or money is a temporary nuisance. Where the nuisance is temporary, damages to property affected by the nuisance are recurrent and may be recovered from time to time until the nuisance is abated. * * *

Further, being charged with the duty of protecting property rights against damage from a nuisance, a court of equity will on application of the person injured, enjoin the nuisance. * * * This is especially true where the nuisance is classed as "temporary." Seldom, if ever, will an award of damages, standing alone, be an adequate remedy where the nuisance gives every promise of continuing and is one that can be corrected by the expenditure of labor or money. However, in this case the chancellor denied plaintiffs' application for injunctive relief, giving as his reason "that an injunction would be too harsh a remedy." This conclusion was predicated on the chancellor's finding that the lagoon, as located and maintained, was a permanent nuisance—that is, one that the City of Martin could not correct by the expenditure of labor and money and that a consequent result of an injunction would be the denial to the City of Martin of a needed sewage lagoon. As heretofore noted, the nuisance that is the subject of this action, in fact, is one that can be corrected by the expenditure of time and labor. * * * In view of past inaction on the part of the City of Martin, we are of the opinion that an injunction should issue from the Chancery Court of Weakley County requiring the City of Martin to take all reasonable steps to terminate odors from the lagoon, including but not limited to the twice daily operation of a motorboat over the surface of the lagoon to churn and break up surface matter and the addition of enzymes in an amount sufficient to effect the speedy reduction of waste material without the presence of offensive odors.

Evidence of damage to appellants' real property from the nuisance was directed to proving the depreciation in its market value. This was in the mistaken belief that the nuisance was, as found by the chancellor, permanent in nature. The measure of damages for a temporary nuisance is the injury to the value of the use and enjoyment of the property, which is usually shown by evidence of the extent that the rental value of the property is diminished by the nuisance. The chancellor's award of damages, being predicated on the wrong measure, was improper and the Court of Appeals acted correctly in setting aside the award. The Court of Appeals also dismissed appellants' action, which we think was error. Appellants demonstrated that they are entitled to the aid of a court of equity in the abatement of a nuisance. They also showed that the nuisance interfered with the use and enjoyment of their property. They are entitled to damages for the loss of this use and enjoyment. * * *

The judgment of the Court of Appeals dismissing the action is reversed. The cause is remanded to the Chancery Court of Weakley County for the entry and enforcement of a mandatory injunction directed to the abatement of the nuisance, and for the taking of proof on the issue of damages. Costs of the appeal are adjudged against both parties equally.

ESCOBAR v. CONTINENTAL BAKING COMPANY

Appeals Court of Massachusetts, 1992.
33 Mass.App.Ct. 104, 596 N.E.2d 394.

DREBEN, JUSTICE.

The plaintiffs purchased a three-decker house on Purchase Street in New Bedford adjacent to land on which the defendant operates a bakery distribution center. Bakery deliveries are made in trucks and tractor trailers, and, in order to insure the freshness of the product, some deliveries occur between the hours of midnight and 7:00 A.M. Contending that the noise from the trucks is a nuisance, the plaintiffs brought this action to enjoin the nighttime (early morning) deliveries to the site. A judge of the Superior Court denied injunctive relief, finding that the utility of the defendant's conduct far outweighs the harm to the plaintiffs. Instead, he awarded $36,000 in damages, not for the diminution in value of the plaintiffs property, as none was shown, but for the "nuisance which has affected their sleep." The award was to compensate them "for all past, present and future damages they are likely to undergo."

In this appeal by the defendant, we must consider whether, under circumstances where an injunction is too severe a remedy, damages may be awarded, and, if so, whether they may be recovered by the plaintiffs in this case. To be decided is whether it is reasonable to require that a cost—the harm to the plaintiffs—of the defendant's socially desirable activity be borne by the defendant. We hold that, while there are some situations where damages may be awarded, the recovery of damages in this case is not appropriate.

In contending that the judge's findings establish that its activities do not constitute a nuisance, the defendant recognizes that "[t]he law of nuisance affords no rigid rule to be applied in all instances. It is elastic. It undertakes to require only that which is fair and reasonable under all the circumstances." Stevens v. Rockport Granite Co., 216 Mass. 486, 488, 104 N.E. 371 (1914). What the defendant fails to acknowledge is that, under the current law of nuisance, the denial of an injunction is not always a precedent for the denial of damages. Even where the utility of the defendant's conduct outweighs the gravity of the harm, a court may conclude, in some circumstances, that "a cost of carrying on that activity should be borne by the defendant; therefore, the activity is a nuisance, justifying a tort action for damages." Prosser & Keeton, Torts § 88A, at 631 (5th ed. 1984). See also id. § 89, at 641. As stated in comment d, Restatement (Second) of Torts § 822 (1977), "It may be reasonable to continue an important activity if payment is made for the harm it is causing but unreasonable to initiate or continue it without paying." See also id. § 826 comment f; Gilbert v. Showerman, 23 Mich. 447, 456 (1871); DeBlois v. Bowers, 44 F.2d 621, 624 (D.Mass.1930); Boomer v. Atlantic Cement Co., 26 N.Y.2d 219, 226, 309 N.Y.S.2d 312, 257 N.E.2d 870 (1970).

While there has been no explicit adoption of this concept by Massachusetts decisions, the focus in our cases on the balance of equities and what is reasonable under the circumstances, as well as the flexibility of relief afforded, leads us to conclude that the Supreme Judicial Court would concur in this approach. For example, in Pendoley v. Ferreira, 345 Mass. 309, 315, 187 N.E.2d 142 (1963), Justice Cutter, writing for the court, determined that, while the plaintiffs were entitled to have the offensive operation (a piggery) terminated, an injunction should be delayed to allow for a reasonable adjustment of the defendant's affairs. During the period of delay, additional payments were to be made to the plaintiffs for the harm caused. We see little difference in principle in allowing a defendant to continue its operations for a longer or more permanent time but with a concurrent obligation to pay a plaintiff for the loss.

Before recounting the facts found by the judge, we point out that we do not consider ourselves bound by his conclusion that it was unreasonable for the defendant to act as it did without paying for the harm that was inflicted on the plaintiffs. Whether a nuisance exists is factually based. Strachan v. Beacon Oil Co., 251 Mass. 479, 485, 146 N.E. 787 (1925). The finding of a nuisance, however, embraces not only factual determinations but is also "a ruling as to what facts are sufficient in law to constitute a nuisance under the circumstances disclosed." Kasper v. H.P. Hood & Sons, Inc., 291 Mass. 24, 25, 196 N.E. 149 (1935). It "is a sufficiently mixed question of law and fact to permit an appellate court to resolve the issue at least where [as here] the action below was tried to the court." Melrose Hous. Authy. v. New Hampshire Ins. Co., 402 Mass. 27, 31 n. 4, 520 N.E.2d 493 (1988), quoting with approval the opinion of the Appeals Court in the same case, 24 Mass.App.Ct. 207, 215, 507 N.E.2d 787 (1987), which in turn quoted from Cook v. Avien, Inc., 573 F.2d 685, 697 (1st Cir.1978).

We turn to the facts as found by the judge and occasionally quote from his findings. Continental Baking Company's facility and the plaintiffs' adjacent three-decker house are both located on Purchase Street, a major north-south traffic route in New Bedford. "The neighborhood surrounding the plaintiffs' property has been commercial, busy and fairly noisy for decades." Also abutting the plaintiffs' building are a parking lot and a large commercial laundry that causes noise and emits odors. Trains run on railroad tracks next to, and parallel with, Purchase Street. Within two blocks of the plaintiffs' building are a major six-lane highway (Route 195), a major east-west traffic route (Coggeshall Street), and an all-night Sunoco gasoline station.

The defendant's building has been used in connection with the baking industry since 1915. Acquired by the defendant in 1926, the building was operated until 1965 as both a bakery and a distribution facility. From 1965 on, the property was used as a site for distribution of bakery products, and, until 1980, it also housed a thrift store where the defendant conducted retail sales. After the termination of its baking and retail operations, the defendant's activities generated less nighttime noise than before.

The defendant's use of the building has always entailed nighttime activities. The nighttime schedule of deliveries between 12:00 midnight and 7:00 A.M. has been in effect since at least 1963. After 10:00 P.M. and before 11:30 A.M., deliveries to the New Bedford facility only take place once a night. The purpose of these deliveries is to maximize freshness, "the single most important attribute in the bakery business."

Products having a wholesale value of seven million dollars and a retail value of nearly nine million dollars are distributed annually from the New Bedford facility, where the defendant employs thirty-eight persons. Because freshness is important in order to be competitive, an injunction prohibiting nighttime deliveries would necessitate relocation of the defendant's plant. It would cost the defendant approximately $1.7 million to build a new distribution site.

The plaintiffs knew there was a bakery business next door when they bought their property for $35,900 in 1977.[2] The 1977 price reflected the property's location and the defendant's business activities.

Applying a balancing test of harm to the plaintiffs and hardship to the defendant, the judge found that injunctive relief was inappropriate because, as we indicated earlier, "the utility of the defendant's conduct far outweighs the harm done to the plaintiffs." See Restatement (Second) of Torts § 826. He found, however, that the sleep of the plaintiffs was affected and that the plaintiffs had suffered damage due to the unreasonable interference with their use and enjoyment of their property. As compensation, the judge awarded them $36,000 to cover all past, present, and future damages.

While our cases have not discussed the factors which determine whether the plaintiff or the defendant should bear the loss to the plaintiff from conduct which is sufficiently in the social interest that it should not be enjoined, we think the same (or similar) considerations which have traditionally informed our nuisance determinations should also be applicable in deciding whether the less severe remedy of damages should be awarded. This is consistent with what Prosser and Keeton suggest as some of the relevant factors:

"(1) the amount of the harm resulting from the interference;

"(2) the relative capacity of the plaintiff and the defendant to bear the loss by way of shifting the loss to the consuming public at large as a cost of doing business or by other means such as some type of insurance;

"(3) the nature of the plaintiff's use of his property;

"(4) the nature of the defendant's use of his property;

"(5) the nature of the locality;

2. Jose Escobar testified that at the time of trial their property was worth $155,000. He also testified that he conducts a siding business there with three trucks.

"(6) priority in time as to the respective activities of the plaintiff and the defendant in the area." Prosser & Keeton, Torts § 88, at 630.

We also find instructive the authors' examples:

"Those who build residences in a rural area, and beyond the limits of a city and zoning regulations and the protection thus afforded, do so for many reasons, but they may justly and fairly be required to accept certain hazards of so doing. Moreover, if an industrial enterpriser first arrived in an area and plaintiff at a modest price purchased a tract for residential use, the fact that his use and enjoyment for such a purpose is substantially affected is not, generally speaking, a sufficient justification for relief." Ibid.

Applying these or analogous considerations to the findings of the judge, we conclude that this is not a case where it is reasonable to impose upon the defendant the cost of the noise encountered by the plaintiffs. While the plaintiffs have suffered some physical discomforts, they have obtained considerable benefits by coming to the area. They purchased the property at a price that reflected its location and the defendant's adjacent business; the property has increased considerably in value, see note 2, supra, and has, as Jose Escobar testified, special value to him as he can store his materials and trucks on the property and can maintain his construction business from the site. When they purchased the property, the plaintiffs were aware of the bakery business and that the area was, in large measure, commercial.

In determining whether a nuisance exists, the "character of the locality is a circumstance of great importance." Kasper v. H.P. Hood & Sons, Inc., 291 Mass. at 27, 196 N.E. 149. Moreover, while coming to a nuisance in itself does not bar relief, it, too, is a significant factor in determining what is fair and reasonable. "No one can move into a quarter given over to foundries and boiler shops and demand the quiet of a farm." Stevens v. Rockport Granite Co., 216 Mass. at 488, 104 N.E. 371. There is here no suggestion that the neighborhood is changing or becoming less industrial, see id. at 489, 104 N.E. 371; Pendoley v. Ferreira, 345 Mass. at 310, 187 N.E.2d 142, or that by withholding damages the court is preventing changes in the locale thereby "arrogat[ing to the defendant] a good deal of the value of the adjoining land." Cf. Richmond Bros., Inc. v. Hagemann, 359 Mass. 265, 268, 268 N.E.2d 680 (1971), quoting from a predecessor draft to Restatement (Second) of Torts, § 840D, comment b. Although the judge made no findings concerning the relative capacity of the plaintiffs and the defendant to reduce the effects of the noise, Escobar in testifying acknowledged that he did not use an air conditioner in the summer and also indicated that he did not think the defendant's offer to build a wall and a cover over its trucking activities would be helpful.

In sum, we conclude that there was error in the award of damages. The judgment for the plaintiffs is reversed and judgment is to enter for the defendant.

So ordered.

Note

The *Escobar* court refers to the "coming to the nuisance" doctrine. The history of this concept is set forth in Weida v. Ferry, 493 A.2d 824, 827 (R.I.1985) (verdict for defendant in nuisance action reversed due to erroneous jury instruction regarding assumption of the risk):

> "The defense is called the doctrine of coming to the nuisance, and at common law it was defined thus:
>
> > 'If my neighbor makes a tan-yard so as to annoy and render less salubrious the air of my house or gardens, the law will furnish me with a remedy: but if he is first in possession of the air, and I fix my habitation near him, the nuisance is of my own seeking, and may continue.' 2 Blackstone, Commentaries on the Laws of England 402 (17th ed. 1830).
>
> "The doctrine has been modified so that one's coming to the nuisance no longer acts as an absolute bar to recovering damages in a nuisance action. This modification came from a recognition that an absolute bar to a finding of nuisance would, in effect, give the offending activity a perpetual servitude upon the land of its neighbors without the payment of any compensation. * * * We believe that one's coming to the nuisance is simply one factor that may be considered in determining whether or not a defendant's or a respondent's conduct was an unlawful interference with a neighbor's real estate. Prosser and Keeton, The Law of Torts 635 (5th ed. 1984)."

The policy considerations behind the "minority view" are set forth in Jerry Harmon Motors, Inc. v. Farmers Union Grain Terminal Ass'n., 337 N.W.2d 427, 431–32 (N.D.1983):

> "We cannot disregard the obvious fact that our state is not as densely populated as many of the states which comprise or follow the majority view. North Dakota has many open spaces available which many of the industrial eastern states do not enjoy. We must also consider what role the alleged nuisance activity has with the general business activities of the community and state, which are primarily farming and agricultural. * * * Grain elevators and feed-grinding businesses are needed and support the farming and agricultural activities of this state. * * *
>
> "We therefore conclude that any individual or corporation or partnership that comes to an alleged nuisance has a heavy burden to establish liability."

While Massachusetts is not a "coming to a nuisance" state, how important was the concept in the resolution of *Escobar?*

HALL v. WOOD

Supreme Court of Mississippi, 1983.
443 So.2d 834.

ROBERTSON, JUSTICE, for the Court:

I.

This is a diffused surface waters case. In 1979 Leo Hall and members of his family purchased and cleared a 20 acre tract of land in southwest

Jackson. Almost immediately diffused surface waters flowing across the skinned land began depositing excessive amounts of silt, sediment and pollution into nearby Lake Catherine. Owners of property abutting Lake Catherine have brought suit and the Chancery Court has enjoined the Halls, prohibitorily and mandatorily, to cease and correct their pollution and destruction of Lake Catherine.

The Halls have appealed charging primarily that the injunction denies them the use of their property for legitimate purposes. In the context of the facts of this case and the damage caused to Lake Catherine, we hold that the stripping of the Hall lands without taking adequate measures to prevent erosion was not a legitimate use of the Halls' property. Accordingly, with only a modification in form to be explained below, we affirm.

* * *

The Halls' 20 acre tract is zoned commercial. Hall acquired it for commercial development purposes. In the summer of 1979 Hall employed land clearers to remove all trees, vegetation and undergrowth. By August of 1979 the land had been completely stripped. The theretofore existing contours of the land were not altered, and no erosion prevention measures were taken at that time.

Hall had been engaged in negotiations with a major retail department store firm. He contemplated a sale of the property to this firm and others for development as a shopping center. Insofar as the record reflects, the tight money economy prevailing in 1979 resulted in the parties with whom Hall was negotiating abandoning their interest in the 20 acre tract in question. Hall was stuck with the property and remains so.

On April 30, 1982, the Lake Catherine Plaintiffs commenced this civil action. In a nutshell they charged that the Halls had been negligent in the use of their adjoining property to the northwest and that this negligence had proximately caused substantial damage to Lake Catherine and their respective property rights therein. The Lake Catherine Plaintiffs further alleged that the damage was continuing. They demanded prohibitory injunctive relief restraining the Halls from any further deposits of silt or sediment into Lake Catherine as well as mandatory injunctive relief that the Halls restore Lake Catherine as nearly as practicable to its former condition. Plaintiffs further demanded monetary damages as well as a lien on the Halls' property to secure their performance of the requested injunctive relief. The Halls denied these allegations and demands for relief.

* * *

[W]e hold that upper landowners such as Hall are entitled to make reasonable use of their land. Where there is a reasonable likelihood of damage to the property of lower landowners, however, upper landowners are required to do whatever is reasonable to minimize the damage. * * * On the liability phase of this case, we affirm.

IV.

A.

With one exception to be explained below, the relief portion of the chancellor's decree will likewise be affirmed.

To begin with, the proof of damage to individual landowners was sufficiently diffused so that the chancellor was wholly correct in denying actual damages. Besides, it is clear from this record that actual damages will do the Lake Catherine Plaintiffs little good. They want their lake restored. As soon as is practicable, they want to be able to enjoy the waters their properties adjoin and include.

We emphasize that an injunction is an equitable remedy. It must be tailored to meet the exigencies of the situation. It must be clear in that the party enjoined is entitled to know what he is expected to do or to refrain from doing. It must be practical in that it must be susceptible of compliance without undue hardship and reasonably likely to achieve the desired end.

In the Final Decree of September 1, 1982, Hall was mandatorily enjoined:

> (a) to do whatever is necessary to stop the erosion from the subject property into Lake Catherine, and (b) to do whatever is necessary to remove from Lake Catherine all silt which has eroded into Lake Catherine from the subject property.

The essence of the injunction is mandatory, although the "stop any further erosion" part has prohibitory trappings.

* * *

Mandatory injunctions should be granted only where that which they demand is reasonably practicable. A mandatory injunction requiring "a practical impossibility" should never issue. The expense and hardship to the party enjoined should also be considered. That these may be substantial counsels caution and restraint.

The uncontradicted evidence in the record reflects that remedial measures are practicable.

Consider first so much of the injunction as enjoins Hall to act to prevent further unreasonable pollution of Lake Catherine. The evidence makes clear that heavy fertilization and seeding coupled with terracing would substantially slow down the flow of water off of Hall's property. A debris basin or sediment control structure constructed at the lower end of the property would keep much sediment out of the lake. In short, corrective measures are feasible.

The Lake Catherine Plaintiffs established that cleanup was also practicable. The water level will have to be lowered before the silt may be removed. This cost of the cleanup operation was estimated at $50,000. Hall offered no evidence suggesting impracticability of cleanup.

Applying to the facts of a given case the important considerations counseling restraint when mandatory injunctive relief is sought inevitably requires judgment calls. Suffice it to say here that the judgment that mandatory injunctive relief was practicable and was the only practicable remedy was well within the evidence and the chancellor's discretion. Under these circumstances, we decline to disturb the chancellor's decision.

B.

On the matter of the content of the specific injunction issued, we applaud the wisdom of the chancellor's recognition that no court under such circumstances should "try * * * to spell out exactly what should be done to stop the erosion". We emphasize that his failure in this regard in no way runs afoul of our long established rule that mandatory injunctions must be clear and explicit on their face so that the party enjoined will be distinctly informed as to what he is enjoined from doing or what he is commanded to do. Nor did the chancellor depart from our current rule found in Rule 65(d)(2), Miss.R.Civ.P., which in pertinent part provides:

> Each order granting an injunction * * * shall be specific in terms; [and] shall describe in reasonable detail and not by reference to the complaint or other document the act or acts sought to be restrained; * * *

When ordering the achievement of ends necessarily reached only through the employment of scientific or engineering techniques, courts of equity should be particularly cautious. An overly precise specification of *means* will generally be beyond judicial competence in fact or in law. What should and ought be done is the very clear specification of the *end* to be achieved. The party enjoined should then be directed to proceed with reasonable dispatch.

The court should be as clear as it reasonably can be in specifying the end which the party enjoined must achieve. On the other hand, it ordinarily will be appropriate to leave the party enjoined maximum flexibility with regard to the *means* of achieving the *end.*

The Plaintiffs in whose favor the injunction is issued have an interest in seeing the work proceed with dispatch. Ordinarily, they have no legitimate interest in the methodology employed. They are entitled to a judicial specification of means only if the means selected by the party enjoined does not substantially achieve the desired end within a reasonable period of time.

C.

The general form of the chancellor's injunction is correct, within the evidence, and will not be disturbed. In one respect, however, the injunction must here be modified.

The final decree provides that Hall shall be deemed to have complied with the injunction

> when Jack Winstead shall have certified to this Court that such work has been completed to his satisfaction.

Winstead was the Hinds County ASC Agent who testified as an expert witness at trial. There is nothing wrong with the court designating an independent expert to serve as an overseer or advisor regarding compliance with work such as that Hall has been enjoined to undertake. The chancellor, however, did not have the authority to delegate to Mr. Winstead what is essentially a judicial responsibility, i.e., certification of compliance with the injunction.

Ironically, the decree and particularly the part we here hold to be error, was drafted by the attorneys, not the chancellor. While it is no doubt of great assistance to the trial judges of this state to have attorneys draft, and consent to the form of, final judgments and decrees, the trial judge himself must independently evaluate and consider the provisions of any such decree and make such corrections as may be appropriate.

D.

Finally Hall challenges that portion of the chancellor's decree as impresses his 20 acre tract with a lien to secure his performance of the injunctive provisions of the decree. Hall's argument, in essence, is that the chancellor had no such lien creating power because there is no reported case in which any such power has been exercised. Hall recognizes that the Chancery Court, where it grants a money judgment, has the power to impress a lien to secure payment of that judgment, as in alimony and child support matters. He urges, on the other hand, that the chancellor has no power to impress a lien to secure compliance with a mandatory and prohibitory injunction.

The remedial powers of our chancellors are sufficient to vindicate the claims and interests of all litigants. Those powers are as broad as equity and justice require. Those powers have always been marked by flexibility and expansiveness so that appropriate remedies may be decreed to satisfy the needs of the particular case. The chancellor's remedial powers are marked by plasticity. Equity jurisdiction permits innovation that justice may be done. That there is no precedent for the precise relief sought is of no consequence.

Courts of equity have all remedial powers necessary to the particular case, except those that are expressly forbidden by law. Accordingly, we look to our law to see if impression of a lien to enforce compliance with an injunction is a power forbidden to the chancellor by our law. We find no statutory or decisional impediment to such power, nor is there apparent in juridical logic any rationale under which this power ought be denied our chancellors.

In holding that the chancellor had the authority to impress a lien, we have taken only the first step. The exercise of such remedial authorities as are committed to our chancellors is ultimately a matter of sound discretion. If the authority exists, we will interfere with the exercise of the authority only where it is demonstrated that the discretion has clearly been abused. No such showing of abuse has been made. On this assignment of error, we affirm.

Affirmed as Modified.

Notes

1. Why did the defendant in *Hall* want the decree to be more specific? In Bishop Processing Co. v. Davis, 213 Md. 465, 132 A.2d 445 (1957), the court

permanently enjoined the defendant "from so using and employing [its] property * * * as to result in the escape of noxious or offensive gases and odors which will affect the complainants * * * in the rightful use and enjoyment of [their] properties." The defendant claimed:

> "that the decree signed by the Chancellors was too general in its terms; that the decree should have specifically pointed out the things that the appellant was required to do and to refrain from doing. In other words, the appellant would have preferred the Court to direct it to do, and not to do, certain things; then, if it complied with the Court's commands, it would not be in contempt of the Court's order, whether the desired *result* was accomplished or not.
>
> "It is pointed out in the *Gathmann* case, *supra,* 190 Md. 359, 360, 58 A.2d 656, that each case must be determined upon its own facts; that it is inadvisable to be too specific in the prohibition first decreed; that in a nuisance case such as the one before us general decrees should be passed with only such specific prohibitions as appear to provide the only remedies; and that the offending party should be permitted to adopt such measures as it sees fit to accomplish the desired result. The decree in that case further pointed out that if the measures so taken are inadequate or insufficient, further application to the Court can be made and the decree made more specific if necessary."

2. Courts of equity have "inherent authority to appoint nonjudicial officers to carry out judicial functions." Prohosky v. Prudential Ins. Co. of America, 584 F.Supp. 1337, 1351 (N.D.Ind.1984). The *Hall* court could have appointed a monitor to supervise the enforcement of the injunction. *Id.*

3. The *Hall* court encourages innovation in the drafting of equitable decrees. One of the most innovative decrees that has come to our attention was drafted by a district judge in Miller v. Cudahy Co., 592 F.Supp. 976 (D.Kan.1984). *Miller* is a case in which over forty landowner-farmers and their lessees sought to recover damages and injunctive relief arising from salt pollution of the fresh-water aquifer underlying their lands. The court held the defendants liable for $3.06 million in temporary damages and a permanent injunction against future pollution. It also entered an award for $10 million in punitive damages. The court stated further, however, that "were the defendants to make a conscientious, good-faith, and realistic effort to address and remedy, within a reasonable time, the pollution presently existing in the aquifer, such an effort would be extremely relevant to this Court's assessment of the defendants' state of mind and to the appropriateness of the award of punitive damages. * * * In the exercise of its broad equitable powers, this Court concludes that the ends of substantial justice would best be served by holding the final judgment as to the punitive damages award temporarily in abeyance, pending the defendants' good-faith efforts to define and remedy the pollution they have caused." Id. at 1008. After three years no feasible plan had been presented and the court declined to remit any of the punitive damages award. Moreover, the district judge received the following mild admonition from the Court of Appeals for the Tenth Circuit:

> "[T]his case points up some of the problems inherent in trial courts using their equitable jurisdiction to attempt to oversee solutions to problems such as the cleanup of the aquifer. The court's attempt to fashion an equitable remedy which would result in the cleansing of the aquifer was

well-intentioned, and we have no reason to question the court's statements that 'the actions proposed went to the nature of the relief [plaintiffs] were seeking, and were consistent with the relief requested' and that the court was attempting 'to fashion a remedy which truly rectified the wrong, not merely compensated for it.' * * * However, during the post trial phase the parties addressed other matters only tangentially related to cleanup plans * * * and as the court candidly admitted, * * * a court supervised remedial program was simply not feasible."

Miller v. Cudahy Co., 858 F.2d 1449, 1459 (10th Cir.1988).

LUNDA v. MATTHEWS

Court of Appeals of Oregon, 1980.
46 Or.App. 701, 613 P.2d 63.

RICHARDSON, PRESIDING JUDGE.

This is an appeal from a judgment in favor of plaintiffs, private landowners, granting damages and injunctive relief in an action for trespass and private nuisance against defendants who operate a cement plant. The evidence viewed in the light most favorable to plaintiffs, who are aided by the verdict, shows the following.

In 1959 plaintiffs purchased their property in a residential/recreational area of LaPine. In 1970, after husband retired, they built a home there and began using the property as their residence. One of the plaintiffs' purposes in moving to LaPine was the clean air. In 1976 defendants constructed the LaPine Readi–Mix Plant about 180 feet north of plaintiffs' house in an area zoned M–2 Industrial. * * *

In 1978 defendants added a cement storage silo to their plant. After the silo was constructed defendants began to receive large shipments of dry cement rather than the bagged cement they previously used. The dry cement shipments arrive about every 10 days by tractor-trailer. Deliveries are often at night. The dry cement is blown into the silo from the trailer. As it is blown in, clouds of cement dust permeate the air. This dust is so thick that one cannot see the outline of trees in the area. During the pumping process, vibrators shake the cement down inside the silo. If this process fails, a jack hammer is used to pound on the sides of the silo to pack the cement. The unloading process is very noisy. It takes about two hours to unload a trailer.

The plant begins its operations around 7:00 a.m. but has been known to start as early as 4:00 a.m. Usually five truckloads of ready-mix concrete are carried out of the plant each day. Trucks loaded with gravel also make deliveries to the plant. The gravel is dumped onto the ground and then is loaded into the cement trucks to be mixed with the cement and water.

These various trucks all pass directly by plaintiffs' residence, raising dust which blows into plaintiffs' home. The defendants generally do not water the access road until after 5:30 in the evening when the delivery trucks are washed out. The Department of Environmental Quality contacted defendants after plaintiffs lodged a complaint and cautioned defendants to water more frequently.

Plaintiffs' first count in trespass complained that the cement dust, road dust, noise pollution and diesel fumes emanating from defendants' readi-mix plant interfered with the exclusive possession of their land. They also complained that defendants' use of their property unreasonably interfered with the use and enjoyment of plaintiffs' property and created a private nuisance. In addition to diminished land values, plaintiffs sought damages for inconvenience, annoyance, physical discomfort and mental distress. They also sought injunctive relief.

The jury returned a verdict for $5,000 damages and the court, by way of injunction, required defendants to water the roadway and plant area traversed by motor vehicles to the extent necessary to control the dust, and enjoined defendants from operating the plant or receiving deliveries between the hours of 10:00 p.m. and 6:00 a.m. and all day on Sunday.

* * *

[The appellate court found that there was sufficient evidence to support the verdict on both the trespass and the private nuisance causes of action.]

Finally, defendants argue that the operation of their plant was reasonable as a matter of law because they had secured an air contaminant discharge permit from the Department of Environmental Quality and they had not been cited for violation of the fallout standards. Conformance with pollution standards does not preclude a suit in private nuisance, ORS 468.100(4); Renken v. Harvey Aluminum (Incorporated), *supra,* 266 F.Supp. at 175–76.

In assignment of error number three, defendants argue that their motion to strike plaintiffs' allegations of inconvenience, annoyance, physical discomfort and mental distress should have been granted.

Distinct from or in addition to damages compensating plaintiffs for the diminution in property value as a result of a nuisance, it is proper to award consequential damages for discomfort, annoyance, inconvenience and personal injury. Consequential damages are also recoverable in actions for trespass. D. Dobbs, Remedies 344 (1973).

In their fifth assignment of error, which we will consider here, defendants contend that plaintiff husband's testimony concerning the worsening of his bronchitis and emphysema was inadmissible, and that the claims in plaintiffs' complaint for husband's illnesses should have been stricken. Defendants argue that the standard to establish whether a nuisance exists depends on whether the defendants' use of their property would interfere with an ordinary, reasonable person's use and enjoyment of his property, and since defendant is physically ill he is not a person of ordinary sensibilities, citing Aldridge v. Saxey, 242 Or. 238, 248, 409 P.2d 184 (1965).

What the defendants fail to realize is that once facts are introduced which could establish a nuisance based on an interference with a normal, reasonable person's use and enjoyment of land, a particularly susceptible plaintiff may recover for physical discomfort from the effects of that nuisance separately and distinctly from the damage to his property.

Plaintiffs may also recover for mental anguish which is the direct result of defendants' trespass, Douglas v. Humble Oil, 251 Or. 310, 445 P.2d 590 (1968). The anguish suffered may be the result of a continuous invasion of plaintiffs' property over a long period of time. Senn v. Bunick, 40 Or.App. 33, 39, 594 P.2d 837, *rev. den.* 287 Or. 149 (1979). Likewise, damages for emotional distress may be recovered in actions for nuisance where the injury is the result of defendants' interference with the use and enjoyment of plaintiffs' land. Edwards v. Talent Irrigation District, 280 Or. 307, 310 n. 4, 570 P.2d 1169 (1977).

The question is one of the sufficiency of the proof that the anguish was caused by defendants' trespass or the nuisance defendants created. Plaintiffs testified that they were very concerned over the loss in value of their home because they are retired and on a fixed income. They also were distressed because they had moved from the Willamette Valley to escape the air pollution only to have this purpose frustrated by defendants' pollution of the area. Further, they testified that they suffered anguish in not being able to be out of doors and enjoy their yard and flowers. Finally, they were agitated over the potential health hazard of continually breathing the dust-laden air. Any anguish plaintiffs suffered is causally linked to their concern over the effects of defendants' trespass and the resulting nuisance. The allegation of emotional distress, annoyance, inconvenience and aggravation of husband's illness was properly submitted to the jury.

* * *

Finally, in assignment of error number six, defendants argue that the court erred in granting injunctive relief. Many of the arguments defendants raise are the same as those discussed under the second assignment of error. There is evidence that defendants caused substantial harm to plaintiffs' interest in the exclusive possession of their land and in its use and enjoyment. There is ample evidence to support a finding that defendants acted unreasonably in the sense that the harm to plaintiffs was greater than they should be required to bear.

The injunction balanced the needs and interests of the parties. It did not close down defendants' business. It only enjoined defendants from operating during nighttime hours and imposed the condition that defendants water the road to prevent excessive road dust. The injunction only restricts defendants from operating their plant at such times and in such a manner as would unreasonably interfere with plaintiffs' use and enjoyment of their property.

Affirmed.

Note

For another interesting example of a "tailored" injunction, *see* Eva Community Association, Inc. v. Buchanan, 1991 WL 241159 (Tenn.App.1991), where the court rejected a permanent injunction against defendant operating a mussel shell purchasing business in a residential area near a lake, but nevertheless approved a "modified" version of it:

> "The defendants in the present case are operating a lawful business and have attempted to operate it in as unobtrusive a manner as possible.

While the record indicates that the business does somewhat interfere with the neighbors' use and enjoyment of their property, the interference is not extreme and is limited to normal business hours. Therefore, we do not believe that the facts of this case warrant completely enjoining the defendants from operating their mussel shell purchasing business. We believe that a more appropriate remedy is to order the defendants to do everything possible to eliminate the offensive aspects of the operation of their business. This includes requiring the defendants to take any steps which will reduce the noise coming from their business. The defendants are further required to see that the mussel shell divers do not park their vehicles in a manner which blocks the road or in any way causes traffic congestion in the area. We also hold that the defendants are permitted to operate their business only during the daylight hours throughout the years. Finally, we believe that the defendants should continue to do everything possible to operate the business in a manner consistent with the local health codes and standards and to continue to do everything necessary to make sure that odors, insects and rodents do not become a problem. Since the institution of our decision may require court supervision for a limited period of time to oversee the defendants' complaints with the modified injunction, the trial court might find it beneficial to appoint a master to oversee the imposition of this order.

"We find that the trial court correctly held that the operation of the defendants' business constitutes a nuisance. We hold, however, that the circumstances surrounding this case do not support the Chancellor's decision permanently enjoining the defendants from operating their mussel shell purchasing business. Therefore, the Chancellor's order permanently enjoining the defendants from operating their mussel shell purchasing business is modified. The defendants are required to take any possible affirmative steps to reduce the noise produced by the operation of their business and to see that the mussel shell divers do not park their vehicles in a way which obstructs traffic in the area. Finally, the defendants are permitted to operate their business only during the daylight hours."

BOOMER v. ATLANTIC CEMENT CO.

New York Court of Appeals, 1970.
26 N.Y.2d 219, 309 N.Y.S.2d 312, 257 N.E.2d 870, 40 A.L.R.3d 590.

BERGAN, JUDGE. Defendant operates a large cement plant near Albany. These are actions for injunction and damages by neighboring land owners alleging injury to property from dirt, smoke and vibration emanating from the plant. A nuisance has been found after trial, temporary damages have been allowed; but an injunction has been denied.

The public concern with air pollution arising from many sources in industry and in transportation is currently accorded ever wider recognition accompanied by a growing sense of responsibility in State and Federal Governments to control it. Cement plants are obvious sources of air pollution in the neighborhoods where they operate.

But there is now before the court private litigation in which individual property owners have sought specific relief from a single plant operation. The threshold question raised by the division of view on this appeal is whether the court should resolve the litigation between the parties now before it as equitably as seems possible; or whether, seeking promotion of the general public welfare, it should channel private litigation into broad public objectives.

A court performs its essential function when it decides the rights of parties before it. Its decision of private controversies may sometimes greatly affect public issues. Large questions of law are often resolved by the manner in which private litigation is decided. But this is normally an incident to the court's main function to settle controversy. It is a rare exercise of judicial power to use a decision in private litigation as a purposeful mechanism to achieve direct public objectives greatly beyond the rights and interests before the court.

Effective control of air pollution is a problem presently far from solution even with the full public and financial powers of government. In large measure adequate technical procedures are yet to be developed and some that appear possible may be economically impracticable.

It seems apparent that the amelioration of air pollution will depend on technical research in great depth; on a carefully balanced consideration of the economic impact of close regulation; and of the actual effect on public health. It is likely to require massive public expenditure and to demand more than any local community can accomplish and to depend on regional and interstate controls.

* * *

The cement making operations of defendant have been found by the court at Special Term to have damaged the nearby properties of plaintiffs in these two actions. That court, as it has been noted, accordingly found defendant maintained a nuisance and this has been affirmed at the Appellate Division. The total damage to plaintiffs' properties is, however, relatively small in comparison with the value of defendant's operation and with the consequences of the injunction which plaintiffs seek.

The ground for the denial of injunction, notwithstanding the finding both that there is a nuisance and that plaintiffs have been damaged substantially, is the large disparity in economic consequences of the nuisance and of the injunction. This theory cannot, however, be sustained without overruling a doctrine which has been consistently reaffirmed in several leading cases in this court and which has never been disavowed here, namely that where a nuisance has been found and where there has been any substantial damage shown by the party complaining an injunction will be granted.

The rule in New York has been that such a nuisance will be enjoined although marked disparity be shown in economic consequence between the effect of the injunction and the effect of the nuisance.

The problem of disparity in economic consequence was sharply in focus in Whalen v. Union Bag & Paper Co., 208 N.Y. 1, 101 N.E. 805. A pulp mill entailing an investment of more than a million dollars polluted a stream in which plaintiff, who owned a farm, was "a lower riparian owner". The economic loss to plaintiff from this pollution was small. The court, reversing the Appellate Division, reinstated the injunction granted by the Special Term against the argument of the mill owner that in view of "the slight advantage to plaintiff and the great loss that will be inflicted on defendant" an injunction should not be granted (p. 2, 101 N.E. p. 805). "Such a balancing of injuries cannot be justified by the circumstances of this case", Judge Werner noted (p. 4, 101 N.E. p. 805). He continued: "Although the damage to the plaintiff may be slight as compared with the defendant's expense of abating the condition, that is not a good reason for refusing an injunction" (p. 5, 101 N.E. p. 806).

Thus the unconditional injunction granted at Special Term was reinstated. The rule laid down in that case, then, is that whenever the damage resulting from a nuisance is found not "unsubstantial", viz., $100 a year, injunction would follow. This states a rule that had been followed in this court with marked consistency (McCarty v. Natural Carbonic Gas Co., 189 N.Y. 40, 81 N.E. 549; Strobel v. Kerr Salt Co., 164 N.Y. 303, 58 N.E. 142; Campbell v. Seaman, 63 N.Y. 568).

* * *

Although the court at Special Term and the Appellate Division held that injunction should be denied, it was found that plaintiffs had been damaged in various specific amounts up to the time of the trial and damages to the respective plaintiffs were awarded for those amounts. The effect of this was, injunction having been denied, plaintiffs could maintain successive actions at law for damages thereafter as further damage was incurred.

The court at Special Term also found the amount of permanent damage attributable to each plaintiff, for the guidance of the parties in the event both sides stipulated to the payment and acceptance of such permanent damage as a settlement of all the controversies among the parties. The total of permanent damages to all plaintiffs thus found was $185,000. This basis of adjustment has not resulted in any stipulation by the parties.

This result at Special Term and at the Appellate Division is a departure from a rule that has become settled; but to follow the rule literally in these cases would be to close down the plant at once. This court is fully agreed to avoid that immediately drastic remedy; the difference in view is how best to avoid it.

One alternative is to grant the injunction but postpone its effect to a specified future date to give opportunity for technical advances to permit defendant to eliminate the nuisance; another is to grant the injunction conditioned on the payment of permanent damages to plaintiffs which would compensate them for the total economic loss to their property present and future caused by defendant's operations. For reasons which will be developed the court chooses the latter alternative.

If the injunction were to be granted unless within a short period—*e.g.*, 18 months—the nuisance be abated by improved methods, there would be no assurance that any significant technical improvement would occur.

The parties could settle this private litigation at any time if defendant paid enough money and the imminent threat of closing the plant would build up the pressure on defendant. If there were no improved techniques found, there would inevitably be applications to the court at Special Term for extensions of time to perform on showing of good faith efforts to find such techniques.

Moreover, techniques to eliminate dust and other annoying by-products of cement making are unlikely to be developed by any research the defendant can undertake within any short period, but will depend on the total resources of the cement industry nationwide and throughout the world. The problem is universal wherever cement is made.

For obvious reasons the rate of the research is beyond control of defendant. If at the end of 18 months the whole industry has not found a technical solution a court would be hard put to close down this one cement plant if due regard be given to equitable principles.

On the other hand, to grant the injunction unless defendant pays plaintiffs such permanent damages as may be fixed by the court seems to do justice between the contending parties. All of the attributions of economic loss to the properties on which plaintiffs' complaints are based will have been redressed.

The nuisance complained of by these plaintiffs may have other public or private consequences, but these particular parties are the only ones who have sought remedies and the judgment proposed will fully redress them. The limitation of relief granted is a limitation only within the four corners of these actions and does not foreclose public health or other public agencies from seeking proper relief in a proper court.

It seems reasonable to think that the risk of being required to pay permanent damages to injured property owners by cement plant owners would itself be a reasonably effective spur to research for improved techniques to minimize nuisance.

The power of the court to condition on equitable grounds the continuance of an injunction on the payment of permanent damages seems undoubted.

The damage base here suggested is consistent with the general rule in those nuisance cases where damages are allowed. * * *

* * *

Thus it seems fair to both sides to grant permanent damages to plaintiffs which will terminate this private litigation. The theory of damage is the "servitude on land" of plaintiffs imposed by defendant's nuisance. (See United States v. Causby, 328 U.S. 256, 261, 262, 267, 66 S.Ct. 1062, 90 L.Ed. 1206, where the term "servitude" addressed to the land was used by Justice Douglas relating to the effect of airplane noise on property near an airport.)

The judgment, by allowance of permanent damages imposing a servitude on land, which is the basis of the actions, would preclude future recovery by plaintiffs or their grantees.

This should be placed beyond debate by a provision of the judgment that the payment by defendant and the acceptance by plaintiffs of permanent damages found by the court shall be in compensation for a servitude on the land.

Although the Trial Term has found permanent damages as a possible basis of settlement of the litigation, on remission the court should be entirely free to re-examine this subject. It may again find the permanent damage already found; or make new findings.

The orders should be reversed, without costs, and the cases remitted to Supreme Court, Albany County to grant an injunction which shall be vacated upon payment by defendant of such amounts of permanent damage to the respective plaintiffs as shall for this purpose be determined by the court.

JASEN, JUDGE (dissenting). I agree with the majority that a reversal is required here, but I do not subscribe to the newly enunciated doctrine of assessment of permanent damages, in lieu of an injunction, where substantial property rights have been impaired by the creation of a nuisance.

It has long been the rule in this State, as the majority acknowledges, that a nuisance which results in substantial continuing damage to neighbors must be enjoined. (Whalen v. Union Bag & Paper Co., 208 N.Y. 1, 101 N.E. 805; Campbell v. Seaman, 63 N.Y. 568). To now change the rule to permit the cement company to continue polluting the air indefinitely upon the payment of permanent damages is, in my opinion, compounding the magnitude of a very serious problem in our State and Nation today.

* * *

The specific problem faced here is known as particulate contamination because of the fine dust particles emanating from defendant's cement plant. The particular type of nuisance is not new, having appeared in many cases for at least the past 60 years. (*See* Hulbert v. California Portland Cement Co., 161 Cal. 239, 118 P. 928 [1911].) It is interesting to note that cement production has recently been identified as a significant source of particulate contamination in the Hudson Valley. This type of pollution, wherein very small particles escape and stay in the atmosphere, has been denominated as the type of air pollution which produces the greatest hazard to human health. We have thus a nuisance which not only is damaging to the plaintiffs, but also is decidedly harmful to the general public.

I see grave dangers in overruling our long-established rule of granting an injunction where a nuisance results in substantial continuing damage. In permitting the injunction to become inoperative upon the payment of permanent damages, the majority is, in effect, licensing a continuing wrong. It is the same as saying to the cement company, you may continue to do harm to your neighbors so long as you pay a fee for it. Furthermore, once such permanent damages are assessed and paid, the incentive to alleviate the wrong would be eliminated, thereby continuing air pollution of an area without abatement.

* * *

This kind of inverse condemnation may not be invoked by a private person or corporation for private gain or advantage. Inverse condemnation should only be permitted when the public is primarily served in the taking or impairment of property. The promotion of the interests of the polluting cement company has, in my opinion, no public use or benefit.

Nor is it constitutionally permissible to impose servitude on land, without consent of the owner, by payment of permanent damages where the continuing impairment of the land is for a private use. This is made clear by the State Constitution (art. I, § 7, subd. [a]) which provides that "[p]rivate property shall not be taken for *public use* without just compensation" (emphasis added). It is, of course, significant that the section makes no mention of taking for a *private* use.

* * *

I would enjoin the defendant cement company from continuing the discharge of dust particles upon its neighbors' properties unless, within 18 months, the cement company abated this nuisance.

It is not my intention to cause the removal of the cement plant from the Albany area, but to recognize the urgency of the problem stemming from this stationary source of air pollution, and to allow the company a specified period of time to develop a means to alleviate this nuisance.

I am aware that the trial court found that the most modern dust control devices available have been installed in defendant's plant, but, I submit, this does not mean that *better* and more effective dust control devices could not be developed within the time allowed to abate the pollution.

Moreover, I believe it is incumbent upon the defendant to develop such devices, since the cement company, at the time the plant commenced production (1962), was well aware of the plaintiffs' presence in the area, as well as the probable consequences of its contemplated operation. Yet, it still chose to build and operate the plant at this site.

In a day when there is a growing concern for clean air, highly developed industry should not expect acquiescence by the courts but should instead plan its operations to eliminate contamination of our air and damage to its neighbors.

Accordingly, the orders of the Appellate Division, insofar as they denied the injunction, should be reversed, and the actions remitted to Supreme Court, Albany County to grant an injunction to take effect 18 months hence, unless the nuisance is abated by improved techniques prior to said date.

FULD, C.J., and BURKE and SCILEPPI, JJ., concur with BERGAN, J. BREITEL and GIBSON, JJ., taking no part.

Notes

1. An excellent discussion of the Restatement (Second) of Torts § 826 (1977), which defines an intentional nuisance, appears in Carpenter v. Double

R Cattle Co., Inc., 105 Idaho 320, 669 P.2d 643 (App.1983) (adopting Restatement (Second) of Torts), rev'd, 108 Idaho 602, 701 P.2d 222 (1985).

"The Second Restatement, like its predecessor, divides [private] nuisances into two groups: (a) 'intentional and unreasonable' invasions of another's interest in the use and enjoyment of property, and (b) invasions which are 'unintentional' but otherwise actionable under general tort principles. Second Restatement at § 822.

"The first category is broader than the term 'intentional' at first glance might suggest. Section 825 of the Second Restatement explains that an invasion is 'intentional' if the actor knows that the invasion is resulting, or is substantially certain to result, from his activity. Thus, the purpose of an activity, such as a feedlot, may not be to invade its neighbors' interests in the use and enjoyment of their property; but the invasion is 'intentional' within the meaning of the Second Restatement if the proprietors of the activity know that such an invasion is resulting—or is substantially certain to result—from the intended operation of their business. * * *

"The Second Restatement treats such an 'intentional' invasion as a nuisance if it is 'unreasonable.' Section 826 of the Second Restatement now provides two sets of criteria for determining whether this type of nuisance exists:

> An intentional invasion of another's interest in the use and enjoyment of land is unreasonable if
>
> (a) the gravity of the harm outweighs the utility of the actor's conduct, or
>
> (b) the harm caused by the conduct is serious and the financial burden of compensating for this and similar harm to others would not make the continuation of the conduct not feasible.

* * *

"The Second Restatement clearly has rejected the notion that if an activity's utility exceeds the harm it creates, the activity is not a nuisance and therefore is free from all liability in damages or for injunctive relief. *See* Pendergrast v. Aiken, 293 N.C. 201, 236 S.E.2d 787 (1977) (adopting Tentative Draft 18 of the Second Restatement). It discards those earlier authorities which had responded to the problem of disparate economic consequences of injunctions by narrowing the concept of nuisance. * * *

* * *

"[The Second Restatement recognizes] that utility of the activity alleged to be a nuisance is a proper factor to consider in the context of injunctive relief; but that damages may be awarded regardless of utility. Evidence of utility does not constitute a defense against recovery of damages where the harm is serious and compensation is feasible. Were the law otherwise, a large enterprise, important to the local economy, would have a lesser duty to compensate its neighbors for invasion of their rights than would a smaller business deemed less essential to the community. * * *

"[The Second Restatement also recognizes] the fundamental difference between making an activity compensate those whom it harms, and forcing the activity to discontinue or to modify its operations. The damage question goes to a person's basic right in tort law to recover for harm inflicted by another. The injunction question is broader; it brings into play the interest of other persons who may benefit from the activity. Comparative benefits and hardships must be weighed in determining whether injunctive relief is appropriate. * * *

"The Second Restatement deals effectively with the problem of 'externalities' identified in the ALI proceedings. Where an enterprise externalizes some burdens upon its neighbors, without compensation, our market system does not reflect the true cost of products or services provided by that enterprise. Externalities distort the price signals essential to the proper functioning of the market.

"This problem affects two fundamental objectives of the economic system. The first objective, commonly called 'efficiency' in the economic theory, is to promote the greatest aggregate surplus of benefits over the costs of economic activity. The second objective, usually termed 'equity' or 'distributive justice,' is to allocate these benefits and costs in accordance with prevailing societal values. The market system best serves the goal of efficiency when prices reflect true costs; and the goal of distributive justice is best achieved when benefits are explicitly identified to the correlative costs.

"Although the problem of externalities affects both goals of efficiency and distributive justice, these objectives are conceptually different and may imply different solutions to a given problem. In theory, if there were no societal goal other than efficiency, and if there were no impediments to exchanges of property or property rights, individuals pursuing their economic self-interests might reach the most efficient allocation of costs and benefits by means of exchange, without direction by the courts. *See* Coase, The Problem of Social Cost, 3 J.L. & ECON. 1 (1960). However, the real world is not free from impediments to exchanges, and our economic system operates within the constraints of a society which is also concerned with distributive justice. Thus, the courts often are the battlegrounds upon which campaigns for efficiency and distributive justice are waged.

"[The history of nuisance law] has reflected the differing emphases upon efficiency and distributive justice. As noted, the English system of property law placed a preeminent value upon property rights. It was thus primarily concerned with distributive justice in accord with those rights. For that reason the English system favored the injunction as a remedy for a nuisance, regardless of disparate economic consequences. However, when the concept of nuisance was incorporated into American law, it encountered a different value system. Respect for property rights came to be tempered by the tort-related concept of fault, and the demands of a developing nation placed greater emphasis upon the economic objective of efficiency relative to the objective of distributive justice. The injunction fell into disfavor. The reaction against the injunction, as embodied in the First Restatement, so narrowed the concept of nuisance itself that it rendered the courts impotent to deal with externalities generated by enterprises of great utility. This reaction was excessive; neither efficiency nor distributive justice has been well served.

"In order to address the problem of externalities, the remedies of damages and injunctive relief must be carefully chosen to accommodate the often competing goals of efficiency and distributive justice. *See generally* Polinsky, Resolving Nuisance Disputes: The Simple Economics of Injunctive and Damage

Remedies, 32 Stan.L.Rev. 1075 (1980); Ellickson, Alternatives to Zoning: Covenants, Nuisance Rules, and Fines as Land Use Controls, 40 U.Chi.L.Rev. 681 (1973). * * * * Section 826(a) of the Second Restatement allows both injunctions and damages to be employed where the harm created by an economic activity exceeds its utility. Section 826(b) allows the more limited remedy of damages alone to be employed where it would not be appropriate to enjoin the activity but the activity is imposing harm upon its neighbors so substantial that they cannot reasonably be expected to bear it without compensation."

2. The complexity of the balancing process that a court of equity undertakes in determining whether to enjoin a nuisance is illustrated by Harrison v. Indiana Auto Shredders Co., 528 F.2d 1107, 1109–1125 (7th Cir.1975):

> "This is an appeal from a judgment of the United States District Court for the Southern District of Indiana in a nuisance action, permanently enjoining appellant—Indiana Auto Shredders Company from operating its shredding plant for the recycling of automobiles in the Irish Hill section of Indianapolis, Indiana. * * * The suit was filed by appellee—Russell Harrison (d/b/a Indiana Coldweld Company) and some 33 other 'claimants' who reside or work in the Irish Hill section, alleging: (1) that the dust, vibration, and noise generated by the company's shredding plant constituted a common law and statutory nuisance under Indiana law by damaging property and endangering the health and safety of residents and workers in the area; and (2) that the company's shredding plant violated various local air pollution regulations.
>
> * * *
>
> "For reasons stated below, we reverse the judgment of the district court.
>
> * * *
>
> "Weighing the desire for economic and industrial strength against the need for clean and livable surroundings is not easily done, especially because of the gradations in quality as well as quantity that are involved. * * *
>
> * * *
>
> "The problem of balancing the equities in this case, however, was compounded by the fact that the company was not the ordinary industrial polluter. Usually, industrial polluters bring only their proprietary rights to be balanced on the scale opposite the community interests in a cleaner environment. The polluter asks the court to give due weight to the contributions that the business enterprise makes to the community by its economic achievements: payroll, taxes, investment of profits. Although when contrasted with the direct damage caused by uncontrolled pollution, such contributions may seem indirect, they are nonetheless entitled to serious consideration. No court could lightly decide to shut down a business that was the sole or principal livelihood of a community's citizens. Economic and property interests are entitled to significant weight. But

* *See also* Cooter, Unity in Tort, Contract, and Property: The Model of Precaution, 73 Calif.L.Rev. 1 (1985); Epstein, Nuisance Law: Corrective Justice and Its Utilitarian Constraints, 8 J.Legal Stud. 49 (1979).

here, the Indiana Auto Shredders Company makes more than only those economic contributions to the Indianapolis community; it is making a direct contribution toward improving the environment and conserving its natural resources by the recycling of abandoned automobiles. In curtailing the company's operations, the court below chose a very serious course of action. It is our view that such a course of action must be based upon conspicuous facts and reasonable standards of law.

"At the outset, one notes that environmental litigation of this type, whether based upon the Indiana nuisance statute or the common law of nuisance, logically will involve two stages of adjudication. First, the court or trier of fact will determine whether the facts alleged actually constitute a nuisance and a nuisance of what type. Second, having determined the nature of the alleged nuisance, the court will fashion relief appropriate to the equities of the case. Each of these two stages implicate their own legal standards.

* * *

"Ordinarily a permanent injunction will not lie unless (1) either the polluter seriously and imminently threatens the public health or (2) he causes non-health injuries that are substantial and the business cannot be operated to avoid the injuries apprehended. Thus the particular situation facts of each pollution nuisance case will determine whether a permanent injunction should be issued. When a business' offensive activities fall short of that standard, only the combination of both reckless disregard of substantial annoyances caused to adjoining property owners plus the impossibility of mitigating the offensive characteristics of the business will justify the granting of permanent injunctive relief.

"Turning then to the instant case, the decision to permanently close the Indiana Auto Shredders Company was made in error. Although the record indicates that industrial wastes are generated beyond the confines of the property, such facts are not supportive of permanent injunctive action unless injury to health, safety, or welfare is shown. All of the testimony as to appellant's violation of the regulations of the Division of Public Health and Hospital Corporation of Marion County, Indiana, and the Indiana State Board of Health has been negative. The testimony of the authorities and scientific experts was that no violation of state or local health and safety regulations has occurred. Even the claimants' own scientific tests show compliance. Thus the findings of the district court as to violations of the zoning ordinance regarding the emission of particulate matter, earth vibrations, sound, and odorous matter in such quantities as to endanger the public health and safety are clearly erroneous. Under these circumstances and in the absence of any proof of the substantiality of the damage or the incorrigibility of the shredder's operation, the permanent injunction must be ordered withdrawn.

* * *

"This is not to say that those features of the appellant's operation that are found to be offensive should not be remedied. We only say that the offender shall have time to correct the evil. If the appellant does not correct the infractions presently existing within a reasonable period, the district court may take action that will require the appellant so to do.

Likewise, on remand, if the district court deems it advisable to have the appraisal of a neutral expert as to the air contamination, he may proceed to obtain one.

"[The *Harrison* court also authorized the trial court to assess loss of use damages for a nonpermanent nuisance.]"

3. Compare the balancing of the hardships in nuisance cases with the balancing test applied in trespass cases regarding encroachments. *See* Merrill, Trespass, Nuisance, and the Costs of Determining Property Rights, 14 J. Legal Stud. 13 (1985).

4. The power of a court of equity to enter a conditional injunction is discussed in Baldwin v. McClendon, 292 Ala. 43, 288 So.2d 761 (1974):

> "Under a prayer for general relief, a court of equity has power to mold its relief to meet the equities developed in the trial * * *. Where a court of equity assumes jurisdiction for injunctive relief, it will retain the bill for all purposes necessary to a complete determination and settlement of the matters involved, though they be purely of a legal nature. May v. Lowery, 214 Ala. 230, 107 So. 67."

5. Conditional decrees have been sought as an alternative remedy in actions to enjoin encroachments. *See* Olson v. Lindberg, 286 N.W.2d 692 (Minn.1979) (plaintiff prayed for a mandatory injunction to remove an encroachment or, alternatively, for equitable damages; court ordered payment of equitable damages).

6. In *Boomer,* the majority declined to enter an experimental decree. Similarly, in Madison v. Ducktown Sulphur, Copper & Iron Co., 113 Tenn. 331, 83 S.W. 658 (1904), the court balanced the hardships and denied small farmers an injunction against the devastating effects of sulphurous gases produced by two great copper smelters in southeastern Tennessee, relegating the complainants to damages. The court found that the defendants "have been and are pursuing the only known method by which these plants can be operated and their business successfully carried on; that the open-air roast heap is the only method known to the business or to science by means of which copper ore of the character mined by the defendants can be reduced; that the defendants have made every effort to get rid of the smoke and noxious vapors, one of the defendants having spent $200,000 in experiments to this end, but without result.

"It is found in substance, that, if the injunctive relief should be granted, the defendants will be compelled to stop operations, and their property will become practically worthless, the immense business conducted by them will cease, and they will be compelled to withdraw from the state. It is a necessary deduction from the foregoing that a great and increasing industry in the state will be destroyed, and all of the valuable copper properties of the state become worthless." (83 S.W. 658 at page 660). Further, the court emphasized, this would result in great losses of employment, payrolls, taxes and local purchases of supplies.

Then the State of Georgia entered the picture, because of the wholesale destruction of forests, orchards and crops in five counties. It brought suit against the same two copper companies, in the Supreme Court of the United States, as a matter of original jurisdiction. After final hearing, injunction was granted. Georgia v. Tennessee Copper Co., 206 U.S. 230, 27 S.Ct. 618, 51 L.Ed.

1038 (1907). The court envisaged the status of the state as quasi-sovereign, not as property owner. "Some peculiarities necessarily mark a suit of this kind. If the state has a case at all, it is somewhat more certainly entitled to specific relief than a private party might be. It is not lightly to be required to give up sovereign rights for pay * * *. This court has not quite the same freedom to balance the harm that will be done by an injunction against that of which the plaintiff complains, that it would have in deciding between two subjects of a single political power." (206 U.S. 230 at pages 237–238, 27 S.Ct. 618 at page 619). As a consequence of the injunction, experiments were conducted under neutral scientific inspectors appointed by the Court which led to new production processes and to regulation of the volume of sulphur content in the fumes, adjusted seasonally and with variations in wind, humidity, temperature and pressure. Georgia v. Tennessee Copper Co., 237 U.S. 474, 35 S.Ct. 631, 59 L.Ed. 1054 (1915); 240 U.S. 650, 36 S.Ct. 465, 60 L.Ed. 846 (1916). Two results followed. One was the reduction in the harmful character of the fumes by more than fifty percent. The other was the evolution of a new commercial byproduct, sulphuric acid. This was a pioneer development in the industry. *See* I.W. Haynes, American Chemical Industry, A History 263 (1954); Bulletin, U.S. Bureau of Mines 84 (1915).

SPUR INDUSTRIES, INC. v. DEL E. WEBB DEVELOPMENT CO.

Supreme Court of Arizona, 1972.
108 Ariz. 178, 494 P.2d 700.

CAMERON, VICE CHIEF JUSTICE.

From a judgment permanently enjoining the defendant, Spur Industries, Inc., from operating a cattle feedlot near the plaintiff Del E. Webb Development Company's Sun City, Spur appeals. * * * Although numerous issues are raised, we feel that it is necessary to answer only two questions. They are:

1. Where the operation of a business, such as a cattle feedlot, is lawful in the first instance, but becomes a nuisance by reason of a nearby residential area, may the feedlot operation be enjoined in an action brought by the developer of the residential area?
2. Assuming that the nuisance may be enjoined, may the developer of a completely new town or urban area in a previously agricultural area be required to indemnify the operator of the feedlot who must move or cease operation because of the presence of the residential area created by the developer?

* * *

It is clear that as to the citizens of Sun City, the operation of Spur's feedlot was both a public and a private nuisance. They could have successfully maintained an action to abate the nuisance. Del Webb, having shown a special injury in the loss of sales, had standing to bring suit to enjoin the nuisance. Engle v. Clark, 53 Ariz. 472, 90 P.2d 994 (1939). The judgment of the trial court permanently enjoining the operation of the feedlot is affirmed.

MUST DEL WEBB INDEMNIFY SPUR?

A suit to enjoin a nuisance sounds in equity and the courts have long recognized a special responsibility to the public when acting as a court of equity * * *.

In addition to protecting the public interest, however, courts of equity are concerned with protecting the operator of a lawfully, albeit noxious, business from the result of a knowing and willful encroachment by others near his business.

In the so-called "coming to the nuisance" cases, the courts have held that the residential landowner may not have relief if he knowingly came into a neighborhood reserved for industrial or agricultural endeavors and has been damaged thereby:

> "Plaintiffs chose to live in an area uncontrolled by zoning laws or restrictive covenants and remote from urban development. In such an area plaintiffs cannot complain that legitimate agricultural pursuits are being carried on in the vicinity, nor can plaintiffs, having chosen to build in an agricultural area, complain that the agricultural pursuits carried on in the area depreciate the value of their homes. The area being *primarily agricultural,* any opinion reflecting the value of such property must take this factor into account. The standards affecting the value of residence property in an urban setting, subject to zoning controls and controlled planning techniques, cannot be the standards by which agricultural properties are judged. * * *"

Dill v. Excel Packing Company, 183 Kan. 513, 525, 526, 331 P.2d 539, 548, 549 (1958). * * * Were Webb the only party injured, we would feel justified in holding that the doctrine of "coming to the nuisance" would have been a bar to the relief asked by Webb, and, on the other hand, had Spur located the feedlot near the outskirts of a city and had the city grown toward the feedlot, Spur would have to suffer the cost of abating the nuisance as to those people locating within the growth pattern of the expanding city. * * *

We agree, however, with the Massachusetts court that:

> "The law of nuisance affords no rigid rule to be applied in all instances. It is elastic. It undertakes to require only that which is fair and reasonable under all the circumstances. In a commonwealth like this, which depends for its material prosperity so largely on the continued growth and enlargement of manufacturing of diverse varieties, 'extreme rights' cannot be enforced. * * *" Stevens v. Rockport Granite Co., 216 Mass. 486, 488, 104 N.E. 371, 373 (1914).

There was no indication in the instant case at the time Spur and its predecessors located in western Maricopa County that a new city would spring up, full-blown, alongside the feeding operation and that the developer of that city would ask the court to order Spur to move because of the new city. Spur is required to move not because of any wrongdoing on the part of Spur, but because of a proper and legitimate regard of the courts for the rights and interests of the public.

Del Webb, on the other hand, is entitled to the relief prayed for (a permanent injunction), not because Webb is blameless, but because of the damage to the people who have been encouraged to purchase homes in Sun City. It does not equitably or legally follow, however, that Webb, being entitled to the injunction, is then free of any liability to Spur if Webb has in fact been the cause of the damage Spur has sustained. It does not seem harsh to require a developer, who has taken advantage of the lesser land values in a rural area as well as the availability of large tracts of land on which to build and develop a new town or city in the area, to indemnify those who are forced to leave as a result.

Having brought people to the nuisance to the foreseeable detriment of Spur, Webb must indemnify Spur for a reasonable amount of the cost of moving or shutting down. It should be noted that this relief to Spur is limited to a case wherein a developer has, with foreseeability, brought into a previously agricultural or industrial area the population which makes necessary the granting of an injunction against a lawful business and for which the business has no adequate relief.

It is therefore the decision of this court that the matter be remanded to the trial court for a hearing upon the damages sustained by the defendant Spur as a reasonable and direct result of the granting of the permanent injunction. Since the result of the appeal may appear novel and both sides have obtained a measure of relief, it is ordered that each side will bear its own costs.

Affirmed in part, reversed in part, and remanded for further proceedings consistent with this opinion.

HAYS, C.J., STRUCKMEYER and LOCKWOOD, JJ., and UDALL, RETIRED JUSTICE.*

Notes

1. In a provocative article, Professor Rabin advocates a new approach to resolving private nuisance disputes that puts an increased emphasis on the use of conditional injunctions:

> "When the light from a racetrack owned by one person interferes with an outdoor movie theater owned by another, what is the proper resolution of the conflict? Traditionally, courts have assumed such a question to be a simple one. If the interference did not constitute a nuisance, the cinema owner would have no legal remedy. She would have to tolerate the interference or ameliorate its effects at her own expense, such as by shielding the cinema from the lights. If the interference constituted a 'nuisance,' a court would issue an injunction forcing the track owner to shade his lights or otherwise to protect the cinema at his own expense.
>
> "Professors Calabresi and Melamed have identified two additional alternatives in a recent stimulating article.[3] First, a court could award the cinema owner damages for future harm, while denying an injunction against the track owner.[4] This article suggests that a court generally

* For an analysis of the *Spur* case, see Note, 38 Mo.L.Rev. 135 (1973).

3. Calabresi & Melamed, Property Rules, Liability Rules and Inalienability: One View of the Cathedral, 85 Harv.L.Rev. 1089 (1972).

4. *E.g.,* State v. Board of Education, 116 N.J.Super. 305, 282 A.2d 71 (1971) (Board recovered cost of air conditioning and sound proofing to buffer the noise of adjacent highway). The leading modern case illustrating

should enforce the right to damages by issuing an injunction against the track owner that would be dissolvable upon his payment of the damages. Such an injunction is one form of what may be called a conditional injunction. The measure of damages probably would be the cost to the cinema owner of erecting a shield against the light, as this would be required of her by the duty to avoid adverse consequences. Second, a court could issue an injunction requiring the track owner to shade his lights, conditional upon the cinema owner's paying the cost.[5] This remedy is another form of conditional injunction.

"Four alternative dispositions, therefore, are available in a nuisance action. Which alternative should be used, and under what circumstances, are the subjects of this article. * * *

* * *

III

PROPOSED–SOLUTION

"Courts too often confuse the question of 'who should pay for it?' with the question of 'what should be done?' The questions are distinct and require separate treatment. The question of who should pay can be answered only with reference to the criterion of fairness, involving an assessment of relative moral fault. In contrast, the second question should be resolved by the criterion of efficiency.

"The procedure here proposed for resolving private nuisance cases involves two steps. The first step would be to determine who is morally more blameworthy for the existence of the conflict. That person should bear the expense of resolving the conflict. This should satisfy the fairness criterion. The second step in the proposed procedure would be to determine how the conflict can be resolved with least expense. This resolution of the conflict would satisfy the efficiency criterion. As a result, the person at fault would pay the cost of resolving the conflict caused by the nuisance in the most efficient manner. This result would be both fair and efficient.

"The following chart summarizes the solutions that the proposed procedure would yield for variations of the hypothetical posed earlier.

Resolving Land Use Conflicts to Optimize Fairness and Efficiency

	PARTY AT FAULT	
	Track Owner	**Cinema Owner**
MOST EFFICIENT SOLUTION	Court Order: Track owner enjoined from interfering with cinema unless he pays damages equal to	Court Order: Track owner enjoined from interfering with cinema if cinema owner pays track

the trend toward awarding damages rather than an injunction in nuisance cases is Boomer v. Atlantic Cement Co., 26 N.Y.2d 219, 309 N.Y.S.2d 312, 257 N.E.2d 870 (1970). *See also* Harrison v. Indiana Auto Shredders Co., 528 F.2d 1107 (7th Cir.1975) * * *.

Of course, damages for past interference would be appropriate whether or not an injunction is issued.

5. Apparently, the only case that has adopted this remedy is Spur Indus. Inc. v. Del E. Webb Dev. Co., 108 Ariz. 178, 494 P.2d 700 (1972).

		PARTY AT FAULT	
		Track Owner	**Cinema Owner**
MOST EFFICIENT SOLUTION		Court Order: least expensive solution.	Court Order: owner the cost of compliance.*
Physical changes less expensive than abandoning either use.	Shading track lights cheaper.	*Track owner will shade lights at his expense, complying with the injunction.*	*Cinema owner will pay track owner cost of installing shades, and track owner will install them in compliance with injunction.*
	Shielding cinema cheaper.	*Track owner will pay damages to cinema owner, measured by cost of shielding cinema, thereby lifting the injunction.*	*Cinema owner will build a light shield at her own expense rather than enforce an injunction.**
Physical changes more expensive than abandoning either use.	Abandoning track cheaper.	*Track owner will abandon track.*	*Cinema owner will pay track owner cost of abandoning track, and injunction will be imposed.*
	Abandoning cinema cheaper.	*Track owner will pay damages to cinema owner, measured by profits lost because of abandonment of cinema. Injunction will be lifted and cinema abandoned.*	*Cinema owner will abandon cinema, and injunction will not be imposed.**

* Of course, where the cinema owner is at fault, and the efficient solution is either shielding or abandoning the cinema, the cinema owner will not attempt to enforce her right to an injunction conditional upon her payment of the track owner's cost of compliance.

"The procedure suggested here departs from the traditional method of analysis used in nuisance cases. Under the traditional method the court simply determines whether the interference is a nuisance. If the court finds that it is, the remedy is an unconditional injunction. If the court finds that it is not, an injunction is refused. Occasionally, a court will award damages but refuse an injunction. Such cases are explainable by reference to the doctrine of comparative hardship. Only rarely does a plaintiff receive an injunction that is dissolvable if the defendant pays damages. And apparently in only one case has a plaintiff obtained an injunction conditional on her paying defendant the cost of his compliance. This article contends that these rarely used conditional injunctions should become the usual remedies, and the other remedies should become the rarities. Such conditional injunctions will promote economic efficiency more effectively without sacrificing fairness."

Rabin, Nuisance Law: Rethinking Fundamental Assumptions, 63 Va.L.Rev. 1299, 1300, 1309–11 (1977).*

2. Although the conditional decrees developed by the courts in *Boomer* and *Spur* have been favored by commentators who engage in economic analysis, Professor Polinsky has compared the damages and injunctive remedies and has concluded that neither is clearly superior:

"The resolution of nuisance disputes may, following Calabresi and Melamed,[6] be viewed as involving two steps. First, a determination must be made as to who is entitled to prevail. The polluter can be granted the right to pollute, or the pollutee can be granted the right to be free from pollution. Then, in the language of Calabresi and Melamed, a decision must be made whether to protect the entitlement by a 'property rule' or a 'liability rule.' The former grants the holder of the entitlement an

* Reprinted with permission of the Virginia Law Review Association and Fred B. Rothman & Co.

6. Calabresi & Melamed, Property Rules, Liability Rules, and Inalienability: One View of the Cathedral, 85 Harv.L.Rev. 1089 (1972).

injunction, while the latter awards him damages determined by some collective authority such as a court. Thus, in their framework, there are four possible types of solutions, depending on who is given the entitlement and how it is protected.[7]

"Most recent legal commentaries on nuisance law have strongly recommended the use of damages rather than injunctions.[8] Whether court decisions also favor the damage remedy is unclear, although many commentators perceive a trend in this direction.[9] Three arguments have been suggested for this preference; I will refer to these as the extortion, strategic behavior, and 'bonus payment' arguments.

"The first argument against injunctive remedies is that they allow the plaintiff to 'extort' the defendant. This possibility arises whenever the potential cost that enforcement of the injunction would impose on the defendant exceeds the loss borne by the plaintiff if the activity in question occurs. Suppose, for example, that operation of a plant injures a pollutee by $1,000 while the polluter would lose $10,000 in profits if the plant were shut down by an injunction. Because the defendant may be willing to pay up to his entire potential profit to prevent the shutdown, the plaintiff might be able to exact compensation well in excess of his actual damages. Under a damage remedy, however, the court dictates the plaintiff's compensation—presumably $1,000 in this example—leaving no scope for extortion.

"Note that the extortion argument relates to the goal of distributional equity, not economic efficiency. In the previous example, it is efficient for the plant to continue to operate since the gains are $10,000 while the costs are only $1,000. If, because of the threat of an injunction, the polluter pays the pollutee $9,000 in order to continue operating, this may be inequitable, but it is not inefficient.

"The second argument against injunctive remedies—the strategic behavior argument—concerns the consequences for economic efficiency of *unsuccessful* extortion. Strategic behavior consists of bargaining conduct in which a party, perhaps misperceiving his opponent's bargaining position, holds out for a settlement that is never reached (or that is reached after undue delay or negotiation cost). Under an injunctive remedy, strategic behavior may prevent the parties from reaching an efficient resolution of the dispute. In the previous example, the plaintiff might hold out for $8,000 while the defendant, also behaving strategically, might refuse to pay

7. These solutions are a property rule with the entitlement held by the polluter; a property rule with the entitlement held by the pollutee; a liability rule with the entitlement held by the polluter; and a liability rule with the entitlement held by the pollutee.

8. *See, e.g.,* Ellickson, Alternatives to Zoning: Covenants, Nuisance Rules, and Fines as Land Use Controls, 40 U.Chi.L.Rev. 681, 738–48 (1973); Rabin, Nuisance Law: Rethinking Fundamental Assumptions, 63 Va.L.Rev. 1299, 1309–48 (1977); Comment, Internalizing Externalities: Nuisance Law and Economic Efficiency, 53 N.Y.U.L.Rev. 219, 228–40 (1978).

9. The leading modern American cases illustrating the use of damage remedies are Boomer v. Atlantic Cement Co., 26 N.Y.2d 219, 257 N.E.2d 870, 309 N.Y.S.2d 312 (1970), and Spur Indus., Inc. v. Del E. Webb Dev. Co., 108 Ariz. 178, 494 P.2d 700 (1972). English courts apparently favor injunctive relief relative to damages. Ogus & Richardson, Economics and the Environment: A Study of Private Nuisance, 36 Cambridge L.J. 284, 308–09 (1977). But recently there may have been "[s]ome easing in the judicial attitude" with regard to this preference. *Id.* at 310 (citing Miller v. Jackson and Another, [1977] 3 W.L.R. 20).

anything over $5,000. As a result, the plaintiff might enforce the injunction and shut down the defendant's plant (at least for some period). In contrast, a damage award seems to overcome strategic behavior problems because the defendant does not have to obtain the consent of the plaintiff. In the example, the defendant presumably would choose to pay any court-determined damage award under $10,000 and keep his plant in operation.

"The third argument for damage remedies—the 'bonus payment' argument—is offered less frequently than the other two arguments. Once it has been decided to use a damage remedy for either of the other reasons, it is possible to pursue additional distributional goals by making the defendant's liability more or less than the plaintiff's actual damages. In the example, suppose the plaintiff is poorer than the defendant and a more equal distribution of income is desired. The damage award could be augmented by a 'bonus payment' to achieve the precise amount of redistribution preferred. If redistribution by other means—such as the income tax system—is costlier (in an efficiency sense), then using a damage remedy to achieve this end may be appropriate. Under the injunctive remedy, on the other hand, distributional outcomes are uncertain. For example, extortion may lead the defendant to pay the plaintiff any amount between $1,000 and $10,000. The actual sum will depend on the parties' relative bargaining strengths. Alternatively, strategic behavior may lead to enforcement of the injunction, forcing the defendant to shut down, with a loss of $10,000 to him and a gain of $1,000 in pollution damage avoided to the plaintiff.

"These three arguments amount to the proposition that damage remedies are better able to achieve the efficient outcome (by avoiding strategic behavior) and to promote the desired distributional outcome (by avoiding extortion and allowing bonus payments). This article will demonstrate, however, that in realistic circumstances the preference for damage remedies is not always justified. In terms of achieving efficiency, it will be shown that damage remedies are just as susceptible to strategic behavior problems as injunctive remedies when, realistically, courts cannot correctly determine actual damages. And in terms of achieving distributional equity, it will be shown that damage remedies are not nearly as flexible distributionally as is usually presumed. Damage remedies are still preferable in some circumstances, but injunctive remedies are superior in other circumstances. By systematically exploring the relative merits of the remedies in different situations, I hope to provide a better understanding of when each should be used.

* * *

"The basic conclusions of the article can be briefly stated as follows: In the best of all possible worlds—cooperative behavior, costless redistribution, and perfect information—injunctive and damage remedies are equally desirable. The presence of strategic behavior alone does not change this conclusion. However, if it is also costly to redistribute income, the remedies are no longer equivalent. When there are a small number of litigants in these circumstances, neither remedy is generally preferable. When there are a large number of litigants, however, the damage remedy is superior. Finally, and most realistically, if the courts also have imperfect information, neither remedy is generally preferable. Depending on what information is available, either the injunctive or the damage remedy may be more desirable in any specific instance. Given the presence of these complications, the view that damage remedies are generally superior is not supported."

Polinsky, Resolving Nuisance Disputes: The Simple Economics of Injunctive and Damage Remedies, 32 Stan.L.Rev. 1075, 1076–80 (1980).*

3. The "coming to the nuisance" doctrine operates as an absolute defense to an action for injunctive relief in a minority of jurisdictions, just as it bars an action for damages. *See supra* p. 540. Most courts, however, treat it as only one factor to be considered along with many others in balancing the hardships to determine whether to grant an injunction. *E.g.,* McQuade v. Tucson Tiller Apartments, Ltd., 25 Ariz.App. 312, 543 P.2d 150 (1975). For an economic analysis of the "coming to the nuisance" doctrine, see Wittman, First Come, First Served: An Economic Analysis of "Coming to the Nuisance," 9 J.Legal Stud. 557 (1980).

As you read the next case, consider the impact of the "right to farm" statutes on the majority rule regarding the "coming to the nuisance" doctrine.

HERRIN v. OPATUT

Supreme Court of Georgia, 1981.
248 Ga. 140, 281 S.E.2d 575.

GREGORY, JUSTICE.

In October, 1977 the defendants purchased a 57–acre tract of "pasture" land in Atkinson County, with the intention of establishing an egg farm. Subsequently, 26 chicken layer houses were built and on March 15, 1979, 40,000 chickens were brought in. The defendants began transacting business under the trade name, "Frances Egg Farm." The record discloses that, at the time plaintiffs instituted this lawsuit, over 500,000 chickens were housed at the Frances Egg Farm.

In April, 1980, plaintiffs, primarily residents of the area surrounding the Frances Egg Farm, filed suit against the defendants, alleging that they are "plagued by flies and offensive odors" emanating from the Frances Egg Farm. Plaintiff "Guest Pond, Inc.", alleged that the defendants are draining wastes from their egg farm into plaintiff's pond, with the result that many of the fish are dying. Plaintiffs prayed that the Frances Egg Farm be declared a nuisance and enjoined from further business activity.

Defendants denied that the flies created a problem, stating that they took elaborate precautions to kill all of the flies attracted to their operation, including daily use of a fly insecticide fogging system and fly bait placed "at strategic locations on the farm." Defendants subsequently filed a motion to dismiss on the ground that plaintiffs' claim is barred by Code Ann. §§ 72–107 and 72–108.

After an evidentiary hearing, the trial court granted defendants' motion to dismiss.

Plaintiffs appeal, alleging that the trial court erred in finding that their claim is barred by Code Ann. §§ 72–107 and 72–108. We agree and reverse.

(1) In 1980 the General Assembly enacted Code Ann. §§ 72–107 and 72–108. Code Ann. § 72–107 expresses the "legislative * * * declaration of policy" behind Code Ann. § 72–108. These statutes provide:

> "It is the declared policy of the State to conserve and protect and encourage the development and improvement of its agricultural land for the production of food and other agricultural products. When nonagricultural land uses extend into agricultural areas, agricultural operations often become the subject of nuisance suits. As a result, agricultural operations are sometimes forced to cease operations. Many others are discouraged from making investments in farm improvements. It is the purpose of this law [§§ 72–107, 72–108] to reduce the loss to the State of its agricultural resources by limiting the circumstances under which agricultural operations may be deemed to be a nuisance."

Code Ann. § 72–107, Ga.Laws 1980, p. 1253.

> "No agricultural or farming operation, place, establishment, or facility, or any of its appurtenances, or the operation thereof, shall be or shall become a nuisance, either public or private, as a result of changed conditions in or around the locality of such agricultural or farming operation, place, establishment, or facility if such agricultural or farming operation, place, establishment, or facility has been in operation for one year or more."

Code Ann. § 72–108, Ga.Laws, 1980, pp. 1253–1254.

Defendants take the position that only two issues are relevant in determining whether Code Ann. § 72–108 applies to bar a nuisance action brought against an agricultural facility. First, they posit, the trial court must find that the challenged facility is an "agricultural or farming operation" within the meaning of the statute. Next the court must determine whether this facility has been in operation for one year prior to the institution of the lawsuit; if the court finds that the facility meets both requirements, Code Ann. § 72–108 provides that the operation may not be abated as a nuisance.*

We cannot accept this expansive interpretation of the statute. We do agree with the defendants that the clear intent of the legislature, set out in Code Ann. § 72–107, is to "conserve and protect and encourage" the development of farm land and the agricultural resources of this state. However, the General Assembly chose to extend this protection to a limited, but increasingly occurring, situation, i.e., the extension of "nonagricultural land uses * * * into agricultural areas." Recognizing that the advent of what is commonly called "urban sprawl" into what have tradi-

* The defendant's position had been adopted by the court in Born v. Exxon Corp., 388 So.2d 933 (Ala.1980). *See generally* Grossman & Fischer, Protecting the Right to Farm: Statutory Limits on Nuisance Actions Against the Farmer, 1983 Wis.L.Rev. 95, 124–25.

tionally been agricultural areas often subjects agricultural operations to nuisance suits by the new landowners, the legislature undertook to protect certain existing agricultural facilities from such lawsuits. Code Ann. § 72–108 sets out the requirements which a farming operation must meet in order to be afforded this protection. Reducing Code Ann. § 72–108 to its most essential terms, we read it as providing that "[n]o agricultural * * * facility * * * shall be * * * a nuisance * * * as a result of changed conditions in the locality of such * * * facility * * * if [it] * * * has been in operation for one year or more." In order for the statute to apply to protect a given agricultural facility, that facility must first show that it is or has become a nuisance "as a result of changed conditions in * * * the locality of [its] operation." To construe the meaning of this language, Code Ann. §§ 72–107 and 72–108 must be read together. Doing so, we conclude that "changed conditions in * * * the locality" of the facility refers solely to the extension of nonagricultural land uses, residential or otherwise, into existing agricultural areas. In arriving at this conclusion, we recognize that Code Ann. § 72–108 presupposes the challenged facility is operating in a manner that makes it a nuisance which, but for the statute, could be abated. While the facility is located in an isolated or largely agricultural area, however, it is likely that there will be few attempts to enjoin its operation. It is, as Code Ann. § 72–107 acknowledges, "[w]hen nonagricultural land uses extend into agricultural areas [that] agricultural operations often become the subject of nuisance suits." Thus, it is not a change in the nature of the facility itself which has caused the operation to become a nuisance, but changes in the uses of the surrounding land in ways that are incompatible with the existing agricultural facility: the newcomers then seek to enjoin the facility from doing what it has always done. Thus, the facility is or becomes a nuisance "as a result of changed conditions in or around the locality" of the agricultural facility. The legislature has chosen, as a matter of policy, to exempt the agricultural facility in this situation from being declared a nuisance *if* the facility has been in operation for one year prior to the "changed conditions * * * in the locality." Of course, that which may constitute a nuisance regardless of urban sprawl, such as polluting a stream, is never protected by the statute since such activity does not become a nuisance as a result of "changed conditions in the surrounding locality."

Defendants argue, however, that the legislature did not intend to restrict the application of Code Ann. § 72–108 to this singular situation. Rather, they urge that the legislature also intended to protect "changed conditions" or growth in the nature of the agricultural facility itself. By way of illustration they posit that land which has always been "agricultural in nature" (such as their pasture land) is protected by the statute when it is (1) "improved" in a manner consistent with its agricultural nature (e.g., developed into an egg farm), and (2) the "improvement" remains in effect for one year before a lawsuit is filed. Defendants insist that the pre-existing "agricultural nature" of their land and uninterrupted operation for one year entitles them to protection under Code Ann. § 72–108 regardless of whether they constructed their egg farm before or after nonagricultural uses had been made of the areas surrounding their land. Taken to its logical conclusion, this line of reasoning would permit the construction of an agricultural facility on vacant land centered in a developed, urban area which, after operating for one year, could never be abated as a nuisance. Clearly, this is not what the legislature sought to protect against. Code Ann. § 72–107 states that the "purpose of this law" is to reduce the loss of agricultural resources by "*limiting the circumstances* under which agricultural operations may be deemed to be a nuisance." [Emphasis supplied]. The statute does not provide, as defendants suggest, that any agricultural facility which remains in operation for one year can thereafter never be abated as a nuisance.

What the statute requires is that the agricultural facility sought to be enjoined have been in existence at least one year prior to the change in conditions in the locality in order to receive protection. Therefore, in determining whether an agricultural facility is insulated under § 72–108 from abatement as a nuisance, the court must inquire (1) whether the operation is an "agricultural facility" within the meaning of the statute; (2) whether the nuisance action is being brought "as a result of changed conditions in the locality of the facility" and (3) whether the facility has been in operation for one year or more prior to the changed conditions in the surrounding locality.

In this case defendants' egg farm falls within the purview of Code Ann. § 5–2903, defining "poultry and poultry products" as agricultural commodities and is, thus, an agricultural facility. Turning to the question of whether this nuisance suit has arisen "as a result of changed conditions" in the locality surrounding defendants' egg farm, we note that the parties have stipulated that plaintiffs were making nonagricultural uses of their lands prior to the establishment of defendants' egg farm. Consequently, if defendants' facility is a nuisance, it is not so "as a result of changed conditions in the locality" within the meaning of Code Ann. § 72–108. Nor has defendants' egg farm been in operation for one year prior to the change in conditions in the surrounding locality. As noted above, it is clear that the "changed conditions in the * * * locality" surrounding defendants' egg farm occurred before construction of the egg farm began. Contrary to defendants' position, it is not significant that the egg farm remained in operation for one year prior to the institution of this lawsuit.

This is not a case where plaintiffs' nonagricultural uses of their land have encroached upon defendants' existing egg farm. Nor do we find that defendants' situation is one which the legislature intended to protect under Code Ann. § 72–108. Consequently, we hold that the trial court erred in finding that plaintiffs' complaint was barred by this provision, and in granting defendants' motion to dismiss.

Notes

1. "Right to farm" statutes have been enacted since 1978 in at least 37 states. Grossman & Fischer, Protecting the Right to Farm: Statutory Limits on Nuisance Actions Against the Farmer, 1983 Wis.L.Rev. 95, 118 n. 108. Their purpose is to protect farmers and farming operations from nuisance liability. Although the language of the statutes varies, "most provide in essence that when the plaintiff has come to the nuisance, the defendant

agricultural operation either is not, or is presumed not to be, a nuisance." *Id.* at 117. *See also* Steffens v. Keeler, 200 Mich.App. 179, 503 N.W.2d 675 (1993) (pig farmer defendant who moves across from residential plaintiff has defense under "right to farm" statute where surrounding area is still largely residential).

For a discussion of the environmental and constitutional implications of the right to farm statutes, see Grossman & Fischer, Protecting the Right to Farm: Statutory Limits on Nuisance Actions Against the Farmer, 1983 Wis. L.Rev. 95. The authors also propose a model right to farm statute. *Id.* at 163–65.

2. How would the *Spur* case, *supra* p. 560 have been decided under Georgia's right to farm statute? *See* Comment, The Arizona Agricultural Nuisance Protection Act, 1982 Ariz.St.L.J. 689, 721–22 (1982).

HOBBS v. SMITH

Supreme Court of Colorado, 1972.
177 Colo. 299, 493 P.2d 1352.

HODGES, JUSTICE.

The Court of Appeals affirmed a trial court judgment which granted an injunction prohibiting the continuation of circumstances which constituted a private nuisance. The petitioner * * * [contends] that when legislative authorities, by zoning ordinances, permit an act or a particular use of land, a court has no authority to enjoin a public or private nuisance naturally resulting therefrom. * * *

The trial court found that the petitioner kept one to two horses in the backyard of her home, which was located in a residential section of Jefferson County. A Jefferson County Zoning Ordinance permitted the keeping of two horses on petitioner's property. The trial court found that petitioner was exercising all reasonable skill and care in maintaining the property where the animals were kept and that no health regulations were being violated. However, the trial court also found that flies were attracted to the general area by the horses and that noxious odors therefrom permeated the area. It was found that the respondents suffered a substantial interference with the use and enjoyment of their property which adjoined petitioner's property. The trial court ruled that while the keeping of horses did not violate the zoning ordinance, it did constitute a nuisance in fact (per accidens) and therefore, there was a proper basis for granting an injunction prohibiting the keeping of horses on the petitioner's property. It has been held that a lawful use may become a nuisance in fact or per accidens by reason of locality, surroundings, or other circumstances. Robichaux v. Huppenbauer, 258 La. 139, 245 So.2d 385.

In its opinion, affirming the trial court's judgment, the Court of Appeals held that even though zoning regulations permit an act to be done, and the act is being done with reasonable care and skill, the courts may grant relief where it is found that the acts complained of constitute a nuisance per accidens, and that to hold otherwise would be to state that the legislative body may license a nuisance.

* * *

Judgment affirmed.

PRINGLE, C.J., and DAY and KELLEY, JJ., dissent.

DAY, JUSTICE (dissenting):

I respectfully dissent.

I hasten to add my fears that the precedent of the majority decision could curtail the effective gains which have been made in creating legislative awareness of good long-range land use planning. When the legislative authority has validly declared that a given activity is lawfully permitted in a particular zone, and the activity is lawfully conducted, to permit the courts to enjoin the use provides a judicial veto of proper, valid legislative functions.

I submit the better reasoned position to take is that land use regulations are best conceived by the legislative branch under its constitutional exercise of police power whereby there is afforded broad application for the public good. The court should not act to set aside or prevent that which the legislative branch has determined to be permitted. This will seriously affect long-range land use planning.

Such planning has salutory two-fold aspects. One provides for orderly growth; the other provides for the possibility of citizens finding a place in which to live and enjoy their own particular tastes. * * * There have been conceived in many states equine country clubs for persons who enjoy horseback riding, jumping, polo, etc. In such developments citizens can build and live and indulge in their recreational hobby. People who do not have similar tastes should not and probably would not establish a home in such an environment. * * *

I would reverse the trial court injunction.*

Notes

1. The impact of zoning on an action to enjoin a nuisance is described in D. Dobbs, Handbook on the Law of Remedies 363 (1973): **

> "In a good many instances the activity of the defendant, which the plaintiff seeks to enjoin as a nuisance, is the kind of activity permitted by a zoning ordinance or license or special statute. Most courts faced with this situation hold that zoning ordinances do not protect a nuisance from injunction merely by authorizing the general kind of use. The zoning ordinance is, of course, relevant in such cases as indicating something of the present and probable future character of the neighborhood, but it does not prevent an injunction by its bare existence. These rules seem reasonable, because though zoning ordinances do legitimize the authorized businesses within the prescribed areas, they seem to legitimize general models, not particular methods of operation. Much the same attitude is taken where the defendant has procured a license to operate his plant, or shows he has complied with administrative regulations addressed to his business.

* Accord: Allison v. Smith, 695 P.2d 791 (Colo.App.1984) (activity that complies with zoning ordinance may constitute a private nuisance if there is substantial interference with plaintiff's use and enjoyment.)

** Reprinted with permission of West Publishing Co.

> "Several courts have followed the 'minority view' to the effect that an injunction will not issue against a nuisance if the activity is one authorized by a zoning ordinance or statute."

2. California, one of the minority jurisdictions, has codified the zoning defense in section 731a of the Code of Civil Procedure:

> **"§ 731a. Injunction in Industrial or Commercial Zones or Airports**
>
> "Whenever any city, city and county, or county shall have established zones or districts under authority of law wherein certain manufacturing or commercial or airport uses are expressly permitted, except in an action to abate a public nuisance brought in the name of the people of the State of California, no person or persons, firm or corporation shall be enjoined or restrained by the injunctive process from the reasonable and necessary operation in any such industrial or commercial zone or airport of any use expressly permitted therein, nor shall such use be deemed a nuisance without evidence of the employment of unnecessary and injurious methods of operation. Nothing in this act shall be deemed to apply to the regulation and working hours of canneries, fertilizing plants, refineries and other similar establishments whose operation produce offensive odors."

The California cases applying the statute to private nuisance actions are discussed in Sierra Screw Products, Inc. v. Azusa Greens, Inc., 88 Cal.App.3d 358, 151 Cal.Rptr. 799 (1979) (mandatory injunction granted requiring defendant to redesign two holes on properly zoned golf course so that golf balls would not fall on plaintiff's adjoining property).

Is the California statute applicable to actions for damages, or only to actions for injunctive relief? *See* Wilson v. Interlake Steel Co., 32 Cal.3d 229, 185 Cal.Rptr. 280, 649 P.2d 922 (1982).

How does the California statute compare with Georgia's right to farm statute, quoted in *Herrin, supra* p. 563? Does either statute apply to trespass actions? *See generally* Comment, Remedies for Intangible Intrusions: The Distinction Between Trespass and Nuisance Actions Against Lawfully Zoned Businesses in California, 17 U.C.D.L.Rev. 389 (1983).

3. Assume that you have a client whose residence has a solar system which includes collectors on the roof to supply energy for heat and hot water. Your client wants to enjoin the planned construction of a house on an adjacent lot to the south of your client's lot. If the house is located as planned, it will comply with all of the relevant zoning ordinances and deed restrictions, but it will cause a shadowing effect on the solar collectors that will reduce the efficiency of the system and may seriously damage it. What procedure would you advise your client to follow? What is the likelihood of success on the merits? Would the outcome be different, depending upon whether the case were governed by *Hobbs* or by section 731a of the California Code of Civil Procedure? Those issues were considered in Prah v. Maretti, 108 Wis.2d 223, 321 N.W.2d 182 (1982), a landmark decision by Justice Shirley Abrahamson:

> "After filing his complaint, the plaintiff moved for a temporary injunction to restrain and enjoin construction by the defendant. In ruling on

that motion the circuit court heard testimony, received affidavits and viewed the site.

* * *

"The circuit court denied plaintiff's motion for injunctive relief, declared it would entertain a motion for summary judgment and thereafter entered judgment in favor of the defendant.

* * *

"As to the claim of private nuisance the circuit court concluded that the law of private nuisance requires the court to make 'a comparative evaluation of the conflicting interests and to weigh the gravity of the harm to the plaintiff against the utility of the defendant's conduct.' The circuit court concluded: 'A comparative evaluation of the conflicting interests, keeping in mind the omissions and commissions of both Prah and Maretti, indicates that defendant's conduct does not cause the gravity of the harm which the plaintiff himself may well have avoided by proper planning.' * * *

* * *

"The private nuisance doctrine has traditionally been employed in this state to balance the conflicting rights of landowners, and this court has recently adopted the analysis of private nuisance set forth in the Restatement (Second) of Torts. CEW Mgmt. Corp. v. First Federal Savings & Loan Association, 88 Wis.2d 631, 633, 277 N.W.2d 766 (1979). The Restatement defines private nuisance as 'a nontrespassory invasion of another's interest in the private use and enjoyment of land.' Restatement (Second) of Torts sec. 821D (1977). The phrase 'interest in the private use and enjoyment of land' as used in sec. 821D is broadly defined to include any disturbance of the enjoyment of property. * * *

"Although the defendant's obstruction of the plaintiff's access to sunlight appears to fall within the Restatement's broad concept of a private nuisance as a nontrespassory invasion of another's interest in the private use and enjoyment of land, the defendant asserts that he has a right to develop his property in compliance with statutes, ordinances and private covenants without regard to the effect of such development upon the plaintiff's access to sunlight. In essence, the defendant is asking this court to hold that the private nuisance doctrine is not applicable in the instant case and that his right to develop his land is a right which is *per se* superior to his neighbor's interest in access to sunlight. This position is expressed in the maxim 'cujus est solum, ejus est usque ad coelum et ad infernos,' that is, the owner of land owns up to the sky and down to the center of the earth. The rights of the surface owner are, however, not unlimited. U.S. v. Causby, 328 U.S. 256, 260–1, 66 S.Ct. 1062, 1065, 90 L.Ed. 1206 (1946).

"The defendant is not completely correct in asserting that the common law did not protect a landowner's access to sunlight across adjoining property. At English common law a landowner could acquire a right to receive sunlight across adjoining land by both express agreement and under the judge-made doctrine of 'ancient lights.' Under the doctrine of ancient lights if the landowner had received sunlight across adjoining property for a specified period of time, the landowner was entitled to continue to receive unobstructed access to sunlight across the adjoining property. Under the doctrine the landowner acquired a negative prescriptive easement and could prevent the adjoining landowner from obstructing access to light.

"Although American courts have not been as receptive to protecting a landowner's access to sunlight as the English courts, American courts have afforded some protection to a landowner's interest in access to sunlight. American courts honor express easements to sunlight. American courts initially enforced the English common law doctrine of ancient lights, but later every state which considered the doctrine repudiated it as inconsistent with the needs of a developing country. * * *

"Many jurisdictions in this country have protected a landowner from malicious obstruction of access to light (the spite fence cases) under the common law private nuisance doctrine. * * *

* * *

"We therefore hold that private nuisance law, that is, the reasonable use doctrine as set forth in the Restatement, is applicable to the instant case. Recognition of a nuisance claim for unreasonable obstruction of access to sunlight will not prevent land development or unduly hinder the use of adjoining land. It will promote the reasonable use and enjoyment of land in a manner suitable to the 1980's. That obstruction of access to light might be found to constitute a nuisance in certain circumstances does not mean that it will be or must be found to constitute a nuisance under all circumstances. The result in each case depends on whether the conduct complained of is unreasonable.

"Accordingly we hold that the plaintiff in this case has stated a claim under which relief can be granted. * * *

"The defendant asserts that even if we hold that the private nuisance doctrine applies to obstruction of access to sunlight across adjoining land, the circuit court's granting of summary judgment should be affirmed.

"Although the memorandum decision of the circuit court in the instant case is unclear, it appears that the circuit court recognized that the common law private nuisance doctrine was applicable but concluded that defendant's conduct was not unreasonable. The circuit court apparently attempted to balance the utility of the defendant's conduct with the gravity of the harm. Sec. 826, Restatement (Second) of Torts (1977). The defendant urges us to accept the circuit court's balance as adequate. We decline to do so.

"The circuit court concluded that because the defendant's proposed house was in conformity with zoning regulations, building codes and deed restrictions, the defendant's use of the land was reasonable. This court has concluded that a landowner's compliance with zoning laws does not automatically bar a nuisance claim. Compliance with the law 'is not the controlling factor, though it is, of course, entitled to some weight.' Bie v. Ingersoll, 27 Wis.2d 490, 495, 135 N.W.2d 250 (1965). The circuit court also concluded that the plaintiff could have avoided any harm by locating his own house in a better place. Again, plaintiff's ability to avoid the harm is a relevant but not a conclusive factor. *See* secs. 826, 827, 828, Restatement (Second) of Torts (1977).

"Furthermore, our examination of the record leads us to conclude that the record does not furnish an adequate basis for the circuit court to apply the proper legal principles on summary judgment. The application of the reasonable use standard in nuisance cases normally requires a full exposition of all underlying facts and circumstances. Too little is known in this case of such matters as the extent of the harm to the plaintiff, the suitability of solar heat in that neighborhood, the availability of remedies to the plaintiff, and the costs to the defendant of avoiding the harm.

* * *

"For the reasons set forth, we reverse the judgment of the circuit court dismissing the complaint and remand the matter to circuit court for further proceedings not inconsistent with this opinion." *

How would the Wisconsin Supreme Court have decided *Prah* if it had applied Professor Rabin's analysis, *supra* pp. 562–64? *See* Recent Development, Casting a Shadow on a Solar Collector—A Cause of Action Recognized; An Alternative Resolution Framework Suggested, 68 Cornell L.Rev. 941 (1983).

2. *Public Nuisance and Statutory Remedies*

ARMORY PARK NEIGHBORHOOD ASSOCIATION v. EPISCOPAL COMMUNITY SERVICES IN ARIZONA

Supreme Court of Arizona, In Banc., 1985.
148 Ariz. 1, 712 P.2d 914.

FELDMAN, JUSTICE.

On December 11, 1982, defendant Episcopal Community Services in Arizona (ECS) opened the St. Martin's Center (Center) in Tucson. The Center's only purpose is to provide one free meal a day to indigent persons. Plaintiff Armory Park Neighborhood Association (APNA) is a non-profit corporation organized for the purpose of "improving, maintaining and insuring the quality of the neighborhood known as Armory Park Historical Residential District." The Center is located on Arizona Avenue, the western boundary of the Armory Park district. On January 10, 1984, APNA filed a complaint in Pima County Superior Court, seeking to enjoin ECS from operating its free food distribution program. The complaint alleged that the Center's activities constituted a public nuisance and that the Armory Park residents had sustained injuries from transient persons attracted to their neighborhood by the Center.

* *See generally* Lungren, Solar Entitlement: A Proposed Legislative Model, 4 J. Energy L. & Pol'y 171 (1983); Note, Obtaining Access to Solar Energy: Nuisance, Water Rights, and Zoning Administration, 45 Brooklyn L.Rev. 357 (1979); Comment, Solar Energy and Restrictive Covenants: The Conflict Between Public Policy and Private Zoning, 67 Calif.L.Rev. 350 (1979); Comment, Obstruction of Sunlight as a Private Nuisance, 65 Calif.L.Rev. 94 (1977); Note, An Integrated Approach to Solar Access, 34 Case W.Res. L.Rev. 367 (1983–84); Comment, Solar Rights and Restrictive Covenants: A Microeconomic Analysis, 7 Fordham Urb.L.J. 283 (1979): Note, Prah v. Maretti: Solar Rights and Private Nuisance Law, 16 J.Mar.L.Rev. 435 (1983); Note, A Private Nuisance Remedy for Obstruction of Solar Access, 48 Mo. L.Rev. 769 (1983); Note, Prah v. Maretti: Deficiencies of a Nuisance Law Cause of Action for Obstruction of Solar Access, 78 Nw. U.L.Rev. 861 (1983).

The superior court held a hearing on APNA's application for preliminary injunction on March 6 and 7, 1984. At the commencement of the hearing, the parties stipulated that * * * there is no issue concerning any State, County, or Municipal zoning ordinance, or health provision, before the Court. And, the Court may find that defendants are in compliance with the same. The residents then testified about the changes the Center had brought to their neighborhood. Before the Center opened, the area had been primarily residential with a few small businesses. When the Center began operating in December 1982, many transients crossed the area daily on their way to and from the Center. Although the Center was only open from 5:00 to 6:00 p.m., patrons lined up well before this hour and often lingered in the neighborhood long after finishing their meal. The Center rented an adjacent fenced lot for a waiting area and organized neighborhood cleaning projects, but the trial judge apparently felt these efforts were inadequate to control the activity stemming from the Center. Transients frequently trespassed onto residents' yards, sometimes urinating, defecating, drinking and littering on the residents' property. A few broke into storage areas and unoccupied homes, and some asked residents for handouts. The number of arrests in the area increased dramatically. Many residents were frightened or annoyed by the transients and altered their lifestyles to avoid them.

Based on the hearing testimony, the trial court granted the preliminary injunction and denied ECS' motion to dismiss. In its order, the court noted that ECS could be enjoined because its activities constituted both a public and a private nuisance. After its motion for reconsideration was denied, ECS filed a special action in the court of appeals, and shortly thereafter filed a notice of appeal from the order granting the injunction. The court of appeals consolidated the proceedings and stayed enforcement of the trial court's order pending a final decision.

A divided court of appeals reversed the trial court's order. * * * We granted review in this case because of the importance of the following questions:

1) When does a voluntary association have standing to bring an action for public nuisance on behalf of its members?

2) May a lawful business be enjoined for acts committed off its premises by clients who are not under its control or direction?

3) Is it necessary to plead and prove a zoning or criminal violation by the defendant, or may a lawful activity be enjoined because the manner in which it is conducted is unreasonable and therefore constitutes a public nuisance?

Now considered a tort, a public nuisance action originated in criminal law. Early scholars defined public nuisance as "an act or omission 'which obstructs or causes inconvenience or damage to the public in the exercise of rights common to all her Majesty's subjects.'" PROSSER, W. AND W.P. KEETON, HANDBOOK ON THE LAW OF TORTS, § 90, at 643 (5th ed. 1984), quoting Stephen, General View of the Criminal Law in England 105 (1890). The sole remedy was criminal prosecution. Prosser, supra, § 86, at 618.

Historically, the remedy for a private nuisance was an action "upon the case," as it was an injury consequential to the act done and found its roots in civil law. PEARCE, E. AND D. MESTON, HANDBOOK ON THE LAW RELATING TO NUISANCES 2 (1926). A private nuisance is strictly limited to an interference with a person's interest in the enjoyment of real property. The Restatement defines a private nuisance as "a nontrespassory invasion of another's interest in the private use and enjoyment of land." RESTATEMENT (SECOND) OF TORTS § 821D. A public nuisance, to the contrary, is not limited to an interference with the use and enjoyment of the plaintiff's land. It encompasses any unreasonable interference with a right common to the general public. RESTATEMENT, supra, § 821B. * * *

Thus, a nuisance may be simultaneously public and private when a considerable number of people suffer an interference with their use and enjoyment of land. See Spur Industries, 108 Ariz. at 184, 494 P.2d at 706. The torts are not mutually exclusive. Some of plaintiff's members in this case have suffered an injury to the use and enjoyment of their land. Any reference to both a public and a private nuisance by the trial court was, we believe, merely a recognition of this well-accepted rule and not error. However, both because plaintiff did not seek relief under the theory of private nuisance and because that theory might raise standing issues not addressed by the parties, we believe plaintiff's claim must stand or fall on the public nuisance theory alone.

Defendant argues that the Association has no standing to sue and that, therefore, the action should be dismissed. The trial court disagreed and defendant claims it erred in so doing. Two standing questions are before us. The first pertains to the right of a private person, as distinguished from a public official, to bring a suit to enjoin the maintenance of a public nuisance. The original rule at common law was that a citizen had no standing to sue for abatement or suppression of a public nuisance since such inconvenient or troublesome offences [sic], as annoy the whole community in general, and not merely some particular persons; and therefore are indictable only, and not actionable; as it would be unreasonable to multiply suits, by giving every man a separate right of action, by what damnifies him in common only with the rest of his fellow subjects. IV BLACKSTONE COMMENTARIES 167 (1966). It was later held that a private individual might have a tort action to recover personal damages arising from the invasion of the public right. Y.B. 27 Hen. VIII, Mich, pl. 10, cited in RESTATEMENT, supra, § 821C comment a. However, the individual bringing the action was required to show that his damage was different in kind or quality from that suffered by the public in common. PROSSER, supra, § 90, at 646; HARPER & JAMES, THE LAW OF TORTS § 1.23, at 64–5 (1956).

The rationale behind this limitation was two-fold. First, it was meant to relieve defendants and the courts of the multiple actions that might follow if every member of the public were allowed to sue for a common wrong. Second, it was believed that a harm which affected all members of the public equally should be handled by public officials. RESTATEMENT, supra, § 821C comment a. See also Engle v. Clark, 53 Ariz. 472, 90 P.2d

994 (1939). Considerable disagreement remains over the type of injury which the plaintiff must suffer in order to have standing to bring an action to enjoin a public nuisance. However, we have intimated in the past that an injury to plaintiff's interest in land is sufficient to distinguish plaintiff's injuries from those experienced by the general public and to give the plaintiff-landowner standing to bring the action.

* * *

We hold, therefore, that because the acts allegedly committed by the patrons of the neighborhood center affected the residents' use and enjoyment of their real property, a damage special in nature and different in kind from that experienced by the residents of the city in general, the residents of the neighborhood could bring an action to recover damages for or enjoin the maintenance of a public nuisance.

Defendant claims that its business should not be held responsible for acts committed by its patrons off the premises of the Center. It argues that since it has no control over the patrons when they are not on the Center's premises, it cannot be enjoined because of their acts. We do not believe this position is supported either by precedent or theory.

In Shamhart v. Morrison Cafeteria Co., 159 Fla. 629, 32 So.2d 727 (1947), the defendant operated a well frequented cafeteria. Each day customers waiting to enter the business would line up on the sidewalk, blocking the entrances to the neighboring establishments. The dissenting justices argued that the defendant had not actually caused the lines to form and that the duty to prevent the harm to the plaintiffs should be left to the police through regulation of the public streets. The majority of the court rejected this argument, and remanded the case for a determination of the damages. See, also, Reid v. Brodsky, 397 Pa. 463, 156 A.2d 334 (1959) (operation of a bar enjoined because its patrons were often noisy and intoxicated; they frequently used the neighboring properties for toilet purposes and sexual misconduct); Barrett v. Lopez, 57 N.M. 697, 262 P.2d 981, 983 (1953) (operation of a dance hall enjoined, the court finding that "mere possibility of relief from another source [police] does not relieve the courts of their responsibilities"); Wade v. Fuller, 12 Utah 2d 299, 365 P.2d 802 (1961) (operation of drive-in cafe enjoined where patrons created disturbances to nearby residents); McQuade v. Tucson Tiller Apartments, 25 Ariz.App. 312, 543 P.2d 150 (1975) (music concerts at mall designed to attract customers enjoined because of increased crowds and noise in residential area).

Under general tort law, liability for nuisance may be imposed upon one who sets in motion the forces which eventually cause the tortious act; liability will arise for a public nuisance when "one person's acts set in motion a force or chain of events resulting in the invasion." RESTATEMENT, supra, § 824 comment b. We hold, therefore, that defendant's activity may be enjoined upon the showing of a causal connection between that activity and harm to another.

The testimony at the hearing establishes that it was the Center's act of offering free meals which "set in motion" the forces resulting in the injuries to the Armory Park residents. * * *

Since the rules of a civilized society require us to tolerate our neighbors, the law requires our neighbors to keep their activities within the limits of what is tolerable by a reasonable person. However, what is reasonably tolerable must be tolerated; not all interferences with public rights are public nuisances. As Dean Prosser explains, "[t]he law does not concern itself with trifles, or seek to remedy all of the petty annoyances and disturbances of everyday life in a civilized community even from conduct committed with knowledge that annoyance and inconvenience will result." PROSSER, supra, § 88, at 626. Thus, to constitute a nuisance, the complained-of interference must be substantial, intentional and unreasonable under the circumstances. RESTATEMENT, supra, § 826 comment c and § 821F. Our courts have generally used a balancing test in deciding the reasonableness of an interference. See McQuade v. Tucson Tiller Apartments, supra.

The trial judge did not ignore the balancing test and was well aware of the social utility of defendant's operation. * * * The evidence of the multiple trespasses upon and defacement of the residents' property supports the trial court's conclusion that the interference caused by defendant's operation was unreasonable despite its charitable cause.

The common law has long recognized that the usefulness of a particular activity may outweigh the inconveniences, discomforts and changes it causes some persons to suffer. We, too, acknowledge the social value of the Center. Its charitable purpose, that of feeding the hungry, is entitled to greater deference than pursuits of lesser intrinsic value. It appears from the record that ECS purposes in operating the Center were entirely admirable. However, even admirable ventures may cause unreasonable interferences. See e.g., Assembly of God Church of Tahoka v. Bradley, 196 S.W.2d 696 (Tex.Civ.App.1946). We do not believe that the law allows the costs of a charitable enterprise to be visited in their entirety upon the residents of a single neighborhood. The problems of dealing with the unemployed, the homeless and the mentally ill are also matters of community or governmental responsibility.

ECS argues that its compliance with City of Tucson zoning regulations is a conclusive determination of reasonableness. We agree that compliance with zoning provisions has some bearing in nuisance cases. We would hesitate to find a public nuisance, if, for example, the legislature enacted comprehensive and specific laws concerning the manner in which a particular activity was to be carried out. Accord RESTATEMENT, supra, § 821B comment f. We decline, however, to find that ECS' compliance with the applicable zoning provisions precludes a court from enjoining its activities. The equitable power of the judiciary exists independent of statute. Although zoning and criminal provisions are binding with respect to the type of activity, they do not limit the power of a court acting in equity to enjoin an unreasonable, albeit permitted, activity as a public nuisance. * * *

ECS argued that there is no criminal violation and that a tort claim for nuisance must be based on such a violation. * * * We are squarely faced, therefore, with the issue of whether a public nuisance may be found in the absence of a statute making specific conduct a crime.

In MacDonald v. Perry, supra, we indicated that the inquiry in a nuisance claim is not whether the activity allegedly constituting the nuisance is lawful but whether it is reasonable under the circumstances. The Restatement states that a criminal violation is only one factor among others to be used in determining reasonableness. That section reads: (1) A public nuisance is an unreasonable interference with a right common to the general public. (2) Circumstances that may sustain a holding that an interference with a public right is unreasonable include the following: (a) Whether the conduct involves a significant interference with the public health, the public safety, the public peace, the public comfort or the public convenience, or (b) whether the conduct is proscribed by a statute, ordinance or administrative regulation, or (c) whether the conduct is of a continuing nature or has produced a permanent or long-lasting effect, and, as the actor knows or has reason to know, has a significant effect upon the public right. (Emphasis supplied.) RESTATEMENT, supra, § 821B. Comment d to that section explains: It has been stated with some frequency that a public nuisance is always a criminal offense. This statement is susceptible of two interpretations. The first is that in order to be treated as a public nuisance, conduct must have been already proscribed by the state as criminal. This is too restrictive * * *. [T]here is clear recognition that a defendant need not be subject to criminal responsibility. RESTATEMENT, supra, § 821B comment d, at 89.

Our earlier decisions indicate that a business which is lawful may nevertheless be a public nuisance.

* * *

We hold, therefore, that conduct which unreasonably and significantly interferes with the public health, safety, peace, comfort or convenience is a public nuisance within the concept of tort law, even if that conduct is not specifically prohibited by the criminal law.

* * *

The trial court's order granting the preliminary injunction is affirmed. By affirming the trial court's preliminary orders, we do not require that he close the center permanently. It is of course, within the equitable discretion of the trial court to fashion a less severe remedy, if possible. The opinion of the court of appeals is vacated. The case is remanded for further proceedings.

HOLOHAN, C.J., GORDON, V.C.J., and HAYS and CAMERON, JJ., concur.

Notes

1. The public nuisance concept has become an increasingly useful device in dealing with environmental pollution and related matters.* Consider, for

* For other cases in which injunctions were obtained against "noise pollution" under a public nuisance theory, *see* People v. Mason, 124 Cal.App.3d 348, 177 Cal.Rptr. 284 (1981)

example, the language of the United States Supreme Court in Illinois v. City of Milwaukee, 406 U.S. 91, 92 S.Ct. 1385, 31 L.Ed.2d 712 (1972), a case in which the state of Illinois sought to have Milwaukee's release of sewage into Lake Michigan enjoined as a public nuisance:

> "The remedy sought by Illinois is not within the precise scope of remedies prescribed by Congress. Yet the remedies which Congress provides are not necessarily the only federal remedies available. 'It is not uncommon for federal courts to fashion federal law where federal rights are concerned.' Textile Workers v. Lincoln Mills, 353 U.S. 448, 457, 77 S.Ct. 912, 918, 1 L.Ed.2d 972. When we deal with air or water in their ambient or interstate aspects, there is a federal common law, as Texas v. Pankey, 10 Cir., 441 F.2d 236, recently held.
>
> "The application of federal common law to abate a public nuisance in interstate or navigable waters is not inconsistent with the Water Pollution Control Act. Congress provided in § 10(b) of that Act that, save as a court may decree otherwise in an enforcement action, 'State and interstate action to abate pollution of interstate or navigable waters shall be encouraged and shall not * * * be displaced by Federal enforcement action.'
>
> * * *
>
> "When it comes to water pollution this Court has spoken in terms of 'a public nuisance,' New York v. New Jersey, 256 U.S. 296, 313, 41 S.Ct. 492, 497, 65 L.Ed. 937; New Jersey v. New York City, 283 U.S. 473, 481, 482, 51 S.Ct. 519, 521, 75 L.Ed. 1176. In Missouri v. Illinois, 200 U.S. 496, 520–521, 26 S.Ct. 268, 269–270, 50 L.Ed. 572, the Court said, 'It may be imagined that a nuisance might be created by a State upon a navigable river like the Danube, which would amount to a *casus belli* for a State lower down, unless removed. If such a nuisance were created by a State upon the Mississippi the controversy would be resolved by the more peaceful means of a suit in this court.'
>
> "It may happen that new federal laws and new federal regulations may in time pre-empt the field of federal common law of nuisance. But until that comes to pass, federal courts will be empowered to appraise the equities of the suits alleging creation of a public nuisance by water pollution. While federal law governs, consideration of state standards may be relevant. * * * Thus, a State with high water quality standards may well ask that its strict standards be honored and that it not be compelled to lower itself to the more degrading standards of a neighbor. There are no fixed rules that govern; these will be equity suits in which the informed judgment of the chancellor will largely govern."

(enjoining noise from bar and restaurant that was located 600–800 feet from residential housing); Burgess v. Omahawks Radio Control Org., 219 Neb. 100, 362 N.W.2d 27 (1985) (enjoining operation of a radio-controlled model aircraft in violation of zoning ordinance).

For commentaries on the use of a public nuisance action in environmental litigation, *see* Bryson & MacBeth, Public Nuisance, The Restatement, Second, Torts, and Environmental Law, 2 Ecology L.Q. 241 (1972); Murphy, Environmental Law: New Legal Concepts In the Antipollution Fight (1971), 36 Mo.L.Rev. 78, 83–84; Raney, Common Law v. Statutory Pollution Abatement: The Texas Attorney General's Dilemma, 19 S.Tex.L.J. 557 (1978); Comment, Acid Rain—The Limitations of Private Remedies, 1983 S.Ill.U.L.J. 515 (1983).

State governments and their agencies have successfully utilized public nuisance theory to obtain injunctions against environmental problems whether or not other statutory criminal or civil penalties were applicable. *See e.g.,* United States ex rel. Scott v. United States Steel Corp., 356 F.Supp. 556 (N.D.Ill.1973) (neither Federal Water Pollution Control Act nor Federal Refuse Act barred injunction on public nuisance theory against discharge of waste water into Lake Michigan); Commonwealth v. Barnes & Tucker Co., 455 Pa. 392, 319 A.2d 871 (1974) (even though statute regulating the area did not authorize injunction to require mine owner to treat acid mine drainage, injunction was available under public nuisance doctrine). *See also* State ex rel. New Mexico Water Quality Control Comm. v. Molybdenum Corp. of America, 89 N.M. 552, 555 P.2d 375 (1976) (river pollution).

2. In Illinois v. City of Milwaukee, 406 U.S. 91, 92 S.Ct. 1385, 31 L.Ed.2d 712 (1972), the court left open the question of whether the result was affected by the passage of the 1972 Amendments to the Water Pollution Control Act. On remand, the lower court concluded that the cause of action had survived the new statute and that injunctive relief was appropriate. 599 F.2d 151 (7th Cir.1979). On appeal, the Supreme Court reversed that decision, holding that the defendant's activities were governed by administrative permits regulating its pollution. 451 U.S. at 320, 101 S.Ct. at 1794. One commentator has observed that nothing in the 1972 Amendments expressly indicates an intention to preempt federal common law, and therefore the Court's holding "seems to have been based on the desire to avoid an independent policymaking role for the courts in an area where Congress had acted." Farber, Equitable Discretion, Legal Duties, and Environmental Injunctions, 45 U.Pitt.L.Rev. 513, 520 (1984).

3. Although zoning generally is not an absolute defense to a public nuisance action, some jurisdictions do recognize zoning as a bar to such a cause of action. For example, in Robinson Brick Co. v. Luthi, 115 Colo. 106, 111, 169 P.2d 171, 173 (1946), the court said,

> "Where the legislative arm of the government has declared by statute and zoning resolution what activities may or may not be conducted in a prescribed zone, it has in effect declared what is or is not a *public nuisance.*"

Id. at 111, 169 P.2d at 173.

Reread California Code of Civil Procedure § 731a, *supra* p. 573, to determine the impact of zoning on a public nuisance action in that state. Consider the policies underlying the approaches taken by Colorado and California with regard to zoning as a defense to a public nuisance action.

4. Historically, the courts have been reluctant to recognize the defenses of laches and estoppel in public nuisance actions brought by a governmental agency on the ground that abating a public nuisance is an exercise of the police power of the State. More recently, however, both defenses have been recognized against governmental plaintiffs in the interest of fairness. For a discussion of this modern trend, see Parcel, Making the Government Fight Fairly: Estopping the United States, 27 Rocky Mtn.Min.L.Inst. 41 (1982); Comment, Equitable Estoppel of the Government, 47 Brooklyn L.Rev. 423 (1981); Comment, Equitable Estoppel of the Government, 79 Colum.L.Rev. 551 (1979); Comment, Estopping the State: Just and Equitable Considerations, 34 Drake L.Rev. 197 (1984–85); Comment, Emergence of an Equitable Doctrine of

Estoppel Against the Government—The Oil Shale Cases, 46 U.Colo.L.Rev. 433 (1975); Note, 22 Howard L.J. 513 (1979) (summarizing cases that have recognized laches as a bar to an action by the government).

5. Under the traditional approach, a private party may not bring a public nuisance action unless he or she has sustained "special injury" or one that is "different in kind" from that suffered by members of the public at large. *See e.g.,* Housing Authority of City and County of San Francisco v. Superior Court, 14 Cal.App.4th 874, 18 Cal.Rptr.2d 218 (1993). Presumably, the purpose of this limitation is to preserve the meaningfulness of the public prosecutor's discretion and to protect defendants from a multiplicity of lawsuits. There is a recent trend to relax this limitation. For example, in Akau v. Olohana Corp., 65 Hawaii 383, 652 P.2d 1130 (1982), the Hawaii Supreme Court held that "a member of the public has standing to sue to enforce the rights of the public [against a public nuisance] even though his injury is not different in kind from the public's generally, if he can show that he has suffered an injury in fact, and that the concerns of a multiplicity of suits are satisfied by any means, including a class action." *See* Restatement (Second) of Torts § 821(c)(2) (1979).

In jurisdictions that continue to require proof of an injury "different in kind" from that sustained by the general public, private parties may prove that they have standing when the act complained of is both a private nuisance and a public nuisance. *See, e.g.,* Newhall Land and Farming Co. v. Superior Court, 19 Cal.App.4th 334, 23 Cal.Rptr.2d 377 (1993); B & W Management, Inc. v. Tasea Inv. Co., 451 A.2d 879 (D.C.App.1982); Town of Rome City v. King, 450 N.E.2d 72 (Ind.App.1983); Frady v. Portland Gen. Elec. Co., 55 Or.App. 344, 637 P.2d 1345 (1981). For example, a smoking factory may well constitute a private nuisance to an adjoining owner in that it unreasonably interferes with the use and enjoyment of his or her real estate and at the same time it may represent to the community at large a public nuisance. Similarly, if pollution of a river destroys fish, "such pollution would constitute a private nuisance where the river flowed through private property and a public nuisance in those areas where the public right to fish was interfered with." Murphy, Environmental Law: New Legal Concepts In the Antipollution Fight, 36 Mo.L.Rev. 78, 84 (1971).*

A few jurisdictions by statute authorize private suits on behalf of the state to enjoin public nuisances even though the private plaintiffs are not specially injured. *See* Note, 80 W.Va.L.Rev. 55, 56 (1977). In addition, some legislation expressly authorizes non-injured private parties to bring injunction suits

* Attempts by private practitioners and professional associations to enjoin the unlawful practice of a profession as a public nuisance illustrate vividly the confusion in applying the "special injury" approach. It would seem, for example, that the illegal practice of medicine may harm the health of the public at large, but it would also injure the private practitioner in the same community both financially and by downgrading the profession in the public eye. Thus, it could be argued that the private practitioner or association suffers an injury that is "special" or "different in kind" from that suffered by the general public. The cases, however, are hardly uniform. For cases which do find standing in these situations, *see* Touchy v. Houston Legal Found., 432 S.W.2d 690 (Tex. 1968) (law); Dempsey v. Chicago Title Ins. Co., 10 Ohio App.3d 281, 462 N.E.2d 184 (1983) (surveying); Cuyahoga County Bar Ass'n v. Gold Shield, Inc., 52 Ohio Misc. 105, 369 N.E.2d 1232 (1975) (law); Boggs v. Werner, 372 Pa. 312, 94 A.2d 50 (1953) (dentistry). *Contra* Massachusetts Soc'y of Optometrists v. Waddick, 340 Mass. 581, 165 N.E.2d 394 (1960) (optometrists); Missouri Veterinary Medical Ass'n v. Glisan, 230 S.W.2d 169 (Mo.App.1950) (veterinary medicine). *See generally* Comment, Competitors' Right to Enjoin Unlicensed Professional Practice, 24 U.Chi.L.Rev. 714, 717–21 (1957).

against certain special types of public nuisance. *See, e.g.,* M.C.L.A. § 14.-528(202) (pollution of air, water and other natural resources); Littleton v. Fritz, 65 Iowa 488, 22 N.W. 641 (1885) (illegal liquor establishments).

6. The relationship between a private and a public nuisance action is explored in United States v. Olin Corp., 606 F.Supp. 1301, 1304–08 (N.D.Ala. 1985), a private nuisance action for an injunction brought after the entry of a consent decree in a public nuisance action brought by Alabama and the United States to enjoin the defendant from polluting the environment with DDT:

> "Olin argues that because Alabama and the United States brought a *parens patriae* action on behalf of its citizens, subsequent suits by individual citizens are barred by res judicata.
>
> "In order for res judicata to have a preclusive effect on subsequent actions, the following elements must be met:
>
> > (1) that the prior judgment must have been rendered by a court of competent jurisdiction;
> >
> > (2) that there must have been a final judgment on the merits;
> >
> > (3) that the parties, or those in privity with them, must be identical in both suits; and
> >
> > (4) that the same cause of action must be involved in both suits. * * *
>
> "Plaintiffs cite several cases for the proposition that private plaintiffs are not barred from bringing a private enforcement action even though their interests were purportedly advanced by the United States in previous litigation that resulted in a consent decree, but plaintiffs cite no cases involving a prior *parens patriae* action. The weight of authority indicates that once a state represents all of its citizens in a *parens patriae* suit, a consent decree or final judgment entered in such a suit is conclusive upon those citizens and is binding upon their rights. * * *
>
> "Plaintiffs argue that the consent decree by its own language mandates a denial of defendant's motion. Paragraph 46 of the consent decree provides that it does not 'have any effect upon rights of persons or entities not parties to this consent decree.' Plaintiffs assert that they are not barred by res judicata because they were neither parties to the consent decree entered in the earlier litigation nor in privity with the parties to the consent decree. Resolution of these arguments turn on whether the prior litigation was in fact a *parens patriae* suit and whether the *Wilhoite* plaintiffs, as citizens of Alabama and the United States, are unnamed parties or privies within the meaning of that doctrine.
>
> "In a proper *parens patriae* suit, the state or federal government is deemed to represent all of its citizens. * * *
>
> "In a recent case, the Supreme Court analyzed the *parens patriae* doctrine in assessing whether a state had standing to sue on behalf of all of its citizens:
>
> > This summary of the case law involving *parens patriae* actions leads to the following conclusions. In order to maintain such an action, the State must articulate an interest apart from the interests of particular private parties, *i.e.,* the State must be more than a nominal party. The State must express a quasi-sovereign interest. Although the

> articulation of such interests is a matter for case by case development—neither an exhaustive formal definition nor a definitive list of qualifying interests can be presented in the abstract—certain characteristics of such interests are so far evident. These characteristics fall into two general categories. First, a State has a quasi-sovereign interest in the health and well-being—both physical and economic—of its residents in general. Second, a State has a quasi-sovereign interest in not being discriminatorily denied its rightful status within the federal system.

Alfred L. Snapp & Son, Inc. v. Puerto Rico, 458 U.S. 592, 607, 102 S.Ct. 3260, 3269, 73 L.Ed.2d 995 (1982). * * * Traditionally, *parens patriae* lawsuits involved a government suing to enjoin alleged nuisances caused by water or air pollution. Alfred L. Snapp & Son, Inc., 458 U.S. at 602, 102 S.Ct. at 3266. *See also* Annot., 42 A.L.R.Fed. 23 (1979 & Supp.1984).

* * *

"Plaintiffs are correct in their assertion that Alabama law would permit individual plaintiffs to bring an action seeking injunctive relief for abatement of a public nuisance. Alabama statutory law is in accord: 'If a public nuisance causes a special damage to an individual in which the public does not participate, such special damage gives a right of action.' Ala.Code § 6–5–123 (1975). Note, however, that the right accrues only to an individual plaintiff who can show harm distinct in kind and degree from that suffered by the public in general. Plaintiffs have not made such a showing.

"Moreover, it is also clear that a private citizen has no action to enjoin a nuisance where an action has already been brought on behalf of the state. 'Were it otherwise, suits might be multiplied to an indefinite extent, so as to create a public evil, in many cases much greater than that which was sought to be redressed.' Duy v. Alabama Western Railroad Co., 175 Ala. 162, 184, 57 So. 724, 731 (1911) (Mayfield, J., dissenting).

"By suing to eliminate the alleged public nuisance created by the presence of DDT pollution which was alleged to have caused injury to the wildlife, natural resources, health and welfare of Alabama residents in the subject area, the court finds that Alabama and the United States were suing in a *parens patriae* capacity as representative of all of its citizens including the *Wilhoite* plaintiffs. With this finding and because the instant plaintiffs are seeking the same relief as that requested and attained by Alabama and the United States in the earlier litigation, the court holds that plaintiffs' injunctive claims are barred by res judicata and that plaintiffs are bound by the terms and provisions of the consent decree."

7. The remedies available in public and private nuisance actions were compared in State *ex rel.* Dresser Industries v. Ruddy, 592 S.W.2d 789, 793 (Mo.1980) (en banc) (public nuisance action brought by the State of Missouri for past pollution of waterways caused by rupture of "dam" of defendant's settling basin, which contained waste from barite mining operation; complaint sought $1,000,000 in actual damages and $2,000,000 in statutory penalties):

> "Actual and punitive damages are permitted in conjunction with the maintenance of suits involving private nuisances. * * * Injunctions or abatements have been the traditional remedies where the state brings suit

for a public nuisance, 66 C.J.S. *Nuisances* § 77 (1950), but the prayer in Count II of the state's petition, admittedly based on the common law, seeks 'damages' only. Neither party has cited any precedent in this state wherein it was declared that 'damages,' absent some statutory authority, were or were not recoverable by public authorities for a public nuisance. Argument is made that such a recovery should follow necessarily, based on the theory that a protectible interest of the state is recognized; that such an interest can be harmed; that a legitimate interest which can be harmed is entitled to a rejuvenating compensation to repair that interest, including past injuries wrongfully caused by a nuisance; that absent such recovery, those causing damage to a public interest suffer no penalty whatever if the 'cause' has been corrected and no private individual can show a 'special' damage; that abatement or injunctive relief in retrospect would be a moot issue and constitute no relief at all. Whether or not actual or punitive damages are appropriate, in any event, would depend on the facts of a particular case. Punitive damages usually follow gross negligence on the part of a defendant or willful or continual perpetration of tortious activity. Absent any relevant factual record, we leave it to the trial court in the first instance, to determine whether or not damages are appropriate or allowable under Count II."

VILLAGE OF WILSONVILLE v. SCA SERV., INC.

Supreme Court of Illinois, 1981.
86 Ill.2d 1, 55 Ill.Dec. 499, 426 N.E.2d 824.

CLARK, JUSTICE:

On April 18, 1977, the plaintiff village of Wilsonville (the village) filed a complaint seeking injunctive relief in the circuit court of Macoupin County. Plaintiffs Macoupin County and the Macoupin County Farm Bureau were granted leave to intervene on April 29, 1977, and May 9, 1977, respectively. They filed complaints substantially similar to the village's complaint. The gravamen of the complaints was that the operation of the defendant's chemical-waste-disposal site presents a public nuisance and a hazard to the health of the citizens of the village, the county, and the State. The Attorney General of Illinois filed a complaint on May 26, 1977, seeking an injunction pursuant to the Environmental Protection Act (Ill.Rev.Stat. 1975, ch. 111½, pars. 1003(d), 1003(n), 1012(d), 1043). * * * Trial began on June 7, 1977, consumed 104 days, and resulted in judgment for the plaintiffs on August 28, 1978. The trial court's judgment order concluded that the site constitutes a nuisance and enjoined the defendant from operating its hazardous-chemical-waste landfill in Wilsonville. It ordered the defendant to remove all toxic waste buried there, along with all contaminated soil found at the disposal site as a result of the operation of the landfill. Further, the court ordered the defendant to restore and reclaim the site. * * *

The Appellate Court for the Fourth District unanimously affirmed the trial court's judgment. (77 Ill.App.3d 618, 33 Ill.Dec. 163, 396 N.E.2d 552.) * * * We affirm.

The record in this matter is over 13,000 pages long. The appellate court opinion sets out many pertinent facts. It is only necessary to summarize them here.

The defendant has operated a chemical-waste landfill since 1977. The site comprises approximately 130 acres, 90 of which are within the village limits of the plaintiff village. The remaining 40 acres are adjacent to the village. The defendant enters into agreements with generators of toxic chemical waste to haul the waste away from the generators' locations. The defendant then delivers it to the Wilsonville site, tests random samples of chemical waste, and then deposits the waste in trenches. There are seven trenches at the site. Each one is approximately 15 feet deep, 50 feet wide, and 250 to 350 feet long. Approximately 95% of the waste materials were buried in 55–gallon steel drums, and the remainder is contained in double-wall paper bags. After the materials are deposited in the trenches, uncompacted clay is placed between groups of containers and a minimum of one foot of clay is placed between the top drum and the top clay level of the trench.

The site is bordered on the east, west, and south by farmland and on the north by the village. The entire site, the village, and much of the surrounding area is located above the abandoned Superior Coal Mine No. 4, which operated from 1917 to 1954. The No. 6 seam of the mine was exploited in this area at a depth of 312 feet. The mining method used to extract coal was the room-and-panel method, whereby about 50% of the coal is left in pillars which provide some support for the earth above the mine. There was testimony at trial by Dr. Nolan Augenbaugh, chairman of the Department of Mining, Petroleum and Geological Engineering at the University of Missouri at Rolla, that pillar failure can occur in any mine where there is a readjustment of stress. * * *

On February 11, 1976, the defendant applied to the IEPA for a permit to develop and operate the hazardous-waste landfill. A developmental permit was issued by the IEPA on May 19, 1976. * * *

The materials deposited at the site include polychlorinated biphenyls (PCBs), a neurotoxic, possibly carcinogenic chemical which it has been illegal to produce in this country since 1979. Due to the extensive use of PCBs in electrical equipment such as transformers, capacitors, and heat-transfer systems, and in hydraulic systems, any PCBs that were produced legally now have to be disposed of when they are no longer in use. * * *

Finally, considerable testimony was adduced, much of it conflicting, as to dust, odors, and spills of chemical waste which have occurred in the village. * * *

We conclude that the evidence in this case sufficiently establishes by a preponderance of the evidence that the chemical-waste-disposal site is a nuisance both presently and prospectively. * * * Moreover, the General Assembly has, since the inception of this suit, passed a statute prohibiting the placement of a hazardous-waste-disposal site above a shaft or tunneled mine. Section 21(g) of the Environmental Protection Act provides:

> "No person shall:
>
> * * *

> (g) Locate a hazardous waste disposal site above an active or inactive shaft or tunneled mine or within 2 miles of an active fault in the earth's crust. * * * (Ill.Rev.Stat.1979, ch. 111½, par. 1021(g).)"

The instant disposal site is above an inactive tunneled mine lying partly within the corporate limits of the village of Wilsonville. Without an express statutory provision stating an act is to have retroactive effect, it can only be applied prospectively. Thus, the defendant cannot be thought to be in violation of the foregoing provision. The fact remains, however, that the instant site, which is intended to be permanent, is located above an inactive tunneled mine.

* * *

The trial court herein concluded that defendant's chemical-waste-disposal site constitutes both a private and a public nuisance. Professor Prosser has defined a private nuisance as "a civil wrong, based on a disturbance of rights in land" (Prosser, Torts sec. 86, at 572 (4th ed. 1971)), and a public nuisance as "an act or omission 'which obstructs or causes inconvenience or damage to the public in the exercise of rights common to all Her Majesty's subjects.' " (Prosser, Torts sec. 88, at 583 (4th ed. 1971) * * *

The defendant herein argues that "[e]ven if some or all of plaintiffs' evidence is deemed believable, the findings of the courts below that [defendant's] conduct constitutes a prospective nuisance must be reversed for failure to * * * balance the reasonableness and utility of the defendant's conduct, the harm to the plaintiff, and the general societal policy toward risk-taking before [a court may] find an actionable nuisance present." The defendant continues that the law of Illinois requires that the circuit court engage in a balancing process before reaching a conclusion that the waste disposal site presents a prospective nuisance. * * * [However], the trial court did engage in a balancing process, as is made clear by the following excerpt from the trial court's memorandum opinion.

> "It is the opinion of the Court that the state of the law is such that nuisance cannot be justified on the ground of necessity, pecuniary interest, convenience or economic advantage.
>
> The Court understands as does counsel that there is a need for disposal of industrial hazardous wastes. However, where disposal of wastes create a nuisance said disposal site may be closed through legal action.
>
> Substantial sums of money have been expended by the defendant in developing and operating the Earthline site at Wilsonville. Not only is the site convenient to nearby industries but it is a profit producer for the defendant. All of these elements are relevant to our economic system but notwithstanding the same it is the opinion of the Court that nuisances cannot be justified on such grounds when we have substantial injury to individual rights, community rights, substantial damage to human beings and other living things.

* * *

> The importance of an industry to the wealth and prosperity of an area does not as a matter of law give to it rights superior to the primary or natural rights of citizens who live nearby. *However, such matters may be considered and have been in this case.*
>
> * * *
>
> In this case the defendant established its chemical waste landfill near the area where persons of the Village had resided for many years. * * *
>
> An industrial waste disposal site in and adjacent to a village means that the hazardous waste disposal operation is near or next to homes, families—children, youth, middle aged and old people—sick people, well people—sensitive persons and anxious and fearful persons. The location of a business has significance in reference to being a nuisance or not being a nuisance." (Emphasis added.)

We think the foregoing indicates that the trial court did carefully engage in a balancing process between the site's social utility and the plaintiffs' right to enjoy their property and not suffer deleterious effects from chemical wastes. Accordingly, the defendant's argument that the trial court did not balance the equities in this case is without merit.

The defendant's next contention is that the courts below were in error when they failed to require a showing of a substantial risk of certain and extreme future harm before enjoining operation of the defendant's site. We deem it necessary to explain that a *prospective* nuisance is a fit candidate for injunctive relief. Prosser states: "Both public and private nuisances require some substantial interference with the interest involved. Since nuisance is a common subject of equity jurisdiction, the damage against which an injunction is asked is often merely threatened or potential; but even in such cases, there must be at least a threat of a substantial invasion of the plaintiff's interests." (Prosser, Torts sec. 87, at 577 (4th ed. 1971).) The defendant does not dispute this proposition; it does, however, argue that the trial court did not follow the proper standard for determining when a prospective nuisance may be enjoined. The defendant argues that the proper standard to be used is that an injunction is proper only if there is a "dangerous probability" that the threatened or potential injury will occur. (*See* Restatement (Second) of Torts sec. 933(1), at 561, comment *b* (1979).) The defendant further argues that the appellate court looked only at the potential consequences of not enjoining the operation of the site as a nuisance and not at the likelihood of whether harm would occur. The defendant assigns error on this basis.

We agree with the defendant's statement of the law, but not with its urged application to the facts of this case. Again, Professor Prosser has offered a concise commentary. He has stated that "[o]ne distinguishing feature of equitable relief is that it may be granted upon the threat of harm which has not yet occurred. The defendant may be restrained from entering upon an activity where it is highly probable that it will lead to a nuisance, although if the possibility is merely uncertain or contingent he may be left to his remedy after the nuisance has occurred." (Prosser,

Torts sec. 90, at 603 (4th ed. 1971).) This view is in accord with Illinois law. * * * In *Fink* the plaintiff sought to enjoin construction of a dam and also the discharge of sewage effluent in a watercourse which flowed past plaintiffs' property. Construction of the dam was not enjoined, but the discharge of effluent was prospectively enjoined. The court stated:

> "While, as a general proposition, an injunction will be granted only to restrain an actual, existing nuisance, a court of equity may enjoin a threatened or anticipated nuisance, where it clearly appears that a nuisance will necessarily result from the contemplated act or thing which it is sought to enjoin. This is particularly true where the proof shows that the apprehension of material injury is well grounded upon a state of facts from which it appears that the danger is real and immediate. While care should be used in granting injunctions to avoid prospective injuries, there is no requirement that the court must wait until the injury occurs before granting relief." (71 Ill.App.2d 226, 281–82, 218 N.E.2d 240.)

We agree.

In this case there can be no doubt but that it is highly probable that the chemical-waste-disposal site will bring about a substantial injury. Without again reviewing the extensive evidence adduced at trial, we think it is sufficiently clear that it is highly probable that the instant site will constitute a public nuisance if, through either an explosive interaction, migration, subsidence, or the "bathtub effect," the highly toxic chemical wastes deposited at the site escape and contaminate the air, water, or ground around the site. That such an event will occur was positively attested to by several expert witnesses. A court does not have to wait for it to happen before it can enjoin such a result. Additionally, the fact is that the condition of a nuisance is already present at the site due to the location of the site and the manner in which it has been operated. Thus, it is only the damage which is prospective. Under these circumstances, if a court can prevent any damage from occurring, it should do so.

* * *

The next issue we consider is whether the trial court erroneously granted a permanent injunction. * * * The second argument raised is that the courts below did not balance the equities in deciding to enjoin the defendant from continuing to operate the waste-disposal site. Defendant cites Harrison v. Indiana Auto Shredders Co. (7th Cir.1975), 528 F.2d 1107, for the proposition that the court must balance the relative harm and benefit to the plaintiff and defendant before a court may enjoin a nuisance. [*See supra* pp. 553–55.] The court concluded in *Harrison* that since the defendant was not in violation of any relevant zoning standards, and since the shredder did not pose an imminent hazard to the public health, the defendant should not be prevented from continuing to operate. The court then ordered that the defendant be permitted a reasonable time to "launder its objectionable features." 528 F.2d 1107, 1125.

This case is readily distinguishable for the reason that the gist of this case is that the defendant is engaged in an extremely hazardous undertaking at an unsuitable location, which seriously and imminently poses a threat to the public health. We are acutely aware that the service provided by the defendant is a valuable and necessary one. We also know that it is preferable to have chemical-waste-disposal sites than to have illegal dumping in rivers, streams, and deserted areas. But a site such as defendant's, if it is to do the job it is intended to do, must be located in a secure place, where it will pose no threat to health or life, now, or in the future. This site was intended to be a *permanent* disposal site for the deposit of extremely hazardous chemical-waste materials. Yet this site is located above an abandoned tunneled mine where subsidence is occurring several years ahead of when it was anticipated. Also, the permeability-coefficient samples taken by defendant's experts, though not conclusive alone, indicate that the soil is more permeable at the site than expected. Moreover, the spillage, odors, and dust caused by the presence of the disposal site indicate why it was inadvisable to locate the site so near the plaintiff village.

Therefore, we conclude that in fashioning relief in this case the trial court did balance relative hardship to be caused to the plaintiffs and defendant, and did fashion reasonable relief when it ordered the exhumation of all material from the site and the reclamation of the surrounding area. The instant site is akin to Mr. Justice Sutherland's observation that "Nuisance may be merely a right thing in a wrong place—like a pig in the parlor instead of the barnyard." Village of Euclid v. Ambler Realty Co. (1926), 272 U.S. 365, 388, 47 S.Ct. 114, 118, 71 L.Ed. 303, 311, quoted in 2 J. Dooley, Modern Tort Litigation, sec. 31.15, at 225 (1977).

* * *

Accordingly, for all the reasons stated, the judgments of the circuit and appellate courts are affirmed and the cause is remanded to the circuit court to enable it to retain jurisdiction to supervise the enforcement of its order.

Notes

1. When a governmental plaintiff brings a public nuisance action, as compared with a case in which a private citizen brings a private nuisance action, the courts do not have "quite the same freedom to balance the harm that will be done by an injunction against that of which the plaintiff complains * * *." Georgia v. Tennessee Copper Co., *supra* p. 556. Therefore, injunctions are more apt to be issued in public nuisance actions. *Id.;* Flacke v. Bio–Tech Mills, Inc., 95 A.D.2d 916, 463 N.Y.S.2d 899 (1983).

2. Actions to enjoin prospective harm may result in the issuance of what some courts call a "qualified injunction." For example, in Salter v. B.W.S. Corp., 290 So.2d 821 (La.1974), the plaintiff sought to enjoin the operation of the defendant's waste disposal business. The court issued a qualified injunction for the following reasons:

> "Suit was filed in this case before the disposition of any waste material. We have only the plans of the defendant and the beginning of its operation. The record establishes that this waste disposal operation can be conducted safely and in a manner not violating the duties of vicinage. However, the consequences of failure to exercise great care to prevent the escape of poisonous materials are so serious (the poisoning of Frazier's

well) that we deem it appropriate to issue a qualified injunction. Although the record shows only that the violation of recommended engineering procedures will result in damage to neighbors, the consequences of escaping poisonous materials are so terrible that the injunctive relief is appropriate.

"The defendant will therefore be enjoined to conduct its operations in compliance with standards recommended by its experts which will prohibit the escape of noxious substances on the property of its neighbors. The right is reserved to plaintiffs to renew their complaint upon the failure of the defendant to comply with such standards."

Id. at 825.

A qualified injunction requires long-term supervision. In another Louisiana case, the trial court's qualified injunction against a landfill operation was dissolved on appeal on the ground that "such an activity can be more appropriately regulated and monitored by an administrative agency designed and staffed to deal with such operations." Acadian Heritage Realty v. City of Lafayette, 451 So.2d 17, 22 (La.App.1984).

ENVIRONMENTAL DEFENSE FUND v. LAMPHIER

United States Court of Appeals, Fourth Circuit, 1983.
714 F.2d 331.

Before WINTER, CHIEF JUDGE, and MURNAGHAN and ERVIN, CIRCUIT JUDGES.

ERVIN, CIRCUIT JUDGE:

The cause of this appeal is a judgment by the district court holding that the defendants violated state and federal antipollution laws and committed a common law nuisance. We discern no merit in the assorted contentions on appeal, and accordingly we affirm.

I.

James and Janet Lamphier are co-owners of a farm in Culpepper County, Virginia. Since 1974 the farm has been headquarters for "Jim's Liquid Waste," a sole proprietorship belonging to James Lamphier and engaged in the business of industrial waste disposal.

In the fall of 1979, the Virginia State Water Control Board ("SWCB") and the State Department of Health ("SDH") learned that Lamphier was transporting various wastes to his farm and disposing of them by land application and lagooning of bulk liquids, and burial of drummed liquids. After visits to the farm, both state agencies ordered Lamphier to cease his disposal activities. On December 5, 1979, the SWCB issued an emergency order requiring Lamphier to contain all runoff from lagoons and land application areas and submit a list of wastes deposited at the facility. Subsequently, the SWCB ordered Lamphier to devise a land reclamation plan and to construct proper facilities for the disposal of septic wastes. In compliance with these orders, Lamphier halted dumping activities (although he continued to receive shipments of wastes through March, 1980) and, sometime after November 5, 1980, submitted a plan for waste containment and land reclamation to both the SWCB and the SDH. The SWCB subsequently approved the plan, but the SDH did not.

In March, 1980, an investigator for the SDH visited the Lamphier farm and found several 55–gallon drums containing solvents buried on the property. On April 11, 1980, the SDH investigator returned along with a special agent of the state police and, armed with a search warrant, collected samples of well waters and of wastes found in numerous barrels. Tests performed on these samples revealed a high degree of flammability, which under regulations of the Resource Conservation and Recovery Act of 1976 ("RCRA"), 42 U.S.C. §§ 6901 *et seq.*, qualified the wastes as hazardous. *See* 40 C.F.R. § 261.21.

* * *

On June 16, 1980, federal officials intervened. Representatives from the Environmental Protection Agency ("EPA") visited the farm to ascertain whether the materials posed an "imminent hazard" warranting immediate action under § 7003 of RCRA, 42 U.S.C. § 6973. Samples taken revealed no imminent hazard, but in the report to the SWCB, Jack Brinkmann of the EPA left open the possibility that other RCRA violations might be present.

* * *

On November 19, 1980, major new RCRA provisions went into effect, requiring all hazardous waste treatment, storage and disposal facilities to register for permits or non-permit interim status and to comply with certain operating standards. Lamphier took no action to obtain an operator's permit.

* * *

The Environmental Defense Fund, Inc. ("EDF") and the Chesapeake Bay Foundation ("CBF"), two private environmental groups, joined the dispute on October 5, 1981, by filing a complaint against Lamphier under the "citizen suit" provision of RCRA, 42 U.S.C. § 6972, alleging violations of RCRA notification and permit requirements, 42 U.S.C. §§ 6930 and 6925. The Commonwealth of Virginia intervened on January 12, 1982, appending several state law charges to EDF and CBF's action. In addition to injunctive relief, the Commonwealth sought response costs under the Comprehensive Environmental Response, Compensation and Liability Act of 1980, 42 U.S.C. §§ 9601 *et seq.*

After a bench trial, the court found the defendants guilty of common law nuisance and of violations of RCRA and Virginia state law. As relief, the court issued an injunction ordering Lamphier henceforth to comply with applicable hazardous waste regulations. The court further ordered the Lamphiers to provide the plaintiffs and plaintiff-intervenors access to the farm for the purpose of monitoring wastes. Fees and costs were also awarded.

II.

* * *

[The court held that the defendant was in violation of federal law.]

III.

Originally, the EDF and CBF sought civil penalties against Lamphier of $25,000 for each day of violation under the citizen suit provision of RCRA, 42 U.S.C. § 6972. However, at trial, the plaintiffs voluntarily dismissed this claim, limiting the remedy sought to an injunction, plus costs and attorneys fees.

Lamphier maintains that once plaintiffs waived their original claim for civil penalties, no jurisdiction remained over claims for statutory and common law injunctive relief, since the citizen suit provision of RCRA, 42 U.S.C. § 6972, does not expressly authorize such relief. Lamphier cites Middlesex County Sewerage Authority v. National Sea Clammers Association, 453 U.S. 1, 14–15, 101 S.Ct. 2615, 2623–2624, 69 L.Ed.2d 435 (1981), for the proposition that "where a statute expressly provides a particular remedy or remedies, a court must be chary of reading others into it." In *Sea Clammers,* a private association brought a claim seeking damages and declaratory and injunctive relief under the citizen suit provision of the Federal Water Pollution Control Act ("FWPCA"), 33 U.S.C. § 1365(a), and federal common law. Section 1365(a) authorizes citizen suits against any person alleged to be in violation of an effluent standard or a government order under the Act and confers on the district court jurisdiction to enforce such standards or orders and to impose any appropriate civil penalties. The question before the Court was whether section 1365(a) additionally permitted suits for private relief—damages and an injunction—as opposed to "private attorneys general" actions to obtain enforcement of federal law through injunctive relief and civil penalties. The Court held that the plain language of the FWPCA did not authorize a private right of action for injunctive and monetary relief. Although 33 U.S.C. § 1365(a) enumerates only civil penalties, the Court presumed the statute authorized private persons to sue for civil injunctions to enforce the regulatory scheme, provided the private plaintiff complied with the notice requirements set out in section 1365(b). But the plaintiffs in *Sea Clammers* ignored these procedures and thus forfeited their claim for injunctive relief as well as losing their quest for a private award of damages.

Sea Clammers is readily distinguishable from the instant case. The private plaintiffs here did not seek an award of damages but rather acted as private attorneys general in seeking the assessment of civil penalties and an injunction against Lamphier. Under the citizen suit provision of RCRA, 42 U.S.C. § 6972, the district court is authorized to enforce RCRA regulations or orders, presumably to the full extent of its legal and equitable powers. 42 U.S.C. § 6972(a). Provided plaintiffs are genuinely acting as private attorneys general rather than pursuing a private remedy, nothing in RCRA, as in the FWPCA, bars injunctive relief. *See* 42 U.S.C. § 6928.[4]

4. From this analysis it follows that the citizen plaintiffs here are not specially entitled to the benefits of substantive relief. We discern a minor trespass on this proposition in the district court's final order, in which Lamphier is directed to provide ongoing access to his property both to the Commonwealth and to the private plaintiffs for the purpose of monitoring wastes. At oral argument, the EDF and CBF conceded that they are not entitled to personal access to Lamphier's property, and we so construe the district court's order. Access is to be granted to the Commonwealth only.

* * *

IV.

Lamphier next attacks the award of injunctive relief requiring future compliance with the registration requirements of RCRA and directing that Lamphier open up his land to monitoring of wastes. He points out the hornbook rule that to obtain injunctive relief, a plaintiff must prove that legal remedies are inadequate, that risk of an irreparable injury exists, and that the balance of equities justifies an injunction. Since the plaintiffs here did not attempt to prove irreparable injury, Lamphier argues that the grant of injunctive relief was improper.

This argument fails on at least two counts. First, the law of injunctions differs with respect to governmental plaintiffs (or private attorneys general) as opposed to private individuals. Where the plaintiff is a sovereign and where the activity may endanger the public health, "injunctive relief is proper, without resort to balancing." Illinois v. Milwaukee, 599 F.2d 151, 166 (7th Cir.1979), *rev'd on other grounds,* 451 U.S. 304, 101 S.Ct. 1784, 68 L.Ed.2d 114 (1981). Second, in cases of public health legislation, the emphasis shifts from irreparable injury to concern for the general public interest:

> It is contended that the government has not shown irreparable injury and that it has an adequate remedy at law * * *. The United States, however, is not bound to conform with the requirements of private litigation when it seeks the aid of the courts to give effect to the policy of Congress as manifested in a statute. It is a familiar doctrine that an injunction is an appropriate means for the enforcement of an Act of Congress when it is in the public interest.

Shafer v. United States, 229 F.2d 124, 128 (4th Cir.1956). This rationale applies equally to state enforcement of federal and state health laws.

Furthermore, 42 U.S.C. § 6928, the enforcement provision of RCRA, explicitly calls for the judicial issuance of injunctions to coerce compliance with the Act's requirements. Where a statute authorizes injunctive relief for its enforcement, plaintiffs need not plead and prove irreparable injury. * * * The injunctive relief impliedly authorized under 42 U.S.C. § 6972(a) was amply warranted in this case.

Lamphier further urges that the injunction issued by the district court was not sufficiently specific to pass legal muster. * * *

In its Memorandum Opinion and Order filed May 14, 1982, the district court ordered that:

> Plaintiffs and Plaintiff–Intervenor and their agents are granted an injunction and they are expressly authorized to enter onto Defendant's property at reasonable times in order to take such samples and make such tests as the Commonwealth deems appropriate. No bond shall be required.

We find no fatal flaw in the terms of this injunction, which merely requires Lamphier to open up his property to state inspection at reasonable times. By the language of the order, Lamphier is fully apprised of what he must do in order to avoid contempt proceedings. The open-ended duration of the injunction is justified by Lamphier's prior lack of cooperation with authorities. Until such time as Lamphier demonstrates abiding compliance with hazardous waste laws, his farm should remain subject to monitoring by health officials.

* * *

For the foregoing reasons, the judgment of the district court is affirmed.*

Notes

1. Preliminary injunctions are also easier to obtain in public nuisance actions brought by a governmental entity to enforce a violation of a zoning statute or permit, as evidenced by IT Corp. v. County of Imperial, 35 Cal.3d 63, 69–72, 196 Cal.Rptr. 715, 719–21, 672 P.2d 121, 122–27 (1983) (action by county for preliminary injunction restraining IT from disposing of unauthorized wastes at its hazardous waste disposal facility):

> "The principal question raised by this appeal concerns the proper standard for the issuance of a preliminary injunction when a governmental entity seeks to enjoin an alleged violation of a zoning ordinance which specifically provides for injunctive relief.
>
> * * *
>
> "This court has traditionally held that trial courts should evaluate two interrelated factors when deciding whether or not to issue a preliminary injunction. The first is the likelihood that the plaintiff will prevail on the merits at trial. The second is the interim harm that the plaintiff is likely to sustain if the injunction were denied as compared to the harm that the defendant is likely to suffer if the preliminary injunction were issued. * * *
>
> "This court has not addressed the question as to whether this two-factor test is the proper rule to apply when a governmental entity seeks to enjoin an alleged violation of a zoning ordinance which provides for injunctive relief.
>
> "IT contends that the injunction was erroneously issued because the trial court did not balance the relative hardships to the parties. * * *
>
> "The County properly points out that once a trial court has determined that the governmental entity will probably succeed at trial in

* *See generally* Hinds, Liability Under Federal Law for Hazardous Waste Injuries, 6 Harv.Envtl.L.Rev. 1 (1982); Murchison, Does NEPA Matter?—An Analysis of the Historical Development and Contemporary Significance of the National Environmental Policy Act, 18 U.Rich.L.Rev. 557 (1984); Schwartz & Hackett, Citizen Suits Against Private Industry Under the Clean Water Act, 17 Nat. Resources Law, 327 (1984); Zalob, Approaches to Enforcement of Environmental Law: An International Perspective, 3 Hastings Int'l & Comp.L.Rev. 299 (1980); Comment, Abating An Eminent Hazard: Injunctive Relief Under the Comprehensive Environmental Response, Compensation and Liability Act of 1980, 32 Buffalo L.Rev. 787 (1983); Comment, The Role of Injunctive Relief and Settlements Superfund Enforcement, 68 Cornell L.Rev. 706 (1983); Comment, A Directory of Federal Regulations to Pollution and Toxic Torts for the Attorney, 6 Glendale L.Rev. 161 (1984); Comment, Emergency Environmental Health Protection in California, 16 U.S.F.L.Rev. 539 (1982) (proposing model statute that authorizes injunction without proof that remedy at law is inadequate).

proving a statutory violation, the court is justified in presuming that public harm will result if an injunction is not issued. The reasoning underlying this argument is sound. Where a legislative body has enacted a statutory provision proscribing a certain activity, it has already determined that such activity is contrary to the public interest. Further, where the legislative body has specifically authorized injunctive relief against the violation of such a law, it has already determined (1) that significant public harm will result from the proscribed activity, and (2) that injunctive relief may be the most appropriate way to protect against that harm. (*See* Paul v. Wadler (1962) 209 Cal.App.2d 615, 625, 26 Cal.Rptr. 341.)

* * *

"On the other hand, IT is correct that an important function of preliminary injunctions—that of preventing serious interlocutory harm to the ultimately successful party—would be thwarted if an *irrebuttable* presumption in favor of the governmental entity were created. A conclusive presumption would fail to protect those defendants who might suffer grave or irreparable immediate harm from the issuance of an injunction even where that harm far outweighs the harm the public might suffer if no injunction were issued.

"It is apparent from the case law and from the considerations underlying the parties' arguments that the purposes of a preliminary injunction are best served in the present circumstances by an adaptation of the traditional test which incorporates elements of both parties' positions. * * *

"Accordingly, the propriety of an injunction must be judged by the following standard. Where a governmental entity seeking to enjoin the alleged violation of an ordinance which specifically provides for injunctive relief establishes that it is reasonably probable it will prevail on the merits, a rebuttable presumption arises that the potential harm to the public outweighs the potential harm to the defendant. If the defendant shows that it would suffer grave or irreparable harm from the issuance of the preliminary injunction, the court must then examine the relative actual harms to the parties."

2. During the past twenty-five years, the federal government has been a major source of environmental legislation. Among the most significant of these statutes are the Clean Air Act. 42 U.S.C.A. § 7401 *et seq.;* the Clean Water Act, 33 U.S.C.A. § 1251 *et seq.;* Safe Drinking Water Act, 42 U.S.C.A. § 300f *et seq.;* Resource Conservation and Recovery Act of 1976, 42 U.S.C.A. § 6901 *et seq.;* Comprehensive Environmental Response, Compensation, and Liability Act [CERCLA], 42 U.S.C.A. § 9601 *et seq.;* Surface Mining Control and Reclamation Act, 30 U.S.C.A. § 1201 *et seq.;* and the National Environmental Policy Act, 42 U.S.C.A. § 4321 *et seq.*

As we have seen earlier, private parties can experience significant standing roadblocks in public nuisance litigation. With respect to much of the foregoing federal legislation, however, Congress has generally been receptive to citizen judicial enforcement. For example, the language of § 505 of the Clean Water Act provides that "[A]ny citizen may commence a civil action on his own behalf–(A) * * * against any person * * * who is alleged to be in violation of * * * an effluent standard or limitation under this chapter or * * * an order issued by the Administrator or state with respect to such a standard or limitation." 33 U.S.C.A. § 1365(a)(2). Moreover, at least a dozen other major federal environmental statutes contain similar grants of standing to private citizens. *See* Z. Plater, R. Abrams & W. Goldfarb, Environmental Law and Policy: Nature, Law and Society 566 (1992).

NATURAL RESOURCES DEFENSE COUNCIL, INC. v. TEXACO REFINING AND MARKETING, INC.

United States Court of Appeals, Third Circuit, 1990.
906 F.2d 934.

Before HIGGINBOTHAM, CHIEF JUDGE, COWEN and NYGAARD, CIRCUIT JUDGES.

OPINION OF THE COURT

COWEN, CIRCUIT JUDGE.

This appeal arises out of a citizen suit filed by the Natural Resources Defense Council, Inc. and the Delaware Audubon Society (collectively referred to hereafter as "the NRDC") under § 505 of the Clean Water Act ("the Act"), 33 U.S.C. § 1365 (1982 and Supp. III), alleging that Texaco Refining and Marketing, Inc. ("Texaco") illegally discharged effluent into the Delaware River at its Delaware City refinery.

* * *

I.

In order "to restore and maintain the chemical, physical, and biological integrity of the Nation's waters," 33 U.S.C. § 1251(a), the Act makes unlawful the discharge of any pollutant into navigable waters except as authorized under specific sections of the Act. *See generally Gwaltney of Smithfield v. Chesapeake Bay Found., Inc.,* 484 U.S. 49, 52–53, 108 S.Ct. 376, 379, 98 L.Ed.2d 306 (1987). One of these is § 402 which establishes the National Pollutant Discharge Elimination System ("NPDES"). 33 U.S.C. § 1342. Under § 402 either the Administrator of the Environmental Protection Agency ("EPA"), or a state which has established its own EPA-approved permit program, may issue a permit allowing effluent discharges in accordance with specified conditions. 33 U.S.C. § 1342(b), (c).

The holder of a state permit is subject to enforcement action by both the EPA and the state for failure to comply with the permit's conditions. 33 U.S.C. § 1319, 1342(b)(7). In addition, private citizens may bring civil actions against any person alleged to be in violation of a state permit if the federal or state agencies have not acted. 33 U.S.C. § 1365(a)(1). The Act allows the court in a citizen suit to order injunctive relief and/or impose monetary penalties. 33 U.S.C. § 1365(a).

The State of Delaware received its NPDES permit delegation from the EPA on April 1, 1974, and issued a permit to Texaco in 1977 allowing it to discharge limited quantities of 19 categories of industrial waste from its Delaware City refinery into the Delaware River. The permit imposes on Texaco both limitations on the amount of pollutants that can be discharged and monitoring requirements.

As required by the Act, the NRDC notified Texaco in March 1988 that they intended to file a citizen suit against the company for 342 permit violations occurring at the Delaware City refinery between January 1983 and October 1987. Subsequently, on May 17, 1988, the NRDC filed a complaint charging Texaco with 354 violations, including some violations that had occurred since October 1987. The NRDC later dropped 11 alleged violations apparently in response to a statute of limitations argument raised by Texaco.

On December 9, 1989, Texaco filed a motion for partial summary judgment based on several grounds * * *. One week later the NRDC filed their own motion for summary judgment on the issue of liability based on the reported parameter exceedances in Texaco's DMRs. In their motion, the NRDC sought declaratory and injunctive relief, and requested a hearing to determine the appropriate amount of damages. * * *

The district court denied Texaco's motion for partial summary judgment reasoning that even if some of the parameter violations alleged by the NRDC were wholly past violations, i.e., not ongoing or likely to recur, the fact that other parameter violations were ongoing at the time the complaint was filed gave the court jurisdiction over all permit violations. *Natural Resources Defense Council, Inc. v. Texaco Refining and Marketing, Inc.*, 719 F.Supp. 281, 287 (D.Del.1989). * * *

The district court granted the NRDC's motion for summary judgment based on the submitted DMRs. * * *

Having established that Texaco violated the Act, the court enjoined the company, its officers, agents, servants, employees, and those persons in active concert or participation with Texaco, and who receive actual notice of the court's order, from violating terms of the new permit which were either carried over from the old permit or were made stricter in the new version. * * *

Texaco now appeals the district court's order denying both its motion for summary judgment and its supplemental motion for summary judgment. In addition, Texaco appeals the district court's order granting the NRDC's motion for summary judgment and the issuance of a permanent injunction against the company. We have jurisdiction over that part of the district court's order granting injunctive relief pursuant to 28 U.S.C. § 1292(a)(1) (1982).

II.

Texaco argues on appeal that the district court erred by applying the wrong standard in determining whether to grant the NRDC's request for a permanent injunction. More specifically, Texaco argues that the court failed to apply traditional equitable principles in reaching its decision to enjoin the company, including placing the burden on the NRDC to prove that irreparable harm would ensue if the injunction was not granted. * * *

Although somewhat unclear, from our reading of the opinion it does appear that the district court presumed irreparable harm from the mere fact that the Act had been violated. * * *

We agree with Texaco that the district court abused its discretion in this case by presuming irreparable harm and not explicitly applying the traditional equitable standard in determining whether an injunction was appropriate for remedying Texaco's violations of the Act. We believe that the United States Supreme Court's decisions in *Weinberger v. Romero–Barcelo,* 456 U.S. 305, 102 S.Ct. 1798, 72 L.Ed.2d 91 (1982), and *Amoco Prod. Co. v. Village of Gambell,* 480 U.S. 531, 107 S.Ct. 1396, 94 L.Ed.2d 542 (1987), establish that equitable principles are not displaced by the Act. Furthermore, every circuit court that has interpreted *Romero–Barcelo* in this context is in accord with our view, as well as numerous district court opinions in this circuit and elsewhere. Finally, we find that the cases relied upon by the district court for its apparently contrary view that an injunction should automatically follow upon a finding of statutory violation are distinguishable from this case.

In *Romero–Barcelo,* the district court found that the Navy had violated the Act by discharging ordnance into the Atlantic Ocean during training operations without first obtaining an NPDES permit from the EPA. *Romero–Barcelo,* 456 U.S. at 307–08, 102 S.Ct. at 1800–01. The court declined to enjoin the training operations, however, and simply ordered the Navy to apply for a permit from the Administrator of the EPA. *Id.* at 310, 102 S.Ct. at 1802. Emphasizing in its opinion the broad discretion a court in equity possesses in deciding appropriate relief, the district court reasoned that the Navy's activities were not causing any appreciable harm to the environment, while injunctive relief would cause grievous, and perhaps irreparable, harm to the Navy and the general welfare. *Id.* The Court of Appeals for the First Circuit reversed and directed the district court to enjoin all Naval training activities until the Navy obtained a permit. The Court of Appeals held that the traditional equitable balancing of interests was inappropriate where there was an absolute statutory duty to refrain from any pollutant discharge until the permit procedure is followed. *Id.* at 310–11, 102 S.Ct. at 1802.

The Supreme Court reversed the Court of Appeals and remanded the case to the appellate court to review the district court's decision under an abuse of discretion standard. The Court noted that it had "repeatedly held that the basis for injunctive relief in the federal courts has always been irreparable injury and the inadequacy of legal remedies." *Id.* at 312, 102 S.Ct. at 1803. The court explained that in each case the court must balance the competing claims of injury and must consider the consequences to each party, and the public, of the granting or withholding of the requested relief. *Id.* Thus, "[t]he grant of jurisdiction to ensure compliance with a statute hardly suggests an absolute duty to do so under any and all circumstances, and a federal judge sitting as chancellor is not mechanically obligated to grant an injunction for every violation of law." *Id.* at 313, 102 S.Ct. at 1803.

The Court cautioned that:

> Of course, Congress may intervene and guide or control the exercise of the courts' discretion, but we do not lightly assume that Congress has intended to depart from established principles. As the Court said in

Porter v. Warner Holding Co., 328 U.S. 395, 398, 66 S.Ct. 1086, 1089, 90 L.Ed. 1332 (1946):

> Moreover, the comprehensiveness of this equitable jurisdiction is not to be denied or limited in the absence of a clear and valid legislative command. Unless a statute in so many words, or by a necessary and inescapable inference, restricts the court's jurisdiction in equity, the full scope of that jurisdiction is to be recognized and applied.

Romero–Barcelo, 456 U.S. at 313, 102 S.Ct. at 1804 (citations omitted).[5] However, the Court found nothing in the Clean Water Act's language, structure or legislative history evidencing Congress' intent to deny courts their traditional equitable discretion. *Id.* at 316–18, 319, 102 S.Ct. at 1805–06, 1807. The Court of Appeals had erroneously focused on the integrity of the permit process rather than on the integrity of the Nation's water, the real purpose of the Act. *Id.* at 314, 102 S.Ct. at 1804.

Similarly in *Amoco Prod. Co. v. Village of Gambell,* 480 U.S. 531, 107 S.Ct. 1396, 94 L.Ed.2d 542 (1987), the Court of Appeals for the Ninth Circuit found that the Secretary of the Interior had likely failed to comply with provisions of the Alaska National Interest Lands Conservation Act ("ANILCA") and directed the district court to grant a preliminary injunction preventing certain oil and gas lease activity. *Id.* at 540–41, 107 S.Ct. at 1401–02. The Ninth Circuit ruled that "injunctive relief is the appropriate remedy for a violation of an environmental statute absent rare or unusual circumstances." *Id.* at 541, 107 S.Ct. at 1402.

The Supreme Court again reversed, "see[ing] nothing which distinguishes *Romero–Barcelo* from the instant case" and finding "no clear indication in [ANILCA] that Congress intended to deny federal district courts their traditional equitable discretion in enforcing the [statute] * * *." *Amoco,* 480 U.S. at 544, 107 S.Ct. at 1403. The Court stated:

> Like the First Circuit in *Romero–Barcelo,* the Ninth Circuit erroneously focused on the statutory procedure rather than on the underlying substantive policy the process was designed to effect—preservation of subsistence resources. The District Court's refusal to issue a prelimi-

5. As an example of legislative intervention, the Court cited *TVA v. Hill,* 437 U.S. 153, 98 S.Ct. 2279, 57 L.Ed.2d 117 (1978). In that case, the Court held that Congress had foreclosed the traditional discretion exercised by a court in equity:

> The statute involved, the Endangered Species Act, 87 Stat. 884, 16 U.S.C. 1531 *et seq.,* required the District Court to enjoin completion of the Tellico Dam in order to preserve the snail darter, a species of perch. The purpose and language of the statute under consideration in *Hill,* not the bare fact of a statutory violation, compelled that conclusion. Section 7 of the Act, 16 U.S.C. § 1536, requires federal agencies to "insure that actions authorized, funded, or carried out by them do not jeopardize the continued existence of [any] endangered species * * * or result in the destruction or modification of habitat of such species which is determined * * * to be critical." The statute thus contains a flat ban on the destruction of critical habitats.

Weinberger v. Romero–Barcelo, 456 U.S. 305, 313–14, 102 S.Ct. 1798, 1804, 72 L.Ed.2d 91 (1982). Since it was conceded that the Tellico Dam would destroy the snail darters' habitat, an injunction had to be issued because "Congress, it appeared to us, had chosen the snail darter over the dam." *Id.* at 314, 102 S.Ct. at 1804. Turning to the Clean Water Act, the Court noted: "That is not the case here. An injunction is not the only means of ensuring compliance [with the Act]." *Id.*

> nary injunction against all exploration activities did not undermine this policy. The District Court * * * expressly found that exploration activities would not significantly restrict subsistence uses. The Court of Appeals did not conclude that this factual finding was clearly erroneous * * *. Instead, the court stated that "irreparable damage is *presumed* when an agency fails to evaluate thoroughly the environmental impact of a proposed action." * * * This presumption is contrary to traditional equitable principles and has no basis in ANILCA. Moreover, the environment can be fully protected without this presumption.

Id. at 544–45, 107 S.Ct. at 1403–04.

Every Court of Appeals, which has considered the question, has interpreted *Romero–Barcelo* and *Amoco to require* a district court to apply the traditional equitable standard before granting an injunction in cases such as this. For example, the Court of Appeals for the Second Circuit, in *Town of Huntington v. Marsh,* 884 F.2d 648 (2d Cir.1989), *cert. denied,* ___ U.S. ___, 110 S.Ct. 1296, 108 L.Ed.2d 473 (1990), found that the "teaching of these [Supreme Court] cases seems clear." *Id.* at 652. "[I]n the area of environmental statutes, the Supreme Court has explicitly rejected the notion that an injunction follows as a matter of course upon a finding of statutory violation." *Id.* at 651. * * *

See also Northern Cheyenne Tribe v. Hodel, 851 F.2d 1152, 1155–56, 1157–58 (9th Cir.1988); *National Wildlife Fed'n v. Burford,* 835 F.2d 305, 318, 323–24 (D.C.Cir.1987); *Commonwealth of Mass. v. Watt,* 716 F.2d 946, 951–53 (1st Cir.1983). *Cf. United States v. Lambert,* 695 F.2d 536, 540 (11th Cir.1983) (without citing *Romero–Barcelo,* the court held that: "Environmental litigation is not exempt from [the] requirement" that the plaintiff must prove "irreparable harm is likely if an injunction is not granted [for a violation of the Act]"). Indeed, district courts both in this circuit, *see, e.g., Public Interest Research Group of N.J., Inc. v. CP Chemicals, Inc.,* 26 E.R.C. 2017 (D.N.J.1987), and in other circuits, *see, e.g., Natural Resources Defense Council, Inc. v. Outboard Marine Corp.,* 692 F.Supp. 801, 821–23 (N.D.Ill.1988), have applied the traditional equitable standard in determining whether to grant preliminary and permanent injunctions for violations of the Act.

The two cases cited by the district court in support of its apparently contrary position are inapposite. In *United States Postal Service v. Beamish,* 466 F.2d 804 (3d Cir.1972), this Court affirmed an injunction by the district court even though the district court had not applied the traditional equitable standard. And, in *Government of Virgin Islands, Dep't of Conservation and Cultural Affairs v. Virgin Islands Paving, Inc.,* 714 F.2d 283 (3d Cir.1983), the NRDC apparently contends—and the district court appears to assume—that this Court reversed the district court's denial of a preliminary injunction because the district court should not have applied the traditional equitable standard in deciding the question. However, both of these cases are distinguishable from the case *sub judice* because the statutes under which the injunctions were sought in *Beamish* and *Virgin Islands* clearly circumscribed the traditional equitable discretion courts possess in granting injunctive relief. In *Beamish,* the postal service provision in question provided that: "the United States district court * * * shall * * * upon a *showing of probable cause* to believe * * * [that 39 U.S.C. § 3005] is being violated, enter a temporary restraining order and preliminary injunction * * *." *Beamish,* 466 F.2d at 806 (quoting from 39 U.S.C. § 3007) (emphasis added). Likewise, in *Virgin Islands,* the statute in question, the Virgin Islands Coastal Zone Management Act of 1978, provided for preliminary injunctive relief upon a "*prima facie showing* of a violation." *Virgin Islands,* 714 F.2d at 284 (quoting from 12 V.I.C. § 913(b)(1)) (emphasis added). In both of these cases, the legislature had effectively intervened through the statute and guided or controlled the exercise of the courts' traditional discretion. Thus, both of these statutes are the type that the Supreme Court distinguished from the Clean Water Act in *Romero–Barcelo. See Romero–Barcelo,* 456 U.S. at 313–14, 102 S.Ct. at 1804–05.

Thus, it is clear to us that a district court may issue a permanent injunction under the Act only after a showing both of irreparable injury and inadequacy of legal remedies, and a balancing of competing claims of injury and the public interest. *Amoco,* 480 U.S. at 544–47, 107 S.Ct. at 1403–05. From our reading of the district court's opinion in this case it is far from certain that such issues were considered and decided upon by the court. Rather, the district court—especially in light of its finding that no violation of the new permit has occurred—appears to have erroneously presumed irreparable harm from the mere fact of statutory violation, thus improperly focusing on the integrity of the permit process rather than the integrity of the Nation's waters. We will remand the case to the district court, therefore, for a proper determination of whether an injunction should issue. However, we do recognize, and so advise the district court on remand, that in applying the traditional equitable standard: "Environmental injury, by its nature, can seldom be adequately remedied by money damages and is often permanent or at least of long duration, *i.e.* irreparable. If such injury is sufficiently likely, therefore, the balance of harms will usually favor the issuance of an injunction to protect the environment." *Amoco,* 480 U.S. at 545, 107 S.Ct. at 1404.

* * *

In summary, we find that the district court erred in issuing a permanent injunction against Texaco without first applying the traditional equitable standard as to when such an order is appropriate. Thus, we will vacate the portion of the district court's order enjoining Texaco not to violate its new NPDES permit and remand this case to the district court to apply the proper standard. Each party to bear its own costs.

Note

1. Professor Plater has written a critique of *Weinberger v. Romero–Barcelo,* suggesting that it is the first case in which the Court has exercised its equitable discretion so as to "override the specific prohibitions of a statute." Plater, Statutory Violations and Equitable Discretion, 70 Calif.L.Rev. 524, 594 (1982). *See also* Comment, Preliminary Injunctive Relief Under the Federal Water Pollution Control Act, 60 Chi.–Kent L.Rev. 123 (1984); Note, 3 Va.J.Nat.Resources L. 347 (1984). Another commentator, in an effort to

restrict the impact of the *Weinberger* decision, distinguishes between four different types of statutory injunctions:

"A typology of statutory injunctions, demonstrating the distinctive relations between different injunctive provisions and underlying legal duties, will serve to obviate some of the confusion. The critical factors in determining the nature of a statutory injunction are its relationship to a defendant's underlying legal duty and the nature of that duty. Based on this analysis, injunctions can be divided into four groups.

"1. *The Enforcement Injunction.* This category involves direct enforcement of an absolute legal duty. In these cases, the defendant is under a legal duty, but refuses to carry out actions that a law-abiding citizen would perform voluntarily. The purpose of the injunction is to force the defendant to do that which the defendant ought to have done without legal compulsion. *TVA v. Hill* is a clear example of this type of injunction. Since the purpose of the injunction is simply to put the defendant in the same position as the law-abiding citizen, balancing the equities is inappropriate. Asking a court to balance the virtues of obedience to the law against the benefits of violating the law is wholly inappropriate.

"2. *The Compliance Injunction.* This category involves cases like *Weinberger,* in which the defendant is in breach of a qualified duty. Once again, the purpose of the injunction is to force the defendant to act as law-abiding citizens voluntarily do, but here the duty does not amount to immediate compliance. Congress did not intend that citizens shut plants as a routine method of meeting permit deadlines. For the same reason, Congress did not expect courts to make this a routine remedy. As before, the remedy tracks the underlying legal duty. In this category, however, there is more room for consideration of burden in defining the underlying duty itself.

"3. *The Ancillary Injunction.* In the preceding two categories, the hypothetical defendant was in breach of a legal duty that was the basis of the injunction. Often, however, the defendant is in breach of a procedural duty. Obviously, the court can order the defendant to apply for a permit, issue an environmental impact statement or comply with some other procedure. The question is the extent to which a court should also enjoin the activity to which the procedure relates. For example, Congress requires agencies engaging in major federal actions with substantial environmental impacts to issue environmental impact statements. The relevant statute does not, however, expressly create a legal duty to refrain from implementing a project until the impact statement is prepared. But it would be futile for a court simply to issue an order to prepare an impact statement while allowing the underlying federal action to proceed. In *Weinberger,* the Navy was not under a direct duty to refrain from discharges while its permit application was pending. Nevertheless, if those discharges had been causing ecological harm, allowing the activity to continue until the permit proceeding had been completed would have undermined the function of the permit process.

* * *

"4. *The Freestanding Injunction.* In each of the previous categories, the injunction was used as a means of enforcing, either directly or indirectly, an underlying statutory duty. Congress sometimes provides, however, for an injunctive proceeding without creating any separate statutory duties to be enforced in the proceeding, as in the emergency provision under the Clean Water Act. Three possible interpretations of such provisions are possible. First, Congress may simply intend that the provision create a federal forum in which state law will be applied. Second, Congress's aim might be that federal courts create a body of federal common law governing these disputes. Third, such provisions may signify that Congress intends injunctive relief to be mandatory once statutory threshold requirements are met. Environmental emergency provisions arguably are intended to trigger creation of a federal common law, but they actually seem to come closer to the mandatory injunction category. The discretion a court has in issuing emergency injunctions relates more to fashioning the most effective form of relief than to balancing the public health against hardship to the defendant.

"One of the reasons for the considerable confusion in the area of statutory injunctions seems to have been a failure to distinguish clearly between these various varieties of statutory injunction. While the typology given here certainly will not resolve all disputes about statutory injunctions, it may provide a clearer framework for settling these disputes."

Farber, Equitable Discretion, Legal Duties, and Environmental Injunctions, 45 U.Pitt.L.Rev. 513, 538–42 (1984).*

2. The application of traditional equitable conditions precedent to injunctive relief will depend on numerous variables: the language and legislative history of the statute in question; whether the injunctive relief being sought is temporary or permanent; and, if an administrative proceeding is involved, its nature and setting. *Compare* Federal Trade Comm. v. Simeon Management Corp., 532 F.2d 708 (9th Cir.1976) (independent judicial examination of the equities required as a condition precedent to granting a temporary injunction against deceptive trade practices under section 53 of the Federal Trade Commission Act) *with* Federal Trade Comm. v. National Comm. on Egg Nutrition, 517 F.2d 485 (7th Cir.1975) (Congress did not intend an independent judicial weighing of the equities under section 53 of the Act). For a thorough consideration of how state courts deal with these issues, *see* Town of Sherberne v. Carpenter, *supra* p. 529.

SECTION 3. INJUNCTIONS AS A LAW ENFORCEMENT TOOL: ENJOINING CRIME AND OTHER WRONGS

GOOSE v. COMMONWEALTH EX REL. DUMMIT, ATTORNEY GENERAL

Court of Appeals of Kentucky, 1947.
305 Ky. 644, 205 S.W.2d 326.

STANLEY, COMMISSIONER. For a number of years a gambling establishment and saloon, called the "Sycamore Cafe," was conducted at 238–240 Central Avenue, in Louisville. The premises are located in an industrial and residential district in the southern part of the city, and across the street from a Railroad Y.M.C.A.

The property is owned by Roscoe Goose. A saloon license was held by J.W. Goose, but it appears a renewal was lately denied. A soft drink and restaurant license was in the name of Luther Goose. They are brothers and were joint proprietors.

Numerous raids by police officers revealed extensive taking of bets on horse races and other forms of gambling with cards, dice and other devices. During the past five years, J. William Goose and Luther Goose were arrested a number of times on charges of suffering gaming on the premises, gambling, disorderly conduct, malicious assault and other offenses. The records show that all of these charges were "filed away" in court, although on a few occasions the defendants paid petty fines for disorderly conduct. Numerous others were arrested at the same place for the same offenses. Most of them were employees conducting the operations, or stooges to "take the rap." * * * It is a sordid record of wide open, flagrant violations of the laws of the state, both felonies and misdemeanors, particularly maintaining premises on which "persons assemble to wager money or anything of value on the result of any horse race." KRS 436.440. In short, there is portrayed a "common gambling house," conducted by common and professional gamblers.

These men confess a general course of criminality at this place. They have in some way been able to set the law at naught and to continue their criminal project. The processes of the criminal courts seem to have broken down in dealing with this place and these men. At least, they have failed to accomplish their primary purposes of protecting society, reforming the wayward and preventing future offenses of the same kind. As a consequence, the Commonwealth has invoked the processes of the court of equity and obtained an injunction against the named persons to abate their use of the property for the unlawful purposes.

* * *

Courts of equity will not ordinarily enjoin the commission of a crime. The statutes themselves are standing injunctions. But the mere fact that the act constituting a nuisance is also a crime does not hinder the use of the civil processes to procure its abatement where the use of property is a part. There may also be a remedy by indictment and upon conviction an abatement by order of the criminal court where the nuisance may be of a continuing character. This remedy is sometimes confused with the other. But there is a clear distinction between enjoining an individual from committing a crime and enjoining him from using his or another's property so as to make it a nuisance to others, and between a proceeding in equity to abate a nuisance and a criminal prosecution to punish the offender for maintaining it. * * *

It is an historic function of courts of equity to grant preventative as well as remedial relief. Irreparable injury to property rights is perhaps the most common of causes for injunctive relief. Surely irreparable injury to public morals and individual character is of as grave concern as mere loss of dollars and cents. The ground of the jurisdiction is the ability of the chancellor to give a more complete and perfect remedy by a perpetual injunction. It is a weapon from the arsenal of equity to be used to protect Society—to meet the social need that continuation of the offenses at a given place shall be repressed. This abatement by injunction, independent of the criminal prosecution, is supported by ancient precedents and modern instances.

Though aimed at the use of specific property, the injunction operates upon the person of those who shall so use it and may be executed by process of contempt. And no subterfuge will be tolerated.

The principal ground upon which the appellants rely for a reversal of the judgment is thus stated:

> "In an action of this character, it is necessary for the Commonwealth to prove that gaming operations were conducted on the premises, but in addition thereto, before injunctive relief can be procured, it is necessary for the Commonwealth to establish other facts showing that the peace and quiet or morals of the community are injured as a result thereof; that dissolute or criminal characters frequent the premises; that residents are forced to come in contact with a lower strata of society or that the health or morals of the public generally are suffering by reason of the actions of appellants."

In short, the contention seems to be that so long as one operates a "den of iniquity," or other demoralizing business in a quiet, peaceful and gentle way he is beyond the pale of the law and should be let alone. This idea may have had its origin in the long ago when the common law of England did not regard ordinary gambling as an offense per se. 24 Am.Jur., Gaming and Prize Contests, secs. 11, 12, 38. It was once regarded in this state that buying of pools on horse races was not within the statute which fixed a penalty against suffering any game on premises at which money was bet. This is not the law now. In these later days all forms of gambling and the promotion thereof are condemned by the statutes (KRS 436.190 to 436.530) except betting through parimutuel machines at race courses under license by the state. KRS 436.480. But at common law a common gambling house was regarded as a common nuisance because of its tendencies to bring together disorderly persons, promote immorality and lead to breaches of the peace.

Stronger and stronger has become the disposition of the legislatures and the courts to extend the law of nuisances to every sort of gambling irrespective of its connection with other offenses, or of its potentiality of spawning them, or of other conditions which brought it within the classification of a nuisance in former days. It long ago ceased to be essential to injunctive redress that the gambling should be in view of the public or that the public be disturbed by noise therefrom. Nor is it requisite to show that dissolute or criminal characters frequent the premises or that respectable citizens have been "forced to come in contact with a lower strata of society", as appellants submit. * * *

Neither principle nor precedent supports the absolution claimed by these defendants. If the moral fiber of its manhood and womanhood is not a state concern, we may ask, what is? The court does not falter for an answer.

The argument of the appellants is not new. It was put to this court nearly forty years ago and deliberately and clearly answered. We did not then and do not now perceive that the arm of justice is too short to protect the people from a vicious enterprise of this sort—from anything which tends to corrupt or destroy their morals and character. * * *

* * *

We have given this case, and the companion cases, the careful consideration which the appellants request and regarded the consequences of affirmance which they suggest, namely, that "Courts of equity will become a cesspool for the trial of similar actions if appellees' contentions are upheld." Not "cesspools" but "filters."

The judgment is affirmed.

STATE v. HATFIELD, 183 Neb. 157, 158 N.W.2d 612 (1968). Suit was filed by a deputy county attorney to enjoin, as a public nuisance, the operation of a cafe in the city of Omaha, known as the "Seventh Ward Improvement Club", which purportedly served as "a gathering place for hoodlums, prostitutes, gamblers, and other disorderly persons." The trial court denied the injunction and this denial was reversed on appeal notwithstanding the apparent absence of statutory authority. The Nebraska Supreme Court said: "The judgment of the district court is reversed and the cause remanded with directions to enter a judgment in favor of the relator. We do not at this time determine the extent of the relief to be granted, but leave that to the sound discretion of the district court.

"The jurisdiction of an equity court to abate a public nuisance exists independent of statute; and it is within the power of the court to do whatever is reasonably necessary to abate the nuisance. State ex rel. Wilcox v. Ryder, 126 Minn. 95, 147 N.W. 953, 5 A.L.R. 1449; State ex rel. Haugan v. Denis, 40 S.D. 219, 167 N.W. 151; State ex rel. Davenport v. Henry (Mo.App.), 270 S.W.2d 88. This includes the power to enjoin the use of the premises for any purpose for a reasonable period of time." *

Note

Contrast the foregoing decisions with the language of Marsland v. Pang, 5 Hawaii App. 463, 701 P.2d 175 (1985), in which the court affirmed the dismissal of an action by a prosecutor to enjoin the operation of a gambling operation as a public nuisance:

> "At common law courts of equity were without authority or jurisdiction to enjoin criminal acts solely on the basis of their criminality. 5 Moore's Federal Practice ¶ 38.24[3] (2d ed. 1984); IV J. Pomeroy, *A Treatise on Equity Jurisprudence*, § 1347 (5th ed. 1941); T. Spelling and J. Lewis, *A Treatise on the Law Governing Injunctions,* § 10 (1926) (hereinafter Spelling and Lewis); Annot., 40 A.L.R. 1145 (1926); 42 Am.Jur.2d

* For a similar holding, see State ex rel. Spire v. Strawberries, Inc., 239 Neb. 1, 473 N.W.2d 428 (1991).

Injunctions § 157 (1969); 58 Am.Jur.2d *Nuisances* § 143 (1971). Equity courts, even now, will not exercise their powers for the purpose of enforcing the criminal laws by restraining criminal acts. Annot., 40 A.L.R., *supra.* However, the common law has always provided a remedy for a nuisance, either by way of an action for damages or an equitable action to restrain the continuance of the wrong, or both, 58 Am.Jur.2d, *supra,* §§ 98, 143, and where equity would otherwise have jurisdiction to enjoin certain conduct, the fact that the legislature has made such conduct a crime does not affect that jurisdiction. 42 Am.Jur.2d, *supra,* §§ 157, 160.

"The historical basis of equity jurisdiction to grant injunctions is the protection of property rights. Spelling and Lewis, *supra,* § 7. Since the inception of that principle, however, equity jurisdiction has expanded to allow issuance of an injunction where there are other appropriate circumstances besides injury to a specific property right. * * *

"Absent the appropriate circumstances as described above, equity courts nonetheless have authority to enjoin acts constituting a nuisance. * * * The accepted definition of nuisance and public nuisance is set forth in Littleton v. State of Hawaii, 66 Haw. 55, 656 P.2d 1336 (1982), as follows:

> A nuisance has been variously defined to mean "that which unlawfully annoys or does damage to another, anything that works hurt, inconvenience, or damage, anything which annoys or disturbs one in the free use, possession, or enjoyment of his property or which renders its ordinary use or physical occupation uncomfortable, and anything wrongfully done or permitted which injures or annoys another in the enjoyment of his legal rights." 58 Am.Jur.2d *Nuisances* § 1 at 555 (1971). As to what constitutes a public nuisance within the meaning of HRS § 46–12, we consider the following statement of the Kansas court to be generally applicable:
>
> > A nuisance, to be a public nuisance, must be in a public place, or where the public frequently congregate, or where members of the public are likely to come within the range of its influence; for, if the act or use of property be in a remote and unfrequented locality, it will not, unless malum in se, be a public nuisance. (citation omitted) * * * If the nuisance affects a place where the public has a legal right to go, and where the members thereof frequently congregate, or where they are likely to come within its influence, it is a public nuisance. [City of Burlington v. Stockwell, 5 Kan.App. 569, 573, 574, 47 P. 988, 989–90 (1897).]

Littleton, supra, at 67, 656 P.2d at 1345.

"However,

'The suppression of nuisances injurious to the public health or morality is among the most important duties of government. The state, in the exercise of its police power, has authority to abate nuisances, and under this power, and subject to constitutional limitations, the legislature has authority to declare what shall be deemed nuisances and to provide for their suppression. *Since nuisance is a term which does not have a fixed content, either at common law or at the present time, compelling reasons of policy require that the responsibility for establishing those standards of*

> *public morality, the violation of which is to constitute nuisances within equity jurisdiction, be left to the legislature.'*

58 Am.Jur.2d, *supra,* § 14 (footnotes omitted) (emphasis added).

"The authority of the legislature adverted to above was deferred to by the California supreme court in People v. Lim, 18 Cal.2d 872, 118 P.2d 472 (1941), where it was said:

> In [the field of nuisances] where the meaning of terms is so vague and uncertain it is a proper function of the legislature to define those breaches of public policy which are to be considered public nuisances within the control of equity.

Id. at 880, 118 P.2d at 476. The California court also stated that it is not the province of the courts of equity to ordain for themselves the power to abate criminal acts by declaring their mere repetition or continuance a public nuisance where the legislature has not seen fit to do so and where the acts do not in fact constitute a public nuisance. *Id.*

"We agree with the California supreme court that absent a statute or valid ordinance declaring activities in violation of general concepts of public policy to be a nuisance or subject to abatement, equity courts generally are without jurisdiction to enjoin such activities unless they in fact constitute a nuisance. *Id.* at 877, 118 P.2d at 475; *see also* Kreling v. Superior Court of Los Angeles County, 18 Cal.2d 884, 118 P.2d 470 (1941); Schur v. Santa Monica, 47 Cal.2d 11, 300 P.2d 831 (1956).

* * *

NUISANCE ABATEMENT IN THIS JURISDICTION

"This jurisdiction has had from very early times until now numerous statutes providing for abatement of particular activities amounting to nuisances. Nevertheless, the supreme court, in Akwai v. Royal Ins. Co., 14 Haw. 533 (1902), held that under the statute authorizing the territorial board of health to abate nuisances, the board was not authorized to destroy that which was not a nuisance or make or declare that to be a nuisance which was not in fact a nuisance. It follows from *Akwai* that, to warrant an injunction where the nuisance is also a crime, there must be proof of what the law denominates a nuisance as distinguished from a mere crime.

* * *

"In the area of criminal law of this jurisdiction, "Keeping a Common Gambling House" was declared to be a "Common Nuisance" and a criminal offense from the time of the Penal Code in 1869, ch. XXXVI, § 1, until repealed in 1972 by the new penal code. Act 9, § 1, 1972 Haw.Sess.Laws 32, 140. Until repealed the prior law specifically authorized prosecution of the criminal offense and abatement of the common nuisance under HRS § 727–14 (1968). Since repeal of the common nuisance statutes, this jurisdiction has been without a general statutory authority for abatement of such nuisances as described therein. Nonetheless, we hold that the circuit courts in equity may enjoin such activities upon a showing that they in fact do constitute a nuisance. * * *

ABATEMENT OF GAMBLING UNDER HRS § 603–23 (1976)[23]

At the outset it should be noted that § 603–23 is a specific grant of power to the circuit courts. It does not confer authorization upon any of the public officers therein enumerated to seek an injunction. That authority must be found elsewhere. The question, here, is whether HRS § 603–23 allows the court to enjoin a public nuisance upon proper allegation in a suit that the prosecutor is authorized to bring. We hold that it does. However, in the instant case, the court correctly dismissed the counts it did under Rule 12(b), HRCP, for failure to state a claim.

A literal reading of § 603–23 leads one to conclude that the circuit courts may enjoin any criminal activity regardless of the kind and extent of injury inflicted or threatened. Such, however, would be in derogation of the common law adopted in this jurisdiction * * *. Courts should not find that the common law has been superseded in the area mentioned by a statute where it does not appear that such was the legislative purpose. State v. Taylor, 49 Haw. 624, 628–29, 425 P.2d 1014, 1018 (1967). Absent such apparent legislative purpose, the common law will be followed. Burns International Service, Inc. v. Department of Transportation, 66 Haw. 607, 611, 671 P.2d 446, 449 (1983). Moreover, in all cases of statutory construction the rule in this jurisdiction is that the primary duty of the court is to ascertain and implement the legislative intent of the statute, and the courts are not limited to the words of the statute. Kaiama v. Aguilar, 67 Haw. ___, 696 P.2d 839 (1985). We find that superseding the common law in the area of nuisance abatement was not the legislative purpose of HRS § 603–23 and the statute is merely declaratory of the common law. * * *

"We read the statute as a declaration by the legislature that, where there is a jurisdictional basis for equity to act to protect the private or public rights of our citizens from irreparable harm, the mere fact that the act complained of may also be subject to criminal penalties will not oust equity's jurisdiction. *In the absence of express legislative intent to forsake the common law rule regarding the limited jurisdiction of equity to interfere with enforcement of criminal laws, we will not do so. See Burns, supra.* Certainly the legislature could not in enacting § 603–23 have intended to deprive an individual of the panoply of rights accorded an accused in a criminal case, even where there was no factual basis for equity's intervention. We do not believe that the legislature intended to put equity courts in the business of enforcing criminal laws or to undermine the right of the accused to a jury trial and proof beyond a reasonable doubt.

"The prosecutor argues that maintaining a gambling house was a nuisance *per se* indictable at common law and abatable in equity. 38 Am.Jur.2d *Gambling* § 118 (1968). *See* Spelling and Lewis, *supra,* § 10. Research indicates, however, that in the majority of states in which gambling houses have been abated as nuisances, the action has been based upon specific statutes providing for such abatement. *See People v. Lim, supra.* As stated above, until 1972 keeping a gambling house was a criminal offense specifically de-

23. HRS § 603–23 reads as follows:

Injunction of violation of laws and ordinances. The circuit courts shall have power to enjoin or prohibit any violation of the laws of the State, or of the ordinances of the various counties, upon application of the attorney general, the director of the office of consumer protection, or the various county attorneys, corporation counsels, or prosecuting attorneys, even if a criminal penalty is provided for violation of the laws or ordinances. Nothing herein limits the powers elsewhere conferred on circuit courts.

clared to be a public nuisance per se and subject to abatement. The legislature not only repealed the statutory offense, but also the basis for abatement as a public nuisance per se. *Consequently, the keeping of a gambling house, which we will assume is the case here, can only be abated on the complaint of the properly authorized public official if it in fact is a public nuisance. See Akwai v. Royal Ins. Co., supra; People v. Lim, supra.*

"A further aspect of a public nuisance is that one may be created where an act or series of acts constitute an obstruction of public rights, or affect the rights enjoyed by citizens as part of the public. *See* 58 Am.Jur.2d, *supra,* § 8; *see also Littleton v. State, supra. There must be some interference with a public right.* A public right is one common to all members of the general public, and is collective in nature. Restatement (Second) of Torts § 821B comment g (1979). Additionally, in determining whether acts or conduct constitute a public nuisance, the location and surroundings are important and are to be considered with the other circumstances of the case. What is a public nuisance in one locality may not be so in another. 58 Am.Jur.2d, *supra,* § 36. *See Littleton v. State, supra.*

* * *

"We hold that in an action to abate activities allegedly constituting a public nuisance, the statutorily authorized public official is required to allege and prove facts constituting a public nuisance independent of the criminal nature of the activity being conducted. Thus, he or she must allege and prove that where conducted the activities constitute a public nuisance in fact. 58 Am.Jur. 2d, *supra,* §§ 8, 10.

"As stated above, the complaint is prolix and imprecise. It does clearly allege ongoing activities of a criminal nature. It also clearly alleges numerous arrests of the individuals named therein with resulting convictions and sentences which apparently have not curbed the activities of those individuals and others at the property in question. However, its thrust is against those activities as criminal activities and nuisances per se, not as public nuisances in fact.

"The complaint alleges that the activities complained of constitute a public, private or mixed nuisance, affecting a considerable number of persons, individually and jointly, by being 'injurious to the public morals and social well-being and fibre of the people of the State of Hawaii.' We perceive those allegations to really be conclusions as to the results of the alleged criminal activities. *See* 5 Wright and Miller, *supra,* § 1218. The law requires allegations sufficient to show a public nuisance in fact. 58 Am.Jur.2d, *supra,* § 172. *People v. Lim, supra.*

"We think the complaint in *People v. Lim, supra,* is illustrative of the basic pleading requirement in a public nuisance case. The action was one to enjoin a gambling house as a public nuisance and preceded the enactment of the California statute authorizing such actions. The complaint sought to use the aegis of the general California statute regarding nuisance abatement. The lower court sustained a demurrer to the complaint. Defendants argued on appeal that the allegations of the complaint merely presented conclusions framed in the language of the statute. The California supreme court held that while defendants were correct in their contention that particular allegations of fact were required, the allegations of the complaint,

> that the gambling house operated by defendants 'draws together great numbers of disorderly persons, disturbs the public peace, brings together idle persons and cultivates dissolute habits among them, creates traffic and fire hazards, and is thereby injurious to health, indecent and offensive to the senses and impairs the free enjoyment of life and property[,]'

were adequate as against a general demurrer.

"In the instant case, the affidavits attached to the complaint indicate that on two different occasions 300–400 people were observed on the premises. On other occasions, approximately 75 people were observed. The affidavits also indicate that on one occasion, twenty motor vehicles were parked on the shoulder of the road and one hundred vehicles on the premises.

"The record shows that Tanaka's consists of five acres of land in Waianae. There is nothing in the complaint to indicate that the crowds, the traffic, or the activities constitute public nuisances as defined above."

STATE v. RED OWL STORES, INC.

Supreme Court of Minnesota, 1958.
253 Minn. 236, 92 N.W.2d 103.

MURPHY, JUSTICE. * * * The complaints of the State of Minnesota seek to restrain the defendant corporations and certain of their officers from the alleged violation of certain provisions of M.S.A. c. 151 relating to the subject of pharmacy. * * * The complaint against the Red Owl Stores, Inc., alleges that it operates a large number of retail food markets; that it is not registered or licensed with the Minnesota Board of Pharmacy to engage in selling at wholesale or at retail drugs and medicines; that it has been unlawfully selling and distributing various "drugs, medicines, chemicals and poisons" in the State of Minnesota, among them being Alka–Seltzer, Anacin, Bromo Seltzer, Bufferin, Pepto–Bismol, Pinex, Murine, Castoria, Ex–Lax, Feen-a-mint, Sal Hepatica, and Vick's Va–Tro–Nol; that such sales are in violation of §§ 151.15 and 151.25. The complaint further alleges that such sales are being made in widespread locations over the State of Minnesota and also:

> "* * * That to attempt to stop each of such sales would require the expenditure of large sums of money by the State of Minnesota, would require the commencement of a great multiplicity of actions throughout the State and would impose a great burden upon the Courts of this State, all without successfully preventing the continued violation of the provisions of the Pharmacy Law and sections 151.15 and 151.25 thereof."

The complaint further alleges that the conduct of the defendants endangers the public health of the people of Minnesota and renders ineffectual the laws of the state for the protection of public health and asks that the defendant be permanently enjoined and restrained from selling at wholesale or retail drugs, medicines, etc., in violation of the section of the statute quoted, including the drugs named herein.

* * *

The trial court held that under § 151.29 violation of the Pharmacy Act was a misdemeanor and that it was the duty of the city attorney of Minneapolis, pursuant to § 151.30, to prosecute the alleged violations referred to in the complaint. The court further held that the remedy provided by criminal prosecution under § 151.29 is exclusive; that the legislature has not authorized injunctive relief to enforce the provisions of the Pharmacy Act; that no attempt has been made by the state to enforce the act by criminal prosecution; and that there is no evidence to prove that a multiplicity of actions would result from enforcement by criminal prosecution. The court concluded that a single prosecution would reach exactly the same number of persons and stores as might be enjoined in this proceeding. The court also found that the defendants are entitled to a trial by jury as to the alleged violations of the provisions of the Pharmacy Act and that these proceedings which seek injunctive relief circumvent the requirements of law and deny to the defendants a trial by which they are entitled to have proof of guilt established beyond a reasonable doubt.

* * *

In support of their contention that the provisions for prosecution of the misdemeanor, §§ 151.29 and 151.30, represent the exclusive remedy reserved to the state for enforcement, the defendants cite numerous statutory provisions to the effect that, where the legislature has intended that equity should lend its aid in support of criminal law, express provision to that effect has been included in the statute. They point out that courts are reluctant to enforce criminal laws by injunction for the reason that "criminal equity" deprives the defendant of a jury trial and substitutes for the definite penalties fixed by the legislature whatever punishment for contempt a particular court may see fit to exact. * * *

* * *

The state relies on Town of Linden v. Fischer, 154 Minn. 354, 357, 191 N.W. 901, 902, involving an action to enjoin an unlicensed dancehall, in which case we stated that, although equity will not ordinarily restrain the commission of a crime by injunction, it will, nevertheless, "interpose its authority in those cases where the threatened act or conduct of the party will amount to a continuing public nuisance as well as a crime. Such would be the result of repeated violations of the by-law in question. It prohibits public dances without a license, and a violation thereof would constitute a crime; at the same time amounting to a continuous public nuisance." The court observed that the punishment imposed under the circumstances would be ineffective and have no deterrent effect, "while the strong arm of equity would result in the complete suppression of the evil sought to be avoided." * * *

From an examination of the authorities it may be said that, where the acts complained of are violations of the criminal law the courts of equity will not on that ground alone interfere by injunction to prevent their commission, since they will not exercise their preventive power for the purpose of enforcing criminal laws by restraining criminal acts. However, courts of equity will interfere by injunction to restrain acts amounting to a public nuisance if they affect public rights or privileges or endanger public health, regardless of whether such acts are denounced as crimes. * * *

It is also apparent that the exercise of the court's equity jurisdiction to grant injunctive relief must depend upon the facts in each particular case. The contending parties in the case before us view the issues from entirely different aspects. To the defendants this action is in essence a criminal prosecution instituted under the guise of an action in equity. The state on the other hand contends that this is a civil action to enforce a public health measure and that the criminal aspect is incidental.

It seems to us that the case before us involves something more than the prosecution of a misdemeanor. It involves the question of whether, under circumstances where the state is without an adequate remedy at law to enforce a measure adopted in the interest of public health, equity jurisdiction is suspended, merely because the measure in question makes no provision for an injunction. On the basis of the record before us, there are two parts to this question: (1) Does the misdemeanor provision of the act fail to provide the state with an adequate remedy at law? (2) Do the acts of the defendants constitute a danger to the public health?

* * *

On the basis of this evidence the trial court was of the view that one prosecution in the city of Minneapolis would accomplish the same result as an injunction. We do not think the record warrants any such conclusion. Aside from the admitted policy of defendant Red Owl to contest enforcement wherever it is instituted, the [defendant] * * * in oral argument before this court, gives us to understand that rather than have a decision which would resolve the questions of law raised by the pleadings they insist upon a jury trial requiring proof beyond a reasonable doubt as to each particular violation. While courts jealously protect the constitutional rights of those charged with criminal offenses, respect for due process does not require that the courts in every instance should ignore other considerations merely because the act complained of may constitute a misdemeanor. The nuisance aspect of the act sought to be enjoined may be considered, as well as its social consequences. Here we are dealing not with an individual charged with an isolated offense but with an alleged widespread violation of a misdemeanor statute which penalizes breach of a law enacted to protect the public health. It should be recognized that for the state to undertake to prosecute each violation in face of resistance over a great area of the state would in effect set at nought the effective and uniform enforcement of the act.

While it is true that the legislature has not provided for injunctive relief, that fact should not place the pharmaceutical board in a position where, in the face of organized resistance, it must rely on one prosecution at a time to accomplish enforcement. We think that under the circumstances it was the duty of the attorney general as an agent of the state to institute injunctive proceedings to accomplish that purpose.

* * *

* * * The statute here was not passed for the purpose of punishing crime; it was primarily enacted for the protection of the public health and welfare, and the criminal sanction included in the act was intended as a deterrent for the purpose of admonishing those engaged in the sale of drugs that they must comply with the terms of the statute and regulations. Under the circumstances the pharmaceutical board could make little progress toward enforcing the act if it was limited to prosecutions to recover the small penalties provided. Upon the record we are satisfied that the state's evidence is sufficient to establish, without evidence to the contrary, that the remedy at law is inadequate.

While the record is not as adequate as it might be with reference to danger to the public health, that defect is not entirely the fault of the state. The state attempted to introduce evidence as to the manner of the sale of drugs by the self-service method in grocery stores and supermarkets. The trial court sustained an objection to this line of evidence, taking the view that the manner of sale had no bearing on the question of injury to the public health and welfare. We think that the court unduly restricted the state in this respect.

* * *

But, even conceding that the state has not on the record established evidence of *specific* harm to the public, we are of the view that the state has a prima facie case, in view of the public policy in our state that the uncontrolled sale of drugs and medicines is inimical to public health.

* * *

Reversed and new trial granted.*

Notes

1. While no precise definition of "public nuisance" is possible, numerous courts have characterized it as the "doing of or the failure to do something that injuriously affects the safety, health, or morals of the public, or works some substantial annoyance, inconvenience or injury to the public generally." United States v. County Board of Arlington County, 487 F.Supp. 137, 143 (E.D.Va. 1979). Indeed, some courts take the position that "where a statute is openly, publicly, repeatedly, continuously, persistently, and intentionally violated a public nuisance is created." State *ex rel.* Turner v. United Buckingham Freight Lines, Inc., 211 N.W.2d 288 (Iowa 1973) (enjoining defendant from future violations of statute regulating truck length and weight). It would be a mistake, however, to view the public nuisance concept as a substitute for the criminal law. As much of the material in this section illustrates, injunctive relief in this context must not only satisfy a variety of equitable conditions precedent, but, in many instances, must surmount significant constitutional,

* This case is discussed in Note, 25 Brook. L.Rev. 340 (1959); Note, 8 Buff.L.Rev. 298 (1959); Note, 28 Ford.L.Rev. 161 (1959).

At the retrial, the trial court found that the products in question were proprietary medicines and not within the prohibitions of the Pharmacy Act. It accordingly denied an injunction. On appeal, the supreme court determined that the preparations were covered by the Act, but held that injunctive relief would not be granted because sale of these drugs in the defendant's stores was not a nuisance or danger to the public health. *See* State v. Red Owl Stores, Inc., 262 Minn. 31, 115 N.W.2d 643 (1962).

legislative and policy hurdles as well. For further analysis of these limitations on the public nuisance concept, see Note, 40 Mo.L.Rev. 145 (1975).

2. Courts have held that the habitual practice of charging usurious interest rates to necessitous borrowers can constitute a public nuisance subject to abatement by injunction. *See, e.g.,* Larson v. State of Alabama *ex rel.* Patterson, Attorney General, 266 Ala. 589, 97 So.2d 776 (1957); State *ex rel.* Beck v. Basham, 146 Kan. 181, 70 P.2d 24 (1937). *Compare* Nash v. State of Alabama *ex rel.* Atty. Gen., 271 Ala. 173, 123 So.2d 24 (1960) (borrowers not necessitous; injunction improper). *See generally* Annot., 83 A.L.R.2d 848 (1960). The public nuisance doctrine has been extended in one case to allow injunctive relief against usurious revolving charge accounts, notwithstanding the availability of severe criminal penalties or the apparent absence of necessitous borrowers. *See* State v. J.C. Penney Co., 48 Wis.2d 125, 179 N.W.2d 641 (1970).

3. The public nuisance concept is also often used to enjoin the unauthorized practice of a profession. *See* Arizona State Bd. of Dental Examiners v. Hyder, 114 Ariz. 544, 562 P.2d 717 (1977) (unauthorized practice of dentistry); People *ex rel.* Bennett v. Laman, 277 N.Y. 368, 14 N.E.2d 439 (1938) (practicing medicine without a license); The Florida Bar v. Borges–Caignet, 321 So.2d 550 (Fla.1975) (unauthorized practice of law); State *ex rel.* Meyer v. Weiner, 190 Neb. 30, 205 N.W.2d 649 (1973) (unlicensed real estate practices); State Board of Medical Examiners v. Olson, 295 Minn. 379, 206 N.W.2d 12 (1973) (unauthorized practice of medicine); Dempsey v. Chicago Title Ins. Co., 10 Ohio App.3d 281, 462 N.E.2d 184 (1983) (unlawful practice of surveying). For a rejection of the public nuisance doctrine in this setting, see Massachusetts Society of Optometrists v. Waddick, 340 Mass. 581, 165 N.E.2d 394, 90 A.L.R.2d 1 (1960). *Cf.* State *ex rel.* St. Bd. of Ex. Op. v. Kuhwald, 372 A.2d 214 (Del.Ch.1977) (optometry).

4. Res judicata and collateral estoppel problems are raised when injunctive relief is sought by governmental authorities after a not guilty finding or other disposition favorable to the defendant has been entered in a criminal prosecution. As one court has stated, "the fact that a criminal prosecution fails does not mean that an injunction in the civil courts may not be applied for, even where the criminal charge is based on the same alleged violation as is the petition for injunction." City of New Orleans v. Lafon, 61 So.2d 270 (La.App. 1952). This seems to represent the majority approach. For similar holdings, see Blackmon v. Richmond County, 224 Ga. 387, 162 S.E.2d 436 (1968); City of Girard v. Girard Egg Corp., 87 Ill.App.2d 74, 230 N.E.2d 294 (1967); Town of Natick v. Sostilio, 358 Mass. 342, 264 N.E.2d 664 (1970). Res judicata and collateral estoppel concepts normally are inapplicable because the burden of proof is usually heavier on the prosecution in a criminal case and, thus, it is difficult to identify what was decided in the criminal action. *See also* City of Chicago v. Provus, 115 Ill.App.2d 176, 253 N.E.2d 182 (1969) (estoppel by verdict held applicable to prevent a subsequent injunction action because the ordinance prosecution was considered civil and not criminal).

A related argument is that to permit the injunction action after a prior not guilty determination constitutes unconstitutional double jeopardy because, if a defendant violates the injunction, he or she could then be charged with contempt and be punished for the same offense that was the basis for the criminal acquittal. Normally this contention will fail because the criminal and the injunction proceedings are considered separate offenses. *See, e.g.,* City of New Orleans v. Lafon, 61 So.2d 270 (La.App.1952).

* * *

CITY OF CHICAGO v. FESTIVAL THEATRE CORP.

Supreme Court of Illinois, 1982.
91 Ill.2d 295, 63 Ill.Dec. 421, 438 N.E.2d 159.

WARD, JUSTICE:

This appeal concerns the propriety of a permanent injunction issued by the circuit court of Cook County, by which the court restrained the Festival Theatre Corporation and the theater manager, Paul Liang, from presenting obscene live exhibitions. The appellate court held that issuance of the injunction violated the first amendment to the United States Constitution (U.S. Const., amend. I). (88 Ill.App.3d 216, 43 Ill.Dec. 341, 410 N.E.2d 341.) * * *

The plaintiff, the city of Chicago, filed a complaint for injunctive relief on August 29, 1978. The complaint alleged that the defendants, Festival Theatre Corporation and Liang, on three occasions presented exhibitions that consisted of live sex acts in violation of the criminal obscenity statute (Ill.Rev.Stat.1977, ch. 38, par. 11–20). The city alleged that the performances were harmful to its citizens, and that it had no adequate remedy at law. * * *

The court found that the performances were a public nuisance. The injunction stated:

> "The Court Doth Find: That the live stage performance, as performed at the Festival Theater, 3912 N. Sheridan Road, Chicago, Illinois, is a public nuisance.
>
> Therefore, it is Hereby Ordered that defendants, Festival Theater Corporation and Paul N. Liang, their employees, agents and representatives, are hereby permanently enjoined and restrained, until further order of Court, from performing or permitting the performance of lewd acts of live persons, in violation of applicable City Ordinances and State Statutes, at 3912 N. Sheridan Road, Chicago, Illinois, for the entertainment, sexual arousal, or viewing by and of members of the public. * * *"

The appellate court considered that the city of Chicago had demonstrated that it had no adequate legal remedy. Further, the court recognized that the concept of common law nuisance enabled a court to exercise its equity powers to abate a use of premises harmful to public morals. The court held, however, that the concept of a common law public nuisance was so vague that use of it against obscenity "transgresses the constitutional boundaries * * * which provide that conduct regulated as obscenity must be specifically defined." 88 Ill.App.3d 216, 230, 43 Ill.Dec. 341, 410 N.E.2d 341.

* * *

We * * * hold * * * that obscene stage shows may be enjoined as common law public nuisances.

[E]quitable jurisdiction to abate public nuisances is said to be of "ancient origin," and it exists even where not conferred by statute, where the offender is amenable to the criminal law, and where no property rights are involved. Too, in a common law action, the extent of the concept of public nuisance is not limited to those activities the legislature has declared public nuisances.

A theater presenting obscene performances fits within the common law concept of public nuisance. This court in City of Chicago v. Shaynin (1913), 258 Ill. 69, 72, 101 N.E. 224, stated:

> "Public nuisances, strictly speaking, are such as result from the violation of public rights. Of this class are those intangible injuries that result from the immoral, indecent and unlawful acts of parties that become nuisances by reason of their deleterious influence upon the morals or well being of society. * * * 'A public exhibition of any kind that tends to the corruption of morals, to a disturbance of the peace or of the general good order and welfare of society is a public nuisance. Under this head are included * * * any and all exhibitions the natural tendency of which is to pander to vicious tastes and to draw together the vicious and disorderly members of society.' [1 H. Wood, The Law of Nuisances sec. 68 (3d ed. 1893)] [citations]."

In Stevens v. Morenous (1912), 169 Ill.App. 282, 283, the court reviewed a decree enjoining a stage show alleged to be "of a comic, frivolous and unsavory character * * *." While the court concluded that it was error to have enjoined the show, which did not appear to be obscene or immoral, the court recognized that theaters do become common law nuisances "when they are used for the exhibition of immoral and vicious plays * * *." (169 Ill.App. 282, 285.) * * *

Similarly, because brothels tend to attract lewd persons, disturb the peace and contribute to immorality, they have long been held to be public nuisances *per se* at common law. * * * Due to the similarity between the activities of a brothel and those of a live obscene performance, the court in Commissioner v. Sidne Enterprises, Inc. (1977), 90 Misc.2d 386, 394 N.Y.S.2d 777, held that an establishment offering obscene live nude entertainment was a common law public nuisance.

The appellate court here held, as we have noted, that the concept of public nuisance included obscene stage shows. The defendant does not challenge that holding. The court considered nevertheless that such shows could not constitutionally be enjoined as common law nuisances. The court pointed out that theatrical performances involving nudity do enjoy first amendment protection. * * * The court recognized that obscenity is not expression protected by the first amendment and, therefore, may be regulated. * * * Too, the court acknowledged that civil injunction procedures have been held to be permissible means for regulating obscenity. * * *

The constitutional infirmity in the injunctive procedure, the court concluded, lies in the vagueness of the concept of common law nuisance. State laws regulating obscenity must specifically define the proscribed activity. The Supreme Court in Miller v. California (1973), 413 U.S. 15, 23–25, 93 S.Ct. 2607, 2614–15, 37 L.Ed.2d 419, 430–31, stated:

> "State statutes designed to regulate obscene materials must be carefully limited. [Citation.] As a result, we now confine the permissible scope of such regulation to works which depict or describe sexual conduct. That conduct must be specifically defined by the applicable state law, as written or authoritatively construed. A state offense must also be limited to works which, taken as a whole, appeal to the prurient interest in sex, which portray sexual conduct in a patently offensive way, and which, taken as a whole, do not have serious literary, artistic, political, or scientific value.
>
> "The basic guidelines for the trier of fact must be: (a) whether 'the average person, applying contemporary community standards' would find that the work, taken as a whole, appeals to the prurient interest [citation]; (b) whether the work depicts or describes, in a patently offensive way, sexual conduct specifically defined by the applicable state law; and (c) whether the work, taken as a whole, lacks serious literary, artistic, political, or scientific value. * * * If a state law that regulates obscene material is thus limited, as written or construed, the First Amendment values applicable to the States through the Fourteenth Amendment are adequately protected by the ultimate power of appellate courts to conduct an independent review of constitutional claims when necessary."

The appellate court considered that the concept of public nuisance at common law was too vague to satisfy the requirements stated in *Miller.*

The concept of common law public nuisance does elude precise definition. * * *

The vagueness difficulty, however, may be corrected by restricting the reach of the common law nuisance action to the definition of obscenity in our criminal obscenity statute (Ill.Rev.Stat.1977, ch. 38, par. 11–20(b)). The Supreme Court in *Miller,* in the portion we have quoted above, said that a State law regulating obscenity that is not framed according to the *Miller* definition of obscenity may still be constitutional if it is construed as being limited to the *Miller* guidelines. Courts have resolved problems of vagueness in public nuisance statutes by such a construction. (*E.g.,* People *ex rel.* Busch v. Projection Room Theatre (1976), 17 Cal.3d 42, 56, 500 P.2d 600, 608, 130 Cal.Rptr. 328, 336, cert. denied (1976), 429 U.S. 922, 97 S.Ct. 320, 50 L.Ed.2d 289 (vagueness in public nuisance definition of "indecent, or offensive to the senses" cured by construction in accordance with *Miller* obscenity standard); General Corp. v. State *ex rel.* Sweeton (1975), 294 Ala. 657, 663–64, 320 So.2d 668, 673–74, cert. denied (1976), 425 U.S. 904, 96 S.Ct. 1494, 47 L.Ed.2d 753 (vagueness in statute that, as declaratory of the common law, made "places where lewdness" is conducted public nuisances was overcome by judicial construction in accordance with the constitutional test of obscenity).) Similarly, this court has upheld the constitutionality of our criminal obscenity statute by construing it to be limited to the *Miller* standard. * * * Accordingly, in determining whether a performance is a common law public nuisance because of offense to public morality, courts are to employ the definition of obscenity in our criminal obscenity statute (Ill.Rev.Stat.1977, ch. 38, par. 11–20), as judicially construed, which has been recognized as satisfying constitutional requirements (Ward v. Illinois (1977), 431 U.S. 767, 97 S.Ct. 2085, 52 L.Ed.2d 738). Here, the trial court's decision to issue the injunction was based on its finding that the performances were obscene.

The appellate court erroneously rejected the suggestion that it overcome the problem of vagueness in the concept of common law nuisance by limiting the scope of the action to the definition of obscenity. It said that to do so would usurp the legislature's prerogative to establish policy. The General Assembly, however, has already clearly expressed itself in the area of obscenity. Its determination that obscenity is contrary to public policy and offensive and dangerous to society is reflected in the enactment of the statute making obscenity a crime. That statute in part provides:

> "(a) Elements of the Offense.
>
> A person commits obscenity when, with knowledge of the nature or content thereof, or recklessly failing to exercise reasonable inspection which would have disclosed the nature or content thereof, he:
>
> * * *
>
> (2) Presents or directs an obscene play, dance or other performance or participates directly in that portion thereof which makes it obscene; or
>
> (3) Publishes, exhibits or otherwise makes available anything obscene; or
>
> (4) Performs an obscene act or otherwise presents an obscene exhibition of his body for gain; or
>
> * * *
>
> "(b) Obscene Defined.
>
> A thing is obscene if, considered as a whole, its predominant appeal is to prurient interest, that is, a shameful or morbid interest in nudity, sex or excretion, and if it goes substantially beyond customary limits of candor in description or representation of such matters. A thing is obscene even though the obscenity is latent, as in the case of undeveloped photographs.
>
> * * *
>
> "(d) Sentence.
>
> Obscenity is a Class A misdemeanor. A second or subsequent offense is a Class 4 felony."

Ill.Rev.Stat.1977, ch. 38, par. 11–20.

That conduct may be subject to the sanctions of the criminal law does not, of course, foreclose a common law nuisance abatement action against the conduct. * * *

Moreover, by recognizing that an action may be brought to enjoin as public nuisances live obscene exhibitions, as were involved here, judges are not given liberty to impose their individual tastes or sensitivities upon the public. In determining whether the conduct should be enjoined as obscene, the court has to be guided by "contemporary community standards."

We cannot accept the appellate court's observation that the procedures of a civil nuisance action make it unsuitable in obscenity cases. Specifically, the court noted the absence of a right to a jury trial and suggested that the civil standard of proof might not be appropriate. The Supreme Court has approved the use of adversary civil injunctive proceedings against obscenity. (Paris Adult Theatre I v. Slaton (1973), 413 U.S. 49, 55, 93 S.Ct. 2628, 2634, 37 L.Ed.2d 446, 455.) It has not held that jury trials are necessary in civil obscenity proceedings. (*See* Alexander v. Virginia (1973), 413 U.S. 836, 93 S.Ct. 2803, 37 L.Ed.2d 993; Kingsley Books, Inc. v. Brown (1957), 354 U.S. 436, 443–44, 77 S.Ct. 1325, 1328–30, 1 L.Ed.2d 1469, 1475–76.) We recognize that a jury may be useful in determining whether a performance in a given case is obscene according to contemporary community standards. But we recognize too that in not every case could reasonable minds differ as to whether a performance was obscene. Too, under our civil procedure the court is authorized to call an advisory jury to assist it where the court deems it necessary.

As to the propriety of the civil standard of proof, we would observe that the Supreme Court has recently held that proof beyond a reasonable doubt is not required in a civil public nuisance abatement action involving obscenity. Cooper v. Mitchell Brothers' Santa Ana Theater (1981), 454 U.S. 90, 102 S.Ct. 172, 70 L.Ed.2d 262.

The appellate court held also that the injunction is a prohibited prior restraint on expression. The court said that the circuit court's order listed prohibited activities, such as simulated intercourse. Therefore, the defendant is enjoined from presenting performances that involve the proscribed acts in any form or context. Because arguably one or more of the proscribed acts could be performed in a show that is not obscene, the appellate court concluded that this injunction covers even protected expression.

To support its view that this restraint is improper, the court cited Vance v. Universal Amusement Co. (1980), 445 U.S. 308, 100 S.Ct. 1156, 63 L.Ed.2d 413. There, the Supreme Court held that an injunction under a Texas public nuisance abatement statute would operate as an improper prior restraint. Under the statute a court could enjoin the exhibition of films at theaters that habitually had been used for the showing of obscene movies. The court said:

> "As the District Court and the Court of Appeals construed Art. 4667(a), when coupled with the Texas Rules of Civil Procedure, it authorizes prior restraints of indefinite duration on the exhibition of motion pictures that have not been finally adjudicated to be obscene.

Presumably, an exhibitor would be required to obey such an order pending review of its merits and would be subject to contempt proceedings even if the film is ultimately found to be nonobscene. Such prior restraints would be more onerous and more objectionable than the threat of criminal sanctions after a film has been exhibited, since nonobscenity would be a defense to any criminal prosecution." 445 U.S. 308, 316, 100 S.Ct. 1156, 1161, 63 L.Ed.2d 413, 420–21.

We judge that the injunction here did not present a problem of prior restraint. While the injunction does list a variety of sexual acts, it does not proscribe the performance of those acts in all contexts and unconditionally. The order says that the defendants are "permanently enjoined and restrained * * * from performing or permitting the performance of lewd acts of live persons, *in violation of applicable City Ordinances and State Statutes* * * * for the entertainment, sexual arousal, or viewing by and of members of the public; including, but not limited to, the following of such acts: * * *." (Emphasis added.) Considering the pleadings and issues presented in the circuit court, the applicable State statutes to which the court referred obviously are the obscenity provisions of the Criminal Code. The injunction does no more than order the defendants not to violate the criminal laws against obscenity at the theater. Unlike the order in *Vance,* the defendants here could not be held in contempt unless it were shown that they staged a performance that was obscene. In short, the order did not touch protected expression. Any effect it could have produced relating to the first amendment was no greater than that produced by the obscenity provisions of the Criminal Code.

The injunction here would operate as Mr. Justice White in his dissenting opinion in *Vance* visualized (mistakenly, the majority considered) the operation of the injunction issued under the Texas statute. He believed that any injunction issued under the statute would be considered to incorporate the terms of the *Miller* obscenity test. He stated:

"Hence an Art. 4667(a) injunction would not by its terms forbid the exhibition of any materials protected by the First Amendment and would impose no greater functional burden on First Amendment values than would an equivalent—and concededly valid—criminal statute. It simply declares to the exhibitor that the future showing of obscene motion pictures will be punishable. It is true that an Art. 4667(a) injunction is issued by a court of law while a criminal statute is imposed by a legislature. Yet this distinction seems irrelevant for First Amendment purposes." 445 U.S. 308, 321–22, 100 S.Ct. 1156, 1164, 63 L.Ed.2d 413, 424 (White, J., dissenting).

Justice White also saw no constitutional difficulties in the procedures for any contempt action based on an injunction. Because those procedures would include the requirement of notice to the defendant and a judicial hearing in which the burden is on the party seeking to suppress the films to show a violation of the injunction, which would include proof of the obscenity of the films exhibited, he said "such procedures would fully satisfy the requirements of our cases." 445 U.S. 308, 323, 100 S.Ct. 1156, 1165, 63 L.Ed.2d 413, 425 (White, J., dissenting). *

Although we have found no constitutional defect in the injunction, we do consider that it was improvidently granted. A nuisance action involves two inquiries: (1) whether the activity complained of is in fact a nuisance; and, if it is, (2) whether an injunction against the activity is an appropriate remedy. We have already seen that a common law nuisance action may be brought against a theater operator who is conducting live obscene performances. Still, an injunction should not, without more, be issued against the operators of such a theater, as seemingly was done here.

It is a principle of equity that an injunction will not issue except where there is no adequate remedy at law. * * * Here, the activity complained of was the presenting of live obscene exhibitions, and those conducting such exhibitions are amenable to prosecution under the criminal obscenity laws. We deem that issuance of the injunction was error because it was not shown that criminal prosecution fails to afford an adequate remedy for the harm caused.

As we have previously noted, the fact that the activity complained of in a public nuisance action may give rise to a criminal prosecution does not foreclose the bringing of the action for equitable relief. The criminality of the conduct is a relevant factor, however, in determining whether an injunction should issue. * * * The purpose of giving equity jurisdiction in public nuisance actions is to offer remedies more complete than those available at law. * * * To permit a public body to obtain an injunction in a public nuisance action where there is an equally effective criminal law against the conduct would give rise to strong policy objections, such as were advanced in Commonwealth v. Stratton Finance Co. (1941), 310 Mass. 469, 38 N.E.2d 640. There, the court, in decrying any general use of equity in aid of criminal statutes, stated:

> "The objections to 'criminal equity' are that it deprives the defendant of his jury trial; that it substitutes for the definite penalties fixed by the Legislature whatever punishment for contempt a particular judge may see fit to exact; that it is often no more than an attempt to overcome by circumvention the supposed shortcomings of jurors; and that it may result, or induce the public to believe that it results, in the arbitrary exercise of power and in 'government by injunction.' These objections are substantial. They should cause a court to hesitate to extend the use of the injunction into the criminal field without express legislative sanction." 310 Mass. 469, 474, 38 N.E.2d 640, 643.

For a legal remedy to be deemed adequate, "the remedy 'must be clear, complete, and as practical and efficient to the ends of justice and its prompt administration as the equitable remedy.'" * * * This court has consistently recognized that the criminal law is not such a remedy where it is shown ineffective to prevent the continuance of the nuisance. (City of Chicago v. Cecola (1979), 75 Ill.2d 423, 27 Ill.Dec. 462, 389 N.E.2d 526

* For a more extensive discussion of the prior restraint issue, see Mayton, Toward a Theory of First Amendment Process: Injunctions of Speech, Subsequent Punishment and the Costs of the Prior Restraint Doctrine, 67 Cornell L.Rev. 245, 274–77 (1982).

(maximum fine of $200 insufficient to dissuade defendants from maintaining establishment offering sexual massages); Village of Spillertown v. Prewitt (1961), 21 Ill.2d 228, 171 N.E.2d 582 (defendant, having been arrested twice, claimed before village board he would continue stripmining despite imposition of fines under ordinance); People *ex rel.* Kerner v. Huls (1934), 355 Ill. 412, 189 N.E. 346 (criminal prosecution inadequate remedy where defendant's statements showed that he would pay statutory penalties but still not submit his cattle for tuberculin test); People *ex rel.* Dyer v. Clark (1915), 268 Ill. 156, 108 N.E. 994 (numerous criminal convictions of keeper of brothel did not deter her from continuing the activity).

It was not shown here that criminal prosecution would not lend a remedy as clear, complete, practical, and effective as the equitable remedy. * * *

The injunction issued was coextensive with the criminal statute, so it did not seek to affect conduct beyond the reach of the statute. There is no contention by the city of Chicago that conviction and imposition of penalties available under the criminal obscenity law, which makes the first offense a misdemeanor and a second offense a felony, would be ineffective to deter the defendants' activities. The injunction was issued within a few months of even the first arrest at the theater and before the criminal proceedings were completed. It is not claimed that this is a case where a risk to public health would require expedited action by a court acting through its equity powers. We do not hold that an injunction action may not be hereafter brought against the defendants. We judge only that in this action it was not shown that criminal prosecution would be an inadequate remedy.

Thus, a common law nuisance action may be maintained against a theater operator presenting live exhibitions that are obscene under our criminal law of obscenity. An injunction, though, should not issue unless criminal prosecution is shown to be an inadequate remedy.

For the reasons given, the judgment of the appellate court that reversed the circuit court is affirmed.*

Notes

1. A court that is responsive to a defendant's first amendment claim may either rule that the defendant's conduct is protected by the amendment or may

* For two other cases holding that obscenity may be characterized as a common law public nuisance, see People *ex rel.* Busch v. Projection Room Theater, 17 Cal.3d 42, 550 P.2d 600, 130 Cal.Rptr. 328 (1976), *cert. denied,* 429 U.S. 922, 97 S.Ct. 320, 50 L.Ed.2d 289 (1976); City of Minot v. Central Ave. News, Inc., 308 N.W.2d 851 (N.D.1981), *appeal dismissed,* 454 U.S. 1117 (1981) (allowing injunction against specific material adjudged obscene, but refusing to close the establishment from which the obscene material was disseminated for one year). *See also* Napro Dev. Corp. v. Town of Berlin, 135 Vt. 353, 376 A.2d 342 (1977). *See generally* Comment, Enjoining Obscenity as a Public Nuisance and the Prior Restraint Doctrine, 84 Colum.L.Rev. 1616 (1984); Comment, Regulation of Obscenity through Nuisance Statutes and Injunctive Remedies—The Prior Restraint Dilemma, 19 Wake Forest L.Rev. 7 (1983); Note, Injunctions Entered Pursuant to Public Nuisance Obscenity Statutes and the Doctrine of Prior Restraints, 61 Wash.U.L.Q. 775 (1983); Annot. 50 A.L.R.3d 969 (1973) (exhibition of obscene motion pictures as nuisance); Annot., 5 A.L.R.3d 1158 (1966) (modern concept of obscenity).

avoid the issue by narrowly defining what constitutes a public nuisance. *See, e.g.,* People *ex rel.* Carey v. Route 53 Drive–In, 45 Ill.App.3d 81, 3 Ill.Dec. 613, 358 N.E.2d 1298 (1976) (avoidance of the First Amendment issue by refusing to define outdoor motion picture that portrayed sexual scenes as a public nuisance).

2. States increasingly are looking to the public nuisance injunction as a significant weapon against obscenity. Consider the following analysis of this trend:

> "Despite the inclusion of obscenity as a common law nuisance, the use of nuisance doctrine as a major weapon against obscenity is a product mainly of the last decade. The use of nineteenth century nuisance doctrine to restrict expression raises significant constitutional problems not present in the regulation of other common law public nuisances such as drugs or gambling. Since free speech is a 'transcendent value,' the definitions and procedures of any doctrine used to curtail it should be subject to close scrutiny. A nuisance standard that merely determines whether the effect on speech is reasonable fails to provide such rigorous examination. Sweeping common law nuisance formulations about indecent displays and corruption of morals are suspect because they could easily restrict protected speech. This concern is heightened by the problem of distinguishing between protected and unprotected speech. There is no longer a public consensus, in either broad definitions or specific instances, that certain sexual material is unacceptable. Therefore, isolating obscene speech requires an unpredictable weighing of subjective factors that renders the process inevitably vague by practical standards.
>
> "Despite these criticisms, states searching for more effective methods of curtailing the distribution of pornography have sought to regulate adult bookstores and theaters through nuisance law. * * * Generally speaking, three kinds of nuisance statutes have been applied to obscenity cases. Two of them, the so-called Red Light laws and general public nuisance abatement statutes, do not explicitly refer to obscenity; hence, courts have had to interpret their language broadly to include obscenity within their strictures, and most courts have rejected attempts to apply such laws to pornography.
>
> "The third kind of nuisance law, the modern moral nuisance abatement statute, is drafted with obscenity specifically in mind. In the last decade, several states have passed such laws or have amended their old nuisance laws to cover obscenity, thereby removing all doubts of legislative intent. These statutes have generally incorporated the *Miller* definition of obscenity. The blanket injunction and padlock provisions of these statutes, although aimed specifically at obscenity, are similar to the classic Red Light laws, under which certain establishments—mainly houses of prostitution or gambling—could be permanently banned or shut down for the good of the community.
>
> "The padlock order is the most effective and arguably most suppressive sanction that can be authorized against an adult bookstore or theater. Once an establishment is found to have purveyed obscene material, an injunction may be issued closing down the entire premises for a specified period, usually a year. The closure order usually can be lifted if the owner posts a bond for the full value of the property and demonstrates that the

nuisance will not recur. A padlock order declares that the store or theater *itself,* in addition to the obscene material, is a nuisance.

* * *

"Most courts that have considered moral nuisance abatement laws providing for padlock orders have either construed the padlock provision as inapplicable to sexually explicit material, thereby avoiding any constitutional issue, or have struck down the provision flatly on constitutional grounds. In so doing, these courts generally have assumed that padlock orders are prior restraints without engaging in substantial analysis under prior restraint doctrine."

Note, Pornography, Padlocks and Prior Restraints, The Constitutional Limits of the Nuisance Power, 58 N.Y.U.L.Rev. 1478, 1485–89 (1983) (analyzing padlock order and concluding that it "is too blunt an instrument to withstand first amendment scrutiny").* *See also* Rendleman, Civilizing Pornography: The Case for an Exclusive Obscenity Nuisance Statute, 44 U.Chi.L.Rev. 509 (1977).

2. To what extent may a bookstore be ordered closed based on past sexual conduct on the premises rather than on the content of what is being sold? In Arcara v. Cloud Books, Inc., 478 U.S. 697, 106 S.Ct. 3172, 92 L.Ed.2d 568 (1986), the United States Supreme Court, 6–3, upheld the use of an injunction to close an adult bookstore where illicit sexual activities were occurring. The injunction issued pursuant to a New York statute that defined places of "lewdness, assignation or prostitution" as "public health nuisances". According to the Court,

"This Court has applied First Amendment scrutiny to a statute regulating conduct which has the incidental effect of burdening the expression of a particular political opinion. *United States v. O'Brien.* * * *

"We have also applied First Amendment scrutiny to some statutes which, although directed at activity with no expressive component, impose a disproportionate burden upon those engaged in protected First Amendment activities. In Minneapolis Star & Tribune v. Minnesota Commissioner of Revenue, 460 U.S. 575, 103 S.Ct. 1365, 75 L.Ed.2d 295 (1983), we struck down a tax imposed on the sale of large quantities of newsprint and ink because the tax had the effect of singling out newspapers to shoulder its burden. We imposed a greater burden of justification on the State even though the tax was imposed upon a nonexpressive activity, since the burden of the tax inevitably fell disproportionately—in fact, almost exclusively—upon the shoulders of newspapers exercising the constitutionally protected freedom of the press. Even while striking down the tax in *Minneapolis Star,* we emphasized: 'Clearly, the First Amendment does not prohibit all regulation of the press. It is beyond dispute that the States and the Federal Government can subject newspapers to generally applicable economic regulations without creating constitutional problems.'

"The New York Court of Appeals held that the *O'Brien* test for permissible governmental regulation was applicable to this case because the closure order sought by petitioner would also impose an incidental burden upon respondents' bookselling activities. That court ignored a

* Reprinted with permission of *New York University Law Review.*

crucial distinction between the circumstances presented in *O'Brien* and the circumstances of this case: unlike the symbolic draft card burning in *O'Brien,* the sexual activity carried on in this case manifests absolutely no element of protected expression. In *Paris Adult Theatre,* we underscored the fallacy of seeking to use the First Amendment as a cloak for obviously unlawful public sexual conduct by the diaphanous device of attributing protected expressive attributes to that conduct. First Amendment values may not be invoked by merely linking the words 'sex' and 'books.'

"Nor does the distinction drawn by the New York Public Health Law inevitably single out bookstores or others engaged in First Amendment protected activities for the imposition of its burden, as did the tax struck down in *Minneapolis Star.* As we noted in *Minneapolis Star,* neither the press nor booksellers may claim special protection from governmental regulations of general applicability simply by virtue of their First Amendment protected activities. If the city imposed closure penalties for demonstrated Fire Code violations or health hazards from inadequate sewage treatment, the First Amendment would not aid the owner of premises who had knowingly allowed such violations to persist. * * *

"It is true that the closure order in this case would require respondents to move their bookselling business to another location. Yet we have not traditionally subjected every criminal and civil sanction imposed through legal process to 'least restrictive means' scrutiny simply because each particular remedy will have some effect on the First Amendment activities of those subject to sanction. Rather, we have subjected such restrictions to scrutiny only where it was conduct with a significant expressive element that drew the legal remedy in the first place, as in *O'Brien,* or where a statute based on a nonexpressive activity has the inevitable effect of singling out those engaged in expressive activity, as in *Minneapolis Star.* This case involves neither situation, and we conclude the First Amendment is not implicated by the enforcement of a public health regulation of general application against the physical premises in which respondents happen to sell books."

State decisions before and after *Arcara* have reached similar results. *See, e.g.,* State ex rel. Roszmann v. Lions Den, 89 Ohio App.3d 775, 627 N.E.2d 629 (1993); State v. Tenth District Court of Appeal, 63 Ohio St.3d 354, 588 N.E.2d 116 (1992); Commonwealth v. Croatan Books, Inc., 228 Va. 383, 323 S.E.2d 86 (1984). Contra: People ex rel. Arcara v. Cloud Books, Inc., 68 N.Y.2d 553, 510 N.Y.S.2d 844, 503 N.E.2d 492 (1986) (upon remand from Supreme Court in *Arcara,* the New York Court of Appeals held that closure of bookstore violated owner's rights of free expression under the New York constitution).

3. The public nuisance concept has been used successfully in regulating massage parlors, "health spas", live sexual entertainment and related activities. *See generally* Annot., 80 A.L.R.3d 1020 (1976) (massage parlor as nuisance). Unlike the bookstore or motion picture theatre setting, these cases more clearly involve physical conduct and, consequently, the First Amendment is a less significant concern. The cases are numerous. *See, e.g.,* People *ex rel.* Hicks v. Sarong Gals, 27 Cal.App.3d 46, 103 Cal.Rptr. 414 (1972) (lewd unclothed dancing); City of Chicago v. Geraci, 30 Ill.App.3d 699, 332 N.E.2d 487 (1975) ("masturbatory massage parlor"); Commissioner of the Dept. of Buildings of the City of New York v. Sidne Enterprises, Inc., 90 Misc.2d 386,

394 N.Y.S.2d 777 (1977) (topless and bottomless dancing); City of Chicago v. Cecola, 75 Ill.2d 423, 27 Ill.Dec. 462, 389 N.E.2d 526 (1979) (masturbatory massage parlor). *Contra* City of Revere v. Aucella, 369 Mass. 138, 338 N.E.2d 816 (1975) (nude "go-go" dancing).

Whatever the inclination of courts to issue injunctions in such cases, it is crucially important to define precisely the objectionable activity. For example, an injunction directed against the entire business of the massage parlor or health club will often be invalidated as "overbroad." For a judicial admonition on the necessity of separating the acts creating the public nuisance from other permissible activity, see Health Clubs, Inc. v. State *ex rel.* Eagan, 338 So.2d 1324 (Fla.App.1976).

UNITED STATES v. SUPERPHARM CORPORATION

United States District Court, Eastern District of New York, 1981.
530 F.Supp. 408.

COSTANTINO, DISTRICT JUDGE.

This is an action under the Federal Food, Drug and Cosmetic Act ("the Act") 21 U.S.C. § 301 et seq. to enjoin alleged violations of the Act and for other forms of relief. The suit, initiated in January, 1981, contends that Superpharm Corporation ("Superpharm"), and Norman E. Rubin, president of Superpharm, engaged in the manufacture and distribution of a human drug, furosemide, in the absence of approval by the Food and Drug Administration ("FDA"). Specifically, defendants are alleged to be violating drug approval provisions that prohibit the marketing of "new drugs", 21 U.S.C. § 321(p), in interstate commerce without FDA approval. See 21 U.S.C. §§ 331(d) and 355(a).

On January 9, 1981 this court issued a restraining order prohibiting the further manufacture or sale of this drug unless and until approval is obtained from the FDA. Upon mutual consent of the parties, this order remains in effect pending the outcome of this decision. Although settlement discussions ensued and numerous issues resolved, the parties have been unable to settle whether this court has the authority to order the recall of drug products improperly marketed in interstate commerce. Thus, this issue is now before the court.

The Government maintains that this court has the authority pursuant to section 302 of the Act, 21 U.S.C. § 332, to order a recall. Section 302 provides in pertinent part that: the district courts of the United States * * * shall have jurisdiction, for cause shown, to restrain violations of Section 301 of this Title * * * (emphasis supplied). In addition, the Government contends that the court's general equitable power also authorizes the issuance of a recall order. (Citing Mitchell v. DeMario Jewelry, Inc., 361 U.S. 288, 80 S.Ct. 332, 4 L.Ed.2d 323 (1960); Porter v. Warner Co., 328 U.S. 395, 66 S.Ct. 1086, 90 L.Ed. 1332 (1945).)

* * *

An examination of the Act itself reveals that Congress specifically did not include a judicially ordered recall remedy when the Act was passed. It did, however, provide a threefold enforcement scheme: (1) injunctive relief,

21 U.S.C. § 332; (2) criminal prosecution, 21 U.S.C. § 333; and (3) seizure, 21 U.S.C. § 334. Moreover, in reading the legislative history behind the Act when passed in 1938, it is clear that Congress considered seizures to be the most drastic remedy, and that the injunction remedy was included to temper the hardship inherent in seizures: In some cases it should avoid the hardship and expenses to litigants in seizure cases. In many instances seizure is a harsh remedy and should be discouraged * * * In many instances it is believed * * * injunctions can be used with equal effectiveness and with less hardship. H.R.Rep. No. 2139, 75th Cong., 3d Sess. 3–4 (1938). Thus, injunctive relief was obviously viewed as a means to alleviate the hardship seizure might cause to manufacturers, and given this orientation, it is difficult to conclude that Congress intended Section 302(a) to authorize judicial recalls. United States v. C.E.B. Products, Inc., 380 F.Supp. 664, 668 (N.D.Ill.1974).

In effect, the Government is asking this court to do something that the FDA itself cannot do. While there are provisions in the FDA regulations which provide for recalls, recalls cannot be ordered by the FDA, see 21 CFR § 7.40(a), as they are usually undertaken voluntarily, 21 CFR § 7.40(a), at the request of the FDA. 21 CFR § 7.40(b). See generally 21 CFR § 7.1 et seq. The authorized vehicle for FDA removal of goods from the marketplace is the seizure remedy. 21 U.S.C. § 334. It is simply not within the FDA's stated authority to order a manufacturer to recall its own goods.

If for medical and public safety reasons the FDA believes the removal of the restrained pharmaceutical product is imperative, they have the seizure remedy at their disposal. To order a recall under the Act would be an unwarranted act of judicial legislation because the FDA, through the Government, and/or the Government itself, would have yet another method of attacking the allegedly illegal distributions of drugs without being restricted by either the Act or the regulations promulgated thereunder. Recalls are simply not within the enforcement powers of the Act, and the court perceives no reason to expand the remedies currently in effect by including such a remedy. See United States v. C.E.B. Products, Inc., supra; see also National Confectioners Assoc. v. Califano, 569 F.2d 690 (D.C.Cir.1978).

In the alternative, the Government argues that the court's inherent equitable power includes the power to order a recall. In support, the Government cites two Supreme Court cases, Mitchell v. DeMario Jewelry, Inc., supra; Porter v. Warner Co., 328 U.S. 395, 66 S.Ct. 1086, 90 L.Ed. 1332 (1945), which admittedly contain persuasive language. Upon an examination of the cases, however, it appears that the use of the court's equitable power in those cases was necessary to accomplish the purposes of the legislation, and absent such power, the statutes would have been unenforceable.

In Mitchell v. DeMario, supra, the court exercised its equitable powers to order the reimbursement of lost wages to employees who had lost their positions after bringing suit under the Fair Labor Standards Act of 1938 ("FLSA"). The effectiveness of the FSLA's enforcement, as structured by Congress, was completely dependent on employees' coming forward to reveal labor abuses. In the absence of judicially-mandated reimbursement for the lost wages of these employees awaiting reinstatement (as provided by § 15(a)(3) of the FLSA), the purposes of the FLSA clearly would have been frustrated. The DeMario court recognized the need to act in equity so as to enact more fully the purposes and powers of the FLSA.

Similar reimbursement actions were deemed to be within the court's equitable powers of relief in Porter v. Warner Co., 328 U.S. 395, 66 S.Ct. 1086, 90 L.Ed. 1332 (1945), relied on in DeMario. The Supreme Court in Warner so held in order to implement fully the provisions of the Emergency Price Control Act of 1942 ("EPCA"), which set maximum rents that landlords could charge. The Warner court ordered reimbursement for those tenants who had come forward to protest their landlord's violation of the EPCA.

Clearly, it must be acknowledged that in DeMario and Warner, the use of the court's equitable powers was necessary for the realistic enforcement of the specific provisions in the respective statutes. In DeMario, no employee would come forward to reveal FLSA abuses; in Warner, no tenant would reveal his landlord's illegal rents. The Supreme Court's decisions in these cases were obviously concerned with protecting those who come forward to expose violations of the law and without whom enforcement would have been impossible. To rely on these cases for the general proposition that a court may, in its exercise of its equitable powers, grant relief other than that explicitly provided for, is to ignore the legislative and policy background for both the DeMario and Warner decisions.

In the instant case, resort to ancillary remedies through equitable powers is unnecessary to enforce the spirit, as well as the letter, of the Act. The FDA's statutory remedies provide for sufficient means to enforce the Act, and the legislative history and the Act itself manifest a reluctance to expand enforcement powers to the point where they are punitive. See H.R.Rep. No. 2139, 75th Cong., 3d Sess. 3–4 (1938). Moreover, the seizure remedy exists if the FDA perceives a potential public danger which must be rectified immediately, or if the manufacturer or distributor refuses to remove the illegal product from the market. Although the court's duty is heightened when, in a case such as this, the public interest is involved, the Government and the FDA have the tools at their disposal to solve the problem and there is no need to attempt to add to those powers when not necessary. No resort to, or expansion of, the court's equitable power is needed to remove these drugs from interstate commerce. See United States v. C.E.B. Products, Inc., supra; contra United States v. K–N Enterprises, Inc., 461 F.Supp. 988 (N.D.Ill.1978).

Accordingly, the Government's request for an order recalling the drugs from the marketplace is denied.*

* *Accord* United States v. X–Otag Plus Tablets, 441 F.Supp. 105 (D.Colo.1977). *See also* Herbold Laboratory, Inc. v. United States, 413 F.2d 342 (9th Cir.1969) (federal district courts not permitted to enjoin violations of Federal Trade Commission's cease and desist orders). *See generally* Weeda, FDA Seizure and Injunction Actions: Judicial Means of Protecting the Public Health, 35 Food Drug Cosm.L.J. 112 (1980); Comment, Products Liability Class Suits for Injunctive Relief Under Federal Rule 23, 47 Fordham L.Rev. 49 (1978).

Note

Compare the reasoning of the principal case with the language of United States v. Barr Laboratories, Inc., 812 F.Supp. 458, 489 (D.N.J.1993):

> "The court may recall any drug product found to be manufactured in violation of the Act that has been released to the public for distribution. * * * Although not authorized expressly in the Act, this remedy is consistent with the broad equitable relief powers district courts enjoy. * * * Any other rule would allow [defendant] to use its channels of distribution to shield adulterated products from the Court's remedial arm, thereby frustrating the purpose of the Act."

In addition, consider the approach of the California Supreme Court in People v. Superior Court, 9 Cal.3d 283, 107 Cal.Rptr. 192, 507 P.2d 1400 (1973):

> "This is a civil action by the Attorney General against various sellers of encyclopedias and similar publications by door-to-door solicitation, charging false and misleading advertising (Bus. & Prof.Code, § 17500). The complaint prays, inter alia, that defendants be ordered to offer each customer who has been solicited by a fraudulent sales presentation the opportunity to rescind his contract, return the products, and obtain a refund. * * *
>
> "At the time the complaint was filed Business and Professions Code section 17535 provided that false or misleading advertising 'may be enjoined' in an action by the Attorney General, but was silent as to the power of the trial court to order restitution in such a proceeding. On the other hand the statute did not restrict the court's general equity jurisdiction 'in so many words, or by necessary and inescapable inference.' (Porter v. Warner Co., 328 U.S. 395, 398, 66 S.Ct. 1086, 90 L.Ed. 1332, 1337 (1946).) In the absence of such a restriction a court of equity may exercise the full range of its inherent powers in order to accomplish complete justice between the parties, restoring if necessary the *status quo ante* as nearly as may be achieved. * * * In particular, in an action by the Attorney General under section 17535 a trial court has the inherent power to order, as a form of ancillary relief, that the defendants make or offer to make restitution to the customers found to have been defrauded."

SECTION 4. INTERFERENCE WITH CONSTITUTIONAL RIGHTS

A. LEGAL RELIEF

MEMPHIS COMMUNITY SCHOOL DISTRICT v. STACHURA

Supreme Court of the United States, 1986.
477 U.S. 299, 106 S.Ct. 2537, 91 L.Ed.2d 249.

JUSTICE POWELL.

This case requires us to decide whether 42 U.S.C. § 1983 authorizes an award of compensatory damages based on the factfinder's assessment of the value or importance of a substantive constitutional right.

I

Respondent Edward Stachura is a tenured teacher in the Memphis, Michigan, public schools. When the events that led to this case occurred, respondent taught seventh-grade life science, using a textbook that had been approved by the School Board. The textbook included a chapter on human reproduction. During the 1978–1979 school year, respondent spent six weeks on this chapter. As part of their instruction, students were shown pictures of respondent's wife during her pregnancy. Respondent also showed the students two films concerning human growth and sexuality. These films were provided by the County Health Department, and the Principal of respondent's school had approved their use. Both films had been shown in past school years without incident.

After the showing of the pictures and the films, a number of parents complained to school officials about respondent's teaching methods. These complaints, which appear to have been based largely on inaccurate rumors about the allegedly sexually explicit nature of the pictures and films, were discussed at an open School Board meeting held on April 23, 1979. Following the advice of the School Superintendent, respondent did not attend the meeting, during which a number of parents expressed the view that respondent should not be allowed to teach in the Memphis school system.[1] The day after the meeting, respondent was suspended with pay. The School Board later confirmed the suspension, and notified respondent that an "administration evaluation" of his teaching methods was underway. No such evaluation was ever made. Respondent was reinstated the next fall, after filing this lawsuit.

Respondent sued the School District, the Board of Education, various Board members and school administrators, and two parents who had participated in the April 23 School Board meeting. The complaint alleged that respondent's suspension deprived him of both liberty and property without due process of law and violated his First Amendment right to academic freedom. Respondent sought compensatory and punitive damages under 42 U.S.C. § 1983 for these constitutional violations.

At the close of trial on these claims, the District Court instructed the jury as to the law governing the asserted bases for liability. Turning to damages, the court instructed the jury that on finding liability it should award a sufficient amount to compensate respondent for the injury caused by petitioners' unlawful actions:

> "You should consider in this regard any lost earnings; loss of earning capacity; out-of-pocket expenses; and any mental anguish or emotional distress that you find the Plaintiff to have suffered as a result of conduct by the Defendants depriving him of his civil rights." App. 94.

1. One member of the School Board described the meeting as follows:

> "At this time, the public was in a total uproar and completely out of control * * *. People were hollering and shouting and the statement was made from the public that if Mr. Stachura was allowed to return in the morning, they would be there to picket the school.
>
> "At this point of total panic, [the School Superintendent] stated in order to maintain peace in our school district, we would suspend Mr. Stachura with full pay and get this mess straightened out." * * *

In addition to this instruction on the standard elements of compensatory damages, the court explained that punitive damages could be awarded, and described the standards governing punitive awards.[2] Finally, at respondent's request and over petitioners' objection, the court charged that damages also could be awarded based on the value or importance of the constitutional rights that were violated:

> "If you find that the Plaintiff has been deprived of a Constitutional right, you may award damages to compensate him for the deprivation. Damages for this type of injury are more difficult to measure than damages for a physical injury or injury to one's property. There are no medical bills or other expenses by which you can judge how much compensation is appropriate. In one sense, no monetary value we place upon Constitutional rights can measure their importance in our society or compensate a citizen adequately for their deprivation. However, just because these rights are not capable of precise evaluation does not mean that an appropriate monetary amount should not be awarded.
>
> "The precise value you place upon any Constitutional right which you find was denied to Plaintiff is within your discretion. You may wish to consider the importance of the right in our system of government, the role which this right has played in the history of our republic, [and] the significance of the right in the context of the activities which the Plaintiff was engaged in at the time of the violation of the right." *Id.,* at 96.

The jury found petitioners liable,[3] and awarded a total of $275,000 in compensatory damages and $46,000 in punitive damages.[4] * * *

In an opinion devoted primarily to liability issues, the Court of Appeals for the Sixth Circuit affirmed, holding that respondent's suspension had violated both procedural due process and the First Amendment. *Stachura v. Truszkowski,* 763 F.2d 211 (1985). Responding to petitioners' contention that the District Court improperly authorized damages based solely on the value of constitutional rights, the court noted only that "there was ample proof of actual injury to plaintiff Stachura both in his effective discharge * * * and by the damage to his reputation and to his professional career as a teacher. Contrary to the situation in *Carey v. Piphus,* 435 U.S. 247, 98 S.Ct. 1042, 55 L.Ed.2d 252 (1978) * * *, there was proof from which the jury could have found, as it did, actual and important damages." *Id.,* at 214.

We granted certiorari limited to the question whether the Court of Appeals erred in affirming the damages award in the light of the District Court's instructions that authorized not only compensatory and punitive

2. Petitioners do not challenge the award of punitive damages in this Court.

3. The jury found petitioners liable based both on the alleged deprivation of procedural due process and on the alleged violation of respondent's First Amendment rights.

4. The bulk of the award was against the School Board, which was assessed $233,750 in compensatory damages. Three of the individual defendants were each assessed $8,250, while six others were each charged $2,750. Nine individual defendants were assessed punitive damages, ranging from $1,000 to $15,000.

damages, but also damages for the deprivation of "any constitutional right." [5] 474 U.S. 918, 106 S.Ct. 245, 88 L.Ed.2d 254 (1985). We reverse, and remand for a new trial limited to the issue of compensatory damages.

II

Petitioners challenge the jury instructions authorizing damages for violation of constitutional rights on the ground that those instructions permitted the jury to award damages based on its own unguided estimation of the value of such rights. Respondent disagrees with this characterization of the jury instructions, contending that the compensatory damages instructions taken as a whole focused solely on respondent's injury and not on the abstract value of the rights he asserted.

We believe petitioners more accurately characterize the instructions. The damages instructions were divided into three distinct segments: (i) compensatory damages for harm to respondent, (ii) punitive damages, and (iii) additional "compensat[ory]" damages for violations of constitutional rights. No sensible juror could read the third of these segments to modify the first. On the contrary, the damages instructions plainly authorized—in addition to punitive damages—two distinct types of "compensatory" damages: one based on respondent's actual injury according to ordinary tort law standards, and another based on the "value" of certain rights. We therefore consider whether the latter category of damages was properly before the jury.

III

A

We have repeatedly noted that 42 U.S.C. § 1983 [8] creates " 'a species of tort liability' in favor of persons who are deprived of 'rights, privileges, or immunities secured' to them by the Constitution." *Carey v. Piphus,* 435 U.S. 247, 253, 98 S.Ct. 1042, 1047, 55 L.Ed.2d 252 (1978), quoting *Imbler v. Pachtman,* 424 U.S. 409, 417, 96 S.Ct. 984, 988, 47 L.Ed.2d 128 (1976). * * * Accordingly, when § 1983 plaintiffs seek damages for violations of constitutional rights, the level of damages is ordinarily determined according to principles derived from the common law of torts. * * *

Punitive damages aside,[9] damages in tort cases are designed to provide "*compensation* for the injury caused to plaintiff by defendant's breach of

5. Since our decision in *Carey v. Piphus,* 435 U.S. 247, 98 S.Ct. 1042, 55 L.Ed.2d 252 (1978), several of the Courts of Appeals have concluded that damages awards based on the abstract value of constitutional rights are proper, at least as long as the right in question is substantive. * * * See also Love, Damages: A Remedy for the Violation of Constitutional Rights, 67 Calif.L.Rev. 1242 (1979). Other courts have determined that our reasoning in *Carey* forecloses such awards. * * *

8. Section 1983 reads:

"Every person who, under color of any statute, ordinance, regulation, custom, or usage, of any State or Territory or the District of Columbia, subjects, or causes to be subjected, any citizen of the United States or other person within the jurisdiction thereof to the deprivation of any rights, privileges, or immunities secured by the Constitution and laws, shall be liable to the party injured in an action at law, suit in equity, or other proper proceeding for redress."

9. The purpose of punitive damages is to punish the defendant for his willful or malicious conduct and to deter others from similar behavior. * * * In *Smith v. Wade,* 461 U.S. 30, 103 S.Ct. 1625, 75 L.Ed.2d 632 (1983), the Court held that punitive damages may be available in a proper § 1983 case. As

duty." 2 F. Harper, F. James, & O. Gray, Law of Torts § 25.1, p. 490 (2d ed. 1986) (emphasis in original), quoted in *Carey v. Piphus, supra,* 435 U.S., at 255, 98 S.Ct., at 1047. See also *Bivens v. Six Unknown Federal Narcotics Agents,* 403 U.S. 388, 395, 397, 91 S.Ct. 1999, 2004, 2005, 29 L.Ed.2d 619 (1971); *id.,* at 408–409, 91 S.Ct., at 2010–2011 (Harlan, J., concurring in judgment). To that end, compensatory damages may include not only out-of-pocket loss and other monetary harms, but also such injuries as "impairment of reputation * * *, personal humiliation, and mental anguish and suffering." *Gertz v. Robert Welch, Inc.,* 418 U.S. 323, 350, 94 S.Ct. 2997, 3012, 41 L.Ed.2d 789 (1974). See also *Carey v. Piphus, supra,* 435 U.S., at 264, 98 S.Ct., at 1052 (mental and emotional distress constitute compensable injury in § 1983 cases). Deterrence is also an important purpose of this system, but it operates through the mechanism of damages that are *compensatory*—damages grounded in determinations of plaintiffs' actual losses. * * * Congress adopted this common-law system of recovery when it established liability for "constitutional torts." Consequently, "the basic purpose" of § 1983 damages is "*to compensate persons for injuries* that are caused by the deprivation of constitutional rights." *Carey v. Piphus,* 435 U.S., at 254, 98 S.Ct., at 1047 (emphasis added). * * *

Carey v. Piphus represents a straightforward application of these principles. *Carey* involved a suit by a high school student suspended for smoking marijuana; the student claimed that he was denied procedural due process because he was suspended without an opportunity to respond to the charges against him. The Court of Appeals for the Seventh Circuit held that even if the suspension was justified, the student could recover substantial compensatory damages simply because of the insufficient procedures used to suspend him from school. We reversed, and held that the student could recover compensatory damages only if he proved actual injury caused by the denial of his constitutional rights. *Id.,* at 264, 98 S.Ct., at 1052. We noted: "Rights, constitutional and otherwise, do not exist in a vacuum. Their purpose is to protect persons from injuries to particular interests * * *." *Id.,* at 254, 98 S.Ct., at 1047. Where no injury was present, no "compensatory" damages could be awarded.

The instructions at issue here cannot be squared with *Carey,* or with the principles of tort damages on which *Carey* and § 1983 are grounded. The jurors in this case were told that, in determining how much was necessary to "compensate [respondent] for the deprivation" of his constitutional rights, they should place a money value on the "rights" themselves by considering such factors as the particular right's "importance * * * in our system of government," its role in American history, and its "significance * * * in the context of the activities" in which respondent was engaged. App. 96. These factors focus, not on compensation for provable injury, but on the jury's subjective perception of the importance of constitutional rights as an abstract matter. *Carey* establishes that such an ap-

in punitive damages instructions used in this case explained, however, such damages are available only on a showing of the requisite intent. App. 94–95 (authorizing punitive damages for acts "maliciously, or wantonly, or oppressively done"); *Smith v. Wade, supra,* at 51, 103 S.Ct., at 1637.

* * *

proach is impermissible. The constitutional right transgressed in *Carey*—the right to due process of law—is central to our system of ordered liberty. * * * We nevertheless held that *no* compensatory damages could be awarded for violation of that right absent proof of actual injury. *Carey,* 435 U.S., at 264, 98 S.Ct., at 1052. *Carey* thus makes clear that the abstract value of a constitutional right may not form the basis for § 1983 damages.[11]

Respondent nevertheless argues that *Carey* does not control here, because in this case a *substantive* constitutional right—respondent's First Amendment right to academic freedom—was infringed. The argument misperceives our analysis in *Carey.* That case does not establish a two-tiered system of constitutional rights, with substantive rights afforded greater protection than "mere" procedural safeguards. We did acknowledge in *Carey* that "the elements and prerequisites for recovery of damages" might vary depending on the interests protected by the constitutional right at issue. *Id.,* at 264–265, 98 S.Ct., at 1053. But we emphasized that, whatever the constitutional basis for § 1983 liability, such damages must always be designed "to *compensate injuries* caused by the [constitutional] deprivation." *Id.,* at 265, 98 S.Ct., at 1053 (emphasis added).[13] * * * That conclusion simply leaves no room for noncompensatory damages measured by the jury's perception of the abstract "importance" of a constitutional right.

Nor do we find such damages necessary to vindicate the constitutional rights that § 1983 protects. See n. 11, *supra.* Section 1983 presupposes that damages that compensate for actual harm ordinarily suffice to deter constitutional violations. *Carey, supra,* 435 U.S., at 256–257, 98 S.Ct., at 1043 ("To the extent that Congress intended that awards under § 1983 should deter the deprivation of constitutional rights, there is no evidence that it meant to establish a deterrent more formidable than that inherent in the award of compensatory damages"). Moreover, damages based on the "value" of constitutional rights are an unwieldy tool for ensuring compli-

11. We did approve an award of nominal damages for the deprivation of due process in *Carey.* 435 U.S., at 266, 98 S.Ct., at 1053. Our discussion of that issue makes clear that nominal damages, and not damages based on some undefinable "value" of infringed rights, are the appropriate means of "vindicating" rights whose deprivation has not caused actual, provable injury:

"Common-law courts traditionally have vindicated deprivations of certain 'absolute' rights that are not shown to have caused actual injury through the award of a nominal sum of money. By making the deprivation of such rights actionable for nominal damages without proof of actual injury, the law recognizes the importance to organized society that those rights be scrupulously observed; but at the same time, it remains true to the principle that substantial damages should be awarded only to compensate actual injury or, in the case of exemplary or punitive damages, to deter or punish malicious deprivations of rights." *Ibid.* (footnote omitted).

13. *Carey* recognized that "the task * * * of adapting common-law rules of damages to provide fair compensation for injuries caused by the deprivation of a constitutional right" is one "of some delicacy." *Id.,* at 258, 98 S.Ct., at 1049. We also noted that "the elements and prerequisites for recovery of damages appropriate to compensate injuries caused by the deprivation of one constitutional right are not necessarily appropriate to compensate injuries caused by the deprivation of another." *Id.,* at 264–265, 98 S.Ct., at 1053. See also *Hobson v. Wilson,* 237 U.S.App.D.C., at 279–281, 737 F.2d, at 61–63. This "delicate" task need not be undertaken here. None of the parties challenges the portion of the jury instructions that permitted recovery for actual harm to respondent, and the instructions that *are* challenged simply do not authorize compensation for injury. We therefore hold only that damages based on the "value" or "importance" of constitutional rights are not authorized by § 1983, because they are not truly compensatory.

ance with the Constitution. History and tradition do not afford any sound guidance concerning the precise value that juries should place on constitutional protections. Accordingly, were such damages available, juries would be free to award arbitrary amounts without any evidentiary basis, or to use their unbounded discretion to punish unpopular defendants. Cf. *Gertz,* 418 U.S., at 350, 94 S.Ct., at 3012. Such damages would be too uncertain to be of any great value to plaintiffs, and would inject caprice into determinations of damages in § 1983 cases. We therefore hold that damages based on the abstract "value" or "importance" of constitutional rights are not a permissible element of compensatory damages in such cases.

B

Respondent further argues that the challenged instructions authorized a form of "presumed" damages—a remedy that is both compensatory in nature and traditionally part of the range of tort law remedies. Alternatively, respondent argues that the erroneous instructions were at worst harmless error.

Neither argument has merit. Presumed damages are a *substitute* for ordinary compensatory damages, not a *supplement* for an award that fully compensates the alleged injury. When a plaintiff seeks compensation for an injury that is likely to have occurred but difficult to establish, some form of presumed damages may possibly be appropriate. See *Carey,* 435 U.S., at 262, 98 S.Ct., at 1051; cf. *Dun & Bradstreet, Inc. v. Greenmoss Builders,* 472 U.S. 749, 760–761, 105 S.Ct. 2939, 2946, 86 L.Ed.2d 593 (1985) (opinion of POWELL, J.); *Gertz v. Robert Welch, Inc., supra,* 418 U.S., at 349, 94 S.Ct., at 3011. In those circumstances, presumed damages may roughly approximate the harm that the plaintiff suffered and thereby compensate for harms that may be impossible to measure. As we earlier explained, the instructions at issue in this case did not serve this purpose, but instead called on the jury to measure damages based on a subjective evaluation of the importance of particular constitutional values. Since such damages are wholly divorced from any compensatory purpose, they cannot be justified as presumed damages.[14] Moreover, no rough substitute

14. For the same reason, *Nixon v. Herndon,* 273 U.S. 536, 47 S.Ct. 446, 71 L.Ed. 759 (1927), and similar cases do not support the challenged instructions. In *Nixon,* the Court held that a plaintiff who was illegally prevented from voting in a state primary election suffered compensable injury. Accord, *Lane v. Wilson,* 307 U.S. 268, 59 S.Ct. 872, 83 L.Ed. 1281 (1939). This holding did not rest on the "value" of the right to vote as an abstract matter; rather, the Court recognized that the plaintiff had suffered a particular injury—his inability to vote in a particular election—that might be compensated through substantial money damages. See 273 U.S., at 540, 47 S.Ct., at 446 ("the petition * * * seeks to recover for private damage").

Nixon followed a long line of cases, going back to Lord Holt's decision in *Ashby v. White,* 2 Ld.Raym. 938, 92 Eng.Rep. 126 (1703), authorizing substantial money damages as compensation for persons deprived of their right to vote in particular elections. *E.g., Wiley v. Sinkler,* 179 U.S. 58, 65, 21 S.Ct. 17, 20, 45 L.Ed. 84 (1900); *Wayne v. Venable,* 260 F. 64, 66 (CA8 1919). Although these decisions sometimes speak of damages for the value of the right to vote, their analysis shows that they involve nothing more than an award of presumed damages for a nonmonetary harm that cannot easily be quantified:

"In the eyes of the law th[e] right [to vote] is so valuable that damages are presumed from the wrongful deprivation of it without evidence of actual loss of money, property, or any other valuable thing, and the amount of the damages is a question peculiarly appropriate for the determination of the jury, because each member of the jury has personal knowledge of the value of the right." *Ibid.*

for compensatory damages was required in this case, since the jury was fully authorized to compensate respondent for both monetary and nonmonetary harms caused by petitioners' conduct.

Nor can we find that the erroneous instructions were harmless. * * *

* * *

Although the verdict specified an amount for punitive damages, it did not specify how much of the remaining damages was designed to compensate respondent for his injury and how much reflected the jury's estimation of the value of the constitutional rights that were infringed. The effect of the erroneous instruction is therefore unknowable, although probably significant: the jury awarded respondent a very substantial amount of damages, none of which could have derived from any monetary loss.[15] It is likely, although not certain, that a major part of these damages was intended to "compensate" respondent for the abstract "value" of his due process and First Amendment rights. For these reasons, the case must be remanded for a new trial on compensatory damages.

IV

The judgment of the Court of Appeals is reversed, and the case is remanded for further proceedings consistent with this opinion.

It is so ordered.

JUSTICE BRENNAN and JUSTICE STEVENS join the opinion of the Court and also join JUSTICE MARSHALL's opinion concurring in the judgment.

JUSTICE MARSHALL, with whom JUSTICE BRENNAN, JUSTICE BLACKMUN, and JUSTICE STEVENS join, concurring in the judgment.

I agree with the Court that this case must be remanded for a new trial on damages. Certain portions of the Court's opinion, however, can be read to suggest that damages in § 1983 cases are necessarily limited to "out-of-pocket loss," "other monetary harms," and "such injuries as 'impairment of reputation * * *, personal humiliation, and mental anguish and suffering.'" See *ante,* at 2543. I do not understand the Court so to hold, and I write separately to emphasize that the violation of a constitutional right, in proper cases, may itself constitute a compensable injury.

The appropriate starting point of any analysis in this area is this Court's opinion in *Carey v. Piphus,* 435 U.S. 247, 98 S.Ct. 1042, 55 L.Ed.2d 252 (1978). In *Carey,* we recognized that "the basic purpose of a § 1983 damages award should be to compensate persons for injuries caused by the deprivation of constitutional rights." *Id.,* at 254, 98 S.Ct., at 1047; see

See also *Ashby v. White, supra,* at 955, 92 Eng.Rep., at 137 (Holt, C.J.) ("As in an action for slanderous words, though a man does not lose a penny by reason of the speaking [of] them, yet he shall have an action"). The "value of the right" in the context of these decisions is the money value of the particular loss that the plaintiff suffered—a loss of which "each member of the jury has personal knowledge." It is *not* the value of the right to vote as a general, abstract matter, based on its role in our history or system of government. Thus, whatever the wisdom of these decisions in the context of the changing scope of compensatory damages over the course of this century, they do not support awards of noncompensatory damages such as those authorized in this case.

15. Throughout his suspension, respondent continued to receive his teacher's salary.

ante, at 2542–2543. We explained, however, that application of that principle to concrete cases was not a simple matter. 435 U.S., at 257, 98 S.Ct., at 1048. "It is not clear," we stated, "that common-law tort rules of damages will provide a complete solution to the damages issue in every § 1983 case." *Id.,* at 258, 98 S.Ct., at 1049. Rather, "the rules governing compensation for injuries caused by the deprivation of constitutional rights should be tailored to the interests protected by the particular right in question—just as the common-law rules of damages themselves were defined by the interests protected in various branches of tort law." *Id.,* at 259, 98 S.Ct., at 1050.

Applying those principles, we held in *Carey* that substantial damages should not be awarded where a plaintiff has been denied procedural due process but has made no further showing of compensable damage. We repeated, however, that "the elements and prerequisites for recovery of damages appropriate to compensate injuries caused by the deprivation of one constitutional right are not necessarily appropriate to compensate injuries caused by the deprivation of another." *Id.,* at 264–265, 98 S.Ct., at 1053. We referred to cases that support the award of substantial damages simply upon a showing that a plaintiff was wrongfully deprived of the right to vote, without requiring any further demonstration of damages. *Id.,* at 264–265, n. 22, 98 S.Ct., at 1052–1053, n. 22.

Following *Carey,* the Courts of Appeals have recognized that invasions of constitutional rights sometimes cause injuries that cannot be redressed by a wooden application of common-law damages rules. In *Hobson v. Wilson,* 237 U.S.App.D.C. 219, 275–281, 737 F.2d 1, 57–63 (1984), cert. denied, 470 U.S. 1084, 105 S.Ct. 1843, 85 L.Ed.2d 142 (1985), which the Court cites, *ante,* at 2544, and n. 13, plaintiffs claimed that defendant Federal Bureau of Investigation agents had invaded their First Amendment rights to assemble for peaceable political protest, to associate with others to engage in political expression, and to speak on public issues free of unreasonable government interference. The District Court found that the defendants had succeeded in diverting plaintiffs from, and impeding them in, their protest activities. The Court of Appeals for the District of Columbia Circuit held that that injury to a First Amendment-protected interest could itself constitute compensable injury wholly apart from any "emotional distress, humiliation and personal indignity, emotional pain, embarrassment, fear, anxiety and anguish" suffered by plaintiffs. 237 U.S.App.D.C., at 280, 737 F.2d, at 62 (footnotes omitted). The court warned, however, that that injury could be compensated with substantial damages only to the extent that it was "reasonably quantifiable"; damages should not be based on "the so-called inherent value of the rights violated." *Ibid.*

I believe that the *Hobson* court correctly stated the law. When a plaintiff is deprived, for example, of the opportunity to engage in a demonstration to express his political views, "[i]t is facile to suggest that no damage is done." *Dellums v. Powell,* 184 U.S.App.D.C. 275, 303, 566 F.2d 167, 195 (1977). Loss of such an opportunity constitutes loss of First Amendment rights " 'in their most pristine and classic form.' " *Ibid.,* quoting *Edwards v. South Carolina,* 372 U.S. 229, 235, 83 S.Ct. 680, 683, 9

L.Ed.2d 697 (1963). There is no reason why such an injury should not be compensable in damages. At the same time, however, the award must be proportional to the actual loss sustained.

The instructions given the jury in this case were improper because they did not require the jury to focus on the loss actually sustained by respondent. Rather, they invited the jury to base its award on speculation about "the importance of the right in our system of government" and "the role which this right has played in the history of our republic," guided only by the admonition that "[i]n one sense, no monetary value we place on Constitutional rights can measure their importance in our society or compensate a citizen adequately for their deprivation." App. 96. These instructions invited the jury to speculate on matters wholly detached from the real injury occasioned respondent by the deprivation of the right. Further, the instructions might have led the jury to grant respondent damages based on the "abstract value" of the right to procedural due process—a course directly barred by our decision in *Carey.*

The Court therefore properly remands for a new trial on damages. I do not understand the Court, however, to hold that deprivations of constitutional rights can never themselves constitute compensable injuries. Such a rule would be inconsistent with the logic of *Carey,* and would defeat the purpose of § 1983 by denying compensation for genuine injuries caused by the deprivation of constitutional rights.

Notes

1. Justice Powell said, "When a plaintiff seeks compensation for an injury that is likely to have occurred but difficult to establish, some form of presumed damages may possibly be appropriate." *Stachura,* 477 U.S. at 311. To what type of injury is he referring? He is not referring to injury from a violation of procedural due process. *See* Carey v. Piphus, 435 U.S. 247, 98 S.Ct. 1042, 55 L.Ed.2d 252 (1978), discussed in *Stachura.* He does mention presumed damages in the context of voting rights violations. *Stachura,* 477 U.S. at 311 n. 14. What is the difference between injury from procedural due process violations and voting rights violations? *See* Love, Presumed General Compensatory Damages in Constitutional Tort Litigation: A Corrective Justice Perspective, 49 Wash. and Lee L.Rev. 67 (1992) (voting rights and procedural due process rights violations distinguishable, *inter alia,* on ground that procedural due process violations are capable of being cured by injunctive relief, leaving only emotional distress as the remaining injury).

2. The possibility of awarding presumed damages has not been foreclosed by the courts. *See* Baumgardner v. Secretary, 960 F.2d 572, 583 (6th Cir. 1992); Walje v. City of Winchester, 827 F.2d 10, 12–13 (6th Cir.1987).

3. In a case decided after *Carey,* the Supreme Court explicitly authorized the recovery of punitive damages in constitutional tort litigation "when the defendant's conduct is motivated by evil motive or intent, or when it involves reckless or callous indifference to the federally protected rights of others." Smith v. Wade, 461 U.S. 30, 56, 103 S.Ct. 1625, 1640, 75 L.Ed.2d 632 (1983).

4. A plaintiff who prevails in a § 1983 constitutional tort action may be allowed "a reasonable attorney's fee as part of the costs" under 42 U.S.C.A. § 1988, enacted as the Civil Rights Attorney's Fees Awards Act of 1976. The Supreme Court has ruled that 42 U.S.C.A. § 1988 does not allow attorneys' fees

to be recovered from a governmental entity when a plaintiff sues government employees only in their personal capacities and prevails. It noted that:

* * *

"Personal-capacity suits seek to impose personal liability upon a government official for actions he takes under color of state law. See, *e.g.*, Scheuer v. Rhodes, 416 U.S. 232, 237–238, 94 S.Ct. 1683, 1686–1687, 40 L.Ed.2d 90 (1974). Official-capacity suits, in contrast, 'generally represent only another way of pleading an action against an entity of which an officer is an agent.' Monell v. New York City Dept. of Social Services, 436 U.S. 658, 690 n. 55, 98 S.Ct. 2018, 2035 n. 55, 56 L.Ed.2d 611 (1978). As long as the governmental entity receives notice and an opportunity to respond, an official-capacity suit is, in all respects other than name, to be treated as a suit against the entity. It is *not* a suit against the official personally, for the real party in interest is the entity. Thus, while an award of damages against an official in his personal capacity can be executed only against the official's personal assets, a plaintiff seeking to recover on a damages judgment in an official-capacity suit must look to the governmental entity itself. * * *

"With this distinction in mind, it is clear that a suit against a government official in his or her personal capacity cannot lead to imposition of fee liability upon the governmental entity. A victory in a personal-capacity action is a victory against the individual defendant, rather than against the entity that employs him. Indeed, unless a distinct cause of action is asserted against the entity itself, the entity is not even a party to a personal-capacity lawsuit and has no opportunity to present a defense. That a plaintiff has prevailed against one party does not entitle him to fees from another party, let alone from a non-party. Yet that would be the result were we to hold that fees can be recovered from a governmental entity following victory in a personal-capacity action against government officials."

Kentucky v. Graham, 473 U.S. 159, 105 S.Ct. 3099, 3103–3107, 87 L.Ed.2d 114 (1985).*

5. The effectiveness of damages as a remedy for the violation of constitutional rights is severely impaired by the immunities accorded to public officials and governmental entities. Professor Christina Whitman, in a thought-provoking article, has suggested that instead of presuming that damages are the "ordinary" form of relief for constitutional torts, the courts should regard injunctions as the preferred remedy. Whitman, Constitutional Torts, 79 Mich. L.Rev. 5 (1980). If a plaintiff's procedural due process rights are at issue, is an injunction a more effective remedy than damages under *Carey*?

B. INJUNCTIVE RELIEF

WEYENBERG v. MENASHA

United States District Court, Eastern District of Wisconsin, 1975.
401 F.Supp. 801.

MYRON L. GORDON, DISTRICT JUDGE.

This is the plaintiff's motion for a temporary restraining order pursuant to Rule 65, Federal Rules of Civil Procedure. I conclude that the plaintiff's application for temporary relief should be granted.

* *See generally* Note, Surveying the Law of Fee Awards Under the Attorney's Fees Awards Act of 1976, 59 Notre Dame L.Rev. 1293 (1984).

* * *

The plaintiff's verified complaint seeks, among other things, injunctive relief restraining the defendants from removing him as the superintendent of police of the town of Menasha without first providing him with a hearing consistent with the requirements of the due process clause of the fourteenth amendment. Monetary relief is also sought by the plaintiff, but allegations pertaining to such claim are not germane to the instant motion and will not be discussed in this opinion.

To obtain a temporary restraining order, the plaintiff must bear the burden of demonstrating that: (1) there is a strong probability of success on the merits; (2) he will suffer irreparable harm if interim relief is not granted; (3) there is no manifest danger of substantial harm to other parties. * * *

I am satisfied that the plaintiff's first and second claims for relief are likely to succeed on the merits. The first claim alleges a denial of due process in the plaintiff's termination as police superintendent. Such claim is allegedly actionable directly under the Constitution and under 42 U.S.C.A. § 1983, with jurisdiction predicated upon 28 U.S.C.A. §§ 1331 and 1343(3), respectively. The second claim alleges a denial of equal protection in that procedural protections afforded to certain Wisconsin police department employees pursuant to Wis.Stat. § 62.13(5) (1973) are not available to the plaintiff.

From the formal resolution of the town board of Menasha dated July 27, 1970, it appears that the plaintiff's contract of employment as superintendent of police is terminable at the will of the board. Thus, I do not believe it likely that the plaintiff will be able to prove that he had a property interest in continuing as police superintendent which is protectable under the due process clause.

Nevertheless, I believe that the minutes of the town board meetings of May 25, 1975, and August 1, 1975, demonstrate that the plaintiff was subjected to state action which infringed his rights under the fourteenth amendment. The following quotation from the minutes of the August 1, 1975, board meeting makes it probable that the elimination of the plaintiff's job as police superintendent at the May 25, 1975, meeting may have been motivated by the existence of charges likely to involve the alleged misconduct or incompetence of the plaintiff:

> "Motion was made by [the defendant] Mr. Unkefer and seconded by [the defendant] Mr. Page, that the responsibility and order for the Police Department, will be given to Mr. Robert C. Weyenberg, and that he will be a patrolman at a salary of $12,000 per year, with no overtime, *until this issue is settled* or a new person is hired.

"Amended by Mr. Page, *if Mr. Weyenberg is judged innocent,* the difference in salary would be made up, not to include overtime, for the pertinent period.

"Amendment carried.

"Motion carried." (Emphasis added).

Under these circumstances, I believe the plaintiff is likely to prevail on his claim that the elimination of his job called into question his good name, honor and integrity, thus requiring the defendants to provide him with a due process hearing. Board of Regents of State Colleges v. Roth, 408 U.S. 564, 573, 92 S.Ct. 2701, 33 L.Ed.2d 548 (1972); Wisconsin v. Constantineau, 400 U.S. 433, 437, 91 S.Ct. 507, 27 L.Ed.2d 515 (1971). Such hearing requires that the following protections be provided: (1) written notice of the charges; (2) disclosure of the evidence supporting the charges; (3) an opportunity to be heard in person and to present witnesses and evidence; (4) the right to confront and cross-examine witnesses; (5) a neutral and detached decisionmaker; and (6) a written statement of the decisionmaker as to the evidence relied upon and the reasons for his findings and conclusions. * * *

In addition to the protections described above, the plaintiff is likely to be entitled to the further protections offered by Wis.Stat. § 62.13(5) as a matter of fourteenth amendment equal protection. * * * Thus, the plaintiff cannot be permanently discharged or replaced until he has had a hearing at which he is permitted the aid of counsel and the right to subpoena witnesses.

I am not only persuaded that the plaintiff is likely to succeed on the merits in view of the foregoing, but I am also convinced that the plaintiff will suffer irreparable harm if injunctive relief is not granted. Until the plaintiff is provided with an opportunity to defend his reputation, he is unfairly burdened with a serious impediment to his ability to seek new employment, should that become necessary. Also, his standing in the community has been imperiled.

Moreover, I have no difficulty concluding that the defendants will not be unduly burdened by providing the plaintiff with an adequate hearing before they endeavor permanently to replace the plaintiff as the head of the Menasha police department.

Finally, although the plaintiff urges that he should be returned to his position as superintendent of police pending a hearing, I believe that the better course is to permit the plaintiff to retain his job as a Menasha police officer and to receive the same pay and benefits to which he was entitled as the police superintendent. This would leave the plaintiff in substantially the same position as one who is suspended with pay.

* * *

[U]ntil such time as this matter can be heard on the plaintiff's motion for a preliminary injunction, the defendants are hereby temporarily restrained as follows: The defendants shall hereafter provide the plaintiff the wages and other employment benefits to which he was entitled when he last held the position of superintendent of police of the town of Menasha, and the defendants shall not permanently replace the plaintiff as superintendent of the Menasha police department regardless of the title given to any such replacement, until such time as the defendants provide to the plaintiff a pretermination hearing consistent with this opinion. * * *

Note

State and local public officials enjoy either absolute or qualified immunities from liability for damages under § 1983, but these immunities are irrelevant in actions for injunctive relief. Local governmental entities are not immune from liability for damages under § 1983, and they may be sued directly for injunctive relief as well. State governmental entities are immune from suit in federal court under the eleventh amendment, but state officials may be sued in federal court in their official capacities for *prospective* injunctive relief. Pennhurst State School & Hospital v. Halderman, 465 U.S. 89, 104 S.Ct. 900, 79 L.Ed.2d 67 (1984); Edelman v. Jordan, 415 U.S. 651, 94 S.Ct. 1347, 39 L.Ed.2d 662 (1974); *Ex parte* Young, 209 U.S. 123, 28 S.Ct. 441, 52 L.Ed. 714 (1908). *See generally* Nahmod, Civil Rights and Civil Liberties Litigation (1979).

MORGAN v. McDONOUGH

United States Court of Appeals, First Circuit, 1976.
540 F.2d 527.

Before COFFIN, CHIEF JUDGE, MCENTEE and CAMPBELL, CIRCUIT JUDGES.

LEVIN H. CAMPBELL, CIRCUIT JUDGE.

This appeal was filed on December 10, 1975, by the Boston School Committee (the Committee) from orders of the district court designating a temporary receiver for South Boston High School and ordering the transfer, without reduction in pay, of certain of its staff. The question before us is whether under the extraordinarily difficult and troubled circumstances confronting the School in the fall and early winter of 1975, the district court exceeded its powers in entering such orders. The instant appeal does not deal with how long such a receivership may properly last.

First integrated by court order in 1974 ("Phase I"), the South Boston High School was serving a racially mixed enrollment in 1975–76 under Phase II, a city wide desegregation plan formulated by the district court and upheld on appeal to this court. Morgan v. Kerrigan, 530 F.2d 401 (1st Cir.), *cert. denied,* 426 U.S. 935, 96 S.Ct. 2648, 49 L.Ed.2d 386 (1976). In November, 1975, the plaintiffs, representing a class of all black Boston public school students and parents, moved to close the School, alleging that black students there were being denied a peaceful, integrated and nondiscriminatory education. Following a lengthy hearing and several visits to the School, the district court found plaintiffs' basic allegations to be correct, but declined to close the School, ordering instead that it be placed in the temporary receivership of the court, effective December 10, 1975. The court first named as receiver a senior official of the Boston School Department, who was, in fact, the assistant superintendent for the district within which the School was located, but on January 9, 1976, after this appeal was filed, the court appointed Boston's Superintendent of Schools,

Marion J. Fahey, as temporary receiver in place of the previous receiver. The stated purpose of the receivership was to effectuate as soon as possible "such changes in the administration and operation of South Boston High School as are necessary to bring the School into compliance with the student desegregation plan dated May 10, 1975 [Phase II], and all other remedial orders entered by the court in these proceedings, *e.g.*, desegregation of faculty and staff." The court directed the receiver to (1) arrange for the transfer of the School's headmaster, full-time academic administrators, and football coach, without reduction in compensation, benefits, or seniority; (2) evaluate the qualifications of all faculty and educational personnel and arrange the transfer and replacement of whomever he sees fit for the purposes of desegregation, without reduction in compensation, benefits, or seniority; (3) file a plan with the court for the renovation of the School; (4) try to enroll non-attending students and establish catch-up classes; and (5) make recommendations to the court relative to certain provisions of the plan. It is the receivership order and the foregoing directions, including especially those for transfer of staff, which are the subject of this appeal.

As the district court's primary orders requiring South Boston High School and other Boston schools to be desegregated have been reviewed and sustained, *see Morgan v. Kerrigan, supra,* the time is no longer ripe to consider arguments against Phase II itself. The questions now before us are simply whether the lower court properly determined that plaintiff's rights under the desegregation plan were being violated at South Boston High School, and if so, whether the temporary remedies ordered were reasonable and lawful. We answer these questions in the affirmative. Given the lawfulness of the court's desegregation decrees, there is little question that it had the power to take reasonable steps to ensure compliance therewith and to protect the students attending the city's desegregated schools. The evidence here does not show that the court went beyond what might reasonably be considered necessary to cope with a grave threat to the desegregation plan and to the safety and rights of the black students at South Boston High School.

II

Conditions at South Boston High School which resulted in the challenged receivership and transfer orders are described in the district court's oral and written findings, based on a week-long evidentiary hearing and on affidavits and personal visits to the School.

* * *

The district court's central impression was that the services provided at South Boston High were "primarily custodial and only incidentally educational." The court characterized the atmosphere as not so much filled with racial tension, or even any tension, as with a "pervasive lassitude and emptiness." * * *

The district court's findings indicate that, as the court concluded, black students attending the School were not receiving a "peaceful, desegregated education". Rather they were subject to insult, intimidation and continued segregation. * * * Doubtless the difficulty stemmed in no small measure from intentional conduct by private organizations and individuals in the South Boston community. But difficult as was the position of school officials, there was reason to believe that conditions could have been, and still could be, ameliorated by them, and that their active and passive conduct contributed to the grave situation so clearly at odds with the court's prior decrees. * * *

The question thus boils down to the propriety of the relief that was ordered. A district court's power to fashion and effectuate desegregation decrees is broad and flexible, and the remedies may be "administratively awkward, inconvenient, and even bizarre". Swann v. Charlotte–Mecklenburg Board of Education, 401 U.S. 1, 15–16, 28, 91 S.Ct. 1267, 1282, 28 L.Ed.2d 554 (1971). Remedial devices should be effective and relief prompt. * * * While a receivership has been instituted only once in a reported desegregation case, Turner v. Goolsby, 255 F.Supp. 724 (S.D.Ga. 1966), receiverships are and have for years been a familiar equitable mechanism. *See* Fed.R.Civ.P. 66; 4 Pomeroy, Equity Jurisprudence § 1330 *et seq.* (Symons ed. 1941). They are commonly a vehicle for court supervision of distressed businesses, but have not been limited to that role. The Supreme Court indicated many years ago that a receiver might take charge of a company to enforce compliance with the antitrust laws. * * * Receiverships and court-appointed officials with some of the same functions as the receiver here have been approved in other contexts. *See, e.g.,* Inmates of Attica Correctional Facility v. Rockefeller, 453 F.2d 12, 25 (2d Cir.1971). * * * Masters have been used extensively to formulate plans and recommendations, one of the present receiver's chief functions. * * * Finally, there is precedent for a district court having desegregation responsibilities to order personnel shifts. * * *

We thus find nothing impermissible *per se* about any of the actions the court took. The test is one of reasonableness under the circumstances. To be sure, direct judicial intervention in the operation of a school system is not to be welcomed, and it should not be continued longer than necessary. But if in extraordinary circumstances it is the only reasonable alternative to noncompliance with a court's plan of desegregation, it may, with appropriate restraint, be ordered. * * *

The receivership here was a means to enlist without delay top Boston School Department leadership to work in conjunction with the court on the troubles of the School. The court utilized the device to ensure priority attention by senior administrators, under court supervision, to South Boston High's unique problems. The more usual remedies—contempt proceedings and further injunctions—were plainly not very promising, as they invited further confrontation and delay; and when the usual remedies are inadequate, a court of equity is justified, particularly in aid of an outstanding injunction, in turning to less common ones, such as a receivership, to get the job done. * * *

Had the School Committee then in office been cooperative, a voluntary approach might have summoned similar resources without need for a formal receivership. However, the then School Committee had continuously resisted desegregation, and its leaders had advised the court on more than one occasion that they would obey nothing but direct orders. The court had reasonable cause, therefore, to discount the likelihood of effective cooperation. It also had reason to fear that even direct orders to that Committee would, as in the past, be met by resistance, subterfuge, or, at very least, delay. * * * Finally, it bears emphasizing that the principal alternative being suggested to the receivership order was to order that South Boston High be closed. That alternative would not only have involved the abandonment of a large and useful facility but would have necessitated the planning, expense, and inconvenience of finding places for some 2000 students. Without expressing any opinion on the propriety of ordering the School closed, it can be said that the district court demonstrated both restraint and wisdom in selecting the receivership option. For all of the foregoing reasons, therefore, we see the district court's action not as excessive but as reasonably tailored to carrying out the court's responsibilities.

Nor do we find unreasonable the transfer of the headmaster, coach and other staff. Apart from finding overt resistance to the segregation plan by the coach, the court also noted adverse faculty attitudes and a lack of leadership by the School administration in implementing the plan. Given the situation that had developed at the School under existing leadership, the court was entitled to conclude that a change in command was indicated. The change tied into the appointment of the receiver, giving the latter, in conjunction with the court, the opportunity, after study, to bring in administrators and perhaps faculty that seemed best able to cope with the extraordinary difficulties and pressures at the School.

It is true that the court's actions, while not reaching beyond the professional School Department, supplanted the supervisory authority of the elected Committee in this area. However, judicial desegregation necessarily involves some displacement of decision-making powers, as we have already witnessed in other aspects of this case, *e.g.*, drawing of district lines, teacher hiring, and so on. * * * The extent of the court's power is limited to what is required to ensure students their right to a non-segregated education, but within that parameter it may do what reasonably it must. * * *

Here, contrary to the Committee's assertions, we find no evidence of any intrusion by the district court upon the School Committee's right to determine "educational philosophy" except as that philosophy might impermissibly encourage a racially separate school system. The "limited, general purpose of said receivership", as the lower court stated, is only to bring the School into compliance with the desegregation plan and orders. As the receiver is the Superintendent of Schools, we can see little danger that the receivership will introduce educational policies contrary to those prevailing in the system as a whole. * * *

We would, however, add a *caveat.* Obviously the substitution of a court's authority for that of elected and appointed officials is an extraordinary step warranted only by the most compelling circumstances. Those circumstances here were the failure of local officials to give effect to the court's desegregation orders in a meaningful manner. The receivership should last no longer than the conditions which justify it make necessary, and the court's utilization of the receivership must not go beyond the constitutional purposes which the device is designed to promote. We have no doubt that the district court will exercise appropriate restraint in this respect and, in particular, will give thought to appropriate conditions under which the receivership can be terminated at the earliest opportunity consistent with the rights of children and parents to a peaceful non-segregated education.

Affirmed.*

Notes

1. The development of the structural injunction, which seeks to reorganize an ongoing social institution, is viewed from a critical perspective in Nagel, Separation of Powers and the Scope of Federal Equitable Remedies, 30 Stan. L.Rev. 661, 661–663 (1978): *

> "In recent years, both popular and academic [2] attention has begun to focus on the innovative and expansive remedies that federal courts have utilized with increasing frequency, especially against state governments. These forms of relief raise the question whether the judiciary has begun to tolerate in itself a blending of functions that would never be tolerated in another branch of government. Federal district courts largely have as-

* The trend toward using masters and receivers in civil rights litigation is described in Comment, The Wyatt Case: Implementation of a Judicial Decree Ordering Institutional Change, 84 Yale L.J. 1338, 1340–1347 (1975): **

** Reprinted by permission of The Yale Law Journal Company and Fred B. Rothman & Company from The Yale Law Journal, Vol. 84, pp. 1138, 1340–1347.

"In devising techniques for implementation of institutional change, courts have sought to make the judicial process more available to the institution's residents, thus partially insulating them from the control of the institution. Courts have also sought means to obtain independent, reliable information about what is going on in the institution to subject the institution's professed expertise to the scrutiny of other experts, and to 'open up' the institutional bureaucracy by giving staff at all levels access to the court.

"To accomplish this, the judiciary has drawn on its authority to fashion 'appropriate instruments required for the performance of [its] duties,' including the power to appoint judicial officers. In addition to employing traditional remedies, such as the appointment of masters or receivers, courts have fashioned several new ones.

"One novel judicial approach has combined the factfinding role of the traditional master and the supervisory role of the traditional receiver to form a 'hybrid' master to aid in the implementation of structural injunctions. For example, in Pennsylvania Association for Retarded Children v. Pennsylvania, two masters, one an attorney and one a special educator, were charged with both evaluating and implementing a plan drafted by the state to provide a suitable public education for retarded children. * * *

"Another new implementation technique used by the courts has been the assignment of monitors * * * appointed simply to observe the implementation process and report their observations to the court.

"A third method of implementation has involved the judicial appointment of ombudsmen to hear inmate complaints and grievances, conduct investigations, and make recommendations to the court. Unlike masters and monitors, which are envisioned as temporary, interim measures to aid in the implementation of decrees until compliance is achieved, ombudsmen have sometimes been included as part of the substantive relief, *i.e.*, part of the restructuring of the institution." *See also* Levine, The Authority of Remedial Special Masters in Federal Institutional Reform Litigation: The History Reconsidered, 17 U.C.D.L.Rev. 753 (1984).

2. *E.g.*, O. Fiss, Injunctions (1972); Chayes, The Role of the Judge in Public Law Litigation, 89 Harv.L.Rev. 1281 (1976); Hill, Constitutional Remedies, 69 Colum.L.Rev. 1109 (1969); Johnson, The Constitution and the Federal District Judge, 54 Tex.L.Rev. 903 (1976) * * *. [Footnotes 196–99 from the original.]

sumed the duties of administering a state mental health system[4] and a state prison.[5] Many federal courts are intimately involved with operating public school systems, and one court has placed a public high school directly under judicial control. For some years, of course, courts have mandated state apportionment schemes. One court has ordered the reorganization of an entire city government. In short, courts have exercised traditionally executive functions by appointing executive and quasi-executive officers responsible to the judiciary and by determining administrative processes in elaborately detailed decrees; they have exercised legislative functions by setting policy standards for the operation of state and federal programs, including the setting of budgetary requirements. * * *

"Not surprisingly, perhaps, in light of the judiciary's institutional needs and biases, the Supreme Court has held that the constitutional doctrine of separation of powers has no bearing on the problem of defining the limits of federal courts' equitable powers against state governments.[12] The more extreme implications of this position are unacceptable by nearly any standard. As applied at the federal level, the fundamental assumption behind separation of powers is that because no branch of government can be trusted in its use of power, the power of each branch must be limited by some degree of functional specialization.

"The federal judiciary is not immune from the need for limitations based on functional differentiation." *

2. Professor Owen Fiss, engaging in a thoughtful analysis of the structural injunction, has made the following observations in The Civil Rights Injunction 86–93 (1978): **

"The injunction became the primary remedy in civil rights litigation for a very special set of reasons, and it remains to be seen whether those reasons are generalizable.

"One set of reasons is technocratic—civil rights litigation presented the courts with technical tasks that could not be performed by remedies other than the injunction, or that could not be performed as well. The conversion of the dual school systems to unitary school systems is a prime example. From a purely technocratic perspective the injunction seemed ideally suited. In contrast to damage judgments or criminal prosecutions, the injunction could more easily accommodate the group nature of the claim, it could provide the requisite specificity and continuing supervision

4. Wyatt v. Stickney, 344 F.Supp. 373 (M.D.Ala.1972), aff'd in part sub nom. Wyatt v. Aderholt, 503 F.2d 1305 (5th Cir.1974).

5. Pugh v. Locke, 406 F.Supp. 318 (M.D.Ala.1976), aff'd in relevant part sub nom. Newman v. Alabama, 559 F.2d 283 (5th Cir.1977); Holt v. Sarver, 309 F.Supp. 362 (E.D.Ark.1970), aff'd, 442 F.2d 304 (8th Cir. 1971).

12. Elrod v. Burns, 427 U.S. 347, 352 (1976) * * *.

* Structural injunctions have been praised and criticized by a wide range of commentary. Eisenberg, Section 1983: Doctrinal Foundations and an Empirical Study, 67 Cornell L.Rev. 482 (1982); Eisenberg & Yeazell, The Ordinary and Extraordinary in Institutional Litigation, 93 Harv.L.Rev. 465 (1980); Fletcher, The Discretionary Constitution: Institutional Remedies and Judicial Legitimacy, 91 Yale L.J. 63 (1982); Gewirtz, Remedies and Resistance, 92 Yale L.J. 585 (1983); Jones, Federal Court Remedies: The Creative Use of Potential Remedies Can Produce Institutional Change, 27 How.L.J. 879 (1984); Nagel, Controlling the Structural Injunction, 7 Harv.J.L. & Pub.Pol'y 395 (1984); Resnick, Managerial Judges, 96 Harv.L.Rev. 376 (1982); Rudenstine, Institutional Injunctions, 4 Cardozo L.Rev. 611 (1983).

** Reprinted with permission of the Indiana University Press.

over long periods of time, and it introduced a desired degree of softness—it had a prospective quality, and directives could easily be modified as the courts enhanced their understanding of the constitutional goal and how that goal might be achieved. All this seemed essential for structural reformation.

"Similarly, when the demand was to compensate for the systematic and thorough wrongs of slavery, the Jim Crow era, or the more subtle, and recent, forms of discrimination, cash payments seemed peculiarly inadequate. * * * The inadequacy stemmed from the group nature of the underlying claim and a belief that only in-kind benefits would effect a change in the status of the group.

"The injunction was also well suited for the preventive needs of civil rights litigation. To a large extent this litigation was aimed at government officials, and it was fair to presume that they are not as sensitive to the prospect of damage judgments as the businessman working within a competitive framework. Moreover, in contrast to both damage judgments and criminal prosecutions, the injunction is capable of speaking only to the future, and with great specificity. * * *

"The second reason for the primary of the injunction in civil rights litigation is more normative. It turns not so much on the content of the injunction and the technical advantages it brings as on the allocation of power implicit in the injunctive process. The injunctive process essentially allocates power to the citizen-grievant (the power of initiation) and to the judiciary (the power of decision). Such an allocation of power was favored because it seemed essential to the success of the civil rights claim.

* * *

"The allocation of power of initiation to the individual citizen needs no strenuous justification; it readily accords with the American traditions of individualism (in the antigovernmental sense). But the allocation of the power of decision to the judiciary requires a very special justification—it is at odds with our democratic traditions. This justification was lacking with the labor injunction; the same was true with the anti-Progressivism injunction, and in that instance the antidemocratic objection was strengthened by a claim that the decisional agency (the judges) lacked 'scientific expertise.' In the case of the civil rights injunction, however, this special justification for the allocation to the judiciary could be found in the doctrine of 'minority rights.'

* * *

"The essential lesson of the civil rights injunction is not that we should supplant one remedial hierarchy with another. * * * Rather, the civil rights injunction teaches that we should move to a nonhierarchical conception of remedies. It teaches that the choice of remedy should not turn on generalized propositions—couched in the obscure but colorful language of history—about which remedies are favored and which are disfavored. It should instead turn upon an appreciation of the technical advantages of each remedy and a judgment, made in light of the substantive claim, about the desirability of the allocation of power that is implicit in each remedial system. * * *

* * *

"The structural injunction entails a relationship of long duration between the judge and the social institution, a series of interventions, either increasing the specificity or modifying previously issued decrees, inviting or permitting participation by amici, such as the Department of Justice, or possibly even creating new agencies to assist in the policing of performance. An auxiliary bureaucratic structure is often created. In economic terms this behavioral pattern is costly. Of even greater concern is its impact on the judicial role. The structural injunction tends to accentuate the personification inherent in the injunctive process and to make it difficult for the judge to maintain the umpireal posture. The judge is brought perilously close, so it is claimed, to breaching the line between administration and law.

"These considerations—the consumption of resources and even more, the role transformation—render plausible the possibility of a right without a remedy—that the court will decline to issue a structural injunction even though that is by far the best remedy, or for that matter the only remedy. * * *

"I acknowledge these concerns, and yet I do not concede their persuasiveness. I do not believe the structural injunction should be put beyond the reach of the courts. [E]ven if the role transformations inherent in the structural decree are considered a cost and are aggregated with the economic ones, they do not become insurmountable: they only call for more urgent justification. Extraordinary injunctions may require extraordinary claims. What gives legal claims such a special status, the entitlement to be considered 'extraordinary,' is the special nature of the substantive claim—the systematic denial of important rights to a social group. Thus the departures from the standard models of judicial behavior are ultimately justified and determined by underlying substantive rights."

For a recent example of a broad injunction appointing a receiver to take over and manage a state jail, *see* Shaw v. Allen, 771 F.Supp. 760 (S.D.W.Va. 1990).

NORCISA v. BOARD OF SELECTMEN OF PROVINCETOWN

Supreme Judicial Court of Massachusetts, 1975.
368 Mass. 161, 330 N.E.2d 830.

QUIRICO, JUSTICE.

This is an appeal by the defendants, the board of selectmen of Provincetown (selectmen) and their agent, from a decree entered by the judge of the Probate Court for Barnstable County, apparently acting under G.L. c. 231A, §§ 1, 2, and under G.L. c. 215, § 6, as appearing in St.1963, c. 820, § 1, declaring that the plaintiff and her retail clothing business in the town of Provincetown (town) are not within the scope of G.L. c. 101, §§ 1–12, the Transient Vendor Statute, and ordering that the town and its agents, servants, and employees "are hereby restrained and permanently enjoined from enforcing * * * any of the provisions of Mass.G.L. c. 101, §§ 1–12, against the Petitioner or the retail business she operates." This appeal was first entered in the Appeals Court and we then transferred it to this court, acting on our own motion. G.L. c. 211A, § 10(A), inserted by St.1972, c. 740, § 1. Prior to the commencement of this suit in equity, a criminal complaint had issued in the Second District Court of Barnstable County charging the plaintiff with violating G.L. c. 101, §§ 6, 8. This criminal complaint was still pending when the decree appealed from issued. The obvious purpose and effect of the decree was to enjoin the pending criminal prosecution. We reverse.

The facts apparently relied on by the judge in issuing the final decree were contained in a document signed by attorneys for both the plaintiff and the defendants, entitled "Agreed Statement of Facts." It appears from this document that sometime late in 1973 the plaintiff, who was a resident of Provincetown, opened a retail clothing business in that town under the name of The Town Crier Wearhouse. At the time she opened her business, the plaintiff was informed by the agent for the selectmen "that she would not be able to open and operate her business unless she paid to Provincetown a license fee of two hundred dollars ($200.00), furnished a bond of five hundred dollars ($500.00), to the Commonwealth, and applied for both a state and town Transient Vendor's License, all of the above pursuant to and authorized by G.L. c. 101, § 3."

General Laws c. 101, § 3, requires that anyone "before commencing business in the commonwealth as a transient vendor" shall apply for a State license, good for one year, to do business as a transient vendor, subject to local rules and regulations. * * * A "transient vendor" is defined as "any person, either principal or agent, who engages in a temporary or transient business in the commonwealth selling goods, wares or merchandise, either in one locality or in traveling from place to place." G.L. c. 101, § 1. "Temporary or transient business" is further defined as "any exhibition and sale of goods, wares or merchandise which is carried on in any tent, booth, building or other structure, unless such place is open for business during usual business hours for a period of at least twelve consecutive months." G.L. c. 101, § 1.

The plaintiff's position as stated in the "Agreed Statement of Facts" is that she was not a transient vendor at the time the selectmen sought to categorize her as one, that she had not been a transient vendor in the past, and that she would not be a transient vendor in the future. * * * The defendants' position, in the court below as well as in their brief here, has been "that under the terms of the statute petitioner is required to take out a transient vendor's license unless she *has been* 'open for business during usual business hours for a period of at least twelve consecutive months' " (emphasis added).

* * *

At one time, it was common for courts to express the view that an equity court had no "jurisdiction" to enjoin a criminal prosecution. * * *

In this Commonwealth, however, it was early established that courts with general equity powers have the power to restrain criminal prosecutions. * * *

As pointed out in the *Shuman* case, the occasions when an equity court may properly enjoin a criminal prosecution remain the exception to the "general rule" of nonintervention. Some of the basic policy reasons underlying the rule of nonintervention were well-expressed by the Supreme Court of Hawaii: "Courts of equity are not constituted to deal with crimes and criminal proceedings. They have no power to punish admitted offenders of a challenged penal statute after holding it to be valid, or to compensate those injured by the violations thereof while the hands of the officers of the law have been stayed by injunction. To that extent such courts are incapable of affording a complete remedy. Equity, therefore, takes no part in the administration of the criminal law. It neither aids, restrains, nor obstructs criminal courts in the exercise of their jurisdiction. Ordinarily a court of equity deals only with civil cases involving property rights where it can afford a complete remedy by injunctive relief. Hence it does not interfere in the enforcement of penal statutes even though invalid unless there be exceptional circumstances and a clear showing that an injunction is urgently necessary to afford adequate protection to rights of property so as to circumvent great and irreparable injury until the validity of the particular penal statute is sustained." Liu v. Farr, 39 Hawaii 23, 35–36 (1950).

Both the *Shuman* and *Liu* cases quoted above indicated that equity would act only to protect "property rights" from irreparable damage by criminal prosecution. In the leading case of Kenyon v. Chicopee, 320 Mass. 528, 70 N.E.2d 241 (1946), however, we largely rejected the personal rights-property rights distinction as a factor in considering whether an injunction should issue. * * *

The plaintiff variously claims that G.L. c. 101, §§ 1–12, is either unconstitutional on its face or as applied, or that the statute, properly construed, does not apply to her at all. In accordance with these claims, she asserts that she cannot be prosecuted for failure to comply with the statute. If we assume, again without deciding the question, that the plaintiff indeed cannot properly be prosecuted under this statute, the issue resolves itself simply to whether the available defenses to the District Court criminal complaint amount to an adequate remedy at law. In the circumstances of this case, we think they plainly do.

In both the *Shuman* and *Kenyon* cases, the question was considered whether, in the circumstances of those cases, the defense to the criminal prosecution provided an adequate remedy at law. Since the injunction was denied in the former case and granted in the latter, it is instructive to compare them.

In the *Shuman* case, six merchants alleged that the defendant chief of police of Northampton threatened to prosecute them for conducting a business without a license, which they claimed they were not obligated to obtain. The plaintiffs' bill sought to make out a case of irreparable damage and inadequacy of legal remedy by alleging, inter alia, that it would take several months to obtain a decision on the case from an appellate court and that in the intervening period the loss of profits and advantageous business relations would cause the plaintiffs great and irreparable damage. To these averments, a demurrer was sustained. This court upheld the sustaining of the demurrer. After noting that in the event of multiple, oppressive, and wrongful prosecutions, an injunction might properly issue, we said: "A possibility that complaints may be lodged against six persons is not enough under these circumstances to make out a case of multiplicity. The allegations as to repeated complaints are not sufficient to warrant the inference that the courts of this commonwealth will countenance continued and oppressive prosecutions when once a genuine test case open to fair question has been presented and is on its way to final decision." 229 Mass. at 229, 118 N.E. at 256 (1918). We further rejected any notion that our courts of criminal jurisdiction could not protect the rights in question: "[The bill] assumes that one innocent of any infraction of the law will be found guilty by the district court and by the superior court, a presumption which as matter of law cannot be indulged, at least upon such general allegations. The allegations as to property damage are nothing more than the ordinary averments which might be made by anybody engaged in business, undertaking a branch of commercial adventure believed by the officers charged with enforcing the law to be in contravention of some penal statute confessedly valid in itself. Simply that one is in business and may be injured in respect of his business by prosecution for an alleged crime, is no sufficient reason for asking a court of equity to ascertain in advance whether the business as conducted is in violation of a penal statute." 229 Mass. at 230, 118 N.E. at 256 (1918).

In the *Kenyon* case, by contrast, we reversed interlocutory decrees sustaining demurrers where the bill alleged that members of Jehovah's Witnesses had been repeatedly, on different dates, arrested, prosecuted, and convicted under an unconstitutional ordinance. * * * We observed: "The plaintiffs' rights are of the most fundamental character. According to the bill they have been violated repeatedly. It is plain that the legal remedies by defending against repeated complaints and bringing successive actions for malicious prosecution or false arrest are not adequate." 320 Mass. at 534, 70 N.E.2d at 245 (1946).

In the present case, the plaintiff is the subject of a complaint charging a single violation of the statute. She avers that the statute is either unconstitutional on its face or as applied, or that, properly construed, it is inapplicable to her. These averments, of course, would, if established, each constitute a complete defense to the violation charged. We repeat here a passage from a United States Supreme Court case which applies equally to the matter before us: "It is a familiar rule that courts of equity do not ordinarily restrain criminal prosecutions. No person is immune from prosecution in good faith for his alleged criminal acts. Its imminence, even though alleged to be in violation of constitutional guarantees, is not a ground for equity relief since the lawfulness or constitutionality of the statute or ordinance on which the prosecution is based may be determined as readily in the criminal case as in a suit for injunction. * * * It does not appear from the record that petitioners have been threatened with any injury other than that incidental to every criminal proceeding brought lawfully and in good faith, or that a * * * court of equity by withdrawing the determination of guilt from the * * * [criminal] courts could rightly afford petitioners any protection which they could not secure by prompt trial and appeal pursued to this Court." Douglas v. Jeannette, 319 U.S. 157, 163–164, 63 S.Ct. 877, 881, 87 L.Ed. 1324 (1943).

In general, we believe the Federal policy of ordinarily refusing to enjoin pending State criminal prosecutions is sound. This policy, based partly on principles of Federal–State comity and partly on the general equitable principles we have summarized in this opinion, * * * prohibits equitable interference with criminal prosecutions absent "very special circumstances." *Younger v. Harris, supra,* at 45, 91 S.Ct. 746. "Very special circumstances" may be merely a shorthand way of requiring a stricter application of general equitable principles, for example, that no injunction will issue unless the plaintiff will suffer irreparable and immediate injury without it. But however the concept is phrased, the necessity of defending a single criminal prosecution rarely, if ever, justifies issuance of the injunction.

* * *

[The court also concluded that declaratory relief was unavailable. For further consideration of declaratory relief in this context, see Chapter 5 *infra.*]

For the reasons given above, the injunction and declaratory relief should not have been granted. The final decree is reversed and a new judgment is to be entered dismissing the bill.

So ordered.

Note

The principal case is representative of a strong judicial sentiment against enjoining criminal prosecution, at least in the absence of exceptional circumstances, such as prosecutorial harrassment and bad faith. Professor Dobbs has articulated succinctly the reasons behind this rule:

> "If the injunction-seeker has a good defense, he can usually present it in the criminal proceeding itself, perhaps even obtain a dismissal in an early probable cause hearing. While and injunction may be a preferable remedy for any number of reasons, the normal rules of criminal procedure may be thought to require that courts keep hands off the criminal process. If the court hears all the evidence in the injunction suit and decides the prosecution can proceed, then all the evidence will be produced again before another judge in the criminal suit. If the evidence is not heard in the injunction suit, the question may be abstract and not suitable for a final determination. Either way, it seems better to use the criminal process unless its use can be shown to be a wrong and also one that threatens important rights of the plaintiff."

D. Dobbs, Law of Remedies 176 (2d Ed.1993).

Where a person is confronted by a threatened prosecution, it is arguable that injunction suits should receive somewhat more favorable treatment. In such a situation, the injunction suit does not duplicate an already commenced criminal action. Moreover, a person whose actions may be inhibited by a statute may wish to challenge its constitutionality: "If he has already violated it, he can do so in the criminal prosecution that ensues. However, he should not be forced to violate a statute in order to discover whether it can validly limit his activities. * * * If the plaintiff is in real need of determining his rights so that his full freedom of action can be assured on the one hand and his freedom from prosecution can be assured on the other, there is no very obvious reason why the courts of the state should not determine the constitutionality of the statute in an equity suit to enjoin its prosecution." D. Dobbs, Handbook on the Law of Remedies 114 (1973). Nevertheless, courts continue to require a showing of irreparable injury and, in some instances, that property or commercial interests are threatened. *See, e.g.,* S.S. Kresge Co. v. Davis, 277 N.C. 654, 178 S.E.2d 382 (1971); State v. Logue, 376 S.W.2d 567 (Tex.1964). The standard is relaxed a bit when the plaintiff claims a violation of the first amendment, as discussed in Spartacus Youth League v. Board of Trustees of Illinois Indus. Univ., 502 F.Supp. 789, 796–97 (N.D.Ill.1980) (action by youth organization challenging university regulations governing sale and distribution of literature at student union) (preliminary injunction granted):

> "The standard for justiciability determinations is '* * * whether the facts alleged * * * show that there is a substantial controversy, between parties having adverse legal interests, of sufficient immediacy and reality to warrant * * *' judicial review. Maryland Casualty Co. v. Pacific Coal & Oil Co., 312 U.S. 270, 273, 61 S.Ct. 510, 512, 85 L.Ed. 826 (1941). The test is an imprecise one, with only the opposite poles of the factual continuum providing clear guidance. A plaintiff need not invariably wait until he has been directly subjected to a law or policy before he brings a judicial challenge, but he cannot go to court simply by showing that a regulation exists and that he believes it will be enforced against him. National Student Association v. Hershey, 412 F.2d 1103, 1110 (D.C.Cir.1969). Between these principles fall the majority of the cases, where the probability of several contingencies must be evaluated on a case-by-case basis: '* * * the likelihood that the complainant will disobey the law, the certainty that such disobedience will take a particular form, any present injury occasioned by the threat of prosecution, and the likelihood that a prosecution will actually ensue.' Regional Rail Reorganization Act Cases, 419 U.S. 102, 143 n. 29, 95 S.Ct. 335, 358, 42 L.Ed.2d 320 (1974).
>
> "In the First Amendment area, however, a somewhat relaxed standard of uncertainty is applicable. Injury to First Amendment rights may result from the threat of enforcement itself, since it may chill the plaintiff's ardor and eliminate his desire to engage in protected expression. Dombrowski v. Pfister, 380 U.S. 479, 85 S.Ct. 1116, 14 L.Ed.2d 22 (1965); 13 Wright, Miller & Cooper, Federal Practice & Procedure § 3532, at 245 n. 29 (1975). 'The threat of sanctions may deter their [First Amendment rights'] exercise almost as potently as the actual application of sanctions.' *Dombrowski v. Pfister, supra;* NAACP v. Button, 371 U.S. 415, 433, 83 S.Ct. 328, 338, 9 L.Ed.2d 405 (1963). Although not every chill will create a justiciable controversy, it may be enough that the plaintiff raises 'a credible threat of enforcement and plausible allegations of intent or desire to engage in the threatened activities * * *' *Hershey, supra,* 412 F.2d at 1111–12."

MITCHUM v. FOSTER

Supreme Court of the United States, 1972.
407 U.S. 225, 92 S.Ct. 2151, 32 L.Ed.2d 705.

MR. JUSTICE STEWART delivered the opinion of the Court.

The federal anti-injunction statute provides that a federal court "may not grant an injunction to stay proceedings in a State court except as expressly authorized by Act of Congress, or where necessary in aid of its jurisdiction, or to protect or effectuate its judgments." An Act of Congress, 42 U.S.C.A. § 1983, expressly authorizes a "suit in equity" to redress "the deprivation," under color of state law, "of any rights, privileges, or immunities secured by the Constitution. * * * " The question before us is whether this "Act of Congress" comes within the "expressly authorized" exception of the anti-injunction statute so as to permit a federal court in a § 1983 suit to grant an injunction to stay a proceeding pending in a state court. This question, which has divided the federal courts, has lurked in the background of many of our recent cases, but we have not until today explicitly decided it.

I

The prosecuting attorney of Bay County, Florida, brought a proceeding in a Florida court to close down the appellant's bookstore as a public nuisance under the claimed authority of Florida law. The state court entered a preliminary order prohibiting continued operation of the bookstore. After further inconclusive proceedings in the state courts, the appellant filed a complaint in the United States District Court for the Northern District of Florida, alleging that the actions of the state judicial and law enforcement officials were depriving him of rights protected by the First and Fourteenth Amendments. Relying upon 42 U.S.C.A. § 1983, he asked for injunctive and declaratory relief against the state court proceedings, on the ground that Florida laws were being unconstitutionally applied by the state court so as to cause him great and irreparable harm. A single federal district judge issued temporary restraining orders, and a three-judge court was convened pursuant to 28 U.S.C.A. §§ 2281 and 2284.* After a hearing, the three-judge court dissolved the temporary restraining orders and refused to enjoin the state court proceeding, holding that the "injunctive relief sought here as to the proceedings pending in the Florida courts does not come under any of the exceptions set forth in Section 2283. It is not expressly authorized by Act of Congress, it is not necessary in the aid of this court's jurisdiction and it is not sought in order to protect or effectuate any judgment of this court." Mitchum v. Foster, 315 F.Supp.

* Until 1976, any such injunction suit had to comply with the requirements of the Three–Judge Federal Court Act, 28 U.S.C.A. § 2281, which specified that federal suits to enjoin the enforcement of state legislation on constitutional grounds be heard by a three judge federal panel. Under the 1976 legislation, a three judge court is required only in actions "challenging the constitutionality of the apportionment of any state-wide legislative body" and in certain other relatively limited situations. *See* C. Wright, Handbook on the Law of Federal Courts 297 (1983). Consequently, it is no longer necessary to examine the substantial complexities of that statute when considering a federal court challenge to a state proceeding.

1387, 1389. An appeal was brought directly here under 28 U.S.C.A. § 1253 and we noted probable jurisdiction.

II

In denying injunctive relief, the District Court relied on this Court's decision in Atlantic Coast Line Railroad v. Brotherhood of Locomotive Engineers, 398 U.S. 281, 90 S.Ct. 1739, 26 L.Ed.2d 234. The Atlantic Coast Line case did not deal with the "expressly authorized" exception of the anti-injunction statute, but the Court's opinion in that case does bring into sharp focus the critical importance of the question now before us. For in that case we expressly rejected the view that the anti-injunction statute merely states a flexible doctrine of comity, and made clear that the statute imposes an absolute ban upon the issuance of a federal injunction against a pending state court proceeding, in the absence of one of the recognized exceptions * * *.

It follows, in the present context, that if 42 U.S.C.A. § 1983 is not within the "expressly authorized" exception of the anti-injunction statute, then a federal equity court is wholly without power to grant any relief in a § 1983 suit seeking to stay a state court proceeding. In short, if a § 1983 action is not an "expressly authorized" statutory exception, the anti-injunction law absolutely prohibits in such an action all federal equitable intervention in a pending state court proceeding, whether civil or criminal, and regardless of how extraordinary the particular circumstances may be.

* * *

III

The anti-injunction statute goes back almost to the beginnings of our history as a Nation. In 1793, Congress enacted a law providing that "[no] writ of injunction be granted [by any federal court] to stay proceedings in any court of a state. * * *" Act of March 2, 1793, 1 Stat. 335. The precise origins of the legislation are shrouded in obscurity, but the consistent understanding has been that its basic purpose is to prevent "needless friction between state and federal courts." Oklahoma Packing Co. v. Oklahoma Gas & Elec. Co., 309 U.S. 4, 9, 60 S.Ct. 215, 218, 84 L.Ed. 447. The law remained unchanged until 1875, when it was amended to permit a federal court to stay state court proceedings that interfered with the administration of a federal bankruptcy proceeding. The present wording of the legislation was adopted with the enactment of Title 28 of the United States Code in 1948.

Despite the seemingly uncompromising language of the anti-injunction statute prior to 1948, the Court soon recognized that exceptions must be made to its blanket prohibition if the import and purpose of other Acts of Congress were to be given their intended scope. So it was that, in addition to the bankruptcy law exception that Congress explicitly recognized in 1875, the Court through the years found that federal courts were empowered to enjoin state court proceedings, despite the anti-injunction statute, in carrying out the will of Congress under at least six other federal laws. These covered a broad spectrum of congressional action: (1) legislation providing for removal of litigation from state to federal courts, (2) legislation limiting the liability of shipowners, (3) legislation providing for federal interpleader actions, (4) legislation conferring federal jurisdiction over farm mortgages, (5) legislation governing federal habeas corpus proceedings, and (6) legislation providing for control of prices.

In addition to the exceptions to the anti-injunction statute found to be embodied in these various Acts of Congress, the Court recognized other "implied" exceptions to the blanket prohibition of the anti-injunction statute. One was an *"in rem"* exception, allowing a federal court to enjoin a state court proceeding in order to protect its jurisdiction of a *res* over which it had first acquired jurisdiction. Another was a "relitigation" exception, permitting a federal court to enjoin relitigation in a state court of issues already decided in federal litigation. Still a third exception, more recently developed permits a federal injunction of state court proceedings when the plaintiff in the federal court is the United States itself, or a federal agency asserting "superior federal interests."

In Toucey v. N.Y. Life Ins. Co., 314 U.S. 118, 62 S.Ct. 139, 86 L.Ed. 100, the Court in 1941 issued an opinion casting considerable doubt upon the approach to the anti-injunction statute reflected in its previous decisions. The Court's opinion expressly disavowed the "relitigation" exception to the statute, and emphasized generally the importance of recognizing the statute's basic directive "of 'hands off' by the federal courts in the use of the injunction to stay litigation in a state court." 314 U.S., at 132, 62 S.Ct., at 143. The congressional response to *Toucey* was the enactment in 1948 of the anti-injunction statute in its present form in 28 U.S.C.A. § 2283, which, as the Reviser's Note makes evident, served not only to overrule the specific holding of *Toucey,* but to "restore the basic law as generally understood and interpreted prior to the Toucey decision."

We proceed, then, upon the understanding that in determining whether § 1983 comes within the "expressly authorized" exception of the anti-injunction statute, the criteria to be applied are those reflected in the Court's decisions prior to *Toucey.* A review of those decisions makes reasonably clear what the relevant criteria are. In the first place, it is evident that, in order to qualify under the "expressly authorized" exception of the anti-injunction statute, a federal law need not contain an express reference to that statute. As the Court has said, "no prescribed formula is required; an authorization need not expressly refer to § 2283." Amalgamated Clothing Workers of America v. Richman Brothers Co., 348 U.S. 511, 516, 75 S.Ct. 452, 455, 99 L.Ed. 600. Indeed, none of the previously recognized statutory exceptions contains any such reference. Secondly, a federal law need not expressly authorize an injunction of a state court proceeding in order to qualify as an exception. Three of the six previously recognized statutory exceptions contain no such authorization. Thirdly, it is clear that, in order to qualify as an "expressly authorized" exception to the anti-injunction statute, an Act of Congress must have created a specific and uniquely federal right or remedy, enforceable in a federal court of equity, which could be frustrated if the federal court were not empowered to enjoin a state court proceeding. This is not to say that in order to come within the exception an Act of Congress must, on its face and in every one of its provisions, be totally incompatible with the prohibition of the anti-injunction statute. The test, rather, is whether an Act of Congress, clearly creating a federal right or remedy enforceable in a federal court of equity, could be given its intended scope only by the stay of a state court proceeding.

With these criteria in view, we turn to consideration of 42 U.S.C.A. § 1983.

IV

* * *

Section 1983 was a product of a vast transformation from the concepts of federalism that had prevailed in the late 18th century when the anti-injunction statute was enacted. The very purpose of § 1983 was to interpose the federal courts between the States and the people, as guardians of the people's federal rights—to protect the people from unconstitutional action under color of state law, "whether that action be executive, legislative or judicial." *Ex parte* Virginia, 100 U.S. 339, 346, 25 L.Ed. 676. In carrying out that purpose, Congress plainly authorized the federal courts to issue injunctions in § 1983 actions, by expressly authorizing a "suit in equity" as one of the means of redress. And this Court long ago recognized that federal injunctive relief against a state court proceeding can in some circumstances be essential to prevent great, immediate, and irreparable loss of a person's constitutional rights. *Ex parte* Young, 209 U.S. 123, 28 S.Ct. 441, 52 L.Ed. 714; *cf.* Truax v. Raich, 239 U.S. 33, 36 S.Ct. 7, 60 L.Ed. 131; Dombrowski v. Pfister, 380 U.S. 479, 85 S.Ct. 1116, 14 L.Ed.2d 22. For these reasons we conclude that, under the criteria established in our previous decisions construing the anti-injunction statute, § 1983 is an Act of Congress that falls within the "expressly authorized" exception of that law.

In so concluding, we do not question or qualify in any way the principles of equity, comity, and federalism that must restrain a federal court when asked to enjoin a state court proceeding. These principles, in the context of state criminal prosecutions, were canvassed at length last Term in Younger v. Harris, 401 U.S. 37, 91 S.Ct. 746, 27 L.Ed.2d 669, and its companion cases. They are principles that have been emphasized by this Court many times in the past.

* * * Today we decide only that the District Court in this case was in error in holding that, because of the anti-injunction statute, it was absolutely without power in this § 1983 action to enjoin a proceeding pending in a state court under any circumstances whatsoever.

The judgment is reversed and the case is remanded to the District Court for further proceedings consistent with this opinion. It is so ordered.

MR. JUSTICE POWELL and MR. JUSTICE REHNQUIST took no part in the consideration or decision of this case.

[The concurring opinion of MR. CHIEF JUSTICE BURGER, with whom MR. JUSTICE WHITE and MR. JUSTICE BLACKMUN joined, is omitted.]

Notes

1. Because § 2283 has been interpreted to apply only to pending proceedings, it would not bar an injunction suit against a threatened state court action. *See* Dombrowski v. Pfister, 380 U.S. 479, 484 n. 2, 85 S.Ct. 1116, 1119 n. 2, 14 L.Ed.2d 22 (1965); C. Wright, A. Miller & E. Cooper, Federal Practice and Procedure § 4222 (1978). In Leiter Minerals v. United States, 352 U.S. 220, 77 S.Ct. 287, 1 L.Ed.2d 267 (1957), the Supreme Court held that § 2283 did not prohibit injunction suits against state proceedings where the United States sought the injunction. *Accord* Equal Employment Opportunity Commission v. Levi Strauss & Co., 515 F.Supp. 640 (N.D.Ill.1981) (federal agency as plaintiff). During the same term the Court decided *Mitchum v. Foster,* it extended the *Leiter* decision to permit suits against state proceedings brought by the N.L.R.B. *See* N.L.R.B. v. Nash–Finch Co., 404 U.S. 138, 92 S.Ct. 373, 30 L.Ed.2d 328 (1971). For a discussion of some of the broader implications of both the *Mitchum* and *Nash–Finch Co.* cases, *see* Note, 86 Harv.L.Rev. 207 (1972). The anti-injunction statute also is inapplicable if the proceedings in the state court are not of a judicial nature. *See* Lynch v. Household Finance Corp., 405 U.S. 538, 92 S.Ct. 1113, 31 L.Ed.2d 424 (1972) (state prejudgment garnishment statute held not "judicial").

The holding in *Mitchum* that § 1983 injunction suits are not barred by the anti-injunction statute is especially significant because substantial numbers of suits to enjoin pending state proceedings (including criminal proceedings) are brought under § 1983. Consequently, the *Mitchum* decision significantly reduces the practical impact of the anti-injunction statute. *See* Comment, 42 Mo.L.Rev. 559, 574–575 (1977). *See generally* Redish, The Anti–Injunction Statute Reconsidered, 44 N.W.U.L.Rev. 717 (1977).

2. *Mitchum* addresses the question of whether a federal court may enjoin state court proceedings. In Donovan v. City of Dallas, 377 U.S. 408, 84 S.Ct. 1579, 12 L.Ed.2d 409 (1964) and General Atomic Co. v. Felter, 434 U.S. 12, 98 S.Ct. 76, 54 L.Ed.2d 199 (1977), the court held that a state court may not enjoin either pending or prospective in personam actions in federal courts because states cannot limit the jurisdiction of federal courts. There is disagreement, however, as to whether this rule prevents a state court from enjoining a federal court action in order to protect the state court's jurisdiction over property brought under its control by proceedings in rem or quasi in rem. *Compare* Meridian Investing & Development Corp. v. Suncoast Highland Corp., 628 F.2d 370 (5th Cir.1980) *with* Moody v. State *ex rel.* Payne, 351 So.2d 552 (Ala.1977). *See also* C. Wright, Law of Federal Courts 276–77 (4th ed. 1983). In addition, there may also be some question whether the *Donovan* rule extends to courts that are not mandated by the Constitution, such as the Canal Zone Federal District Court. *See* Crawley v. Bauchens, 57 Ill.2d 360, 312 N.E.2d 236 (1974) (issue raised, but injunction denied on other grounds).

3. In Eddy *ex rel.* Pfeifer v. Christian Science Bd. of Directors, 62 Ill.App.3d 918, 19 Ill.Dec. 781, 379 N.E.2d 653 (1978), the plaintiff attempted to relitigate issues that had already been resolved by the court. The plaintiff's *pro se* complaint alleged that Ralph W. Cessna did not teach a primary class in accordance with the church manual bylaw requiring that the class be taught from the chapter entitled "Recapitulation" in the book "Science and Health with Key to the Scriptures" by Mary Baker Eddy. The circuit court dismissed the complaint and enjoined the plaintiff from pursuing related litigation in both

the Illinois and federal courts. The appellate court voided the injunction against litigating in the federal courts, citing *Donovan* and *General Atomic Co., supra* note 2. The court then addressed the other issue:

> "The injunction restraining plaintiff from instituting or proceeding with related actions in the State courts stands on a different footing. We believe it is clear that the court had the power to enter such an order under appropriate circumstances. * * *
>
> "It is well settled that Illinois courts may restrain the maintenance of vexatious and harassing litigation. (Bowman v. Lake County Public Building Commission, 31 Ill.2d 575, 203 N.E.2d 129 (1964). * * * Although plaintiff may be sincere in his feeling that a wrong has been committed, it is apparent that unless enjoined he may continually attempt to evade the clear mandate of this court. Furthermore, because his actions are filed *pro se* and consist of lengthy documents whose language is often hard to follow, his litigation becomes even more burdensome to the court and opposing litigants. Therefore, we find that the court did not abuse its discretion by issuing an injunction."

Id. at 920, 379 N.E.2d at 655.*

The *Eddy* case represents a traditional use of the equitable Bill of Peace to restrain numerous actions at law when they are being used to harass or vex the plaintiff or when such actions are pending in inferior courts where complete relief cannot be obtained. *See* H. McClintock, Equity § 179 (2nd ed. 1948). *See also* Muka v. New York State Bar Ass'n, 120 Misc.2d 897, 466 N.Y.S.2d 891 (1983) (non-lawyer law school graduate who had previously filed "hundreds of actions" against defendant and countless other state and federal judges and other officials enjoined from filing further civil actions against defendant unless represented by counsel); Rudnicki v. McCormack, 210 F.Supp. 905 (D.R.I.1962) (plaintiff enjoined from further litigation against state or federal judges and their employees unless permission of court is obtained). *Cf.* Hill v. Estelle, 423 F.Supp. 690 (S.D.Tex.1976) (injunction against prisoners to prevent repetitious frivolous suits). *Compare* In re Davis' Custody, 248 N.C. 423, 103 S.E.2d 503 (1958) (Bill of Peace not available to husband to enjoin former spouse from challenging prior child custody agreement). For an example of a legislative attempt to deal with the problem, see West's Cal.Civ.Pro.Code §§ 391–391.6, which authorizes a court on motion to require that a plaintiff who is designated as a "vexatious litigant" provide security as a condition for suit. *See* In re Shieh, 17 Cal.App.4th 1154, 21 Cal.Rptr.2d 886 (Cal.App.1993) (attorney who was determined to be a "vexatious litigant" under foregoing statute enjoined from filing new litigation without leave of court).**

* Federal courts are also empowered to enjoin relitigation of an issue. For an excellent discussion of the justifications for occasionally issuing an injunction, rather than relying exclusively on res judicata and collateral estoppel to protect the prevailing party, see Michigan v. City of Allen Park, 573 F.Supp. 1481, 1488 (E.D.Mich.1983) ("The interests of repose, finality of judgments, protection of defendants from unwarranted harassment, and concern for maintaining order in the court's dockets have been deemed sufficient * * * to warrant such a prohibition against relitigation of claims.").

** More complex problems are raised where the party seeks the Bill of Peace to enjoin separate actions by multiple parties. For example, if it were determined that the one against whom the claims were made was negligent, issues of contributory negligence, proximate cause, and damages could arise in each case, "and those issues would require separate determination with respect to each claim either in actions at law or in the suit in equity." H. McClintock, Equity 487 (2d ed.

4. A state court that has acquired jurisdiction over the parties may enjoin them from proceeding with another action in a different state. Huff v. Huff, 69 N.C.App. 447, 317 S.E.2d 65 (1984) (divorce proceeding). Similarly, one federal district court has the power to enjoin a litigant before it from proceeding in another federal district court. Barclaysamerican/Commercial, Inc. v. Consumer Indus., Inc., 585 F.Supp. 1340 (W.D.N.C.1984). However, "the situation could arise in which one court entered an injunction restraining the litigant from proceeding in the other forum and the other forum issued a counter-injunction enjoining the litigant from seeking enforcement of the prior injunction. The result of the injunctions would only serve to undermine the integrity of two United States District Courts if they engaged in this unseeming battle. The time, therefore, to dispose of this unsavory spectacle of judicial disorder is when it begins. As Justice Holmes succinctly stated, '[u]niversal distrust creates universal incompetence.' Graham v. United States, 231 U.S. 474, 480, 34 S.Ct. 148, 151, 58 L.Ed. 319 (1913)." *Id.* at 1342. For reasons of necessity as well as comity, then, courts of coordinate jurisdiction rarely issue injunctions designed to restrict the exercise of the other's jurisdiction. Ordinarily the forum court will require the plaintiff to show that the defendant's conduct in bringing the foreign action constitutes fraud, gross wrong or oppression. *See* Crawley v. Bauchens, 57 Ill.2d 360, 312 N.E.2d 236 (1974).

OHIO CIVIL RIGHTS COMMISSION v. DAYTON CHRISTIAN SCHOOLS, INC.

Supreme Court of the United States, 1986.
477 U.S. 619, 106 S.Ct. 2718, 91 L.Ed.2d 512.

MR. JUSTICE REHNQUIST delivered the opinion of the Court.

Appellee Dayton Christian Schools, Inc. (Dayton), and various individuals brought an action in the United States District Court for the Southern District of Ohio under 42 U.S.C. § 1983 [42 USCS § 1983], seeking to enjoin a pending state administrative proceeding brought against Dayton by appellant Ohio Civil Rights Commission (Commission). Dayton asserted that the Free Exercise and Establishment Clauses of the First Amendment prohibited the Commission from exercising jurisdiction over it or from punishing it for engaging in employment discrimination. The District Court refused to issue the injunction on grounds that any conflict between the First Amendment and the administrative proceedings was not yet ripe, and that in any case the proposed action of the Commission violated neither the Free Exercise Clause nor the Establishment Clause of the First Amendment, as made applicable to the States by the Fourteenth Amend-

1948). Moreover, many courts have evidenced the feeling that the right to jury trial is particularly important to the law plaintiffs. *Id.*

Compare American Lead Corp. v. Davis, 111 Ind.App. 242, 38 N.E.2d 281 (1941) *with* Yuba Consolidated Gold Fields v. Kilkeary, 206 F.2d 884 (9th Cir.1953). See the classic work, Chafee, Bills of Peace with Multiple Parties, 45 Harv.L.Rev. 1297 (1932).

To a great extent the problems of multiple claim and multiple party litigation have been alleviated by modern procedural codes and rules. Provision in these codes and rules for class actions, joinder of parties and consolidation as well as the enactment of declaratory judgment statutes have substantially taken over the role of the Bill of Peace. *See, e.g.,* Federal Rules of Civil Procedure, rules 19, 23 and 42 (28 U.S.C.A.). For a discussion of many of these devices, see Developments in the Law—Multiparty Litigation in the Federal Courts, 71 Harv.L.Rev. 874 (1958).

ment. The Court of Appeals for the Sixth Circuit reversed, holding that the exercise of jurisdiction and the enforcement of the statute would impermissibly burden appellees' rights under the Free Exercise Clause and would result in excessive entanglement under the Establishment Clause. We postponed the question of jurisdiction pending consideration of the merits. 474 U.S. 978, 106 S.Ct. 379, 88 L.Ed.2d 332 (1985). We now conclude that we have jurisdiction, and we reverse, holding that the District Court should have abstained under our cases beginning with Younger v. Harris, 401 U.S. 37, 91 S.Ct. 746, 27 L.Ed.2d 669 (1971).

Dayton is a private nonprofit corporation that provides education at both the elementary and secondary school levels. It was formed by two local churches, the Patterson Park Brethren Church and the Christian Tabernacle, and it is regarded as a "nondenominational" extension of the Christian education ministries of these two churches. Dayton's corporate charter establishes a board of directors (board) to lead the corporation in both spiritual and temporal matters. * * * The charter also includes a section entitled "Statement of Faith," which serves to restrict membership on the board and the educational staff to persons who subscribe to a particular set of religious beliefs. The Statement of Faith requires each board or staff member to be a bornagain Christian and to reaffirm his or her belief annually in the Bible, the Trinity, the nature and mission of Jesus Christ, the doctrine of original sin, the role of the Holy Ghost, the resurrection and judgment of the dead, the need for Christian unity, and the divine creation of human beings.

The board has elaborated these requirements to include a belief in the internal resolution of disputes through the "biblical chain of command." The core of this doctrine, rooted in passages from the New Testament, is that one Christian should not take another Christian into courts of the State. Teachers are expected to present any grievance they may have to their immediate supervisor, and to acquiesce in the final authority of the board, rather than to pursue a remedy in civil court. The board has sought to ensure compliance with this internal dispute resolution doctrine by making it a contractual condition of employment.

Linda Hoskinson was employed as a teacher at Dayton during the 1978–1979 school year. She subscribed to the Statement of Faith and expressly agreed to resolve disputes internally through the biblical chain of command. In January 1979, she informed her principal, James Rakestraw, that she was pregnant. After consulting with his superiors, Rakestraw informed Hoskinson that her employment contract would not be renewed at the end of the school year because of Dayton's religious doctrine that mothers should stay home with their preschool age children. Instead of appealing this decision internally, Hoskinson contacted an attorney who sent a letter to Dayton's superintendent, Claude Schindler, threatening litigation based on state and federal sex discrimination laws if Dayton did not agree to rehire Hoskinson for the coming school year.

Upon receipt of this letter, Schindler informed Hoskinson that she was suspended immediately for challenging the nonrenewal decision in a manner inconsistent with the internal dispute resolution doctrine. The board reviewed this decision and decided to terminate Hoskinson. It stated that the sole reason for her termination was her violation of the internal dispute resolution doctrine, and it rescinded the earlier nonrenewal decision because it said that she had not received adequate prior notice of the doctrine concerning a mother's duty to stay home with her young children.

Hoskinson filed a complaint with appellant Ohio Civil Rights Commission (Commission), alleging that Dayton's nonrenewal decision constituted sex discrimination, in violation of Ohio Rev.Code Ann. § 4112.02(A) (Supp. 1985), and that its termination decision penalized her for asserting her rights, in violation of Ohio Rev.Code Ann. § 4112.02(I) (Supp.1985). The Commission notified Dayton that it was conducting a preliminary investigation into the matter, and repeatedly urged Dayton to consider private settlement, warning that failure to do so could result in a formal adjudication of the matter.

The Commission eventually determined that there was probable cause to believe that Dayton had discriminated against Hoskinson based on her sex and had retaliated against her for attempting to assert her rights in violation of §§ 4112(A) and (I). Pursuant to Ohio Rev.Code Ann. § 4112.05(B) (Supp.1985), it sent Dayton a proposed Conciliation Agreement and Consent Order that would have required Dayton to reinstate Hoskinson with backpay, and would have prohibited Dayton from taking retaliatory action against any employee for participating in the preliminary investigation. The Commission warned Dayton that failure to accede to this proposal or an acceptable counteroffer would result in formal administrative proceedings being initiated against it. When Dayton failed to respond, the Commission initiated administrative proceedings against it by filing a complaint. Dayton answered the complaint by asserting that the First Amendment prevented the Commission from exercising jurisdiction over it since its actions had been taken pursuant to sincerely held religious beliefs.

While these administrative proceedings were pending, Dayton filed this action against the Commission in the United States District Court for the Southern District of Ohio under 42 U.S.C. § 1983 [42 USCS § 1983], seeking a permanent injunction against the state proceedings on the ground that any investigation of Dayton's hiring process or any imposition of sanctions for Dayton's nonrenewal or termination decisions would violate the Religion Clauses of the First Amendment. App. 118–120. The Commission filed a motion to dismiss, arguing, inter alia, that the District Court should refrain from enjoining the administrative proceedings based on federal abstention doctrines. * * * It also filed various documents defending its action on the merits.

Without addressing the abstention argument, the District Court refused to issue the injunction. 578 F.Supp. 1004 (1984). The Court of Appeals for the Sixth Circuit reversed, as previously noted, holding that the exercise of such jurisdiction would violate both the Free Exercise Clause and the Establishment Clause of the First Amendment. 766 F.2d 932 (1985).

* * *

Having taken jurisdiction over the decision below, we now turn to whether the District Court should have exercised jurisdiction over the case itself. We conclude that the District Court should have abstained from adjudicating this case under Younger v. Harris, 401 U.S. 37, 91 S.Ct. 746, 27 L.Ed.2d 669 (1971), and later cases.

In Younger v. Harris, supra, we held that a federal court should not enjoin a pending state criminal proceeding except in the very unusual situation that an injunction is necessary to prevent great and immediate irreparable injury. We justified our decision both on equitable principles, id., at 43, 91 S.Ct. 746, 27 L.Ed.2d 665 and on the "more vital consideration" of the proper respect for the fundamental role of States in our federal system. Id., at 44, 91 S.Ct. 750. Because of our concerns for comity and federalism, we thought that it was

> "perfectly natural for our cases to repeat time and time again that the normal thing to do when federal courts are asked to enjoin pending proceedings in state courts is not to issue such injunctions." Id., at 45, 91 S.Ct. 751 (emphasis added).

We have since recognized that our concern for comity and federalism is equally applicable to certain other pending state proceedings. We have applied the Younger principle to civil proceedings in which important state interests are involved. Huffman v. Pursue, Ltd., 420 U.S. 592, 95 S.Ct. 1200, 43 L.Ed.2d 482 (1975); Juidice v. Vail, 430 U.S. 327, 97 S.Ct. 1211, 51 L.Ed.2d 376 (1977); Trainor v. Hernandez, 431 U.S. 434, 97 S.Ct. 1911, 52 L.Ed.2d 486 (1977); Moore v. Sims, 442 U.S. 415, 423, 99 S.Ct. 2371, 60 L.Ed.2d 994 (1979). We have also applied it to state administrative proceedings in which important state interests are vindicated, so long as in the course of those proceedings the federal plaintiff would have a full and fair opportunity to litigate his constitutional claim. We stated in Gibson v. Berryhill, 411 U.S. 564, 576–577, 93 S.Ct. 1689, 36 L.Ed.2d 488 (1973), that "administrative proceedings looking toward the revocation of a license to practice medicine may in proper circumstances command the respect due court proceedings." Similarly, we have held that federal courts should refrain from enjoining lawyer disciplinary proceedings initiated by state ethics committees if the proceedings are within the appellate jurisdiction of the appropriate State Supreme Court. Middlesex County Ethics Committee v. Garden State Bar Assn., 457 U.S. 423, 102 S.Ct. 2515, 73 L.Ed.2d 116 (1982). Because we found that the administrative proceedings in Middlesex were "judicial in nature" from the outset, id., at 432–434, 102 S.Ct. 2515, 73 L.Ed.2d 116, it was not essential to the decision that they had progressed to state-court review by the time we heard the federal injunction case.

We think the principles enunciated in these cases govern the present one. We have no doubt that the elimination of prohibited sex discrimination is a sufficiently important state interest to bring the present case within the ambit of the cited authorities. We also have no reason to doubt that Dayton will receive an adequate opportunity to raise its constitutional claims. Dayton contends that the mere exercise of jurisdiction over it by the state administrative body violates its First Amendment rights. But we have repeatedly rejected the argument that a constitutional attack on state procedures themselves "automatically vitiates the adequacy of those procedures for purposes of the Younger–Huffman line of cases." Moore, supra, at 427, n. 10, 60 L.Ed.2d 994, 99 S.Ct. 2371. Even religious schools cannot claim to be wholly free from some state regulation. Wisconsin v. Yoder, 406 U.S. 205, 213, 92 S.Ct. 1526, 32 L.Ed.2d 15 (1972). We therefore think that however Dayton's constitutional claim should be decided on the merits, the Commission violates no constitutional rights by merely investigating the circumstances of Hoskinson's discharge in this case, if only to ascertain whether the ascribed religious-based reason was in fact the reason for the discharge.

Dayton also contends that the administrative proceedings do not afford the opportunity to level constitutional challenges against the potential sanctions for the alleged sex discrimination. In its reply brief in this Court, the Commission cites several rulings to demonstrate that religious justifications for otherwise illegal conduct are considered by it. See, e.g., In re St. Mary of the Falls, No. 948 (1975). Dayton in turn relies on a decision of the Supreme Court of Ohio, Mobil Oil Corp. v. Rocky River, 38 Ohio St.2d 23, 26, 309 N.E.2d 900, 902 (1974), in which that court held that a local zoning commission could not consider constitutional claims. But even if Ohio law is such that the Commission may not consider the constitutionality of the statute under which it operates, it would seem an unusual doctrine, and one not supported by the cited case, to say that the Commission could not construe its own statutory mandate in the light of federal constitutional principles. Cf. NLRB v. Catholic Bishop of Chicago, 440 U.S. 490, 99 S.Ct. 1313, 59 L.Ed.2d 533 (1979). In any event, it is sufficient under Middlesex, supra, at 436, 73 L.Ed.2d 116, 102 S.Ct. 2515, that constitutional claims may be raised in state-court judicial review of the administrative proceeding. Section 4112.06 of Ohio Rev.Code Ann. (1980) provides that any "respondent claiming to be aggrieved by a final order of the commission * * * may obtain judicial review thereof." Dayton cites us to no Ohio authority indicating that this provision does not authorize judicial review of claims that agency action violates the United States Constitution.

The judgment of the Court of Appeals is therefore reversed, and the case remanded for further proceedings consistent with this opinion.

[An opinion by JUSTICE STEVENS concurring in the judgment, which JUSTICES BRENNAN, MARSHALL and BLACKMUN join, is omitted]

Notes

1. The philosophical underpinnings of the "Our Federalism" doctrine were described by the Supreme Court in Younger v. Harris, 401 U.S. 37, 43–45, 91 S.Ct. 746, 750–751, 27 L.Ed.2d 669 (1971):

> "The precise reasons for this longstanding public policy against federal court interference with state court proceedings have never been specifically identified but the primary sources of the policy are plain. One is the basic doctrine of equity jurisprudence that courts of equity should not act, and particularly should not act to restrain a criminal prosecution, when the moving party has an adequate remedy at law and will not suffer irrepara-

ble injury if denied equitable relief. The doctrine may originally have grown out of circumstances peculiar to the English judicial system and not applicable in this country, but its fundamental purpose of restraining equity jurisdiction within narrow limits is equally important under our Constitution, in order to prevent erosion of the role of the jury and avoid a duplication of legal proceedings and legal sanctions where a single suit would be adequate to protect the rights asserted. This underlying reason for restraining courts of equity from interfering with criminal prosecutions is reinforced by an even more vital consideration, the notion of 'comity,' that is, a proper respect for state functions, a recognition of the fact that the entire country is made up of a Union of separate state governments, and a continuance of the belief that the National Government will fare best if the States and their institutions are left free to perform their separate functions in their separate ways. This, perhaps for lack of a better and clearer way to describe it, is referred to by many as 'Our Federalism,' and one familiar with the profound debates that ushered our Federal Constitution into existence is bound to respect those who remain loyal to the ideals and dreams of 'Our Federalism.' The concept does not mean blind deference to 'States Rights' any more than it means centralization of control over every important issue in our National Government and its courts. The Framers rejected both these courses. What the concept does represent is a system in which there is sensitivity to the legitimate interests of both State and National Governments, and in which the National Government, anxious though it may be to vindicate and protect federal rights and federal interests, always endeavors to do so in ways that will not unduly interfere with the legitimate activities of the States. It should never be forgotten that this slogan, 'Our Federalism,' born in the early struggling days of our Union of States, occupies a highly important place in our Nation's history and its future."

2. The *Younger* or "Our Federalism" bar is inapplicable unless a state proceeding is pending. *See* Zablocki v. Redhail, 434 U.S. 374, 379 n. 5, 98 S.Ct. 673, 677 n. 5, 54 L.Ed.2d 618 (1978). For an analysis of the complexities of what constitutes a "pending" proceeding, see C. Wright, A. Miller & E. Cooper, Federal Practice and Procedure § 4253 (1978). A prosecutor can avoid the *Younger* problem in the threatened prosecution setting, however, simply by filing the state prosecution after the initiation of the federal injunction suit, but before "any proceedings of substance on the merits have taken place in federal court." Hicks v. Miranda, 422 U.S. 332, 95 S.Ct. 2281, 45 L.Ed.2d 223 (1975). As to when the federal action becomes a "proceeding of substance," consider the following recent Supreme Court explanation:

> "Whether issuance of [a] temporary restraining order [is] a substantial federal court action or not, issuance of [a] preliminary injunction certainly [is]. *See* Doran v. Salem Inn, Inc., 422 U.S. 922, 929–931, 95 S.Ct. 2561, 2566–2567, 45 L.Ed.2d 648 (1975). A federal court action in which a preliminary injunction is granted has proceeded well beyond the 'embryonic stage,' *id.,* at 929, 95 S.Ct., at 2566, and considerations of economy, equity, and federalism counsel against *Younger* -abstention at that point."

Hawaii Housing Authority v. Midkiff, 467 U.S. 229, 104 S.Ct. 2321, 81 L.Ed.2d 186 (1984).

It is important to emphasize that while the absence of a pending state proceeding avoids a *Younger* problem, a party seeking injunctive relief against state enforcement needs to be able to establish *at least* some likelihood or threat of enforcement by state authorities in order to avoid having the suit dismissed for want of a "case or controversy" under Article III of the United States Constitution: "When plaintiffs do not claim that they have ever been threatened with prosecution, that a prosecution is remotely possible, they do not allege a dispute susceptible to resolution by a federal court." Babbitt v. United Farm Workers Nat. Union, 442 U.S. 289, 99 S.Ct. 2301, 60 L.Ed.2d 895 (1979).

3. To what extent does *Younger* apply to civil suits generally? Doubts in the lower courts as to whether *Younger* ever applied in a civil action solely between private parties, (*see* Diaz v. Strathis, 576 F.2d 9 (1st Cir.1979)), were settled by Pennzoil Co. v. Texaco, Inc., 481 U.S. 1, 107 S.Ct. 1519, 95 L.E.2d 1 (1987), which held that the federal courts should not have entertained an injunction suit challenging the constitutionality of a Texas appeal bond statute in an on-going case between private litigants in the Texas courts. The Supreme Court reasoned that the state's interest in the enforceability of judgments of its courts was comparable to its interest in the enforceability of judicial orders by civil contempt proceedings held in Juidice v. Vail, 430 U.S. 327, 97 S.Ct. 1211, 51 L.Ed.2d 376 (1977), to justify invocation of *Younger*. The majority opinion, however, disclaimed any rule that "Younger abstention is always appropriate whenever a civil proceeding is pending in a state court." 481 U.S. at 14 n. 12. In concurring in the judgment, Justice Brennan stated that the merits should have been decided, and the validity of the statute upheld on the merits. He adhered to his oft-stated view "that Younger is, in general, inapplicable to civil proceedings, especially when the plaintiff brings a § 1983 action alleging violation of federal constitutional rights." He argued that the "State's interest in this case is negligible." 481 U.S. at 19.

On the other hand, two years later, in New Orleans Public Service, Inc. v. Council of the City of New Orleans, 491 U.S. 350, 109 S.Ct. 2506, 105 L.Ed.2d 298 (1989) the Court stressed that not all civil proceedings are subject to the Younger doctrine. That case held that *Younger* did not bar a federal injunction and declaratory judgment action by a utility against a city rate-making proceeding. The Court stated:

> "Although our concern for comity and federalism has led us to expand the protection of Younger beyond state criminal proceedings, * * * and even to civil proceedings involving certain orders that are uniquely in furtherance of the state courts' ability to perform their judicial functions, [*see Juidice* and *Pennzoil*] it has never been suggested that Younger requires abstention in deference to a state judicial proceeding reviewing legislative or executive action.
>
> "While we have expanded Younger beyond criminal proceedings, and even beyond proceedings in courts, we have never extended it to proceedings that are not 'judicial in nature.' *See* Middlesex County Ethics Comm. v. Garden State Bar Ass'n. * * * ('It is clear beyond doubt that the New Jersey Supreme Court considers its bar disciplinary proceedings as "judicial in nature." As such, the proceedings are of a character to warrant federal-court deference'). *See also* Ohio Civil Rights Comm'n v. Dayton Christian Schools, Inc., * * * ('Because we found that the administrative

proceedings in Middlesex were "judicial in nature" from the outset, * * * it was not essential to the decision that they had progressed to state-court review by the time we heard the federal injunction case'). The Council's proceedings in the present case were not judicial in nature."

491 U.S. at 367–370.

To what extent does the *Younger* doctrine bar federal declaratory injunction actions as well as injunctive relief? For a detailed consideration of this issue, *see* pp. 365–75 supra.

For further examination of the *Younger* rule, *see* King, Federal Injunctive Relief Against Pending State Civil Proceedings: Younger Days Are Here Again, 44 La.L.Rev. 967 (1984); Redish, The Doctrine of Younger v. Harris: Deference in Search of a Rationale, 63 Cornell L.Rev. 463 (1978); Soifer & Macgill, The Younger Doctrine: Reconstructing Reconstruction, 55 Tex.L.Rev. 1141 (1971); Weinberg, The New Judicial Federalism, 29 Stan.L.Rev. 1191 (1977); Ziegler, A Reassessment of the Younger Doctrine in Light of the Legislative History of Reconstruction, 1983 Duke L.J. 987; Comment, "Our Federalism"—The Limitation of Younger—Samuels and Their Progeny on Federal Intervention in State Court Proceedings, 42 Mo.L.Rev. 559 (1977).

4. There are other "abstention doctrines" which, while seemingly less firmly fixed and less confined to specific remedial settings than either the anti-injunction statute or the *Younger* doctrine, nevertheless can sometimes bar federal court intervention in pending state proceedings. Two of these are referred to as "Pullman abstention" (first enunciated in Railroad Commission of Texas v. Pullman Co., 312 U.S. 496, 61 S.Ct. 643, 85 L.Ed. 971 (1941)) and "Burford abstention" (as articulated in Burford v. Sun Oil Co., 319 U.S. 315, 63 S.Ct. 1098, 87 L.Ed. 1424 (1943)). The Supreme Court recently explained the *Pullman* concept as follows:

> "In [*Pullman*], this Court held that federal courts should abstain from decision when difficult and unsettled questions of state law must be resolved before a substantial federal constitutional question can be decided. By abstaining in such cases, federal courts will avoid both unnecessary adjudication of federal questions and needless friction with state policies * * *. *Id.*, 312 U.S., at 500, 61 S.Ct., at 645. However, federal courts need not abstain on *Pullman* grounds when a state statute is not 'fairly subject to an interpretation which will render unnecessary' the federal constitutional question. *Pullman* abstention is limited to uncertain questions of state law because '[a]bstention from the exercise of federal jurisdiction is the exception, not the rule.' Colorado River Water Conservation Dist. v. United States, 424 U.S. 800, 813, 96 S.Ct. 1236, 1244, 47 L.Ed.2d 483 (1976).

Hawaii Housing Authority v. Midkiff, 467 U.S. 229, 236, 104 S.Ct. 2321, 2327, 81 L.Ed.2d 186 (1984).*

* *See also* Brockett v. Spokane Arcades, Inc., ___ U.S. ___, 105 S.Ct. 2794, 86 L.Ed.2d 394 (1985). *Brockett* involved a state moral nuisance law passed by the Washington legislature and challenged four days later on First Amendment grounds. The Court of Appeals for the Ninth Circuit held the statute unconstitutional on its face. The Supreme Court reversed and remanded, holding that partial rather than facial invalidity was the correct course. Justice O'Connor, in her concurring opinion, pointed out that the challenge in federal court had been brought so quickly that the state of Washington had not yet had a chance to construe the challenged statute.

A recent federal district court decision described *Burford* abstention as follows:

> "[In *Burford,* the Supreme Court] held that the district court should have abstained on a difficult issue of state regulation because of the complexity of the state law issue, the expertise of the state court, the predominance of local issues, and the need for coherent state doctrine in the area. Such an abstention is appropriate where the importance of the issues of state law transcend the result in the individual case. These cases involve administrative regulation of areas of state interest, such as oil exploration, *see Burford, supra,* state eminent domain, *see* Louisiana Power & Light Co. v. Thibodaux, 360 U.S. 25, 79 S.Ct. 1070, 3 L.Ed.2d 1058 (1959), and railroad passenger service, *see* Alabama Public Service Commission v. Southern Railway, 341 U.S. 341, 71 S.Ct. 762, 95 L.Ed. 1002 (1951). These cases involve interpretation of state law and in these cases the courts fear that federal intervention would disrupt state efforts to create coherent policy with regard to matters of substantial state interest."

Adams v. Attorney Registration and Disciplinary Commission of the Supreme Court of Illinois, 600 F.Supp. 390, 396 (N.D.Ill.1984). For further consideration of *Pullman* and *Burford* abstention, *see* New Orleans Public Service, Inc. v. Council of the City of New Orleans, 491 U.S. 350, 109 S.Ct. 2506, 105 L.Ed.2d 298 (1989).

SECTION 5. INTERFERENCE WITH DIGNITY INTERESTS

A. SUBSTITUTIONARY RELIEF

1. Damages

D. DOBBS, THE LAW OF REMEDIES

623, 626–27, 631 (2d ed. 1993).*

§ 7.1 Dignitary Invasions Generally

§ 7.1(1) Background and Scope

"The injuries considered in this chapter can be called dignitary injuries or injuries to the personality. This means that, though economic or physical loss may be associated with the injury in some cases, the primary or usual concern is not economic at all, but vindication of an intangible right.

She would have applied *Pullman* abstention to vacate, stating in part:

"[T]he Court of Appeals asserted that *Pullman* abstention should 'almost never' apply where a state statute is challenged on First Amendment grounds 'because the constitutional guarantee of free expression is, quite properly, always an area of particular federal concern.' 725 F.2d, at 488. This Court has never endorsed such a proposition. *See* Babbitt v. United Farm Workers National Union, 442 U.S. 289, 306–312 (1979). On the contrary, even in cases involving First Amendment challenges to a state statute, abstention may be required 'in order to avoid unnecessary friction in federal-state relations, interference with important state functions, tentative decisions on questions of state law, and premature constitutional adjudication.' *Id.,* at 306."

Id. at 2805.

* Reprinted with permission of West Publishing Co.

"Many dignitary claims are recognized torts that involve some confrontation with the plaintiff in person or some indirect affront to his personality—assault, battery, false imprisonment, malicious prosecution, intentional infliction of mental distress, libel and slander, invasion of privacy, and alienation of affections are all in this category. In addition, these torts have their statutory and constitutional analogues so that essentially the same sort of interests may be protected under a variety of statutes, including federal or state civil rights statutes. Dignitary interests may also be vindicated incidentally, in the course of protecting some other interest, as where mental distress damages are awarded incident to some other tort.

"All these dignitary harms may cause economic harm as well as affront to personality. If so, economic damages may be recovered. However, in a great many of the cases, the only harm is the affront to the plaintiff's dignity as a human being, the damage to his self-image, and the resulting mental distress.

* * *

§ 7.2 Remedies for Defamation

§ 7.2(1) Substantive Background

"The law of defamation attempts to protect the plaintiff's interest in reputation through the torts of libel and slander. The law is unusually complex. It is also closely related to such slightly different torts as privacy invasion and malicious prosecution, and it is quite easily confused with commercial disparagement or trade libel.

"Both libel and slander require a 'publication' or communication by the defendant to someone other than the plaintiff. Libel is traditionally written, tangible or permanent defamation; slander is traditionally oral, intangible, or impermanent. One important consequence of the distinction between libel and slander was that substantial recoveries could be allowed in most libel cases without proof of any loss at all. This is the doctrine of presumed or general damages. It did not apply to ordinary slander cases; pecuniary loss was required in those.

"The common law of defamation imposed a kind of strict liability upon publishers or communicators of material that was derogatory to others. Even if the publisher reasonably believed the material was true, he could be held liable. Although truth was a defense, along with some other 'privileges,' the burden was upon the defendant to persuade the jury that the defamatory publication was true in the substance of its sting.

* * *

§ 7.2(11) Economic Damages

"Although defamation is very largely a dignitary harm or harm to personality, defamation may also proximately cause economic losses. If such losses are adequately proven, they are recoverable items of damages. The same causal elements logically necessary to support a claim of reputational loss are logically necessary to support the claim of economic loss.

"Specifically, the plaintiff who prevails in a defamation claim is entitled to show that the defamation disrupted an employment or business relationship with another, so that the plaintiff lost wages and fringe benefits, commission income, profits or customers, or contract or business opportunities, and entitled to recover such items if they are properly proven.

* * *

"The plaintiff is also entitled to recover medical expenses reasonably incurred when mental distress or physical ill-health is a proximate result of the defamation.

"All economic loss is special damage and subject to the requirement that the loss be proven with reasonable certainty and that it be limited to losses that are not reasonably avoidable."

STUMP v. GATES

United States District Court, District of Colorado, 1991.
777 F.Supp. 808, aff'd without precedential value, 986 F.2d 1429 (1993).

CARRIGAN, JUDGE.

[Children of a man found dead of a gunshot wound by his wife filed a 42 U.S.C. § 1983 suit against some city and county officers claiming, *inter alia,* that improper investigation denied them access to the courts. The plaintiffs also asserted pendant state claims, including an action for defamation. Only the defamation claim discussion is included.]

In their sixth claim, the plaintiffs allege defamation resulting from the defendants' publication of police and coroner reports that Lawrence Ocrant's death was a suicide. Those publications allegedly have impaired the plaintiffs' reputation and standing in the community. Defendants argue that the sixth claim must be dismissed because: (1) the publications were not of and concerning the plaintiffs; and (2) no special damages have been pleaded.

A defamatory communication tends to subject a person to public hatred, contempt or ridicule, or causes him or her to be shunned or avoided. *Walters v. Linhof,* 559 F.Supp. 1231, 1236 (D.Colo.1983); *Fort v. Holt,* 508 P.2d 792, 794 (Colo.App.1973). It injures a person's reputation and reflects poorly upon his or her character. *Id.* (both cites).

Written defamation is libel. The elements of a libel claim are: (1) a written defamatory statement of and concerning the plaintiff; (2) published to a third party; (3) with the publisher's fault amounting to at least negligence; and (4) either actionability of the statement irrespective of special damages or the existence of special damages caused by the publication.[8] *Walters,* 559 F.Supp. at 1235.

Libel is characterized either as *per se* or *per quod.* To be libelous *per se,* a statement:

8. I note that, for purposes of the sixth claim, the plaintiffs are not "public figures," and therefore proof of actual malice is not required. *See Walters,* 559 F.Supp. at 1235 (one does not become public figure merely because media attention attracted).

> "must contain defamatory words *specifically directed at the person claiming injury,* which words must, on their face, and without the aid of intrinsic proof, be unmistakably recognized as injurious." *Lininger v. Knight,* 123 Colo. 213, 226 P.2d 809, 813 (Colo.1951) (emphasis added); *see also Inter–State Detective Bureau, Inc. v. Denver Post, Inc.,* [29 Colo.App. 313] 484 P.2d 131, 133 (Colo.App.1971).

Libel *per se* is actionable without an allegation of actual damages. *Inter–State Detective,* 484 P.2d at 133. A court decides the legal question whether a writing constitutes libel *per se. Id.; Lininger,* 226 P.2d at 813.

Any libel that, unlike libel *per se,* does not carry a defamatory imputation on its face is libel *per quod* which is actionable only where special damages are pleaded. *See, e.g., Lind v. O'Reilly,* 636 P.2d 1319, 1321 (Colo.App.1981); *Inter–State Detective,* 484 P.2d at 133. Libel *per quod* exists where the person to whom the defamatory statement applies can only be ascertained by introducing extrinsic proof. *Lind,* 636 P.2d at 1320.

"Special damages" are limited to specific monetary losses that a plaintiff incurs because of the defamatory publication. *Id.* at 1321. They do not include injuries to a plaintiff's reputation or feelings which do not result in monetary loss. *Id.* Rather special damages must result "from conduct of a person other than the defamer or the one defamed and must be legally caused by the defamation." *Id. (citing* Restatement (Second) of Torts § 575, comment (b)).

In light of the above legal standards, I cannot conclude that the allegedly defamatory statement constitutes libel *per se.* Publication of the conclusion of the police and coroner that Lawrence Ocrant's death was a "probable suicide" is a statement specifically directed at the *deceased,* not the plaintiffs. While that statement may reflect on the family's name, it is not itself a writing that tends to hold the plaintiffs up to public hatred, contempt or ridicule. Nor does it reflect adversely on their character or reputations.

Thus, if the alleged defamation constitutes libel at all, it must meet the standards of *libel per quod.* Plaintiffs, however, have failed to plead special damages. (*See* amended complaint, p. 12–13). Accordingly the sixth claim alleging defamation must be dismissed.

DUN & BRADSTREET, INC. v. GREENMOSS BUILDERS, INC.

Supreme Court of the United States, 1985.
472 U.S. 749, 105 S.Ct. 2939, 86 L.Ed.2d 593.

JUSTICE POWELL announced the judgment of the Court and delivered an opinion, in which JUSTICE REHNQUIST and JUSTICE O'CONNOR joined.

In Gertz v. Robert Welch, Inc., 418 U.S. 323, 94 S.Ct. 2997, 41 L.Ed.2d 789 (1974), we held that the First Amendment restricted the damages that a private individual could obtain from a publisher for a libel that involved a matter of public concern. More specifically, we held that in these circumstances the First Amendment prohibited awards of presumed and punitive damages for false and defamatory statements unless the plaintiff shows "actual malice," that is, knowledge of falsity or reckless disregard for the truth. The question presented in this case is whether this rule of *Gertz* applies when the false and defamatory statements do not involve matters of public concern.

I

Petitioner Dun & Bradstreet, a credit reporting agency, provides subscribers with financial and related information about businesses. All the information is confidential; under the terms of the subscription agreement the subscribers may not reveal it to anyone else. On July 26, 1976, petitioner sent a report to five subscribers indicating that respondent, a construction contractor, had filed a voluntary petition for bankruptcy. This report was false and grossly misrepresented respondent's assets and liabilities. That same day, while discussing the possibility of future financing with its bank, respondent's president was told that the bank had received the defamatory report. He immediately called petitioner's regional office, explained the error, and asked for a correction. In addition, he requested the names of the firms that had received the false report in order to assure them that the company was solvent. Petitioner promised to look into the matter but refused to divulge the names of those who had received the report.

After determining that its report was indeed false, petitioner issued a corrective notice on or about August 3, 1976 to the five subscribers who had received the initial report. The notice stated that one of respondent's former employees, not respondent itself, had filed for bankruptcy and that respondent "continued in business as usual." Respondent told petitioner that it was dissatisfied with the notice and it again asked for a list of subscribers who had seen the initial report. Again petitioner refused to divulge their names.

Respondent then brought this defamation action in Vermont state court. It alleged that the false report had injured its reputation and sought both compensatory and punitive damages. The trial established that the error in petitioner's report had been caused when one of its employees, a seventeen year old high school student paid to review Vermont bankruptcy pleadings, had inadvertently attributed to respondent a bankruptcy petition filed by one of respondent's former employees. Although petitioner's representative testified that it was routine practice to check the accuracy of such reports with the businesses themselves, it did not try to verify the information about respondent before reporting it.

After trial, the jury returned a verdict in favor of respondent and awarded $50,000 in compensatory or presumed damages and $300,000 in punitive damages. Petitioner moved for a new trial. It argued that in *Gertz v. Robert Welch, Inc., supra,* at 349, 94 S.Ct., at 3011, this Court had ruled broadly "that the States may not permit recovery of presumed or punitive damages, at least when liability is not based on a showing of knowledge of falsity or reckless disregard for the truth," and it argued that the judge's instructions in this case permitted the jury to award such damages on a lesser showing. The trial court indicated some doubt as to whether *Gertz* applied to "non-media cases," but granted a new trial "[b]ecause of * * * dissatisfaction with its charge and * * * conviction that the interests of justice require[d]" it. App. 26.

The Vermont Supreme Court reversed. 143 Vt. 66, 461 A.2d 414 (1983). Although recognizing that "in certain instances the distinction between media and nonmedia defendants may be difficult to draw," the court stated that "no such difficulty is presented with credit reporting agencies, which are in the business of selling financial information to a limited number of subscribers who have paid substantial fees for their services." *Id.,* at 73, 461 A.2d, at 417. Relying on this distinguishing characteristic of credit reporting firms, the court concluded that such firms are not "the type of media worthy of First Amendment protection as contemplated by New York Times [Co. v. Sullivan, 376 U.S. 254, 84 S.Ct. 710, 11 L.Ed.2d 686 (1964),] and its progeny." 143 Vt., at 73–74, 461 A.2d, at 417–418. It held that the balance between a private plaintiff's right to recover presumed and punitive damages without a showing of special fault and the First Amendment rights of "nonmedia" speakers "must be struck in favor of the private plaintiff defamed by a nonmedia defendant." *Id.,* at 75, 461 A.2d, at 418. Accordingly, the court held "that as a matter of federal constitutional law, the media protections outlined in *Gertz* are inapplicable to nonmedia defamation actions." *Ibid.,* 461 A.2d, at 75.

Recognizing disagreement among the lower courts about when the protections of *Gertz* apply, we granted certiorari. 464 U.S. 959, 104 S.Ct. 389, 78 L.Ed.2d 334 (1983). We now affirm, although for reasons different from those relied upon by the Vermont Supreme Court.

* * *

III

In *New York Times Co. v. Sullivan, supra,* the Court for the first time held that the First Amendment limits the reach of state defamation laws. That case concerned a public official's recovery of damages for the publication of an advertisement criticizing police conduct in a civil rights demonstration. As the Court noted, the advertisement concerned "one of the major public issues of our time." *Id.,* at 271, 84 S.Ct., at 721. Noting that "freedom of expression *upon public questions* is secured by the First Amendment," *id.,* at 269, 84 S.Ct., at 720 (emphasis added), and that "debate *on public issues* should be uninhibited, robust, and wide-open," *id.,* at 270, 84 S.Ct., at 721 (emphasis added), the Court held that a public official cannot recover damages for defamatory falsehood unless he proves that the false statement was made with " 'actual malice'—that is, with knowledge that it was false or with reckless disregard of whether it was false or not," *id.,* at 280, 84 S.Ct., at 726. In later cases, all involving public issues, the Court extended this same constitutional protection to libels of public figures, *e.g.,* Curtis Publishing Co. v. Butts, 388 U.S. 130, 87 S.Ct. 1975, 18 L.Ed.2d 1094 (1967), and in one case suggested in a plurality opinion that this constitutional rule should extend to libels of any individual so long as the defamatory statements involved a "matter of public or general interest," Rosenbloom v. Metromedia, Inc., 403 U.S. 29, 44, 91 S.Ct. 1811, 1820, 29 L.Ed.2d 296 (1971) (opinion of Brennan, J.).

In Gertz v. Robert Welch, Inc., 418 U.S. 323, 94 S.Ct. 2997, 41 L.Ed.2d 789 (1974), we held that the protections of *New York Times* did not extend as far as *Rosenbloom* suggested. *Gertz* concerned a libelous article appearing in a magazine called American Opinion, the monthly outlet of the John Birch Society. The article in question discussed whether the prosecution of a policeman in Chicago was part of a Communist campaign to discredit local law enforcement agencies. The plaintiff, Gertz, neither a public official nor a public figure, was a lawyer tangentially involved in the prosecution. The magazine alleged that he was the chief architect of the "frame-up" of the police officer and linked him to Communist activity. Like every other case in which this Court has found constitutional limits to state defamation laws, *Gertz* involved expression on a matter of undoubted public concern.

In *Gertz,* we held that the fact that expression concerned a public issue did not by itself entitle the libel defendant to the constitutional protections of *New York Times.* These protections, we found, were not "justified solely by reference to the interest of the press and broadcast media in immunity from liability." 418 U.S., at 343, 94 S.Ct., at 3008. Rather, they represented "an accommodation between [First Amendment] concern[s] and the limited state interest present in the context of libel actions brought by public persons." *Ibid.* In libel actions brought by private persons we found the competing interests different. Largely because private persons have not voluntarily exposed themselves to increased risk of injury from defamatory statements and because they generally lack effective opportunities for rebutting such statements, *id.,* at 345, 94 S.Ct., at 3009, we found that the State possessed a "strong and legitimate * * * interest in compensating private individuals for injury to reputation." *Id.,* at 348–349, 94 S.Ct., at 3011. Balancing this stronger state interest against the same First Amendment interest at stake in *New York Times,* we held that a State could not allow recovery of presumed and punitive damages absent a showing of "actual malice." Nothing in our opinion, however, indicated that this same balance would be struck regardless of the type of speech involved.

IV

We have never considered whether the *Gertz* balance obtains when the defamatory statements involve no issue of public concern. To make this determination, we must employ the approach approved in *Gertz* and balance the State's interest in compensating private individuals for injury to their reputation against the First Amendment interest in protecting this type of expression. * * *

We have long recognized that not all speech is of equal First Amendment importance.[5] It is speech on " 'matters of public concern' " that is

5. This Court on many occasions has recognized that certain kinds of speech are less central to the interests of the First Amendment than others. Obscene speech and "fighting words" long have been accorded no protection. Roth v. United States, 354 U.S. 476, 483, 77 S.Ct. 1304, 1308, 1 L.Ed.2d 1498 (1957); Chaplinsky v. New Hampshire, 315 U.S. 568, 571–572, 62 S.Ct. 766, 769, 86 L.Ed. 1031 (1942); *cf.* Harisiades v. Shaughnessy, 342 U.S. 580, 591–592, 72 S.Ct. 512, 519–520, 96 L.Ed. 586 (1952) (advocating violent overthrow of the government is unprotected speech); Near v. Minnesota *ex rel.*

"at the heart of the First Amendment's protection." First National Bank of Boston v. Bellotti, 435 U.S. 765, 776, 98 S.Ct. 1407, 1415, 55 L.Ed.2d 707 (1978), quoting Thornhill v. Alabama, 310 U.S. 88, 101, 60 S.Ct. 736, 743, 84 L.Ed. 1093 (1940). * * * In contrast, speech on matters of purely private concern is of less First Amendment concern. 461 U.S., at 146–147, 103 S.Ct., at 1689–1690. As a number of state courts, including the court below, have recognized, the role of the Constitution in regulating state libel law is far more limited when the concerns that activated *New York Times* and *Gertz* are absent. * * *

* * *

While such speech is not totally unprotected by the First Amendment, *see* Connick v. Myers, 461 U.S., at 147, 103 S.Ct., at 1690, its protections are less stringent. In *Gertz,* we found that the state interest in awarding presumed and punitive damages was not "substantial" in view of their effect on speech at the core of First Amendment concern. 418 U.S., at 349, 94 S.Ct., at 3011. This interest, however, *is* "substantial" relative to the incidental effect these remedies may have on speech of significantly less constitutional interest. The rationale of the common law rules has been the experience and judgment of history that "proof of actual damage will be impossible in a great many cases where, from the character of the defamatory words and the circumstances of publication, it is all but certain that serious harm has resulted in fact." W. Prosser, Law of Torts § 112, p. 765 (4th ed. 1971); *accord, Rowe v. Metz, supra,* 425–426, 579 P.2d, at 84; Note, Developments in the Law—Defamation, 69 Harv.L.Rev. 875, 891–892 (1956). As a result, courts for centuries have allowed juries to presume that some damage occurred from many defamatory utterances and publications. Restatement of Torts § 568, comment b, at 162 (1938) (noting that Hale announced that damages were to be presumed for libel as early as 1670). This rule furthers the state interest in providing remedies for defamation by ensuring that those remedies are effective. In light of the reduced constitutional value of speech involving no matters of public concern, we hold that the state interest adequately supports awards of presumed and punitive damages—even absent a showing of "actual malice." [7]

Olson, 283 U.S. 697, 716, 51 S.Ct. 625, 631, 75 L.Ed. 1357 (1931) (publication of troop ship sailings during war time may be enjoined). In the area of protected speech, the most prominent example of reduced protection for certain kinds of speech concerns commercial speech. Such speech, we have noted, occupies a "subordinate position in the scale of First Amendment values." Ohralik v. Ohio State Bar Assn., 436 U.S. 447, 456, 98 S.Ct. 1912, 1918, 56 L.Ed.2d 444 (1978). It also is more easily verifiable and less likely to be deterred by proper regulation. Virginia Pharmacy Bd. v. Virginia Consumer Council, 425 U.S. 748, 771–772, 96 S.Ct. 1817, 1830–1831, 48 L.Ed.2d 346 (1976). Accordingly, it may be regulated in ways that might be impermissible in the realm of noncommercial expression. *Ohralik, supra,* at 456, 98 S.Ct., at 1918; Central Hudson Gas & Elec. v. Public Serv. Comm'n, 417 U.S. 557, 562–563, 100 S.Ct. 2343, 2349, 2350, 65 L.Ed.2d 341 (1980).

7. The dissent, purporting to apply the same balancing test that we do today, concludes that even speech on purely private matters is entitled to the protections of *Gertz. Post,* at 2960. Its "balance," however, rests on a misinterpretation. In particular, the dissent finds language in *Gertz* that, it believes, shows the State's interest to be "irrelevant." *See post,* at 2964. It is then an easy step for the dissent to say that the State's interest is outweighed by even the reduced First Amendment interest in private speech.

V

The only remaining issue is whether petitioner's credit report involved a matter of public concern. In a related context, we have held that "[w]hether * * * speech addresses a matter of public concern must be determined by [the expression's] content, form, and context * * * as revealed by the whole record." *Connick v. Myers,* 461 U.S., at 147–148, 103 S.Ct., at 1690. These factors indicate that petitioner's credit report concerns no public issue. It was speech solely in the individual interest of the speaker and its specific business audience. This particular interest warrants no special protection when—as in this case—the speech is wholly false and clearly damaging to the victim's business reputation. Moreover, since the credit report was made available to only five subscribers, who, under the terms of the subscription agreement, could not disseminate further, it cannot be said that the report involves any "strong interest in the free flow of commercial information." There is simply no credible argument that this type of credit reporting requires special protection to ensure that "debate on public issues [will] be uninhibited, robust, and wide-open." *New York Times Co. v. Sullivan,* 376 U.S., at 270, 84 S.Ct., at 720.

In addition, the speech here, like advertising, is hardy and unlikely to be deterred by incidental state regulation. It is solely motivated by the desire for profit, which, we have noted, is a force less likely to be deterred than others. Arguably, the reporting here was also more objectively verifiable than speech deserving of greater protection. In any case, the market provides a powerful incentive to a credit reporting agency to be accurate, since false credit reporting is of no use to creditors. Thus, any incremental "chilling" effect of libel suits would be of decreased significance.

VI

We conclude that permitting recovery of presumed and punitive damages in defamation cases absent a showing of "actual malice" does not violate the First Amendment when the defamatory statements do not involve matters of public concern. Accordingly, we affirm the judgment of the Vermont Supreme Court.

It is so ordered.

Gertz, however, did not say that the state interest was "irrelevant" in absolute terms. Indeed, such a statement is belied by *Gertz* itself, for it held that presumed and punitive damages were available under some circumstances. 418 U.S., at 349, 94 S.Ct., at 3011. Rather, what the *Gertz* language indicates is that the State's interest is not substantial relative to the First Amendment interest in *public speech.* This language is thus irrelevant to today's decision.

The dissent's "balance," moreover, would lead to the protection of all libels—no matter how attenuated their constitutional interest. If the dissent were the law, a woman of impeccable character who was branded a "whore" by a jealous neighbor would have no effective recourse unless she could prove "actual malice" by clear and convincing evidence. This is not malice in the ordinary sense, but in the more demanding sense of *New York Times.* The dissent would, in effect, constitutionalize the entire common law of libel.

CHIEF JUSTICE BURGER, concurring in the judgment.

In Gertz v. Robert Welch, Inc., 418 U.S. 323, 94 S.Ct. 2997, 41 L.Ed.2d 789 (1974), contrary to well-established common law prevailing in the states, a divided Court held that a private plaintiff in a defamation action cannot recover for a published falsehood unless he proves that the defendant was at least negligent in publishing the falsehood. The Court further held that there can be no "presumed" damages in such an action and that the private plaintiff cannot receive "punitive" damages unless it is established that the publication was made with "actual malice," as defined in New York Times v. Sullivan, 376 U.S. 254, 84 S.Ct. 710, 11 L.Ed.2d 666 (1964).

* * *

The single question before the Court today is whether *Gertz* applies to this case. The plurality opinion holds that *Gertz* does not apply because, unlike the challenged expression in *Gertz,* the alleged defamatory expression in this case does not relate to a matter of public concern. I agree that *Gertz* is limited to circumstances in which the alleged defamatory expression concerns a matter of general public importance, and that the expression in question here relates to a matter of essentially private concern. I therefore agree with the plurality opinion to the extent that it holds that *Gertz* is inapplicable in this case for the two reasons indicated. No more is needed to dispose of the present case.

I continue to believe, however, that *Gertz* was ill-conceived, and therefore agree with Justice White that *Gertz* should be overruled. I also agree generally with Justice White's observations concerning *New York Times v. Sullivan. New York Times,* however, equates "reckless disregard of the truth" with malice; this should permit a jury instruction that malice may be found if the defendant is shown to have published defamatory material which, in the exercise of reasonable care, would have been revealed as untrue. But since the Court has not applied the literal language of *New York Times* in this way, I agree with Justice White that it should be reexamined. The great rights guaranteed by the First Amendment carry with them certain responsibilities as well.

Consideration of these issues inevitably recalls the aphorism of journalism attributed to the late Roy Howard that, "too much checking on the facts has ruined many a good news story."

JUSTICE WHITE, concurring in the judgment.

Until New York Times v. Sullivan, 376 U.S. 254, 84 S.Ct. 710, 11 L.Ed.2d 666 (1964), the law of defamation was almost exclusively the business of state courts and legislatures. Under the then prevailing state libel law, the defamed individual had only to prove a false written publication that subjected him to hatred, contempt or ridicule. Truth was a defense; but given a defamatory false circulation, general injury to reputation was presumed; special damages, such as pecuniary loss and emotional distress, could be recovered; and punitive damages were available if common-law malice were shown. General damages for injury to reputation were presumed and awarded because the judgment of history was that "in many cases the effect of defamatory statements is so subtle and indirect that it is impossible directly to trace the effects thereof in loss to the person defamed." Restatement of Torts § 621, Comment a, p. 314 (1938). The defendant was permitted to show that there was no reputational injury; but at the very least, the prevailing rule was that at least nominal damages were to be awarded for any defamatory publication actionable per se. This rule performed

> "[A] vindicatory function by enabling the plaintiff publicly to brand the defamatory publication as false. The salutary social value of this rule is preventive in character since it often permits a defamed person to expose the groundless character of a defamatory rumor before harm to the reputation has resulted therefrom." *Id.* § 569, Comment b, p. 166.

Similar rules applied to slanderous statements that were actionable per se.[1]

New York Times v. Sullivan was the first major step in what proved to be a seemingly irreversible process of constitutionalizing the entire law of libel and slander. Under the rule announced in that case, a public official suing for libel could no longer make out his case by proving a false and damaging publication. He could not establish liability and recover any damages, whether presumed or actually proved, unless he proved "malice", which was defined as a knowing falsehood or a reckless disregard for the truth. 376 U.S., at 280, 84 S.Ct., at 726. Given that proof, however, the usual damages were available, including presumed and punitive damages. This judgment overturning 200 years of libel law was deemed necessary to implement the First Amendment interest in "uninhibited, robust, and wide-open" debate on public issues. *Id.,* at 270, 84 S.Ct., at 720. * * *

* * *

I joined the judgment and opinion in *New York Times.* I also joined later decisions extending the *New York Times* standard to other situations. But I came to have increasing doubts about the soundness of the Court's approach and about some of the assumptions underlying it. I could not join the plurality opinion in *Rosenbloom,* and I dissented in *Gertz,* asserting that the common-law remedies should be retained for private plaintiffs. I remain convinced that *Gertz* was erroneously decided. I have also become convinced that the Court struck an improvident balance in the *New York Times* case between the public's interest in being fully informed about public officials and public affairs and the competing interest of those who have been defamed in vindicating their reputation.

In a country like ours, where the people purport to be able to govern themselves through their elected representatives, adequate information about their government is of transcendent importance. That flow of intelligence deserves full First Amendment protection. Criticism and assessment of the performance of public officials and of government in

1. At the common law, slander, unlike libel, was actionable per se only when it dealt with a narrow range of statements; those imputing a criminal offense, a venereal or loathsome and communicable disease, improper conduct of a lawful business, or unchastity of a woman. Restatement of Torts § 570 (1938). To be actionable, all other slanderous statements required additional proof of special damages other than an injury to reputation or emotional distress. The special damage most often took the form of material or pecuniary loss. *Id.,* § 575 and Comment b, pp. 185–187.

general are not subject to penalties imposed by law. But these First Amendment values are not at all served by circulating false statements of fact about public officials. On the contrary, erroneous information frustrates these values. They are even more disserved when the statements falsely impugn the honesty of those men and women and hence lessen the confidence in government. As the Court said in *Gertz,* "there is no constitutional value in false statements of fact. Neither the intentional lie nor the careless error materially advances society's interest in 'uninhibited, robust, and wide-open' debate on public issues." 418 U.S., at 340, 94 S.Ct., at 3007. Yet in *New York Times* cases, the public official's complaint will be dismissed unless he alleges and makes out a jury case of a knowing or reckless falsehood. Absent such proof, there will be no jury verdict or judgment of any kind in his favor, even if the challenged publication is admittedly false. The lie will stand, and the public continue to be misinformed about public matters. This will recurringly happen because the putative plaintiff's burden is so exceedingly difficult to satisfy and can be discharged only by expensive litigation. Even if the plaintiff sues, he frequently loses on summary judgment or never gets to the jury because of insufficient proof of malice. If he wins before the jury, verdicts are often overturned by appellate courts for failure to prove malice. Furthermore, when the plaintiff loses, the jury will likely return a general verdict and there will be no judgment that the publication was false, even though it was without foundation in reality.[2] The public is left to conclude that the challenged statement was true after all. Their only chance of being accurately informed is measured by the public official's ability himself to counter the lie, unaided by the courts. That is a decidedly weak reed to depend on for the vindication of First Amendment interests—"it is the rare case where the denial overtakes the original charge. Denials, retractions, and corrections are not 'hot' news, and rarely receive the prominence of the original story." *Rosenbloom,* opinion of Brennan, J., 403 U.S., at 46–47, 91 S.Ct., at 1821; *Gertz,* dissenting opinion of Brennan, J., 418 U.S., at 363–364, 94 S.Ct., at 3018–3019.

* * *

Also, by leaving the lie uncorrected, the *New York Times* rule plainly leaves the public official without a remedy for the damage to his reputation. Yet the Court has observed that the individual's right to the protection of his own good name is a basic consideration of our constitutional system, reflecting "our basic concept of the essential dignity and worth of every human being—a concept at the root of any decent system of ordered liberty." *Gertz,* 418 U.S., at 341, 94 S.Ct., at 3008, quoting Rosenblatt v. Baer, 383 U.S. 75, 92, 86 S.Ct. 669, 679, 15 L.Ed.2d 597 (1966) (Stewart, J., concurring). The upshot is that the public official must suffer the injury, often cannot get a judgment identifying the lie for what it is, and has very little, if any, chance of countering that lie in the public press.

2. If the plaintiff succeeds in proving a jury case of malice, it may be that the jury will be asked to bring in separate verdicts on falsity and malice. In that event, there could be a verdict in favor of the plaintiff on falsity, but against him on malice. There would be no judgment in his favor, but the verdict on falsity would be a public one and would tend to set the record right and clear the plaintiff's name.

The *New York Times* rule thus countenances two evils: first, the stream of information about public officials and public affairs is polluted and often remains polluted by false information; and second, the reputation and professional life of the defeated plaintiff may be destroyed by falsehoods that might have been avoided with a reasonable effort to investigate the facts. In terms of the First Amendment and reputational interests at stake, these seem grossly perverse results.

* * *

In *New York Times,* instead of escalating the plaintiff's burden of proof to an almost impossible level, we could have achieved our stated goal by limiting the recoverable damages to a level that would not unduly threaten the press. Punitive damages might have been scrutinized as Justice Harlan suggested in *Rosenbloom,* 403 U.S., at 77, 91 S.Ct., at 1836, or perhaps even entirely forbidden. Presumed damages to reputation might have been prohibited, or limited, as in *Gertz.* Had that course been taken and the common-law standard of liability been retained, the defamed public official, upon proving falsity, could at least have had a judgment to that effect. His reputation would then be vindicated; and to the extent possible, the misinformation circulated would have been countered. He might have also recovered a modest amount, enough perhaps to pay his litigation expenses. At the very least, the public official should not have been required to satisfy the actual malice standard where he sought no damages but only to clear his name. In this way, both First Amendment and reputational interests would have been far better served.

* * *

It is interesting that Justice Powell declines to follow the *Gertz* approach in this case. * * * Although Justice Powell speaks only of the inapplicability of the *Gertz* rule with respect to presumed and punitive damages, it must be that the *Gertz* requirement of some kind of fault on the part of the defendant is also inapplicable in cases such as this.

As I have said, I dissented in *Gertz,* and I doubt that the decision in that case has made any measurable contribution to First Amendment or reputational values since its announcement. Nor am I sure that it has saved the press a great deal of money. Like the *New York Times* decision, the burden that plaintiffs must meet invites long and complicated discovery involving detailed investigation of the workings of the press, how a news story is developed, and the state of mind of the reporter and publisher. *See* Herbert v. Lando, 441 U.S. 153, 99 S.Ct. 1635, 60 L.Ed.2d 115 (1979). That kind of litigation is very expensive. I suspect that the press would be no worse off financially if the common-law rules were to apply and if the judiciary was careful to insist that damages awards be kept within bounds. A legislative solution to the damages problem would also be appropriate. Moreover, since libel plaintiffs are very likely more interested in clearing their names than in damages, I doubt that limiting recoveries would deter or be unfair to them. In any event, I cannot assume that the press, as successful and powerful as it is, will be intimidated into withholding news that by decent journalistic standards it believes to be true.

The question before us is whether *Gertz* is to be applied in this case. For either of two reasons, I believe that it should not. First, I am unreconciled to the *Gertz* holding and believe that it should be overruled. Second, as Justice Powell indicates, the defamatory publication in this case does not deal with a matter of public importance. Consequently, I concur in the Court's judgment.*

JUSTICE BRENNAN, with whom JUSTICE MARSHALL, JUSTICE BLACKMUN and JUSTICE STEVENS join, dissenting.

This case involves a difficult question of the proper application of Gertz v. Robert Welch, Inc., 418 U.S. 323, 94 S.Ct. 2997, 41 L.Ed.2d 789 (1974), to credit reporting—a type of speech at some remove from that which first gave rise to explicit First Amendment restrictions on state defamation law—and has produced a diversity of considered opinions, none of which speaks for the Court. Justice Powell's plurality opinion affirming the judgment below would not apply the *Gertz* limitations on presumed and punitive damages to this case; rather, the three Justices joining that opinion would hold that the First Amendment requirement of actual malice—a clear and convincing showing of knowing falsehood or reckless disregard for the truth—should have no application in this defamation action because the speech involved a subject of purely private concern and was circulated to an extremely limited audience. Establishing this exception, the opinion reaffirms *Gertz* for cases involving matters of public concern, *ante,* at 2944, and reaffirms New York Times v. Sullivan, 376 U.S. 254, 84 S.Ct. 710, 11 L.Ed.2d 686 (1964), for cases in which the challenged speech allegedly libels a public official or a public figure. *Ante,* at 2943–2944. Justice White also would affirm; he would not apply *Gertz* to this case on the ground that the subject matter of the publication does not deal with a matter of general or public importance. *Ante,* at 2953 (concurring in the judgment). The Chief Justice apparently agrees with Justice White. *Ante,* at 2948 (concurring in the judgment). The four who join this opinion would reverse the judgment of the Vermont Supreme Court. We believe that, although protection of the type of expression at issue is admittedly not the "central meaning of the First Amendment," 376 U.S., at 273, 84 S.Ct., at 722, *Gertz* makes clear that the First Amendment nonetheless requires restraints on presumed and punitive damage awards for this expression. The lack of consensus in approach to these idiosyncratic facts should not, however, obscure the solid allegiance the principles of *New York Times v. Sullivan* continue to command in the jurisprudence of this Court. * * *

* * *

II

The question presented here is narrow. Neither the parties nor the courts below have suggested that Respondent Greenmoss Builders should be required to show actual malice to obtain a judgment and actual compen-

* *See generally* Hulme, Vindicating Reputation: An Alternative to Damages as a Remedy for Defamation, 30 Am.U.L.Rev. 375 (1981) (recommending declaratory judgment remedy).

satory damages. Nor do the parties question the requirement of *Gertz* that respondent must show fault to obtain a judgment and actual damages. The only question presented is whether a jury award of presumed and punitive damages based on less than a showing of actual malice is constitutionally permissible. *Gertz* provides a forthright negative answer. To preserve the jury verdict in this case, therefore, the opinions of Justice Powell and Justice White have cut away the protective mantle of *Gertz.*

* * *

Even if not at "the essence of self-government," *Garrison v. Louisiana,* 379 U.S., at 74–75, 85 S.Ct., at 216, the expression at issue in this case is important to both our public discourse and our private welfare. That its motivation might be the economic interest of the speaker or listeners does not diminish its First Amendment value. Whether or not such speech is sufficiently central to First Amendment values to require actual malice as a standard of liability, this speech certainly falls within the range of speech that *Gertz* sought to protect from the chill of unrestrained presumed and punitive damage awards. * * *

* * *

* * * Accordingly, Greenmoss Builders should be permitted to recover for any actual damage it can show resulted from Dun & Bradstreet's negligently false credit report, but should be required to show actual malice to receive presumed or punitive damages. Because the jury was not instructed in accordance with these principles, we would reverse and remand for further proceedings not inconsistent with this opinion.

BROWN & WILLIAMSON TOBACCO CORPORATION v. JACOBSON

United States Circuit Court of Appeals, Seventh Circuit, 1987.
827 F.2d 1119, cert. denied, 485 U.S. 993 (1988).

BAUER, CHIEF JUDGE.

[Brown & Williamson Tobacco Corporation, a cigarette manufacturer, sued Walter Jacobson, and CBS, which owned the Chicago television station on which Jacobson was a news anchor, for libel. The central allegation was that Jacobson, who was advertised as one who "pulls no punches", had falsely and maliciously stated that Brown & Williamson had a strategy of selling Viceroy cigarettes to children, which included relating cigarettes to "pot, wine, beer, and sex", and had misrepresented the findings of a Federal Trade Commission staff report concerning Brown & Williamson's advertising.

A jury awarded Brown and Williamson $3,000,000 in compensatory damages and $2,000,000, and $50,000 in punitive damages against CBS and Jacobson, respectively. The District Court Judge reduced the compensatory damage award to $1.00, but upheld the punitive damage award. After holding that the evidence supported a finding that the defendants had acted with malice (*viz.,* with knowledge of the falsity, or reckless disregard for the truth, of the relevant statements), and affirming the judgment as to liability, the United States Court of Appeals for the Seventh Circuit addressed damages issues.]

In general, damage remedies in defamation cases can include: (1) compensatory damages which may be either general or special; (2) punitive or exemplary damages; and (3) nominal damages. * * * In seeking compensatory damages, a plaintiff may attempt to prove "special damage, that is, of directly linking specific [economic] loss to the [defamatory material] by competent evidence." * * * In certain actions in which the defamatory material is characterized as defamatory *per se,* the plaintiff may recover general compensatory damages without proving special damages. This is called the doctrine of presumed damages and it allows the assessment of damages "without proof by the plaintiff that there [has] been any impairment of reputation." *Prosser and Keeton on Torts,* § 116A at 843. Under that doctrine, presumed damages is "an estimate, however rough, of the probable extent of actual loss a person had suffered and would suffer in the future, even though the loss could not be identified in terms of advantageous relationships lost, either from a monetary or enjoyment-of-life standpoint." The doctrine of presumed damages applies to this case because the libelous material prejudiced Brown & Williamson in its trade or business in a manner that is " 'so obviously and naturally hurtful to [Brown & Williamson] that proof of [its] injurious character can be, and is, dispensed with.' " * * * At trial, Brown & Williamson did not attempt to prove special damages but relied instead on the doctrine of presumed damages. The jury returned a verdict of $3,000,000 in compensatory damages which in this case is composed only of presumed damages. The district court reduced the compensatory damage award to $1.00. 644 F.Supp. at 1260–65. Brown & Williamson appeals that decision.

Punitive damages may also be awarded under Illinois law by a jury when a public figure such as Brown & Williamson proves that a defendant has defamed it with actual malice. * * * The purpose of punitive damages, of course, is to punish the defendant for the improper conduct and to deter him from any future transgressions. The jury awarded $2,050,000 in punitive damages against CBS and Jacobson and the district court upheld the award. 644 F.Supp. at 1260–65. In this court, CBS and Jacobson challenge the punitive damage award as both excessive and inappropriate.

A. Compensatory Damages

During the damage portion of the bifurcated trial, Brown & Williamson introduced a variety of evidence intended to show that its reputation had been harmed by Jacobson's statement. First, Brown & Williamson's general counsel testified that after the broadcast there were calls from the field sales force indicating that their contacts were asking "how in the world could Brown & Williamson have done such a thing." Second, a department sales manager for Brown & Williamson testified that sales managers in the Chicago area had received negative comments from distributors, retailers, and consumers. The reports he received indicated that the sales staff had been disrupted in their normal activities by questions from retailers and consumers about the broadcast. Third, the former Vice President of Marketing for Brown & Williamson testified that the company had a reputation it cared about and that he believed that Viceroy's customers care about the reputation of the company from which they buy cigarettes. He also testified that the company's reputation among governmental entities was important because the cigarette industry is such a closely regulated industry. Fourth, the company introduced evidence that the Perspective (including its rebroadcasts) was seen by over 2.5 million people in the Chicago area. In addition, over two million people read a 1984 article in the *Saturday Evening Post* which repeated some of the most damaging portions of the Perspective. Brown & Williamson also argued that the Perspective was especially devastating because Chicago area viewers believe that Jacobson's Perspectives are reliable.

Although Brown & Williamson asked the jury for $7,000,000 dollars in compensatory damages, the jury was only willing to award $3,000,000. In setting aside the award, the district court relied primarily on the failure of Brown & Williamson to put forth any evidence that "Viceroy lost sales, lost a distributor, lost profits, or had an employee quit or stop working as effectively and enthusiastically as he used to, or that any individual stopped smoking Viceroys." 644 F.Supp. at 1261. The court concluded that "[Brown & Williamson] clearly did not prove any actual damages * * *." *Id.*

* * *

In addition to the failure to prove any pecuniary damages, the court cited two other reasons for its decision to reduce the damage award to $1.00. First, the court held that under Illinois law, substantial damages are not presumed. * * * Second, the court found that any residual effect of the broadcast was greatly reduced if not eliminated by the jury's verdict in favor of Brown & Williamson and the accompanying publicity.[10]

The district court incorrectly relied on Brown & Williamson's failure to prove any actual damages such as lost sales. As noted above, under Illinois law, Brown & Williamson could choose, as it did, to forego any proof of special damages and seek to recover compensatory damages under the doctrine of presumed damages. * * * Brown & Williamson is entitled in this case to recover under the doctrine of presumed damages because Jacobson's Perspective was libelous *per se.* * * *

It is true that the harm to Brown & Williamson's reputation cannot be measured easily. * * * As the Tenth Circuit recently stated, "[a]scertainment of presumed general damages is difficult at best and unavoidably includes an element of speculation." *Sunward Corporation v. Dun & Bradstreet, Inc.,* 811 F.2d 511, 538 (10th Cir.1987).[11] Nonetheless, pre-

10. The court was correct in holding that testimony that employees were emotionally upset is not relevant because a corporation is not capable of mental suffering, which ordinarily will be an important component of an individual's damage award for libel. *See Gertz v. Robert Welch, Inc.,* 680 F.2d 527, 540 (7th Cir.1982), *cert. denied,* 459 U.S. 1226, 103 S.Ct. 1233, 75 L.Ed.2d 467 (1983). Although a corporation is not capable of mental suffering, it is of course still entitled to be compensated for damage to its reputation.

11. Ascertainment of actual damages is often not much easier. This is why it "has been the experience and judgment of history that 'proof of actual damage will be impossible in a great many cases * * * ' W. Prosser, Law of Torts § 112 * * * As a result, courts for centuries have allowed juries to presume that some damage occurred from many de-sumed general damages are permissible under Illinois law and under the United States Constitution. * * *

Brown & Williamson also challenges the district court's conclusion that media coverage of its victory at trial was "fair" and therefore it "ameliorates whatever injury Brown & Williamson might have * * * suffered." * * * In addition, even if the media coverage could be characterized as fair, it does not necessarily mean that the effect of the libelous statements will be ameliorated. For example, much of the post-verdict publicity reported Jacobson's vehement denials of the charges and included assurances by the defendants that, like many libel defendants, they would be victorious in the appellate court. Moreover, some of the commentary that occurred in the wake of the verdict questioned the correctness of the verdict and included some suggestions that the defendants had lost simply because they were "out-lawyered." We conclude that the district court erroneously relied on the post-verdict publicity in setting aside the damage award.

In striking the compensatory damage award, the district court also relied on a statement in an Illinois appellate court decision that substantial damages are not presumed. 644 F.Supp. at 1261 (citing *Bloomfield v. Retail Credit Co.,* 14 Ill.App.3d 158, 302 N.E.2d 88 (1st Dist.1973)). * * *

* * *

We read the holding in *Costello* [v. Capital Cities Communications, 153 Ill.App.3d 956, 106 Ill.Dec. 154, 505 N.E.2d 701 (1987)] as advising an appellate court to give some deference to the jury's determination of presumed damages while also considering whether it considers the jury award of presumed damages excessive. If it finds the award excessive, the court may exercise its discretion and reduce the award to what it considers a more appropriate figure. One obvious factor in deciding how much deference to give a jury verdict on presumed damages is the extent to which the court believes that the jury may have been carried away by passion and prejudice. * * * In this case, the jury appears not to have been carried away by passion and prejudice. Brown & Williamson asked for $7,000,000 in presumed damages but the jury only awarded $3,000,000. Brown & Williamson asked for $10,100,000 in punitive damages but the jury awarded only $2,050,000. At the very least, both of these awards indicate that the jury was not mere putty in the hands of the plaintiff.

* * *

Although the jury did conscientiously fulfill its duty in this case, we are hesitant to uphold the entire award. Illinois law requires appellate courts to examine jury awards under the doctrine of presumed damages with great care to determine whether they are "substantial" or within an acceptable range. * * * We hold that an award of $1,000,000 in compensatory

famatory utterances and publications * * *. This rule furthers the state interest in providing remedies for defamation by ensuring that those remedies are effective." *Dun & Bradstreet, Inc. v. Greenmoss Builders, Inc.,* 472 U.S. 749, 760–61, 105 S.Ct. 2939, 2946, 86 L.Ed.2d 593 (1985) (plurality opinion). The reason for such a rule is illustrated by this case. Even if Brown & Williamson were able to show that there was a decline in Viceroy sales after Jacobson's Perspective, it would be extremely difficult to prove that the decline was the result of the libelous broadcast. * * *

damages is appropriate in this case. The $1,000,000 in presumed damages is sizable but on the facts of this case it is not "substantial" under Illinois law. We grant that it is difficult to draw a distinction but that in effect is what the *Costello* court calls for in applying the test. Unlike *Costello,* this broadcast was made not in a relatively small community but in one of the largest television markets in the country. The defamatory material here was not published once but was broadcast four separate times and was seen by a total viewership of approximately 2.5 million people. It was delivered on what was the most popular news broadcast in Chicago and was delivered by a veteran journalist who was trusted by the public and promoted by his employer as someone who "always leaves you informed." Moreover, the text of the broadcast carried a very substantial sting that must have hurt both the reputation of Brown & Williamson and its parent company (which as CBS's counsel pointed out at trial owns one of the most respected department stores in Chicago). In addition, the libelous material was a television broadcast and not a newspaper editorial. Television is a more intense and more focused medium. It allows the libeler to come into peoples' homes and deliver essentially in person a powerful libelous statement using various voice inflections to add power to the message. Television also allows for the use of graphics to emphasize the libelous material. * * *

We recognize that this is a very inexact and somewhat arbitrary process. Nonetheless, the process is inherent in the doctrine of presumed damages. An appellate court must, under Illinois law, use its judgment in determining the extent to which a jury award of presumed damages will be upheld. Our judgment is $1,000,000.

B. Punitive Damages

Punitive damages are available under Illinois law when a plaintiff has proven actual malice. * * * Several factors can be considered by the jury in arriving at a punitive damage award. First, and most importantly for purposes of this case, the jury was entitled to consider the amount of attorney's fees incurred by the plaintiff in bringing the libel action. * * * Second, the jury was entitled to take into account the defendants' wealth. * * * Finally, because the purpose of punitive damages is deterrence, the jury was entitled to consider evidence of post-verdict recalcitrance in determining the punitive damage award. * * *

Taking only the first two factors into account, we conclude that the district court's decision upholding the jury's punitive damage award was clearly correct. Brown & Williamson's attorney's fees were $1,360,000 prior to post-trial motions. Jacobson's net worth including his contract with CBS was over $5,000,000, while CBS's net worth was approximately one and one-half billion dollars. The punitive damage award of $50,000 against Jacobson is a modest one considering his net worth. *See Brown,* slip op. at 10. It might provide some deterrent value without being destructive. In light of the attorney's fees that Brown & Williamson incurred and CBS's substantial net worth, the $2,000,000 award against CBS is reasonable. The award might provide some deterrence to future misconduct and yet will not burden CBS with a debt that it cannot easily discharge.

V.

One of the most important functions of the court system in the United States is to protect the freedom of the press. * * * [W]e are forced to conclude that this case does not involve freedom of the press. * * *

Affirmed in Part, Reversed in Part.

Notes

1. What legislative solution do you think Justice White would propose? What, if any, would you propose?

2. The court in *Jacobson* says that the doctrine of presumed damages enables a plaintiff to recover general compensatory damages without proving special damages. But it is possible to prove actual damages without proving special damages. What would Brown & Williamson Tobacco Corporation have received if the jury had not found malice? In fact, if no malice has been proved, Gertz v. Robert Welch, Inc., 418 U.S. 323, 94 S.Ct. 2997, 41 L.Ed.2d 789 (1974), requires proof of actual damages, with or without proof of special damages, in lieu of presumed damages.

3. Based on the United States Supreme Court's decision in *Gertz* the Maryland Court of Appeals held that presumed and punitive damages based on negligent defamation were ruled out as a constitutional matter even in a suit by a private figure. Jacron Sales Co. v. Sindorf, 276 Md. 580, 350 A.2d 688 (1976); Hearst Corp. v. Hughes, 297 Md. 112, 466 A.2d 486 (1983). The Maryland Court stressed that damages for "actual injury" due to defamation, including intangible injury such as emotional distress, still were recoverable.

After the United States Supreme Court in Dun & Bradstreet held that *Gertz* was not properly so construed, and thus removed the First Amendment basis for the Maryland rulings, a Judge of a lower Maryland appellate court urged that the holdings of *Jacron* and *Hearst* should be revisited. Hanlon v. Davis, 76 Md.App. 339, 545 A.2d 72 (1988); Gooch v. Maryland Mechanical Systems, Inc., 81 Md.App. 376, 567 A.2d 954, 964–66 (1990) (dissenting opinion). The Maryland Court of Appeals, however, declined to review the latter case, see 573 A.2d 807 (1990).

Can that result be explained as (1) a sub silentio determination to apply the Maryland Constitution differently than the United States Supreme Court applies the First Amendment; or (2) a change in the common law to do away with presumed damages, whether or not it is required by any constitutional provision; or (3) a judgment that presumed damages are essentially duplicative of intangible damages which remain awardable?

Do you favor such a shift away from allowing presumed damages?

4. In Masson v. The New Yorker Magazine, Inc., 960 F.2d 896 (9th Cir.1992) (applying California law), the court rejected the "incremental harm" doctrine, that if the incremental harm imposed by false statements adds only nominally to the harm from non-actionable statements in a publication, the false statements are not actionable. *Accord,* Liberty Lobby, Inc. v. Anderson, 746 F.2d 1563, 1568 (D.C.Cir.1984) (per Scalia, J.), *vacated on other grounds,*

477 U.S. 242, 106 S.Ct. 2505, 91 L.Ed.2d 202 (1986), denouncing the doctrine as a "bad idea", resting on the "assumption that one's reputation is a monolith, which stands or falls in its entirety". The Supreme Court had held, in remanding *Masson* to the Ninth Circuit, that there was no constitutional requirement for such a rule, Masson v. New Yorker Magazine, Inc., ___ U.S. ___, 111 S.Ct. 2419, 2436, 115 L.Ed.2d 447 (1991).

Could the incremental harm doctrine nonetheless be revived as a theory to limit damages?

TACKET v. DELCO REMY DIVISION OF GENERAL MOTORS CORPORATION

United States Court of Appeals, Seventh Circuit, 1991.
937 F.2d 1201.

Before BAUER, CHIEF JUDGE, CUDAHY and COFFEY, CIRCUIT JUDGES.

BAUER, CHIEF JUDGE.

According to the age-old children's rhyme, "Sticks and stones may break your bones, but names can never hurt you." Plaintiff-appellee Thomas Tacket and the law of defamation, however, argue otherwise. According to Tacket, another mellifluous rhyme, one that read "TACKET TACKET WHAT A RACKET," when painted on the inside wall of General Motors', Anderson, Indiana, assembly plant and allowed to remain there for seven or eight months, defamed him and irreparably damaged his reputation.

In this appeal, we revisit a case that we remanded to the district court in 1987. In the instant appeal, we are asked to review the district court's decision that the jury properly could award Tacket $100,000 for the damages he suffered due to the display of the five-word rhyme. Applying settled law from both the state of Indiana and this circuit, we find that Tacket failed to prove the requisite "special damages," and therefore, his award must be reversed.

I.

* * * Tacket alleged that his reputation was irreparably damaged by the sign described above, which was written and displayed by managerial employees of General Motors. * * *

The evidence revealed the following: Thomas Tacket was an employee at Delco Remy Division of General Motors ("Delco") in Anderson, Indiana. Tacket was first employed by Delco in 1971, and rose to the level of night superintendent in 1983. In February 1985, Delco's Anderson facility was working on a generator production contract entitled the "9–S1 Project." A problem arose concerning the attainment of wooden shipping crates. Ed Spearman, one of Tacket's subordinates, suggested that "S & T Specialties" provide the needed crates. Tacket received requisition forms for the crates and processed them during off-duty hours. Both he and Spearman signed the forms.

Some time later, the union representing Delco's workers discovered that Delco was buying the crates from an outside supplier and protested the "out-sourcing" of work that Delco's own staff could have performed. The union also discovered that Spearman was the "S", and suspected that Tacket was the "T", of "S & T Specialties". (The crates were being constructed in Spearman's garage.) Delco promptly suspended both Spearman and Tacket pending an investigation. Delco ultimately fired Spearman, but concluded that it had insufficient evidence to discharge Tacket. He returned to work on April 9, 1985, but his relationship with the workers had soured. Delco thereafter transferred him to a "quality assurance team" with the same rank and salary but with fewer subordinates.

Upon learning of the out-sourcing, the workers spread rumors about Spearman and Tacket. At some point, a sign approximately 3′ x 30′ appeared inside the plant proclaiming the infamous rhyme "TACKET TACKET WHAT A RACKET." This sign stayed up for two to three days during Tacket's suspension. A second, smaller sign approximately 1′ x 4′ proclaiming the same message was stenciled on the inside wall of the plant (*see* photo at *Tacket I,* 836 F.2d at 1044) and remained there for at least seven months.

On the issue of damages, Tacket offered the testimony of Frank Connolly, a psychologist, who diagnosed Tacket to have suffered a psychiatric illness known as depressive neurosis. * * *

At the close of the evidence, the district court instructed the jurors that Tacket could prove damage from the sign in two ways: 1) if the sign were found to impute a crime or to prejudice him in his profession, then injury to his reputation would be established; or, 2) if the sign did not impute such things, then the jury was instructed that the plaintiff could recover only if "special damages" were proven. Special damages were defined as the loss of something having economic or pecuniary value, or the loss of a benefit that has an indirect financial value to the plaintiff. Special interrogatories were given to the jury to aid their deliberations.

The jury returned a verdict for the plaintiff in the amount of $100,000. The jury indicated on its special verdict form that the sign did not tend to damage the plaintiff's reputation without regard to extrinsic circumstances, but that it did defame the plaintiff when considered with other facts. The jury further found that Delco intentionally and unreasonably failed to remove that sign (thereby "publishing" it), and that plaintiff exercised proper care for the protection of his own interests.

Delco then moved to set aside the verdict, arguing that the jury's finding that the sign did not defame Tacket without consideration of extrinsic facts, coupled with Tacket's alleged failure to plead and prove "special damages," mandated entry of judgment in its favor. In its Order of July 6, 1989, the district court determined that Indiana libel law allowed recovery of proven psychological injuries as part of special damages, and permitted Tacket to amend his pleadings to conform them to the evidence. * * * Delco appealed.

II.

* * *

Though Delco presents several claims on appeal, only one issue concerns us today: whether Tacket, under Indiana law, adequately proved special damages. In order to resolve this dispute, we need first consider the broader outlines of defamation law in Indiana. As the district court appropriately noted, defamation, defined as holding a person up to ridicule, scorn or contempt, *See Black's Law Dictionary* at 417 (6th ed. 1990), is comprised of two related torts: libel and slander. Libel generally is concerned with defamatory communications of a permanent sort, such as printed matter, films, and art work. Slander, on the other hand, involves transitory, ephemeral communications, such as speech, gestures, and sign language. *See generally* Prosser and Keeton, *The Law of Torts* 785–97 (5th ed. 1984) ("[L]ibel is that which is communicated by the sense of sight, or perhaps also by touch or smell, while slander is that which is communicated by the sense of hearing.").

In addition to these related torts, the law of defamation includes certain categories and labels. In its July 6, 1989 Order, the district court ably reviewed the history of defamation law and discussed the meaning of the labels "*per se*" and "*per quod.*" For our purposes, suffice it to say that defamation *per se* involves words (whether slanderous or libellous) which, by themselves and without reference to extrinsic circumstances, injure the reputation of the person to whom they are applied, whereas defamation *per quod* requires an allegation of facts and circumstances, aside from the words contained in the publication, to show how the words damage the plaintiff. *Black's Law Dictionary* at 417. It generally is agreed that words, whether they be in the form of libel or slander, and which are defamatory *per se* or *per quod,* are actionable without allegation and proof of any special harm if they: a) impute to another the commission of a crime; b) impute to another a loathsome disease; c) impute unchastity to a woman; or d) tend to injure another in his trade or profession. *Gibson v. Kincaid,* 140 Ind.App. 186, 221 N.E.2d 834, 843 (1967) (Faulconer, J., concurring).

In libel actions, it was well-established by the beginning of the nineteenth century that any libel was actionable *per se,* meaning that it was actionable without the necessity of pleading and proving that the plaintiff suffered any harm from the defamatory writing. Prosser and Keeton, *supra,* at 795. As time passed, however, a sharp disagreement developed about the need to prove special damages in libel *per quod* cases—that is, in cases where the publication became defamatory only to those who were aware of defamatory facts extrinsic to the matter published. *Id.* Because the jury's special verdict made clear that they found the small, painted sign defamatory only when extrinsic circumstances were taken into account, it is undisputed that libel *per quod* is implicated in this case. Thus, the crucial questions are whether libel *per quod* requires pleading and proof of special damages under Indiana law, and, if so, whether Tacket accomplished these tasks in this case. We will consider each question in turn.

The Indiana courts have restated the following general rule on many occasions:

> If a communication is defamatory *per se,* then nominal damages will be presumed by the court and need not be specially pleaded; however, in the absence of words actionable *per se,* special damages must be alleged in the complaint * * *. When we say that words are actionable only upon proof of "special" damage, we mean special in the sense that it must be supported by specific proof, as distinct from the damage assumed to follow in the case of libel *per se,* or libel *per quod* which falls into one of the four special categories * * *. In other words, special damages must be proved in the case of slander or libel *per quod* that does not involve the imputation of a crime, a loathsome disease, unchastity, or injury to the plaintiff's business, profession, trade or office.

* * * Thus, libel *per quod* under Indiana law requires that both extrinsic defamatory facts and special damages be pleaded and proved. *See Agnew v. Hiatt,* 466 N.E.2d 781, 782 (Ind.App.1984) (holding that if an alleged defamation is not defamatory *per se,* "special damages must be alleged in the complaint"); *Gibson,* 221 N.E.2d at 836–37 (affirming judgment for defendants in a defamation case on the grounds that no special damages were proven).

Given that special damages are required to be pleaded and proved in Indiana libel *per quod* cases, we turn to the next question: whether Tacket has done so in this case. To resolve this issue, we must determine what constitutes "special damages." As noted above, the district court instructed the jury that special damages mean that Tacket must show some economic or pecuniary loss, or the loss of a benefit that places on Tacket an indirect financial burden. Yet, in its July 6 Order, the district court interpreted Indiana law "to allow recovery of any damage, pecuniary or otherwise, that is specially pleaded and proved to be a proximate result of the complained of circumstances in a defamation case." The district court determined that, because Tacket showed a specific, psychiatric injury resulting from the sign, he need not demonstrate any pecuniary loss.

We disagree with the district court's interpretation of Indiana law. * * * Tacket's evidence of psychological injury simply does not fall within the class of special damages.

* * *

Tacket's burden was to show damages that are "pecuniary in nature" and that "have been actually incurred as a natural and proximate consequence of the wrongful act." *Stanley v. Kelley,* 422 N.E.2d 663, 668 (Ind.App.1981). *Accord,* C. McCormick, *Damages* § 114 (1935) ("The 'special damage' required in defamation cases must be some material or pecuniary injury. Injury to reputation without more, humiliation, mental anguish, physical sickness—these do not suffice."). In the instant case, Tacket presented no evidence of any pecuniary loss. Instead, he demonstrated that he suffered emotional distress and psychological injury. But such maladies, however painful to Tacket, are only general damages—the kind that routinely follow a defamation. Injury to the plaintiff's reputation and standing in the community, personal humiliation, and mental anguish and suffering are the sort of damages that the law presumes to be the natural result of the publication; they are not special damages. *Stanley,* 422 N.E.2d at 668–69.

* * *

III.

For the foregoing reasons, we find Tacket's evidence of psychological injury insufficient to demonstrate the special damages necessary to uphold the jury's award. * * * The order of the district court denying Delco's motion for judgment notwithstanding the verdict is, therefore, Reversed. We VACATE the judgment on the verdict, and REMAND this case to the district court to enter judgment for Delco, each party to bear its own costs.

CUDAHY, CIRCUIT JUDGE, dissenting.

It is, to say the least, disheartening—and perhaps even productive of a depressive neurosis—to see the scholarly efforts of a district court judge to make sense of Indiana libel law set at naught. I agree with Judge McKinney that "[t]here is no precedential or jurisprudential reason to allow a libel plaintiff to call witnesses to specially prove his business losses, but to disallow expert and other testimony to prove his psychological injuries." Dist.Ct.Op. at 13.

The majority seems to be mired in the jurisdictional conflicts between the ecclesiastical and the common law courts of the sixteenth century. The ecclesiastical courts regarded defamation as a sin and punished it with a penance. For a considerable period of time, therefore, the common law courts held that, unless "temporal" damage could be proved, defamation was a "spiritual" matter to be left to the Church. *See* Prosser, *The Law of Torts* 772; *see also* Veeder, *The History and Theory of the Law of Defamation,* 3 Colum.L.Rev. 546 (1903). Perhaps the majority, too, views a psychological diagnosis as in the "spiritual" realm and thus beyond our competence.

In fact, psychologists may not have really added much to what in another day would have been perceived as a problem of the spirit, best left to ecclesiastical attention. But, *given modern postulates and perspectives,* I see no reason to equate what purports to be a scientific diagnosis threatening adverse economic consequences (through lowered job performance) with a mere presumption of mental anguish and emotional distress. This is the equation, however, that the majority makes. Despite the scientific trappings of expert testimony, the majority is unwilling to factor these matters of the "spirit" into its calculations.

* * *

By seeking to interpret Indiana law as congruent with modern concepts of psychology as a science, the district court has hit upon a perfectly acceptable basis for abandoning jurisdictional distinctions of the sixteenth century that have, as far as I can see, no current utility. The majority, on the other hand, adopts a view which might regard proof even of irreversible psychosis as a mere restatement of mental anguish and emotional distress. For a psychosis, too, is a thing of the spirit (albeit an evil one).

I therefore respectfully dissent.

O'HARA v. STORER COMMUNICATIONS, INC.

California Court of Appeal, Fourth District, 1991.
231 Cal.App.3d 1101, 282 Cal.Rptr. 712.

TODD, ASSOCIATE JUSTICE.

In this consolidated appeal arising from a lawsuit against Storer Communications, Inc. (Storer), which at the time owned television Channel 39 and was operating the station under the call letters of KCST–TV, San Diego, we consider the issue of special damages in defamation actions. Naomi O'Hara sued Storer for slander, and, in a trial limited to special damages, a jury awarded her $300,000. Storer appeals, claiming (1) O'Hara presented no evidence of special damages under the Restatement Second of Torts and evidence of emotional distress was improperly admitted during the trial and (2) therefore, the verdict was excessive and the result of passion and prejudice. O'Hara also appeals, contending (1) it was error to restrict the trial to special damages on the basis she failed to make an adequate demand for a retraction pursuant to Civil Code [1] section 48a and (2) she is entitled to prejudgment interest.

FACTS

On October 12, 1983, Channel 39 broadcast a news report that named O'Hara as "an alleged prostitute" in the company of then-San Diego County Supervisor Paul Eckert. O'Hara in fact was not a prostitute; rather, she was a witness in a grand jury investigation of police involvement in a prostitution ring. The Channel 39 reporter made the error after reading a newspaper article about the grand jury investigation and transposing O'Hara's name with that of the alleged prostitute.

At the time, O'Hara was 44 years old and a free-lance public relations person, who had moved to California in the late 1970's from Kentucky, where she had volunteered in a wide spectrum of community activities. After living for a time in Los Angeles, she moved to San Diego and, in the early 1980's, embarked on a career in promotions and marketing, working at various times for Seaport Village, Agua Caliente Race Track and Marina Village. She was paid $1,200 to $1,500 a month by Seaport Village, $600 a week by Agua Caliente and $2,000 for the first month by Marina Village and $750 a month thereafter.

On November 2, 1983, O'Hara's attorney wrote Channel 39 and requested he be contacted so that a retraction could be discussed. The letter said in part: "I want a retraction published, but ONLY after it has been discussed first with me." On November 3, 1983, the television station's attorney telephoned O'Hara's attorney and it was agreed the station would send O'Hara's attorney transcripts of various broadcasts aired by the station pertaining to O'Hara for his review. The transcripts were sent by Federal Express the following day. The next communication between the attorneys took place on November 15, 1983, when O'Hara's attorney returned a previously placed telephone call. The station's attorney asked whether O'Hara's attorney had a proposed retraction; O'Hara's

1. All statutory references are to the Civil Code unless otherwise specified.

attorney responded that he needed to discuss the matter with his client. On December 7, 1983, the station's attorney telephoned O'Hara's attorney, who said he would call back. Neither the station nor its attorney heard from O'Hara or her attorney again until August 13, 1984, when O'Hara's attorney sent a letter demanding compensation in the amount of $2,500,-000.

On October 12, 1984, O'Hara filed her complaint, stating four different causes of action: defamation, intentional infliction of emotional distress, negligence and invasion of privacy. The complaint alleged that Channel 39's broadcast of October 12, 1983, was slanderous because "it imputed to [O'Hara] the reference of being charged with a crime and a want of chastity."

* * *

DISCUSSION

Central to both appeals is section 48a, which reads in pertinent part as follows:

> "1. In any action for damages for the publication of a libel in a newspaper, or of a slander by radio broadcast, plaintiff shall recover no more than special damages unless a correction be demanded and be not published or broadcast, as hereinafter provided. Plaintiff shall serve upon the publisher, at the place of publication or broadcaster at the place of broadcast, a written notice specifying the statements claimed to be libelous and demanding that the same be corrected. Said notice and demand must be served within 20 days after knowledge of the publication or broadcast of the statements claimed to be libelous.
>
> "2. If a correction be demanded within said period and be not published or broadcast in substantially as conspicuous a manner in said newspaper or on said broadcasting station as were the statements claimed to be libelous, in a regular issue thereof published or broadcast within three weeks after such service, plaintiff, if he pleads and proves such notice, demand and failure to correct, and if his cause of action be maintained, may recover general, special and exemplary damages; provided that no exemplary damages may be recovered unless plaintiff shall prove that defendant made the publication or broadcast with actual malice and then only in the discretion of the court or jury, and actual malice shall not be inferred or presumed from the publication or broadcast.
>
> "* * *
>
> "4. As used herein, the terms 'general damages,' 'special damages,' 'exemplary damages' and 'actual malice,' are defined as follows:
>
> "(a) 'General damages' are damages for loss of reputation, shame, mortification and hurt feelings;
>
> "(b) 'Special damages' are all damages which plaintiff alleges and proves that he has suffered in respect to his property, business, trade, profession or occupation, including such amounts of money as the

> plaintiff alleges and proves he has expended as a result of the alleged libel, and no other;"

The constitutionality of section 48a was upheld in *Werner v. Southern Cal. etc. Newspapers* (1950) 35 Cal.2d 121, 216 P.2d 825, with the Supreme Court finding the danger of excessive recoveries of general damages in defamation actions and the public interest in free dissemination of news justify the limitation of recovery for defamation to special damages when a retraction has not been demanded and refused.

I

We first consider O'Hara's contention that the trial court erred in finding she had failed to comply with section 48a and Storer had not refused to broadcast a correction. The contention is without merit.

[discussion omitted]

II

Having established that O'Hara did not comply with section 48a in making a proper demand for retraction, it follows that under the statute she was limited to proving special damages at trial. Hence, we next consider Storer's assignments of error with respect to evidence of damages presented at trial: (1) O'Hara did not present any evidence of special damages; and (2) the trial court improperly allowed evidence of emotional distress to be presented to the jury.

Subdivision 4(b) of section 48a defines special damages as follows:

> "[A]ll damages which plaintiff alleges and proves that he has suffered in respect to his property, business, trade, profession or occupation, including such amounts of money as the plaintiff alleges and proves he has expended as a result of the alleged libel, and no other;"

O'Hara presented three types of evidence concerning the damage to her livelihood: (1) she suffered a loss of clients unexplained by any other source; (2) McDaniel was concerned over the adverse publicity concerning O'Hara; and (3) the defamation caused a psychic injury that incapacitated her, rendering her unable to work, giving McDaniel a reason for failing to hire her.

It is clear that under California law, a loss of clients following defamation is evidence of recoverable special damages. * * *

* * *

O'Hara presented evidence of such damages with her business calendars for 1982 and 1983 which chronicled substantial business activity before the slanderous broadcast and none whatsoever thereafter, as well as her testimony that after the slanderous broadcast she no longer received phone calls about work.

Next, we assess the effect of O'Hara's testimony that McDaniel told her the adverse publicity was part of his reason for not hiring her. * * * This evidence fits the classical definition of special damage in a defamation case—a business loss suffered by the plaintiff as a result of damage to her reputation. * * *

However, the question remains whether O'Hara's evidence that the defamation rendered her incapable of working constituted special damages under section 48a. The distinction between general damages and special damages is universally recognized: General damages are damages that courts believe generally flow from the kind of substantive wrong done by the defendant. Special damages, on the other hand, include items of loss that are more or less peculiar to the particular plaintiff in that the plaintiff actually suffered the loss in the specific amount. Two limitations apply to special damages: (1) they must be proved to a reasonable certainty; and (2) no special damages are recoverable if they are deemed remote. Here, we must consider the differences between general damages and special damages in the context of defamation actions and section 48a.

Storer argues that none of the witnesses presented by O'Hara * * * testified as to special damages because O'Hara's inability to work does not constitute special damages. In essence, McDaniel's deposition testimony was that he observed some of the effects of the defamation on O'Hara—the shaking of her hands and lack of confidence—and this observation was one reason he did not hire her.

Thus is posed a question never clearly decided by any court in California. May evidence of psychic injury or emotional distress be shown as the cause of special damage where one's business income is diminished because others became aware of the defamed plaintiff's condition? We conclude it may, contrary to Storer's argument, this conclusion does not conflict with the position of the Restatement Second of Torts. Section 622A of the Restatement Second of Torts provides: "Defamation is a legal cause of special harm to the person defamed if (a) it is a substantial factor in bringing about the harm, and (b) there is no rule of law relieving the publisher from liability because of the manner in which the publication has resulted in the harm."

In several states outside this jurisdiction, it has long been established that a plaintiff's own distress or illness caused by the defamation cannot constitute special damages. * * *

While Storer argues the general law of defamation does not permit a plaintiff's emotional injury to bottom a claim of special damages, we are unpersuaded. Under the specific language of section 48a, one's loss of employment due to obvious emotional instability certainly results in a loss to "property, business, trade, profession or occupation" as set out in the statute. In O'Hara's case, substantial evidence supported the jury verdict she had suffered monetary damage through inability to work as a direct and proximate result of the defamation. We have examined the history of the enactment of section 48a by the Legislature and of its amendment in 1945, and find nothing to indicate an intent to limit special damage as argued by Storer. Under the plain meaning of the unambiguous words of the statute, we hold O'Hara has proved special damages. * * *

* * *

III

Storer contends the $300,000 verdict was excessive and there was insufficient evidence to justify it. The contention is without merit.

[discussion omitted]

* * * Given this evidence and the six years between the slanderous broadcast and the trial, we find the $300,000 verdict is adequately supported by the record and reject the argument it is excessive and a result of passion.

IV

O'Hara contends the trial court erred in denying her prejudgment interest under section 3291. The contention has merit.

Section 3291 permits the recovery of prejudgment interest in actions "to recover damages for personal injury sustained by any person resulting from or occasioned by the tort of any other person, corporation * * *." The court's authority to make such an award is predicated on the plaintiff having made an offer under Code of Civil Procedure section 998 to settle the case which the defendant had not accepted before trial or within 30 days, whichever occurs first, and the plaintiff then obtaining a more favorable judgment. Here, O'Hara made a statutory settlement demand less than the judgment.

* * *

Here, the issue presented is whether O'Hara's action for defamation is one "to recover damages for personal injury." We first look at the nature of the tort. "[D]efamation is an invasion of the interest in reputation and good name * * *. A defamatory communication usually has been defined as one which tends to hold the plaintiff up to hatred, contempt or ridicule, or to cause him to be shunned or avoided. This definition is certainly too narrow * * *. Defamation is rather that which tends to injure 'reputation' in the popular sense; to diminish the esteem, respect, goodwill or confidence in which the plaintiff is held, or to excite adverse, derogatory or unpleasant feelings or opinions against him." (Prosser & Keeton, Torts (5th ed. 1984) § 111, pp. 771–773, fns. omitted.) A defamation claim thus seeks to vindicate decidedly personal interests. As such, defamation is a personal injury within the meaning of section 3291.

* * *

Storer contends O'Hara's verdict did not represent personal injury damages but rather property damages and therefore the trial court was correct in refusing to award prejudgment interest under section 3291. Storer argues that O'Hara, by virtue of her failure to adequately request a retraction under section 48a, was restricted to special damages and precluded from recovering general damages under that statute. Given the definitions of special damages and general damages contained in section 48a, Storer claims O'Hara's award constituted compensation for property injuries. We are not persuaded. Section 48a represents a legislative determination that the danger of excessive recoveries in defamation actions, as well as the public interest in free dissemination of news, justifies restricting recovery to special damages when a retraction has not been demanded and refused. (*Werner, supra,* 35 Cal.2d 121, 216 P.2d 825.) Section 48a has not changed the nature of the tort of defamation from a personal injury into a property injury, but rather has placed a limit on the type of damages that can be recovered if the plaintiff does not properly seek a retraction.

DISPOSITION

The judgment is reversed insofar as it denied prejudgment interest. The matter is remanded to the superior court with [directions] that the judgment be amended to include prejudgment interest pursuant to section 3291. In all other respects, the judgment is affirmed.

KREMER, P.J., concur.

AMOS, ASSOCIATE JUSTICE, dissenting.

While I concur with part I of the majority opinion, I disagree with the reasoning and conclusions in part II. The primary issue in part II is whether special damages, as defined in Civil Code section 48a, subdivision (4)(b), includes loss of income from O'Hara's inability to work as a result of illness, depression or emotional distress caused by defamation. The majority concludes it does. I disagree and would reverse for the reasons set forth below.

Prior to the taking of evidence, the trial court ruled that it would allow testimony of O'Hara's emotional state and depression "* * * for the purpose of showing the plaintiff's inability to work." The court further clarified its position during trial when it stated, "* * * if they found a potential employer that says, 'Look, I wanted to hire this lady but I couldn't because of her disability,' that then proves special damages."

Numerous witnesses testified regarding O'Hara's inability to work. Dr. Koshkarian testified O'Hara had acute symptoms of anxiety and depression coupled with a lack of self-confidence. * * *

* * *

The law of defamation was developed to protect one's reputation. To recover damages plaintiff should first be required to establish injury to reputation through either presumption or proof. (Prosser & Keeton, Torts, (5th ed. 1984) § 116A, p. 844.)

The California retraction statutes eliminate general and exemplary damages when a plaintiff fails to demand a retraction. * * * While these statutes severely limit the damages available to a plaintiff, they have been upheld as constitutional and are designed to prevent excessive damages and further the public interest in the free dissemination of news. * * * In his dissent in *Werner,* Justice Carter noted, "It is a rare situation where a plaintiff can trace and prove the special damage he has suffered from libelous matter printed in a newspaper or spoken over the radio about him. This does not mean that he may not have suffered sharply—but it does mean that he may never hear of business opportunities which would have been his *had the 'libelous stain' not appeared on his name plate.*" (*Id.* at p. 142, 216 P.2d 825; emphasis added.) Special damages are damages which a plaintiff suffers to his property, business, trade, profession or occupation caused by this "libelous stain" or injury to his reputation, not damages resulting from the plaintiff's emotional state.

Texts on defamation indicate special damages must flow directly from the injury to reputation and not from the effects of defamation such as illness. (Sack, Libel, Slander, and Related Problems (1980) § VII.2.2., pp. 345–346.) Mental distress, even if it results in physical illness, is not sufficient to justify an award of special damages. (Smolla, Law of Defamation (4th ed. 1991) § 9.07, pp. 9–15.)

The Restatement Second of Torts section 575, comments *b* and *c*, discusses special damages and states in part:

> "*b. Special harm.* Special harm, as the words are used in this Chapter, is the loss of something having economic or pecuniary value * * *.
>
> * * *
>
> "Special harm must result from the conduct of a person other than the defamer or the one defamed and must be legally caused by the defamation. It is, however, immaterial whether the harmful action is taken because the person who takes it believes the defamation, or because he is unwilling to deal or to associate with *one whose reputation has been impaired by it. Loss of reputation* alone is not enough to make the defamer liable under the rule stated in this Section unless it *is reflected in some kind of economic or pecuniary loss.* So too, lowered social standing and its purely social consequences are not sufficient. Thus the fact that a slander has caused the person defamed to lose caste in the eyes of his friends and so has deprived him of many pleasant social contacts is not special harm. If, however, *the loss of reputation results in material loss* capable of being measured in money, the fact that the lowered social standing resulting from the slander itself causes the acts that produce the loss does not prevent the tangible loss from being special harm.
>
> "*c. Emotional distress.* Under the traditional rule, the emotional distress caused to the plaintiff by his knowledge that he has been defamed is not special harm; and this is true although the distress results in a serious illness * * *." (Emphasis added.)

Allowing special damages for emotional distress is contrary to the position taken by the Restatement. The Restatement follows the traditional rule that the special damage must flow from the loss of reputation, not emotional harm. Under the Restatement, the loss of income must result from a third party's knowledge of the defamation.

The traditional rule is followed in other states. * * *

* * *

To be consistent with the traditional rules, section 48a, subdivision 4(b) must be interpreted to allow as special damages for loss of income only those losses caused by a third party's conduct resulting from the third party's knowledge of the defamation. There is no evidence to suggest that when the Legislature adopted section 48a or modified it by changing from "actual" to "special" damages in 1945 it intended to expand the traditional rule. Section 48a is a limitation, not an expansion, of the rules providing damages to a defamed party. While one can sympathize with O'Hara, under the present state of the law, without a demand for retraction, she is not entitled to damages resulting from her inability to work caused by her emotional problems irrespective of whether these emotional problems or their physical manifestations observed by a third party caused her to lose a job.

Nor can I conclude that the testimony of Cravens, Maloney and Wood was merely harmless, even if McDaniel's testimony, or O'Hara's version of McDaniel's testimony, is considered evidence of special damages. The testimony of her emotional state and her refusal to accept job offers clearly impacted the jury. O'Hara's counsel utilized the Wood testimony in closing argument to establish her potential earning capacity to be $50,000 per year. The jury awarded $300,000 which appears to be her earning capacity times the six-year period for which she sought loss of income.

I agree that if O'Hara could establish the decline in her business resulted from the publication of the slanderous statement this would constitute special damages. The court did not limit her to that theory of proof. It allowed her to prove special damages resulting from her inability to work caused by emotional distress. This was error. Accordingly, I would reverse.

Questions

1. If you had been a judge on the California Court of Appeal, would you have joined the majority or dissenting opinion? Why?

2. If Naomi O'Hara had not lost any income, what would have happened to her defamation claim? What happened to the claims in Stump v. Gates, supra, p. 675 and *Tacket?* What type of damages would the plaintiffs in *Stump* and *Tacket* have had to allege? Are medical bills special damages?

3. Are *Tacket* and *O'Hara* reconcilable?

2. Restitution

NOSSEN v. HOY

United States District Court, Eastern District of Virginia, 1990.
750 F.Supp. 740.

MEMORANDUM

MERHIGE, DISTRICT JUDGE.

The parties are before the Court on Defendant's Motion to Transfer and Defendant's Motion to Dismiss. The parties have fully briefed these issues and they are ripe for decision. This Court has diversity jurisdiction over this matter pursuant to 28 U.S.C. § 1332(a)(1).

BACKGROUND

This is an action for the unlawful appropriation of Plaintiff Richard Nossen's name, reputation and work, for conversion of Nossen's property, and for quasi-contract. Nossen, a Virginia citizen, is former Assistant Director of the Internal Revenue Service's Criminal Investigation Division. He is an expert in the field of detection and investigation of financial crimes. He has authored two works in his field: *The Seventh Basic Investigative Technique* and *Determination of Undisclosed Financial Interest.* These books, according to Defendant's pleadings, were published for and by the United States Government, which holds the rights to them.

Defendant Michael Hoy, a citizen of the State of Washington and sole proprietor of Loompanics Unlimited, is a self-described publisher of "controversial and unusual books." He engages in mail order sales of the books he publishes; some of these sales occur in Virginia. Among the books advertised for sale in the 1990 Loompanics catalogue is a publication entitled *Advanced Investigative Techniques for Private Financial Records,* by Richard A. Nossen. This book is a combined reprinting of Nossen's two works. In the book, authorship is specifically attributed to Nossen, whose brief biography appears on the publication's second page. A full page advertisement for the book appears on page three of the catalogue and Hoy has advertised the book in numerous other catalogues. Hoy's advertisement of the book, and its consequent sale for profit, all occurred without Nossen's knowledge, consent or permission.

Nossen alleges that Hoy promotes his publications to those who may wish to engage in criminal activity. He further alleges that Hoy intentionally distorted the characterization of Nossen's works attempting to make sales to his clientele. Nossen alleges that Hoy's activity has led the public to believe that Nossen approves of Hoy's publications and alleges that, as a result of Hoy's appropriation of his name and reputation, Nossen has suffered embarrassment, mental distress and damage to his professional reputation. Nossen alleges that Hoy's actions have and will continue absent intervention from this Court.

Based on these allegations, Nossen has filed suit against Hoy for the unauthorized use of his name pursuant to Virginia Code § 8.01–40, for the unlawful conversion of Nossen's property (his name, reputation and work), and for quasi-contract for the alleged unjust enrichment achieved by Hoy with the use of Nossen's property.

* * *

B. The Quasi–Contract Contract

Defendant Hoy moves to dismiss Nossen's action for quasi-contract for failure to state a claim. Hoy argues that courts may imply a contract-in-fact only where one person has enriched himself at the expense of another and that, in this case, Nossen has not alleged the loss of a benefit. In addition, Hoy asserts that an action for quasi-contract can succeed only based on joint dealings of the parties and that where, as here, the parties have not dealt with each other, no such action can stand. Hoy confuses the concepts of implied-in-fact contract and quasi-contract.

The implied-in-fact contract is a true contract, containing all of the elements that construct an enforceable agreement. It differs from an actual contract in that the parties have not reduced it to a writing or to an oral agreement; rather, the court infers the implied-in-fact agreement from the course of conduct of the parties. In contrast, a quasi-contract is not a contract at all but rather an equitable remedy thrust upon the recipient of a benefit under conditions where that receipt amounts to unjust enrichment. See *Marine Dev. Corp. v. Rodak,* 225 Va. 137, 300 S.E.2d 763, 766 (1983); C. Kaufman, *Corbin on Contracts,* § 19, at 50 (Supp.1989) (discussing distinction between implied-in-fact agreement and quasi-contract). At issue here is only the latter concept.

The quasi-contract is a plaintiff's remedy at law when the facts establish that a defendant has been unjustly enriched at the expense of the plaintiff, but where the facts fail to establish that the parties established any form of agreement. To establish a quasi-contract a plaintiff generally must show three elements: (1) A benefit conferred on the defendant by the plaintiff; (2) Knowledge on the part of the defendant of the conferring of the benefit; and (3) Acceptance or retention of the benefit by the defendant in circumstances that render it inequitable for the defendant to retain the benefit without paying for its value. See *Corbin on Contracts,* § 19, at 50 (citing *Alaska Sales and Serv., Inc. v. Millet,* 735 P.2d 743 (Alaska 1987)). Both Virginia and Washington recognize the quasi-contract action to recover unjust enrichment. For Virginia law, see *Kern v. Freed Co.,* 224 Va. 678, 299 S.E.2d 363, 365 (1983) (quasi-contract insures "that a man shall not be allowed to enrich himself unjustly at the expense of another"). For Washington law, see *Lynch v. Deaconess Medical Center,* 113 Wash.2d 162, 776 P.2d 681 (1989); *Family Medical Bldg., Inc. v. State Dep't of Social & Health Servs.,* 104 Wash.2d 105, 702 P.2d 459 (1985).

The facts alleged by Nossen are sufficient to state a claim for quasi-contract. Nossen alleges that Hoy has received a benefit from the use of Nossen's property: his name and reputation. Hoy therefore, allegedly has received a benefit from Nossen without having paid fair consideration and therefore—allegedly—has been unjustly enriched. In addition, Nossen has alleged that Hoy had knowledge of the benefit and has accepted and retained the benefit under circumstances that would make it unfair for him to not pay fair value for its use. To the extent Nossen alleges that Hoy used his name and reputation absent permission and knowingly received a benefit from that use, Nossen states a claim for quasi-contract under both Virginia and Washington law.

Furthermore, the modern trend is to recognize actions for quasi-contract based on a "reasonable expectation theory." Under this doctrine, one of three things must be true to recover in quasi-contract: (1) The plaintiff had a reasonable expectation of payment; (2) The defendant should reasonably have expected to pay; or (3) Society's reasonable expectations of security of person and property would be defeated by nonpayment. See *Provident Life & Acc. Ins. v. Waller,* 906 F.2d 985, 993 (4th Cir.1990); *Corbin on Contracts,* § 19A, at 59. Because Nossen has alleged that Hoy should have expected to pay for the use of Nossen's name and reputation, Nossen also has stated a claim for quasi-contract.

Conclusion

For the foregoing reasons, this Court will deny Defendant's Motion to Transfer and will deny Defendant's Motion to Dismiss the Conversion

Count and the Quasi-Contract Count, insofar as they pertain to Defendant's alleged use of Plaintiff's name and reputation. The Court will grant Defendant's Motion to Dismiss to the extent that it pertains to the alleged use of Plaintiff's work.

An appropriate Order will issue.

Note

The approach of the *Nossen* Court should not surprise those who are generally familiar with basic restitution notions. It would appear to be perfectly obvious that one may enrich himself or herself by virtue of conduct which is defamatory, or violates some other dignitary interest such as the right of privacy whether the latter be thought of in terms of a "right to be let alone" or the market value of one's name or likeness (usually referred to as one's "right of publicity"). This assumes, of course, that the conduct in question is wrongful in the sense of not being sheltered by the constitutionally protected freedoms in this area. The United States Supreme Court has held that the Constitution in its First and Fourteenth Amendments does not prevent a state from protecting plaintiff's right of publicity and "the rationale for [protecting the right of publicity] is the straightforward one of preventing unjust enrichment * * *." * Zacchini v. Scripps-Howard Broadcasting Co., 433 U.S. 562, 576, 97 S.Ct. 2849, 53 L.Ed.2d 965 (1977).

In what is perhaps the most perceptive and scholarly comment upon the potential for restitution relief in this area Professor Kenneth York, in an article written thirty-five years ago, made this observation with respect to the exercise in semantics which occupied much of the time of the courts which considered the restitution possibility in the dignitary area: "[I]t is necessary only to go back to the factual matter of enrichment * * * [and if] it exists, restitution necessarily follows irrespective of what different courts would call the wrong." York, "Extension of Restitutional Remedies," 4 U.C.L.A. Law Review 499 (1957) at 539.

It is something of a surprise, therefore, to discover how few cases have sought restitution relief for this kind of wrong, and how the result in those few cases which are reported almost uniformly discouraged resort to restitution remedies in the dignitary area. Hart v. E.P. Dutton & Co., 197 Misc. 274, 93 N.Y.S.2d 871 (1949) aff'd, 277 App.Div. 935, 98 N.Y.S.2d 773, reconsideration denied, 277 App.Div. 962, 99 N.Y.S.2d 1014 (1950) is illustrative.

In *Hart* the plaintiff, Merwin Hart, in 1949, sued the publisher of a 1943 book entitled "Under Cover" on the ground that it had libelously referred to him as a traitor to the United States during World War II. Rather than seeking damages for defamation, which had a one year statute of limitations, Hart sought to recover the defendant's profits in a quasi-contract action with a six year statute of limitations. The Court said:

> "As was stated in *Miller v. Schloss,* supra, 'A quasi or constructive contract rests upon the equitable principle that a person shall not be allowed to enrich himself unjustly at the expense of another' and is created when 'because [of] the acts of the parties' a person is possessed of money or property which in equity or good conscience he should not retain. The

* The Court quotes Kalven, "Privacy in Tort Law—Were Warren and Brandeis Wrong," 31 Law & Contemp. Prob. 326, 331 (1966).

application of this rule requires inquiry, not only into the acts of the defendant, but also the acts of the plaintiff. One who publishes a libel, especially if done maliciously, as charged in this complaint, is guilty of conduct which makes him liable for damages. An action for damages affords the plaintiff full compensation for any injuries which he has suffered. In addition to compensatory damages he may recover punitive damages if proper foundation is established by the proof. The law requires that a plaintiff must bring his action to recover such damages within one year. It would seem that it is not equitable and just to permit a person, who has been the subject of a libellous article published in a book, to acquiesce in or permit the sale and distribution of such book to continue for a period of nearly six years without taking any steps whatsoever to protest or stop the sale and distribution of the book and then to maintain an action for the profits derived from the sale and distribution of the book. The publication of a book entails great expense and effort on the part of the publisher and the profits derived therefrom are due in large measure to elements outside of the printed matter contained therein. To permit such an action as the plaintiff has brought, under the circumstances alleged in the complaint, would have the effect of making the publisher for a period of years, the servant of the plaintiff, who, despite his failure to avail himself of a complete legal remedy, may now assert a right to the fruits of the defendant's labor and investment even beyond that which may flow from the alleged libel. Such a situation would be inequitable and would result in the unjust enrichment of the plaintiff. Under such circumstances no contract should be 'implied in law' requiring the defendant to account to the plaintiff for profits derived from the publication of the book." *

See also Cason v. Baskin, 159 Fla. 31, 30 So.2d 635 (1947).

A rare exception is the approach taken by the Court of Appeals in Georgia in Cabaniss v. Hipsley, 114 Ga.App. 367, 151 S.E.2d 496 (1966). There the court, reversing in part and granting a new trial in part, stated that the plaintiff had a potentially protectible right in her name and likeness "where there was an appropriation for the defendant's benefit use or advantage upon which to predicate liability. * * * Recovery under this theory ["quasi-contract"] is measured by the unjust enrichment of the defendant and not by the injury to plaintiff's feelings or reputation (and we assume, but do not decide, to plaintiff's own commercial interests)." (151 S.E.2d, at 506). The court granted a new trial because the record did not contain evidence of the benefit obtained by the defendant as a result of this invasion of the plaintiff's rights. This aspect of restitution relief in this area is considered in greater detail below.

GREENSPAN v. OSHEROFF

Supreme Court of Virginia, 1986.
232 Va. 388, 351 S.E.2d 28.

* * *

[While Dr. Osheroff was hospitalized for depression at the instance of his young associate, Dr. Greenspan, he attempted to take over Dr. Osher-

* This fact situation is typical of those in which an appreciation of the option of electing the quasi-contract claim (where other remedies otherwise available are barred for one reason or another) may make recovery possible. See text at p. 307, *supra*.

off's dialysis practice. When Dr. Osheroff returned to the practice, Dr. Greenspan attempted to interfere with Dr. Osheroff's ability to practice medicine by calling a Department Chief of a hospital which then suspended Dr. Osheroff's hospital privileges until the hospital conducted a hearing, after which the privileges were reinstated. Dr. Greenspan also had patients, while undergoing dialysis treatment, sign forms saying that they would not accept treatment from Dr. Osheroff.]

Dr. Osheroff and Osheroff, Inc. brought this suit in equity against Dr. Greenspan, Dr. Tolkan, Nurse Hess, and Prince William Dialysis Facility, Inc. Counts I and II alleged that the defendants had willfully and maliciously undertaken to injure the complainants in their reputation, trade, business or profession in violation of Code §§ 18.2–499 and 18.2–500. Count III alleged defamation. Count IV alleged malicious interference with the contractual relations existing between the complainants and NMC [National Medical Care, Inc., a corporation operating dialysis centers]. Count V sought the imposition of a constructive trust upon the profits of Prince William Dialysis Facility, Inc. [operated by Dr. Greenspan]. Count VI alleged common-law interference with business, reputation and both existing and prospective physician-patient relationships. The bill prayed for treble damages, injunctive relief, attorneys fees, and the constructive trust mentioned above.

* * *

Under Counts I and II, the chancellor found that neither Dr. Tolkan nor Nurse Hess had entered into a malicious conspiracy to injure Dr. Osheroff, and that they were therefore not liable for treble damages under Code §§ 18.2–499 and 18.2–500. Dr. Greenspan, on the other hand, was found to have been motivated by a malicious desire to harm Dr. Osheroff and his professional corporation in their business or profession. Because he did not conspire or combine with any other person to accomplish this end, the court found no violation of Code § 18.2–499(a). The court did, however, find Dr. Greenspan guilty of attempting to procure others to participate in a conspiracy prohibited by Code § 18.2–499(a), and therefore concluded that Dr. Greenspan was in violation of Code § 18.2–499(b), which prohibits such attempts. Assessing damages pursuant to Code § 18.2–500, the court awarded compensatory damages of $184,804, trebled to $554,412, plus $90,000 in attorneys fees and costs against Dr. Greenspan. No error has been assigned to the quantum of attorneys fees, but Dr. Greenspan challenges the entire award under Counts I and II on appeal.

Under Count III, the court found no malice on Dr. Tolkan's part, but found that Nurse Hess had uttered an unprivileged and defamatory statement to a newspaper and assessed $5,000 damages against her. That award is not before us on appeal. The court awarded $10,000 in compensatory damages and $20,000 in punitive damages against Dr. Greenspan in favor of Dr. Osheroff for defamation, but provided that those damages would not be in addition to the damages assessed under Counts I, II, and VI.

Under Count IV, the court found for the defendants. Under Count V, the court imposed a constructive trust in favor of both complainants on one-half of the profits to be derived from the Prince William Dialysis Facility until the judgment under Counts I and II is paid in full. Under Count VI, the court awarded the complainants compensatory damages of $184,804 and punitive damages of $369,608 against Dr. Greenspan, but provided that these would not be in addition to the damages awarded under Counts I, II, and III.

* * *

We find no error in the chancellor's assessment of damages under Code § 18.2–500. Dr. Osheroff introduced the testimony of an expert economist who calculated the income loss sustained as a result of the opening of the Prince William Dialysis Center and the patients taken by Drs. Greenspan and Tolkan. For the years 1980 through 1985, this amounted to $824,-662.00, discounted to a present value of $535,270. The chancellor disagreed with the economist's projection of these losses over a six-year period, and concluded, based upon the historic growth of the practice, that Dr. Osheroff could fairly be expected to rebuild his practice in three years. A three-year projection, discounted to present value, produced the court's assessment of actual damages of $184,804. We find nothing unreasonable in this approach. As the chancellor noted, the award is roughly equivalent to the loss of professional fees for the thirty patients actually lost during the first year, for twenty such patients the second year, for ten the third year, and none thereafter. That rate of growth is reasonably related to the history of the practice as shown by the evidence.

Because the awards of damages made under Counts III and VI are included within, and are not in addition to, the award of treble damages made under Counts I and II, our affirmance of the latter renders moot any further consideration of the arguments on appeal relating to defamation and tortious interference with contractual relationships. It is necessary to consider the propriety of the constructive trust imposed on one-half the profits of the Prince William Dialysis Center under Count V, however, because the appeal bond may be insufficient to satisfy the judgment in full and the constructive trust may come into play in order to satisfy the judgment for damages.

The chancellor found that Dr. Osheroff could have obtained the necessary waivers in order to establish a dialysis facility in Prince William County with the consent of NMC. It clearly would have been in his interest to do so. There was no direct evidence on this point, but the chancellor's finding is based upon an inference warranted by the circumstantial evidence concerning Dr. Osheroff's relationship with NMC and the success of his practice. The chancellor further found that Dr. Greenspan had a fiduciary obligation to Dr. Osheroff and his professional corporation arising out of the employer-employee relationship between them as well as Dr. Greenspan's explicit assumption of a duty to take care of Dr. Osheroff's practice during his illness. The chancellor concluded that, in establishing the Prince William Dialysis Center in competition with Dr. Osheroff's practice, after applying for a certificate of need on Dr. Osheroff's stationery and purportedly for Dr. Osheroff's benefit, Dr. Greenspan had breached his fiduciary duty to exercise the utmost faith and loyalty to his employer. Because Dr. Greenspan stood to profit from that breach, the chancellor found, by clear and convincing evidence, that the imposition of a constructive trust was warranted upon the profits of the instrumentality which was the product of Dr. Greenspan's breach of fiduciary duty. The chancellor took the view that if Dr. Greenspan had in fact established the Prince William facility in compliance with his fiduciary duty, he and Dr. Osheroff would have operated it as equal partners. The constructive trust was, therefore, imposed only on that half of the profits which would rightfully have accrued to Dr. Osheroff.

A constructive trust is created by operation of law and is independent of the intention of the parties. It may arise from breach of a fiduciary duty as well as from actual fraud or unconscionable conduct amounting to constructive fraud. *Leonard v. Counts,* 221 Va. 582, 588–90, 272 S.E.2d 190, 195–196 (1980); *Porter v. Shaffer,* 147 Va. 921, 928–29, 133 S.E. 614, 616 (1926). The evidence necessary to support the imposition of a constructive trust must be clear, definite, and convincing. *Sutton v. Sutton,* 194 Va. 179, 185, 72 S.E.2d 275, 278 (1952).

In *Horne v. Holley,* 167 Va. 234, 240, 188 S.E. 169, 172 (1936), we said:

> It is well settled that where one person sustains a fiduciary relation to another he can not acquire an interest in the subject matter of the relationship adverse to such other party. If he does so equity will regard him as a constructive trustee and compel him to convey to his associate a proper interest in the property or to account to him for the profits derived therefrom. (Citations omitted).

Applying the foregoing principles to the facts before us, we find the chancellor's imposition of a constructive trust in favor of the complainants upon one half the profits of the Prince William Dialysis Center, until the judgment is paid in full, to be proper.

Because we find no error in the decree appealed from, it will be

Affirmed.

Notes

1. The *Greenspan* opinion is interesting in particular because it imposed a constructive trust on one-half the defendant's profits from a particular dialysis facility until payment of the judgment for damages based upon a remedy theory seeking recovery for defendant-physician's injury to, *inter alia,* plaintiff-physician's professional name and reputation. The damages in question were assessed based upon violation of a Virginia statute which provided relief for such a violation in the form of both compensatory damages and a recovery of the "profits" enjoyed by the wrongdoer as a consequence of the violation. The Supreme Court did not find it necessary to rule on the finding of the Trial Court that the plaintiff had also proven a right to damages at law based upon defamation because that court had ruled that the damages to which the plaintiff was entitled for that violation were included in the damages awarded on the other statutory counts and would not be cumulative. There is, however, no reason to suppose that the Court would not have ruled that the profits to

which the constructive trust applied were equally available to apply to the damages award for defamation.

This case is, therefore, a somewhat novel use of the conventional constructive trust form of restitution relief to aid in securing the payment of damages for violation of important dignitary interests.

The case also illustrates a successful effort to show what part of the defendant's total profits from his professional activities were the results of a wrongful disparagement of the plaintiff. The Supreme Court approved the finding by the trial court of an amount of wrongfully acquired profits (from the total of the profits earned by the defendant during the period in question) based upon the number of patients acquired by defendant by virtue of the wrongful conduct and the charge for services to them.

It is not clear how helpful this approach will be for those plaintiffs who face a seemingly more difficult task of proving what portion of the defendant's total financial return from the transaction in question may be said to consist of a "benefit" that was at the expense of or, to put it another way, was taken from, the plaintiff. It was the burden of this task which caused Professor Palmer to say the following concerning the possibility of restitution relief for violations of dignitary interests such as the right of privacy: "[Recovery will be difficult when] one considers the nature of the interest interfered with and the manner of interference, that there was no interest which went to the defendant on which a market value could be placed * * * [a]nd as to recovery of profits, there would be a virtually insurmountable difficulty in ascertaining the portion of the profits attributable to the parts of the [for example] book which constituted an invasion of privacy." (I G. Palmer, Law of Restitution (1978) at 129). (*See* Cason v. Baskin, 155 Fla. 198, 20 So.2d 243 (1944) (where the Court expresses similar concern in a case involving publication of a book containing an allegedly disparaging biographical sketch of plaintiff). Would that be a valid concern in Hart v. E.P. Dutton & Co., discussed in the note after the *Nossen* case?

The problem is similar to that faced by the plaintiff who has co-habited with the defendant for a period of time without marriage during which the defendant accumulated an estate which arguably is the result, at least in part, of the effort and support of the plaintiff and the plaintiff seeks to recover a part of that gain or "benefit.". Some of those cases in which the plaintiff was successful were discussed at an earlier point. (*See* text at pp. 316–17, *supra*).

Another approach is suggested by the practice which is followed in those cases where the wrongdoer, who has enriched himself by virtue of the wrongful conduct in question, is made the defendant in an action to obtain an accounting. There the burden of proof, and thus the risk of non-persuasion, is placed upon the wrongdoer, the defendant, who admittedly has been enriched in some amount. This approach, which was suggested by Professor York in the article quoted above, also has been used in the co-habitation cases. (*See* text at pp. 316–17, *supra*).

Professor Palmer in his treatise, *Law of Restitution*, comments on a recent opinion denying a request for an accounting for profit realized from the wrongful use of the commercial rights relating to the name, reputation and likeness of the comedians, Laurel and Hardy, in these terms:

"In Price v. Hal Roach Studios, 400 F.Supp. 836 (S.D.N.Y.1975), applying New York law, the court held that plaintiffs were not entitled to an accounting of profits realized from interference with the right of publicity. An accounting of profits is available in New York, the court held, only where there is a fiduciary relationship between the parties. This is comparable to allowing the common law forms of action to determine a party's substantive rights. The substantive question is whether the defendant is unjustly enriched when he profits through the wrongful use of the plaintiff's name and likeness. If he is, the profit should be recoverable. When the only feasible means of administering such a recovery is through a suit in equity for an accounting, that is the form of relief a court should give. * * * [For example,] a California statute providing a cause of action that survives the death of the person in question also authorizes recovery of 'any profits from the unauthorized use that are attributable to the use.' Cal.Civ.Code § 990." (1990 Supp., Note 30a at p. 46).

Where the defendant's conduct has been sufficiently egregious, as in cases involving fiduciary fraud, equity routinely takes away from the defendant all the traceable benefits from the conduct in question no matter what the relation to the plaintiff. (See text at pp. 331–34, *supra.*) Such an approach would seem to be readily justified in those cases in this area where the plaintiff was required to, or could, prove actual malice. (See text at pp. 676–92, *supra.*)

2. Some states have adopted legislation designed to allow recovery from a criminal of the benefit received from aiding in the publication of an account of the criminal conduct in question, and for allocation of the sum recovered to the victims or their families. Such legislation would appear to offer some consolation to the families for the publicity and remorse that results from having had a family member who was a victim of the defendant and is now to be the subject of the profit-making publication or presentation in question. What statute can be enacted after the Supreme Court's holding in the next case?

SIMON & SCHUSTER, INC. v. MEMBERS OF THE NEW YORK STATE CRIME VICTIMS BOARD

Supreme Court of the United States, 1991.
___ U.S. ___, 112 S.Ct. 501, 116 L.Ed.2d 476.

JUSTICE O'CONNOR delivered the opinion of the Court.

New York's "Son of Sam" law requires that an accused or convicted criminal's income from works describing his crime be deposited in an escrow account. These funds are then made available to the victims of the crime and the criminal's other creditors. We consider whether this statute is consistent with the First Amendment.

* * *

This case began in 1986, when the Board first became aware of the contract between petitioner Simon & Schuster and admitted organized crime figure Henry Hill.

B

Looking back from the safety of the Federal Witness Protection Program, Henry Hill recalled: "At the age of twelve my ambition was to be a gangster. To be a wiseguy. To me being a wiseguy was better than being president of the United States." N. Pileggi, Wiseguy: Life in a Mafia Family 19 (1985) (hereinafter Wiseguy). Whatever one might think of HIll, at the very least it can be said that he realized his dreams. After a career spanning 25 years, Hill admitted engineering some of the most daring crimes of his day, including the 1978–1979 Boston College basketball point-shaving scandal, and the theft of $6 million from Lufthansa Airlines in 1978, the largest successful cash robbery in American history. Wiseguy 9. Most of Hill's crimes were more banausic: He committed extortion, he imported and distributed narcotics, and he organized numerous robberies.

Hill was arrested in 1980. In exchange for immunity from prosecution, he testified against many of his former colleagues. Since his arrest, he has lived under an assumed name in an unknown part of the country.

In August 1981, Hill entered into a contract with author Nicholas Pileggi for the production of a book about Hill's life. The following month, Hill and Pileggi signed a publishing agreement with Simon & Schuster. Under the agreement, Simon & Schuster agreed to make payments to both Hill and Pileggi.

* * *

The result of Hill and Pileggi's collaboration was Wiseguy, which was published in January 1986. The book depicts, in colorful detail, the day-to-day existence of organized crime, primarily in Hill's first-person narrative. Throughout Wiseguy, Hill frankly admits to having participated in an astonishing variety of crimes.

* * *

From Henry Hill's perspective, however, the publicity generated by the book's success proved less desirable. The Crime Victims Board learned of Wiseguy in January 1986, soon after it was published.

C

On January 31, the Board notified Simon & Schuster: "It has come to our attention that you may have contracted with a person accused or convicted of a crime for the payment of monies to such person."

* * *

The Board reviewed the book and the contract, and on May 21, 1987, issued a Proposed Determination and Order. The Board determined that Wiseguy was covered by § 632–a of the Executive Law, that Simon & Schuster had violated the law by failing to turn over its contract with Hill to the Board and by making payments to Hill, and that all money owed to Hill under the contract had to be turned over to the Board to be held in escrow for the victims of Hill's crimes. The Board ordered Hill to turn over the payments he had already received, and ordered Simon & Schuster to turn over all money payable to Hill at that time or in the future.

Simon & Schuster brought suit in August 1987, under 42 U.S.C. § 1983, seeking a declaration that the Son of Sam law violates the First Amendment and an injunction barring the statute's enforcement. After the parties filed cross-motions for summary judgment, the District Court found the statute consistent with the First Amendment. 724 F.Supp. 170 (SDNY 1989). A divided Court of Appeals affirmed. *Simon & Schuster, Inc. v. Fischetti,* 916 F.2d 777 (CA2 1990).

Because the Federal Government and most of the States have enacted statutes with similar objectives, see 18 U.S.C. § 3681; Note, *Simon & Schuster, Inc. v. Fischetti:* Can New York's Son of Sam Law Survive First Amendment Challenge?, 66 Notre Dame L.Rev. 1075, 1075, n. 6 (1991) (listing state statutes), the issue is significant and likely to recur. We accordingly granted certiorari, 498 U.S. ___, 111 S.Ct. 950, 112 L.Ed.2d 1039 (1991), and we now reverse.

* * *

A statute is presumptively inconsistent with the First Amendment if it imposes a financial burden on speakers because of the content of their speech.

* * *

The Son of Sam law is such a content-based statute. It singles out income derived from expressive activity for a burden the State places on no other income, and it is directed only at works with a specified content. Whether the First Amendment "speaker" is considered to be Henry Hill, whose income the statute places in escrow because of the story he has told, or Simon & Schuster, which can publish books about crime with the assistance of only those criminals willing to forgo remuneration for at least five years, the statute plainly imposes a financial disincentive only on speech of a particular content.

* * *

The Son of Sam law establishes a financial disincentive to create or publish works with a particular content. In order to justify such differential treatment, "the State must show that its regulation is necessary to serve a compelling state interest and is narrowly drawn to achieve that end." *Arkansas Writers' Project,* 481 U.S., at 231, 107 S.Ct., at 1728.

* * *

The Board disclaims, as it must, any state interest in suppressing descriptions of crime out of solicitude for the sensibilities of readers. See Brief for Respondents 38, n. 38. As we have often had occasion to repeat, " '[T]he fact that society may find speech offensive is not a sufficient reason for suppressing it. * * *' "

* * *

The Board thus does not assert any interest in limiting whatever anguish Henry Hill's victims may suffer from reliving their victimization.

There can be little doubt, on the other hand, that the State has a compelling interest in ensuring that victims of crime are compensated by those who harm them.

* * *

The State likewise has an undisputed compelling interest in ensuring that criminals do not profit from their crimes. Like most if not all States, New York has long recognized the "fundamental equitable principle," *Children of Bedford v. Petromelis,* 77 N.Y.2d, at 727, 570 N.Y.S.2d, at 460, 573 N.E.2d, at 548, that "[n]o one shall be permitted to profit by his own fraud, or to take advantage of his own wrong, or to found any claim upon his own iniquity, or to acquire property by his own crime." *Riggs v. Palmer,* 115 N.Y. 506, 511–512, 22 N.E. 188, 190 (1889). The force of this interest is evidenced by the State's statutory provisions for the forfeiture of the proceeds and instrumentalities of crime. See N.Y.Civ.Prac.Law §§ 1310–1352 (McKinney Supp.1991).

The parties debate whether book royalties can properly be termed the profits of crime, but that is a question we need not address here. For the purposes of this case, we can assume without deciding that the income escrowed by the Son of Sam law represents the fruits of crime. We need only conclude that the State has a compelling interest in depriving criminals of the profits of their crimes, and in using these funds to compensate victims.

The Board attempts to define the State's interest more narrowly, as "ensuring that criminals do not profit from storytelling about their crimes before their victims have a meaningful opportunity to be compensated for their injuries." Brief for Respondents 46. Here the Board is on far shakier ground. The Board cannot explain why the State should have any greater interest in compensating victims from the proceeds of such "storytelling" than from any of the criminal's other assets * * *

* * *

As a means of ensuring that victims are compensated from the proceeds of crime, the Son of Sam law is significantly overinclusive. As counsel for the Board conceded at oral argument, the statute applies to works on *any* subject, provided that they express the author's thoughts or recollections about his crime, however tangentially or incidentally. See Tr. of Oral Arg. 30, 38; see also App. 109. In addition, the statute's broad definition of "person convicted of a crime" enables the Board to escrow the income of any author who admits in his work to having committed a crime, whether or not the author was ever actually accused or convicted. § 632–a(10)(b).

These two provisions combine to encompass a potentially very large number of works. Had the Son of Sam law been in effect at the time and place of publication, it would have escrowed payment for such works as The Autobiography of Malcolm X, which describes crimes committed by the civil rights leader before he became a public figure; Civil Disobedience, in which Thoreau acknowledges his refusal to pay taxes and recalls his experience in jail; and even the Confessions of Saint Augustine, in which the author laments "my past foulness and the carnal corruptions of my soul," one instance of which involved the theft of pears from a neighboring vineyard. See A. Haley & Malcolm X, The Autobiography of Malcolm X 108–125

(1964); H. Thoreau, Civil Disobedience 18–22 (1849, reprinted 1969); The Confessions of Saint Augustine 31, 36–37 (Franklin Library ed. 1980).

* * *

The Federal Government and many of the States have enacted statutes designed to serve purposes similar to that served by the Son of Sam law. Some of these statutes may be quite different from New York's, and we have no occasion to determine the constitutionality of these other laws. We conclude simply that in the Son of Sam law, New York has singled out speech on a particular subject for a financial burden that it places on no other speech and no other income. The State's interest in compensating victims from the fruits of crime is a compelling one, but the Son of Sam law is not narrowly tailored to advance that objective. As a result, the statute is inconsistent with the First Amendment.

The judgment of the Court of Appeals is accordingly

Reversed.

JUSTICE BLACKMUN, concurring in the judgment.

I am in general agreement with what the Court says in its opinion. I think, however, that the New York statute is underinclusive as well as overinclusive and that we should say so. Most other States have similar legislation and deserve from this Court all the guidance it can render in this very sensitive area.

JUSTICE KENNEDY, concurring in the judgment.

The New York statute we now consider imposes severe restrictions on authors and publishers, using as its sole criterion the content of what is written. The regulated content has the full protection of the First Amendment and this, I submit, is itself a full and sufficient reason for holding the statute unconstitutional. In my view it is both unnecessary and incorrect to ask whether the State can show that the statute " 'is necessary to serve a compelling state interest and is narrowly drawn to achieve that end.' "

Notes

1. Is Snepp v. United States, 444 U.S. 507, 100 S.Ct. 763, 62 L.Ed.2d 704 (1980) reconcilable with *Simon & Schuster*? In *Snepp* a former CIA employee published a book entitled "Decent Interval" about CIA activities in Vietnam without obtaining prepublication clearance from the CIA as required by his contracts with the Agency. The Supreme Court upheld a constructive trust on Snepp's proceeds from the book, discussing the First Amendment arguments in a footnote:

> "The Court of Appeals and the District Court rejected each of Snepp's defenses to the enforcement of his contract. 595 F.2d 926, 931–934 (CA4 1979); 456 F.Supp., at 180–181. In his petition for certiorari, Snepp relies primarily on the claim that his agreement is unenforceable as a prior restraint on protected speech.
>
> "When Snepp accepted employment with the CIA, he voluntarily signed the agreement that expressly obligated him to submit any proposed publication for prior review. He does not claim that he executed this agreement under duress. Indeed, he voluntarily reaffirmed his obligation

when he left the Agency. We agree with the Court of Appeals that Snepp's agreement is an 'entirely appropriate' exercise of the CIA Director's statutory mandate to 'protec[t] intelligence sources and methods from unauthorized disclosure,' 50 U.S.C. § 403(d)(3). 595 F.2d, at 932. Moreover, this Court's cases make clear that—even in the absence of an express agreement—the CIA could have acted to protect substantial government interests by imposing reasonable restrictions on employee activities that in other contexts might be protected by the First Amendment. The Government has a compelling interest in protecting both the secrecy of information important to our national security and the appearance of confidentiality so essential to the effective operation of our foreign intelligence service. See *infra,* at 766. The agreement that Snepp signed is a reasonable means for protecting this vital interest."

2. Can First Amendment rights be relinquished by contract but not by murder? Are national security interests *sui generis*?

3. Can a prohibition against profiting in any way from a crime be made as part of a criminal sentence? *See* sentencing of Katherine Ann Power, The Washington Post, Nov. 25, 1993, p. A3. If the prohibition is made as part of a plea bargain is it contractual and therefore enforceable?

4. Is the Son of Sam statute restitutionary? The N.Y. statute sets up a fund to reimburse victims for their losses and, therefore, is not purely restitutionary.

B. SPECIFIC RELIEF: INJUNCTION

KRAMER v. THOMPSON

United States Court of Appeals, Third Circuit, 1991.
947 F.2d 666.

Before BECKER, NYGAARD and ALITO, CIRCUIT JUDGES.

OPINION OF THE COURT

BECKER, CIRCUIT JUDGE.

These appeals, from various injunctive orders and a damages judgment of the district court for the Eastern District of Pennsylvania in a bizarre libel case founded upon our diversity jurisdiction, present the interesting question under Pennsylvania law of the ability of a judge to enjoin future libels and to compel the retraction of past libels. For the reasons that follow, we will reverse the district court's orders enjoining defendant/appellant Richard Thompson from publishing further libels against plaintiff/appellee Steven M. Kramer, his former lawyer, and ordering Thompson to retract past libelous statements. The judgment awarding damages will be reversed and remanded for a new trial on damages for the reasons set forth in a companion opinion filed this day.

I. FACTS AND PROCEDURAL HISTORY

The parties' relationship began in July 1982, when Thompson retained Kramer to bring a securities fraud claim against Thompson's former broker, Prudential–Bache, Inc. No question was raised by Thompson concerning Kramer's stewardship for the next three years. Indeed, during this time, Thompson wrote on several occasions praising Kramer's performance.[1] Then, in the fall of 1985, Kramer was contacted by an F.B.I. agent to whom Thompson previously had complained about his investment losses at Prudential–Bache. The agent asked Kramer whether the stocks at issue were completely worthless. Kramer responded that Thompson had purchased the stocks for roughly $120,000 and later had sold them for approximately $15,000. Thus, while informing the agent that Thompson had suffered a very substantial loss, Kramer also informed the agent that technically the stocks were not worthless. When Thompson learned of this conversation, however, he became enraged, and accused Kramer of deliberately dissuading the F.B.I. from investigating the matter. The parties' relationship deteriorated rapidly thereafter and, in October 1985, Thompson discharged Kramer as his counsel.

Seeking to ensure that he ultimately would be compensated for his services, Kramer refused to return the case files to Thompson until the latter agreed to deposit the proceeds of any future judgment or settlement with the court pending resolution of the attorney's fees issue. Thompson would not agree, and Kramer secured an order from the district court which provided that any funds recovered would be placed in escrow, and that the fee dispute would be arbitrated. Kramer then made the case files available to Thompson and his new counsel.

On February 4, 1986, Thompson wrote to the Disciplinary Board of the Pennsylvania Supreme Court (the "Disciplinary Board") alleging that Kramer had failed to represent him effectively in the Prudential–Bache action.[2] At about the same time, Thompson began writing a series of critical and accusatory letters about Kramer to various private attorneys, federal judges, F.B.I. agents, federal and state prosecutors, newspapers, and television stations in the Philadelphia area.[3] With varying degrees of repetition, these letters alleged that Kramer: (1) had "thrown" Thompson's case; (2) had deliberately destroyed certain documents related to the case; (3) had used drugs and was a member of the highly publicized "Yuppie Drug Ring" organized by Philadelphia dentist Lawrence Lavin;[4] (4) was connected to organized crime; and (5) had committed arson on his own car. Kramer demanded a retraction, but Thompson refused.

Kramer thereupon brought a libel action against Thompson in the Court of Common Pleas of Philadelphia County. Undaunted by Kramer's suit, Thompson continued his letter-writing campaign. The court eventually entered a default judgment on the issue of liability against Thompson for failure to comply with discovery.

After the default judgment was entered against him, Thompson ceased to write critically about Kramer for approximately two years. In early

1. Thompson is a self-employed exporter of pumps and other equipment and a self-styled consumer activist, who writes frequently under the letterhead of the "Thompson–American Anti–fraud League."

2. On April 8, 1986, the Disciplinary Board dismissed Thompson's complaint.

3. Thompson sent a total of at least 160 separate letters to 60 different individuals or entities.

4. Thompson's apparent basis for this accusation was Kramer's representation of several minority shareholders of WMOT Enterprises, Inc., a company which had been infiltrated and bilked of funds by one of Lavin's co-conspirators.

1989, however, Thompson became aware of a suit filed by Kramer in federal district court against Mano Arco, a garage that had performed repair work on Kramer's car. Kramer's suit alleged that Mano Arco's negligent workmanship had been responsible for the fire that engulfed his car while it was travelling on the New Jersey Turnpike. Thompson took it upon himself to contact, first by phone and then by letter, the lawyer for Mano Arco. After informing the lawyer of his view that Kramer had committed arson on his own car, Thompson resumed his accusations that Kramer had thrown Thompson's securities fraud case, and that he was involved in the Yuppie Drug Ring and the underworld. Thompson's letter to Mano Arco's attorney purported to be copied to the state Disciplinary Board, the federal judge hearing the case, The *Philadelphia Inquirer,* the United States Justice Department, and Kramer.

Kramer then filed the instant libel action in the United States District Court for the Eastern District of Pennsylvania, alleging diversity of citizenship. Thompson filed an answer, naming thirteen third-party defendants and asserting counterclaims for libel and slander, legal malpractice, obstruction of justice, malicious prosecution, and civil RICO violations. The district court later dismissed the third-party defendants and the counterclaims, and imposed sanctions on Thompson with respect to one of the third-party defendants.

Trial commenced on April 2, 1990. Having determined that Thompson's statements were *per se* libelous in that they were false and made in reckless disregard of their truth or falsity, the court directed a verdict for Kramer at the close of Kramer's case—i.e., without hearing Thompson's defense on the issue of liability. The court restricted the scope of Thompson's case to evidence relevant to the calculation of compensatory and punitive damages. * * *

The jury ultimately awarded Kramer $100,000 in compensatory and $38,000 in punitive damages, and the district court entered judgment accordingly on April 10, 1990. The court simultaneously entered a permanent injunction, prohibiting Thompson from making further statements about Kramer of the type adjudged libelous, and ordering him to write letters of retraction to all persons who had received prior libelous communications. Thompson's post-trial motions for judgment n.o.v. and for a new trial were denied. Thompson filed a timely notice of appeal.

After learning that Thompson had failed to send all the retraction letters required by the court's permanent injunction, Kramer moved to hold Thompson in contempt of court. Although declining to hold Thompson in civil contempt, the district court, *inter alia,* again ordered him to make the appropriate retractions.

Shortly thereafter, Thompson submitted a petition, which he later amended, seeking leave to appear as *amicus curiae* in the case of *Matthews v. Freedman,* Appeal No. 89–2112, then pending before this court. *Matthews* involved an appeal by Kramer of sanctions imposed on him by a district court in a matter unrelated to his litigation with Thompson. Thompson's petition contained renewed accusations that Kramer had "thrown" his case, was associated with the Yuppie Drug Ring, and generally was guilty of perjury, forgery, fraud, and extortion. In the petition, Thompson also repudiated the prior retraction letter that the district court had "forced" him to write. Thompson sent copies of his petition to the Disciplinary Board, U.S. Attorney's Office, F.B.I., I.R.S., and lawyers associated with the *Matthews* case.

Kramer filed a second motion to hold Thompson in contempt. This time, the district court declared Thompson in civil contempt of the permanent injunction, and ordered that he be confined and fined $500 per day until he purged himself of contempt by withdrawing all statements and court filings related to the *Matthews* case. Thompson then drafted, and the court edited and approved, the required letter of withdrawal. The court also ordered Thompson to advise the Clerk of this court, in regard to the instant appeal, that he had "admitted under oath in the trial of this matter that he defamed Steven Kramer and promised the jury, before verdict, that he apologized and would not in the future make such statements as were accused as defamatory by plaintiff."

On August 24, 1990, the district court entered an expanded injunction prohibiting Thompson from contacting any person with whom Kramer conducts his business. Thompson filed a second notice of appeal with this court (No. 90–1640), which was consolidated with Thompson's pending appeal. We granted expedited argument, but refused Thompson's motion to stay enforcement of the injunction pending disposition of his appeal. After hearing argument, however, we stayed enforcement of the injunction, pending that disposition.

II. Discussion

Thompson appeals from a variety of orders of the district court, raising numerous allegations of error. * * * We will limit our inquiry in this opinion to the challenges to the permanent injunction entered by the district court against Thompson after trial and to that injunction's subsequent enforcement and expansion.

As discussed above, this injunction essentially provided Kramer with two forms of equitable relief, in addition to the $138,000 in damages awarded by the jury. First, the court, threatening civil contempt, enjoined Thompson initially from issuing new statements of the type found libelous, and ultimately from contacting anyone with whom Kramer does business. Second, the injunction required Thompson to retract or withdraw various previously issued libelous statements and court filings. Thompson argues that the permanent injunction thus had the effect of "prohibiting and mandating" speech in violation of the First Amendment to the United States Constitution and Article I, section 7 of the Pennsylvania Constitution. We will consider separately Thompson's challenges to the prohibitory injunction and to the retraction order.

A. *Injunction Against Further Defamatory Statements*

It is axiomatic in this diversity case that the injunction cannot stand if it contravenes *either* the United States or Pennsylvania Constitutions. Because Thompson presses his claim principally by reference to the Pennsylvania Constitution, we will begin our analysis there. * * *

Thompson relies primarily upon *Willing v. Mazzocone,* 482 Pa. 377, 393 A.2d 1155 (1978), which he argues is on all fours with the instant dispute, and which stands for the proposition that the Pennsylvania Constitution does not tolerate an injunction against libelous speech. Although we ultimately conclude that *Willing* differs in important respects from the instant dispute, the factual and legal contours of the two cases are sufficiently similar to merit a detailed comparison.

In 1968, defendant Helen Willing retained plaintiffs Carl Mazzocone and Charles Quinn, who practiced law together, to represent her in a worker's compensation claim. The two lawyers successfully obtained a settlement for Willing, from which she collected disability benefits for several years. In addition to their fee, Mazzocone and Quinn deducted $150 from the settlement as costs of the case. They claimed, and their records verified, that the money had been paid to one Dr. Robert DeSilverio, a psychiatrist who had been retained to testify on Willing's behalf.

At some point, for an unknown reason (and contrary to all available evidence), Willing came to believe that Mazzocone and Quinn had diverted for their own benefit $25 of the $150 allegedly paid to Dr. DeSilverio. For two days in 1975, Willing marched in protest in an area adjacent to the court buildings at City Hall in Philadelphia where the Court of Common Pleas, before which Mazzocone and Quinn practiced, was located. While marching, Willing wore a "sandwich-board" sign around her neck and on which she had written:

LAW–FIRM
of
QUINN–MAZZOCONE
Stole money from me—and
Sold-me-out-to-the
INSURANCE COMPANY

To attract attention while marching, Willing pushed a shopping cart bearing an American flag, continuously rang a cow bell, and blew on a whistle.

Mazzocone and Quinn attempted unsuccessfully to discourage Willing from further public protest. The two then filed a complaint in equity in the Court of Common Pleas of Philadelphia County seeking an injunction against further demonstration. The court found that there was no factual basis for Willing's defamatory protest, but noted that "either by reason of eccentricity or an even more serious mental instability," Willing could not be convinced that she had not been defrauded. 393 A.2d at 1157. The court enjoined Willing from further demonstration or picketing and from "carrying placards which contain defamatory and libelous statements and or uttering, publishing and declaring defamatory statements against [Mazzocone and Quinn]." *Id.*

On appeal, the Superior Court of Pennsylvania affirmed the injunction, although narrowing it somewhat so as to prohibit Willing only from "uttering or publishing statements to the effect that Mazzocone and Quinn, Attorneys-at-Law stole money from her and sold her out to the insurance company." *Mazzocone v. Willing,* 246 Pa.Super. 98, 369 A.2d 829, 834 (1976). In affirming the injunction, the Superior Court openly rejected the "traditional view that equity does not have the power to enjoin the publication of defamatory matter." *Id.,* 369 A.2d at 831 (citations omitted).[12] The court noted that four reasons traditionally have been offered to justify equity's refusal to enjoin defamation:

> (1) equity will afford protection only to property rights; (2) an injunction would deprive the defendant of his right to a jury trial on the issue of the truth of the publication; (3) the plaintiff has an adequate remedy at law; and (4) an injunction would be unconstitutional as a prior restraint on freedom of expression.

Id. The court then went on to state that "the logic and soundness of these reasons have been severely criticized by numerous commentators,"[13] and that "[o]ur own analysis compels us to conclude that blind application of the majority view to the instant case would be antithetical to equity's historic function of maintaining flexibility and accomplishing total justice whenever possible." *Id.* The court then reviewed each of the four traditional justifications.

12. The origin of this common-law precept is generally traced to Lord Eldon's *dicta* in *Gee v. Pritchard,* 2 Swans. 402, 36 Eng. Rep. 670 (1818), as adopted in the United States in *Brandreth v. Lance,* 8 Paige 24 (N.Y.Ch.1839). These decisions reflected a distrust of equitable jurisdiction over libel, traceable, in part, to the Star Chamber which "once exercised the power of cutting off the ears, branding the foreheads, and slitting the noses of the libellers of important personages * * * and [which] was [also] * * * in the habit of restraining the publication of such libels by injunction." *Brandreth,* 8 Paige at 26. *See generally Kwass v. Kersey,* 139 W.Va. 497, 81 S.E.2d 237, 242 (1954) (reviewing rationale for evolution of common-law rule). As an out-growth of *Gee* and *Brandreth,* libel plaintiffs in the United States generally have been limited to legal relief in the form of money damages.

13. The first assault on the common law's refusal to enjoin a defamation was led by Dean Roscoe Pound, *see* Pound, *Equitable Relief Against Defamation and Injuries to Personality,* 29 Harv.L.Rev. 640 (1916), who apparently became so convinced of the wisdom and inevitability of abandoning the rule that he and Professor Chafee published a casebook detailing the emerging trend, *see* R. Pound and Z. Chafee, *Cases on Equitable Relief Against Defamation and Injuries to Personality* (1930). Pound's work has spawned a considerable body of literature over the years which has criticized the common-law rule, lamented the inadequacy of money damages as a remedy for defamation, and advocated a variety of alternative equitable remedies including declaratory judgment, right of reply, voluntary or mandatory retraction, injunction, and arbitration. *See generally* Long, *Equitable Jurisdiction to Protect Personal Rights,* 33 Yale L.J. 115 (1923); Chafee, *Possible New Remedies for Errors in the Press,* 60 Harv.L.Rev. 1 (1946); Donnelly, *The Right of Reply: An Alternative to an Action for Libel,* 34 Va.L.Rev. 867 (1948); Leflar, *Legal Remedies for Defamation,* 6 Ark.L.Rev. & B. Ass'n J. 423 (1952); Note, *Developments in the Law of Defamation,* 69 Harv.L.Rev. 875 (1956) [hereinafter Note, *Developments in Defamation*]; Note, *Developments in the Law of Injunctions,* 78 Harv. L.Rev. 994 (1965) [hereinafter Note, *Developments in Injunctions*]; Note, *Vindication of the Reputation of a Public Official,* 80 Harv. L.Rev. 1730 (1967); Bertelsman, *Injunctions Against Speech and Writing: A Re-Evaluation,* 59 Ky.L.J. 319 (1970); Note, *Corporate Defamation and Product Disparagement: Narrowing the Analogy to Personal Defamation,* 75 Colum.L.Rev. 963 (1975); Hulme, *Vindicating Reputation: An Alternative to Damages As a Remedy for Defamation,* 30 Am.U.L.Rev. 375 (1981); Gold, *Does Equity Still Lack Jurisdiction to Enjoin a Libel or Slander?,* 48 Brook.L.Rev. 231 (1982); Barron, *The Search for Media Accountability,* 19 Suffolk U.L.Rev. 789 (1985); Franklin, *A Declaratory Judgment Alternative to Current Libel Law,* 74 Cal.L.Rev. 809 (1986); Leval, *The No-Money, No-Fault Libel Suit: Keeping Sullivan in its Proper Place,* 101 Harv.L.Rev. 1287 (1988); Wissler, Bezanson, Cranberg & Soloski, *Why Current Libel Law Doesn't Work and What Judges Can Do About It,* 27 Judges' J. 29 (1988); and Dienes, *Libel Reform: An Appraisal,* 23 U.Mich.J.L.Ref. 1 (1989).

First, the court noted that the Pennsylvania Supreme Court had expressly repudiated the maxim that equity will protect property rights but not personal rights. *Id.* (citing *Everett v. Harron,* 380 Pa. 123, 110 A.2d 383 (1955)).[14] Pennsylvania apparently is now in line with the Restatement and the vast majority of other jurisdictions in this regard. *See Kenyon v. City of Chicopee,* 320 Mass. 528, 70 N.E.2d 241, 244 (1946); *see generally* Restatement (Second) of Torts § 937 comment (a) (1969); Gold, *supra* note 13, at 236–37; Note, *Developments in Injunctions, supra* note 13, at 998–1000. *But see Murphy v. Daytona Beach Humane Society,* 176 So.2d 922, 924 (Fla.App.1965) (denying injunction against defamation based on traditional view that equity will not protect rights of personality).

Second, the Superior Court reasoned that the argument that a defendant has a right to a jury determination as to the truth of a publication[15] "loses all persuasion * * * in those situations where the plaintiff has clearly established before a judicial tribunal that the matter sought to be enjoined is both defamatory and false." 369 A.2d at 831. Because there was no doubt that Willing's sign was both false and malicious, the Superior Court reasoned that "[t]o refuse injunctive relief under the circumstances of this case on the grounds that defendant would be denied a jury trial is to elevate form over substance." *Id.* 369 A.2d at 832.

Third, the Superior Court challenged the precept that plaintiffs do not need equitable relief because they have an adequate remedy at law for

14. The differential protection provided in equity for property and personal rights was a particular source of annoyance for Dean Pound:

> If a threatened tort involves injury to property for which the legal remedy is inadequate * * * preventive relief is normally available. But if an injury to personality is threatened, wholly destructive of plaintiff's dearest interest, we are told that his only recourse is the legal remedy of damages although no pecuniary measure can possibly be applied to the interest and no pecuniary standard to the wrong. May we give any reasons other than purely historical for a doctrine which at first blush is so arbitrary and unjust? Do the rules which our books still announce upon this subject rest upon any basis more legitimate than unintelligent adherence to the *dicta* of a great judge in the pioneer case? May we put this corner of the law in the order of reason by making the rules thereof conform to the general principle of concurrent jurisdiction where the legal remedy for a legal right is inadequate or by showing sound reason why, in this one spot, that general principle should not obtain?

Pound, *supra* note 13 at 640–41. * * *

15. The notion of the right to a jury determination as to the libelous nature of speech apparently originated with Fox's Libel Act, 32 Geo. II, c. 60, § 1 (1792), which stated:

> On every such trial the jury sworn to try the issue may give a general verdict of guilty or not guilty upon the whole matter put in issue * * * and shall not be required or directed by the Court or judge * * * to find the defendant * * * guilty merely on the proof of publication by such defendant * * * of the paper charged to be a libel * * *.

Prior to Fox's Act, English judges had determined whether a particular statement was libelous; the jury merely determined whether there had been publication of the statement. *See* Leflar, *supra* note 13, at 434 n. 37. Fox's Act thus expanded the jury's role, a development which was transplanted to America when many of the states subsequently patterned their respective constitutional and statutory provisions governing libel upon the Act, *see* Note, *Developments in Defamation, supra* note 13, at 944. Since this time, numerous courts have referred to the right to a jury trial in denying injunctions against defamation, generally reasoning that the jury provides a safeguard against judicial censorship of speech. *See Schmoldt v. Oakley,* 390 P.2d 882, 886 (Okl.1964). *See generally* Annotation, *Injunction as Remedy Against Defamation of Person,* 47 A.L.R.2d 715, 727–28 [§ 5b] (1956) (citing cases).

damages.[16] In particular, the Superior Court reasoned that Mazzocone and Quinn did *not* have an adequate remedy at law because: (1) the value of their professional and personal reputations, and the diminution in that value resulting from Willing's libel, were difficult to prove and measure; (2) given Willing's apparent mental instability, it was reasonable to assume that she would continue to libel the plaintiffs, necessitating a multiplicity of damage actions on their behalf; and (3) Willing was indigent, rendering any action for damages a "pointless gesture" in any event.[17] 369 A.2d at 832. In light of these factors, the Superior Court concluded that Mazzocone and Quinn did not have an adequate remedy at law.

Fourth, although the Superior Court acknowledged that the argument that an injunction against defamation is an unconstitutional prior restraint on free expression "is by far the most cogent of all the reasons offered in support of the traditional view," [19] it reasoned that not all restrictions on speech constitute prior restraints. 369 A.2d at 832. Invoking Justice Frankfurter's opinion in *Kingsley Books, Inc. v. Brown,* 354 U.S. 436, 441–42, 77 S.Ct. 1325, 1327–28, 1 L.Ed.2d 1469 (1957), the court maintained instead that "a pragmatic and modern rather than a theoretical and historical approach" should be employed in determining what constitutes a

16. This precept is also of considerable vintage:

> The adequate remedy rule well reflected Chancery's subordinate position as it developed in medieval England against the background of the established courts of law. Equity was a "gloss" on the law; its sole justification for assuming jurisdiction was that traditional legal remedies and procedures could not offer the plaintiff satisfactory relief.

Note, *Developments in Injunctions, supra* note 13, at 997 (citations omitted). Although law and equity have been merged in most jurisdictions, the adequate remedy rule continues to be cited frequently as a ground for denying injunctive relief against defamation. *See Alberti v. Cruise,* 383 F.2d 268 (4th Cir. 1967); Annotation, *Injunction as Remedy Against Defamation of Person,* 47 A.L.R.2d 715, 724–25 [§ 4a] (1956) (and cases cited therein).

17. The adequate remedy at law rationale for denying injunctions against defamations has been rejected or criticized in numerous reported decisions and in the literature. *See generally Dino de Laurentiis Cinematografica, S.p.A. v. D–150, Inc.,* 366 F.2d 373, 375–76 (2d Cir.1966); *Menard v. Houle,* 298 Mass. 546, 11 N.E.2d 436, 437 (1937); *Murphy,* 176 So.2d at 927 (Wigginton, J. specially concurring); Note, *Developments in Injunctions, supra* note 13, at 1000–04; Bertelsman, *supra* note 13, at 320; Gold, *supra* note 13, at 262. These cases and articles generally adopt the modern view, reflected in the Restatement (Second) of Torts § 936 (1969), that the availability of legal remedies is merely one of the factors to be considered in determining the appropriateness of an injunction against a threatened tort.

19. *See Konigsberg v. Time, Inc.,* 288 F.Supp. 989 (S.D.N.Y.1968) ("To enjoin any publication, no matter how libelous, would be repugnant to the First Amendment to the Constitution."); *Krebiozen Research Foundation v. Beacon Press, Inc.,* 334 Mass. 86, 93, 134 N.E.2d 1, 6 (1956) ("[T]he constitutional protection of free speech and public interest in the discussion of many issues greatly limit the areas in which the power to grant injunctive relief may or should be exercised in defamatory cases."); *Northwestern Pac. R. Co. v. Lumber & Sawmill Workers' Union,* 31 Cal.2d 441, 189 P.2d 277, 282 (1948) ("[Equity] will not restrain the commission of a libel or slander, for that is prior censorship—a basic evil denounced by the constitutions of the United States and California in protecting freedom of speech and press."). *See generally* Annotation, *Injunction as Remedy Against Defamation of Person,* 47 A.L.R.2d 715, 726–27 (1956) ("The most formidable obstacle to the grant of injunctive relief against personal defamation in this country has been the feeling of the courts that to allow such relief would infringe the constitutionally guaranteed freedoms of speech and of the press by setting up what would be, at least potentially, a system of judicial censorship."); Bertelsman, *supra* note 13 at 323 ("[T]he constitutional problem of prior restraint * * * has proved to be the most formidable obstacle to the granting of injunctive relief in cases involving speech or writing.").

prior restraint. 369 A.2d at 832–33. As explicated by the Superior Court, this pragmatic approach should attempt to weigh, on a case-by-case basis, the likelihood that the alleged defamatory statements were true, the magnitude of the harm done to the plaintiff if the speech is not restrained, the adequacy of legal remedies, and, most importantly, whether the public interest will be disserved by suppressing the speech. *Id.* 369 A.2d at 833–34 (citations omitted). Under this pragmatic approach, the court concluded, the injunction against Willing should not be considered an unconstitutional prior restraint.

The Supreme Court of Pennsylvania reversed, essentially refuting the reasoning of the Superior Court on two grounds. 482 Pa. 377, 393 A.2d 1155 (1978). First, invoking Blackstone and referencing the pernicious English Licensing Acts, * * * the Supreme Court noted that the Commonwealth of Pennsylvania long has rejected any prior restraint on the exercise of speech as reflected in Article I, section 7 of the Pennsylvania Constitution and in the Court's own decision in *Goldman Theatres v. Dana,* 405 Pa. 83, 173 A.2d 59, *cert. denied,* 368 U.S. 897, 82 S.Ct. 174, 7 L.Ed.2d 93 (1961).

Second, the Supreme Court addressed the Superior Court's argument that Mazzocone and Quinn did not have an adequate remedy at law because Willing was indigent and unable to satisfy a damages action. In unequivocal terms, the Supreme Court stated that Willing's constitutional rights should not be contingent upon her financial status.

The Supreme Court added that, as a matter of common-law precedent, the Superior Court had been wrong in assuming that Willing's indigency in any way was relevant to determining whether Mazzocone and Quinn had an adequate remedy at law.

* * *

In short, *Willing* may be summarized as follows. The Superior Court was presented with a case which, in its view and that of many of the commentators, cried out for reexamining the common-law precept that equity will not enjoin a defamation. The Superior Court, after carefully considering each of the traditional justifications for the precept, found one no longer viable and the remaining three unpersuasive given the certainty that Willing's statements were false, the likelihood that she would continue to issue libelous statements, her inability to satisfy a damages judgment, and the fact that the public had little interest in the speech at issue. The Supreme Court, however, stood firmly behind the traditional bar to equitable relief, holding essentially that Willing's constitutional rights to uncensored speech and trial by jury were paramount even though, as a practical matter, she would be immune to a damages action after the speech was issued.

Given the similarities between *Willing* and the instant dispute, and the Pennsylvania Supreme Court's flat rejection of the Superior Court's avoidance of the traditional rule against enjoining defamation, it arguably would be appropriate to overturn the district court's injunction against Thompson without further elaboration. We believe, however, contrary to Thompson's assertions, that there is a material difference between the two cases that makes further analysis unavoidable.

As noted previously, *Willing* originated when Mazzocone and Quinn filed a suit in equity in the Court of Common Pleas of Philadelphia seeking to enjoin Willing's defamatory protest. The two lawyers never sought damages, nor did a jury ever pass upon the veracity of Willing's statements. The Common Pleas judge, satisfied that the statements obviously lacked foundation and that Willing was mentally imbalanced, issued the injunction based entirely upon his view of the situation and his equitable powers. Thompson, by contrast, was enjoined from further defamatory speech as an adjunct to Kramer's successful action at law for damages. Because the district court directed a verdict in Kramer's favor on the issue of liability, leaving to the jury only the issue of damages, we recognize that it is not entirely accurate to state that Thompson was afforded a jury determination as to the veracity of his statements. However, since the directed verdict is functionally equivalent to a jury award, at least in theory Thompson's comments were found to be libelous after a full and fair jury trial.

The existence of a jury trial is a potentially crucial distinction between *Willing* and this case. Two of the three traditional reasons for barring equity from enjoining a defamation, as described by the Pennsylvania Supreme Court in *Willing,* are obviated once a jury has determined that the enjoined statements are indeed libelous. First, it obviously cannot be said that a defendant has been denied the right to a jury determination of the veracity of his statements if a judge issues an injunction against further statements *after* a jury has determined that the same statements are untrue and libelous. Second, not all injunctions against speech constitute prior restraints. The United States Supreme Court has held repeatedly that an injunction against speech generally will not be considered an unconstitutional prior restraint if it is issued after a jury has determined that the speech is not constitutionally protected. *See, e.g., Pittsburgh Press Co. v. Pittsburgh Comm'n on Human Rel.,* 413 U.S. 376, 390, 93 S.Ct. 2553, 2561, 37 L.Ed.2d 669 (1973) ("The special vice of a prior restraint is that communication will be suppressed, either directly or by inducing excessive caution in the speaker, before an adequate determination that it is unprotected by the First Amendment."). The Pennsylvania cases appear to be in accord. Because libelous speech is not protected by either the United States or the Pennsylvania Constitutions, * * * it follows that, once a jury has determined that a certain statement is libelous, it is not a prior restraint for the court to enjoin the defendant from repeating that statement.

Mindful of our responsibility to predict how the Pennsylvania Supreme Court would decide this case under its laws and Constitution, the case appears to be reducible to the following question: Would the Pennsylvania Supreme Court have upheld the injunction against Willing if Mazzocone and Quinn had first obtained a jury determination that her statements were libelous? Stated more broadly, would the Pennsylvania Supreme Court be willing to permit an exception to the rule that equity will not enjoin a defamation in cases where there already has been a jury determination that the defendant's statements were libelous?

Although this is apparently a question of first impression under Pennsylvania law, it has been considered in other jurisdictions. To begin with, our research reveals four Missouri cases that suggest in *dicta* that an injunction can issue against further publication of defamatory statements once the plaintiff had secured a jury verdict. *See Flint v. Hutchinson Smoke Burner Co.,* 110 Mo. 492, 19 S.W. 804, 806 (1892); *Wolf v. Harris,* 267 Mo. 405, 184 S.W. 1139, 1141–42 (1916); *Ryan v. Warrensburg,* 342 Mo. 761, 117 S.W.2d 303, 308 (1938); *Downey v. United Weatherproofing Inc.,* 363 Mo. 852, 253 S.W.2d 976, 983 (1953). * * *

In 1975, the Supreme Courts of Ohio and Georgia became the first courts clearly to adopt this exception to the general rule that equity will not enjoin a defamation. See *O'Brien v. University Community Tenants Union,* 42 Ohio St.2d 242, 327 N.E.2d 753 (1975); *Retail Credit Co. v. Russell,* 234 Ga. 765, 218 S.E.2d 54 (1975). *O'Brien* was instituted by a landlord who claimed that he was being defamed and blacklisted by a tenants' group. The landlord secured a jury determination that certain statements were libelous and then sought and obtained an injunction against further libel. The Supreme Court of Ohio affirmed the injunction stating:

> Once speech has judicially been found libelous, if all the requirements for injunctive relief are met, an injunction for restraint of continued publication of that same speech may be proper. The judicial determination that specific speech is defamatory must be made prior to any restraint.

327 N.E.2d at 756.

In *Retail Credit,* the plaintiff, the subject of a credit report containing statements adjudged libelous by a jury, obtained a permanent injunction prohibiting the defendant from republishing the libelous statements.

Nearly a decade later, the Minnesota Supreme Court followed suit in *Advanced Training Systems v. Caswell Equipment Co.,* 352 N.W.2d 1 (Minn.1984). That court held:

> A judicial tribunal has, after full adversarial proceedings, found that defendant's criticism of [plaintiff's] equipment constituted 'false or misleading' product disparagement * * * Other courts have also upheld the suppression of libel, so long as the suppression is limited to the precise statements found libelous *after* a full and fair adversary proceeding. We therefore hold that the injunction below, limited as it is to material found either libelous or disparaging after a full jury trial, is not unconstitutional and may stand.

352 N.W.2d at 11 (citations omitted).

We find the reasoning and policies undergirding these cases quite persuasive. But that is not dispositive here. Our function is to look, as best we can, into the minds of the members of the Pennsylvania Supreme Court, and to ascertain their likely disposition of this case. Although the prediction is difficult, the available evidence leads us to the conclusion that the Pennsylvania Supreme Court would overturn the injunction against prospective libel issued by the district court against Thompson. In reaching this conclusion, we are persuaded by five factors.

First, the maxim that equity will not enjoin a libel has enjoyed nearly two centuries of widespread acceptance at common law. The welter of academic and judicial criticism of the last seventy years has, in truth, done little more than chip away at its edges. In any event, as evidenced by the Pennsylvania Supreme Court's unqualified rejection of the Superior Court's "modern" view in *Willing,* Pennsylvania would appear firmly bound to the traditional rule. This may well be due to the extraordinary reverence and solicitude with which the Commonwealth of Pennsylvania has viewed the right of free expression, tracing back to the experiences in England of its founder William Penn and carried forward in the Commonwealth's various Constitutions. * * *

Second, although an exception to the general rule has been recognized in several cases where there has been a jury determination of the libelous nature of specific statements, we would do well not to overstate the degree of acceptance that has been accorded to this exception. For the better part of this century, this exception existed, as best we can determine, only in Missouri, and there based entirely on a single line of *dicta.* That three state supreme courts have affirmatively adopted the exception in the last two decades may represent the trickle that presages the collapse of the common-law dam. But, for now, it remains a trickle. And as far as we can tell, the Pennsylvania Supreme Court is more likely to plug the holes in the dam than to contribute to its destruction.

Third, even if we thought that the Pennsylvania Supreme Court might be inclined to adopt the jury determination exception, we doubt that this is the case in which it would do so. The district court in this case took the decidedly unusual step of directing a verdict on the issue of liability against Thompson before he put on a defense, finding that the statements were so patently libelous that no justification or defense could possibly exist. In theory, of course, a directed verdict at law is tantamount to a jury verdict. From the defendant's perspective, however, a directed verdict is indistinguishable from the decree of a court sitting in equity. Given the fear of judicial censorship that has pervaded this area of jurisprudence, and the almost talismanic significance that the case law attaches to the decisions of juries, we think it likely that, even if the Pennsylvania Supreme Court were willing to adopt this exception, it would do so only when there *actually* has been a jury determination regarding the libelous nature of the defendant's statements.

Fourth, and perhaps most importantly, we believe that the Pennsylvania Supreme Court would not adopt the jury determination exception if confronted with this case because, as *Willing* pointedly suggests, that Court continues to place great emphasis on the adequate remedy doctrine as a bar to equitable relief. Indeed, even a jury determination that particular statements are libelous does not address the traditional notion that equity should not intervene where legal remedies (i.e., damages) are adequate, either in practice or even just in theory.

Whether or not that court would have felt less passionately about the adequate remedy rule had it been satisfied that the rights to trial by jury and free speech were not also implicated is difficult to discern. In the end, we can do no more than take the *Willing* court's words at face value. * * *

Fifth and finally, we note that this case presents a stronger case than *Willing* for denying equitable relief. Unlike Willing, there has been no showing that Thompson is indigent (the record suggests that he is moderately affluent), or that the threat of future damages is inadequate to deter him or to compensate Kramer. Therefore, even under the liberal standards for granting equitable relief urged by the Superior Court in *Willing,* 393 A.2d at 1158, an injunction probably would be inappropriate in this case. And certainly, given the Pennsylvania Supreme Court's rigid adherence to the traditional adequate remedy rule, Kramer's prospects for securing an injunction from that court seem slim.

For the foregoing reasons, we will reverse those portions of the district court's orders that enjoined Thompson from repeating the statements deemed libelous and from communicating with anyone doing business with Kramer.

B. Mandatory Retraction and Withdrawal of Prior Statements and Court Filings

We need not tarry very long over those portions of the district court's orders that sought to force Thompson to write letters of retraction to recipients of prior libelous statements and to withdraw libelous court filings. We have reviewed the available literature and reported decisions. Although the notion of *compelled* retraction occasionally has been advanced in the literature, we have not found a single case in which such a remedy has been awarded.

To our knowledge, the only two cases that even remotely come close to addressing mandatory retraction are *Miami Herald Publishing Co. v. Tornillo,* 418 U.S. 241, 94 S.Ct. 2831, 41 L.Ed.2d 730 (1974), and *Coughlin v. Westinghouse Broadcasting and Cable, Inc.,* 689 F.Supp. 483 (E.D.Pa. 1988). In *Miami Herald,* the Supreme Court was called upon to assess the constitutionality of a Florida statute that provided a so-called "right of reply" to political candidates whose personal or official records were assailed by the media. Under the statute, newspapers were required to print, free of cost to the candidate, and subject to punishment if they refused, any reply that a candidate wished to make to the newspapers' charges. The Court declared the statute unconstitutional stating:

> [T]he Court has expressed sensitivity as to whether a retraction or requirement constituted the compulsion exerted by government on a newspaper to print that which it would not otherwise print. The clear implication has been that no such compulsion to publish that which " 'reason' tells them should not be published" is unconstitutional. A responsible press is an undoubtedly desirable goal, but press responsibility is not mandated by the Constitution and like many other virtues cannot be legislated.

Miami Herald, 418 U.S. at 256, 94 S.Ct. at 2838–39 (citations omitted).

A "right of reply" differs from a mandatory retraction in that the former merely requires the defamer to provide space for a reply, whereas the latter requires the defamer to mouth or pen the words the plaintiff would have him say. As such, the unconstitutionality of compelled retraction would seem to follow *a fortiori* from the Court's declaration that Florida's "right of reply" statute is unconstitutional.

Coughlin is also somewhat related to our inquiry. There, a policeman, who claimed that he had been defamed by a television station, wrote the management of the station demanding retraction, but was rebuffed. Apparently unable to prove that the statements had been made with sufficient recklessness to support a typical damages action for libel, the policeman sought damages invoking the novel theory that the station had breached a common-law duty under Pennsylvania law to retract what it later knew to be false. * * *

Judge Pollak reviewed the authorities speaking to the constitutionality of mandatory retraction, focusing on *Miami Herald* * * *. He concluded, in *dicta,* that "[m]y view of the matter is that a carefully crafted retraction statute could well be constitutional." *Id.* at 489. Judge Pollak denied the plaintiff's claim, however, concluding that even if mandatory retraction would survive constitutional scrutiny, such a cause of action properly should originate with the Pennsylvania legislature, not the courts. *Id.* at 490. We agree.

In sum, we find no support for the various retractions and withdrawals forced upon Thompson by the district court. Consequently, those orders of the district court compelling such retractions and withdrawals, and the associated contempt citations, must be reversed.

III. CONCLUSION

For the foregoing reasons, we will reverse those portions of the orders of the district court, * * * that permanently enjoined defendant from uttering libelous statements, mandated the retraction or withdrawal of past libelous statements, held defendant in civil contempt, and awarded plaintiff attorney's fees arising out of contempt proceedings. * * *

BINGHAM v. STRUVE

New York Supreme Court, Appellate Division, 1992.
184 A.D.2d 85, 591 N.Y.S.2d 156.

Before SULLIVAN, J.P., and WALLACH, KUPFERMAN and KASSAL, JJ.

PER CURIAM.

Plaintiffs, A. Walker Bingham III and his wife, Nicolette P. Bingham, commenced this action on or about February 7, 1991, seeking a permanent injunction and money damages for alleged libel and intentional infliction of emotional distress. For the reasons that follow, we modify the orders of the IAS court to the extent of granting plaintiffs' motion for a preliminary injunction and directing *in camera* inspection and conditional discovery of defendant's divorce records.

This litigation arose from the repeated oral and written communications of defendant, Catherine T.A. Struve, to plaintiffs' family members, business associates, neighbors, and former colleagues, which charge, *inter alia,* that plaintiff-husband raped her in 1953, when she was a 19–year–old librarian, and he a 24–year–old first-year law student, at Harvard Law School. The allegedly libelous communications, which started in or about December 1989 with letters and telephone calls, took a new form in August 1991, when defendant began to picket in front of plaintiffs' apartment building in Manhattan. The hand-lettered sandwich board which she wore on these almost daily occasions proclaimed as follows:

ATTENTION RESIDENTS OF 19 EAST 72ND ST.
A. WALKER BINGHAM 3 RAPED ME AND
IS NOW SUING ME FOR LIBEL

It is undisputed that plaintiff-husband and defendant had a youthful affair, which commenced in 1953 and ended in 1955, and that for the next 30 years they lived separate lives. Defendant married in 1965, had two children, and was divorced in 1984. Plaintiff-husband was also married, first in the 1950's, which marriage ended in divorce, and then to plaintiff-wife in 1967. He has three children.

After a chance encounter between plaintiff-husband and defendant in 1983, a second affair began and lasted until 1989 when, defendant contends, the memory of the alleged rape, which she had repressed for 36 years, was unlocked. Defendant states that she then realized that this was why she had been depressed and dysfunctional for years, and that it accounted for her inability to pursue a career and succeed in her marriage. It is defendant's further claim that, by publicizing her charges against plaintiff-husband, she will be able to come to terms with the traumatic event and heal emotionally, a process that requires an admission of guilt and expression of remorse from plaintiff-husband.

The law is well-established that a party seeking preliminary injunctive relief must demonstrate a likelihood of ultimate success on the merits, irreparable harm in the absence of injunctive relief, and a weighing of equities in his favor (*Little India Stores, Inc. v. Singh,* 101 A.D.2d 727, 728, 475 N.Y.S.2d 38; *Bashein v. Landau,* 96 A.D.2d 479, 465 N.Y.S.2d 178). A judicial determination regarding likelihood of success on the merits does not, as the IAS court stated, amount to a pre-determination of the issues. Rather, "the showing of a *likelihood* of success * * * must not be equated with the showing of a *certainty* of success" on the merits [emphasis in original] (*Tucker v. Toia,* 54 A.D.2d 322, 326, 388 N.Y.S.2d 475; *Parkmed Co. v. Pro–Life Counselling, Inc.,* 91 A.D.2d 551, 553, 457 N.Y.S.2d 27).

Here, the undisputed evidence was sufficient to demonstrate a likelihood of plaintiffs' ultimate success. Plaintiffs established a prima facie case of libel on the merits, since the offending statements injure plaintiff-husband's reputation and good name, and otherwise expose him to "public contempt, scorn, obloquy, ridicule, shame or disgrace", and "induce an evil opinion of him in the minds of right-thinking persons" (*Lawlor v. Gallagher Presidents' Report, Inc.,* 394 F.Supp. 721, 726 [S.D.N.Y.1975], remanded, 538 F.2d 311 [2d Cir.1976]; *Privitera v. Town of Phelps,* 79 A.D.2d 1, 3,

435 N.Y.S.2d 402). In contrast, defendant's charge of a 38–year–old rape is unsupported by any objective evidence or corroborating testimony, as is, necessarily, its accompanying claim of repressed memory. Indeed, the allegation of rape is seriously challenged by the *undisputed* fact that the 1953 affair continued for two years after its occurrence, and that defendant had a second, six-year affair with plaintiff-husband 30 years later.

Further, defendant's credibility is likely to be hampered by the shocking and, again, unsupported accusations of a sexual nature with which she has impugned the morals of plaintiff-husband's 89–year–old mother and plaintiff-wife, and by the various contradictions contained in documents authored by defendant, including a claim that she bore plaintiff-husband's child in the 1950's, and a subsequent denial that she had ever made such a claim.

Defendant's attempt to continue her offending communications as protected free speech under the First Amendment and its New York State Constitution analogue, Article One, Section Eight, must fail. Constitutional free speech protections are intended to encourage "debate on public issues [that is] uninhibited, robust, and wide-open" (*New York Times Co. v. Sullivan,* 376 U.S. 254, 270, 84 S.Ct. 710, 721, 11 L.Ed.2d 686). Distinctions are drawn where, as here, the defamatory speech does not advance such societal interests and, indeed, concerns a private individual (*Gertz v. Robert Welch, Inc.,* 418 U.S. 323, 344, 94 S.Ct. 2997, 3009, 41 L.Ed.2d 789). Moreover, these protections are not absolute (*Nebraska Press Association v. Stuart,* 427 U.S. 539, 570, 96 S.Ct. 2791, 2808, 49 L.Ed.2d 683). As noted in *Gitlow v. State of New York,* 268 U.S. 652, 666, 45 S.Ct. 625, 630, 69 L.Ed. 1138, "the freedom of speech * * * secured by the Constitution, does not confer an absolute right to speak or publish, without responsibility, whatever one may choose" (*see also, Angel v. Levittown Union Free School Dist. No. 5,* 171 A.D.2d 770, 772, 567 N.Y.S.2d 490).

In assessing plaintiffs' entitlement to a preliminary injunction, we have further concluded that the potential harm caused by defendant's continued communications and the picketing of plaintiffs' home is irreparable, as it is capable of injuring plaintiff-husband's standing and reputation in all aspects of his personal and professional life, and of inflicting serious psychological and emotional damage to both plaintiffs, as well as to their family members. Such harm is not readily compensable in damages.

We have also weighed the relative hardship that may be suffered by defendant if the preliminary injunction is granted, and conclude that the degree of harm to be caused to plaintiffs if the conduct continues unabated far exceeds any which may be caused to defendant if her picketing and other communications are enjoined pending the trial.

With respect to the production of defendant's sealed divorce records, it is our conclusion that defendant's allegations that plaintiff-husband deprived her of "any chance for a happy marriage" and so traumatized her that she lost the "possibility of intimacy and friendships with either sex", render these records potentially relevant to the instant proceeding. We are cognizant, however, that the interests of defendant's former husband may be affected, and it is, accordingly, the directive of this Court that the records be examined *in camera* for materiality and relevance to this litigation, and that discovery rulings be tailored to meet any reasonable objections raised by defendant's former spouse.

Finally, it is the view of this Court that plaintiffs have failed to put forth a sufficiently compelling reason to overcome the strong public policy of favoring open judicial proceedings (Judiciary Law § 4; *Herald Co. Inc. v. Weisenberg,* 89 A.D.2d 224, 226, 455 N.Y.S.2d 413, *aff'd* 59 N.Y.2d 378, 465 N.Y.S.2d 862, 452 N.E.2d 1190; *Anonymous v. Anonymous,* 158 A.D.2d 296, 297, 550 N.Y.S.2d 704).

Accordingly, the order, * * * which denied plaintiffs' motion for a preliminary injunction and for closure of all proceedings and a sealing of the record, should be modified, on the law and in the exercise of discretion, to grant plaintiffs' motion for a preliminary injunction, and otherwise affirmed, without costs; and the order of said court, entered July 23, 1991, which, *inter alia,* granted defendant's motion for a protective order, and denied plaintiffs' cross-motion to compel production of sealed records pertaining to defendant's 1985 divorce, should be modified, on the law and in the exercise of discretion, to grant plaintiffs' cross-motion, to the extent that said records will be produced for *in camera* inspection, with notice and opportunity to be heard accorded to defendant's former spouse before any discovery determinations are made, and otherwise affirmed, without costs.

Order, Supreme Court, New York County, entered October 7, 1991, which denied plaintiffs' motion for a preliminary injunction and for closure of all proceedings and sealing the record, is modified, on the law and in the exercise of discretion, to grant plaintiffs' motion for a preliminary injunction, and otherwise affirmed, without costs; and the order of said court, entered July 23, 1991, which, *inter alia,* granted defendant's motion for a protective order, and denied plaintiffs' cross motion to compel production of sealed records pertaining to defendant's 1985 divorce, is modified, on the law and in the exercise of discretion, to grant plaintiffs' cross motion, to the extent that said records will be produced for in camera inspection, with notice and opportunity to be heard accorded to defendant's former spouse before any discovery determinations are made, and otherwise affirmed, without costs.

All concur.

Notes

1. While the property right-personal right distinction is usually no longer a bar to injunctive relief, courts may nevertheless refuse relief because of a variety of other considerations. Sometimes the denials may be based on traditional equitable concepts, such as adequacy of the legal remedy. Oftentimes, a refusal to grant an injunction may be couched in traditional equitable maxims that tend to mask the underlying constitutional or policy concerns. A good example of this is Sixty–Seventh Minnesota State Senate v. Beens, 406 U.S. 187, 92 S.Ct. 1477, 32 L.Ed.2d 1 (1972), where the Supreme Court, in reversing a lower court order reducing the size of the Minnesota state legislature, seemed to emphasize limits on the remedial powers of equity as well as expressing its constitutional and federalism concerns. At other times courts

will rely overtly on such non-equitable considerations. Much of the defamation and privacy material in this section exemplifies this approach.

The material in this section also emphasizes the practicability concerns that sometimes preclude the issuance of injunctive relief. These are not unique to injunctions and are treated extensively in the chapter on specific performance of contracts. *See* Chapter 5 *infra.* Practicability concerns include (1) a court's reluctance or inability to supervise or become significantly involved in the policing of the injunction; and (2) the futility of utilizing an injunction to force unwilling parties to continue a strained personal relationship. While the property right-personal right distinction will not normally bar injunctive relief, the more a case involves personal or societal concerns, as opposed to tangible property interests, the more practicability becomes a potential obstacle to the injunctive remedy.

2. Are *Kramer* and *Bingham* reconcilable? Should it make a difference that *Kramer* involves permanent injunctive relief while the *Bingham* plaintiff seeks only a preliminary injunction? Or does that fact make the cases even more difficult to reconcile? Is it relevant that *Bingham* more than *Kramer* involves sensitive matters of personal privacy?

3. The general hesitancy on the part of equity to grant injunctive relief against defamation has undoubtedly been buttressed by the series of United States Supreme Court decisions imposing First Amendment limitations on the recovery of damages in defamation cases involving public officials and public figures. Moreover, even where there is some chance of a damage recovery under the foregoing standards, injunctive relief will still be extremely difficult to obtain because of a pervasive judicial hostility toward prior restraints.

Judicial reluctance to enjoin defamation has not gone unchallenged by the commentators. For a well-reasoned analysis that criticizes the Pennsylvania Supreme Court in *Mazzacone* and espouses the view that "to enjoin a defendant in a proper case from continuing a campaign of vilification would not be incompatible with either equitable tradition or constitutional doctrine," see Gold, Does Equity Still Lack Jurisdiction to Enjoin a Libel or Slander?, 48 Brooklyn L.Rev. 231, 262 (1982).

4. Traditionally, injunctive relief has been more available in the trade libel area than in personal reputation defamation cases. For example, in perhaps the most graphic business defamation cases, courts have enjoined dissatisfied car owners from painting lemons or white elephants on automobiles so as to identify them as having been sold by the plaintiffs. *See, e.g.,* Carter v. Knapp Motor Co., 243 Ala. 600, 11 So.2d 383 (1943); Menard v. Houle, 298 Mass. 546, 11 N.E.2d 436 (1937). *But cf.* Schmoldt v. Oakley, 390 P.2d 882 (Okl.1964). This greater willingness to enjoin trade libel "reflects a recognition by the courts that, apart from the inadequacy of the damage remedy to protect the plaintiff's needs, the defendant's claim to jury trial and to protection against prior restraint on speech is not compelling. The facts are often undisputed, and jury trial is not necessary to protect free speech, since judges are not likely to be prejudiced against communication of this sort." Developments in the Law—Injunctions, 78 Harv.L.Rev. 994, 1010 (1965).

This distinction may have been diminished by recent constitutional developments in the "commercial speech" area. In an early case, Valentine v. Chrestensen, 316 U.S. 52, 62 S.Ct. 920, 86 L.Ed. 1262 (1942), the United States Supreme Court stated that the constitution imposes no restraint on government with respect to regulating "purely commercial advertising." From this statement the theory developed that expression "tainted by some commercial element was second class speech, undeserving of first amendment protection." Comment, Prior Restraints and Restrictions on Advertising After Virginia Pharmacy Board: The Commercial Speech Doctrine Reformulated, 43 Mo. L.Rev. 64 (1978). However, in a series of more recent decisions, the United States Supreme Court has rejected the theory and made it clear that commercial speech, like other speech and expression, is protected by the First Amendment. *See* Peel v. Attorney Registration and Disciplinary Comm'n of Illinois, 496 U.S. 91, 110 S.Ct. 2281, 110 L.Ed.2d 83 (1990); Shapero v. Kentucky Bar Ass'n, 486 U.S. 466, 108 S.Ct. 1916, 100 L.Ed.2d 475 (1988); Zauderer v. Office of Disciplinary Counsel of the Supreme Court of Ohio, 471 U.S. 626, 105 S.Ct. 2265, 85 L.Ed.2d 652 (1985); Linmark Associates, Inc. v. Township of Willingsboro, 431 U.S. 85, 97 S.Ct. 1614, 52 L.Ed.2d 155 (1977); Bates v. State Bar of Arizona, 433 U.S. 350, 97 S.Ct. 2691, 53 L.Ed.2d 810 (1977); Virginia State Bd. of Pharmacy v. Virginia Citizens Consumer Council, Inc., 425 U.S. 748, 96 S.Ct. 1817, 48 L.Ed.2d 346 (1976). *See generally* J. Nowack, R. Rotunda & J. Young, Constitutional Law 1011–1035 (4th ed. 1991).

Nevertheless, the degree of First Amendment protection for commercial speech is not as substantial as that afforded other types of speech activity. The following commentary is an appropriate description of the current state of constitutional protection afforded commercial speech:

> "It appears that the [Supreme Court] will prohibit states from banning the truthful conveyance of commercial information but that they will allow the state a much greater leeway in protecting against false, deceptive or misleading practices. The lower the informational content of the regulated speech, the greater latitude the Court will give the government in drafting such regulations."

J. Nowack, R. Rotunda & J. Young, Constitutional Law 1034 (4th ed. 1991).

Since "false" commercial speech remains constitutionally unprotected, this arguably may provide a basis for continuing to sanction injunctive relief against trade libel, even though the First Amendment prohibits other types of defamation from being similarly enjoined. Nevertheless, in contrast to the earlier cases involving disgruntled automobile purchasers, more recent commercial defamation decisions rely heavily on the prior restraint concept to deny injunctive relief. *See e.g.,* Degroen v. Mark Toyota–Volvo, Inc., 811 P.2d 443 (Colo.App.1991) (attempt to enjoin picketing of auto dealership by disgruntled father of purchaser constituted an invalid prior restraint under 1st Amendment); Franklin Chalfont Associates v. Kalikow, 392 Pa.Super. 452, 573 A.2d 550 (1990) (attempt by developer-homeseller to enjoin use of signs and peaceful picketing by home purchasers that disparaged developer and its product held to be unconstitutional prior restraint); Paradise Hills Associates v. Procel, 1 Cal.Rptr.2d 514 (Cal.App.1991) (preliminary injunction against home purchasers denied on prior restraint grounds at least where developer did not allege that purchasers' statements were false); Pittman v. Cohn Communities, Inc., 240 Ga. 106, 239 S.E.2d 526 (1977) (injunctive relief denied on First Amendment grounds against home purchasers who placed signs in their yards stating "BEFORE YOU BUY IN SUNWOOD TALK TO THIS DISSATISFIED OWNER"). Should a court be more suspicious of an action to enjoin the "commercial" speech of disgruntled consumer than it is of an attempt to suppress such speech by a product seller? On the other hand, shouldn't a court be concerned about activities that are aimed at "blackmailing" or otherwise coercing a seller into compliance with a consumer's unwarranted demand?

GALELLA v. ONASSIS

United States Court of Appeals, Second Circuit, 1973.
487 F.2d 986.

Before SMITH, HAYS and TIMBERS, CIRCUIT JUDGES.

J. JOSEPH SMITH, CIRCUIT JUDGE:

Donald Galella, a free-lance photographer, appeals from a summary judgment dismissing his complaint against three Secret Service agents for false arrest, malicious prosecution and interference with trade (S.D.N.Y., Edward C. McLean, Judge), the dismissal after trial of his identical complaint against Jacqueline Onassis and the grant of injunctive relief to defendant Onassis on her counterclaim * * *. Galella raises the First Amendment as an absolute shield against liability to any sanctions. The judgments dismissing the complaints are affirmed; the grant of injunctive relief is affirmed as herein modified. * * *

Galella is a free-lance photographer specializing in the making and sale of photographs of well-known persons. Defendant Onassis is the widow of the late President, John F. Kennedy, mother of the two Kennedy children, John and Caroline, and is the wife of Aristotle Onassis, widely known shipping figure and reputed multimillionaire. John Walsh, James Kalafatis and John Connelly are U.S. Secret Service agents assigned to the duty of protecting the Kennedy children under 18 U.S.C.A. § 3056, which provides for protection of the children of deceased presidents up to the age of 16.

Galella fancies himself as a "paparazzo" (literally a kind of annoying insect, perhaps roughly equivalent to the English "gadfly.") Paparazzi make themselves as visible to the public and obnoxious to their photographic subjects as possible to aid in the advertisement and wide sale of their works.

Some examples of Galella's conduct brought out at trial are illustrative. Galella took pictures of John Kennedy riding his bicycle in Central Park across the way from his home. He jumped out into the boy's path, causing the agents concern for John's safety. The agents' reaction and interrogation of Galella led to Galella's arrest and his action against the agents; Galella on other occasions interrupted Caroline at tennis, and invaded the children's private schools. At one time he came uncomfortably close in a power boat to Mrs. Onassis swimming. He often jumped and postured around while taking pictures of her party notably at a theater opening but also on numerous other occasions. He followed a practice of bribing apartment house, restaurant and nightclub doormen as well as romancing a family servant to keep him advised of the movements of the family.

After detention and arrest following complaint by the Secret Service agents protecting Mrs. Onassis' son and his acquittal in the state court, Galella filed suit in state court against the agents and Mrs. Onassis.

Galella claimed that under orders from Mrs. Onassis, the three agents had falsely arrested and maliciously prosecuted him, and that this incident in addition to several others described in the complaint constituted an unlawful interference with his trade.

Mrs. Onassis answered denying any role in the arrest or any part in the claimed interference with his attempts to photograph her, and counterclaimed for damages and injunctive relief, charging that Galella had invaded her privacy, assaulted and battered her, intentionally inflicted emotional distress and engaged in a campaign of harassment.

* * *

Certain incidents of photographic coverage by Galella, subsequent to an agreement among the parties for Galella not to so engage, resulted in the issuance of a temporary restraining order to prevent further harassment of Mrs. Onassis and the children. Galella was enjoined from "harassing, alarming, startling, tormenting, touching the person of the defendant * * * or her children * * * and from blocking their movements in the public places and thoroughfares, invading their immediate zone of privacy by means of physical movements, gestures or with photographic equipment and from performing any act reasonably calculated to place the lives and safety of the defendant * * * and her children in jeopardy." Within two months, Galella was charged with violation of the temporary restraining order; a new order was signed which required that the photographer keep 100 yards from the Onassis apartment and 50 yards from the person of the defendant and her children. Surveillance was also prohibited.

* * *

After a six-week trial the court dismissed Galella's claim and granted relief to both the defendant and the intervenor. Galella was enjoined from (1) keeping the defendant and her children under surveillance or following any of them; (2) approaching within 100 yards of the home of defendant or her children, or within 100 yards of either child's school or within 75 yards of either child or 50 yards of defendant; (3) using the name, portrait or picture of defendant or her children for advertising; (4) attempting to communicate with defendant or her children except through her attorney.

* * *

[The court then concluded that the dismissal of Galella's claim against the Secret Service agents had been proper because they were entitled to official immunity.]

* * *

Discrediting all of Galella's testimony the court found the photographer guilty of harassment, intentional infliction of emotional distress, assault and battery, commercial exploitation of defendant's personality, and invasion of privacy. Fully crediting defendant's testimony, the court found no liability on Galella's claim. Evidence offered by the defense showed that Galella had on occasion intentionally physically touched Mrs. Onassis and her daughter, caused fear of physical contact in his frenzied attempts to get their pictures, followed defendant and her children too closely in an automobile, endangered the safety of the children while they were swimming, water skiing and horseback riding. Galella cannot successfully challenge the court's finding of tortious conduct.

Finding that Galella had "insinuated himself into the very fabric of Mrs. Onassis' life * * *" the court framed its relief in part on the need to prevent further invasion of the defendant's privacy. Whether or not this accords with present New York law, there is no doubt that it is sustainable under New York's proscription of harassment.

Of course legitimate countervailing social needs may warrant some intrusion despite an individual's reasonable expectation of privacy and freedom from harassment. However the interference allowed may be no greater than that necessary to protect the overriding public interest. Mrs. Onassis was properly found to be a public figure and thus subject to news coverage. *See* Sidis v. F.R. Publishing Corp., 113 F.2d 806 (2d Cir.), *cert. denied,* 311 U.S. 711, 61 S.Ct. 393, 85 L.Ed. 462 (1940). Nonetheless, Galella's action went far beyond the reasonable bounds of news gathering. When weighed against the *de minimis* public importance of the daily activities of the defendant, Galella's constant surveillance, his obtrusive and intruding presence, was unwarranted and unreasonable. If there were any doubt in our minds, Galella's inexcusable conduct toward defendant's minor children would resolve it.

Galella does not seriously dispute the court's finding of tortious conduct. Rather, he sets up the First Amendment as a wall of immunity protecting newsmen from any liability for their conduct while gathering news. There is no such scope to the First Amendment right. Crimes and torts committed in news gathering are not protected. * * * There is no threat to a free press in requiring its agents to act within the law.

* * *

Injunctive relief is appropriate. Galella has stated his intention to continue his coverage of defendant so long as she is newsworthy. * * *

The injunction, however, is broader than is required to protect the defendant. Relief must be tailored to protect Mrs. Onassis from the "paparazzo" attack which distinguishes Galella's behavior from that of other photographers; it should not unnecessarily infringe on reasonable efforts to "cover" defendant. Therefore, we modify the court's order to prohibit only (1) any approach within twenty-five (25) feet of defendant or any touching of the person of the defendant Jacqueline Onassis; (2) any blocking of her movement in public places and thoroughfares; (3) any act foreseeably or reasonably calculated to place the life and safety of defendant in jeopardy; and (4) any conduct which would reasonably be foreseen to harass, alarm or frighten the defendant.

Note

An injunction was also issued against intrusive conduct in Kramer v. Downey, 680 S.W.2d 524 (Tex.Civ.App.1984). The plaintiff, a married man, had had an extramarital affair with the defendant. After he ended the brief affair, she "began a pattern of conduct to thrust herself into his presence and otherwise to disrupt his domestic and professional life." *Id.* at 525. The plaintiff was granted an injunction analogous to that used in domestic relations cases to minimize friction between estranged couples. In addition, the plaintiff was awarded $1,000 in actual damages and $25,000 in exemplary damages, of which $13,500 were remitted. For a discussion of the damages recoverable in actions for invasion of privacy, see Ellis, Damages and the Privacy Tort: Sketching a "Legal Profile," 64 Iowa L.Rev. 1111 (1979).

CARSON v. HERE'S JOHNNY PORTABLE TOILETS, INC.

United States Court of Appeals, Sixth Circuit, 1983.
698 F.2d 831.

Before KENNEDY, CIRCUIT JUDGE, BROWN and SWYGERT, SENIOR CIRCUIT JUDGES.

BAILEY BROWN, SENIOR CIRCUIT JUDGE.

This case involves claims of unfair competition and invasion of the right of privacy and the right of publicity arising from appellee's adoption of a phrase generally associated with a popular entertainer.

Appellant, John W. Carson (Carson), is the host and star of "The Tonight Show," a well-known television program broadcast five nights a week by the National Broadcasting Company. Carson also appears as an entertainer in night clubs and theaters around the country. From the time he began hosting "The Tonight Show" in 1962, he has been introduced on the show each night with the phrase "Here's Johnny." This method of introduction was first used for Carson in 1957 when he hosted a daily television program for the American Broadcasting Company. The phrase "Here's Johnny" is generally associated with Carson by a substantial segment of the television viewing public. In 1967, Carson first authorized use of this phrase by an outside business venture, permitting it to be used by a chain of restaurants called "Here's Johnny Restaurants."

Appellant Johnny Carson Apparel, Inc. (Apparel), formed in 1970, manufactures and markets men's clothing to retail stores. Carson, the president of Apparel and owner of 20% of its stock, has licensed Apparel to use his name and picture, which appear on virtually all of Apparel's products and promotional material. Apparel has also used, with Carson's consent, the phrase "Here's Johnny" on labels for clothing and in advertising campaigns. In 1977, Apparel granted a license to Marcy Laboratories to use "Here's Johnny" as the name of a line of men's toiletries. The phrase "Here's Johnny" has never been registered by appellants as a trademark or service mark.

Appellee, Here's Johnny Portable Toilets, Inc., is a Michigan corporation engaged in the business of renting and selling "Here's Johnny" portable toilets. Appellee's founder was aware at the time he formed the corporation that "Here's Johnny" was the introductory slogan for Carson on "The Tonight Show." He indicated that he coupled the phrase with a second one, "The World's Foremost Commodian," to make "a good play on a phrase."

Shortly after appellee went into business in 1976, appellants brought this action alleging unfair competition, trademark infringement under federal and state law, and invasion of privacy and publicity rights. They sought damages and an injunction prohibiting appellee's further use of the phrase "Here's Johnny" as a corporate name or in connection with the sale or rental of its portable toilets.

After a bench trial, the district court issued a memorandum opinion and order, Carson v. Here's Johnny Portable Toilets, Inc., 498 F.Supp. 71 (E.D.Mich.1980), which served as its findings of fact and conclusions of law. The court ordered the dismissal of the appellants' complaint.

* * *

[The court first affirmed the district court's holding that Carson had no valid claim for unfair competition or trademark infringement.]

The appellants also claim that the appellee's use of the phrase "Here's Johnny" violates the common law right of privacy and right of publicity. The confusion in this area of the law requires a brief analysis of the relationship between these two rights.

In an influential article, Dean Prosser delineated four distinct types of the right of privacy: (1) intrusion upon one's seclusion or solitude, (2) public disclosure of embarrassing private facts, (3) publicity which places one in a false light, and (4) appropriation of one's name or likeness for the defendant's advantage. Prosser, Privacy, 48 Calif.L.Rev. 383, 389 (1960). This fourth type has become known as the "right of publicity." Factors Etc., Inc. v. Pro Arts, Inc., 579 F.2d 215, 220 (2d Cir.1978), *cert. denied,* 440 U.S. 908, 99 S.Ct. 1215, 59 L.Ed.2d 455 (1979); *see* Zacchini v. Scripps–Howard Broadcasting Co., 433 U.S. 562, 572, 97 S.Ct. 2849, 2855, 53 L.Ed.2d 965 (1977). Henceforth we will refer to Prosser's last, or fourth, category as the "right of publicity."

Dean Prosser's analysis has been a source of some confusion in the law. His first three types of the right of privacy generally protect the right "to be let alone," while the right of publicity protects the celebrity's pecuniary interest in the commercial exploitation of his identity. *Zacchini, supra,* 433 U.S. at 573, 97 S.Ct. at 2856. *See generally* The Right of Publicity—Protection for Public Figures and Celebrities, 42 Brooklyn L.Rev. 527 (1976). Thus, the right of privacy and the right of publicity protect fundamentally different interests and must be analyzed separately.

We do not believe that Carson's claim that his right of privacy has been invaded is supported by the law or the facts. Apparently, the gist of this claim is that Carson is embarrassed by and considers it odious to be associated with the appellee's product. Clearly, the association does not appeal to Carson's sense of humor. But the facts here presented do not, it appears to us, amount to an invasion of any of the interests protected by the right of privacy. In any event, our disposition of the claim of an invasion of the right of publicity makes it unnecessary for us to accept or reject the claim of an invasion of the right of privacy.

The right of publicity has developed to protect the commercial interest of celebrities in their identities. The theory of the right is that a celebrity's identity can be valuable in the promotion of products, and the celebrity has an interest that may be protected from the unauthorized commercial exploitation of that identity. In Memphis Development Foundation v. Factors Etc., Inc., 616 F.2d 956 (6th Cir.), *cert. denied,* 449 U.S. 953, 101 S.Ct. 358, 66 L.Ed.2d 217 (1980), we stated: "The famous have an exclusive legal right during life to control and profit from the commercial use of their name and personality." *Id.* at 957.

The district court dismissed appellants' claim based on the right of publicity because appellee does not use Carson's name or likeness. 498 F.Supp. at 77. It held that it "would not be prudent to allow recovery for a right of publicity claim which does not more specifically identify Johnny Carson." 498 F.Supp. at 78. We believe that, on the contrary, the district court's conception of the right of publicity is too narrow. The right of publicity, as we have stated, is that a celebrity has a protected pecuniary interest in the commercial exploitation of his identity. If the celebrity's identity is commercially exploited, there has been an invasion of his right whether or not his "name or likeness" is used. Carson's identity may be exploited even if his name, John W. Carson, or his picture is not used.

In Motschenbacher v. R.J. Reynolds Tobacco Co., 498 F.2d 821 (9th Cir.1974), the court held that the unauthorized use of a picture of a distinctive race car of a well known professional race car driver, whose name or likeness were not used, violated his right of publicity.

* * *

In Ali v. Playgirl, Inc., 447 F.Supp. 723 (S.D.N.Y.1978), Muhammad Ali, former heavyweight champion, sued Playgirl magazine under the New York "right of privacy" statute and also alleged a violation of his common law right of publicity. The magazine published a drawing of a nude, black male sitting on a stool in a corner of a boxing ring with hands taped and arms outstretched on the ropes. The district court concluded that Ali's right of publicity was invaded because the drawing sufficiently identified him in spite of the fact that the drawing was captioned "Mystery Man." The district court found that the identification of Ali was made certain because of an accompanying verse that identified the figure as "The Greatest." The district court took judicial notice of the fact that "Ali has regularly claimed that appellation for himself." *Id.* at 727.

In Hirsch v. S.C. Johnson & Son, Inc., 90 Wis.2d 379, 280 N.W.2d 129 (1979), the court held that use by defendant of the name "Crazylegs" on a shaving gel for women violated plaintiff's right of publicity. Plaintiff, Elroy Hirsch, a famous football player, had been known by this nickname.

* * *

In this case, Earl Braxton, president and owner of Here's Johnny Portable Toilets, Inc., admitted that he knew that the phrase "Here's Johnny" had been used for years to introduce Carson. * * * That the "Here's Johnny" name was selected by Braxton because of its identification with Carson was the clear inference from Braxton's testimony irrespective of such admission in the opening statement.

We therefore conclude that, applying the correct legal standards, appellants are entitled to judgment. The proof showed without question that appellee had appropriated Carson's identity in connection with its corporate name and its product.

CORNELIA G. KENNEDY, CIRCUIT JUDGE, dissenting.

I respectfully dissent from that part of the majority's opinion which holds that appellee's use of the phrase "Here's Johnny" violates appellant Johnny Carson's common law right of publicity. While I agree that an individual's identity may be impermissibly exploited, I do not believe that the common law right of publicity may be extended beyond an individual's name, likeness, achievements, identifying characteristics or actual performances, to include phrases or other things which are merely associated with the individual, as is the phrase "Here's Johnny." The majority's extension of the right of publicity to include phrases or other things which are merely associated with the individual permits a popular entertainer or public figure, by associating himself or herself with a common phrase, to remove those words from the public domain.

* * *

[N]either policy nor case law supports the extension of the right of publicity to encompass phrases and other things merely associated with an individual as in this case. I would affirm the judgment of the District Court on this basis as well.

Notes

1. Vanna White, of "Wheel of Fortune" game show fame, sued Samsung Electronics America, Inc. alleging that a Samsung print advertisement depicting a robot attired in a wig and gown standing next to a Wheel of Fortune type game board violated her common law right of publicity under California law. A panel of the Court of Appeals for the Ninth Circuit, on a 2–1 vote, relied on *Carson* in reversing a trial court entry of summary judgment in favor of Samsung. *See* White v. Samsung Electronics America, Inc., 971 F.2d 1395 (9th Cir.1992). A petition for an en banc rehearing was denied. See White v. Samsung Electronics America, Inc., 989 F.2d 1512 (9th Cir.1993). In dissenting from the latter denial, Judge Kozinski, in an opinion joined by two of his colleagues, stated:

> "The ad that spawned this litigation starred a robot dressed in a wig, gown and jewelry reminiscent of Vanna White's hair and dress; the robot was posed next to a Wheel-of-Fortune-like game board. *See* Appendix. The caption read 'Longest-running game show. 2012 A.D.' The gag here, I take it, was that Samsung would still be around when White had been replaced by a robot.
>
> "Perhaps failing to see the humor, White sued, alleging Samsung infringed her right of publicity by 'appropriating' her 'identity.' Under California law, White has the exclusive right to use her name, likeness, signature and voice for commercial purposes. Cal.Civ.Code § 3344(a); Eastwood v. Superior Court, 149 Cal.App.3d 409, 417, 198 Cal.Rptr. 342,

347 (1983). But Samsung didn't use her name, voice or signature, and it certainly didn't use her likeness. The ad just wouldn't have been funny had it depicted White or someone who resembled her—the whole joke was that the game show host(ess) was a robot, not a real person. No one seeing the ad could have thought this was supposed to be White in 2012.

"The district judge quite reasonably held that, because Samsung didn't use White's name, likeness, voice or signature, it didn't violate her right of publicity. 971 F.2d at 1396–97. Not so, says the panel majority: The California right of publicity can't possibly be limited to name and likeness. If it were, the majority reasons, a 'clever advertising strategist' could avoid using White's name or likeness but nevertheless remind people of her with impunity, 'effectively eviscerat[ing]' her rights. To prevent this 'evisceration,' the panel majority holds that the right of publicity must extend beyond name and likeness, to any 'appropriation' of White's 'identity'—anything that 'evoke[s]' her personality. *Id.* at 1398–99.

"But what does 'evisceration' mean in intellectual property law? Intellectual property rights aren't like some constitutional rights, absolute guarantees protected against all kinds of interference, subtle as well as blatant. They cast no penumbras, emit no emanations: The very point of intellectual property laws is that they protect only against certain specific kinds of appropriation. I can't publish unauthorized copies of, say, *Presumed Innocent;* I can't make a movie out of it. But I'm perfectly free to write a book about an idealistic young prosecutor on trial for a crime he didn't commit. So what if I got the idea from *Presumed Innocent?* So what if it reminds readers of the original? Have I 'eviscerated' Scott Turow's intellectual property rights? Certainly not. All creators draw in part on the work of those who came before, referring to it, building on it, poking fun at it; we call this creativity, not piracy.

"The majority isn't, in fact, preventing the 'evisceration' of Vanna White's existing rights; it's creating a new and much broader property right, a right unknown in California law. It's replacing the existing balance between the interests of the celebrity and those of the public by a different balance, one substantially more favorable to the celebrity. Instead of having an exclusive right in her name, likeness, signature or voice, every famous person now has an exclusive right to *anything that reminds the viewer of her.* After all, that's all Samsung did: It used an inanimate object to remind people of White, to 'evoke [her identity].' 971 F.2d at 1399.

"Consider how sweeping this new right is. What is it about the ad that makes people think of White? It's not the robot's wig, clothes or jewelry; there must be ten million blond women (many of them quasi-famous) who wear dresses and jewelry like White's. It's that the robot is posed near the 'Wheel of Fortune' game board. Remove the game board from the ad, and no one would think of Vanna White. *See* Appendix. But once you include the game board, anybody standing beside it—a brunette woman, a man wearing women's clothes, a monkey in a wig and gown—would evoke White's image, precisely the way the robot did. It's the 'Wheel of Fortune' set, not the robot's face or dress or jewelry that evokes White's image. The panel is giving White an exclusive right not in what she looks like or who she is, but in what she does for a living.

"This is entirely the wrong place to strike the balance. Intellectual property rights aren't free: They're imposed at the expense of future creators and of the public at large. Where would we be if Charles Lindbergh had an exclusive right in the concept of a heroic solo aviator? If Arthur Conan Doyle had gotten a copyright in the idea of the detective story, or Albert Einstein had patented the theory of relativity? If every author and celebrity had been given the right to keep people from mocking them or their work? Surely this would have made the world poorer, not richer, culturally as well as economically.

* * *

"The intellectual property right created by the panel here has none of these essential limitations: No fair use exception; no right to parody; no idea-expression dichotomy. It impoverishes the public domain, to the detriment of future creators and the public at large. Instead of well-defined, limited characteristics such as name, likeness or voice, advertisers will now have to cope with vague claims of 'appropriation of identity,' claims often made by people with a wholly exaggerated sense of their own fame and significance. * * * Future Vanna Whites might not get the chance to create their personae, because their employers may fear some celebrity will claim the persona is too similar to her own. The public will be robbed of parodies of celebrities, and our culture will be deprived of the valuable safety valve that parody and mockery create.

"Moreover, consider the moral dimension, about which the panel majority seems to have gotten so exercised. Saying Samsung 'appropriated' something of White's begs the question: *Should* White have the exclusive right to something as broad and amorphous as her 'identity'? Samsung's ad didn't simply copy White's schtick—like all parody, it created something new. True, Samsung did it to make money, but White does whatever she does to make money, too; the majority talks of 'the difference between fun and profit,' 971 F.2d at 1401, but in the entertainment industry fun *is* profit. Why is Vanna White's right to exclusive for-profit use of her persona—a persona that might not even be her own creation, but that of a writer, director or producer—superior to Samsung's right to profit by creating its own inventions? Why should she have such absolute rights to control the conduct of others, unlimited by the idea-expression dichotomy or by the fair use doctrine?

"Finally, I can't see how giving White the power to keep others from evoking her image in the public's mind can be squared with the First Amendment. Where does White get this right to control our thoughts? The majority's creation goes way beyond the protection given a trademark or a copyrighted work, or a person's name or likeness. All those things control one particular way of expressing an idea, one way of referring to an object or a person. But not allowing *any* means of reminding people of someone? That's a speech restriction unparalleled in First Amendment law.

"What's more, I doubt even a name-and-likeness-only right of publicity can stand without a parody exception. The First Amendment isn't just about religion or politics—it's also about protecting the free development of our national culture. Parody, humor, irreverence are all vital components of the marketplace of ideas. The last thing we need, the last thing the

First Amendment will tolerate, is a law that lets public figures keep people from mocking them, or from 'evok[ing]' their images in the mind of the public. 971 F.2d at 1399.

"The majority dismisses the First Amendment issue out of hand because Samsung's ad was commercial speech. *Id.* at 1401 & n. 3. So what? Commercial speech may be less protected by the First Amendment than noncommercial speech, but less protected means protected nonetheless. Central Hudson Gas & Elec. Corp. v. Public Serv. Comm'n, 447 U.S. 557, 100 S.Ct. 2343, 65 L.Ed.2d 341 (1980). And there are very good reasons for this. Commercial speech has a profound effect on our culture and our attitudes. Neutral-seeming ads influence people's social and political attitudes, and themselves arouse political controversy. 'Where's the Beef?' turned from an advertising catchphrase into the only really memorable thing about the 1984 presidential campaign. Four years later, Michael Dukakis called George Bush 'the Joe Isuzu of American politics.'

"In our pop culture, where salesmanship must be entertaining and entertainment must sell, the line between the commercial and noncommercial has not merely blurred; it has disappeared. Is the Samsung parody any different from a parody on Saturday Night Live or in Spy Magazine? Both are equally profit-motivated. Both use a celebrity's identity to sell things—one to sell VCRs, the other to sell advertising. Both mock their subjects. Both try to make people laugh. Both add something, perhaps something worthwhile and memorable, perhaps not, to our culture. Both are things that the people being portrayed might dearly want to suppress.

* * *

"Commercial speech is a significant, valuable part of our national discourse. The Supreme Court has recognized as much, and has insisted that lower courts carefully scrutinize commercial speech restrictions, but the panel totally fails to do this. The panel majority doesn't even purport to apply the *Central Hudson* test, which the Supreme Court devised specifically for determining whether a commercial speech restriction is valid. The majority doesn't ask, as *Central Hudson* requires, whether the speech restriction is justified by a substantial state interest. It doesn't ask whether the restriction directly advances the interest. It doesn't ask whether the restriction is narrowly tailored to the interest. *See id.* at 566, 100 S.Ct. at 2351. These are all things the Supreme Court told us—in no uncertain terms—we must consider; the majority opinion doesn't even mention them.

"Process matters. The Supreme Court didn't set out the *Central Hudson* test for its health. It devised the test because it saw lower courts were giving the First Amendment short shrift when confronted with commercial speech. *See Central Hudson,* 447 U.S. at 561–62, 567–68, 100 S.Ct. at 2348–49, 2352. The *Central Hudson* test was an attempt to constrain lower courts' discretion, to focus judges' thinking on the important issues—how strong the state interest is, how broad the regulation is, whether a narrower regulation would work just as well. If the Court wanted to leave these matters to judges' gut feelings, to nifty lines about 'the difference between fun and profit,' 971 F.2d at 1401, it could have done so with much less effort.

> "Maybe applying the test would have convinced the majority to change its mind; maybe going through the factors would have shown that its rule was too broad, or the reasons for protecting White's 'identity' too tenuous. Maybe not. But we shouldn't thumb our nose at the Supreme Court by just refusing to apply its test."

Id. at 1514–1521.

Suppose Judge Kozinski's First Amendment analysis is correct. Would an action for injunctive relief raise more serious constitutional questions than a suit for damages?

2. If Barbara Reynolds, who looks like Jacqueline Kennedy Onassis, is photographed by Christian Dior–New York, Inc. for purposes of advertising Dior products, may Jacqueline enjoin the use of Barbara's face by bringing a cause of action for appropriation? For an affirmative answer, *see* Onassis v. Christian Dior–New York, Inc., 122 Misc.2d 603, 472 N.Y.S.2d 254 (1984).

3. What if *Time* or *Newsweek* planned to publish an unflattering photograph of Jacqueline Kennedy Onassis (taken by Galella) as part of an election year story on the history of the Kennedy clan? Assuming that Galella snapped the photograph in compliance with the injunction that appears on p. 740, *supra,* could Jacqueline Kennedy Onassis obtain an injunction prohibiting publication of the photograph by the defendant magazine? Consider the next excerpt in answering this question.

NOTE, RIGHT OF PRIVACY—AVAILABILITY OF INJUNCTIVE RELIEF FOR INVASIONS OF PRIVACY, 39 Mo.L.Rev. 647 (1974) *: "The two remaining types of privacy invasions, public disclosure of embarrassing private facts and publicity placing the plaintiff in a false light in the public eye, share the basic set of characteristics that dominate courts' decisions on whether to grant or withhold injunctive relief. Cases arising in this area must involve a publication, in the generic sense, of facts or implications to the public. Both in that respect, and in the nature of the resulting injury, these two categories of invasions bear more than a passing resemblance to the tort of defamation. It is that resemblance which is responsible for much of the confusion and occasional injustice that mar the protection of this aspect of the right of privacy.

"The general rule of equity in such cases is easily stated: There is a heavy presumption against any enjoining of speech or writing. The reasons normally given for denial of injunctions against invasions of privacy by publication are (1) adequacy of legal remedy, (2) equity's limitation to the protection of property rights, and (3) fear of violating constitutional rights of freedom of speech and the press and the right to jury trial.[149] It would seem that in most situations the adequacy of a legal remedy is a fact question, with no prescribed resolution; and the property right-personal right distinction no longer carries the weight in courts of equity that it once did. Accordingly, the substantive issue is whether there are constitutional barriers to enjoining publications which interfere with privacy rights.

"Two principal constitutional arguments are typically raised in opposition to the use of injunctions as a remedy for invasions of privacy by publication:

149. *See* Bertelsman, Injunctions Against Speech and Writing: A Re-evaluation, 59 Ky. L.J. 319 (1971); *cf.* Annot., 47 A.L.R.2d 715 (1956).

the traditional prior restraint doctrine, as delineated in *Near v. Minnesota;* [150] and the special privilege accorded publications about public officials and persons involved in newsworthy events, as developed in *New York Times Co. v. Sullivan* [151] and its progeny. As a strict rule of law, the greater obstacle to the imposition of equitable relief would appear to be presented by the *Near* decision, in which the Supreme Court held impermissible an attempt to prohibit future publications by the defendants in a particular vein on the basis of past publications of allegedly defamatory material. There was no explicit language in the opinion which purported to limit its applicability to the protection of only newsworthy or political items. Consequently, *Near* is frequently cited as an absolute bar to enjoining *any* publication, regardless of content or purpose.

"Alternatively, there is no clear statement of intent to apply the *Near* doctrine to every situation involving a publication of some sort. It is arguable that the doctrine of prior restraint should be a relevant consideration in the general first amendment area only when there is a threat of a *system* of governmentally sanctioned censorship, whereby *all* future communicative publications of a given type are sought to be prohibited or restricted. The *Near* decision itself grew out of such a factual setting; it was the state's restrictive policy which the Court found constitutionally objectionable.[152] No such danger of suppression of ideas is present when a private effort is made to enjoin future publications of personal or embarrassing material not in the public interest. In the private sphere injunctive actions are concerned with *specific* acts or statements which have been made in the past and which alone would be prevented in the future. Broad censorship of a general *type* of statement or publication need not be involved.

"There has yet been no Supreme Court ruling which conclusively rejects such an argument. In *Organization for a Better Austin v. Keefe,* the Court held unconstitutional an injunction against 'passing out pamphlets, leaflets or literature of any kind, and from picketing' by the defendant community organization, which sought to expose and discourage the plaintiff realtor's 'blockbusting' tactics. The plaintiff asserted that past distributions of leaflets had invaded his right of privacy; but the Court emphasized that defendant's leaflets were informational in nature, concerned with a matter of legitimate public interest. 'Respondent thus carries a heavy burden of showing justification for the imposition of such a restraint. He has not met that burden.' The Court did not suggest, however, that the burden would be impossible to meet. In a separate context the Supreme Court has recognized that 'the right of every person "to be let alone" must be placed in the scales with the right of others to communicate.' [153] The mere incantation of the ritual words 'prior restraint' should not force an immediate denial of injunctive relief in true privacy cases without a realistic appraisal of the probable results in each case.

"The second line of cases which limit the availability of injunctive relief in the privacy area begins with *New York Times Co. v. Sullivan.* The Supreme

150. 283 U.S. 697 (1931).

151. 376 U.S. 254 (1964).

152. *Cf.* New York Times Co. v. United States, 403 U.S. 713 (1971). In the Pentagon Papers case, the Supreme Court held the issuance of an injunction against publication, as sought by the *federal government,* to be an invalid prior restraint.

153. Rowan v. United States P.O. Dep't., 397 U.S. 728, 736 (1970).

Court in *New York Times* held that a public official could not recover for defamation absent a showing that the defendant made the statement with knowledge that it was false or with reckless disregard of its truth or falseness. Subsequent decisions extended basically the same test to 'public figures.' A further extension was made, in *Time, Inc. v. Hill,*[154] an action brought under the New York right of privacy statute, by the application of the 'actual malice' test to private individuals temporarily elevated to the status of public figures through their involvement in a newsworthy event of legitimate interest to the public. The Court's policy decision in these cases was based on the social need, underlying the constitutional right to free speech and a free press, for open, unencumbered exchange of ideas and criticism, free from the 'chilling effect' of the fear of possible liability for inadvertent mistakes. The Court in effect applied a balancing test, and found the social interest in maintaining an open forum for speech to outweigh the individual's interest in always being able to have a cause of action for defamation, where the subject matter of the defamation was in the public eye.

"The argument for that approach is less pleasing when it is applied across the board to a privacy action. A factor in the decision to balance against the interests of the defamed person is the idea that the injury to reputation caused by defamatory speech can be cured by more speech; a person's reputation can be restored, in theory, by the opportunity to make a convincing reply to his attacker. But the right of privacy is meant to protect the interest in keeping certain private facts out of the public eye, a completely separate concept from the preservation of reputation. No amount of extra speech can ever restore the solitude and privacy of a person after being exposed as a reformed prostitute[155] or having a detailed account of his private life spread across the pages of a national magazine.[156] But in spite of this 'misapplication of first amendment theory to the law of privacy,'[157] it has emerged as the backbone of the general rule prohibiting injunctive relief for invasions of privacy by publication.

"This is not to say, however, that the rule is an absolute bar to injunctions. There are very real situations in which an individual may be held up to a false light in the public eye, without legitimate reason to be so placed before the public; yet no element of exchange of ideas in the public forum is present. Without the requisite use of speech to pass pertinent information into the public sphere, the doctrine of *New York Times* should not attach. Given such a situation, once a plaintiff establishes a definite injury to his interest in privacy and the inability of legal remedies to restore him to his former position, courts should, and usually will, grant an injunction to protect his privacy. A common example of a nonconstitutionally protected publication which places a person in a false light is the presence of the person's picture in a 'rogue's gallery' after his arrest did not terminate in conviction. There is an increasing willingness among courts to enjoin the continued exhibition of pictures of innocent persons

154. 385 U.S. 374 (1967). Although ostensibly a privacy action, alleging that plaintiffs were placed in a false light in the public eye, the same issue was involved as in the pure defamation cases: the liability for false statements made in the context of an event or person within the public interest.

155. Melvin v. Reid, 112 Cal.App. 285, 297 P. 91 (1931).

156. Sidis v. F–R Pub. Corp., 113 F.2d 806 (2d Cir.), cert. denied, 311 U.S. 711 (1940).

157. Nimmer, The Right to Speak from Times to Time: First Amendment Theory

to the public,[158] or even to compel the return of photographs or fingerprints if no conviction has resulted.[159] But courts will still commonly refuse an injunction as unnecessary if the public won't in fact see the photographs.[160]

* * *

"Where the constitutional considerations implicit in *New York Times* are not present, there is no reason to impose the actual malice test. The argument follows that when those same constitutional considerations are not present, publications which expose an individual to glaring and underserving attention should be subject to injunction, in the same manner that unwarranted physical intrusions may be enjoined. Courts have, on occasion, enjoined some of the more outrageous excursions into plaintiffs' private lives, on the theory that there can be no legitimate public need to know of such matters.[161] There is nothing in the *Time* and *Gertz* decisions to preclude a similar finding today."

Note

Courts have been somewhat more willing to enjoin privacy invasions involving threatened disclosures of private facts than to grant injunctive relief against defamation. Perhaps justification can be found in the protection of privacy afforded by contemporary constitutional law in several contexts. While the constitutional right to privacy only provides protection against the government, the privacy values it represents are reflected in the tort actions for invasion of privacy and provide a substantial counterweight to First Amendment prior restraint concerns. Moreover, as one commentator has observed (in describing the interests of the press):

> "From a number of additional perspectives, * * * the privacy tort of public disclosure is more manageable and less offensive to speech and press concerns than either defamation or many other, presently accepted, limitations on expression. The loss of public information, for example, will be substantially less in the privacy than in the defamation setting because the remedy will involve purging only identifying detail or information; defamation, on the other hand, may require excising facts that are more likely to be the substance of the expression itself rather than merely a dramatization of an idea, and will more generally be linked narrowly to the need for credibility as an element of the impact of an item than is characteristic of public disclosures."

Applied to Libel and Misapplied to Privacy, 56 Calif.L.Rev. 935, 958–61 (1968).

158. *See* Menard v. Mitchell, 430 F.2d 486 (D.C.Cir.1970); T.N.G. v. Superior Court, 4 Cal.3d 767, 484 P.2d 981, 94 Cal. Rptr. 813 (1971).

159. *See* Eddy v. Moore, 5 Wash.App. 334, 487 P.2d 211 (1971) (finding constitutional right of privacy; police must show compelling reason for retention of fingerprints); cf. Henry v. Looney, 65 Misc.2d 759, 317 N.Y.S.2d 848 (1971). *See* McCutcheon, Constitutional Law—Right of Privacy—A Constitutional Right to Return of Fingerprints and Photographs on Acquittal, 37 Mo. L.Rev. 709 (1972).

160. *See* Kolb v. O'Connor, 14 Ill.App.2d 81, 142 N.E.2d 818 (1957); Miller v. Gillespie, 196 Mich. 423, 163 N.W. 22 (1917) (arrest records).

161. *See* Bazemore v. Savannah Hosp., 171 Ga. 257, 155 S.E. 194 (1930) (parents of malformed child stated cause of action to enjoin hospital from distributing pictures of the child); Clavman v. Bernstein, 38 Pa.D. & C. 543 (Phila.Co.1939). [See Commonwealth v. Wiseman, 356 Mass. 251, 249 N.E.2d 610 (1969), cert. denied, 398 U.S. 960, 90 S.Ct. 2165, 26 L.Ed.2d 546 (1970). Discussed in 70 Colum.L.Rev. 359 (1970). Ed.]

Bezanson, Public Disclosures as News: Injunctive Relief and Newsworthiness in Privacy Actions Involving the Press, 64 Iowa L.Rev. 1061, 1080 (1979) *

SCHUTZ v. SCHUTZ

Supreme Court of Florida, 1991.
581 So.2d 1290.

KOGAN, JUSTICE.

We have for review Schutz v. Schutz, 522 So.2d 874 (Fla. 3d DCA 1988), in which the district court affirmed a post-dissolution order which the petitioner contends requires her to affirmatively express feelings and beliefs which she does not have in violation of her first amendment right of free expression. Although we approve the result reached below, our decision is based on a more narrow construction of the challenged order than that urged by the petitioner and accepted by the district court.

A brief summary of the facts leading up to the order at issue is sufficient for our purposes. A final judgment dissolving the six-year marriage of petitioner, Laurel Schutz (mother) and respondent, Richard R. Schutz (father) was entered by the trial court on November 13, 1978. Although custody of the parties' minor children was originally granted to the father, the final judgment was later modified in 1979. Under the modified judgment, the mother was awarded sole custody of the children, and the father was both granted visitation rights and ordered to pay child support.

As noted by the trial court, the ongoing "acrimony and animosity between the adult parties" is clear from the record. The trial court found that in February 1981 the mother moved with the children from Miami to Georgia without notifying the father. After moving, the mother advised the father of their new address and phone number. Although the father and children corresponded after the move, he found an empty house on the three occasions when he traveled to Georgia to visit the children. The father was not notified that after only seven months in Georgia the mother and children had returned to Miami. Four years later in 1985, upon discovering the children's whereabouts, the father visited the children only to find that they "hated, despised, and feared" him due to his failure to support or visit them. After this visit, numerous motions concerning visitation, custody and support were filed by the parties.

After a final hearing on the motions, the trial court found that "the cause of the blind, brainwashed, bigoted belligerence of the children toward the father grew from the soil nurtured, watered and tilled by the mother." The court further found that "the mother breached every duty she owed as the custodial parent to the noncustodial parent of instilling love, respect and feeling in the children for their father." The trial court's findings are supported by substantial competent evidence.

Based on these findings, the trial court ordered the mother "to do everything in her power to create in the minds of [the children] a loving, caring feeling toward the father * * * [and] to convince the children that it is the mother's desire that they see their father and love their father." The court further ordered that breach of the obligation imposed "either in words, actions, demeanor, implication or otherwise" would result in the "severest penalties * * *, including contempt, imprisonment, loss of residential custody or any combination thereof."

Although the district court construed the above quoted portions of the order to require the mother to "instruct the children to love and respect their father," 522 So.2d at 875, it concluded that she was not " 'protected' by the first amendment from a requirement that she fulfil her legal obligation to undo the harm she had already caused." Id.

We begin our analysis by noting our agreement with the district courts of appeal that have found a custodial parent has an affirmative obligation to encourage and nurture the relationship between the child and the noncustodial parent. See Schutz v. Schutz, 522 So.2d at 875; Gardner v. Gardner, 494 So.2d 500, 502 (Fla. 4th DCA 1986), appeal dismissed, 504 So.2d 767 (Fla.1987); In re Adoption of Braithwaite, 409 So.2d 1178, 1180 (Fla. 5th DCA 1982). This duty is owed to both the noncustodial parent and the child. This obligation may be met by encouraging the child to interact with the noncustodial parent, taking good faith measures to ensure that the child visit and otherwise have frequent and continuing contact with the noncustodial parent and refraining from doing anything likely to undermine the relationship naturally fostered by such interaction.

Consistent with this obligation, we read the challenged portion of the order at issue to require nothing more of the mother than a good faith effort to take those measures necessary to restore and promote the frequent and continuing positive interaction (e.g., visitation, phone calls, letters) between the children and their father and to refrain from doing or saying anything likely to defeat that end. There is no requirement that petitioner express opinions that she does not hold, a practice disallowed by the first amendment. Coca–Cola Co. v. Department of Citrus, 406 So.2d 1079, 1087 (Fla.1981) ("the state may never force one to adopt or express a particular opinion"), appeal dismissed, 456 U.S. 1002, 102 S.Ct. 2288, 73 L.Ed.2d 1297 (1982); see Wooley v. Maynard, 430 U.S. 705, 97 S.Ct. 1428, 51 L.Ed.2d 752 (1977) (states' interest insufficient to outweigh individual's first amendment right to avoid being courier of state motto); West Virginia State Board of Education v. Barnette, 319 U.S. 624, 642, 63 S.Ct. 1178, 1187, 87 L.Ed. 1628 (1943) (state cannot "prescribe * * * matters of opinion or force citizens to confess by word or act their faith therein").

Under this construction of the order, any burden on the mother's first amendment rights is merely "incidental."[2] Therefore, the order may be sustained against a first amendment challenge if "it furthers an important or substantial governmental interest * * * and if the incidental restriction

2. The burden is "incidental" because the state interests which are furthered by the order are "unrelated to the suppression of free expression." United States v. O'Brien, 391 U.S. 367, 377, 88 S.Ct. 1673, 1679, 20 L.Ed.2d 672 (1968).

on alleged First Amendment freedoms is no greater than is essential to the furtherance of that interest." United States v. O'Brien, 391 U.S. 367, 377, 88 S.Ct. 1673, 1679, 20 L.Ed.2d 672 (1968). Accordingly, we must balance the mother's right of free expression against the state's parens patriae interest in assuring the well-being of the parties' minor children. However, as with all matters involving custody of minor children, the interests of the father and of the children, which here happen to parallel those of the state, must also factor into the equation.

In this case, the court, acting on behalf of the state as parens patriae, sought to resolve the dispute between the parties in accordance with the best interests of their children by attempting to restore a meaningful relationship between the children and their father by assuring them unhampered, frequent and continuing contact with him. See § 61.13(2)(b)1, Fla.Stat. (1985) (the court shall determine all matters relating to custody of minor children in accordance with the best interests of each child and it is the public policy of this state to assure a minor child frequent and continuing contact with both parents after marriage has been dissolved); id. § 61.13(3)(a) ("frequent and continuing contact with the nonresidential parent" is generally considered to be in best interest of child). In resolving the matter, the court also properly considered the father's constitutionally protected "inherent right" to a meaningful relationship with his children,[3] a personal interest which in this case is consistent with the state's interest in promoting meaningful family relationships. See id. § 61.001(2)(a) (one of the purposes of chapter 61 is to "safeguard meaningful family relationships").

There is no question that the state's interest in restoring a meaningful relationship between the parties' children and their father, thereby promoting the best interests of the children, is at the very least substantial. Likewise, any restriction placed on the mother's freedom of expression is essential to the furtherance of the state's interests because affirmative measures taken by the mother to encourage meaningful interaction between the children and their father would be for naught if she were allowed to contradict those measures by word or deed.

Moreover, as evinced by this record, the mother as custodial parent has the ability to undermine the association to which both the father and the parties' children are entitled. Frazier v. Frazier, 109 Fla. 164, 169, 147 So. 464, 466 (1933) (recognizing a noncustodial parent's "inherent right" to "enjoy the society and association of [his or her] offspring, with reasonable opportunity to impress upon them a father's or a mother's love and affection in their upbringing"); § 61.13(2)(b)1 (minor child is assured frequent and continuing contact with both parents). Therefore, not only is the incidental burden placed on her right of free expression essential to the

3. Frazier v. Frazier, 109 Fla. 164, 172, 147 So. 464, 467 (1933) (noncustodial father is "entitled to have and enjoy [child's] society for a reasonably sufficient length of time each year to enable him to inculcate in her mind a spirit of love, affection and respect for her father," if such is not contrary to best interest of child); see Michael H. v. Gerald D., 491 U.S. 110, 109 S.Ct. 2333, 2342, 105 L.Ed.2d 91 (1989) (parent-child relationship which develops within the unitary family is constitutionally protected); Quilloin v. Walcott, 434 U.S. 246, 254–55, 98 S.Ct. 549, 554–55, 54 L.Ed.2d 511 (1978) ("the relationship between parent and child is constitutionally protected").

furtherance of the state's interests as expressed in chapter 61, but also it is necessary to protect the rights of the children and their father to the meaningful relationship that the order seeks to restore.

Accordingly, construing the order as we do, we find no abuse of discretion by the trial court, nor impermissible burden on the petitioner's first amendment rights. Although we do not approve the district court's construction of that portion of the order under review, nor the analysis employed below, the result reached is approved.[4]

It is so ordered.

SHAW, C.J., and OVERTON, McDONALD and BARKETT, JJ., concur.

GRIMES, J., concurs in part and dissents in part with an opinion.

[Dissent and concurring opinion of GRIMES, J., omitted].

Notes

1. What practicability problems do you see with the district court order in *Schutz*? To what extent does the "narrower" order approved by the Florida Supreme Court obviate those problems? Are you bothered by an order against the mother that prohibits "saying anything" that will defeat the end "of frequent and positive interaction between the children and the father"?

2. Injunctive relief is frequently sought in disputes between former spouses concerning the surname of the children of the marriage. The maxim that equity will protect property, but not personal, rights has been virtually abandoned in the name-change context. Moreover, the universal standard guiding courts in this area is the best interests of the child. *See e.g.,* In re Grimes, 530 Pa. 388, 609 A.2d 158 (1992) and authorities cited therein. *See generally* Annot., 92 A.L.R.3d 1091 (1979). The more controversial issue, however, is whether the father has a special or presumptive interest in the child's use of his surname. Consider, in this regard, the language of the Oklahoma Supreme Court in Tubbs v. Harrison, 620 P.2d 384, 386–87 (Okl.1980):

> "It is generally recognized that a father has a protectible claim in the continued use by the child of the paternal surname in accordance with the usual custom, even though the mother may be the custodial parent. The paternal interest has been alluded to by various terms—a natural right, a fundamental right, a primary or time-honored right, a common-law right, a protectible interest and even a legal right. It has been protected by a variety of procedural devices. While the authorities appear somewhat divided, the better view is that a non-custodial father whose paternal bond remains unsevered has a recognized interest in the child's continued use of his surname.
>
> "Various courts have taken the position that to deprive a child of his father's surname is a serious and far-reaching action. This is so because a name, in addition to furnishing a means of identifying a person, signifies a particular relationship. The paternal surname is said to have a tendency to identify the relationship between a father and his children whether it is bestowed as a matter of law or centuries-old custom. It has been recog-

4. We decline to reach the other issues raised that were summarily rejected by the court below.

nized that change of a child's paternal surname may foster an unnatural barrier between the father and the child and erode a relationship that should be nurtured. Some authorities believe that whenever the parents of a child are divorced and the custody is in the mother, the remaining bond between the father and child is at best tenuous and may be further weakened, if not utterly destroyed, by a change of the minor's surname. Rights in a parental bond have been variously classified as 'essential rights' 'basic civil rights', 'fundamental rights' and 'personal rights' more precious than those of property. The interest comprised within the parental bond is the subject of constitutional protection under both the Due Process and Equal Protection Clauses."

Compare the approach to the foregoing problem adopted by the Supreme Court of California in *In re* Marriage of Schiffman, 28 Cal.3d 640, 643–647, 169 Cal.Rptr. 918, 925, 620 P.2d 579, 583–84 (1980):

"Surnames have been used at least since the Norman Conquest. In early days they were derived from individual reputations, characteristics, occupations, or places of birth and residence and were not passed from generation to generation. The custom of patrilineal succession seems to have been a response to England's medieval social and legal system, which came to vest all rights of ownership and management of marital property in the husband. '[T]he inheritance of property was often contingent upon an heir's retention of the surname associated with that property.' (Note, The Controversy Over Children's Surnames: Familial Autonomy, Equal Protection and the Child's Best Interests, 1979 Utah L.Rev. 303, 305. * * *

"At common law a married woman had little legal identity apart from her husband's. After marriage, custom dictated that the wife give up her surname and assume the husband's. She could no longer contract or litigate in her own name; nor could she manage property or earn money. (Babcock, Freedman, Norton & Ross, Sex Discrimination and the Law (1975) pp. 561–563.) Allowing the husband to determine the surname of their offspring was part of that system, wherein he was sole legal representative of the marriage, its property, and its children.

"Today those bases for patrimonial control of surnames have virtually disappeared. * * *

* * *

"It is argued that rules preferring the paternal surname are justified because they formalize long-standing custom, provide a convenient and certain surname system, make official record-keeping simpler, and minimize confusion and difficulty with public and private bureaucracies. (Utah Note, at pp. 307–308.) Moreover, courts and commentators have pointed out that identification with the paternal surname may give the child a healthy sense of family as well as ethnic and religious identity and also maintain her or his rightful link with an absent or noncustodial father. (*Id.,* at pp. 321–325.)

"None of those concerns mandates retention of the father's preference. Surnames now may be changed in many situations, and the patrilineal rule has hardly been absolute. Our record-keeping and genealogical systems cope well with the truly significant number of individuals and families that already deviate from the biological-patrilineal norm. We see no reason why these systems cannot accommodate to a fairer standard for resolving disputes between biological parents.

"Further, the changing family patterns that are recognized and encouraged by the Uniform Parentage Act support the conclusion that once-accepted assumptions about 'family identity' and 'noncustodial fathers' are losing force. To the extent that understandable concerns do arise in particular cases, cannot they be fully considered in the context of the 'child's best interest' test?

* * *

"We conclude that the rule giving the father, as against the mother, a primary right to have his child bear his surname should be abolished. Henceforth, as in parental custody disputes, the sole consideration when parents contest a surname should be the child's best interest. * * *

"Under the test thus revised the length of time that the child has used a surname is to be considered. * * * If, as here, the time is negligible because the child is very young, other facts may be controlling. For instance, the effect of a name change on preservation of the father-child relationship, the strength of the mother-child relationship, and the identification of the child as part of a family unit are all pertinent. The symbolic role that a surname other than the natural father's may play in easing relations with a new family should be balanced against the importance of maintaining the biological father-child relationship. '[T]he embarrassment or discomfort that a child may experience when he bears a surname different from the rest of his family' should be evaluated."

For the view that the "paternal surname is neither a fundamental right nor a law of nature" and espousing a "dual naming system [which] would protect for each parent the symbolic value of the child's surname," see Comment, Like Father, Like Child: The Rights of Parents In Their Childrens' Names, 70 Va.L.Rev. 1313, 1354 (1984). For a comprehensive discussion of the issues raised in *Tubbs* and *Schiffman, see* MacDougall, The Right of Women to Name Their Children, 3 Law & Inequality 91, 131–59 (1985).

LYON v. IZEN

Appellate Court of Illinois, 1971.
131 Ill.App.2d 594, 268 N.E.2d 436.

In her complaint filed in April 1970 plaintiff alleged that she has been married to Samuel S. Lyon and that they have been successful partners in the practice of medicine; that some time prior to September 1964 the plaintiff and her husband hired defendant as a laboratory technician, and defendant "thereafter began a steady course of conduct toward plaintiff's husband with the deliberate intent of alienating the affection of plaintiff's husband"; that in connection with their medical practice the plaintiff and her husband maintained a complete telephone service; that in February 1969 after repeated calls from defendant at short intervals and unusual hours, plaintiff was obliged to discontinue her telephone service; and that in December 1969 and March 1970 defendant continued making such telephone calls. The complaint also alleges that as a result of defendant's conduct plaintiff and her husband have lived separate and apart since May 1968; that plaintiff and her husband intend to resume living together but that defendant's actions are designed to prevent such a reconciliation. Finally, plaintiff alleges that because of the defendant's behavior, her business is interfered with in that she is unable to maintain adequate phone service, she is irritable and nervous and has lost the consortium, affection, society and services of her husband.

Plaintiff's husband did not join in this complaint nor is he named a defendant.

Based on plaintiff's verified complaint and defendant's motion to dismiss, the trial court, without hearing testimony, denied defendant's motion and ordered the issuance of the temporary injunction.

Defendant contends that the trial court erred in entering the temporary injunction. The courts of our state have long recognized a distinction between property or pecuniary rights and personal rights in applying equity jurisdiction. Injury to property, whether actual or prospective, is the foundation upon which the jurisdiction of a court of equity rests. Sheridan v. Colvin, 78 Ill. 237; People v. McWeeney, 259 Ill. 161, 102 N.E. 233; People v. Prouty, 262 Ill. 218, 104 N.E. 387; and O'Brien v. Matual, 14 Ill.App.2d 173, 144 N.E.2d 446. Plaintiff's complaint does not allege any pecuniary loss but claims that the defendant, by her behavior, has alienated the affection of plaintiff's husband and has thereby deprived plaintiff of his consortium, society and marital services. In Siegall v. Solomon, 19 Ill.2d 145, 149, 166 N.E.2d 5, 7, the court stated: "It is, however, the modern view that rights of a husband in his wife's affections and society are not property within the due process clause. * * *" Therefore, the rights of the plaintiff to her husband's affection and society, which are alleged to have been violated by the defendant in the instant case, are not property rights which can be governed by injunction, and the injunction must therefore be reversed.

Defendant also argues that the temporary injunction is too broad in scope and that the injunctive relief cannot be applied with any practical success by the trial court. In Hoffmann v. Hoffmann, 59 Ill.App.2d 459, 208 N.E.2d 579, the trial court issued an injunction enjoining the defendant from "doing or threatening to do any act calculated to prevent or interfere with a reconciliation of Eugene V. Hoffmann and Elizabeth Hoffmann or other amicable adjustment of this suit." On appeal the trial court's order was reversed and the cause was remanded with directions to vacate the order. As the court stated at page 462, 208 N.E.2d at page 581:

> The injunction is couched in broad general language, in violation of the requirement that an injunction order should set forth the acts enjoined with such particularity that the party enjoined can understand precisely what is forbidden. City of Kankakee v. N.Y.C.R.R. Co., 387 Ill. 109, 55 N.E.2d 87; Evans v. Johnston, 300 Ill.App. 78, 20 N.E.2d 841; 28 Am.Jur., Injunctions, § 293 (1959).

In Snedaker v. King, 111 Ohio St. 225, 145 N.E. 15, the plaintiff-wife also sought an injunction to restrain defendant from seeing, speaking, communicating or associating with plaintiff's husband at plaintiff's home or elsewhere, so as to prevent plaintiff's husband from giving to plaintiff his love, affection, companionship, conjugal relation or support. The trial court ordered that an injunction issue against the defendant. However, on appeal the court held that the injunction decree should have been denied. As the court stated at page 228, 145 N.E. at pages 16–17:

> The decree in this case is an extreme instance of government by injunction. It attempts to govern, control, and direct personal relations and domestic affairs. Among other restrictions placed upon the defendant by this decree is that of remaining away from any place where plaintiff's husband may be, and from interfering with plaintiff's efforts to communicate with her husband, and with her efforts to regain his love, esteem, support, and conjugal relation.
>
> * * *
>
> Such extension of the jurisdiction of equity to regulate and control domestic relations, in addition to the legal and statutory remedies already provided, in our opinion is not supported by authority, warranted by sound reason, or in the interest of good morals or public policy. The opening of such a wide field for injunctive process, enforceable only by contempt proceedings, the difficulty if not impossibility of such enforcement, and the very doubtful beneficial results to be obtained thereby, warrant the denial of such a decree in this case, and require a modification of the judgment in that respect.

In the instant case we believe that the temporary injunction order is too broad in scope and that enforcement of this injunction by the court would be extremely difficult and impractical.

Defendant also contends (1) that a court of equity will not grant injunctive relief where the plaintiff has an adequate remedy at law and (2) that plaintiff has pleaded conclusions and not facts in her complaint. However, it is unnecessary to discuss these contentions based on our prior findings.

The order of the trial court granting the issuance of the temporary injunction is reversed; the order denying defendant's motion to dismiss the complaint is reversed and the cause remanded for further proceedings not inconsistent with this opinion.

Reversed and remanded with directions.

ENGLISH, P.J., and LORENZ, J., concur.

Notes

1. *Lyons* illustrates that an occasional court still purports to rely on the "personal-property right" distinction in denying injunctive relief. Is this wise? What do you think was the court's primary reason for reversing the trial court's grant of an injunction?

2. "Equitable relief by way of injunction against the defendants for interference with marital relations is not often sought and is probably impractical. * * * [Most] courts have generally denied such injunctions as a serious infringement of personal freedom of the other spouse and beyond the appropri-

ate reach of equity." W. Keeton, D. Dobbs, R. Keeton, D. Owen, Prosser & Keeton on the Law of Torts 923–24 (5th ed. 1984).

3. At least half of the states have abolished or seriously limited damage actions for alienation of affections by statute. *Id.* at 930. Should these statutes have any effect on injunctive relief in such jurisdictions? Should they cut in favor of equitable relief on the ground that there is no longer an adequate legal remedy? Or should they cast doubt on whether an underlying right exists for equity to protect? *See* Henley v. Rockett, 243 Ala. 172, 8 So.2d 852 (1942) (injunctive relief available notwithstanding statute); Devine v. Devine, 20 N.J.Super. 522, 90 A.2d 126 (1952) ("The plaintiff has no adequate remedy at law since the enactment of the 'Heart Balm' statute. * * * The statute is to be strictly construed and not stretched to cover more than its plain language would justify; and there is nothing in the statute that would prohibit a suit for injunctive relief as distinguished from a suit for money damages.")

For further examples of similar cases, see Logan v. Davidson, 282 Ala. 327, 211 So.2d 461 (1968) (wife's request for injunction to enjoin another woman from alienating husband's affections granted, affirmed). Latham v. Karger, 267 Ala. 433, 103 So.2d 336 (1958) (same); Kilgrow v. Kilgrow, 268 Ala. 475, 107 So.2d 885 (1958) (injunction to restrain wife from interfering with husband's attempt to send child to school of husband's faith, reversed); White v. Thomson, 324 Mass. 140, 85 N.E.2d 246 (1949) (injunctive relief against alienation of affections will not be granted in Massachusetts); Hadley v. Hadley, 323 Mich. 555, 36 N.W.2d 144 (1949) (injunction against wife associating with other men, denied); Rose v. Aaron, 345 Mich. 613, 76 N.W.2d 829 (1956) (error to enjoin other man from receiving gifts from, associating with or visiting plaintiff's wife); Diamond v. Diamond, 372 Pa. 562, 94 A.2d 569 (1953) (dismissal of wife's bill to enjoin husband from committing adultery with named person, affirmed).

See also Bennett, Injunctive Protection of Personal Interests—A Factual Approach, 1 La.L.Rev. 665 (1939); Moreland, Injunctive Control of Family Relations, 18 Ky.L.J. 207 (1930); Developments in the Law—Injunctions, 78 Harv.L.Rev. 994, 1006–1007 (1965).

MARQUETTE v. MARQUETTE

Court of Appeals of Oklahoma, 1984.
686 P.2d 990.

REYNOLDS, JUDGE:

Jeff L. Marquette appeals trial court's orders of October 13, 1982, and November 19, 1982, restraining him from abusing, injuring, threatening or harassing his ex-wife, Julie M. Marquette. Trial court entered both orders under the Protection from Domestic Abuse Act, 22 O.S.Supp.1983 § 60 *et seq.*

Appellant and Appellee were divorced on September 10, 1982. Appellee was given custody of the parties' two young sons. On October 13, 1982, Appellee filed a petition for [a] protective order.[2] She gave the following reasons for requesting the protective order:

2. 22 O.S.Supp.1983 § 60.2 provides a sample petition. Tulsa County used this sample and provided it to Appellee. This form simplified the petitioning process since,

> continued harassment & assault following the divorce granted Sept. 10, 1982. Throws children's clothes, shoes, toys, & children at me. Verbal threats are made to me in front of the children. I am afraid of being harmed as I have in the past. And afraid of emotional damage these scenes are doing to my children.

Appellee requested the court to enter an emergency ex parte order.[3] The court granted her request, and set a show cause hearing on November 1, 1982. The ex parte order prohibited Appellant from abusing, injuring, visiting, communicating with, or threatening Appellee. It also instructed Appellant not to abuse or injure the minor children.

Appellant filed a demurrer and motion to dismiss on October 26, 1982. The hearing was passed by agreement from November 1 to November 3, 1982. On November 3, 1982, trial court modified the ex parte order to provide Appellant with specific visitation hours. Full hearing was again continued until November 19, 1982. * * * Following trial on November 19, 1982, trial court entered a mutual protective order.[5]

* * *

We address the justiciability of this appeal as an initial matter. The ex parte order of October 13, 1982, expired at the trial on November 19, 1982. The protective order issued after the trial expired at the end of one year. * * * The expiration of the orders renders the controversy moot, and therefore, nonjusticiable, unless it comes within an exception to the mootness doctrine.

Oklahoma recognizes two exceptions to the mootness doctrine: (1) when the appeal presents a question of broad public interest, and (2) when the challenged event is "capable of repetition yet evading review."

Domestic violence has wide-ranging ramifications [9] and can certainly be characterized as an issue of broad public interest. Further, under the ex

for the most part, Appellee was able to check the appropriate box.

3. 22 O.S.Supp.1983 § 60.2(B) (Petition for Protective Order):

5. (Check A or B)

(A) ☐ The victim is in immediate and present danger of abuse from the defendant and an emergency ex parte order is necessary to protect the victim from serious harm. The plaintiff requests the following relief in the emergency ex parte order: (check one or more)

☐ Order the defendant not to abuse or injure the victim.

☐ order the defendant not to visit, assault, molest, harass or otherwise interfere with the victim.

☐ order the defendant not to threaten the victim.

☐ order the defendant to leave the residence located at ______ on or before ______

☐ ____________________

(describe other relief that plaintiff requests)

(B) ☐ The plaintiff does not request an emergency ex parte order.

5. The Act does not specifically provide for such an order, nor was it requested by Appellant at trial. However, since Appellee does not raise the question of its validity as to her, we will not consider it on appeal.

9. Taub, Ex Parte Proceedings in Domestic Violence Situations: Alternative Frameworks for Constitutional Scrutiny, 9 Hofstra L.Rev. 95 (1980); Note, The Battered Wife's Dilemma: To Kill or Be Killed, 32 Hastings L.J. 895 (1980).

parte order of October 13, 1982, Appellant was effectively denied his parental visitation since he could not communicate with his ex-wife, the custodial parent. This denial is likely to reoccur in future cases, yet evade review under ex parte orders. We find that both exceptions to the mootness doctrine can be invoked on Appellant's behalf.

* * *

Appellant urges the Act is criminal in nature, and he was entitled to the protections allowed in criminal proceedings. * * *

In the absence of any legislative history, it is reasonable to assume the passage of the Act is a result of increased public awareness regarding the serious nature of domestic violence.[11] The Legislature has attempted to remedy this problem by providing immediate, as well as long-range, protection for the victims of domestic abuse.

We find the remedy provided is civil, not criminal, in nature for the following reasons. "A criminal action is one prosecuted by the State as a party, against a person charged with a public offense, for the punishment thereof." "Every other action is a civil action." The Act provides that the complaining party be the victim of the abuse, unless the victim is a minor or incompetent. In that event, an adult household member may petition on behalf of the minor or incompetent. The State is not a party to this action, and the defendant is not charged with a public offense. * * *

The only "criminal" aspect of the Act is the penalty provision contained in § 60.6:

> Any person who has been served with an ex parte or final protective order and is in violation of such protective order, *upon conviction* shall be guilty of a misdemeanor and shall be punished by a fine of not more than One Thousand Dollars ($1,000.00) or by a jail term of not more than one (1) year, or both. Ex parte and final protective orders shall include notice of these penalties. [Emphasis added.]

This penalty provision does not overshadow the substance of the Act. On the whole, this Act merely creates an additional framework through which the court may exercise its long recognized equitable power to grant restraining and injunctive orders in extraordinary circumstances. * * * Trial court did not err when it used the "preponderance of the evidence" test at the November 19 trial.

Appellant contends [the] trial court erred by overruling his demurrer to Appellee's petition for protective order. He alleges the language of the petition does not rise to the level of domestic abuse as defined by statute. The Act defines domestic abuse as: "a. causing or attempting to cause serious physical harm, or b. threatening another with imminent serious physical harm * * *." 22 O.S.Supp.1983 § 60.1. * * * Appellee's petition alleged harassment, assault, throwing children, verbal threats, and fear of harm. "Serious bodily injury" has been defined as that which would "give rise to apprehension of danger to life, to health or limbs." Hall v. State,

11. *See, e.g.*, Note, Restraining Order Legislation For Battered Women: A Reassessment, 16 U.S.F.L.Rev. 703 (1982); Comment, Domestic Relations: Post-Marital Squabbles and the Harassing Ex-Spouse, 28 Ok.L.Rev. 404 (1975); *See* note 9, *supra.*

309 P.2d 1096 (Okl.Crim.1957). We will not give a "blood and guts" interpretation to the requirement of "serious physical harm". We find the language of the petition was sufficient to withstand a general demurrer.

* * *

Appellant's final assertion of error alleges denial of due process under the October 13 ex parte order. The due process guarantee is intended to protect an individual against arbitrary acts of the government. Appellant was effectively denied his right to visit his children from October 13 until November 3. This occurred because he could not communicate with his ex-wife, the custodial parent.

This interference with Appellant's visitation rights is significant. Appellant alleges this right has been violated without procedural due process. We do not take the interference with parental visitation lightly, but we note that such interference can only occur for a total of ten days prior to the deprived parent receiving a full hearing. This infringement must be balanced against the government's interest in issuing the order and the risk of erroneous deprivation under existing procedures.[23]

The State's interest in providing this protection to the victims of domestic abuse is apparent. The legislation promotes the health, safety and general welfare of its citizens. Domestic violence has become a problem of considerable magnitude.

> The consequences of allowing battering to continue can be serious. Experts believe that domestic violence is likely to escalate in cyclical fashion, at times resulting in the woman's death. Women caught in the cycle of abuse may, in the process of defending themselves, kill their assailant. Children exposed to such patterns of violence not only may suffer immediate emotional distress, but also may reproduce their parents' behavior patterns as adults.[24]

Temporary restraining orders issued without notice have survived constitutional attack. *See, e.g.* United States v. Spilotro, 680 F.2d 612 (9th Cir.1982); State v. B Bar Enterprises, Inc., 133 Ariz. 99, 649 P.2d 978 (Ariz.1982). The Act provides the following procedures prior to issuance of the ex parte order. An ex parte order is not issued unless good cause is shown by petitioner at a hearing held by the court. Only then may the court issue such order as is necessary to protect the victim from immediate and present danger of domestic abuse. Under the 1983 version of the Act, a hearing must be held within ten days after the petition is filed regardless of whether an ex parte order has been issued. Although there is always some chance of erroneous deprivation, the trial court will have opportunity to judge the credibility of the petitioner prior to issuing the order. The court may be able to see first hand the evidence of domestic violence.

23. Mathews v. Eldridge, 424 U.S. 319, 96 S.Ct. 893, 47 L.Ed.2d 18 (1976); State *ex rel.* Williams v. Marsh, [626 S.W.2d 223 (Mo. 1982) (en banc)]; *See also* Taub, *supra* note 9 at 107.

24. Taub, *supra,* note 9, p. 96 (footnotes omitted); *see also* note 11 *supra.*

Carefully considering all the above factors, we find the procedural safeguards employed under the Act prior to the issuance of an ex parte order, coupled with the state's interest in securing immediate protection for abused victims, of sufficient weight to meet Appellant's due process challenge.

* * *

We hold the trial court properly exercised its authority under the Act.

Affirmed.

Notes

1. Many courts issue injunctions against acts of spousal violence, harassment and molestation in connection with divorce and related proceedings. *See e.g.,* Carpenter v. Carpenter, 252 So.2d 591 (Fla.App.1971); Keller v. Keller, 158 N.W.2d 694 (N.D.1968); *Contra* Kapneck v. Kapneck, 31 Md.App. 410, 356 A.2d 572 (1976) (divorce court lacks "equitable jurisdiction" to issue such orders). Moreover, practicability concerns are rarely an overt consideration in such cases.

2. During the 1970's, "forty-nine states and the District of Columbia * * * enacted new legislation to provide legal remedies to victims of domestic violence." Lerman, A Model State Act: Remedies for Domestic Abuse, 21 Harv.J. on Legis. 61, 61–62 & n. 1 (1984) (comprehensive list of new laws). *See also* Comment, Spouse Abuse: Proposal For a New Rule of Thumb, 17 U.Rich.L.Rev. 633, 645 (1983). *See, e.g.,* West's Ann.Cal.Civ.Code § 4359; Smith Hurd Ann.Ill.Stat. ch. 69, § 25; Minn.Stat.Ann. § 518B.01; Mo.Rev. Stat. § 455.010 *et seq.;* Or.Rev.Stat. 107.700; Purdon's Pa.Stat. Tit. 35 § 10182. For an excellent analysis of the Pennsylvania and California statutes, see Comment, Restraining Order Legislation for Battered Women: A Reassessment, 16 U.S.F.L.Rev. 703 (1982). *See generally* Fain, Conjugal Violence: Legal and Psychological Remedies, 32 Syracuse L.Rev. 497 (1981); Gottlieb & Johnson, Reform in Kansas Domestic Violence Legislation, 31 U.Kan.L.Rev. 527 (1983) (discussing empirical evidence regarding implementation of reform); Lerman, Protection of Battered Women: A Survey of State Legislation, 6 Women's Rts. L.Rep. 27 (1980); Waits, The Criminal Justice System's Response to Battering: Understanding the Problem, Forging the Solutions, 60 Wash.L.Rev. 267 (1985) (describing the battering relationship, its impact on both parties to the relationship, and its effect on children); Note, Domestic Violence: Legislative and Judicial Remedies, 2 Harv. Women's L.J. 167 (1979); Note, Duties and Enforcement Mechanisms for the Rights of Battered Women, 16 Suffolk U.L.Rev. 937 (1982).

3. In *Marquette,* a prior divorce decree had already awarded custody of the couple's children to their mother. Thus, the ex parte order interfered only with the father's visitation rights. Suppose, however, divorce has not yet occurred and there has been no prior adjudication as to custody. Domestic abuse acts commonly authorize the use of ex parte orders to deprive one parent of temporary child custody. Do such orders raise more serious due process concerns? Consider the analysis of the Minnesota Supreme Court in Baker v. Baker, 494 N.W.2d 282 (Minn.1992):

> "The requirements of due process are flexible and call for such procedural protections as the particular situation demands. The main

factors to consider are: (1) the private interests to be affected by the official action; (2) the risk of erroneous deprivation of these interests and the probable value of additional safeguards; and (3) the government interests involved. Mathews v. Eldridge, 424 U.S. 319, 335, 96 S.Ct. 893, 903, 47 L.Ed.2d 18 (1976).

"There are two potentially protected 'private interests' at issue here: (1) the exclusion from a shared dwelling; (2) the liberty interest of a parent in custody of his or her children. In addition to restraining the respondent from committing acts of domestic abuse, the temporary order may exclude the respondent from a shared dwelling, or from the residence or place of employment of the petitioner. Minn.Stat. § 518B.01, subd. 7(a).

"The *ex parte* order in this case also granted temporary custody of the infant to the petitioner, with visitation to the respondent. While both parents have strong interests in the custody and enjoyment of their child, a parent's love and affection must yield to considerations of the child's welfare. State v. Whaley, 246 Minn. 535, 75 N.W.2d 786, 791 (1956). * * * [T]he Domestic Abuse Act recognizes the preeminence of the child's welfare by allowing an award of temporary custody only 'on a basis which gives primary consideration to the safety of the victim or the children.' Minn.Stat. § 518B.01, subd. 6(a)(3).

"The second *Mathews* factor goes to the risk of erroneous deprivation of the private interests and the probable value of additional safeguards. Mathews, 424 U.S. at 335, 96 S.Ct. at 903. We conclude that the Domestic Abuse Act provides extensive procedural safeguards which guard against such error. The *ex parte* order must be based upon an application for an order for protection supported by a sworn affidavit alleging specific facts and circumstances of past abuse. Minn.Stat. § 518B.01, subd. 4(b). Only judges or referees may issue such orders. *Id.* at subd. 3. The *ex parte* order is very short term, *id.* at subd. 7(b) and the respondent must be given notice of the full hearing. *Id.* at subd. 5(a). The only additional procedural safeguard possible would be a requirement of notice to the respondent before an order was granted. This would result in unnecessary and possibly dangerous time delays.

"Finally, we must consider the third *Mathews* factor, the government interests involved. While at first blush, it may seem that the interest at issue here is a purely private one, that is, individual freedom from further domestic assault, it is also true that the general public has an extraordinary interest in a society free from violence, especially where vulnerable persons are at risk. This is the reason that criminal prosecutions are brought in the name of the state, for example.

"In another key case, Fuentes v. Shevin, 407 U.S. 67, 92 S.Ct. 1983, 32 L.Ed.2d 556 (1972), the Supreme Court discussed the characteristics of the 'extraordinary situations' which justify postponing notice and opportunity for hearing. First, the deprivation of the property interest must be 'directly necessary to secure an important governmental or general public interest.' *Id.* at 91, 92 S.Ct. at 2000. Second, there must be 'a special need for very prompt action.' *Id.* Third, the state must keep strict control over the process by limiting its authorization to a government official acting under 'the standards of a narrowly drawn statute.' *Id.*

"We believe that the domestic abuse situation shares these characteristics with other situations where *ex parte* relief has been allowed. First, it is not necessary to recite again the state's strong interest in preventing violence in a domestic setting. Second, inasmuch as the statute requires an allegation of an 'immediate and present danger of domestic abuse,' Minn.Stat. § 518B.01, subd. 7(a), there can be no argument that a special need for prompt action is shown. Finally, the statute is very narrowly drawn and, of course, compliance with its terms must be determined by a district court judge or other judicial officer before *ex parte* relief is available.

"After reviewing the application of both the general *Mathews* factors and the more specific *Fuentes* factors to these facts, we conclude that there is no due process violation in the granting of *ex parte* relief pursuant to the Domestic Abuse Act."

Other courts have been equally unsympathetic to due process challenges to ex parte restraining orders in the domestic abuse context. *See e.g.,* Sanders v. Shephard, 185 Ill.App.3d 719, 133 Ill.Dec. 712, 541 N.E.2d 1150 (1989); State ex rel. Williams v. Marsh, 626 S.W.2d 223 (Mo.1982); Grant v. Wright, 222 N.J.Super. 191, 536 A.2d 319 (App.Div.1988); Schramek v. Bohren, 145 Wis.2d 695, 429 N.W.2d 501 (App.1988); Blazel v. Bradley, 698 F.Supp. 756 (W.D.Wis. 1988).

WARFIELD v. PENINSULA GOLF & COUNTRY CLUB

California Court of Appeal, First District, 1989.
214 Cal.App.3d 646, 262 Cal.Rptr. 890.

OPINION

RACANELLI, P.J.—In this case concerning sexual discrimination in a country club membership, we review the propriety of the trial court's dismissal of plaintiff's first amended complaint after sustaining defendants' demurrer without leave to amend.

Procedural Background

In 1970, Richard and Mary Ann Warfield, as husband and wife, acquired a regular family membership in the Peninsula Golf and Country Club, a nonprofit, privately owned and operated, social and recreational club. The initial membership payment and regular monthly fees were paid with community property funds. Mary Ann and her children regularly used the club facilities and participated in its social events.

In February 1981, Richard and Mary Ann obtained an interlocutory decree of dissolution of marriage; the property settlement agreement awarded Mary Ann the family membership at Peninsula Golf and Country Club.

In May 1981, the board of directors of the club, upon ascertaining that Richard no longer wished to maintain his membership, voted to terminate the Warfield membership under section 7.5 of the bylaws, whereby a regular family membership may be issued to an adult male only. Thereafter, the board (as required under the bylaws) tendered a redemption fee check to Mary Ann, which she refused to accept.

On November 2, 1981, Mary Ann filed a complaint for damages and injunctive relief against Peninsula Golf and Country Club and its board of directors as defendants. The multicount complaint alleged violations of Civil Code section 51 (Unruh Civil Rights Act); violations of * * * the common law right to fair procedure; discrimination based upon sex and a request for a preliminary and permanent injunction.

In January 1982, the trial court issued a preliminary injunction enjoining defendant from terminating plaintiff's rights and privileges in the club. In February 1982, the court sustained defendant's demurrer with leave to amend as to all causes of action except those concerning due process, fair procedure and declaratory relief.

* * *

The trial court sustained defendant's second demurrer without leave to amend as to all counts, and judgment of dismissal was entered on May 10, 1982. Following denial of plaintiff's postjudgment motions, plaintiff appealed from the judgment entered.

Discussion

* * *

II.

Applicability of Unruh Civil Rights Act

Plaintiff's major contention on appeal is that the trial court erred in sustaining the demurrer to the causes of action for violation of the Unruh Civil Rights Act (Act) on the ground that defendant was not a business establishment.

Civil Code section 51, as amended, prohibits sexual discrimination by any "business establishment." The statute provides in pertinent part: "All persons within the jurisdiction of this state are free and equal, and no matter what their sex, race, color, religion, ancestry, national origin, or blindness or other physical disability are entitled to the full and equal accommodations, advantages, facilities, privileges, or services in all business establishments of every kind whatsoever."

The Act has been construed as "this state's bulwark against arbitrary discrimination in places of public accommodation" and without which "facilities in private ownership, but otherwise open to the public, would be free under state law to exclude people for invidious reasons like sex, religion, age, and even race." (*Isbister v. Boys' Club of Santa Cruz, Inc.* (1985) 40 Cal.3d 72, 75 [219 Cal.Rptr. 150, 707 P.2d 212].)

The core question whether defendant is a "business establishment" within the meaning of the Act does not lend itself to a formula-like solution under the more traditional public-private classification scheme.

* * *

In its initial construction of the statute, as amended in 1959, the Supreme Court declared "that the term 'business establishments' was used in the broadest sense reasonably possible." (*Burks v. Poppy Construction*

Co. (1962) 57 Cal.2d 463, 468 [20 Cal.Rptr. 609, 370 P.2d 313]; accord *Isbister v. Boys' Club of Santa Cruz, Inc., supra,* 40 Cal.3d at p. 76.) More recently, the court reasoned that the broadened scope of business establishments in the amended version of the statute indicated a legislative intent "to include therein all formerly specified private and public groups or organizations that may reasonably be found to constitute 'business establishments of every type whatsoever.'" The court then proceeded to explain: "Although our cases so far have all dealt with profit-making entities, we see no reason to insist that profit-seeking be a *sine qua non* for coverage under the act. Nothing in the language or history of its enactment calls for excluding an organization from its scope simply because it is nonprofit. [Citation.]" (*O'Connor v. Village Green Owners Assn.* (1983) 33 Cal.3d 790, 795–796 [191 Cal.Rptr. 320, 662 P.2d 427].)

Thus, defendant's two-pronged argument for automatic exclusion as a business establishment under the Act (nonprofit status and elimination of "private groups" from the legislation) is wholly unpersuasive.

Accepting plaintiff's allegations at face value, defendant would appear to possess certain businesslike characteristics as discussed in several recent California cases. (See, e.g., *Isbister v. Boys' Club of Santa Cruz, Inc., supra,* 40 Cal.3d 72; *Rotary Club of Duarte v. Board of Directors* (1986) 178 Cal.App.3d 1035 [224 Cal.Rptr. 213], affd. *sub nom. Bd. of Dirs. of Rotary Int'l v. Rotary Club* (1987) 481 U.S. 537 [95 L.Ed.2d 474, 107 S.Ct. 1940] [upholding application of goods and services criteria to determine business establishment]; *Curran v. Mount Diablo Council of the Boy Scouts* (1983) 147 Cal.App.3d 712 [195 Cal.Rptr. 325, 38 A.L.R.4th 607], app. dism. (1984) 468 U.S. 1205 [82 L.Ed.2d 873, 104 S.Ct. 3574].) [5]

Plaintiff alleged, inter alia, that defendant operates a restaurant and bar and recreational facilities for its members and their guests and also leases its facilities to others. The furnishing of goods and services to members was considered in *Curran* and *Rotary Club* to be essential elements defining a business establishment. (See also dis. opn. of Mosk, J., in *O'Connor v. Village Green Owners Assn., supra,* 33 Cal.3d at p. 802.)

Moreover, the allegations concerning defendant's operation of a bar and restaurant and recreational facilities (presumably, a golf course, tennis courts, swimming pool and "pro" shops) give rise to an implication that some members will use the facilities for purposes of business meetings or entertainment with fees and related expenses paid or reimbursed by their employer.

5. In *Isbister,* the Supreme Court held that the Boys' Club of Santa Cruz was a business establishment covered by the Act in that it was a place of public accommodation with recreational facilities open to the community generally (with females excepted) and that such facilities were the club's principal activity and reason for existence. (40 Cal.3d 72.)

In *Rotary Club,* the Second District Court of Appeal held that both Rotary International (a nonprofit, worldwide organization) and the local club were business establishments within the meaning of the Act. The court concluded that the club was not private and was engaged in providing goods, services and facilities. (178 Cal.App.3d 1035.)

In *Curran,* a judgment of dismissal following sustaining of a demurrer was reversed, based in part on a determination that plaintiff's allegations reflected that defendant Boy Scouts had certain "businesslike attributes." (147 Cal.App.3d 712.)

In addition, the court in *Rotary Club* recognized that there are "substantial business benefits" gained by belonging to an organization such as Rotary which are to be considered "when deciding whether an organization is bound by the Unruh Act." (*Rotary Club of Duarte v. Board of Directors, supra,* 178 Cal.App.3d at p. 1055.)

Thus, plaintiff's pleaded allegations, if proved, could qualify defendant club as a "business establishment" within the broad interpretation of that clause under the Act.

III.

Interference with Protected Associational Rights of Private Clubs

Defendant vigorously argues, however, that not only is it exempted from the Act by reason of its "private" club status, but that attempted enforcement against it will impermissibly interfere with its right to discriminate in associations as guaranteed under the First Amendment as earlier interpreted by the United States Supreme Court. (*Griswold v. Connecticut* (1965) 381 U.S. 479 [14 L.Ed.2d 510, 85 S.Ct. 1678], citing *Bell v. Maryland* (1964) 378 U.S. 226 [12 L.Ed.2d 822, 84 S.Ct. 1814].)

However, as defendant candidly acknowledges, the right to associational privacy is not without qualification (*Evans v. Newton* (1966) 382 U.S. 296 [15 L.Ed.2d 373, 86 S.Ct. 486]) and is subject to a balancing process. "The right to associate for expressive purposes is not, however, absolute. Infringements on that right may be justified by regulations adopted to serve compelling state interests, unrelated to the suppression of ideas, that cannot be achieved through means significantly less restrictive of associational freedoms." (*Roberts v. United States Jaycees* (1984) 468 U.S. 609, 623 [82 L.Ed.2d 462, 475, 104 S.Ct. 3244]; accord *Bd. of Dirs. of Rotary Int'l v. Rotary Club, supra,* 481 U.S. at p. 549 [95 L.Ed.2d at pp. 486–487, 107 S.Ct. at p. 1947] and *New York State Club Ass'n v. City of New York* (1988) 487 U.S. 1, 14, fn. 5 [101 L.Ed.2d 1, 17, 108 S.Ct. 2225, 2235].)

As noted by the *Rotary Club* court: "The ill effects of discrimination against the individual as well as on society are well recognized. Our nation's Supreme Court in *Roberts v. United States Jaycees* (1984) 468 U.S. 609 [82 L.Ed.2d 462, 104 S.Ct. 3244], succinctly stated that it 'has frequently noted that discrimination based on archaic and overbroad assumptions about the relative needs and capacities of the sexes forces individuals to labor under stereotypical notions that often bear no relationship to their actual abilities. It thereby both deprives persons of their individual dignity and denies society the benefits of wide participation in political, economic, and cultural life.' (*Id.,* at p. 625 [82 L.Ed.2d at p. 476].)" (*Rotary Club of Duarte v. Board of Directors, supra,* 178 Cal.App.3d at p. 1062.)

In *Roberts,* the Supreme Court described two types of protected associational rights: intimate (family) relations and expressive. (*Roberts v. United States Jaycees, supra,* 468 U.S. at pp. 617–623 [82 L.Ed.2d at pp. 470–475].) In determining that Minnesota's requirement that the Jaycees' organization admit women as regular members did not abridge the members' expressive associational rights, the court at the same time expressed its concern over any laws that would operate as direct restraints on freedom of expression. (*Id.,* at p. 628 [82 L.Ed.2d at p. 478].) A similar two-part framework was adopted in assessing First Amendment claims raised in *Rotary International* and the facial attack on the New York City ordinance prohibiting discrimination by private clubs meeting the size and services criteria specified under the local law. In *Rotary International,* the court held that the application of business establishment criteria under the Act to Rotary International and the Duarte, California Rotary Club does not violate the members' First Amendment associational rights. (*Bd. of Dirs. of Rotary Int'l v. Rotary Club, supra,* 481 U.S. at p. 548 [95 L.Ed.2d at p. 486, 107 S.Ct. at p. 1948].)

The associational rights defendant asserts are subject to the same kind of factual inquiry applicable to a determination of other defendants' privacy status. "Whether the 'zone of privacy' established by the First Amendment extends to a particular club or entity requires a careful inquiry into the objective characteristics of the particular relationships at issue. [Citations.]" (*Bd. of Dirs. of Rotary Int'l v. Rotary Club, supra,* 481 U.S. at p. 547, fn. 6 [95 L.Ed.2d at p. 486, 107 S.Ct. at p. 1947].) In the context of examining intimate associational rights, the *Roberts* court noted that "factors that may be relevant include size, purpose, policies, selectivity, congeniality, and other characteristics that in a particular case may be pertinent." (468 U.S. at p. 620 [82 L.Ed.3d at p. 473].)

Although defendant has consistently argued that its membership is selective and restricted, plaintiff has also alleged that defendant's facilities are open to the public, at least in the form of guest use and rental. Of course, at this stage of the proceedings, there is no record proof that some membership applications are actually rejected under a selective screening process or that criteria other than financial ability are used. The crucially important issues of degree of exclusivity maintained and the nature of the intimate or expressive associational rights involved are matters properly subject to proof.

In summary, in light of our analysis of the principles which apply, we conclude that plaintiff has properly alleged facts sufficient to state a cause of action for violation of the Unruh Civil Rights Act.

IV.

Denial of Right to Fair Procedure and Due Process

Plaintiff also contends the trial court erred in sustaining the demurrer to her cause of action alleging denial of her right to fair procedure and due process under both the common law and the California Constitution. Our review of the relevant decisional law supports plaintiff's basic contention.

Under the *Marinship–Pinsker* [10] line of cases, certain private entities are required to use fair procedure in excluding persons from membership because "[they] possess substantial power either to thwart an individual's pursuit of a lawful trade or profession, or to control the terms and

10. *James v. Marinship Corp.* (1944) 25 Cal.2d 721 [155 P.2d 329, 160 A.L.R. 900] (closed shop trade union may not arbitrarily maintain closed membership) and *Pinsker v. Pacific Coast Society of Orthodontists* (1974) 12 Cal.3d 541 [116 Cal.Rptr. 245, 526 P.2d 253] (professional association under common law duty to employ fair procedure in denying application for membership).

conditions under which it is practiced." (*Ezekial v. Winkley* (1977) 20 Cal.3d 267, 272 [142 Cal.Rptr. 418, 572 P.2d 32].) Plaintiff alleged that, as a self-supporting real estate agent, she was dependent on the business she acquired, including significant contact sources through use of the club facilities. She further alleged that she received no notice of fair hearing before the termination of her valuable property interest in Peninsula Golf and Country Club.

Defendant replies that the right to fair procedure can only arise in the context of an organization holding a power of monopoly over a trade or profession, such as a labor union or a professional society. Defendant also contends no facts are alleged showing that denial of club membership adversely impacts plaintiff's fundamental right to pursue her chosen profession. Defendant further argues plaintiff lacks standing to assert a claim of arbitrary expulsion because she never possessed title to a club membership.

Although most of the recent decisions concerning the right to fair procedure have arisen in the context of trade union or professional membership claims,[11] the Supreme Court's language has been much broader in scope:

> "However, the application of the common law rule does not depend on the existence of 'monopoly' power. (E.g., *Ascherman II, supra,* 45 Cal.App.3d at p. 511 [availability of other nearby hospitals no bar to claim for wrongful denial of staff privileges]; *Ascherman I, supra,* 39 Cal.App.3d at p. 650, fn. 9 [same].) The judicial inquiry, rather, has consistently been focused on the practical power of the entity in question to affect substantially an important economic interest. Plaintiff has alleged such power in the matter before us." (*Ezekial v. Winkley, supra,* 20 Cal.3d at p. 277.) The *Ezekial* court also concluded: "The underlying theme of these [expulsion] decisions, variously stated, is that membership in an association, with its associated privileges, once attained, is a valuable interest which cannot be arbitrarily withdrawn. Thus, they comport with the broader principle that one on whom an important benefit or privilege has already been conferred may enjoy legal protections not available to an initial applicant for the same benefit. (See, e.g., *Bixby v. Pierno, supra,* 4 Cal.3d at p. 146.)" (*Id.,* at p. 273; see *Curran v. Mount Diablo Council of the Boy Scouts, supra,* 147 Cal.App.3d at pp. 720–725.)

Viewing the allegations broadly, plaintiff possessed the *benefits and privileges* of membership in the club even though the certificate of membership was issued in the name of her former husband. Nor does defendant deny plaintiff's legal use of and access to the benefits and privileges of club membership before the marital dissolution. The allegations raise viable factual issues concerning plaintiff's property interest in the club membership, purchased and maintained with community property funds and

11. The right to fair procedure was originally held to apply to mutual benefit societies and other fraternal and social groups. (See, e.g., *Taboada v. Sociedad Espanola etc.* (1923) 191 Cal. 187, 191 [215 P. 673, 27 A.L.R. 1508]; *Von Arx v. San Francisco G. Verein* (1896) 113 Cal. 377, 379–380 [45 P. 685]; *Supreme Lodge, etc. v. L.A. Lodge No. 386* (1917) 177 Cal. 132, 136 [169 P. 1040].)

awarded to her as a community property interest under the integrated property settlement agreement. Accordingly, the order sustaining the demurrer to the pleaded cause of action was erroneous.

* * *

Disposition

We reverse the order or judgment of dismissal based upon the order sustaining demurrer as to plaintiff's causes of action alleging violation of the Unruh Civil Rights Act and denial of the right of fair procedure * * *.

NEWSOM, J., and HOLMDAHL, J., concurred.

Notes

1. Traditionally, equity courts have been reluctant to intervene in membership disputes of private associations, clubs, professional and religious organizations and honorary societies. What practicability concerns are reflected in this reluctance? Today, judicial intervention in this area is increasing substantially. There are several reasons for this. First, to the extent that the private organization is significantly involved with the government, it may be treated as the "state" for 14th Amendment purposes and its membership practices thus become subject to constitutional scrutiny. More important, contemporary legislation, as reflected in *Warfield,* often prohibits many private associations from engaging in a wide variety of discriminatory practices. *See e.g.,* Beynon v. St. George–Dixie Lodge No. 1743, Benevolent & Protective Order of Elks, 854 P.2d 513 (Utah 1993) (prohibition on female Elks barred by state statute on "regulation of enterprises"). Finally, irrespective of such legislation, equity courts are much more inclined to intervene in the affairs of a private association where admission practices affect the excluded person's ability to earn a livelihood. A succinct statement to this effect is in Falcone v. Middlesex County Medical Society, 34 N.J. 582, 170 A.2d 791, 89 A.L.R.2d 952 (1961), where the court said: "When courts originally declined to scrutinize admission practices of membership associations they were dealing with social clubs, religious organizations and fraternal associations. Here the policies against judicial intervention were strong and there were no significant countervailing policies. When the courts were later called upon to deal with trade and professional associations exercising virtually monopolistic control, different factors were involved. The intimate personal relationships which pervaded the social, religious and fraternal organizations were hardly in evidence and the individual's opportunity of earning a livelihood and serving society in his chosen trade or profession appeared as the controlling policy consideration."

2. It is also much more common for a court to intervene where there has been an expulsion from membership, as opposed to a refusal to admit. This is largely because the expelled member can assert certain rights that are unavailable to his or her counterpart seeking admission. For example, the expelled member may claim: (1) the deprivation of some property interest of the member; (2) the breach of a contractual relationship; or (3) tortious interference with the member's relationship with the organization. *See* Chafee, The Internal Affairs of Associations Not for Profit, 43 Harv.L.Rev. 991, 999–1010 (1930). Is *Warfield* an admission or exclusion case?

While courts frequently intervene in expulsion situations to compel a private association to follow its own rules, this is not invariably the case. Consider, for example, the language of the New Jersey Supreme Court in reversing a lower court order reinstating a member of a masonic order who had been expelled from his lodge for alleged misappropriation of lodge funds: "In determining whether an organization is bound by its established procedures, we would again balance the organization's interest in autonomy and its reasons for straying from its rules against the magnitude of interference with the member's interest in the organization and the likelihood that the established procedure would safeguard that interest." Rutledge v. Gulian, 93 N.J. 113, 459 A.2d 680 (1983).

3. Consider the implications of Zelenka v. Benevolent and Protective Order of the Elks, 129 N.J.Super. 379, 324 A.2d 35 (1974). In that case a New Jersey appellate court ruled that it was error for the Chancery Court to have refused to order reinstatement of an expelled member who, without the prior authorization of the Grand Exalted Ruler, had published a letter to the editor calling for an end to the organization's "white male" membership requirement. The court stated:

> "We can take judicial notice that the Elks order, comprising about 1½ million members, is one of the most widely located fraternal organizations in the country and that membership in it is highly prized in many communities. There is justification for inferring deep interest in his membership by the present plaintiff, a former head of his lodge. The personal value to plaintiff of his membership in the order thus calls for an evaluation of his relational interests, weighed against the assertion by the order of a constitutional right of selectivity in the private associations of its members.
>
> * * *
>
> "The most searching recent analysis of the general subject, 'Developments in the Law—Judicial Control of Actions of Private Associations,' 76 Harv.L.Rev. 983 *et seq.* (1963) persuasively observes:
>
>> '* * * a court can most confidently adjudicate cases where the group imposes sanctions to enforce a rule or policy which prohibits or inhibits the performance by the individual of a duty or function for the performance of which the state normally relies on individual initiative. The role of the member as a responsible citizen—voter, witness, petitioner to the legislature—is protected.' [at 1006]
>
> "The parties are in agreement that the issue here is not whether defendants were justified in expelling plaintiff for urging a change in the order's membership criteria. It is agreed that that was not the basis for the action, but rather plaintiff's expressing *any* opinion publicly on the matter at all, whether for or against the membership rule, without complying with the lodge regulation requiring approval of the expression by the Grand Exalted Ruler. Defendants urge that their policy against 'public washing of private organizational linen' is a justified one and that plaintiff voluntarily sacrificed his right of unqualified freedom of speech to that extent when he joined the order. It may be observed, however, that the

pertinent statute of the order does not preclude public expression by a member concerning a fraternal matter if one man—the Grand Exalted Ruler—approves, and such approval is left to that official's absolute discretion.

"There is probably no right more fundamental to the liberties of the people and to the successful functioning of the democratic system than that of individual freedom of expression. Undoubtedly that right is qualified in numerous respects by our public laws, and it is similarly qualified in respect of its exercise in the course of one's participation in the activities of private associations. A member of a Republican club, for example, could not expect to be allowed by the courts to campaign for a Democratic candidate and nevertheless remain immune to expulsion from the club for cause.

"In the present case, however, defendants profess not to be concerned over plaintiff's espousal of reform of their membership policies. Moreover, nothing in the order's basic purposes and objects, as we read them expressed in the preamble of its constitution, appears to be offended by a member's public plea for support by fellow members on an issue of the significance of racial qualifications for membership in the order without obtaining advance approval by the national head of the order. Nor do defendants contend to the contrary.

"The question devolves, then, to one of offense to general public policy in a regulation of the character under consideration. We are not here faced with a regulation enjoining secrecy as to lodge ritual, or imposing restrictions on public discussion by members of matters of peculiar concern to the lodge or order, such as the amount of initiation or other fees or the times and places of meetings, etc., with respect to which there is no general public interest or concern. On the other hand, the matter of racial qualifications for membership in an organization as large, as widespread and as socially significant as the Elks, albeit a private voluntary organization, is a subject conspicuously touching what interests and concerns the general public. *See, e.g.,* Brunson v. Rutherford Lodge, 128 N.J.Super. 66, 319 A.2d 80 (Law Div.1974).

"The public policy undergirding the principle of free discussion of issues of such broad public interest as that mentioned, entirely independently of its constitutional sanction in respect of state abridgement, appears to us to far outweigh the private interest of defendants in restricting public discussion of such an issue by their members to those instances in which advance approval is vouchsafed by a single official at national headquarters."

4. To what extent should principles governing private associations be applicable to expulsion of students by private colleges and universities? Consider in this regard the language of Harvey v. Palmer College of Chiropractic, 363 N.W.2d 443, 444–45 (Iowa App.1984):

"Although the due process clause of the fourteenth amendment is applicable only to state action, '[t]he requirements imposed by the common law on private universities parallel those imposed by the due process clause on public universities.' Abbariao v. Hamline University School of Law, 258 N.W.2d 108, 113 (Minn.1977). Courts have analyzed the relationship between a student and a private university under several legal theories, including the law of contracts and the law of associations. Neither theory fits perfectly and, therefore, should not be rigidly applied. * * * It is clear, however, that a private university may not expel a student arbitrarily, unreasonably, or in bad faith.

"Courts are reluctant to intervene in cases involving dismissal for academic deficiencies since such decisions are within the expertise of the school; but dismissals for disciplinary reasons are more closely scrutinized by the courts.

"In Tedeschi v. Wagner College, 49 N.Y.2d 652, 661, 404 N.E.2d 1302, 1306, 427 N.Y.S.2d 760, 765, a student had been suspended for both academic and nonacademic reasons. However, she was not accorded a hearing before the Student–Faculty Hearing Board as required by the published college guidelines for student suspensions and dismissals. The New York Court of Appeals found it unnecessary to belabor the legal theory most applicable to the student-college relationship. The court held:

> Whether by analogy to the law of associations, on the basis of a supposed contract between university and student, or simply as a matter of essential fairness in the somewhat one-sided relationship between the institution and the individual, we hold that when a university has adopted a rule or guideline establishing the procedure to be followed in relation to suspension or expulsion that procedure must be substantially observed.

Id. at 660, 404 N.E.2d at 1306, 427 N.Y.S.2d at 764. The court reinstated the plaintiff as a student unless prior to the opening of the fall term she had been disciplined in accordance with established procedures.

"A similar result was reached by a federal district court applying New Jersey law in Clayton v. Trustees of Princeton University, 519 F.Supp. 802 (D.N.J.1981). In that case the plaintiff was accused of changing a test answer during a lab practical. He was convicted by the Princeton Honor Committee and suspended from school for one year. *Id.* at 803. After analyzing the New Jersey law of associations the court concluded:

> Certainly the proposition that once an organization has established rules for itself it must follow them is not a radical proposition. Princeton voluntarily promulgated the procedures that Mr. Clayton claims it violated in suspending him. It is not unreasonable to hold Princeton to the requirement of substantial compliance with these procedures.

Id. at 806. The court found there was a material dispute of fact over whether plaintiff had been accorded the procedural protections to which he was entitled under school regulations and, therefore, denied the cross-motions for summary judgment."

SECTION 6. INTERFERENCE WITH THE PERSON

A. SUBSTITUTIONARY RELIEF

1. *Basic Categories of Recovery*

D. DOBBS, THE HORNBOOK OF THE LAW OF REMEDIES

647–648 (2d ed. 1993).*

§ 8.1 Damages for Personal Injury

§ 8.1(1) Elements of Damages for Personal Injury

Compensation Elements Generally

"*Compensatory, lump-sum awards.* The traditional theory is that, except for punitive damages imposed as punishment for more serious wrongdoings, awards for personal injury are aimed at compensating the victim or making good the losses proximately resulting from the injury. Personal injury awards are lump-sum awards; unlike workers' compensation awards, they are not paid out in weekly or monthly sums. For this reason all damages for personal injury, including damages expected to accrue in the future, traditionally must be proved and calculated at the trial.[2]

"*Elements.* Plaintiffs prove three basic elements of recovery in personal injury actions. (1) Time losses. The plaintiff can recover loss [of] wages or the value of any lost time or earning capacity where injuries prevent work. (2) Expenses incurred by reason of the injury. These are usually medical expenses and kindred items. (3) Pain and suffering in its various forms, including emotional distress and consciousness of loss.

"*Permanent or future harm.* One characteristic or attribute of each element of damage is that it may be permanent, or if not permanent, may continue to cause harm for some period in the future. Permanency and continuation of harm in the future are not logically elements of harm in themselves. They are not losses but they are characteristics that reflect the degree of loss which the plaintiff suffers. If an injury is permanent or will continue in the future, the plaintiff may lose time from her job, may have additional medical expense, or may suffer pain long after the trial is over. The plaintiff is entitled to recover for such future losses with respect to each of the elements. Proof of future loss may be especially difficult or uncertain in many cases, however. In addition, adjustments must be made when future losses are estimated to account for inflation and the effects of prepayment.

"*Elements apply in injury claims generally.* Although details may differ in particular jurisdictions, the basic elements just listed are always

* Reprinted with permission of West Publishing Co.

2. Periodic payment statutes and structured settlements may provide for payment of damages over a period of time, but nevertheless rely primarily on an up-front determination of the amount of damages. See § 8.5(5) below.

recognized as recoverable items in some form, not only in the various states, but also under federal tort systems such as the FELA[7] and Jones Act.[8] The same elements are recognized as recoverable in any kind of tort claim for personal injury. Pain and suffering, for example, is equally recoverable in a strict products liability claim, in an ordinary negligence case, and in a civil rights action. Even wrongful death actions, with their statutory peculiarities, take into account the same general kinds of elements of damage and the same general kinds of adjustments in the award. The identity of the elements in all tort cases flows from the compensatory theory of recovery. That is, since the law attempts to measure compensation for losses, differences in losses require a different recovery but differences in the tort that leads to those losses do not."

McDONALD v. UNITED STATES

United States District Court, Middle District of Pennsylvania, 1983.
555 F.Supp. 935.

CONABOY, DISTRICT JUDGE.

[The court found that the plaintiff's injuries were caused by the swine influenza vaccination that she received. As a result she was entitled to receive damages pursuant to the Federal Tort Claims Act and the Swine Flu Act.]

B. APPLICABLE LAW AND MEASURE OF RECOVERY

In an action brought under the Federal Tort Claims Act, it is "the law of the state where the act or omission occurred" which provides the applicable standards of substantive liability. 28 U.S.C. § 1346(b); * * * Since the Swine Flu Act incorporates by reference the liability provisions of the Federal Tort Claims Act, state law standards also apply to claims brought pursuant to the Swine Flu Act. * * * Lucy McDonald received her swine flu vaccination in Pittston, Pennsylvania and, therefore, the Pennsylvania law of damages for personal injuries governs the extent of the Defendant's liability in this action. * * *

In Pennsylvania, the courts have consistently held that "damages are to be compensatory to the full extent of the injury sustained." * * * Under this state's law, a plaintiff is entitled to be compensated for all past medical expenses reasonably and necessarily incurred and all future medical expenses reasonably likely to be incurred for the treatment and care of his injuries; past lost earnings and lost future earning capacity; and past, present and future pain and suffering. * * * A plaintiff in Pennsylvania must only prove these elements of damage with reasonable certainty. * * * See also *Story Parchment Co. v. Paterson Parchment Paper Co.*, 282 U.S. 555, 562, 51 S.Ct. 248, 250, 75 L.Ed. 544 (1931) (reasonable certainty rule bars only those damages which "are not the certain result of the

7. 45 U.S.C.A. § 51. See, reflecting damage elements, Chesapeake & O.R. Co. v. Carnahan, 241 U.S. 241, 243, 36 S.Ct. 594, 594, 60 L.Ed. 979 (1916) (FELA damages include pain and mental anguish, bodily injury, pecuniary loss including "loss of power and capacity for work" and its effect upon plaintiff's future).

8. 46 U.S.C.A. § 688. See, reflecting damage elements, Allen v. Seacoast Products, Inc., 623 F.2d 355 (5th Cir.1980) (pain, earning power, medical).

wrong, not * * * those damages which are definitely attributable to the wrong and only uncertain in respect of their amount.").

1. *Past Medical Expenses*

The parties have stipulated that the reasonable and necessarily incurred past medical expenses related to Lucy McDonald's present illness total $56,645.18.[47]

2. *Future Medical Expenses*

It was unequivocally confirmed by every physician testifying in this case that Lucy McDonald's primary medical deficits of lower extremity paraplegia and bowel and bladder dysfunction are now permanent. As a result of this debilitating condition, she will require, among other things, the constant care and treatment of professionally trained medical personnel in order to prevent the serious complications sometimes associated with her present illness, such as prolonged hospitalization, surgical intervention, and inordinately expensive therapy. At trial and in an earlier report, Dr. Rhamy outlined the essential treatment, its cost, and some of the prophylactic measures which should be taken in an effort to care for and rehabilitate the Plaintiff over the remaining years of her life. In this regard, the Court finds that based on the United States Life Expectancy Tables, Lucy McDonald's present life expectancy is approximately 40 years. Dr. Rhamy expressly indicated that with the appropriate medical attention he has recommended, Lucy McDonald can expect to attain this normal life expectancy. In calculating an award for the future medical expenses to which the Plaintiff is entitled to in this case, we have divided this element of damages into four areas: medical treatment, nursing care, miscellaneous equipment and devices, and architectural changes in the Plaintiff's house. We will address these items *seriatim.*

a. *Medical Treatment*

The Plaintiff does and must continue to take numerous medications for problems related to her present neurological and urological condition. The total lifetime costs of these medications is $33,499.00.

In an effort to prevent osteoporosis of the bones, a common phenomenon in paraplegics, regular orthopedic evaluations must be undertaken at a cost of $100.00 per year and $4,000.00 over the Plaintiff's lifetime. As an additional orthopedic measure, an award of $7,200.00 will be made for the reasonable likelihood of future surgery to correct para-articular calcification of the hip joints, which occurs in one-half of all paraplegics.

With respect to the Plaintiff's skin condition, Dr. Rhamy testified that it is very likely, a 68% chance, that the Plaintiff will develop additional decubiti over the sacral part of her body. He estimated the cost of treatment, including possible surgery, to range from $16,500.00 to $68,000.00. The Court will award $16,500.00 for such future care.

47. See Plaintiff's Exhibit # 360 for a detailed breakdown of the specific items of damage under this category.

Lucy McDonald's urological condition will require the closest monitoring and the most frequent treatment because of her permanent bowel and bladder dysfunction. * * * [T]he Court will approve most of the urological treatment recommendations and award $135,550.00 as damages for such requirements. The total amount of the medical treatment expenses is therefore $197,749.00.

b. Nursing Care

As previously noted, the testimony at trial was, in the Court's view, persuasive in demonstrating that the Plaintiff will require continual nursing care throughout her lifetime to prevent and treat the potential serious complications of her disease. The issue that arises, however, for the Court's determination in awarding damages is the degree or type of nursing care which is reasonably necessary for the Plaintiff. Several options were referred to at trial.

At the outset, the Court rejects the government's proposal regarding institutionalized care or apartment-type community living for the handicapped for Lucy McDonald. These options were suggested by the Defendant's expert economist, Dr. George Reavy, solely from an economic standpoint and were unsupported by any medical evidence establishing them as feasible alternatives for this particular Plaintiff. On the other hand, Plaintiff herself testified that it is very important for her to stay in her present home; she describes it as being the "family homestead" and the gathering place for her brothers and sisters and their families. Dr. Turchetti, a psychiatrist, opined that such alternatives as proffered by the government would be markedly detrimental to the Plaintiff's emotional condition. He stated that to Lucy McDonald her present home represents security and to strip her away from this would be "cruel". * * * Dr. Rhamy also testified that, in his opinion, an extended care treatment center would not be conducive to the normal interpersonal relationship of a husband and wife. Based on this uncontradicted medical testimony and in a compassionate sense of fairness to the plight of the Plaintiff, the Court concludes that the Defendant's proposals are not a reasonable solution to this Plaintiff's present and future nursing care needs.

Dr. Rhamy testified as to two alternatives, a "low" and "high" nursing care plan for the Plaintiff. The "low" plan consisted of a licensed practical nurse (LPN) for one eight-hour shift and a helper or nurse's aid for the other 16 hours of the day, seven days of the week. The "high" alternative would be an LPN on an around the clock basis, seven days of the week.

* * *

* * * Nurse Harring presented a schedule of nursing care for the Plaintiff which, considering all the medical testimony presented regarding the Plaintiff's present physical status and her future medical needs, the Court finds to be the most feasible option in this case. This plan consists of: (1) the services of a RN for one eight-hour shift per day for five days of the week (40 hours per week); (2) the services of an LPN for one eight-hour shift for seven days of the week (56 hours per week); and (3) the services of a nurse's aide or helper for the remaining shift during the week

and the extra shift on the weekends (72 hours per week). Nurse Harring also testified that the reasonable and average eight-hour shift rate in this geographical area for an RN is $75.00 and for an LPN is $65.00. It was earlier established by Dr. Rhamy that the nurse's aide or helper would be a minimum wage worker at a present rate of $3.35 per hour. Computing these hourly figures over the life expectancy of the Plaintiff, the Court will award $2,228,096.00 as damages for the reasonable future cost of necessary nursing care for the Plaintiff.[56]

c. *Miscellaneous Equipment and Devices*

As previously referred to, the Plaintiff's present life expectancy is approximately 40 years. The uncontroverted testimony of several of Plaintiff's expert medical witnesses, specifically Drs. Rhamy, Lichtenfeld and Poser and Nurse Harring, established that at present and over the course of her entire lifetime Lucy McDonald will require numerous items of paraplegic equipment to assist her in maintaining a state of optimum physical health. * * *

The final item listed, the van, deserves brief comment. Dr. Rhamy and Nurse Harring testified specifically as to the necessity of this mode of transportation for a paraplegic, especially one with a bowel and bladder disorder. Plaintiff is unable to move independently, or even easily with assistance, from her wheelchair into a regular automobile. As a result, at times the ordeal of the transfer process not only physically tires her but it also causes undue pressure upon her bladder and involuntary urination. Dr. Rhamy as well as Dr. Turchetti noted that a van would be important for Lucy McDonald's emotional well-being also, in that it would greatly facilitate her access to numerous social activities and thereby assist her in regaining some of the self-esteem and respect she now so obviously lacks. Dr. Rhamy poignantly described the Plaintiff's present status as a "prisoner in her own house." * * * The Plaintiff herself testified that a van would be most useful for these daily activities and would also enable she and Francis to resume taking weekend trips to visit friends and relatives as they did prior to her disability.

Under these circumstances, we believe that the necessary cost for a hydraulic-lift van, as established by Dr. Rhamy and unchallenged by the Defendant, is a proper element of damages in the instant case.

d. *Necessary Architectural Changes in Plaintiff's House*

The Court received into evidence at trial a report prepared by Richard Hardy, an architect, in the firm of Pyros & Sanderson, Wilkes–Barre, Pennsylvania, outlining proposed alterations to the McDonald home to suitably accommodate Lucy in her present condition. The total estimated cost of this project is $77,000.00. The propriety of the architectural changes is consistent with the testimony of Drs. Rhamy and Lichtenfeld and Nurse Harring, and was not contradicted by the testimony of any

56. The weekly cost under this nursing plan is $1,071.20; thus, the yearly figure would be $55,702.40 and, accordingly, calculating this yearly rate over the 40 year life expectancy of the Plaintiff produces the sum of $2,228,096.00. We believe this to be a conservative amount since no doubt the cost of nursing care will greatly escalate over the next forty years.

defense witnesses. After examining the specifics of this plan, the Court finds that the recommendations and estimates contained therein are both reasonable and necessary to enable the Plaintiff to adjust as conveniently as possible to her paraplegic lifestyle.[59]

3. *Lost Earnings*

The testimony on this issue was presented by Dr. Andrew Verzilli, Professor of Economics, Drexel University, on behalf of the Plaintiff, and by Dr. George C. Reavy, Economic Consultant, University of Scranton, for the Defendant.

a. Wages

There was no dispute in this case that the amount of the past lost wages sustained by the Plaintiff from December, 1976 until the date of trial was $44,800.00.

Under Pennsylvania law, "[w]hen an injury is a permanent one, one which will cause a loss or lessening of future earning power, a recovery may be had for the probable loss of future earnings." *Kaczkowski v. Bolubasz,* [491 Pa. 561, 566 n. 7, 421 A.2d 1027 (1980)] quoting McCormick, *Damages* at 299 (20th reprint 1975). * * *

On this issue of Lucy McDonald's lost future earnings, there was disagreement between the expert economists on the initial factor of the Plaintiff's work-life expectancy. Dr. Verzilli's calculations were based on an assumed retirement age of 65, an approximately 26 year future work life period. Dr. Reavy's projection of a 15.19 year work life expectancy for the Plaintiff, on the other hand, was founded upon the U.S. Department of Labor, Tables for Working Life for Men and Women (1977).

The Plaintiff argues that the utilization of these tables in this case would be inappropriate because they unjustly interdict a consideration of her particular economic condition. At trial, Dr. Reavy, upon cross-examination, indicated that one of the principal contributing factors to the shortened work life expectancy of a female, as reflected in these tables, is the prospect of child-bearing and the concomitant departure from the work force by a woman. In this case, however, the McDonalds did not have any children at the time Lucy, then 33, contracted GBS and, as a result of this illness, it is exceedingly unlikely they ever will. Moreover, as noted, shortly after the onset of her disease, the Plaintiff's husband, Francis, was seriously injured and remains physically disabled for social security purposes. The Plaintiff also testified that she enjoyed her work at Lee Manufacturing and would have continued there if not for her illness. On this latter point, Leo Gutstein, the owner of Lee Manufacturing, testified that Lucy was a valued employee and a presser position would have remained available to her if she did not become disabled.

59. Mr. Hardy also outlined and estimated the cost of constructing a new one-story custom home as an alternative to remodeling the McDonald's present home. Such a project would cost approximately $135,665.00; however, as noted previously, the Plaintiff has no desire to nor is it psychologically advisable for her to vacate the present family residence.

In determining the Plaintiff's "probable" loss of future earnings in light of these circumstances, particularly her husband's inability to provide an income for the household, the Court concludes that the Plaintiff would have remained in the work force until age 65. Thus, her present work life expectancy is 26 years.

With respect to the Plaintiff's future earnings figure, both economic experts, relying upon the testimony of Mr. Gutstein, used an average annual figure of $13,650.00. Specifically, Mr. Gutstein testified that if Lucy was presently employed as a presser in his facility, she would be earning $7.50 per hour and working an estimated 35 hours per week. Computed over a 52 week period, these wages translate into an annual salary of $13,650.00. The Court accepts this as a reasonable method of arriving at the Plaintiff's annual earnings figure.

The Plaintiff also seeks an upward adjustment of this yearly amount by a 2% productivity factor in accordance with the standards set forth by the Supreme Court of Pennsylvania in *Kaczkowski v. Bolubasz, supra.* * * *

In this case, Dr. Verzilli, the Plaintiff's economist, testified that based on the Plaintiff's actual earning history at Lee Manufacturing and the testimony of Leo Gutstein, the owner of Lee Manufacturing, a 2% productivity factor for the Plaintiff would be appropriate. Mr. Gutstein testified that despite some industry declines, his business has grown substantially from the time period of 1976 to the present. He attributes this to diversification of his business through the addition of more product lines. In terms of productivity of his employees, he stated that Lee Manufacturing has made substantial capital expenditures for automated equipment, which has resulted in: (1) production being greater with a consistent work force, and (2) his shops and its employees earning substantially above the industry standards. Finally, in his role as financial planner for the company, he estimated that the future growth of Lee Manufacturing, exclusive of inflation, would be 3 to 5 percent annually. Additionally, Dr. Verzilli stated that this two percent figure is actually lower than the Plaintiff's past growth rate from 1970 to 1976. He further noted that it would be unrealistic to assume no growth in the Plaintiff's future earnings.

Dr. Reavy, the Defendant's economist, was of the opinion that no productivity factor increase was warranted in this case. In determining this, he measured the percentage change in the Plaintiff's hourly wage rate in 1973 of $4.43 per hour, to the present estimated rate of $7.50 per hour. He determined that although this indicated a 69.3% increase in the Plaintiff's hourly wage rate, when compared to the rise in the consumer price index of 120.4% for the same time period, he concluded that there had been no real growth in the Plaintiff's wages. The Court is of the view, however, that this method of comparison does not accurately reflect the *Kaczkowski* Court's concept of productivity or "merit" increases. See *id.* at 565 n. 5, 421 A.2d 1027. It should be borne in mind that the consumer price index is the government's measure of inflation, the impact of which has already been taken into account with future interest rates under the total offset approach of *Kaczkowski.*[63] The inflation figure, therefore, should not be the sole factor considered in the computation of a productivity component, a "separate and distinct phenomena" which is "controlled by different variables than the inflationary factor." *Id.* at 570, 565 n. 5, 421 A.2d 1027. As noted above, a consideration of future wage or productivity increases should be based on such factors as the age, experience, skill, and education of the individual as well as, we believe, the future economic condition of the particular industry or company with which the individual would have been employed if not for the permanent injuries sustained. See 54 Temp.L.Q. 576, 586–87 n. 81. Such an analysis entails, by necessity, an *ad hoc* case-by-case determination.

In view of the testimony adduced by the Plaintiff's expert economist and by her former employer, the Court finds that a proper foundation has been laid in this case to justify the requested 2% productivity factor adjustment in the amount of Plaintiff's lost future earnings. While we recognize, as did the court in *Kaczkowski,* that such an award "may be subject to a degree of speculation", nonetheless, we also share that tribunal's view that "it is exceedingly more accurate to assume that the future will not remain stagnant with the past." *Id.* at 580, 421 A.2d 1027.[64] The Plaintiff's future lost earning capacity in this case is therefore $437,209.00.

With respect to fringe benefits, both economists agreed that this item constitutes a significant portion of the financial package for a worker and has traditionally been considered as part of compensation. In this case, Dr. Verzilli opined that a 20% adjustment to earnings should be made to account for such benefits. He reached this conclusion by examining the union (ILGWU) contract relative to Lee Manufacturing Company for the years 1979 through 1982, which establishes and identifies the contributions based on the worker's payroll that would be provided by the employer, on behalf of its employees, for three types of benefits: (1) a health and welfare fund; (2) a retirement fund; and (3) a health services plan. Dr. Reavy, however, examined these documents and concluded that an appropriate value for these benefits would be approximately 5% of earnings. After careful consideration of the testimony of both the economic experts and after reviewing the relevant sections of the union contract and other documents submitted, the Court finds that a reasonable estimate of the value of fringe benefits in this case is 15 percent of past and future lost earnings, or $72,301.35.

b. Household Services

The Plaintiff also seeks compensation for the past and future value of the daily household services she is unable to perform because of her illness.

63. [The theoretical premise of this decision is that future inflation and future interest rates are presumed to be equal and cancel one another. The application of the "total offset" rule has been held to be appropriate in an action brought under the Swine Flu Act. *Barnes v. United States,* 685 F.2d 66, 70 (3d Cir.1982).]

64. In Posner, *Economic Analysis of Law* (2d ed. 1977), the author comments that in general a 3% productivity factor would be the appropriate figure to utilize in computing lost future earnings. He further notes that such average annual increases are "felt even in industries where productivity is not increasing secularly: employe[r]s in such industries must raise wages to levels competitive with those in other industries or lose their work force." *Id.* at 147, n. 5.

* * * Considering the particular factual circumstances of this case, however, the Court finds that such an award would not be appropriate.

The Plaintiff did testify that presently she is able to do some cooking, cleaning and laundry, albeit in a limited capacity. Apparently the remainder of these household tasks has previously been undertaken by her husband, Francis, who has been required to stay at home at all times to care for Lucy. There was no indication from the testimony that the McDonalds have incurred any additional expenses for such services from the onset of the Plaintiff's disabilities until trial and, thus, we believe there is no basis for a monetary award for this time period.

Several factors persuade the Court that an award for the future value of household services would also be inappropriate in this case. These include: (1) the Plaintiff's husband's ability to perform these chores, especially since he will not be working and moreover, will no longer be required to provide "nursing care" for the Plaintiff; (2) Lucy's increased ability to undertake these tasks in view of the proposed architectural changes in the McDonald home for which compensation has been granted by the Court; and (3) the capability of a minimum wage-worker, for which sufficient damages have also been awarded to employ under the nursing care category heretofore discussed, to render some assistance with these services. With these considerations in mind, the Court concludes that the value of the Plaintiff's household services is not a compensable element of damages in this case.

The total lost earnings of the Plaintiff are as follows:

Past Earnings	$ 44,800.00
Future Earning Capacity	437,209.00
Fringe Benefits	72,301.35
TOTAL	$554,310.35

4. *Pain and Suffering*

The final element of damages to be awarded is compensation for the past, present and future pain and suffering of the Plaintiff as a result of her affliction with GBS. * * * Under Pennsylvania law, such an award should include compensation for a Plaintiff's physical pain and suffering, as well as for any mental anguish, inconvenience, disfigurement, humiliation and the loss of enjoyment of life. * * * The nature of pain and suffering is such that there is no legal yardstick by which to measure accurately reasonable compensation for it, * * * thus, we are confronted with the unenviable task of dispassionately translating "such catastrophic human loss as [the Plaintiff] suffered into money damages. In this process systematic logic is not helpful and precision is not achievable." *Frankel v. Heym,* [466 F.2d 1226, 1228 (3d Cir. 1972)].

In view of the Court's previous discussion, there is no need to set forth in detail the devastation that has beset Lucy McDonald as a result of the swine flu vaccine. She presently is and will permanently continue to be totally dependent on others for virtually every intimate aspect of her everyday life. She will require extensive future medical care but, even with this, she is highly susceptible to infection and illness. She will never again be able to walk or engage in any activity requiring the use of her lower extremities; her legs are simply useless. She has been unable in the past six years to attend church or any social activities for fear of becoming incontinent. She has become, in Dr. Lichtenfeld's words, a "prisoner to her physical condition, humiliation and embarrassment." Additionally, the job she enjoyed and the career she looked forward to are gone. More importantly, the joys of motherhood, a prospect she so fondly embraced, will never be known to her. Even a normal marital relationship with her husband is now impossible. Quite naturally, there has been an extreme transformation in Lucy McDonald's emotional well-being—from an affable, happy-go-lucky active person to an invalid, greatly disturbed by acute depression and a severe loss of self-esteem and dignity. Reflecting her religious background, Lucy ascribes the present torment to her "penance on earth."

Under these circumstances, we believe that a substantial award as compensation for Lucy McDonald's pain and suffering is warranted. In so doing, we share the sentiments of the Court in *Barnes* [v. United States, 685 F.2d 66 (3d Cir. 1982)] that "[m]oney is not a substitute for what she and her family have lost, but nevertheless Congress provided for such an eventuality in the legislation creating the National Swine Flu Immunization Program of 1976 * * *." 516 F.Supp. at 1390. The sum of $600,000.00 is awarded as just and reasonable compensation for pain and suffering.

A summary of the damages (rounded off to dollars) to be awarded the Plaintiff is as follows:

Past Medical Expenses	$ 56,645.00
Future Medical Expenses	
a. Medical Treatment	197,749.00
b. Nursing Care	2,228,096.00
c. Miscellaneous Equipment	257,670.00
d. Architectural Changes	77,000.00
Lost Earnings	554,310.00
Pain and Suffering	600,000.00
TOTAL	$3,971,470.00

5. *Delay Damages*

As an additional element of compensation, the Plaintiff requests an award of delay damages pursuant to Pennsylvania Rule of Civil Procedure 238.[69] Section 2674 of the Federal Tort Claims Act (FTCA) provides, in pertinent part, that:

69. Rule 238 provides, in relevant part:

(a) Except as provided in subdivision (e), in an action seeking monetary relief for bodily injury, death or property damage, or any combination thereof, the court * * * shall (1) add to the amount of compensatory damages * * * in the court's decision in a nonjury trial, damages for delay at ten (10) percent per annum, not compounded, which shall become part of the award, verdict or decision; (2) compute the damages for delay from the date the plaintiff filed the initial complaint in the action or from a date one year after the accrual of the cause

> The United States shall be liable, respecting the provisions of this title relating to tort claims, in the same manner and to the same extent as a private individual under like circumstances, *but shall not be liable for interest prior to judgment or for punitive damages.* (emphasis added).

As previously noted, the Swine Flu Act provides that a claim for any injury sustained from the swine flu program must be brought directly against the United States under the procedures of the Federal Tort Claims Act. * * *

* * *

With respect to the question in this case, the "plain language" of the Swine Flu Act, as noted above, similarly requires that the liability of the United States be limited to the "same extent" as in any other action under the FTCA. See 42 U.S.C. § 247b(k)(2)(A). Such explicit statutory direction compels this Court to conclude that encompassed within this congressional limitation is the prohibition against prejudgment interest, as set forth in section 2674 of the FTCA. It is well settled that interest prior to judgment is not recoverable in other actions brought pursuant to the Federal Tort Claims Act. * * *

This apparently is an issue of first impression, as revealed by the briefs of both litigants as well as our independent research. We do note, however, that our Court of Appeals has recognized the applicability of the "punitive damages" bar of section 2674 in a Swine Flu Act case. * * * In view of such recognition, we can discern no sound reason why our appellate court would not also adopt the prohibition against prejudgment interest portion of that same statute, 28 U.S.C. § 2674, as the "controlling legal precept" in Swine Flu Act cases.

* * *

IX. Conclusion

The Court is not unaware of the unusual length of this Opinion. We are mindful too of the exceptional size of the award of damages. But we are equally cognizant of, and deeply impressed with, the enormous impact of the Plaintiff's extensive injuries. No smaller award could adequately compensate her since her total life, as well as her body, has been drastically and permanently crippled. We have tried, then, in fairness to both parties, to be thorough and complete in laying out our reasoning and analysis of the testimony and the evidence presented in this case.

* * *

> of action, whichever is later, up to the date of the award, verdict or decision.
>
> * * *
>
> (e) If a defendant at any time prior to trial makes a written offer of settlement in a specified sum with prompt cash payment to the plaintiff, and continues that offer in effect until commencement of trial, but the offer is not accepted and the plaintiff does not recover by award, verdict or decision, exclusive of damages for delay, more than 125 percent of the offer, the court * * * shall not award damages for delay for the period after the date the offer was made.

Counsel for the Plaintiff has filed an affidavit in which he states that at no time did he or his client receive any offer of settlement from the Defendant either in written or oral form (Document # 89).

An appropriate Order constituting the Court's Verdict in this case will be entered.

Notes

1. Should different actuarial tables be used for women and men to measure anticipated number of working years? *See* D. Dobbs, The Law of Remedies, § 8.5(2), at 677–79 (2d ed. 1993).

2. Should the inability to have children be a compensable loss? If so, how should it be measured?

3. Could the court in *McDonald* have relied upon the FTCA's bar on punitive damages, rather than its bar on prejudgment interest, in refusing to apply the Pennsylvania "delay" statute? Consider the next case.

MOLZOF v. UNITED STATES

Supreme Court of the United States, 1992.
___ U.S. ___, 112 S.Ct. 711, 116 L.Ed.2d 731.

JUSTICE THOMAS delivered the opinion of the Court.

This case requires us to determine the scope of the statutory prohibition on awards of "punitive damages" in cases brought against the United States under the Federal Tort Claims Act, 28 U.S.C. §§ 2671–2680.

I

Petitioner Shirley Molzof is the personal representative of the estate of Robert Molzof, her late husband. On October 31, 1986, Mr. Molzof, a veteran, underwent lung surgery at a Veterans' Administration hospital in Madison, Wisconsin. After surgery, he was placed on a ventilator. For some undisclosed reason, the ventilator tube that was providing oxygen to him became disconnected. The ventilator's alarm system also was disconnected. As a result of this combination of events, Mr. Molzof was deprived of oxygen for approximately eight minutes before his predicament was discovered. Because of this unfortunate series of events, triggered by the hospital employees' conceded negligence, Mr. Molzof suffered irreversible brain damage, leaving him permanently comatose.

Mr. Molzof's guardian ad litem filed suit in District Court under the Federal Tort Claims Act (FTCA or Act) seeking damages for supplemental medical care, future medical expenses, and loss of enjoyment of life. Respondent (the Government) admitted liability, and the case proceeded to a bench trial on the issue of damages. The District Court determined that the free medical care being provided to Mr. Molzof by the veterans' hospital was reasonable and adequate, that Mrs. Molzof was satisfied with those services and had no intention of transferring Mr. Molzof to a private hospital, and that it was in Mr. Molzof's best interests to remain at the veterans' hospital because neighboring hospitals could not provide a comparable level of care. In addition to ordering the veterans' hospital to continue the same level of care, the court awarded Mr. Molzof damages for supplemental care—physical therapy, respiratory therapy, and weekly doctor's visits—not provided by the veterans' hospital.

The District Court refused, however, to award damages for medical care that would duplicate the free medical services already being provided by the veterans' hospital. Similarly, the court declined to award Mr. Molzof damages for loss of enjoyment of life. Mr. Molzof died after final judgment had been entered, and Mrs. Molzof was substituted as plaintiff in her capacity as personal representative of her late husband's estate.

The United States Court of Appeals for the Seventh Circuit affirmed the District Court's judgment. 911 F.2d 18 (1990). The Court of Appeals agreed with the District Court that, given the Government's provision of free medical care to Mr. Molzof and Mrs. Molzof's apparent satisfaction with that care, any award for future medical expenses would be punitive in effect and was therefore barred by the FTCA prohibition on "punitive damages." *Id.*, at 21. With respect to the claim for Mr. Molzof's loss of enjoyment of life, the Court of Appeals stated that Wisconsin law was unclear on the question whether a comatose plaintiff could recover such damages. *Ibid.* The court decided, however, that "even if Wisconsin courts recognized the claim for loss of enjoyment of life, in this case it would be barred as punitive under the Federal Tort Claims Act," *ibid.*, because "an award of damages for loss of enjoyment of life can in no way recompense, reimburse or otherwise redress a comatose patient's uncognizable loss * * *." *Id.*, at 22. We granted certiorari to consider the meaning of the term "punitive damages" as used in the FTCA. 499 U.S. ____, 111 S.Ct. 1305, 113 L.Ed.2d 239 (1991).

II

Prior to 1946, the sovereign immunity of the United States prevented those injured by the negligent acts of federal employees from obtaining redress through lawsuits; compensation could be had only by passage of a private bill in Congress. * * * The FTCA replaced that "notoriously clumsy," system of compensation with a limited waiver of the United States' sovereign immunity. * * * In this case, we must determine the scope of that waiver as it relates to awards of "punitive damages" against the United States. The FTCA provides in pertinent part as follows:

> "The United States shall be liable, respecting the provisions of this title relating to tort claims, in the same manner and to the same extent as a private individual under like circumstances, *but shall not be liable* for interest prior to judgment or *for punitive damages*." 28 U.S.C. § 2674 (emphasis added).

As this provision makes clear, in conjunction with the jurisdictional grant over FTCA cases in 28 U.S.C. § 1346(b), the extent of the United States' liability under the FTCA is generally determined by reference to state law. * * *

Nevertheless, the meaning of the term "punitive damages" as used in § 2674, a federal statute, is by definition a federal question. * * * Petitioner argues that "§ 2674 must be interpreted so as to permit awards against the United States of those state-law damages which are intended by state law to act as compensation for injuries sustained as a result of the tort, and to preclude awards of damages which are intended to act as punishment for egregious conduct." * * * The Government, on the other hand, suggests that we define "punitive damages" as "damages that are in excess of, or bear no relation to, compensation." * * * Thus, the Government contends that any damages other than those awarded for a plaintiff's *actual* loss—which the Government narrowly construes to exclude damages that are excessive, duplicative, or for an inherently noncompensable loss, *id.,* at 22—are "punitive damages" because they are punitive *in effect.*

We agree with petitioner's interpretation of the term "punitive damages," and conclude that the Government's reading of § 2674 is contrary to the statutory language. Section 2674 prohibits awards of "punitive damages," not "damage awards that may have a punitive effect." "Punitive damages" is a legal term of art that has a widely accepted common-law meaning; "[p]unitive damages have long been a part of traditional state tort law." *Silkwood v. Kerr–McGee Corp.,* 464 U.S. 238, 255, 104 S.Ct. 615, 625, 78 L.Ed.2d 443 (1984). Although the precise nature and use of punitive damages may have evolved over time, and the size and frequency of such awards may have increased, this Court's decisions make clear that the concept of "punitive damages" has a long pedigree in the law. "It is a well-established principle of the common law, that in actions of trespass and all actions on the case for torts, a jury may inflict what are called exemplary, punitive, or vindictive damages upon a defendant, having in view the enormity of his offense rather than the measure of compensation to the plaintiff." * * *

Legal dictionaries in existence when the FTCA was drafted and enacted indicate that "punitive damages" were commonly understood to be damages awarded to punish defendants for torts committed with fraud, actual malice, violence, or oppression. See, *e.g.,* Black's Law Dictionary 501 (3d ed. 1933); The Cyclopedic Law Dictionary 292 (3d ed. 1940). * * * The common law definition of "punitive damages" focuses on the nature of the defendant's conduct. As a general rule, the common law recognizes that damages intended to compensate the plaintiff are different in kind from "punitive damages."

A cardinal rule of statutory construction holds that:

> "[W]here Congress borrows terms of art in which are accumulated the legal tradition and meaning of centuries of practice, it presumably knows and adopts the cluster of ideas that were attached to each borrowed word in the body of learning from which it was taken and the meaning its use will convey to the judicial mind unless otherwise instructed. In such case, absence of contrary direction may be taken as satisfaction with widely accepted definitions, not as a departure from them." *Morissette v. United States,* 342 U.S. 246, 263, 72 S.Ct. 240, 250, 96 L.Ed. 288 (1952).

* * *

The Government's interpretation of § 2674 appears to be premised on the assumption that the statute provides that the United States "shall be liable only for compensatory damages." But the first clause of § 2674, the provision we are interpreting, does not say that. What it clearly states is that the United States "shall not be liable * * * for punitive damages."

The difference is important. The statutory language suggests that to the extent a plaintiff may be entitled to damages that are not legally considered "punitive damages," but which are for some reason above and beyond ordinary notions of compensation, the United States is liable for them "in the same manner and to the same extent as a private individual." These damages in the "gray" zone are not by definition "punitive damages" barred under the Act. In the ordinary case in which an award of compensatory damages is subsequently reduced on appeal, one does not say that the jury or the lower court mistakenly awarded "punitive damages" above and beyond the actual compensatory damages. It is simply a matter of excessive or erroneous compensation. Excessiveness principles affect only the amount, and not the nature, of the damages that may be recovered. The term "punitive damages," on the other hand, embodies an element of the defendant's conduct that must be proved before such damages are awarded.

* * *

* * * The Government contends that the second clause of § 2674 "confirms the compensatory purpose of the statute and demonstrates that Congress intended to define 'punitive damages' by contrasting them with 'actual or compensatory damages.'" Brief for the United States 18–19 (footnote omitted). This argument is undermined, however, not only by the fact that "punitive damages" is a legal term of art with a well-established common law meaning, but also by the Government's own statement that, although the second clause defines "actual or compensatory damages" as "the pecuniary injuries resulting from such death," the "pecuniary injuries" standard does not apply in determining compensatory damages in any other kind of tort suit against the United States. *Id.*, at 19, n. 13. Given this concession, which we agree to be a correct statement of the law, the second clause of § 2674 cannot be read as proving so much as the Government claims.

The Government's interpretation of "punitive damages" would be difficult and impractical to apply. Under the Government's reading, an argument could be made that Mr. Molzof's damages for future medical expenses would have to be reduced by the amount he saved on rent, meals, clothing, and other daily living expenses that he did not incur while hospitalized. Otherwise, these duplicative damages would be "punitive damages" because they have the effect of making the United States pay twice. The difficulties inherent in attempting to prove such offsets would be enormous. That the Government has refused to acknowledge the practical implications of its theory is evidenced by its representations at oral argument that, as a general matter, it is willing to accept state-law definitions of compensatory awards for purposes of the FTCA, Tr. of Oral Arg. 28, and that "there are very few circumstances" in which States have authorized damages awards that the Government would challenge as punitive. *Id.*, at 38.

The Government's reading of the statute also would create problems in liquidated damages cases and in other contexts in which certain kinds of injuries are compensated at fixed levels that may or may not correspond to a particular plaintiff's actual loss. At oral argument, however, the Government disclaimed that extension of its theory, see *id.,* at 28, 35, and instead asserted that its position was that state compensatory awards are recoverable under the Act so long as they are a "reasonable" approximation of the plaintiff's actual damages. *Id.,* at 36. We agree that § 2674 surely does not prohibit any compensatory award that departs from the actual damages in a particular case. But the Government's restrictive reading of the statute would involve the federal courts in the impractical business of determining the actual loss suffered in each case, and whether the damages awarded are a "reasonable" approximation of that loss.

* * *

We conclude that § 2674 bars the recovery only of what are *legally* considered "punitive damages" under traditional common-law principles. This reading of the statute is consistent with the language of § 2674 and the structure of the Act, and it provides courts with a workable standard for determining when a plaintiff is improperly seeking "punitive damages" against the United States. Our interpretation of the term "punitive damages" requires us to reverse the Court of Appeals' decision that Mrs. Molzof is not permitted to recover damages for her husband's future medical expenses and his loss of enjoyment of life. It is undisputed that the claims in this case are based solely on a simple negligence theory of liability. Thus, the damages Mrs. Molzof seeks to recover are not punitive damages under the common law or the FTCA because their recoverability does not depend upon any proof that the defendant has engaged in intentional or egregious misconduct and their purpose is not to punish. We must remand, however, because we are in no position to evaluate the recoverability of those damages under Wisconsin law. Cf. *Sheridan v. United States,* 487 U.S. 392, 401, and n. 6, 108 S.Ct. 2449, 2455, and n. 6, 101 L.Ed.2d 352 (1988). It may be that under Wisconsin law the damages sought in this case are not recoverable as compensatory damages. This might be true because Wisconsin law does not recognize such damages, or because it requires a setoff when a defendant already has paid (or agreed to pay) expenses incurred by the plaintiff, or for some other reason. These questions were not resolved by the lower courts.

III

The judgment of the Court of Appeals is reversed, and the case is remanded for further proceedings consistent with this opinion.

Notes

1. How does a court distinguish between punitive and compensatory damages?

2. Should the district court have applied the collateral source rule and awarded to the plaintiff the value of the past medical expenses that had been received? *See* p. 233, *supra,* for a discussion of the collateral source rule.

3. Should Molzof's estate recover for loss of enjoyment of life? Does it matter whether or not a plaintiff is comatose? Should loss of enjoyment of life and pain and suffering be separate measurements? How should they be

measured? For a discussion of these issues *see* D. Dobbs, The Law of Remedies, § 8.1(4) (2d ed. 1993).

2. *Loss of Earning Capacity*

EARL v. BOUCHARD TRANSPORTATION COMPANY, INC.

United States District Court, Eastern District of New York, 1990.
735 F.Supp. 1167 *modified*, 917 F.2d 1320 (2d Cir. 1990).

WEINSTEIN, DISTRICT JUDGE.

Plaintiff James Earl, a 66 year-old former tugboat deck hand, brings an action against his employer under the Jones Act, 46 U.S.C.App. § 688, and general maritime law for injuries suffered as a result of two separate accidents in 1984. As a consequence of his injuries he claims he was forced to retire on May 16, 1985, approximately a month before turning 62. He claims damages for, *inter alia,* loss of future earnings on the grounds that, absent injury, he would have continued to work at least an additional three years and five weeks—that is, until his 65th birthday, if not longer.

After a three day trial, the jury found for plaintiff and awarded him a total of $855,000 in damages, of which $425,000 was attributed to lost earnings suffered as a result of the second accident. Defendant moves for a new trial or remittitur.

There exists at least some evidence to support a finding that Earl, absent the accident, would have been able to work past the age of 62 and that he would have done so. Regardless of his pre-accident intentions, it is apparent that plaintiff's earning capacity—or work-capital—was permanently impaired or depleted as a result of his injuries.

Theoretically the human working machine can last (with some decreases in effectiveness through illness and decrepitude)—and thus has economic value—almost to the point of death. As a matter of law, then, an award taking into account any loss of value due to injury or death caused by a tortfeasor, can take into account even this residual and declining loss of value up to the time of predicted death. There is a considerable effort in a shrinking labor market to keep older people employed beyond the usual date of retirement. *See* Lewin, *Too Much Retirement Time? A Move is Afoot to Change It,* N.Y. Times, Apr. 22, 1990, § 1, at 1, col. 1. In fact, realities of the labor market in an industrial-commercial world make it unlikely that the last possible moment of a worker's time would be purchased by an employer. Moreover, as age increases, the probability that the worker may claim total disability, using the injury as justification for not pushing himself or herself to work probably increases.

These subtle nuances between loss of full work-capital value at one end of the spectrum and malingering at the other are generally best left to the judgment of the community as reflected in the jury's verdict. In computing the full value of a tort victim's depleted work-capital the jury may consider a variety of factors that differ from plaintiff to plaintiff, such as past earnings, the marketplace value of an individual's skills, the availability of suitable employment, and average work-life expectancy as projected by government statistical tables. This value may be affected as a result of particularized evidence bearing on a plaintiff's pre-accident intentions and proclivities. For example, if the jury credited evidence that before being injured a plaintiff had intended to retire early, a reduction of the full value of an award would be justified under the doctrine of mitigation of damages, which requires tort victims to find alternative employment whenever possible. The award may be increased to the full or close to full value if, on the other hand, the jurors believed that a plaintiff was likely to work beyond that age at which the statistical tables or their common sense experience would normally predict retirement.

Where a jury verdict seems lopsidedly to favor one side or the other, the court has the obligation to require some equalization. This is such a case. Defendant's contention that there was no loss of earning capacity is unfounded. Nevertheless, for the reasons discussed below, defendants' motion for remittitur as to the award for future loss of earnings must be granted since an excessive award was made. Other adjustments are referred to below.

I. Background

A. *The Parties' Claims*

Earl claimed that he injured his right elbow in an August 29, 1984 accident and that he injured his ankle and reinjured his elbow in a second accident on December 13, 1984. Both accidents occurred while he was working on the Marion C. Bouchard, a tugboat owned by plaintiff's employer, defendant Bouchard Transportation Co. Plaintiff contended, and the jury found, that both accidents occurred as a result of the employer's negligence and the unseaworthiness of the tugboat.

As a consequence of the first accident, Earl claimed he was unable to work for two weeks. It was undisputed that he was unable to work for 11 days after the second accident. He returned to work approximately a month later, in early 1985, but claimed that his injuries eventually forced him to retire on May 16, 1985—three years and five weeks before his planned retirement at age 65.

Evidence adduced by defendants at trial indicated that plaintiff's intention prior to the accidents had been to retire in June of 1985 when he turned 62 years of age. Captain Kenneth Bekkelund of the Marion C. Bouchard testified that it had been common knowledge prior to Earl's December 1984 accident that he "was looking forward to retiring and talked of it frequently." Bekkelund testified that none of the crew had been surprised when plaintiff retired in May 1985. A member of the tugboat crew testified that Earl said nothing about being unable to work when he called to announce his retirement. Defendants also claimed that Earl had communicated his intention to retire to the family doctor treating him for the ankle injury even before the doctor had formally certified that Earl was "not fit for duty."

Plaintiff testified that he "would probably have retired * * * at 65." He denied having spoken about early retirement plans to his captain or fellow crew members. With regard to his doctor, Earl acknowledged that while he may have "discussed the possibility" of retiring, he did not recall having informed his physician of any definite plan to do so. In his closing argument, plaintiff's counsel presented the jury with two possible scenarios: retirement at age 65 as plaintiff testified was his intention, or retirement at age 67, based on the average work-life expectancy of a then–62 year old man. In its charge to the jury the court presented the issue of retirement age as one of disputed fact.

B. Remittitur

The $425,000 awarded for the loss of prospective earnings can be upheld only if the record contained evidence that plaintiff had the intention and ability to work past the age of 70, or, if not, could nonetheless have reasonably expected to receive an enormous—and unprecedented—increase in wages during the twilight years of his career as a deck hand. The record supports neither proposition.

* * *

II. APPLICABLE LAW

In this Jones Act case, federal law—that is, both judge-made general maritime law and federal statutory law—governs. * * *

* * *

In a recent Jones Act case the trial court observed that "[d]amages in tort cases are designed to provide reparation for the injury caused [because] the 'cardinal principle of damages in Anglo–American law is that of *compensation* for the injury caused to plaintiff by defendant's breach of duty.' " * * *

Neither the Jones Act nor the FELA includes any reference to the items of damages that are recoverable. * * * A Jones Act claimant, like any other tort victim bringing an action pursuant to state decisional or federal law, is entitled to full compensation, including damages for loss or impairment of earning capacity. * * *

III. DEPLETION OF WORK–CAPITAL

"An injury that reduces the period of work-life expectancy deprives the worker of the value of work-capital." * * * Unlike the plaintiff in *Rummo,* the life-expectancy of the plaintiff in the case at bar was not shortened. His work expectancy was, the jury found, reduced. While fortunately not terminal, James Earl's injuries were nonetheless permanently and fully disabling and, according to the jury, prevented him from working.

Regardless of whether or not a plaintiff would have exercised the choice to work as long as he could have, he or she is entitled to damages "measured by the extent to which [plaintiff's] capacity for earnings has been reduced." Restatement (Second) of Torts § 924 comment c. *See also* 2 S. Speiser, C. Krause & A. Gans, *The American Law of Torts* § 8:27, at 630. In effect, the " 'economic horizon of the [plaintiff] has been shortened because of the injuries.' "

There is no requirement that an injured plaintiff even be employed at the time of the accident in order to recover for impairment of earning capacity. * * * *See also Gault v. Monongahela Power Co.,* 159 W.Va. 318, 223 S.E.2d 421, 426–27 (1976) (although plaintiff had ostensibly retired, he had intended to return to work as pipefitter and was therefore entitled to damages for impairment of earning capacity).

Earning capacity is determined by what a plaintiff "*could* have earned even if he or she never worked to that capacity in the past." 2 M. Minzer, J. Nates, C. Kimball, D. Axelrod & R. Goldstein, *Damages in Tort Actions* § 10.22[3][a] (citations omitted). As a California appellate court has observed, "[i]mpairment of the capacity or power to work is an injury separate from the actual loss of earnings." * * *

This principle is most clearly illustrated by cases involving injured students, homemakers, and infants. *See, e.g., Feldman v. Allegheny Airlines, Inc.,* 524 F.2d 384, 388 (2d Cir.1975) (in determining future earnings of college-educated 25 year old woman who was unemployed when killed in plane crash, fact finder properly considered fact that she had been capable of working full-time for forty years until she was 65, had planned to attend law school and would have continued to work part-time for an estimated eight years while raising children); *Pucino v. Crete,* No. 89–644, 1990 WL 21303 (N.D.N.Y. Feb. 28, 1990) (LEXIS, Genfed library, Dist. file) (future earnings of aviation student killed while in last year of college are to be determined by wages he could have been expected to make as pilot over course of his pre-accident work-life expectancy); *Kavanaugh v. Nussbaum,* 129 A.D.2d 559, 514 N.Y.S.2d 55 (2d Dep't 1987) (injured infant's future earning capacity calculated using work-life expectancy of person having normal statistical life and work-life expectancies), *aff'd as modified on other grounds,* 71 N.Y.2d 535, 528 N.Y.S.2d 8, 523 N.E.2d 284 (1988); *Ward v. La. & Ark. Railway,* 451 So.2d 597, 608 (La.App.2d Cir.1984) (injured high school student entitled to recover for loss of earning capacity even though she had not as yet entered work force); *Grimes v. Haslett,* 641 P.2d 813, 818 n. 3 (Ala.1982) ("The right of an injured homemaker to recover for impaired earning capacity regardless of whether she was employed before the injury exemplifies the distinction between an award for lost earnings and an award for lost earning capacity.").

At most, some courts have required that the plaintiff have been *employable* or *potentially* employable, rather than actually employed at the time of the accident. For example, in *Espana v. United States,* 616 F.2d 41 (2d Cir.1980), the court of appeals observed that tort victims such as housewives or students who, prior to injury, have not earned as much as they could in the marketplace, are entitled to recover damages for loss of full-time earning capacity. *Id.* at 43 n. 2. In contrast, the court found that a plaintiff who had attempted and was unable before his accident to find full-time employment was not entitled to full-time compensation. *Id.* at 43–44. * * *

The conceptual difference between the loss of earning capacity and the loss of actual wages is also illustrated by cases holding that the injured party is not barred from recovering for loss of earning capacity even if he or she earns as much as or more than before the injury. * * * The rationale behind this seemingly paradoxical result is consistent with the concept of lost earning capacity, for "by having one less trade at his disposal the injured Plaintiff has a reduction in future employability." * * *

Nor does the ability to recover for impaired earning capacity even where there is no actual wage loss necessarily undermine the doctrine of mitigation of damages. Under this doctrine, a Jones Act claimant, like other tort victims, has an obligation to mitigate damages where possible by finding other employment. * * * Nonetheless, the plaintiff who does so may still recover a reduced award provided the diminution of his or her work-capital is reflected in the smaller number of employment options available to that person as a result of injury. *But see Alferoff v. Casagrande,* 122 A.D.2d 183, 504 N.Y.S.2d 719, 721 (2d Dep't 1986) (student may not recover for diminution of earning capacity in intended profession as cosmetologist since post-injury job as receptionist paid higher salary).

In the case at bar, plaintiff's announced plan, as testified to by defense witnesses, to retire at age 62, if it had been credited, would have been strong evidence of malingering. It could have shown that in fact he had not lost any of his work capital—*e.g.,* the ability to earn money in the marketplace—and that he had refused or otherwise failed to mitigate his damages. It is clear, however, that the jury believed plaintiff to be completely disabled as a result of his accident, and thus exempt from the obligation to mitigate damages by continuing to work as a deck hand or by seeking other employment.

IV. Determining Work-Life Expectancy

Courts have varied in their approaches to calculating work-life expectancy. The Supreme Court, discussing the calculation of future loss of income in the Longshore and Harbor Workers' Compensation Act, 33 U.S.C. § 901 *et seq.,* observed that

> [t]he lost stream [of income's] length cannot be known with certainty * * *. Given the complexity of trying to make an exact calculation, litigants frequently follow the relatively simple course of assuming that the worker would have continued to work up until a specific date certain.

Jones & Laughlin Steel Corp. v. Pfeifer, 462 U.S. 523, 533–34, 103 S.Ct. 2541, 2548–49, 76 L.Ed.2d 768 (1983). *See, e.g., Andrulonis v. United States,* 724 F.Supp. 1421, 1517 & n. 604 (N.D.N.Y.1989) (court assumes, for convenience and in absence of statistical basis for either plaintiff's or defendant's proffer, that plaintiff would have worked to age 65).

In general "[t]he admissibility of evidence regarding future earning capacity is within the wide discretion of the trial judge." For example, trial courts have considered the likelihood that economic downturns in a particular industry would have resulted in lower wages in future years, as well as the likelihood that a given plaintiff would have been impervious to such economic vicissitudes. *See, e.g., Pretre v. United States,* 531 F.Supp. 931, 935 (E.D.Mo.1981) (although defendant established that plaintiff would have been laid off due to his seniority ranking four years after being injured, court found he would have sought similar work and ordered him compensated for loss of earning capacity, "not merely for the loss of income from any particular job"). *Compare, e.g., Masinter v. Tenneco Oil Co.,* 867 F.2d 892, 899 (5th Cir.1989) (based on evidence of subsequent reduction in work force and in absence of evidence showing that longshoreman plaintiff would have been retained, it was not clearly erroneous for trial court to decide that plaintiff in future would have earned only 75% of his past earnings) *with Connecticut National Bank v. Omi Corp.,* 733 F.Supp. 14 (S.D.N.Y.1990) (awarding full compensation for future loss of earnings despite showing that there was a general loss of seamen's jobs after seaman's death where widow claimed that she and decedent would have moved to area where shipping industry was healthiest).

In the absence of a mandatory retirement policy, a wide range of evidence bearing on retirement is admissible in the discretion of the trial court. Evidence regarding the pre-accident intentions of the plaintiff is often highly probative. *See, e.g., O'Shea v. Riverway Towing Co.,* 677 F.2d 1194, 1198 (7th Cir.1982) (court credits 57 year-old former ship cook's testimony that she had intended to work until age 70); * * *.

The weight given such testimony of a desire and ability to work long beyond the average is, of course, left to the trier of fact. *See, e.g., Kaylor v. Amerada Hess Corp.,* 141 A.D.2d 331, 528 N.Y.S.2d 845, 846 (1st Dep't 1988) (seaman not entitled to recover for future impairment of earning capacity despite stated intention to return to higher paying seagoing job when he currently held shore job and in recent years had worked primarily in shore jobs); *Rosenbaum v. Lefrak Corp.,* 80 A.D.2d 337, 438 N.Y.S.2d 794, 799 (1st Dep't 1981) (rejecting as a dubious and unsupported assumption, plaintiff's claim that he would not have retired at age 62, but would have continued to work as carpenter until age 72).

In circumstances where there is no particularized information regarding a plaintiff's pre-accident intentions or other relevant characteristics, there appear to be no established rules in this circuit. * * *

Statistical charts, such as the mortality tables and work-life expectancy tables prepared by the United States Department of Labor, compile averages and are often deemed authoritative, particularly in the absence of contradictory particularized evidence. * * *

These tables are not binding on the fact finder. * * * Moreover, the statistical charts are updated on average every 10 years and therefore exhibit a lag in reflecting changing work and mortality patterns.

In the instant case the issue of plaintiff's retirement intentions was fully litigated. The jury obviously credited Earl's testimony. Unfortunately, it went far beyond that which could reasonably be inferred from the evidence. Even when viewed in the light most favorable to the plaintiff, the record does not support an award based upon a projected pre-accident work-life expectancy of 70 or more years—an assumption required by the jury award. Plaintiff's own testimony contradicts his claim that a statistical work-life expectancy of a 62 year old man—that is, a work-life expectancy of age 67—should be accepted. A retirement age of 65, on the other hand, has some support in the record and appears to be fair in view of all of the circumstances. It stretches the record as far as possible to favor the plaintiff and the jury's award.

V. CALCULATING DAMAGES

Once the injured victim proves that he or she could have been gainfully employed, it is necessary to show with sufficient certainty the amount of damages. More is involved in computing the value of the diminution of work-capital " 'than comparing the amount earned before and after the injury.' " * * * It has long been the practice in New York, for example, to allow juries to consider the possibility that an injured victim would have advanced through promotions and thus be entitled to a recovery higher than that indicated by an average of his past earnings. * * * *Metz v. Great Atlantic and Pacific Tea Company,* 30 Misc.2d 258, 215 N.Y.S.2d 175, 181 (Sup.Ct.1961) (permanent substitute school teacher had legal right to become permanent teacher and, despite lack of intent to do so, was entitled to recover higher amount). The Supreme Court has observed, "[a]s in all damages awards for tortious injury, '[i]nsistence on mathematical precision would be illusory and the judge or juror must be allowed a fair latitude to make reasonable approximations guided by judgment and practical experience.' " *Sea–Land Services, Inc. v. Gaudet,* 414 U.S. 573, 590, 94 S.Ct. 806, 817, 39 L.Ed.2d 9 (1974) (citation omitted). Nonetheless, the trier of fact must not be left to speculate and to unreasonably inflate an award.

In determining damages for the diminution in the plaintiff's earning capacity, courts have normally utilized an "oversimplified formula * * * which seeks to determine what the [plaintiff's] earnings would have been had he survived in good health, multiplied by [plaintiff's] work life expectancy with the resultant dollar figure arrived at, then discounted to the present value." * * * In cases such as that at bar, past earnings—in the absence of unusual proven circumstances—serve as a dependable and adequate guide to future loss.

Earl was employed full-time before the accidents and there was no indication that he would or could have "retooled" at the age of 62 to go into a higher paying field. Any speculation that he might have been the beneficiary of an increase in wages is in effect cancelled out by the not-insubstantial possibility that he had never intended to work past age 62.

A. *Computations*

The reduced award was computed as follows, giving plaintiff every benefit of the doubt:

1) $105,000 was allowed for lost wages, based upon an average of $37,468.72 for five previous years, with a 25% agreed upon tax rate, making net loss of earnings $87,006.15. Fringe benefits were agreed on as $5,784.00 per year, or $17,908.15 for the three years and five weeks. The total is $104,914.30, rounded off to $105,000.00. There was no proof of increases in future wage rates. No allowance for discount was made because the judgment was entered after the probable date of retirement. No interest was sought for delayed payment, except as indicated in 3), below.

2) Pain and suffering and lost pleasure awards were exaggerated. An award of $100,000 for five years past is allowed. Assuming a possible additional life expectancy of 14 years an additional amount of $280,000 is permitted. The total is $380,000.

3) Maintenance and cure and interest factors were computed without objection at a rate most favorable to plaintiff in the sum of $40,000. This amount included past and future medical expenses. *See Kratzer v. Capital Marine Supply, Inc.,* 490 F.Supp. 222, 229 (M.D.La.1980) (" 'Cure' is payment for medical, therapeutic and hospital expenses [up to that point where maximum cure has been achieved].").

The total award that could possibly be justified is $525,000.00. This sum seems excessive, but it allows maximum effect to the jury's exceptionally sympathetic verdict for the plaintiff.

CONCLUSION

Unless plaintiff agrees to a remittitur to $525,000.00, a new trial is granted.

Notes

1. What if an injured plaintiff had intended to retire at age 62 and, but for the injury would have done so and then discovered a preference for work and taken a post retirement job?

2. What is the scope of the duty to mitigate? Compare Walmsley v. Brady, 793 F.Supp. 393, 394, 395 (D.R.I.1992) with Burke v. Safeway Stores, Inc., 554 So.2d 184, 190 (La.App. 2d Cir.1989). In *Walmsley* the court decided to instruct the jury as follows:

> "Defendants have argued that plaintiff, a veterinarian, has failed to mitigate the damages of lost earning capacity she allegedly sustained from this accident. According to defendants, plaintiff can practice veterinary medicine in a modified form, without performing extensive amounts of surgery, or by serving as an administrative veterinarian in charge of an animal clinic. Plaintiff contends that she trained for, and had always intended to pursue, a surgery-intensive career in equine medicine. Further, plaintiff argues that because her disability has foreclosed her ability to pursue her chosen career path, she is entitled to compensation for lost earnings regardless of her potential earnings in a field she would not have entered but for the accident.
>
> * * *
>
> "While it may be true that Dr. Walmsley's career as a veterinarian of some sort is not ended, it may be just as true that she no longer can practice the variety of veterinary medicine for which she has been trained. It would not be unreasonable for a jury to decide that a physician has a right to practice in the particular field of medicine he or she has chosen, as opposed to practicing in *any* field of medicine.[1] The jury in this case must

1. An analogy can be drawn to damage mitigation requirements under Title VII of the Civil Rights Act of 1964. When an employee is wrongfully terminated or denied promotion in violation of Title VII, she is obliged to mitigate damages (if possible) by seeking employment "substantially equiva-

be entrusted with the ultimate decision regarding this plaintiff's entitlement to lost earnings compensation.

"Accordingly, this Court shall instruct the jury, in essence, as follows:

> As to loss of earnings, if you find the defendants liable, the plaintiff is entitled to recover for such loss of earnings as have resulted from her inability to work because of the injuries sustained. Therefore, in awarding damages, if any, you may consider the extent to which the plaintiff has proved loss of earnings resulting from her inability to work because of the injuries sustained, and the extent to which she has proved that she will lose earnings in the future resulting from her inability to work as a consequence of having sustained such injuries. Loss of earnings relates to the field in which the plaintiff was trained. If she can no longer practice in the specialized field in which she had planned to practice, you must then inquire and determine whether or not such a deprivation has resulted in a loss of earning capacity when juxtaposed against what she can do now as a veterinarian. The plaintiff is not required to mitigate damages to such an extent as to alter her professional career path to an unreasonable degree. As to reasonableness, the plaintiff is not required to accept alternative employment even though she could earn more money in said employment, provided that the higher paying job is unreasonably different from her chosen occupation."

Do you agree? In *Burke* the court said:

> "The evidence in this case wholly supports the trial court's conclusion that the plaintiff is disabled from returning to those vocations in which she has education and experience. She simply does not have the manual dexterity in her left index finger necessary to be a secretary or cosmetologist. Plaintiff's rehabilitation expert testified that without retraining or reeducation the plaintiff would be relegated to performing jobs at or near minimum wage with little or no opportunity for advancement or promotion. To avoid this stagnation, he recommended that the plaintiff pursue a degree in English in order to become a school teacher.
>
> "Dr. Bettinger testified that if plaintiff's losses were calculated over her work life expectancy taking what she could expect to earn as a legal secretary and subtracting what she could earn as a minimum wage clerical worker, the loss would be more than double the loss calculated on his more conservative, rehabilitation approach. We find no fault with this approach which will place plaintiff in a position to earn wages at least comparable to those she could have expected to earn in the occupation for which she was

lent" to the position she had previously held or sought.

> "Substantially equivalent employment" is employment that affords virtually identical promotional opportunities, compensation, job responsibilities, working conditions, and status * * * [i]f the former employee cannot find substantially equivalent employment, he may "lower his sights" and accept noncomparable employment. Title VII, however, "does not require that a person remain employed despite dissatisfaction."

Weaver v. Casa Gallardo, Inc., 922 F.2d 1515, 1527 (11th Cir.1991) (citing Sellers v. Delgado Community College, 839 F.2d 1132, 1138 (5th Cir.1988); EEOC v. Guardian Pools, Inc., 828 F.2d 1507, 1511 (11th Cir.1987)). While the instant case is premised not on Title VII, but on personal injury and negligence, I feel a damage mitigation analogy is not inappropriate.

trained and was pursuing at the time of the accident, and at the same time will not extend her economic loss past the rehabilitation period.

"However, defendants contend that the plaintiff should have either attempted to find some type of employment or begun to pursue her degree before trial as a means of mitigating her damages. We agree.

"The effect of the trial court judgment is to award plaintiff lost wages for a period of approximately eight years, three years before trial and five years after trial. The plaintiff could have either obtained a minimum wage job or begun her studies before the date of trial. In fact, she began to pursue her education at one point but dropped out due to her child's illness. Since we agree with the trial court that the pursuit of a degree is appropriate for this plaintiff and during that period the plaintiff will not be able to work, we will allow for her five years of future losses to run from the date of trial as the trial court ruled. But, we will reduce her past economic losses by a sum that she could have earned had she obtained employment in a minimum wage job. Therefore, we will reduce her award for past economic losses of $45,937, which did not take into account her residual earning capacity during that period, by $33,095 to $12,842 to reflect sums that she could have earned in a minimum wage job. The trial court's award for future economic losses of $67,191 will not be disturbed."

Are they inconsistent? Should the plaintiff's leaving school to take care of a sick child negate damages for that period? Had she been working might she have had accrued leave?

3. In Veazey v. State Farm Mutual Auto Ins., 587 So.2d 5, 8 (La.App. 3d Cir.1991) the court said:

"With reference to point one, the record establishes that plaintiff was at least qualified to do minimum wage work, even if only as a car-hop at a drive-in fast food place. As to point two, it does not seem to us that a minimum wage worker should be bound by a rule requiring showing of availability of minimum wage work in her specific area of habitation. We live in an era when employment follows jobs and not the other way around."

Should costs of relocation be awarded?

4. Consider the discussion in Bernard v. Royal Ins. Co., 586 So.2d 607, 615–17 (La.App. 4th Cir.1991):

"Ms. Bernard testified that she received a B.S. degree in biology from Xavier University in 1983. From 1983 to 1985 she was a substitute teacher for the Orleans Parish School Board. Shortly before the accident (age 24) she interviewed with the Orleans Parish Lead Poison and Prevention Center to start work for about $12,600 per year. Ms. Bernard considered a full-time job in the Orleans school system and contemplated 'some time in the future' going to medical school. She never applied to graduate school.

"In her deposition on November 11, 1989, Ms. Bernard stated that she planned to work at the Lead Prevention Center for a year or two and obtain a master's and doctorate degree in public health. She considered applying to medical school.

"Michael Andry, Director of Special Health Programs for the New Orleans Department of Health, confirmed that he interviewed Ms. Bernard shortly before the accident. She applied for a Civil Service laboratory position which paid $12,564 yearly and he hired her. Mr. Andry said that she told him of her plan to attend graduate school.

"Ellen Boston, Asst. Dean of Tulane School of Public Health and Tropical Medicine and Director of Admissions, reviewed Ms. Bernard's resume and transcripts. She testified that Ms. Bernard was qualified to become a tropical medicine graduate student and probably as a candidate for a doctorate.

"Athena Porter, a high school friend, testified that Ms. Bernard planned to work in the health department until she could save money for graduate school and to pursue a medical degree. Yolanda Bourgeois, a college friend, testified that Ms. Bernard's plans included work in public health to obtain funds for medical school.

* * *

"Ms. Bernard cites two cases to support the award. In Socorro v. Orleans Levee Board, 561 So.2d 739 (La.App. 4th Cir.1990), aff'd in part and rev'd in part 579 So.2d 931 (La.1990), the claimant was a freshman at Delgado College. The issue was the appropriate work life expectancy figures to compute future loss of earning capacity. Mr. Socorro's award of $338,000 was premised on his finishing college because he was a college student when he was injured. Ms. Bernard had not enrolled in a graduate program during the more than two years after she received her undergraduate degree.

"In Lee v. USAA Casualty Insurance Company, 540 So.2d 1083 (La. App. 1st Cir.1989), writs denied 542 So.2d 514 and 515 (La.1989), the 16–year–old junior high school honor student planned a career as a financial consultant. The economist based his calculations on the assumption that plaintiff would finish college with a math degree. The $706,200 jury award for lost future earnings was affirmed. Ms. Bernard received a college degree two years before the accident and was 24 years old. Whether Ms. Bernard would enter the graduate level or pursue a doctorate degree is far more speculative than a junior high honor student finishing college.

"The defendants cite Shackman v. Daigle, 447 So.2d 629 (La.App. 4th Cir.1984). A 43–year–old mother returned to college and was in her sophomore year when a neck injury precluded her from completing college and going to work as a psychiatric nurse. The issue was whether the trial court (which determined there was no disability) correctly refused to allow plaintiff's vocational rehabilitation expert to testify concerning loss of future wages. This Court stated that the expert's 'plotting of plaintiff's future was too speculative' and 'provided no basis for a claim for future wages.' *Id.* at 631.

"In Molbert v. Toepfer, 540 So.2d 577 (La.App. 3rd Cir.1989), aff'd 550 So.2d 183 (La.1989), a 28–year–old college engineering student with average grades, worked for his father in construction. An economist projected future economic loss based on plaintiff obtaining a degree and working as a mechanical engineer. The testimony was uncontroverted, but the trial court awarded $600,000, far less than the range given by the expert.

[Louisiana's] Third Circuit affirmed and noted that plaintiff had not earned a degree or worked as a mechanical engineer prior to the accident.

"Dr. Wolfson's projections are premised on the highly speculative assumption that Ms. Bernard would eventually obtain a doctorate in tropical medicine. She graduated in May, 1983 from Xavier University with a B.S. degree. At the time of the accident (1985) Ms. Bernard had taken no steps to begin a graduate program. She did not work in her specialty or at a full-time job from May, 1983 until July, 1985. Ms. Bernard's only employment after college was as a substitute teacher for two years and she did not remember whether she earned enough money to file a tax return. In her 1987 deposition she stated (as an aside) that she considered going to medical school 'some time in the future'. In her 1989 deposition she mentioned that she intended to seek a graduate degree in public health.

"The record convinces us that the jury abused its discretion. There is no evidence or indication that Ms. Bernard would complete a master's program and earn a doctorate degree. She made no effort to initiate a graduate career. Thus, Dr. Wolfson's calculation of $1,630,415 was based on very unrealistic assumptions. We must lower the award to the highest reasonable award under the circumstances.

"Dr. Wolfson's alternative calculations are based on the plausible assumption that Ms. Bernard would work in a laboratory, a position she accepted just prior to her accident. Her salary would have been $12,600, she would receive promotions over the years, and future loss of earnings would be $867,833."

Do you agree that future lost earning capacity beyond working in a laboratory is too speculative for someone two years out of college who has not yet started advanced studies?

5. How do you measure damages for lost earning capacity for someone who is unemployed? Does Simmons v. City of Monroe, 588 So.2d 1357, 1360, 1362 (La.App.2d Cir.1991) give you guidance?

"On April 2, 1987 plaintiff, Leon Simmons, drove to the Monroe City Hall for the purpose of paying his water bill. As plaintiff climbed the steps leading to the front door of the building, he stepped on a candy bar, slipped and fell. Plaintiff sued defendant, City of Monroe, for injuries received in the fall.

* * *

"Dr. Gilbert testified that since the fall plaintiff would not be capable of working at a physical type of job. Plaintiff was unemployed when his accident occurred. His previous employment was with Sears in its warehouse for nine years. The Sears job required physical labor and ended when the warehouse closed. Plaintiff also worked a second job as an overhead crane operator for O'Neal's which ended when the company moved to Shreveport. Between these two jobs, plaintiff was employed on a full-time basis for more than 40 hours per week. After these jobs ended, plaintiff worked as a cook, painter and carpenter.

"Even if a plaintiff is unemployed at the time of an injury, he is entitled to an award for impairment or diminution of earning power.

Earning capacity is not necessarily determined by actual loss. Damages may be assessed for the deprivation of what an injured plaintiff could have earned. Such damages are calculated on the person's ability to earn money rather than on what he actually earned before the injury. The theory is that the injury has deprived the plaintiff of a capacity which he would have been entitled to enjoy even though he may never have profited from it. Awards for lost earning capacity are inherently speculative and are intrinsically difficult to calculate. Factors to be considered in determining a proper award for lost earning capacity are plaintiff's physical condition before injury, past work history and consistency thereof, amount plaintiff probably would have earned absent the injury and probability that plaintiff would have continued to have earned wages over the remainder of his working life."

6. For a discussion of the consequence of plaintiff's obligation to pay income taxes *see* D. Dobbs, The Law of Remedies, § 8.6(4) (2d ed. 1993).

3. *Loss of Consortium*

BELCHER v. GOINS

Supreme Court of Appeals of West Virginia, 1990.
184 W.Va. 395, 400 S.E.2d 830.

McHugh, Justice:

The primary issue presented in this case is whether this jurisdiction recognizes a child's claim for loss or impairment of parental consortium, against a tortfeasor for nonfatal, negligently inflicted injuries sustained by the parent. We believe the Circuit Court of McDowell County answered the certified questions correctly in part and incorrectly in part. While this Court herein recognizes such a claim by a minor child, or by a handicapped child of any age who is dependent upon the injured parent, the plaintiff here was not a minor or handicapped child at the time the cause of action accrued. Accordingly, we remand this case with directions for the trial court to enter judgment for the defendant on the claim in question.

I.

Phyllis Belcher, mother of the plaintiff, Stephanie L. Belcher, was injured when the car she was driving was negligently struck head-on by a car driven by the defendant, Sherry L. Goins. Phyllis Belcher's claim against the defendant has been settled and dismissed with prejudice.

At the time of the collision the plaintiff was over eighteen years of age but resided in her mother's home with her mother. The plaintiff was not in or near her mother's car at the time of the collision.

As a count in her amended complaint, the plaintiff sought recovery from the defendant for "loss of love, companionship, and consortium of and from her mother," for mental anguish and for nursing and household services provided by the plaintiff to her mother after her mother was injured.

* * *

II.

A.

Traditionally, at common law "consortium" was defined as consisting of the alliterative trio of (1) services, (2) society and (3) sexual relations, and the husband was entitled to recover damages from a tort-feasor when *one or more* of these elements of the relationship with his wife were lost or impaired due to an injury to her. * * *

Similarly, "parental consortium" refers to the relationship between parent and child and is the right of the child to the intangible benefits of the companionship, comfort, guidance, affection and aid of the parent. * * * As a leading text writer has stated, it is useful to refer to the parent-child relationship, as well as the husband-wife relationship, as constituting consortium; the important aspects of the parent-child relationship, apart from the parent's duty of pecuniary support, are the intangibles which follow from living together as a family, including the affection, society, companionship, the mutual learning and the moral support given and received. 1 H. Clark, *The Law of Domestic Relations in the United States,* § 12.1, at 651 (2d ed. 1987).

The legislature of this state has recognized the validity of a claim by family members, including minor children, for damages for loss of consortium, including mental anguish, in cases involving the wrongful death of a family member.[4] The wrongful death statute allows distribution of net damages, including noneconomic damages, to those persons named in the decedent's will, or, if there be no will, to those persons who would be the decedent's heirs or next of kin under the laws of descent and distribution. * * * Net damages distributable to these family members "include ... damages for the following: (A) Sorrow, mental anguish, and solace which may include society, companionship, comfort, guidance, kindly offices and advice of the decedent; [and] (B) compensation for reasonably expected loss of * * * (ii) services, protection, care and assistance provided by the decedent[.]" *W.Va.Code,* 55–7–6(c)(1)(A) & (B)(ii) [1989].

B.

There is a split of authorities as to whether a minor child has a legally cognizable claim for loss or impairment of parental consortium, against a tortfeasor who negligently injures, but does not kill, the minor child's parent. Adhering to the early common-law rule, most state courts have refused to recognize such a claim. * * *

* * *

4. In the wrongful death context, compensatory damages awarded for loss of these intangibles are often referred to as "solatium."

C.

Several reasons typically have been offered to deny recognition of a parental consortium claim in a nonfatal injury case: (1) the weight of precedent refuses to recognize such a claim; (2) courts should defer to the legislature in this area; (3) double recovery; (4) multiplicity of actions; (5) difficulty of assessing the amount of damages; (6) increased liability insurance costs; (7) adverse effect on family relations; and (8) exposure to potentially unlimited liability. Virtually all of the courts recognizing a parental consortium claim in a nonfatal injury case address these matters. This Court believes each of these reasons are unpersuasive. We address each of these points in order.

First, this Court is more concerned with the persuasiveness of precedent than with the weight of precedent. While thirteen of the twenty-two state courts of last resort which have decided this issue since 1980 have denied a claim for parental consortium in a nonfatal injury case, we are not bound by the mere weight of judicial precedent but rather by the rule which embodies the more persuasive reasoning. * * * This Court concludes that the analysis of those decisions which have recognized a parental consortium claim in a nonfatal injury case, * * * is more persuasive than the analysis of those decisions which have rejected that claim.

Second, with respect to deferral to the legislature, in addition to observing that *the analogous claim for spousal consortium was judicially created,* we echo the sentiments of the Vermont court in *Hay:*

> The argument that this Court should prohibit the present claim for parental consortium from going to a jury because the issue is more appropriate for legislative resolution is wholly unpersuasive; such an argument ignores our responsibility to face a difficult legal question and accept judicial responsibility for a needed change in the common law. This Court has often met changing times and new social demands by expanding outmoded common law concepts.
>
> * * * When confronted with these difficult and complex issues, this Court did not shirk its duty and retreat into the safe haven of deference to the legislature * * *. One of the principal purposes of the [common] law of torts is to compensate people for injuries they sustain as a result of the negligent conduct of others.

145 Vt. at 543–44, 496 A.2d at 945 (citations omitted). Virtually all of the other courts recognizing the claim at issue also *expressly* refused to defer to the legislature for substantially the same reasons.

* * *

We also reject the third major reason for denying a claim of parental consortium in a nonfatal injury case, specifically, double recovery. The argument is that, as a practical matter, juries already award damages for loss or impairment of parental consortium in a nonfatal injury case as an undisclosed part of the *parent's* recovery of noneconomic damages. This argument, however, actually is support for open recognition of the minor child's action. The double recovery problem is easily eliminated by limiting the injured *parent's* recovery in this area to the loss or impairment of the parent's *pecuniary* ability to support the child; similarly, the *child's* cause of action would be limited to the loss of the parent's *society,* companionship and the like. * * * Rather than having juries make blind calculations of the minor child's loss in determining an award to the parent, the minor child's loss would be argued openly in court and the jury would be instructed to consider the minor child's loss separately. * * *

Moreover, this same argument as to double recovery would apply also to spousal consortium (the physically injured spouse's award might include an undisclosed amount for the other spouse's consortium loss or impairment). As in a parental consortium case, in a spousal consortium case the jury should be instructed as to the distinctive types of damages of the parties. We will assume that juries follow the court's instructions, including these instructions.

The fourth major reason for denying a parental consortium claim in a nonfatal injury case, namely, multiplicity of actions, is likewise unsound as a reason for totally denying such a claim. Virtually all of the courts recognizing this type of claim address this argument by requiring joinder of the minor children's parental consortium claims with the injured parent's claim, unless that is not feasible. We adopt this approach, too.

* * *

Fifth, we find unpersuasive the argument that the claim at issue should not be recognized because of the difficulty in assessing the amount of damages. A factfinder's calculation of damages for a minor child's loss of parental consortium is not any more difficult than the calculation necessary for indeterminate damages in other actions, such as for spousal consortium in a nonfatal injury case, spousal or parental consortium in a wrongful death case or for pain and suffering in a nonfatal injury case. As an adjunct to this argument, it has been contended that monetary compensation will not enable the minor child to regain what was lost (the society, companionship and the like) when the parent was seriously injured. This Court agrees with the following response to that contention:

> Although a monetary award may be a poor substitute for the loss of a parent's society and companionship, it is the only workable way that our legal system has found to ease the injured party's tragic loss. We recognize this as a shortcoming of our society, yet we believe that allowing such an award is clearly preferable to completely denying recovery. * * *

Another reason advanced for denying recognition of a parental consortium claim in a nonfatal injury case is that recognition of such a claim would increase the liability insurance costs to society. We are unswayed by this assertion and concur with these comments:

> [P]roperly, the provision and cost of such [liability] insurance varies with potential liability under the law, not the law with the cost of insurance.
>
> * * * No doubt there are genuine wrongs that courts are ill suited to set right, and others that do not merit the social costs of litigation. But if these costs are to be the reason for denying an otherwise

> meritorious cause of action, that is one judgment to be made by legislatures rather than by courts.

* * *

A seventh reason offered for opposing recognition of the claim in question is that each of the minor children likely would attempt to magnify the quality of his or her relationship with the parent *vis-a-vis* the other minor children in order to enhance his or her own damage award. The same situation is present, however, in wrongful death actions. * * *

Finally, there is the fear of exposure to liability to a potentially unlimited number of people who could claim and prove a loss or impairment of consortium because of the close relationship with the physically injured person. This fear is unfounded:

> In an era of ever-increasing caseloads in both the trial and appellate courts of this state, and where our society is being increasingly criticized for its propensity for litigation, the recognition of a new cause of action is not a step which we take lightly. However, it is the rights of the new class of plaintiffs, and the desire to see justice made available within our legal system, which are of paramount importance.

The "new class of plaintiffs" which we recognize here is *limited* to minor children, as well as physically or mentally handicapped children of any age who are dependent upon the injured parent physically, emotionally and financially. Because of the *crucial* role of the parent in these *vitally important* relationships, damages are almost certain to be inflicted when a tortfeasor interferes with these relationships by seriously injuring the parent physically.

We note that two state courts of last resort, namely, those in Arizona and Washington, * * * have allowed recovery of parental consortium damages by any adult child, as well as by a minor child, in a case involving nonfatal injury to the parent. There is some logic to that approach, in that adult children, too, may suffer a real loss when the parent-child relationship is disturbed by the tortious infliction of physical injuries upon the parent. We note also that the West Virginia wrongful death statute allows recovery of parental consortium damages by adult, as well as by minor, children. Nevertheless, due to the very broad impact of extending this new common-law claim to all adult children, this Court at this time declines to follow the Arizona and Washington opinions in this regard.

* * *

D.

Having examined precedents elsewhere and having addressed the concerns related to recognition of a claim for parental consortium in a case involving nonfatal injuries sustained by the parent, this Court now turns to precedent within this jurisdiction. * * *

* * *

E.

Based upon all of the above, we state our holdings. First, "parental consortium" refers to the intangible benefits to a minor child arising from his or her relationship with such child's natural or adoptive parent. It includes society, companionship, comfort, guidance, kindly offices and advice of such parent and the protection, care and assistance provided by the parent. Consistent with the wrongful death statute, *W.Va.Code,* 55–7–6, as amended, parental consortium also includes sorrow and mental anguish concerning the impairment of the relationship.

Second, any minor child, or a physically or mentally handicapped child of any age who is dependent upon his or her natural or adoptive parent physically, emotionally and financially, may maintain a cause of action for loss or impairment of parental consortium, against a third person who seriously injures such child's parent, thereby severely damaging the parent-child relationship. To the extent that *Wallace v. Wallace,* 155 W.Va. 569, 184 S.E.2d 327 (1971), is inconsistent herewith, it is overruled.

We wish to point out that a minor or handicapped child's claim for loss or impairment of parental consortium is different from a claim for negligent infliction of emotional distress. Negligent infliction of emotional distress usually requires that the plaintiff witness a physical injury to a closely related person, suffer mental anguish that manifests itself as a physical injury and the plaintiff must be within the zone of danger so as to be subject to an unreasonable risk of bodily harm created by the defendant. * * * In contrast, a minor or handicapped child's claim for loss or impairment of parental consortium does not require that such child be within the zone of danger. Consortium claims are *sui generis.*

III.

The third certified question, *see supra* section I., raises the issue of whether parental consortium includes the value of nursing, domestic or household services provided by a child to the injured parent. We hold that this item is not an element of parental consortium.

The courts recognizing a parental consortium claim in a nonfatal injury case do not include as an element of such consortium the value of these or any other services provided by a child to the injured parent. Instead, the injured *parent* would be entitled to claim recovery of the value of such services provided by a child or by anyone else providing such services with or without charge. Thus, "parental consortium" does not include the value of nursing, domestic or household services provided by a minor or handicapped child to the injured parent.

IV.

The plaintiff here was not a minor or handicapped child at the time the cause of action accrued. Accordingly, having answered the certified questions, we remand this case with directions for the trial court to enter judgment for the defendant on this claim.

Certified questions answered; case remanded with directions.

Notes

1. For another point of view *see* Butz v. World Wide, Inc., 492 N.W.2d 88 (N.D.1992):

"Defendants World Wide, Inc., and Cass Oil Co. appeal from part of a judgment entered on April 27, 1992, by the district court, awarding Plaintiff Rose Marie Butz (Rose) the sum of $30,000 in damages for her loss of spousal consortium. Plaintiffs Scott Butz, Dawn Butz, and Robert Butz (the Butz children) cross-appeal from a portion of the same district court judgment dismissing their claim for loss of parental consortium. We affirm.

"On June 15, 1984, Charles Butz, Jr., husband of Rose and father of the Butz children, was severely injured in a boating accident. He was riding on a 'Super Tube' that was being pulled behind a boat on a lake. While on the 'Super Tube,' he collided with another boat parked along the shore, causing his injuries. The 'Super Tube' was manufactured by World Wide, Inc., and sold by Cass Oil Co.

"On January 15, 1985, Charles Butz, Jr., commenced an action in district court against World Wide, Inc., and Cass Oil Co. (World Wide) for the personal injuries sustained in the accident. On June 2, 1987, the jury returned a verdict for Charles Butz, Jr., in excess of $500,000. That judgment was affirmed by this Court in Butz v. Werner, 438 N.W.2d 509 (N.D.1989). Neither Rose nor the Butz children asserted their prospective loss of consortium claims in Charles Butz, Jr.'s personal injury action.

"On May 2, 1990, Rose and the Butz children brought their loss of consortium claims against World Wide, nearly three years subsequent to the entry of the jury verdict. World Wide moved for summary judgment of dismissal of both Rose's loss of spousal consortium claim and the Butz children's loss of parental consortium claim. World Wide contended that North Dakota does not recognize a cause of action for loss of parental consortium; further, any claim for loss of consortium must mandatorily be joined with the original personal injury action, or thereafter be barred.

* * *

"In its 'Findings of Fact, Conclusions of Law and Order for Judgment,' the district court awarded Rose the stipulated $30,000 in damages for her loss of spousal consortium. The district court dismissed the Butz children's claim for loss of parental consortium.

* * *

"We conclude that this is the best approach to loss of consortium claims in North Dakota, and in the future we will require joinder when possible. In the future, if the 'deprived' party fails to join the claim, that party must offer the court a compelling reason for non-joinder or it will be dismissed with prejudice. Absent a compelling reason, non-joinder will result in an absolute bar to any loss of consortium claim asserted after the conclusion of the underlying action of the 'impaired' party.

We will not, however, apply this new declaration of law to the case at bar. To do so would be unduly burdensome and unfair to the Plaintiffs in this case who have had little warning that this might be our view of what is appropriate. Rather, we will utilize the 'Sunburst Doctrine' and apply the present decision prospectively.

* * *

"Having decided that compulsory joinder does not apply to the case at bar, and therefore the judgment of the district court is affirmed in respect to Rose's claim, we now proceed to consider whether or not children have a cause of action for loss of parental consortium. We hold that they do not.

"We have considered this issue before in Hastings v. James River Aerie No. 2337, Etc., 246 N.W.2d 747 (N.D.1976), and Morgel v. Winger, 290 N.W.2d 266 (N.D.1980). These holdings are clearly contrary to the Butz children's claim. Both of the cases are still binding precedent in North Dakota, and control the issue before the Court.

"The Butz children assert that the *Hastings* and *Morgel* cases are outdated due to subsequent occurrences in the area of law which they address.

* * *

"The Butz children also contend that our earlier decisions in Hopkins v. McBane, 427 N.W.2d 85 (N.D.1988), First Trust Co. v. Scheels Hardware, 429 N.W.2d 5 (N.D.1988), and Jacobs v. Anderson Bldg. Co., 430 N.W.2d 558 (N.D.1988), strengthen their claim for loss of parental consortium. They believe that the three foregoing cases are indicative of some type of extensive trend which is broadening the spectrum for loss of consortium claims. Once again, we must disagree. The decisions in those cases permitted parents recovery for loss of their children's society, comfort, and companionship. Parents were an already-existing class of plaintiffs in wrongful death and personal injury actions for children; however, such 'nonpecuniary' damages were not previously recoverable. *McBane* and its progeny did not expand the class of plaintiffs, it merely expanded the damages which could be recovered in wrongful death or personal injury cases. Thus, the argument that *McBane* and its progeny allow children to bring an action for loss of parental consortium is overbroad and unpersuasive.

"We continue to believe the ten reasons for denying children a cause of action for loss of parental consortium, set out in the annotation found at 69 A.L.R.3d 528,[4] quoted with approval in *Hastings,* are still valid. Furthermore, we believe our rationale in *Morgel* remains a sound interpretation of the law.

> 'We agree with the California Court which, in Borer v. American Airlines, Inc., 19 Cal.3d 441, 138 Cal.Rptr. 302, 563 P.2d 858, 862

4. 69 A.L.R.3d 528, has currently been superseded by 11 A.L.R.4th 549. The new Annotation enumerates the very same ten reasons for denying children a cause of action for loss of parental consortium. They are:

> "(1) the absence of any enforceable claim on the child's part to the parent's services, (2) the absence of precedents, (3) the uncertainty and remoteness of the damages involved, (4) the possible overlap with the parent's recovery, (5) the multiplication of litigation, (6) the possibility of upsetting settlements made with parents, (7) the danger of fabricated actions, (8) the increase in insurance costs, (9) the public policy expressed in some jurisdictions in the enactment of 'heart balm' statutes, and (10) family problems arising from segregated awards to children."

11 A.L.R.4th at 553–54.

(1977), said that the question of a child's right to recover for loss of parental consortium is one of policy. Because we believe that the question is one of policy, *we conclude that the birth of the child's cause of action for loss of parental consortium should be attended to by the Legislature as its obstetrician.'*

Morgel, 290 N.W.2d at 267 (emphasis added).

"For the foregoing reasons, we affirm the judgment of the district court."

See also Monias v. Endal, 330 Md. 274, 623 A.2d 656, 661 (1993) (Maryland does not recognize a child's right to loss of consortium of an injured parent). *But see* Reagan v. Vaughn, 804 S.W.2d 463 (Tex.1990) (Texas recognizes the right of all children, minor and adult, to loss of consortium of an injured parent).

4. *Wrongful Death and Survival Statutes*

D. DOBBS, THE LAW OF REMEDIES

§ 8.3(1), at 670 (2d ed. 1993).*

"*Three rules.* Three distinct and basic common law rules bore on recovery of damages in death cases. These rules remain important today as the reasons for modern statutory changes. These rules were: (1) If the tortfeasor died after committing a tort against his victim, the victim's claim died as well. (2) If the tort *victim* died, his cause of action was at an end, 'drowned,' in the larger matter of a crime against the Crown. (3) The victim's survivors had no independent claim of their own against the tortfeasor for the loss of their support or for their grief and sorrow. There has never been any good explanation for all these rules."

What is the difference between a wrongful death statute and a survival statute? What survives in a survival statute? Consider the following cases:

NELSON v. AMERICAN NATIONAL RED CROSS

United States District Court, District of Columbia, 1993.
815 F.Supp. 501.

JACKSON, DISTRICT JUDGE.

On February 8, 1985, James Nelson, Sr., a 58–year old florist, underwent an elective splenectomy at Georgetown University Hospital ("Georgetown") in Washington, D.C. to correct a bleeding disorder of the skin and mucous membranes. When he hemorrhaged postoperatively, his blood loss was replaced with multiple units of blood and blood products obtained by the hospital from the blood bank operated by the District of Columbia chapter of the American National Red Cross. One of the units was later learned to have been contaminated with the human immunodeficiency virus ("HIV").

On March 15, 1991, Nelson died of acquired immunodeficiency syndrome ("AIDS") at John Hopkins Hospital, Baltimore, Maryland, the disease having been derived from the transfusion he had received at Georgetown six years earlier.

On March 9, 1992, Nelson's son, as personal representative of his father's estate, brought the instant action against the American National Red Cross, its local affiliate, and Georgetown University Hospital, as the suppliers of the tainted blood, under the District of Columbia's Wrongful Death Act and its Survival Statute, to recover damages resulting from the events culminating in his father's death.

Plaintiff contends that, although the ELISA test to detect directly the presence of HIV antibodies in blood did not become available until March, 1985, both the risk of contracting AIDS through blood transfusions, and simple if less efficacious modalities of blood-donor screening and alternative treatments for Nelson's condition, had been well known to the American Red Cross and Georgetown for several years prior to February, 1985, and that each in its own way had therefore been negligent in failing to employ them to avert that risk in Nelson's case.

The defendants have moved to dismiss the complaint or for summary judgment, on limitations grounds. They assert that any action to recover for their alleged negligence expired, at the latest, in October, 1989, three years after Nelson learned that he had been "injured" (i.e., infected), even giving plaintiff the benefit of the so-called "discovery rule." Plaintiff responds that, if it is "injury" to a victim that starts the statute running, then Nelson's injury did not occur until AIDS overtook him in 1990. Moreover, even if Nelson is deemed to have been actionably "injured" when he received the tainted blood, and the statute commenced to run when he learned of it some months later, Nelson did not have—and may never have had—the knowledge essential to put him on notice that his time within which to make a claim for it was limited, namely, as the D.C. Court of Appeals has put it in one case, "some evidence of wrongdoing" on the part of the prospective defendants. * * *

I.

The record before the Court establishes that, in early fall of 1986, some 19 months after Nelson's operation, the local chapter of the Red Cross informed Nelson's physician at Georgetown that the donor of one of the units of blood with which Nelson had been transfused in February, 1985, had subsequently tested positive for the HIV antibody. The physician in turn notified Nelson, who met in person with the doctor on October 3rd, was tested himself, and told on October 10th that he, too, had tested HIV positive.

II.

The District of Columbia Survival Statute, D.C.Code § 16–2701 (1981) saves an extant right of action "in whose favor it has accrued for any cause" for posthumous enforcement by a decedent's estate. If the "cause" is a personal injury done to the decedent while he was alive, the "right of action" is governed for limitations purposes by D.C.Code § 12–301(8) (1981), which provides that such actions "may not be brought after the expiration of [three years] from the time the right to maintain the action accrues." * * * Under controlling District of Columbia precedents the right to maintain an action for injury to the person "accrues" when "injury result[s]" from a prospective defendant's wrongful conduct. * * * But when "the fact of injury [is] not readily apparent and ... might not become apparent for several years after the incident causing injury ha[s] occurred," * * *, the District of Columbia courts follow the "discovery rule" by which the limitations period will not commence to run until the injury ought to be apparent, or "when the plaintiff knows or through the exercise of due diligence should have known of the injury." * * *

* * *

This Court concludes, as defendants contend, that the cause of action which plaintiff seeks to pursue here under the District of Columbia's Survival Statute is time-barred. Nelson was "injured," for limitations purposes, when he received the pathogenic transfusion, as surely so as if he had been administered a poison or struck a blow. He "discovered," as did the defendants, that he had been infected in October of 1986. He also knew how, when and by whom the infecting agent had been procured and introduced into his body. And he knew that the consequences were likely to be lethal. A tragedy had befallen him for which he was himself entirely innocent. "Wrongdoing" by someone was more than a hypothetical possibility.

* * *

III.

The plaintiff's wrongful death claim here, however, is not so manifestly untimely. The District of Columbia Wrongful Death Act, D.C.Code § 16–2701 (1981) provides that a death caused by the "wrongful act" of another gives rise to an action for damages for the benefit of the decedent's surviving dependent next-of-kin if the "wrongful act" is such as would have entitled the decedent to have maintained such an action had his death not ensued. The applicable period of limitations is "one year after the death of the person injured." D.C.Code § 16–2702 (1981). This action was filed within the year following Nelson's death, but defendants contend that because Nelson himself was time-barred at his death, so too is plaintiff as his personal representative; in other words, because Nelson was not "entitled" to maintain the action when "death ensued," neither is his personal representative whose rights, they say, are derivative of, and no larger than, his decedent's.

Plaintiff correctly observes, however, that the Wrongful Death Act was enacted by the legislature to protect interests of persons other than the victim in his own vitality, specifically, the interests of his spouse and next-of-kin who have also, by reason of his death, sustained a loss the law regards as compensable. The cause of action it creates is not derivative but, rather, a new and independent cause of action which is not constrained by any temporal limits on the enforceability by the decedent himself of his own rights respecting the same injury at the time of his death.

There is, it appears, no controlling decision of the District of Columbia Court of Appeals on the issue, and both plaintiff and defendants cite a multitude of cases from other jurisdictions in support of the construction they say this Court must give to the District of Columbia's version of the Wrongful Death Act. Older cases from the U.S. Court of Appeals for the District of Columbia Circuit, however, suggest that the construction favored by the plaintiff is the appropriate construction, * * * and is apparently in accord with the majority rule throughout the country of those courts having construed similar versions of Lord Campbell's Act. *See* W. Page Keeton, *Prosser and Keeton on the Law of Torts* § 127, at 957 (5th ed. 1984); Restatement (Second) of Torts § 899 cmt. c (1979).

Such a conclusion does not alleviate a legitimate concern for the judicial system's ability to resolve death claims which are stale in fact while nevertheless viable under the statute of limitations. A timely action for wrongful death might theoretically be predicated upon a defendant's conduct ancient in the extreme if only the suit follows death within the ensuing year. It is, however, the legislature's exclusive prerogative to provide the prophylaxis of a statute of absolute repose, as it has done in other cases, *see, e.g.,* D.C.Code § 12–310 (1981), if that is to be the policy of the forum. This federal court certainly may not do so.

For the foregoing reasons, it is, therefore, this 11th day of March, 1993,

Ordered, that defendants' motion to dismiss the complaint or for summary judgment is granted in part and denied in part; and it is

Further Ordered, that Counts II, IV and VI of plaintiff's amended complaint are dismissed with prejudice.

RUSSELL v. INGERSOLL–RAND CORPORATION

Supreme Court of Texas, 1992.
841 S.W.2d 343.

HECHT, JUSTICE.

If an individual's action for personal injuries would have been barred by limitations at the time of his death, are actions based upon the same wrongful conduct, brought by his heirs, legal representatives or estate under the Survival Statute, TEX.CIV.PRAC. & REM.CODE § 71.021, and by his beneficiaries under the Wrongful Death Statute, TEX.CIV.PRAC. & REM.CODE §§ 71.001–.011, also barred by limitations? Both the district court and the court of appeals answered this question affirmatively. 795 S.W.2d 243. We agree.

I

In 1981, Donnon Russell was diagnosed as suffering from chronic obstructive pulmonary disease caused by exposure to silica during his employment for many years as a sandblaster and painter. In 1982, Russell filed suit to recover damages for his injuries. In amended pleadings, Russell named a total of 14 defendants who he alleged manufactured and distributed products containing silica that he had used in his work. In 1988, before the case could come to trial, Russell died. Five weeks later, Russell's widow and four children[1] filed an amended petition naming

1. Russell's widow is Betty Parr Russell. His four children are Norma Lynn Coker, Gail Lee Harrah, Jeannie Marie Bourgoin and Dennis O'Neal Russell.

themselves as plaintiffs and claiming damages on behalf of Russell's estate and for his death. Plaintiffs also added seven defendants whom Russell had never sued himself, who are respondents in this Court.[2]

Respondents moved for summary judgment on the ground that plaintiffs' claims against them are barred by limitations. In their last amended petition in the trial court plaintiffs asserted claims based on strict liability, negligence, gross negligence, misrepresentation, and breach of warranty. Respondents argue that the causes of action against them accrued either in 1981 when Russell's condition was first diagnosed, or no later than 1982 when he filed suit. Had Russell sued respondents immediately before his death, his claims would have been barred by limitations.[3] Respondents contend that plaintiffs' actions are derivative of Russell's and are therefore likewise barred.

Plaintiffs argue that while their actions are in some sense derivative of Russell's, the sole statute of limitations applicable to their claims under the survival and wrongful death statutes is Tex.Civ.Prac. & Rem.Code § 16.-003(b), which states: "A person must bring suit not later than two years after the day the cause of action accrues in an action for injury resulting in death. The cause of action accrues on the death of the injured person." Based upon this statute, plaintiffs argue that they had two years from Russell's death to file their claims, even if Russell's own claims for the same injury would have been barred at the time he died.

The district court granted summary judgment for respondents and severed it from plaintiffs' claims against the defendants which Russell timely sued. The court of appeals affirmed. 795 S.W.2d 243.

II

At common law, an individual's action for personal injuries did not survive his death. * * * The Legislature has abrogated this rule by Tex.Civ.Prac. & Rem.Code § 71.021, which states:

Survival of Cause of Action

(a) A cause of action for personal injury to the health, reputation, or person of an injured person does not abate because of the death of the injured person or because of the death of a person liable for the injury.

(b) A personal injury action survives to and in favor of the heirs, legal representatives, and estate of the injured person. The action

2. Respondents are Ingersoll–Rand Co., McKenzie Equipment Co., Schramm, Inc., Cooper Industries, Inc., Joy Manufacturing Co., IC Group Inc., and Sullair Corp.

3. The statutes of limitations applicable to these causes of actions are two or four years. Tex.Civ.Prac. & Rem.Code §§ 16.-003(a), 16.004; Tex.Bus. & Com.Code § 2.725. Plaintiffs contend that fact issues remain as to when the causes of action against respondents accrued, precluding summary judgment. More specifically, plaintiffs argue that the discovery rule operates to delay accrual of the causes of action against respondents until Russell could reasonably have determined that they were among the parties at fault. Generally, however, "limitations begin to run when the fact of injury is known", *Moreno v. Sterling Drug, Inc.*, 787 S.W.2d 348, 351 (Tex.1990), not when the alleged wrongdoers are identified. There is no question on the record before us that Russell's actions accrued no later than 1982, when he filed suit.

survives against the liable person and the person's legal representatives.

(c) The suit may be instituted and prosecuted as if the liable person were alive.

By this statute, a decedent's action survives his death and may be prosecuted in his behalf. The survival action, as it is sometimes called, is wholly derivative of the decedent's rights. The actionable wrong is that which the decedent suffered before his death. The damages recoverable are those which he himself sustained while he was alive and not any damages claimed independently by the survival action plaintiffs (except that funeral expenses may also be recovered if they were not awarded in a wrongful death action). * * * Any recovery obtained flows to those who would have received it had he obtained it immediately prior to his death—that is, his heirs, legal representatives and estate. Defenses that could have been raised against a claim by the injured person may also be raised against the same claim asserted by the person's heirs and estate. * * *

It follows from these general principles that if a decedent's action would have been barred by limitations had it been asserted immediately prior to his death, a survival action based upon the same alleged wrong is likewise barred. If the decedent's action would not have been barred, the running of the limitations period is tolled by the decedent's death for up to one year. Tex.Civ.Prac. & Rem.Code § 16.062. * * *

III

Wrongful death actions are also derivative of the decedent's rights. Such actions are creatures of statute abrogating the common law rule that no cause of action may be brought for the death of another person. * * * As initially passed, our Wrongful Death Statute provided in part:

> Sec. 1. [W]hensoever the death of any person may be caused by wrongful act, neglect, unskilfulness or default, and the act, neglect, unskilfulness or default is such as would (if death had not ensued) have entitled the party, injured, to maintain an action for such injury, then and in every such case the person who would have been liable if death had not ensued, shall be liable to an action for damages, notwithstanding the death of the person injured * * *.
>
> * * *
>
> Sec. 3. The action shall be brought within one year after the death of such deceased.

Act approved Feb. 2, 1860, 8th Leg., R.S., ch. 35, § 1, 1860 Tex.Gen.Laws 32, 4 H. Gammel, Laws of Texas 1394 (1898). Sections 1 and 3 were amended and separated in 1879. Section 1 was changed to read in part: "The wrongful act, negligence, carelessness, unskillfulness or default mentioned * * * must be of such character as would, if death had not ensued, have entitled the party injured to maintain an action for such injury." Tex.Rev.Civ.Stat. art. 2900 (1879). Section 3 was moved from the wrongful death provisions to a general limitations provision which prescribed that certain actions be brought within one year, including: "Actions for injuries done to the person of another where death ensued from such injuries". Tex.Rev.Civ.Stat. art. 3202(4) (1879). The 1879 provision added: "the cause of action shall be considered as having accrued at the death of the party injured." *Id.* In 1897, the limitations period was changed from one to two years. Act approved Mar. 4, 1897, 25th Leg., R.S., ch. 14, 1897 Tex.Gen.Laws 12, 12; 10 H. Gammel Laws of Texas 1066, 1066 (1898). The language establishing the cause of action remained in substantially the same form, becoming article 4672 of the Texas Revised Civil Statutes of 1925, and in 1985, section 71.003(a) of the Texas Civil Practice and Remedies Code, Act of May 17, 1985, 69th Leg., R.S., ch. 959, § 1, 1985 Tex.Gen.Laws 3242, 3296, which is in effect today. The two-year limitations period has also remained constant, and is now codified at Tex.Civ. Prac. & Rem.Code § 16.003(b).

Currently, the Wrongful Death Statute allows an action by a decedent's beneficiaries "only if the individual injured would have been entitled to bring an action for the injury if he had lived." Tex.Civ.Prac. & Rem. Code § 71.003(a). * * *

* * *

For 132 years, since Texas first created an action for wrongful death, this Court has allowed the action only if the decedent could have maintained suit for his injuries immediately prior to his death. * * *

Plaintiffs, however, argue that the defense of limitations is an exception to the rule that a wrongful death action is derivative. They base this argument on the second sentence of the statute of limitations for wrongful death actions, which states that "[t]he cause of action accrues on the death of the injured person." Tex.Civ.Prac. & Rem.Code § 16.003(b). Because a wrongful death action does not accrue until the death of the injured person, plaintiffs argue, even if the decedent's own cause of action is then barred, the wrongful death action is not.

We do not agree that section 16.003(b) must be read as an exception to section 71.003(a). Section 16.003(b) sets the time when a wrongful death action accrues, if it exists. It does not, however, provide that there is always an action to accrue. The Wrongful Death Statute allows an action by a decedent's beneficiaries "only if the individual injured would have been entitled to bring an action for the injury if he had lived." Tex.Civ. Prac. & Rem.Code § 71.003(a).

* * *

It is wrong to say, as one of the dissents does, that our decision penalizes the families of people who die lingering deaths. A person whose injuries result in death is entitled, while he is alive, to sue and recover damages from those liable for his injuries. The defendant against whom judgment is rendered is not required to respond again in damages to the family of the injured person after he dies. And the defendant who is exonerated of liability to the injured person is not required to defend against the same claims by the person's family following his death. The families of injured persons are not penalized in such circumstances. Neither are they penalized when they are precluded from suing because a decedent, in his lifetime, chose not to sue until his own claims were barred by limitations. We have not, as one of the dissents states, placed wrongful death beneficiaries in the impossible situation of being required to file suit before the death of which they complain. We hold only, in the words of section 71.003(a), that they are entitled to sue "only if the individual injured would have been entitled to bring an action for the injury if he had lived."

To adopt the plaintiffs' position in this case would greatly relax the statute of limitations for death cases. By their reading of section 16.003(b), statutory beneficiaries are allowed to sue within two years of a death, even if the action which allegedly caused the death occurred five, ten, twenty or more years earlier. This would thwart the very purpose of limitations, which is to require that actions be brought within a reasonable, prescribed period after a wrong occurs.

* * *

To try to show that the defense of limitations is different from other defenses to wrongful death actions, the dissents rely on two commentators, who purport only to state the majority rule in American jurisdictions,[11] the Restatement (Second) of Torts, which conflicts with the first Restatement of Torts,[12] and a few cases.[13] But the more authoritative view, and probably the more prevalent, is that if a decedent's action would be barred by limitations, then so would a wrongful death action. Construing a federal statute, the United States Supreme Court stated in *Michigan Central R.R. v. Vreeland,* 227 U.S. 59, 70, 33 S.Ct. 192, 196, 57 L.Ed. 417 (1913):

> [A]s the foundation of the right of action [for wrongful death] is the original wrongful injury to the decedent, it has been generally held that the new action is a right dependent upon the existence of a right in the decedent immediately before his death to have maintained an action for his wrongful injury.

Settled precedent of this Court and other courts in Texas, representing consistent statutory construction for more than a century, supports our conclusion that there should be no exception for limitations to the general rule providing that our statutory wrongful death claim is essentially derivative in nature. The weight of authority in other jurisdictions, unsurprisingly, reaches the same result. A single exception for limitations is logically inconsistent, in fact, with the principle underlying limitations—

11. W. Page Keeton et. al., Prosser and Keeton on the Law of Torts § 127, at 957 (5th ed. 1984); William L. Prosser, The Law of Torts § 127, at 911 (4th ed. 1971); Leon Green, *The Texas Death Act,* 26 Tex.L.Rev. 461, 461, 463 (1948).

12. Restatement (Second) of Torts § 899 cmt. c, at 442 (1979) ("Under most wrongful death statutes, the cause of action is a new and independent one, accruing to the representative or to surviving relatives of the decedent only upon his death; and since the cause of action does not come into existence until the death, it is not barred by prior lapse of time, even though the decedent's own cause of action for the injuries resulting in death would be barred."); Restatement of Torts § 899 cmt. c, at 524–26 (1939) ("A cause of action for death is complete when death occurs; since, however, the decedent in his lifetime had a cause of action, the cause of action for death does not come into existence if before the death the action for the tortious conduct has been barred by the lapse of time.").

13. [citations omitted]

that actions should be timely asserted or not at all—since it would permit wrongful death beneficiaries to sue within two years of the death of their family member, regardless of how long before his death he may have been injured.

For all these reasons, we hold that the defense of limitations bars the wrongful death action against the respondents in this case as a matter of law.

* * *

We therefore affirm the judgment of the court of appeals.

Concurring and dissenting opinion by DOGGETT, J., joined by MAUZY, J.

Concurring and dissenting opinion by GAMMAGE, J. [omitted]

Notes

1. Which approach do you agree with?

2. In the District of Columbia if James Nelson, Sr. had brought suit but died before judgment, what would happen to the suit? Consider the District of Columbia survival statute:

§ 12–101. Survival of rights of action.

On the death of a person in whose favor or against whom a right of action has accrued for any cause prior to his death, the right of action, for all such cases, survives in favor of or against the legal representative of the deceased.

3. In the District of Columbia if James Nelson, Sr. had brought suit and recovered before he died, for what types of damages would he have recovered? What would that have done to his son's wrongful death suit? Consider the District of Columbia wrongful death statute.

§ 16–2701. Liability; damages; prior recovery as precluding action.

When, by an injury done or happening within the limits of the District, the death of a person is caused by the wrongful act, neglect, or default of a person or corporation, and the act, neglect, or default is such as will, if death does not ensue, entitle the person injured, or if the person injured is married, entitle the spouse, either separately or by joining with the injured person, to maintain an action and recover damages, the person who or corporation that is liable if death does not ensue is liable to an action for damages for the death, notwithstanding the death of the person injured, even though the death is caused under circumstances that constitute a felony.

The damages shall be assessed with reference to the injury resulting from the act, neglect, or default causing the death, to the spouse and the next of kin of the deceased person; and shall include the reasonable expenses of last illness and burial. Where there is a surviving spouse, the jury shall allocate the portion of its verdict payable to the spouse and next of kin, respectively, according to the finding of damage to the spouse and next of kin. If, in a particular case, the verdict is deemed excessive the trial judge or the appellate court, on appeal of the cause, may order a reduction of the verdict. An action may not be maintained pursuant to this chapter if the party injured by the wrongful act, neglect, or default has recovered damages therefor during his life.

Most state statutes do not explicitly bar a wrongful death suit if the decedent had recovered for injuries later resulting in death. Consider the analysis of the United States Supreme Court in an admiralty action:

"England's Lord Campbell's Act, the first wrongful death statute, permits recovery 'whensoever the Death of a Person shall be caused by [the] wrongful Act * * * of another and the Act * * * is such as would (if Death had not ensued) have entitled the Party injured to maintain an Action and recover Damages in respect thereof * * *.' Early English cases interpreting the Act held that this language conditioned wrongful death recovery upon the existence of an actionable cause of the decedent at his death; if the deceased had reduced his claim to judgment and settled with or released his tortfeasor, and therefore up to the time he died could not have maintained a further action for his injuries, his dependents could have no cause of action for his wrongful death. Since Lord Campbell's Act became the prototype of American wrongful death statutes, most state statutes contained nearly identical language and have been similarly interpreted by state courts. Though the federal wrongful death statutes do not contain the same controversial language, the FELA, at least, has been held to be 'essentially identical with' Lord Campbell's Act, * * * and therefore similar restrictions have been placed on FELA wrongful death recovery.

"[New maritime wrongful death remedies are not so restricted.] Since the policy underlying the remedy is to insure compensation of the dependents for *their* losses resulting from the decedent's death, the remedy should not be precluded merely because the decedent, during his lifetime, is able to obtain a judgment for his own personal injuries. * * *

* * *

"[Collateral estoppel will prevent the plaintiffs in a wrongful death action] 'from attempting to relitigate the issue of the support due from the decedent's future wages.' "

Sea–Land Services, Inc. v. Gaudet, 414 U.S. 573, 94 S.Ct. 806, 812–14, 818, 39 L.Ed.2d 9 (1974).

4. For a different twist on the interaction of a survival statute and a wrongful death statute *see* King v. National Spa and Pool Institute, Inc., 607 So.2d 1241, 1246 (Ala.1992):

"Specifically, we hold that the survival statute, Ala.Code 1975, § 6–5–462, means exactly what its plain language states, that '*all* personal claims upon which an action has been filed * * * survive in favor of and against personal representatives * * *.' (Emphasis supplied.) The fact that the injury that serves as the basis for the personal injury action later gives rise to a wrongful death claim does not extinguish the original personal injury claim.

"This means that the holdings in *Elam, Mattison,* and *Parker,* supra, and Carroll v. Florala Memorial Hospital, Inc., 288 Ala. 118, 257 So.2d 837 (1972), are also overruled to the extent that those holdings relied on the rule that a personal injury action does not survive the plaintiff's death if a wrongful death claim could be based on the same injury. The rule that a plaintiff substituted for a deceased plaintiff must file an entirely new complaint in order to recover for wrongful death is therefore no longer the law. Should the plaintiff die as a result of the injuries alleged in the original personal injury suit, the properly substituted personal representative may amend the original complaint to add a wrongful death claim.

"The law in the case before us and in all similar cases pending at the time of this decision is that the original personal injury action survives the death of the plaintiff just as if the injury had not caused the death. Under the Alabama Rules of Civil Procedure, the plaintiff can, and should be allowed to, present both the personal injury claim and the wrongful death claim to the finder of fact.

"In addition to our interpretation of legislative intent within the context of modern pleading and practice and the plain meaning of Ala.Code 1975, § 6–5–462, our holding that the wrongful death statute does not limit the survival statute rests on two other bases. First, our cases have long recognized that the common law rule that death ended the decedent's ability to sue and be sued is not the law in our state. The clearest example that death is no longer a bar as it was at common law is the survival statute discussed above. See also Ex Parte Holsonback, 236 Ala. 265, 182 So. 28 (1938); King v. Pearce, 14 Ala.App. 628, 71 So. 656 (1916). As noted earlier, a wrongful death claim for punitive damages payable to the heirs is not the same action as a personal injury claim for compensation based on injuries that cause death."

5. The following questions illustrate the difference between a wrongful death statute and a survival statute.

a. D hits P and P breaks an arm. Who can sue whom for what cause of action?

b. D hits P and P dies instantly. Who can sue whom for what cause of action?

c. D hits P and P breaks an arm, and later dies from internal injuries sustained in the attack by D. Who can sue whom for what cause of action?

d. D hits P and P breaks an arm, and later dies from an illness unrelated to D's attack? Who can sue whom for what cause of action?

e. D hit P and P breaks an arm. D later dies. Who can sue whom for what cause of action?

6. The types of damages that can be recovered in either a survival action or a wrongful death action vary widely from jurisdiction to jurisdiction. Consider Simmons v. Hartford Ins. Co., 786 F.Supp. 574, 579, 581 (E.D.La.1992):

"Plaintiffs argue that Macey Simmons' parents should be able to recover for Macey's loss of enjoyment of future life or 'hedonic damages' as a result of her death.

* * *

"This Court is only aware of one state, Connecticut, that has construed its death remedy to allow compensation for hedonic damages. Katsetos v. Nolan, 170 Conn. 637, 368 A.2d 172, 183 (1976). *See* McClurg, *supra,* 66 Notre Dame Law Rev. at 95; Note, 'Hedonic Damages for

Wrongful Death: Are Tortfeasors Getting Away with Murder?,' 78 Geo.L.J. 1687, 1693 (1990). In addition, the Seventh Circuit and a few federal district courts have allowed hedonic damages in death cases under 42 U.S.C. § 1983. Sherrod v. Berry, 827 F.2d 195 (7th Cir.1987), rehearing on other grounds, 856 F.2d 802 (7th Cir.1988) (en banc); Heath v. City of Hialeah, 560 F.Supp. 840, 841 (S.D.Fla.1983). Thus, the concept of allowing hedonic damages in wrongful death cases is far from widely accepted.

"It is well-settled under Louisiana law that the elements of damage that can be claimed in a wrongful death action are loss of love and affection, loss of services, loss of support, medical expenses and funeral expenses. *See, e.g.,* Archie v. Board of Supervisors of Louisiana State University, 543 So.2d 1348, 1353 (La.App. 1st Cir.1989); Domangue v. Eastern Airlines, Inc., 542 F.Supp. 643, 646 (E.D.La.1982). This is consistent with the plain language of art. 2315.2, which allows the survivors to recover 'damages which *they* sustained as a result of the [decedent's] death.'

"The Louisiana Supreme Court has never explicitly said that hedonic damages are not allowed in wrongful death cases. However, in the *Pierre* case, *supra,* the Louisiana First Circuit interpreted the above statutory language as precluding recovery of hedonic damages under the wrongful death statute. 515 So.2d at 618. This is consistent with the prevailing view, that wrongful death statutes were meant to compensate the survivors for their losses, not for the decedent's losses.

"It would be unjustifiable for this Court to suggest that the Louisiana Supreme Court would approve of hedonic damages in wrongful death actions when (1) no Louisiana court has ever allowed it, and (2) it would contradict the plain meaning of the statute. Defendants' summary judgment motion on this issue must be granted."

See also D. Dobbs, The Law of Remedies, §§ 8.3(2), 8.3(3) (2d ed. 1993).

7. For a discussion of jurisdictions that do and do not recognize wrongful pregnancy, wrongful birth, and wrongful life as causes of action and the remedial issues for the jurisdictions that do, *see* D. Dobbs, The Law of Remedies, § 8.2 (2d ed. 1993).

5. *Tort "Reform"*

D. DOBBS, THE LAW OF REMEDIES

§ 8.8 (2d ed. 1993).*

"SUMMARY

"*The tort reform movement.* Limitations on the kinds of harm for which damages may be awarded at all, or on the amount of recovery, are not new in tort law. But the tort reform movement of the 1980s was a large, systematic and sustained movement to impose a number of new limitations on liability. That movement was a renewal and a broadening of an earlier effort which was intended to limit medical malpractice liabilities.

"Both waves of tort reform argued that a crisis had erupted because claims had increased in volume and amount, that insurance costs were

* Reprinted with permission of West Publishing Co.

excessive as a result, that insurance was not even available in some instances, and that some valuable goods or services were being driven from the market by the threat of tort liability. The tort reform movement was a political effort to reduce tort liability by a variety of means, with the expectation that reduced liability would mean reduced insurance premiums and sufficient financial safety to engage in production of appropriate goods and services.

"*Tort reform changes.* Tort reform initiatives of the 1980s produced a wide range of enactments. Some statutes attacked the substantive tort law rules by changing rules of liability or adding defenses. Others launched procedural initiatives, limiting joint and several liability or imposing more stringent statutes of limitations. Many of the tort reform packages affected remedies, notably by modifying the collateral source rule by instituting periodic payment systems, and by limiting punitive damages in some instances.

"The most direct attack on the plaintiff's claim has been to impose a 'cap' or dollar limit on the amount that can be recovered. As a direct limit on recoverable damages, this is a new thing in the law and quite distinct even from those few cases in which the legislature created a special cause of action and placed a dollar limit on it.[7] The idea of a direct dollar cap on damages is even more strongly opposed to the common law, which attempted to provide compensation for injury and to estimate that compensation on a case by case basis.

"*Types of statutes.* Statutes imposing direct caps on damages differ along two lines of cleavage. *First,* they differ as to the kind of claim or defendant to which they apply. Some apply only to cases involving particular subject matter, such as those involving medical malpractice. *Second,* they differ as to the kind or element of damage that is subject to a cap. Some caps apply only to damages for pain and suffering or other intangible damages. An indirect cap may be imposed by shunting certain cases out of the tort system altogether, much as workers' compensation does, or by setting up a public compensation system to handle larger claims. By 1990, some kind of direct cap had been imposed in at least half the states, though in some cases the statute has been held to be unconstitutional.

"**TYPES OF DAMAGES CAPPED**

"*(1) Noneconomic limits only.* Many of the statutes limit or cap recovery of 'noneconomic', 'general', or non-pecuniary damages, but leave the plaintiff a full recovery for all actual pecuniary harms. The noneconomic cap limits damages for pain and suffering, loss of consortium, and mental distress.[9] Some states have also capped punitive damages.[10]

"*(2) Limit on recovery of actual damages.* Some statutes go far beyond the first group by limiting the recovery of damages for pecuniary or "economic" harm as well as for intangible harms. Statutes which contain

7. *E.g.,* W.Va.Code, § 57–7A–2 ($2500 cap on special liability of parents for certain acts of children).

9. *E.g.,* West's Ann.Cal.Civ.Code § 3333.2.

10. *See,* upholding a punitive damages cap, Bagley v. Shortt, 261 Ga. 762, 410 S.E.2d 738 (1991).

these absolute limits, however, usually apply only to a specified group of defendants, such as health care providers.[11]

"*(3) Dual caps.* Some statutes impose two caps—first on noneconomic damages, and second on total recovery.[12]

"Types of Cases or Defendants to Which Cap Applies

"*(1) Application to cases generally.* Perhaps a dozen statutes by 1990 had been enacted to cap damages in personal injury cases generally, subject sometimes to relatively narrow exceptions.[13] When the statute applies to personal injury cases generally, it usually imposes a cap only on noneconomic damages.

"*(2) Application of specified claims or defendants.* The remainder of the statutes apply a cap to specified claims, most commonly to claims against health care providers,[14] governmental entities,[15] alcohol providers [16] and other groups [17] which had been generally favored at common law by limited duty rules or by immunities.

"Indirect Caps and Substitute Compensation Systems

"Caps are imposed indirectly when a public compensation scheme with a non-tort measure of recovery is substituted for tort liability. The Federal Childhood Vaccine Injury Act provides a semi-compulsory, strict-liability compensation system for certain vaccine injuries with substantial but not unlimited compensation.[18] California has enacted a similar statute to cover

11. *E.g.,* West's Colo.Rev.Stat.Ann. § 13–64–302 ($1 million cap on medical malpractice damages of any kind); La.Rev.Stat. 1299.42(B) (total cap $500,000 plus interest and costs); West's Ann.Ind.Code 16–9.5–2–2 ($100,000 for a single health care provider, but added compensation systems); Va.Code § 8.01–581.15 ($1 million).

12. *E.g.,* West's Colo.Rev.Stat.Ann. § 13–21–102.5 ($250,000 on non-economic damages in any injury case) *and* West's Colo.Rev. Stat.Ann. § 13–64–302 ($1 million cap on medical malpractice damages of any kind).

13. Alaska Stat. 09–17.010 (500,000); West's Colo.Rev.Stat.Ann. § 13–21–102.5 (250,000); Haw.Rev.Stat.Ann. § 663–8.7 (375,000); Idaho Code § 6–1603 (400,000); Md.Code, Cts. & Jud.Proc.Code § 11–108 (350,000); Minn.Stat.Ann. § 549.23 (400,-000); N.H.Rev.Stat.Ann. 508:4–d (875,000); Or.Rev.Stat. 18.560 (500,000). As to those held unconstitutional, see segment "Constitutionality" below.

14. *E.g.,* Ala.Code § 6–5–544 (400,000); West's Ann.Cal.Civ.Code § 3333.2 (250,000); West's Colo.Rev.Stat.Ann. § 13–64–302 ($1,000,00); LSA–Rev.Stat. 1249.42 (100,-000/500,000); West's Ann.Ind.Code 16–9.5–2–2 (100,000); Mass.Gen.Laws Ann. ch. 231, § 60h (500,000); M.C.L.A. § 27a.1483 (225,-000); Vernon's Ann.Mo.Stat. § 538.210 ($350,000 for noneconomic damages) (passed 1986); N.M.Stat.Ann. § 41–5–6 (500,000); Ohio Rev.Code § 2307.43 (200,000); S.D.Codified Laws 21–3–12 (1,000,000); Utah Code Ann. 78–14–7.1 (250,000); Va.Code § 8.01–581.15 (1,000,000); W.Va.Code, 55–7b–8 (1,000,000); Wis.Stat.Ann. 893.55(4)(d) (1,000,000).

15. Me.Rev.Stat.Ann. § 8105 ($300,000 cap on all claims against government entity or employees); Mont.Code Ann. 2–9–108 ($750,000 for public entity, scheduled to terminate June 30, 1991).

16. Utah Code Ann. 32A–14–1(4) ($100,-000 cap).

17. S.D.Codified Laws 33–55–210 ($200,-000 cap on "actual damages" recovery from charitable organization and this recovery bars suit against the negligent employee as well).

18. 42 U.S.C.A. § 300aa–1. The plaintiff is compelled to seek an award under the scheme before resorting to tort law. The plaintiff may then take the cash in hand and waive the rest or he may reject the certain award and hope for a tort judgment. The drafters obviously have in mind that the plaintiff will ordinarily accept the substitute scheme. The idea is that this protection will help to guarantee that vaccine makers will not be forced from the market by tort liability. See generally Victor Schwartz & Liberty Mashigian, National Childhood Vaccine Injury Act of 1986: An Ad Hoc Remedy or a

any prospective injury from an AIDS vaccine.[19] Some state statutes provide a cap on damages against health care providers but then add a public compensation scheme on top of the cap to guarantee the victim additional recovery when damages exceed the cap.[20]

"CONSTITUTIONALITY

"*Statutes unconstitutional.* A fair number of states have found cap statutes to be unconstitutional on various grounds including denial of due process and equal protection,[21] especially where the statute capped damages for an interest group such as health care providers and where no substitute compensation scheme was provided.[22] Sometimes the statute has been found unconstitutional on rather narrow or local grounds not necessarily convincing to outsiders, as in a decision that caps on damages somehow interfered with jury trial rights.[23] But the most central argument against the caps for health care providers is that if there is a crisis for health care

Window for the Future?, 48 Ohio St.L.J. 387 (1987).

19. West's Ann.Cal.Health & Safety Code §§ 199.48–199.51. In some instances tort liability against the vaccine maker is preserved. Where it is not, the plaintiff must claim against the state-created fund. But the fund compensation, although it caps damages, allows up to $550,000 in pain and suffering claims.

20. *See, e.g.,* Williams v. Kushner, 549 So.2d 294 (La.1989) (reflecting a cap of $100,000 against health care providers with an added claim against a public compensation fund, which in turn was capped at $400,000). The Virginia Birth–Related Neurological Injury Compensation Act, Va.Code Ann. § 38.2–5001 covers a narrow range of birth-related injuries with the object of maintaining available insurance for obstetricians, providing for strict liability against a state-created fund, which in turn is created by assessments against medical professionals generally. See, describing the system, Note, Innovative No–Fault Tort Reform for an Endangered Specialty, 74 Va.L.Rev. 1487 (1988). See also comments in Epstein, Market and Regulatory Approaches to Medical Malpractice: The Virginia Obstetrical No–Fault Statute, 74 Va.L.Rev. 1451 (1988); O'Connell, Pragmatic Constraints on Market Approaches: A Response to Professor Epstein, 74 Va.L.Rev. 1475 (1988). Cf. 40 Pa.Stat. § 1301.701 (providers to purchase insurance only for $100,000 per occurrence, state fund to cover excess).

21. Smith v. Department of Insurance, 507 So.2d 1080 (Fla.1987); Wright v. Central Du Page Hospital Ass'n, 63 Ill.2d 313, 347 N.E.2d 736, 80 A.L.R.3d 566 (1976); Kansas Malpractice Victims Coalition v. Bell, 243 Kan. 333, 757 P.2d 251 (1988); Carson v. Maurer, 120 N.H. 925, 424 A.2d 825, 12 A.L.R.4th 1 (1980) (medical malpractice damages cap); Brannigan v. Usitalo, 134 N.H. 50, 587 A.2d 1232 (1991) (general personal injury damages cap); Morris v. Savoy, 61 Ohio St.3d 684, 576 N.E.2d 765 (1991); Lucas v. United States, 757 S.W.2d 687 (Tex.1988); Sofie v. Fibreboard Corp., 112 Wash.2d 636, 771 P.2d 711, 780 P.2d 260 (1989). See also White v. State, 203 Mont. 363, 661 P.2d 1272, 43 A.L.R.4th 1 (1983) (governmental entity cap unconstitutional); Condemarin v. University Hospital, 775 P.2d 348 (Utah 1989) (governmental liability limits unconstitutional as applied to university hospital, divided court). See Annotation, Validity and construction of state statutory provisions relating to limitations on amount of recovery in medical malpractice claim and submission of such claim to pretrial panel, 80 A.L.R.3d 583 (1977).

22. *See* Lucas v. United States, 757 S.W.2d 687 (Tex.1988).

23. Sofie v. Fibreboard Corp., 112 Wash.2d 636, 771 P.2d 711, 780 P.2d 260 (1989) (state constitution's jury trial right). The claim that the jury must decide the measure of damages does not seem in line with the usual notion that the law prescribes the remedy and its measure. *See* Boyd v. Bulala, 877 F.2d 1191 (4th Cir.1989) (rejecting the argument that caps interfere with federal jury trial rights); cf. Davis v. Omitowoju, 883 F.2d 1155 (3d Cir.1989) (also rejecting jury trial argument, on ground that federal jury trial rights guarantee the jury against interference by judge, not against legislation); Peters v. Saft, 597 A.2d 50 (Me. 1991) ("Although it is conceivable that a statute could limit the measure of tort damages so drastically that it would result in a denial of the right to trial by jury and the denial of a remedy, the $250,000 cap before us is not such a measure. In the present context, the right 'to a jury trial means that, with respect to those questions of fact that the substantive law makes material, the party has the right to have a determination made by the jury' ").

providers, the problem is theirs and not that of an individual victim of their negligence; and that while government might provide assistance to the providers, the individual victim should not be forced to do so.[24]

"*Statutes constitutional.* Although the caps appear to be invoked to aid the tortfeasor at the expense of the victim, they have been upheld in important decisions,[25] especially where the legislature seems to have sought to provide the victim with substitutes for full tort compensation.[26] Where the statute merely caps damages for intangible harm, there may be justifications quite different from those aimed at aiding a special group of defendants, because intangible harms are hard to measure and because their unmeasurable nature may in effect compel all citizens to pay the high costs for goods and services.[27] The constitutionality of a cap is probably also easier to sustain when the statute merely provides protection for a defendant which was once immune altogether, as in the case of a public entity.[28] Similarly, where the legislature creates a cause of action that did not previously exist, courts are likely to sustain legislative caps.[29]

* * *

"There are also likely to be issues about how caps are to be applied in cases of multiple injuries by one defendant and cases of multiple defendants causing one injury. Many of the statutes attempt to address some of these issues, but their exact scope will probably leave room for more litigation.

24. *See* Carson v. Maurer, 120 N.H. 925, 424 A.2d 825, 12 A.L.R.4th 1 (1980); Morris v. Savoy, 61 Ohio St.3d 684, 576 N.E.2d 765, 771 (1991) (denial of due process: "[I]t is irrational and arbitrary to impose the cost of the intended benefit to the general public solely upon a class consisting of those most severely injured by medical malpractice" (quoting an unreported case).

25. Davis v. Omitowoju, 883 F.2d 1155 (3d Cir.1989); Franklin v. Mazda Motor Corp., 704 F.Supp. 1325 (D.Md.1989); Fein v. Permanente Medical Group, 38 Cal.3d 137, 211 Cal.Rptr. 368, 695 P.2d 665 (1985), cert. denied, 474 U.S. 892, 106 S.Ct. 214, 88 L.Ed.2d 215 (1985); Potomac Elec. Power Co. v. Smith, 79 Md.App. 591, 558 A.2d 768 (1989) (constitutional at least in death cases); Etheridge v. Medical Center Hospitals, 237 Va. 87, 376 S.E.2d 525 (1989).

26. *See* Lucas v. United States, 757 S.W.2d 687 (Tex.1988) (no viable quid pro quo for the seriously injured victim of medical malpractice). The *Lucas* court thought it "significant" "that in two of the jurisdictions in which damages caps were upheld, the fact that alternative remedies were provided weighed heavily in the decision," Id. at 691, citing Johnson v. St. Vincent Hospital, Inc., 273 Ind. 374, 404 N.E.2d 585, 601 (1980); Sibley v. Board of Supervisors of Louisiana, 462 So.2d 149, 156 (La.1985). In Williams v. Kushner, 549 So.2d 294 (La.1989) the court upheld a cap on the public compensation fund, but did not address the cap on liability of a private health care provider.

27. Cf. Schweich v. Ziegler, Inc., 463 N.W.2d 722 (Minn.1990) ("underwriting challenges" presented by such damages; upholding cap of $400,000 on various intangible injury damages, including loss of consortium, on attack regarded as similar to due process attack under state law and on standards similar to minimal scrutiny standard).

28. *See* Annotation, Validity and construction of statute or ordinance limiting the kinds or amount of actual damages recoverable in tort action against governmental unit, 43 A.L.R.4th 19 (1986). Contra, holding such a statute unconstitutional, White v. State, 203 Mont. 363, 661 P.2d 1272, 43 A.L.R.4th 1 (1983); cf. Condemarin v. University Hospital, 775 P.2d 348 (Utah 1989) (governmental cap unconstitutional as applied to university hospital).

29. *See* Potomac Elec. Power Co. v. Smith, 79 Md.App. 591, 558 A.2d 768 (1989); Owen v. Meserve, 381 Mass. 273, 408 N.E.2d 867, 870 (1980), cert. denied, 449 U.S. 1082, 101 S.Ct. 866, 66 L.Ed.2d 806 (1981) (death actions); cf. Peters v. Saft, 597 A.2d 50 (Me. 1991) (where liability of alcohol server was not established, legislature could rationally impose liability and cap it).

"EFFECTS

"At this writing extensive data about the effect of caps is not available. But the most obvious effects are likely to be that recoveries will be reduced and that reduced recoveries may serve the purposes of the tort reform movement by making insurance more readily available and affordable.

"At the same time, by cutting liability, the tort reform statutes may have several other less obvious effects. One might be that deterrence levels are reduced too far, even if they were too high before; in other words, the caps might not be pegged at the best level for optimum safety even if caps in principle are a good idea. Another is that since the plaintiff's claim is pursued by lawyers paid on contingent fees, a reduction of potential damages will reduce the fee. A reduced fee will almost certainly mean that some complicated cases will simply be too costly to pursue. This has led to the proposal that if caps are imposed, lawyer's fees should then be paid by the losing defendant.[32]

"Effects might be quite different depending on whether the statute caps all damages or only intangible damages. There is no way to determine the appropriate dollar award for intangible harm and no guarantee that present awards are even remotely "accurate" by any standard. Awards of hundreds of thousands for a broken arm cannot be shown to offer the proper level of deterrence; nor can they be shown to be the right amount of compensation. So the statutes which cap intangible damages of this kind might represent no reduction in appropriate levels of deterrence. And, for much the same reason, awards of nonpecuniary damages may have a compulsory insurance effect or a 'tort tax' effect, because they probably help drive up the cost of goods and services to everyone, including the very poor. In this state of affairs, it has been argued that after some minimum amount of intangible damages are provided, it might be best to let people buy first party insurance if they felt it worth their while to be assured of payments for pain.[33] But even if this is correct, intangible damages like others serve a function in financing litigation, so that capping these damages, however justified in theory, may preclude appropriate recoveries because no one can afford to sue in expensive cases with caps. Again, however, a cap with an attorney fee award would present a different picture.

"All the effects of caps will not be clear for some time. Some of the effects may turn out to be a surprise. For example, courts which are now reluctant to permit open-ended emotional distress damages might find it easier to support a broader tort rule for recovery if a cap set an upper limit. It may turn out that although recoveries will not be as high as in the past, there may be more of them. No one knows all the effects of this new legislative venture in caps; perhaps no one even knows for sure that they will narrow the total costs of defense.

32. *See* Hicks, Statutory Damage Caps Are an Incomplete Reform: A Proposal for Attorney Fee Shifting in Tort Actions, 49 La.L.Rev. 763 (1989).

33. *See* Schwartz, Proposals for Products Liability Reform: A Theoretical Synthesis, 97 Yale L.J. 353 (1988).

"ALTERNATIVES

"Because the problems of open-ended awards are indeed substantial, some kinds of caps deserve serious consideration. But because flat caps are in the nature of things arbitrary and not even-handed, other forms of setting limits will probably be developed. Schedules are used for the estimation of pecuniary loss in a number of situations, sometimes directly as in the case of workers' compensation, and sometimes indirectly, as where a physician converts a limited motion in a limb to a percentage disability which in turn can be converted into a highly conventionalized dollar figure.[34]

"There are now proposals on the floor for development of several types of schedules for limiting (and guaranteeing) the award of non-pecuniary awards. One type of schedule would use variable limits on damages, depending on stated levels of injury, and age grouping of the plaintiff.[36] The limits could be based on past experience with the same type of claim or could be based on some other judgment about the appropriate amount. Other types of schedules are possible. No doubt comparisons could be made with sentencing 'guidelines' adopted for federal criminal sentencing,[37] and also with the 'grids' used in social security disability determinations.[38] Very probably these options will be debated and refined, with due effort to avoid building bias or discrimination into the schedules. If non-pecuniary awards are to be limited, those limits may be found in the future through some means other than flat caps."

B. RESTITUTION

Can someone profit from injuring someone else? A tortfeasor who murders to inherit or receive insurance proceeds would gain, but typically a constructive trust or statutory remedy is imposed to disgorge the gain. *See* D. Dobbs, The Law of Remedies, §§ 6.7 and 8.9 at 689–90 (2d ed. 1993). What if a notorious murderer writes about the crimes? Should the murderer be permitted to retain the gain from the sale of a book or movie? *See* Simon & Schuster, Inc. v. Members of the New York State Crime Victims Board, ___ U.S. ___, 112 S.Ct. 501, 116 L.Ed.2d 476 (1991), printed *supra* p. 710.

C. SPECIFIC RELIEF: INJUNCTION

A tortfeasor cannot be enjoined to undo physical injury or death because such injury cannot be undone. Can a tortfeasor be enjoined from committing further injury? Can a suspected potential tortfeasor be enjoined from committing a first tort? How effective would such injunctions

34. *See* Pryor, Flawed Promises: A Critical Evaluation of the American Medical Association's Guides to the Evaluation of Permanent Impairment (Book Review), 103 Harv. L.Rev. 964 (1990) (reviewing American Medical Ass'n, Guides to the Evaluation of Permanent Impairment (1988)).

36. *See* Bovbjerg, Sloan & Blumstein, Valuing Life and Limb in Tort: Scheduling "Pain and Suffering", 83 Nw.U.L.Rev. 908 (1989).

37. *See* Mistretta v. United States, 488 U.S. 361, 109 S.Ct. 647, 102 L.Ed.2d 714 (1989) (upholding the statutory requirement of determinate sentence under guidelines against a delegation and separation of powers arguments).

38. *See* 20 C.F.R. Pt. 404, Subpt. P, App. 2 (4–1–89 ed.).

be? *See* Marquette v. Marquette, 686 P.2d 990 (Okl.App.1984), printed *supra* p. 760.

Chapter 7

REMEDIES FOR CONTRACTUAL RELATIONSHIPS—BREACH, MISTAKE, MISREPRESENTATION AND REFORMATION

SECTION 1. BASIC PRINCIPLES

A. REMEDIES AFFIRMING THE CONTRACT

If two parties have contracted but one party breaches, the nonbreaching party may choose to "affirm" the contract and sue the breaching party either for damages or for specific performance. By affirming the contract, the nonbreaching party is recognizing the existence and validity of the contract. The following sections discuss the options for measuring damages, the criteria necessary for specific performance, and the theories supporting the "right to breach" in the ordinary course.

Later sections will discuss the nonbreaching party's options if it does not "affirm" the contract.

1. Damages

FREUND v. WASHINGTON SQUARE PRESS, INC.

Court of Appeals of New York, 1974.
34 N.Y.2d 379, 357 N.Y.S.2d 857, 314 N.E.2d 419.

SAMUEL RABIN, JUDGE.

In this action for breach of a publishing contract, we must decide what damages are recoverable for defendant's failure to publish plaintiff's manuscript. In 1965, plaintiff, an author and a college teacher, and defendant, Washington Square Press, Inc., entered into a written agreement which, in relevant part, provided as follows. Plaintiff ("author") granted defendant ("publisher") exclusive rights to publish and sell in book form plaintiff's work on modern drama. Upon plaintiff's delivery of the manuscript, defendant agreed to complete payment of a nonreturnable $2,000 "advance". Thereafter, if defendant deemed the manuscript not "suitable for publication", it had the right to terminate the agreement by written notice within 60 days of delivery. Unless so terminated, defendant agreed to publish the work in hardbound edition within 18 months and afterwards in paperbound edition. The contract further provided that defendant would pay royalties to plaintiff, based upon specified percentages of sales. (For example, plaintiff was to receive 10% of the retail price of the first 10,000 copies sold in the continental United States.) If defendant failed to publish within 18 months, the contract provided that "this agreement shall terminate and the rights herein granted to the Publisher shall revert to the Author. In such event all payments theretofore made to the Author shall belong to the Author without prejudice to any other remedies which the Author may have." * * *

Plaintiff performed by delivering his manuscript to defendant and was paid his $2,000 advance. Defendant thereafter merged with another publisher and ceased publishing in hardbound. Although defendant did not exercise its 60–day right to terminate, it has refused to publish the manuscript in any form.

Plaintiff commenced the instant action * * * and initially sought specific performance of the contract. The Trial Term Justice denied specific performance but, finding a valid contract and a breach by defendant, set the matter down for trial on the issue of monetary damages, if any, sustained by the plaintiff. At trial, plaintiff sought to prove: (1) delay of his academic promotion; (2) loss of royalties which would have been earned; and (3) the cost of publication if plaintiff had made his own arrangements to publish. The trial court found that plaintiff had been promoted despite defendant's failure to publish, and that there was no evidence that the breach had caused any delay. Recovery of lost royalties was denied without discussion. The court found, however, that the cost of hardcover publication to plaintiff was the natural and probable consequence of the breach and, based upon expert testimony, awarded $10,000 to cover this cost. It denied recovery of the expenses of paperbound publication on the ground that plaintiff's proof was conjectural.

The Appellate Division, (3 to 2) affirmed, finding that the cost of publication was the proper measure of damages. In support of its conclusion, the majority analogized to the construction contract situation where the cost of completion may be the proper measure of damages for a builder's failure to complete a house or for use of wrong materials. The dissent concluded that the cost of publication is not an appropriate measure of damages and consequently, that plaintiff may recover nominal damages only.* We agree with the dissent. In so concluding, we look to the basic purpose of damage recovery and the nature and effect of the parties' contract.

It is axiomatic that, except where punitive damages are allowable, the law awards damages for breach of contract to compensate for injury caused

* Plaintiff does not challenge the trial court's denial of damages for delay in promotion or for anticipated royalties.

by the breach—injury which was foreseeable, i.e., reasonably within the contemplation of the parties, at the time the contract was entered into. * * * Money damages are substitutional relief designed in theory "to put the injured party in as good a position as he would have been put by full performance of the contract, at the least cost to the defendant and without charging him with harms that he had no sufficient reason to foresee when he made the contract." (5 Corbin, Contracts, § 1002, pp. 31–32; 11 Williston, Contracts [3d ed.], § 1338, p. 198.) In other words, so far as possible, the law attempts to secure to the injured party the benefit of his bargain, subject to the limitations that the injury—whether it be losses suffered or gains prevented—was foreseeable, and that the amount of damages claimed be measurable with a reasonable degree of certainty and, of course, adequately proven. (See, generally, Dobbs, Law of Remedies, p. 148; see, also, Farnsworth, Legal Remedies for Breach of Contract, 70 Col.L.Rev. 1145, 1159.) But it is equally fundamental that the injured party should not recover more from the breach than he would have gained had the contract been fully performed. (Baker v. Drake, 53 N.Y. 211, 217; see, generally, Dobbs, Law of Remedies, p. 810.)

Measurement of damages in this case according to the cost of publication to the plaintiff would confer greater advantage than performance of the contract would have entailed to plaintiff and would place him in a far better position than he would have occupied had the defendant fully performed. Such measurement bears no relation to compensation for plaintiff's actual loss or anticipated profit. Far beyond compensating plaintiff for the interests he had in the defendant's performance of the contract—whether restitution, reliance or expectation (see Fuller & Perdue, Reliance Interest in Contract Damages, 46 Yale L.J. 52, 53–56) an award of the cost of publication would enrich plaintiff at defendant's expense.

Pursuant to the contract, plaintiff delivered his manuscript to the defendant. In doing so, he conferred a value on the defendant which, upon defendant's breach, was required to be restored to him. Special Term, in addition to ordering a trial on the issue of damages, ordered defendant to return the manuscript to plaintiff and plaintiff's restitution interest in the contract was thereby protected. (Cf. 5 Corbin, Contracts, § 996, p. 15.)

At the trial on the issue of damages, plaintiff alleged no reliance losses suffered in performing the contract or in making necessary preparations to perform. Had such losses, if foreseeable and ascertainable, been incurred, plaintiff would have been entitled to compensation for them. * * *

As for plaintiff's expectation interest in the contract, it was basically twofold—the "advance" and the royalties. (To be sure, plaintiff may have expected to enjoy whatever notoriety, prestige or other benefits that might have attended publication, but even if these expectations were compensable, plaintiff did not attempt at trial to place a monetary value on them.) There is no dispute that plaintiff's expectancy in the "advance" was fulfilled—he has received his $2,000. His expectancy interest in the royalties—the profit he stood to gain from sale of the published book—while theoretically compensable, was speculative. Although this work is not plaintiff's first, at trial he provided no stable foundation for a reasonable estimate of royalties he would have earned had defendant not breached its promise to publish. In these circumstances, his claim for royalties falls for uncertainty. * * *

Since the damages which would have compensated plaintiff for anticipated royalties were not proved with the required certainty, we agree with the dissent in the Appellate Division that nominal damages alone are recoverable. * * * Though these are damages in name only and not at all compensatory, they are nevertheless awarded as a formal vindication of plaintiff's legal right to compensation which has not been given a sufficiently certain monetary valuation. * * *

In our view, the analogy by the majority in the Appellate Division to the construction contract situation was inapposite. In the typical construction contract, the owner agrees to pay money or other consideration to a builder and expects, under the contract, to receive a completed building in return. The value of the promised performance to the owner is the properly constructed building. In this case, unlike the typical construction contract, the value to plaintiff of the promised performance—publication—was a percentage of sales of the books published and not the books themselves. Had the plaintiff contracted for the printing, binding and delivery of a number of hardbound copies of his manuscript, to be sold or disposed of as he wished, then perhaps the construction analogy, and measurement of damages by the cost of replacement or completion, would have some application.

Here, however, the specific value to plaintiff of the promised publication was the royalties he stood to receive from defendant's sales of the published book. Essentially, publication represented what it would have cost the defendant to confer that value upon the plaintiff, and, by its breach, defendant saved that cost. The error by the courts below was in measuring damages not by the value to plaintiff of the promised performance but by the cost of that performance to defendant. Damages are not measured, however, by what the defaulting party saved by the breach, but by the natural and probable consequences of the breach *to the plaintiff*. In this case, the consequence to plaintiff of defendant's failure to publish is that he is prevented from realizing the gains promised by the contract—the royalties. But, as we have stated, the amount of royalties plaintiff would have realized was not ascertained with adequate certainty and, as a consequence, plaintiff may recover nominal damages only.

Accordingly, the order of the Appellate Division should be modified to the extent of reducing the damage award of $10,000 for the cost of publication to six cents, but with costs and disbursements to the plaintiff.

RESTATEMENT (SECOND) OF CONTRACTS

§ 344 (1981).*

"**§ 344. Purposes of Remedies**

"Judicial remedies under the rules stated in this Restatement serve to protect one or more of the following interests of a promisee:

(a) his 'expectation interest,' which is his interest in having the benefit of his bargain by being put in as good a position as he would have been in had the contract been performed,

(b) his 'reliance interest,' which is his interest in being reimbursed for loss caused by reliance on the contract by being put in as good a position as he would have been in had the contract not been made, or

(c) his 'restitution interest,' which is his interest in having restored to him any benefit that he has conferred on the other party."

BURNHAM, CONTRACT DAMAGES IN MONTANA PART II: RELIANCE AND RESTITUTION

45 Mont.L.Rev. 1, 2–3 (1984).**

"The three interests are illustrated by the following example. A agrees to build a house for B for $50,000, of which $5000 represents A's profit. If B breaches before any performance by A, A's only remedy is the expectation interest, $5000. If B breaches after A has expended $30,000, A's reliance interest is $30,000 and A's expectation interest is $35,000. If A has conferred on B a benefit worth $36,000, A's restitution interest is $36,000.

* * *

[T]he interests in contract actions overlap with the interests served by the other two branches of the law of obligations, tort and restitution. Reliance, in serving the injured party's interest in being restored to the status quo, performs the same function in tort actions. And restitution, in serving the injured party's interest in recovering benefits unjustly retained, performs the same function in actions based on unjust enrichment."

A. FARNSWORTH, CONTRACTS

839–45 (1990).**

"**§ 12.1 Purposes of Remedies.** Why do people keep their promises? Sometimes the reason has little to do with the legal remedies available to the promisee of a broken promise. One may simply regard keeping promises as the 'right' thing to do. Or one may fear that if one breaks one's promise the promisee will not keep the return promise, that the promisee and others will not deal with one in the future, or that one's general reputation will suffer.

"It might be supposed that the law would add to these extra-legal compulsions a system of sanctions of its own, designed to compel promisors to keep their promises. Somewhat surprisingly, our system of contract remedies rejects, for the most part, compulsion of the promisor as a goal. It does not impose criminal penalties on one who refuses to perform one's promise, nor does it generally require one to pay punitive damages. Our system of contract remedies is not directed at *compulsion* of *promisors* to *prevent* breach; it is aimed, instead, at *relief* to *promisees* to *redress* breach. Its preoccupation is not with the question: how can promisors be made to keep their promises? Its concern is with a different question: how can people be encouraged to deal with those who make promises? The result may sometimes be to compel a promisor to keep one's promise, but this is only the incidental effect of a system designed to serve other ends. Perhaps it is more consistent with free enterprise to promote the use of contract by encouraging promisees to rely on the promises of others instead of by compelling promisors to perform their promises. In any event, along with the celebrated freedom to make contracts goes a considerable freedom to break them as well.

"How do courts encourage promisees to rely on promises? Ordinarily they do so by protecting the expectation that the injured party had when making the contract by attempting to put the injured party in as good a position as the party would have been in had the contract been performed, that is, had there been no breach. The interest measured in this way is called the *expectation interest* and is said to give the injured party the 'benefit of the bargain.' [6] The expectation interest is based not on the injured party's hopes at the time he made the contract, but on the actual value that the contract would have had to the injured party had it been performed. The expectation of the foolishly optimistic landowner who contracted to have an oil well dug is not the gusher that the landowner hoped for but the dry well that actually would have resulted. Since the circumstances at the time for performance, rather than those at the time of the making of the contract, are determinative, changes in the market adverse to the promisee that occur between the time of making and the time for performance diminish the promisee's expectation interest.

* * *

"At times, a court will enforce a promise by protecting the promisee's reliance instead of his expectation. The injured party may, for example, have changed position in reliance on the contract by incurring expenses in preparation or in performance. In that case, the court may attempt to put

6. For a statement of the expectation interest, see UCC 1–106(1) ("remedies provided by this Act shall be liberally administered to the end that the aggrieved party may be put in as good a position as if the other party had fully performed"). The seminal article on the expectation, reliance, and restitution interests is Fuller and Perdue, The Reliance Interest in Contract Damages (pts. 1, 2), 46 Yale L.J. 52, 373 (1936, 1937). *See* Restatement Second § 344; Birmingham, Notes on the Reliance Interest, 60 Wash.L.Rev. 217 (1985); Hudec, Restating the "Reliance Interest," 67 Cornell L.Rev. 704 (1982). For general discussions of contract damages, *see* Cooter & Eisenberg, Damages for Breach of Contract, 73 Calif.L.Rev. 1432 (1985); Farnsworth, Legal Remedies for Breach of Contract, 70 Colum.L.Rev. 1145 (1970); Vernon, Expectancy Damages for Breach of Contract: A Primer and a Critique, 1976 Wash.U.L.Q. 179.

the injured party back in the position in which that party would have been had the contract not been made. The interest measured in this way is called the *reliance interest.* It is useful to distinguish two kinds of reliance. The first, reliance that consists of preparation for and performance under the contract in question, has been called 'essential' reliance. It includes whatever is, in a sense, the 'price' that a party must pay for what it is to receive under the contract. The second, reliance that consists of preparations for collateral transactions that a party plans to carry out when the contract in question is performed, has been called 'incidental' reliance. Consider a contract to build a store. If the owner repudiates after the builder has spent money on architect's drawings, labor, and materials, these expenditures are essential reliance. If the builder repudiates after the owner has spent money in buying a stock of goods and hiring employees, these expenditures are incidental reliance. In either case the reliance interest is ordinarily smaller than the expectation interest because, while the expectation interest takes account of the injured party's lost profit as well as his reliance, the reliance interest includes nothing for his lost profit. In this connection it is important to understand that the law has not generally recognized yet another kind of reliance that consists in foregoing opportunities to make other contracts. In the example given, the builder may have passed up another job, and the owner may have passed up the possibility of hiring another builder in reliance on their contract. But the difficulties of proving this are obvious, and courts have not been receptive to claims based on this kind of reliance. Situations in which damages have been measured by the reliance interest have characteristically been those in which damages measured by the full expectation are for some reason regarded as inappropriate and the court turns to the reliance interest as a lesser included component that will give a measure of relief.

* * *

"Sometimes a court will recognize a third interest in cases of breach of contract by granting restitution to the injured party. However, the object of restitution is not the enforcement of a promise, but an entirely distinct goal—the prevention of unjust enrichment. The focus is on the party in breach rather than on the injured party, and the attempt is to put the party in breach back in the position in which that party would have been had the contract not been made. The party in breach is required to disgorge what that party has received in money or services by, for example, returning the benefit to the injured party that conferred it. The interest of the injured party that is measured in this way is called the *restitution interest.* It is ordinarily smaller than either the expectation interest or the reliance interest. Although recovery measured by either of those interests takes account of cost incurred in conferring a benefit on the party in breach, the restitution interest includes neither the injured party's lost profit nor the part of that party's expenditures in reliance that conferred no benefit on the party in breach.

"For a simple illustration of the three interests—expectation, reliance, and restitution—consider a contract by a builder to build a building on an owner's land for $100,000. If it would have cost the builder $90,000 to build the building, and the owner repudiates the contract before the builder has done anything in reliance on it, the builder's only loss is the $10,000 profit that the builder would have made. This is the builder's expectation interest, since this is the amount it will take to put the builder in as good a position as if the contract had been performed. Since the builder has done nothing in reliance and no benefit has been conferred on the owner, the builder's reliance and restitution interests are both zero. If, however, the owner does not repudiate until the builder has spent $60,000 of the $90,000 it would have cost to build it, the builder's expectation interest is now $70,000, since this is the amount it will take to put the builder in as good a position as if the contract had been performed. The builder's reliance interest is now $60,000, the amount spent on past performance. And if the benefit to the owner of the partly finished building is, say, $40,000, the builder's restitution interest is now $40,000.

"What types of remedies are available to protect these interests?

"§ 12.2 **Types of Remedies.** The judicial remedies available for breach of contract can be characterized as 'specific' or 'substitutional.' Relief is said to be specific when it is intended to give the injured party the very performance that was promised, as when the court orders a defaulting seller of goods to deliver them to the buyer. Relief is said to be 'substitutional' when it is intended to give the promisee something in substitution for the promised performance, as when the court awards a buyer of goods money damages instead of the goods.

"Judicial remedies for breach of contract can also be characterized as either 'legal' or 'equitable,' depending on whether, before the merger of law and equity, they were available in the common law courts or in courts of equity. The principal legal remedy to enforce a promise is a judgment awarding a sum of money. This is usually substitutional relief, as when the sum is damages to compensate the injured party for breach; but it may also be specific, as when the sum is an amount due under the contract. The principal equitable remedy to enforce a contract is an order requiring specific performance of the contract or enjoining its nonperformance. This is specific relief.

"Similar distinctions can be drawn among remedies designed to prevent unjust enrichment. Restitution may be accomplished by a legal remedy, a judgment awarding a sum of money. This is usually substitutional, as when the sum is an amount considered equal to the value of the benefit conferred on the party in breach. But it may also be specific, as when the sum is an amount that the injured party paid to the party in breach and that constitutes the very benefit conferred. Restitution may also be accomplished by an equitable remedy, an order requiring the return of property. This is specific relief.

"Other remedies in contract cases include replevin of a chattel, cancellation or reformation of a writing, and issuance of a declaratory judgment. Arbitration, a nonjudicial remedy, may also be available. Moreover, in some circumstances a party to a contract is empowered to protect itself or to obtain satisfaction by methods not involving recourse to a court, such as retaking goods or foreclosing on security."

The following sections of the Restatement (Second) of Contracts (1981) * list limitations on recovery of contract damages. Why are those limitations imposed?

"§ 351. Unforeseeability and Related Limitations on Damages

"(1) Damages are not recoverable for loss that the party in breach did not have reason to foresee as a probable result of the breach when the contract was made.

"(2) Loss may be foreseeable as a probable result of a breach because it follows from the breach

(a) in the ordinary course of events, or

(b) as a result of special circumstances, beyond the ordinary course of events, that the party in breach had reason to know.

"(3) A court may limit damages for foreseeable loss by excluding recovery for loss of profits, by allowing recovery only for loss incurred in reliance, or otherwise if it concludes that in the circumstances justice so requires in order to avoid disproportionate compensation.

"§ 352. Uncertainty as a Limitation on Damages

"Damages are not recoverable for loss beyond an amount that the evidence permits to be established with reasonable certainty.

"§ 353. Loss Due to Emotional Disturbance

"Recovery for emotional disturbance will be excluded unless the breach also caused bodily harm or the contract or the breach is of such a kind that serious emotional disturbance was a particularly likely result.

"§ 355. Punitive Damages

"Punitive damages are not recoverable for a breach of contract unless the conduct constituting the breach is also a tort for which punitive damages are recoverable."

2. *Specific Performance*

D. DOBBS, HORNBOOK ON THE LAW OF REMEDIES

805 (2d ed. 1993).**

Specific Performance Generally

"*Elements in grant or denial of relief.* One remedy that fulfills the plaintiff's expectancy interest is specific performance. It may at the same time serve certain restitutionary functions.[1] A specific performance decree

1. See Levmore and Stuntz, Remedies and Incentives in Private and Public Law: A Comparative Essay, 1990 Wis.L.Rev. 483, 487. Specific performance against a defendant who threatens to breach in order to gain greater profits by contracting elsewhere pre-

is a court order compelling the defendant to perform the contract. The main advantage to the plaintiff is that it provides the very performance contracted for, not a money substitute. This remedy is almost routinely available to enforce contracts for the purchase of land. In other cases, the court's decision to grant or deny specific performance is ordinarily a product of several considerations—practicalities, equities and hardships.

"Under the traditional views, specific relief will be denied when (1) the legal remedy is regarded as adequate or the plaintiff is not subjected to irreparable harm by the breach; (2) the hardship to the defendant outweighs the plaintiff's legitimate interest in specific performance; (3) the "equities" or ethical considerations favor the defendant; for example, specific relief may be denied because the contract is too one-sided, because the plaintiff is estopped or has unclean hands, because the plaintiff delayed too long in pursuing the claim, or because remedies are not 'mutual'; (4) specific performance is deemed impractical because it will require too much judicial supervision or for other reasons. Equitable defenses like hardship, unfairness, laches and others, theoretically work to deny specific performance but to leave open the remedies 'at law' for damages."

RESTATEMENT (SECOND) OF CONTRACTS

§§ 359–60 (1981). *

"§ 359. Effect of Adequacy of Damages

"(1) Specific performance or an injunction will not be ordered if damages would be adequate to protect the expectation interest of the injured party.

* * *

"Comment:

"*a. Bases for requirement.* The underlying objective in choosing the form of relief to be granted is to select a remedy that will adequately protect the legally recognized interest of the injured party. If, as is usually the case, that interest is the expectation interest, the remedy may take the form either of damages or of specific performance or an injunction. As to the situation in which the interest to be protected is the restitution interest, see § 373.

"During the development of the jurisdiction of courts of equity, it came to be recognized that equitable relief would not be granted if the award of damages at law was adequate to protect the interests of the injured party. There is, however, a tendency to liberalize the granting of equitable relief by enlarging the classes of cases in which damages are not regarded as an adequate remedy. This tendency has been encouraged by the adoption of the Uniform Commercial Code, which 'seeks to further a more liberal attitude than some courts have shown in connection with the specific performance of contracts of sale.' Comment 1 to Uniform Commercial

vents the gain and is thus analogous to disgorgement.

Code § 2–716. In accordance with this tendency, if the adequacy of the damage remedy is uncertain, the combined effect of such other factors as uncertainty of terms (§ 362), insecurity as to the agreed exchange (§ 363) and difficulty of enforcement (§ 366) should be considered. Adequacy is to some extent relative, and the modern approach is to compare remedies to determine which is more effective in serving the ends of justice. Such a comparison will often lead to the granting of equitable relief. Doubts should be resolved in favor of the granting of specific performance or injunction.

* * *

"§ 360. Factors Affecting Adequacy of Damages

"In determining whether the remedy in damages would be adequate, the following circumstances are significant:

"(a) the difficulty of proving damages with reasonable certainty,

"(b) the difficulty of procuring a suitable substitute performance by means of money awarded as damages, and

"(c) the likelihood that an award of damages could not be collected."

D. DOBBS, THE LAW OF REMEDIES

§ 12.8(2) (2d ed. 1993).*

§ 12.8(2) The Adequacy Test

The Traditional Adequacy Test

"*Old and new.* The chief disputes about specific performance today center on its availability. Contract remedies are traditionally money remedies rather than coercive remedies. This is in line with the tradition that equity remedies are usually to be awarded with care or even reluctance. Some commentators today have proposed that specific performance be granted whenever the plaintiff prefers it, without regard to the adequacy test. Others think the adequacy test is already dead and that it actually has little or no effect in the cases. It is certainly true that while older statements of the test sounded quite rigid, contemporary applications of the test are usually liberal. Many courts today would apparently permit specific relief whenever there seems to be any kind of special need for or substantial advantage to it,[1] so long as there are no countervailing factors.

* * *

* Reprinted with permission of West Publishing Co.

1. Both courts and commentators have observed the general willingness to find the legal remedy inadequate. E.g., Osborne v. Bullins, 549 So.2d 1337 (Miss.1989).

One symptom of the liberalization that may not be obvious to the casual reader is the increased use of a positive rather than a negative formula in discussing the test. Guinness–Harp Corp. v. Joseph Schlitz Brewing Co., 613 F.2d 468 (2d Cir.1980) ("New York follows the general rule that specific performance is available where there is no adequate monetary remedy"); Castle v. Cohen, 840 F.2d 173 (3d Cir.1988) ("If there is no adequate remedy at law, a court of equity may, in its discretion, grant specific performance").

Rethinking the Adequacy Test

"*Merger of law and equity eliminates one basis.* A number of important contemporary scholars have attacked the adequacy test in specific performance cases and sometimes in injunction cases as well. Others have sought to defend it. Although the critics do not speak with one voice, their stance is possible largely because the judicial system itself has changed so that one of the grounds that might support the adequacy test no longer exists.

"The adequacy test originated in a system quite unlike anything we see today. Law courts were physically and historically separate from equity courts, staffed by different judges from different intellectual traditions and to some extent with different loyalties and ideals. In that system it was impolitic at best for one court to interfere too much with another's business. When equity did interfere with law, it was wise to enter disclaimers of respect, of which the adequacy test was one.

"None of this is relevant in most of today's courts. Almost all courts of general jurisdiction enjoy legal and equitable powers combined. The judge who presides is both judge and chancellor. The adequacy test is not required or even relevant to smooth over a potential conflict of jurisdictions. So the most obvious historical purpose of the adequacy test no longer justifies using it to bar specific performance.

"*The Laycock position.*[28] Professor Laycock has set forth at length a view consistent with the idea that merger of law and equity eliminates the need for the adequacy test. He believes that, presumptively, injunctive relief of all kinds should be granted as readily as damages are granted, but in addition he believes that courts in fact do that in the great majority of cases. The adequacy test, in his assessment of the cases, is expressed in words but not in deeds. For him, the adequacy test has already been reduced from a solemn giant among the equity rules to a pernicious imp. Yet the imp continues to create needless litigation and to focus attention of the courts and the lawyers on the elements of a case that do not need solution rather than on the elements that do, leading to confusion and sometimes to bad results as well. The best thing to do about it is to get rid of it altogether.[29]

"*The Yorio position.* Attackers want to take the adequacy test literally, because, like most other doctrines, if it is taken literally it is easier to attack. Defenders of the adequacy test want to see it, as lawyers and judges see many other doctrines, as an incomplete formula, perhaps defective, perhaps still in the making, but in any event not to be read literally. Once the literal shell is cast off, they seem to say, the basically sound core can stand revealed.

28. All of the positions summarized here are scholarly and complex, and any summary must necessarily be inadequate and to that extent misleading. I apologize to all the authors whose immense labors are here reduced to simple statements.

29. D. Laycock, The Death of the Irreparable Injury Rule (1991); Laycock, The Death of the Irreparable Injury Rule, 103 Harv.L.Rev. 687 (1990).

"Professor Yorio's argument seems to be in this vein. He argues in favor of an adequacy test as a step in the cost-benefit analysis that should always accompany the choice of a remedy. If specific performance will cost the defendant, the courts and society more than it will (legitimately) benefit the plaintiff, then damages may be the rightly preferred remedy, if that remedy is adequate. If damages are adequate, it would be hard to justify imposing extra costs to make specific performance work, and Professor Yorio believes that a defendant's resistance to specific performance is good evidence that it would be more costly than damages.[30] Seen in this light, the test as envisioned by Professor Yorio is surely defensible, but if so perhaps the adequacy test should be reformulated to Professor Yorio's specifications to sharpen our perceptions about what is in issue.[31]

"*Economic arguments.* Some economic thinkers have supported the adequacy test because it approximates the kinds of remedies parties would themselves bargain for. One buying a unique item would probably bargain for specific performance, but one buying wheat futures would be satisfied (and might prefer) damages. The adequacy test obtains this same result without requiring the parties to bargain about it.[32] Others have attacked the adequacy test on economic grounds. Professor Schwartz has argued that damages remedies are often 'undercompensatory' because aggrieved plaintiffs cannot prove all damages or for other similar reasons and that specific performance would tend to satisfy the goal of complete "compensation" [33] and create an efficiency in doing so.[34]

"The argument for free grant of specific performance has led to subsidiary economic debates. For instance, economic thinkers have debated whether routine specific performance would [35] or would not [36] discourage the right amount of effort by the plaintiff to minimize damages. A less significant argument speculates about the relative costs of proving up the specific performance case as compared to the relative costs of proving up the damages case.

"One economic debate that literature has treated as important is whether routine grant of specific performance would undermine the policy of efficient breach. This segment of the debate has sometimes turned in part on whether, presented with a more valuable opportunity, the defendant might be able to 'renegotiate' or buy his way out of the plaintiff's contract, so that he could proceed with a better deal elsewhere. On this point, the costs of renegotiation become central to the debaters' guess: will

30. Edward Yorio, Contract Enforcement: Specific Performance and Injunctions, § 2.3 (1989).

31. Professor Laycock agrees that the Yorio standard is a good one, but thinks it is simply not the (literal) adequacy test. See Laycock, The Death of the Irreparable Injury Rule, 103 Harv.L.Rev. 687, 695 (1990).

32. See Kronman, Specific Performance, 45 U.Chi.L.Rev. 351 (1978).

33. As to whether compensation should be defined so broadly, see § 12.2(1) above. As to whether compensation should be considered to be the only goal of contract remedies, see Edward Yorio, Contract Enforcement: Specific Performance and Injunctions § 2.3 (1989).

34. Schwartz, The Case for Specific Performance, 89 Yale L.J. 271 (1979).

35. Goetz & Scott, The Mitigation Principle: Toward a General Theory of Contractual Obligation, 69 Va.L.Rev. 967 (1983).

36. Ulen, The Efficiency of Specific Performance: Toward a Unified Theory of Contract Remedies, 83 Mich.L.Rev. 341, 389–92 (1984).

they be so high as to discourage some productive breaches?[37] Whatever the merits of these arguments, the adequacy test does not seem to provide a solution, because, as Professor Laycock has pointed out,[38] the adequacy test does not generally prevent specific performance in favor of the buyer when supply is short—the case in which efficient breach is most likely to be in issue. And where the goods are 'truly fungible,' it may not much matter whether specific performance is available or not, since either party in that event could buy in the market.[39]

"*The freedom of contract solution.* As some commentators have recognized,[40] much of the debate lies in the realm of hypothesis, and there is very little data about most of the costs involved. The area of dispute would be much reduced if the parties were free to bargain for liquidated damages in any amount or, if they chose, specific performance. If courts put no restraints on such bargains beyond the obvious ones that the agreed remedy must not have been secured by fraud or unconscionable processes, the parties could 'bargain in' to a specific performance regime if they chose. That would leave mainly the question whether it would be more efficient to allow parties to 'bargain in' or more efficient to institute a specific performance regime and let them 'bargain out' of it if they chose. If the law of contracts remedies adopted a free bargaining posture, most of the preferences of the debaters on both sides would be at least largely satisfied."

3. *Efficient Breach and Broken Promises*

D. DOBBS, THE LAW OF REMEDIES

29–35 (2d ed. 1993).*

§ 1.9 Remedial Analysis: Counting Costs and Benefits

Choosing Remedies in the Light of Costs and Benefits

"To impose a remedy is to impose costs and to create benefits. Any remedy, including injunctive and other non-money remedies, will impose costs upon the defendant. Any effective remedy will also create benefits for the plaintiff. Remedies may also impose costs upon or provide benefits for third persons or the public.

"In choosing between two remedies (or two measures of a single remedy), courts usually attempt to choose a remedy that will approximately vindicate the plaintiff's right. But costs and benefits of a remedy must also be considered. A remedy that costs more than the benefit it provides may be an inefficient means of vindicating the plaintiff's right. Because rights are more important than efficiencies in some cases, a costly, inefficient

37. See Goetz & Scott, The Mitigation Principle: Toward a General Theory of Contractual Obligation, 69 Va.L.Rev. 967 (1983).

38. Laycock, The Death of the Irreparable Injury Rule, 103 Harv.L.Rev. 687, 769 (1990).

39. See Narasimhan, Modification: The Self–Help Specific Performance Remedy, 97 Yale L.J. 61 (1987) (summarizing arguments and doubting that specific performance should be routinely granted).

40. Ulen, The Efficiency of Specific Performance: Toward a Unified Theory of Contract Remedies, 83 Mich.L.Rev. 341, 402–03 (1984).

remedy is not necessarily 'wrong.' But judges will want to consider the alternatives before inflicting a remedy that costs more to the defendant than it is worth to the plaintiff. So counting costs and benefits of remedies is worthwhile. This section introduces some of the problems to be considered when remedies are selected with costs and benefits in mind.

"Economic analysis is important in legal thought.[2] Perhaps that analysis is most effective in helping to determine how rights are assigned in the first place, but it cannot be disregarded in choosing remedies * * *. The modest goal of this section is to illustrate some ways in which lawyers and judges may compare remedial options by counting the costs and benefits of each proposed remedy. It also suggests some situations in which counting costs and benefits may itself be too expensive or even irrelevant.

Efficiency

"Efficiency as maximizing human satisfactions. Economist-lawyers sometimes say that economic efficiency only means a respect for human wants. Goods have value because human beings want them. Economic value is thus viewed as a reflection of human desires, and efficiency is merely a word used to talk about maximizing human satisfaction. For instance, suppose that you build your house on the wrong lot by mistake and the owner proposes to remedy the matter by forcing its removal, which will substantially destroy the house. Even though the house is built in violation of the plaintiff's property rights, it has value to human beings. Destruction of the house is 'inefficient' enough to make us consider whether other remedies will suffice.

"The Pareto superior idea of efficiency. What counts as maximizing human satisfactions? You could measure human satisfaction or utility solely in terms of wealth. Some economic thinkers do indeed emphasize wealth maximization as a measure of efficiency because wealth can be measured more readily than increased subjective satisfactions. A more general definition of efficiency is called Pareto superior efficiency. This type of efficiency is said to occur if, as a result of the transaction (or judicial decision) no one is worse off and at least one person is better off. Worse off and better off require comparisons to something. Usually people mean worse off or better off in comparison to no transaction at all.

"It may not be possible to show that any transaction is in fact Pareto superior or otherwise efficient.[6] Nor is it entirely clear that Pareto

2. Economic analysis of law, or law and economics, has developed primarily since the early 1970s and has produced legions of writers, as well as work ranging from homey example to high theory. For a general introduction see Richard Posner, Economic Analysis of Law (3d ed. 1986) (a non-technical, understandable book by the best-known proponent of economic analysis); A. Mitchell Polinsky, An Introduction to Law and Economics (1983) (short and readable).

6. See Hovenkamp, Positivism in Law and Economics, 78 Calif.L.Rev. 815 (1990) (Pareto analysis has "almost no application to real world policymaking because its conditions are never satisfied"); Calabresi, The Pointlessness of Pareto: Carrying Coase Further, 100 Yale L.J. 1211 (1991) (arguing that when all relevant costs are considered, including the cost of change, Pareto superior conditions cannot be met).

In the limited world of litigation, Pareto comparisons may be possible because we accept a platform of assumptions or positive conventions from which to launch them. But even this platform may not provide a suffi-

superior ideas of efficiency can be readily translated to decisions of courts about remedies, as distinct from decisions about rights. Most economic analysis is really about the efficiency of assigning underlying rights to one person or another rather than about the relative efficiency of remedies in a practical litigation context. However, a rough application of the idea to remedies might be intelligible. If two remedies both vindicate the plaintiff's right, but one costs more than the other, the more costly remedy is less efficient. The defendant is worse off in comparison to the more efficient remedy.

"*The Kaldor–Hicks test of efficiency.* Efficiency is not a simple idea. Economists also recognize other types of efficiency that are important in economic analysis and in philosophical arguments about the merits of efficiency goals.[7] Instead of measuring efficiency by the Pareto superior definition, you could use the Kaldor–Hicks test: whether the proposed allocation of resources (or remedy), as compared to the alternative, will make at least one person better off in such a degree that the gain will be sufficient to compensate all persons who are made worse-off.

"The Kaldor–Hicks test for efficiency, as it might be applied in litigation or remedial analysis, seems to emphasize satisfactions measurable in money or wealth. The Pareto superior test allows one person to veto the proposed change with the claim 'I will be worse off.' Kaldor–Hicks does not; it adds up total gains and subtracts total losses. Kaldor–Hicks applied in a remedies context would require us to evaluate all interests in dollars. Such a test of efficiency is hard to use effectively when the plaintiff claims an injunction on the ground that dollars will not adequately vindicate her rights.

"Suppose the defendant, to save the cost of using a longer and less risky route, is trucking toxic wastes through a neighborhood full of children where there is also an increased risk of overturned trucks which might allow the toxic material to escape. The risk is small and the savings great enough to pay the potential damages as discounted by the probability of their occurrence. The Kaldor–Hicks idea of efficiency might tell the judge to refuse an injunction against the trucking of toxic materials through a residential neighborhood. The judge would be required to estimate the neighborhood plaintiffs' prospective damages in dollars, and also to convert the plaintiffs' present fears into dollars. Yet the plaintiffs in the neighborhood might prefer to do without the dollars and recover their sense of peace

cient foundation when the plaintiff claims to have subjective valuations of entitlements in issue, as where the owner of an ordinary alley cat claims, "My cat is worth a million dollars to me."

7. Jules Coleman neatly outlines these definitions in Coleman, Efficiency, Utility, and Wealth Maximization, 8 Hofstra L.Rev. 509 (1980). They are: (1) Pareto superior: compared to the alternative, no one is worse off by the allocation of resources in question and at least one person is better off. (2) Pareto optimal: no further reallocation of resources can make one person better off without making another worse off; (3) Kaldor–Hicks efficiency: compared to the alternative, the allocation of resources under consideration will make at least one person better off in such a degree that the gain will be sufficient to compensate all persons who are made worse-off. With Kaldor–Hicks compare

and safety.[8]

"Efficiency vs. right. Lawyers are quick to point out that a decision that is efficient in some economic sense may also be unfair or require a redistribution of resources that offends our sense of rightness. Some such apparently efficient decisions might even turn out to be inefficient if human satisfaction or "welfare" is not measured solely in dollars. Some economists have been thinking along similar lines.[9] If these criticisms are sound, it means that at times it may be important to discard the "efficient" solution. Yet, within the practical limitations imposed in litigation and in some particular cases, it is still desirable to do the best we can to estimate costs and benefits in trying to solve remedies problems.

"Efficiency in selecting a remedy: the painting sale example. How does this efficiency idea work in choosing among remedies or measures of a single remedy?

"Suppose the plaintiff, Paloma, operates an art gallery and has contracted to purchase a painting from Dufy for $10,000. She is certain she can resell it to Mrs. Momar for $15,000, although she has no contract to do so. Dufy, however, decides to keep the painting for himself and refuses to go through with the sale to Paloma. The plaintiff may sue for damages for breach of the contract, but she might also consider suing for specific performance. If the plaintiff wanted the painting for her own aesthetic satisfaction, her claim for specific performance would be especially appealing because a recovery of damages would not give her the same satisfaction. Because she wanted the painting only to re-sell, however, her wants can be satisfied by paying her the resale price less the contract price for the painting. If the defendant values the painting more than he values the $5,000, he would prefer to pay the damages. The plaintiff's wants, on the other hand, would be equally satisfied either by receiving the painting for resale or receiving the $5,000.

"In this example, the court can seek efficiency or maximum human satisfaction in its choice between the damages remedy and the specific performance remedy. At least on the surface, it looks as if the damages remedy tends to produce the more total satisfaction of the parties than the specific performance remedy. The plaintiff will be just as well off with damages because it will give her the same 'profit' she would have made upon resale. The defendant will be better off because, although he must pay $5,000 for breach of contract, he retains something he now values more than he values that amount of money, namely, the painting. Only if one felt vindictive about mind-changing promisors would it be desirable to minimize the defendant's satisfaction.[10]

the discussion in the paragraph "Efficient breach" below.

8. A broader form of the criticism of Kaldor–Hicks is that it embodies a double assumption that each dollar awarded is worth the same as each other dollar and that a dollar awarded to P is worth the same to her as the dollar taken from D. See Hovenkamp, Positivism in Law and Economics, 78 Calif.L.Rev. 815 (1990).

9. See Cirace, A Synthesis of Law and Economics, 44 Sw.L.J. 1139 (1990).

10. Some cases for comparison or contrast are Groves v. John Wunder Co., 205 Minn. 163, 286 N.W. 235, 123 A.L.R. 502 (1939) and Peevyhouse v. Garland Coal & Min. Co., 382 P.2d 109 (Okl.1962), aff'd on

"Counting costs and benefits, however, is at best difficult. Conventions or practicalities may limit the costs and benefits that can be counted. In the painting example, remember that the plaintiff buyer was intending to re-sell the painting to Mrs. Momar. We have no obvious way of comparing Mrs. Momar's loss of satisfaction with the reneging seller's gain in satisfaction when the sale is stopped. Nor is it clear that we should do so. The impracticality of measuring costs and benefits to all people and throughout all time may induce us to accept as a convention what some thinkers accept as an article of faith: that if Mrs. Momar's disappointment is great enough, she will offer enough money to buy the painting from the reneging seller. In that case, the total satisfaction would again be maximized.[11]

"Economic thinkers differ among themselves about particular solutions. Some might disagree that the award of damages in the painting example would be more efficient; [12] some might even seek to shift the focus away from traditional notions of efficiency in order to consider more explicitly proper distribution of goods,[13] fairness, or even right for right's sake. The point of the present discussion, however, is not to reach an ultimate conclusion about the relative efficiency of the damages and the specific performance remedy. It is rather to point out that from a remedies point of view, the desire to maximize human satisfaction arises when the lawyer or judge must choose between remedies or between measures or adjustments of them. It also serves to show that the satisfactions protected by considering costs and benefits are not necessarily limited to pecuniary satisfactions. In the painting example, the reneging seller's aesthetic interests and the disappointed gallery owner's pecuniary interests are both protected.[14]

"*Efficient breach.* An idea of efficient breach of contract is tucked away below the surface in the painting example. The idea of efficient

rehearing, 382 P.2d 116 (Okl.1963), cert. denied, 375 U.S. 906, 84 S.Ct. 196, 11 L.Ed.2d 145 (1963), both discussed in § 12.19(1) below.

11. In this scenario, suppose that Mrs. Momar believes she will have more than $20,000 satisfaction from owning the painting. The reneging seller, remember, has kept the painting by paying the gallery owner's expected profit of $5,000. Momar can offer $20,000 to the reneging seller. If he accepts the offer, Momar improves her satisfaction level because the painting is worth more to her. The reneging seller improves his satisfaction, too. We know that because he would not sell unless he regarded the $20,000 cash as worth more to him than the painting. If the reneging seller refuses to sell for what Momar will pay, then we know that he gets more than $20,000 satisfaction from the painting, so the painting stays home where it produces the most total satisfaction. Dr. Pangloss would love it, and so, for a while, would Candide. It is the best of all possible worlds.

12. Cf. Schwartz, The Case for Specific Performance, 89 Yale L.J. 271 (1979). Schwartz argued in favor of specific performance as a routinely available remedy on the ground that if it was the plaintiff's preferred remedy it would provide better compensation for breach and would generate efficiencies for that reason. See also § 12.8(2) below.

13. Calabresi, The Pointlessness of Pareto: Carrying Coase Further, 100 Yale L.J. 1211 (1991); Cirace, A Synthesis of Law and Economics, 44 Sw.L.J. 1139 (1990) (efficiency by any standard does not correlate "to wealth maximization because the total amount of wealth a society generates depends upon both the efficiency and the distribution of income").

14. The efficiency of the solution does not turn on whether the owner wants the painting for his own aesthetic satisfaction or because he has a better sales opportunity elsewhere. The point is only that subjective and personal satisfactions are equally protected by the efficiency analysis.

breach excites controversy. The notion is that sometimes a contract *should* be breached to achieve efficiency in the sense of maximum satisfactions as shown by measurable economic gains. The efficient breach idea does not relieve the defendant from liability for his breach. On the contrary, it regards the breach as efficient only if the breaching party can earn or save enough by breaching to pay all of the damages caused by that breach and then pays those damages.

"*The music group example.* Suppose that three young people in a small city form a music group. After a few successful appearances in local establishments, they sign a three-year record contract with a local recording studio. The group cuts a record and the studio distributes it according to contract, but the studio's resources are limited; it cannot provide national distribution or publicity. Given its limited resources, the studio can expect to make no more than $10,000 per year and the music group can expect even less. Nevertheless, the record falls into the hands of a national record company, which is impressed with the group's talent and offers the group hundreds of thousands of dollars for a contract. The national contract would provide the group with an opportunity for national recognition and distribution. But the local recording studio objects, claiming that the group is already bound by a contract with the local studio. Should it be permitted to enjoin the music group from accepting the offer from the national company? Or alternatively, to reap some or all of the national profits? Or should the local recording studio be limited to a recovery of its actual damages under the contract, not more than $10,000 a year?

"*Applying efficient breach ideas to the music group case.* The efficient breach idea says that the music group should breach the contract with the local studio, using the gains from the new contract to pay the damages. Such a result would comport with the Kaldor–Hicks notion of efficiency.[15] The group will enjoy increased opportunities and a chance to exploit its talent, the national company will reap business profits, and audiences will reap greater enjoyment through wider exposure of the group. The local studio is not worse off, because its lost profits have been compensated for by the damages payment. If the local studio were allowed to enjoin the music group from performing nationally, or to effectively inhibit that performance by imposing punitive damages on the group or on the national company, the group, the national company, and the potential audience would all be worse off, but the local studio would be no better off. The world's wealth, as measured by the development of the musical talent and the price people pay for it, would be less.

"*Arguments against efficient breach.* One argument often raised against efficient breach notions is that the local studio (in this example) ought to be entitled to a share of the surplus that breach makes possible. If a court were to issue an injunction against the national contract, the national company would have to buy out the local studio. The local studio would charge enough to give it some share in the new-found value. But

15. Kaldor–Hicks efficiency is achieved whether or not the group's gains are used to pay damages. Even so, arguments for efficient breach do not propose to relieve the music group from liability for damages.

unless a contract right is equivalent to a property right, it is not so clear that the victim of breach should be entitled to share in the surplus created by the breach. In this example, it is not the studio's talent, not its investment, not its labor, and not its publicity or distribution that will produce the gains of the new deal. A second point, and one much discussed, is that the costs of bargaining and buying out the old contract—renegotiation costs—may be so high that the national company will drop the deal altogether. So if you want to preserve the benefits of efficient breach, you may want to avoid taxing the opportunity that leads to the breach by compelling a costly buyout.

"Most people can think of several reasons to question the efficient breach idea. Some say it is immoral because the group has made a promise and should be required to keep it, or at least not to profit by its breach.[17] Some might say that at least when the parties contract about property rather than services, the buyer acquires a kind of equitable property interest as soon as the contract is signed and so should enjoy any profits the seller makes from re-selling at a higher price. In the painting example, if Dufy simply sold the painting to a new buyer instead of to Paloma, you could view the case as almost like a conversion of a painting that equitably belongs to Paloma.[18]

"Other critics might argue that the breach victim never recovers full damages, so that fair conditions for essential breach never occur.[19] Still others argue that although efficiency might result if you measure it in money, you might get a different answer if you measured it in total utility. In the music group case maybe more people achieve more satisfaction if the contract is breached, but maybe not in some other examples. Suppose in the painting hypothetical that Dufy reneges on his contract to sell to Paloma because a Mr. Getty gives him $20,000 for it. Although Mr. Getty paid more than Paloma or Mrs. Momar could afford, the breach and sale to Getty may not have increased satisfactions at all unless you are willing to say that satisfactions are measured only in the money payment. (Mr. Getty might let only his rich friends see the painting while anyone would be allowed to see it in Mrs. Momar's house.)

"Economic thinkers do not fully agree about the role for efficient

17. Some promises are as this argument assumes, but commercial promises that are not specifically performable are usually construed to mean something like "I will perform as stated in this contract, else pay legal damages." If the defendant has promised only to perform or pay, there is no immorality if he chooses the second option rather than the first.

18. This is a kind of equitable conversion reasoning. It is occasionally applied to real property to permit the would-be purchaser to take the gains made by the reneging seller, see § 12.7(4) below. It is a formal conception that may express results, not a reason for regarding the contract right as property.

19. One form of this argument is that some elements of damages are almost never recoverable in civil suits. The plaintiff usually must pay her own attorney fees, for example. So far as the argument against efficient breach relies on this proposition, it seems better addressed to the rule against attorney fee recovery. Another form of the argument is that some losses cannot be compensated in money because they are subjective or too difficult to prove. But the plaintiff is fully compensated according to the terms of the contract if she recovers either the performance promised or the legal damages; she may have other losses, but they are not losses the defendant agreed to cover.

breach, if any.[20] Perhaps much depends on the underlying assumptions of the parties; perhaps something depends on the facts of individual cases. But if efficient breach ideas apply in any cases, it pays lawyers and judges to consider the costs in all cases.

B. THE MUTUALITY OF REMEDY CONCEPT

BLEECHER v. CONTE

Supreme Court of California, 1981.
29 Cal.3d 345, 213 Cal.Rptr. 852, 698 P.2d 1154.

BIRD, CHIEF JUSTICE.

This case involves a land sale agreement with a liquidated damages clause which, upon the buyers' breach of contract, limited the seller's remedy to possession of any plans or reports prepared at the buyers' request and expense. The court must decide: (1) whether the buyers' promise was illusory and, therefore, failed to bind the parties to the legal obligations of a valid contract; and (2) whether the buyers were entitled to specific performance even though the seller waived that remedy in the liquidated damages clause.

* * *

[The plaintiffs entered into a contract to purchase 40 acres of property for $150,000 for a condominium development with defendant, "an experienced businesswoman." The buyers agreed to "do everything in their power to expedite the recordation of the final map," and the escrow was scheduled to close on the day after the final tract map was recorded. The form contract contained the following liquidated damages clause:

> The parties consider it impracticable or extremely difficult to fix the actual damages in the event Buyer does not fulfill its obligations hereunder; therefore, the parties agree that payment to Seller of the sum of *all plans and reports* as liquidated damages shall constitute Seller's sole remedy in the event of any material breach by Buyer hereunder. Seller hereby expressly waives any and all right seller may now or hereafter have to specific performance hereof.

Shortly after the contract was signed, the defendant refused to proceed with the agreement unless the buyers would pay the entire purchase price before the end of the calendar year. The buyers sued for specific performance.]

At the trial, Mrs. Conte defended her actions by asserting that: (1) she had never agreed to an open-ended escrow; (2) the agreement was void because it imposed no legal obligation on the buyers; and (3) she could not be forced to specifically perform because of the nature of the liquidated damages clause. The presence in this clause of one party's waiver of the

20. See Harrison, Egoism, Altruism, and Market Illusions: The Limits of Law and Economics, 33 U.C.L.A.L.Rev. 1309 (1986) (doubting values and assumptions of some economic analysis); A. Polinsky, An Introduction to Law and Economics, 32–36 (1983) (right amount of efficient breach might lead to the wrong amount of efficient investment in reliance on the contract).

specific performance remedy precluded, she claimed, specific performance of the agreement for either party.

The trial court rejected her arguments and entered judgment for the plaintiffs. The court ordered Mrs. Conte to place the deed to the property in escrow and to sign the escrow instructions. Plaintiffs were ordered to proceed with diligence to obtain and record a tract map within a period of six months, unless the court modified its ruling. This appeal by the seller followed.

II.

The first issue to be decided is whether the agreement lacked mutuality of obligation and, therefore, was unenforceable. A bilateral contract is one in which there are mutual promises given in consideration of each other. * * * [The court concluded that, because the buyers had expressly promised "to do everything in their power to expedite the recordation of the final map," there was mutuality of obligation.]

The only real issue before this court is whether the presence of the liquidated damages clause affected the *remedy* to which the buyers were entitled. Thus, the court must decide whether the buyers were prevented from obtaining specific performance because the liquidated damages clause stated that the seller waived that remedy if the buyers failed to perform their duties.

For many years this view was adopted by the courts. One party to a contract could not obtain specific performance if that remedy was unavailable to the other party. However, the Restatement of Contracts rejected this rule. "The fact that the remedy of specific enforcement is not available to one party is not a sufficient reason for refusing it to the other party." (Rest., Contracts, § 372, subd. (1). *See also* 7 Witkin, Summary of Cal.Law (8th ed. 1974) pp. 5274–5276.)

The comment to section 372 is instructive. "The substantial purpose of all attempted rules requiring mutuality of remedy is to make sure that the defendant will not be compelled to perform specifically without good security that he will receive specifically the agreed equivalent in exchange." (Rest., Contracts, § 372, com. a on subd. (1), at p. 678.) Section 373 of the Restatement recognized that "[s]pecific enforcement may properly be refused if a substantial part of the agreed exchange for the performance to be compelled is as yet unperformed and its concurrent or future performance is not well secured to the satisfaction of the court."

In 1969, the California Legislature discarded the rigid and outdated requirement of mutuality of remedy with respect to specific performance. Civil Code section 3386 was amended to provide that "[n]otwithstanding that the agreed counterperformance is not or would not have been specifically enforceable, specific performance may be compelled if: [¶] (a) Specific performance would otherwise be an appropriate remedy; and [¶] (b) The agreed counterperformance has been substantially performed or its concurrent or future performance is assured or, if the court deems necessary, can be secured to the satisfaction of the court." (*See* Stats.1969, ch. 156, § 1, p. 410.) [1]

Under existing precedent, a trial court may include terms in a decree which adjust the equities between the parties so as to bring about substantial justice. In this manner, the courts can ensure that counterperformance by a party seeking specific performance will be forthcoming.

In the present case, the seller contends that the trial court exceeded its jurisdiction when it "remade" the contract. However, this argument mischaracterizes what the trial court actually did. As entered, the judgment simply imposed a reasonable time limit of six months within which the buyers were to complete their performance under the agreement. This can scarcely be characterized as a rewriting of the contract.

The seller argues, without the benefit of any authority, that the trial court should have required the buyers to post security for their future performance in an amount equal to the cost of obtaining the necessary reports and the tract map. Unfortunately, the seller fails to demonstrate the necessity for such a requirement and ignores the fact that the trial court reserved jurisdiction to make supplemental orders.

In summary, the seller's waiver of her right to specific performance in the liquidated damages clause did not prevent the buyers from compelling the specific performance of this land sale agreement.

* * *

The judgment of the trial court is affirmed.

Notes

1. The classic statement of the traditional mutuality of remedy doctrine appears in E. Fry, Specific Performance § 286 (1st ed. 1858): "A contract to be specifically enforced by the Court must be mutual, that is to say, such that it might, at the time it was entered into, have been enforced by either of the parties against the other of them. When, therefore, whether from personal incapacity to contract, or the nature of the contract, or any other cause, the contract is incapable of being enforced against one party, that party is generally incapable of enforcing it against the other, though its execution in the latter way might in itself be free from the difficulty attending its execution in the

1. The California Law Revision's official comment to section 3386, as amended, provides:

Comment—Law Revision Commission

"This section is amended to eliminate the requirement that, to obtain specific performance, the plaintiff be 'compellable specifically to perform everything to which the [defendant] is entitled under the same obligation.' The amendment substitutes the rules of the Restatement of Contracts that (1) specific enforcement should not be denied in an appropriate case solely because of a lack of 'mutuality of remedies' and (2) that such enforcement may be denied if the defendant's receipt of the counterperformance is not assured and cannot be secured to the satisfaction of the court. * * * With respect to subdivision (b), the assurance or security that the defendant will receive the agreed counterperformance may be provided by the plaintiff's past conduct, by his economic interest in performing, or by granting a conditional decree or requiring the plaintiff to give security for his performance. * * *

"The section as amended achieves the only reasonable objective of the mutuality of remedies rule formerly stated by the section and developed in the case law: It assures that the defendant will not be forced to perform without receiving the agreed counterperformance from the plaintiff."

former." * The doctrine is still followed to some extent in approximately 25 jurisdictions. Richards, Mutuality of Remedy—A Call for Reform, 13 Mem.St. U.L.Rev. 1, 10 (1982).

For a valuable analysis of California case law under a statutory mutuality of remedy doctrine, see Note, Mutuality of Remedy in California Under Civil Code Section 3386, 19 Hast.L.J. 1430 (1968).

2. In the states that still apply the mutuality of remedy doctrine, there are various times for determining mutuality:

> "Lord Justice Fry took the position in his original statement of the rule of mutuality of remedy in 1858 that in order for the mutuality requirement to be satisfied, it must have existed at the time of the formation of the contract. That is, there must be no bar, other than the adequacy of the legal remedy, to specific performance of the contract by either party at the time the contract is made. * * *
>
> "As critics and recognized exceptions to the rule became more numerous, Pomeroy offered a modification. After stating the Fry version of the mutuality rule, Pomeroy noted that the rule 'is open to so many exceptions that it is of little value as a rule.' But because of the general recognition that the doctrine of mutuality had obtained in the courts of equity, Pomeroy attempted a restatement that would be less encumbered with exceptions.
>
>> If at the time of the filing of the bill in equity, the contract being yet executory on both sides, the defendant, himself free from fraud or other personal bar, could not have the remedy of specific performance against the plaintiff, then the contract is so lacking in mutuality that equity will not compel the defendant to perform but will leave the plaintiff to his remedy at law.
>
> By making this change in the doctrine, requiring mutuality of remedy only at the time suit was filed and only when the defendant was free from fault, Pomeroy was able to reconcile most of the generally recognized exceptions to the rule.
>
> "A small minority of jurisdictions have allowed an even later point in time for satisfaction of the prerequisite of mutuality of remedy. The courts in those states have held that 'mutuality of remedy is sufficient if it exists at the time of entry of the decree, or even at the time of the enforcement of the decree.'
>
> "The justification for determining mutuality at the time of suit is that the defendant has no legitimate complaint, based on lack of mutuality of remedy at the time of contracting, if he is assured of mutuality of remedy at the time that the plaintiff seeks a decree ordering the defendant to specifically perform his side of the bargain. Although this approach sounds plausible, it overlooks the possibility that such a rule might afford the plaintiff an opportunity to speculate on the contract. The applicability of the negative mutuality of remedy defense presupposes that the defendant is unable to obtain specific performance of the contract against the

* As to mutuality of remedy, see 5A A. Corbin, Contracts §§ 1178–1204 (1964); D. Dobbs, Handbook on the Law of Remedies § 2.4 (1973); Durfee, Mutuality in Specific Performance, 20 Mich.L.Rev. 289 (1922); Richards, Mutuality of Remedy—A Call for Reform, 13 Mem.St.U.L.Rev. 1 (1982).

plaintiff, for whatever reason, at the time it was made. According to the mutuality of remedy rule as stated by Fry, such a contract would not be specifically enforceable by the plaintiff.

"By contrast, the Pomeroy modification in some cases permits the plaintiff at his choosing to remove the obstacle to the defendant's right to specific performance and to satisfy thereby the mutuality requirement and thus become eligible to seek specific performance of the contract. Under Pomeroy's modification, which requires only that mutuality exist at the time of suit, the contract would be transformed into a type of option contract—enforceable at the option of the plaintiff."

Richards, Mutuality of Remedy—A Call for Reform, 13 Mem.St.U.L.Rev. 1, 15–16 (1982).*

3. The states that no longer recognize the mutuality of remedy doctrine adhere to the position set forth in Restatement (Second) of Contracts § 363 (1981): **

"§ 363. Effect of Insecurity as to the Agreed Exchange

"Specific performance or an injunction may be refused if a substantial part of the agreed exchange for the performance to be compelled is unperformed and its performance is not secured to the satisfaction of the court.

"Comment:

"*a. Importance of security.* The rule stated in this Section is intended to make sure that a party is not compelled to render his own performance without receiving substantially the agreed exchange from the other party. * * * Even if performance by the party in breach would have been due under the contract before that of the injured party, such security is desirable since, after controversy has developed, the risk of non-performance is increased. In some situations, the injured party may already have so far partly performed and so committed his funds and labor that his own self-interest furnishes adequate security. In other situations, however, it will be reasonable, in the exercise of judicial discretion, to require the injured party to furnish further security.

"*b. Means of securing performance.* The desired security can often be afforded by the terms of the order itself. If performance by the injured party is already due or will be due simultaneously with the performance of the party in breach, the order may be made conditional on the injured party's rendition of his performance. * * * If performance by the injured party is not due under the contract until after performance by the party in breach or is not due until an undetermined time, the injured party may nevertheless consent to have the order conditioned on his simultaneous performance, and even absent his consent it may be just to require him to perform simultaneously if he is to be granted equitable relief rather than damages. In such situations a discount may be allowed to compensate the injured party for the advancement in the time for his performance. * * *

"If it is impossible to assure performance by the injured party, an order may be refused, especially if there is reason to fear that the injured

* Reprinted with permission of the Memphis State University Law Review.

party will not perform. For example, a contract to render personal service exclusively for one employer will not be indirectly enforced by an injunction against serving another employer unless the court is convinced that the employer is ready and willing to perform his part of the contract.

* * *

"c. *'Mutuality of remedy.'* It has sometimes been said that there is a requirement of 'mutuality of remedy.' However, the law does not require that the parties have similar remedies in case of breach, and the fact that specific performance or an injunction is not available to one party is not a sufficient reason for refusing it to the other party. The rationale of the supposed requirement of 'mutuality of remedy' is to make sure that the party in breach will not be compelled to perform without being assured that he will receive any remaining part of the agreed exchange from the injured party. It is therefore enough if adequate security can be furnished."

C. REMEDIES DISAFFIRMING THE CONTRACT: RESCISSION AND RESTITUTION (WITH ELECTION OF CONTRACT RELATED REMEDIES)

JONES v. BOHN

Supreme Court of South Dakota, 1981.
311 N.W.2d 211.

FOSHEIM, JUSTICE.

This action was brought by the plaintiffs, Eugene and Barbara Jones, on alternative counts of rescission, breach of warranty and negligence. The trial court found for the plaintiffs based on their claim of rescission. The defendants, Charles and Judith Bohn, appeal. We affirm.

This controversy relates to a home in Pierre, South Dakota, which appellees purchased from the appellants. Subsequent to the purchase, the house became uninhabitable due to severe settling problems.

* * *

[T]he appellees, by letter dated November 7, 1978, rescinded the contract, tendered back the house, and demanded repayment of their purchase money from the appellants.

* * *

The appellees based their action for rescission on SDCL 53–11–2, alleging material failure of consideration through fault of the defendants, and fraud by misrepresentation.

At the outset we briefly note that an action for rescission may be brought as a legal * * * or as an equitable action * * *. If the action is in equity, the rescission is accomplished by court decree. When an action is brought * * * [as a legal action], however, the rescission has already been accomplished by the unilateral act of one of the parties to the contract. The rescinding party brings the legal action for rescission to enforce his rights arising from the rescission. * * * Since the present action is a legal action on a rescission, we must determine whether the appellees' rescission complied with statutory [and usual] requirements.*

The trial court found that the plaintiffs were reasonably diligent in exercising their rights to rescind. The appellees rescinded by letter dated November 7, 1978. That was shortly after discovering the facts which justified the rescission. That letter also contained the required offer to restore. In light of these facts it is clear that the appellees met the * * * requirements of rescission.

The court concluded that plaintiff rescinded the contract as of November 19, 1978 and that there was a substantial failure of consideration because of the settling. Conclusion of law No. 2 states that "[a]s between the parties to the sale of the house, the fault for the failure of consideration is that of the Bohns, although the Court is not making any decision in this conclusion of law as to the possible liability to the Bohns of other parties." The trial court's decision is therefore seemingly based on * * * [the rule] which allows rescission of a contract "[i]f through the fault of the party as to whom he rescinds, the consideration for his obligation fails in whole or in part."

* * *

The judgment is affirmed.

KNAEBEL v. HEINER

Supreme Court of Alaska, 1983.
663 P.2d 551.

CONNOR, JUSTICE.

This appeal is from a superior court judgment denying Jeffrey Knaebel rescission of a reorganization agreement between appellant, Knaebel, and appellees, Lawrence Heiner and E.R. Chipp.

In 1970, Knaebel and Heiner, both mining engineers, and Chipp, a geologist, founded Resource Associates of Alaska, Inc. (hereinafter referred to as "RAA"). RAA is a close corporation which conducts mineral explorations for itself and on behalf of clients. All three founders worked for the corporation in various capacities. From 1970 until April 1979, Knaebel was president and general manager of the corporation. Chipp, Heiner and Knaebel each owned approximately 30% of the corporation's outstanding stock.

By 1978, the corporation had offices in Fairbanks, Anchorage and Colorado. At that time RAA encountered numerous problems in Colorado where the business was expanding rapidly. Knaebel moved to Colorado to supervise the corporation's business there. This move resulted in increased tensions between the parties. In February 1979, Chipp offered to sell his interest in RAA for $250,000. Heiner proposed that he and Knaebel purchase Chipp's share of the corporation. Knaebel did not want to break up the relationship between these parties, and he refused Heiner's proposition. Reorganization discussions then began.

* Citations to individual sections of the statute are omitted.

* * *

On April 2, 1979, the parties finally agreed that Knaebel would form a Type D reorganization. The assets of RAA were divided pursuant to the agreement. Knaebel received cash and properties and contracted to serve as a consultant for $4,667 a month. In accordance with the terms of the agreement, Knaebel resigned as chief officer of the corporation. The three partners then began to draft the Type D reorganization plan. A dispute arose over the legality of the reorganization plan when tax counsel advised Knaebel that it contained many defects. The dispute was not resolved and Knaebel subsequently sought rescission of the reorganization agreement in the superior court.

Numerous issues are raised by both appellant and appellees. Of those, we address the following: * * * (2) Is Knaebel entitled to seek equitable rescission?

* * *

RIGHT TO RESCISSION

Appellees contend that Knaebel is not entitled to seek equitable rescission because: (1) Knaebel has an adequate remedy at law, (2) Knaebel seeks equity with "unclean hands," and (3) Knaebel did not, before seeking rescission, return to RAA the proceeds he received pursuant to the reorganization agreement.

We decline to adjudicate the merits of these defenses as the trial court is best qualified to make such determinations. * * * However, because these issues arise frequently in the trial courts, we set forth the following general rules to provide guidance.

One who seeks the interposition of equity must generally show that he either has no remedy at law or that no legal remedy is adequate. * * *

Although "[t]here is no general formula for determining when a legal remedy is inadequate * * *, there are some common patterns in the cases." D. Dobbs, Handbook on the Law of Remedies § 2.5, at 57 (1973). Dobbs mentions four types of cases in which damages may not provide an adequate remedy: (1) when the thing that plaintiff has been deprived of is unique and irreplaceable, (2) when a legal remedy would require that the plaintiff bring more than one lawsuit, (3) when the defendant is insolvent, and (4) when the amount of damages is highly speculative. *Id.* The trial court shall decide on remand whether the facts of Knaebel's case indicate that damages would be an inadequate remedy.

Next we address the appellees' contention that Knaebel is not entitled to seek rescission because he does so with "unclean hands."

The equitable maxim, "He who comes into equity must come with clean hands," has been interpreted as meaning that, "since equity tries to enforce good faith in defendants, it no less stringently demands the same good faith from plaintiffs." Chaffee, Some Problems of Equity 1 (1950). In order to successfully raise the defense of "unclean hands," the defendant must show: (1) that the plaintiff perpetrated some wrongdoing; and (2) that the wrongful act related to the action being litigated. *Id.* Although " 'equity does not demand that its suitors shall have led blameless lives,' as to other matters, it does require that they shall have acted fairly and without fraud or deceit *as to the controversy in issue.*" * * *

Appellees claim that Knaebel made an illegal loan to himself in early 1980. However, the accuracy of this allegation was not shown at trial. On remand, the trial court shall make all necessary findings regarding alleged wrongdoing by Knaebel. Absent such findings, appellees' allegation of unclean hands is untenable. * * *

Finally we address the appellees' contention that Knaebel must return the proceeds he received pursuant to the reorganization agreement before he may seek equitable rescission.

Rescission *at law* is a suit based upon rescission already accomplished. At law the court has nothing to do with the rescission itself; it is only involved if a subsequent suit is brought by plaintiff to recover what he gave to defendant pursuant to the rescinded transaction. D. Dobbs, *supra,* § 4.8, at 292–93.

"Restoration or tender [of the benefits received under the transaction being rescinded] before suit is a necessary element in legal rescission, but is wholly superfluous as a prerequisite to the commencement of a suit in equity for rescission or cancellation." Lightner v. Karnatz, 258 Mich. 74, 241 N.W. 841, 842 (Mich.1932). * * *

Equitable rescission differs from rescission at law in that it is not conditioned upon restoration of benefits, nor does it require an offer of restoration. *Lightner v. Karnatz,* 241 N.W. at 842.

> "Since rescission is not accomplished 'in equity' until the court so decrees, *the plaintiff has no obligation before suit to make restitution* of goods or money he received from the defendant * * * [since the court has the] capacity to protect the defendant by its decree and to condition rescission upon full restoration.
>
> This does not mean that the plaintiff is entitled to get back what he gave and keep what he got, too. It means only that *he need not make formal tender before suit.*"

D. Dobbs, *supra,* § 4.8, at 294 (emphasis added).

Because Knaebel seeks equitable rescission rather than legal rescission, we hold, as a matter of law, that neither restoration nor tender is required by Knaebel before suit.

* * *

Reversed and Remanded.

Notes

1. "In general, the law courts required the plaintiff [who sought rescission at law rather than in equity] to return or attempt to return benefits received before commencing the action, whereas in equity restitution of such benefits to the defendant was worked out in the decree itself. Although the

rule at law produces unnecessarily harsh results, courts have nonetheless adhered to it in a significant number of modern decisions. * * *

* * *

"* * * There is no modern justification for this unneeded distinction between law and equity. And, law or equity aside, there is no justification for the refusal to reach a decision on the merits of the case, particularly since the tender required of the plaintiff is in almost all instances an empty gesture. That is, if the defendant intends to contest the plaintiff's claim on the merits, he will nearly always reject the tender, which leaves the situation as it was before the tender. And finally, even though the defendant were prepared to accept the tendered return, while saving his right to contest the claim on the merits [in order to avoid the conclusion that he/she acceded to the rescission], a well-advised plaintiff can forestall such return by making the tender conditional on satisfaction of his restitution claim." I G. Palmer, Law of Restitution (1978) at pp. 482–84.

2. In some situations, there will be practical problems making it difficult or impossible for the party seeking rescission to restore that which was received from the defendant. In Gordon v. Tafe, 121 N.H. 250, 250–51, 428 A.2d 892, 893–94 (1981) the Court, while affirming a refusal of rescission relief because the parties could not be restored, substantially, to the status quo, made this statement concerning the restoration obligation:

> "Furthermore, this court has recognized that the general principle that the parties must be put in the same situation in which they stood at the time the contract was entered into cannot be taken in a strict literal sense. Otherwise 'no contract could be rescinded after there has been a change of possession, because the parties could not be put in the same situation in which they were before the contract.' Concord Bank v. Gregg, 14 N.H. 331, 338 (1842). As a practical matter absolute and literal restoration is not required if all that is reasonably possible and demanded by the equities is done. * * *"

The manner in which the courts have dealt with a variety of situations where restoration "in a strict literal sense" was not possible is discussed by Professor Dobbs in D. Dobbs, Law of Remedies, (2d ed. 1993) at 464–66 and by Professor Palmer in I G. Palmer, Law of Restitution (1978), § 3.11.

3. The Uniform Commercial Code has eliminated the requirement that a buyer return or offer to return goods before suing for restitution. I G. Palmer, *supra,* note 2, at 299.

4. As a result of the merger of law and equity, some states, including New York, have enacted statutes abolishing the distinction between the tender requirements in actions for legal and equitable rescission:

> NEW YORK CIVIL PRACTICE LAW AND RULES, sec. 3004. "A party who has received benefits by reason of a transaction that is void or voidable because of fraud, misrepresentation, mistake, duress, infancy or incompetency, and who, in an action or by way of defense or counterclaim, seeks rescission, restitution, a declaration or judgment that such transaction is void, or other relief, whether formerly denominated legal or equitable, dependent upon a determination that such transaction was void or voidable, shall not be denied relief because of a failure to tender before judgment restoration of such benefits; but the court may make a tender of

restoration a condition of its judgment, and may otherwise in its judgment so adjust the equities between the parties that unjust enrichment is avoided." *

LOWE v. LYM

Court of Appeals of Idaho, 1982.
103 Idaho 259, 646 P.2d 1030.

WALTERS, CHIEF JUDGE.

This is an appeal from a summary judgment granting rescission of a land sale transaction [in which the buyers alleged that fraud and misrepresentation occurred in the sale]. We affirm the entry of the judgment in favor of the sellers but remand for redetermination of the amount of monetary recovery by the buyers.

The buyers, Russell and Caryn Lowe, purchased real property located in Bannock County from John and Terry Lym. Following payment of the purchase price and receipt of the deed, the buyers applied for a building permit for construction of a residence on the property. Issuance of the permit was denied by county authorities on the basis that the property was part of a subdivision which had not been properly platted and approved.

* * *

The district court's determination to grant summary judgment was based upon communications between the parties occurring subsequent to the closing of the land sale transaction, and prior to the commencement of the litigation by the buyers. The sale transaction was closed in October, 1976. By the following June, the buyers had been refused the building permit. That month the attorney for the buyers made written demand upon the sellers. After stating that the buyers were unable to obtain a building permit because the property purchased from the sellers was enclosed in an illegal subdivision, the letter recited:

> Accordingly, demand is hereby made upon you for the return of all sums of money paid by Mr. Lowe, together with all interest and for damages he has incurred, including an amount for an attorney fee.
>
> *You are further notified that Mr. Lowe hereby rescinds his contract of purchase.* * * *
>
> Your immediate reply is expected, and unless we hear from you, further legal action will be instituted. (Emphasis supplied.)

Seven months later, on January 24, 1978, the attorney for the sellers responded. His letter to the buyers' attorney stated:

> I am in receipt of your letter of June 24, 1977, to Mr. John Lym *whereby Mr. Ed Lowe rescinds his contract of purchase* for lands purchased from Mr. Lym in the Gibson Jack area of Bannock County, Idaho. * * *

* For the effects of the statute in the New York courts, see Patterson, Improvements in the Law of Restitution, 40 Cornell L.Q. 667, 670–75 (1955). This and other statutory alterations of the tender requirement are discussed in D. Dobbs, *supra,* note 2, at 465–66.

> *Please be advised that Mr. Lym accepted the rescission of the contract of purchase. * * * Mr. Lym considers the contract rescinded* thereby making him the owner of said parcel of property with merely a determination of the amount of money paid to Mr. Lowe left to be made. If this sum cannot be agreed upon by March 1, 1978, we will ask a court of competent jurisdiction to determine the amount which should be paid over to Mr. Lym. (Emphasis supplied.)

In the summary judgment proceedings, the sellers contended the letter from the buyers' attorney constituted an "offer" to rescind the transaction, and that their responsive letter constituted an "acceptance" of the offer. The district court agreed.

* * *

We affirm the judgment of the district court, although not upon the "offer and acceptance" theory found by the court in its order granting summary judgment. Rather, we affirm on the basis of mutual consent to rescission.

Our analysis begins with the recognition that this case does not involve an attempted rescission of an existing, executory contract between the parties. Here the land sale transaction was completed. The sellers had received the purchase price, the buyers had received a deed to the property, and nothing remained to be performed by either of them. Fully executed contracts, however, may be rescinded by the parties, by returning them to the status quo they occupied prior to the executed contract. Executed contracts "under which the chose is vested" ordinarily can be rescinded only by mutual consent or judicial decree.

The mutuality of assent to rescind a transaction can arise in at least two ways. It may arise from offer and acceptance, or from demand followed by agreement or acquiescence.

> "Mutual assent may be by offer to rescind and acceptance by the other party, but the offer on the one side must be accepted on the other, before its withdrawal, and one party to a contract cannot abrogate or rescind it by merely giving notice to the other of its intention so to do. *However, where a party, even without right, claims to rescind a contract, if the other party agrees to the rescission or does not object thereto and permits it to be rescinded, the rescission is by mutual consent.*"

17A C.J.S. *Contracts* § 389, at 466 (1963). (Emphasis supplied.)

Here the letter of the buyers did not specifically tender an *offer* to rescind; rather, it explicitly served notice that the buyers "hereby rescind" the contract, and it made demand for recovery of certain amounts of money. The letter did encourage a reply but did not purport to invite an *acceptance* of the terms stated in the letter. Although the sellers responded by "accepting" the rescission, they also specifically declared that they, too, considered the contract rescinded. This conduct falls within the rule last stated above, that where a party, without right, claims to rescind a contract and the other party agrees or does not object thereto and permits it to be rescinded, the rescission is by mutual consent. *Id.*

Thus, there was mutual assent to rescission before the suit was filed by the buyers. The terms of the rescission superceded the terms of the original contract.

> The rescission of a contract is in itself a new contract; it is the substitution of a new agreement for the old. The mutual rights of the parties are determined by the terms of their rescission agreement. Where a contract has been rescinded by mutual consent, the parties are, as a general rule, restored to their original rights with relation to the subject matter, and they are entitled to be placed in status quo as far as possible. All rights under the rescinded contract are terminated, and the parties are discharged from their obligations thereunder. No claim or action for breach can be maintained thereafter. * * *

17A C.J.S. *Contracts* § 392, at 471–472 (1963).

* * *

Whether a rescission by consent has been effected is one of law for the court, where the facts are admitted or clearly established. In our view the facts clearly establish that the parties mutually consented to a rescission, prior to the filing of suit. The district court properly, although upon a different analysis, also determined as a matter of law that there was a rescission and that the sellers were therefore entitled to summary judgment.

* * *

We conclude that the buyers are correct as to the second point raised, i.e., that the judgment was incomplete. In the summary judgment, the district court provided for return to the buyers of the purchase price, the award of interest, and the allowable attorney fees. To that extent, the entry of summary judgment was proper. The court did not, however, address the amount of damages necessary to restore the buyers to the status quo, nor did the court address the taxes or assessments paid, if any, which would be recoverable by the buyers upon rescission of the land sale transaction. These issues remain to be determined. The matter will therefore be remanded to the district court for determination of those items and any additional recovery to which the buyers may be entitled, to restore them, as far as possible, to the status quo. * * *

* * *

The judgment granting rescission is affirmed and the matter is remanded for further proceedings consistent with this opinion.

Note

The contract in *Lowe* was for a sale of land and the purchase had been closed by delivery of a deed and the payment of the purchase price. In such situations involving fully executed contracts for the sale of an interest in land there can be no rescission *at law,* as the *Lowe* court observes. Rescission relief, if available, must be by equity decree or as a consequence of a new contract between the parties in which they agree to undo the land sale transaction and restore the *status quo ante.* The latter option, of course, also is available with respect to contracts which are not for the sale of land, whether the agreement be executed or executory. The *Lowe* court discusses two methods by which such a contract to rescind a prior contract can be made.

The extent to which special limitations restrict the right to rescission and restitution, whether at law or in equity, because the subject matter of the contract is land, is considered in I G. Palmer, Law of Restitution 1978, §§ 4.17–4.19; see, also, text, *infra,* pp. 999–1006.

COON v. SCHOENEMAN

Court of Civil Appeals of Texas, 1972.
476 S.W.2d 439.*

GUITTARD, JUSTICE.

This suit was brought by the builder of eleven houses against the owner of the lots upon which they were built to recover a share of the profits from their sale, and in the alternative for the reasonable value of his services as builder. At the trial plaintiff abandoned his claim for profits and sought to recover the value of his services. The trial court excluded evidence of the value of his services and sustained defendant's motion for instructed verdict. Plaintiff appeals, contending that the trial court erred in refusing to permit proof of the elements of *quantum meruit* and in refusing to submit issues on *quantum meruit.*

The question is whether proof of an express contract for compensation as a share of profits excludes recovery for value of services, where there is evidence that defendant's breach of the contract prevented plaintiff from completing it. We hold that plaintiff could elect to recover the value of his services and was entitled to go to the jury on his alternative plea.

The question turns on the distinction between damages and restitution as remedies for breach of contract. Damages is the amount which would put plaintiff in as good position as if the contract had been performed by both parties. It gives him the benefit of his bargain, including any profit he would have made, and is determined by the contract price, less any amount saved by his being excused from further performance. Restitution is the amount which would put plaintiff in as good a position as he would have been in if no contract had been made. It restores to plaintiff the value of what he parted with in performing the contract. 5 Corbin, Contracts §§ 996, 1102 (1964). When defendant has committed a breach of contract which is serious enough to excuse plaintiff from performing further, plaintiff is entitled to elect between these remedies. Restatement, Contracts § 347, and comment b following (1932); 5 Corbin, *op. cit. supra,* §§ 1104, 1109. He may pursue both remedies in the same suit by alternative pleadings and make his election at the trial. 5 Corbin, *op. cit. supra,* § 1110 at 590. The remedy of restitution, which is normally pursued by an action in *quantum meruit* for reasonable value of services rendered, is not under these circumstances an action upon an implied or quasi-contract, as in a case where there is no express contract and plaintiff sues for reasonable value of services accepted by defendant. It is rather an alternative

* This case is also considered at p. 1064.

remedy for breach of an express contract.* *Id.* § 1106. The measure of such restitution is the value of plaintiff's services on the market rather than the benefit to defendant. *Id.* § 1107.

An important limitation on the right of a plaintiff to elect between the remedies of damages and restitution is that when plaintiff's performance of the whole or a separable part of the contract entitles him to compensation in an agreed amount or at an agreed rate, he is limited to the compensation specified in the contract. This rule is stated in Restatement, Contracts §§ 350, 351 (1932) as follows:

> "§ 350. The remedy of restitution in money is not available to one who has fully performed his part of a contract, if the only part of the agreed exchange for such performance that has not been rendered by the defendant is a sum of money constituting a liquidated debt; but full performance does not make restitution unavailable if any part of the consideration due from the defendant in return is something other than a liquidated debt.
>
> "§ 351. Restitution is not available as a remedy with respect to any performance by the plaintiff for which a definite part of the consideration was apportioned in the contract as its equivalent in exchange, if
>
> (a) the consideration so apportioned has been rendered in full, or
>
> (b) it is a liquidated sum of money."

This limitation is reasonable because if plaintiff has obligated himself to perform services for a certain amount, and he has already earned that amount, it is just to measure his compensation by the amount he agreed to take for such services. 5 Corbin, *op. cit. supra* §§ 1110, 1111. The authorities relied on by defendant fall into this category. They hold that upon performance of an express contract for the rendition of services for a certain price, the contract fixes the measure of compensation and precludes recovery in *quantum meruit* for the value of services rendered. On the other hand, in cases where plaintiff's complete performance has been prevented by defendant's breach, Texas authorities support the first rule above stated, that plaintiff may elect either to recover his damages under the contract or treat the contract as rescinded and recover the reasonable value of his work in *quantum meruit.*

Application of these principles to the present case brings us to the conclusion that plaintiff's evidence raised issues for the jury as to breach by defendant preventing his further performance and the reasonable value of his services. The only evidence is the testimony of plaintiff Harold Coon. He testified that defendant Frank Schoeneman had told him he had certain lots in Irving and Arlington and that he needed somebody to build houses on them. Schoeneman proposed that Coon build the houses, Schoeneman would finance them, they would get a third person to sell them, and they

* *See* I G. Palmer, The Law of Restitution § 4.1, at 365–66 (1978) ("quasi-contract" is appropriate to describe the plaintiff's remedy in this situation). *Compare* Childres & Garamello, The Law of Restitution and the Reliance Interest in Contracts, 64 Nw.U.L.Rev. 433 (1969).

would split the profits three ways. Coon agreed and started building. After he had built seven houses in Irving, including six "model homes," and had started four in Arlington, Schoeneman told him the rest of the Irving lots had been sold and proposed that Coon proceed with the project in Arlington on a different deal, which was that Coon would pay him $350 a house, Schoeneman would furnish the lots, and Coon would get all the profit. Coon agreed, with the understanding that he would have five houses under construction or ready for sale continuously and that no lots would be sold to other builders in the immediate area. Schoeneman agreed to these conditions. When Coon had finished four houses on the Arlington lots and was ready to start a fifth, he discovered that Schoeneman had sold the rest of the lots and other contractors were preparing to build on lots next to the houses Coon had built. Coon built no more houses on Schoeneman's lots. Schoeneman said he would send Coon his part of the profits from the houses that were built, but he sold the houses and never gave Coon any of the proceeds. Coon never received anything for his work.

Defendant objected to plaintiff's testimony concerning the value of his services on the ground that the proof established an express agreement to share profits and plaintiff was limited to recovery of such profits. The objection was sustained, and plaintiff gave his testimony concerning the value of his services in the form of a bill of exceptions. At the close of plaintiff's direct testimony the trial court sustained defendant's motion to instruct a verdict in his favor on the ground that plaintiff had shown only that there was a verbal agreement to share profits, but had not shown that there were any profits.

Since the trial court instructed a verdict for defendant, we must view the evidence in the light most favorable to plaintiff. Viewing Coon's testimony in that light, we conclude that a jury would have been justified in finding that Schoeneman breached the contract by selling off the Arlington lots contrary to his agreement that he would allow Coon to keep five houses ready for sale or under construction and would not sell lots to other contractors in the immediate area. Coon was thus prevented by Schoeneman's breach from building any more houses. Though the oral contract, as described by Coon, is not definite as to how many houses Coon was entitled to build, it did give him the right to build at least five and to be free from competition by other builders on Schoeneman's lots in the immediate area. On Schoeneman's breach of that agreement, Coon was entitled under the above authorities either to sue for his damages under the contract, including his share of profits on the houses he had built and the profits he would have made on other houses, or to treat the contract as rescinded and recover the reasonable value of his services.

We have considered whether the contract was divisible and the consideration apportionable, so that on completion and sale of each house plaintiff became entitled to compensation in a liquidated amount for his share of the profit and should be limited to that amount. Probably the contract is not divisible, since six of the houses in Irving were "model homes," which presumably were not expected to be sold at as much profit as others to be built. The mere fact that there is a contract rate of payment per unit of performance does not make the contract divisible, since the parties may not have been willing to contract separately for each unit. *5 Corbin, op. cit. supra* § 1111 at 593. However, we conclude that the divisibility of the contract does not matter, since even if the profits were apportionable to each house, the amount was not liquidated. It depended on the sale price and the various factors making up the cost. Consequently, under the rule stated in either § 350 or § 351 of the Restatement, plaintiff was not limited to the contract measure of compensation.

The case is analogous to one in which the agreed exchange for services is something other than a determinable amount of money, such as property or an interest in the business. In that case even a plaintiff who has fully performed may recover the reasonable value of his services rather than the value of what was promised to him. Coens v. Marousis, 275 Pa. 478, 119 A. 549 (1923); *5 Corbin, op. cit. supra* § 1110 at 587. This rule seems to be based on the idea that since plaintiff cannot obtain his specific *quid pro quo* under the contract, and proof of its value may be difficult, he should not be limited to recovery of damages but should be able to recover the reasonable value of his services by way of restitution. Likewise, in this case, since defendant repudiated the contract and prevented plaintiff from continuing performance, plaintiff is entitled to elect his remedy of restitution, and should not be required to assume the burden of establishing the profit on the sale of each of eleven houses in order to recover compensation for his services.

One of the problems here is that both of the oral contracts described by plaintiff provided for compensation in terms of profit, and, therefore, contractual compensation was contingent on the existence of profits, which were not proved. Thus defendant contends that plaintiff failed to prove that he was entitled to any compensation at all. The question is whether the contingent character of the contractual compensation renders unavailable the alternative remedy of restitution, so that plaintiff is without remedy for defendant's breach unless he can prove that profits were realized in the past, or would have been realized in the future if the contract had been fully performed.

In our opinion the contingent nature of the contractual compensation does not affect the plaintiff's right to restitution upon defendant's material breach of the contract. Proof that no profits were made on the houses sold would not establish that no profits would have been realized if defendant had complied with the contract. Presumably, greater profits were anticipated from sale of subsequent houses than from the "model homes." Moreover, defendant's principal breach was his sale of adjacent lots to competing builders. Such a breach may in itself have prevented any profit on the four houses in Arlington or may have reduced the amount of profit, but proof would be difficult. The party who has wrongfully prevented the other party from completing the contract should not benefit from his own wrong. Consequently, we hold that even though the contractual compensation was contingent on profits, the same rule of restitution applies as in other cases where defendant's breach has prevented further performance by plaintiff. Plaintiff should have his election to treat the contract as rescinded and recover the reasonable value of his services.

* * *

Reversed and remanded.

Notes

1. Where the defendant's conduct constitutes a "material breach," the plaintiff ordinarily will elect between rescission/restitution damages and damages for breach of contract and, where appropriate, for specific performance. If the plaintiff rescinds the agreement, quasi-contract relief ordinarily will be available where the plaintiff has performed in part, although the manner of measuring the amount recoverable may vary depending on several factors. If the plaintiff "affirms" the contract and sues for damages, the plaintiff will seek to prove both "reliance" damages (out-of-pocket losses sustained in the course of performance) and "expectation" damages (lost benefits, including, possibly, profits directly traceable to defendant's failure to perform). Fuller and Perdue, The Reliance Interest in Contract Damages, 46 Yale L.J. 52, 73 (1936); Childres and Garamella, The Law of Restitution and the Reliance Interest in Contract, 64 Nw.U.L.Rev. 433 (1969); 5 A. Corbin, Contracts § 992 (1964). *See also* pp. 831–839, *supra*. The latter rule is designed to place the plaintiff in as good a position as if there had been performance by the defendant.

The plaintiff has the burden of showing with reasonable certainty the profits which would have been earned had the defendant performed in those cases where the contract is "affirmed" and expectation damages are sought. This presents a real challenge to the attorney whose client is engaged in a type of venture in which there are typically many failures. Professor Corbin has drawn attention to a great variety of situations of this nature in which counsel for the plaintiff may nonetheless satisfy this requirement. Examples include actions for profits which would have been earned if (1) a fishing boat had been delivered, or (2) title and possession had been transferred to a going business, or (3) oil drilling equipment had been delivered. *See* 5 A. Corbin, Contracts § 1022 (1964).

2. There are a number of grounds for rescinding a contractual agreement, including material breach, failure of consideration, mistake, duress, undue influence and fraud. The question arises of how to measure the plaintiff's restitution recovery for the benefit conferred upon the other party prior to the act justifying rescission. Several means of measuring "benefit" might be utilized: the market value of what was received; increase in market value of the property upon which the improvement was made; particular value to the defendant (which might include a portion of profits or of the proceeds of any disposition); the plaintiff's costs in conferring the benefit; or the price, if any, fixed by the contract for the performance creating the benefit. Generally, in restitution cases where monetary relief is sought, the method chosen for measuring the benefit reflects the nature of the defendant's conduct. I G. Palmer, The Law of Restitution § 5.1 (1978). In some instances, such as mutual mistake, there is no greater "fault" by one party than by the other; but where the right to rescind is based upon a "material breach" by the defendant, fault lies with the defendant. The defendant's breach might have been either wilful (because it had been within his or her power to perform) or unavoidable (in the sense that it was beyond his or her power to prevent). Where the case involves rescission for wilful breach, the defendant's reprehensible conduct arguably should give the plaintiff the benefit of whichever theory results in the

larger recovery, without regard to contract limits. According to the prevailing view the contract price does not limit the amount of restitutionary relief. I G. Palmer, The Law of Restitution § 4.4 (1978). *Compare* Childres and Garamello, The Law of Restitution and the Reliance Interest in Contract, 64 Nw. U.L.Rev. 433 (1969).

3. The rule discussed by the Court in *Coon* limits the plaintiff's right to rescind a contract and sue for restitution in those situations where the contract is fully performed except for the defendant's obligation to pay the sum specified in the contract and the breach complained of consists of a failure to do so. There, as the Court notes, the plaintiff's sole remedy for breach is to sue for the contract price. This limitation upon the right to rescind does not apply, as a general matter, where the defendant's obligation upon which a claim of breach is made is other than one simply to pay the price specified in the contract, or in those cases where the basis for seeking rescission is some form of conduct other than breach such as misrepresentation. *See,* I G. Palmer, §§ 4.3 at 383 and 3.3 at 236.

4. Where rescission and restitution are available, and relief on this basis is awarded, the courts as a general matter do not limit the plaintiff's recovery in quasi-contract to the contract price, nor is it material to the restitution claim that plaintiff would have suffered a loss had the contract been performed. *Id.,* at 389–90. *Compare,* Childres and Garamello, The Law of Restitution and the Reliance Interest in Contract, 64 Nw.U.L.Rev. 433 (1969).

May the plaintiff recover the gains derived by defendant from use of whatever performance may have been received from plaintiff? See, I G. Palmer, Law of Restitution (1978) § 4.9.

ROYAL v. PARADO

District Court of Appeal of Florida, 1985.
462 So.2d 849.

SMITH, JUDGE.

Appellants seek reversal of a final judgment rescinding a quitclaim deed and quieting title to certain parcels of land located in St. Johns County, Florida. We affirm the trial court's jurisdiction, but find error on other issues, and vacate the final judgment and remand for further proceedings.

The issues are * * * (3) whether the court erred in granting rescission [by an equity decree] of appellee's deed to appellants, especially since there was no finding of fraud on the part of appellants, and the judgment does not return them to their status quo. We find error in the court's ruling on the latter two issues, requiring reversal.

I—FACTS

* * *

* * * [I]n 1979 the parties began discussions of a possible arrangement whereby appellee would convey the easterly one-half of her land to appellants, in exchange for a promise from the appellants that they would live on the conveyed property and provide care and attention to appellee for the rest of her life. Apparently, appellee had a dread of living her later life in a

nursing home, and hence was willing to give up possession of a portion of her property in exchange for assurances that this would never come to pass.

As a result of these discussions, on August 1, 1980, appellee conveyed the easterly one-half of her property to the appellants. In order to provide a residence for themselves, appellants then borrowed approximately $33,000 from the Beach Federal Savings and Loan Association, Jacksonville Beach, mortgaging the property conveyed by appellee as security, and commenced construction of a residence on the eastern half of the property at issue here. The total investment by appellants in the residence was $74,178.

* * *

Two significant events (characterized by the trial court as "shocking") took place on August 12, 1981. First, Lillian Mack Emerson and appellant Carole Royal went to the savings and loan association where appellee conducted her banking business, and attempted to cash certain certificates of deposit, in the amount of $85,000, which were owned jointly in the names of appellee, Mrs. Emerson, and appellant Carole Royal. The attempt was unsuccessful, however, because on the preceding day a freeze had been placed on the certificates of deposit by appellee after she had discovered that the certificates were missing from her safety deposit box. * * *

The second August 12, 1981 incident also involves Mrs. Emerson and the appellants. Mrs. Emerson petitioned the Circuit Court of St. Johns County for an emergency mental evaluation of the appellee pursuant to Section 394.463, Florida Statutes, advising the deputy clerk of court that appellee was in need of long-term convalescent care and emergency evaluation. Appellants Carole and James Royal accompanied Mrs. Emerson to the courthouse, where they signed two affidavits in support of Mrs. Emerson's petition. As a result of the petition, appellee was transported by the St. Johns County Sheriff's Department to Flagler Hospital, St. Augustine. Appellee was evaluated—and immediately released—when neither the intake examiner nor the clinical psychologist could find any basis for detention or treatment of appellee. No evidence was introduced at trial that appellee had ever received treatment for mental or emotional problems.

* * *

V—Rescission

Finally, appellants contend that the trial court erred in granting rescission [based on the facts stated above]. Although we do not foreclose the granting of rescission, we do agree that the judgment as rendered improperly grants such relief. As a rule, a court of equity will ordinarily rescind an instrument only for fraud, accident or mistake, and not because of the mere want or failure of consideration; an action for damages at law is usually considered adequate where failure of consideration exists. Here, the trial court's order and subsequent final judgment predicates the granting of the remedy of rescission on failure of consideration occasioned by appellants' actions culminating in the events of August 12, 1981. The trial court did not make a specific factual finding that appellants were guilty of fraud. It appears, therefore, that the remedy applied does not coincide with the trial court's findings. It is unclear to us, however, whether the trial court upon re-examination of the evidence in the light of applicable legal principles might nevertheless find rescission justified in this case.

The facts recited by the trial court suggest fraudulent inducement as a possible alternate ground for rescission. This ground for rescission exists where at the time of execution of a contract, the party promising to perform an act in the future has a secret undisclosed intent not to carry it out, but fraudulently represents that he will perform as an inducement to the other party to enter into the contract. The rule, which may be applicable to the facts in the case at bar, is well recognized where a deed is executed in consideration of an agreement by the grantee to support the grantor. Where the grantee had no intention of carrying out the agreement, this constitutes a fraud vitiating the conveyance. * * * Here, the trial court found that the appellants provided nominal care and attention to appellee after June 1981, when the new house was substantially completed. The trial court also found that the "shocking" character of appellants' actions of August 12, 1981, in effect nullified all previous efforts of appellants in providing care and attention to appellee. Arguably, these actions were sufficiently egregious to raise a presumption of fraudulent inducement under the authorities above cited. However, whether rescission is justified under this theory is a matter we leave to the further consideration of the trial judge on remand.

In the event the trial court, on remand, continues to opt for rescission as the appropriate remedy here, considering all the circumstances, one further matter must be addressed. As previously noted, appellants complain (and rightly so, as the facts recited demonstrate), that the final judgment does not return them to their status quo. The law is well settled that a condition precedent to the granting of the remedy of rescission is that the other party be returned to his status quo. Generally, a contract will not be rescinded even for fraud when it is not possible for the opposing party to be put back into his pre-agreement status quo condition. Moreover, a party who makes good faith improvements to the land to be returned to another is entitled to compensation to the extent that the improvements have added value to the returned property. It is manifestly clear that the judgment did not return appellants to their status quo, for they not only made improvements to appellee's property for which no compensation was received, they were also ordered to continue making mortgage payments on a residence they no longer are able to occupy and from which they can derive no benefit.

Finally, we direct that on remand the trial court be guided by the rule that the court should go no further than is reasonably necessary to balance fully the equities flowing between the parties, and in exercising its discretion should grant relief appropriate to the wrongs suffered, or as may be reasonably called for by the circumstances of the case.

Accordingly, the judgment below is affirmed in part, and reversed in part, and the cause is remanded to the trial court for further proceedings consistent with this opinion.

NORTON v. POPLOS,* 443 A.2d 1 (1982). The plaintiff seller sought specific performance of a contract for the sale of certain real estate. The defendant buyer counterclaimed for rescission, cancellation of the deed and restitution on the ground that the sale had been induced by a material misrepresentation of which the seller was unaware at the time it was made.

In granting the defendant the equitable relief sought the Court stated:

* * *

A.

Essentially, the equitable remedy of rescission results in abrogation or "unmaking" of an agreement, and attempts to return the parties to the *status quo.* Common grounds for rescission of a contract for the sale of real property include fraud, misrepresentation and mistake. 8A *Thompson on Real Property* § 4465 pp. 366, 367 (1963). But in addition to rescission for fraudulent misrepresentation, *Williston on Contracts* § 1487 p. 322 (3rd Ed.1970), rescission also may be granted under certain circumstances for innocent misrepresentations made by a seller. Thus, as stated by Professor Williston:

> "It is not necessary, in order that a contract may be rescinded for fraud or misrepresentation, that the party making the misrepresentation should have known that it was false. Innocent misrepresentation is sufficient for though the representation may have been made innocently, it would be unjust and inequitable to permit a person who has made false representations, even innocently, to retain the fruits of a bargain induced by such representations."

Williston, supra, at § 1500, pp. 400, 401. Similarly, the recently promulgated *Restatement 2d of Contracts,* § 164, states that,

> "If a party's manifestation of assent is induced by either a fraudulent *or material* misrepresentation by the other party upon which the recipient is justified in relying, the contract is voidable by the recipient." (Emphasis added.)

See also Restatement 1st of Contracts, § 476 (1932). Most American jurisdictions which have addressed this issue appear to recognize that an innocent material misrepresentation by a vendor which induces the sale of the property is ground for rescission of the contract. *Thompson, supra,* § 4472, pp. 401, 402. In addition to ordering rescission, a court will generally direct that a down payment by a buyer be returned on a theory of restitution. *See Restatement 1st of Restitution,* § 55 (1937); *Dobbs, Handbook on the Law of Remedies,* § 4.1, p. 222 (1973).

A misrepresentation need not be in the form of written or spoken words. Stated simply, a misrepresentation is merely an "assertion not in accordance with the facts," *Restatement 2d of Contracts,* § 159, and such an assertion may be made by conduct as well as words. *Id.* Comment a. And although a statement or assertion may be facially true, it may constitute an actionable misrepresentation if it causes a false impression as to the true state of affairs, and the actor fails to provide qualifying information to cure the mistaken belief.

* This case also is considered at p. 1006, infra.

* * *

Finally, we consider several other matters raised in the appeal.

In the *Norton* case the Supreme Court of Delaware stated as follows with respect to defenses based upon a "merger clause": "Poplos argues that Norton's claim is barred by a 'merger' clause which, in essence, states that the parties have read and understood the contract and that 'they do not rely on any written or oral representations not expressly written in [the] contract.' It is clear, however, that a merger clause does not preclude a claim based upon fraudulent misrepresentations.* Slater v. Berlin, D.C.Mun.Ct.App., 94 A.2d 38, 43 (1953); Ortel v. Upper Ashburton Realty Co., Md.Ct.App., 171 Md. 678, 190 A. 239, 242 (1937). The law is not quite so clear, however, with respect to the effect of such a clause on an innocent or honest misrepresentation. Although we are aware of authority to the contrary, *cf.* Wilkinson v. Carpenter, Or.Supr., 276 Or. 311, 554 P.2d 512 (1976), we follow the better rule which is this: even if a sales contract contains a merger clause, a buyer may rescind the contract if it resulted from an innocent but material misrepresentation by a seller. As the Rhode Island Supreme Court has stated:

> '[T]he availability of the remedy of rescission is motivated by the obvious inequity of allowing a person who has made an innocent misrepresentation to retain the fruits of the bargain induced thereby. If we are to permit a party to rescind a contract as a result of an innocent misrepresentation, the "boiler plate" found in the merger clause shall not bar the use of this remedy.' * * * " (443 A.2d 1, at 4).

Note

Actionable misrepresentation may occur in a variety of other situations. These include: (1) failure to disclose that the contracting party is in fact the undisclosed agent of another (Walker v. Galt, 171 F.2d 613 (5th Cir.1948)); (2) failure to reveal pertinent material facts where a fiduciary duty of loyalty is owed to the other party, or a relationship of trust and confidence exists between them (Moon v. Phipps, 67 Wash.2d 948, 411 P.2d 157 (1966)); (3) lack of intent to perform the promise given as consideration for a contract as illustrated by the *Royal* case; see, California Conserving Co. v. D'Avanzo, 62 F.2d 528 (2d Cir.1933); Entron, Inc. v. General Cablevision of Palatka, 435 F.2d 995 (5th Cir.1970) (failure to perform promised consideration evidences state of mind at time of contracting).

Opinions ordinarily are not a basis for rescission for misrepresentation. Restatement of Restitution § 8(3) (1937). There are exceptions, however, as when the "opinion" is given "in bad faith" (Stern v. Satra Corp., 539 F.2d 1305 (2d Cir.1976)) or by one purporting to be an expert. Restatement of Restitution § 8(3)(b) (1937). The traditional approach has treated a misrepresentation of law as necessarily involving an opinion and, consequently, as not providing a basis for rescission. *See* Restatement of Restitution § 55 (1937). However the courts have found a variety of special circumstances justifying

* This is the general rule. *See* I G. Palmer, Law of Restitution § 3.20 (1978).

reliance and rescission where the statement of law was misleading. Illustrative are Sainsbury v. Pennsylvania Greyhound Lines, Inc., 183 F.2d 548 (4th Cir.1950) (representation of law by a lawyer acting as a claims adjuster); Dushane v. Kazmierczak, 192 Misc. 23, 79 N.Y.S.2d 293 (1948), aff'd, 274 App.Div. 1025, 86 N.Y.S.2d 480 (1948) ("implied representation" of law by board of education to teacher); Fawcett v. Sun Life Assur. Co., 135 F.2d 544 (10th Cir.1943) (representation of law by insurer with "superior knowledge").

HEAD & SEEMANN, INC. v. GREGG

Court of Appeals of Wisconsin, 1981.
104 Wis.2d 156, 311 N.W.2d 667.*

VOSS, PRESIDING JUDGE.

Bettye Gregg fraudulently induced Head & Seemann, Inc. to sell her a home in Brookfield. She occupied the home for five months but was subsequently ejected by a court order. In the action on the claim from which this appeal comes, Head & Seemann sought damages for the five months lost use of the property. At issue was whether a defrauded party who obtains rescission and restitution of real estate may also recover rental value and out-of-pocket expenses for the period of lost possession. The trial court held that the election of remedies doctrine barred an additional action for rental value and out-of-pocket expenses. Because we do not believe that rescission and an action for damages are inconsistent remedies, we reverse.

Defendant Bettye J. Gregg offered to buy a Brookfield home from plaintiff corporation. She represented, verbally and in writing, that she had $15,000 to $20,000 of equity in another home and would pay this amount to plaintiff after selling the other home. She knew, however, that she had no such equity. Relying on these intentionally fraudulent representations, plaintiff accepted defendant's offer to buy, and the parties entered into a land contract. After taking occupancy, defendant failed to make any of the contract payments. Plaintiff's investigation then revealed the fraud.

Plaintiff commenced this action seeking one of two alternative forms of relief. Based on the fraud, plaintiff sought rescission, ejectment and recovery for five months of lost use of the property and out-of-pocket expenses. Alternatively, based on defendant's breach of contract, plaintiff sought rescission, foreclosure and ejectment.

The trial court granted partial summary judgment for plaintiff, rescinding the contract for fraud. The court ordered ejectment but stayed the order for two weeks pending defendant's voluntary removal. The court also obtained plaintiff's stipulation that, if defendant removed herself within the two weeks, the plaintiff's claim for damages would be dismissed. Defendant failed to vacate the property, and the court entered an interlocutory judgment of ejectment.

* The Wisconsin Supreme Court affirmed the decision and adopted the Court of Appeals opinion as its own. 107 Wis.2d 126, 318 N.W.2d 381 (1982).

Defendant later sought dismissal of the damages claim based on the election of remedies doctrine. The court determined that the judgment for ejectment was an election of remedies barring recovery of damages and, therefore, dismissed the cause of action based on fraud. On appeal, this court certified this case to the Wisconsin Supreme Court to resolve the conflict in case law. The certification was denied.

Plaintiff contends that it is entitled to recover for the lost use of the property and out-of-pocket expenses during defendant's possession of the property. It contends that recovery for these items, in addition to the rescission and return of the real estate, is necessary to restore plaintiff to his status before the fraud and execution of the contract. Since these "damages" would only restore plaintiff to its previous position and would not give plaintiff the purchase price or the benefit of the bargain, plaintiff argues that the remedies are not inconsistent, and the doctrine of election of remedies should not be applied. We agree.

The election of remedies doctrine is an equitable principle barring one from maintaining inconsistent theories or forms of relief. Bank of Commerce v. Paine, Webber, Jackson & Curtis, 39 Wis.2d 30, 36–39, 158 N.W.2d 350, 352–53 (1968). Its underlying purpose is to prevent double recovery for the same wrong. *Id.* at 36, 158 N.W.2d at 352; D. Dobbs, Handbook on the Law of Remedies § 1.5, at 14 (1973). The label "election of remedies" is frequently used as a cloak for an estoppel or ratification where, for example, it bars a suit for rescission of a contract *subsequent* to some act of affirmance of the contract. *See, e.g.,* Beers v. Atlas Assurance Co., 231 Wis. 361, 285 N.W. 794 (1939). Wisconsin courts have been attempting to restrict the doctrine to reduce its harsh effects. * * *

The classic application of the election of remedies doctrine is that a defrauded party has the election of either rescission or affirming the contract and seeking damages. First National Bank & Trust Co. v. Notte, 97 Wis.2d 207, 225, 293 N.W.2d 530, 539 (1980). The choice is forced with respect to alternative theories in a single lawsuit because of inconsistency of both rescinding and affirming the contract.

Thus, it superficially appears that if a claimant chooses to seek rescission, he may not sue for damages. But the word "damages," like the label "election of remedies," impedes rather than aids the inquiry into the types of relief appropriate in a given case. Rescission is always coupled with restitution: the parties return the money, property or other benefits so as to restore each other to the position they were in prior to the transaction. In the case of fraud or misrepresentation, the victim has the priority of restoration, and if a loss must be borne, the wrongdoer bears it. *See* First National Bank & Trust Co. v. Notte, 97 Wis.2d at 225–26, 293 N.W.2d at 539.

This case presents a crucial question dealing with the nature of restitution. At issue is whether restitution to a rescinding fraud victim includes everything he has reasonably paid out or given up in the transaction or only includes what the other party has actually received.[1] Two Wisconsin cases provide contradictory answers.

1. Under the second possibility in which the victim gets only what the other party received, the victim's expenditures paid to third parties would not be included in his recovery. [Footnote by the Court.]

In Carpenter v. Mason, 181 Wis. 114, 193 N.W. 973 (1923), plaintiff entered into a land contract in reliance on defendant's fraudulent statements. The trial court entered judgment of rescission and ordered recovery of the money paid toward the purchase plus $140 for plaintiff's costs in moving from another state as a result of the fraud. The Wisconsin Supreme Court disallowed the moving costs. The court stated that placing the parties *in status quo* "does not mean that the parties are to be restored to the situation which existed previous to their entering into the contract." *Id.* at 116, 193 N.W. at 974. It means, the court indicated, only that each party must return what he has actually received. Defendants did not receive plaintiff's expenditures for moving. "To require them to restore more than they received would be to permit the plaintiff to recover *damages for breach of the contract.* The plaintiff does not affirm the contract but disaffirms it and seeks rescission. He may not do both." *Id.* (emphasis added).

Interestingly, a later case contradicting *Carpenter* also involved moving expenses incurred in reliance on misrepresentations and the resulting bargain. In Schnuth v. Harrison, 44 Wis.2d 326, 171 N.W.2d 370 (1969), plaintiff was fraudulently induced to buy into and to operate a business and to take a lease. In granting rescission and restitution, the trial court included awards for travel expenses, moving expenses (over $1,700) and salary the plaintiff never received. This time, the supreme court affirmed. "All these items were aimed at making the plaintiff whole and were properly awarded as items of damage needed to place him in the same position he was in before the contract." *Id.* at 339, 171 N.W.2d at 377–78.

Thus, the two cases give different answers to whether restitution is measured by the victim's actual loss or by what the wrongdoer actually received (whenever the two measures are not the same). *Schnuth* did not cite *Carpenter,* and no other Wisconsin case has criticized *Carpenter.* The instant plaintiff seeks "damages" of the restitutionary nature involved in the two conflicting cases. Under *Carpenter,* plaintiff would be barred from part or all of the monetary award he seeks on the theory that defendant received only the land or perhaps only the land and its use but not other expenses, while *Schnuth* would apparently permit the entire award.

Two possible theories can reconcile the disparities in the two cases. The first is that Wisconsin, in the *Schnuth* case, rejected the election of remedies doctrine. The other theory is that actions for rescission and restorative damages are not inconsistent.

The Abandonment of Election of Remedies Doctrine

One method of reconciling the *Carpenter* case and the *Schnuth* case is by concluding that Wisconsin has abandoned the election of remedies doctrine. *Carpenter v. Mason* has become a somewhat infamous horror story cited as a good reason why the election of remedies doctrine ought to be abolished:

> The best example that I can recall to show the need for the fraud statute [abolishing election of remedies in fraud cases in New York] is a case decided in Wisconsin during an earlier boom period. * * * The trial court allowed all three items, but the Supreme Court of Wisconsin sternly rejected the claim for moving expenses, not on the ground that they were not proximate damages resulting from the defendant's wrong, but on the ground that the plaintiff had elected to disaffirm the contract and therefore could not recover damages for deceit.
>
> What substantial reason can be given for such a decision? Did not the defendants' wrong proximately cause the plaintiff all of the losses that he sustained? Did not the plaintiff allege and prove all of the facts necessary to entitle him to all of the items of recovery claimed? Was there any *duplication* of items of recovery? Certainly not. Was the defendant misled prejudicially by the plaintiff's suing to get his money "back," and also his money paid out for moving? No prejudicial reliance appears. Then is not the doctrine of election of remedies here merely a requirement of formal consistency? To satisfy this requirement *fully* it would seem that, in order to recover his moving expenses, the plaintiff would have to "affirm" the voidable contract, pay to the defendants the balance due on the contract price (thus sending "good money" after "bad") and then sue the wrongdoers to obtain judgment for his total expenditures. This would be "true" affirmance, angelic consistency. (It might also be construed as a complete condonation of the fraud!) But the nineteenth century courts that enjoyed the logic-chopping of the election doctrine were usually not so strict as to require the defrauded party to perform his *executory promises* to the fraud-doer in order to be able to recover damages for the deceit. [Footnotes omitted, emphasis in original.]

Patterson, Improvements in the Law of Restitution, 40 Cornell L.Q. 667, 679–80 (1955). Professor Dobbs' criticism of *Carpenter* and its election doctrine appears in his hornbook, *Remedies* § 1.5, at 14–15 and § 9.4, at 633–34.

A host of commentators support elimination of the election of remedies doctrine. A common theme is that the doctrine substitutes labels and formalism for inquiry into whether double recovery results in *fact.* The rigid doctrine goes to the other extreme, actually resulting in the under-compensation of fraud victims and the protection of undeserving wrong-doers. *See, e.g., id.;* I G. Palmer, Law of Restitution §§ 3.9–3.10 (1978); Hine, Election of Remedies, a Criticism, 26 Harv.L.Rev. 707 (1913); Annot., Rescission of Contract as Affecting Right to Recover Damages for Fraud in Procuring It, 120 A.L.R. 1154 (1939). *Cf.* Roberts v. Sears, Roebuck & Co., 573 F.2d 976 (7th Cir.), cert. denied, 439 U.S. 860, 99 S.Ct. 179, 58 L.Ed.2d 168 (1978) (awarding rescission of patent assignment plus $1,000,000 for defendant's past profits; no inconsistency or double recovery because rescission protects future rights while money compensates past injury for fraud).

The Uniform Commercial Code eliminates the election doctrine with respect to sales of goods.

At least two states have eliminated the formal doctrine by statute. California Civil Code § 1692 (West) provides in part:

> A claim for damages is not inconsistent with a claim for relief based upon rescission. The aggrieved party shall be awarded complete relief, including restitution of benefits, if any, conferred by him as a result of the transaction and any consequential damages to which he is entitled; but such relief shall not include duplicate or inconsistent items of recovery.

See also N.Y.Civ.Prac.Law § 3002(e) (McKinney) (in cases of fraud or misrepresentation).*

It appears that the commentators and the modern trend of the law support abandonment of the formalistic shell of the doctrine of election of remedies. The law can prevent windfalls to claimants without going overboard by requiring that fraud victims bear part of the loss, absolving defrauding parties of their proper responsibility.

Elimination of the formal doctrine would permit courts to focus on the rule of one satisfaction and deemphasize theoretical consistency of remedies. In the instant case, plaintiff might have its rescission and consequential damages for the *tort* of fraud or deceit. Since the tort system is designed to make one whole to the extent possible through a monetary award, plaintiff would receive such damages in tort which in addition to return of the land would restore it to its preinjury position. *See* sec. 402.721, Stats. No double recovery would result in this case.

Although the trend in law appears to support abandoning the election doctrine, no case indicates that this, in fact, has been done in Wisconsin. The *Schnuth* case did not end the use of the election of remedies doctrine in Wisconsin, it merely gave a different description of restitution.

RESCISSION AND RESTORATIVE DAMAGES AS CONSISTENT REMEDIES

A second approach to reconciling the two cases is to retain the formal election of remedies doctrine but clearly define rescission and restorative damages as entirely consistent with each other and therefore not subject to election. We believe this is what *Schnuth* intended.

Other state courts have adopted this approach. In Jennings v. Lee, 105 Ariz. 167, 461 P.2d 161 (1969), plaintiff not only obtained rescission and return of her real estate but also $11,000 for the real estate agent's commission she paid as well as sums sufficient to release two mortgages she executed.

> Her recovery of this money is *not inconsistent with the rule that a party may not rescind and recover damages in the same suit.* That rule

* N.Y.C.P.L. § 3002(e) reads as follows:

Claim for damages and rescission. A claim for damages sustained as a result of fraud or misrepresentation in the inducement of a contract or other transaction, shall not be deemed inconsistent with a claim for rescission or based upon rescission. In an action for rescission or based upon rescission the aggrieved party shall be allowed to obtain complete relief in one action, including rescission, restitution of the benefits, if any, conferred by him as a result of the transaction, and damages to which he is entitled because of such fraud or misrepresentation; but such complete relief shall not include duplication of items of recovery. [Footnote by the Court.]

> is designed to prevent a defrauded party from both repudiating the contract and then suing on it only to *gain the benefit of the bargain.* There is ample authority that a defrauded party may not only receive back the consideration he gave, but also may recover any sums that are necessary to restore him to his position prior to the making of the contract.

Id. at 173, 461 P.2d at 167 (emphasis added). *See also* Kent Homes v. Frankel, 128 A.2d 444 (D.C.Ct.App.1957) (awarding commuting costs).

Many other cases recognize that "disaffirmance" of damages only rules out "expectation" damages—the benefit of the bargain—and distinguish restitutionary "damages."

> Damages for restitution are different from damages for breach of contract; and the former are permissible to restore the plaintiff to his former position when rescission is granted because of fraud. Several other states allow the recovery of restitutionary damages along with rescission when fraud or misrepresentations is the cause of the claim. We believe that restitutionary damages conform with the purpose of rescission, which is to put the defrauded party back in as good a position as he occupied before entering the contract. Consequently, we hold that such damages may be awarded along with rescission.

Robison v. Katz, 94 N.M. 314, 320, 610 P.2d 201, 207 (1980). In equity, the court makes the calculated adjustments necessary to do complete justice. If complete justice requires that damages be awarded with the rescission, the court will award them. Atkins v. Beasley, 544 S.W.2d 505, 507 (Tex.Civ.App.1976) (restitutionary damages for cost of drilling an oil well, not damages at law).

Two clear forms of restitutionary awards are recoverable when coupled with rescission: The first is "reasonable expenditures in reliance on the bargain." Bodenhamer v. Patterson, 278 Or. 367, 377, 563 P.2d 1212, 1218 (1977) (road and septic tank expenditures which did not enhance value of land); *accord,* Hammac v. Skinner, 265 Ala. 9, 89 So.2d 70 (1956) (moving expenses). The second is the rent or use value of the real estate during the other's possession.

Even in situations where the buyer is defrauded and entitled to the rescission, he or she must ordinarily pay rental value to the seller. This provides *a fortiori* support for the above authorities.

In the instant case, plaintiff seeks rental value and incidental expenses as part of restitution, items clearly recoverable under the great weight of authority. We believe that *Schnuth* recognized the position that rescission and restorative damages are consistent remedies which work together to restore the injured party to his precontract position. For this reason, restorative damages, which in this case is rent, should be allowed in addition to rescission. The two are not inconsistent remedies.

Order reversed.

Notes

1. *Head* was an action for *equitable* rescission brought by a seller of real property. In Isaacs v. Bokor, 566 S.W.2d 532 (Tenn.1978), the plaintiff was a

buyer of real estate who had tendered a reconveyance of the property (along with the improvements) to the seller and then had brought an action for *legal* rescission based on mutual mistake. The court held that the plaintiff could recover restorative damages in addition to recovering the purchase price:

> "[I]t is too narrow a view to state that a vendee, upon rescission, is limited strictly to the purchase price which he paid for the property. Where he has changed his position and made improvements, he may well be entitled to recover for their value, although, in attempting to restore the parties to their former status, courts may require the vendee to account to the vendor for the use or rental value of the property, to convey improvements to him, and to restore to the vendor anything of value which the vendee has received from him in the rescinded transaction."

Id. at 540.

2. The question in cases such as *Head* is whether the party with a right to rescind for fraudulent misrepresentation who elects to do so, whether in law or equity, is limited to the quasi-contract restitution relief to which he is, of course, entitled, or may he recover other damages as well? The quasi-contract damages would be measured by the amount of the benefit conferred by the rescinding party on the other party, whereas the damage claim would be based upon the non-duplicative losses (other than "expectation damages" in the form of lost profits) incurred as a result of the defendant's tortious conduct. See, generally, I G. Palmer, Law of Restitution, 1978 §§ 3.9–3.10.

WALRAVEN v. MARTIN

Court of Appeals of Michigan, 1983.
123 Mich.App. 342, 333 N.W.2d 569.

ALLEN, JUDGE.

Must a plaintiff make an election between inconsistent theories of recovery before proceeding to trial? The trial court, in an order dated June 8, 1981, held yes, requiring plaintiff to elect to proceed in equity against defendants Martin and Samuels for rescission or to proceed against all of the defendants at law for damages resulting from the alleged fraud committed upon him. The action was stayed by the trial court per the parties' stipulation and the order was certified by the court as final for purposes of appeal under GCR 1963, 518.2. Plaintiff appeals as of right. We reverse.

In July, 1978, plaintiff purchased a business, Bill's Cafe, which is located in Bay City, from defendants Martin and Samuels, the owners. The property was listed by the sellers with defendant Kenneth Warner, a real estate broker for defendant Warner Realty, Inc. * * * Upon taking possession of the premises and after beginning remodeling, plaintiff discovered that the city would be constructing a sewer in the area of Bill's Cafe and, as a result, streets and sidewalks would be torn up, the parking lot would be unavailable at times, utilities would be cut off for periods of time, and the traffic on the streets bordering the restaurant would be interrupted.

By letter dated August 18, 1978, plaintiff offered to rescind the transaction and demanded repayment of the down payment and reimbursement for remodeling and other expenses. Rescission was denied by Martin and Samuels. However, on November 2, 1978, plaintiff reconveyed the property to Martin and Samuels by quitclaim deed pursuant to an agreement signed by the sellers and plaintiff. The agreement provided that restoration of the premises to Martin and Samuels would not constitute a release or waiver of any rights of plaintiff arising out of the transaction, including an action for breach of contract, rescission and fraud, nor would restoration constitute acceptance by the sellers of a rescission of the contract.

* * *

[Plaintiff filed a complaint against Martin and Samuels for rescission based on fraud or, in the alternative, for damages resulting from the fraudulent concealment of information concerning the sewer project. Plaintiff also sought to recover damages from Warner and Warner Realty, Inc.]

Two weeks before trial, defendants Warner and Warner Realty, Inc. filed a motion to require plaintiff to make an election of remedies. After oral arguments and submission of briefs, the motion was granted in an order dated June 8, 1981. The order required plaintiff to choose between proceeding against Martin and Samuels in equity for rescission, with the result that all other defendants would be dismissed, or to proceed against all defendants for damages resulting from the alleged fraud committed upon him.

This case requires us to consider the continued viability of the common law doctrine of election of remedies.[1] It has long been stated that a party who elects to proceed on one theory of recovery is *thereafter* barred from asserting any inconsistent remedy. Ielmini v. Bessemer National Bank, 298 Mich. 59, 298 N.W. 404 (1941); Gloeser v. Moore, 284 Mich. 106, 278 N.W. 781 (1938). Generally, the doctrine applies only where two or more inconsistent remedies were available and the party has actually chosen and pursued the one to the exclusion of the other. *Ielmini v. Bessemer National Bank, supra,* 298 Mich. pp. 66–67, 298 N.W. 404. That situation is in contrast to the instant case where the aggrieved party has not yet chosen one remedy to the exclusion of the other. The inconsistency in the present case stems from plaintiff's request for rescission of the contract, and plaintiff's request for damages resulting from fraud committed on him, which involves affirmance of the contract.

Plaintiff herein, by seeking inconsistent remedies simultaneously, has not "elected" a remedy. Nevertheless, several cases from other jurisdictions support defendants' claim that the trial court may compel an election between inconsistent remedies at any stage of the proceedings. 25 Am.Jur. 2d, Election of Remedies, § 31, pp. 673–674. However, no Michigan case is cited therein for such proposition. Furthermore, while we have found dicta

1. Numerous articles have been written about the election doctrine; none are favorable. *See,* Fraser, Election of Remedies: An Anachronism, 29 Okla.L.Rev. 1 (1976); Patterson, Improvements in the Law of Restitution, 40 Cornell L.Q. 667 (1955); Yerkes, Election of Remedies in Cases of Fraudulent Misrepresentation, 26 S.Cal.L.Rev. 157 (1953); Note, Election of Remedies: A Delusion?, 38 Colum.L.Rev. 292 (1938); Hine, Election of Remedies, A Criticism, 26 Harv. L.Rev. 707 (1913); Dobbs, Remedies, § 1.5 p. 13; I G. Palmer, Law of Restitution (1978) § 3.10, p. 283. [Footnotes by the Court.]

that election of inconsistent remedies may be compelled at any stage of the proceedings (Willard v. Shekell, 236 Mich. 197, 206, 210 N.W. 260 [1926]), we have found no Michigan case prohibiting the simultaneous pursuit of inconsistent remedies. In fact, the only Michigan case directly in point held that the plaintiff should not have been required to elect between a count in rescission and a count for breach of contract.

Modern rules of civil procedure, the election of remedy doctrine expressed in the current legal periodicals cited earlier, and the Supreme Court's decision in Gruskin v. Fisher, 405 Mich. 51, 273 N.W.2d 893 (1979), lead us to conclude that plaintiff may simultaneously pursue all of his remedies against the sellers and other defendants herein regardless of legal consistency, *so long as plaintiff is not awarded double recovery.* While defendants emphasize the basic repugnance of allowing plaintiff to "blow hot and cold" at the same time, the inconsistency only involves legal theories of recovery. Under rescission plaintiff would be required to restore all benefits received and would be entitled to the purchase price of the restaurant and consequential damages, Mock v. Duke, 20 Mich.App. 453, 174 N.W.2d 161 (1969), whereas his actual damages, which are the same regardless of which defendant committed the fraud upon him, consist of plaintiff's loss of the bargain measured by the difference between the actual value of the property and its value if it had been as represented. Hubert v. Joslin, 285 Mich. 337, 346, 280 N.W. 780 (1938); Barker v. Fordville Land Co., 264 Mich. 95, 96–97, 249 N.W. 491 (1933). There is no inconsistency in the factual basis plaintiff relies upon in support of each theory. We believe it unfair to require plaintiff to choose which theory to proceed under prior to trial since res judicata would prevent him from proceeding under his alternative theory should the first choice prove unsuccessful. We also note that defendants are adequately protected from the plaintiff's changing course in midstream by our doctrines of equitable estoppel, waiver, accord and satisfaction and res judicata.

Several other jurisdictions have rejected the election prior to trial doctrine by caselaw, or by statute.[7] Our rejection of election prior to trial is consistent with Michigan's rules of civil procedure. Under GCR 1963, 111, every pleading is a simple, concise statement of the facts on which relief can be granted on any sustainable legal theory regardless of consistency and whether based on legal or equitable grounds or both.[8]

"Declaratory relief, in cases of actual controversy, may be claimed. Relief in the alternative or of several different types may be demanded.

* * *

7. N.Y. CPLR § 3002(e) (McKinney) states that in any case based on fraud, claims for rescission, based on rescission or for damages shall not be deemed inconsistent and the aggrieved party shall be allowed to obtain complete relief in one action, but such complete relief shall not include duplication of benefits. Ga.Code § 3–114 states that a plaintiff may pursue any number of consistent or inconsistent remedies against the same person or different persons until he shall obtain a satisfaction from some of them. *See also,* UCC § 2–703, which eliminates the election doctrine in sale-of-goods cases.

8. In contrast to today's system of fact pleading, the election doctrine developed during a time of theory pleading and the division of courts of law and equity.

"(2) Inconsistent claims or defenses are not objectionable, and when a party is in doubt as to which of 2 or more statements of fact is true, he may allege them in the alternative. A party may also state as many separate claims or defenses as he has regardless of consistency and whether based upon legal or equitable grounds or upon both." GCR 1963, 111.1(3) and 111.9(2).

Further, the plaintiff may join as many defendants as may be liable in one action, GCR 1963, 206, and GCR 1963, 505.2 and 509.3 give the trial court discretion to bifurcate trial and control the sequence of proof so as to facilitate complex trials and the determination of judge and jury issues.

* * *

We reiterate that, while plaintiff is entitled to complete relief, he is not entitled to double recovery. Hence, if verdicts are eventually returned against the sellers, defendants Martin and Samuels, for both rescission and damages, judgment may be entered on only one since these are alternative measures of plaintiff's loss. If judgment for damages is entered against the sellers, the other defendants may be held jointly and severally liable if a verdict is rendered against them. However, if judgment for rescission is entered against the sellers, the other defendants may only be held liable to the extent that the rescission judgment has failed to restore the status quo (because of the sellers' insolvency or otherwise).

Reversed and remanded for further proceedings. Costs to plaintiff.*

LENAWEE COUNTY BD. OF HEALTH v. MESSERLY

Supreme Court of Michigan, 1982.
417 Mich. 17, 331 N.W.2d 203.

RYAN, JUSTICE.

In March of 1977, Carl and Nancy Pickles, appellees, purchased from appellants, William and Martha Messerly, a 600–square–foot tract of land upon which is located a three-unit apartment building. Shortly after the transaction was closed, the Lenawee County Board of Health condemned the property and obtained a permanent injunction which prohibits human habitation on the premises until the defective sewage system is brought into conformance with the Lenawee County sanitation code.

We are required to determine whether appellees should prevail in their attempt to avoid this land contract on the basis of mutual mistake and failure of consideration. We conclude that the parties did entertain a mutual misapprehension of fact, but that the circumstances of this case do not warrant rescission.

I

The facts of the case are not seriously in dispute. In 1971, the Messerlys acquired approximately one acre plus 600 square feet of land. A three-unit apartment building was situated upon the 600–square–foot portion. The trial court found that, prior to this transfer, the Messerlys' predecessor in title, Mr. Bloom, had installed a septic tank on the property

* See pp.305–6, *supra*, as to "election."

without a permit and in violation of the applicable health code. The Messerlys used the building as an income investment property. * * *

After inspecting the property, Mr. and Mrs. Pickles executed a new land contract with the Messerlys on March 21, 1977. It provided for a purchase price of $25,500. A clause was added to the end of the land contract form which provides:

> "17. Purchaser has examined this property and agrees to accept same in its present condition. There are no other or additional written or oral understandings."

Five or six days later, when the Pickleses went to introduce themselves to the tenants, they discovered raw sewage seeping out of the ground. Tests conducted by a sanitation expert indicated the inadequacy of the sewage system. The Lenawee County Board of Health subsequently condemned the property and initiated this lawsuit in the Lenawee Circuit Court against the Messerlys as land contract vendors, and the Pickleses, as vendees, to obtain a permanent injunction proscribing human habitation of the premises until the property was brought into conformance with the Lenawee County sanitation code. The injunction was granted, and the Lenawee County Board of Health was permitted to withdraw from the lawsuit by stipulation of the parties.

When no payments were made on the land contract, the Messerlys filed a cross-complaint against the Pickleses seeking foreclosure, sale of the property, and a deficiency judgment. Mr. and Mrs. Pickles then counterclaimed for rescission against the Messerlys. * * * In count one, Mr. and Mrs. Pickles alleged failure of consideration. * * *

After a bench trial, the court concluded that the Pickleses had no cause of action against * * * the Messerlys * * * as there was no fraud or misrepresentation. This ruling was predicated on the trial judge's conclusion that none of the parties knew of Mr. Bloom's earlier transgression or of the resultant problem with the septic system until it was discovered by the Pickleses, and that the sanitation problem was not caused by any of the parties. The trial court held that the property was purchased "as is", after inspection and, accordingly, its "negative * * * value cannot be blamed upon an innocent seller". Foreclosure was ordered against the Pickleses, together with a judgment against them in the amount of $25,943.09.

Mr. and Mrs. Pickles appealed from the adverse judgment. The Court of Appeals * * * reversed the finding of no cause of action on the Pickleses' claims against the Messerlys. Lenawee County Board of Health v. Messerly, 98 Mich.App. 478, 295 N.W.2d 903 (1980). It concluded that the mutual mistake[5] between the Messerlys and the Pickleses went to a basic, as opposed to a collateral, element of the contract, and that the parties intended to transfer income-producing rental property but, in actuality, the vendees paid $25,500 for an asset without value.

5. Mr. and Mrs. Pickles did not allege mutual mistake as a ground for rescission in their pleadings. However, the trial court characterized their failure of consideration argument as mutual mistake resulting in failure of consideration. [Footnotes by Court.]

II

We must decide initially whether there was a mistaken belief entertained by one or both parties to the contract in dispute and, if so, the resultant legal significance.

A contractual mistake "is a belief that is not in accord with the facts". 1 Restatement Contracts, 2d, § 151, p. 383. The erroneous belief of one or both of the parties must relate to a fact in existence at the time the contract is executed. Richardson Lumber Co. v. Hoey, 219 Mich. 643, 189 N.W. 923 (1922); Sherwood v. Walker, 66 Mich. 568, 580, 33 N.W. 919 (1887) (Sherwood, J., dissenting). That is to say, the belief which is found to be in error may not be, in substance, a prediction as to a future occurrence or non-occurrence. * * *

The Court of Appeals concluded, after a *de novo* review of the record, that the parties were mistaken as to the income-producing capacity of the property in question. 98 Mich.App. 487–488, 295 N.W.2d 903. We agree. The vendors and the vendees each believed that the property transferred could be utilized as income-generating rental property. All of the parties subsequently learned that, in fact, the property was unsuitable for any residential use.

* * *

A contract may be rescinded because of a mutual misapprehension of the parties, but this remedy is granted only in the sound discretion of the court. Harris v. Axline, 323 Mich. 585, 36 N.W.2d 154 (1949). Appellants argue that the parties' mistake relates only to the quality or value of the real estate transferred, and that such mistakes are collateral to the agreement and do not justify rescission, citing A & M Land Development Co. v. Miller, 354 Mich. 681, 94 N.W.2d 197 (1959).

In that case, the plaintiff was the purchaser of 91 lots of real property. It sought partial rescission of the land contract when it was frustrated in its attempts to develop 42 of the lots because it could not obtain permits from the county health department to install septic tanks on these lots. This Court refused to allow rescission because the mistake, whether mutual or unilateral, related only to the value of the property.

> "There was here no mistake as to the form or substance of the contract between the parties, or the description of the property constituting the subject matter. The situation involved is not at all analogous to that presented in Scott v. Grow, 301 Mich. 226, 3 N.W.2d 254, 141 A.L.R. 819 (1942). There the plaintiff sought relief by way of reformation of a deed on the ground that the instrument of conveyance had not been drawn in accordance with the intention and agreement of the parties. It was held that the bill of complaint stated a case for the granting of equitable relief by way of reformation. In the case at bar plaintiff received the property for which it contracted. The fact that it may be of less value than the purchaser expected at the time of the transaction is not a sufficient basis for the granting of equitable relief, neither fraud nor reliance on misrepresentation of material facts having been established." 354 Mich. 693–694, 94 N.W.2d 197.

Appellees contend, on the other hand, that in this case the parties were mistaken as to the very nature of the character of the consideration and claim that the pervasive and essential quality of this mistake renders rescission appropriate. They cite in support of that view Sherwood v. Walker, 66 Mich. 568, 33 N.W. 919 (1887), the famous "barren cow" case. In that case, the parties agreed to the sale and purchase of a cow which was thought to be barren, but which was, in reality, with calf. When the seller discovered the fertile condition of his cow, he refused to deliver her. In permitting rescission, the Court stated:

> "It seems to me, however, in the case made by this record, that the mistake or misapprehension of the parties went to the whole substance of the agreement. If the cow was a breeder, she was worth at least $750; if barren, she was worth not over $80. * * * "

As the parties suggest, the foregoing precedent arguably distinguishes mistakes affecting the essence of the consideration from those which go to its quality or value, affording relief on a per se basis for the former but not the latter. * * *

However, the distinctions which may be drawn from *Sherwood* and *A & M Land Development Co.* do not provide a satisfactory analysis of the nature of a mistake sufficient to invalidate a contract. Often, a mistake relates to an underlying factual assumption which, when discovered, directly affects value, but simultaneously and materially affects the essence of the contractual consideration. It is disingenuous to label such a mistake collateral. * * *

Appellant and appellee both mistakenly believed that the property which was the subject of their land contract would generate income as rental property. The fact that it could not be used for human habitation deprived the property of its income-earning potential and rendered it less valuable. However, this mistake, while directly and dramatically affecting the property's value, cannot accurately be characterized as collateral because it also affects the very essence of the consideration. "The thing sold and bought [income generating rental property] had in fact no existence". Sherwood v. Walker, 66 Mich. 578, 33 N.W. 919.

We find that the inexact and confusing distinction between contractual mistakes running to value and those touching the substance of the consideration serves only as an impediment to a clear and helpful analysis for the equitable resolution of cases in which mistake is alleged and proven. Accordingly, the holdings of *A & M Land Development Co.* and *Sherwood* with respect to the material or collateral nature of a mistake are limited to the facts of those cases.

Instead, we think the better-reasoned approach is a case-by-case analysis whereby rescission is indicated when the mistaken belief relates to a basic assumption of the parties upon which the contract is made, and which materially affects the agreed performances of the parties. 1 Restatement Contracts, 2d, § 152, pp. 385–386.[11] Rescission is not available, however,

11. Section 152 delineates the legal significance of a mistake.

"§ 152. When Mistake of Both Parties Makes a Contract Voidable

to relieve a party who has assumed the risk of loss in connection with the mistake. 1 Restatement Contracts, 2d, §§ 152, 154, pp. 385–386, 402–406.[12]

All of the parties to this contract erroneously assumed that the property transferred by the vendors to the vendees was suitable for human habitation and could be utilized to generate rental income. The fundamental nature of these assumptions is indicated by the fact that their invalidity changed the character of the property transferred, thereby frustrating, indeed precluding, Mr. and Mrs. Pickles' intended use of the real estate. Although the Pickleses are disadvantaged by enforcement of the contract, performance is advantageous to the Messerlys, as the property at issue is less valuable absent its income-earning potential. Nothing short of rescission can remedy the mistake. Thus, the parties' mistake as to a basic assumption materially affects the agreed performances of the parties.

Despite the significance of the mistake made by the parties, we reverse the Court of Appeals because we conclude that equity does not justify the remedy sought by Mr. and Mrs. Pickles.

Rescission is an equitable remedy which is granted only in the sound discretion of the court. * * *

In cases of mistake by two equally innocent parties, we are required, in the exercise of our equitable powers, to determine which blameless party should assume the loss resulting from the misapprehension they shared. Normally that can only be done by drawing upon our "own notions of what is reasonable and just under all the surrounding circumstances".

Equity suggests that, in this case, the risk should be allocated to the purchasers. We are guided to that conclusion, in part, by the standards announced in § 154 of the Restatement of Contracts 2d, for determining when a party bears the risk of mistake. See fn. [12]. Section 154(a) suggests that the court should look first to whether the parties have agreed to the allocation of the risk between themselves. While there is no express assumption in the contract by either party of the risk of the property becoming uninhabitable, there was indeed some agreed allocation of the risk to the vendees by the incorporation of an "as is" clause into the contract which, we repeat, provided:

"(1) Where a mistake of both parties at the time a contract was made as to a basic assumption on which the contract was made has a material effect on the agreed exchange of performances, the contract is voidable by the adversely affected party unless he bears the risk of the mistake under the rule stated in § 154.

"(2) In determining whether the mistake has a material effect on the agreed exchange of performances, account is taken of any relief by way of reformation, restitution, or otherwise."

12. "§ 154. When a Party Bears the Risk of a Mistake

"A party bears the risk of a mistake when

"(a) the risk is allocated to him by agreement of the parties, or

"(b) he is aware, at the time the contract is made, that he has only limited knowledge with respect to the facts to which the mistake relates but treats his limited knowledge as sufficient, or

"(c) the risk is allocated to him by the court on the ground that it is reasonable in the circumstances to do so."

> "Purchaser has examined this property and agrees to accept same in its present condition. There are no other or additional written or oral understandings."

That is a persuasive indication that the parties considered that, as between them, such risk as related to the "present condition" of the property should lie with the purchaser. If the "as is" clause is to have any meaning at all, it must be interpreted to refer to those defects which were unknown at the time that the contract was executed.[15] Thus, the parties themselves assigned the risk of loss to Mr. and Mrs. Pickles.[16]

We conclude that Mr. and Mrs. Pickles are not entitled to the equitable remedy of rescission and, accordingly, reverse the decision of the Court of Appeals.

Notes

1. Mistake has been variously defined as an "erroneous idea" (S. Williston, Contracts § 1535 (3rd ed. 1970)), "mistaken thoughts" (3 A. Corbin, Contracts § 597 (1960)), and "a state of mind not in accord with the facts." Restatement of Restitution § 6 (1937). A mistake of fact has conventionally been deemed to be actionable if both parties "assumed" the same state of facts to exist, bargained on that basis and ultimately agreed upon consideration which reflects those assumptions. When the mistake is later discovered, it seems appropriate to undo the transaction because the expectations of both parties were not realized. The Restatement of Restitution § 6, comment c (1937) distinguishes between "mistake" and "ignorance": "There may be ignorance of a fact without mistake as to it, since mistake imports advertence to facts and one is ignorant of many facts as to which he does not advert. However, mistake is always based upon ignorance which leads to a belief in the existence of non-existing things or the non-existence of existing things." The Restatement also distinguishes between a state of mind and actionable conduct: "Neither ignorance, which leads to mistake, nor mistake itself can be the sole basis of an action * * * It is only where the mistake leads to conduct that legal consequences are affected and that mistake becomes operative as a ground for legal relief." *Id.*

With respect to risk assumption as to possible mistakes by express contract terms such as a statement that the sale is "as is," see II G. Palmer, Law of Restitution, 1978 § 12.5 (1978).

2. 3 A. CORBIN, CONTRACTS §§ 604, 634–38 (1960).* "A mistake as to the area of land that is the subject of a contract of sale may be such as to require remedy. If the contract was for the sale at a specified price per acre, justice may require an abatement in the price in proportion to the deficiency or

15. An "as is" clause waives those implied warranties which accompany the sale of a new home, Tibbitts v. Openshaw, 18 Utah 2d 442, 425 P.2d 160 (1967), or the sale of goods. M.C.L. § 440.2316(3)(a); M.S.A. § 19.2316(3)(a). Since implied warranties protect against latent defects, an "as is" clause will impose upon the purchaser the assumption of the risk of latent defects, such as an inadequate sanitation system, even when there are no implied warranties.

16. An "as is" clause does not preclude a purchaser from alleging fraud or misrepresentation as a basis for rescission. See 97 A.L.R.2d 849. However, Mr. and Mrs. Pickles did not appeal the trial court's finding that there was no fraud or misrepresentation, so we are bound thereby.

an additional payment for the excess. Even though the agreed price was by the tract, and not by the acre, its amount may have been determined with reference to a basic assumption of a specific area. Whether or not such was the case is a question of fact, and may be a difficult one. When such was the assumption, and the error is material, the court should award an appropriate remedy. If the difference in area is so great as to cause a substantial degree of frustration of the purpose for which the land was bought, the buyer should be awarded a rescission if he seeks it. For less important differences the remedy is proportionate abatement in price, this taking the form of restitution if the price has been paid. Sometimes, the remedy may well be a decree giving the defendant a choice between rescission and his repairing the deficiency by an abatement or a payment or even an additional conveyance.

"If the sale was strictly by the tract, in gross, and the price was not determined at so much per unit of area, the fact that a mistake was made as to area will probably be held to be immaterial. If the mistake did not affect the price, and did not otherwise cause the making of the sale, the contract stands as made."

3. The cases in this section have focused on misrepresentation, mutual mistake, contract breach and inadequacy of consideration as possible grounds for rescission. Other potential justifications for rescission include duress. See, Odorizzi v. Bloomfield School Dist., 246 Cal.App.2d 123, 54 Cal.Rptr. 533 (1966) and undue influence (see text at pp. 1152–58, *infra.*)

4. There can be no rescission relief in the case of a "unilateral", rather than a "mutual", mistake by one of the parties in the course of contract formation if the other party is unaware of the mistaken assumption. (*See,* II G. Palmer, Law of Restitution 1978, §§ 12.3, 12.4.). Where such knowledge of the other's mistake is present, the contract will be rescinded and restitution granted. This is often characterized as "fraudulent conduct", although it will justify rescission relief but not recovery on a theory of the tort of fraud and deceit. II G. Palmer, Law of Restitution 1978, § 12.3. Where, there is a mistake in reducing an agreement to writing (a mistake in "integration") and one party is aware that the writing does not in fact state that which both parties agreed would be its terms, it is sometimes said that there has been "fraudulent" conduct on the part of the party who is aware of the other party's mistaken impressions as to the writing's content. While for a "unilateral mistake" of this nature there can be no rescission, there may be a basis for asking a court of equity to "reform" the writing by ordering the execution of another writing which does reflect the terms agreed upon. D. Dobbs, Law of Remedies § 9.5 (2d ed. 1993) at 716.

A quite different situation is presented where, for example, one party simply makes a payment to, or confers a benefit in another form upon, another party due to a mistaken assumption that there was a duty to do so, or by virtue of mistaken identity. Such situations, of course, do not involve mistakes, whether mutual or unilateral, in contract formation. The mistake lay in conferring the unsolicited benefit upon the party where, had the party known the true facts, he would not have done so. For this type of "unilateral mistake" restitution relief is usually available. Such restitution claims are considered in II G. Palmer, Law of Restitution 1978 § 11.2; see text at pp. 1163–66, *infra.*

5. Whether self-induced, as in the case of "mutual mistake," or brought about by reprehensible conduct by the other party in cases involving intentional, reckless or innocent misrepresentation, or by virtue of a mistake left uncorrected where there is knowledge of the other party's mistaken state of mind, "the underlying mistake * * * [must] be, in some sense material" if rescission relief is to be awarded. Shore Builders, Inc. v. Dogwood, Inc., 616 F.Supp. 1004 (D.Del.1985), at 1016; Alabi v. DHL Airways, Inc., 583 A.2d 1358, 1362 (Del.Super.1990) (discussing the position of the Restatement (Second) of Contracts, § 164 that "materiality" in the usual sense is not required for rescission relief where the mistake is the result of a "fraudulent" misrepresentation). *See, also,* I G. Palmer, Law of Restitution (1978) § 3.19 at 351–52 where Professor Palmer develops the notion that the rigor of the "materiality" requirement depends upon the nature of the conduct which brings about the mistake in question.

HUTCHISON v. PYBURN

Court of Appeals of Tennessee, 1977.
567 S.W.2d 762.

DROWOTA, JUDGE.

This is a case involving fraud in the sale of realty in which plaintiffs-vendees were awarded both rescission of the deed and punitive damages by the Chancery Court of Davidson County. Since the case is before us without a bill of exceptions, our recitation of the facts follows the allegations of plaintiffs-appellees and the findings of the Chancellor.

In January of 1973, plaintiffs William and Jo Lynn Hutchison purchased a house and lot from defendants Robert and Carol Pyburn for $24,000.00. Of this amount, $23,500.00 represented a loan from Home Federal Savings & Loan Association which was secured by a deed of trust. Defendant Jack Williams built the house and sold the property to the Pyburns, and his brother defendant John Williams, was real estate agent for the Pyburns in the sale of the property to plaintiffs. In July of 1973, plaintiffs noticed seepage from their sewage disposal system, investigated, and discovered that their property had not been approved as a home site by the Metropolitan Board of Health because it lacked the requisite topsoil to sustain the septic tank and overflow field needed for sewage disposal. Further, the Metropolitan Department of Codes Administration had been informed of the problem, and had issued a building permit to defendant Jack Williams only by mistake. Evidently defendant Pyburn had become aware of the sewage problem after purchasing the property from Williams and had prevailed on Williams to release him from his obligation to purchase it, whereupon Pyburn and Williams negotiated the sale to plaintiffs.

Plaintiffs brought suit, alleging that the defendants Pyburn and Williams knew of the property's condition and that there was no practical means of correcting it at the time of the sale. They charged that defendants' failure to inform them of the sewage problem amounted to fraud and deceit, and that the condition of the property represented a breach of the warranties contained in the deed. The Chancellor dismissed the case against defendant John Williams, but entered a decree in favor of plaintiffs against the Pyburns and Jack Williams. The decree allowed plaintiffs rescission of the contract, incidental damages in the form of expenses incurred in connection with the property, moving costs, and attorney's fees, from all of which was deducted the reasonable rental value of the property for the period of plaintiffs occupancy. In addition to the sum due plaintiffs in incidental damages, which was set at $3,168.94, the Chancellor assessed $5,000.00 in punitive damages against the defendants and made a specific finding that defendants' misrepresentation was fraudulent. * * *

* * *

Defendants also assert that the trial court erred in awarding punitive damages for misrepresentations incident to a contract when rescission of the contract and deed was also decreed. * * *

Punitive or exemplary damages are awarded to punish a defendant for his wrongful conduct and to deter others from similar conduct in the future. * * * They are awarded in cases of fraud, malice, gross negligence, or oppression, or in similar cases involving wilful misconduct. * * * Such damages relate to the nature of the defendant's actions in inflicting or causing the injury rather than to the extent of the injury that results. * * *

In Tennessee it is established that courts of equity are empowered to award punitive damages. Jones v. Morrison, 62 Tenn.App. 50, 458 S.W.2d 434 (1970); Gill v. Godwin, 59 Tenn.App. 582, 442 S.W.2d 661 (1967); Kneeland v. Bruce, 47 Tenn.App. 136, 336 S.W.2d 319 (1960). *Kneeland* was an injunction action by a plaintiff who had been fraudulently induced to sign two mortgage notes and trust deeds and had consequently lost her property to a *bona fide* purchaser. Both compensatory and punitive damages were awarded. The court upheld the latter award with the statement that Chancery Courts have jurisdiction to give punitive damages "in proper cases." 336 S.W.2d at 325. In *Gill,* the defendant fraudulently induced the plaintiff to undertake an obligation, secured by a mortgage, to have defendant erect a building on plaintiff's vacant lot. Defendant's only purpose in doing so was to take the lot by foreclosure. In upholding an award of punitive damages, the court found that the authority of Chancery Courts to make such an award was established "in actions involving fraud." 442 S.W.2d at 663. Thus, in Tennessee an award of punitive damages is permissible in equity, and fraud is proper conduct by defendant on which to base such an award.

One objection raised to the award of punitive damages in this case is that it is inconsistent with rescission of the deed under the doctrine of election of remedies. That doctrine estops a plaintiff who has clearly chosen to pursue one of two inconsistent and irreconcilable remedies from later resorting to the other. Barger v. Webb, 216 Tenn. 275, 391 S.W.2d 664 (1965); Barnes v. Walker, 191 Tenn. 364, 234 S.W.2d 648 (1950). The "essential element" here is "that the remedies be inconsistent." Holder v. Martin, 219 Tenn. 165, 407 S.W.2d 461, 465 (1966). A good example of such inconsistency is furnished by *Barger, supra,* in which plaintiff's acceptance of a settlement in her suit for conversion against a bank that had repossessed her property was held an election that estopped her from later suing for a statutory remedy under the statute that then regulated repossession under conditional sales contracts. Since allowance of the statutory remedy would have provided double redress for a single wrong, it was found inconsistent with the cause of action for conversion in which plaintiff had gained a settlement. There is no such inconsistency, however, between the remedy of rescission and an award of punitive damages. The latter, as we have already noted, is designed to penalize and deter, and results from the nature of defendant's conduct rather than from the harm it causes. The character of punitive damages, then, is in no wise inconsistent with rescission and its concomitant remedies of restitution and incidental damages. The latter are all aimed at *redressing* the harm done the plaintiff and, while this means they may be considered inconsistent with a remedy such as compensatory damages, which also aims at redress but by a different method, they may not be so considered with respect to the *deterrent* sanction of punitive damages. Thus, plaintiffs' choice of rescission as a means of redress is not inconsistent with their request for punitive damages and does not estop them from making that request.

Similarly, punitive damages do not conflict with the theoretical aim of equitable rescission, which is to return the parties to the status in which they were prior to the transaction. That aim is simply one approach to redressing the wrong done to plaintiff, an approach that differs from that of compensatory damages, which are intended to redress the wrong by directly compensating the plaintiff for what he has lost. But again, punitive damages are not intended to redress the plaintiff's wrong, but to make an example of the defendant's conduct. Since they thus relate to considerations totally different from those of rescission, punitive damages neither frustrate rescission's redressing of plaintiff's wrong by return of the parties to the *status quo,* nor are they inconsistent with it.

Cases often announce the rule that there must be proof of "actual damages" before punitive damages may be awarded. * * * The cases are unclear, however, as to the meaning of "actual damages" in this context. It has been logically suggested that the phrase should mean no more than that the plaintiff cannot get punitive damages without proving a valid cause of action, that is, without showing that he has been legally injured in some way, which is really a roundabout way of saying that there can be no cause of action for punitive damages alone. *See* Dobbs, Remedies § 3.9 at 208–10 (1973); 22 Am.Jur.2d Damages § 241 (1965). However, probably because injury to the plaintiff is asserted as a cause of action for compensatory damages in most cases in which punitive damages are asked, courts sometimes seem to view the "actual damages" rule as requiring proof or award of compensatory damages as a basis for punitive damages. * * *

[Some Tennessee cases], applied broadly, would allow recovery of punitive damages if plaintiff, in addition to showing the requisite degree of bad conduct and intent by defendant, could merely prove his entitlement to injunctive relief or nominal damages. But we need not go so far here in construing "actual damages" not to mean strictly an award of compensatory damages. Returning to the case before us, we hold simply that plaintiffs' proof of their entitlement to rescission of the deed, refund of the purchase price, and incidental damages such as moving expenses, shows sufficient harm and loss to them to satisfy the "actual damages" prerequisite to recovery of punitive damages in Tennessee.

Finally, defendants point to a proposition which we agree is the general rule in Tennessee and elsewhere: punitive damages may not be recovered in an action for breach of contract. *See* Bland v. Smith, 197 Tenn. 683, 277 S.W.2d 377 (1955); Johnson v. Woman's Hospital, 527 S.W.2d 133 (Tenn. App.1975). This case, however, is not one for breach of contract, for plaintiffs asked that the contract be made a nullity by rescission. Further, the pleadings and memorandum of the trial court indicate that the main thrust of the action is a claim of fraud and misrepresentation against all the defendants, although an additional claim of breach of warranty was asserted against the Pyburns, with whom plaintiffs were in privity. Thus, regardless of any overtones of contract that may appear in this suit, there also clearly exists here a cause of action against all defendants for the sort of tortious misconduct required as a basis for recovery of punitive damages. For this reason, such a recovery cannot be defeated by the rule that punitive damages are unavailable in contract actions.

We are aware of no case ruling on the availability of punitive damages in the precise context of the remedy of rescission and incidental damages presented here, and we realize that the Tennessee cases holding punitive damages available in equity also have generally been ones in which ordinary compensatory damages were awarded. *See Jones, supra; Gill, supra.* After examining the question closely, however, we are unable to perceive any good reason to preclude the award of punitive damages in a suit for equitable rescission and incidental damages such as this one. Indeed, logic compels us to hold that, as a matter of law, punitive damages are available in such a case if the plaintiff can demonstrate the requisite degree of bad conduct and intent on the part of the defendant.

Affirmed.

On Petition to Rehear

In denying the petition, we emphasize * * * that our approach advances two related and sound policies. One is not unduly to burden the plaintiff, who is the wronged party, in making his choice of redress between rescission and compensatory damages by forbidding him to couple a request for punitive damages with rescission, which may often provide a smaller recovery than compensatory damages to begin with. The other is to prevent the plaintiff's choice of redress from allowing the defendant, who is the wrongdoer, to escape the punishment that the law of punitive damages imposes for certain types of conduct.

Note

It appears that an increasing number of jurisdictions are permitting the recovery of punitive damages in actions for rescission based on fraud. Berry v. McLeod, 124 Ariz. 346, 604 P.2d 610 (1979) (proof of "special damages" required as prerequisite to punitive damages); Jahn v. Brickey, 168 Cal.App.3d 399, 214 Cal.Rptr. 119 (1985); Robison v. Katz, 94 N.M. 314, 610 P.2d 201

(1980). In *Jahn,* the court also permitted the plaintiff to recover for emotional distress. *See also* D. Dobbs, Law of Remedies 447–48 (2d ed. 1993).

D. REFORMATION

1. *Grounds for Reformation* *

METZLER v. BOLEN

United States District Court, District of North Dakota, 1956.
137 F.Supp. 457.

REGISTER, DISTRICT JUDGE. This is an action for reformation of a Contract for Deed, for specific performance and damages. The case was tried to the Court without a jury.

Much of the evidence admitted consists of exhibits.

In September, 1950, plaintiff [Metzler] and defendant [Bolen] entered into a contract for deed whereby defendant agreed to sell, and plaintiff agreed to purchase, the northeast quarter of section 25 in township 155 north of range 95 west of the 5th principal meridian in Williams county, North Dakota. The agreement was dated ______ day of September, 1950, was signed and acknowledged by the plaintiff on September 16, 1950, and thereafter was signed and duly delivered by the defendant. It is in the usual form, except as to the following provision which was typed therein by E.C. Rudolph (attorney for plaintiff) prior to the execution thereof:

> "The second party herein shall have unto himself 6½% [6¼%] of 50% of oils, metals, minerals found in, under, or upon said land herein described, but he agrees to join with first party, on the same terms as he (1st party) accepts drilling rights given to any drilling Co., which first party selects."

The "second party" referred to therein is the plaintiff, Mr. Harold Metzler.

Prior to the preparation of this agreement by Mr. Rudolph, the parties hereto had communicated with each other, over a period of years, concerning the purchase or rental by the plaintiff of the land involved in this lawsuit. * * *

* * *

In defendant's letter of September 9, 1950, to Mr. E.C. Rudolph appears the following:

> "Enclosed is an abstract showing title in the M & M Bank. My deed has been recorded from them. The taxes became delinquent and I purchased the same thru tax title, but the abstractor wrote me that the County retained ½ of the mineral and oil rights. If this land is ever

* For general references, see 13 S. Williston, Contracts §§ 1547–1556, 1568A, 1581–1594 (3d ed. 1970); 3 A. Corbin, Contracts §§ 597–621 (1960); III G. Palmer, The Law of Restitution §§ 13.1–13.19 (1978); Restatement (Second) Contracts § 155 (1981); Palmer, The Effect of Misunderstanding on Contract Formation and Reformation Under the Restatement of Contracts Second, 65 Mich.L.Rev. 33 (1966); Newman, Relief for Mistake in Contracting, 54 Cornell L.Rev. 232 (1969); Rabin, A Proposed Black-Letter Rule Concerning Mistaken Assumptions in Bargain Transactions, 45 Tex.L.Rev. 1273 (1967); Note, Reformation of Instruments in Louisiana, 30 Tul.L.Rev. 486 (1956).

> drilled for oil, my understanding is that fee owner must give up to the Co. drilling all but 12½%. I'll give him 6¼%. That is ½ of what I will own if the land is drilled, i.e. ½ of the 12½% int. You can easily check on the abstract, as the title rests largely on mortgages, and the Tax Title cut them all out of having an interest in the title."

This letter was in possession of Mr. Rudolph at the time he prepared the executed Contract for Deed (Exhibit 4) and was the basis for the provisions therein which have hereinbefore been quoted.

Plaintiff in his Complaint and with reference to said quoted provision alleges in part as follows:

> "That said provision in said Contract for Deed did not express the true Agreement between the Plaintiff, Harold Metzler, and the Defendant, R.J. Bolen; that the agreement between the Plaintiff and the Defendant was that the Defendant would convey to the Plaintiff all surface rights and an undivided fifty per cent (50%) interest in and to all the oil, gas, metals, and other minerals that the Defendant owned in the land described in this Complaint and said Contract for Deed; that at the time said Agreement was entered into it was believed mistakenly by the party preparing the Contract for Deed to be the fact that Williams County owned 50% of the oil, gas, metals and other minerals in said land", and
>
> "That said Contract for Deed through and by a mistake of fact does not express the true agreement between the parties to said Contract for Deed."

* * *

There is no claim by the plaintiff that defendant, R.J. Bolen, was guilty of fraud or misrepresentation. It is noted that, upon request, abstract of title was forwarded by the defendant to plaintiff, that defendant advised the plaintiff as to information he had received from the abstractor, and that full disclosure was made to the best of his knowledge, concerning his title.

Doubtless, at the time of the execution of the Contract for Deed, both parties believed that Williams County did own 50% of all of the oil, gas and minerals in and under said land. * * * [However, the Supreme Court of North Dakota] decided that such reservation [by the county] was void, and that the tax deed from the County to the purchaser conveyed all right, title and interest of the County to the premises involved. Therefore, defendant was actually the owner of all of the oil, gas and minerals in and under said premises.

The sole question involved herein is whether, because of such mistaken belief on the part of both parties to the Contract concerning the extent of defendant's interest in said oil, gas and minerals, plaintiff is entitled to the relief asked for.

* * *

To justify reformation on the ground of mistake, the mistake must have been made in the drawing of the instrument and not in the making of the contract which it evidences. A mistake as to the existing situation, which leads either one or both of the parties to enter into a contract which they would not have entered into had they been apprised of the actual facts, will not justify reformation. It is not what the parties would have intended if they had known better, but what did they intend at the time, informed as they were. Russell v. Shell Petroleum Corporation, 10 Cir., 66 F.2d 864.

Williston on Contracts, Vol. 3, Sec. 1549, states the rule as follows:

> "If, because of mistake as to an antecedent or existing situation, the parties make a written instrument which they might not have made, except for the mistake, the court cannot reform the writing into one which it thinks they would have made, but in fact never agreed to make." * * *

Before reformation of contract can be had there must have been in effect an agreement which written instrument evidences, and mistake relied upon must have been in drafting of instrument, not in making of contract. * * *

> "If the instrument as executed expresses the agreement of the parties, it is no ground for reformation that in arriving at such agreement, both parties labored under the same misconception. * * *" 4 Tiffany, Real Property, Third Edition, Sec. 985, p. 79.

A presumption arises from the instrument itself that it fully and clearly sets forth the true agreement of the parties, and where the mistake in such instrument is denied, the burden is on the party alleging the mistake to prove that the written instrument does not fully or truly state the agreement that the parties intended to make—and parol evidence of such alleged mutual mistake, as a basis for the modification of a written instrument must be clear, satisfactory, specific and convincing.

Not only has the plaintiff failed to sustain his burden of proving mutual mistake by clear, satisfactory, specific and convincing evidence, but, in the opinion of this Court, the evidence is to the contrary. The specific provisions of the contract involved were typed into the contract by plaintiff's attorney, at the time of a conference with the plaintiff, and with plaintiff's full knowledge, understanding and approval. The provisions were definite, specific, unambiguous and in accordance with the specific offer of the defendant contained in the latter's letter. There was no mistake as to the language of the contract; nothing intended to be inserted was omitted by mistake. No mistake occurred in reducing to writing the contract upon which the parties had agreed. The mistake complained of related to the extent of defendant's interest in the oil, gas and minerals—a matter which entered into the minds of the parties in formulating their agreement. However, it is the opinion of this Court that the minds of the contracting parties did meet upon the proposition expressed in the writing, and that the actual contract was as expressed therein; that is, that the written contract itself expressed the true intention of the parties which existed at that time.

* * *

For the reasons hereinbefore stated, judgment will be for the defendant. Findings, Conclusions and Order in accordance herewith will be prepared and submitted by counsel for the defendant. It will be so ordered.*

JENSEN v. MILLER

Supreme Court of Oregon, 1977.
280 Or. 225, 570 P.2d 375.

LENT, JUSTICE.

Plaintiffs sued to quiet title to a strip of land. Defendants counterclaimed for reformation of the contract and deed by which plaintiffs had conveyed to the defendants unimproved land, contending the disputed strip is part of the realty they purchased from the plaintiffs although not described in the contract and deed. The trial court decreed reformation of the legal description of the subject realty in the contract and deed to include the disputed strip and awarded defendants attorney fees. Plaintiffs appeal. We affirm.

* * *

The facts found by the trial court may be summarized as follows: In 1969 the parties contracted for sale of land by plaintiffs to defendants. During negotiations prior to making the contract, plaintiffs showed defendants the land and, in particular, pointed out as the eastern boundary of the land to be sold a line which had been brush-cut and marked by a surveyor hired by plaintiffs for this purpose. Hereinafter this line will be referred to as the "brush line." An earnest money agreement preceded the making of the land-sale contract.

* * *

* * * Plaintiffs and defendants thereafter made a land-sale contract, and when defendants had performed thereunder, plaintiffs executed and delivered to them a warranty deed. Both instruments contained a legal description that placed plaintiffs' eastern boundary line about 67 feet west of the brush line. This was due to an error made by the plaintiffs' surveyor some five years prior to the sale. That error was unknown to any of the parties at that time.

During the period 1969 to 1973, defendants, with plaintiffs' "encouragement and assistance," made improvements in the disputed strip. The error in the original survey was not discovered until a new survey was made in 1973. The trial court found that, considering the oral testimony and the earnest money agreement description, one in light of the other, the parties intended the brush line to be the eastern boundary line of the land sold. It further found that there was a mutual, material mistake, that defendants were not grossly negligent in making such a mistake, and in fact did so in reliance upon plaintiffs' representations, and that such

* This case is discussed in Note, 35 Tex. L.Rev. 263 (1956). Accord: King v. Talcott, 80 Or.App. 701, 723 P.2d 1058 (1986).

reliance was justified. Finally, the trial court found that defendants had expended $1,500 in reasonable attorney fees in the suit below.

Plaintiffs assert two assignments of error: first, that the trial court erred in reforming the legal description of the land in the contract and deed * * *. The first assignment amounts to a contention that the quantum of evidence produced by the defendants to show mutual mistake was insufficient to support the decree of reformation. Our first inquiry must be to determine the nature and quantum of proof necessary to support a decree of reformation of a contract.

The parties seeking reformation of a written contract must establish, by the appropriate quantum of proof, (1) that there was an antecedent agreement to which the contract can be reformed; (2) that there was a mutual mistake or a unilateral mistake on the part of the party seeking reformation and inequitable conduct on the part of the other party; and (3) that the party seeking reformation was not guilty of gross negligence. * * *

Defendants offered evidence in support of each of these three elements, and the trial court found it sufficient to support a decree of reformation. The quantum of proof necessary to support a decree of reformation has been described in widely differing terms by this court, but it is agreed by all that "[a] mere preponderance of the evidence does not suffice." *Kontz v. B.P. John Furniture Corp.*, 167 Or. 187, 205, 115 P.2d 319, 326 (1941). The parties below and on appeal appear to have accepted this general statement, and therefore we do not review its validity.*

In the instant case, the first element, that of an antecedent agreement, is established without question. We find, as the trial court did, that the evidence clearly establishes that the initial agreement of the parties was that the brush line would represent the eastern boundary of the land sold by the plaintiffs to the defendants.

The element of mutual mistake, while perhaps less clearly established and subject to directly contradictory evidence by the interested parties, was in our judgment supported by convincing testimony. The trial judge, who observed the testimony firsthand, resolved this conflict in favor of the defendants, and, as stated above, this finding is entitled to great weight. We decline to reverse the trial court on this point.

Finally, defendants must prove the negative element, that the mistake on their part was not due to their *gross* negligence. The evidence, as adduced at trial and found by the trial court, fully supports this allegation to any necessary degree. Plaintiffs were not only responsible, at least vis-

* This court has variously labeled the quantum of evidence necessary to support the reformation of a written contract as "clear and convincing * * * with a high degree of probability." *Ray v. Ricketts,* 235 Or. 243, 250, 383 P.2d 52, 55 (1963); "clear and unequivocal," *Moyer et ux v. Ramseyer et al.*, 226 Or. 122, 135, 359 P.2d 407 (1961); "clear, satisfactory and convincing," *Weatherford v. Weatherford,* 199 Or. 290, 297, 257 P.2d 263, 260 P.2d 1097 (1953); "high degree of cogency," *Kontz v. B.P. John Furniture Corp.*, 167 Or. 187, 205, 115 P.2d 319 (1941); "clearest and most satisfactory," *DeTweede v. Barnett Estate,* 160 Or. 406, 414, 85 P.2d 361 (1939); "clear and satisfactory," id. at 415, 85 P.2d 361; and "very high degree of cogency," *Southeast Port. L. Co. v. Heacock et al.*, 128 Or. 248, 259, 275 P. 28 (1929).

a-vis the defendants, for the error of the surveyor whom they had employed; they refused to have the property resurveyed in 1969, instead hiring the same surveyor to draw the boundary line based on the original survey. Indeed, when faced with an indication that there was something wrong, plaintiffs continually reassured defendants that they would get substantially what they had bargained for. Defendants, as found by the trial court, were entitled to rely on plaintiffs' representations. Even if they were not, such reliance would not constitute negligence so gross as to deny them the equitable relief they sought. * * *

Plaintiffs also assign as error the trial court's award of attorney fees to defendants. * * *

Plaintiffs, however, contend that by the complete performance of this contract, full payment by the defendants and delivery of the warranty deed by the plaintiffs, the contract was merged into the deed and the provision allowing attorney fees was extinguished.

The doctrine of merger, in this context, provides that "the deed supersedes the contract as to all its provisions made pursuant to the terms of the latter." *City of Bend v. Title & Trust Co.*, 134 Or. 119, 127, 289 P. 1044, 1047 (1930). The doctrine is subject, however, to the important qualification that contractual provisions which are not embodied in the deed are superseded only if the parties *intended* to surrender them. Id.

* * *

The determination of this intention is a matter of fact to be adduced from the evidence at trial. * * *

In the present case, we find that the defendants did not intend to extinguish their right to contractual attorney fees by accepting the warranty deed in view of the fact that the defect in the deed itself was unknown to either party at the time of its delivery. * * *

A second qualification to the doctrine of merger is when "through fraud or relievable mistake the grantee has been induced to accept something different from what the contract required." * * * The trial court reformed the contract based on mutual mistake, and we affirm that ruling. The deed, prior to reformation, gave the defendants "something different [and less] than what the contract required"; therefore, the doctrine of merger has no application.

* * *

* * * The trial court did not err in making such an award.

Affirmed.

13 S. WILLISTON, CONTRACTS § 1552 (3d ed. 1970).* Effect of Parol Evidence Rule on Reformation.

> "The right of reformation, wherever allowed, is necessarily an invasion or limitation of the parol evidence rule, since when equity reforms a writing, it enforces an oral agreement at variance with the

* Reprinted with permission of The Lawyers Co-operative Publishing Co.

writing which the parties had agreed upon as a memorial of their bargain.

"This limitation is necessary to work justice, and there seems no more reason to object to it in case of reformation than in case of rescission for fraud or for mistake. It is understood that to warrant reformation or rescission, the court must be persuaded by the clearest kind of evidence that a mistake has been made by both parties, or in some cases by one, or that some other basis exists upon which relief should be granted.

"In either case, unless the mistake precludes the existence of a contract at law, it should not be denied that the writing correctly states the actual contract or conveyance which has been made, but since it is inequitable to allow the enforcement of it, and, since justice requires the substitution of another in its place, equity gives relief, where reformation is appropriate, and to that end, generally and necessarily admits any relevant parol or other extrinsic evidence.

"This is fully recognized so far as executed transactions are concerned irrespective of whether the relief sought is rescission or reformation, and also where the question concerns the rescission of executory contracts." *

REYNOLDS v. WOOD, 219 N.C. 626, 14 S.E.2d 642 (1941). Action by purchaser for recovery of price paid for lot no. 198, to which vendor had no title. Counterclaim for reformation of the deed so as to convey lot no. 196, which vendor did own, alleging a mutual mistake in the description in that plaintiff intended to purchase and defendant intended to convey lot no. 196. The Municipal Court overruled plaintiff's motion to dismiss the counterclaim, and ordered the deed reformed as prayed. The Superior Court, on a review of the evidence, reversed and the Supreme Court affirmed, saying: "We do not think there was evidence to support the finding [in the Municipal Court] that there was a mutual mistake in the description of the lot conveyed so as to entitle the defendant to the equity of reformation. All the evidence is to the effect that the plaintiff wished to purchase lot no. 198 and not lot no. 196, and that she had no intention of purchasing lot no. 196. There is no evidence that the parties had gone upon the premises, or that they had mistakenly inserted a different description of the lot intended to be conveyed. At the time plaintiff offered to purchase lot no. 198 it was erroneously supposed that defendant owned that lot. There was no meeting of the minds of the parties as to the purchase of lot no. 196, and plaintiff did not agree to purchase that lot, and does not wish to do so. The court cannot, under the guise of reformation, enforce a contract which the parties themselves have not made." *See* 3 A. Corbin, Contracts § 614 (1960).

Notes

1. The Restatement of Contracts 2d § 155 (1981) states that reformation will be given for "any" failure to express the agreement and without regard to

* *See* Palmer, Reformation and the Parol Evidence Rule, 65 Mich.L.Rev. 833 (1967); Restatement (Second) Contracts § 155 (1981); 3 A. Corbin, Contracts § 580 (1960).

whether there was a "material variance" which some courts have considered necessary for reformation. *See,* III G. Palmer, The Law of Restitution (1978) § 13.1.

2. It is often said that a reformation decree "relates back" to the date of the execution of the writing in question. While this is the usual effect, reformation will not be allowed to impair the rights of innocent purchasers who have bought between the date of the mistake in integration and that of the reformation order. III G. Palmer, The Law of Restitution (1978) § 13.1.

3. The standard of proof required in reformation actions is set forth in Aetna Ins. Co. v. Paddock, 301 F.2d 807 (5th Cir.1962), where the insured sought reformation of an insurance policy on the ground of mutual mistake (approving jury charge in following terms):

> " 'To set aside and reform or correct that instrument in which a mutual mistake is alleged, it must be shown by clear and convincing evidence, and by that term is meant the witnesses to a fact must be found to be credible and that the facts to which they have testified are distinctly remembered and the details thereof narrated exactly and in due order and that the testimony be clear, direct and weighty and convincing, so as to enable you to come to a clear conviction without hesitancy of the truth of the precise facts in issue * * *' " Compare Frierson v. Sheppard, 201 Miss. 603, 29 So.2d 726 (1947) (reformation of mineral right and royalty transfers. "All of our pronouncements, as to the degree of evidence required to secure the reformation of an instrument, are exclusively to the effect that such modification must be sustained by proof beyond a reasonable doubt." *Accord* Economou v. Economou, 136 Vt. 611, 399 A.2d 496 (1979). *Frierson* is criticized in Note, 19 Miss.L.J. 363 (1948). See the discussion of this problem of proof in Note, 33 Tex.L.Rev. 968 (1955).

4. The uniform requirement of a burden of proof higher than that which is customary in civil actions reflects a judicial awareness that the reformation remedy, while designed to prevent a party from enjoying the benefits of fraud or mistake in integration, may be resorted to in an effort to avoid performance where the writing correctly states the actual contract. Reformation actions may, and often do, become mere "swearing matches." Sims v. Wilson, 255 Ark. 465, 501 S.W.2d 214 (1973) (dissenting opinion). One party's word against that of the other ordinarily fails to satisfy the burden of proof for reformation and "corroborative evidence" supporting the assertions of the party seeking reformation is necessary. Ingram v. Forrer, 563 P.2d 181 (Utah 1977); Rolph v. McGowan, 20 Wash.App. 251, 579 P.2d 1011 (1978).

5. The question may arise of whether the party against whom reformation relief is awarded can be held in breach of the contract actually agreed upon (and now imposed by court decree) based on that party's conduct prior to the issuance of the reformation decree. For example, in Miscione v. Bishop, 130 Ariz. 371, 636 P.2d 149 (1981) the plaintiffs had sold certain real estate to the defendants. The oral agreement called for a down payment of $3,000. Due to mutual mistake, the written agreement called for no down payment; the price was to be paid in ten equal annual payments of $1,075. The latter sum was tendered by the buyers to the sellers in conformance with the unreformed agreement. The sellers then brought an action for reformation. The court ruled that the sellers were entitled to reformation of the agreement so as to require a down payment of $3,000. The plaintiffs then contended that the

reformation "related back to the execution of the promissory note." Consequently, the plaintiffs asserted, the defendants were in violation of the agreement when they tendered $1,075, rather than $3,000. The court recognized that reformation relates back for such purposes as defeating the rights of intervening creditors who do not have the standing of purchasers for value without notice. However, the court ruled that a party to the contract could not be held in breach because that party had tendered performance as required by the unreformed contract.

BUCK v. MOUNTAIN STATES INVESTMENT CORP.

Supreme Court of New Mexico, 1966.
76 N.M. 261, 414 P.2d 491.

COMPTON, JUSTICE. This is an action for reformation of an insurance policy and to recover for the loss by fire of household goods and other items while in transit from Texas to New Mexico. * * *

On January 16, 1963, pursuant to several telephone conversations, Mr. Buck and the solicitor agent for Mountain States Investment Corporation, acting as agent of the appellant, Western Fire and Casualty Company, met at the agent's office in Albuquerque and entered into an oral contract whereby the agent agreed to have issued to the appellee an insurance policy in the amount of $8,000.00, to be effective from August 16, 1963 to August 31, 1963, insuring against loss by fire the appellee's household goods and effects and fifty trash receptacle units while in transit from Bryan, Texas to Albuquerque, New Mexico. The premium of $48.00 for the policy was paid by the appellee and a binder was issued to him by the solicitor agent who represented the binder to be in conformity with their oral agreement. The appellee thereupon put the binder into his pocket without reading it and proceeded immediately to Bryan, Texas with his employer, a Mr. Huff, in the latter's automobile. The household goods were loaded onto a rented trailer hitched to Mr. Huff's car. On August 19, 1963, while en route to Albuquerque, all of the items, which the court found to be valued at $4,000.00, were totally destroyed by fire. Appellant's agent was immediately notified of the loss, but liability was denied on the ground that the policy issued by the appellant provided insurance coverage for shipment by truck only.

On conflicting testimony the court found that the oral agreement was for coverage of the household goods and trash receptacle units by any method of transportation selected by appellee; that the binder issued was represented to appellee by the agent to conform to the oral agreement; that the agent misrepresented the coverage of the insurance binder; and that the appellee relied upon these representations to his loss.

The court further found that the insurance policy issued by the appellant pursuant to the order of its agent neither conformed to the oral agreement nor to the binder issued by its agent; that the appellee was never advised by either the appellant or its agent that the policy as issued differed in its terms from the oral agreement although the appellant knew that the terms of the policy were materially different from the agreement between the agent and the appellee. The court then concluded that the policy should be reformed to provide coverage of the household goods and effects against loss by fire while in transit from Bryan, Texas to Albuquerque, by whatsoever means of transportation chosen by the appellee. Judgment was entered accordingly and the insurance company appeals. No appeal is taken from a judgment dismissing the action with prejudice against the agent.

The appellee testified that at the time of the negotiations prior to the preparation of the written contract, it was understood and agreed by him and the agent that the insurance to be issued would cover transportation of the goods by automobile, trailer, truck or other means of conveyance; that he relied upon the agent's representations that the binder expressed their oral agreement and that the insurance policy would conform thereto. Appellee's testimony was corroborated by Mr. Huff who was with appellee when he applied for the coverage.

But the binder issued to the appellee by the agent provided for coverage of household goods and fifty receptacle trash units being shipped "by truck." The policy of insurance thereafter issued by the appellant provided coverage on the household goods and effects while in transit in a rental truck under the control of certain types of shippers, such as a railway company, railway express company, or common carrier. No coverage whatever was included for the trash receptacle units. The policy was not received by the agent until after the loss had been reported to it, and was never delivered to the appellee nor seen by him until the time of trial.

The substance of a single point relied upon by the appellant for reversal of the judgment is that there are only two grounds upon which reformation of a contract may be granted, i.e., (a) a mutual mistake of the parties, or (b) a mistake by one of the parties accompanied by fraud on the part of the other party, and since the trial court did not make findings on either of these issues, its judgment is unsupported by the findings.

It is well established in this jurisdiction, and generally, that a court of equity may grant reformation of a contract where either by mutual mistake of the parties, or through mistake on the part of one party and fraud or inequitable conduct on the part of the other party, the written instrument drafted to evidence a contract fails to express the real agreement and intentions of the parties. * * *

As we view the findings in this case, while they do not expressly find either mutual mistake or fraud, implicit is a finding of inequitable conduct both on the part of the appellant and its agent.* An agent's conduct need not be characterized as fraud in order to warrant reformation of an insurance policy. In Portella v. Sonnenberg, 74 N.J.Super. 354, 181 A.2d 385, reformation was granted where an agent, with knowledge of the insured's request for complete liability coverage on a department store, remained silent about the exclusion of elevators and failed to write the policy so plainly that its examination by the insured would bring home the

* Compare Layh v. Jonas, 96 Idaho 688, 535 P.2d 661 (1975), discussing reformation based upon "fraudulent misrepresentation" by an insurance agent as to coverage of an existing group medical insurance policy.

exclusion. The court declined to call the agent's conduct fraudulent but rather a lack of good faith and fair dealing. * * *

* * * We evaluate the evidence with regard to inequitable conduct on the part of the appellant and its agent as clear, convincing and satisfactory. * * *

Lastly, the appellant contends that the reformation of the contract of insurance here results in an illegal contract and, therefore, the relief sought should have been denied. * * *

* * *

A court of equity will not withhold relief where it is necessary in the interest of justice and of sound public policy to enforce a contract which is inhibited by statute, but is not declared void, provided the parties are not in pari delicto. Baldwin v. Equitable Life Assurance Society of United States, 252 Iowa 639, 108 N.W.2d 66, and cases cited therein. We do not find, nor has there been pointed out to us, any provision in our applicable insurance statutes which declares as void policies issued in violation thereof.

The judgment should be affirmed. It is so ordered.*

CARMODY, C.J., and NOBLE, J., concur.

Notes

1. There is deceptive conduct justifying reformation where a term agreed upon was omitted from the writing but one party read the agreement to the other as if it were present (Crewe v. Blackmon, 289 S.C. 229, 345 S.E.2d 754 (1986)), or where the parties agree as to the terms to be included but one party changes a term without the knowledge of the other. Waite v. Salestrom, 201 Neb. 224, 266 N.W.2d 908 (1978).

2. Reformation for fraud or inequitable conduct (because one party is aware of the mistake in *integration*) should not be confused with the rescission remedy where there is mistake of fact on one side and knowledge of that mistake on the other. The latter affords no basis for reformation because of the absence of the essential element of a prior oral agreement to which the writing may be made to conform. For example, in McConnell v. Pickering Lumber Corp., 217 F.2d 44 (9th Cir.1954), the court said:

> "Appellants concede that it is essential in cases of asserted mutual mistake to show an antecedent agreement to which the writing can be reformed. But they say that such is not the rule in the case of unilateral mistake, although they confess having found no California authority so holding. * * *
>
> "A study of the local decisions cited in the briefs, together with others which we have consulted, leaves us wholly unconvinced of the soundness of appellants' thesis. These cases have uniformly involved factual situations

* *See also* Brandwein v. Provident Mut. Life Ins. Co., 3 N.Y.2d 491, 168 N.Y.S.2d 964, 146 N.E.2d 693 (1957) (alleged misrepresentation that plaintiff's right to "vested" insurance collection fees would be recorded in the official records of the defendant corporation: reformation of the "records" granted). The case is discussed in Notes, 44 Cornell L.Q. 124, 27 Ford.L.Rev. 125 (1958).

whereby the contract as reformed corresponded with a prior agreement between the parties."

3. A fundamental element of reformation relief is an oral "agreement" to which to conform the writing in order to have it reflect the manifested intent of the parties. This does not mean, however, that reformation is inappropriate where the parties "do not intend an agreement to become binding until put in writing, or have crystallized negotiations into agreement only 'at the moment of executing the written contract'." III G. Palmer, The Law of Restitution (1978) § 13.2, at 8. There appears to be some question as to whether the drafters of the Restatement (Second) of Contracts agree with Professor Palmer. *See* Restatement (Second) of Contracts § 155, comment a (1981).

4. The question of whether there was a pre-existing "oral agreement" to which to conform the writing arose in Mutual of Omaha Ins. Co. v. Russell, 402 F.2d 339 (10th Cir.1968), cert. denied, 394 U.S. 973 (1969). It was contended that one party to the negotiations, in this instance the insurer, had a duty to speak and give certain information to the plaintiff insured. Had the duty been discharged, it was argued, the parties ultimately would have reached a different oral understanding than that which was reached. The plaintiff wanted to reform the writing to conform to this oral agreement that "might have been" reached. The appellate court reversed the trial court, which had allowed reformation:

> "Thus the whole case boils down in reality to one question: Did Insurer have a duty to tell the Assured that several insurance policies were available and to explain fully the provisions and limitations of those policies? Without this supposed duty (and its breach) the District Judge would have had no basis for judge-reformation of the contract to conform to a regular straight flight insurance policy which Insurer was offering for sale.* * * *

5. Insurance contracts provide a fertile field for reformation litigation. The contracts themselves usually are long, varied, and often technical in language. The insured suffers a loss or is confronted with a claim which the insured "thought" was covered. The company takes the position that the policy does not provide coverage. The insured then sues to reform the policy so that it states the coverage "assured" by the agent who issued it. Suits of this nature are increasing in number and the courts seem to be sympathetic to the insureds in those cases where the issuing agent testifies that the claimed assurances were indeed made to the insured. Warner v. Continental Cas. Co., 534 P.2d 695 (Okl.App.1975). *Compare* Rempel v. Nationwide Life Ins. Co., 471 Pa. 404, 370 A.2d 366 (1977) (reformation decreed when the agent denied having given such assurance).

Reformation has been awarded even in situations where it is shown that, had the contested coverage been requested from the insurance company's home office, it would have been refused since neither the defendant company nor any other insurer wrote policies with the coverage in question. Johnson v. United

* *See also,* Stowe Township v. Standard Life Ins. Co., 507 F.2d 1332 (3d Cir.1975).

Investors Life Ins. Co., 263 N.W.2d 770 (Iowa 1978). *See,* Keeton, Insurance Law Rights at Variance With Policy Provisions, 83 Harv.L.Rev. 961 (1970).

6. Many insurance policies contain "incontestability clauses." These provide that the "policy shall be incontestable after it has been in force [for a specified period] * * * except for any nonpayment of premiums and * * * [certain other provisions, and] if the insured's age has been misstated, any amount payable by the Company shall be such as the premium would have purchased at the correct age." It is generally held that, while the provision will prevent rescission relief to the issuer on the basis of alleged misrepresentations by the insured in applying for the coverage, it does not bar reformation for a scrivener's error which, for example, causes the policy coverage to be stated to be "$50,000" instead of $5,000. Mutual Life Ins. Co. v. Simon, 151 F.Supp. 408 (S.D.N.Y.1957); Schaefer v. California–Western States Life Ins. Co., 262 Cal.App.2d 840, 69 Cal.Rptr. 183 (1968).

SCOTT v. GROW

Supreme Court of Michigan, 1942.
301 Mich. 226, 3 N.W.2d 254.

STARR, JUSTICE. Plaintiff appeals from an order granting defendant's motion to dismiss her bill of complaint.

On November 8, 1939, plaintiff filed bill of complaint alleging, in substance, that she is the residuary legatee under the "purported last will and testament of Judson P. Grow," who died April 2, 1939; that such will has been offered for probate and certain objections to its admission having been filed, the matter was certified to the circuit court for Oakland county, in chancery, and is there awaiting trial. Plaintiff further alleged that * * * [Judson Grow and his wife, Grace Grow, had deeded four parcels of land to plaintiff (for the sole purpose of releasing Grace Grow's dower rights) and then had obtained a divorce on October 11, 1937. The plaintiff had executed a quit claim deed of the four parcels back to the Grows on October 12, describing them as "tenants by the entireties and not as joint tenants." The plaintiff alleged that the parties to the deed and the scrivener had intended a conveyance making the parties "joint tenants" and not "tenants in common." Grace died on April 13, 1938, and Judson remained in possession of the property until his death on April 2, 1939. The complaint claimed that, on Judson's death, the title to the property held by Judson Grow (as survivor) passed to her as the residuary legatee under his will. The plaintiff then alleged that the defendant, Russell Grow, claimed "an undivided one-half title and interest" in the land as legatee under the will of Grace Grow. The plaintiff asked the court to reform the deed of October 12, 1937, "so as to truly represent the intentions of the parties thereto," and further requested that the court quiet title in her against the defendant, Russell Grow.*

* However, reformation has been denied in some instances where the parties agree that the instrument they have chosen (*e.g.,* a particular form to create a security interest) is the one they wish to use but it is subsequently discovered that the instrument in question will not permit the desired result. The distinction appears to be between the situation where the parties agree upon the "objective" of using an effective legal instrument without negotiating over the choice of instruments (reformation proper), and that where a con-

* * * The trial court filed opinion for dismissal of plaintiff's bill of complaint and on April 15, 1940, entered order of dismissal. Plaintiff appeals from such order.

The trial court based its opinion upon the conclusions (1) that plaintiff cannot invoke the aid of a court of equity to reform and correct a mistake in the deed of October 12, 1937, from plaintiff to Judson P. Grow and Grace Burton Grow, because such deed was voluntary and without consideration; (2) that, as plaintiff claims as residuary legatee under the will of Judson P. Grow, she cannot contradict the terms of such deed; and (3) that an alleged mistake as to the legal consequence of a known fact is not a basis for relief in equity.

* * *

The question is: Does plaintiff's bill of complaint properly allege facts which, if assumed to be true, entitle plaintiff to the relief sought?

In her bill plaintiff alleged, in effect, that all parties made a mutual mistake in the preparation of the deed of October 12, 1937, in that the phrase describing the grantees "as tenants by entireties and not as joint tenants" did not carry out and effectuate the intention and purpose of the parties. On the ground of mutual mistake, plaintiff seeks to reform and correct such deed, so as to designate the grantees "as joint tenants and not tenants in common."

Judson P. Grow and Grace Burton Grow were divorced October 11, 1937, and were not husband and wife when the deed to them was executed October 12, 1937. Such grantees, not being husband and wife, could not take an estate by the entireties; they could take either as tenants in common or as joint tenants. 3 Comp.Laws 1929, § 12964 (Stat.Ann. § 26.44). Therefore, the phrase in the deed describing the grantees, Judson P. Grow and Grace Burton Grow, "as tenants by entireties and not as joint tenants," is clearly ambiguous, assuming that the allegations in the bill of complaint are true, and does not carry out the intention and purpose of the parties.

* * *

We cannot agree with defendant's contention that the alleged mutual mistake in describing the grantees "as tenants by entireties and not as joint tenants" does not create a basis for equitable relief.

* * *

> "Where a written instrument fails to express the intention of the parties because of a mutual mistake as to the interpretation or legal effect of the words of the writing, though there is no misapprehension as to what words have been used, reformation is allowed. It is not necessary, moreover, in order to establish a mistake which may be reformed that it should be shown that particular words were misunder-

sideration of the various types of instruments which might be used is part of the negotiation process and both parties elect to use a particular type of instrument (reformation improper). *See* III G. Palmer, The Law of Restitution § 13.4 (1978). [Footnote by the Court]

stood. 'It is sufficient that the parties had agreed to accomplish a particular object by the instrument to be executed, and that the instrument as executed is insufficient to effectuate their intention.' " 5 Williston on Contracts, Rev.Ed., p. 4423, § 1585, quoting from Leitensdorfer v. Delphy, 15 Mo. 160, 167, 55 Am.Dec. 137.

The following illustration is given in the Restatement of the Law of Restitution, p. 204, § 51:

> "A agrees to sell and B agrees to buy a half-interest in Blackacre owned in fee by A. The parties agree that the incidents of a tenancy in common shall follow, although they do not know the legal terminology. A executes a conveyance by which B becomes a joint tenant. A is entitled to a reformation of the deed to correspond to the agreement."

* * *

The rule enunciated in cases cited by defendant that equity will not grant relief for mistake as to the legal effect of the entire instrument has no application to the instant case in which equity could, on the allegations in plaintiff's bill, which are assumed to be true, decree reformation on the ground that the parties made a mutual mistake as to the legal import and meaning of the technical words "as tenants by entireties and not as joint tenants."

* * *

We are satisfied that plaintiff's bill of complaint, assuming the facts therein alleged to be true, states a cause of action and ground for equitable relief.

* * *

The order entered April 15, 1940, dismissing plaintiff's bill of complaint is hereby set aside, and the case is remanded for further proceedings in accordance with this opinion. Plaintiff shall have costs.*

Notes

1. The long-standing rule of equity allowing reformation where the "intent" of the parties is clear, but an inapt legal term was used to achieve the end "intended," was stated by the United States Supreme Court in Philippine Sugar Estates Dev. Co. v. Government of the Phillipine Islands, 247 U.S. 385, 38 S.Ct. 513, 62 L.Ed. 1177 (1918), in the following language:

> "It is well settled that courts of equity will reform a written contract where, owing to mutual mistake, the language used therein did not fully or accurately express the agreement and intention of the parties. The fact that interpretation or construction of a contract presents a question of law and that, therefore, the mistake was one of law is not a bar to granting relief."

2. The question of whether reformation relief may be available to reform a "general release" of personal injury claims in order to limit its application to the claims against the other party to the instrument, and prevent its applica-

* *Contra* Burke v. Lee, 225 Ark. 564, 283 S.W.2d 689 (1955) (reformation denied on somewhat similar facts). *See generally,* 3 A. Corbin, Contracts § 616, at 749 (1960).

tion to third parties who also may be "jointly and severally liable" for the injury, is discussed in III G. Palmer (1978), §§ 13.19(a) and 12.22(b). *See, also,* Alexander v. Kirkham, 365 So.2d 1038 (Fla.App.1978); Alabama Farm Bureau Ins. Co. v. Hunt, 519 So.2d 480 (Ala.1987).

3. In a number of instances, reformation has been considered appropriate where the writing in the form executed by the parties was illegal or unenforceable, or had an undesired effect upon the rights of third parties. For example, some courts have shown a willingness to "reform" ("blue-pencil") and order specific performance of a restrictive covenant which was found to be unreasonable, contrary to public policy, and therefore unenforceable as written. Justin Belt Co. v. Yost, 502 S.W.2d 681 (Tex.1973). The Supreme Court of New Hampshire refused to reform a restrictive covenant in an employment contract in Smith, Batchelder & Rugg v. Foster, 119 N.H. 679, 406 A.2d 1310 stating:

"Although the master erred in stating that he had no authority to reform the overly broad restrictive covenants, *Solari Industries, Inc. v. Malady, supra,* his error is harmless because the plaintiff was not prejudiced by the ruling. Daniels v. Barker, 89 N.H. 416, 420, 200 A. 410, 415 (1938). The plaintiff is not entitled to reformation because the master found that it failed to sustain its burden of proving good faith in the execution of the employment contracts." *Id.* at 685, 406 A.2d at 1313–14.

Other illustrative cases are Turney v. Roberts, 255 Ark. 503, 501 S.W.2d 601 (1973) (interest provision provided a rate which was usurious until reformed); Krenz v. Medical Protective Co., 57 Wis.2d 387, 204 N.W.2d 663 (1973) (general release provision released all parties jointly and severally liable until reformed); Dickey v. Barnes, 268 Or. 226, 519 P.2d 1252 (1974) (instrument violated the statute regulating condominiums until reformed); Stoltz, Wagner & Brown v. Duncan, 417 F.Supp. 552 (W.D.Okl.1976) (provision violated the rule against perpetuities until reformed pursuant to Oklahoma statute that allowed reformation where appropriate "to give effect to general intent" of the creator of the interest); McPherson v. First & Citizens Nat. Bank, 240 N.C. 1, 81 S.E.2d 386 (1954) (the court indicated a willingness, if unborn children could be effectively represented, to reform an irrevocable inter vivos trust so as to eliminate a violation of the rule against remoteness of vesting).

JONES v. STAR CREDIT CORP.

Supreme Court of New York, Nassau County, Pt. 3, 1969.
59 Misc.2d 189, 298 N.Y.S.2d 264.

SOL M. WACHTLER, JUSTICE. On August 31, 1965 the plaintiffs, who are welfare recipients, agreed to purchase a home freezer unit for $900 as the result of a visit from a salesman representing Your Shop At Home Service, Inc. With the addition of the time credit charges, credit life insurance, credit property insurance, and sales tax, the purchase price totalled $1,234.80. Thus far the plaintiffs have paid $619.88 toward their purchase. The defendant claims that with various added credit charges paid for an extension of time there is a balance of $819.81 still due from the plaintiffs. The uncontroverted proof at the trial established that the freezer unit, when purchased, had a maximum retail value of approximately $300. The question is whether this transaction and the resulting contract could be considered unconscionable within the meaning of Section 2–302 of the Uniform Commercial Code which provides in part:

> "(1) If the court as a matter of law finds the contract or any clause of the contract to have been unconscionable at the time it was made the court may refuse to enforce the contract, or it may enforce the remainder of the contract without the unconscionable clause, or it may so limit the application of any unconscionable clause as to avoid any unconscionable result.
>
> "(2) When it is claimed or appears to the court that the contract or any clause thereof may be unconscionable the parties shall be afforded a reasonable opportunity to present evidence as to its commercial setting, purpose and effect to aid the court in making the determination. L.1962, c. 553, eff. Sept. 27, 1964."

There was a time when the shield of "caveat emptor" would protect the most unscrupulous in the marketplace—a time when the law, in granting parties unbridled latitude to make their own contracts, allowed exploitive and callous practices which shocked the conscience of both legislative bodies and the courts.

The effort to eliminate these practices has continued to pose a difficult problem. On the one hand it is necessary to recognize the importance of preserving the integrity of agreements and the fundamental right of parties to deal, trade, bargain, and contract. On the other hand there is the concern for the uneducated and often illiterate individual who is the victim of gross inequality of bargaining power, usually the poorest members of the community.

Concern for the protection of these consumers against overreaching by the small but hardy breed of merchants who would prey on them is not novel. The dangers of inequality of bargaining power were vaguely recognized in the early English common law when Lord Hardwicke wrote of a fraud, which "may be apparent from the intrinsic nature and subject of the bargain itself; such as no man in his senses and not under delusion would make." * * *

The law is beginning to fight back against those who once took advantage of the poor and illiterate without risk of either exposure or interference. From the common law doctrine of intrinsic fraud we have, over the years, developed common and statutory law which tells not only the buyer but also the seller to beware. This body of laws recognizes the importance of a free enterprise system but at the same time will provide the legal armor to protect and safeguard the prospective victim from the harshness of an unconscionable contract.

Section 2–302 of the Uniform Commercial Code enacts the moral sense of the community into the law of commercial transactions. It authorizes the court to find, as a matter of law, that a contract or a clause of a contract was "unconscionable at the time it was made", and upon so finding the court may refuse to enforce the contract, excise the objectionable clause or limit the application of the clause to avoid an unconscionable result. * * *

There is no reason to doubt, moreover, that this section is intended to encompass the price term of an agreement. * * *

Fraud, in the instant case, is not present; nor is it necessary under the statute. The question which presents itself is whether or not, under the circumstances of this case, the sale of a freezer unit having a retail value of $300 for $900 ($1,439.69 including credit charges and $18 sales tax) is unconscionable as a matter of law. The court believes it is.

* * *

Having already paid more than $600 toward the purchase of this $300 freezer unit, it is apparent that the defendant has already been amply compensated. In accordance with the statute, the application of the payment provision should be limited to amounts already paid by the plaintiffs and the contract be reformed and amended by changing the payments called for therein to equal the amount of payment actually so paid by the plaintiffs.*

Notes

1. Apart from this largely unexplored innovation in Section 2–302 of the U.C.C., there is scant authority for "reforming" a contract which is found to be unreasonably costly to one of the parties by a judgment altering the consideration in order to make the consideration "fairer." ** Perhaps the most interesting is National Presto Industries, Inc. v. United States, 167 Ct.Cl. 749, 338 F.2d 99 (1964), cert. denied, 380 U.S. 962 (1965). This case is discussed in Notes, 65 Colum.L.Rev. 542 (1965); 53 Geo.L.J. 826 (1965); 114 U.Pa.L.Rev. 306 (1965).

2. There are other situations where, due to the special circumstances in question, the court gives what it calls "reformation" relief to avoid an inequitable result that would result from an award of a conventional form of relief (usually rescission) and, in some instances, to avoid unjust enrichment. These cases do not fit into the traditional pattern of reformation cases because the court is not simply conforming the writing to an earlier oral agreement. *See, e.g.,* Wright v. Heizer Corp., 503 F.Supp. 802 (N.D.Ill.1980) (notes evidencing a loan by a corporate controller to the corporation he controlled had been obtained as part of certain conduct in violation of the controller's duty to the corporation; the notes in question were "reformed," by alteration of their terms, in the course of unraveling the several transactions involved in a manner that would protect the corporation's current interests); Thomas v. Satfield Co., 363 Mich. 111, 108 N.W.2d 907 (1961) (lease between two

* *See also* Block v. Ford Motor Credit Co., 286 A.2d 228, 10 UCC Reporting Service 139 (D.C.App.1972) (acceleration clause recovery limited to face amount of contract and accrued finance charges, less payment made); Frostifresh Corp. v. Reynoso, 52 Misc.2d 26, 274 N.Y.S.2d 757 (1966), *rev'd in part,* 54 Misc.2d 119, 281 N.Y.S.2d 964 (1967); I.R. Anderson, Uniform Commercial Code §§ 2–302:14, 2–302:15 and 2–302:23 (2d ed. 1970); Hester, Deceptive Sales Practices and Form Contracts—Does the Consumer Have a Private Remedy?, Duke L.J. 831 (1968); D. Dobbs, Handbook On The Law of Remedies § 10.7 (1973).

** *See* III G. Palmer, The Law of Restitution § 13.9, at 55–60 (1978).

corporations with interlocking directors in contravention of directors' fiduciary duties not cancelled, but "reformed" by reducing the amount of the rent).

2. *Defenses to Reformation*

WEHNER v. SCHROEDER

Supreme Court of North Dakota, 1984.
354 N.W.2d 674.

GIERKE, JUSTICE.

* * *

LACHES

The Tormaschys argue that the doctrine of laches should bar the Wehners' action [to reform a deed to add a reservation of mineral rights] which was brought 31 years after the deed was executed.

Laches does not arise from a delay or lapse of time alone, but is such a delay in enforcing one's right as to work a disadvantage to another. * * * This Court has often stated that in addition to the time element, the party against whom laches is sought to be invoked must be actually or presumptively aware of his rights and must fail to assert them against a party who in good faith permitted his position to become so changed that he could not be restored to his former state. * * * Furthermore, the general rule is that "laches do not commence to run against an action for the reformation of an instrument, until the fraud or mistake had been or ought to have been discovered." Annot., 106 A.L.R. 1338, 1345 (1937).

The trial court determined, on the basis of this Court's previous decision in *Wehner,* that the Wehners' action accrued in 1978 when they discovered that the warranty deed did not contain the mineral reservation. The trial court found that nothing occurred between 1978 and July 1981, when the suit was brought, to prejudice the Tormaschys in defending against the action. We have reviewed the record in this case and conclude that the trial court did not err in determining that the doctrine of laches did not bar the Wehners' action.

ESTOPPEL

The Tormaschys contend that the Wehners should be estopped from asserting their title to the 50 percent mineral interests.

The rule for determining whether or not a party should be estopped from asserting their title to property was first set out by this Court in Gjerstadengen v. Hartzell, 9 N.D. 268, 275–276, 83 N.W. 230, 232 (1900):

> "The rule as to the requisites of an estoppel in pais as applied to the title to realty which appeals to us as the most equitable to all parties is that announced by Field, J., in Boggs v. Mining Co., 14 Cal. [279] on page 367. He said: 'It is undoubtedly true that a party may in many instances be concluded by his declarations or conduct, which have influenced the conduct of another to his injury. The party is said in such cases to be estopped from denying the truth of his admissions. But to the application of this principle with respect to the title of

property it must appear: First, that the party making the admission by his declaration or conduct was apprised of the true state of his own title; second, that he made the admission with the express intention to deceive, or with such careless and culpable negligence as to amount to constructive fraud; third, that the other party was not only destitute of all knowledge of the true state of the title, but of the means of acquiring such knowledge; and, fourth, that he relied directly upon such admission, and will be injured by allowing its truth to be disproved. * * * There must be some degree of turpitude in the conduct of a party before a court of equity will estop him from the assertion of his title; the effect of the estoppel being to forfeit his property, and transfer its enjoyment to another.' "

Thus, a party seeking to rely on estoppel must not only lack actual knowledge regarding the true state of title, but must also be destitute of the means of acquiring such knowledge. A public record is such a means. Gilbertson v. Charlson, 301 N.W.2d 144, 148 (N.D.1981).

In the prior appeal in this case, this Court determined that an examination of the title abstract would have disclosed the discrepancy between the two instruments executed by the Wehners and the Schroeders, and should have made the Tormaschys aware of the potential problem and caused them to investigate further. Thus, the Tormaschys were not destitute of the means of acquiring knowledge of the state of the title from the public record. The trial court did not err in determining that the Wehners were not estopped from asserting their title in this case.

* * *

The Tormaschys also assert that before the Wehners are entitled to reformation, they must show that they were free from negligence in creating the problem for which the reformation is sought. The Wehners' failure to read the documents before signing them, the Tormaschys claim, should bar the Wehners from being granted reformation in this case.

Generally, the negligent failure of the complaining party to read an instrument before signing it does not, in itself, bar reformation. 66 Am.Jur.2d Reformation of Instruments § 83 (1973); Restatement (Second) of Contracts § 157 comment b (1981). This rule has also been applied to reformation of real estate instruments. 66 Am.Jur.2d Reformation of Instruments §§ 84 and 85 (1973); Annot., 81 A.L.R.2d 7, §§ 12 and 13 (1962 & Later Case Service). It has also been stated that "[w]here the parties entrust to an attorney or scrivener the duty of preparing a deed or other document in accord with their agreement, and he, by his own mistake or fraud, embodies in it stipulations and conditions other than those agreed upon, the party against whom it is sought to be enforced may have it reformed, although he signed it without reading it." 66 Am.Jur.2d Reformation of Instruments § 85 (1973).

We believe that in order to bar reformation under these particular circumstances, the fault of the party requesting relief must amount "to a failure to act in good faith and in accordance with reasonable standards of fair dealing." Restatement (Second) of Contracts, § 157 (1981). The trial court applied this test and noted in its memorandum opinion that the Wehners' negligence in not reading the deed before they signed it did "not rise to a high degree because one is entitled to rely on the product of an attorney." The trial court found no evidence that the Wehners failed to act in good faith or in accordance with reasonable standards of fair dealing. We have reviewed the record in this case and cannot say that the trial court erred in this regard.

* * *

Finally, the Tormaschys appear to argue that reformation based on mutual mistake should be allowed only in actions between the original contracting parties. However, the general rule is that reformation of a written instrument will be allowed as against the original parties to the instrument and all those who claim under said parties in privity, with the exception of bona fide purchasers or encumbrancers for value and without notice. * * * In the previous appeal in this action, this Court determined that the Tormaschys were not third-party bona fide purchasers. *Wehner, supra,* 335 N.W.2d at 566.

For the reasons stated in this opinion, the judgment is affirmed.

[Dissent of PEDERSON, J., omitted.]

3. *Statute of Frauds.*

2 A. CORBIN, CONTRACTS

§ 340, at 193–98 (1960).*

REFORMATION GRANTED FOR MISTAKE, BUT NOT TO REMEDY INCOMPLETENESS OR FILL INTENTIONAL GAPS.

"Cases where a writing is erroneous because of fraud, accident, or mistake must be clearly distinguished from those where there has never been any writing at all or where an existing writing does not accord with the oral agreement because the parties did not intend that it should. In thousands of cases they do not intend to reduce the agreement to writing; and in others, they know well enough that an informal note or memorandum does not state all that was agreed. In these cases, whether they have made an enforceable agreement or not, the absence of a complete and accurate writing is not due to fraud, accident, or mistake; and neither party is entitled to relief [from the statute of frauds] on such a ground.

"Furthermore, although a memorandum in writing is made that is insufficient to satisfy the requirements of the statute, it may be exactly the memorandum that the parties intended to make. They may have left out a necessary description because the subject matter was not entirely agreed upon or because they did not know that a better description would be necessary. They may have made an insufficient memorandum merely because they never heard of the statute of frauds and were ignorant of its

* Reprinted with permission of Yale University.

requirements. Here there may be ignorance of fact or law; but there is no fraud and the face of the document contains no mistaken expression.

"The problem of what constitutes such fraud or mistake as will justify an equitable remedy presents a few special aspects in statute of frauds cases. It may be noted, first, that the refusal to perform a promise is not fraud. Equity would not grant a remedy merely because a party promised to sign a memorandum sufficient to satisfy the statute of frauds and has failed to do so. Further, the mere fact that a memorandum is insufficient to satisfy the statute is not in itself a sufficient ground for relief. In the absence of fraud or mistake, convincingly proved, equity would not decree reformation merely to supply essential provisions of the contract that are not contained in the memorandum signed by the party to be charged. If equity would thus supply a memorandum whenever the parties have failed to do so, the statute of frauds would be largely nullified. It is only in cases where the signing of a sufficient memorandum has been prevented by fraud, or where a document has been drawn up by the parties as a memorial of their oral agreement, but fails to be a correct one by reason of accident or mistake, that reformation can be properly asked.* In such cases, the great weight of authority is to the effect that reformation will be decreed and that the contract as corrected in accordance with the oral agreement will be specifically enforced. The fact that the contract is executory and that there has not been a part performance is not regarded as a good reason for denying equitable relief.

"In several cases where the subject was given much consideration, the court has refused to decree reformation of a written contract or memorandum and then to decree the specific performance of the contract as it has been reformed. They have been willing to decree rescission or cancellation as in the case of deeds of conveyance, freely admitting proof of the oral agreement for this purpose; but they have not been willing to enforce affirmatively an agreement that was not sufficiently evidenced by the written memorandum that the parties executed. These courts are undoubtedly correct in observing that specific enforcement of the reformed agreement is in substance the affirmative enforcement of an oral contract of which the parties have made no sufficient memorandum. Without doubt, the majority of courts granting such remedies generally are aware of this; but they have felt that they were carrying out the chief purposes for which the statute was passed, even though in the individual case they might seem to be going counter to its express letter.

"Some high courts, however, while recognizing that the statute of frauds does not limit equity powers, also incline to assert that the requirements of the statute are satisfied by the corrected writing supposedly constructed under coercion by the court. The corrected memorandum, if actually corrected and signed, no doubt satisfies the statute with respect to

* *See* David v. Tucker, 196 Neb. 575, 244 N.W.2d 197 (1976) (memorandum reformed to add a provision for "a 29 percent down payment with the balance payable in equal annual installments.")

subsequent enforcement; but the operative facts inducing equity to compel the correction were the antecedent oral agreement and not the subsequent memorandum by relation back."

The Restatement (Second) of Contracts § 156 (1981) has taken the position that an essential term may be added by reformation, thus abandoning its earlier position and adopting Professor Corbin's approach.

4. Party seeking reformation was not a party to the execution of the instrument sought to be reformed.

The courts generally have agreed that the donee under an inter vivos gift instrument, *after* the death of the donor, may obtain reformation of the instrument. Hazlett v. Bryant, 192 Tenn. 251, 241 S.W.2d 121 (1951); Note, 22 Tenn.L.Rev. 566 (1952); Note, 4 Vand.L.Rev. 326 (1951). *See* Reina v. Erassarret, 103 Cal.App.2d 258, 229 P.2d 92 (1951) (action against the surviving husband of the donor); Note, 25 S.Cal.L.Rev. 212 (1952); Reinberg v. Heiby, 404 Ill. 247, 88 N.E.2d 848 (1950) (action against a codonee); Note, 34 Minn.L.Rev. 698 (1949). These cases and notes reflect the equitable factors and the diverse views involved. There is general agreement, however, that the donee may not have relief against the donor while the donor is living. *See* Comment, 58 Mich.L.Rev. 90 (1959).

Reformation relief also is available to either the promissor or the beneficiary in the case of third party beneficiary contracts. III G. Palmer, The Law of Restitution § 13.19 (1978).

The traditional rule is that there can be no reformation of a will. This was considered in Carpenter v. Tinney, 420 S.W.2d 241 (Tex.Civ.App.1967):

"In American Jurisprudence it is said that validity of a will or any part of it is not affected by mistake of fact or law inducing execution of the will, unless fraud or undue influence was perpetrated upon the testator. 57 Am.Jur., Wills, sec. 375, p. 272.

"Generally a mistake of fact or law, in the absence of fraud or undue influence, will not defeat the probate of a will, even though the testator would or might have made a different will if there had been no such mistake inducing the testator to make the will. It is also the general rule that courts have no right to vary or modify the terms of a will or to reform it even on grounds of mistake. 95 C.J.S. Wills § 586, p. 713."

See D. Dobbs, Handbook on the Law of Remedies § 11.6, at 752 (1973).

However, in Matter of Snide, 52 N.Y.2d 193, 418 N.E.2d 656, 437 N.Y.S.2d 63 (1981), where both husband and wife, intending to execute mutual wills at a common execution ceremony, executed by mistake the will intended for the other, an exception was recognized and reformation awarded after the death of the husband. This case is discussed in Langbein & Waggoner, Reformation of Wills on the Ground of Mistake: Change of Direction in American Law?, 130 U.Pa.L.R. 521 (1982).

SECTION 2. CONTRACTS RELATING TO PERSONAL PROPERTY (SALE OF GOODS)

A. LEGAL REMEDY: DAMAGES

1. Action by Buyer

a. Goods Not Received Or Accepted

AZTEC CORPORATION v. TUBULAR STEEL, INC.

Court of Appeals of Texas, 14th District, 1988.
758 S.W.2d 793.

MURPHY, JUSTICE.

The dispute underlying this appeal concerned a sale of goods.

* * *

Tubular is a Missouri corporation specializing in the wholesale distribution of steel tubular goods, including pipe used in oil field operations. In November 1981 Tubular received an order from its customer, Peabody World Trade, to supply 22,060 feet of 7–inch outside diameter, 29–pound pipe with long thread and couple. The pipe was to be accompanied by mill papers, certifying the physical and chemical composition of the pipe. The end finish on the pipe was critical in order that its segments could be screwed together for use in the oil field.

In attempting to fill the Peabody order according to its specifications, Tubular salesmen called several sources, including Aztec, a Louisiana corporation specializing in the purchase and sale of pipe. Mr. Ken Chalaire, Aztec's operations manager, quoted Tubular a price of $29.23 per foot to supply the pipe to which Tubular orally agreed. A written purchase order was then mailed to Aztec, reciting the quantity, price and specifications and other requisites, such as mill papers and thread protectors.

* * *

[T]he pipe that arrived at the port of Houston did not meet the specifications of the purchase order and was rejected by Peabody. Fortunately, Tubular was able to find pipe that conformed to Peabody's specifications for $29.79 per foot, or $67,325. When Tubular was unable to obtain a refund from Aztec or LaBouve of $64,739 paid for the nonconforming goods, it sued for its cost of cover and incidental expenses incurred in disposing of the pipe.

In response to special issues, the jury found that Ken Chalaire was acting as the agent for Aztec Corporation, that Aztec did enter into a contract with Tubular to supply pipe, that Aztec warranted that the pipe would have long thread and couple and would have accompanying mill papers, that Aztec failed to deliver pipe conforming to its contract or warranties, that such failure was a proximate cause of damage to Tubular, * * * and that $35,000 would compensate Tubular for its damage.

* * *

Aztec's contentions are based upon the duty of an injured party to mitigate damages. Tubular, Aztec argues, could have and should have had the pipe ends rethreaded in a machine shop for approximately $5,000. Aztec's argument ignores the fact that the pipe would still have lacked the mill certificates essential to the contract; it ignores the fact that there were tight time constraints of which Aztec was aware; and it ignores the fact that unrefuted evidence showed that Tubular had tried to mitigate damages by selling the pipe but was unsuccessful. It further ignores applicable law regarding buyers' remedies upon rightful rejection of nonconforming goods.

Applicable sections of the Texas Business and Commerce Code (Texas UCC) provide that where there is support in the evidence, aggrieved buyers are entitled to the following remedies:

§ 2.711 Buyer's Remedies in General; Buyer's Security Interest in Rejected Goods

(a) Where * * * the buyer rightfully rejects * * * with respect to any goods involved, * * * the buyer may cancel and * * * in addition to recovering so much of the price as has been paid

(1) "cover" and have damages under the next section [Section 2.712] as to all the goods affected whether or not they have been identified to the contract.

* * *

(c) On rightful rejection or justifiable revocation of acceptance a buyer has a security interest in goods in his possession or control for any payments made on their price and any expenses reasonably incurred in their inspection, receipt, transportation, care and custody and may [hold] such goods and resell them in like manner as an aggrieved seller (Section 2.706).

§ 2.712 "Cover"; Buyer's Procurement of Substitute Goods

(a) After a breach within the preceding section the buyer may "cover" by making in good faith and without unreasonable delay any reasonable purchase of or contract to purchase goods in substitution for those due from the seller.

(b) The buyer may recover from the seller as damages the difference between the cost of cover and the contract price together with an[y] incidental or consequential damages as hereinafter defined (Section 2.715) but less expenses saved in consequence of the seller's breach.

§ 2.715 Buyer's Incidental and Consequential Damages

(a) Incidental damages resulting from the seller's breach include expenses reasonably incurred in inspection, receipt, transportation and care and custody of goods rightfully rejected, any commercially reason-

> able charges, * * * and any other reasonable expenses incident to the delay or other breach.

Tex.Bus. & Com.Code Ann. §§ 2.711, 2.712, 2.715 (Tex.UCC) (Vernon 1968).

Under section 2.711(a), upon a finding of liability, an aggrieved buyer is entitled to recover as much of the contract price as he has paid. Section 2.711 *et seq.* establish the exclusive means for modifying the amount of recovery sought under the Texas UCC. Damages may exceed the price paid upon findings by the jury of cost of cover exceeding contract price (§§ 2.711 and 2.712) and by findings of incidental or consequential damages (§§ 2.712 and 2.715). Conversely, damages must be reduced by the amount of profit derived from the buyer's resale of the goods. Section 2.711(c) gives the aggrieved buyer a security interest in the goods and a right to possession pending their sale or seller's repayment of contract price paid. Any sale must be made in good faith and conducted in a commercially reasonable manner. Tex.Bus. & Com.Code Ann. §§ 2.706 and 2.711 (Tex.UCC) (Vernon 1968). In addition to challenging buyer's evidence on the amount he was paid, a defendant seller could attack the buyer's good faith, the commercial reasonableness of the sale, or the amount derived from sale. An aggrieved buyer may retain the goods for collateral and offer them for sale. In the event that the buyer (now a section 2.711 secured party) is unsuccessful in finding a purchaser for the collateral, the Texas UCC does not permit that he be charged with the value of the collateral as a set off to his recovery. Therefore, in determining damages a jury may not consider the fact that the buyer retained possession of the goods. Nonconforming goods are by definition goods other than those ordered; those that do not sell are more likely a liability to the secured party than an asset. Furthermore, there is no Texas UCC provision requiring that a buyer of nonconforming goods rework or refabricate the goods to make them conform to the original contract between the parties.

At trial Tubular presented evidence to show its damages under the applicable Texas UCC provisions as follows:

Recovery of price paid under contract § 2.711	$64,739.00
Cost of cover minus contract price ($67,325.40 − 64,739.00) § 2.712	2,586.40
Incidental expenses §§ 2.712 and 2.715	3,400.00
TOTAL	$70,725.40

These amounts were uncontroverted.

Evidence documenting the cost of cover came in during the testimony of a disinterested witness, a former employee, now a competitor of Tubular. An interested witness, Tubular's president, James Morgan, testified as to the incidental expenses of transportation and storage. Although the evidence was uncontroverted, the jury could have disbelieved the documentary evidence and testimony on cost of cover and incidental expenses. By awarding Tubular less than the uncontroverted amount paid under the contract, the jury determined the amount of each to be nothing. The trier of fact is the sole judge of the credibility of the witnesses. * * * A jury may or may not believe a witness's testimony in whole or in part. We cannot substitute our judgment for that of the jury and order additur with respect to these two elements of recovery. * * * Although the evidence would have supported the award of damages for cost of cover and incidental expenses, the award of unliquidated damages could be corrected only by granting a new trial. Such has not been prayed for by Tubular.

A different situation exists with respect to the amount paid under the contract. That amount was conclusively established. As with the evidence presented on cost of cover, proof of payment in full of the contract price was well documented by Tubular's exhibits and was admitted through the testimony of a disinterested witness. The jury findings that a contract existed, that Aztec failed to deliver goods conforming to that contract, and that such failure was a proximate cause of damages establish as a matter of law that Tubular was entitled to recovery as an aggrieved buyer under the applicable provisions of the Texas UCC. As described above, the starting point for determining the amount of this recovery was the uncontroverted amount paid by Tubular under the contract. If the jury had believed that, although a contract existed, *no* payment was made under the contract, the jury finding would have been a minimum of zero and a maximum of $5,986.40 (the sum of the other two elements of damage: cost of cover and incidental expenses). The finding of $35,000 by the jury can only indicate that it believed that some amount was paid on the contract, but the dollar amount found has no support in the evidence. A jury shall not substitute a finding of its own creation for a fact conclusively established under the evidence. *See* Tex.R.Civ.P. 226a; Callejo v. Brazos Elec. Power Coop., 755 S.W.2d 73 (Tex.1988).

The sole evidence presented as to the amount paid under the contract was $64,739. Aztec's defense to the suit was two-fold: it denied liability and testified that Tubular could have remade and used the nonconforming goods. It did not contest the amount paid. The only evidence which a jury might properly consider to reduce the recovery of the full amount paid on the contract would be evidence that a sale of the goods resulted in a set off or evidence that the unsuccessful sale was not conducted in good faith and in a commercially reasonable manner so as to realize the full and proven value of the nonconforming goods. No such evidence was presented. Testimony that Tubular could have had the pipe ends rethreaded was not competent evidence to reduce the buyer's recovery under section 2.711.

We hold that Tubular's damages in the amount of $64,739 were established as a matter of law. Judgment n.o.v. is authorized under Rule 301 of the Texas Rules of Civil Procedure when a directed verdict would have been proper. After the jury determined liability, a directed verdict would have been proper as to the amount paid under the contract to be recovered, leaving to the jury only the issues of cost of cover and incidental damages. * * * Tubular's cross point is sustained with respect to recovery of the full amount paid on the contract; it is denied with respect to cost of cover and incidental expenses.

The judgment of the trial court is affirmed as modified.

Notes

1. Damages should put plaintiff Tubular in what position? What damages would do that, and what UCC sections authorize those damages? Note that the general provisions of the U.C.C. in § 1–106 are consistent with the principles discussed in the first section of this chapter. Section 1–106(1) provides: "The remedies provided by this Act shall be liberally administered to the end that the aggrieved party may be put in as good a position as if the other party had fully performed but neither consequential or special nor penal damages may be had except as specifically provided in this Act or by other rule of law."

2. What were the direct damages? What do the incidental damages represent? What would consequential damages be and why didn't plaintiff seek them?

3. How did Tubular mitigate its damages? How did Aztec claim Tubular should have mitigated its damages? Do you agree with Aztec?

4. When the court increased the jury's award for one type of damage but not others, was the court's reasoning internally inconsistent? Does it affect your answer that Tubular did not seek consequential damages?

5. U.C.C. § 2–712(1) provides that "the buyer may 'cover' by making in good faith and without unreasonable delay any reasonable purchase of or contract to purchase goods in substitution for those due from the seller." May a purchaser cover by producing internally the goods that the seller did not deliver? If so, may that buyer recover the costs of production as well as the profits it would have made had it produced goods for sale to others? *See* Dura-Wood Treating Co. v. Century Forest Indus., 675 F.2d 745 (5th Cir.1982) *cert. denied*, 459 U.S. 865, *appeal aft. remand,* 694 F.2d 112 (5th Cir.1982) (buyer may cover by producing goods internally but cannot collect costs of production and foregone profits if those are greater than the cost of purchasing goods from an outside source).

KOENEN v. ROYAL BUICK COMPANY

Court of Appeals of Arizona, 1989.
162 Ariz. 376, 783 P.2d 822.

ROLL, JUDGE.

Defendant Royal Buick Company (Royal Buick) appeals from a judgment entered in favor of Thomas Koenen in connection with an alleged breach of contract involving a limited edition automobile. Because sufficient evidence was presented that Koenen entered into a contract with Royal Buick and that Royal Buick breached that contract, we affirm.

FACTS

In September 1986, Thomas Koenen learned from automobile literature that General Motors planned to manufacture 500 special editions of the Buick Regal Grand National automobile. The vehicle, dubbed the Grand National Experimental (GNX) was the quickest limited production car in the United States at that time. The GNX, like the Grand National, was available only in black and had a 3.8 turbo-charged fuel-injected hand-built motor. The GNX, however, had additional features including an intercooled turbo-charged V–6 engine with special body, special tires and suspension, and special wheels. The GNX was featured on the cover of *Autoweek* and *Popular Mechanics.*[1]

Several months before Royal Buick, a Tucson-based automobile dealership, received official notification that it would receive one of the 500 GNX autos, Koenen contacted salesperson William Yalen at Royal Buick. Koenan, along with his father and brother, collected cars under the name of Koenen Classic Cars. Their collection was stored in an air-conditioned California warehouse. Koenen had previously conducted transactions with Royal Buick and Yalen. In March 1986, Koenen purchased a 1986 Grand National from Royal Buick for cash. Yalen was the salesperson. In August 1986, Koenen purchased a 1987 Grand National through Yalen from Royal Buick for cash.

In November 1986, Koenen went to Yalen and told him that he wished to buy a GNX. Koenen showed Yalen current literature regarding Buick's plan to offer a limited number of this special edition. During discussions with Yalen and new car sales manager Robert Sagar, Koenen agreed to pay the window sticker price for the vehicle, that is, the price placed on the car at the factory.

In December 1986, Royal Buick General Manager Tom Bird orally agreed to sell the GNX to Gary Gerovac. No purchase order was completed, however. On January 5, 1987, Jeff Buchner signed a purchase order agreement to purchase a GNX from Royal Buick. Although Buchner offered to give Royal Buick a $1000 deposit in connection with the purchase order, he was told that a $100 deposit was satisfactory. At that time, sales manager Sagar assured Buchner that he was "first in line."

On February 16, 1987, a purchase order form was signed by Koenen, Yalen, and Sagar regarding the GNX. The document contained the notation:

> Order is not binding on Seller until accepted in writing by officer, or Sales-manager of Seller, and until Purchaser's credit has been approved.

The purchase order also contained the notation "Price and Availability To Be Determined?" Koenen was listed on the form as the purchaser. Koenen told Sagar and Yalen that he was willing to pay up to $30,000 if that was the sticker price. Sagar and Yalen told Koenen that no one else had made a deposit and that Koenen was number one to receive a GNX. Koenen gave Yalen a check for $500 as a deposit for the GNX but asked that the check not be cashed. On February 17, 1987, Royal Buick filled out a purchase order form for David Woon and accepted a $500 deposit from him for purchase of the GNX. On February 20, 1987, Koenen replaced the February 16, 1987 check with a $500 check from his father.

In a letter dated April 21, 1987, General Motors notified Royal Buick that it would receive one GNX. The window sticker price for the vehicle

1. Mandel, "Speedway Born," *Autoweek,* Feb. 16, 1987, at 63; Allen, "Speed Thrills," *Popular Mechanics,* March 1987, at 63.

was $29,290. Royal Buick General Manager Tom Bird placed a market value of $44,900 on the vehicle. Yalen contacted Koenen to see if Koenen wanted to bid on the vehicle.

On May 8, 1987, Royal Buick returned the deposits to Koenen, Buchner, and Woon. When Buchner received the letter, he contacted Sagar to protest. Sagar asked Buchner if he would be interested in bidding on the vehicle. Royal Buick received the GNX in September 1987. Royal Buick placed a price of $44,900 on the vehicle. Bird testified as to the process by which he arrived at the $44,900 figure:

> Q Who came up with the price?
>
> A I did.
>
> Q And how did you come up with that price?
>
> A In doing a little search as to what the cars were bringing around the country, that that [sic] seemed to be somewhat of a mean figure.
>
> Q About $45,000?
>
> A Right. We wanted to be a little cheaper than anybody else, so we cut it down a hundred dollars.
>
> Q Four hundred?
>
> A Forty-four nine.
>
> Q Forty-four nine?
>
> A I was being facetious in that last comment, but it was forty-four nine.

In April 1988, Royal Buick sold the vehicle for $39,750 to an Oklahoma physician.

Procedural History

Koenen received Royal Buick's May 8, 1987 letter informing him that he would not be able to purchase the GNX. The letter included a check in the amount of Koenen's $500 deposit, but Koenen declined to cash the check. Koenen proceeded to file a civil complaint alleging breach of contract on the part of Royal Buick. As part of the complaint, Koenen sought a temporary restraining order preventing Royal Buick from selling the GNX. By stipulation of the parties, Royal Buick agreed not to sell the vehicle. On November 30, 1987, a preliminary injunction was denied and Royal Buick was permitted to sell the GNX.

Koenen's complaint against Royal Buick was joined with a complaint filed by Buchner, who also sought damages based upon Royal Buick's refusal to sell the GNX to him.

The matter was tried to the court without a jury. The trial court awarded Koenen and Buchner $15,610 each, representing the difference between the manufacturer's suggested retail price ($29,290) and the fair market value of the automobile ($44,900).

ISSUES ON APPEAL

* * *

Enforceability of the Contract

Royal Buick argues that no enforceable contract was entered between Koenen and Royal Buick for the sale of the GNX.

* * *

The evidence supports the trial court's finding that the purchase order constituted a contract.

Statute of Frauds

Royal Buick next argues that the purchase order fails to satisfy the requirements of the statute of frauds. A.R.S. § 47–2201(A) * * *.

* * *

The purchase order was sufficient to indicate that a contract for sale existed between Koenen and Royal Buick.

Parol Evidence

Royal Buick next argues that the trial court erred in permitting the introduction of parol evidence to contradict the terms of the purchase agreement.

* * *

Royal Buick admits that the price and availability terms are ambiguous. Where a writing is ambiguous, extrinsic evidence will be admitted to explain it. * * *

Royal Buick argues that the writing indicates that the price had not been determined. Koenen maintains that the price was arrived at because he offered to pay the manufacturer's suggested retail price and although that price was yet to be determined, the formula was accepted by Royal Buick. We agree.

* * *

Legality of Contract

Royal Buick next argues that the contract for the sale of the car was void because Koenen planned on transporting the vehicle to California in violation of California Health and Safety Code § 43151(a). * * * However, simply because Koenen, with his father and brother, stores vehicles in a warehouse located in California does not establish that Koenen operates an established place of business in California. In addition, the record indicates that Koenen would not have driven the vehicle but merely placed it in storage. * * * Even assuming that the California statute could operate so as to negate an Arizona contract for the sale of a car, no evidence was presented that Koenen intended to use, register, or sell the vehicle in California. In addition, there was no evidence that the car did not comply with California standards. We find the contract was valid.

Proof of Damages

Finally, Royal Buick argues that the trial court should have computed damages as the difference between the cost to cover the loss and the contract price, and that Koenen failed to prove the cost of cover.

The UCC permits a buyer to elect the remedy when damaged by the actions of the seller. A.R.S. § 47–2711. Here, Koenen elected the difference between the fair market value and the contract price. A.R.S. § 47–2713.

Koenen's father purchased a GNX for the family collection from another source. No evidence was introduced as to the purchase price of that particular vehicle. Royal Buick argues that because Koenen's father succeeded in obtaining a GNX from a different source, Koenen suffered no damages or, alternatively, that Koenen was required to introduce evidence as to the purchase price for the other GNX so that the court would be able to determine the fair market value of the GNX which Koenen was unable to purchase from Royal Buick.

We disagree. First, the fact that Koenen's father purchased a substitute vehicle is not dispositive. If the father's purchase was proven to be a reasonable substitute for the contracted car then the measure of damages would be the difference between the cost of cover and the contract price. No evidence shows that the vehicle was purchased specifically to substitute for the lost bargain under the Royal Buick contract. The car was purchased in April or May 1988, some 11 or 12 months after Royal Buick repudiated the contract. Also, Koenen testified that even after acquiring the GNX, he was still possibly in the market for another one.

"The burden of proof as to mitigation of damages is on the party asserting the requirement." * * * Royal Buick failed to introduce any evidence that the father's purchase substituted for the Royal Buick contract or that the purchase of that car in any way mitigated the damages under the contract. Therefore, Royal Buick cannot claim that the buyer elected the remedy of cover. * * *

Royal Buick also argues that Koenen was required to introduce evidence as to the purchase price for the other GNX so the court could determine the fair market value of the contracted GNX. We disagree. A.R.S. § 47–2713 requires that market price be determined at the time the buyer learned of the breach. Royal Buick breached its contract with Koenen on May 8, 1987. Evidence of the purchase price of a GNX one year later is not dispositive of the fair market value of the vehicle in 1987. Significantly, when the Royal Buick general manager testified regarding the fair market value of the GNX which Royal Buick was selling, he testified that he surveyed Buick dealerships and determined that $45,000 was a fair market value for the GNX. This concession by Royal Buick could certainly be considered by the trial court.

The trial court correctly computed damages as the difference between the fair market value and the contract price. Sufficient evidence was presented to support the trial court's conclusion that $44,900 was the market value of the vehicle.

We affirm.

ATTORNEYS' FEES

A.R.S. § 12–341.01 authorizes an award to the successful party in any contested action arising out of contract. Section 12–341.01 applies to appeals as well as trials. * * * Appellee Koenen is awarded attorneys' fees incurred in the defense of this appeal.

Notes

1. How were Koenen's direct damages different from Tubular's direct damages?

2. Why weren't Koenen's damages measured by the difference between cover and the contract price? Should they have been? Can a plaintiff recover incidental and consequential damages without attempting to cover? *See* R.B. Matthews, Inc. v. Transamerica Transp. Services, Inc., 945 F.2d 269, 275–276 (9th Cir.1991) (case remanded to see if buyer of drop frame trailers had opportunity to cover after seller breached contract; if not, consequential damages improper).

3. Why wasn't the later car purchase considered to be cover?

4. If the buyer does not cover and the seller's breach was anticipatory, that is, before performance is due, may the buyer wait until performance is due to measure the difference between the market price and the contract price? What if the market price for the undelivered goods is rising during that time? *See* Cosden Oil & Chemical Co. v. Karl O. Helm Aktiengesellschaft, 736 F.2d 1064, 1072 (5th Cir.1984) (buyer of polystyrene who chose not to cover after anticipatory breach during rising market must measure the market "at the time he could have covered—a reasonable time after repudiation.")

5. The buyer's remedies under the Uniform Commercial Code are also described in Productoro E Importadora De Papel v. Fleming, 376 Mass. 826, 383 N.E.2d 1129 (1978):

> "The Uniform Commercial Code provides an aggrieved buyer two alternative remedies when the seller repudiates or withholds delivery as TMI did here. *See* G.L. c. 106, § 2–711. The buyer may recover his economic loss measured by the difference between the market price and the contract price. G.L. c. 106, § 2–713. The buyer may instead effect 'cover' by procuring substitute goods and may then recover the difference between the cover and contract prices. G.L. c. 106, § 2–712. In either case, the buyer may also recover the incidental and foreseeable consequential damages he incurred because of the seller's breach. G.L. c. 106, § 2–715. Also in either case, the buyer's damage recovery is to be reduced by the expenses he avoided by not having to perform the contract. G.L. c. 106, §§ 2–712(2), 2–715(1).
>
> "The apparent purpose of each of the alternative damage remedies is to place the aggrieved buyer in the same position as performance would have done. *See* G.L. c. 106, § 1–106(1). When the buyer effects cover, as PIPSA did in this case, and subsequently recovers damages under § 2–712, he ends up in possession of equivalent goods and out of pocket in the amount he would have expended to obtain conforming goods from the defaulting seller under the contract. J. White & R. Summers, Uniform Commercial Code § 6–3, at 176–177 (1972). Calculation of cover damages

under § 2.712 should, therefore, embody three steps. First, the judge should determine the aggregate difference between the cover price and the contract price. Second, the damage award should be increased by the incidental and consequential damages recoverable under § 2–715. Third, the award should be reduced, even to extinction, by the expenses that the breach enabled the buyer to avoid. *E.g.,* Barbarossa & Sons v. Iten Chevrolet, Inc., Minn., 265 N.W.2d 655 (1978)."

6. The concept of cover did not appear in the Uniform Sales Act. It was first introduced in the Uniform Commercial Code, and serves two purposes: "it enables the buyer to make reasonable substitute purchases and to recover the cost thereof rather than the difference between market value and contract price and, at the same time, protects the seller from consequential damages which could have been mitigated by the purchase of substitute goods." Gerwin v. Southeastern California Ass'n of Seventh Day Adventists, 14 Cal.App.3d 209, 92 Cal.Rptr. 111 (1971). Essentially, "the cover rules are an expression of the general duty to mitigate damages and usually the same principles apply." S.J. Groves & Sons Co. v. Warner Co., 576 F.2d 524, 528 (3d Cir.1978).

JEWELL–RUNG AGENCY, INC. v. THE HADDAD ORGANIZATION, LTD.

United States District Court,
Southern District of New York, 1993.
814 F.Supp. 337.

ROBERT P. PATTERSON, Jr., District Judge.

Plaintiff Jewell–Rung Agency, Inc. ("Jewell–Rung"), seeks damages in excess of $350,000 for the defendant's alleged breach of contract. Defendant The Haddad Organization, Ltd. ("Haddad"), moves for summary judgment on the issue of damages and to strike portions of the affidavits of Donald Jewell and Leo McGinity, submitted by Plaintiff in opposition to summary judgment, on the ground that they do not comply with Fed. R.Civ.P. 56(e). Plaintiff cross-moves based on Rule 56(e) for an order striking portions of the affidavit of Neal Robson, submitted in support of Defendant's motion for summary judgment. For the reasons set forth below, Plaintiff's motion to strike is denied, Defendant's motion to strike is granted in part and denied in part, and Defendant's motion for summary judgment is denied.

* * *

BACKGROUND

Jewell–Rung is a Canadian corporation engaged in the business of importing and selling men's clothing at wholesale. Haddad is a New York corporation that manufactures men's outerwear sold under the "Lakeland" label.

In 1990, Jewell–Rung ordered samples of Lakeland men's outerwear from Haddad so that it might seek orders for this clothing from Canadian retailers. Haddad supplied Jewell–Rung with the ordered samples, which Jewell–Rung used to obtain orders from customers in Canada.

In January of 1991, Jewell–Rung placed an initial purchase order with Haddad for 2,325 garments of Lakeland men's outerwear, having a total listed price of approximately $250,000 in American currency, for the Fall 1991 season. By February 1991, Plaintiff had taken orders for 372 of these garments at a wholesale price of $107,506 in Canadian currency.

* * *

Plaintiff alleges that Haddad's acceptance of its January 1991 purchase order created a binding contract, which Haddad subsequently breached by failing to fill the purchase order and entering into its exclusive distributorship agreement with Olympic. Plaintiff further alleges that because it did not learn of Haddad's alleged breach until February of 1991, it was unable to fill its customers' orders for Lakeland goods for the Fall 1991 season or to obtain a substitute line of men's outerwear and, as a result, sustained over $350,000 in damages.

For the purposes of this summary judgment motion only, Defendant Haddad concedes that its acceptance of Jewell–Rung's January 1991 purchase order created a binding contract and that Haddad's agreement with Olympic constituted a breach of that contract. The defendant seeks summary judgment with respect to damages on three grounds: (1) Plaintiff's failure to mitigate damages bars any recovery; (2) Plaintiff's refusal to cover prohibits recovery of consequential damages; and (3) alternatively, any recovery by Plaintiff of lost profits must be limited to the profits derived from the orders already placed by Plaintiff's customers at the time of Defendant's breach of contract.

DISCUSSION

* * *

II. Motion for Summary Judgment

Summary judgment is appropriate if the evidence offered demonstrates that there is no genuine issue as to any material fact and the moving party is entitled to judgment as a matter of law.

* * *

A. *The availability of damages in general*

New York's Uniform Commercial Code provides that a buyer may recover damages for a seller's breach of a contract of sale by either of two methods. N.Y.U.C.C. § 2–711(1). The buyer may either "cover" and obtain damages under N.Y.U.C.C. § 2–712, or recover damages for non-delivery as provided under N.Y.U.C.C. § 2–713.

It is undisputed that Jewell–Rung, the buyer in this case, did not "cover" and may seek damages under section 2–713 only. This section provides that "the measure of damages for non-delivery or repudiation by the seller is the difference between the market price at the time when the buyer learned of the breach and the contract price together with any incidental and consequential damages * * *, but less expenses saved in consequence of the seller's breach."

Haddad asserts that at the time when Jewell–Rung learned of the alleged breach of contract, Olympic offered to sell Jewell–Rung Lakeland outerwear to fill all of its orders at the contract price to which Jewell–Rung and Haddad had agreed. According to Haddad, the market price of the goods at the time when the buyer learned of the breach was therefore equivalent to the contract price, and the buyer is deemed to have suffered no damage under section 2–713.

Plaintiff has, however, demonstrated the existence of a genuine issue of fact as to whether Olympic actually offered to supply Jewell–Rung with the same goods at the same price agreed upon by Haddad. * * *

The submission by each party of competent but conflicting accounts as to the nature of any offers made by Olympic to Jewell–Rung presents a genuine issue of material fact as to the available market price for the Lakeland goods at the time of Defendant's alleged breach of contract.

Haddad further contends that the existence of this genuine issue of fact as to price is immaterial to Plaintiff's claim for damages because Plaintiff concedes that it would have rejected Olympic's offer to sell it substitute goods at any price. Plaintiff maintains that purchasing and selling Lakeland goods manufactured by Olympic would have operated to the detriment of its own sales of competing lines of outerwear in the future. Haddad asserts that Plaintiff's refusal to buy from Olympic constitutes a breach of its duty to mitigate damages and therefore bars recovery in this action.

Haddad's argument boils down to an assertion that Plaintiff's failure to effect cover bars recovery of damages under section 2–713. However, the Uniform Commercial Code makes clear that "cover" is an alternative to the relief authorized under section 2–713, *see* N.Y.U.C.C. § 2–711(1), and that failure of a buyer to effect cover "does not bar him from any other remedy." *Id.* at § 2–712(3). "Recovery of damages based on market price fluctuation under Section 2–713 is not * * * contingent upon the buyer's attempting to cover." *Kashi v. Gratsos,* 790 F.2d 1050, 1056 (2d Cir.1986). Accordingly, Plaintiff's failure to purchase substitute goods from Olympic or any other seller does not preclude recovery of damages for Haddad's alleged breach of contract.

B. The availability of consequential damages

Haddad maintains that Jewell–Rung's failure to effect cover bars it from recovering consequential damages. Although N.Y.U.C.C. § 2–712(3) explicitly states that "[f]ailure of the buyer to effect cover * * * does not bar him from any other remedy," the Official Comment to this section of the Uniform Commercial Code cautions that it must be read in conjunction with section 2–715(2)(a). *See* N.Y.U.C.C. § 2–712 Official Comment at 645 (McKinney 1964). Section 2–715(2)(a) limits consequential damages to losses "which could not reasonably be prevented by cover or otherwise."

As previously stated, Jewell–Rung does not dispute that it did not attempt to effect cover. However, a genuine issue of material fact exists as to whether Jewell–Rung's failure to seek cover was reasonable under the circumstances.

Jewell–Rung provides several reasons why it did not seek cover. In explaining why it did not buy goods from Olympic, Jewell–Rung states that it had the following concerns: that its customers would not be satisfied with the quality of Lakeland goods manufactured by Olympic, which specializes in the production of lower-priced clothing for discounters and department stores, Jewell Aff. at ¶¶ 8–10, 14; that supplying its customers with outerwear manufactured by Olympic for the Fall 1991 season would provide Olympic with an entree to those customers for all of the next season's goods, *id.* at ¶ 16; and that purchasing goods from Olympic would place it at the complete mercy of a competitor for the timely supply of goods, *id.* at ¶ 23 n. 4.

Jewell–Rung further points out that it had no source other than Olympic for Lakeland goods, which were not fungible but were "branded goods, manufactured from specific patterns and specific styles." *Id.* at ¶ 23. In addition, Jewell–Rung alleges that substitutions for Lakeland goods were not available that late in the purchasing cycle, and that it was in fact unable to find a replacement line for two seasons. *Id.* at ¶ 25.

Based upon the reasons put forth by Jewell–Rung for its failure to cover, this Court cannot say at this time that such failure to cover was unreasonable as a matter of law. The cases cited by Defendant, *Happy Dack Trading Co. v. Agro–Industries, Inc.,* 602 F.Supp. 986 (S.D.N.Y.1984), and *Hilord Chem. Corp. v. Ricoh Elecs., Inc.,* 875 F.2d 32 (2d Cir.1989), are factually distinguishable. In *Happy Dack,* the Court denied recovery of lost profits because the plaintiffs failed to effect cover as to a fungible good, i.e. resin, that was available on the open market. *Happy Dack,* 602 F.Supp. at 994. Specific brands and styles of clothing, such as the Lakeland goods at issue here, are not so fungible. *See Texpor Traders, Inc. v. Trust Co. Bank,* 720 F.Supp. 1100, 1114 (S.D.N.Y.1989). In *Hilord Chem. Corp.,* the Court did not actually decide that the plaintiff had unreasonably failed to cover; it held only that the trial court should have instructed the jury on the issue of cover in light of testimony that specific sources of substitute goods were available to the plaintiff. *Hilord Chem. Corp.,* 875 F.2d at 38.

Accordingly, the defendant's motion for summary judgment is also denied insofar as it seeks to bar recovery for consequential damages.

C. Limitation on recovery of lost profits

In the alternative, Haddad asserts that any lost profits awarded to Jewell–Rung should be limited to those derived from confirmed orders placed by Jewell–Rung's customers at the time of the alleged breach.

Under New York law, recovery of lost profits has three prerequisites. First, the party seeking lost profits must demonstrate "with certainty that such damages have been caused by the breach and, second, the alleged loss must be capable of proof with reasonable certainty." *Kenford Co. v. County of Erie,* 67 N.Y.2d 257, 502 N.Y.S.2d 131, 132, 493 N.E.2d 234, 235 (1986). Third, "there must be a showing that the particular damages were fairly within the contemplation of the parties to the contract at the time it was made." *Id.; accord Care Travel Co. v. Pan American World Airways, Inc.,* 944 F.2d 983, 994 (2d Cir.1991).

Before any evidence of lost profits is presented in this matter, Haddad asks the Court to rule as a matter of law that lost profits, with the exception of anticipated payments for garments already ordered by retailers at the time of breach, are incapable of proof with reasonable certainty. Haddad makes two arguments in support of this position.

First, Haddad cites *Texpor Traders,* 720 F.Supp. at 1114, *Wullschleger & Co. v. Jenny Fashions, Inc.,* 618 F.Supp. 373, 378 (S.D.N.Y.1985), and *Harbor Hill Lithographing Corp. v. Dittler Bros., Inc.,* 76 Misc.2d 145, 348 N.Y.S.2d 920, 924 (Sup.Ct.Nassau Cty.1973), for the proposition that in the case of a wholesaler, lost profits are restricted to those pertaining to confirmed orders of resale. None of these cases comes close to establishing such a per se rule. Each case merely limits recovery of lost profits after the plaintiff has presented evidence and failed to demonstrate a reasonable basis for calculating lost profits other than those derived from confirmed orders that were in place at the time of breach.

Second, Haddad maintains that lost profits are rarely appropriate where the injured party is a new business because such damages are by nature highly speculative. When a "new business" seeks to recover lost profits, "a stricter standard" of proof is required "for the obvious reason that there does not exist a reasonable basis of experience upon which to estimate lost profits with the requisite degree of reasonable certainty." *Kenford Co.,* 502 N.Y.S.2d at 132, 493 N.E.2d at 235; *accord Care Travel Co.,* 944 F.2d at 993. This heightened standard of proof for new businesses indicates that new ventures will have difficulty demonstrating lost profits; it does not mean that new businesses should be denied an opportunity to present their evidence of such damages at trial.

Whether Jewell–Rung is in fact a "new business" within the meaning of *Kenford Co.* is itself unclear. It is new to the business of selling Lakeland products in Canada, but its experience as a wholesaler of men's clothing in Canada is evidence of its viability as an enterprise and could, for example, yield evidence as to previous patterns of profit on resale of similar lines of clothing.

Accordingly, Defendant's request to limit recovery of lost profits to confirmed orders of resale is denied at this time.

Notes

1. What was plaintiff seeking as damages?

2. What arguments did defendant make for denying, as a matter of law, plaintiff's consequential damages and what were the court's responses?

3. The court gave three requirements that must be met before consequential damages may be recovered by the plaintiff. Defendant only addressed two of those requirements. What was the one not addressed and why do you think it was not raised?

4. Must the plaintiff cover? If not, what happens?

5. How would you try to settle this case at this point? What arguments for settlement would you make for both parties?

6. As *Jewell–Rung* stated, the right to recover consequential damages under the Uniform Commercial Code is conditioned upon the traditional common law requirements that such damages must be proved to be caused by the breach, proved with reasonable certainty, and shown to be "within the contemplation of the parties to the contract at the time it was made." 814 F.Supp. at 342. U.C.C. § 2–715(2) provides "Consequential damages resulting from the seller's breach include (a) any loss resulting from general or particular requirements and needs of which the seller at the time of contracting had reason to know and which could not reasonably be prevented by cover or otherwise; and (b) injury to person or property proximately resulting from any breach of warranty." *Compare* Gerwin v. Southeastern California Association of Seventh Day Adventists, 14 Cal.App.3d 209, 92 Cal.Rptr. 111 (1971) (action for specific performance or damages for failure to sell bar fixtures and equipment; lost profits for new business disallowed because plaintiff attempted to conceal identity from defendant at time of contracting and failed to prove both the occurrence and extent of lost profits with reasonable certainty) *and* Bockman Printing & Services, Inc. v. Baldwin–Gregg, Inc., 213 Ill.App.3d 516, 157 Ill.Dec. 630, 572 N.E.2d 1094, 1101 (1 Dist.1991) (defendants had no reason to know that plaintiff would contract for more business based on contract with defendants to design and manufacture a machine to fold papers since past two attempts to build such a machine had failed) *with* Sweco, Inc. v. Continental Sulfur and Chem., 808 S.W.2d 112, 117 (Tex.App.1991) (seller of sulphur grinding machine expressly warranted production per hour and anticipated that production; testimony of amount of profit per ton was sufficient to uphold jury verdict for lost profits for sulphur not produced). *See generally* Note, An Economic Approach to Hadley v. Baxendale, 62 Neb.L.Rev. 157 (1983); Annot., 96 A.L.R.3d 299 (1979).

b. Goods Accepted, But Defective

REYNOLDS METALS CO. v. WESTINGHOUSE ELEC. CORP.

United States Court of Appeals, Fifth Circuit, 1985.
758 F.2d 1073.

Before THORNBERRY, REAVLEY, and HIGGINBOTHAM, CIRCUIT JUDGES.

PATRICK E. HIGGINBOTHAM, CIRCUIT JUDGE:

Westinghouse Electric Corporation challenges a judgment for damages entered following a jury's determination that Westinghouse breached a contract with Reynolds Metals Company. Westinghouse argues that Reynolds' contract claim was barred by disclaimers of warranty, that in any event there was no breach, and that Reynolds failed to give the required notice before suing on its claim. We reject these arguments but conclude that Westinghouse's challenge to the damage award itself is well-founded because the amounts awarded included consequential damages not recoverable under the parties' agreement. We therefore affirm the jury's finding of breach but remand for a new trial on the issue of damages.

I

In early 1970, Reynolds solicited bids for the sale of certain electrical equipment needed by its San Patricio plant in Corpus Christi, Texas.

Westinghouse responded to the solicitation with a series of bids that were finalized in a full proposal to Reynolds offering to manufacture the desired equipment—a large electric transformer unit—for approximately $250,-000.00. This price included not only the machinery itself, but also a "competent Westinghouse service engineer" who was to be present "for two full days * * * during equipment check or startup." The proposal warranted the machinery for one year from the date of shipment and made those warranty terms the exclusive remedy of the purchaser; that is, Westinghouse disclaimed all warranties not expressed in its proposal and excluded any liability to Reynolds for "special, indirect, incidental or consequential damages" that might be sustained in the event of a breach of the sales contract or warranty.

Reynolds accepted the Westinghouse proposal with a purchase order. * * *

The only significant addition to the parties' agreement was made in January of 1971, while manufacture of the transformer unit was still in progress. Reynolds determined that the equipment would not be put into operation until well after shipment and therefore requested an extension of the one-year warranty. Westinghouse agreed and extended the warranty for an additional twelve months "based upon storage during the first twelve months, * * * [for] a net total price of $2,637.00." The warranty extension at this price was made dependent upon several conditions, including "inspection of all equipment prior to start-up, and start-up supervision by the Westinghouse Industrial Systems Department." The cost of such supervision was to be borne by Reynolds in addition to the warranty extension price, with credit to be given Reynolds for cost of the two days of start-up assistance provided for in the original agreement.

The equipment was shipped in July of 1971 and was stored in a protected location at the San Patricio plant until its installation in the spring of 1973. Reynolds hired a local electrical contractor to perform most of this work under the supervision of a Reynolds engineer, Ken Younger, and installation was substantially completed by late February. At that point Westinghouse engineer David Reindl arrived at the plant for final inspection and start-up of the equipment. Reindl had a degree in electrical engineering, but apparently lacked extensive experience with transformer units of the type being installed, and more importantly, considered it his responsibility to "technically assist" rather than to "supervise" Reynolds in the installation of the purchased equipment. Despite the alleged confusion over his responsibilities, Reindl worked with Younger over the following two months until most problems with the unit were resolved, and the equipment was placed in service in late April.

Although no deficiencies in Reindl's performance of his duties were evident at the time he rendered his services, he apparently failed to install properly the system for detection of ground current in the transformer. * * *

The equipment had an expected life-span of twenty to thirty years, but on April 11, 1974, less than a year after it was put into service, the transformer unit failed. The problem, according to Reynolds' experts, was two-fold. The failure itself was the result of the assertedly improper design of a compression ring in the transformer. That design allegedly caused continuous burning in the transformer from the time of installation and somewhat more serious burning on April 11, when excessive power demands were allegedly made on the transformer. The ground detection system described above contributed to the problem, according to Reynolds' experts, in that some of the low-level burning, and certainly the high-level burning on April 11, should have been detected by a properly installed ground alarm system before significant damage was done.

The transformer was shipped to Westinghouse's repair facility in Houston immediately after the April 11 incident, and at about the same time Reynolds made a warranty claim to Westinghouse based on the failure of the equipment. Westinghouse denied the claim on the ground that its warranty had expired, and Reynolds paid the repair bill on the equipment, which totalled $109,284.82. Reynolds did not otherwise level a claim against Westinghouse on the basis of this incident until it filed suit in state court in April 1976. Westinghouse timely removed to federal court based on diversity of citizenship.

Reynolds alleged causes of action in negligence, strict liability, contract, and warranty, but because the negligence and strict liability claims were barred by the applicable statutes of limitation, the case proceeded to trial under theories of warranty and contract. The primary dispute was whether Westinghouse's warranty disclaimers and limitations on liability applied, and in the event that they did, whether warranty protection commenced on the date of shipment of the equipment in 1971 or upon completion of the installation of the equipment in 1973.

At the close of all the evidence the district court granted an instructed verdict in favor of Westinghouse on nearly all issues. * * *

The district court's instructed verdict left Reynolds' breach of contract claim as the only theory of recovery with merit. The contract claim centered on the alleged failure of Westinghouse to send a "competent" Westinghouse service engineer "to supervise" installation of the transformer as called for by the sales contract. Although the district court interpreted Westinghouse's surviving warranty disclaimers to exclude any warranties, express or implied, relating to services supplied incidental to the sale of the equipment, the court concluded that these warranty disclaimers did not necessarily bar a breach of contract claim based on the services of David Reindl, the engineer supplied by Westinghouse. The court reasoned that given Reindl's limited qualifications and prior experience, his apparent misconception that he was obligated to assist rather than supervise installation of the transformer, and his work at the San Patricio plant, a jury could conclude that Westinghouse had completely failed to fulfill its contractual obligation to provide a competent service engineer to supervise installation of the purchased equipment. In short, the court concluded that the evidence could support more than a claim for breach of warranty because the alleged deficiencies in Reindl's services arguably constituted a total failure of performance.

Despite strenuous objections by Westinghouse, the case was submitted to the jury on this contract theory. The jury found that Westinghouse failed to send a competent service engineer as required by the contract, and that this failure was a proximate cause of all of Reynolds' damages. The district court then entered judgment in favor of Reynolds in the amount of $109,284.82, the figure stipulated by the parties as the cost to repair the transformer, together with pre-judgment interest. Westinghouse timely filed this appeal.

II

We are persuaded that the district court was correct in submitting the breach of contract claim to the jury and that the jury's finding of breach was adequately supported by the evidence. We nevertheless reverse the district court's decision to award damages for the breach on the basis of the amounts Reynolds paid Westinghouse to repair the transformer because, causation problems aside,[6] the costs to repair the equipment are not the appropriate measure of damages here.

1

Westinghouse advances [two] lines of attack on Reynolds' contract theory of recovery. The first is that a claim based on Reindl's performance under the contract can be none other than a claim for a breach of warranty for services supplied incidental to the sale of the equipment. Because the district court ruled that any such warranty was effectively disclaimed in Westinghouse's general disclaimer of warranty, Westinghouse urges that any contractual claim arising out of the services provided necessarily was barred as well. We disagree. If Westinghouse had provided a competent engineer to supervise installation of the transformer, and that engineer had not performed as expected, there would be a breach of warranty but not a total failure of performance. In contrast, if Reindl did not even qualify as a "competent" engineer and did not believe that it was his duty "to supervise" Reynolds in the installation, then by supplying him Westinghouse failed to perform at all as promised under the contract. Such a failure would constitute a total failure of performance, a breach of contract for which the warranty disclaimer would not protect Westinghouse, or at least the jury was entitled to so conclude on this record.

A related argument of Westinghouse, that the contract did not impose upon it any *obligation* to provide an engineer to supervise the installation of the equipment, and therefore that Reindl's allegedly inadequate supervision could not have been a breach, is more persuasive. * * *

The district court, however, had no opportunity to consider this argument, because Westinghouse did not raise the point until it brought

6. Westinghouse correctly points out that under Reynolds' breach of contract theory, Westinghouse could not possibly be liable for all of the repairs performed on the transformer. Reynolds' experts explained that there was a design flaw that caused burning within the transformer, and that the flaw was a primary cause of Reynolds' damages. The breach of contract, Westinghouse's failure to inspect and supervise properly the installation of the ground alarm system, then, only caused those extra damages resulting from Reynolds' failure to discover the burning early on in the life of the transformer, not the entire costs of repair.

this appeal. * * * We refuse to entertain theories raised for the first time on appeal. * * *

2

The district court correctly found that Westinghouse's disclaimer of liability for special, indirect, incidental, and consequential damages was part of the parties' contract. Cognizant of the need to enforce this limitation, the district court excluded costs of transporting the transformer to and from Houston for repairs and excluded all lost profits claims by Reynolds. Westinghouse argues that the district court failed to give full effect to this limitation, however, because the court awarded Reynolds the cost to repair its transformer as damages for the found breach. Such damages, Westinghouse argues, are also consequential damages which may not be recovered under the agreement. We agree.

The law of contract, whether under the common law or the Uniform Commercial Code, generally authorizes damages for breach in the amount of the expectancy interest of the wronged party. That is, the rules for contract damages are intended to place the victim of the breach in the same position he would have occupied had the breach not occurred. There are three principal elements to such damages: (1) general difference-in-value losses—the difference in value to the wronged party of the performance or goods tendered and the performance or goods as promised under the contract; (2) incidental losses—costs incurred in a reasonable effort, whether successful or not, to avoid losses caused by the breach; and (3) consequential losses—items such as lost profits or injuries to person or property foreseeably caused by the breach.

While incidental losses are often readily identifiable as an item of contract damages, difference-in-value losses are sometimes difficult to separate from those which are consequential. Distinguishing the latter items is not ordinarily important in contract cases, given the general principle that all expectancy damages are recoverable. But whenever the parties have, as here, excluded consequential damages by agreement, the court must be careful to limit the damage award to the difference-in-value component of the contract claim and must not include damages for that which would otherwise be compensable as consequential losses.

Professors White and Summers explain the problem and the proper implementation of the consequential damages limitation with the following illustration:

> [I]n Russo v. Hilltop Lincoln–Mercury, 479 S.W.2d 211, 10 U.C.C. 768 (Mo.App.1972), defective wiring caused a fire which destroyed the buyer's new automobile. The court awarded the buyer the full purchase price of the automobile without identifying that portion of the price which represented recovery for consequential damages. Only the difference between the automobile's warranted and actual value at the time of acceptance could be recovered as general damages under 2–714(2). The defective wiring system reduced the actual value of the automobile at the time of acceptance below the purchase price, but the defect did not render the automobile worthless as of the acceptance date. A large part of the fire damage was therefore consequential.

> Had the parties excluded consequentials by contract, the court would have had to identify the value differential component of the buyer's total loss.

J. White & R. Summers, Uniform Commercial Code § 10–4 at 386–87 (2d ed. 1980).

Applying this limitation in calculating the damages recoverable in the case at bar, we rely on Tex.Bus. & Com.Code § 2.714 (Vernon 1968)—the damages provision in the U.C.C. most analogous to the failure of performance claim here [8]—and the analogy provided by Professors White and Summers in the sale of goods case described above. Section 2.714(b) tells us that the general difference-in-value damages to which Reynolds is entitled for Westinghouse's failure to provide a competent service engineer to install the purchased equipment is the difference in value to Reynolds at that time of the services provided and those promised. Presumably such damages would be determinable in terms of the fee that would have been charged Reynolds by a competent and properly prepared service engineer less the market value of the services that Reindl provided.

We recognize that it was a foreseeable consequence of Westinghouse's breach of contract that the alarm system might fail to detect ground current. It was also foreseeable that this failure might in turn permit burning within the transformer to occur unbeknownst to Reynolds and thus exacerbate the damage done to the transformer if short circuiting occurred. Such foreseeable damages are ordinarily recoverable under an expectancy theory, but they are nevertheless *consequential* losses and do not reflect the difference-in-value damages attributable to the original breach of contract. The proximate cause inquiry submitted to the jury here therefore cast too broad a net and captured more than those damages compensable under the contract. * * * In order to give effect to the consequential damages limitation agreed to by these parties, there must be a new trial on the issue of damages.[3]

III

In sum, we affirm the jury's finding of a breach of contract, but conclude that the losses compensable under the agreement did not include

8. § 2.714 provides as follows:

Buyer's Damages Breach in Regard to Accepted Goods

(a) Where the buyer has accepted goods and given notification (Subsection (c) of Section 2.607) he may recover as damages for any non-conformity of tender the loss resulting in the ordinary course of events from the seller's breach as determined in any manner which is reasonable.

(b) The measure of damages for breach of warranty is the difference at the time and place of acceptance between the value of the goods accepted and the value they would have had if they had been as warranted, unless special circumstances show proximate damages of a different amount.

(c) In a proper case any incidental and consequential damages under the next section may also be recovered.

3. In light of our decision on the proper measure of damages, we also vacate the district court's award of pre-judgment interest. Westinghouse raises several attacks on that award in this appeal, but we express no opinion on the merit of those arguments. We note only that the issue of entitlement to prejudgment interest under Texas law is a slippery problem at best and that this court has pending before it an appeal involving the issue. In the present case we leave the matter for the district court to decide in the first instance on remand.

costs of repair. We therefore remand for a new trial on the issue of damages.*

Notes

1. What damages might Reynolds Metal Company have recovered from Westinghouse if Reynolds had been able to establish a breach of warranty and if there had been no disclaimers in the contract between the parties? What damages would be recoverable under U.C.C. § 2–714 if someone purchased an automobile that turned out to be a "lemon," and the seller could not repair the car properly, despite repeated efforts? ** Would it matter whether the buyer had purchased the car primarily for business or for personal use? Consider the sections of the Restatement (Second) of Contracts (1981) regarding consequential damages at p. 839, *supra* in answering these questions.

2. The measure of recovery for loss of use damages in an action for breach of warranty under the Uniform Commercial Code is discussed in Murray v. Holiday Rambler, Inc., 83 Wis.2d 406, 432–35, 265 N.W.2d 513, 525–27 (1978) ("lemon" motor home):

> "The jury awarded the plaintiffs $2,500 for loss of use of the motorhome from the date of revocation of acceptance, August 15, 1974, to the date of the verdict. * * *
>
> "However, we are of the opinion that the plaintiffs have not sustained their burden of proof with regard to loss of use damages in the amount of $2,500. Consequential damages need not be shown with mathematical precision. Official Comment 4, sec. 2–715, UCC. Nevertheless, the burden of proving consequential damages is on the buyer, Official Comment 4, sec. 2–715, UCC; he must prove by credible evidence to a reasonable certainty that such damages were suffered and must prove, at least to a reasonable probability, the amount of these damages. * * *
>
> "Here, there was evidence with regard to the period of time during which the motorhome was unusable, and with regard to the approximate rental cost of a replacement motorhome, but there was no evidence of the extent to which the motorhome would have been used by the plaintiffs if it had not been defective.
>
> "Mr. Murray testified that he was unable to use the motorhome from January 30, 1974, to March 10, 1974, and the motorhome apparently remained unusable for much of the period from March 10th to July, 1974. Although the plaintiffs made a fishing trip in the motorhome in May without much trouble, they were forced to shorten the Colorado trip by one week as a result of the problems with the vehicle, and the vehicle was not used for any additional trips prior to the trial. It had been driven only once or twice, over a four-mile route between the plaintiffs' former resi-

* *See generally* Samuels, The Unconscionability of Excluding Consequential Damages under the Uniform Commercial Code When No Other Meaningful Remedy Is Available, 43 U.Pitt.L.Rev. 197 (1981); Shanker, Retreat to Progress: A Proposal to Eliminate Damage Awards for Loss of Business Profits, 85 Com.L.J. 83 (1980).

** For a discussion of this issue, see McGrady v. Chrysler Motors Corp., 46 Ill. App.3d 136, 4 Ill.Dec. 705, 360 N.E.2d 818 (1977) (plaintiff purchased a "lemon" automobile; total repair charges were $907; jury awarded $17,314.60 actual damages and $2,685.40 punitive damages; plaintiff offered to remit $10,000; court entered judgment against defendant for $7,314.60 (the exact purchase price) and denied punitive damages; affirmed on appeal).

dence and a new residence, and Mr. Murray had lived in it for approximately one week while they were moving.

"There was testimony that the rental cost of a comparable vehicle was approximately $155 per week plus eight cents per mile traveled. However, there was no evidence that the Murrays had in fact rented a replacement. Although Mr. Murray testified that the motorhome was purchased '* * * to go on trips, use it for vacations and fishing and whatever you use one for,' there was no evidence of the extent to which it would have been used. * * *

"Damages for loss of use of a recreational vehicle should be founded upon credible evidence of the use which would have been made of the vehicle if not for the defects, or upon evidence of expenses actually incurred as a result of the vehicle's inoperability. Such losses should not be calculated simply by reference to the number of days the vehicle sits idle, absent evidence that the vehicle would have been in use for the entire period.

"The only definite testimony concerning lost use of the motorhome was to the effect that the Colorado trip was cut short by one week. * * *

"Based upon our review of the evidence bearing upon loss of use of the motorhome, we determine that $500 is a reasonable sum to award the plaintiffs for loss of the use of the vehicle."

GEM JEWELERS, INC. v. DYKMAN

New York Supreme Court, Appellate Division, 1990.
160 A.D.2d 1069, 553 N.Y.S.2d 890.

LEVINE, JUSTICE.

* * *

In August 1984 plaintiff entered into an agreement with defendant Columbia–Art Store Equipment Company (hereinafter defendant) for the construction and installation of new, custom-designed jewelry cabinets, cases and fixtures for plaintiff's retail jewelry store in the City of Gloversville, Fulton County, for a total price of $36,000. The items were to be built in accordance with plans and specifications drawn by a California-based designer specializing in jewelry stores who had been retained to design the renovation of plaintiff's store. Cabinets, cases and fixtures were installed in the fall of 1984. After paying over $32,000 on the contract, plaintiff wrote to defendant's president in May 1986 complaining of the workmanship and of the fact that solid cherry hardwood cases were "ordered and paid * * * for", but "we received [only] veneered particle board". Defendant's president responded by denying that there were any defects and suggested that the unpaid balance was sufficient to cover any unsatisfactory items. Plaintiff subsequently brought this action for breach of contract, breach of warranty and fraud. Defendant counterclaimed for $3,000, representing the alleged unpaid balance on the contract. After dismissal of plaintiff's fraud cause of action, the case proceeded to trial, at the conclusion of which the jury found in plaintiff's favor, awarding

$40,000 in damages and rejecting defendant's counterclaim. This appeal by defendant ensued.

* * *

[D]efendant argues that reversal was required because Supreme Court erred in its instructions on damages. The parties had agreed that, since the contract items had been accepted by plaintiff, the damage issue was controlled by U.C.C. 2–714. Under that section of the UCC, a buyer can recover damages "for any non-conformity of tender the loss resulting * * * from the seller's breach as determined in any manner which is reasonable" (U.C.C. 2–714[1]). However, the measure of damages for breach of warranty "is the difference * * * between the value of the goods accepted and the value they would have had if they had been as warranted, unless special circumstances show proximate damages of a different amount" (U.C.C. 2–714[2]). The reference to value in U.C.C. 2–714(2) is to the fair market value of the goods (*see,* 4 Anderson, Uniform Commercial Code § 2–714:5, at 471 [3d ed]).

In its instructions to the jury on plaintiff's breach of contract cause of action, Supreme Court charged alternative measures of damages, i.e., the "actual cost of making the goods meet the requirements of the contract", and "the difference in value between the goods as accepted and the value of the goods had they been in conformance with the contract". Charging damages for breach of warranty, the court adhered to the language of U.C.C. 2–714(2). Supreme Court then directed the jury to select a reasonable measure of damages. Defendant excepted to that portion of the charge which permitted the jury to award damages on the basis of cost to correct, and also excepted on the same ground to the court's supplemental charge on the general definition of damages, in response to the jury's request. Defendant claims that, in this case, the evidence only supported an award of damages based upon the difference between the value of the goods as accepted and their value had they been as warranted. It is asserted that Supreme Court's departure from this measure of damages in its charge was prejudicial, in that it invited the jury to compensate plaintiff on the basis of the replacement costs for solid wood cabinets and cases, an unacceptable standard under U.C.C. 2–714. Again, we disagree.

* * * First, plaintiff's evidence clearly showed that the cabinets and cases called for under the agreement were custom-designed specifically for plaintiff's store and further supported the inference that solid wood was specifically required for aesthetic reasons, as communicated to defendant; thus, special circumstances existed justifying a departure from the ordinary standard of damages based upon the difference between value of the goods as accepted and value as warranted. As this case can be found to involve unique goods not bought and sold on the open market, it can reasonably be concluded that the standard breach of warranty measure of damages under U.C.C. 2–714(2) was inadequate * * *. While Supreme Court's instructions could have been more explicit regarding such special circumstances, any deficiency was not preserved by defendant's exception to the submission to the jury of any measure of damages other than one based upon the value of the goods as accepted and value as warranted. Under the

foregoing special circumstances, cost of replacement was a proper measure of damages under U.C.C. 2–714(2) * * *.

Moreover, particularly in the case of goods not regularly traded on the open market, replacement cost is a proper method of determining the value of goods as warranted under U.C.C. 2–714(2). * * * Thus, the jury could validly have used the replacement cost of solid cherry wood cabinets and cases in making its award, even if no alternative measure of damages had been submitted to it by Supreme Court.

Defendant also argues that the jury's award of $40,000 to plaintiff was excessive. We find that there is evidence substantially supporting this amount. Specifically, there was testimony that the cost in 1984 to replace the cabinets, cases and fixtures with items conforming to the contract was approximately $44,000. The designer of the cabinets and cases, who saw them in plaintiff's store in May 1986, described their appearance as "horrible", and plaintiff's qualified expert appraiser described them as made of "a very thin veneer on a pressed board * * * of a sawdust composition" with the veneer "bubbling and peeling" on many cases and colors that did not match. The jury, therefore, could reasonably have concluded that the value of the contract items as supplied by defendant was not more than their salvage value in 1984 as used fixtures, as testified to by plaintiff's expert. Thus, damages of $40,000 were not excessive, despite being more than the contract price.

* * *

Judgment affirmed, with costs.

Notes

1. In *Gem Jewelers* does the court need the discussion of inadequacy of the "ordinary standard" of breach of warranty damages? Where do you usually see such a discussion? How do cases involving tortious interference with personal property use cost of repair to measure damages? *See* pp. 382–410 *supra*. Should the measurement of diminution in value be different in contract cases than in tort cases?

2. Note that Gem Jewelers received more than it had contracted to pay. Was that a windfall?

3. If a wholesaler who buys defective goods has to reduce the resale price of those goods to the buyer who had contracted to purchase the goods, is that reduction the U.C.C. § 2–714(2) "difference at the time and place of acceptance between the value of the goods accepted and the value they would have had if they had been warranted". Carbontek Trading Co., Ltd. v. Phibro Energy, Inc., 910 F.2d 302 (5th Cir.1990) says it is. Do you agree? How does that case compare with Transoil (Jersey) Ltd. v. Belcher Oil Co., 950 F.2d 1115 (5th Cir.) (buyer of oil with higher vanadium content than provided in contract cannot use price at which it sold the nonconforming oil as evidence of the value of the oil received because that price may have reflected a collapse of the market for oil), *cert. denied,* ___ U.S. ___, 113 S.Ct. 90, 121 L.Ed.2d 53 (1992).

2. *Action by Seller*

SPRAGUE v. SUMITOMO FORESTRY COMPANY, LTD.

Supreme Court of Washington, En Banc, 1985.
104 Wash.2d 751, 709 P.2d 1200.

DORE, JUSTICE.

This action involves a claim by Clyde Sprague against Sumitomo Forestry Company, Ltd. for breach of contract arising from Sumitomo's unconditional cancellation of a log purchase contract.

* * *

Via a special verdict form, the jury found (1) that there was no mutual rescission; (2) that there was a breach and no waiver; (3) that the contract price was $197,204 and the resale price was $144,924 with net contractual damages of $52,280; (4) that Sprague sustained incidental damages of $216,498 for the following items: (a) cost of refinancing, $39,674; (b) extra transportation cost, $5,612; (c) loss of revenue on Flip Blowdown not covered by contract, $9,121; (d) loss of logging time, 11 weeks, $171,200; and (e) cost of moving tower, $2,115.

The major thrust of Sumitomo's appellate argument here is that Sprague did not give the requisite notice of intention to resell the canceled goods as required by RCW 62A.2–706(3) and, therefore, Sprague is not entitled to recover the difference between the contract price and the resale price.

RESALE PRICE DIFFERENTIAL

The catalogue of a seller's remedies in a breach of contract case governed by the sale of goods provisions of the Uniform Commercial Code is found in RCW 62A.2–703. In the present case, the catalogue of available remedies can quickly be reduced to two; these are:

(1) resale and recovery under RCW 62A.2–706, or

(2) recovery of the difference between the contract price and the market price under RCW 62A.2–708(1).

At trial Sprague apparently proceeded, pursuant to RCW 62A.2–706, to recover as damages the difference between the resale price and contract price. RCW 62A.2–706(1) provides that if the seller acts in good faith and in a commercially reasonable manner, he may recover the difference between the resale price and the contract price, together with any incidental damages allowed under RCW 62A.2–710, less expenses saved.

RCW 62A.2–706(2) goes on to permit resale at public or private sale. Of critical importance here is the requirement of RCW 62A.2–706(3) which provides that where an aggrieved seller resells goods which are the subject of a breach at a private sale, he must give the buyer "reasonable notification of his intention to resell."

In response to his failure to give specific notice of intention to resell, and in support of his judgment, Sprague argues: that the lack of notice was an affirmative defense which the buyer failed to plead, or that the buyer, from all the surrounding facts and circumstances, knew or should have known that the seller was going to resell the logs.

We deal first with whether the buyer needed to plead affirmatively as a defense the admitted lack of actual notice. This issue has not been previously addressed in Washington and only a few courts have reached this issue. Notice has been termed a "prerequisite" and a "condition precedent" to section 2–706 damage claims. * * * The burden of showing compliance with the notice requirement has been placed on the seller. * * *.

Williston has analyzed the issue as follows:

> Assuming that the seller has an affirmative duty to meet the requirements of § 2–706, a showing by the seller of compliance with this section would make it unnecessary for the buyer to raise a defense of lack of notice. All the buyer need do is show contradictory evidence of the seller's statement that he gave notice of his intention to resell.

3 A. Squillante & J. Fonseca, *Williston on Sales* § 24–7, at 418 (4th ed. 1974). This analysis, which finds notice as a prerequisite to bringing the claim, fits well with Washington law on affirmative defenses. CR 8(c) enumerates certain specific affirmative defenses which must be pleaded, but includes a general clause "and any other matter constituting an avoidance or affirmative defense." While this language is very general, it clearly contemplates matters which are in avoidance or are a specific affirmative defense. It would follow, therefore, that if notice of intent to resell is part of the seller's prima facie case, then lack of such notice would not have to be affirmatively denied.

To recover under RCW 62A.2–706, Sprague was required to give notice of intent to resell. This is an element of the seller's right to invoke the remedies of RCW 62A.2–706. Therefore, the buyer need not plead as an affirmative defense those elements which seller must prove.

Next, can the notice requirement be satisfied by the fact that the buyer knew or should have known that the seller intended to resell? From the plain language of RCW 62A.2–706, the giving by the seller of notice of intention to resell is a specific requirement to entitle seller to claim as damages the difference between resale price and the contract price. The words of subsection (3) are precise: "the seller *must* give the buyer reasonable notification of his intention to resell." (Italics ours.) RCW 62A.2–706(3).

Sprague contends Sumitomo knew or should have known that Sprague would make a resale and hold Sumitomo liable for the difference in resulting recovery. Thus, he argues that there was substantial compliance with the notice requirement. Sprague would have us hold that his filing of a lawsuit is sufficient notice. Whether such filing could ever be adequate notice is not before us. Factually, what is before us is a complaint that alleges a breach of contract and subsequent damages. It gives no notice of the remedy claimed other than damages. It was not an adequate substitute for the statutorily required notice of intent to resell.

MARKET PRICE DIFFERENTIAL

It is a general rule of appellate practice that the judgment of the trial court will not be reversed when it can be sustained on any theory, although different from that indicated in the decision of the trial judge. *Cheney v. Mountlake Terrace,* 87 Wash.2d 338, 552 P.2d 184 (1976). Although the jury verdict cannot be upheld under the resale method of determining damages, we find that the record supports the verdict under the alternate method of establishing damages, computed by measuring the difference between the market price and the contract price as provided in RCW 62A.2–708. This provision states:

> (1) Subject to subsection (2) and to the provisions of this Article with respect to proof of market price (RCW 62A.2–723), the measure of damages for non-acceptance or repudiation by the buyer is the difference between the market price at the time and place for tender and the unpaid contract price together with any incidental damages provided in this Article (RCW 62A.2–710), but less expenses saved in consequence of the buyer's breach.
>
> (2) If the measure of damages provided in subsection (1) is inadequate to put the seller in as good a position as performance would have done then the measure of damages is the profit (including reasonable overhead) which the seller would have made from full performance by the buyer, together with any incidental damages provided in this Article (RCW 62A.2–710), due allowance for costs reasonably incurred and due credit for payments or proceeds of resale.

It is fundamental under RCW 62A.2–703 and the sections that follow that an aggrieved seller is not required to elect between damages under RCW 62A.2–706 and 62A.2–708. RCW 62A.2–703 cumulatively sets forth the remedies available to a seller upon the buyer's breach. The pertinent commentary thereto indicates specifically that the remedies provided are cumulative and not exclusive and that as a fundamental policy Article 2 of the U.C.C. rejects any doctrine of election of remedy.

The seller has the burden of proof with respect to market price or market value. A seller cannot avail himself of the benefit of RCW 62A.2–708 when he has not presented evidence of market price or market value. However, the resale price of goods may be considered as appropriate evidence of the market value at the time of tender in determining damages pursuant to RCW 62A.2–708. * * *

While, admittedly, Sprague's resale came after the time for tender, it can still be utilized as a market price. * * * RCW 62A.2–723(2) states:

> (2) If evidence of a price prevailing at the times or places described in this Article is not readily available the price prevailing within any reasonable time before *or after* the time described or at any other place which in commercial judgment or under usage of trade would serve as a reasonable substitute for the one described may be used, * * *.

(Italics ours.)

The court is granted a "reasonable leeway" (Official Comments to RCWA 62A.2–723) in measuring market price. During the trial of this action, not only was there testimony to the effect that in an effort to mitigate damages, respondent Sprague sold the Flip Blowdown logs to five purchasers at private sales in 1981 and 1982, there was also testimony that the market price remained at the same level as at the time and place of tender in late 1980.

The net contractual damages of $52,280 ($197,204 contract price—$144,924 resale price) which was awarded respondent under the jury verdict thus equaled the measure of damages available under RCW 62A.2–708(1). We affirm this award.

Incidental Damages

Sprague is entitled also to incidental damages. RCW 62A.2–708 provides that the seller is entitled to the difference between the market price and contract price "together with any incidental damages provided in this Article (RCW 62A.2–710), but less expenses saved in consequence of the buyer's breach." Incidental damages are defined in RCW 62A.2–710 as follows:

> Incidental damages to an aggrieved seller include any commercially reasonable charges, expenses or commissions incurred in stopping delivery, in the transportation, care and custody of goods after the buyer's breach, in connection with return or resale of the goods or otherwise resulting from the breach.

At trial, the jury found that respondent sustained incidental damages of $216,498 for the following items: (a) cost of refinancing, $39,674; (b) extra transportation cost, $5,612; (c) loss of revenue on Flip Blowdown not covered by contract, $9,121; (d) loss of logging time, 11 weeks, $171,200; and (e) cost of moving tower, $2,115.

Sumitomo contends that some of these items are not incidental damages but more properly classified as consequential. Consequential damages are *not* allowed except as specifically provided in RCW Title 62A or by other rule of law. RCW 62A.1–106. Washington Comment to section 2–710 indicates that consequential damages are denied to sellers under the Uniform Commercial Code. RCWA 62A.2–710.

The distinction between consequential and incidental damages was made in *Petroleo Brasileiro, S.A. Petrobras v. Ameropan Oil Corp.*, 372 F.Supp. 503, 508 (E.D.N.Y.1974):

> While the distinction between the two is not an obvious one, the Code makes plain that incidental damages are normally incurred when a buyer (or seller) repudiates the contract or wrongfully rejects the goods, causing the other to incur such expenses as transporting, storing, or reselling the goods. On the other hand, *consequential damages* do not arise within the scope of the immediate buyer-seller transaction, but rather *stem from losses incurred by the non-breaching party in its dealings, often with third parties,* which were a proximate result of the breach, and which were reasonably foreseeable by the breaching party at the time of contracting.

(Citations omitted. Italics ours.)

We find that the loss of logging time is an inappropriate item of incidental damages. Sprague's damage claim for loss of logging time is essentially a claim for lost profits on a contract with Mt. Baker Plywood. In *Petroleo Brasileiro,* the court stated that "consequential damages do not arise within the scope of the immediate buyer-seller transaction [as do incidental damages], but rather stem from losses incurred by the non-breaching party in its dealings, often with third parties * * *" *Petroleo Brasileiro,* at 508. Applying this test to Sprague's claim for loss of logging time, Sprague's loss clearly did not arise within the scope of his contract with Sumitomo; instead, Sprague incurred this loss as a consequence of his delay in performing his contract with Mt. Baker Plywood, a third party. The fact that Sumitomo's conduct proximately caused Sprague's loss is irrelevant to this analysis. The focus is upon losses arising within the scope of the immediate contract. Accordingly, Sprague's loss can only be characterized as consequential. Therefore, the judgment awarded Sprague is reduced by $171,200.

The remaining costs are not seriously contested by appellant and appear to be appropriate items of incidental damages.

* * *

The judgment is reduced by $171,200 to eliminate an improper element of damages. As modified, the judgment is affirmed.

Notes

1. In what position was plaintiff seeking to be put, and was he? What U.C.C. sections were involved? Why did the court not award resale price differential damages? Was the court internally inconsistent in its reasoning when it affirmed the verdict on another theory?

2. Under the Uniform Sales Act, the resale price was evidence of the market price. R. Alderman, A Transactional Guide to the Uniform Commercial Code 374–75 (2d ed. 1983). Does the Uniform Commercial Code "increase the importance of the resale price by making it a conclusive test of the value of the rejected goods if the resale has been conducted in good faith and in a commercially reasonable manner"? *Id.*

3. Note that section 2–706 is the counterpart to the buyer's remedy of cover. Professor Eisenberg has argued convincingly that a seller who resells under § 2–706 should be precluded from recovering contract-market differential damages when the market price is lower than the resale price, just as a buyer who covers is limited to cover damages when the market price is higher than the cover price. Eisenberg, The Responsive Model of Contract Law, 36 Stan.L.Rev. 1107, 1141–44 (1984). That conclusion was upheld in Tesoro Petroleum Corp. v. Holborn Oil Co., Ltd., 145 Misc.2d 715, 547 N.Y.S.2d 1012 (1989). There plaintiff had contracted to sell gasoline at $1.30 per gallon, sold it a few days after defendant's breach for $1.10 per gallon but sought damages measured by the difference between the contract price and the market price at the time of breach of $.80 per gallon. The market for gasoline had taken a sudden, sharp drop. Plaintiff argued that § 2–703 gave it a choice between § 2–706 and § 2–708. The court said "granting [plaintiff] the $3,000,000 additional recovery that it seeks would result in a windfall which cannot be said to have been in the contemplation of the parties at the time of their negotia-

tions, and would be inconsistent with the policy of the Code * * * ". *Id.* at 1016.

4. As the court in *Sprague* noted, the resale in § 2–706 must be made in good faith and be commercially reasonable. This requirement has prohibited a plaintiff from collecting damages based on a resale price of iron scrap to its sister corporation at a noticed public sale when a previously held private sale of scrap that had been identified to the breached contract had yielded a higher resale price. Afram Export Corp. v. Metallurgiki Halyps, S.A., 592 F.Supp. 446 (E.D.Wis.1984), aff'd in part, rev'd in part, 772 F.2d 1358 (7th Cir.1985). *See also* Apex Oil Co. v. Belcher Co. of New York, Inc., 855 F.2d 997 (2d Cir.1988). In *Apex,* heating oil on a ship destined for defendant was sold shortly after defendant's breach, but plaintiff claimed resale damages for oil sold later, at a lower price. The Second Circuit said "at least with respect to fungible goods, identification for the purposes of a resale transaction does not necessarily require that the resold goods be the exact goods that were rejected or repudiated." *Id.* at 1002. But it held that "The rule that a 'resale should be made as soon as practicable after * * * breach', * * * should be stringently applied where, as here, the resold goods are not those originally identified to the contract. In such circumstances, of course, there is a significant risk that the seller, who may perhaps have already disposed of the original goods without suffering any loss, has identified new goods for resale in order to minimize the resale price and thus to maximize damages." *Id.* at 1007.

What happens if the plaintiffs in both *Afram Export* and *Apex Oil* could have sold their goods to the defendants and also to the subsequent buyers? This issue is explored in the cases that follow.

NEUMILLER FARMS, INC. v. CORNETT

Supreme Court of Alabama, 1979.
368 So.2d 272.

SHORES, JUSTICE.

Jonah D. Cornett and Ralph Moore, Sellers, were potato farmers in DeKalb County, Alabama. Neumiller Farms, Inc., Buyer, was a corporation engaged in brokering potatoes from the growers to the makers of potato chips. The controversy concerns Buyer's rejection of nine loads of potatoes out of a contract calling for twelve loads. A jury returned a verdict of $17,500 for Sellers based on a breach of contract. Buyer appealed. We affirm.

From the evidence, the jury could have found the following:

On March 3, 1976, the parties signed a written contract whereby Sellers agreed to deliver twelve loads of chipping potatoes to Buyer during July and August, 1976, and Buyer agreed to pay $4.25 per hundredweight. The contract required that the potatoes be United States Grade No. 1 and "chipt [sic] to buyer satisfaction." As the term was used in this contract, a load of potatoes contains 430 hundredweight and is valued at $1,827.50.

Sellers' potato crop yielded twenty to twenty-four loads of potatoes and Buyer accepted three of these loads without objection. At that time, the market price of chipping potatoes was $4.25 per hundredweight. Shortly thereafter, the market price declined to $2.00 per hundredweight.

When Sellers tendered additional loads of potatoes, Buyer refused acceptance, saying the potatoes would not "chip" satisfactorily. Sellers responded by having samples of their crop tested by an expert from the Cooperative Extension Service of Jackson County, Alabama, who reported that the potatoes were suitable in all respects. After receiving a letter demanding performance of the contract, Buyer agreed to "try one more load." Sellers then tendered a load of potatoes which had been purchased from another grower, Roy Hartline. Although Buyer's agent had recently purchased potatoes from Hartline at $2.00 per hundredweight, he claimed dissatisfaction with potatoes from the same fields when tendered by Sellers at $4.25 per hundredweight. Apparently the jury believed this testimony outweighed statements by Buyer's agents that Sellers' potatoes were diseased and unfit for "chipping."

Subsequently, Sellers offered to purchase the remaining nine loads of potatoes from other growers in order to fulfill their contract. Buyer's agent refused this offer, saying " * * * 'I'm not going to accept any more of your potatoes. If you load any more I'll see that they're turned down.' * * * 'I can buy potatoes all day for $2.00.' " No further efforts were made by Sellers to perform the contract.

At the time of Buyer's final refusal, Sellers had between seventeen and twenty-one loads of potatoes unharvested in their fields. Approximately four loads were sold in Chattanooga, Tennessee; Atlanta, Georgia; and local markets in DeKalb County. Sellers' efforts to sell their potato crop to other buyers were hampered by poor market conditions. Considering all of the evidence, the jury could properly have found that Sellers' efforts to sell the potatoes, after Buyer's final refusal to accept delivery, were reasonable and made in good faith.

This case presents three questions: 1) Was Buyer's refusal to accept delivery of Sellers' potatoes a breach of contract? 2) If so, what was the proper measure of Sellers' damages? and 3) Was the $17,500 jury verdict within the amount recoverable by Sellers under the proper measure of damages?

§ 7–2–703, Code of Alabama 1975 (UCC), specifies an aggrieved seller may recover for a breach of contract "Where the buyer *wrongfully* rejects * * * goods * * *." (Emphasis Added) We must determine whether there was evidence from which the jury could find that the Buyer acted wrongfully in rejecting delivery of Sellers' potatoes.

A buyer may reject delivery of goods if either the goods or the tender of delivery fails to conform to the contract. § 7–2–601, Code of Alabama 1975. In the instant case, Buyer did not claim the tender was inadequate. Rather, Buyer asserted the potatoes failed to conform to the requirements of the contract; i.e., the potatoes would not chip to buyer satisfaction.

The law requires such a claim of dissatisfaction to be made in good faith, rather than in an effort to escape a bad bargain. * * * A claim of dissatisfaction by a merchant-buyer of fungible goods must be evaluated using an objective standard to determine whether the claim is made in good faith. Because there was evidence that the potatoes would "chip" satisfactorily, the jury was not required to accept Buyer's subjective claim to the contrary. A rejection of goods based on a claim of dissatisfaction, which is not made in good faith, is ineffectual and constitutes a breach of contract for which damages are recoverable.

We next consider the proper measure of damages under the UCC. One of the remedies available to aggrieved sellers is the recovery of "* * * damages for nonacceptance (section 7–2–708) * * *." § 7–2–703, Code of Alabama 1975.

The measure of damages available through § 7–2–708, Code of Alabama 1975, is:

> "(1) Subject to subsection (2) and to the provisions of this article with respect to proof of market price (section 7–2–723), the measure of damages for nonacceptance or repudiation by the buyer is the difference between the market price at the time and place for tender and the unpaid contract price together with any incidental damages provided in this article (section 7–2–710), but less expenses saved in consequence of the buyer's breach.
>
> "(2) If the measure of damages provided in subsection (1) is inadequate to put the seller in as good a position as performance would have done then the measure of damages is the profit (including reasonable overhead) which the seller would have made from full performance by the buyer, together with any incidental damages provided in this article (section 7–2–710), due allowance for costs reasonably incurred and due credit for payments or proceeds of resale."

Buyer contends the jury verdict was excessive in view of § 7–2–708(1), Code of Alabama 1975. Based on a "per hundredweight" calculation, Buyer suggests the proper damage formula would be the difference between the contract price ($4.25 per hundredweight) and the "market price at the time and place for tender" (stipulated to be $2.00 per hundredweight); netting damages of $2.25 per hundredweight of potatoes in the rejected nine loads. We disagree.

On its face, the Code restricts the use of the subsection (2) measure of damages to those cases in which "* * * the measure of damages provided in subsection (1) is inadequate to put the seller in as good a position as performance would have done * * *." It is implicit within this provision, however, that, in order to employ the damage formula of subsection (1), there must not only exist a market for the contracted goods, but also the aggrieved seller must have a legal obligation to enter that market in his effort to avoid the foreseeable adverse consequences of buyer's breach of contract. Unless there is both a market and an obligation to enter it, the subsection (1) measure of damages is functionally inadequate and the aggrieved seller may seek redress through application of the measure of damages provided in subsection (2). * * *

In the instant case, at least some market for potatoes existed; but we must consider whether Sellers had a legal obligation to sell the rejected nine loads of potatoes in that market. * * *

Generally, the damages recoverable by a nonbreaching party will be measured as though that party had made a reasonable effort to avoid the foreseeable adverse consequences of the breach. In doing so, however, the nonbreaching party is not required to expose himself to undue risk, expense or humiliation. * * *

The jury apparently concluded that, although Sellers made reasonable and diligent efforts to sell as many loads as possible, only four loads of potatoes could be sold of the seventeen to twenty-one loads in Sellers' fields, at the time of tender. To expect Sellers to give priority to selling those potatoes allocated to Buyer's contract, rather than selling the unallocated portion of their inventory, would be to require them to forego an advantageous opportunity and sacrifice a substantive right. Such is not the law. Had Sellers' inventory consisted solely of the potatoes allocated to Buyer's contract or had Sellers failed to act reasonably to sell their entire inventory, they would have failed to meet the obligation imposed by the avoidable consequences rule. However, under the circumstances here presented, Sellers had no obligation to enter the market with those potatoes allocated to Buyer's contract. Absent such a legal obligation, the measure of damages provided in § 7–2–708(1), *supra,* is inadequate. Sellers may recover damages as measured by § 7–2–708(2), Code of Alabama 1975.

The contested portion of Sellers' contract calls for the payment of $4.25 per hundredweight of potatoes contained in nine loads, each of which contained 430 hundredweight; totaling $16,447.50. Additionally, Sellers claim interest of $1,480.20 for eighteen months, and $62.00 freight expenses incurred due to Buyer's breach. They contend that the total amount which they might have recovered was $17,989.78; and that the jury verdict should stand, because it does not exceed this amount.

The subsection (2) damage formula allows Sellers to recover "* * * the profit (including reasonable overhead) * * * from full performance by the buyer * * * incidental damages provided in this article (section 7–2–710), due allowance for costs reasonably incurred and due credit for payments or proceeds of resale." Under the facts of this case, we need not consider the ramification upon the subsection (2) damage formula of "due credit for payments," or "proceeds of resale." We now consider whether the jury's verdict is compatible with a damage award based on Sellers' "profit (including reasonable overhead)," "costs reasonably incurred" and "incidental damages" provided in § 7–2–710, Code of Alabama 1975.

The proper application of the subsection (2) measure of damages has received reflective consideration in R. Childres & R. Burgess, Seller's Remedies: The Primacy of UCC 2–708(2), 48 N.Y.U.L.Rev. 833 (1973). The authors define profit as "* * * an economic term, expressed in dollar amounts, representing the excess of that received [or which ought to have been received] over that expended in the business transactions or operations, the latter being also expressed in dollar amounts." *Childres & Burgess, supra* at 838.

The total amount expended in performance of a contract is composed of "fixed costs" and "variable costs." The "fixed costs," sometimes called "overhead," are those relatively stable expenses which are essential to performance and which continue even if the performance of a specific contract is temporarily halted. Recovery of overhead, to the extent that it is reasonably incurred, is specifically allowed as part of the award for profit by subsection (2). *Childres & Burgess, supra* at 846.

The "variable costs" are those expenses, incurred in reliance on the contract, which may be identified to a specific contract and which, if the contract were not to be performed, could be avoided. This element usually includes such items as the costs of material and labor which go directly to the production of the contract goods. If the breach occurs at a time when the aggrieved seller has already incurred variable costs, recovery for these damages is allowable as part of "costs reasonably incurred" under subsection (2). *Childres & Burgess, supra* at 860. We note, however, that the variable costs which an aggrieved seller might have avoided by diligent and reasonable efforts are not "reasonably incurred" and may not be recovered under § 7–2–708(2), *supra.*

Suffice it to say that there is evidence in the record from which the jury could reasonably conclude that the Sellers substantially performed their part of the bargain and had incurred substantially all of the expenses incidental to performance on their part. This being so, the jury's verdict of $17,500 was within those damages recoverable by Sellers as a consequence of Buyer's breach of contract.

Affirmed.

Notes

1. In *Neumiller Farms,* the court allowed the plaintiff to recover prejudgment interest. For a discussion of prejudgment interest *see* pp. 225–229 *supra.*

2. Section 2–708(2) was written to change the law governing the damages recoverable by a "components seller":

> "A components seller is a seller who agrees to assemble or manufacture contract goods for a buyer. If the buyer breaches the contract before the goods are finished and the components seller reasonably elects not to complete production, courts and commentators generally agree that the seller is entitled to recover lost profits under 2–708(2).[76] This is a departure, however, from the common law and the Uniform Sales Act.
>
> "Common law courts generally awarded lost profits only to sellers of specially ordered goods. If there was a ready market for the goods the seller was limited to recovery of the contract price-market price differential. In addition, under the Uniform Sales Act it was required that the seller have access to a ready market. A seller electing not to complete

76. *See, e.g.,* Unique Sys., Inc., 622 F.2d 373; Nobs Chem., 616 F.2d 213; Neumiller Farms, Inc., 368 So.2d 272; Bead Chain Mfg. Co., 183 Conn. 266, 439 A.2d 314; Cesco Mfg. Corp. v. Norcross, Inc., 7 Mass.App. 837, 391 N.E.2d 270 (1979); Timber Access Indus. Co. v. U.S. Plywood–Champion Papers, Inc., 263 Or. 509, 503 P.2d 482 (1972); Detroit Power Screwdriver, 25 Mich.App. 478, 181 N.W.2d 828; Chicago Roller Skate Mfg. Co. v. Sokol Mfg. Co., 185 Neb. 515, 177 N.W.2d 25 (1970); J. White & R. Summers, [Handbook of the Law Under the Uniform Commercial Code § 7–13 (2d ed. 1980)]. *But see* Goetz & Scott, Measuring Sellers' Damages: The Lost–Profits Puzzle, 31 Stan.L.Rev. 323 (1979); Peters, Remedies For Breach of Contracts Relating to the Sale of Goods Under the Uniform Commercial Code: A Roadmap For Article Two, 73 Yale L.J. 199 (1963).

performance could recover lost profits under Uniform Sales Act section 64(4) by showing that he could not make substitute contracts on the open market.

"Legislative history indicates that 2–708(2) was intended to apply in cases where a components seller reasonably ceases manufacture after learning of the breach. In its 1949 draft form, 2–708 did not indicate whether it was intended to supply a remedy for the components seller. In the 1954 revision, language was added to the section, unaccompanied by official explanation, which was designed to incorporate an appropriate measurement for salvage cases: 'due allowance for costs reasonably incurred and *due credit for* payments or *proceeds of resale.*' According to the drafters, this clause was added to clarify the right of the seller to realize junk value when it is manifestly useless to complete the operation of manufacture. Section 2–708(2) is tailored to fit the components seller who has reasonably ceased manufacture and attempts to salvage the contract materials he has on hand.

"The crucial question for lost profit recovery is whether the components seller's decision not to complete the goods was reasonable. The seller 'in the exercise of reasonable commercial judgment' and 'for the purposes of avoiding loss and of effective realization' may under 2–704 either 'complete the manufacture * * * or cease manufacture and resell [the goods] for scrap or salvage value * * *.' Completion makes the goods available for resale under 2–706, the seller's primary remedy, or if resale is impracticable, allows the seller to bring an action under 2–709 for the contract price. Once the components seller completes the goods after the breach, his status as a components seller is no longer relevant to the determination of which remedies are available to him. He is then in the same position as any other seller who is left in possession of completed goods after the breach.

"One commentator interprets 2–704 in language resembling the common law mitigation of damages doctrine.[77] According to Professor Harris, a seller's decision not to complete the goods should be deemed reasonable unless the seller knew or should have known that this decision would enhance his damages and a decision to complete would not unreasonably impair or harm his other interests.

"The most important criterion for determining whether the components seller's decision not to complete the goods was reasonable is the availability of a resale market for the goods. The absence of a resale market makes the measures in 2–706 and 2–708(1) inapplicable. The contract-resale measure in 2–706 cannot apply when the seller cannot resell the goods. The absence of a resale market also precludes application of the contract-market formula of 2–708(1). Moreover, in most situations, a commercially reasonable seller would not incur the expenses necessary to complete performance only to bring an action for the full contract price under 2–709.[78] Therefore, if the seller fails to find an available market in which to mitigate his damages, he may recover lost profits under 2–708(2).

77. Harris, A Radical Restatement of the Law of Seller's Damages: Sales Act and Commercial Code Results Compared, 18 Stan. L.Rev. 66, 72 (1965).

78. *See supra* note 32 (text of U.C.C. § 2–709).

Normally the buyer should not be liable for expenses the seller incurs toward completion

"Cases which present the least difficulty to courts evaluating components sellers' damage claims are those involving specially manufactured goods.[79] When the goods are specially manufactured, the absence of a resale market induces a salvage decision under 2–704(2). Courts uniformly agree that 2–708(2) is the only appropriate measure of damages in this situation.[80] The breaching buyer is the only market for a seller of specially manufactured goods. As the Connecticut Supreme Court stated in Bead Chain Manufacturing Co. v. Saxton Products, Inc., 'a seller of uncompleted components whose market is composed solely of the buyer in breach cannot adequately measure his damages in any other way.'

"Lost profit recovery due to the lack of a market is not limited to those situations where the lack of a market is attributable to the uniqueness of the goods. For example, in Unique Systems, Inc. v. Zotos International, Inc.,[81] the seller contracted to develop and manufacture a commercial hairspray system for a buyer. The buyer repudiated the contract before placing any orders. The court found that there was no market price because the buyer's anticipatory breach prevented the seller from producing the system in marketable quantities. The contract-market measure of damages was therefore inadequate and the seller was awarded lost profits.".

Note, Seller's Recovery of Lost Profits for Breach of a Sales Contract: Uniform Commercial Code Section 2–708(2), 11 Wm. Mitchell L.Rev. 227, 238–41 (1985).*

NATIONAL CONTROLS, INC. v. COMMODORE BUSINESS MACHINES, INC.

California Court of Appeal, First District, 1985.
163 Cal.App.3d 688, 209 Cal.Rptr. 636.

SCOTT, ASSOCIATE JUSTICE.

Respondent National Controls, Inc. (NCI) brought an action for breach of contract against appellant Commodore Business Machines, Inc. (Commo-

after being informed of the breach. In certain circumstances, however, the seller may make a commercially reasonable decision to complete the contract goods and then find that no market exists by the time the goods are completed. Because the seller's decision was reasonable at the time, the seller should recover the full contract price. However, "[i]t will take a persuasive lawyer to convince a court that it should not measure the 2–704 decision by hindsight when the plaintiff, having completed, finds himself unable to resell." J. White & R. Summers, *supra* note 30, § 7–5, at 263 (footnote omitted).

79. Specially manufactured goods are goods produced to the buyer's specifications and for which there exists no market but the buyer in breach. *See, e.g.,* Neumiller Farms, Inc., 368 So.2d at 275–76 (some market for chipping potatoes existed but seller had no obligation to give priority to selling those potatoes allocated to buyer's contract); Bead Chain Mfg. Co., 183 Conn. at 278–79, 439 A.2d at 320 (specially manufactured electronic parts); Industrial Circuits Co. v. Terminal Communications, Inc., 26 N.C.App. 536, 537, 216 S.E.2d 919, 920 (1975) (printed circuit boards). *See generally* Childress & Burgess, Seller's Remedies: The Primacy of U.C.C. § 2–708(2), 48 N.Y.U.L.Rev. 833, 876–77 (1983); J. White & R. Summers, *supra* note 2, § 7–5.

80. *See, e.g.,* Anchorage Centennial Dev. Co. v. Van Wormer & Rodrigues, Inc., 443 P.2d 596, 599 (Alaska 1968); *Bead Chain Mfg. Co.,* 183 Conn. at 278–79, 439 A.2d at 320; *Detroit Power Screwdriver,* 25 Mich. at 486–88, 181 N.W.2d at 832–33; *Chicago Roller Skate Mfg. Co.,* 185 Neb. at 517–18, 177 N.W.2d at 27.

81. 622 F.2d 373.

dore). After a court trial, judgment was entered awarding NCI over $280,000 in damages, and Commodore has appealed.

I

NCI manufactures electronic weighing and measuring devices. Among its products is the model 3221 electronic microprocessor technology load cell scale (the 3221), which is designed to interface with a cash register for use at check-out stands. NCI sells the 3221 to cash register manufacturers, also termed original equipment manufacturers, or O.E.M.s. NCI does not maintain an inventory stock of the scales, but builds them to specific order by an O.E.M. The 3221 is a standard unit, which is modified by NCI to meet the specifications of each O.E.M. with respect to cash register compatibility, paint, and logo.

* * *

On March 31, 1981, in a phone conversation with Wiggins, Rogers placed a firm order for 900 scales: 50 to be delivered in May, 150 in June, 300 in July, and 400 in August. Wiggins and Rogers agreed on quantity, price, and delivery schedule. * * *

Delivery was made to Commodore of the first 200 units, and 300 units were ready to ship in June of 1981. As of that date, the remaining 400 units of the order were nearly complete. However, Commodore accepted only the first 50 scales, and did not accept or pay for the remaining 850 units. Thereafter, all of the 850 units were resold to National Semiconductor, an existing O.E.M. customer. NCI's vice president and general manager in charge of its Florida manufacturing facility testified that in 1980 and 1981, the plant had the production capacity to more than double its output of 3221's.

Among its findings and conclusions, the trial court concluded that the terms of the parties' contract were those established during their telephone discussions prior to and on March 31, 1981. * * *

The court also found that NCI was a "lost volume seller" who was entitled to recover the loss of profit it would have made on the sale of the 850 units to Commodore, notwithstanding its subsequent resale of those units to another customer.

* * *

III

Commodore also contends that the trial court erred when it relied on section 2708, subdivision (2), to award NCI damages by way of lost profits. In a related argument, Commodore contends that if lost profits were the proper measure of damages, it was entitled under the plain language of section 2708 to credit for the proceeds of NCI's resale of the contract goods to National Semiconductor.

Damages caused by a buyer's breach or repudiation of a sales contract are usually measured by the difference between the resale price of the goods and the contract price, as provided by Uniform Commercial Code section 2–706. When it is not appropriate to use this difference to measure the seller's loss (as when the goods have not been resold in a commercially reasonable manner), the seller's measure of damages is the difference between the market and the contract prices as provided in Uniform Commercial Code section 2–708, subdivision (1). Ordinarily, this measure will result in recovery equal to the value of the seller's bargain. However, under certain circumstances this formula is also not an adequate means to ascertain that value, and the seller may recover his loss of expected profits on the contract under subdivision (2) of Uniform Commercial Code section 2–708. (3 Hawkland, Uniform Commercial Code Series (1982–1984) §§ 2–708—2–708:04.)

Section 2708[(2)] provides: * * *

> "(2) If the measure of damages provided in subdivision (1) is inadequate to put the seller in as good a position as performance would have done then the measure of damages is the profit (including reasonable overhead) which the seller would have made from full performance by the buyer, together with any incidental damages provided in this division (Section 2710), due allowance for costs reasonably incurred and due credit for payments or proceeds of resale."

When buyers have repudiated a fixed price contract to purchase goods, several courts elsewhere have construed subdivision (2) of Uniform Commercial Code section 2–708 or its state counterpart to permit the award of lost profits under the contract to the seller who establishes that he is a "lost volume seller," *i.e.,* one who proves that even though he resold the contract goods, that sale to the third party would have been made regardless of the buyer's breach. The lost volume seller must establish that had the breaching buyer performed, the seller would have realized profits from two sales. (*See* Goetz & Scott, Measuring Sellers' Damages: The Lost–Profits Puzzle (1979) 31 Stan.L.Rev. 323, 326.)

In Neri v. Retail Marine Corporation, [30 N.Y.2d 393, 285 N.E.2d 311, 334 N.Y.S.2d 165 (1972)], seller contracted to sell a new boat, which it ordered and received from its supplier. The buyer then repudiated the contract. Later, seller sold the boat to another buyer, for the same price. The court relied on Uniform Commercial Code section 2–708, subdivision (2), to award the seller its lost profits under the contract, reasoning that the record established that market damages would be inadequate to put the seller in as good a position as performance would have done. The court drew an analogy to an auto dealer with an inexhaustible supply of cars. A breach of an agreement to buy a car at a standard price would cost that dealer a sale even though he was able to resell the car at the same price. In other words, had the breaching buyer performed, seller would have made two sales instead of one. (*Id.,* at pp. 312–315.)

While the seller in *Neri* was a retailer, the lost volume seller rule is also applicable to manufacturers. (Nederlandse, etc. v. Grand Pre–Stressed Corp., [466 F.Supp. 846 (E.D.N.Y.1979), aff'd 614 F.2d 1289 (2d Cir. 1979)]). In *Nederlandse,* seller, a manufacturer of steel strand, brought an action against buyer for breach of an agreement to purchase approximately 1,180 metric tons of strand. Defendant had accepted only about 221 tons, and repudiated the remaining 958 tons, of which 317 tons had been already produced by seller. Seller resold the 317 tons to various third party purchasers. (*Id.,* at p. 849.)

The court held that seller was entitled to lost profits under Uniform Commercial Code section 2–708, subdivision (2), and that no set-off would be allowed for profits earned through the sales to third parties. The evidence established that seller had sufficient production capacity to supply not only the 1,180 tons required by the contract, but also the 317 tons sold to third parties. The fact that seller was a manufacturer rather than a retailer, and that he produced only to order rather than maintaining an inventory, was of no significance in determining the applicability of Uniform Commercial Code section 2–708. (*Id.,* at pp. 853–854.)

Commodore accurately points out that the lost volume seller rule has been criticized by some commentators as overly simplistic. (Goetz & Scott, *supra,* 31 Stan.L.Rev. 323, 330–354.) Nevertheless, those courts considering the question have held that Uniform Commercial Code section 2–708 does allow lost profits to a "lost volume seller" and that criticism has not resulted in any revision of the section.

Commodore also contends that if NCI was entitled to lost profits under the contract, Commodore should have received credit for the proceeds of the resale.

The literal language of section 2708, subdivision (2), does provide some support for that contention: "If the measure of damages provided in subdivision (1) is inadequate to put the seller in as good a position as performance would have done then the measure of damages is the profit (including reasonable overhead) which the seller would have made from full performance by the buyer, *together with * * * due credit for payments or proceeds of resale.*" (Emphasis added.) However, courts elsewhere have uniformly held that the underscored language does not apply to a lost volume seller. (*See* Teradyne, Inc. v. Teledyne Industries, Inc., [676 F.2d 865 (1st Cir.1982)]).

As the court in Snyder v. Herbert Greenbaum & Assoc., Inc., [38 Md.App. 144, 380 A.2d 618 (1977)] explained, "Logically, lost volume status, which entitles the seller to the § 2–708(2) formula rather than the formula found in § 2–708(1), is inconsistent with a credit for the proceeds of resale. The whole concept of lost volume status is that the sale of the goods to the resale purchaser could have been made with other goods had there been no breach. In essence, the original sale and the second sale are independent events, becoming related only after breach, as the original sale goods are applied to the second sale. To require a credit for the proceeds of resale is to deny the essential element that entitles the lost volume seller to § 2–708(2) in the first place—the mutual independence of the contract and the resale.

> "Practically, if the 'due credit' clause is applied to the lost volume seller, his measure of damages is no different from his recovery under § 2–708(1). Under § 2–708(1) he recovers the contract/market differential and the profit he makes on resale. If the 'due credit' provision is applied, the seller recovers only the profit he makes on resale plus the difference between the resale price and the contract price, an

almost identical measure to § 2–708(1). If the 'due credit' clause is applied to the lost volume seller, the damage measure of 'lost profits' is rendered nugatory, and he is not put in as good a position as if there had been performance." (*Id.,* at p. 625.)

In this case, the evidence was undisputed that in 1980 and 1981, NCI's manufacturing plant was operating at approximately 40 percent capacity. The production of the 900 units did not tax that capacity, and the plant could have more than doubled its output of 3221's and still have stayed within its capacity. That evidence was sufficient to support the court's findings that NCI had the capacity to supply both Commodore and National Semiconductor, and that had there been no breach by Commodore, NCI would have had the benefit of both the original contract and the resale contract. Accordingly, the trial court correctly determined that NCI was a lost volume seller, that the usual "contract price minus market price" rule set forth in subdivision (1) of section 2708 was inadequate to put NCI in as good a position as performance would have done, and that NCI was therefore entitled to its lost profits on the contract with Commodore, without any set-off for profits on the resale to National Semiconductor.

Judgment is affirmed.*

Notes

1. One method of calculating "lost profits (including reasonable overhead)" under section 2–708(2) is to deduct from the contract price the "direct costs" that are attributed to contract performance. Under this formula, it is critical that direct costs be distinguished from overhead. *See* Teradyne, Inc. v. Teledyne Indus., Inc., 676 F.2d 865, 869–70 (1st Cir.1982); Scullin Steel Co. v. PACCAR, Inc., 748 S.W.2d 910, 912–15 (Mo.App.1988).

2. If the amount of the "lost volume seller's" profits are ascertainable at the time of the buyer's breach, prejudgment interest is recoverable. Comeq, Inc. v. Mitternight Boiler Works, Inc., 456 So.2d 264, 269 (Ala.1984) (prejudgment interest awarded); Autonumerics, Inc. v. Bayer Industries, Inc., 144 Ariz. 181, 696 P.2d 1330 (App.1984) (prejudgment interest denied).

3. The Seventh Circuit has a three part test for identifying a lost volume seller. *See* R.E. Davis Chemical Corp. v. Diasonics, Inc., 924 F.2d 709, 711 (7th Cir.1991):

> "We held that in order to qualify as a lost volume seller, a plaintiff must establish the following three factors:
>
> (1) that it possessed the capacity to make an additional sale,
>
> (2) that it would have been profitable for it to make an additional sale, and
>
> (3) that it probably would have made an additional sale absent the buyer's breach."

4. For a discussion of the type of evidence which indicates a seller is *not* a lost volume seller, *see* Bill's Coal Co. v. Board of Public Utilities, 887 F.2d 242, 245 (10th Cir.1989).

* For an excellent summary of the cases decided under section 2–708(2) of the Uniform Commercial Code, *see* Sebert, Remedies under Article Two of the Uniform Commercial Code, 130 U.Pa.L.Rev. 360, 383–407 (1981).

5. The defendant in *National Controls* was a merchant. Would the remedy imposed in *National Controls* be equally appropriate if the defendant were a consumer? To put this question into perspective, consider the following hypothetical:

> Buyer, a law school student, contracts with seller, a local stereo dealer, to purchase a stereo set, to be delivered one month later, for $750. Before the factory has begun to fill Buyer's order, Buyer repudiates the contract. Seller's factory cost for the stereo set ordered by Buyer is $450. Seller may purchase as many stereo sets from the manufacturer as it can sell.

Although an application of the "lost volume seller" rule would permit Seller to recover "lost profits (including reasonable overhead)" from Buyer, few retailers in fact attempt to recover such damages from breaching consumers. Eisenberg, The Bargain Principle and Its Limits, 95 Harv.L.Rev. 741, 797–98 (1982). Both Professors Eisenberg and Goldberg suggest that a cancellation charge would be a preferable remedy under these circumstances. *Id.;* Goldberg, An Economic Analysis of the Lost–Volume Retail Seller, 57 So.Cal.L.Rev. 283 (1984).

NOBS CHEMICAL, U.S.A., INC. v. KOPPERS CO., INC.

United States Court of Appeals, Fifth Circuit, 1980.
616 F.2d 212.

Before CHARLES CLARK, RONEY and HENDERSON, CIRCUIT JUDGES.

HENDERSON, CIRCUIT JUDGE:

Koppers Company contracted with the plaintiffs, Nobs Chemical, U.S.A., Inc. (hereinafter referred to as "Nobs") and Calmon–Hill Trading Corporation (hereinafter referred to as "Calmon–Hill") to purchase 1000 metric tons of cumene.[1] Koppers breached the contract. Nobs and Calmon–Hill brought suit in United States District Court for the Southern District of Texas, and the case was tried before the court sitting without a jury.

The district court found that the plaintiffs had arranged to purchase the cumene in Brazil for $400.00 a ton and to expend $45.00 per ton for the cost of transporting the cumene to the defendant, for a total expense of $445,000.00. Koppers agreed to buy the cumene for $540,000.00. The court applied Tex.Bus. & Com.Code § 2.708(b) (Vernon), and determined that the plaintiffs were entitled to recover their lost profits, $95,000.00 ($540,000.00 minus $445,000.00). The district court ruled that the plaintiffs could not recover the extra $25.00 per ton they allegedly were forced to pay their Brazilian supplier when the price per ton increased because their total order with the supplier was reduced from 4,000 metric tons to 3,000 metric tons because of Koppers' breach. The court decided this lost quantity discount amounted to consequential damages and was, therefore, not recoverable.

Nobs and Calmon–Hill appeal the measure of damages applied by the district court, and, assuming it is correct, they challenge the computation of

1. Cumene is "a colorless oily hydrocarbon * * * used as an additive for high-octane motor fuel. * * *" Webster's Third New International Dictionary 553 (1966).

those damages. The defendant, Koppers, cross-appeals, also claiming that the district court's calculation of damages under the lost profits method was incorrect.

We first turn to the issue of whether the district court was correct in applying the lost profits measure of damages to the plaintiffs' loss.

According to Tex.Bus. & Com.Code Ann. § 2.708 (Vernon)

> (a) * * * the measure of damages for non-acceptance or repudiation by the buyer is the difference between the market price at the time and place for tender and the unpaid contract price together with any incidental damages provided in this chapter (Section 2.710), but less expenses saved in consequence of the buyer's breach. * * *

The plaintiffs urge that subsection (a) should govern in this case. Because the market value of cumene dropped to between $220.40 and $264.48 a metric ton at the time of the breach, the plaintiffs contend that they should recover the difference between the contract price ($540,000.00) and the market price (between $220,400.00 and $264,480.00), substantially more than the $95,000.00 awarded them under subsection (b).

* * *

Because there does not appear to be any law directly on point, we take the liberty of looking to those more learned on the subject of the Uniform Commercial Code. Professors White and Summers, recognizing that § 2.708(b) is not the most lucid or best-drafted of the sales article sections, decided that the drafters of the Uniform Commercial Code intended subsection (b) to apply to certain sellers whose losses would rarely be compensated by the subsection (a) market price-contract price measure of damages, and for these sellers the lost profit formula was added in subsection (b). One such type of seller is a "jobber," who, according to the treatise writers, must satisfy two conditions: "[f]irst, he is a seller who never acquires the contract goods. Second, his decision not to acquire those goods after learning of the breach was not commercially unreasonable. * * * " J. White & R. Summers, Uniform Commercial Code § 7–10, at 228 (1972) (hereinafter cited as "White & Summers"). Nobs and Calmon–Hill clearly fit this description. The plaintiffs never acquired the goods from their Brazilian supplier, and, as White and Summers point out, an action for the purchase price or resale was therefore unavailable. *See* Tex.Bus. & Com. Code Ann. §§ 2.703, 2.704, 2.706, 2.709 (Vernon). *See also* American Metal Climax, Inc. v. Essex International, Inc., 16 U.C.C.Rep. 101, 115 (S.D.N.Y.1974) ("[C]ompensatory damages as provided in the contract-market formula of § 2–708(1) [§ 2.708(a)] are realistic only where the seller continues to be in a position to sell the product to other customers in the market.").

The plaintiffs argue, however, that in this case the measure of damages under subsection (a) would adequately compensate them and therefore, according to the terms of subsection (a), subsection (b) does not control. This is an intriguing argument. It appears that the drafters of § 2.708(a) did not consider the possibility that recovery under that section may be *more than* adequate. White & Summers, *supra,* § 7–12, at 232–233.

It is possible that the code drafters intended subsection (a) as a liquidated damage clause available to a plaintiff-seller regardless of his actual damages. There have been some commentators who agree with this philosophy. *See* C. Goetz & R. Scott, Measuring Sellers' Damages: the Lost–Profits Puzzle, 31 Stan.L.Rev. 323, 323–324 n. 2 (1979); E. Peters, Remedies for Breach of Contracts Relating to the Sale of Goods Under the Uniform Commercial Code: A Roadmap for Article Two, 73 Yale L.J. 199, 259 (1963). But, this construction is inconsistent with the code's basic philosophy, announced in Tex.Bus. & Com.Code Ann. § 1.106(a) (Vernon), which provides "that the aggrieved party may be put in as good a position as if the other party had fully performed" but not in a better posture. White & Summers, *supra,* § 7–12, at 232. * * * Moreover, White and Summers conclude that statutory damage formulas do not significantly affect the practices of businessmen and therefore "breach deterrence," which would be the purpose of the statutory liquidated damages clause, should be rejected in favor of a standard approximating actual economic loss. White & Summers, *supra,* § 7–12, at 232. No one insists, and we do not think they could, that the difference between the fallen market price and the contract price is necessary to compensate the plaintiffs for the breach. Had the transaction been completed, their "benefit of the bargain" would not have been affected by the fall in market price, and they would not have experienced the windfall they otherwise would receive if the market price-contract price rule contained in § 2.708(a) is followed. Thus, the premise contained in § 1.106 and Texas case law is a strong factor weighing against application of § 2.708(a).[3]

Our conclusion that the district court was correct in applying § 2.708(b) brings us to the second issue—was it error for the district court to refuse to award the plaintiffs the additional $75,000.00, which they were required to pay when they lost their quantity discount?

We believe the trial court was correct in declining to award the plaintiffs the extra $75,000.00.[4] Under § 2.708(b), in addition to profit, the seller may recover "incidental damages" and "due allowance for costs reasonably incurred." The code does not provide for the recovery of consequential damages by a seller. Tex.Bus. & Com.Code Ann. § 1.106(a) (Vernon); Petroleo Brasileiro, S.A. v. Ameropan Oil Corp., 372 F.Supp. 503, 508 (E.D.N.Y.1974); *Cf.* Tex.Bus. & Com.Code Ann. § 2.715 (Vernon) (buyer's remedies). "Incidental damages" are defined in Tex.Bus. & Com.Code Ann. § 2.710 (Vernon) as "any commercially reasonable charges, expenses or commissions incurred in stopping delivery, in the transportation, care and custody of goods after the buyer's breach, in connection with return or resale of the goods or otherwise resulting from the breach." The

3. White and Summers' condition forcing the damage formula of subsection (b) on the plaintiff-seller. They would require the defendant to prove that the measure of damages in subsection (a) would overcompensate the plaintiff. We do not find this to be a problem here, as the figures themselves refute any contention that the market price-contract price rule is anything but over-adequate compensation for the plaintiffs. [J. White & R. Summers, Uniform Commercial Code, § 7–12, at 232–233 (1972)].

4. Because we find that these expenses were not recoverable under § 2.708(b), it is unnecessary to decide whether the district court correctly termed these costs "consequential damages."

draftsmen's comment to the section states that the purpose is to "authorize reimbursement of the seller for expenses reasonably incurred by him as a result of the buyer's breach." We think it is clear that § 2.710 was intended to cover only those expenses contracted by the seller after the breach and occasioned by such things as the seller's need to care for, and, if necessary, dispose of, the goods in a commercially reasonable manner. *See,* Guy H. James Construction Co. v. L.B. Foster Co., No. 17,473 (Tex.Civ. App.1979) (cost of replacing material in stock for resale recoverable as incidental damages); Cesco Mfg. Corp. v. Norcross, Inc., ___ Mass.App. ___, 391 N.E.2d 270, 27 U.C.C.Rep. 126 (Mass.App.1979) (incidental damages awarded for storage and moving of goods wrongfully rejected); Lee Oldsmobile v. Kaiden, 32 Md.App. 556, 363 A.2d 270, 20 U.C.C.Rep. 117 (1976) (commissions paid to salesman and broker on resale, floor plan interest on cost of car between breach of contract for sale of car and resale, and transportation expenses recoverable as incidental damages); Harlow & Jones, Inc. v. Advance Steel Co., 424 F.Supp. 770 (E.D.Mich.1976) (charges for storage and handling of goods after breach recoverable as incidental damages); Neri v. Retail Marine Corp., 30 N.Y.2d 393, 334 N.Y.S.2d 165, 285 N.E.2d 311, 10 U.C.C.Rep. 950 (1972) (proper incidental damages include storage, upkeep, finance charges and insurance for boat after buyer breached contract for sale); Bache & Co. v. International Controls Corp., 339 F.Supp. 341 (S.D.N.Y.), aff'd 469 F.2d 696 (2d Cir.1972) (seller can recover as incidental damages commissions due him as result of buyer's breach); Hudgens v. Bain Equip. & Tube Sales, Inc., 459 S.W.2d 873 (Tex.Civ.App.1970) (expense of recovering and transporting goods not paid for awarded); *Cf.,* Industrial Circuits Co. v. Terminal Communications, Inc., 26 N.C.App. 536, 216 S.E.2d 919, 17 U.C.C.Rep. 996 (1975) ("bill back" charges which resulted when buyer failed to order a certain quantity not allowed).

Equally as clear is the premise that this lost discount is not a "cost reasonably incurred" within the meaning of § 2.708(b), which has been defined as "an amount equal to what he [the seller] has expended for performance of the contract that will now be valueless." White & Summers, *supra,* § 7–13, at 236. The extra $25.00 per ton does not fall within this definition, most obviously because it was not an expense necessary to the performance of the contract. Rather, it was simply an extra benefit the sellers did not receive from their supplier by reason of the buyer's breach.

* * *

Affirmed.

Notes

1. The issue posed by *Nobs Chemical Co.* is whether market differential damages should set a floor under the plaintiff's recovery. For a cogent discussion of this issue, see Eisenberg, The Responsive Model of Contract Law, 36 Stan.L.Rev. 1107, 1138–44 (1984): *

"[S]ome commentators have argued that market-price damages should set a floor under the plaintiff's recovery and that often such a floor can

* Reprinted with permission of the Stanford Law Review.

only be justified under a standardized approach to damages.[77] I shall show in this section that in all but a few cases a market-price damages floor is justified even under an individualized approach, and that in those few remaining cases, market-price damages should not be awarded.

"*Breach by the buyer.* Let us begin with the following hypothetical, taken from an article by David Simon, who in turn drew upon an example in *Restatement (First):*

> [*Stock Problems.*] *A* contracts to sell to *B* 1000 shares of stock owned by *A,* at a price of $10 per share. The shares are freely traded in the market. On the delivery date, when the market price is $6 per share, *B* breaches and refuses to accept delivery. *A* does not supply any proof that he sold at $6 per share or suffered any other actual loss.

In analyzing this hypothetical, Simon argues that *A* should recover $4,000, and suggests that under an individualized approach *A* would recover $4,000 only if he could prove that as a result of *B's* breach he was compelled to sell the stock at $6 per share or less. The argument is right, but the suggestion is wrong. Simon here confuses a wealth effect and an income effect. If *A* did not sell the stock at $6 per share or less, he may not have realized a $4,000 loss in income, but he has clearly lost $4,000 in wealth, and therefore should recover that amount under an individualized approach regardless of what he did with his stock. Call the corporation whose stock is involved *C.* Since *C's* stock is homogeneous and freely traded, there is no legal connection between the *C* stock that *A* owned on the contract date and the *C* stock he must deliver to *B.* Suppose, for example, *A* had not owned any *C* stock on the contract date. He still could have acquired 1,000 *C* shares on the delivery date, used those shares to fill his contract with *B,* and increased his wealth by $4,000. As it happens, *A* did own 1,000 shares of *C* stock on the contract date, but no rule of law required *A* to fill his contract with *B* by delivering those particular shares. On the contrary, *A* was perfectly free to go into the market on the delivery date, buy 1,000 new shares of *C* stock, turn a $4,000 profit by filling his contract with the new shares, and retain his old *C* stock. Indeed, market-price damages are calculated as if *A* did just that: Under the market-price measure, a seller does not recover the difference between the contract price and his original cost for the commodity, but rather the difference between the contract price and the market price of the commodity at the date of the breach. As a result of *B's* breach, *A* lost the opportunity to turn a $4,000 profit by buying *C* stock on the delivery date and selling it to *B.* Under an individualized approach, therefore, *A* is entitled to $4,000 damages regardless of what he did with his old 1,000 *C* shares after *B's* breach.

* * *

"In short, under an individualized approach *A* should recover $4,000 without showing that he sold his stock at $6 per share or less. Indeed, *A* should recover $4,000 even if, by reason of a later market rise, he sold his *C* stock at more than $6 per share, or even if *A* still owned his *C* stock at the time of trial and it was then worth $10 per share. To put the matter

77. *See* Simon, A Critique of the Treatment of Market Damages in the Restatement (Second) of Contracts, 81 Colum.L.Rev. 80 (1981); Simon & Novack, Limiting the Buyer's Market Damages to Lost Profits: A Challenge to the Enforceability of Market Contracts, 92 Harv.L.Rev. 1395 (1979).

more generally, in any contract for the sale of a readily marketable homogeneous commodity, the seller always incurs damages at least equal to the spread between contract price and market price, because, had performance occurred, he could always have turned a profit equal to that spread by filling the contract through a contemporaneous market purchase. Accordingly, even under an individualized approach, market-price damages should always set a floor under the seller's recovery in contracts for the sale of such a commodity, except where the seller himself forgoes the market-price measure by identifying goods to the contract and reselling them promptly for the very purpose of fixing damages.

"Difficulties may arise, however, where the commodity is differentiated. Essentially, these difficulties involve two sorts of cases. In the first type, the seller has made a contract to purchase the commodity from a third person, and the price under that contract exceeds the market price at the time of breach. Take, for example, the following hypothetical, also drawn from an illustration used by Simon:

> *Third–Party Supplier.* *A* contracts to sell to *B* a used grinding mill for $10,000. *A* had previously contracted to purchase the mill from *C* for $8,000. On the delivery date the market value of the mill is $6,000. *B* refuses to accept delivery.

Normally, *A* should recover damages of $4,000, representing the swing between making a $2,000 profit, by buying the mill at $8,000 and selling at $10,000, and incurring a $2,000 loss, by buying for $8,000 a mill worth only $6,000. Suppose, however, that *C* excuses *A* from performing, so that *A* does not incur the $2,000 loss. Should *A* then be limited to damages of $2,000 lost profit? Simon argues that $4,000 market-price damages are still appropriate. To analyze this problem, we must ask why *C* would excuse *A*. One possibility is that *C* expects something in return, such as reciprocal treatment in future dealings. In that case, the excuse is not cost-free to *A*, and while the precise cost must be indeterminate, it can be presumptively valued at $2,000. Or, *C* may give up his claim against *A* as a compassionate act to relieve the hardship caused by *B's* breach. In that case, if *A* is made whole by a $4,000 judgment against *B*, he would be morally obliged to pass through $2,000 of that amount to *C*. Indeed, *A* may implicitly promise to make such a pass-through. If *B* pays *A* $4,000 and *A* does what he should, therefore, both *A* and *C* would end up just where they would have been if *B* had performed. In both these cases, damages of $4,000 would be justified under individualized principles.

"On the other hand, *C* may release *A* because *C* values the mill at $8,000 or more. Since a used grinding mill is relatively differentiated, the $6,000 market price is likely to be derived by extrapolating from sales of similar mills. *C* may place a special value on his own mill because, say, it has special characteristics suited to his needs, or it is already installed, or he knows it is not a lemon. Here *C* will expect nothing more of *A*, *A* will have lost wealth of only $2,000, and damages of $2,000 will put *A* where he would have been if *B* had performed. Similarly, suppose that *A* settles *C's* claim for $1,000, incurring legal expenses of $500 in the process. Here too, *C* presumably expects nothing more from *A*, and under an individualized approach *A* should recover only $3,500 ($2,000 lost profit plus $1,500 out-of-pocket costs).

"Simon argues that in cases like the *Third–Party Supplier* hypothetical the seller should recover $4,000 regardless of the circumstances 'to deter breach * * *, to enable the market to function in an orderly and predictable fashion, to avoid burdensome complications of proof, to simplify and make uniform the law, to provide a readily predictable result for businessmen * * *, and to facilitate settlements.' The emphasis on deterring breach runs counter to the traditional contract-law approach that damages should be based not on deterrence but on compensation. In any event, expectation damages will not fail to deter breach merely because they are measured in an individualized manner. The remaining arguments, which are those invoked in support of any kind of standardized contract-law rule, unrealistically exaggerate the difficulty of administering individualized damage rules in the present context."

2. Note the language used in Union Carbide Corp. v. Consumers Power Co., 636 F.Supp. 1498, 1501 (E.D.Mich.1986) in following *Nobs Chemical:*

"[Union Carbide's claims ignore] the question of what measure of damages is appropriate where market price damages greatly over-compensate the seller vis-a-vis what it would receive if the contract had been performed. Presumably, Union Carbide would claim the seller somehow deserved this exorbitant award as the premium for standing ready to perform in the face of the buyer's breach.

"This position is contrary to the clear intention of the UCC that remedies should place the parties in the same position as if the contract had been performed. U.C.C. § 1–106 * * *."

3. Two commentaries on seller's remedies under the Uniform Commercial Code conclude that the Code *as construed by the courts* provides appropriate remedies. Schlosser, Damages for the Lost–Volume Seller: Does an Efficient Formula Already Exist? 17 U.C.C.L.J. 238 (1985); Note, Seller's Recovery of Lost Profits for Breach of a Sales Contract: Uniform Commercial Code Section 2–708(2), 11 Wm. Mitchell L.Rev. 227 (1985).

JELEN AND SON, INC. v. BANDIMERE

Supreme Court of Colorado, en banc, 1990.
801 P.2d 1182.

JUSTICE ERICKSON delivered the Opinion of the Court.

* * *

I

Samson Bandimere owned property in Jefferson County, which consisted of approximately four acres, two large warehouse-type buildings, and several small buildings. From the late 1970s until September 1985, Bandimere rented space on the land to a succession of tenants engaged in mining-related business operations including the alleviation and recovery of precious metals. The last tenant defaulted in 1985, and Bandimere took possession of the property, some equipment, and barrels of chemicals on the premises, to offset the money owed for back rent. Bandimere testified that he was unsure what some of the equipment was, or what the barrels contained, other than liquids or chemicals of some type. Bandimere was told, however, by one of the ex-tenants that he probably had "an EPA problem" with the barrels. There were approximately 30–40 fifty-five gallon barrels, most without lids and many that were corroded or leaking. Some of the barrels had labels, but many did not.

Bandimere did not have the contents of the barrels examined by experts, but sought to sell the equipment and barrels as a single lot. In December 1985, Bandimere contacted Michael Jelen, the president of Jelen and Son, which specialized in the purchase and resale of mining equipment. Jelen examined the items on Bandimere's property, and agreed to exchange a compressor Bandimere wanted for the materials, equipment, and barrels on the premises and $3,500. * * *

Bandimere also testified that Jelen agreed to retrieve the equipment and barrels from Bandimere's property, although Jelen disputed that claim. Regardless of the original understanding, some time in late December Bandimere agreed, in a telephone conversation with Jelen, to deliver the items to one of Jelen's properties located on North Indiana Street in Jefferson County.

Approximately one month later, on the morning of January 28, 1986, Bandimere loaded the barrels on two flatbed trucks, and he and an employee drove to Jelen's property intending to make delivery of the barrels, many of which were still leaking and open. As Bandimere approached Jelen's property, he apparently got lost and turned around in the parking lot of the local fire department, approximately one block from Jelen's yard. The fire marshall, Henry Binder, happened to glance out his window and noticed the trucks with liquid splashing out of the barrels. Binder was an acquaintance of the Jelens, and contacted Rosemary Jelen after he saw the trucks enter her property. After being told Michael Jelen was out of town, and that she was not expecting delivery of any barrels, Binder and two Jefferson County sheriffs went to the Jelen yard to investigate. When Bandimere said that he did not know what the chemicals were, Binder called for a hazardous materials expert and restricted access to the area. The barrels were subsequently found to contain, among other things, acid and potassium cyanide that, when combined, produce hydrocyanic acid, a deadly gas.

Both the trucks and barrels were impounded. Jelen refused to accept the barrels containing the chemicals or hazardous material, and the authorities determined they were Bandimere's responsibility. With the assistance of Arvada's hazardous material team, the barrels were stabilized and their contents cleaned-up. The chemicals were eventually sent to a mining company. Bandimere was cited with criminal charges for causing a hazardous waste incident, but those charges were subsequently dismissed after Bandimere agreed to pay all costs associated with the clean-up of the materials.

In August 1987, Bandimere filed suit against Jelen claiming it was Jelen's refusal to accept the barrels that caused Bandimere to be held responsible for the clean-up costs. Trial was to a jury, which returned a verdict in favor of Bandimere and awarded damages, including attorney fees spent by Bandimere to defend against the criminal charges.

Jelen appealed to the court of appeals, which affirmed the jury verdict and award with the exception of the attorney fees. The court held, *inter alia,* that "[i]n breach of contract cases, the breaching party is liable in damages for all natural and proximate consequences of the breach which could have been reasonably anticipated at the time of the execution of the contract * * * includ[ing] those assessed here: the cost of clean-up and disposal * * *." The court found, "Bandimere's transportation of the chemicals was in direct response to Jelen's refusal to pick them up and his suggestion that Bandimere deliver them himself."

II

The sales of goods in Colorado is controlled by Title 4, Article 2, C.R.S. (1973 & 1990 Supp.), which substantially adopts the Uniform Commercial Code (U.C.C.).

Although in contention at trial, we assume for the purposes of this review that there was a contract between the parties that included the exchange of the barrels of chemicals in issue, some other equipment and materials, and $3,500 for a compressor valued at $17,500. Under the contract, as originally written, Jelen was to retrieve the chemicals and all other equipment from Bandimere at Bandimere's place of business. Our assumption is based on the instructions to the jury requiring the jury to find that there was a contract, that Jelen agreed to purchase the chemicals, that Jelen authorized Bandimere to deliver the chemicals, and that Bandimere suffered damages as a result of Jelen's breach if Bandimere was to recover damages. The jury verdict for Bandimere would be inconsistent with any other findings of fact. *See Knapp v. Hurd,* 100 Colo. 537, 68 P.2d 557 (1937).

III

Under the Uniform Commercial Code, consideration for goods may be payable in money, goods, realty, or otherwise. § 4–2–304, 2 C.R.S. (1973). "If it is payable in whole or in part in goods, each party is a seller of the goods which he is to transfer." *Id.* In this case, Bandimere is a seller of the chemicals, and his rights under the U.C.C. are limited to those of a seller against a breaching buyer. Even if Jelen did breach the contract, Bandimere's remedies are limited to those provided by section 4–2–703. Once Jelen breached the contract by not accepting the goods, Bandimere could:

(a) Withhold delivery of such goods;

(b) Stop delivery by any bailee as hereafter provided (section 4–2–705);

(c) Proceed under section 4–2–704 respecting goods still unidentified to the contract;

(d) Resell and recover damages as hereafter provided (section 4–2–706);

(e) Recover damages for nonacceptance (section 4–2–708) or in a proper case the price (section 4–2–709);

(f) Cancel.

Id. Bandimere did not clearly invoke any of the above remedies, but instead based his claim directly on section 4–2–710. Regardless of whether Bandimere relied on section 4–2–706 or 4–2–708, section 4–2–710 operates in the same manner:

> Incidental damages to an aggrieved seller include any commercially reasonable charges, expenses, or commissions incurred in stopping delivery, in the transportation, care, and custody of goods *after* the buyer's breach, in connection with return or resale of the goods, or otherwise resulting from the breach.

Id. (emphasis added).

A

The trial court allowed evidence of attorney fees paid by Bandimere to go before the jury. The court of appeals reversed, holding that attorney fees were not proper incidental damages. We agree.

Most commentators and courts find that section 4–2–710 does not include attorney fees as incidental damages. * * * We agree with this view and hold that absent other statutory or contractual provisions to the contrary, attorney fees are not incidental damages under section 4–2–710.

B

Bandimere argues there was a contractual relationship and that two breaches were committed by Jelen. The first breach, according to Bandimere, occurred when Jelen requested Bandimere to deliver the goods. The second breach occurred when Bandimere attempted to deliver the goods and Jelen rejected them. Bandimere concedes, however, that he agreed to deliver the chemicals after the telephone call from Jelen requesting that he do so. Such an agreement, even if not a valid contract modification, represents a waiver by Bandimere of the delivery terms. § 4–2–209(4), 2 C.R.S. (1973) ("Although an attempt at modification or rescission does not satisfy the requirements of subsection (2) or (3) of this section [that the statute of frauds must be satisfied], it can operate as a waiver."). A waiver can be shown by "unequivocal conduct or statements betraying an intent to relinquish known rights." *United States v. Santa Fe Eng'rs, Inc.,* 515 F.Supp. 512, 515 (D.Colo.1981); *see also Lease Fin., Inc. v. Burger,* 40 Colo.App. 107, 114, 575 P.2d 857, 862 (1977); *Farmers Elevator Co. v. Anderson,* 170 Mont. 175, 178–81, 552 P.2d 63, 65–66 (1976) (voluntary relinquishment of a known right, claim, or privilege).

After the delivery terms were waived by Bandimere, Jelen no longer had a legal duty to retrieve the chemicals from Bandimere's property. The trial court and court of appeals concluded that a breach did occur when Jelen refused to accept the chemicals after Bandimere attempted delivery. * * * Even assuming that the terms of the contract were breached, Bandimere would still not be entitled to damages under the U.C.C.

C

The court of appeals allowed damages for clean-up costs incurred by Bandimere. Rather than look to the U.C.C., however, the court of appeals relied on a pre-code case, *Uinta Oil Refining Co. v. Ledford,* 125 Colo. 429,

244 P.2d 881 (1952), in which we stated that the breaching party is liable for all foreseeable damages that were the "natural and proximate consequence of a breach thereof." *Id.* at 434, 244 P.2d at 885. The seller's remedies are now controlled by the U.C.C., however, and Bandimere's damages in contract must flow, if at all, from the code. As we have previously stated, under the facts before us, Bandimere's recovery must be under section 4–2–710.

By holding that Bandimere could recover damages that were the consequence of Jelen's breach, the court of appeals blurred the distinction between U.C.C. seller's and buyer's remedies. Section 4–2–715 specifically allows buyers to recover consequential damages resulting from the seller's breach. § 4–2–715(2), 2 C.R.S. (1973). There is no corresponding provision in the code allowing the seller to recover consequential damages.[5] "Reading the explicit grant in 2–715 together with the restriction in 1–106, courts have concluded that the drafters did not intend to give the seller consequential damages. The courts seem also to have concluded that the words 'or otherwise resulting from the breach' in 2–710 itself do not authorize recovery of consequential damages." 1 White & Summers, *supra,* at 382. *See also Petroleo Brasileiro, S.A. Petrobras v. Ameropan Oil Corp.,* 372 F.Supp. 503 (E.D.N.Y.1974) [hereinafter *Petroleo*].

In *Petroleo,* the district court stated:

> While the distinction between the two is not an obvious one, the Code makes plain that incidental damages are normally incurred when a buyer (or seller) repudiates the contract or wrongfully rejects the goods, causing the other to incur such expenses as transporting, storing, or reselling the goods. On the other hand, consequential damages do not arise within the scope of the immediate buyer-seller transaction, but rather stem from losses incurred by the nonbreaching party in its dealings, often with third parties, which were a proximate result of the breach, and which were reasonably foreseeable by the breaching party at the time of the contracting.

Id. at 508. The expenses at issue in *Petroleo* were fines levied against the plaintiff-seller by the Brazilian government as a result of the defendant-buyer's failure to pay for oil he received from the seller. The court held that those penalties could not be properly characterized as "incidental" damages under section 2–710. *Id.* at 509. Other courts agree with that formulation. *Bill's Coal Co. v. Board of Pub. Utils. of Springfield,* 887 F.2d 242 (10th Cir.1989) (incidental costs do not include those expended in preparation for litigation); *Stokes v. Roberts,* 289 Ark. 319, 711 S.W.2d 757 (1986) (had sellers never entered into the contract, they still would have been obligated); *S.C. Gray, Inc. v. Ford Motor Co.,* 92 Mich.App. 789, 286 N.W.2d 34 (1979) (interest on loans taken out to maintain seller's business until buyer paid him are not incidental damages); *Sprague v. Sumitomo*

5. Section 4–1–106(1) declares:

> The remedies provided by this title shall be liberally administered to the end that the aggrieved party may be put in as good a position as if the other party had fully performed, *but neither consequential or special nor penal damages may be had except as specifically provided in this title or by any other rule of law.*

(Emphasis added.)

Forestry Co., 104 Wash.2d 751, 709 P.2d 1200 (1985) (that loss was proximately caused by buyer's breach is irrelevant).

Bandimere's damages were not incidental to Jelen's refusal to accept delivery of the chemicals, but instead were incurred as a result of improper storage, handling, and transportation of hazardous materials and his subsequent dealings with a third party: the State of Colorado. Just as the fines levied against the seller in *Petroleo* could not be fairly characterized as incidental damages, the costs Bandimere agreed to pay the state for reimbursement cannot be recovered as incidental costs under section 4–2–710. That those costs may have been levied against Bandimere as a proximate consequence of Jelen's failure to claim ownership of the chemicals is not relevant since the focus of section 4–2–710 is upon damages arising within the scope of the immediate contract. *See, e.g., Sprague,* 104 Wash.2d at 757, 709 P.2d at 1206.

In addition, the damages did not arise as a result of the breach, as they must to be characterized as incidental under section 4–2–710. *See* 1 White & Summers, *supra,* at 381; *Serna, Inc. v. Harman,* 742 F.2d 186 (5th Cir.1984). The invoice or contract drawn up by Jelen and Bandimere contained no delivery terms, except an ambiguous term "F.O.B. Golden," which might have applied to the chemicals or instead to Bandimere's compressor. Bandimere agreed to deliver the chemicals after being requested to do so by Jelen, but Jelen had no control over how Bandimere chose to make that delivery. It was Bandimere's decision to load open, corroded, and leaking barrels of hazardous material on two flatbed trucks and drive them to Jelen's yard, and the damages Bandimere incurred were in consequence of unreasonably transporting the materials. *See N.L. Indus., Inc. v. Department of Transp.,* 901 F.2d 141, 144 (D.C.Cir.1990). Jelen was under no obligation to accept delivery of the barrels under the circumstances.

IV

We conclude that the court of appeals correctly reversed the jury award of attorney fees against Jelen in favor of Bandimere. We hold, however, that the court of appeals erred in upholding the remainder of the jury award to Bandimere.

Accordingly, we reverse the award of consequential damages to Bandimere and return this case to the court of appeals with directions to remand to the trial court to enter judgment for the defendant, Jelen and Son, Inc.

Lohr, J., does not participate.

Notes

1. Why do you think the U.C.C. does not permit sellers to recover consequential damages? Do you agree?

2. How would you characterize the contract in *Jelen* so that the plaintiff could get consequential damages? What if the compressor had been defective?

3. For what proposition does *Jelen* cite *Sprague,* the first case in this part.

4. What if Jelen and Son had said they were backing out of the contract before anything had been transported, and Bandimere had paid a hazardous waste company to transport and store the chemicals. What direct and other damages could Bandimere have recovered. *Cf.* A1 Ferro Commodities Corp. v. Tube City Iron and Metal Co., 728 F.Supp. 1158, 1165–66 (E.D.Pa.1990) (plaintiff seller entitled to incidental damages for the storage of scrap steel after defendant buyer's repudiation of the contract and prior to the resale of the scrap) aff'd, 914 F.2d 241 (3d Cir.1990).

B. RESTITUTION

MELMS v. MITCHELL

Supreme Court of Oregon, 1973.
266 Or. 208, 512 P.2d 1336.

McAllister, Justice.

This is a suit for rescission of a contract in which defendant agreed to sell and plaintiffs to purchase a cordwood business, including hardwood stumpage growing on defendant's land and certain equipment used in cutting and hauling the wood. Defendant appeals from a decree of rescission and a money judgment for plaintiffs. Plaintiffs cross-appeal, contending that they were entitled to recover certain items of damage not allowed by the trial court.

* * *

The day after the contract was signed the plaintiffs took over the wood business and commenced to cut and sell wood from defendant's property. Plaintiff Ells devoted full time to the business and Melms worked part time. From the beginning they encountered difficulties and were never able to cut and sell enough wood to make a profit. Because of the lack of income Ells quit cutting wood full time late in December 1969, but Melms continued to carry on the business for another month.

In the meantime defendant became dissatisfied with the way plaintiffs were cutting wood and with their failure to account, to his satisfaction, for the wood as they cut it. By letter dated January 18, 1970, defendant suspended plaintiffs' cutting rights and stated that the cutting rights would be terminated as of February 18 unless certain conditions specified in the letter were met. On January 26, 1970, plaintiff Melms called on defendant and notified him that plaintiffs were rescinding the contract. Defendant refused to agree to a rescission.

Plaintiffs then filed this suit, alleging in their complaint that they were induced to enter the contract by certain material misrepresentations made by defendant, and praying for a decree of rescission. * * *

* * *

We are of the opinion that the evidence shows that defendant's representation as to the quantity of dry wood available was both false and material. * * *

Although the trial court held otherwise, we are of the opinion that this transaction is governed by the Sales Article of our Commercial Code (ORS Chapter 72). * * * The contract in the present case covered certain equipment and existing inventory of cut wood, as well as wood to be cut. The trial court was of the opinion that the contract was, however, not a sale of goods, but a contract for the sale of a going business. The written contract is headed "Sale of Wood Business," but the entire purchase price is allocated by its terms among the various items of tangible property which are within the statutory definitions of goods. * * *

Many of the principles of law governing this case were considered in Lanners v. Whitney, 247 Or. 223, 428 P.2d 398 (1967), which involved material misrepresentations of the condition of an aircraft. We determined that ORS 72.6080 was applicable. That section provides:

> "(1) The buyer may revoke his acceptance of a lot or commercial unit whose nonconformity substantially impairs its value to him if he has accepted it
>
> * * *
>
> "(b) without discovery of such nonconformity if his acceptance was reasonably induced either by the difficulty of discovery before acceptance or by the seller's assurances.
>
> "(2) Revocation of acceptance must occur within a reasonable time after the buyer discovers or should have discovered the ground for it and before any substantial change in condition of the goods which is not caused by their own defects. It is not effective until the buyer notifies the seller of it."

In *Lanners,* as in this case, the buyer notified the seller, after learning of the misrepresentation, that he considered the contract at an end. * * *

Defendant contends that plaintiffs' notice was not proper, because it included a demand for damages, and because plaintiffs offered only to return the "equipment", and did not mention the gasoline and the cut wood which had been included in the sale. * * * The Code does not include a requirement that a buyer who seeks to recover the purchase price must restore what he has received under the contract. We have no doubt, however, that such restoration is encompassed within the concept of revocation of acceptance, and that equitable principles, which supplement the Code's provisions, demand that a buyer seeking cancellation on the grounds of misrepresentation should return what he has received. See ORS 71.1030; 2 Anderson, Uniform Commercial Code 422.

This court has followed the rule that a plaintiff who seeks rescission in equity need not prove a prior tender or offer to restore the benefits received under the contract because, by resorting to equity, he indicates his willingness to do equity. The demand for damages did not render plaintiffs' revocation ineffective. The Code provides that the remedy of cancellation does not preclude recovery of damages in appropriate cases:

> "Remedies for material misrepresentation or fraud include all remedies available under ORS 72.1010 to 72.7250 for nonfraudulent

breach. Neither rescission or a claim for rescission of the contract for sale nor rejection or return of the goods shall bar or be deemed inconsistent with a claim for damages or other remedy." ORS 72.7210

If plaintiffs' notice was inadequate for a failure to offer to return all goods purchased under the contract upon payment of a proper amount, plaintiffs' submission to the jurisdiction of equity constitutes an adequate offer to do so.

Defendants also contend that plaintiffs' notice was not timely. What is a "reasonable time" under ORS 72.6080(2), *supra,* depends upon the facts of the particular case. *See* ORS 71.2040(2). The Official Comments to UCC 2–608 (ORS 72.6080) state, as to revocation of acceptance:

> "* * * Since this remedy will be generally resorted to only after attempts at adjustment have failed, the reasonable time period should extend in most cases beyond the time in which notification of breach must be given, beyond the time for discovery of non-conformity after acceptance and beyond the time for rejection after tender." Comment 4 to UCC 2–608.

Under the circumstances of this case, we cannot hold that plaintiffs allowed an unreasonable length of time to pass before notifying defendant of their revocation. * * *

Defendant also contends that plaintiffs, in January, were in default under the contract, and therefore were not entitled to rescind. We have reviewed the evidence with care, and we agree with the trial court's finding that plaintiffs were not in default. * * *

The remaining questions raised by the parties have to do with the amount of the judgment. The trial court allowed the plaintiffs $2,350, the total purchase price [which had been paid by plaintiff buyer, when the contract was entered into.] plus interest at six percent from January 26, 1970 (the date of notice of revocation), plus $792 representing storage expense for the equipment at the rate of $1.50 per day from January 26 to the date of trial. Defendant objects to the allowance of interest and storage charges.

ORS 82.010 provides that interest at the legal rate is payable on all moneys after they become due. Applying this statute in rescission cases, this court has held that the money paid by a rescinding purchaser is due on the date its return is demanded, and that interest is properly allowed from that date. * * * In the present case, although notice of revocation of acceptance was given on January 26, plaintiffs did not make an effective offer to return the goods upon refund of the purchase price until they filed their complaint. Under these circumstances, we are of the opinion that both the interest and the storage charges should begin to run on the date the complaint was filed rather than on January 26 as held by the trial court.

Plaintiffs contend that they are entitled to recover the cost of "cover"—the dry wood they had to buy in order to fill their customers' orders—under ORS 72.7120, which provides:

> "(1) After a breach within ORS 72.8110 the buyer may 'cover' by making in good faith and without unreasonable delay any reasonable purchase of or contract to purchase goods in substitution for those due from the seller.
>
> "(2) The buyer may recover from the seller as damages the difference between the cost of cover and the contract price together with any incidental or consequential damages as defined in ORS 72.7150, but less expenses saved in consequence of the seller's breach."

Plaintiffs purchased 20 cords of cut dry wood for $303. Their contract with defendant called for payment of $2.50 a cord for stumpage. The difference between the cost of cover and the contract price is $253–$303, less $50 for 20 cords at $2.50. From this figure the statute provides for a deduction for "expenses saved in consequence of the seller's breach." Plaintiffs, when they purchased cut wood in order to fill their orders, were saved the expense of cutting and handling wood on defendant's land. There is no evidence of plaintiffs' own cutting and handling costs. The only evidence on this subject is that defendant, while he operated the business, estimated his expenses at $10 a cord for cutting and $5 a cord for other expenses. If plaintiffs' costs were similar, the expenses saved by buying 20 cords of cut wood would have been $300, or more than the difference between the cost of cover and the contract price. In short, the record does not show that plaintiffs suffered any damage by reason of their purchase of cut dry wood as cover.

Plaintiffs also argue that they are entitled to recover, as consequential damages under ORS 72.7150(2), the wages they lost in order to devote their time to the cordwood business and their anticipated profits which failed to materialize. The lost wages are not a consequence of defendant's misrepresentation and cannot be recovered. If the quantity of dry wood had been as defendant represented, plaintiffs would have had to either give their own time to the business or hire others to do so.

Plaintiffs' real complaint is that the business failed to make a profit. We have no doubt that lost profits may, as plaintiffs contend, be recovered as consequential damages under ORS 72.7150(2) in proper cases, but we find no basis for such an award in the present case. Both of the plaintiffs were inexperienced in the cordwood business. Although the record does provide some evidence of defendant's profit per cord while he was operating the business, we cannot assume that plaintiffs' failure to make the same profit was due entirely or primarily to the lack of a sufficient quantity of available dry wood. Considering the type of business involved, plaintiffs' inexperience, and the lack of detailed evidence on cost and profit factors, the record is insufficient to support an award for loss of anticipated profits. * * *

The decree will be modified to provide that plaintiffs shall recover interest and storage charges from the date the complaint was filed; except as modified, the decree of the trial court is affirmed.

Notes

1. *Personal property contracts where the Uniform Commercial Code does not apply.* If the contract is for a sale of personal property such as chattels the

vendor with a cause based upon *misrepresentation* may rescind by giving notice to that effect and making a legally sufficient tender. A vendor who has delivered the property to the vendee may then bring a replevin action on the theory that his rescission avoided the vendor's transfer of title to the vendee. Should the vendee refuse to return the chattel to which the plaintiff now has a claim to both title and a right of possession, this conduct may be the basis of a conversion action forcing a sale to the defendant. Recovery of goods and chattels for the buyer's *breach* was generally denied at common law. Some older cases held that quasi-contract would not lie in the situation where a party has wrongful possession of a chattel, but has not disposed of it. If the property were sold by the vendee, quasi-contract would then lie to recover the proceeds of the sale. If there is a basis for equity jurisdiction, such as, for example, where fiduciary fraud is involved, the plaintiff may have the benefit of a constructive trust, or lien and, possibly, an accounting in equity. A breach of contract, without more, is generally considered inadequate for equity jurisdiction purposes except, perhaps, in certain cases where title has passed to the contract breaker, and the tendency, today, is to treat misrepresentations not involving fiduciary misconduct in connection with a sale of personal property in the same manner except in special situations such as those involving corporate shares. The vendee who rescinds, on the other hand, is usually regarded as having an adequate remedy by suit in quasi-contract. In most jurisdictions the vendee also may have the benefit of an equitable lien as security for recovery of this restitution relief.

These remedies options are discussed by Professor Palmer in I Law of Restitution (1978) §§ 3.16, 4.7 and 3.13.

2. *The general approach to restitution under the U.C.C.* It was traditionally characteristic of rescission relief at law in the case of personal property that the rescinding party must give notice and tender a restoration of the benefits received, with a resulting loss of the right to consequential damages, and, in particular, lost profits because of the implications of the "election of remedies doctrine". As noted in a recent article comparing the common law and the U.C.C. approaches to rescission and restitution:

> "The Uniform Commercial Code changes all of these rules. The buyer has a right to return nonconforming goods when the Code standards for return are met, the right to do so is not found in equity, and the buyer is not forced to an election of remedies [nor is "tender" required, as noted by the *Melms* court]. In addition to returning the goods, the buyer is entitled to his other damages, including consequential damages. Conversely, where the circumstances do not permit the buyer to return the goods, an action for breach of warranty may still be available.
>
> "The Code approach to the buyer's right to return the goods revolves around the remedies of rejection and revocation of acceptance. In essence, the buyer has a right to reject the goods until he has accepted them. Once the goods have been accepted, the buyer's right to return the goods depends upon whether he can meet the standards established for revocation of acceptance. Rejection is a more advantageous buyer's remedy because the standard for the return of the goods is easier to satisfy. Prior to acceptance, a buyer theoretically may reject goods for nonconformity, however minor it may be. * * *

> "Once the goods have been accepted, the buyer may only return the goods if he can show that their value has been substantially impaired. Not only is the standard for return a more difficult one for the buyer to meet, but the buyer also has the burden of proving that the standard has been met." Wallach, "The Buyer's Right to Return Unsatisfactory Goods—The Uniform Commercial Code Remedies of Rejection and Revocation of Acceptance," 20 Washburn L.J. 20, 20–21 (1980) *:

The U.C.C., in the case of breach, for all practical purposes eliminates the election of remedies doctrine by making reliance and consequential damages available in connection with restitution, which include loss of expected profits. (U.C.C. §§ 2–711, 2–712, 2–713, 2–721 and 2–313 (1962)). The Code takes a similar position, as a practical matter, regarding the election doctrine where the right to restitution is based upon misrepresentation rather than breach. In some contexts where the Code permits the undoing of the contract it avoids use of the term "rescission" although, of course, that is often the basis for allowing recourse to one or more of these remedies. *See, e.g.*, §§ 2–608 and 2–711 (buyer's right to return goods because of seller's breach.) I G. Palmer, Law of Restitution (1978) § 3.9.

The Code provides for restitution in a variety of ways and situations. The principal means are recovery in quasi-contract, the right to retain or repossess the goods in question together with provision for statutory possessory liens by buyer and seller (which may be foreclosed by either public or private sales) and, in some special circumstances, the right to the benefits of tracing. With respect to the latter, and the benefits of the constructive trust and equitable lien, see, I G. Palmer, Law of Restitution (1978) at 338–39.

3. *Vendor's restitution remedies under the U.C.C.* A vendor's restitution rights under the Code depend, in large measure, upon whether the basis for seeking relief is misrepresentation or breach of contract.

In the case of a *breach* of *contract* claim, where the transaction was a "credit sale", a vendor is restricted to recovery of the contract price if there has been full performance by delivery to the buyer. (See § 2–703). If there were no delivery, or title were retained, the vendor may then refuse to perform and claim restitution. Such a vendor with possession may have, in effect, a lien upon the goods. (§§ 9–503, 9–505 and 2–706).

In the case of a "cash sale," on the other hand, the vendor may retain, or take steps to repossess, the goods when payment is refused and treat the contract as terminated. (§ 2–507). The vendor would, in that event, also be entitled to what is, in effect, a lien. (§ 2–706).

In the case of a claim against the vendee based upon *misrepresentation*, rather than breach, the vendor's remedies depend upon the nature of the fraud in question. If there were a misrepresentation by the vendee as to solvency, or there were insolvency in fact at the time of delivery, the goods may be recovered if there is a demand for their return within ten days after receipt by the buyer. (§ 2–702(2)). The ten day limit does not apply, however, if the vendor relies, as a basis for claiming deception, upon a written representation of solvency made to the vendor in question within three months prior to the date of delivery. (*Id.*).

* Reprinted with permission of the Washburn Law Journal.

Should the vendor, on the other hand, rely upon an actionable misrepresentation not related to insolvency he/she may assert the right to reclaim the goods by the use of the appropriate possessory remedy, recover in quasi-contract as well as, it would appear, claim the benefit of tracing in equity. I G. Palmer, Law of Restitution (1978) at § 3.17.

4. *Vendee's restitution rights under the U.C.C.* The right of a vendee who has accepted delivery because of a failure to discover a breach due to the nonconformity of the goods depends upon whether the vendee can meet the standard for revoking the acceptance. This, in turn, depends upon whether there has been a substantial impairment of the value of the goods as a result of the vendor's breach. (See, I G. Palmer, Law of Restitution (1978) at 490). These limitations governing the right to return the goods were emphasized in the excerpt from the Wallach article quoted in Note 1, above.

If there were no delivery to the vendee, delivery were justifiably refused, or the goods were rightly returned, the buyer may claim restitution of payments on the price as well as other damages. (§§ 2–711; 2–601). The buyer with the privilege of returning the goods also may claim a lien upon them to secure restitution of his payments on price, and certain expenses related to handling the goods, but not to secure other damages claims. (§§ 2–721; 2–711; 2–706).

The vendee basing a claim upon *misrepresentation* rather than breach, by way of contrast, as a general matter may recover in quasi-contract the amount of any payments made, as well as other appropriate damages as emphasized by the Court in Melms v. Mitchell. (See §§ 2–721; 2–711). Such a buyer with possession may have a buyer's lien upon the goods to secure payment. The buyer, unlike the seller with a comparable lien, is required to account with respect to the proceeds of the sale. (§§ 2–706(6); 2–711, comments 1 and 2). This disparity in treatment has been criticized by Professor Palmer. (I. Palmer, Law of Restitution (1978) at 496–97 and 310–12).

C. SPECIFIC PERFORMANCE

1. *Action by Seller*

ROYAL JONES & ASSOCIATES, INC. v. FIRST THERMAL SYSTEMS, INC.

District Court of Appeal of Florida, 1990.
566 So.2d 853.

ZEHMER, JUDGE.

Royal Jones & Associates, Inc., appeals from a final judgment of the lower court finding that it breached a contract with First Thermal Systems, Inc., and awarding damages to First Thermal Systems, Inc., in the amount of the contract price pursuant to section 672.709, Florida Statutes (1987). Because the goods under the contract were specially manufactured for Royal Jones, were not suitable for sale to others in the ordinary course of First Thermal's business, and it appeared that any efforts on behalf of First Thermal to resell the goods would have been unavailing, we affirm.

On October 4, 1988, Royal Jones ordered three steel rendering tanks from First Thermal for use in its business of constructing rendering plants. Under the terms of the contract, First Thermal would manufacture the tanks according to Royal Jones's specifications for a price of $64,350. Royal Jones was to receive the tanks at First Thermal's place of manufacture in Chattanooga, Tennessee. Royal Jones failed to appear at First Thermal's plant to take delivery of the tanks, refused to accept shipment of the tanks, and refused to pay the contract price. As of the date of the trial, the tanks were still being held for Royal Jones at First Thermal's plant.

The lower court found that Royal Jones had breached the contract, and that the only testimony before it was that the goods were specially manufactured for Royal Jones and were not suitable for sale in the ordinary course of First Thermal's business. Concluding that mitigation of damages was not a viable defense, the court entered judgment for First Thermal, pursuant to section 672.709, awarding First Thermal the contract price of $64,350, interest to the date of trial in the amount of $8,630.56, and attorney's fees and costs in the amount of $3,528.07.

Section 672.709(1)(b) provides that when the buyer fails to pay the price for goods as it becomes due, the seller may recover, together with incidental damages, the price "[o]f goods identified to the contract if the seller is unable after reasonable effort to resell them at a reasonable price or the circumstances reasonably indicate that such effort will be unavailing." Royal Jones contends that the lower court erred in awarding First Thermal the full contract price as damages for the tanks pursuant to section 672.709, because there was no evidence presented at trial that either First Thermal was unable to resell the tanks after making a reasonable effort to do so, or that the circumstances reasonably indicated that such effort would be unavailing. In reply, First Thermal contends that there was uncontroverted testimony at trial that the tanks were specially manufactured for Royal Jones and that any efforts at resale would have been unavailing.

While there are no Florida appellate decisions interpreting section 672.709 that would be applicable to these circumstances, cases from other jurisdictions support the lower court's decision to award First Thermal the full contract price. Thus, in *FMI, Inc. v. RMAX, Inc.*, 286 S.C. 343, 333 S.E.2d 360 (1985), the court held that where there was evidence that the seller specially manufactured goods for the buyer, the buyer failed to pay for those goods, and the seller had no other customer to which to sell the goods, such evidence was sufficient to warrant submitting to the jury the issue of whether any effort to resell the goods would be unavailing. 333 S.E.2d at 362. * * *

[W]e hold that the trial court did not err in awarding First Thermal the full contract price as damages, because the evidence presented at trial by First Thermal was sufficient to meet its burden of proving that the circumstances reasonably indicated that any effort to resell the tanks would have been unavailing. There was testimony at trial that First Thermal specially manufactured the tanks for Royal Jones according to drawings supplied by Royal Jones and that First Thermal had not taken any steps to resell the tanks because it did not know how to market or resell rendering tanks. First Thermal proved that any effort at resale would have been unavailing because these were the only rendering tanks First Thermal ever made, the tanks were manufactured according to Royal Jones's specifications, First Thermal had no other customers to which it could resell the tanks, and it was unaware how the tanks could have been marketed for resale. Also, the tanks were built without needed internal components and to a special size in accordance with Royal Jones's specifications and could not be used as rendering tanks without special engineering to which First Thermal had no access. Finally, there was testimony that the tanks had only scrap value to First Thermal of about $700 if they were processed for a scrap dealer. This evidence was sufficient to shift the burden to Royal Jones to show that any effort at resale would not have been unavailing, or that the tanks had some potential market value beyond the salvage value claimed by First Thermal. *See FMI, Inc.; Tracor, Inc.* However, Royal Jones presented no evidence to the contrary at trial, and the lower court did not err in awarding First Thermal the full contract price pursuant to section 672.709.

Royal Jones next contends that allowing First Thermal to recover the contract price, while allowing it to keep the rendering tanks, amounts to an impermissible double recovery on the part of First Thermal, citing *Page Avjet v. Cosgrove Aircraft Svc.,* 546 So.2d 16 (Fla. 3d DCA 1989). In *Page Avjet,* the Third District Court of Appeal held that the trial court erred in permitting the seller to recover the purchase price of a turbine *and* to retain the turbine that the buyer had returned to the seller without considering the buyer's defenses of set-off and return of the turbine. 546 So.2d at 17–18. The court stated that "to permit [the seller] to retain both the turbine and the purchase price would constitute an impermissible double recovery." 546 So.2d at 17–18.

First Thermal contends that section 672.709(2) permits it to hold the tanks prior to collecting on the judgment. Section 672.709(2) provides that:

> [w]here the seller sues for the price he must hold for the buyer any goods which have been identified to the contract and are still in his control except that if resale becomes possible he may resell them at any time prior to collection of the judgment. The net proceeds of any such resale must be credited to the buyer and payment of the judgment entitles him to any goods not resold.

Section 672.709(2) permits First Thermal to hold the tanks for Royal Jones's credit prior to collection of the judgment and requires First Thermal to credit Royal Jones with the net proceeds of any resale of the tanks made prior to collection on the judgment or to turn over any tanks not resold upon Royal Jones's payment of the judgment. First Thermal has reaffirmed its willingness to turn the tanks over to Royal Jones upon payment. Consequently, there is no impermissible double recovery. The *Page Avjet* decision is not applicable to these circumstances.

Finding no error in the trial court's ruling, the judgment is affirmed.

Notes

1. The remedies available to a seller under the Uniform Commercial Code are described as follows by Professor Eisenberg:

> "The obligation of a buyer of goods is normally limited to the payment of money. As a result, if the buyer breaches, the seller's actual expectation can normally be satisfied without taking his subjective value into account, provided the seller's remedies are individualized. Pre-Code law usually limited the seller to standardized market-price damages. In parallel to its treatment of buyers, the Code perpetuated this remedy but also introduced several individualized alternatives. First, the Code supplied the seller with a counterpart to the buyer's remedy of cover. Under section 2–706, if the buyer defaults the seller may resell the goods and, if he does so in good faith and in a commercially reasonable manner, he can recover the difference between the resale price and the contract price. Second, the Code supplied the seller with a counterpart to the buyer's remedies of specific performance and replevin. Under section 2–709(1), the seller can recover the price of goods identified to the contract if, after reasonable effort, he cannot resell at a reasonable price, or if the circumstances reasonably indicate that he will be unable to do so."

Eisenberg, The Responsive Model of Contract Law, 36 Stan.L.Rev. 1107, 1136 (1984).*

The seller's action under section 2–709(1) is correctly described as an action for specific performance because, after paying the price, the buyer is entitled to any unsold goods. Specific performance is an equitable action, and there is no right to a jury trial in actions for equitable relief. *See* Chapter 9 *infra.*

2. Section 2–709 allows the seller to recover incidental damages, as defined by section 2–710:

> "Incidental damages to an aggrieved seller include any commercially reasonable charges, expenses or commissions incurred in stopping delivery, in the transportation, care and custody of goods after the buyer's breach, in connection with return or resale of the goods or otherwise resulting from the breach."

Section 2–710 has been interpreted to allow the recovery of prejudgment interest on the unpaid price. Atlas Concrete Pipe, Inc. v. Roger J. Au & Son, Inc., 467 F.Supp. 830 (E.D.Mich.1979), rev'd on other grounds, 668 F.2d 905 (6th Cir.1982). *See also* Associated Metals & Minerals Corp. v. Sharon Steel Corp., 590 F.Supp. 18 (S.D.N.Y.1983), *aff'd,* 742 F.2d 1431 (2d Cir.1983).

2. *Action by Buyer*

CUMBEST v. HARRIS

Supreme Court of Mississippi, 1978.
363 So.2d 294.

WALKER, JUSTICE, for the Court:

This is an appeal from an order of the Chancery Court of Jackson County, Mississippi, dismissing appellant Cumbest's bill of complaint.

The sole question presented is whether the personal property, which was the subject of the controversy, is of such peculiar, sentimental or

* Reprinted with permission of the Stanford Law Review.

unique value as to come within the exception to the general rule that a chancery court will not ordinarily decree specific performance of a contract involving personal property.

Cumbest's bill of complaint and exhibits attached thereto aver, among other things, that on May 19, 1976, Donald Ronnie Cumbest and Bedford Harris, respectively, contracted for the sale and purchase of certain hi-fi equipment via a bill of sale. An option agreement was also signed on the same date allowing Cumbest to repurchase the audio equipment on or before 5:00 p.m., Monday, June 7, 1976. The language of these two instruments is clear and unambiguous and both were signed and notarized.

The complainant averred that the transaction was intended to be a loan, in substance, and that the audio equipment was to serve as collateral. It also states that from early morning on Monday, June 7, 1976, until late that evening every effort humanly possible was made to pay the required amount of money to the defendant. The defendant purposely avoided meeting with him at various places during the day, thereby fraudulently and deliberately evading the receipt of the money as contracted for in The Option to Repurchase Agreement. In desperation the complainant deposited the required amount of money with the defendant's landlord on the evening of June 7, 1976, and approximately a week later initiated this lawsuit seeking equitable relief. * * *

The amended complaint further averred that the complete assemblage of the audio equipment took several years for the appellant to acquire and because of the unique nature and irreplaceability of much of the equipment the court should assert jurisdiction of the case and grant such equitable relief as it deems appropriate. Finally, the complainant prays for the defendant to be enjoined against the disposition, sale or removal of the property and for the court to mandate specific performance of the contract to reconvey.

The chancellor allowed a hearing solely on the question of whether the property was of such sentimental value or so unique as to come within the exception to the general rule that the chancery court will not ordinarily decree specific performance of a contract involving personal property.

Cumbest was the only witness to testify at the proceeding. The property involved was a stereo system allegedly valued at $10,000. The system consisted of twenty separate parts accumulated over a period of fifteen years. There was testimony that Cumbest had acquired experience in stereophonic and recording equipment over the years by working in hi-fi stores in Oxford and Gulfport. He also did some recording of a professional nature. According to him, the items involved were a part of a recording studio which consisted of carefully matched parts, rather than a mere stereo set as contended by the defendant. The parts involved could not function alone, and could not be matched to just any standard stereo system. Cumbest testified that many of the integral parts of the system could no longer be replaced, *e.g.*, the main reel to reel recorder; a stereo quadraphonic four channel logic decoder which, according to Cumbest, was originally on order for two years; a stereo three channel crossover preamplifier with base boost and turn over frequency control; some speaker components, and the particular diamond needle in the turntable system. Other equipment was personally designed and built by Cumbest himself. He testified that he purchased the parts and assembled the speakers to accommodate his particular system, and that the cabinets were designed and handmade by him after extensive study and research to meet the needs of his particular system.

* * *

In other testimony he pointed out that even those items which are still available are of the type which require special order purchases and that in obtaining them originally there were six months to two years waiting periods. As to sentimental value, Cumbest testified:

> As far as the snetimental [sic] value of the equipment, it is very great, blood, sweat and tears have gone into it, I spent 15 years acquiring it piece by piece and I would never seel [sic] it at any price.

Defendant put on no witnesses to contradict Cumbest's testimony.

As the chancellor recited in his order, the general rule is that, ordinarily, specific performance will not be decreed if the subject matter of the contract sought to be enforced is personalty. However, this general principle is subject to several well recognized exceptions, such as: (1) Where there is no adequate remedy at law; (2) Where the specific articles or property are of peculiar, sentimental or unique value; and (3) Where due to scarcity the chattel is not readily obtainable. 81 C.J.S. Specific Performance §§ 81–83 (1977). These exceptions are partly founded on the principle of the inadequacy of a remedy at law and the remedy may, in a proper case, be allowed where damages are not readily ascertainable.

> "The tests to determine whether or not specific performance of a contract should be granted are the same in case of contracts for the sale of personalty as in the case of contracts for the sale of realty, namely, whether the damages for the breach are the equivalent of the promised performance, and whether the remedy at law is inadequate." 81 C.J.S. Specific Performance § 80 (1977).

Such equitable relief is justified by the fact that the legal remedy of replevin is subject to defects of procedure which prevent the successful plaintiff from invariably recovering possession of the chattel. There is also considerable authority, old and new, showing liberality in the granting of an equitable remedy. 11 Williston Contracts § 1419 (3d ed. 1968); Miss. Code Ann. § 75–2–716 (1972).

In the present case, there was uncontradicted testimony that some components of the system were irreplaceable. Other components were replaceable but only with difficulty and long waiting periods. Additionally, Cumbest testified that the system was acquired over a fifteen-year span and that he personally designed and built parts of it specifically to match that particular system. Based on that testimony, we must conclude the property had both a unique value and falls into the category of property which is not readily obtainable due to scarcity.

For the above reasons, we hold that the chancellor erred in not finding that the property was sufficiently unique to justify the equitable jurisdiction of a chancery court. The cause will be remanded for a hearing on the merits.

Notes

1. Section 2–716 of the Uniform Commercial Code, which is cited by the *Cumbest* court, gives the buyer of goods an action for specific performance:

> "(1) Specific performance may be decreed where the goods are unique or in other proper circumstances.
>
> "(2) The decree for specific performance may include such terms and conditions as to payment of the price, damages, or other relief as the court may deem just.
>
> "(3) The buyer has a right of replevin for goods identified to the contract if after reasonable effort he is unable to effect cover for such goods or if the circumstances reasonably indicate that such effort will be unavailing. * * *
>
> "Official Comment
>
> "1. The present section continues in general prior policy as to specific performance and injunction against breach. However, without intending to impair in any way the exercise of the court's sound discretion in the matter, this Article seeks to further a more liberal attitude than some courts have shown in connection with the specific performance of contracts of sale.
>
> "2. In view of this Article's emphasis on the commercial feasibility of replacement, a new concept of what are 'unique' goods is introduced under this section. Specific performance is no longer limited to goods which are already specific or ascertained at the time of contracting. The test of uniqueness under this section must be made in terms of the total situation which characterizes the contract. Output and requirements contracts involving a particular or peculiarly available source or market present today the typical commercial specific performance situation, as contrasted with contracts for the sale of heirlooms or priceless works of art which were usually involved in the older cases. However, uniqueness is not the sole basis of the remedy under this section for the relief may also be granted 'in other proper circumstances' and inability to cover is strong evidence of 'other proper circumstances' ".* **

2. In *Cumbest,* the court held that the plaintiff was entitled to specific performance because the goods were unique. Other examples of unique personal property include (1) the "Miss New Mexico–USA" title (Patrick v.

** *See generally* Annot., 26 A.L.R.4th 294 (1983) (specific performance of sale of goods under U.C.C. § 2–716). For the drafting history of section 2–716 and summaries of the cases decided under the Uniform Commercial Code, see Axelrod, Specific Performance of Contracts for Sales of Goods: Expansion or Retrenchment in the 1980's, 7 Vt.L.Rev. 249 (1982); Greenberg, Specific Performance under Section 2–716 of the Uniform Commercial Code: "A More Liberal Attitude" in the "Grand Style," 17 New Eng.L.Rev. 321 (1982); Schmitt & Pasterczyk, Specific Performance under the Uniform Commercial Code: Will Liberalism Prevail?, 26 DePaul L.Rev. 54 (1976).

Miss New Mexico–USA Universe Pageant, 490 F.Supp. 833 (W.D.Tex.1980)); (2) stock in a closely held corporation (Burns v. Gould, 172 Conn. 210, 374 A.2d 193 (1977)); (3) an astronomical clock (Ruddock v. First National Bank, 201 Ill.App.3d 907, 147 Ill.Dec. 310, 559 N.E.2d 483 (1990)); (4) a liquor license (Borough of Jefferson v. Century III Associates, U.S.S., 498 Pa. 57, 444 A.2d 665 (1982)); and, (5) "Albert's Famous Mexican Hot Sauce" business, including the hot sauce formula and goodwill (Madariaga v. Morris, 639 S.W.2d 709 (Tex.App.1982)).*

3. The Uniform Commercial Code also authorizes specific performance when the goods are unique only in light of the buyer's individual or subjective preferences:

a. In Schweber v. Rallye Motors, Inc., 12 U.C.C.Rep.Serv. 1154 (N.Y.Sup. Ct.1973), the plaintiff ordered a Rolls Royce Corniche from the defendant. One year later, the contract was cancelled. The plaintiff claimed the cancellation was prompted by the dealer's statement that it would be impossible to obtain a car of the desired style and color. The dealer contended that the plaintiff initiated the cancellation when he learned of a price increase. In any event, a few days later, the automobile which the plaintiff had ordered appeared in the dealer's showroom. When the plaintiff demanded its sale to him, he was informed that it had already been sold to Zara Contracting Co. The plaintiff then brought an action against the dealer for specific performance and requested a preliminary injunction restraining the defendant from selling or transferring the automobile pending the trial of the case:

> "Defendants contend that * * * plaintiff has no cause of action against the defendants and even if he did, it could only be for damages, and not specific performance, because the subject matter, the Rolls Royce Corniche, is not unique, that approximately 100 convertible automobiles of this type are sold in the United States each year, and therefore, it is not an appropriate subject for specific performance. Furthermore, defendants argue that they have offered to sell to plaintiff a similar automobile, but with a different interior design, and defendants therefore conclude that the only remedy of the plaintiff, in any event, would be an action for damages.
>
> "The court, at this time, is not required to pass upon the contested issue as to whether the cancellation of the contract was induced by defendants' fraudulent representations. * * * The question before the court now is whether a temporary injunction should lie under the circumstances, or whether plaintiff should be relegated to an action for damages.
>
> "Prior to the effective date of the Uniform Commercial Code (Sept. 27, 1964), the remedy of specific performance was limited under section 149 of the Personal Property Law. The latter section authorized such relief, 'Where the seller has broken a contract to deliver *specific or ascertained goods.*' In interpreting the statute, the courts had consistently held that automobiles, or other items, which were purchased under contracts for future delivery, could not be the subject of specific performance. (Gellis v. Falcon Buick Co., 191 Misc. 566; Kalisgi v. Grole Motors, 69 N.Y.S.2d 645; Goodman v. Henry Caplan, Inc., 188 Misc. 242). However, with the advent

* *See* 5A A. Corbin, Contracts 1148 (1964); Note, Recent Trends in the Specific Enforcement of Contracts to Sell Securities, 51 Mich. L.Rev. 408 (1953). For an interesting case involving a vendor seeking specific performance of a contract to sell corporate shares, see Hurley v. Thomas, 169 So.2d 519 (Fla. App.1964).

of the Uniform Commercial Code, § 2–716 relating to specific performance, the language requiring 'specific or ascertained goods' was eliminated. * * *

"Specific performance under subdiv. 1, of § 2–716 UCC may be decreed 'where the goods are unique, *or in other proper circumstances.*'

"The court believes that the circumstances herein justify the relief of specific performance and accordingly grants the motion for the temporary injunction provided: (a) that plaintiff post a surety bond in the sum of $5,000 for all damages which may be sustained by defendants by reason of this injunction * * *."

b. Compare Paloukos v. Intermountain Chevrolet Co., 99 Idaho 740, 588 P.2d 939 (1978), in which the court denied specific performance to the buyer of a Chevrolet pickup truck after the defendant dealer failed to deliver "because of a product shortage":

> "Paloukos alleged no facts suggesting anything unique about the pickup involved. The market value of such a vehicle is readily ascertainable and Paloukos' pleadings indicate no reason why damages would not be adequate relief. Moreover, the sole remaining defendant in this case, Intermountain, is a dealer, not a manufacturer, of automobiles. Paloukos does not allege that Intermountain is in possession of a conforming pickup which it could sell him. Indeed, the record suggests quite the contrary. It is well established that the courts will not order the impossible, such as ordering the seller under a sales contract to sell to the buyer that which the seller does not have."

c. In King Aircraft Sales, Inc. v. Lane, 68 Wash.App. 706, 846 P.2d 550 (1993) the court held that specific performance was appropriate for two airplanes even though there were others available because these were "rare in terms of their exceptional condition." *Id.* at 553. Because the planes had been sold the trial court awarded damages and the court of appeals affirmed, rejecting the argument that because specific performance had been sought, no damages could be awarded. The court noted, with respect to specific performance, that:

> "The UCC, like its predecessor, the Uniform Sales Act, does not expressly require that the remedy at law be inadequate in order to invoke specific performance. However, the stated intent of the drafters of the UCC was to continue 'in general prior policy as to specific performance and injunction against breach', and also 'to further *a more liberal attitude* than some courts have shown' toward specific performance. (Emphasis added.) Official Comment 1, RCW 62A.2–716.
>
> "Nevertheless, there is a split of authority among those jurisdictions which have considered whether a buyer's remedy at law must be inadequate before specific performance can be granted.
>
> * * *
>
> "We find the liberal interpretation urged by the UCC drafters to be entirely consistent with the common law of our state. Prior to adoption of the UCC, our cases did not always require the absence of a legal remedy before awarding specific performance nor did these cases require the goods to be absolutely 'unique.' "

Id. at 554–55.

4. Although the Uniform Commercial Code does not explicitly state that adequacy of the legal remedy precludes specific performance, "such a position is implicit in the Code's emphasis on cover as its principal buyer's remedy." Greenberg, Specific Performance under Section 2–716 of the Uniform Commercial Code: "A More Liberal Attitude" in the "Grand Style," 17 New Eng.L.Rev. 321, 352 (1982). Section 2–716(3) also conditions a buyer's right of replevin on the inability to effect cover. *E.g.,* T and T Air Charter, Inc. v. Duncan Aircraft Sales, 566 So.2d 361 (Fla.App.1990) (writ of replevin erroneously issued by trial judge because buyer did not show reasonable efforts to cover or that efforts would be unavailing). The New York Law Revision Commission's suggestion that subsection (3) be extended unconditionally to any goods identified to the contract "was rejected as extending the buyer's right to specific relief well beyond traditional limits, without any useful social purpose." Greenberg at 339. As a result, replevin is now "less readily available under the Code than it was under a similar provision in the Uniform Sales Act." *Id.* Nevertheless, buyers occasionally request replevin. *E.g.,* Big Knob Fire Co. v. Lowe & Moyer Garage, Inc., 338 Pa.Super. 257, 487 A.2d 953 (1985) (buyer replevied goods identified to the contract from seller's creditor).

5. Usually a plaintiff proves the inadequacy of the legal remedy by establishing that the goods are unique or that cover is impracticable. The legal remedy may also be inadequate, however, if the plaintiff must bring successive suits in order to enforce it. For example, in Teague v. Springfield Life Insurance Co., 55 N.C.App. 437, 439–41, 285 S.E.2d 860, 862–63 (1982), the court ordered specific performance of a contract to make monthly payments of disability benefits:

> "Under the facts of this case, plaintiff's remedy at law is inadequate. Defendant's persistent refusal to pay disability benefits under the contract contemplates 'successive lawsuits to recover in a piecemeal fashion the sums due,' at great hardship to the plaintiff whose livelihood now depends on the performance of the contract. *Moore, supra,* 297 N.C. at 18, 252 S.E.2d at 738. The Court's reasoning in *Moore* is persuasive when applied to the present case:
>
> > Equity 'seeks to reach and do complete justice where courts of law, through the inflexibility of their rules and want of power to adapt their judgments to the special circumstances of the case, are incompetent so to do.' Zebulon v. Dawson, 216 N.C. 520, 522, 5 S.E.2d 535, 537 (1939).
>
> * * *
>
> The adequacy of the remedy at law must be evaluated in a relative sense, treating the contract in a particular case 'as one of a class, and the inquiry is whether, in agreements generally of that kind, the terms or relations of the parties are such that the legal remedy of damages is adequate or inadequate.' *Pomeroy's Specific Performance of Contracts,* § 27, pp. 89–90 (3d ed. 1926). The *Restatement of the Law of Contracts,* § 361, p. 646 sets forth the factors involved in the determination of the adequacy of remedies at law when specific performance of a contract is sought. Subsections (c) and (e) are pertinent to our consideration. Subsection (c) focuses on 'the difficulty, inconvenience, or impossibility of obtaining a duplicate or substantial equivalent of the promised performance by means of money awarded as damages.'

> * * * Subsection (e) focuses on 'the probability that full compensation cannot be had without multiple litigation.' This factor goes to the heart of the inadequacy of plaintiff's remedy at law as discussed *supra* and, in an appropriate situation, is a sound basis for the granting of equitable relief.

297 N.C. at 16–18, 252 S.E.2d at 737–38. When applied to the facts of this case, the logic in *Moore* supports a holding that plaintiff is entitled to specific performance of the contract so long as he is disabled within the terms of the contract. This the trial court sought to do in its judgment. The factor of judicial economy, while not controlling, is certainly worthy of consideration in determining the issue in question."

See also Chattin v. Chattin, 245 Va. 302, 427 S.E.2d 347 (1993) (specific performance ordered for spousal support and other provisions of separation agreement because legal remedy of successive suits inadequate).

6. A contract provision for liquidated damages may not afford an "adequate legal remedy," even though it is valid, and therefore a liquidated damages clause does not automatically preclude specific performance. Restatement (Second) of Contracts § 361 (1981).

7. May a court order specific performance if the plaintiff does not seek it? *See* Merkes v. Mapston, 257 Mont. 408, 849 P.2d 210 (1993). There the plaintiff had agreed to sell some trucks to defendant for $29,500, and had agreed to take $24,000 and a truck that plaintiff had previously sold defendant for $5500. When the defendant did not deliver the truck, the plaintiff sued for money damages. The trial court ordered the plaintiff to accept the truck. The Supreme Court of Montana held that the trial court did not have authority to order specific performance.

8. Note that because specific performance is an equitable remedy, equitable defenses are available. *See* pp. 125–138 *supra*.

LACLEDE GAS CO. v. AMOCO OIL CO.

United States Court of Appeals, Eighth Circuit, 1975.
522 F.2d 33.

ROSS, CIRCUIT JUDGE.

The Laclede Gas Company (Laclede), a Missouri corporation, brought this diversity action alleging breach of contract against the Amoco Oil Company (Amoco), a Delaware corporation. It sought relief in the form of a mandatory injunction prohibiting the continuing breach or, in the alternative, damages. The district court held a bench trial on the issues of whether there was a valid, binding contract between the parties and whether, if there was such a contract, Amoco should be enjoined from breaching it. It then ruled that the "contract is invalid due to lack of mutuality" and denied the prayer for injunctive relief. The court made no decision regarding the requested damages. Laclede Gas Co. v. Amoco Oil Co., 385 F.Supp. 1332, 1336 (E.D.Mo.1974). This appeal followed, and we reverse the district court's judgment.

On September 21, 1970, Midwest Missouri Gas Company (now Laclede), and American Oil Company (now Amoco), the predecessors of the parties to this litigation, entered into a written agreement which was designed to provide central propane gas distribution systems to various residential developments in Jefferson County, Missouri, until such time as natural gas mains were extended into these areas. * * *

* * * [T]he agreement placed certain duties on both Laclede and Amoco. Basically, Amoco was to "[i]nstall, own, maintain and operate * * * storage and vaporization facilities and any other facilities necessary to provide [it] with the capability of delivering to [Laclede] commercial propane gas suitable * * * for delivery by [Laclede] to its customers' facilities." Amoco's facilities were to be "adequate to provide a continuous supply of commercial propane gas at such times and in such volumes commensurate with [Laclede's] requirements for meeting the demands reasonably to be anticipated in each Development while this Agreement is in force." Amoco was deemed to be "the supplier," while Laclede was "the distributing utility."

For its part Laclede agreed to "[i]nstall, own, maintain and operate all distribution facilities" from a "point of delivery" which was defined to be "the outlet of [Amoco] header piping." Laclede also promised to pay Amoco "the Wood River Area Posted Price for propane plus four cents per gallon for all amounts of commercial propane gas delivered" to it under the agreement.

Since it was contemplated that the individual propane systems would eventually be converted to natural gas, one paragraph of the agreement provided that Laclede should give Amoco 30 days written notice of this event, after which the agreement would no longer be binding for the converted development.

Another paragraph gave Laclede the right to cancel the agreement. * * *

There was no provision under which Amoco could cancel the agreement.

* * *

During the winter of 1972–73 Amoco experienced a shortage of propane and voluntarily placed all of its customers, including Laclede, on an 80% allocation basis, meaning that Laclede would receive only up to 80% of its previous requirements. Laclede objected to this and pushed Amoco to give it 100% of what the developments needed. Some conflict arose over this before the temporary shortage was alleviated.

Then, on April 3, 1973, Amoco notified Laclede that its Wood River Area Posted Price of propane had been increased by three cents per gallon. Laclede objected to this increase also and demanded a full explanation. None was forthcoming. Instead Amoco merely sent a letter dated May 14, 1973, informing Laclede that it was "terminating" the September 21, 1970, agreement effective May 31, 1973. It claimed it had the right to do this because "the Agreement lacks 'mutuality.' "[1]

1. While Amoco sought to repudiate the agreement, it resumed supplying propane to the subdivisions on February 1, 1974, under the mandatory allocation guidelines promul-

The district court felt that the entire controversy turned on whether or not Laclede's right to "arbitrarily cancel the Agreement" without Amoco having a similar right rendered the contract void "for lack of mutuality" and it resolved this question in the affirmative. We disagree with this conclusion and hold that settled principles of contract law require a reversal.

* * *

II.

Since he found that there was no binding contract, the district judge did not have to deal with the question of whether or not to grant the injunction prayed for by Laclede. He simply denied this relief because there was no contract. Laclede Gas Co. v. Amoco Oil Co., *supra,* 385 F.Supp. at 1336.

Generally the determination of whether or not to order specific performance of a contract lies within the sound discretion of the trial court. However, this discretion is, in fact, quite limited; and it is said that when certain equitable rules have been met and the contract is fair and plain "specific performance goes as a matter of right." Miller v. Coffeen, 365 Mo. 204, 280 S.W.2d 100, 102 (1955), quoting, Berberet v. Myers, 240 Mo. 58, 77, 144 S.W. 824, 830 (1912). (Emphasis omitted.)

With this in mind we have carefully reviewed the very complete record on appeal and conclude that the trial court should grant the injunctive relief prayed. We are satisfied that this case falls within that category in which specific performance should be ordered as a matter of right.

Amoco contends that four of the requirements for specific performance have not been met. Its claims are: * * * (2) the remedy of specific performance would be difficult for the court to administer without constant and long-continued supervision; (3) the contract is indefinite and uncertain; and (4) the remedy at law available to Laclede is adequate. * * *

* * *

While a court may refuse to grant specific performance where such a decree would require constant and long-continued court supervision, this is merely a discretionary rule of decision which is frequently ignored when the public interest is involved. *See, e.g.,* Joy v. St. Louis, 138 U.S. 1, 47, 11 S.Ct. 243, 34 L.Ed. 843 (1891).

Here the public interest in providing propane to the retail customers is manifest, while any supervision required will be far from onerous.

Section 370 of the Restatement of Contracts (1932) provides:

> Specific enforcement will not be decreed unless the terms of the contract are so expressed that the court can determine with reasonable certainty what is the duty of each party and the conditions under which performance is due.

gated by the Federal Energy Administration under the Federal Mandatory Allocation Program for propane. It is agreed that this is now being done under the contract.

We believe these criteria have been satisfied here. * * * Amoco is to supply all the propane which is reasonably foreseeably required, while Laclede is to purchase the required propane from Amoco and pay the contract price therefor. The parties have disagreed over what is meant by "Wood River Area Posted Price" in the agreement, but the district court can and should determine with reasonable certainty what the parties intended by this term and should mold its decree, if necessary, accordingly. Likewise, the fact that the agreement does not have a definite time of duration is not fatal since the evidence established that the last subdivision should be converted to natural gas in 10 to 15 years. This sets a reasonable time limit on performance and the district court can and should mold the final decree to reflect this testimony.

It is axiomatic that specific performance will not be ordered when the party claiming breach of contract has an adequate remedy at law. This is especially true when the contract involves personal property as distinguished from real estate.

However, in Missouri, as elsewhere, specific performance may be ordered even though personalty is involved in the "proper circumstances." Mo.Rev.Stat. § 400.2–716(1); Restatement of Contracts, *supra,* § 361. And a remedy at law adequate to defeat the grant of specific performance "must be as certain, prompt, complete, and efficient to attain the ends of justice as a decree of specific performance." National Marking Mach. Co. v. Triumph Mfg. Co., 13 F.2d 6, 9 (8th Cir.1926).

One of the leading Missouri cases allowing specific performance of a contract relating to personalty because the remedy at law was inadequate is Boeving v. Vandover, 240 Mo.App. 117, 218 S.W.2d 175, 178 (1949). In that case the plaintiff sought specific performance of a contract in which the defendant had promised to sell him an automobile. At that time (near the end of and shortly after World War II) new cars were hard to come by, and the court held that specific performance was a proper remedy since a new car "could not be obtained elsewhere except at considerable expense, trouble or loss, which cannot be estimated in advance." *

We are satisfied that Laclede has brought itself within this practical approach taken by the Missouri courts. As Amoco points out, Laclede has propane immediately available to it under other contracts with other suppliers. And the evidence indicates that at the present time propane is readily available on the open market. However, this analysis ignores the fact that the contract involved in this lawsuit is for a long-term supply of propane to these subdivisions. The other two contracts under which Laclede obtains the gas will remain in force only until March 31, 1977, and April 1, 1981, respectively; and there is no assurance that Laclede will be

* *Boeving* was followed by the court in Sedmak v. Charlie's Chevrolet, Inc., 622 S.W.2d 694 (Mo.Ct.App.1981), an action to specifically enforce a contract to sell one of a limited number of Corvette automobiles manufactured to commemorate the selection of the Corvette as the Pace Car for the Indianapolis 500. The seller had refused to deliver the car to the plaintiff for the contract price of $15,000, insisting instead that the plaintiff bid on it. The court acknowledged that the Pace Car was "not unique in the traditional legal sense," since 6,000 Pace Cars had been manufactured. However, the court ordered specific performance because the limited edition was "in short supply and great demand," making it "difficult, if not impossible" to cover.

able to receive any propane under them after that time. Also it is unclear as to whether or not Laclede can use the propane obtained under these contracts to supply the Jefferson County subdivisions, since they were originally entered into to provide Laclede with propane with which to "shave" its natural gas supply during peak demand periods. Additionally, there was uncontradicted expert testimony that Laclede probably could not find another supplier of propane willing to enter into a long-term contract such as the Amoco agreement, given the uncertain future of worldwide energy supplies. And, even if Laclede could obtain supplies of propane for the affected developments through its present contracts or newly negotiated ones, it would still face considerable expense and trouble which cannot be estimated in advance in making arrangements for its distribution to the subdivisions.

Specific performance is the proper remedy in this situation, and it should be granted by the district court.

Conclusion

For the foregoing reasons the judgment of the district court is reversed and the cause is remanded for the fashioning of appropriate injunctive relief in the form of a decree of specific performance * * *.*

Notes

1. In Weathersby v. Gore, 556 F.2d 1247 (5th Cir.1977), the buyer of cotton under an exclusive output contract brought an action for specific performance after the seller gave notice of cancellation, expressing an intent to sell his cotton elsewhere. The court declined to grant specific performance:

> "Far predating Mississippi's adoption of the Uniform Commercial Code, but indicating the reasons why specific performance is not suitable here, is Scott v. Billgerry, 40 Miss. 119 (1866). Billgerry was the purchaser of seventy-five bales of cotton from Scott. The purchase price of $3900 was paid at the time the contract was entered. Upon Scott's subsequent refusal to deliver, Billgerry sought specific performance. Though the court was not referring to an output contract but rather to the simple purchase of cotton bales, the language is equally applicable here:
>
> > 'It is altogether immaterial whether there was a sale of certain specific bales of cotton, or an agreement to sell and deliver a certain number of bales out of a particular lot, or a general agreement to sell and deliver a certain number of bales, without any designation of the specific bales, or of the particular lot out of which they are to come. All such cases depend upon the same general principle. The rule is, not to entertain jurisdiction in equity for a specific performance of agreements respecting goods, chattels, stock, choses in action, and other things of a personal nature, unless, under the particular circumstances of the case, there can be no adequate compensation in damages at law.' *Id.* at 140.

* *See generally* Greenberg, Specific Performance under Section 2–716 of the Uniform Commercial Code: "A More Liberal Attitude" in the "Grand Style," 17 New Eng. L.Rev. 321, 347–52 (1982); Speidel, Court–Imposed Price Adjustment Under Long–Term Supply Contracts, 76 Nw.U.L.Rev. 369 (1981).

"The adoption of the Uniform Commercial Code by Mississippi does not suggest the considerations expressed in *Scott v. Billgerry* are now to be rejected. Other than to indicate that the Code is intended to 'further a more liberal attitude than some courts have shown in connection with the specific performance of contracts of sale,' the comments accompanying UCC § 2–716 are of little guidance. The comments also state that '[o]utput and requirements contracts involving a particularly or peculiarly available source of market present today the typical commercial specific performance situation,' but the interpretation of this language appears to range from suggesting all output contracts should be specifically enforceable to a mere observation that output contracts form a suitable factual background in most cases in which specific performance may be sought.

"The general rule applicable when specific performance is requested has been stated in Roberts v. Spence, 209 So.2d 623, 626 (Miss.1968): 'Specific performance of a contract will not be awarded where damages may be recovered and the remedy in a court of law is adequate to compensate the injured party.' Considering the reluctance expressed in Roberts to authorization of the specific performance remedy, we hold that the Mississippi Supreme Court would apply a restrictive reading of § 75–2–716. A similar interpretation of the Code provision was adopted by the Georgia Supreme Court in Duval & Co. v. Malcom, 233 Ga. 784, 214 S.E.2d 356 [16 UCC Rep. 1217] (1975). There a buyer attempted to get specific performance of a cotton output contract entered into with a cotton farmer. Specific performance was rejected with the statement damages would be sufficient unless cotton could not be obtained in the open market. Thus the Georgia court, as did the Mississippi Supreme Court in *Austin,* [336 So.2d 745 (1976)], would have permitted specific performance if the buyer could not otherwise obtain the needed cotton. Absent this fact, specific performance was not an available remedy. The Georgia court gave considerable attention to the Code language that specific performance should be permitted when goods are unique and 'in other proper circumstances.' The vague language was held not to authorize wholesale granting of the remedy when output contracts were involved. The remedy of damages—the difference between the market price at the time of the breach and the contract price—adequately compensated the buyer for his inability to procure the cotton from the farmer with whom he had contracted. *Cf.* R.L. Kimsey Cotton Co., Inc. v. Ferguson, 233 Ga. 962, 214 S.E.2d 360 [16 UCC Rep. 1223] (1975). Likewise Weathersby was adequately protected from any damages occasioned by Gore's breach of the contract, if any occurred. He could have acquired additional cotton on the open market when Gore informed him he would no longer perform under the contract. He did not do so and thus, if entitled to damages at all, must settle for the difference between the contract and the market price at the time Gore cancelled. *See* Miss.Code Ann. § 75–2–712 (1973)."

2. Consider the following terms of a contract between a cotton marketing association and its membership:

"15. (a) Inasmuch as the remedy at law would be inadequate; and inasmuch as it is now and ever will be impracticable and extremely difficult to determine the actual damage resulting to the Association, should the Grower fail so to sell and deliver all of his cotton, the Grower hereby agrees to pay to the Association for all cotton delivered, sold, consigned or marketed by or for him other than in accordance with the terms hereof, the sum of five cents per pound as liquidated damages for the breach of this contract; all parties agreeing that this contract is one of a series dependent for its true value upon the adherence of each and all the growers to each and all of the said contracts.

"(b) The Grower agrees that in the event of a breach or threatened breach by him of any provisions regarding delivery of cotton, the Association shall be entitled to an injunction to prevent breach or further breach hereof and to a decree for specific performance hereof; and the parties agree that this is a contract for the purchase and sale of personal property under special circumstances and conditions, and that the buyer cannot go to the open market and buy cotton to replace any which the Grower may fail to deliver."

In Staple Cotton Cooperative Ass'n v. Pickett, 326 So.2d 337 (La.1976), the court enforced the terms of the above contract by ordering specific performance against a grower who had not yet marketed his crop. However, the court said that the plaintiff would have been entitled to specific performance even if there had been no contract provision authorizing the remedy.

No provision in the Uniform Commercial Code and no section of the Restatement (Second) of Contracts expressly denies the parties to a contract the right to contract for specific performance. Nevertheless, it is generally assumed that courts will not be bound by such contractual stipulations because the decision to grant specific performance calls for the exercise of equitable judicial discretion. Restatement (Second) of Contracts §§ 357–58 (1981).

For a summary and critique of the current case law concerning the validity of a contractual provision that purports to give one party a right to specific performance, see Kronman, Specific Performance, 45 U.Chi.L.Rev. 351, 371–73 (1978). *See also* Martin v. Sheffer, 102 N.C.App. 802, 403 S.E.2d 555 (1991) and Frank LeRoux, Inc. v. Burns, 4 Wash.App. 165, 480 P.2d 213 (1971) (Section 2–719(1)(a) of the Uniform Commercial Code implicitly authorizes a contractual agreement for specific performance).

3. Contrary to the outcome in *Weathersby* and *Duval,* most courts ordered specific performance of the contracts to supply cotton when cotton prices tripled in 1973. Important factors in these decisions were the resale of cotton to third parties,* the general unavailability of substitute cotton,** and harm to the cooperative marketing association in the event of a member's failure to abide by the agreement to sell.*** Thus the cotton cases represent a continuation of earlier cases which held that contracts for the sale of a grower's output are specifically enforceable when there is a lack of available substitutes.****

* R.N. Kelly Cotton Merchant, Inc. v. York, 379 F.Supp. 1075 (M.D.Ga.1973), *aff'd per curiam,* 494 F.2d 41 (5th Cir.1974); Mitchell–Huntley Cotton Co. v. Waldrep, 377 F.Supp. 1215 (N.D.Ala.1974); Austin v. Montgomery, 336 So.2d 745 (Miss.1976). *See also* Ace Equip. Co. v. Aqua Chem., Inc., 73 Pa.D. & C.2d 300, 20 U.C.C.Rep.Serv. 392 (1975) (specific performance granted to buyer of transformer who had arranged to resell it at a substantial profit).

** Mitchell–Huntley Cotton Co. v. Waldrep, 377 F.Supp. 1215 (N.D.Ala.1974) (characterized cotton as "unique and irreplaceable").

*** Carolinas Cotton Growers Ass'n v. Arnette, 371 F.Supp. 65 (D.S.C.1974).

**** Campbell Soup Co. v. Wentz, 172 F.2d 80 (3d Cir.1948) (carrots; contract not specifically enforced due to unconscionability); Hunt Foods v. O'Disho, 98 F.Supp. 267 (N.D.Cal.1951) (peaches; contract specifically enforced); Curtice Bros. Co. v. Catts, 72 N.J.Eq. 831, 66 A. 935 (1907) (tomatoes; con-

SECTION 3. CONTRACTS RELATING TO REAL PROPERTY

A. DAMAGES

The two most widely employed remedies for breaches of real estate sale contracts are damages and specific performance. An award of damages usually contemplates that the vendor will keep the property, or will sell it to someone else. An order of specific performance, on the other hand, is predicated on his conveying it to the contract purchaser, who will pay the full agreed price. In general, either buyer or seller may seek either remedy if the other party breaches.

Loss of bargain damages are traditionally measured as the difference between the contract price and the market value of the land on the date of breach. Under this measure, the vendor can obtain nothing if the property's value is higher than the contract price, while the purchaser can recover nothing if the property is worth less than the contract amount. But the "pure" loss of bargain computation may be only the beginning of a total claim for damages, as the following case and notes illustrate.

DONOVAN v. BACHSTADT

Supreme Court of New Jersey, 1982.
91 N.J. 434, 453 A.2d 160.

[Defendant Bachstadt contracted to sell real estate to plaintiffs Donovans for $58,900. The contract provided that Bachstadt would finance $44,000 by way of a purchase money mortgage, thus helping the Donovans avoid the necessity of bank financing, which at the time was available only at very high interest rates. Under applicable usury statutes, the purchase money mortgage could not have borne an interest rate exceeding 10.5%. It developed that Bachstadt did not have and could not obtain good title to the property.]

When defendant could not obtain marketable title, the Donovans commenced this suit for compensatory and punitive damages. As previously observed the trial court granted plaintiffs' motion for summary judgment. It was indisputable that the defendant had breached the agreement. The only issue was damages. The trial court held that plaintiffs were entitled under N.J.S.A. 2A:29–1 to recovery of their costs for the title search and survey. Plaintiffs had apparently in the interim purchased a home in Middlesex County and obtained a mortgage loan bearing interest at the rate of 13¼% per annum. Plaintiffs sought the difference between 10½% and 13¼% as compensatory damages, representing their loss of the benefit of the bargain. The trial court denied recovery because the contract was for the sale of the property and the financing "was only incidental to the basic concept."

The Appellate Division reversed. 181 N.J.Super. 367, 437 A.2d 728 (1981). It held that N.J.S.A. 2A:29–1 was declarative of the general

tract specifically enforced). *See also* Ferry–Morse Seed Co. v. Food Corn, Inc., 729 F.2d 589 (8th Cir.1984) (seed corn; mandatory preliminary injunction granted).

common law right to recover consequential damages for breach of a contract and that the statute modified the preexisting law, which limited a realty purchaser to recovery of his deposit upon a seller's breach due to a defective title. The court concluded the statute intended that the general law of damages for breach of a contract applies and stated that the difference in interest rates could be the basis for a measure of damages depending on whether the plaintiffs "have entered into a comparable transaction for another home * * * or are likely to do so in the near future * * *." Id. at 376, 437 A.2d 728. The Appellate Division cautioned that any award of future damages should represent the true life of the mortgage and be reduced to present value. Further, the plaintiffs should be held to a duty to mitigate. Lastly, if the proofs should demonstrate that plaintiffs have not purchased and are not likely to purchase a home in the near future, their damages would be remote and speculative. The cause was remanded for a plenary hearing.

I

The initial inquiry is whether plaintiffs are entitled to compensatory damages. We had occasion recently to discuss the measure of damages available when a seller breaches an executory contract for the sale of real property. St. Pius X House of Retreats v. Diocese of Camden, 88 N.J. 571, 582–87, 443 A.2d 1052 (1982). We noted that New Jersey follows the English rule, which generally limits a buyer's recovery to the return of his deposit unless the seller wilfully refuses to convey or is guilty of fraud or deceit. The traditional formulation of the English rule has been expressed by T. Cyprian Williams, an English barrister, as follows:

> Where the breach of contract is occasioned by the vendor's inability, without his own fault, to show a good title, the purchaser is entitled to recover as damages his deposit, if any, with interest, and his expenses incurred in connection with the agreement, but not more than nominal damages for the loss of his bargain. [T.C. Williams, The Contract of Sale of Land 128 (1930)]

In *St. Pius* we found no need to reexamine the English rule, though we raised the question whether the American rule that permits a buyer to obtain benefit of the bargain damages irrespective of the nature of the reasons for the seller's default might not be more desirable.

* * *

We are satisfied that the American rule is preferable. The English principle developed because of the uncertainties of title due to the complexity of the rules governing title to land during the eighteenth and nineteenth centuries. Oakley, "Pecuniary Compensation for Failure to Complete a Contract for the Sale of Land," 39 Cambridge L.J. 58, 69 (1980). At that time the only evidence of title was contained in deeds which were in a phrase attributed to Lord Westbury, "difficult to read, disgusting to touch, and impossible to understand." The reason for the English principle that creates an exception to the law governing damages for breaches of executory contracts for the sale of property is no longer valid, and the exception should be eliminated. *Cessante ratione legis, cessat et ipsa lex* (the reason for a law ceasing, the law itself ceases). See Fox v. Snow, 6 N.J. 12, 14, 22–23, 76 A.2d 877 (1950) (Vanderbilt, C.J., dissenting). Indeed in England the rule has been modified by placing the burden of proof on the vendor to establish that he has done everything within his power to carry out the contract. Malhotra v. Choudhury, [1978] 3 W.L.R. 825; [1979] 1 All E.R. 186 (C.A.).

Whether titles are clear may be ascertained by record searches. See N.J.S.A. 46:21–1; Jones, "The New Jersey Recording Act—A Study of its Policy," 12 Rutgers L.Rev. 328, 329–30 (1957). Moreover, limitation periods may be applicable. See N.J.S.A. 2A:14–30; 13A N.J. Practice (Lieberman, Abstracts and Titles) § 1643 at 140 (3d ed. 1966). Thus, it is standard practice for title examiners to search the back title for 60 years and until a warranty deed is found in the chain of title. Palamarg Realty Co. v. Rehac & Piatkowski, 80 N.J. 446, 460, 404 A.2d 21 (1979). Further the parties may insert appropriate provisions in their agreements protecting them from title defects so that to a very large extent sellers may control the measure of redress.

There is no sound basis why benefit of the bargain damages should not be awarded whether the subject matter of the contract is realty or personalty. Serious losses should not be borne by the vendee of real estate to the benefit of the defaulting vendor. This is particularly so when an instalment purchase contract is involved that extends over a period of years during which the vendee makes substantial payments upon the principal, as well as extensive improvements to the property.

The innocent purchaser should be permitted to recover benefit of the bargain damages irrespective of the good or bad faith of the seller. Contract culpability depends on the breach of the contractual promise. 4A Corbin, Contracts §§ 943–44, at 806–08 (1951). Where, as here, the seller agreed that title would be marketable, the seller's liability should depend upon his breach of that promise.

Many commentators have advocated the adoption of the American rule. 11 S. Williston, A Treatise on the Law of Contracts § 1399 at 524 (3d ed. 1968); 5A Corbin on Contracts § 1097 at 523 (1964); D. Dobbs, Handbook on the Law of Remedies § 12.8 at 835–36 (1973); 3 American Law of Property § 11.67 at 168 (1952). English commentators have also sharply criticized the English rule and advocated permitting the buyer to recover damages for loss of profit. Oakley, supra, at 70; Sydenham, "The Anomalous Rules in Bain v. Fothergill," 41 The Conveyancer and Property Lawyer 341 (1977). Many states now follow the American rule. 5A Corbin, supra, § 1098 at 525–35; 11 S. Williston, supra, at 524–28.

The English rule is consistent with the limitation on recovery in suits on a covenant for breach of warranty [in a deed]. The damages for a buyer, who has taken title and is ousted because the title is defective, are limited to the consideration paid and interest thereon. Gerbert v. Trustees, 59 N.J.L. 160, 180, 35 A. 1121 (E. & A.1896). There appears to be no real difference between that situation and one where the vendor who does not have good title refuses to convey. In both cases the buyer loses the property because of a defect in the title. The fact that one sues for breach of a warranty covenant does not justify depriving a buyer of compensatory damages to which he is justly entitled when the seller breaches the contract of sale. Professor Corbin has suggested that any inconsistency in this respect should be resolved by awarding full compensatory damages when the action is for breach of warranty. 5A Corbin, supra, § 1098, at 533. Moreover, an anomaly already exists, for our courts have acknowledged that a buyer may recover such damages upon a showing of the seller's bad faith. See Ganger v. Moffett, 8 N.J. 73, 83 A.2d 769 (1951).

We are satisfied that a buyer should be permitted to recover benefit of the bargain damages when the seller breaches an executory contract to convey real property. Here the defendant agreed to convey marketable title. He made that bargained-for promise and breached it and is responsible to the plaintiff for the damages occasioned thereby. The next question is how to compute those compensatory damages.

II

Judicial remedies upon breach of contract fall into three general categories: restitution, compensatory damages and performance. Separate concepts undergird each of these remedial provisions. The rationale for restitution is to return the innocent party to his status before the contract was executed. Compensatory damages are intended to recompense the injured claimant for losses due to the breach, that is, give the innocent party the benefit of the bargain. Performance is to effect a result, essentially other than in terms of monetary reparation, so that the innocent party is placed in the position of having had the contract performed. We have now adopted the American rule providing for compensatory damages upon the seller's breach of an executory contract to sell realty and we must examine the appropriate elements that should properly be included in an award.

"Compensatory damages are designed 'to put the injured party in as good a position as he would have had if performance had been rendered as promised.' 5 Corbin, Contracts § 992, p. 5 (1951)." 525 Main Street Corp. v. Eagle Roofing Co., 34 N.J. 251, 254, 168 A.2d 33 (1961); see also Giumarra v. Harrington Heights, Inc., 33 N.J.Super. 178, 196, 109 A.2d 695 (App.Div.1954), aff'd o.b., 18 N.J. 548, 114 A.2d 720 (1955); E. Farnsworth, Contracts 839 (1982). What that position is depends upon what the parties reasonably expected. It follows that the defendant is not chargeable for loss that he did not have reason to foresee as a probable result of the breach when the contract was made. Hadley v. Baxendale, 9 Exch. 341, 5 Eng.Rul.Case 502, (1854); accord Crater v. Binninger, 33 N.J.L. 513 (E. & A.1869). The oft-quoted language in Hadley for this proposition is:

> Where two parties have made a contract, which one of them has broken, the damages which the other party ought to receive, in respect of such breach, should be such as may fairly be considered either arising naturally, i.e., according to the usual course of things, from such breach of contract itself, or such as may reasonably be supposed to have been in the contemplation of both parties at the time they made the contract, as the probable result of the breach of it. [5 Eng.Rul.Case at 504]

See Restatement (Second) of Contracts § 351 (1981); see also Weiss v. Revenue Building & Loan Ass'n, 116 N.J.L. 208, 210, 182 A. 891 (E. & A.1936). Further the loss must be a reasonably certain consequence of the breach although the exact amount of the loss need not be certain. Kozlowski v. Kozlowski, 80 N.J. 378, 388, 403 A.2d 902 (1979); Tessmar v. Grosner, 23 N.J. 193, 203, 128 A.2d 467 (1957).

The specific elements to be applied in any given case of a seller's breach of an executory agreement to sell realty may vary in order to achieve the broad purposes of reparations; some items, however, will almost invariably exist. Thus the purchaser will usually be entitled to the return of the amount paid on the purchase price with interest thereon. Costs and expenses incurred in connection with the proposed acquisition, such as for the title search and survey, would fall in the same category. The traditional test is the difference between the market price of the property at the time of the breach and the contract price. Ganger v. Moffett, 8 N.J. 73, 79, 83 A.2d 769 (1951); King v. Ruckman, 24 N.J.Eq. 298 (Ch.), aff'd, 24 N.J.Eq. 556 (E. & A.1873). See cases cited in annotation, "Measure of recovery by vendee under executory contract for purchase of real property where vendor is unable to convey," 48 A.L.R. 12, 15–17 (1927). Under this standard the buyer who had taken possession before title passed would be entitled to recover for improvements he made that increased the value of the property. Sabaugh v. Schrieber, 87 Ind.App. 588, 162 N.E. 248 (1928).

The difference between market and contract price may not be suitable in all situations. Thus where a buyer had in turn contracted to sell the realty, it is reasonable to measure his damages in terms of the actual lost profit. See Bonhard v. Gindin, 104 N.J.L. 599, 142 A. 52 (E. & A.1928) (awarding the consideration paid, search fees, taxes and assessments paid, and lost profits from a sale to a third person); see also Giumarra v. Harrington Heights, 33 N.J.Super. 178, 109 A.2d 695 (App.Div.1954) (awarding contract buyer of realty lost profits in action against contract buyer's assignee). What the proper elements of damage are depend upon the particular circumstances surrounding the transaction, especially the terms, conditions and nature of the agreement.

The plaintiffs here assert that their damages are equivalent to the difference in interest costs incurred by them in purchasing a different home at another location. This claim assumes that the financial provision of the contract concerning the purchase money mortgage that the defendant agreed to accept was independent and divisible from the purchase of the land and house. The defendant contends that he did not agree to loan these funds in connection with the purchase of some other property, but that this provision was incidental to the sale of the house. Neither position is entirely sound. This financing was an integral part of the transaction. It can be neither ignored nor viewed as an isolated element.

The relationship of the financing to the purchase of a home has changed in recent years. As interest rates rose and the availability of first mortgage funds was sharply reduced, potential homeowners, though desirous of purchasing homes, found financing difficult to obtain. The seller's acceptance of a purchase money mortgage became an important factor in effecting a sale. See Rand, "Home Resale Market: Pattern Shift," N.Y. Times, March 22, 1981, § 11, at 18, col. 3. In evaluating a contract such a financial arrangement could play an important part in determining price. The rise in interest rates, the expense of mortgage credit and the availability of funds has rendered traditional methods of financing acquisition of homes impractical. Walleser, "The Changing Complexion of Home Mortgage Financing in America," 31 Drake L.Rev. 1, 2 (1981). Favorable vendor financing could lead to increased market value. Only then might a buyer be able to purchase. Iezman, "Alternative Mortgage Instruments: Their Effect on Residential Financing," Real Est.L.J. 3, 4 (1981). The importance of a seller's purchase money mortgage to the overall agreement to convey property was recognized in King v. Ruckman, 24 N.J.Eq. 298 (Ch.), aff'd, 24 N.J.Eq. 556 (E. & A.1873). The seller agreed to convey certain property and to accept as part of the purchase price a purchase money mortgage with 6% interest payable in five annual installments. The seller refused to convey. The buyer obtained a final decree for specific performance including the purchase money mortgage. The Chancery Court's view of the mortgage confirmed by the Court of Errors and Appeals on review was:

> The benefit accruing to the purchaser from having time for the payment of the bulk of the principal, and of the rate agreed on for interest, is apparent. It is a material ingredient of the bargain, as much so in reality, though not in degree, as the price, and cannot be withheld from the purchaser in this case by the willful misconduct of the vendor, for the sole benefit of the vendor himself. [24 N.J.Eq. at 303]

The interest rate is not sufficiently discrete to calculate damages in terms of it alone under these circumstances.

In some circumstances interest rate differentials are an appropriate measure of damages. Where the buyer has obtained specific performance, but because of the delay has incurred higher mortgage rates, then his loss clearly should include the higher financing cost. Godwin v. Lindbert, 101 Mich.App. 754, 300 N.W.2d 514 (1981), is illustrative. The buyers lost their commitment for a mortgage with an interest rate of 8¾% when the seller refused to convey. The buyers succeeded in obtaining specific performance but were compelled to borrow funds at 11½%. They were awarded the difference reduced to present value. See also Reis v. Sparks, 547 F.2d 236 (4th Cir.1976). Moreover, we are not unmindful of the possibility that a buyer might demonstrate that a lending institution's commitment to advance the funds initially at a certain interest rate was due to the buyer's financial condition. The particular realty might well be a secondary and incidental consideration for the loan. Therefore an interest differential occasioned by the seller's default might be a proper factor in fixing damages where the buyer shortly thereafter purchased another property financed at a higher interest rate.

This is not such a situation. The defendant's motive was to sell a house and not to lend money. In measuring the plaintiffs' loss there should be a determination of the fair market value of the property and house that could be acquired with a purchase money mortgage in the principal amount of $44,000 at an interest rate of 10½% (no appeal was taken from the judgment of reformation) for a 30–year term. The valuation should be at the time the defendant failed to comply with the judgment of specific performance. The plaintiffs would be entitled to the difference between $58,900 and that fair market value. If the fair market value was not more than the contract price, the plaintiffs would not have established any damage ascribable to the loss of the bargain. They are also entitled to their expenditures for the survey, search, and counsel fees for services rendered in preparation of the aborted closing. The plaintiffs have hitherto received the return of the deposit.

Notes

1. The English rule, discussed in Donovan, limiting the purchaser to restitutionary recovery when the seller's title is defective but the seller has acted in good faith, is followed in about half the American jurisdictions. However, it does not apply if the vendor breaches the contract, even in good faith, for reasons unrelated to his title. *See* Beard v. S/E Joint Venture, 321 Md. 126, 581 A.2d 1275 (1990), for a thorough discussion of this issue.

Suppose the contract itself restricts the buyer's remedy to restitution. If the seller acted in bad faith, can the buyer still get loss-of-bargain damages? The court so held in Wolofsky v. Waldron, 526 So.2d 945 (Fla.App.1988).

2. How is "fair market value" determined for purposes of the "loss of bargain" rule? With single family dwellings, the primary approach is to utilize recent sales of comparable properties in the geographical area. Suppose, however, we are dealing with commercial or residential rental real estate. How is fair market value determined? Consider the following analysis:

> "Fair market value of the property is the price at which it would change hands between a willing buyer and seller, neither being under any compulsion to consummate the sale. Ohio Casualty Insurance Co. v. Ramsey (1982), Ind.App., 439 N.E.2d 1162, 1167, *trans. denied.* In *Ohio Casualty,* we set out three well recognized methods of determining a property's fair market value taken by eminent domain:
>
> > '(1) the current *cost of reproducing* the property less depreciation from all sources; (2) the "*market data* " approach or value indicated by recent sales of comparable properties in the market, and (3) the "*income-approach,*" or the value which the property's net earning power will support based upon the capitalization of net income. This three-approach means of reaching market value is usually combined. It is stated in American Institute of Real Estate Appraisers. "The Appraisal of Real Estates" (3d ed.) at page 66: " * * * In the majority of his assignments, the appraiser utilizes all three approaches. *On occasion he may believe the value indication from one approach will be more significant than from the other two,* yet he will use all three as a check against each to test his own judgment." All three methods have been judicially approved.' "

Annon II, Inc. v. Rill, 597 N.E.2d 320, 326–27 (Ind.App.1992).

3. In addition to the traditional loss-of-bargain damages, available to a buyer only if the property's value is higher than the contract price, what other elements of damage ("incidental" or "consequential") might an innocent buyer attempt to recover?

(a) Expenditures for title examination, survey, and attorneys' fees in preparation for the closing? *See Donovan, supra.*

(b) Airfare for travel to negotiate and execute the contract which the seller subsequently breached? See Fountain v. Mojo, 687 P.2d 496 (Colo. App.1984).

(c) Additional rent, taxes, mortgage interest, and other carrying costs at her present location while she locates and purchases substitute property?

(d) Loss of particularly favorable financing from a bank or savings association, no longer available as a result of interest rate changes? See Wall v. Pate, 104 N.M. 1, 715 P.2d 449 (1986).

(e) The cost of leasing temporary quarters elsewhere, including rent, advertising for a place to lease, and the expense of moving to the leased premises? *See* Gorzelsky v. Leckey, 402 Pa.Super. 246, 586 A.2d 952 (1991).

If these items are recoverable as damages, should they (or any of them) be offset by the fact that the purchaser still has the purchase money, and may have earned interest on it (if it was to have been paid in cash) or has saved the interest which she would have paid on it (if she intended to borrow it)? *See* ULTA § 2–514. Should they be offset by general declines in property values, so that the purchaser can subsequently obtain similar property at a lower cost?

4. Consider the damages recoverable by the seller when the buyer breaches. The traditional measure of loss-of-bargain damages measures the property's market value as of the date of the breach, but as the *Donovan* case suggests, this may not be a fair or relevant date. Frequently the seller will be forced to put the property back on the market and may wait for months or even years before another buyer is found. In a declining market, the ultimate sale price may be much lower than the value on the date of the breach. Assuming that the seller has continued to make a diligent effort to resell, shouldn't the actual resale price be the relevant value for purposes of computing damages? The court so held in Kuhn v. Spatial Design, Inc., 245 N.J.Super. 378, 385–86, 585 A.2d 967, 970 (1991), following the rule for sales of goods found in U.C.C. §§ 2–706, –708 and in ULTA §§ 504–507:

"A rule that restricts damages for breach of a contract to buy real estate to the difference between contract price and value at the time of breach (plus expenses) works fairly only in a static market. A damage rule works fairly in a declining market only if it takes account of slowing sales and falling values. In such cases, where the seller puts the property back on the market and resells, the measure is not contract price less value at the time of breach, but rather the resale price, if it is reasonable as to time, method, manner, place and terms. These are matters for the factfinder, who may or may not conclude from the evidence that what actually occurred after breach by way of resale was reasonable and thus provides an accurate measure of damages.

"We adopt, for these purposes, the essence of the sellers' damage rules provided for sellers of goods in the Uniform Commercial Code, *N.J.S.A.* 12A:2–706 and 708, and adapted for sellers of real estate in §§ 504–507 of the Uniform Land Transactions Act (ULTA), which New Jersey has not adopted. We adopt these rules because they take account of the effect of changing market conditions in sound ways which New Jersey's reported decisions have not yet taken into account.

"Where a buyer of real estate wrongfully rejects, repudiates or materially breaches as to a substantial part of the contract, the seller may resell in a manner that is reasonable as to method, manner, time, place and terms. The defaulting buyer must have reasonable notice of the time after which resale will take place. If the resale is a public sale, the defaulting buyer must have notice of the time and place, and may buy. The seller may then recover the amount by which the unpaid contract price and any incidental and consequential damages exceed the resale price, less expenses avoided because of the buyer's breach. *See* ULTA § 2–504, 13 *U.L.A.* 552 (1977); *N.J.S.A.* 12A:2–706."

5. A further reason the courts may prefer to rely on the actual reselling price as the pertinent measure of value is that otherwise they must act on the basis of appraisal testimony, which is notoriously imprecise. For example, in Askari v. R & R Land Co., 179 Cal.App.3d 1101, 225 Cal.Rptr. 285 (1986), the appraisers for the two parties were $400,000 apart in their estimates of value as of the trial date—an amount which was 32% of the original contract price of $1.25 million. Such variations in appraisals are not unusual, and scarcely build one's confidence in the measurement of damages.

6. Consider now the "incidental" and "consequential" damages recoverable by a seller. Should they include the following?

(a) Carrying costs of the property until it is resold (assuming continuing reasonable efforts to resell)? Such costs might include property taxes, insurance, utilities, and maintenance. See Mueller v. Johnson, 60 Wash. App. 683, 806 P.2d 256 (1991); Allen v. Enomoto, 228 Cal.App.2d 798, 803–804, 39 Cal.Rptr. 815 (1964) (approving these items). But see Quigley v. Jones, 255 Ga. 33, 334 S.E.2d 664 (1985), refusing to allow the vendor damages for taxes, insurance, utilities, repairs, or loss of use of the sales proceeds, during the time he attempted to remarket the property.

(b) Interest on existing mortgage loans on the property until it is resold?

(c) Interest income the seller expected to earn on the purchase price, or on purchase-money mortgage financing he was obligated under the contract to provide to the purchaser? See Askari v. R & R Land Co., 179 Cal.App.3d 1101, 225 Cal.Rptr. 285 (1987) (approving recovery of lost interest on purchase-money financing); Van Moorlehem v. Brown Realty Co., 747 F.2d 992 (10th Cir.1984) (denying recovery for interest seller expected to earn on cash purchase price).

(d) The cost of a second real estate broker's commission on the resale, if the seller was obliged to pay a commission on the first sale even though it did not close? See Mueller v. Johnson, 60 Wash.App. 683, 806 P.2d 256 (1991) (approving this item). Other resale expenses (e.g., advertising) would presumably be treated similarly.

(e) Increased tax liability as a result of changes in the tax laws occurring between the scheduled closing under the original contract and the date of a later resale? See Morgan v. Tzung, 278 Cal.Rptr. 221 (1991) (Cal.Ct.App. ordered not published, Rule 976, Cal.Rules of Ct.) (denying recovery).

See generally ULTA § 2–507; R. Cunningham, W. Stoebuck, and D. Whitman, Property § 10.3 (2d Ed.1993). Should these items be recoverable for the entire time period to the date of resale (again, assuming reasonable efforts to resell), or merely to the date of breach? Should it matter whether the seller's land was tied up in litigation with the buyer (perhaps with a *lis pendens* filed) so that, as a practical matter, the property could not be resold until the litigation was concluded? See Morgan v. Tzung, supra.

Suppose the value of the property rises during the period the seller is attempting to remarket it, and he sells it for more than the original contract price. Should this increase offset his recovery of incidental or consequential damages? Askari v. R & R Land Co., supra, so holds; contra, see Turner v. Benson, 672 S.W.2d 752 (Tenn.1984).

What about the use value of the property during the period the seller is attempting to resell? If the seller in fact lets the property to a tenant during the interim, it seems obvious that the rent collected should offset the seller's claim for incidental and consequential damages. Should a similar result follow, with an offset for fair rental value, if the seller continues to use the land himself? Or suppose the seller does not in fact use the property, but it remains available and adaptable to the seller's use?

7. Even if the contract is eventually performed, either under a decree of specific performance or voluntarily (but after an unjustified delay), should the non-breaching party also be permitted to recover some or all of the elements mentioned in the above notes as damages? See Dato v. Mascarello, 197 Ill.App.2d 847, 145 Ill.Dec. 411, 557 N.E.2d 181 (1989) (where purchaser breached and was ordered to specifically perform, vendor could also recover damages for interest on purchase money mortgage purchaser should have been paying, and for vendor's carrying costs of the property, during the period of delay); Shelter Corp. of Canada, Ltd. v. Bozin, 468 So.2d 1094 (Fla.App.1985) (where vendor breached and was ordered to specifically perform, it could recover damages for interest and taxes, but only to the extent offset by purchaser's claim for damages for loss of fair rental value); III Lounge, Inc. v. Gaines, 227 Neb. 585, 419 N.W.2d 143 (1988); Annot., 74 A.L.R.2d 578 (1960). Cf. McCoy v. Alsup, 94 N.M. 255, 609 P.2d 337 (App.1980).

B. RESTITUTION

UTEMARK v. SAMUEL

District Court of Appeal, 1953.
118 Cal.App.2d 313, 257 P.2d 656.

SHINN, PRESIDING JUSTICE.

In this action plaintiffs had judgment for the rescission* of a contract to purchase unimproved land for $10,000. The reason for the rescission was that while plaintiffs performed and offered to perform their agreement, the defendants refused to perform and to give a deed upon tender of the purchase price.

* Rescission is also considered in Ch. 4, *supra*.

The date of the agreement was September 14, 1946, and the date of the judgment, January 24, 1952. During this interval plaintiffs were in possession and made valuable improvements, consisting of the construction of a shop for a welding business, and the installation of a small office building.

The court rendered an interlocutory decree May 17, 1950, by which rescission was decreed and a referee was appointed to take evidence and report upon: (1) the reasonable value of the usage of the land while plaintiffs were in possession; (2) the present market value of the land and buildings; (3) the value of the buildings apart from the land; (4) the cost to plaintiffs of construction of the building; (5) the value of the buildings removed from the land and the feasibility and cost of removal; (6) knowledge of defendants at the time of the sale as to the uses plaintiffs intended to make of the property. The referee reported: (1) that the reasonable value of the use of the land, unimproved, was $50 per month; (2) the reasonable value of the use of the land after it was improved by plaintiffs was $286 per month; (3) the present market value of the land with the buildings was $11,650; the value of the office building was $250; (4) there were no other improvements which would enhance the value of the land; (5) the value of the office building removed from the land was $250; (6) the fair market value of the shop building was $6,400; (7) he could not determine whether it would be feasible to remove the shop building.

The court found: (1) $10,000 was a fair price for the land at the time of the purchase; (2) plaintiffs had complied, and offered to comply, with the agreement; (3) defendants failed and refused to convey the land; (4) plaintiffs gave due notice of rescission and offered to make restoration; (5) plaintiffs had paid $6,419.30 on the contract price, $508.42 as taxes, and a real estate commission of $500; (6) cost of the improvements placed on the land by plaintiffs was $12,154.41 (these items total $19,582.13); (7) the value of the shop building was $6,400, and of the office building, $250; (8) present value of the land and improvements was $11,650; (9) the rental value of the land from September 14, 1946 to July 14, 1947, was $50 per month, or $500; the rental value of the land and shop building from July 14, 1947 to December 1, 1947, was $1,810; for the land and shop from January 1, 1948 to December 31, 1948, $2,600, and from January 1, 1949 to August 30, 1951, $135 a month, or $4,320. According to these figures the total rental value was $8,230. The court then added $6,419.30, the amount paid on the contract, $508.42 taxes paid, $500 commission paid, $6,400 the present value of the shop building, and $250 the value of the office building, making a total of $14,077.72. From this sum was deducted $8,230 as the value of the use of the land and buildings, leaving a balance of $5,847.73, the amount for which plaintiffs were given judgment, which was declared to be a lien on the land.

Plaintiffs were ordered to pay $500 as half of the fee fixed for the referee, and defendants were ordered to pay the other half. The amount of the fee was declared to be a lien on the land.

Plaintiffs appeal on a clerk's transcript. Their principal contentions are that the court erred in not restoring them to their original position by giving them judgment for the sums they had expended under the agreement, including the reasonable cost of their improvements which became attached to the land, and that it was error to require them to pay a part of the fee of the referee.

We shall discuss first the use by the court of the market value of the improvements at the time of trial as a basis for reimbursement of plaintiffs for their expenditures upon the land. As already noted, the cost of the improvements was found to be $12,154.41, and their present value of $6,650. By the judgment plaintiffs were compelled to lose the difference of $5,504.41.

The statutory law on the subject is § 3408 of the Civil Code: "On adjudging the rescission of a contract, the court may require the party to whom such relief is granted to make any compensation to the other which justice may require." We think it is safe to say that the invariable rule is that one who has rescinded his contract to purchase land is entitled to receive as a part of his detriment caused by the seller's breach the cost of permanent improvements which he has placed upon the land in good faith. Mr. Williston says (Rev.Ed.Vol. 5, p. 4136): "So where a vendor wrongfully refuses a conveyance to a purchaser in possession, the latter may recover what he has paid the vendor and also what he has expended in improvements on the land and not merely the increased value of the land by virtue of the improvement. That is, the law should impose on the wrongdoing defendant a duty to restore the plaintiff's former status, not merely to surrender any enrichment or benefit that he may unjustly hold or have received; though if the market value or, in the absence of a market value, the benefit to the defendant of what has been furnished exceeds the cost or value to the plaintiff, there is no reason why recovery of this excess should not be allowed."

Defendants have not brought to our attention any case in which the court required the defaulting seller, upon rescission, to pay only the amount by which the improvements enhanced the value of the property, regardless of the reasonable cost expended by the buyer thereon. Defendants merely argue that the court had power to adjust the equities between the parties, but this does not satisfy. The authority expressed in § 3408 of the Civil Code is one that must be exercised in accordance with settled principles of law and equity. In the absence of evidence, and of any finding of bad faith on the part of plaintiffs, or improvidence or recklessness in making the expenditures or improvements, it was error not to allow plaintiffs judgment for the amount found to have been expended by them, since it must be presumed that they acted in good faith. There was no finding that the building was not suitable for uses which were permitted under zoning regulations which affected the property, all of which were specified in the findings.

It appears to have been the purpose of the court to place the *defendants* in *status quo* regardless of any loss *plaintiffs* might suffer, but it was the plaintiffs, not the defendants, who were entitled to be restored to their former position. This is the purpose of rescission. Equity is solicitous that the innocent party who rescinds be not made to suffer. It exercises no such solicitude for the wrongdoer who has brought about a situation in which one or the other must lose. When defendants elected not to convey the property they necessarily elected to take the consequences, which meant restoration of plaintiffs to the position they were in at the time they entered into the agreement.

Insofar as the fees of the referee are concerned, we must say initially that the record does not disclose any good reason for a reference of the issues. It appears to have been made for the benefit of defendants. Plaintiffs were interested only in the amount of money which they had expended, which would seem to have been a simple matter for the court to determine. All the other questions submitted to the referee pertain to the rental value, the present value of the land with the improvements, and the improvements separated from the land, and the determination of these questions had relation only to the defendants' theory, adopted by the court, that the defendants should not be required to pay on account of the improvements any more than their market value at the time of trial. The parties were entitled to the time of the court without extra expense, in the absence of reasonable necessity for a reference. So far as the findings go, if there was necessity, it appears to have been caused by the defendants. The matter of the referee's fees should be re-examined and the charge reapportioned. If plaintiffs were prepared to prove the cost of their improvements expeditiously, and without wasting the time of the court, they should have been permitted to do so without a reference. If they were not so prepared, or if they agreed to the reference, they should be charged with a share of the reasonable expense of the reference proportionate to the time consumed before the referee in hearing their evidence. Where the parties have not agreed upon a different rate of compensation, the fees of a referee are $5 per day. Code Civ.Proc. § 1023. We may add that there is nothing in the findings to explain or justify a fee of $1,000 for the services of the referee. Neither can we understand how the land, found to be worth $10,000, plus the improvements worth $6,650, could be found to have a present value of only $11,650, although these were all immaterial findings.

Defendants were entitled to offset the reasonable rental value of the unimproved land against any sums due from them. They were not entitled to receive as a credit the value of the use of the improvements installed by plaintiffs. Also, the rental from January 1 to December 31, 1948, of $2,600, or $216.66 per month, was based upon a finding that plaintiffs earned in their business in that year $26,000, and that ten per cent of it was a reasonable rental. This was not a proper criterion of rental value.

In their closing brief plaintiffs, for the first time, make the claim that they should have been allowed interest on the money they had paid out on the contract, for taxes and a broker's commission. No reason being shown for not raising the point in the opening brief, it does not deserve consideration. Graner v. Hogsett, 84 Cal.App.2d 657, 191 P.2d 497. We may say, however, that interest should have been allowed, Kane v. Ott, 73 Cal.App. 124, 128, 238 P. 126, and that it is one of the matters to be considered by the trial court in balancing the equities. A considerable discretion rests with that court in determining "what justice may require," in the way of compensation due from plaintiffs upon rescission of their purchase. But when plaintiffs are given interest on their money, there will yet be other matters to consider. One question would be whether the amount to be paid by defendants as the cost of the improvements should be reduced by the amount of normal depreciation of the buildings. Plaintiffs have had the use of them, and if defendants are to be charged with the original cost it would not be inequitable to reduce the cost figure by the amount of normal depreciation or deterioration due to use. Such matters are within the discretion of the trial court. We therefore confine our opinion to the questions of law which we have discussed. We may add, however, that the record discloses no reason for not allowing plaintiffs their costs of suit.

The judgment is affirmed insofar as it decrees a rescission of the agreement of purchase and denies relief to defendants on their cross-complaint; in all other respects it is reversed for further proceedings.

PARKER WOOD and VALLEE, JJ., concur.

Note

If the vendee plaintiff of real property in *Utemark v. Samuel* had received title (contrary to what transpired there), the right to rescind would depend upon the basis for the claim for this relief. If it were *fraud,* rescission relief would be available without regard to whether the contract were executory, or executed, as suggested by the note which follows the next principal case. By contrast, the courts, as a general matter, deny rescission relief to a vendee to whom title has been conveyed where the complaint is based upon *breach* of contract due to a title defect. The vendee's remedies are then said to be "merged in the deed" and, consequently the vendee is limited to a claim for damages based upon title warranties. This limitation, however, does not apply where a vendor's title undertaking, or promise, is not merged in the deed, or where the contract is executory and title has not been conveyed to the vendee.

The vendee who does rescind after making improvements or payments on the purchase price may ask the equity court to impose a lien upon the property to satisfy claims based upon these outlays and would be required to account for the value of use, as well as other, benefits during occupancy as was required in *Utemark.* These vendee remedies are discussed in I Palmer, Law of Restitution (1978) §§ 3.14, 3.15, 4.17 and 4.18.

NORTON v. POPLOS * 443 A.2d 1 (Del.1982). The plaintiff seller sought specific performance of a contract for the sale of certain real estate. The defendant buyer counterclaimed for rescission, cancellation of the deed and restitution on the ground that the sale had been induced by a material misrepresentation of which, however, the seller was unaware at the time it was made.

The Supreme Court of Delaware ruled that there could be rescission and restitution even though the misrepresentation relied upon was "innocent" and therefore, not tortious, and remanded the case to the trial court for a finding with respect to that possibility.

The court discussed the misrepresentation issue, and the relevance of the provision in the contract which stated there are no "written or oral representations" not expressed in the contract (a so-called "merger clause") as follows:

> "Essentially, the equitable remedy of rescission results in abrogation or 'unmaking' of an agreement and attempts to return the parties to the

* This case also is considered at p. 872, *supra.*

status quo. Common grounds for rescission of a contract for the sale of real property include fraud, misrepresentation and mistake. 8A *Thompson on Real Property* § 4465 pp. 366, 367 (1963). But in addition to rescission for fraudulent misrepresentation, *Williston on Contracts* § 1487 p. 322 (3rd Ed.1970), rescission also may be granted under certain circumstances for innocent misrepresentations made by a seller. Thus, as stated by Professor Williston:

> 'It is not necessary, in order that a contract may be rescinded for fraud or misrepresentation, that the party making the misrepresentation should have known that it was false. Innocent misrepresentation is sufficient for though the representation may have been made innocently, it would be unjust and inequitable to permit a person who has made false representations, even innocently, to retain the fruits of a bargain induced by such representations.'

Williston, supra, at § 1500, pp. 400, 401. Similarly, the recently promulgated *Restatement 2nd of Contracts,* § 164, states that,

> 'If a party's manifestation of assent is induced by either a fraudulent *or material* misrepresentation by the other party upon which the recipient is justified in relying, the contract is voidable by the recipient.' (Emphasis added.)

See also Restatement 1st of Contracts, § 476 (1932). Most American jurisdictions which have addressed this issue appear to recognize that an innocent material misrepresentation by a vendor which induces the sale of the property is ground for rescission of the contract. *Thompson, supra,* § 4472, pp. 401, 402. In addition to ordering rescission, a court will generally direct that a down payment by a buyer be returned on a theory of restitution. *See Restatement 1st of Restitution,* § 55 (1937); *Dobbs, Handbook on the Law of Remedies,* § 4.1, p. 222 (1973).

"A misrepresentation need not be in the form of written or spoken words. Stated simply, a misrepresentation is merely an 'assertion not in accordance with the facts.' *Restatement 2nd of Contracts,* § 159, and such an assertion may be made by conduct as well as words. *Id.* Comment a. And although a statement or assertion may be facially true, it may constitute an actionable misrepresentation if it causes a false impression as to the true state of affairs, and the actor fails to provide qualifying information to cure the mistaken belief.

* * *

"Finally, we consider several other matters raised in the appeal.

* * *

"Poplos argues that Norton's claim is barred by a 'merger' clause which, in essence, states that the parties have read and understood the contract and that "they do not rely on any written or oral representations not expressly written in [the] contract." It is clear, however, that a merger clause does not preclude a claim based upon fraudulent misrepresentations.* Slater v. Berlin, D.C.Mun.Ct.App., 94 A.2d 38, 43 (1953); Ortel v. Upper Ashburton Realty Co., Md.Ct.App., 171 Md. 678, 190 A. 239,

* This is the general rule. See, I G. Palmer, Law of Restitution (1978) § 3.20.

242 (1937). The law is not quite so clear, however, with respect to the effect of such a clause on an innocent or honest misrepresentation. Although we are aware of authority to the contrary, *cf.* Wilkinson v. Carpenter, Or.Supr., 276 Or. 311, 554 P.2d 512 (1976), we follow the better rule which is this: even if a sales contract contains a merger clause, a buyer may rescind the contract if it resulted from an innocent but material misrepresentation by a seller. As the Rhode Island Supreme Court has stated:

> '[T]he availability of the remedy of rescission is motivated by the obvious inequity of allowing a person who has made an innocent misrepresentation to retain the fruits of the bargain induced thereby. If we are to permit a party to rescind a contract as a result of an innocent misrepresentation, the boiler plate found in the merger clause shall not bar the use of this remedy.'

Halpert, supra, 267 A.2d at 735.

* * *

"For the reasons stated herein, the judgment is affirmed in part, reversed in part and the case is remanded for such proceedings consistent herewith as the Court of Chancery deems necessary." *

Notes

1. Rescission relief is routinely awarded to both the vendor and the vendee in land sale contracts where there is a claim of *fraud* without regard to whether the contract of sale has been executed and title transferred. Where the title has passed the assistance of equity may be needed in order to return title to the vendor. This was to be achieved, in *Norton,* by a decree cancelling the deed conveying the property to the vendee. The vendee would be required to account for any benefits received by virtue of occupancy but could also make a restitution claim for the value of improvements. In the latter event, where it is the wrongdoing party who seeks to recover for the benefits conferred, the value of the improvements, if restitution is to be allowed, should be determined by the method giving the lowest value to them.

Where, by way of contrast, a vendor seeks rescission relief based upon *breach* of contract, rather than fraud, neither quasi-contract relief, nor specific restitution relief in equity, is available if title has passed to the vendee. The vendor in such situations is left to sue on the contract for the contract price. In some jurisdictions the vendor may also ask the court to impose a lien upon the property to which the vendee has title to secure payment of the unpaid purchase price. If title has not passed the vendor who complains of a material breach may rescind and seek restitution relief accordingly. There may be no incentive to do so, however, because foreclosure of his vendor's lien, or terminating (rather than "rescinding") the contract and seeking to retain as damages any payments made by the vendee on the contract price, may be more attractive options. *See,* generally, I G. Palmer, Law of Restitution (1978) §§ 3.15 and 4.19.

2. Actionable misrepresentation may occur in a variety of other situations. These include: (1) failure to disclose that the contracting party is in fact the undisclosed agent of another (Walker v. Galt, 171 F.2d 613 (5th Cir.1948));

* This note material, along with the principal case, was also considered at pp. 873–74, *supra.*

(2) failure to reveal pertinent material facts where a fiduciary duty of loyalty is owed to the other party, or a relationship of trust and confidence exists between them (Moon v. Phipps, 67 Wash.2d 948, 411 P.2d 157 (1966)); (3) lack of intent to perform the promise given as consideration for a contract (California Conserving Co. v. D'Avanzo, 62 F.2d 528 (2d Cir.1933)); Entron, Inc. v. General Cablevision of Palatka, 435 F.2d 995 (5th Cir.1970) (failure to perform promised consideration evidences state of mind at time of contracting).

Opinions ordinarily are not a basis for rescission for misrepresentation. Restatement of Restitution § 8(3) (1937). There are exceptions, however, as when the "opinion" is given "in bad faith" (Stern v. Satra Corp., 539 F.2d 1305 (2d Cir.1976)) or by one purporting to be an expert. Restatement of Restitution § 8(3)(b) (1937). The traditional approach has treated a misrepresentation of law as necessarily involving an opinion and, consequently, as not providing a basis for rescission. *See* Restatement of Restitution § 55 (1937). However the courts have found a variety of special circumstances justifying reliance and rescission where the statement of law was misleading. Illustrative are Sainsbury v. Pennsylvania Greyhound Lines, Inc., 183 F.2d 548 (4th Cir.1950) (representation of law by a lawyer acting as a claims adjuster); Dushane v. Kazmierczak, 192 Misc. 23, 79 N.Y.S.2d 293 (1948), *aff'd,* 274 App.Div. 1025, 86 N.Y.S.2d 480 (1948) ("implied representation" of law by board of education to teacher); Fawcett v. Sun Life Assur. Co., 135 F.2d 544 (10th Cir.1943) (representation of law by insurer with "superior knowledge").*

C. SPECIFIC PERFORMANCE

1. *Suits by Buyer or Seller*

CENTEX HOMES CORP. v. BOAG

Superior Court of New Jersey, Chancery Division, 1974.
128 N.J.Super. 385, 320 A.2d 194.

[Centex constructed a condominium project in New Jersey which, when completed, would include six 31–story buildings containing more than 3600 units. The Boags signed a contract to purchase a condominium unit for $73,700, but shortly thereafter Mr. Boag was transferred by his employer to Chicago. The Boags stopped payment on the check they had given as earnest money, and refused to complete the purchase. Centex then brought this action for specific performance, or in the alternative, for liquidated damages in the amount of the earnest money.]

* * *

[U]nder a condominium housing scheme each condominium apartment unit constitutes a separate parcel of real property which may be dealt with in the same manner as any real estate. Upon closing of title the apartment unit owner receives a recordable deed which confers upon him the same rights and subjects him to the same obligations as in the case of traditional forms of real estate ownership, the only difference being that the condominium owner receives in addition an undivided interest in the common elements associated with the building and assigned to each unit. See the Condominium Act, N.J.S.A. 46:8B–1 et seq.; 15 Am.Jur.2d, Condominiums

* See, also, p. 873, *supra.*

and Cooperative Apartments, at 977 et seq.; Note, 77 Harv.L.Rev. 777 (1964).

Centex urges that since the subject matter of the contract is the transfer of a fee interest in real estate, the remedy of specific performance is available to enforce the agreement under principles of equity which are well-settled in this state. * * *

The principle underlying the specific performance remedy is equity's jurisdiction to grant relief where the damage remedy at law is inadequate. The text writers generally agree that at the time this branch of equity jurisdiction was evolving in England, the presumed uniqueness of land as well as its importance to the social order of that era led to the conclusion that damages at law could never be adequate to compensate for the breach of a contract to transfer an interest in land. Hence specific performance became a fixed remedy in this class of transactions. See 11 Williston on Contracts (3d ed. 1968) § 1418A; 5A Corbin on Contracts § 1143 (1964). The judicial attitude has remained substantially unchanged and is expressed in *Pomeroy* as follows:

> * * * in applying this doctrine the courts of equity have established the further rule that in general the legal remedy of damages is inadequate in all agreements for the sale or letting of land, or of any estate therein; and therefore in such class of contracts the jurisdiction is always exercised, and a specific performance granted, unless prevented by other and independent equitable considerations which directly affect the remedial right of the complaining party * * * [1 Pomeroy, Equity Jurisprudence (5th ed. 1941), § 221(b)]

While the inadequacy of the damage remedy suffices to explain the origin of the vendee's right to obtain specific performance in equity, it does not provide a *rationale* for the availability of the remedy at the instance of the vendor of real estate. Except upon a showing of unusual circumstances or a change in the vendor's position, such as where the vendee has entered into possession, the vendor's damages are usually measurable, his remedy at law is adequate and there is no jurisdictional basis for equitable relief. But see Restatement, Contracts § 360, comment c.[2] The early English precedents suggest that the availability of the remedy in a suit by a vendor was an outgrowth of the equitable concept of mutuality, i.e., that equity would not specifically enforce an agreement unless the remedy was available to both parties. See the discussion in Stoutenburgh v. Tompkins, 9 N.J.Eq. 332, 342–346 (Ch.1853); 4 Pomeroy, Equity Jurisprudence (5th ed. 1941), § 1405; Annotation, 65 A.L.R. 7, 40 (1930); Jones v. Newhall, 115

2. The Restatement's reasoning, as expressed in § 360, comment c amounts to the inconsistent propositions that (1) because the vendor may not have sustained any damage which is actionable at law, specific performance should be granted, and (2) he would otherwise sustain damage equal to the loss of interest on the proceeds of the sale. Yet loss of interest is readily measurable and can be recovered in an action at law, and to the extent that the vendor has sustained no economic injury, there is no compelling reason for equity to grant to him the otherwise extraordinary remedy of specific performance. At the end of the comment, the author suggests that the vendor is entitled to specific performance because that remedy should be mutual, a concept which is substantially rejected as a decisional basis in §§ 372 and 373 of the Restatement.

Mass. 244, 15 Am.Rep. 97, 103 (Sup.Jud.Ct.1874); Comment, 10 Villanova L.Rev. 557, 568–569 (1965).

So far as can be determined from our decisional law, the mutuality of remedy concept has been the prop which has supported equitable jurisdiction to grant specific performance in actions by vendors of real estate. * * *

Our present Supreme Court has squarely held, however, that mutuality of remedy is not an appropriate basis for granting or denying specific performance. Fleischer v. James Drug Store, 1 N.J. 138, 62 A.2d 383 (1948); see also, Restatement, Contracts § 372; 11 Williston, Contracts (3d ed. 1968), § 1433. The test is whether the obligations of the contract are mutual and not whether each is entitled to precisely the same remedy in the event of a breach. In *Fleischer* plaintiff sought specific performance against a cooperative buying and selling association although his membership contract was terminable by him on 60 days' notice. Justice Heher said:

> And the requisite mutuality is not wanting. The contention contra rests upon the premise that, although the corporation "can terminate the contract only in certain restricted and unusual circumstances, any 'member' may withdraw at any time by merely giving notice."
>
> Clearly, there is mutuality of obligation, for until his withdrawal complainant is under a continuing obligation of performance in the event of performance by the corporation. It is not essential that the remedy of specific performance be mutual. * * * The modern view is that the rule of mutuality of remedy is satisfied if the decree of specific performance operates effectively against both parties and gives to each the benefit of a mutual obligation. * * *
>
> The fact that the remedy of specific enforcement is available to one party to a contract is not in itself a sufficient reason for making the remedy available to the other; but it may be decisive when the adequacy of damages is difficult to determine and there is no other reason for refusing specific enforcement. Restatement, Contracts (1932), sections 372, 373. It is not necessary, to serve the ends of equal justice, that the parties shall have identical remedies in case of breach. [at 149, 62 A.2d at 388]

The disappearance of the mutuality of remedy doctrine from our law dictates the conclusion that specific performance relief should no longer be automatically available to a vendor of real estate, but should be confined to those special instances where a vendor will otherwise suffer an economic injury for which his damage remedy at law will not be adequate, or where other equitable considerations require that the relief be granted. Cf. Dover Shopping Center, Inc. v. Cushman's Sons, Inc., 63 N.J.Super. 384, 394, 164 A.2d 785 (App.Div.1960). As Chancellor Vroom noted in King v. Morford, 1 N.J.Eq. 274, 281–282 (Ch.Div.1831), whether a contract should be specifically enforced is always a matter resting in the sound discretion of the court and

> * * * considerable caution should be used in decreeing the specific performance of agreements, and * * * the court is bound to see that it really does the complete justice which it aims at, and which is the ground of its jurisdiction.

Here the subject matter of the real estate transaction—a condominium apartment unit—has no unique quality but is one of hundreds of virtually identical units being offered by a developer for sale to the public. The units are sold by means of sample, in this case model apartments, in much the same manner as items of personal property are sold in the market place. The sales prices for the units are fixed in accordance with [a] schedule filed by Centex as part of its offering plan, and the only variance as between apartments having the same floor plan (of which six plans are available) is the floor level or the building location within the project. In actuality, the condominium apartment units, regardless of their realty label, share the same characteristics as personal property.

From the foregoing one must conclude that the damages sustained by a condominium sponsor resulting from the breach of the sales agreement are readily measurable and the damage remedy at law is wholly adequate. No compelling reasons have been shown by Centex for the granting of specific performance relief and its complaint is therefore dismissed as to the first count.

Notes

1. The court in *Centex* makes a good deal of the fact that the condominium units were numerous and very similar. What relevance does this fact have to the *vendor's* right to specific performance? See Notes, 48 Temp.L.Q. 847 (1975); 43 U.Cin.L.Rev. 935 (1974). See ULTA § 2–506, which would often produce a result similar to *Centex.* Recall our earlier discussion about the difficulty of measuring loss of bargain damages on the basis of the testimony of appraisers. If Centex Homes had sought damages instead of specific performance, would it have had this difficulty? Given the fact that it had an ongoing sales program and a clearly-defined price schedule for its condominium units, would it not have been able to establish their current market value easily and reliably? Moreover, would not its success (or lack of success) in that sales program make it quite easy to estimate how long it would take Centex to remarket the unit the Boag's refused to buy, and for that matter, what the cost of remarketing it would be? Do you suppose these factors influenced the court in reaching its conclusion that specific performance was unnecessary?

2. Other recent cases casting doubt on the usual assumption that a vendor may have specific performance as a matter of course include Seabaugh v. Keele, 775 S.W.2d 205 (Mo.App.1989); Wolf v. Anderson, 334 N.W.2d 212 (N.D.1983); and Perron v. Hale, 108 Idaho 578, 701 P.2d 198 (1985). The last case, which seems to go much farther than *Centex,* contains the following language:

> "this Court has denied specific performance of a land sale contract when the "reasons assigned by the authorities for the rule applied in land contract cases are not convincing when applied to the facts of the case * * * * " Suchan v. Rutherford, 90 Idaho 288, 295, 410 P.2d 434, 438 (1966) (vendor of farm denied specific performance). This denial of specific

performance in particular land sale contracts cannot be distinguished on the basis that the remedy is not as readily available to vendors as it is to purchasers. * * * Rather, *Suchan* has been most often cited by this Court and others for the proposition that even though the case involves a land sale contract, specific performance may nevertheless be denied in particular circumstances within the discretion of the court. * * *

"*Suchan v. Rutherford, supra,* states that 'in each case equity must consider all factors affecting the availability of the remedy [of specific performance].' 90 Idaho at 298, 410 P.2d at 440. The factors which *Suchan* considered in denying specific performance were that: common irrigated farmland in Idaho is not necessarily unique and the market value is easily ascertainable; denial of specific performance would not deprive vendor of investment since the contract was not for cash, but a long term installment contract; specific performance of the long term contract would be difficult to enforce and might be unjust, oppressive or unconscionable over the long term of the contract; and, vendor was living on the property and there were no rental, depreciation, or enhancement values to complicate a damages formulation since vendor had sued only thirty-seven days after execution of the contract. Based on these particular facts, the court concluded that damages were adequate and enforcement of specific performance would be inequitable. In *Watkins v. Paul, supra,* the court denied specific performance to the holders of an option since the proposed purchasers had no 'unique purpose' in obtaining the land but merely wanted to 'resell it for profit.' 95 Idaho at 501, 511 P.2d at 783.

"None of the factors in *Suchan* or *Watkins,* or similar factors, exist in the present case. Rather, the evidence presents other factors which militate for the grant of specific performance. The house is of a unique construction. It is located in a seasonal recreation area with a limited marketing season. The trial court found that 'the house has deteriorated during this litigation because of [the] lack of occupancy * * * [which] is entirely the responsibility of the [buyers].' This deterioration would affect the market value and, in addition, a rental value would complicate a damages formulation. The buyers had the lower level of the house altered and partially finished to their particular desires, and buyers had done substantial damage to the walls upstairs and down while attempting to discover building defects. The agreement was for a cash sale which can be easily enforced. The buyers presented no evidence that specific performance would be unjust or oppressive. The evidence shows that at least one of the buyers had bought and sold property several times, and the buyers apparently had sufficient cash (the proceeds from the sale of the Nevada property) to purchase the house. Faced with these factors, we conclude that the trial court properly exercised its discretion in granting specific performance to the sellers."

3. Should the holding of *Centex* apply to a specific performance action by a *purchaser?* Assume the unit is one of hundreds of virtually identical units in a large condominium project. Is the lack of uniqueness enough to deny the purchaser's claim? At least two recent cases have refused to apply the reasoning of *Centex* to purchasers, and have granted them specific performance. See Pruitt v. Graziano, 215 N.J.Super. 330, 521 A.2d 1313 (1987); Giannini v. First National Bank of Des Plaines, 136 Ill.App.3d 971, 91 Ill.Dec. 438, 483 N.E.2d 924 (1985). Why are purchasers different from sellers in this respect?

In *Giannini,* the successor in interest of a developer of a large condominium project decided to refrain from filing a condominium declaration on certain of the buildings, and to place them in rental service instead. However, Giannini had signed a contract to purchase a unit in one of these buildings, and sued for specific performance. The defendant claimed that specific performance was impossible because the "property" did not exist (since the building had not officially been converted to condominium status). The court rejected this argument and ordered specific performance. It also noted that Giannini's legal remedies were literally "inadequate" because the original developer of the project had become insolvent and been dissolved, with the real estate having been transferred to the lending institution which had held the mortgage on it.

4. Unlike the *Centex* and *Perron* courts, most courts routinely grant specific performance for either party. *See, e.g.,* BD Inns v. Pooley, 218 Cal.App.3d 289, 266 Cal.Rptr. 815 (1990). Even if the vendor cannot fully perform (for example, because he does not own all the land contracted for, or it is subject to some encumbrance) the purchaser can still (if she wishes) get specific performance with an abatement of the price. *See, e.g.,* Rosenthal v. Sandusky, 35 Colo.App. 220, 533 P.2d 523 (1975); III Am.L.Prop. § 11.69 (1952); Note, Specific Performance with Abatement, 24 Okl.L.Rev. 495 (1971).

5. Earlier we considered the enforcibility of liquidated damages provisions in the context of contracts for the sale of chattels. See pp. 264–271 supra. Here, however, the focus is on the extent to which such clauses limit the availability of equitable relief. More specifically, to what extent does the presence of a liquidated damages provision prohibit the granting of specific performance? Consider Professor Dobbs' analysis of this issue:

> "If the liquidated damage clause by its terms specifies a deposit or a stipulated sum as the sole remedy for the plaintiff, or declares that its payment terminates the obligations of the parties, then of course the plaintiff cannot have specific performance any more than he could have actual damages; the remedy would be limited to the stipulated damages. But if the liquidated damages clause is not the sole remedy and not intended to give the defendant the option of buying out of the contract at the price specified, specific performance remains an option for the plaintiff. A liquidated damages or forfeiture clause that limits the liability of one party does not necessarily limit the liability of the other. The land buyer whose only liability upon default is to lose his earnest money deposit may still have specific performance against the seller unless the seller's liability is also limited by the agreement.
>
> "But even if, as a matter of contract interpretation, the liquidated damages clause did not foreclose specific performance, courts at one time worried that provision for liquidated damages might be inconsistent with the underlying premises of specific performance. If a land buyer or seller provides for liquidated damages, it may seem that the contract only signifies money, not a unique thing, hence that specific performance should be or could be denied. This view attaches too much significance both to the liquidated damages clause and to specific adequacy rules. Some courts have avoided the impact of this view by finding that the clause was not a true liquidated damages clause. But such a ruling is distortive. The easy answer is that even if the adequacy test is still dominant, the option to use liquidated damages might be a prudent provision to have at the time the

contract is made and one not at all inconsistent with a genuine desire to enforce the contract for its unique qualities. So the presence of a non-exclusive liquidated damages clause does not in itself preclude specific performance. The liquidated damages clause precludes specific performance only if the clause was intended to be an exclusive remedy."

3. D. Dobbs, Law of Remedies 268–69 (2d Ed.1993).*

6. Sometimes a court will deny specific performance because the contract is insufficiently certain. This issue was discussed at length in Barry M. Dechtman, Inc. v. Sidpaul Corp., 89 N.J. 547, 552–53, 446 A.2d 518, 521 (1982):

> "The oft-stated rule is that the terms of the contract must be definite and certain so that the court may decree with some precision what the defendant must do. 11 Williston, Contracts (3 ed. Jaeger), § 1414 at 810; 5A Corbin, Contracts (2 ed. 1964), § 1174 at 278. Whether the contract meets the test need not depend upon a literal reading. The court must also examine the situation of the parties and the accompanying circumstances to ascertain the meaning of the agreement. * * * Seeming difficulties of enforcement due to uncertainties attributable to language may vanish in the light of practicalities and a full understanding of the parties' intent. Reasonable certainty of the terms is sufficient. The two leading authorities on contracts have cautioned against refusal to order specific performance because of an apparent uncertainty in the terms of the contract. Professor Williston states:
>
> > It seems probable that the difficulty regarding uncertainty has been overemphasized; certainly, it should not be allowed to hamper or restrict equitable relief further than necessity requires. [11 *Williston, supra,* § 1424 at 819]
>
> Professor Corbin agrees:
>
> > There are cases in which the court has made a mountain out of a molehill and refused a decree that might well have been granted. Apparent difficulties of enforcement that arise out of uncertainties in expression often disappear in the light of courageous common sense and reasonable implications of fact. [5A *Corbin, supra,* at 283]"

Some courts require a greater degree of certainty when the plaintiff is seeking specific performance than when the plaintiff sues for damages. *E.g.,* Fox v. Sails at Laguna Club Dev. Corp., 403 So.2d 456 (Fla.App.1981) (denying claim for specific performance and remanding for consideration of cause of action for damages); Homart Devel. Co. v. Sigman, 868 F.2d 1556 (11th Cir.1989).

7. There are a variety of situations where specific performance may be denied and the plaintiff left to other remedies. These include:

> (a) If the vendor has resold the land to a purchaser who had no notice of the prior contract, the court will not force the innocent purchaser to give up the land in order to award specific performance to the original buyer. *See* Krantz v. Donner, 285 So.2d 699 (Fla.App.1973). On the other hand, where a subsequent purchaser takes with notice of the prior contract, she will lose the land if the original purchaser insists on specific performance. Frankel v. Northeast Land Co., 391 Pa.Super. 226, 570 A.2d 1065 (1990).

(b) Both specific performance and other remedies may be denied if there are precedent or concurrent conditions which have not been satisfied or if the plaintiff is in substantial breach.

(c) If the purchaser was buying the land for the purpose of immediate resale at a profit, its supposed uniqueness arguably is of little importance to him and damages is sometimes considered an adequate remedy. *See* Watkins v. Paul, 95 Idaho 499, 511 P.2d 781 (1973); cf. Chan v. Smider, 31 Wash.App. 730, 644 P.2d 727 (1982); Brenner, Specific Performance of Contracts for the Sale of Land Purchased for Resale or Investment, 24 McGill L.J. 513 (1978); McClintock Equity § 60 (2d Ed.1948). However, where the purchaser has already entered into a resale contract, is there a sound policy argument for granting specific performance of the original contract?

8. In 1984 the California legislature amended West's Ann.Cal.Civil Code § 3387 to provide that damages are conclusively presumed inadequate to compensate a purchaser of a single-family dwelling who intends to occupy it, while in other cases of contract breach by vendors, damages are merely presumed to be inadequate. Is this a form of consumerism? Are houses really more unique, or in some other relevant way different, than commercial or agricultural property?

9. Even when specific performance is ordered, a court may give a judgment for damages as well to compensate the innocent party for the delay or for other harms which have ensued since the date the contract should have been performed. *See, e.g.,* Woliansky v. Miller, 146 Ariz. 170, 704 P.2d 811 (App. 1985) (damages for deterioration to improvements on the land during five year delay); Bravo v. Buelow, 168 Cal.App.3d 208, 214 Cal.Rptr. 65 (1985) (damages resulting from rise in cost to purchaser of constructing a house on the land). Numerous cases in recent years have awarded damages for the higher cost of mortgage financing which the purchaser must pay because interest rates have risen during the period of delay; *see, e.g.,* Appollo v. Reynolds, 364 N.W.2d 422 (Minn.App.1985); Hutton v. Gliksberg, 128 Cal.App.3d 240, 180 Cal.Rptr. 141 (1982). See Garland, Purchaser's Interest Rate Increase: Caveat Venditor, 27 N.Y.L.Sch.L.Rev. 745 (1982); Note, 12 Seaton Hall L.Rev. 916 (1982); R. Cunningham, W. Stoebuck & D. Whitman, Property § 10.5 nn. 20–22 (2d Ed.1993).

10. If the seller does not own all the property covered by the contract, the purchaser may wish, and can generally obtain, specific performance with an abatement of the price to reflect the shortage in the land. *See, e.g.,* Burk v. Hefley, 32 Ark.App. 133, 798 S.W.2d 109 (1990); Ewing v. Bissell, 105 Nev. 488, 777 P.2d 1320 (1989). The same principle is applied if the seller owns only a fractional undivided interest in the property he contracted to sell; see Chastain v. Schomburg, 258 Ga. 218, 367 S.E.2d 230 (1988).

11. If the vendor breaches but refuses to return the purchaser's earnest money, some states give her a "vendee's lien" on the property to secure its recovery. *See* Sparks v. Charles Wayne Group, 568 So.2d 512 (Fla.App.1990) (purchaser may file a notice of lis pendens in support of his vendee's lien). Unless the contract is recorded (which is unlikely), a conveyance by the vendor to a good faith purchaser without notice of the contract will free the land of the lien. *See* State Sav. & Loan Ass'n v. Kauaian Development Co., 50 Hawaii 540, 445 P.2d 109 (1968); cf. In re Pearl, 40 B.R. 860 (Bkrtcy.D.N.J.1984). *See*

ULTA § 2–512, which provides for recordation of a "notice of lien" by the purchaser.

12. Suppose the vendor not only agrees to sell Blackacre, but also to finance part of the purchase price by taking back from the purchaser a promissory note and a purchase money mortgage. In essence, the vendor is agreeing to make a loan to the purchaser for part of the purchase price. Will a court grant specific performance of this promise? Traditionally, many courts have been unwilling to grant borrowers specific performance of agreements to lend money on the theory that breaches of such contracts can always be fully compensated in damages. *See e.g.,* Rogers v. Challis, 27 Beav. 175, 54 Eng.Rep. 68 (Ch.1859); City Centre One Associates v. Teachers Insurance and Annuity Ass'n of America, 656 F.Supp. 658 (D.Utah 1987); Bechtold Paving, Inc. v. City of Kenmare, 446 N.W.2d 19 (N.D.1989). However, this rule is hardly followed uniformly. Consider, in this regard, the language of Bregman v. Meehan, 479 N.Y.S.2d 422 (Sup.Ct.1984), where the court granted the purchaser's request for specific performance of a purchase money mortgage:

> "A review of the facts and analysis set forth, *supra,* reflects there is considerable difficulty in fairly evaluating the real extent of the plaintiffs' harm in this case. An accurate calculation of damages in cases concerned with mortgage lending now involves complexities not foreseen 100 years ago. D.C. Draper, The Broken Commitment: A Modern View of the Mortgage Lender's Remedy, 59 Cornell L.Rev. 418, 429 (Nov.–Mar. 1973–1974). It is not the same as in 1859, when *Roger v. Challis* was decided, and the court could say with equanimity 'There is a mere matter of calculation, and a jury would easily assess the amount of damages which the Plaintiff has sustained.'
>
> "The prior analysis also illustrates that a money judgment on the purchase money mortgage in this case would be substantially unfair to either plaintiff or defendant, depending upon the method of calculation employed, as compared to requiring specific performance of that mortgage obligation. The problem arises primarily because interest rates in recent years have been subject to unusual fluctuations, and rate trends are not predictable even with reasonable probability. This fact is demonstrated by the varying discount rates employed by courts over even a brief period of years. *Compare* Reis v. Sparks, 547 F.2d 236 [4th Cir.1976] using 5% *with* Hutton v. Gliksberg, 128 Cal.App.3d 240, 180 Cal.Rptr. 141 [2d Dist.1982] applying 14%. These are problems beyond this Court's control.
>
> "Thus, in recent years, there has been a noticeable erosion of the rule that a borrower cannot obtain specific performance on an agreement to lend money. Rather, specific performance has been granted, particularly when the loan relates to the sale of real property. * * *
>
> "As one authority has stated, a purchase money mortgage such as this, given by a seller at lower than commercially available rates, is usually for the purpose of encouraging a sale. It generally indicates that a buyer has agreed either to pay a higher price than he would otherwise have paid, or a price he could not otherwise afford absent the purchase money mortgage. In return, as here, the buyer has the benefit of relatively lower mortgage payments and a much smaller down payment than could be achieved with more traditional financing. Ominsky, Creative Mortgaging: PMMS,

Wraps and Various Participations, 14 Real Estate Rev. 74, 75 (Spring 1984). * * *

"[I]t is highly unlikely these plaintiffs will find another lender willing to give them a $60,000 second mortgage at 12% with a 15 year term, prepayment rights and a balloon payment. The principal amount, the term, and the prepayment right may all be different, making the substitute performance too costly or otherwise unacceptable. One authority has stated that 'specific performance is the only realistic protection available for the borrower's expectation interest, since only specific performance can protect against all the intangible and immeasurable losses occasioned by a broken commitment.' M.J. Mehr and L.A. Kilgore, Enforcement of the Real Estate Loan Commitment: The Improvement of the Borrower's Remedies, 24 Wayne L.Rev. 1011, 1034. That is true in this case."

See generally Brannon, Enforceability of Mortgage Loan Commitments, 18 Real Prop.Prob. & Tr.J. 724 (1983); Annot. 82 A.L.R.3d 1116 (1978).

RESTATEMENT (SECOND) OF CONTRACTS

§ 364 (1981) *

"§ 364. Effect of Unfairness

"(1) Specific performance or an injunction will be refused if such relief would be unfair because

"(a) the contract was induced by mistake or by unfair practices,

"(b) the relief would cause unreasonable hardship or loss to the party in breach or to third persons, or

"(c) the exchange is grossly inadequate or the terms of the contract are otherwise unfair. * * *

"Comment;

"*a. Types of unfairness.* Courts have traditionally refused equitable relief on grounds of unfairness or mistake in situations where they would not necessarily refuse to award damages. Some of these situations involve elements of mistake (§§ 152, 153), misrepresentation (§ 164), duress (§ 175) or undue influence (§ 177) that fall short of what is required for avoidance under those doctrines. Others involve elements of impracticability of performance or frustration of purpose that fall short of what is required for relief under those doctrines. Still others involve elements of substantive unfairness in the exchange itself or in its terms that fall short of what is required for unenforceability on grounds of unconscionability (§ 208). The gradual expansion of these doctrines to afford relief in an increasing number of cases has resulted in a contraction of the area in which this traditional distinction is made between the availability of equitable and legal relief. Nevertheless, the discretionary nature of equitable relief permits its denial when a variety of factors combine to make enforcement of a promise unfair, even though no single legal doctrine alone would make the promise unenforceable. Such general equitable doctrines as those of laches and 'unclean hands' supplement the rule stated in this Section."

HILTON v. NELSEN

Supreme Court of Minnesota, 1979.
283 N.W.2d 877.

BRUCE C. STONE, JUSTICE.

This is an appeal from the order of the district court awarding plaintiff specific performance of a contract for the sale of farmland and damages. We affirm in part, reverse in part, and remand for a new trial at law on the issue of damages.

In September 1974, defendants Dale and Geraldine Nelsen entered into negotiations for the sale of their 720-acre farm to plaintiff, Irvin Hilton, a Missouri real estate investor who had come to defendants' real estate agency, Phelps Farm Sales, looking for farm situations and investment opportunities in northwestern Minnesota. The rather lengthy and complex contract that was eventually entered into was drafted by Hilton's attorney, although some of the provisions were suggested by the Nelsens after several hours of discussion between the parties. The Nelsens were not represented by an attorney until after they had signed the contract.

The contract, dated October 4, 1974, provided generally for the sale of the property to Hilton for $180,000. * * * Although the Nelsens thought they had signed a contract for deed, the agreement provided for title and possession to pass at closing.

Because the purchaser's performance was contingent on his ability to obtain an owner's title insurance policy without exceptions, Nelsen saw an attorney in March 1975 to help him clear certain title defects. After being advised by his attorney that the agreement was not a contract for deed, Nelsen instructed his attorney to tell Hilton that he would not close unless he had a contract for deed. On March 28, Nelsen's attorney sent Hilton's attorney a letter to this effect; the latter replied that if the Nelsens refused to close, Hilton would sue for specific performance as provided by the remedies clause of the contract.[1] Nelsen's attorney then advised Nelsen to attempt to close. * * *

The Nelsens were able to clear the defects in title, except for a real estate mortgage, a reservation of mineral rights by the State of Minnesota, and easements for existing public roads and underground telephone cables. At the end of April 1975, the Nelsens bought and moved to a farm in Nebraska. On May 7 or 8, 1975, Nelsen called Hilton from Nebraska and advised him that he was ready to close.

The evidence was in dispute as to this telephone conversation; the Nelsens claimed that Hilton demanded a reduction of $16,000 to close, and

1. The contract provided that "all * * * parties who have signed said contract agree that in the event should [sic] any said party refuse to close said contract, that Purchaser shall have available to him the remedy of specific performance or damages at law, at Purchaser's option."

Hilton claimed that he could not recall such a conversation. * * * Nelsen, believing that Hilton had defaulted, returned to Minnesota and made no further attempt to close. Nelsen farmed the land in 1975 but lost the crop.

In February 1976, Hilton's attorney wrote to notify Nelsen that Hilton would be ready to close on May 1, 1976, the last closing date on the contract. * * * The next day, Nelsen's attorney wrote to Hilton's attorney informing him that Nelsen had decided not to sell the farm. Hilton then instructed his attorney to bring this action, which was filed on May 17, 1976.

Meanwhile, some time in April 1976, Phelps told Hilton that Nelsen's mortgage was about to be foreclosed. Hilton * * * successfully bid $67,-000—the amount of the unpaid balance on the mortgage—and purchased it subject to the 1–year right of redemption. Nelsen continued to occupy and work the land throughout 1976.

On May 23, 1977, pursuant to a conversation with a law partner of Nelsen's attorney, defendant Lyle Mandt agreed to purchase the Nelsen farm by redeeming the mortgage. * * * The Nelsens gave a quitclaim deed to Mandt and Mandt gave Nelsen an option to repurchase the property by January 1, 1978, for $121,074.05. Nelson farmed the property in 1977.

The trial court sitting without a jury found that the Nelsens had breached the contract, ordered specific performance for the plaintiff against both the Nelsens and Mandt, and ordered that plaintiff be allowed to deduct from the downpayment in the original agreement the sum of $39,600, representing the fair and reasonable rental value of the property during the years 1976 and 1977.

* * *

2. Specific Performance

Because the trial court's factual findings are reasonably supported by the evidence, they are not clearly erroneous and must be affirmed. Rule 52.01, Rules of Civil Procedure. Thus, we affirm the findings that the sellers materially breached the contract by their repudiation by letter on April 28, 1976, and their failure to close on May 1, 1976. However, it does not automatically follow that Hilton is entitled to specific performance of the contract, as ordered by the trial court. * * * In this case, a combination of the following factors convinces us that ordering specific performance is not an appropriate exercise of the court's equitable discretion:

(a) Purchaser Hilton did not intend to farm or homestead on the land, but rather intended to rent the property to a tenant farmer. Because any equivalent parcel of Minnesota farmland would serve these investment purposes, the uniqueness of the land is less weighty here as a factor calling for specific performance, especially if damages at law are an adequate remedy for the sellers' breach. In this case, the plaintiff has not detrimentally changed his position in reliance upon the sellers' performance to such an extent that specific performance is necessary or a damages remedy inadequate. The plaintiff may easily be compensated in damages for losses occasioned by this contractual relationship.

(b) There were elements of unfairness, or at least overreaching, in the contract itself. * * *

First, the contract lacked mutuality of remedy. Although that alone will not render specific performance inequitable, mutuality is one element which may be considered in determining whether to award specific performance. * * *

Here, according to the contractual provisions, the sellers' only remedy in the event of default by the purchaser would be the retention of $2,500 earnest money as liquidated damages. If the sellers defaulted, however, the purchaser could elect either specific performance or damages as a remedy. * * *

Second, the contract was subject to unilateral termination by the purchaser for a variety of reasons. * * *

Third, the payment terms evidenced overreaching by the purchaser. Of a total contract price of $180,000, the purchaser need only pay $2,500 into escrow as an earnest deposit and $49,700 cash upon closing—a total of $52,200 paid when the title transferred. The remaining $127,800 was to be financed by a part-purchase money note secured by a 10–year mortgage or deed of trust to the sellers. Prior to the end of the 10th year, the sellers' only return would be interest on the unpaid amount at 7 percent annually plus $2,000 a year in the 6th through 9th year of the contract. Thus, apart from interest, the sellers would receive during 9 years and 11 months only $60,200 toward property worth $180,000, while the purchaser would be receiving rental income on the land which, the trial court found, had a median rental value of approximately $20,000 per year. * * *

(c) The testimony in evidence indicated that the basic terms of the contract were misunderstood by the defendants. Significantly, the defendant-sellers were not represented by an attorney in negotiations with plaintiff-purchaser. The contract, which was lengthy and complex, was drafted and explained to the Nelsens by the plaintiff's attorney. * * * Only when the Nelsens consulted an attorney for assistance in clearing the title did they learn that the contract was not a contract for deed, as they had thought it was. The Nelsens erroneously understood that May 1, 1975, was the *only* closing date under the contract. They also thought, incorrectly, that Hilton's initial payment would pay off their mortgage. * * *

(d) Circumstances have arisen since the formation of the contract which further undermine the fairness of specific performance. * * * Third-party interests have intervened by way of Mandt's redemption of the property. Mandt now has legal and equitable title to the property. There was no finding that Mandt had personal knowledge of Hilton's rights under the October 4, 1974, contract. The contract for sale was not recorded, and Mandt testified that he had no knowledge of the contract. If he did not, specific performance of the contract would necessarily be subject to Mandt's property rights.

In light of the totality of the circumstances discussed above, we conclude that, as a matter of law, this contract is not one which the court in its equitable discretion may specifically enforce. Plaintiff must seek his remedy at law. We do not mean to suggest that any one of the factors discussed above is necessarily sufficient to render specific performance inequitable. Considering them together, however, we feel compelled to the decision we have reached, which is necessarily limited to the narrow facts presented here.

3. Damages

Having concluded that the contract is not specifically enforceable and that plaintiff's remedy is at law, we need not reach the question of whether an allowance for lost rents was properly awarded by the trial court, which sat in equity rather than at law. Accordingly, we reverse the judgment and, because the first trial was in equity, remand this case for a new trial at law on the question of damages.[5] The parties, of course, may demand a jury trial on this issue.[6]

Affirmed in part, reversed in part, and remanded.*

BEST v. CULHANE

Missouri Court of Appeals, 1984.
677 S.W.2d 390.

Kelly, P., Judge.

Dolan Company Sales, Inc., instituted this interpleader action seeking a determination as to which of the defendants, John J. Culhane and Phyllis S. Culhane, husband and wife, or Earl Best, Sr. and Bonnie Best, husband and wife, were entitled to 100 shares of Union Electric stock deposited with it as escrow agent pursuant to a Sales Contract on a home and 150 acre farm in Pike County, Missouri. The Bests filed an Answer to the Interpleader action admitting that they and the Culhane's had entered into a Sales Contract for the sale of the Pike County acreage, but denying the other allegations in said Petition for Interpleader. The Bests also filed a "counterclaim" against the Culhanes seeking specific performance of the Sales Contract for the purchase of the Pike County acreage.

The Culhanes filed a First Amended Answer to the Petition in Interpleader denying that they had entered into the Sales Contract with the Bests for the purchase of the Pike County Tract. * * *

5. The measure of damages was not argued before the trial court or on appeal. However, without so holding, we observe that the measure of damages appears to be the difference between the market value of the land on May 1, 1976, and the contract price of $180,000, plus such additional expenses as the purchaser may reasonably have incurred to that date in a bona fide attempt to comply with the contract.

6. The record is not clear as to whether jury trial was waived on all issues below. Regardless, our decision that the contract is not specifically enforceable requires a new opportunity to elect a jury trial.

* *See generally* Eisenberg, The Bargain Principle and Its Limits, 95 Harv.L.Rev. 741, 748–85 (1982); Farber, Contract Law and Modern Economic Theory, 78 Nw.U.L.Rev. 303 (1983); Kratovil, The Restatement (Second) of Contracts and the UCC: A Real Property Law Perspective, 16 J.Mar.L.Rev. 287, 290–99 (1983) (discussing section 2–302 of the Uniform Commercial Code); Schwartz, The Case for Specific Performance, 89 Yale L.J. 271, 273, 298–303, 306 (1979) ("defenses to requests for specific performance that rest on unfairness of contract terms or prices and that differ from the defenses in actions at law should be eliminated"); Shedd, Real Estate Transactions and the Principles of Unconscionability, 13 Real Est.L.J. 334 (1985).

The Culhanes also filed an Answer to the Bests' "counterclaim" admitting that they had deposited the stock with Dolan, but denying all of the other allegations in Bests' "counterclaim" for specific performance. They further alleged that if the court should find a contract between them and the Bests, that * * * the Bests, as an inducement to cause them to enter into the contract, had misrepresented to them that 40 acres of the farm was tillable and 70 acres was for pasture, when in fact, this was not so and the Bests knew this and made said representations with the intent to deceive and defraud them and that to enforce specific performance of the contract under these circumstances would be inequitable, unfair, and unjust.

After a bench trial the court found: that the Bests and the Culhanes entered into a valid contract for the sale of real estate on February 4, 1981; * * * that the real estate was represented to contain 40 acres tillable and 70 acres of pasture and that Earl Best, Sr. furnished said figures to William Babbitt, the Bests' representative, whereas the real estate actually contained 18 acres tillable and 29 acres pasture; that the difference between the tillable acres and pasture acres as represented and as they actually exist is a substantial variance; * * * that the Culhanes had a right, under the circumstances, to void the contract between themselves and the Bests; that the Culhanes were relying on income from the tillable acres and pasture acres, as represented by the Bests, to help pay for the real estate which was the subject of the contract of February 4, 1981; * * * that the contract between the Bests and the Culhanes is not capable of being performed because there is not the 40 tillable acres and the 70 acres pasture as represented. The Bests' petition for specific performance was denied and dismissed and Dolan was ordered to return the 100 shares of Union Electric Company stock to the Culhanes.

* * *

Appellants contend that the misrepresentations concerning the amount of tillable and pasture acreage were not material misrepresentations but were mere opinions regarding non-material matters which the Culhanes had no right to rely on. They equate the statements in the listing contract, that there were 40 tillable acres and 70 acres of pasture, to "puffing."

Specific performance of a realty purchase contract is not a matter of strict right, but rests in the trial court's discretion. * * *

A "misrepresentation" is an assertion that is not in accord with the facts. *Restatement (Second) of Contracts,* § 159 (1979). A misrepresentation is material if it would be likely to induce a reasonable person to manifest his assent, or if the maker knows that it would be likely to induce the recipient to do so. *Restatement (Second) of Contracts,* § 162(2) (1979).

There can be little doubt from the evidence that the statements in the listing contract relative to the tillable acreage and the pasture acreage were not in accord with the facts. There was substantial evidence that these figures were furnished to Dolan by Mr. Best. There is a question whether the Bests came into equity with clean hands. In his treatise, *Equity Jurisprudence,* § 400 (4th Ed.1918), Pomeroy limits the application of this principle to cases where the plaintiff's unconscientious actions relate to the subject matter of the lawsuit and where plaintiff's conduct in entering into the contract is "* * * unconscientious or unjust, or marked by a want of good faith." *Pomeroy, supra,* § 399. The common law of Missouri also supports the "unclean hands" doctrine. * * * In the case before us for decision the conduct of the appellants was unconscientious in allowing the acreage of tillable and pasture acreage to be misrepresented and such conduct may be characterized as "concealment of important facts even though not fraudulent." Said conduct relates to the subject matter of the lawsuit, i.e. the real estate. The trial court's denial of specific performance in this case, is not an abuse of discretion because the Bests came into court seeking equity with unclean hands.

Another ground for the denial of specific performance in the circumstances of this case is that the evidence shows that the contract was entered into by mutual mistake. The Bests never farmed the land themselves; rather, their neighbor, Mr. Johns, farmed the land. Even were we to assume that the Bests did not know the actual acreage available for farming or pasturage, nevertheless, before furnishing these acreage figures to Mr. Babbitt of Dolan they should have ascertained the accuracy of those figures. Had they done so they would have learned that the acreage was not as stated. While the Culhanes may have been mistaken in relying on the figures set out in the listing contract, whether they were opinions or facts, their mistake was made possible, intentionally or not, by the acts or omissions of the Bests. On the plainest principles of justice, such error prevents a specific enforcement of the agreement. * * * The court in [Public Water Supply District of Pemiscot County No. 1 v. Fowlkes, 497 S.W.2d 642, 649 (Mo.Ct.App.1966)] said: "The mistake of fact to justify refusal of specific performance need not be such as would avoid a contract at law, or even such as would justify rescission or reformation of the contract."

The trial court's judgment and the briefs on appeal present the issues so as to support a theory of misrepresentation and mistake in the inducement to contract. Appellants, in support of their argument that the stated acreage available for tillage and pasturage were merely opinions, cite cases involving the valuation of property in which a buyer might well expect a seller would over-estimate. However, these cases are inapposite to misrepresentation of acreage where the seller is in a superior position to know the true acreage than is the purchaser. * * *

We believe this principle of law is applicable to this case where the Culhanes were depending upon income from the tillable and pasture acreage to help pay the mortgage they would have to arrange to finance the purchase of the property.

* * *

Judgment affirmed.*

* *Accord Wilson v. Thomason,* 406 So.2d 871 (Ala.1981) (denying specific performance to buyer who disguised his true identity; seller would not have signed contract if she had known that buyer was a member of the Devil's Disciples motorcycle club); Smith v. Fer-

Notes

1. The defense of unclean hands is an equitable defense, suggesting that the plaintiff who is not entitled to equitable relief might nevertheless be able to obtain legal relief. Consider, for example, the following passage from Finnerty v. Reed, 2 Mass.App.Ct. 846, 312 N.E.2d 578 (1974):

> "* * * The evidence shows that the plaintiff's son, who acted as the plaintiff's agent for the sale, admitted that the defendant specifically asked him if there were restrictions on the lot, that at that time he knew of the restriction in the deed to the plaintiff's predecessor in title which barred issuance of a building permit until the lot had been 'approved for an individual sewerage disposal system by the Board of Health,' and that he did not disclose the existence of that restriction in response to the defendant's inquiry. The unsuitability of the lot in this respect could and did in fact thwart what the plaintiff's son knew to be the defendant's sole purpose in purchasing the lot. The evidence falls short of showing misrepresentation of a material fact; but even if we assume that the contract is good at law, it does not follow that it will be specifically enforced in equity. It is a universally recognized principle, that a court of equity will not decree specific performance of a contract when it would be inequitable to do so. Specific performance may be refused when a contract is 'hard and unreasonable, so that enforcement of it would be oppressive to the defendant, or where there has been [a] misrepresentation by the plaintiff on a material point, or other unfair conduct, although it may not be sufficient to invalidate the contract * * *.' Chute v. Quincy, 156 Mass. 189, 191, 30 N.E. 550, 551 (1892). *See also* Shikes v. Gabelnick, 273 Mass. 201, 206–207, 173 N.E. 495 (1930); Freedman v. Walsh, 331 Mass. 401, 406, 119 N.E.2d 419 (1954). As the plaintiff has not, in our opinion, shown himself to be entitled to specific performance, the judge was not in error in dismissing the bill. The final decree is to be modified by striking the first paragraph and, as so modified, is affirmed."

Accord Stachnik v. Winkel, 394 Mich. 375, 230 N.W.2d 529 (1975); Carmen v. Fox Film Corp., 269 Fed. 928 (2d Cir.1920).

Compare Frank and Endicott, Defenses in Equity and "Legal Rights," 14 La.L.Rev. 380–381 (1954):* "The books are full of expressions to the effect that the law will do dirty work which a 'court of conscience' is too refined to touch. Here are typical examples: * * * 'Even though the plaintiff's conduct has not been such as to cause a court to refuse him a judgment for damages * * * it may be such as to disentitle him to the remedy of specific performance.' * * *

"The precise question for analysis here is whether the distinction in law implicit in these quotations is also a distinction in fact. The rule of law obviously contemplates that there may be a legal remedy which survives a rejection of the equitable claim. Does such a remedy actually exist?

"To find out the practical value of that remedy at law, we have examined 350 reported cases in which the defenses of clean hands, inadequacy of

guson, 622 P.2d 1086 (Okla.Ct.App.1980) (jury found in favor of plaintiff on defendant's allegations of fraud, but court denied specific performance to plaintiff on grounds that plaintiff's conduct precluded equitable relief even if contract were valid at law).

* Reprinted with permission of Louisiana Law Review.

consideration, hardship and misrepresentation have been raised in the past ten years.

* * *

"Of the 350 'pure conscience' cases, 150 most clearly turned on clean hands, inadequacy of consideration, hardship or misrepresentation. Letters were sent to counsel of record inquiring as to the subsequent history of these 150 cases. Fifty-six responses were received. While the sample is too small to permit of firm conclusions, the results are sufficiently suggestive to be worth reporting as a possible starting point for analysis by others.

"The fifty-six surviving cases were utterly diverse, involving specific performance and injunction, tort and contract. Yet in one respect they were uniform: In every instance, an equitable defeat was a total defeat. In no instance did the defeated claimant gain anything by virtue of any reserved legal rights; in only two instances did he so much as try."

2. A few courts have applied the unclean hands doctrine in actions for damages. Three arguments support these decisions: "(1) the merger of law and equity; (2) equitable and legal remedies are many times equally harsh; and (3) conduct not warranting an equitable remedy does not warrant a legal remedy either." Note, The Application of the Clean Hands Doctrine in Damages Actions, 57 Notre Dame Law. 673 (1982). *See also* pp. 131–136 *supra*.

FITZGERALD v. O'CONNELL

Supreme Court of Rhode Island, 1978.
120 R.I. 240, 386 A.2d 1384.

KELLEHER, JUSTICE.

This is an appeal from the denial by a Superior Court justice, after a hearing, of the plaintiffs' complaint seeking specific performance of a contract to sell real estate. The trial justice based his denial on his findings that the plaintiffs were guilty of laches by not acting with reasonable diligence to secure their rights and dismissed their complaint.

In an undated, sealed agreement the Fitzgeralds agreed to purchase, and Gertrude S. O'Connell to sell, a parcel of unimproved real estate on Binney Street in Newport, Rhode Island. The parcel abuts other real estate owned by the Fitzgeralds, who wished to enlarge their own property. Under the terms of the purchase and sales agreement, the purchase price was $500. The Fitzgeralds paid $250 upon execution of the agreement and were to pay the balance upon delivery of the deed at the closing, which was to take place on October 24, 1963.

Gertrude O'Connell died on July 19, 1963, and by will devised an undivided two-thirds interest in the property to her son, Jay K. O'Connell, and his wife, defendant Cathleen D. O'Connell, as joint tenants. The remaining one-third interest was devised to her two granddaughters, defendants Linda O'Connell and Anne O'Connell.

Sometime in September 1963, the Fitzgeralds forwarded a check for $250, representing the balance of the purchase price, to Jay O'Connell who, along with his wife Cathleen, was acting as co-executor of his mother's estate. This check was never cashed. Mr. O'Connell later advised the

Fitzgeralds that he was going to rip up the check as a gift to their newly born twins.

Approximately a year later the Fitzgeralds asked Mr. O'Connell when the conveyance could be completed. Mr. O'Connell replied that his mother's estate was "a little mixed up" and that he would let them know when the transfer could be taken care of. The Fitzgeralds' attorney inquired of the attorney representing the estate of Gertrude O'Connell as to when the estate would be in a position to carry out the purchase and sales agreement and was advised that the conveyance would have to wait until the probate proceedings were completed. Two years later, in October 1966, Mr. O'Connell died, and his wife Cathleen, as joint tenant, acquired his interest in the real estate. After waiting a "respectful" period of time, the Fitzgeralds contacted Cathleen O'Connell, advised her of the purchase and sales agreement, and asked to be notified when the estate was settled. According to the Fitzgeralds, Mrs. O'Connell did not dispute the agreement in any way.

The first and final account for the estate of Gertrude S. O'Connell was allowed on July 9, 1970. The lien on the property of the State of Rhode Island for inheritance taxes due from the estate of Jay K. O'Connell was not discharged until February 21, 1972.

Sometime later the Fitzgeralds learned from Cathleen O'Connell that she planned to sell the real estate to a third party. In July 1972, the Fitzgeralds filed a copy of the purchase and sales agreement in the Newport Land Evidence Records. This litigation was commenced in October 1973.

There is no dispute that, but for the O'Connells' defense of laches, the Fitzgeralds would be entitled to a decree ordering the O'Connells to specifically perform the contract of sale. * * *

In their answer the O'Connells asserted that the claim was barred by both the statute of limitations and by the doctrine of laches. In his introductory remarks at the beginning of the trial, the trial justice stated that the defense of laches was really the only issue. In his view the defense of the statute of limitations did not apply "because this is an instrument under seal." Presumably, he meant to say that the general 6–year statute of limitations contained in G.L.1956 (1969 Reenactment) § 9–1–13 did not apply and that the 20–year period applicable to instruments under seal would not bar this claim. * * *

We must first resolve the issue of whether the doctrine of laches may be applied at all. Since 1912 an unquestioned (and perhaps ignored) rule of Rhode Island law has been that suits in equity to compel the conveyance of property are diligently brought if they are brought within the period of limitation fixed by statute. Knowles v. Knowles, 33 R.I. 491, 494, 82 A. 257, 258 (1912). There we held that the defense of laches was "not open" since the suit was brought within the period of limitation. Since the purchase and sales agreement involved here is one under seal, the *Knowles* doctrine would indicate that the Fitzgeralds' claim could never be barred by laches before 1983—regardless of the prejudice to the O'Connells. Not only is this result contrary to what was the majority view at common law prior to the merger of law and equity [4] but insofar as we have been able to discover, it is not followed by any jurisdiction today, save our own. * * *

Having in mind the mid–1960 adoption of the Superior Court Rules of Civil Procedure with its accompanying merger of law and equity and the abolition of the forms of action, whatever may have been the validity or wisdom of the *Knowles* principle, we believe it should no longer be followed. Today in this jurisdiction there is but one form of action, a "civil action," Super.R.Civ.P. 2, and "all civil actions" now have an applicable statute of limitation. Section 9–1–13. Thus, were we to continue to apply the *Knowles* rule, the doctrine of laches could never be invoked: the defense would be unavailable if the statute had not run and unnecessary if it had. Accordingly, we overrule *Knowles* and hold that the defense of laches may be asserted in civil actions seeking equitable relief notwithstanding the fact that the period fixed by the applicable statute of limitations has not expired.

Whether the Fitzgeralds were guilty of laches in prosecuting this cause of action is a question of fact and, in the first instance, one which is committed to the sound discretion of the trial justice. But such discretion is not unlimited and will be reviewed by this court for an abuse thereof. As we have noted many times, mere lapse of time does not constitute laches. It is only where unexplained and inexcusable delay has the effect of visiting prejudice on the other party that the defense may be successfully invoked. This principle was best stated in Chase v. Chase, 20 R.I. 202, 203–04, 37 A. 804, 805 (1897):

> "Laches, in legal significance, is not mere delay, but delay that works a disadvantage to another. So long as parties are in the same condition, it matters little whether one presses a right promptly or slowly, within limits allowed by law; but when, knowing his rights, he takes no steps to enforce them until the condition of the other party has, in good faith, become so changed that he cannot be restored to his former state, if the right be then enforced, delay becomes inequitable and operates as an estoppel against the assertion of the right. The disadvantage may come from loss of evidence, change of title, intervention of equities and other causes, but when a court sees negligence on one side and injury therefrom on the other, it is a ground for denial of relief."

In order to bar the Fitzgeralds' claim because of its staleness, the burden was on the O'Connells to show that the claim was " 'first asserted after an unexplained delay of such great length as to render it difficult or impossible for the court to ascertain the truth of the matters in controversy and do justice between the parties, or as to create a presumption against the existence or validity of the claim, or a presumption that it has been abandoned or satisfied.' " Lombardi v. Lombardi, 90 R.I. at 210, 156 A.2d at 913. While the Fitzgeralds' delay in this case was certainly lengthy (10

4. 2 Lawrence, *Equity Jurisprudence* § 1038 at 1123 (1929); 2 Pomeroy, *Equity Jurisprudence* § 419(b) at 175 (5th ed. 1941); Pomeroy, *Specific Performance of Contracts* § 403 at 855–56, note (e) (3d ed. 1926); Re, *Cases and Materials on Equity and Equitable Remedies* 765 (5th ed. 1975).

years), it was not without explanation. The trial justice, in his decision, implied that the Fitzgeralds had adequately explained the reason why they had not brought suit on the contract from October 1963 to July 1970, the date Gertrude O'Connell's estate was closed. Throughout this period the Fitzgeralds and their attorney made repeated requests of the O'Connells to complete performance of the agreement. Each time they were assured that performance would be forthcoming and were asked to wait until the estate of Gertrude O'Connell was settled. A delay is excusable where it is induced or caused by the adverse party, as by acknowledging the justness of the claim and promising to make good thereon. * * *

The trial justice was of the opinion that the Fitzgeralds should have acted to protect their rights once Gertrude O'Connell's estate was closed in July 1970, even though he acknowledged that the inheritance tax lien of Jay O'Connell's estate remained a cloud on the title until February 1972. Once the inheritance tax lien was cleared in February 1972, the Fitzgeralds waited almost a year and a half (October 1973) before instituting this action. The trial justice apparently felt this year-and-a-half delay to be both unexplained and prejudicial.

We need not decide whether the Fitzgeralds' delay in bringing suit was unexplained and inexcusable, for we believe the O'Connells have failed to show how they have been prejudiced by this delay. The trial justice found that the O'Connells had been prejudiced by two factors: by the payment of $728.48 in property taxes since 1963 and by the increase in the value of the property.[6] The trial justice's reliance on the payment of taxes as sufficient evidence of prejudice is most curious, since the Fitzgeralds offered to reimburse the O'Connells for any taxes paid on the property prior to the commencement of the suit. In short, the Fitzgeralds stood willing to alleviate this prejudicial element, and the trial justice could well have conditioned the grant of specific performance on this fact. * * *

In addition to the taxes which had been paid, the trial justice noted that "there might even be some prejudice going to the present value of the property." Since the Fitzgeralds' delay in asserting their rights from 1963 to 1970 was induced, at least in part, by Jay O'Connell's assurances that performance would be forthcoming as soon as his mother's estate was settled, only the rise in value from 1970 to 1973 could be considered in assessing prejudice. As noted above, no evidence was presented indicating the fair market value of the property prior to 1972. Even assuming the property appreciated from 1970 to 1973, or even from 1963 to 1973, it is hard to see how the O'Connells have been prejudiced thereby. The mere fact that the value of the property contracted for has increased in value will not warrant a refusal to carry out its terms in the absence of circumstances indicating fraud or bad faith. Humble Oil & Refining Co. v. Lennon, 94 R.I. 509, 517, 182 A.2d 306, 311 (1962).

6. A real estate agent in Newport, Rhode Island, testified that, in his opinion, the $2,820 assessed value of the property also represented the fair market value of the property. No evidence was presented regarding the fair market value of the parcel in 1963. The $2,820 figure was established in 1972, when the entire city was reevaluated.

In the past, typical examples of prejudice that have supported the defense of laches have been the loss of evidence, a change of title, or the death of a key witness. Chase v. Chase, 20 R.I. at 204, 37 A. at 805; Lister v. Lister, 47 R.I. 366, 133 A. 437 (1926). Evidence that a defendant expended sums of money in constructing improvements has also been held to be sufficient prejudice to support a finding of laches. Motta v. Gouveia, 84 R.I. 149, 122 A.2d 159. Where the subject matter is speculative and subject to rapid fluctuation in value, such as oil and mining properties, the doctrine of "speculative delay" may bar a claim to ownership if the claimant asserts his interest only after the risk has passed and the value of the property has become apparent. West Los Angeles Institute for Cancer Research v. Mayer, 366 F.2d 220, 228 (9th Cir.1966); McIver v. Norman, 187 Or. 516, 546–47, 213 P.2d 144, 153 (1949).

While there is no hard and fast rule for determining what constitutes sufficient prejudice to invoke the doctrine of laches, we believe the trial justice erred in the instant case. The O'Connells have neither suffered the loss of material evidence nor constructed improvements upon the property. No rights of third parties have been called into question. Nothing in the record suggests that the Fitzgeralds awaited the rise in value of the property before asserting their claim. To the contrary, the Fitzgeralds have, since 1963, stood ready, willing, and able to perform their part of the bargain in order to extend the boundaries of their homestead. In short, the fact that the value of the property has appreciated does not in and of itself convert delay into laches. * * *

The plaintiffs' appeal is sustained, the judgment appealed from is reversed, and the case is remanded to the Superior Court with direction to enter judgment for the plaintiffs.

Notes

1. *Accord* Thirty–Four Corp. v. Sixty–Seven Corp., 15 Ohio St.3d 350, 474 N.E.2d 295 (1984). *Compare* Gaglione v. Cardi, 120 R.I. 534, 388 A.2d 361 (1978) (property rose in value from $20,000 in 1966 to $100,000 in 1972; "plaintiff's unexplained delay in bringing this suit, coupled with the dramatic rise in the value of the parcel, makes this case a proper one for invoking the doctrine of laches"). When the plaintiff seeks specific performance of an option to purchase real estate, the courts are more apt to invoke the defense of laches and deny equitable relief, as illustrated by Schroeder v. Schlueter, 85 Ill.App.3d 574, 575–77, 407 N.E.2d 204, 206–07 (1980):

> "The parties entered into an agreement dated March 31, 1969 which granted to the plaintiff and his former wife, the exclusive right to purchase approximately 200 acres of farmland for the sum of $70,000, conditioned upon the delivery of a notice of election to purchase by '12 noon on December 30, 1969.' The evidence was in conflict as to whether this deadline had been met or missed, and it appears no further action was ever taken to exercise the option. * * * The complaint which initiated this action was filed on March 2, 1978, and at no time prior to that date did the plaintiff assert his rights under the contract. * * *
>
> "The limiting doctrine known as *laches* has been defined repeatedly in this state as such neglect or omission to assert a right, taken in conjunction

with a lapse of time of greater or lesser duration and other circumstances causing prejudice to an adverse party, as will operate to bar relief in equity.

* * *

"[A] marked appreciation or depreciation in the value of the property which is the object of controversy, such that the granting of relief would itself work an inequity, is evidence of injury or prejudice justifying the invocation of *laches.* * * * We believe the rule to be especially applicable where an option contract is concerned because time is a material element of the consideration running to the optionee. * * * In regard to the right at equity to have specific performance of a contract of sale, unreasonable delay coupled with a material advance in value is fatal for equity will not allow a purchaser to remain in the wings gambling on the future rise in price.

"In the case at bar, * * * appellees made significant improvements to the land by clearing wooded areas, improving and monitoring soil conditions and drainage characteristics, all in the interest of their farming operations. Appellant was well aware of these actions since he occupied a portion of the acreage concerned. * * * Meanwhile, its total worth increased from the purchase price of $70,000 to $500,000. * * * It has been held that a party is guilty of *laches,* which ordinarily will defeat whatever rights he may have, when he remains passive while another party 'incurs risk, enters into obligations, or makes expenditures for improvements or taxes.' The present facts are an excellent illustration of the rule. * * *"

2. Laches is also more likely to be a successful defense to an action for specific performance based upon a contract that expressly declares time to be of the essence. *E.g.,* Boyd v. Mercantile Safe Deposit & Trust Co., 28 Md.App. 18, 344 A.2d 148 (1975).

3. It is often stated that statutes of limitation bar legal relief only unless otherwise expressly provided, and that only laches would operate to bar equitable relief, even though analogous legal relief would be barred by the statute. *See* DeFuniak, Handbook of Modern Equity § 24 (1956); Blankenship v. Boyle, 329 F.Supp. 1089 (D.C.D.C.1971). As a practical matter, however, many states have made their statutes of limitation applicable to equity suits, either by express statutory language or by judicial construction. *See, e.g.,* Ludwig v. Scott, 65 S.W.2d 1034 (Mo.1933).

The relationship between the legal defense of the statute of limitations and the equitable defense of laches is discussed in Shell v. Strong, 151 F.2d 909, 911 (10th Cir.1945):

"Lapse of time alone does not constitute laches. Delay will not bar relief where it has not worked injury, prejudice, or disadvantage to the defendant or others adversely interested.

"Since laches is an equitable defense, its application is controlled by equitable considerations. It cannot be invoked to defeat justice, and it will be applied only where the enforcement of the right asserted will work injustice.

"A court of equity is not bound by the statute of limitations, but, in the absence of extraordinary circumstances, it will usually grant or withhold relief in analogy to the statute of limitations relating to actions at law of like character. Under ordinary circumstances, a suit in equity will not be stayed for laches before, and will be stayed after, the time fixed by the analogous statute, but if unusual conditions or extraordinary circumstances make it inequitable to allow the prosecution of a suit after a briefer, or to forbid its maintenance after a longer, period than that fixed by the analogous statute, a court of equity will not be bound by the statute, but will determine the extraordinary case in accordance with the equities which condition it. When a suit is brought within the time fixed by the analogous statute, the burden is on the defendant to show, either from the face of the complaint or by his answer, that extraordinary circumstances exist which require the application of the doctrine of laches. On the other hand, when the suit is brought after the statutory time has elapsed, the burden is on the complainant to aver and prove circumstances making it inequitable to apply laches to his case." *See also* Goodman v. McDonnell Douglas Corp., 606 F.2d 800, 804–05 (8th Cir.1979), cert. denied, 446 U.S. 913 (1980).

2. *The Equitable Conversion Concept*

R. CUNNINGHAM W. STOEBUCK & D. WHITMAN, THE LAW OF PROPERTY 698 (2d Ed.1993).* "During the period between formation and performance of a land sale contract, a variety of events may occur which raise questions about the contract's significance. Some of them have their principal effect on only one of the parties: the death of a party, a judgment obtained against him, or the like. Such events may trigger the operation of legal rules, such as an intestate succession statute or a judgment lien act, which depend on *characterization* of the party's interest as real or personal property. In most American jurisdictions, this characterization is based on the theory of equitable conversion, which holds that once the parties have entered into a contract which equity would specifically enforce, the buyer's interest in the contract is converted into real estate and the seller's interest into personal property. This result is said to follow from the view that equity regards as having been done that which ought to be done, and which equity would order done—namely, the conveyance of the title to the buyer and payment of the price to the seller.**"

The equitable conversion doctrine, if applied literally and consistently, would have a substantial impact on diverse fact situations that have as a common element a contract for the sale of land. How will the doctrine affect the interests of such parties as heirs, devisees and personal representatives when either the vendor or vendee dies prior to the consummation of the contract? How does the doctrine affect creditors of the vendor or vendee? What consequences follow from recognizing the doctrine when

* Reprinted with permission of West Publishing Co.

** The doctrine's modern form originated with Lord Eldon's opinion in Seaton v. Slade, 7 Ves.Jun. 265 (1802); *see* Davis, The Origin of the Doctrine of Equitable Conversion by Contract, 25 Ky.L.Rev. 58 (1936). *See generally* 3 Am.L.Prop. §§ 11.22–.35 (1952); 3A Corbin, Contracts § 667 (1960); Simpson, Legislative Changes in the Law of Equitable Conversion by Contract: I, 44 Yale L.J. 559 (1935).

there has been a casualty loss prior to contract consummation? Although the equitable conversion principle is relevant to other aspects of land sale contracts (such as dower, condemnation, claims regarding rents and profits, and taxation), space considerations dictate that the following material focus on an examination of equitable conversion in the context of the basic questions posed above.

It should be stressed that courts frequently employ the equitable conversion concept indiscriminately to two distinctly different types of land contracts—the earnest money contract (also known as a "binder" or "marketing contract") and the installment land contract (also known as a "contract for deed" or a "long term land contract"). The earnest money contract, which is the one most frequently encountered in this casebook, is used primarily to establish the parties' rights and liabilities during the period of approximately one or two months between the date of the bargain and the date of closing. On the latter date, title passes to the purchaser and security agreements, if any, are consummated. The installment land contract is a substitute for the purchase money mortgage. Both instruments enable the seller to finance the unpaid portion of the real estate purchase price. Under an installment land contract, the purchaser normally takes possession and makes monthly installment payments of principal and interest until the principal balance is paid off. The seller retains legal title until the final payment is made, at which time full title is conveyed to the purchaser. Such contracts may be amortized over time periods as short as a year or as long as twenty years or more. In studying the following material, consider whether the equitable conversion concept, assuming its application is appropriate at all, should be employed in both types of land contract settings.

IN RE THE ESTATE OF McDONOUGH

Appellate Court of Illinois, Third District, 1969.
113 Ill.App.2d 437, 251 N.E.2d 405.

RYAN, JUSTICE. On July 1, 1966, Grace S. McDonough and others entered into a contract to sell certain lots to the City of Macomb. * * * The down payment was made and the payment due July 1, 1967, was likewise made when due.

On March 3, 1967, Grace S. McDonough executed her will, paragraph 4 of which provided:

> "I give and devise to my sister-in-law, Louise McDonough, all of the real estate that I have received through my husband, Robert E. McDonough, by Will or deed, located in McDonough County, Illinois, and owned by me at the time of my death, excepting my dwelling house located at 823 East Calhoun Street in Macomb, Illinois."

The interest which Grace S. McDonough owned in the City lots which were the subject matter of the above contract was acquired by her through the will of her husband, Robert E. McDonough, who had died testate on July 2, 1957. In addition to the acquisition of the interest in the City lots involved in this contract, Grace S. McDonough also acquired under the will of her late husband other real estate located in McDonough County valued at approximately $20,000.

Grace S. McDonough died on December 8, 1967, prior to the final payment under the contract by the City of Macomb. Her will was admitted to probate on January 25, 1968. On July 17, 1968, the City made the final payment under the contract. The sum of $4,732 represents the decedent's share in this final payment. Lloyd N. Schertz individually and as executor of the estate of the decedent filed a petition asking the court whether said sum should be distributed as real property under paragraph 4 of the decedent's will above set forth or whether said sum should be distributed as personal property under the residuary clause of the will.

The trial court held that the sum of $4,732 was personal property and directed the executor to distribute the same to the residuary legatees under the will. We are of the opinion that the trial court was correct.

The question has been raised as to whether or not the doctrine of equitable conversion applied so as to change the nature of the interest of the decedent in the property conveyed to the City from real estate to personalty so that the proceeds from the sale would pass under the will as personal property. We do not believe that the answer to this question alone is determinative of the issues in this case. Neither do we believe that we are confronted with the problem of applying or not applying this equitable doctrine. Rather we are of the opinion that there are two questions presented for the court's determination. The first relates to the question of equitable conversion. Did the contract by this equitable doctrine work a conversion of the decedent's interest in the real estate in question from realty to personalty? The second question relates to the intention of the testator expressed in the will. If the contract did effect a conversion from real property to personalty, who did the testator intend should receive the proceeds of the sale under the terms of her will? Both of these questions must be answered because we feel that if the intent was so indicated in the will, the devisee of the real estate would be entitled to receive the balance due on the contract even though a conversion had been effected.

The doctrine of equitable conversion has been defined to be that change in the nature of property by which, for certain purposes, real estate is considered as personal, and personal estate as real. It is the application of the maximum that equity regards as done that which ought to be done. * * *

In the case now before the court, if a conversion was effected, it was brought about by virtue of the contract dated July 1, 1966 and the conversion would have taken place as of the date of the contract. Shay v. Penrose, 25 Ill.2d 447, 185 N.E.2d 218. The conversion would have been accomplished on July 1, 1966, the date of the contract prior to the execution of the will on March 3, 1967.

By the doctrine of equitable conversion equity has sought to give effect to the intention of the parties involved and not to defeat their intention. The trial judge correctly made this observation in rendering his opinion. If a contrary intention appears, a contrary result must be achieved and equity will not decree a conversion if a contrary intention is evident. Leesman, Resulting Trusts—Equitable Conversion As Applied to Installment Contracts For The Sale of Real Estate (1934) 29 ILR 97. Whether there was a conversion of land into personalty depends upon the contract. An equitable conversion is implied only when the intent is unequivocal and the implication leaves no substantial doubt. In order to work a conversion the contract must be such that a court of equity can specifically enforce it against an unwilling purchaser. Masters v. Masters, 325 Ill. 429, 156 N.E. 481.

The contract with the City of Macomb in addition to providing for the down payment and the payment of the balance of the purchase price in two installments also provided that the buyer was entitled to immediate possession of the real estate subject to existing leases. It provided that the buyer was entitled to collect all rents which thereafter became due from the tenants, that the buyer could remove any buildings of the sellers' which were not under lease and that it could make improvements on the property at any time thereafter, all without the consent of the sellers. The buyer agreed to pay all special assessments levied against the property after the date of the contract. In addition the sellers had executed deeds and deposited them in escrow. This contract is clearly one that can be specifically enforced against an unwilling purchaser, which is a requirement for conversion as announced by the Masters case, *supra.* The contract expresses the intent to transfer the incidents of ownership of the real estate from the sellers to the buyer as of the date of the instrument. This contract appears to be the typical situation for the application of the doctrine of equitable conversion and the application of this doctrine appears to conform to the intent of the parties as manifested in the contract. We hold that on July 1, 1966, an equitable conversion of the decedent's interest in the real estate involved in the contract was effected.

In determining who under the decedent's will is to receive the balance due under the contract, we are not concerned with applying the equitable doctrine or not applying it. As indicated above the conversion was effected by the contract which was executed prior to the decedent's death and prior to the execution of her will. We are rather now concerned with the decedent's intent as to who should receive the balance due on this contract and this intent must be ascertained from the will. Even though there may have been a conversion of the real estate to personalty, if the will indicates that the testator intended that the devisee of real estate should receive the balance due under the contract to sell real estate, this end can be accomplished without holding that the doctrine of equitable conversion will not be applied.

The appellant, Louise McDonough, has cited Wright v. Minshall, 72 Ill. 584 and Covey v. Dinsmoor, 226 Ill. 438, 80 N.E. 998 in support of her position that the doctrine of equitable conversion does not apply in this case. Both of these cases involve specific devises of real estate for which a contract for sale had previously been executed prior to the execution of the will. The *Wright* case involved a devise of "all his real estate, land and appurtenances in Clay County." The *Covey* case involved a devise of a tract of land specifically described. However, it was stated in the will that the devise was "subject to my contract of sale * * *." The court in Rhodes v. Meredith, 260 Ill. 138, 102 N.E. 1063 explained the holding in these two cases by saying at page 144, 102 N.E. at page 1066: "The doctrine of equitable conversion was not allowed to interfere with the clearly expressed intention of the testators." It should be noted that in neither the *Wright* case nor the *Covey* case did the devise convey only that real estate which the decedent owned at death. Since the contracts were made prior to the execution of the will in both cases and since a determination in each of these cases that the property would pass as personalty would totally defeat the devise in the will executed subsequent to the contract, the court held that the intention of the testator was that the proceeds of the sale were to pass to the devisee of the real estate. A contrary determination would have rendered the devise made after the contract was executed meaningless and would completely defeat the devise.

A contrary situation exists in the will now before this court. Although the contract was executed prior to the execution of the will the contract did not involve all of the real estate in McDonough County which the testator had received through her late husband. In addition to the real estate covered by the contract the testator owned some $20,000 worth of real estate in McDonough County which she had received through her late husband. Therefore, if the balance due on the contract is to pass as personal property under the will the provision of the devise now under consideration is not rendered meaningless as would have been the case in the *Wright* and *Covey* cases.

Furthermore, the testator in our case expressed her intent in this devise to transfer to the devisee only so much of the real estate described in paragraph 4 of the will as she owned at the time of her death. This could have been all or none of the real estate so described. This is clearly a different intention than that expressed by the testators in the *Wright* and *Covey* cases.

* * *

In *Rhodes v. Meredith, supra,* the decedent died intestate. Prior to his death he had executed a contract to convey his farm. The court stated 260 Ill. at page 143, 102 N.E. at page 1065:

> "When a valid, enforcible contract has been entered into for the sale of real estate, as between the vendor and vendee equity regards the vendee as the owner of the land and the vendor as the owner of the purchase money, which is personalty. The vendor is regarded as the trustee of the naked legal title for the benefit of the vendee, and the vendee as the trustee of the purchase money for the benefit of the vendor. (citing cases) Where the owner of real estate thus enters into a valid contract for its sale, the nature of his estate under the doctrine of equitable conversion is changed, and the real estate will be regarded as converted into personal property, and, in case of the death of the vendor before the contract is performed, it will be treated as assets in the hands of his personal representative."

There appears to be no reason why the real estate which had been converted to personalty by a contract for sale should pass as personalty in case of intestacy as in the Rhodes case but pass as real estate when a will is involved as the appellant contends in this case, unless the will expresses such an intent. We find no such intent expressed in the will now under consideration.

The decision of the Circuit Court of McDonough County will be affirmed.

Affirmed.

STOUDER, P.J., and ALLOY, J., concur.

Notes

1. When the contract to sell follows a devise by the vendor, courts often apply the equitable conversion principle so that the devisee receives no beneficial interest in the real estate. Sometimes courts reach the same result by holding that a devise is revoked by a subsequent contract to sell the land. *See* Simpson, Legislative Changes in the Law of Equitable Conversion by Contract, 44 Yale L.J. 559, 568–71 (1935).

When the testator is the vendee under a land contract, the application of equitable conversion involves the problem of exoneration. If the vendee has devised land, whether before or after entering into the contract to purchase, and then dies, the devisee under the will receives the vendee-testator's equitable title and the purchase price is paid by the residuary personal estate against which there is a right of exoneration. The result is that the devisee benefits at the expense of the residuary legatees. *See generally* R. Cunningham, W. Stoebuck and D. Whitman, The Law of Property § 10.13 (2d Ed. 1993).

The results reached by the application of the equitable conversion doctrine in the testate succession situations have been reversed or modified in a number of jurisdictions by statute. Consider how the following statutes, which are fairly typical of state legislation in this area, would affect the application of equitable conversion principles:

Missouri Revised Statutes (1969):

474.440. *Bond to convey does not revoke devise.*—A bond, covenant or agreement made for a valuable consideration, by a testator, to convey any property devised or bequeathed in any last will previously made, does not constitute a revocation of the previous devise or bequest, either in law or equity; but the property passes by the devise or bequest, subject to the same remedies on the bond, covenant or agreement, for specific performance or otherwise, against the devisees or legatees, as might be had by law against the heirs of the testator, or his next of kin, if the same had descended to them.

474.450. *Encumbrance does not revoke devise—exoneration, when.*—1. A charge or encumbrance upon any real or personal property, for the purpose of securing the payment of money or the performance of any covenant or agreement, is not deemed a revocation of any will, relating to the same property, previously executed.

2. When any property is specifically devised and at the time of the testator's death is subject to a mortgage, pledge, or other lien created prior

to the execution of the will or created by a mortgage, pledge, or other lien executed after the execution of the will as a renewal, or extension, or refinancing of the debt created prior to the execution of the will, the devisee shall take the property so devised subject to the charge or encumbrance unless the will provides expressly or by necessary implication that such mortgage be otherwise paid, but if the mortgage, pledge or other lien was created after the execution of the will the devisee shall take the property exonerated from the encumbrance unless it appears from the terms of the loan agreement or from the circumstances surrounding the loan transaction that the testator intended that the encumbrance should be paid out of the encumbered property rather than from his general estate.

2. "In most states [equitable conversion] is unimportant when the vendor dies intestate, since the heirs and the next-of-kin are typically the same persons taking the same shares in the property; whether it is seen as realty or personalty is irrelevant." R. Cunningham, W. Stoebuck & D. Whitman, The Law of Property 700 (2d Ed.1993). Nevertheless, in a few states, the realty-personalty distinction continues to be important under intestate succession statutes. For example, the Texas statute provides that where the intestate dies without children, but with a surviving spouse, the latter "shall be entitled to all of the personal estate, and to one-half of the lands of the intestate." Vernon's Ann.Tex.Prob.Code Ann. § 38(b)(2) (1980). For an excellent analysis of the equitable conversion concept in the context of the latter statute, *see* Parson v. Wolfe, 676 S.W.2d 689 (Tex.App.1984).

In almost all states, a judgment creates a lien on the real, but usually not the personal, property of the judgment debtor. *See* D. Epstein, Debtor–Creditor Law 46, 52–3 (2d ed. 1980). While the mechanics of obtaining the lien and its effective date vary somewhat, typically the lien applies to all real estate of the judgment debtor in the county in which the judgment is docketed (entered by a court clerk in an appropriate docket book). The time of docketing usually determines lien priority. Consequently, when the judgment debtor is either a purchaser or a vendor under either type of land contract described earlier, the characterization of the judgment debtor's interest as real or personal property can be crucial in determining the rights of the judgment creditor.

CANNEFAX v. CLEMENT

Supreme Court of Utah, 1991.
818 P.2d 546.

STEWART, JUSTICE:

This case is here on certiorari from a decision of the Utah Court of Appeals which reversed a summary judgment entered by the trial court in favor of Donald and Ruth Clement. Donald and Ruth Clement are judgment creditors of George and Lila Barker, vendors of land under a uniform real estate contract. The issue before the Court is one of first impression: whether a vendor's interest in real property sold by a land sale contract is transformed by the doctrine of equitable conversion into personal property and therefore not subject to a judgment lien pursuant to Utah Code Ann. § 78–22–1 (1987). We hold that a judgment against the vendor of land under a land sale contract does not create a lien against a vendor's interest for purposes of § 78–22–1.

On August 28, 1981, pursuant to a uniform real estate contract, George and Lila Barker contracted to sell certain real property which they owned in fee simple to Diane Hodge. Ms. Hodge recorded notice of that contract on August 31, 1981. The defendants, Donald W. Clement and Ruth L. Clement, obtained and docketed a judgment against the Barkers in August 1985. On September 25, 1985, Ms. Hodge paid the amount remaining on the contract, and the Barkers executed a deed to the property to her. On the same date, Hodge gave a warranty deed to the property to the plaintiffs, Raymond and Debra Cannefax. Both transactions took place at a single real estate closing. The Cannefaxes recorded their deed the next day. Following the closing but before the Cannefaxes recorded their deed, the settlement agent, Surety Title Agency, conducted a title search which disclosed the Clements' judgment against the Barkers. Two years later, the Clements sought to enforce the judgment lien against the property through an execution sale scheduled for September 22, 1987.

The Cannefaxes brought this action to quiet title. The trial court granted summary judgment in favor of the Clements, holding that the judgment created a lien on the property in the amount of $54,464.94, the unpaid amount on the contract on September 25, 1985, the closing date, less the amount of prior encumbrances. The court of appeals reversed and ordered the trial court to enter summary judgment in favor of the Cannefaxes, quieting title to their property. The opinion of the court of appeals is recorded at 786 P.2d 1377 (Utah Ct.App.1990). We affirm.

The issue presented to this Court is whether a vendor's interest in an executory land sale contract is "real property" under Utah Code Ann. § 78–22–1 (1987), so that a judgment docketed against the vendor after the contract is entered into creates a lien against the vendor's interest in the property. Utah Code Ann. § 78–22–1 provides:

> From the time the judgment of the district court * * * is docketed and filed * * * it becomes a lien upon all the real property of the judgment debtor, not exempt from execution, in the county in which the judgment is entered, owned by him at the time or by him thereafter acquired during the existence of said lien * * *. The lien shall continue for eight years unless the judgment is previously satisfied * * * in which case the lien of the judgment ceases.

The court of appeals held that under the doctrine of equitable conversion, a vendor's interest in an executory land sale contract is not real property for purposes of § 78–22–1. *Cannefax v. Clement,* 786 P.2d 1377 at 1379–80 (Utah App.1990). In *Butler v. Wilkinson,* 740 P.2d 1244, 1253–54 (Utah 1987), we reiterated the proposition that under the doctrine of equitable conversion, a *vendee's* equitable interest in an installment land sale contract constitutes real property for purposes of § 78–22–1; however, this Court has not previously decided the nature of the vendor's interest for purposes of the lien statute. We now hold that a vendor's interest in an executory land sale contract is not "real property" as that term is used in § 78–22–1.

Although we have not previously considered the nature of a vendor's interest in an installment land contract, a number of other jurisdictions have. The cases are almost evenly divided, with a slight majority allowing the judgment lien to attach to the vendor's interest. R. Cunningham, W. Stoebuck, & D. Whitman, *The Law of Property* § 10.13, at 701 (1984). *Compare Mooring v. Brown,* 763 F.2d 386 (10th Cir.1985) (applying Colorado law), *First Security Bank v. Rogers,* 91 Idaho 654, 657, 429 P.2d 386, 389 (1967), *May v. Emerson,* 52 Or. 262, 266–67, 96 P. 454, 456 (1908), and *Heath v. Dodson,* 7 Wash.2d 667, 672–73, 110 P.2d 845, 847 (1941) (holding that a judgment lien attaches to a vendor's interest in an executory land contract) *with Snow Bros. Hardware Co. v. Ellis,* 180 Ark. 238, 240–41, 21 S.W.2d 162, 163 (1929), *Hull v. Maryland Casualty Co.,* 79 So.2d 517, 518–19 (Fla.1954), *Bank of Hawaii v. Horwoth,* 71 Haw. 204, ___, 787 P.2d 674, 679 (1990), *Cumming v. First Nat'l Bank,* 199 Iowa 667, 669, 202 N.W. 556, 556 (1925), *Clarence M. Bull, Inc. v. Goldman,* 30 Md.App. 665, 667–68, 353 A.2d 661, 663 (1976), *Marks v. City of Tucumcari,* 93 N.M. 4, 6–7, 595 P.2d 1199, 1201–02 (1979), and *Mueller v. Novelty Dye Works,* 273 Wis. 501, 507, 78 N.W.2d 881, 884 (1956) (holding that a judgment lien does not attach to a vendor's interest in an executory land contract). *See also* 46 Am.Jur.2d *Judgments* § 266 (1969). * * *

In other cases, this Court has previously held that the doctrine of equitable conversion applies to transform a vendor's interest in a land sale contract from a real property interest into a personal property interest. For example, in *Allred v. Allred,* 15 Utah 2d 396, 399, 393 P.2d 791, 792 (1964), the Court stated, "As a general rule an enforceable executory contract of sale has the effect of converting the interest of the vendor of real property to personalty." Also, in *In re Estate of Willson,* 28 Utah 2d 197, 200, 499 P.2d 1298, 1300 (1972), the Court held that a widow could not, for purposes of limiting inheritance taxes, claim an exclusion based upon a dower interest in real property subject to an executory contract of sale. The Court stated that the vendor's interest was " '*no longer real estate* * * * *but personal estate* * * * and if he dies before payment, it goes to his administrators, and not to his heirs.' " *Id.* (emphasis in original) (quoting 1 Pomeroy, *Equity Jurisprudence* 105, 135 (5th ed. 1941)).

Jelco, Inc. v. Third Judicial District Court, 29 Utah 2d 472, 475, 511 P.2d 739, 741 (1973), was a condemnation case which held that the vendee was the equitable owner of property under an executory land contract and therefore entitled to the appreciation in the value of the land occurring after the contract was executed. Although the Court declined to apply equitable conversion in *Reynolds v. Van Wagoner,* 592 P.2d 593, 594 (Utah 1979), it was the *vendor* who sought application of the doctrine rather than the vendee. As the Court noted, the vendor's attempt to alter the contract by relying on equitable conversion was clearly impermissible. Finally, in *Butler v. Wilkinson,* 740 P.2d 1244, 1253–54 (Utah 1987), the Court held that a *vendee's* equitable interest in an installment land sale contract is real property for purposes of § 78–22–1.

The Cannefaxes argue that because this Court held that a vendee's interest in a real estate contract is a real property interest, it must necessarily rule that the vendor's interest is not real property. The court of appeals relied on the above cases and the language in *Butler* which stated that if a vendee has an interest in real estate, by a " 'parity of reasoning' " the vendor is deemed to have converted his real property interest to a monetary or legal interest. *Cannefax,* 786 P.2d at 1380 (quoting *Butler,* 740 P.2d at 1255 n. 5). However, that language from *Butler* was intended only as a general description of the doctrine of equitable conversion. The question of the nature of the vendor's interest was not before the Court in *Butler.* In fact, we also observed in *Butler* that

> the characterization of the vendee as "owner" of the land and of the vendor as having no interest in the land is not wholly accurate. The vendor's retention of the legal title is usually coupled with a contract right to forfeit the vendee's interest and to take back the vendee's interests if the vendee defaults.

740 P.2d at 1255 (citation omitted). We also noted that this characterization of the vendor's interest as a lien is not completely accurate:

> The term "vendor's lien" seems to have stuck even though it is inaccurately used before the vendor parts with the title. Until then, it is not, in fact, a lien at all, but rather a retained interest in the land that is derived from the vendor's retention of the fee title.

740 P.2d at 1256 n. 6 (citation omitted). In other words, the mere fact that the vendee is treated as having a real property interest does not necessarily preclude the vendor from also having such an interest.

* * *

The dissent in the court of appeals opinion also argues that the majority's holding is contrary to the intent of the contracting parties. *Cannefax,* 786 P.2d at 1388 (Bullock, Senior District Judge, dissenting). However, the fact that the contract may have "contemplate[d] a transfer of ownership by deed after all installments have been paid" is irrelevant to construing the judgment lien statute. The true issue is whether the vendor retained a sufficient interest in the property to qualify as "owning real property" for purposes of § 78–22–1.

Section 78–22–1 provides that a judgment becomes a lien upon the real property owned by the judgment debtor at the time of docketing. The position taken by the Clements and the trial court is that the judgment lien attaches to real property to the extent that the contract remains unpaid. This argument is inconsistent with the assertion that the vendor's retained title causes his interest to be real property. If the vendor's retention of legal title were sufficient to constitute real property under § 78–22–1, it follows that the judgment lien should attach to the entire property, subject to prior encumbrances. As this Court recognized in *Belnap v. Blain,* 575 P.2d 696, 699 (Utah 1978), the fact that a judgment debtor has no equity in real property because encumbrances on the property exceed its fair market value does not prevent a judgment lien from attaching to the property, subject to prior encumbrances. The Clements' position, that the lien attaches only to the extent the contract is unpaid, is actually the first step toward applying the doctrine of equitable conversion. That position recognizes that the vendor's true interest is in receiving the unpaid amount on the contract, an interest more akin to personalty than to realty.

The principle underlying *Butler, Allred, Willson,* and *Jelco* is that the vendee of an executory land sale contract holds equitable ownership of the property but not legal title. As stated in *Butler,* the vendor retains the naked legal title, which serves as the basis for forfeiting the vendee's interest and retaking possession if the vendee defaults. 740 P.2d at 1255. In *Belnap,* the Court recognized that a judgment lien does not attach to "bare legal title" to property held by a "trustee of an express, constructive, or resulting trust or [by] an agent or mere conduit for the transfer of title to the true owner." 575 P.2d at 699. Admittedly, the vendor's interest in this case constitutes more than "bare legal title." However, for purposes of § 78–22–1, that interest is more closely analogous to the examples mentioned in *Belnap* than it is to true "ownership of real property" as required by the statute. Although the vendor may forfeit the vendee's interest, he may do so only if the vendee first defaults, an event which is completely out of the hands of the vendor. Furthermore, a vendor who breaches a land sale contract in an attempt to retain the property will be subject to either damages or a decree for specific performance. *See Willson,* 28 Utah 2d at 200, 499 P.2d at 1300. Even though the vendor may retain title to the property, that title is effectively held for the benefit of the vendee, to whom it will pass if the contract is carried out. As stated in *Willson,* "the transfer of legal title and record title [is] dependent only upon the acts and conduct of the buyer." *Id.* In short, the mere retention of title of land subject to a land sale contract does not amount to ownership of real property for purposes of § 78–22–1.

Policy concerns also dictate this result. If a judgment lien could attach to the vendor's interest in an executory land contract, the vendee would be forced to make payments at his or her peril, risking the chance that a subsequent judgment has been docketed after execution of the contract. For example, a vendee who has paid the entire purchase price could still be subject to an execution sale on the purchased property if a judgment was docketed after the contract had been entered into but before all the payments had been made. Because a judgment which has not yet been docketed cannot be uncovered by a title search, such a search can provide no protection to the vendee at the time the contract is entered into. Instead, the vendee would be forced to do a title search before each payment. Even if a judgment lien were discovered in this way, the vendee would be forced to choose whether to pay the vendor or the judgment creditor, thereby risking the possibility of having to pay twice. Therefore, the position which the Clements urge this Court to adopt would make real estate contracts impracticable as an alternative to conventional financing, harming those who are poor credit risks and who are unable to obtain other financing.

However, the Clements also argue that if this Court does not rule that a judgment lien attaches to the debtor's interest in the land contract at the time the judgment is docketed, the Court should at least rule that the lien attaches at the time the vendee has notice of the lien. The Clements assert that the Cannefaxes had notice of the lien at the time they purchased the property from Hodge and that the property is therefore subject to the lien. This contention would require us to rewrite § 78–22–1, which provides that the lien will attach to the property from the time the judgment is docketed. Nothing in the statute supports this construction. Furthermore, the stipulated facts would not support the Clements' argument. The settlement agent did not discover the judgment until after the closing. The judgment debtors then transferred title to Hodge before the discovery of the judgment. Therefore, there was nothing to which the lien could attach. Hodge's transfer of title to the Cannefaxes was therefore also free of the lien.

Our holding does not "place insufficient value in the need to efficiently enforce judgments," as the dissent in the court of appeals argues. *Cannefax,* 786 P.2d at 1389. The need to enforce judgments is not so great that a lien must attach to property in the process of being transferred and to which the vendor's rights are contractually limited. This theory not only places undue emphasis on the method of financing chosen by the contracting parties, but it also unfairly allocates risk to the vendee. This holding does not prevent the judgment creditor from reaching the vendor's interest in the property, either by garnishing payments as they are made or perhaps by executing on the vendor's interest in the contract.

For the above reasons, we hold that the vendor's interest in property subject to an executory real estate contract is not real property for purposes of § 78–22–1 and, therefore, that the judgment creditor's lien did not attach to the vendor's interest. The decision of the court of appeals is affirmed.

HALL, C.J., HOWE, ASSOCIATE C.J., and DURHAM and ZIMMERMAN, JJ., concur.

Notes

1. As *Cannefax* notes, a slight majority of cases, the equitable conversion concept notwithstanding, treat the vendor's interest in an installment land contract as real estate for judgment lien purposes. Under the reasoning of several of these latter cases, the judgment lien "extends to all of the vendor's interest remaining in the land and binds the land to the extent of the unpaid purchase price." First Security Bank of Idaho v. Rogers, 91 Idaho 654, 429 P.2d 386 (1967). Under this approach, the vendor has a real estate interest because she retains legal title to the land until the contract is fully performed and a deed is delivered to the purchaser. Note, 47 Mo.L.Rev. 328, 321 (1982). In order to understand the practical impact of the majority and minority approaches, the following example should be helpful:

> "Suppose that an installment contract vendor was entitled to collect $50,000 over the next four years. X then docketed a $20,000 judgment against vendor in a county where the contract land was located. Y then docketed a $40,000 judgment against vendor in the same county. Y holds an execution sale on the judgment and he purchases at the sale for $40,000. Y clearly paid too much. Under the majority rule the vendor's interest is real estate and thus both judgments were liens on that interest.

Their relative priority is determined by the date each judgment was docketed. Accordingly, since Y's judgment was docketed later than X's, Y purchased the vendor's interest subject to X's unpaid $20,000 lien. On the other hand, if the foregoing fact situation occurs in a minority jurisdiction Y is much better off. In such states the vendor's interest is personalty. As such, a judgment creditor can obtain no interest in it until it is levied upon by the sheriff pursuant to the issuance of a writ of execution. The date of judgment docketing establishes no priority; rather, the first execution sale passes title to the personalty free and clear of any other judgment no matter when it was docketed. Thus, in our example, even though Y's judgment was obtained after X's, Y purchased at the execution sale a title free and clear of any lien in favor of X."

1 G. Nelson and D. Whitman, Real Estate Finance Law 140 (3d Ed.1994).

2. Almost all states hold that the vendee's interest is real estate for purposes of judgment lien legislation and that a creditor who holds a judgment against the vendee thus obtains a valid lien on the vendee's contract interest. *See* 1 G. Nelson & D. Whitman, Real Estate Finance Law 138 (3d Ed.1994). Courts reach this result either by employing equitable conversion or legislative intent.

"The practical implications of this rule can be illustrated by the following hypothetical: Suppose that a vendee has paid off $40,000 of an installment land contract price of $100,000. The land then has a fair market value free and clear of liens of $100,000. Vendee's creditor then dockets a $15,000 judgment against vendee in a county where the contract land is located. Vendee then borrows $30,000 from mortgagee and gives it a mortgage on the contract land, which mortgage mortgagee promptly records. Vendee then defaults on the mortgage and mortgagee forecloses. Because the judgment against the vendee is a valid lien on the vendee's interest and because it was docketed prior to the execution and recordation of the mortgage, the purchaser at the foreclosure sale will buy the vendee's interest subject to the judgment lien.

* * *

"Under the equitable conversion theory, from the time an earnest money or installment land contract is executed, the vendee's interest is considered in equity to be real estate while the vendor's retention of legal title and the right to receive the balance of the purchase price is deemed primarily to be personalty.[4] Other courts eschew the equitable conversion approach and simply hold that the legislature intended that the vendee's interest be treated as real estate for purposes of judgment lien legislation.[5] This statutory construction approach is preferred by these courts because of a concern over the uncertainty of

4. Hume, Real Estate Contracts and the Doctrine of Equitable Conversion in Washington: Dispelling the Ashford Cloud, 7 U.P.S.L.Rev. 233, 240 (1984); Leavell, Love and Nelson, Equitable Remedies and Restitution 356–57 (3d Ed.1980); Bank of Santa Fe v. Garcia, 102 N.M. 588, 698 P.2d 458 (App. 1985); Mutual Building & Loan Association v. Collins, 85 N.M. 706, 516 P.2d 677 (1973); Bartz v. Paff, 95 Wis. 95, 69 N.W. 297 (1896); *cf.,* Westfair Corp. v. Kuelz, 90 Wis.2d 631, 280 N.W.2d 364 (App.1979).

5. Cascade Security Bank v. Butler, 88 Wash.2d 777, 567 P.2d 631 (1977); Joseph v. Donovan, 114 Conn. 79, 157 A. 638 (1931); Hoffman v. Semet, 316 So.2d 649 (Fla.App. 1975); Butler v. Wilkinson, 740 P.2d 1244 (Utah 1987); Note, 47 Mo.L.Rev. 328, 321 (1982).

the equitable conversion concept and the implications its application would create for other areas such as devolution at death, wills and trusts.[6] "

Id. at 139–39.

3. Note that equitable conversion occurs only if there is a contract which equity would specifically enforce. Thus, there is no conversion if, at the relevant time, there is only an unaccepted offer or an unexercised option. Likewise, some courts hold that no conversion if the vendor's title is unmarketable. *See e.g.,* Coe v. Hays, 328 Md. 350, 614 A.2d 576 (1992); Bleckley v. Langston, 112 Ga.App. 63, 143 S.E.2d 671 (1965). A few courts also take the position that no conversion takes place until all the conditions precedent to the transfer of legal title have been satisfied. *See* Sanford v. Breidenbach, 111 Ohio App. 474, 173 N.E.2d 702 (1960).

4. Suppose that during the executory period of the contract, a casualty loss occurs that is the fault of neither party. As a result, the property's value or usefulness is diminished. Which of the parties must absorb the risk or sustain the loss? Stated more specifically, must the buyer complete the purchase despite the loss, or may she rescind or at least insist on a reduction of the price? Here, assuming the contract is silent as to this issue, equitable conversion plays an important role in many states. Because the buyer is deemed to own "real estate" from the time of execution of the contract, the loss is imposed on the buyer. She is subject to a decree of specific performance, even though the real estate has been devalued by the loss. Which party had possession at the time of the loss is said to be irrelevant. *See* 6A Powell, Real Property par. 933 (1979).

Is the equitable conversion approach to risk of loss sound from a policy perspective? Is it consistent with the probable expectation of the parties as to their rights? Does it place the risk on the party who is best able to oversee the property and guard against loss? Does it place the risk on the party who is most likely to carry insurance against it? See Fineberg, Risk of Loss in Executory Contracts for the Sale of Real Property, 14 Colum.J.L. & Soc.Prob. 453 (1979).

Whatever its merits, the doctrine continues to find support in recent risk of loss cases. *See, e.g.,* Continental Ins. Co. v. Brown, 630 F.Supp. 302 (W.D.Va. 1986); Ambrose v. Harrison Mut. Ins. Ass'n, 206 N.W.2d 683 (Iowa 1973); Bleckley v. Langston, 112 Ga.App. 63, 143 S.E.2d 671 (1965). Note, however, that the parties may avoid its application as they wish in their contract. Hence, the litigated cases usually involve situations where risk of loss is not dealt with.

5. A few courts have refused to follow equitable conversion in risk-of-loss cases; they usually place the risk on the seller until legal title or possession is transferred and permit the buyer to rescind, or sometimes to have specific performance with abatement of the price. This approach is sometimes referred to as the "Massachusetts rule." *See* Libman v. Levenson, 236 Mass. 221, 128 N.E. 13 (1920); Anderson v. Yaworski, 120 Conn. 390, 181 A. 205 (1935); Lampesis v. Travelers Ins. Co., 101 N.H. 323, 143 A.2d 104 (1958). Consider the following excerpt from Skelly Oil Co. v. Ashmore, 365 S.W.2d 582, 588 (Mo.1963):

6. *See e.g.,* Cascade Security Bank v. Butler, 88 Wash.2d 777, 567 P.2d 631 (1977).

> "The *non sequitur* involved in the proposition that performance may be had because of the equitable ownership of the land by the vendee, which in turn depends upon the right of performance, is evident. The doctrine of equitable conversion, so far as it is exemplified by the authorities hitherto considered, cannot lead to the result of casting the burden of loss on the vendee, since the *conversion depends upon the question whether the contract should in equity be performed.* In all other cases where the vendee is treated as the equitable owner of the land, it is only because the contract is one which equity first determines should be specifically performed. (Emphasis added.)

See Hume, Real Estate Contracts and the Doctrine of Equitable Conversion in Washington; Dispelling the *Ashford* Cloud, 7 U.Puget Sound L.Rev. 233 (1984).

In a jurisdiction that refuses to follow equitable conversion, what is the result when damage or destruction to the improvements occurs? The Massachusetts answer was given in Hawkes v. Kehoe, 193 Mass. 419, 79 N.E. 766 (1907):

> We are of opinion that in this commonwealth, when, as in this case, the conveyance is to be made of the whole estate, including both land and buildings, for an entire price, and the value of the buildings constitutes a large part of the total value of the estate, and the terms of the agreement show that they constituted an important part of the subject matter of the contract, it is now settled by the decision in Wells v. Calnan, 107 Mass. 514, that the contract is to be construed as subject to the implied condition that it no longer shall be binding if, before the time for the conveyance to be made, the buildings are destroyed by fire. The loss by the fire falls upon the vendor, the owner; and if he has not protected himself by insurance, he can have no reimbursement of this loss; but the contract is no longer binding upon either party. If the purchaser has advanced any part of the price, he can recover it back. * * * If the change in the value of the estate is not so great, or if it appears that the buildings did not constitute so material a part of the estate to be conveyed as to result in an annulling of the contract, specific performance may be decreed, with compensation for any breach of agreement, or relief may be given in damages.

Suppose, in a case involving major damage to the improvements, the purchaser still wants to enforce the contract, but with an abatement of the purchase price to account for the loss. Can she do so under the language above? Is there any sound policy reason to preclude her doing so? Compare Laurin v. DeCarolis Const. Co., 372 Mass. 688, 363 N.E.2d 675 (1977), in which the vendor, during the executory period of the contract, removed trees, shrubs, and gravel from the property. The court cited Libman v. Levenson, supra, in holding the vendor liable for damages. The case is obviously distinguishable from the usual risk-of-loss case in that the damage was a result of the vendor's willful acts, but it seems to suggest that damages might be available even in cases of innocent loss. If this is correct, is it substantially different than granting specific performance with abatement?

6. While the losses which equitable conversion imposes on the purchaser are usually the result of fire or other physical hazards, the risk of changes in the property's legal status is sometimes allocated to the purchaser in the same way. The following are illustrative:

(a) zoning change: Mohave County v. Mohave–Kingman Estates, Inc., 120 Ariz. 417, 586 P.2d 978 (1978); J.C. Penney Co. v. Koff, 345 So.2d 732 (Fla.App.1977); *cf.* Clay v. Landreth, 187 Va. 169, 45 S.E.2d 875 (1948) (contract will not be enforced if zoning change has made property unusable for purchaser's intended purpose).

(b) building code change: Cox v. Supreme Sav. & Loan Ass'n, 126 Ill.App.2d 293, 262 N.E.2d 74 (1970).

(c) eminent domain action: Arko Enterprises, Inc. v. Wood, 185 So.2d 734 (Fla.App.1966); Annot., 27 A.L.R.3d 572 (1969).

7. Suppose the event which causes a loss is also a title defect, such as the imposition by the city of a lien for a sewer improvement assessment. Should this be treated as a breach of the covenant of marketable title (imposing the risk on the seller) or handled under equitable conversion (imposing the risk on the purchaser)? *See* Byrne v. Kanig, 231 Pa.Super. 531, 332 A.2d 472 (1974). The eminent domain cases raise this same issue (although the courts do not always recognize it), since a pending eminent domain action is a defect in marketable title. *See* III Am.L.Prop. § 11.49 n. 52 (1952).

UNIFORM VENDOR AND PURCHASER RISK ACT

§ 1. Risk of Loss. Any contract hereafter made in this State for the purchase and sale of realty shall be interpreted as including an agreement that the parties shall have the following rights and duties, unless the contract expressly provides otherwise:

(a) If, when neither the legal title nor the possession of the subject matter of the contract has been transferred, all or a material part thereof is destroyed without fault of the purchaser or is taken by eminent domain, the vendor cannot enforce the contract, and the purchaser is entitled to recover any portion of the price that he has paid;

(b) If, when either the legal title or the possession of the subject matter of the contract has been transferred, all or any part thereof is destroyed without fault of the vendor or is taken by eminent domain, the purchaser is not thereby relieved from a duty to pay the price, nor is he entitled to recover any portion thereof that he has paid.

Notes

1. As the foregoing statute indicates, risk of loss is sometimes resolved by legislation. Consider, in this regard, the following analysis of two such legislative approaches:

> "The first, the Uniform Vendor and Purchaser Risk Act (UVPRA), was drafted by Professor Williston and promulgated by the Commissioners on Uniform State Laws in 1935; it has been adopted in ten states. The second is Section 2–406 of the Uniform Land Transactions Act (ULTA), adopted by the Commissioners in 1975 but not yet enacted by any legislature. Both take the same basic approach, leaving the risk of loss on the vendor until possession or legal title is transferred to the purchaser. They deny the vendor the right to enforce the contract and compel him to return the buyer's deposit if a material loss occurs while he has the risk. Yet both

> acts leave the law in an uncertain state on several points. They appear to apply only to physical damage and to takings in eminent domain; whether they would influence a court in a case of loss by zoning amendment or other change of legal status is unclear. Both employ the concept of materiality of loss without attempting to define it in dollar or percentage terms. For example, it is by no means obvious whether a $1000 fire in a single-family home would qualify. The UVPRA is also deficient in failing to indicate whether, after a material loss, the purchaser may nonetheless specifically enforce the contract with abatement of the price, and whether, if the loss is nonmaterial and the contract is enforced against the purchaser, he is entitled to a price abatement for the damage. The ULTA answers both of these questions affirmatively. The inadequacies of both of these model acts suggest that neither is an adequate substitute for a competently-drafted contract clause which deals explicitly with all of the matters discussed above."

R. Cunningham, W. Stoebuck & D. Whitman, The Law of Property (2d ed. 1993).*

2. In the vast majority of risk of loss situations, the property is covered by casualty insurance. To what extent should such coverage alter traditional analysis in this area?

"The legal rules governing risk of loss are complicated when the loss is covered by a casualty insurance policy. If there is only one policy and it insures the party on whom the law or the contract imposes the risk of loss, the problems are minimal. But all too often the logic of equitable conversion puts the risk on the buyer when the seller is the only party insured. If the seller recovers the full price for the land and also collects from his insurer, he seems to receive an unwarranted stroke of good fortune. The seller may argue that there is no reason to give the buyer any benefit from the insurance, which is, after all a personal contract of indemnity between insurer and insured. But the seller's windfall has been too much for most modern courts to swallow, and the cases generally permit him to enforce the contract only if he is willing to abate the price to the extent of his insurance recovery. This result, which is often explained as the imposition of a constructive trust on the insurance funds in favor of the purchaser, greatly mitigates the original unfairness of equitable conversion.

"Occasionally a case arises in which the positions of the parties are reversed: the purchaser has insurance, but the risk is on the vendor. Here again is an opportunity for a windfall, this time to the purchaser. Can he collect the insurance proceeds and at the same time escape his contract or buy the land at an abated price? To do so he must meet several objections. First, if he refuses to complete the purchase as is clearly his right, his insurer may argue that he has suffered no loss at all, and that since the insurer's duty was to indemnify his loss, it owes him nothing. This argument has considerable force. Even if the purchaser proceeds with the contract and buys with an abatement of price, the insurer can take much the same position. Moreover, if the insurer pays the claim, the vendor may argue that the insurance was intended for his benefit as well, despite the fact that he was not a named insured; this argument is likely to succeed only if the contract stipulated that the purchaser would carry insurance. The vendor may then insist that the abatement of price owing to the loss be reduced by the insurance proceeds, or if the purchaser defaults on the contract the vendor may seek to recover the insurance proceeds from him."

R. Cunningham, W. Stoebuck & D. Whitman, The Law of Property 707 (2d ed. 1993).**

SECTION 4. CONTRACTS RELATING TO SERVICES

A. LEGAL REMEDY: DAMAGES

1. Action By Buyer

SMITH v. MARK COLEMAN CONSTRUCTION, INC.

District Court of Appeal of Florida, 1992.
594 So.2d 812.

PARKER, JUDGE.

John H. and Sharon A. Smith appeal a final judgment entered in their favor, arguing the award of damages was inadequate. We agree and reverse for a new trial.

The Smiths contracted with appellee, Mark Coleman Construction, Inc., to build a house at a construction price of $266,614. The house, completed in about June 1987, contained numerous defects. On October 28, 1988, the Smiths filed a breach of contract action against Coleman Construction. After a nonjury trial, the trial judge awarded damages for approximately nine items of repairs. This appeal involves only the damages awarded for a hump in the floor of two second-story bedrooms.

Neither party or any witness disputes that prominent humps exist which are obvious to the naked eye. The hump is in the center of the two bedrooms and remains a hump across the floor to the wall in these bedrooms. There is approximately a one and three-eighths inch rise between the height of the floor at the bedroom doorways and the level of the floor at the hump. Apparently the trusses were not sealed properly and the humps appeared when tiles were placed on the roof, causing the trusses to become unaligned. The Smiths discovered the humps three or four months before the completion of the house and brought this to the attention of Coleman Construction. Coleman Construction installed a series of lag bolts to prevent further deterioration of the alignment. The repair, however, did nothing to eliminate the hump, yet Coleman Construction continued construction on the house to completion.

The Smiths attempted to present evidence to support two alternative theories of recovery. The Smiths tried to present the testimony of a real estate appraiser as to the market value of the home with the hump to support their claim that they were entitled to receive an award of the diminution of the market value between a house like theirs with no hump and their house as it existed with a hump in two bedrooms. The trial court

** Reprinted with permission of West Publishing Co.

disallowed this testimony, ruling that such an award was not the proper measure of damages in this case. The Smiths presented the testimony of a general contractor to support their alternative theory of damages which was the cost of removing the hump. Coleman Construction presented the testimony of a general contractor who testified to the cost of disguising the hump effect.

Based upon the trial judge's comments about the amount he would permit the Smiths to recover as to each repair and the total amount awarded in the final judgment, it is clear that the judge awarded $3,640 for a cosmetic masking of the floor defect. We find that award, based upon all the evidence, to be inadequate.

The supreme court, in *Grossman Holdings Ltd. v. Hourihan,* 414 So.2d 1037 (Fla.1982), adopted section 346(1)(a) of the Restatement (First) on Contracts (1932) as the measure of damages for a breach of a construction contract. This subsection provides, in part, as follows:

> (a) For defective or unfinished construction he [the contracting party] can get judgment [from the builder] for either
>
> (i) the reasonable cost of construction and completion in accordance with the contract, if this is possible and does not involve unreasonable economic waste; or
>
> (ii) the difference between the value that the product contracted for would have had and the value of the performance that has been received by the plaintiff, if construction and completion in accordance with the contract would involve unreasonable economic waste.

Hourihan, 414 So.2d at 1039 (quoting Restatement (First) of Contracts § 346(1)(a) (1932)).

The supreme court also cited the following comment to subsection 346(1)(a):

> The purpose of money damages is to put the injured party in as good a position as that in which full performance would have put him; but this does mean he is to be put in the same specific physical position. Satisfaction for his harm is made either by giving him a sum of money sufficient to produce the physical product contracted for or by giving him the exchange value that that product would have had if it had been constructed * * *. Sometimes defects in a complete structure cannot be physically remedied without tearing down and rebuilding, at a cost that would be imprudent and unreasonable. The law does not require damages to be measured by a method requiring such economic waste. If no such waste is involved, the cost of remedying the defect is the amount awarded as compensation for failure to render the promised performance.

Id. (quoting Restatement (First) of Contracts § 346(1)(a) comment (1932)). In short, a party is entitled to recover the cost of repairing a defect so that it is in compliance with the contract or, if that would result in economic waste, the diminution of value between a house built in accordance with the contract and the one actually built. *See also Temple Beth Sholom &*

Jewish Center, Inc. v. Thyne Constr. Corp., 399 So.2d 525 (Fla. 2d DCA 1981).

Applying the *Hourihan* holding to the instant case, we conclude that the trial court erred in precluding the testimony relating to diminution of value. The Smiths presented the testimony of an engineer who testified that he had no suggestion as to a practical method of eliminating the hump. Such a repair would include removing the subflooring, flooring, and ceiling and tracking the exterior end of the truss in order to lower the interior end to the girder. The engineer cautioned that shaving or cutting the truss would be detrimental to the structural integrity of the house.

The Smiths' general contractor expert estimated that the removal of the hump by jacking up the trusses and leveling the floor would cost between $10,000 and $15,000, not including the incidental repairs that such a procedure would necessitate such as repairing the cracks in the interior and exterior walls and fixing the bedroom cabinets. He further testified that he would do the repair based on the time involved and the materials needed. At the time of his testimony, he did not know the extent of labor and materials which would be required because he had not torn up the floor to ascertain exactly what was required to make the repair. The general contractor further testified that he would not undertake such a repair without consulting an engineer. It was his opinion, however, that "anything can be repaired."

The trial judge apparently relied upon the general contractor's testimony in ruling that no economic waste would occur in repairing the hump. Based on the testimony of the engineer and the general contractor, this ruling was in error. The engineer was the only witness competent to testify to the feasibility of such a repair on the structural integrity of the house, and he knew of no way of practically eliminating the hump. Even though the general contractor estimated that he might be able to remove the hump for between $10,000 and $15,000, he did not know the effect of such repair on the structural integrity of the house. Upon initial consideration, it may seem that the Smiths should have presented experts who could testify definitively regarding whether such a repair could be effected and the exact cost for doing so. The Smiths, however, were in a difficult situation because no person could testify competently on this matter unless the person tore up the floor and examined the structure. This court is hesitant to require such a drastic and expensive course of action when Coleman Construction had the opportunity to eliminate the hump months before the house was completed.

Even if this court would find that diminution of value was not a proper measure of damages in this case, there is no substantial, competent evidence to support the amount which the trial judge awarded. Coleman Construction's expert did not testify to any method to eliminate the hump. His recommended methods of repair involved masking the hump to make it less noticeable. His first suggestion was to utilize wood leveling cant strips tapered away from the hump. This method would create a noticeable "step-up" at each bedroom doorway. His alternative suggestion was to utilize multiple coats of a laminate base material and to feather the material out into the hallway to eliminate the "step-up" at the bedroom doorways. The expert testified that the maximum cost to make the repair would be $2,800 plus a thirty percent profit margin. This totals $3,640, the amount the trial court awarded.

We find that the Smiths should not have to accept a final judgment that awards only a cosmetic fix to a noticeable construction defect. The only evidence in the record as to the cost of removing the hump was a minimum of $10,000. Thus, we conclude that the trial court erred in awarding only $3,640 for the removal of the hump. Accordingly, we reverse the final judgment and remand for a new trial on the amount of damages relating to the hump. At a new trial, the Smiths should be awarded either (1) the reasonable cost of removing the hump if it does not involve unreasonable economic waste or (2) if the floor cannot be repaired without creating economic waste, the difference in value of their house with the hump in the floor and the value of a house built in accordance with the contract.

Reversed and remanded for new trial.

RYDER, A.C.J., and LEHAN, J., concur.

RESTATEMENT (SECOND) OF CONTRACTS

§ 348 (1981) *

"§ 348. Alternatives to Loss in Value of Performance

* * *

"(2) If a breach results in defective or unfinished construction and the loss in value to the injured party is not proved with sufficient certainty, he may recover damages based on

"(a) the diminution in the market price of the property caused by the breach, or

"(b) the reasonable cost of completing performance or of remedying the defects if that cost is not clearly disproportionate to the probable loss in value to him.

* * *

"Comment:

* * *

"*c. Incomplete or defective performance.* If the contract is one for construction, including repair or similar performance affecting the condition of property, and the work is not finished, the injured party will usually find it easier to prove what it would cost to have the work completed by another contractor than to prove the difference between the values to him of the finished and the unfinished performance. Since the cost to complete is usually less than the loss in value to him, he is limited by the rule on avoidability to damages based on cost to complete. * * * If he has actually had the work completed, damages will be based on his expenditures if he [has made a reasonable effort to avoid loss].

"Sometimes, especially if the performance is defective as distinguished from incomplete, it may not be possible to prove the loss in value to the injured party with reasonable certainty. In that case he can usually recover damages based on the cost to remedy the defects. Even if this gives him a recovery somewhat in excess of the loss in value to him, it is better that he receive a small windfall than that he be undercompensated by being limited to the resulting diminution in the market price of his property.

"Sometimes, however, such a large part of the cost to remedy the defects consists of the cost to undo what has been improperly done that the cost to remedy the defects will be clearly disproportionate to the probable loss in value to the injured party. Damages based on the cost to remedy the defects would then give the injured party a recovery greatly in excess of the loss in value to him and result in a substantial windfall. Such an award will not be made. It is sometimes said that the award would involve 'economic waste,' but this is a misleading expression since an injured party will not, even if awarded an excessive amount of damages, usually pay to have the defects remedied if to do so will cost him more than the resulting increase in value to him. If an award based on the cost to remedy the defects would clearly be excessive and the injured party does not prove the actual loss in value to him, damages will be based instead on the difference between the market price that the property would have had without the defects and the market price of the property with the defects."

Notes

1. In *Hourihan,* the major case relied upon in *Smith,* a purchaser entered into a contract with a builder for a house to be built on particular lot according to specific plans and specifications. Prior to construction, purchaser discovered that the builder intended to build the house as a "mirror image" of the house specified in the plans. Purchaser protested but the builder erected the mirror image house nonetheless. The purchaser took possession and title to the house and sued for damages. Should purchaser be able recover damages sufficient to reconstruct the house as called for in the original plans and specifications? Or should purchaser be able to obtain diminution in value damages only? Should it be relevant that purchaser could now sell the house at a profit? According to the Florida Supreme Court in *Hourihan,* "damages for a breach of contract should be measured as of the date of the breach. * * * Fluctuations in value after the breach do not affect the nonbreaching party's recovery. Here, it may be possible to demonstrate a difference in value as of the date of delivery between the house the [purchaser] contracted for and the house that [builder] built."

2. The measure of damages in an action by a purchaser of services against a breaching provider is discussed in Eisenberg, The Responsive Model of Contract Law, 36 Stan.L.Rev. 1107, 1155–65 (1984): *

* Reprinted with permission of the Stanford Law Review.

"Suppose now that a contract for the provision of services is breached by the service-provider. As in a breach by a seller of goods, the expectation principle might appear to entitle the injured party to either specific performance or damages measured by the difference between the contract price and the value that he subjectively places on the services. However, specific performance will usually be either impracticable or unavailable for reasons of policy, and direct judicial measurement of the injured party's subjective value presents obvious problems of administration. Nevertheless, the courts usually can protect the injured party's actual expectation by applying an objective but individualized measure, based on the cost required to put the subject matter of the contract into its promised state—a measure generally known as cost of completion. At least where the injured party has actually had the work completed, cost of completion is analogous to cover. Like cover, cost of completion is both objective, since it does not depend on direct measurement of subjective valuation, and individualized, since it depends on the circumstances of the individual case. Moreover, cost of completion, like cover, should normally put the plaintiff in the same position as performance would have done.

"An alternative measure of damages for nonperformance of services is generally known as diminished value. Under this measure, the plaintiff recovers the difference between the market value of the contract's subject matter as it stands, and its market value had the seller performed as promised. Although this measure is essentially standardized, in a market with perfect information, cost-of-completion and diminished-value damages would usually be approximately equal, since the difference between the market value of the subject matter in its actual and promised states should usually equal the cost of transforming the subject matter from one state to the other. * * *

"In certain circumstances, however, the two measures will differ. In some such cases, the courts have limited the recovery to diminished-value damages, over the injured party's objection. * * *

* * *

"[T]he cases applying this principle have spelled out its rationale poorly at best, and the competing rules that have been advanced for imposing the limit are generally unsatisfactory. One rule, reflected in Section 346(1)(a)(i) of *Restatement (First),* is that the court should not award cost of completion if that measure would involve unreasonable economic waste. An award of damages, however, merely redistributes wealth between the parties, and therefore cannot in itself involve waste. While a plaintiff may use the proceeds of a damage recovery to engage in activity the court would regard as wasteful, that has never been a criterion for selecting among damage measures.

"A second rule is that courts should not award cost of completion if damages so measured would be 'grossly and unfairly out of proportion' to the 'result,' 'good,' or 'end' to be attained. * * * Disparity between cost of completion and diminution in market value, however, should not in itself present a ground for refusing cost-of-completion damages. * * *

"A third rule, reflected in some of the commentary, is that the courts should not award cost of completion if that measure would create a windfall. This rule, however, provides no guidance for determining when a windfall would result. If completion is required to satisfy the plaintiff's expectation, it is hard to see why its cost would constitute a windfall. Indeed, limiting the plaintiff's damages to diminution in value may give the defendant a windfall.[120]

"The underlying problem with all three rules is that they attempt to solve an essentially subjective problem with objective tests. The guiding rationale is very simple. The purpose of expectation damages is to put the injured party where he would have been had the contract been performed. Since cost-of-completion damages usually accomplish that objective, this measure should usually be utilized. It need not be utilized, however, where the factfinder is convinced it would not accomplish that objective because both the market and the plaintiff value the difference between the existing and promised states of the contract's subject matter at less than the cost of completion, and the plaintiff therefore would not use a recovery measured by that cost to achieve completion.

* * *

"While the ultimate issue is therefore subjective, the courts should normally determine that issue by looking to objective indicators, particularly whether the subject matter of the contract involved personal rather than strictly commercial interests, or whether strategic considerations, such as location, would lead the plaintiff to assign a value to the subject matter in

120. Many other rules have also been proposed by the commentators. *See, e.g.,* D. Dobbs, *supra* note 58, at 902 (where an owner is interested only in economic value to begin with, the difference between cost of completion and diminished value should be split between the parties); Farnsworth, Legal Remedies for Breach of Contract, 70 Colum.L.Rev. 1145, 1175 (1970) (where there is uncertainty concerning the difference between the value to the owner of the promised and the rendered performance, and cost of completion varies widely from diminished value, the trier of fact should have discretion to fix any figure, not unreasonable under the circumstances, so long as it lies within those two limits); Harris, Ogus & Phillips, *supra* note 62, at 601–10 (courts should award the injured party the value he places on the promised performance); Marschall, Willfulness: A Crucial Factor in Choosing Remedies for Breach of Contract, 24 Ariz.L.Rev. 733 (1982) (the choice between cost of completion and diminished value should turn on whether the breach was willful); Muris, *supra* note 148, at 395–96 (cost of completion should be awarded when (i) the original purchase price exceeds the fair market value at the time of purchase and the cost figure reflects the original cost of production; (ii) cost of completion is less than or equal to diminution in value; (iii) diminution in value is too difficult to calculate with reasonable certainty; or (iv) subjective value is relevant and cost of completion does not grossly exceed the likely subjective value); Yorio, In Defense of Money Damages for Breach of Contract, 82 Colum.L.Rev. 1365, 1388–1423 (1982) (cost of completion should be awarded in all cases, unless the breach was inadvertent or due to changed circumstances; in those cases the innocent party should receive (i) half the difference between cost of completion and diminished value, (ii) half the gain that resulted to the contractor by virtue of the breach, or (iii) at least where the owner has derived no benefit, restitution of amounts paid to the contractor). Most of these rules turn in whole or in part on objective tests, or at least on an attempt to avoid determining subjective intent, and are therefore subject to the same problems as the rules advanced by the courts. Marschall's rule appears to turn on a subjective test—the willfulness of the breach—but as regards nonwillful breaches, Marschall suggests a balancing of the conventional objective factors, such as waste and disproportionality.

Professor Farnsworth has written a second article recommending that when a provider of services has rendered "a defective performance that leaves the injured party with no opportunity to use that party's return performance to obtain a reasonable substitute," the injured party may invoke a restitutionary remedy to disgorge any gain resulting from the breach. Farnsworth, Your Loss or My Gain? The Dilemma of the Disgorgement Principle in Breach of Contract, 94 Yale L.J. 1339 (1985). [Ed.]

its promised state higher than would the market. Thus in *Edgar v. Hosea* the court distinguished between commercial and residential construction, and ruled that in cases involving the latter, damages should be measured by cost of completion, 'since unlike a commercial structure, a dwelling has an esthetic value and must be constructed as the owner wants it, even though the finished dwelling may be just as good.' * * *

"In short, in cases where cost of completion substantially exceeds diminution in value, the analysis should proceed in three steps. First, if the plaintiff has actually paid a third party to have the work completed, damages should always be measured by cost of completion, since we know that cost of completion does not exceed the plaintiff's valuation of the differential between the existing and promised states of the subject matter of the contract. Second, if the plaintiff has not had the work completed, damages should be measured by cost of completion unless the defendant convincingly demonstrates that the plaintiff's valuation of the differential is significantly less than the cost of completion, and that the plaintiff therefore probably does not intend to complete. Third, if such a demonstration is made, damages should normally be measured by the greater of (i) diminution in value or (ii) the plaintiff's valuation of the differential, based, where possible, on the amount he paid for completion, viewed ex ante at the time of contract formation."

3. When an employer sues an employee for breaching a personal services contract, the employer's recovery is measured by the difference between the contract price and the cost of obtaining substitute services. The latter cost may be proven by establishing the cost of cover or, if no substitute is available, by looking to the higher wages that the former employee is earning from a new employer. *E.g.,* Roth v. Speck, 126 A.2d 153 (D.C.1956). *See generally* D. Dobbs, Handbook on the Law of Remedies § 12.26 (1973). Note that if the services are defective, the usual remedy is termination of the employee, rather than damages for the difference between the value of the services actually rendered and the contract price.

4. Incidental and consequential damages are recoverable by a buyer of services, but consequential damages for lost profits caused by a delay in the completion of construction or by a breach of a personal services contract are often very difficult to prove. 3 D. Dobbs, Law of Remedies §§ 12.21, 12.26 (2d ed. 1993). One way to solve this problem is through the use of liquidated damages clauses, and they are widely used and approved by the courts in construction contracts. *Id.* at § 12.21. A common method of protecting an employer against breach of a key employee is a clause providing that the employee will not compete with the employer during the term of the contract. *Id.* at § 12.26.

2. *Action by Seller*

3 D. DOBBS, LAW OF REMEDIES

§ 12.21(2) (2d ed. 1993).*

"An employee wrongfully discharged in violation of contract may recover damages measured by the contract price, less replacement income under the avoidable consequences rules, plus recoverable consequential damages. The recoverable contract price includes both direct wages and other employment benefits. It may, for example, include deferred compensation for past services, such as commissions payable in the future or a future share in the business. It also includes an employer's payments to a retirement benefit fund, at least if the payments would result in benefits to the plaintiff.

"In most states the recovery is based on the full price due for the unexpired term of the contract, subject to the rules for minimizing damages. Where the employee is only guaranteed a specified time period to work after notice, the unexpired term for which compensation is due is the notice period. Where the employee is guaranteed [permanent employment], unless there is good cause for discharge, the effect may be that the employee can recover wages [over] the remainder of her working life, subject only to deductions for avoidable consequences and reductions to present value. An older way of proceeding was to require separate suits for installments as due, and some states still use this rule. Past due installments may still be the only sums due if the contract term has expired when suit is brought or the employee has been reinstated.

"*The first and second rules of avoidable consequences.* The avoidable consequences rules place two limitations on the plaintiff's recovery. Under the first rule the defendant is entitled to a credit for any income the plaintiff actually earns in lieu of the employment income. This rule credits the defendant with realized income even if it was realized in a job that would not count as a substitute.

* * *

" '*Reasonable diligence*'. Courts sometimes speak of the second rule by saying that the plaintiff is expected to use 'reasonable diligence' to find suitable substitute employment. The reasonable diligence statement can be misleading, however. If the plaintiff does exercise reasonable diligence but finds no comparable employment, that fact strongly supports the view that no comparable employment exists and tends to rebut any evidence the defendant may offer to the contrary. The plaintiff's lack of diligence might also corroborate the defendant's evidence that comparable employment existed. But the second rule does not dismiss the plaintiff for lack of diligence. If the defendant fails to prove that comparable employment was available, the plaintiff's lack of diligence does not defeat or reduce her claim. The claim is reduced under the second rule only if suitable substitute employment was available and to the extent that it would have or did provide replacement income.

* * *

"*Suitable, comparable, or substitute employment.* A suitable substitute job must be one that the plaintiff could have obtained with reasonable effort or expense; it must not be 'inferior' work and it must provide the plaintiff with a similar rank or status. In the case of artists or professionals, similar professional experience and exposure is also important in judging suitability of the proposed substitute job. In many instances a similar job in a distant locality will not count as a substitute, although where mobility is a common attribute of particular employment the locality feature might be unimportant. Or what is considered the same locality might be different depending on whether the employee is a high level executive or a school teacher. When the employee can minimize damages only by accepting otherwise suitable re-employment with the defendant, he is usually expected to do so; his damages are reduced if the defendant makes a re-employment offer in good faith."

Note

1. Professor Eisenberg compares the measure of damages recoverable by a seller of goods, a seller of services under a construction contract, and a seller of personal services in Eisenberg, The Responsive Model of Contract Law, 36 Stan.L.Rev. 1107, 1148–55 (1984): *

"The obligation of a buyer of services, like that of a buyer of goods, is normally limited to the payment of money. As in the case of goods, therefore, if the buyer breaches, the seller's actual expectation can normally be satisfied without taking his subjective value into account, provided the seller's remedies are individualized.

"The established formula for measuring damages for breach by a buyer of services is based on the difference between the contract price and the seller's out-of-pocket cost of completion at the time of breach. This formula mirrors the net-proceeds measure afforded a seller of goods under section 2–708(2) of the Uniform Commercial Code. There is, however, an important difference between the rules governing goods cases and services cases. In goods cases, both the formula and its application are individualized, since the section 2–708(2) net-proceeds measure is available only where the breach does not enable the seller to make a replacement sale that he could not otherwise have made. In contrast, in most types of services cases courts have applied the net-proceeds measure in a highly standardized fashion, without regard to the presence of a replacement sale.

"Take, for example, the following hypothetical:

Busy Plumber. Plumber engages in the business of upgrading plumbing in old commercial buildings; he operates at full capacity, and must often turn down jobs. On January 1, Plumber enters into a contract to do a plumbing job for Owner 1 for $6000, the work to begin on February 1 and to be completed in two weeks. On January 30, Owner 1 repudiates the contract. On January 31, Plumber enters into a contract to do a plumbing job for Owner 2 for $7600, the work to begin on February 1 and to be completed in two weeks. Plumber could not have accepted the job with Owner 2 but for the breach by Owner 1. Plumber's out-of-pocket costs for performing his contract with Owner 1 would have been $3400. His out-of-pocket costs for performing his contract with Owner 2 are $2900. Plumber now sues Owner 1.

"In assessing Plumber's recovery, the expectation principle would require the contract with Owner 2 to be taken as an offset, lest damages place him in a better position than performance would have done. In the past, however, the courts have usually not permitted such an offset. * * *

"In striking contrast, in cases where 'personal services' *are* involved—that is, in contracts of employment—if the buyer (employer) breaches, the law reduces the damages of the seller (employee) not only by any replacement wages he actually earns, but by any wages he would have earned had he used reasonable efforts to find a replacement job. This difference between the employment and nonemployment cases is highly anomalous. For one thing, an employment contract is only a special case of a contract for the provision of services. For another, if the law must treat employment contracts differently than other services contracts, one would expect it to be more tenderhearted to employees than to business organizations.

"Two kinds of arguments have been made in support of the traditional no-offset rule applied in nonemployment cases. One follows from a concept of business economics, and the other from a concept of reciprocity. The business-economics argument, advanced by Professor Patterson, is that, 'As an enterpriser, [a] builder may take on an indefinite number of contracts and make a profit on all of them.' [115] This argument is empirically wrong. Factors such as managerial resources, working capital, and bonding limits constrain the number of jobs a contractor can take on. Of course, a contractor often can expand capacity within limits. In most cases, therefore, a buyer's breach may not enable a contractor to make a replacement contract he could not otherwise have made. * * * That is no reason, however, to prohibit the buyer from establishing that, in his case, the breach enabled the seller to take on a replacement job that he could not otherwise have performed.

"The reciprocity argument is that '[i]t would not be just to give the defendant the benefit of a good contract and not charge him with the loss of a bad one when plaintiff had honestly used his skill, time, and capital.' [117] This argument rests on the tacit assumption that the defendant is not liable for the loss on a bad replacement contract. That assumption might be questioned: By way of analogy, if the employer breaks an employment contract and the employee incurs expenses in seeking a replacement job, those expenses are added to the employee's damages even if the search is unsuccessful. In any event, both the seller's damages and the offset should be measured by net proceeds—that is, by the difference between out-of-pocket expenses and the contract price—not by net profits. Many service contracts result in negative net profits, but few will be likely to result in negative net proceeds. It is therefore letting the tail wag the dog to deny an offset for a replacement contract that yields positive net proceeds, on the theory that a defendant should not bear the burden of (an extremely unlikely) replacement contract that yields negative net proceeds. Furthermore, negative-net-proceeds contracts might be distinguished from positive-net-proceeds contracts on the grounds that they are not reasonably foreseeable (because so unlikely), and that they probably result from the seller's lack of skill, which the defendant should not have to subsidize.

115. Patterson, Builder's Measure of Recovery for Breach of Contract, 31 Colum.L.Rev. 1286, 1306 (1931).

117. Grinnell Co. v. Voorhees, 1 F.2d 693 (3d Cir.1924).

"Finally, the reciprocity argument does not square with the courts' treatment of employment contracts in cases where the employee starts his own business during the unexpired term of the breached contract. The general rule is that the employee's recovery is reduced by what he has earned and can reasonably expect to earn in his new business during the unexpired term of the broken agreement. If the reciprocity argument were correct, it would apply to this case as well.

"In short, the rule traditionally applied to nonemployment services contracts is triply anomalous: It is inconsistent with the expectation principle, with the rules governing contracts for the sale of goods, and with the rules governing a kindred class of contracts for the sale of services. Therefore, it is not surprising that the rule seems to be eroding. For example, in *M. & R. Contractors & Builders v. Michael* [121] the court said that if a contractor 'could *not* have worked on another job or project unless he had been discharged from the performance of the defendant's contract, then the gains from the other employment or undertaking must be deducted from [its] damages.[122] Similarly, the comment to section 347 of *Restatement (Second) of Contracts* adopts the rule that if an injured party makes substitute arrangements for the use of resources he would have needed to perform the original contract, the net profit from the substitute arrangements reduces his damages. The comment continues:

> *f. Lost volume.* * * * Since entrepreneurs try to operate at optimum capacity * * * it is possible that an additional transaction would not have been profitable and that the injured party would not have chosen to expand his business by undertaking it had there been no breach. It is sometimes assumed that he would have done so, but the question is one of fact to be resolved according to the circumstances of each case. * * *
>
> > [Illustration] 16. *A* contracts to pave *B's* parking lot for $10,000. *B* repudiates the contract and *A* subsequently makes a contract to pave a similar parking lot for $10,000. *A's* business could have been expanded to do both jobs. *Unless it is proved that he would not have undertaken both, A's* damages are based on the net profit he would have made on the contract with *B,* without regard to the subsequent transaction.[123]

"Suppose now that a seller of services could have obtained a replacement job but did not. This problem has not been worked out in the context of nonemployment contracts, because under the traditional rule replacement jobs were irrelevant in that context. In the context of employment contracts, however, the well-established rule is that the employee has a duty to mitigate, so that wages he could have earned on a replacement job, but did not, will be offset against his recovery. This duty complements the rule that wages the employee actually does earn on a replacement job offset his recovery. Under the latter rule, an employee

121. 215 Md. 340, 138 A.2d 350 (1958).

122. *Id.* at 355, 138 A.2d at 358 (emphasis in original); *see also* Kearsarge Computer, Inc. v. Acme Staple Co., 116 N.H. 705, 709–10, 366 A.2d 467, 471 (1976); McMullen v. Wel–Mil Corp., 23 N.C.App. 736, 209 S.E.2d 507 (1974); 5 A. Corbin, *supra* note 52, §§ 1041, 1094 (1964).

* * *

123. Restatement (Second) of Contracts § 347 comment f (1981) (emphasis added).

who takes a replacement job in effect works for the breaching employer rather than for himself. Unless a duty to take such a job existed, therefore, the offset rule might encourage employees to stand idle. For this reason, the same duty should apply to other sellers of services.

"But what rule determines whether the duty to mitigate has been satisfied? The traditional statement of the duty frames the issue in objective and even standardized terms: The plaintiff has a duty to take a replacement job if it involves 'similar employment, with similar conditions of employment and rank and in the same locality.' However, a job that is objectively comparable, on an abstract level, to the job originally contracted for, may not satisfy the plaintiff for perfectly good reasons, ranging from quality of management to degree of risk. In such a case, a rule that in effect forces the plaintiff to take the replacement job violates the expectation principle because it places him in a worse position than he would have occupied had the defendant performed the original contract, which presumably involved a satisfactory job. A preferable approach, therefore, would be to treat an employee or other seller of services in the same manner as a covering buyer of goods, so that the search for a replacement is tested by a standard of reasonableness, but the substantive decision is tested by a standard of good faith. If the plaintiff failed to make a reasonable search, and if that search would have discovered an objectively comparable job, he should bear the uncertainty of whether he would have accepted the job. If he does make a reasonable search, however, he should not be constrained to accept an alternative job which he in good faith deems unsatisfactory. Like any subjective standard, this test is subject to abuse, but the likelihood of abuse seems small. Given normal economic and psychological needs, few persons are likely to turn down a satisfactory job in favor of inactivity and the *chance* of recovering damages that would put them in no better financial position than would the replacement job. As in the case of cover, motives of self-regard will therefore indirectly control good faith, and in any event, good faith can be directly reviewed by the court.

"The leading case of *Parker v. Twentieth Century–Fox Film Corp.*[129] supports this bifurcated approach to search and decision. Shirley MacLaine had contracted with Fox to play the female lead in *Bloomer Girl* at a minimum compensation of $750,000. Before production started, Fox decided not to produce the picture and offered MacLaine the lead in *Big Country, Big Man* for identical compensation. *Big Country* was to be filmed at the time scheduled for *Bloomer Girl,* but *Bloomer Girl* would have been a musical while *Big Country* would be a dramatic western, and *Bloomer Girl* would have been filmed in California while *Big Country* would be filmed in Australia. Also, the *Bloomer Girl* contract gave MacLaine the power of director and screenplay approval, but the *Big Country* contract provided only that Fox would consult with MacLaine on these issues. MacLaine rejected *Big Country* and brought suit for breach of contract. Fox pleaded that MacLaine, by refusing to accept *Big Country,* had failed to mitigate damages.

"The California Supreme Court affirmed a summary judgment for MacLaine. The court made obeisance to the traditional statement of the mitigation rule by finding that the two roles were not equivalent, and that

129. 3 Cal.3d 176, 474 P.2d 689, 89 Cal. Rptr. 737 (1970).

the changed contract provisions made *Big Country* 'an offer of inferior employment.' The thrust of the opinion, however, went considerably further. First, the court seemed to eviscerate the traditional, standardized test by indicating that any distinction between two jobs would render them different in kind as a matter of law. Second, the court properly drew a sharp distinction between search and decision:

> In the present case defendant has raised no issue of *reasonableness of efforts* by plaintiff to obtain other employment. * * * Despite defendant's arguments to the contrary, no case * * * holds or suggests that reasonableness is an element of a wrongfully discharged employee's option to reject, or fail to seek, different or inferior employment. * * * [132]

* * *

"In summary, if a buyer of services breaches, the seller should recover under an individualized net-proceeds measure of damages. If the seller accepts a replacement job, his net proceeds on that job should offset his recovery against the buyer. The seller should make reasonable efforts to search for such a job, but his decision to reject a replacement job that he finds should be judged by the subjective standard of good faith."

MONGE v. BEEBE RUBBER CO.

Supreme Court of New Hampshire, 1974.
114 N.H. 130, 316 A.2d 549.

LAMPRON, JUSTICE.

Action of assumpsit to recover damages for an alleged breach of an oral contract of employment. Plaintiff was hired in September 1968 at wages of $1.84 per hour to work on a conversion machine in defendant's factory and was allegedly told that if she worked well she would get better jobs with better pay. Plaintiff claims that she was harassed by her foreman because she refused to go out with him and that his hostility, condoned if not shared by defendant's personnel manager, ultimately resulted in her being fired. Trial by jury resulted in a verdict for the plaintiff in the amount of $2,500. * * *

* * *

Plaintiff sued for breach of an employment contract for an indefinite period of time. The employer has long ruled the workplace with an iron hand by reason of the prevailing common-law rule that such a hiring is presumed to be at will and terminable at any time by either party. * * *

The law governing the relations between employer and employee has evolved over the years to reflect changing legal, social and economic conditions. 3A A. Corbin, Contracts § 674 at 205, 206 (1960). In this area "[w]e are in the midst of a period in which the pot boils the hardest and in the process of change the fastest." Although many of these changes have

132. *Id.* at 182 n. 5, 474 P.2d at 693 n. 5, 89 Cal.Rptr. at 741 n. 5 (emphasis in original).

resulted from the activity and influence of labor unions, the courts cannot ignore the new climate prevailing generally in the relationship of employer and employee.

In all employment contracts, whether at will or for a definite term, the employer's interest in running his business as he sees fit must be balanced against the interest of the employee in maintaining his employment, and the public's interest in maintaining a proper balance between the two. We hold that a termination by the employer of a contract of employment at will which is motivated by bad faith or malice or based on retaliation is not in the best interest of the economic system or the public good and constitutes a breach of the employment contract. Such a rule affords the employee a certain stability of employment and does not interfere with the employer's normal exercise of his right to discharge, which is necessary to permit him to operate his business efficiently and profitably.

The sole question on appeal is whether there was sufficient evidence to support the jury's finding that defendant, through its agents, acted maliciously in terminating plaintiff's employment. * * *

The jury could draw the not-so-subtle inference from the evidence before it that the hostility of defendant's foreman and connivance of the personnel manager resulted in [her] discharge. The foreman's overtures and the capricious firing at 2:00 a.m., the seeming manipulation of job assignments, and the apparent connivance of the personnel manager in this course of events all support the jury's conclusion that the dismissal was maliciously motivated.

In our opinion, however, the verdict included elements of damage not properly recoverable. The plaintiff lost 20 weeks employment at an average pay of $70.81 per week. This would account for $1,416.20 of the verdict, leaving $1,083.80 attributable to mental suffering. Such damages are not generally recoverable in a contract action. They could not be found in this case to have resulted from the discharge. Plaintiff had been having difficulty with her husband and had been receiving annoying telephone calls which upset her. She presented no medical testimony. Although she alleged that her discharge caused her mental suffering, her difficulties all preceded the discharge. We therefore remand the case for a new trial unless the plaintiff consents to a reduction of the verdict by the amount of $1,083.80.

Remanded.

Notes

1. Even when a contract provides for job security, the courts have refused to award damages for mental distress caused by the employer's breach:

> "Sharon Valentine seeks to recover mental distress damages arising out of the alleged breach of an employment contract. Valentine claims that, under the contract, she was entitled to job security and the peace of mind that is associated with job security. Because an employment contract providing for job security has a personal element, and breach of such a contract can be expected to result in mental distress, Valentine argues that

she should be able to recover mental distress damages. She also asks for exemplary damages.

"The Court of Appeals affirmed the decision of the trial court dismissing the claims for mental distress and exemplary damages. We affirm.

* * *

"In determining what damages are recoverable, the courts of this state have qualified the general rule, pursuant to which mental distress damages for breach of contract are not recoverable, with a narrow exception. Rather than look to the foreseeability of loss to determine the applicability of the exception, the courts have considered whether the contract 'has elements of personality' and whether the 'damage suffered upon the breach of the agreement is capable of adequate compensation by reference to the terms of the contract.'

"The narrow scope of those verbal formulas appears on consideration of the limited situations in which this Court has allowed the recovery of mental distress damages for breach of contract. In Vanderpool v. Richardson, 52 Mich. 336, 17 N.W. 936 (1883), recovery was allowed for breach of a promise to marry. In Stewart v. Rudner, 349 Mich. 459, 84 N.W.2d 816 (1957), a doctor who failed to fulfill his promise to deliver a child by caesarean section was required to pay mental distress damages. In Miholevich v. Mid–West Mutual Auto Ins. Co., 261 Mich. 495, 246 N.W. 202 (1933), the plaintiff, who was jailed for failure to pay a liability judgment, recovered mental distress damages from an insurer who had failed to pay the judgment.

"Loss of a job is not comparable to the loss of a marriage or a child and generally results in estimable monetary damages. In *Miholevich,* the breach resulted in a deprivation of personal liberty.

"An employment contract will indeed often have a personal element. Employment is an important aspect of most persons' lives, and the breach of an employment contract may result in emotional distress. The primary purpose in forming such contracts, however, is economic and not to secure the protection of personal interests. The psychic satisfaction of the employment is secondary.

"Mental distress damages for breach of contract have not been awarded where there is a market standard by which damages can be adequately determined. Valentine's monetary loss can be estimated with reasonable certainty according to the terms of the contract and the market for, or the market value of, her service. Mental distress damages are not awarded an employee found to have been wrongfully discharged in violation of a collective bargaining agreement.

"We conclude, because an employment contract is not entered into primarily to secure the protection of personal interests and pecuniary damages can be estimated with reasonable certainty, that a person discharged in breach of an employment contract may not recover mental distress damages."

Valentine v. General Am. Credit, Inc., 420 Mich. 256, 261–63, 362 N.W.2d 628, 630–31 (1984).

2. Many courts allow a tort action for a wrongful or retaliatory discharge. *See e.g.,* Gantt v. Sentry Insurance, 1 Cal. 4th 1083, 4 Cal.Rptr.2d 874, 824 P.2d 680 (1992); Adams v. George W. Cochran & Company, 597 A.2d 28 (D.C.App.1991). The differences between tort and contract actions are discussed in Brockmeyer v. Dun & Bradstreet, 113 Wis.2d 561, 574–75, 335 N.W.2d 834, 841 (1983):

> "Whether the cause of action for wrongful discharge should be maintained in tort or contract or both needs to be resolved. Those cases implying a contractual term of good faith dealing sounded in contract. Most, though not all of the public policy exception cases from other states were tort actions. The most significant distinction in our view between the two causes of action in wrongful discharge suits is in the damages that may be recovered. In tort actions, the only limitations are those of 'proximate cause' or public policy considerations. Punitive damages are also allowed. In contract actions, damages are limited by the concepts of foreseeability and mitigation. The remedies established by the majority of Wisconsin wrongful discharge statutes are limited to reinstatement and backpay, contractual remedy concepts. We believe that reinstatement and backpay are the most appropriate remedies for public policy exception wrongful discharges since the primary concern in these actions is to make the wronged employee 'whole'. Therefore, we conclude that a contract action is most appropriate for wrongful discharges."

D. DOBBS, LAW OF REMEDIES

618 (2d Ed.1993). *

"About the same time that exceptions were developing to the 'at will' rule, courts began dealing with important statutory provisions against retaliatory[4] and discriminatory discharges as well as with provisions against other forms of employment discrimination.[5] A patchwork of some complexity has resulted. Common law job rights, federal statutory rights and state statutory rights[6] must all be made to work with each other[7] and also with preexisting systems such as workers' compensation[8] and union-management grievance and arbitration procedures.[9] Because statutes protect against several forms of job discrimination and not merely against

* Reprinted with permission of West Publishing Co.

4. *E.g.,* 42 U.S.C.A. § 7622; 42 U.S.C.A. § 5851; N.Y.—McKinney's Labor Law § 740. See § 6.10(3) below.

5. *E.g.,* 42 U.S.C.A. 2000e et seq. (Title VII of the 1964 Civil Rights Act). See § 6.10(3) below.

6. *E.g.,* Iowa Code Ann. § 601A.6.

7. *See* Froyd v. Cook, 681 F.Supp. 669 (E.D.Cal.1988) (state Fair Employment Housing Act did not preempt or displace state common law wrongful discharge action); Chrisman v. Philips Industries, Inc., 242 Kan. 772, 751 P.2d 140 (1988) (plaintiff contended he was discharged in part because he refused to approve the employer's defective products to be used in nuclear industry, claim held preempted by a federal anti-retaliatory statute dealing with nuclear industry); Lally v. Copygraphics, 85 N.J. 668, 428 A.2d 1317 (1981) (administrative remedy for retaliatory firing attributable to employee's workers' compensation claim does not bar tort suit).

8. *See* Note, Workers' Compensation Exclusivity and Wrongful Termination Tort Damages: An Injurious Tug of War?, 39 Hast.L.J. 1229 (1988).

9. *See* Korn, Collective Rights and Individual Remedies: Rebalancing the Balance after Lingle v. Norge Division of Magic Chef, Inc., 41 Hastings L.J. 1149 (1990).

discharge,[10] they are broader in scope than the present section, which considers discharge and closely analogous actions, such as discriminatory refusal to hire or promote.

"Many strategy issues lurk in these materials, because remedies may be quite different depending on the claim asserted. For example, the common law claims usually do not carry with them any award of attorney fees to the prevailing plaintiff, but the statutory claims routinely provide for such awards.[11] On the other hand, some of the statutory claims did not traditionally permit punitive damages or mental distress damages or even consequential damages, while such damages are recoverable in some common law cases [12] and under other statutes.[13]"

Note

Probably the most important federal legislation dealing with discriminatory discharges and other forms of employment discrimination is Title VII of the 1964 Civil Rights Act. *See* 42 U.S.C.A. § 2000e *et seq.* Important amendments to Title VII contained in the Civil Rights Act of 1991 significantly expanded the remedies available to an aggrieved employee. This is especially the case with emotional distress and punitive damages. These remedial changes to Title VII have been described as follows:

> "Previously, under Title VII a prevailing plaintiff was entitled to injunctive relief, including reinstatement, backpay, lost benefits, attorneys' fees, certain litigation costs, and interest.[55] Under the Civil Rights Act of 1991, a prevailing plaintiff in a claim for intentional discrimination under Title VII also may be entitled to: (1) compensatory damages, including those for emotional pain, suffering, inconvenience, mental anguish, and loss of enjoyment of life; and (2) punitive damages if the plaintiff demonstrates that the employer engaged in discriminatory conduct with malice or with reckless indifference to the employee's federally protected rights.[56] For each complaining party, the amount of compensatory and punitive damages must not exceed:
>
> — $50,000 for employers with more than 14 and fewer than 101 employees; [57]
>
> — $100,000 for employers with more than 100 and fewer than 201 employees;
>
> — $200,000 for employers with more than 200 and fewer than 501 employees; and

10. Wage and hour legislation, labor-management relations legislation for example. Particular statutes of narrow scope may also dictate remedies. 29 U.S.C.A. § 2002 prohibits employers generally from requiring or even requesting employees to take a lie detector test. Section 2005 provides remedies similar to but broader than many of the remedies provided in job discrimination statutes: "legal or equitable relief as may be appropriate, include, but not limited to, employment, reinstatement, promotion, and the payment of lost wages and benefits."

11. *See* § 6.10(4) below.

12. *See* § 6.10(2) below.

13. Under 42 U.S.C.A. §§ 1981 and 1983 in particular.

55. 42 U.S.C. § 2000e–5 (1988).

56. 42 U.S.C. § 1981a (Supp.III 1992).

57. The employer must have the stated number of employees in each of 20 or more calendar weeks in the current or preceding year. These caps may be removed in the future.

— $300,000 for employers with more than 500 employees.[58]

"Significantly, the Act provides that a plaintiff who seeks compensatory or punitive damages may demand a jury trial.[59] A plaintiff may also be granted expert fees as part of an attorney's fee award.[60]

"Under the Act, a defendant will be liable for declaratory and certain injunctive relief and a plaintiff's attorney's fees and costs if a plaintiff proves that race, color, religion, sex, or national origin was a 'motivating factor' for any employment decision, even though other factors also motivated the employment decision, and where the defendant demonstrates that it would have taken the same action absent the impermissible motivation.[61] In those situations, however, a plaintiff is not allowed admission, reinstatement, hiring, promotion, backpay, or compensatory or punitive damages.[62]

"The potential under the Act for the receipt of greater monetary rewards by plaintiffs and their attorneys undoubtedly will cause an increase in the number of discrimination charges and lawsuits filed against employers. In particular, the Act now provides a monetary remedy for sexual harassment victims not dependent on lost compensation. Previously, a sexually harassed employee could receive compensation only for economic losses under Title VII. Since loss of pay often does not accompany harassment, little or no monetary relief was provided for such claims. The possibility of greater financial rewards for plaintiffs and their counsel necessarily results in a substantial increase in employers' financial exposure and makes settlement more difficult.

"Now that plaintiffs can recover for emotional distress, mental anguish, pain and suffering, and may also recoup expert witness fees, plaintiffs are expected increasingly to use experts at trial. This will require employers seriously to consider utilizing experts on their own behalf which will result in more expensive litigation. It also makes trials more complex and more difficult for employers to win."

Haney, Litigation of a Sexual Harassment Case After the Civil Rights Act of 1991, 68 Notre Dame L.Rev. 1037, 1044–45 (1993).*

B. RESTITUTION

COON v. SCHOENEMAN

Court of Civil Appeals of Texas, 1972.
476 S.W.2d 439.

GUITTARD, JUSTICE.

This suit was brought by the builder of eleven houses against the owner of the lots upon which they were built to recover a share of the profits from their sale, and in the alternative for the reasonable value of his services as builder. At the trial plaintiff abandoned his claim for profits and sought to recover the value of his services. The trial court excluded

58. 42 U.S.C. § 1981a(b) (Supp.III 1992).

59. *Id.* § 1981a(c).

60. *Id.* § 1988(b).

61. *Id.* §§ 2000e–2(m), 2000e–5(g)(2)(B).

62. *Id.* § 2000e–5(g)(2)(B).

evidence of the value of his services and sustained defendant's motion for instructed verdict. Plaintiff appeals, contending that the trial court erred in refusing to permit proof of the elements of *quantum meruit* and in refusing to submit issues on *quantum meruit.*

The question is whether proof of an express contract for compensation as a share of profits excludes recovery for value of services, where there is evidence that defendant's breach of the contract prevented plaintiff from completing it. We hold that plaintiff could elect to recover the value of his services and was entitled to go to the jury on his alternative plea.

The question turns on the distinction between damages and restitution as remedies for breach of contract. Damages is the amount which would put plaintiff in as good a position as if the contract had been performed by both parties. It gives him the benefit of his bargain, including any profit he would have made, and is determined by the contract price, less any amount saved by his being excused from further performance. Restitution is the amount which would put plaintiff in as good a position as he would have been in if no contract had been made. It restores to plaintiff the value of what he parted with in performing the contract. 5 Corbin, Contracts §§ 996, 1102 (1964). When defendant has committed a breach of contract which is serious enough to excuse plaintiff from performing further, plaintiff is entitled to elect between these remedies. Restatement, Contracts § 347, and comment b following (1932); 5 Corbin, *op. cit. supra,* §§ 1104, 1109. He may pursue both remedies in the same suit by alternative pleadings and make his election at the trial. 5 Corbin, *op. cit. supra,* § 1110 at 590. The remedy of restitution, which is normally pursued by an action in *quantum meruit* for reasonable value of services rendered, is not under these circumstances an action upon an implied or quasi-contract, as in a case where there is no express contract and plaintiff sues for reasonable value of services accepted by defendant. It is rather an alternative remedy for breach of an express contract.* *Id.* § 1106. The measure of such restitution is the value of plaintiff's services on the market rather than the benefit to defendant. *Id.* § 1107.

An important limitation on the right of a plaintiff to elect between the remedies of damages and restitution is that when plaintiff's performance of the whole or a separable part of the contract entitles him to compensation in an agreed amount or at an agreed rate, he is limited to the compensation specified in the contract. This rule is stated in Restatement, Contracts §§ 350, 351 (1932) as follows:

> "§ 350. The remedy of restitution in money is not available to one who has fully performed his part of a contract, if the only part of the agreed exchange for such performance that has not been rendered by the defendant is a sum of money constituting a liquidated debt; but full performance does not make restitution unavailable if any part of

* *See* I G. Palmer, The Law of Restitution § 4.1, at 365–66 (1978) ("quasi-contract" is appropriate to describe the plaintiff's remedy in this situation). *Compare* Childres & Garamello, The Law of Restitution and the Reliance Interest in Contracts, 64 Nw.U.L.Rev. 433 (1969).

the consideration due from the defendant in return is something other than a liquidated debt.

"§ 351. Restitution is not available as a remedy with respect to any performance by the plaintiff for which a definite part of the consideration was apportioned in the contract as its equivalent in exchange, if

(a) the consideration so apportioned has been rendered in full, or

(b) it is a liquidated sum of money."

This limitation is reasonable because if plaintiff has obligated himself to perform services for a certain amount, and he has already earned that amount, it is just to measure his compensation by the amount he agreed to take for such services. 5 Corbin, *op. cit. supra* §§ 1110, 1111. The authorities relied on by defendant fall into this category. They hold that upon performance of an express contract for the rendition of services for a certain price, the contract fixes the measure of compensation and precludes recovery in *quantum meruit* for the value of services rendered. On the other hand, in cases where plaintiff's complete performance has been prevented by defendant's breach, Texas authorities support the first rule above stated, that plaintiff may elect either to recover his damages under the contract or treat the contract as rescinded and recover the reasonable value of his work in *quantum meruit*.

Application of these principles to the present case brings us to the conclusion that plaintiff's evidence raised issues for the jury as to breach by defendant preventing his further performance and the reasonable value of his services. The only evidence is the testimony of plaintiff Harold Coon. He testified that defendant Frank Schoeneman had told him he had certain lots in Irving and Arlington and that he needed somebody to build houses on them. Schoeneman proposed that Coon build the houses, Schoeneman would finance them, they would get a third person to sell them, and they would split the profits three ways. Coon agreed and started building. After he had built seven houses in Irving, including six "model homes," and had started four in Arlington, Schoeneman told him the rest of the Irving lots had been sold and proposed that Coon proceed with the project in Arlington on a different deal, which was that Coon would pay him $350 a house, Schoeneman would furnish the lots, and Coon would get all the profit. Coon agreed, with the understanding that he would have five houses under construction or ready for sale continuously and that no lots should be sold to other builders in the immediate area. Schoeneman agreed to these conditions. When Coon had finished four houses on the Arlington lots and was ready to start a fifth, he discovered that Schoeneman had sold the rest of the lots and other contractors were preparing to build on lots next to the houses Coon had built. Coon built no more houses on Schoeneman's lots. Schoeneman said he would send Coon his part of the profits from the houses that were built, but he sold the houses and never gave Coon any of the proceeds. Coon never received anything for his work.

Defendant objected to plaintiff's testimony concerning the value of his services on the ground that the proof established an express agreement to share profits and plaintiff was limited to recovery of such profits. The objection was sustained, and plaintiff gave his testimony concerning the value of his services in the form of a bill of exceptions. At the close of plaintiff's direct testimony the trial court sustained defendant's motion to instruct a verdict in his favor on the ground that plaintiff had shown only that there was a verbal agreement to share profits, but had not shown that there were any profits.

Since the trial court instructed a verdict for defendant, we must view the evidence in the light most favorable to plaintiff. Viewing Coon's testimony in that light, we conclude that a jury would have been justified in finding that Schoeneman breached the contract by selling off the Arlington lots contrary to his agreement that he would allow Coon to keep five houses ready for sale or under construction and would not sell lots to other contractors in the immediate area. Coon was thus prevented by Schoeneman's breach from building any more houses. Though the oral contract, as described by Coon, is not definite as to how many houses Coon was entitled to build, it did give him the right to build at least five and to be free from competition by other builders on Schoeneman's lots in the immediate area. On Schoeneman's breach of that agreement, Coon was entitled under the above authorities either to sue for his damages under the contract, including his share of profits on the houses he had built and the profits he would have made on other houses, or to treat the contract as rescinded and recover the reasonable value of his services.

We have considered whether the contract was divisible and the consideration apportionable, so that on completion and sale of each house plaintiff became entitled to compensation in a liquidated amount for his share of the profit and should be limited to that amount. Probably the contract is not divisible, since six of the houses in Irving were "model homes," which presumably were not expected to be sold at as much profit as others to be built. The mere fact that there is a contract rate of payment per unit of performance does not make the contract divisible, since the parties may not have been willing to contract separately for each unit. *5 Corbin, op. cit. supra* § 1111 at 593. However, we conclude that the divisibility of the contract does not matter, since even if the profits were apportionable to each house, the amount was not liquidated. It depended on the sale price and the various factors making up the cost. Consequently, under the rule stated in either § 350 or § 351 of the Restatement, plaintiff was not limited to the contract measure of compensation.

The case is analogous to one in which the agreed exchange for services is something other than a determinable amount of money, such as property or an interest in the business. In that case even a plaintiff who has fully performed may recover the reasonable value of his services rather than the value of what was promised to him. Coens v. Marousis, 275 Pa. 478, 119 A. 549 (1923); *5 Corbin, op. cit. supra* § 1110 at 587. This rule seems to be based on the idea that since plaintiff cannot obtain his specific *quid pro quo* under the contract, and proof of its value may be difficult, he should not be limited to recovery of damages but should be able to recover the reasonable value of his services by way of restitution. Likewise, in this case, since defendant repudiated the contract and prevented plaintiff from continuing performance, plaintiff is entitled to elect his remedy of restitution, and should not be required to assume the burden of establishing the profit on the sale of each of eleven houses in order to recover compensation for his services.

One of the problems here is that both of the oral contracts described by plaintiff provided for compensation in terms of profit, and, therefore, contractual compensation was contingent on the existence of profits, which were not proved. Thus defendant contends that plaintiff failed to prove that he was entitled to any compensation at all. The question is whether the contingent character of the contractual compensation renders unavailable the alternative remedy of restitution, so that plaintiff is without remedy for defendant's breach unless he can prove that profits were realized in the past, or would have been realized in the future if the contract had been fully performed.

In our opinion the contingent nature of the contractual compensation does not affect the plaintiff's right to restitution upon defendant's material breach of the contract. Proof that no profits were made on the houses sold would not establish that no profits would have been realized if defendant had complied with the contract. Presumably, greater profits were anticipated from sale of subsequent houses than from the "model homes." Moreover, defendant's principal breach was his sale of adjacent lots to competing builders. Such a breach may in itself have prevented any profit on the four houses in Arlington or may have reduced the amount of profit, but proof would be difficult. The party who has wrongfully prevented the other party from completing the contract should not benefit from his own wrong. Consequently, we hold that even though the contractual compensation was contingent on profits, the same rule of restitution applies as in other cases where defendant's breach has prevented further performance by plaintiff. Plaintiff should have his election to treat the contract as rescinded and recover the reasonable value of his services.

On oral argument there was discussion of whether the contract created a partnership or joint venture so that plaintiff was not entitled to bring the suit without seeking an accounting of the affairs of the partnership or joint venture. On examination of the record we do not find that the evidence shows as a matter of law that the relationship was a partnership or joint venture. Moreover, the modified contract as applied to the Arlington project was not a profit-sharing arrangement, since Coon was to get all the profits after paying Schoeneman $350 per house. Consequently, plaintiff's claim is not limited to an accounting.

Reversed and remanded.

Notes

1. Where the defendant's conduct constitutes a "material breach," the plaintiff ordinarily will elect between rescission/restitution and damages for breach of contract and, where appropriate, for specific performance. If the plaintiff rescinds the agreement, quasi-contract relief will normally be available where the plaintiff has performed in part, although the manner of measuring the amount recoverable may vary depending on several factors. If the plaintiff

"affirms" the contract and sues for damages, the plaintiff will seek to prove both "reliance" damages (out-of-pocket losses sustained in the course of performance) and "expectation" damages (lost benefits, including, possibly, profits directly traceable to defendant's failure to perform). Fuller and Perdue, The Reliance Interest in Contract Damages, 46 Yale L.J. 52, 73 (1936); Childres and Garamella, The Law of Restitution and the Reliance Interest in Contract, 64 Nw.U.L.Rev. 433 (1969); 5 A. Corbin, Contracts § 992 (1964). The latter rule is designed to place the plaintiff in as good a position as if there had been performance by the defendant.

The plaintiff has the burden of showing with reasonable certainty the profits which would have been earned had the defendant performed. This presents a real challenge to the attorney whose client is engaged in a type of venture in which there are typically many failures. Professor Corbin has drawn attention to a great variety of situations of this nature in which counsel for the plaintiff may nonetheless satisfy this requirement. Examples include actions for profits which would have been earned if (1) a fishing boat had been delivered, or (2) title and possession had been transferred to a going business, or (3) oil drilling equipment had been delivered. *See* 5 A. Corbin, Contracts § 1022 (1964).

ROSENBERG v. LEVIN

Supreme Court of Florida, 1982.
409 So.2d 1016.

OVERTON, JUSTICE.

ON REHEARING AND REARGUMENT

The opinion of June 11, 1981, is vacated and replaced by the following opinion.

OVERTON, JUSTICE.

This is a petition to review a decision of the Third District Court of Appeal, reported as Levin v. Rosenberg, 372 So.2d 956 (Fla.3d DCA 1979). The issue to be decided concerns the proper basis for compensating an attorney discharged without cause by his client after he has performed substantial legal services under a valid contract of employment. We find conflict with our decision in Goodkind v. Wolkowsky, 132 Fla. 63, 180 So. 538 (1938).

We hold that a lawyer discharged without cause is entitled to the reasonable value of his services on the basis of quantum meruit, but recovery is limited to the maximum fee set in the contract entered into for those services. We have concluded that without this limitation, the client would be penalized for the discharge and the lawyer would receive more than he bargained for in his initial contract. In the instant case, we reject the contention of the respondent lawyer that he is entitled to $55,000 as the reasonable value of his services when his contract fee was $10,000. We affirm the decision of the district court and recede from our prior decision in *Goodkind.*

The facts of this case reflect the following. Levin hired Rosenberg and Pomerantz to perform legal services pursuant to a letter agreement which provided for a $10,000 fixed fee, plus a contingent fee equal to fifty percent of all amounts recovered in excess of $600,000. Levin later discharged Rosenberg and Pomerantz without cause before the legal controversy was resolved and subsequently settled the matter for a net recovery of $500,000. Rosenberg and Pomerantz sued for fees based on a "quantum meruit" evaluation of their services. After lengthy testimony, the trial judge concluded that quantum meruit was indeed the appropriate basis for compensation and awarded Rosenberg and Pomerantz $55,000. The district court also agreed that quantum meruit was the appropriate basis for recovery but lowered the amount awarded to $10,000, stating that recovery could in no event exceed the amount which the attorneys would have received under their contract if not prematurely discharged. 372 So.2d at 958.

The issue submitted to us for resolution is whether the terms of an attorney employment contract limit the attorney's quantum meruit recovery to the fee set out in the contract. This issue requires, however, that we answer the broader underlying question of whether in Florida quantum meruit is an appropriate basis for compensation of attorneys discharged by their clients without cause where there is a specific employment contract. The Florida cases which have previously addressed this issue have resulted in confusion and conflicting views.

* * *

The existing case law in this state reflects that this Court is on record as favoring the traditional contract means of recovery. We have, however, inferred in dicta in *Kelner* that quantum meruit may be the proper basis for recovery in a contingent fee contract situation. The First District Court of Appeal in *Sohn* expressly held that quantum meruit is proper in a contingency contract. In the instant case, the Third District Court of Appeal held that quantum meruit is proper where the contingency does not control and limited such quantum meruit recovery to the maximum amount of the contract fee.

There are two conflicting interests involved in the determination of the issue presented in this type of attorney-client dispute. The first is the need of the client to have confidence in the integrity and ability of his attorney and, therefore, the need for the client to have the ability to discharge his attorney when he loses that necessary confidence in the attorney. The second is the attorney's right to adequate compensation for work performed. To address these conflicting interests, we must consider three distinct rules.

Contract Rule

The traditional contract rule adopted by a number of jurisdictions holds that an attorney discharged without cause may recover damages for breach of contract under traditional contract principles. The measure of damages is usually the full contract price, although some courts deduct a fair allowance for services and expenses not expended by the discharged attorney in performing the balance of the contract. *E.g.*, Bockman v. Rorex, 212 Ark. 948, 208 S.W.2d 991 (1948) (fixed fee contract); Tonn v.

Reuter, 6 Wis.2d 498, 95 N.W.2d 261 (1959) (contingency fee contract); *see generally* 1 S. Speiser, Attorneys' Fees §§ 4:24–:36 (1973). Some jurisdictions following the contract rule also permit an alternative recovery based on quantum meruit so that an attorney can elect between recovery based on the contract or the reasonable value of the performed services. *E.g.,* In re Downs, 363 S.W.2d 679 (Mo.1963); French v. Cunningham, 149 Ind. 632, 49 N.E. 797 (1898). *See* 1 S. Speiser, Attorneys' Fees § 4:36 (1973).

Support for the traditional contract theory is based on: (1) the full contract price is arguably the most rational measure of damages since it reflects the value that the parties placed on the services; (2) charging the full fee prevents the client from profiting from his own breach of contract; and (3) the contract rule is said to avoid the difficult problem of setting a value on an attorney's partially completed legal work.

Quantum Meruit Rule

To avoid restricting a client's freedom to discharge his attorney, a number of jurisdictions in recent years have held that an attorney discharged without cause can recover only the reasonable value services rendered prior to discharge. This rule was first announced in Martin v. Camp, 219 N.Y. 170, 114 N.E. 46 (1916), where the New York Court of Appeals held that a discharged attorney could not sue his client for damages for breach of contract unless the attorney had completed performance of the contract. The New York court established quantum meruit recovery for the attorney on the theory that the client does not breach the contract by discharging the attorney. Rather, the court reasoned, there is an implied condition in every attorney-client contract that the client may discharge the attorney at any time with or without cause. With this right as part of the contract, traditional contract principles are applied to allow quantum meruit recovery on the basis of services performed to date. Under the New York rule, the attorney's cause of action accrues immediately upon his discharge by the client, under the reasoning that it is unfair to make the attorney's right to compensation dependent on the performance of a successor over whom he has no control. *See* Tillman v. Komar, 259 N.Y. 133, 135–36, 181 N.E. 75, 76 (1932).

The California Supreme Court, in Fracasse v. Brent, 6 Cal.3d 784, 494 P.2d 9, 100 Cal.Rptr. 385 (1972), also adopted a quantum meruit rule. That court carefully analyzed those factors which distinguish the attorney-client relationship from other employment situations and concluded that a discharged attorney should be limited to a quantum meruit recovery in order to strike a proper balance between the client's right to discharge his attorney without undue restriction and the attorney's right to fair compensation for work performed. The *Fracasse* court sought both to provide clients greater freedom in substituting counsel and to promote confidence in the legal profession while protecting society's interest in the attorney-client relationship.

Contrary to the New York rule, however, the California court also held that an attorney's cause of action for quantum meruit does not accrue until the happening of the contingency, that is, the client's recovery. If no recovery is forthcoming, the attorney is denied compensation. The California court offered two reasons in support of its position. First, the result obtained and the amount involved, two important factors in determining the reasonableness of a fee, cannot be ascertained until the occurrence of the contingency. Second, the client may be of limited means and it would be unduly burdensome to force him to pay a fee if there was no recovery. The court stated that: "[S]ince the attorney agreed initially to take his chances on recovering any fee whatever, we believe that the fact that the success of the litigation is no longer under his control is insufficient to justify imposing a new and more onerous burden on the client." *Id.* at 792, 494 P.2d at 14, 100 Cal.Rptr. at 390.

Quantum Meruit Rule Limited by the Contract Price

The third rule is an extension of the second that limits quantum meruit recovery to the maximum fee set in the contract. This limitation is believed necessary to provide client freedom to substitute attorneys without economic penalty. Without such a limitation, a client's right to discharge an attorney may be illusory and the client may in effect be penalized for exercising a right.

The Tennessee Court of Appeals, in Chambliss, Bahner & Crawford v. Luther, 531 S.W.2d 108 (Tenn.Ct.App.1975), expressed the need for limitation on quantum meruit recovery, stating: "It would seem to us that the better rule is that because a client has the unqualified right to discharge his attorney, fees in such cases should be limited to the value of the services rendered or the contract price, whichever is less." 531 S.W.2d at 113. In rejecting the argument that quantum meruit should be the basis for the recovery even though it exceeds the contract fee, that court said:

> To adopt the rule advanced by Plaintiff would, in our view, encourage attorneys less keenly aware of their professional responsibilities than Attorney Chambliss, * * * to induce clients to lose confidence in them in cases where the reasonable value of their services has exceeded the original fee and thereby, upon being discharged, reap a greater benefit than that for which they had bargained.

531 S.W.2d at 113. Other authorities also support this position.*

Conclusion

We have carefully considered all the matters presented, both on the original argument on the merits and on rehearing. It is our opinion that it is in the best interest of clients and the legal profession as a whole that we adopt the modified quantum meruit rule which limits recovery to the

* For example, Corbin on Contracts, in the chapter dealing with restitution, cites the quantum meruit rule with this limitation with approval. Contracts § 1102 (1980 Supp.) at 207–08. Another commentator stated: "The protection afforded to the client becomes illusory if the discharged attorney's recovery on *quantum meruit* exceeds the contract price." Note, Limiting the Wrongfully Discharged Attorney's Recovery to Quantum Meruit—*Fracasse v. Brent,* 24 Hastings L.Rev. 771, 774 (1973). This comment also appeared in a recent article: "In New York, discharge of an attorney cancels the contract of employment. Thus an attorney can recover the full value of his services, even if it exceeds the contract price. This holding defeats the policy against penalizing the client for exercising his right to discharge an attorney, because he essentially is forced to pay damages for exercising a right." Note, Attorney's Right to Compensation When Discharged Without Cause From a Contingent Fee Contract—*Covington v. Rhodes,* 678 Wake Forest L.Rev. 677, 689–90 (1979). [Footnote is court's.]

maximum amount of the contract fee in all premature discharge cases involving both fixed and contingency employment contracts. The attorney-client relationship is one of special trust and confidence. The client must rely entirely on the good faith efforts of the attorney in representing his interests. This reliance requires that the client have complete confidence in the integrity and ability of the attorney and that absolute fairness and candor characterize all dealings between them. These considerations dictate that clients be given greater freedom to change legal representatives than might be tolerated in other employment relationships. We approve the philosophy that there is an overriding need to allow clients freedom to substitute attorneys without economic penalty as a means of accomplishing the broad objective of fostering public confidence in the legal profession. Failure to limit quantum meruit recovery defeats the policy against penalizing the client for exercising his right to discharge. However, attorneys should not be penalized either and should have the opportunity to recover for services performed.

Accordingly, we hold that an attorney employed under a valid contract who is discharged without cause before the contingency has occurred or before the client's matters have concluded can recover only the reasonable value of his services rendered prior to discharge, limited by the maximum contract fee. We reject both the traditional contract rule and the quantum meruit rule that allow recovery in excess of the maximum contract price because both have a chilling effect on the client's power to discharge an attorney. Under the contract rule in a contingent fee situation, both the discharged attorney and the second attorney may receive a substantial percentage of the client's final recovery. Under the unlimited quantum meruit rule, it is possible, as the instant case illustrates, for the attorney to receive a fee greater than he bargained for under the terms of his contract. Both these results are unacceptable to us.

We further follow the California view that in contingency fee cases, the cause of action for quantum meruit arises only upon the successful occurrence of the contingency. If the client fails in his recovery, the discharged attorney will similarly fail and recover nothing. We recognize that deferring the commencement of a cause of action until the occurrence of the contingency is a view not uniformly accepted. Deferral, however, supports our goal to preserve the client's freedom to discharge, and any resulting harm to the attorney is minimal because the attorney would not have benefited earlier until the contingency's occurrence. There should, of course, be a presumption of regularity and competence in the performance of the services by a successor attorney.

In computing the reasonable value of the discharged attorney's services, the trial court can consider the totality of the circumstances surrounding the professional relationship between the attorney and client. Factors such as time, the recovery sought, the skill demanded, the results obtained, and the attorney-client contract itself will necessarily be relevant considerations.

* * *

It is so ordered.

SUNDBERG, C.J., and BOYD and ALDERMAN, JJ., concur.

ADKINS and MCDONALD, JJ., dissent.

Notes

1. Is it possible that Coon is receiving more than if the contract had been completed? Would the rule applied in *Rosenberg* allow a nonlawyer plaintiff to recover more than the contract price? Most, but not all, jurisdictions allow recovery in restitution to put a nonlawyer plaintiff in a better position than full performance would have done. *See* 3 D. Dobbs, The Law of Remedies § 12.-20(2), at 462–63. Which approach do you favor and why?

2. Suppose an attorney dies prior to the completion of litigation taken on a contingency basis. What should the compensation be for the attorney's services? Read City of Barnsdall v. Curnutt at pp. 1166–1170 *infra.*

PUTTKAMMER v. MINTH

Supreme Court of Wisconsin, 1978.
83 Wis.2d 686, 266 N.W.2d 361.

CONNOR T. HANSEN, JUSTICE.

On November 20, 1974, Victor Puttkammer, d/b/a Asphalt Spraying Co., plaintiff-appellant, commenced this action against the defendant-respondent, Arthur Minth, seeking compensation for improvements made to certain real property owned by Minth. The complaint was subsequently amended, and the material facts alleged in the amended complaint and assumed to be true for purposes of this appeal, are as follows:

The defendant, Minth, is the owner of the Hiawatha Supper Club in Eagle River, Wisconsin, which he leased during 1972 and 1973 to James Piekarski. During the period of the lease, the plaintiff, at the request of Piekarski, resurfaced the access and service areas of the supper club, providing labor and materials with a reasonable value of $2,540, and increasing the value of the property by the same amount.

The defendant was aware that this work was being done and "stood by and acquiesced" in its completion. Piekarski did not pay for the work and was subsequently adjudged bankrupt, with no assets in his estate for the payment of plaintiff. The defendant now has the benefit of the improvements but refuses to pay for them, and the plaintiff has not been paid for any portion of the work.

The complaint further alleges that the plaintiff has exhausted his remedy against Piekarski and that if the defendant is not required to pay for the improvements, he will be unjustly enriched at the plaintiff's expense. The amended complaint therefore prays for damages in the amount of $2,540, plus costs and disbursements.

The defendant demurred to this amended complaint on the ground that it failed to state a cause of action. The trial court sustained the demurrer and denied the plaintiff leave to further amend the complaint.

The issues on this appeal are whether the complaint alleges facts sufficient to state a cause of action and whether the trial court abused its discretion in denying the plaintiff the right to plead over.

* * *

The plaintiff maintains that the complaint states a cause of action in equity for unjust enrichment. The elements of such a cause of action are: (1) a benefit conferred upon the defendant by the plaintiff; (2) an appreciation or knowledge by the defendant of the benefit; and (3) acceptance or retention by the defendant of the benefit under circumstances making it inequitable for the defendant to retain the benefit without payment of its value. * * *

The amended complaint in the present case alleges facts sufficient to satisfy the first and second of these requirements. The complaint alleges that a benefit has been conferred on the defendant in that the value of his property has been enhanced by $2,540. The complaint also alleges appreciation by the defendant of the fact of the benefit, since it is alleged the defendant was aware the work was being performed and stood by and acquiesced in its completion.

The question is whether the complaint alleges facts sufficient to establish, either expressly or by inference, the third requirement: that the benefit was accepted or retained under such circumstances as to make retention of the benefit of the resurfacing, without payment therefor, inequitable.

In an action for unjust enrichment, " ' * * * [r]ecovery is based upon the universally recognized moral principle that one who has received a benefit has the duty to make restitution when to retain such benefit would be unjust.' * * * " It is not enough to establish that a benefit was conferred and retained; the retention must be inequitable.

The law in this state thus recognizes the principle set forth in the Restatement, *Restitution,* sec. 1, Comment c., p. 13, that:

> " * * * Even where a person has received a benefit from another, he is liable to pay therefor only if the circumstances of its receipt or retention are such that, as between the two persons, it is unjust for him to retain it. The mere fact that a person benefits another is not of itself sufficient to require the other to make restitution therefor * * *."

The defendant relies upon a series of cases in which subcontractors, unable to recover from the general contractor with whom they contracted, have sought to recover payment for labor and materials directly from property owners on a theory of unjust enrichment. In these cases, this court has denied recovery and has held that retention of the benefit of the improvements by the owners is not unjust. *Seegers v. Sprague, supra; Gebhardt Bros. Inc. v. Brimmel, supra;* Superior Plumbing Co. v. Tefs, 27 Wis.2d 434, 134 N.W.2d 430; and Utschig v. McClone, 16 Wis.2d 506, 114 N.W.2d 854 (1962). The denial of recovery in the subcontractor cases is attributable to the fact that in such cases the owner has paid, or is obligated to pay, the general contractor for the value of the improvements. Retention of the benefits is therefore equitable. * * *

This "critical factor" is not present here. There is no suggestion that the defendant has paid for the benefits, and the cases cited by the defendant are therefore inapposite.

The plaintiff, on the other hand, relies on two cases sustaining actions by contractors against property owners on the theory of unjust enrichment.

In *Nelson v. Preston, supra,* a plumbing contractor had contracted with a developer, Franklyn Preston, to provide labor and materials in connection with the construction of eight houses. Preston did not own the houses; his mother did. Preston was not a co-owner of the property and was not an agent of his mother, nor did his mother have any part in contracting for the improvements. Nevertheless, this court concluded that the mother would be unjustly enriched if permitted to retain the benefits, and she was therefore required to pay for the work.

The decisive consideration in the *Nelson Case* was the relation between the party at whose instance the work was performed—the son—and the party from whom recovery was sought, the mother. This court emphasized that the mother and son were jointly engaged in developing a subdivision, with the son building houses which were then sold, with the proceeds going to the mother. This court found that there was "a relation * * * between the mother and the son under which services and material procured by the son from the [contractor] were to go into her property and to become of benefit to her." *Nelson, supra,* 262 Wis. at 554, 55 N.W.2d at 921. In view of this relation, this court held that it would be unjust for the mother to retain the benefits of the improvements without paying therefor.

Kelley Lumber Co. v. Woelfel, supra, was an appeal from the overruling of a demurrer. There, the complaint alleged that the plaintiff had sold building supplies to a William Woelfel, who had used them to construct a house. Shortly after selling the house, Woelfel died, and the plaintiff sought to recover the value of the building supplies from Woelfel's widow on a theory of unjust enrichment.

This court held that the complaint stated a cause of action. The house in which the materials were used was located on a lot which had been owned jointly by Mr. and Mrs. Woelfel, and the sale proceeds had been deposited in their joint checking account and had passed to Mrs. Woelfel on her husband's death. Further, the complaint alleged that the widow had "assented" to the use of the materials and had "accepted" them. In *Kelley,* therefore, as in *Nelson,* there was a relationship between the party procuring the work and the party from whom recovery was sought, or an intermingling of their interests such that the services were provided for the benefit of both parties.

In S & M Rotogravure Service, Inc. v. Baer, 77 Wis.2d 454, 252 N.W.2d 913 (1977) as in the present case, a contractor sought to recover in unjust enrichment from a property owner for work done under contract with the owner's lessee. This court upheld the complaint as against a demurrer. In that case, however, the complaint alleged that much of the work had been performed "at the special instance and request" of the property owner; that the owner had approved all plans for the work and all payments therefor; and that the payments were made by checks drawn on the owner's account. *S & M Rotogravure Service, Inc. v. Baer, supra,* 77 Wis.2d, at 461, 252 N.W.2d 913.

Nelson v. Preston, supra; Kelley Lumber Co. v. Woelfel, supra; and *S & M Rotogravure Service, Inc. v. Baer, supra,* are distinguishable from the instant case. Each of those cases was decided on the basis of the special relationship that existed between the party procuring the work and the party retaining the benefits. These relationships were such that it was not inequitable to hold that the work had been for the benefit of both parties. These cases are exceptions to the general rule. They rest on the proposition that interests of the owner and occupant or procurer of services are closely intermingled and the benefits of the transactions are by prearrangement to be shared between them.[1]

The case before us is not such a case. Rather, this case is representative of the usual case in which the owner has no part in initiating the work and is merely a passive beneficiary of the work performed at the instance of another. The unjust enrichment or restitution claim is asserted by one who did the work, and produced an incidental gain to the owner, by merely performing his contract with another and is now dissatisfied because the return promised under the contract is not forthcoming. In a sense it can be said that the contractor, at least to the extent of the gain, seeks to make the owner an insurer of the contract entered into by the defaulting procurer. The fact that the owner knew of the work, acquiesced in its performance and voiced no disapproval of the work, does not make the owner liable. There is no allegation in the instant complaint from which it can reasonably be inferred that the work was done by authority of the owner.

The general rule of the authorities which have come to our attention is summarized in 98 C.J.S. Work & Labor § 42, pp. 779, 780, as follows:

> "* * * [A] landlord or lessee [sic] cannot be held liable for materials furnished and labor performed by plaintiff on the leased premises where plaintiff entered into the undertaking looking only to the tenant or lessee for payment in the absence of anything to show that the landlord ordered the work, or authorized anyone to have it done, or ratified the work after it was done, and notwithstanding the landlord ultimately benefits from the work that was done by reason of his ownership of the property."

In the instant case the complaint does not allege or reasonably imply that the work was ordered or ratified by the defendant; that the plaintiff performed the work expecting to be paid by the defendant; that the plaintiff was prejudiced by any misconduct or fault on the part of the defendant; or that the interests of Piekarski and the defendant were so related or intermingled that it can be said that the contract was executed for the defendant's benefit. The most that can be said from the complaint is that the defendant knowingly acquiesced in the performance of the work. This is insufficient basis to impose liability on one who did not request the

1. Dawson, The Self-Serving Intermeddler, 87 Harv.L.Rev. 1409, 1450 (1974).

work and may not have desired it. The trial court was correct in ruling that the complaint fails to state a cause of action.

However, the plaintiff further argues that rather than entering judgment sustaining the demurrer and dismissing the action on its merits, the trial court should have granted the plaintiff a reasonable opportunity to plead over. * * * In sustaining the demurrer, the trial court stated:

> "Ordinarily, this court when sustaining a demurrer prefers to grant opposing counsel a limited time to amend its pleadings, but with the sustaining of this demurrer and the fact that the contracting tenant has been adjudged bankrupt there seems to be no other options available."

It appears that this refusal to permit the plaintiff to plead over may have been premised on an erroneous view of the law. The trial court correctly stated that retention of the improvements was not inequitable because there had been no showing that the owner needed or wanted the resurfacing. The trial court further stated, however, that *Gebhardt Bros., Inc. v. Brimmel, supra,* "held against unjust enrichment on the grounds that plaintiff was not hired by defendant-owner." This suggests that the trial court's ruling may be based on a misconception that lack of privity precludes the existence of a cause of action for unjust enrichment.

However, this court's decisions establish that privity is not necessary for recovery on a theory of unjust enrichment. * * *

* * *

* * * We believe the plaintiff should have a reasonable opportunity to amend the complaint if he elects to do so and is able to allege facts and circumstances sufficient to show that retention of the benefits by the defendant would be unjust.

Therefore we are obliged to reverse the judgment and remand the cause with directions to sustain the demurrer and grant the plaintiff leave to serve and file an amended complaint within thirty days from the date of remittitur, if he elects to do so.

Judgment reversed and cause remanded.

Note

How should Puttkammer amend his complaint? Consider the following analysis of third party cases:

> "[C]ourts inconsistently provide recovery in cases involving third parties. Third parties are people who have not requested the plaintiff's services, such as people not parties to the contract under which the plaintiff worked. The plaintiff may seek recovery from a third party when the plaintiff cannot recover from the party with whom he originally contracted, often due to that party's insolvency or bankruptcy. The plaintiff also may seek recovery from a third party when the plaintiff repairs property, mistakenly thinking it was his or hers or when the plaintiff mistakenly thinks that he or she has a contract with the third party.

"In third-party cases the court must balance the countervailing considerations of the unjustness of permitting forfeiture against the hardship of making one pay for work that he or she did not ask for and perhaps did not want and could not afford. * * * Currently, the courts tend to grant or deny restitution without weighing these concerns. They make their judgment on incomplete quantum meruit analysis. * * * [C]ourts who terminate analysis because third-party cases contain no request or acceptance elements [should] focus on whether the defendant received a benefit and, if so, comparing the conduct and hardships of the plaintiff and defendant to achieve a just result.

* * *

"In *Idaho Lumber, Inc. v. Buck,*[446] a contractor sought to recover from the owner of the premises the remainder of the contract price for remodeling a funeral home into a restaurant. The contractor had not contracted with the owner, but with the owner's lessee who defaulted on both the lease and the contract and subsequently was discharged in bankruptcy. The contractor sued the owner on a quasi-contract theory for unjust enrichment.

"The court analyzed the claim as a contract implied in law, with classic unjust enrichment language that the defendant's basis for liability was the unjustness of allowing the defendant to retain a benefit received from the plaintiff. The court used, however, two elements not included among the three traditional unjust enrichment elements. The court listed the following three elements: 'A benefit conferred upon the defendant by the plaintiff, appreciation by the defendant of such benefit, and acceptance of such benefit under such circumstances that it would be inequitable for him to retain the benefit without payment of the value thereof.' An unjust enrichment analysis does not require the elements of appreciation and acceptance of the benefit. * * *

"In *Idaho Lumber,* the court found the defendant's acceptance in a convoluted manner, using the fact that the plaintiff performed work on request, albeit not the defendant owner's request, as one of the steps of its reasoning. The court held that the contractor was not a volunteer because he had worked at the request of the lessee, the lease authorized the lessee to make the request, and the owner knew that the lessee would make the improvements and in fact, acquiesced to those improvements. As this was the only discussion of the acceptance element, the court obviously assumed that the defendant's acquiescence constituted acceptance.

"There are some problems with this analysis. Normally, the term acceptance implies that one has an opportunity to reject. No facts in *Idaho Lumber* indicated that the landlord had the authority to reject or stop improvements authorized in the lease. In addition, the court found that the scope of the remodeling and the cost of the work greatly exceeded the amount either party contemplated when they negotiated the lease. The original plan called for $40,000 worth of remodeling. The lessee's repeated changes increased the cost to $106,000. Thus it is hard to believe that the owner acquiesced to improvements so far beyond those contemplated when he authorized the original plan.

446. 710 P.2d 647 (Idaho Ct.App.1984).

"[T]he trial and appellate courts disagreed on the measurement of recovery. The trial court awarded to the plaintiff the percentage of defendant's enhanced value of the property that corresponded with the percentage of plaintiff's costs the bankrupt lessee had not paid. The court of appeals, however, awarded all costs not shown unreasonable, limited by the defendant's gain. The defendant's gain did not limit recovery in *Idaho Lumber* because the gain exceeded the unpaid costs.

"In *Dalton v. Bundy,*[460] a contractor installed vinyl siding on a house pursuant to a contract with the Bundys. He learned, when he tried to collect his fee, that the Bundy's twelve-year-old daughter owned the house, and that the parents were bankrupt. The contractor sued the daughter in quantum meruit for the enhanced value of the house. The court denied the claim because the court found no evidence that the child knowingly accepted or requested the benefit.[462] Although the court presumed that she lived in the house, the court apparently required more in the way of acceptance than merely owning and residing in the house. The court did not state what would constitute acceptance.

* * *

"Use of the defendant's acceptance of the benefit element is problematical. As one can see from these cases, it is difficult to determine what constitutes acceptance because the courts' interpretations vary widely. In *Idaho Lumber,* the fact supporting the acceptance element was the defendant's before-the-fact permission to the lessee that enabled the lessee to contract for improvements. In *Dalton,* the court defined acceptance only by what it was not, finding that ownership and presumed residence in a house at the time the plaintiff was making improvements did not constitute acceptance of those benefits.

"Thus when one compares these two cases, * * * one sees inconsistent results. One sees one court awarding recovery against a landlord who was not in control of the property at the time the improvements were made and another court denying recovery to an owner and occupant of the house who presumably could have ordered that the plaintiff not make improvements. Both courts used the acceptance element in arriving at their decisions. In *Dalton,* the defendant likely had greater opportunity to reject the improvements than did the defendant in *Idaho Lumber,* but the latter court ordered the defendant to pay, while the former court did not. *Idaho Lumber* shows how anything can be found to be an acceptance. *Dalton* shows how anything can be found not to constitute acceptance.

* * *

"Courts could analyze more easily the third-party cases with the proposed two-tiered analysis.

* * *

"If a case lacks one of the request or mutual expectation of payment elements [from the first tier] then the court's analysis should move on to

460. 666 S.W.2d 443 (Mo.App.1984).

462. *Id.* at 445. The court found the daughter's minority irrelevant for the quantum meruit claim, saying that the holding would be the same were she an adult. *Id.*

the second tier. In most third-party cases the request element is absent, so the courts will apply the second tier analysis. That tier, which is used second because it involves concepts that are more difficult and because the first tier can resolve sensibly many quantum meruit cases, uses the three classic unjust enrichment elements: (1) did the defendant obtain a benefit; (2) did the defendant obtain the benefit at the plaintiff's expense; and, (3) is it unjust that the defendant retain the benefit without paying the plaintiff for it.

* * *

"Where the defendant cannot return or stop the work, the concept of acceptance is not useful and often prematurely ends the court's analysis, foreclosing further discussion of unjust enrichment. The court's use of the concept of acceptance of a benefit when the defendant cannot return or prevent the benefit is not useful because the same facts can yield opposite results. One could say either that the defendant accepted the benefit because he actually had the benefit [490] or that he did not accept the benefit because he did not request the benefit.[491] Thus, the courts should not focus on acceptance or a lack of acceptance, and, where finding a lack of acceptance, should not end the analysis.

"Before ruling for the defendant, a court should consider whether it is just for a defendant to retain a benefit without payment. In determining unjustness in a third-party situation where the defendant could not return or prevent the benefit, the court should first inquire into the conduct of the parties. For example, did the plaintiff in *Idaho Lumber* assume the risk that the restauranteur would not be able to pay? Was plaintiff negligent in incurring the costs? In *Dalton,* was the plaintiff negligent in mistaking the authority of the contracting party? Could the defendant, however, have stopped the work? Second, the court should determine whether the defendant is in a position to pay. How liquid is the benefit? Would it be a hardship for the defendant to pay for it? Could the court impose a lien on the property? Can the defendant afford to pay for the benefit? Does the plaintiff's loss outweigh the hardship to defendant in having to pay? The courts do not ask these questions, yet the defendant's possible inability to pay is a major reason that the courts do not award restitution.

"If a court determines that a defendant should disgorge his gain, it must decide how to measure that gain. When the defendant's gain is the same as the reasonable value of the plaintiff's services the court has no problem in measuring recovery. When the defendant's gain is less than the reasonable value of plaintiff's services, the defendant's gain is the appropriate measurement since recovery is only possible in unjust enrichment, which measures recovery as the defendant's gain. The court can no longer view the reasonable value of the plaintiff's services as the defendant's gain because [without a request by the defendant, the defendant] cannot benefit by getting what [was] requested.

* * *

490. *See* Idaho Lumber, Inc. v. Buck, 710 P.2d 647 (Idaho Ct.App.1985).

491. *See* Dalton v. Bundy, 666 S.W.2d 443 (Mo.App.1984).

"When applying this analysis to *Idaho Lumber* one contrasts the plaintiff's possibly negligent conduct with the defendant's presumable inability to stop the work. If these factors could weigh in plaintiff's favor, the court would base recovery on the increased market or rental value of the property due to the improvements. The court did not discuss the defendant's financial ability to pay for the benefit, although this factor is relevant. If the property's rent increased, the defendant realized an actual monetary benefit from plaintiff's work, which could easily be disgorged. Another possibility could be a lien satisfied upon the defendant's eventual sale of the property.

"It is not clear that the plaintiff should *not* have recovered in *Dalton*. First, the defendant might have been able to stop the work. In addition, the court did not compare the conduct of the parties or discuss their relative hardships. Use of the second tier [of analysis] would enable the court to determine whether the defendant was unjustly enriched retaining a benefit."

Kovacic–Fleischer, A Proposal to Simplify Quantum Meruit Litigation, 35 Am.U.L.Rev. 547, 628–641 (1986).*

C. SPECIFIC PERFORMANCE AND INJUNCTIVE RELIEF

CITY STORES COMPANY v. AMMERMAN

United States District Court, District of Columbia, 1967.
266 F.Supp. 766, affirmed, 129 U.S.App.D.C. 325, 394 F.2d 950 (1968).

GASCH, DISTRICT JUDGE.

[Plaintiff, a department store corporation, brought this action against the defendants, builders and developers of a suburban Washington, D.C. shopping center located in northern Virginia, for specific performance of a contract whereby the defendants allegedly promised to offer the plaintiff a lease in the shopping center of one of the major buildings to be constructed in the center on terms at least equal to those offered to other department stores in the center. The court determined first that there was a valid and binding option contract and that the contract was not indefinite for purposes of equitable relief.]

* * *

The question whether a contract which also calls for construction of a building can or should be specifically enforced apparently never has been decided before in this jurisdiction. The parties have cited no cases on this point.

At the outset, it should be noted that where specific performance of such contracts has been granted the essential criterion has not been the nature or subject of the contract, but rather the inadequacy or impracticability of legal remedies. *See* 5 Williston on Contracts § 1423 (Rev.Ed. 1937); 4 Pomeroy's Equity Jurisprudence §§ 1401–1403 (5th Ed.1941). Contracts involving interests in land or unique chattels generally are

* Reprinted with permission of the author and The American University Law Review.

specifically enforced because of the clear inadequacy of damages at law for breach of contract. As Pomeroy says:

> "The foundation and measure of the jurisdiction is the desire to do justice, which the legal remedy would fail to give. * * *
>
> "* * * The jurisdiction depending upon this broad principle is exercised in two classes of cases: 1. Where the subject-matter of the contract is of such a special nature, or of such a peculiar value, that the damages, when ascertained according to legal rules, would not be a just and reasonable substitute for or representative of that subject-matter in the hands of the party who is entitled to its benefit; or in other words, where the damages are *inadequate;* 2. Where, from some special and practical features or incidents of the contract inhering either in its subject matter, in its terms, or in the relations of the parties, it is impossible to arrive at a legal measure of damages at all, or at least with any sufficient degree of certainty, so that *no* real compensation can be obtained by means of an action at law; or in other words, where damages are *impracticable.*"

It is apparent from the nature of the contract involved in this case that even were it possible to arrive at a precise measure of damages for breach of a contract to lease a store in a shopping center for a long period of years—which it is not—money damages would in no way compensate the plaintiff for loss of the right to participate in the shopping center enterprise and for the almost incalculable future advantages that might accrue to it as a result of extending its operations into the suburbs. Therefore, I hold that the appropriate remedy in this case is specific performance.

Some jurisdictions in the United States have opposed granting specific performance of contracts for construction of buildings and other contracts requiring extensive supervision of the court, but the better view, and the one which increasingly is being followed in this country, is that such contracts should be specifically enforced unless the difficulties of supervision outweigh the importance of specific performance to the plaintiff. 5 Williston on Contracts § 1423 (Rev.Ed.1937). This is particularly true where the construction is to be done on land controlled by the defendant, because in that circumstance the plaintiff cannot employ another contractor to do the construction for him at defendant's expense. In the case at bar, the fact that more than mere construction of a building is involved reinforces the need for specific enforcement of the defendants' duty to perform their entire contractual obligation to the plaintiff.

* * *

The defendants contend that the granting of specific performance in this case will confront the court with insuperable difficulties of supervision, but after reviewing the evidence, I am satisfied that the standards to be observed in construction of the plaintiff's store are set out in the Hecht and Woodward & Lothrop leases with sufficient particularity (Plaintiff's Ex. F) as to make design and approval of plaintiff's store a fairly simple matter, if the parties deal with each other in good faith and expeditiously, as I shall hereafter order.

For example, Article VIII, Sec. 8.1, Paragraph (G) of the Hecht lease (the Woodward & Lothrop lease contains a similar provision) says:

> "The quality of (i) the construction, (ii) the construction components, (iii) the decorative elements (including landscaping irrigation systems for the landscaping) and (iv) the furnishings; and the general architectural character and general design, the materials selection, the decor and the treatment values, approach and standards of the Enclosed Mall shall be comparable, at minimum, to the qualities, values, approaches and standards as of the date hereof of the enclosed mall at Topanga Plaza Shopping Center, Los Angeles, California. * * * "

The existing leases contain further detailed specifications which will be identical to those in the lease granted to plaintiff. The site for plaintiff's store has already been settled by the design of the center. Although the exact design of plaintiff's store will not be identical to the design of any other store, it must be remembered that all of the stores are to be part of the same center and subject to its overall design requirements. If the parties are not in good faith able to reach an agreement on certain details, the court will appoint a special master to help settle their differences, unless they prefer voluntarily to submit their disagreements to arbitration.

* * *

[The court then rejected defendant's claims of hardship and waiver and concluded that the plaintiff was entitled to specific performance of a lease on terms equivalent to that offered to the Hecht department store in the shopping center.] *

M. LEO STORCH LIMITED PARTNERSHIP v. EROL'S, INC.

Court of Special Appeals of Maryland, 1993.
95 Md.App. 253, 620 A.2d 408.

BISHOP, JUDGE.

* * *

Storch is the owner of Hilltop Plaza Shopping Center located in Bowie, Maryland. The rentable area of Hilltop Plaza is 116,075 square feet. On August 7, 1984, Hannah Storch, Storch's predecessor, and Erol's entered into an agreement for the lease of a 5,400 square foot portion (4.6522%) of

* For a case illustrating the view that it is impracticable to grant specific performance of a construction contract, see Yonan v. Oak Park Federal Sav. & Loan Ass'n, 27 Ill. App.3d 967, 326 N.E.2d 773 (1975).

For a discussion of the law governing specific performance of construction contracts, see Fran Realty, Inc. v. Thomas, 30 Md.App. 362, 354 A.2d 196 (1976); Axelrod, Judicial Attitudes Toward Specific Performance of Construction Contracts, 7 U.Dayton L.Rev. 33 (1981); Barnick, Expediting Construction by Enjoining Performance, 21 Prac.Law. 59 (July, 1975); Comment, Specific Performance of Construction Contracts—Archaic Principles Preclude Necessary Reform, 47 Notre Dame L.Rev. 1025 (1972). *See generally* Van Hecke, Changing Emphases in Specific Performance, 40 N.C.L.Rev. 1, 13–14 (1961); Annot., 38 A.L.R.3d 1052 (1971).

For an excellent discussion of the use of special masters in specific performance litigation, see Schwartz, The Case for Specific Performance, 89 Yale L.J. 271, 292–96 (1979) (recommending that breaching party bear costs of special master).

the shopping center. Erol's planned to use the leased premises ("Hilltop Erol's") to sell and rent televisions, video cameras, video tape recorders, videotapes, movies, and accessories. The initial term of the lease was five years, beginning October 1, 1984. Erol's exercised its option to renew the lease for an additional five year term, ending September 30, 1994. Erol's rent obligation was fixed—the monthly rent did not fluctuate with Hilltop Erol's monthly gross sales.

Starting in August 1990, Hilltop Erol's averaged 3,000 customers per month. In order to turn a profit, however, Hilltop Erol's was required to average over 5,000 customers per month. Accordingly, Hilltop Erol's operated at a loss; the store projected that it would continue to operate at a loss in 1992. The entire Erol's chain experienced similar difficulties.

* * *

After learning of Erol's intention to close Hilltop Erol's, Storch filed the action *sub judice*. In Count III of the complaint, Storch averred:

> Defendants are bound to operate the leased premises "during the entire term of this Lease with due diligence and efficiency" and to "carry at all times in said premises a stock of merchandise of such size, character and quality as shall be reasonably designed to produce the maximum return to Landlord and Tenant." Defendants are breaching this covenant by closing the Hilltop Plaza store. Plaintiffs are being irreparably injured and will continue to be irreparably injured by defendants' breach.
>
> Wherefore plaintiffs pray that the Court issue a temporary and permanent injunction enjoining defendants closing of the Hilltop Plaza store.

Storch relied on, in part, the "continuous operation clause" found in paragraph nine of the agreement which provides:

> Tenant shall operate all of the leased premises during the entire term of this Lease with due diligence and efficiency so as to produce all of the gross sales which may be produced by such manner of operation, unless prevented from doing so by causes beyond Tenant's control. Subject to inability by reason of strikes or labor disputes, Tenant shall carry at all times in said premises a stock of merchandise of such size, character and quality as shall be reasonably designed to produce the maximum return to Landlord and Tenant.

On February 3, 1992, the trial court denied Storch's motion for *ex parte* injunctive relief, and, instead, issued a show cause order. Three days later, Hilltop Erol's closed. At the time of the hearing on the show cause order (i.e., the hearing on the motion for interlocutory injunctive relief), Hilltop Erol's had been closed for over six weeks; two years, five months remained until Erol's obligation under the lease agreement would terminate.

Pamela Handy ("Handy"), Erol's district manager, testified that each Erol's store requires a manager, assistant manager, two part-time managers and two part-time associates. Erol's managers must be able to control inventory and "shrinkage," review profit and loss reports, work within budgets, and handle payroll, hiring and firing. Erol's employees undergo a ninety-day training class when they are first hired. According to Handy, in order to be successful within the video industry:

> you really need to have some type of movie knowledge; being able to select and help purchase tapes that [Erol's] will select for certain stores. You have to know your customers, what titles are going to rent in a particular store, how many copies you need to buy for that. You need to be able to supply customers with that knowledge; to be able to put a movie in their hands and let them rent.

Handy testified that, in order to reopen Hilltop Erol's, Erol's would have to interview, hire, and train new employees, and would have to purchase five to eight thousand movie titles.

* * *

We hold that the trial court did not abuse its discretion when it denied interlocutory injunctive relief because Storch did not prove a "likelihood of success on the merits."

* * *

Storch is seeking injunctive relief to enforce the continuous operation clause of the lease agreement. Maryland courts have allowed "[i]njunctive relief * * * as the functional equivalent of specific performance." *SECI, Inc.,* 63 Md.App. at 726, 493 A.2d 1100. However, " '[a] suit for an injunction which seeks to accomplish all the purposes of a decree for specific performance is subject to the principles which apply to an application for the latter remedy * * *.' " *Id.* (*quoting Smith v. Myers,* 130 Md. 64, 67, 99 A. 938 (1917)) (alteration in original).

It is well-settled that

> "where [a] contract is, in its nature and circumstances, unobjectionable—or, as it is sometimes stated, fair, reasonable and certain in all its terms—it is as much a matter of course for a court of equity to decree specific performance of it as it is for a court of law to award damages for its breach."

Gross v. J & L Camping & Sports Ctr., Inc., 270 Md. 539, 543–44, 312 A.2d 270 (1973) (*quoting Glendale Corp. v. Crawford,* 207 Md. 148, 154, 114 A.2d 33 (1955)); *see also Maryland–Nat'l Capital Park & Planning Comm'n v. Washington Nat'l Arena,* 282 Md. 588, 615, 386 A.2d 1216 (1978). It is equally settled, however,

> that specific performance will not [ordinarily] be decreed if the performance is of such a character as to make effective enforcement unreasonably difficult or to require such long-continued supervision by the court as is disproportionate to the advantages to be gained from such a decree and to the harm to be suffered in case it is denied.

Edison Realty Co. v. Bauernschub, 191 Md. 451, 460, 62 A.2d 354 (1948); *see also* Restatement (Second) of Contracts § 366 (1979) ("A promise will not be specifically enforced if the character and magnitude of the performance would impose on the court burdens in enforcement or supervision that are disproportionate to the advantages to be gained from enforcement and to the harm to be suffered from its denial."). Although the trial court *may* award injunctive relief notwithstanding the difficulty of enforcement, the failure to grant an injunction under such circumstances does not constitute an abuse of the court's discretion. *See Bauernschub,* 191 Md. at 460, 62 A.2d 354.

* * *

Storch cites *Stamatiades v. Merit Music Serv., Inc.,* 210 Md. 597, 124 A.2d 829 (1956), as the only Maryland appellate court decision addressing the propriety of enforcing, by way of injunction, the continuous operation clause of a lease. In *Stamatiades,* the plaintiff agreed to lend the defendants, proprietors of a restaurant, $3,000 on the condition that they enter into an agreement for the lease of coin-operated amusement devices. The agreement required that three coin-operated devices be installed in defendants' restaurant and that they remain in continuous operation during the term of the lease. Under the agreement, plaintiff was to receive fifty percent of the machines' gross receipts. Further, the agreement prohibited defendants from installing or permitting the installation of similar equipment supplied by anyone other than plaintiff. Defendants also expressly agreed "that a decree might be passed in a suit brought for such purpose enjoining them 'from violating th[e] covenant.'" *Id.* at 602, 124 A.2d 829.

Shortly after the parties entered into the agreement, plaintiff discovered that the machines had been "disconnected and were no longer in use, and either then or thereafter machines furnished by the same competitor whose machines had previously been installed in [defendants'] restaurant were again installed there." *Id.* at 603. Defendants then paid off the $3,000 loan and ordered the removal of plaintiff's machines from the restaurant. After the machines were removed, and after negotiations failed, plaintiff filed suit.

The trial court enjoined the defendants "from placing, or permitting any person or persons other than the plaintiff * * * to place or locate any coin-operated amusement, music or vending machines in the premises." *Id.* at 601, 124 A.2d 829. Storch likens the injunction in *Stamatiades* to one necessary to enforce specifically the continuous operation clause of its lease with Erol's. We fail to see any resemblance.

The injunction in *Stamatiades* prohibited the defendants from doing something—using, in their restaurant, coin-operated amusement, music or vending machines not belonging to the plaintiff. This variety of injunction, one that prohibits the doing of an act, is properly characterized as a "negative" or "prohibitory" injunction. *See Automobile Dealer Resources, Inc. v. Occidental Life Ins. Co.,* 15 N.C.App. 634, 190 S.E.2d 729, 732 (1972). The injunction that Storch seeks *sub judice* would require Erol's to reopen its Hilltop store, hire and train new employees, purchase substantial merchandise, and operate as a retail video operation. This type of injunction is clearly of a "mandatory" nature as it "is intended to restore a status quo and to that end requires a party to perform a positive act." *Id.* *Stamatiades* is, therefore, inapposite.

Storch cites two other cases, *Dover Shopping Ctr., Inc. v. Cushman's Sons, Inc.,* 63 N.J.Super. 384, 164 A.2d 785 (App.Div.1960), and *Lincoln Tower Corp. v. Richter's Jewelry Co.,* 152 Fla. 542, 12 So.2d 452 (1943), to demonstrate that courts have specifically enforced continuous operation clauses of shopping center leases. These cases, however, "are both old * * * and against the weight of authority." *CBL & Assocs., Inc.,* 761 F.Supp. at 812. *See generally* John A. Glenn, Annotation, *Lease of Store as Requiring Active Operation of Store,* 40 A.L.R.3d 971 (1971 & Supp.1992). Several courts have recently rejected *Dover Shopping Ctr., Inc.* and *Lincoln Tower Corp.* and have followed the established principle of equity that

> "* * * '[c]ontracts which by their terms stipulate for a succession of acts, whose performance cannot be consummated by one transaction, but will be continuous, and require protracted supervision and direction, with the exercise of special knowledge, skill, or judgment in such oversight, * * * are not, as a rule, specifically enforced.' Pomeroy on Specific Performance of Contracts, § 312, and cases cited in note 5; Waterman on Specific Performance of Contracts, § 49; *Electric Co. v. Mobile, supra.* [109 Ala. 190, 195, 19 So. 721] * * *."

Lorch, Inc. v. Bessemer Mall Shopping Ctr., Inc., 294 Ala. 17, 310 So.2d 872, 875 (1975) (*quoting Tombigbee Valley R.R. v. Fairford Lumber Co.,* 155 Ala. 575, 47 So. 88 (1908)).

For example, in *New Park Forest Assocs. II v. Rogers Enters., Inc.,* 195 Ill.App.3d 757, 142 Ill.Dec. 474, 552 N.E.2d 1215, *cert. denied,* 133 Ill.2d 559, 149 Ill.Dec. 324, 561 N.E.2d 694 (1990), the plaintiff shopping center brought an action against one of its tenants, seeking a temporary injunction, an order of specific performance, and a permanent injunction to prevent the defendant from closing its store in violation of a continuous operation clause. The lease required defendant to "operat[e] [the] store for the 'sale and repair of better quality jewelry' " and prohibited defendant from " 'vacat[ing] or abandon[ing] the Premises at any time during the Term.' " *Id.* 142 Ill.Dec. at 475, 552 N.E.2d at 1216. The Appellate Court of Illinois held that the plaintiff did not have a likelihood of success on the merits.

> In this case, success on the merits means that the court would order specific performance of the long term lease.
>
> * * *
>
> Generally, Illinois courts have refused to enter mandatory injunctions to enforce contracts "which by their terms call for a succession of acts whose performance can not be consummated by one transaction, and which require protracted supervision and direction. * * * A court of equity will not assume what it can not practically accomplish."

Id. 142 Ill.Dec. at 477, 552 N.E.2d at 1218 (*quoting Grape Creek Coal Co. v. Spellman,* 39 Ill.App. 630, 632 (1891)).

> The contract in this case calls for [defendant's] continuous occupancy and use of the leased space until approximately December 31, 1997, nine years after [plaintiff] first requested an injunction and specific performance. The lease contains numerous detailed provisions

> for hours, signs, displays, painting, common areas and other operational requirements. Even the very purpose of the lease, the operation of a premises for the "sale and repair of better quality jewelry," raises enforcement problems for a court which could be placed in the position of deciding what constitutes "better quality." It is possible, that during the life of a mandatory injunction, the court would never have to enforce any of those terms or judge "better quality." Problems may never arise. If problems did arise, however, the court would find itself in the business of managing a shopping center.

Id. 142 Ill.Dec. at 478–79, 552 N.E.2d at 1219–20.

Similarly, the New York Supreme Court, Appellate Division, held that the plaintiff shopping plaza was not entitled to an order of specific performance in *Grossman v. Wegman's Food Mkts., Inc.*, 43 A.D.2d 813, 350 N.Y.S.2d 484 (N.Y.App.Div.1973). The Court recognized

> that a food store will draw people to a shopping center who will also patronize the other stores and that while the food store is closed the business of the other stores will be diminished. There might well be damage to the other tenants while the food store remains vacant, and, if the vacancy extends over a long period of time, it is possible that a tenant might also vacate its premises with resulting damage to plaintiffs.

Id. 350 N.Y.S.2d at 485. The Court, however, followed an earlier case, *Price v. Herman,* 81 N.Y.S.2d 361 (N.Y.Sup.Ct.1948), *aff'd,* 275 App.Div. 675, 87 N.Y.S.2d 221 (N.Y.App.Div.1949), where it was held that a court would not grant an injunction or order specific performance to enforce a continuous operation clause of a lease " 'requir[ing] the performance of varied and continuous acts, or the exercise of special skill, taste, and judgment, * * * because the execution of the decree would require such constant superintendence as to make judicial control a matter of extreme difficulty.' " *Id.* 81 N.Y.S.2d at 362 * * *.

We conclude "that the decisions denying injunctive relief reflect the modern trend and the majority rule." *8600 Assocs., Ltd. v. Wearguard Corp.,* 737 F.Supp. 44, 46 (E.D.Mich.1990); *see also CBL & Assocs., Inc.,* 761 F.Supp. at 812; *Lorch, Inc.,* 310 So.2d at 876; *Madison Plaza, Inc. v. Shapira Corp.,* 180 Ind.App. 141, 387 N.E.2d 483, 487 (1979). An interlocutory injunction that requires Erol's to reopen its Hilltop store would be of the "mandatory" variety—Erol's would have to interview, hire, train, and oversee management and employees. Handy's testimony makes clear that the day-to-day operations of the store would necessarily include varied and continuous acts that require the exercise of special skill, taste, and judgment. *See Lorch, Inc.,* 310 So.2d at 875; *Grossman v. Wegman's Food Mkts., Inc.,* 350 N.Y.S.2d at 485–86.

Although it is quite possible that, during the life of a mandatory injunction, the court would never have to enforce any of the terms of the continuous operation clause, if problems did arise, the court would find itself in the business of managing a retail video operation. *See Rogers Enters., Inc.,* 142 Ill.Dec. at 479, 552 N.E.2d at 1220. We do not hold that injunctive relief may never be ordered to enforce a continuous operation clause under compelling circumstances. That decision lies within the sound discretion of the trial court. We hold only that the trial court did not abuse its discretion in the case *sub judice* because the injunction could require the continuous supervision of the court over an extended period of time and, therefore, would make "effective enforcement unreasonably difficult." *Bauernschub,* 191 Md. at 460, 62 A.2d 354.

Note

Why do you think lessors commonly put continuous operation clauses in shopping center leases? Why do you think the lessor in *Storch* was so insistent on forcing the tenant to comply when there were only two and a half years remaining on the lease? Why not simply sue for the fixed rent that will accrue over the remainder of the lease term?

Does granting specific performance of a continuous operation clause in a lease entail greater judicial supervision than granting the same remedy in the construction contract context? Would it have made a difference had the court in *Storch* been dealing with a percentage lease—one where the rent is calculated wholly or partially as a percentage of the tenant's gross sales? Would it be relevant to know whether other space in the center was rented on a percentage lease basis?

PINGLEY v. BRUNSON

Supreme Court of South Carolina, 1979.
272 S.Ct. 421, 252 S.E.2d 560.

RHODES, JUSTICE:

This appeal is from an order compelling appellant, Carl Brunson, to fulfill his contract to provide entertainment at respondent's restaurant, and further enjoining him from playing musical instruments for any other establishment during times that would conflict with performance of his contract. We reverse, concluding that neither specific performance nor injunctive relief was a proper remedy for enforcement of appellant's contract for personal services.

During the past several years the appellant, who is an automobile repairman by trade, has been playing the organ as part time employment for various establishments in the Mullins area.

On December 6, 1977, appellant entered into a contract to play the organ for respondent's restaurant for a period of three years. By terms of the contract, appellant agreed to play in respondent's place of business for three designated nights each week and an additional night during certain specified months. For his services, respondent agreed to pay Brunson $50.00 per night. The contract further set out: (1) that the respondent was purchasing musical instruments at the price of $4,262.96 for use by the appellant at his restaurant; and (2) that monthly installments on the cost of the instruments were to be provided by deduction from appellant's pay checks. After payment in full, the instruments were to become the property of the appellant. The contract further provided that any breach by appellant would result in his forfeiting any claim to the instruments.

The appellant commenced performing for respondent on the night of December 6, 1977 and played for nine evenings thereafter. On December 27, appellant did not appear for his performance and has failed and refused to perform in accordance with his contract since that time.

Courts of equity will not ordinarily decree specific performance of a contract for personal services, particularly where the performance of the services contracted for would be continuous over a long period of time. 81 C.J.S. Specific Performance § 96 (1977). This rule has been applied to various personal service contracts including, but not limited to, performance as an actor, a singer, a sales agent, and a ball player. Restatement of Contracts § 379 (1932). On the other hand, where services have a unique and peculiar value, specific performance has been awarded under limited circumstances. 81 C.J.S. Specific Performance, *supra.*

Assuming that a valid contract was effected between the parties, the personal services required of appellant were to be performed on a sustained basis over a three year period. The idea of compelling a close personal association over a protracted period of time after disputes have arisen and loyalty and confidence dissipated has been repugnant to courts facing the situation. 11 S. Williston, Contracts § 1423 (3d ed. W. Jaegar 1968).

The exception allowing specific performance of a personal service contract is confined to instances where the performer possesses unique and exceptional skill or ability in his area of expertise. Even though respondent's witnesses asserted appellant's exceptional talent as a major attraction to an area establishment, the further evidence revealed that five other organists of comparable ability were available for hire in the Mullins area. In this regard, we find the general rule to be that if the subject matter of a contract is such that its substantial equivalent is readily obtainable from others rather than defendant in an exchange for a money payment, this factor will be sufficient to deny specific performance. 5 A. Corbin, Contracts § 1142 (1960). Under the circumstances of the case at bar, we cannot conclude from the evidence that appellant's musical talent is of such a unique quality as to warrant an award of specific performance; instead, the availability of other local organ players persuades us that respondent's remedy was at law and not in equity.

For the foregoing reasons, we conclude that the trial court erred in granting a decree of specific performance, compelling the appellant to comply with terms of his contract for personal services. Likewise in error was the lower court's injunctive relief prohibiting the acceptance by respondent of other employment during specified periods. The contract between appellant and respondent did not contain a covenant not to compete or to perform elsewhere. In the absence of an express negative covenant as a basis for injunctive relief, the general rule is as follows:

> In a number of cases the question has arisen as to whether injunction may issue against the breach of an employment contract by an employee and the furnishing of his services to another, where there is no covenant in the contract to the effect that he is not to enter the employment of another during the term of the contract. As a rule, the

court does not award injunction in the absence of an express negative covenant in the contract.

42 Am.Jur.2d, Injunctions, § 104 (1969).

Reversed.

LEWIS, C.J., and LITTLEJOHN, NESS and GREGORY, JJ., concur.*

Note

The decision in *Pingley* is in accord with the Restatement (Second) of Contracts § 367 (1981): **

"§ 367. Contracts for Personal Service or Supervision

"(1) A promise to render personal service will not be specifically enforced.

"(2) A promise to render personal service exclusively for one employer will not be enforced by an injunction against serving another if its probable result will be to compel a performance involving personal relations the enforced continuance of which is undesirable or will be to leave the employee without other reasonable means of making a living.

"Comment:

"*a. Rationale of refusal of specific performance.* A court will refuse to grant specific performance of a contract for service or supervision that is personal in nature. The refusal is based in part upon the undesirability of compelling the continuance of personal association after disputes have arisen and confidence and loyalty are gone and, in some instances, of imposing what might seem like involuntary servitude. * * * The refusal is also based upon the difficulty of enforcement inherent in passing judgment on the quality of performance. To this extent the rule stated in Subsection (1) is an application of the more general rule on the effect of difficulty of enforcement (§ 366).

* * *

"*c. Availability of injunction.* A contract for personal service is usually exclusive in the sense that it imposes not only a duty to render the service to the other party but also a duty to forbear from rendering it to anyone else. Because specific performance of the duty to render the service is precluded by the rule stated in Subsection (1), the availability of injunctive relief to enforce the duty of forbearance takes on special importance. Subsection (2) indicates

* California Civil Code section 3423 provides that an injunction may not be granted to prevent the breach of a contract unless it is "a contract in writing for the rendition or furnishing of personal services from one to another where the minimum compensation for such service is at the rate of not less than six thousand dollars per annum and where the promised service is of a special, unique, unusual, extraordinary or intellectual character, which gives it peculiar value, the loss of which cannot be reasonably or adequately compensated in damages in an action at law, the performance of which would not be specifically enforced * * *." In 1919, when the legislation was enacted, "the sum of $6,000 a year was more than five times the average national wage of $1,142," which is "equivalent to setting the minimum compensation figure at $100,000" in 1984. Motown Record Corp. v. Brockett, 160 Cal.App.3d 123, 138, 207 Cal.Rptr. 574, 584 (1984) (reversing preliminary injunction against Teena Marie). *See also* KGB, Inc. v. Giannoulas, 104 Cal. App.3d 844, 164 Cal.Rptr. 571 (1980) (refusing to enjoin former employee of radio station from appearing in a chicken suit, the costume that he had worn while appearing as radio station's mascot).

the application of the general rule on injunctive relief stated in § 357(2) to this important situation. Under that general rule, an injunction will not be ordered if the remedy in damages would be adequate (§ 359). Damages are likely to be adequate to protect the employer's interest unless the employee's services are unique or extraordinary, either because of special skill that he possesses or because of special knowledge that he has acquired of the employer's business.

"Even if damages are not adequate, however, an injunction will not be granted if its probable result will be to leave the employee without other reasonable means of making a living. It is not the purpose in granting the injunction to enforce the duty to render the service and, to justify granting it, it should appear that the employee is not being forced to perform the contract as the only reasonable means of making a living. Furthermore, if the probable result of an injunction will be the employee's performance of the contract, it should appear that the employer is prepared to continue the employment in good faith so that performance will not involve personal relations the enforced continuance of which is undesirable. These issues are for the exercise of judicial discretion based on such factors as the character and duration of the service, the probability of the renewal of good relations, the extent to which other remedies are adequate, and the probable hardship that will result from an injunction."

AMERICAN BROADCASTING COMPANIES, INC. v. WOLF

Court of Appeals of New York, 1981.
52 N.Y.2d 394, 438 N.Y.S.2d 482, 420 N.E.2d 363.

COOKE, CHIEF JUDGE.

This case provides an interesting insight into the fierce competition in the television industry for popular performers and favorable ratings. It requires legal resolution of a rather novel employment imbroglio.

The issue is whether plaintiff American Broadcasting Companies, Incorporated (ABC), is entitled to equitable relief against defendant Warner Wolf, a New York City sportscaster, because of Wolf's breach of a good faith negotiation provision of a now expired broadcasting contract with ABC. In the present circumstances, it is concluded that the equitable relief sought by plaintiff—which would have the effect of forcing Wolf off the air—may not be granted.

I.

Warner Wolf, a sportscaster who has developed a rather colorful and unique on-the-air personality, had been employed by ABC since 1976. In February, 1978, ABC and Wolf entered into an employment agreement which, following exercise of renewal option, was to terminate on March 5, 1980. The contract contained a clause, known as a good-faith negotiation and first-refusal provision, that is at the crux of this litigation: "You agree, if we so elect, during the last ninety (90) days prior to the expiration of the extended term of this agreement, to enter into good faith negotiations with us for the extension of this agreement on mutually agreeable terms. You further agree that for the first forty-five (45) days of this renegotiation period, you will not negotiate for your services with any other person or company other than WABC–TV or ABC. In the event we are unable to reach an agreement for an extension by the expiration of the extended term hereof, you agree that you will not accept, in any market for a period of three (3) months following expiration of the extended term of this agreement, any offer of employment as a sportscaster, sports news reporter, commentator, program host, or analyst in broadcasting (including television, cable television, pay television and radio) without first giving us, in writing, an opportunity to employ you on substantially similar terms and you agree to enter into an agreement with us on such terms." * * *

Wolf first met with ABC executives in September, 1979 to discuss the terms of a renewal contract. Counterproposals were exchanged, and the parties agreed to finalize the matter by October 15. Meanwhile, unbeknownst to ABC, Wolf met with representatives of CBS in early October. * * *

On February 1, 1980, after termination of the exclusive period, Wolf and CBS orally agreed on the terms of Wolf's employment as sportscaster for WCBS–TV, a CBS-owned affiliate in New York. During the next two days, CBS informed Wolf that it had prepared two agreements and divided his annual compensation between the two: one covered his services as an on-the-air sportscaster, and the other was an off-the-air production agreement for sports specials Wolf was to produce. The production agreement contained an exclusivity clause which barred Wolf from performing "services of any nature for" or permitting the use of his "name, likeness, voice or endorsement by, any person, firm or corporation" during the term of the agreement, unless CBS consented. The contract had an effective date of March 6, 1980.

Wolf signed the CBS production agreement on February 4, 1980. At the same time, CBS agreed in writing, in consideration of $100 received from Wolf, to hold open an offer of employment to Wolf as sportscaster until June 4, 1980, the date on which Wolf became free from ABC's right of first refusal. The next day, February 5, Wolf submitted a letter of resignation to ABC. * * *

Later in February, Wolf and ABC agreed that Wolf would continue to appear on the air during a portion of the first-refusal period, from March 6 until May 28.

ABC commenced this action on May 6, 1980, by which time Wolf's move to CBS had become public knowledge. The complaint alleged that Wolf, induced by CBS breached both the good-faith negotiation and first-refusal provisions of his contract with ABC. ABC sought specific enforcement of its right of first refusal and an injunction against Wolf's employment as a sportscaster with CBS.

After a trial, Supreme Court found no breach of the contract, and went on to note that, in any event, equitable relief would be inappropriate. A divided Appellate Division, while concluding that Wolf had breached both the good-faith negotiation and first-refusal provisions, nonetheless affirmed on the ground that equitable intervention was unwarranted. There should be an affirmance.

II.

Initially, we agree with the Appellate Division that defendant Wolf breached his obligation to negotiate in good faith with ABC from December, 1979 through March, 1980. * * *

At the same time, there is no basis in the record for the Appellate Division's conclusion that Wolf violated the first-refusal provision by entering into an oral sportscasting contract with CBS on February 4. * * * By its own terms, the right of first refusal did not apply to offers accepted by Wolf prior to the March 5 termination of the ABC employment contract. It is apparent, therefore, that Wolf could not have breached the right of first refusal by accepting an offer during the term of his employment with ABC. * * *

III.

–A–

Courts of equity historically have refused to order an individual to perform a contract for personal services. * * * Originally this rule evolved because of the inherent difficulties courts would encounter in supervising the performance of uniquely personal efforts. * * * During the Civil War era, there emerged a more compelling reason for not directing the performance of personal services: the Thirteenth Amendment's prohibition of involuntary servitude. It has been strongly suggested that judicial compulsion of services would violate the express command of that amendment (Arthur v. Oakes, 63 F. 310, 317; Stevens, Involuntary Servitude by Injunction, 6 Corn.L.Q. 235; Calamari & Perillo, The Law of Contracts [2d ed.], § 16–5). For practical, policy and constitutional reasons, therefore, courts continue to decline to affirmatively enforce employment contracts.

Over the years, however, in certain narrowly tailored situations, the law fashioned other remedies for failure to perform an employment agreement. Thus, where an employee refuses to render services to an employer in violation of an existing contract, and the services are unique or extraordinary, an injunction may issue to prevent the employee from furnishing those services to another person for the duration of the contract. Such "negative enforcement" was initially available only when the employee had expressly stipulated not to compete with the employer for the term of the engagement. Later cases permitted injunctive relief where the circumstances justified implication of a negative covenant. In these situations, an injunction is warranted because the employee either expressly or by clear implication agreed not to work elsewhere for the period of his contract. And, since the services must be unique before negative enforcement will be granted, irreparable harm will befall the employer should the employee be permitted to labor for a competitor.

–B–

After a personal service contract terminates, the availability of equitable relief against the former employee diminishes appreciably. Since the period of service has expired, it is impossible to decree affirmative or negative specific performance. Only if the employee has expressly agreed not to compete with the employer following the term of the contract, or is threatening to disclose trade secrets or commit another tortious act, is injunctive relief generally available at the behest of the employer * * *. Even where there is an express anticompetitive covenant, however, it will be rigorously examined and specifically enforced only if it satisfies certain established requirements (*see, e.g.,* Reed, Roberts Assoc. v. Strauman, *supra,* 40 N.Y.2d at pp. 307–308, 386 N.Y.S.2d 677, 353 N.E.2d 590; Purchasing Assoc. v. Weitz, *supra,* at pp. 272–273; *see, generally,* Calamari & Perillo, The Law of Contracts [2d ed.], §§ 16–19, at pp. 601–602). Indeed, a court normally will not decree specific enforcement of an employee's anticompetitive covenant unless necessary to protect the trade secrets, customer lists or good will of the employer's business, or perhaps when the employer is exposed to special harm because of the unique nature of the employee's services. * * * And, an otherwise valid covenant will not be enforced if it is unreasonable in time, space or scope or would operate in a harsh or oppressive manner. * * * There is, in short, general judicial disfavor of anticompetitive covenants contained in employment contracts. * * *

Underlying the strict approach to enforcement of these covenants is the notion that, once the term of an employment agreement has expired, the general public policy favoring robust and uninhibited competition should not give way merely because a particular employer wishes to insulate himself from competition. * * * Important, too, are the "powerful considerations of public policy which militate against sanctioning the loss of a man's livelihood" * * *. At the same time, the employer is entitled to protection from unfair or illegal conduct that causes economic injury. The rules governing enforcement of anticompetitive covenants and the availability of equitable relief after termination of employment are designed to foster these interests of the employer without impairing the employee's ability to earn a living or the general competitive mold of society.

–C–

Specific enforcement of personal service contracts thus turns initially upon whether the term of employment has expired. If the employee refuses to perform during the period of employment, was furnishing unique services, has expressly or by clear implication agreed not to compete for the duration of the contract and the employer is exposed to irreparable injury, it may be appropriate to restrain the employee from competing until the agreement expires. Once the employment contract has terminated, by contrast, equitable relief is potentially available only to prevent injury from unfair competition or similar tortious behavior or to enforce an express and valid anticompetitive covenant. In the absence of such circumstances, the general policy of unfettered competition should prevail.

IV.

Applying these principles, it is apparent that ABC's request for injunctive relief must fail. There is no existing employment agreement between the parties; the original contract terminated in March, 1980. Thus, the negative enforcement that might be appropriate during the term of employment is unwarranted here. Nor is there an express anticompetitive covenant that defendant Wolf is violating, or any claim of special injury from tortious conduct such as exploitation of trade secrets. In short, ABC seeks to premise equitable relief after termination of the employment upon a simple, albeit serious, breach of a general contract negotiation clause.[7] To grant an injunction in that situation would be to unduly interfere with an individual's livelihood and to inhibit free competition where there is no corresponding injury to the employer other than the loss of a competitive edge. Indeed, if relief were granted here, any breach of an employment contract provision relating to renewal negotiations logically would serve as the basis for an open-ended restraint upon the employee's ability to earn a living should he ultimately choose not to extend his employment.[8] Our public policy, which favors the free exchange of goods and services through established market mechanisms, dictates otherwise.

Equally unavailing is ABC's request that the court create a noncompetitive covenant by implication. Although in a proper case an implied-in-fact covenant not to compete for the term of employment may be found to exist, anticompetitive covenants covering the postemployment period will not be implied.[9] Indeed, even an express covenant will be scrutinized and enforced only in accordance with established principles.

This is not to say that ABC has not been damaged in some fashion or that Wolf should escape responsibility for the breach of his good-faith negotiation obligation. Rather, we merely conclude that ABC is not entitled to equitable relief. Because of the unique circumstances presented, however, this decision is without prejudice to ABC's right to pursue relief in the form of monetary damages, if it be so advised.

Accordingly, the order of the Appellate Division should be affirmed.

FUCHSBERG, JUDGE (dissenting).

I agree with all the members of this court, as had all the Justices at the Appellate Division, that the defendant Wolf breached his undisputed obligation to negotiate in good faith for renewal of his contract with ABC. Where we part company is in the majority's unwillingness to mold an equitable decree, even one more limited than the harsh one the plaintiff proposed, to right the wrong.

* * *

7. Even if Wolf had breached the first-refusal provision, it does not necessarily follow that injunctive relief would be available. Outside the personal service area, the usual equitable remedy for breach of a first-refusal clause is to order the breaching party to perform the contract with the person possessing the first-refusal right (e.g., 5A Corbin, Contracts, § 1197, at pp. 377–378). When personal services are involved, this would result in an affirmative injunction ordering the employee to perform services for plaintiff. Such relief, as discussed, cannot be granted.

8. Interestingly, the negative enforcement ABC seeks—an injunction barring Wolf from broadcasting for CBS—is for a two-year period. ABC's request is premised upon the fact that Wolf and CBS entered into a two-year agreement. Had the agreement been for 10 years, presumably ABC would have requested a 10–year restraint. In short, since it lacks an express anticompetitive clause to enforce, plaintiff seeks to measure its relief in a manner unrelated to the breach or the injury. This well illustrates one of the reasons why the law requires an express anticompetitive clause before it will restrain an employee from competing after termination of the employment.

9. Of course, as discussed, tortious interference with the employer's business by a former employee may sometimes be enjoined absent a noncompetitive covenant.

One need not be in the broadcasting business to understand that the restriction ABC bargained for, and Wolf granted, when they entered into the original employment contract was not inconsequential. The earnings of broadcasting companies are directly related to the "ratings" they receive. This, in turn, is at least in part dependent on the popularity of personalities like Wolf. It therefore was to ABC's advantage, once Wolf came into its employ, especially since he was new to the New York market, that it enhance his popularity by featuring, advertising and otherwise promoting him. This meant that the loyalty of at least part of the station's listening audience would become identified with Wolf, thus enhancing his potential value to competitors, as witness the fact that, in place of the $250,000 he was receiving during his last year with ABC, he was able to command $400,000 to $450,000 per annum in his CBS "deal". A reasonable opportunity during which ABC could cope with such an assault on its good will had to be behind the clause in question.

* * *

In the face of these considerations, the majority rationalizes its position of powerlessness to grant equitable relief by choosing to interpret the contract as though there were no restrictive covenant, express or implied. However, as demonstrated, there is, in fact, an express three-month negative covenant which, because of Wolf's misconduct, ABC was effectively denied the opportunity to exercise. Enforcement of this covenant, by enjoining Wolf from broadcasting for a three-month period, would depart from no entrenched legal precedent. Rather, it would accord with equity's boasted flexibility. * * *

For all these reasons, in my view, literal as well as proverbial justice should have brought a modification of the order of the Appellate Division to include a 90–day injunction—no more and no less than the relatively short and certainly not unreasonable transitional period for which ABC and Wolf struck their bargain.

Notes

1. The majority opinion in *ABC, Inc.* suggests that Wolf still could be held legally responsible for the breach of his good-faith negotiation obligation. What type of relief might ABC seek? *See supra,* pp. 733–36.

2. In Cullman Broadcasting Co., Inc. v. Bosley, 373 So.2d 830 (Ala.1979), a radio station brought an action to obtain injunctive relief and to recover liquidated and punitive damages from the station's former announcer, who had breached a covenant not to compete by accepting employment as a radio announcer at another station. The trial court denied the claim. The appellate court ruled that the covenant was enforceable, but recognized that the one year restriction embodied in the contract had expired:

> "Even though we have decided that the covenant in this case was enforceable, it does not necessarily follow that the trial court improperly denied injunctive relief. The decision regarding injunctive relief is based on a consideration of the nature and character of the employment, the size and condition of the locality to which the prohibition extends, the duration

> of the prohibition and the consideration moving to the employee for his agreement to the restriction.
>
> "If a trial court upon a consideration of the factors noted above, refuses to enjoin an employee from breaching a covenant not to compete, that refusal does not preclude an action by the employer for damages arising out of the employee's breach. Moreover, a stipulation between the parties to a contract as to an amount to be considered liquidated damages in the event of a failure to perform obviates the need for proof of damages."

Id. at 837. In *Cullman,* the liquidated damages clause provided: "The parties hereto recognize that it will be difficult to determine the damages which would be suffered by Employer in the event of a breach of this covenant not to compete and it is therefore agreed by the parties hereto that any such breach by Employee shall entitle Employer to liquidated damages against Employee in the amount of $3,000, and that in addition, Employer shall have such remedies as are in law or equity provided, including, without limitation, any action for specific performance or for injunctive relief."

Id. at 832. *See also* James S. Kemper & Co. Southeast, Inc. v. Cox & Assoc., Inc., 434 So.2d 1380 (Ala.1983) (awarding both injunctive relief and damages for breach of a covenant not to compete).

3. For a further discussion of covenants not to compete, see Blake, Employee Agreements Not to Compete, 73 Harv.L.Rev. 625 (1960); Closius & Schaffer, Involuntary Nonservitude: The Current Judicial Enforcement of Employee Covenants Not to Compete—A Proposal for Reform, 57 S.Cal.L.Rev. 531 (1984); Handler & Lazaroff, Restraint of Trade and the Restatement (Second) of Contracts, 57 N.Y.U.L.Rev. 669 (1982); Kalish, Covenants Not to Compete and the Legal Profession, 29 St. Louis U.L.J. 423 (1985); Kreider, Trends in the Enforcement of Restrictive Employment Contracts, 35 U.Cinn. L.Rev. 16 (1966); Liddle & Gray, Jr., Proof of Damages for Breach of a Restrictive Covenant or Noncompetition Agreement, 9 Empl.Rel.L.J. 455 (1984); Powers, Drafting Non–Compete Covenants: Statutory and Common Law Constraints, 13 Colo.Law. 757 (1984); Rubin & Shedd, Human Capital and Covenants Not to Compete, 10 J.Legal Stud. 93 (1981) (economic analysis); Note, Economic and Critical Analyses of the Law of Covenants Not to Compete, 72 Geo.L.J. 1425 (1984) (critique of Rubin & Shedd); Comment, Employee Restrictive Covenants: Unscrupulous Employees v. Overreaching Employers, 27 S.D.L.Rev. 220 (1982).

As to reasonableness of time and area limitations in post-employment covenants, see annotations in 41 A.L.R.2d 15 (1955) and 43 A.L.R.2d 94 (1955), respectively. As to the same considerations in covenants ancillary to the sale of a business, see annotations in 45 A.L.R.2d 77 (1956) and 46 A.L.R.2d 119 (1956), respectively. There are four basic approaches to overly broad restrictive covenants:

> "1. Deny enforcement of the entire covenant;
>
> "2. The blue pencil approach in which a court will grant enforcement of the covenant if it can blue pencil or strike out objectionable language without changing the impact of the clause;
>
> "3. Reform an overly broad restraint without regard to the severability of contract language; and

"4. Regulation by statute."

Comment, Post Employment Restraints: An Analysis of Theories of Enforcement, and a Suggested Supplement to the Covenant Not to Compete, 17 Tulsa L.J. 155, 156 (1981) (analyzing cases in all 50 states). *See also* Comment, Partial Enforcement of Post–Employment Restrictive Covenants, 15 Colum.J.L. & Soc.Probs. 181 (1979) (approving Restatement (Second) of Contracts § 188(2) (1981)).

The "blue pencil" approach, in any event, will not be applied if the employer is guilty of bad faith or where the covenant suggests that the employer clearly intended to apply oppressive burdens on the employee. Where this is the case, the covenant will not be modified and, instead, will be treated as void. *See e.g.,* Durapin, Inc. v. American Products, Inc., 559 A.2d 1051 (R.I.1989); Hill v. Mobile Auto Trim, Inc., 725 S.W.2d 168 (Tex.1987); Ellis v. James V. Hurson Associates, 565 A.2d 615 (D.C.App.1989); Dryvit System, Inc. v. Rushing, 132 Ill.App.3d 9, 87 Ill.Dec. 434, 477 N.E.2d 35 (1985).

4. It is important to distinguish two types of covenants not to compete. One is a covenant specifying that the seller of a business will not compete with the buyer ("covenant ancillary to the sale of a business"). The other, as in *ABC, Inc.,* specifies that an employee, upon termination of employment, will not compete with his or her former employer. The former covenant has received much more favorable treatment from the courts than the latter. As an Illinois appellate court stated,

> "If the covenant is ancillary to the sale of a business by the covenantor to the covenantee, then all the covenantee must show is that the restriction is reasonable as to time, geographical area and scope of prohibited business activity. If, however the covenant is ancillary only to an employment agreement, the covenantee must show additional special circumstances, such as a near-permanent relationship with his employer's customers and that but for his association with the employer, the former employee would not have had contact with the customers, * * * or the existence of customer lists, trade secrets or other confidential information."

Hamer Holding Group, Inc. v. Elmore, 202 Ill.App. 994, 148 Ill.Dec. 310, 560 N.E.2d 907 (1990). See also, Hamer Holding Group, Inc. v. Elmore, 244 Ill.App.3d 1069, 184 Ill.Dec. 598, 613 N.E.2d 1190 (1993). Indeed, California courts use a state statute as the basis for rejecting the rule of reason in the employment covenant context and for refusing all enforcement of a covenant that completely bars the employee from engaging in a business, trade or profession. *See* West's Ann.Cal.Bus. & Prof.Code § 16600; Bosley Medical Group v. Abramson, 161 Cal.App.3d 284, 207 Cal.Rptr. 477 (1984). Only certain partial limitations on the employee are upheld. *See e.g.,* Campell v. Board of Trustees of Leland Stanford Junior University, 817 F.2d 499 (9th Cir.1987) (if employee's profession was as a "psychologist", a covenant not to use psychological tests did not prevent completely his professional activity; if his profession was characterized "psychological tester", the covenant was void as a complete prohibition on the practice of his profession). On the other hand, another California statute validates reasonable restrictions with respect to the sale of a business or partnership. *See* West's Ann.Cal.Bus. & Prof.Code §§ 16601–16602.

Why do courts and legislatures enforce covenants ancillary to the sale of business more readily than employee covenants? Who is likely to have more bargaining strength, the seller of a business or an employee?

ENDRESS v. BROOKDALE COMMUNITY COLLEGE

Superior Court of New Jersey, Appellate Division, 1976.
144 N.J.Super. 109, 364 A.2d 1080.

Before JUDGES FRITZ, SEIDMAN and MILMED.

The opinion of the court was delivered by

SEIDMAN, J.A.D.

These consolidated appeals are from a judgment in favor of plaintiff reinstating her as a member of the faculty of defendant college with back pay and other benefits, and awarding her damages, both compensatory and punitive, plus counsel fees and costs.

I

On June 27, 1974 plaintiff Patricia H. Endress, an Assistant Professor of Journalism at Brookdale Community College, a public institution of higher learning located in Lincroft, Monmouth County, was discharged from her employment and her contract for the next academic year was rescinded [143] by resolution adopted by the college board of trustees upon the recommendation of the president, [Donald Smith].

The controversy which led to Professor Endress' dismissal and this litigation had its origin in an editorial written by her which appeared in the April 26, 1974 edition of *The Stall,* the student newspaper of which she was the faculty advisor. In substance, it accused the chairman of the board of trustees of a conflict of interest in allegedly making "a deal" whereby his nephew's company received a contract from the college for the furnishing of audio-visual equipment. * * *

In recommending the dismissal to the board of trustees the president of the college asserted as the alleged causes for such action plaintiff's violation of "both the tradition established under Board policy, and the philosophical platform and goals of the College as the same pertain to freedom of the press and student responsibility for the college newspapers," and of the "editorial prerogatives of the student editor and the student staff," in ordering and directing the editor of the newspaper "to publish certain material without his approval," and in causing the publication of "libelous matter contrary to accepted journalistic standards."

Professor Endress thereupon filed a multi-count complaint * * * [alleging] that her employment had been wrongfully terminated, * * * and that she was discharged solely by reason of her exercise of her constitutional right of "freedom of the press, association and speech."

Defendants contended generally that the discharge of Professor Endress and the rescission of her new contract were (we quote from the oral

143. Plaintiff's existing contract would have expired June 30, 1974. The rescinded contract, which would have given her tenure, was for the period July 1, 1974—June 30, 1975.

decision of the trial judge) "all due and proper actions incumbent upon them in the exercise of their duties in their respective capacities, were in no way arbitrary, capricious or conspiratorial, and that the action did not breach any of their respective contractual obligations [with plaintiff]." * * *

At the conclusion of the trial, the judge below, sitting without a jury, entered [a judgment for the plaintiff awarding her $14,121.00 as back pay for the period from July 1, 1974 through June 30, 1975; ordering specific performance of a new employment contract from July 1, 1975 through June 30, 1976; and awarding $10,000 compensatory damages and $70,000 punitive damages for the violation of her constitutional rights.]

* * *

We discern no sound basis for disturbing the holding below that just cause did not exist for dismissing plaintiff from her employment or for rescinding the 1974–1975 contract.

It is evident that at the time of plaintiff's dismissal only three days remained before the existing contract would have expired. Consequently, the substantial relief adjudged below was that plaintiff was entitled to specific performance of the new contract. Additionally, since plaintiff would thereby have acquired tenure, the trial judge also ordered the college to give plaintiff a contract for the year July 1, 1975 to June 30, 1976, with any concomitant salary increment. * * *

The college contends that as the employment contract was one which called for the rendering of personal services by plaintiff, specific performance could not be adjudged. It is settled law, of course, as the trial judge here readily acknowledged, that personal service contracts are generally not specifically enforceable affirmatively. * * *

But we held in Katz v. Gloucester Cty. College Bd. of Trustees, 125 N.J.Super. 248, 250, 310 A.2d 490 (App.Div.1973), that it was no longer open to question that a public agency may neither dismiss from employment nor withhold renewal of a contract from a nontenured public employee for a reason or reasons founded upon the exercise of a constitutionally protected right. *See* Perry v. Sindermann, 408 U.S. 593, 92 S.Ct. 2694, 33 L.Ed.2d 570 (1972); Board of Regents v. Roth, 408 U.S. 564, 92 S.Ct. 2701, 33 L.Ed.2d 548 (1972). * * * Although not clearly articulated below by the trial judge on the dismissal and reinstatement issue, it is thoroughly clear from a reading of the entire opinion that he was of the view, with support in the record, that plaintiff's employment was terminated improperly because of her exercise of First Amendment rights of free speech and press. In such case, the remedy of specific performance is appropriate. In American Ass'n of Univ. Prof. v. Bloomfield College, 136 N.J.Super. 442, 346 A.2d 615 (App.Div.1975), in which we affirmed the trial court's determination that financial exigency was not the bona fide cause for the decision to terminate tenured faculty members, appellants asserted, as they had below, that the remedy of specific performance ran counter to the line of legal precedents denying such relief in cases involving personal service contracts. We found no merit in the argument:

> We agree with the trial judge that the general rule is not inflexible and that the power of a court of equity to grant such a remedy depends upon the factual situation involved and the need for that type of remedy in a particular case. A lack of precedent, or mere novelty, is no obstacle to equitable relief which may be appropriate in a particular fact complex. In view of the uncertainty in admeasuring damages because of the indefinite duration of the contract and the importance of the status of plaintiffs in the milieu of the college teaching profession, it is evident that the remedy of damages at law would not be complete or adequate. * * * The relief granted herein is appropriate to achieve equity and justice. [136 N.J.Super. at 448, 346 A.2d at 618.]

We are entirely satisfied that the trial judge here correctly accorded plaintiff [back pay and specific performance]. * * *

That portion of paragraph 5 of the judgment which awards compensatory damages to plaintiff is modified by reducing the amount to $2500; as modified, it is affirmed.

So much of paragraph 5 of the judgment as awards [$60,000] punitive damages against the individually named trustees is reversed. The award of $10,000 punitive damages against defendant Donald H. Smith is reduced to $2500, and, as modified, that portion of the judgment is affirmed.

The matter is remanded solely for the entry of an amended judgment consistent with the foregoing.*

Notes

1. Under the traditional rule, specific performance is unavailable against an employer who breaches an employment contract. *See* Redgrave v. Boston Symphony Orchestra, Inc., 557 F.Supp. 230 (D.Mass.1983); Barndt v. County of Los Angeles, 211 Cal.App.3d 397, 259 Cal.Rptr. 372 (1989). In the latter case, plaintiff, M.D. sought specific performance of a settlement agreement that entitled plaintiff to be reinstated in the cardiology department of a county hospital. The court rejected the plaintiff's request, noting that the position required "a marked degree of cooperation and goodwill among the parties which an equitable decree cannot regulate." According to the court:

> "It has long been established that a contract to perform personal services cannot be specifically enforced, regardless of which party seeks enforcement. (Poultry Producers etc. v. Barlow (1922) 189 Cal. 278, 288, 208 P. 93; 5A Corbin, Contracts, § 1204, p. 398; Dobbs, Remedies, § 12.25, pp. 929–931.) The rule evolved because of the inherent difficulties courts would encounter in supervising the performance of uniquely personal efforts. 'A fundamental reason why courts will not order specific performance of personal services contracts is because such an order would

* *See also* Findeisen v. North East Indep. School Dist., 749 F.2d 234 (5th Cir.1984), *cert. denied* 105 S.Ct. 2657 (1985) (tenured teacher entitled to pre-termination hearing under procedural due process clause); Henley v. Fingal Public School Dist. # 54, 219 N.W.2d 106 (N.D.1974) (public school teacher claiming wrongful non-renewal entitled to writ of mandamus to compel school district to provide statutory rights). *But see* Schauer v. Jamestown College, 323 N.W.2d 114 (N.D. 1982) (teacher employed by private institution not entitled to a writ of mandate compelling reinstatement). *See generally* Linzer, On the Amorality of Contract Remedies—Efficiency, Equity, and the Second *Restatement,* 81 Colum.L.Rev. 111, 128 (1981) (approving *Endress*).

impose on the courts a difficult job of enforcement and of passing judgment upon the quality of performance. [Citations.] As Corbin observes in his treatise, "An artist does not work well under compulsion, and the court might find it difficult to pass judgment upon the performance rendered." (5A Corbin, *supra,* § 1204, p. 400.)' (Motown Record Corp. v. Brockert (1984) 160 Cal.App.3d 123, 137, 207 Cal.Rptr. 574.) During the Civil War era, there emerged a more compelling reason for not directing the performance of personal services: the Thirteenth Amendment's prohibition of involuntary servitude. (Beverly Glen Music, Inc. v. Warner Communications, Inc. (1986) 178 Cal.App.3d 1142, 1144, 224 Cal.Rptr. 260.) More importantly, however, the common law disfavored specific performance to avoid the friction and social costs that often result when employer and employee are reunited in a relationship that has already failed. (*See* Poultry Producers etc. v. Barlow, *supra,* 189 Cal. at p. 288, 208 P. 93; Rest.2d, Contracts, § 367 comm. (a) at p. 192.) This rationale is particularly applicable where the services to be rendered require mutual confidence among the parties and involve the exercise of discretionary authority. (*See* Rautenberg v. Westland (1964) 227 Cal.App.2d 566, 573, 38 Cal.Rptr. 797.)

* * *

"Whatever remedy the plaintiff in our case may have for recovery of damages for the claimed breach of contract by the county, we think it clear that the settlement agreement contemplates the rendition of personal services which cannot be enforced by an action for specific performance. The public policy against compelling an employer to retain the services of an employee after disputes have arisen and loyalty and confidence have been eroded is particularly applicable here. * * * In light of the personality conflict which plaintiff concedes exists between himself and the chief of the cardiology section, the remedy of specific performance is simply not available to enforce the terms of the settlement agreement."

Id. at 211 Cal.App.3d 403–04, 259 Cal.Rptr. 376–77. Is the Thirteenth Amendment relevant when an *employee* is seeking specific performance? Is involuntary servitude imposed on the employer by awarding such relief?

2. As *Endress* illustrates, when an employer violates a statute or the constitution, courts often reinstate the wrongfully discharged employee and, in the process, award the substantial equivalent of specific performance. *See e.g.,* Brown v. Trustees of Boston University, 891 F.2d 337 (1st Cir.1989) (in reinstating a professor and ordering the grant of tenure, the court noted that "once a university has been found to have impermissively discriminated [because of gender] in making a tenure decision, as here, the University's prerogative to make tenure decisions must be subordinated to the goals embodied in Title VII."); Jeffreys v. My Friend's Place, Inc., 719 F.Supp. 639 (M.D.Tenn. 1989) (employee discharged after reporting for jury duty); Allen v. Autauga County Board of Education, 685 F.2d 1302 (11th Cir.1982) (employee's First Amendment rights violated). If reinstatement is increasingly common in the statutory or constitutional context, why not grant specific performance against all employers who breach an employment contract?

3. In Owens v. Church, 675 S.W.2d 178 (Tenn.App.1984), the court ordered specific performance to the providers of services under a contract whereby the defendant agreed to will all of her property to the plaintiffs,

provided they cared for her for the balance of her life. The court impressed a constructive trust upon the defendant's assets, subject to her right to draw upon them for her reasonable maintenance and care during the remainder of her life.

4. In Crowe v. De Gioia, 203 N.J.Super. 22, 495 A.2d 889 (1985), the court ordered specific performance of an express, oral "palimony" contract whereby the plaintiff agreed to serve as the defendant's companion and housekeeper in exchange for his agreement to support her for the rest of his life and to deed his house to her in the event of his death or the termination of their relationship. After cohabiting with the plaintiff for 20 years, the defendant ended the relationship. In addition to ordering the conveyance of title to the house, the court also awarded the plaintiff the present value of yearly support until the end of her life expectancy (she was 12 years older than the defendant), a lump sum award of $155,642.63, net of taxes.

5. Two commentators who have engaged in economic analysis have reached the conclusion that specific performance should be more readily available as a remedy for breach of contract. Professor Schwartz, like Professor Fiss, recommends that the "inadequacy of legal remedy" doctrine be abolished:

> "The compensation goal of contract law can be achieved by requiring the promisor to pay damages or by requiring the promisor to render the promised performance. Under current law, a promisee is entitled to a damage award as of right but the court retains discretion to decide whether specific performance should be granted. Because specific performance is a superior method for achieving the compensation goal, promisees should be able to obtain specific performance on request. An expanded specific performance remedy would not generate greater transaction costs than the damage remedy involves, nor would its increased use interfere unduly with the liberty interests of promisors. Making specific performance freely available also would eliminate the uncertainty costs of planning and litigation created by the difficulty of predicting whether the remedy will be available. In addition, this reform would reduce the negotiation costs incurred by parties in attempting to create forms of contractual specific performance such as liquidated damage clauses.[96] Further, defenses to requests for specific performance that rest on unfairness of contract terms or prices and that differ from the defenses in actions at law should be

96. This conclusion is similar to the conclusion Professor Fiss reached with regard to injunctions:

> I will urge that the traditional view give way to a nonhierarchical conception of remedies, where there is no presumptive remedy, but rather a context-specific evaluation of the advantages and disadvantages of each form of relief. It should not be necessary to establish the inadequacy of alternative remedies before the injunction becomes available; at the same time, the superiority of the injunction should not be presumed, but rather dependent on an analysis of its technical advantages and the system of power allocation that it implies.
>
> My plea is not confined to the civil rights injunction, but should extend to all types of injunctions.

O. Fiss, The Civil Rights Injunction 6 (1978). Contract remedies also should be "nonhierarchical," so that promisees need not "establish the inadequacy of alternative remedies before" specific performance is available. *Id.* This Article's argument goes further toward authorizing equitable relief than does Professor Fiss's analysis, both because of the clear superiority of specific performance over damages in achieving the compensation goal and because "a context-specific evaluation of the advantages and disadvantages of each form of relief," *id.,* shows that this superiority can usually be purchased at relatively slight, if any, net cost.

eliminated; the grounds for denial of specific performance should be the same as those that now will bar a damage suit. Finally, the defense based on difficulty of supervision should be greatly restricted. If the law is committed to putting disappointed promisees in as good a position as they would have been had their promisors performed, specific performance should be available as a matter of course to those promisees who request it."

Schwartz, The Case for Specific Performance, 89 Yale L.J. 271, 305–06 (1979).* Professor Ulen contends that specific performance should be the routine remedy for breach of contract:

"The reasons for this conclusion may be briefly summarized here. First, if contractual parties are on notice that valid promises will be specifically enforced, they will more efficiently exchange reciprocal promises at formation time. In particular, they will have a stronger incentive than currently exists under the dominant legal remedy to allocate efficiently the risks of loss from breach rather than leaving that task, in whole or in part, to the court or to post-breach negotiations conducted under the threat of a potentially inefficient legal remedy. Second, and perhaps most importantly, specific performance offers the most efficient mechanism for protecting subjective values attached to performance. Thus, it promotes contract breach only if it is efficient, that is, if someone will be better off and no one will be worse off because of the breach. In this regard, specific performance and an expansive enforcement of stipulated remedies constitute integral and inseparable parts of a unified theory of efficient contract remedies. Third, if specific performance were the routine remedy, the post-breach costs of adjusting a contract in order to move the promise to the highest-valuing user would be lower than under the most efficient legal remedy. The central reason for this is that under specific performance the costs of determining various parties' valuation of performance are borne by those parties in voluntary negotiations. This means that the costs of determining willingness-to-pay are borne by those most efficiently placed to determine that amount. Finally, because the costs of ascertaining any subjective values of the innocent party through evidence presented to a court are so high and because, therefore, the possibility of undercompensating the innocent party through a damage remedy is high, specific performance is far less likely to be undercompensatory and far more likely to protect the breachee's subjective valuation than is any other judicially imposed contract remedy."

Ulen, The Efficiency of Specific Performance: Toward A Unified Theory of Contract Remedies, 83 Mich.L.Rev. 341, 365–66 (1984).

JOHNSON v. CALVERT

Supreme Court of California, 1993.
5 Cal.4th 84, 19 Cal.Rptr.2d 494, 851 P.2d 776.

PANELLI, JUSTICE.

Mark and Crispina Calvert are a married couple who desired to have a child. Crispina was forced to undergo a hysterectomy in 1984. Her

* Reprinted by permission of The Yale Law Journal Company and Fred B. Rothman & Company. From The Yale Law Journal, 89 Yale L.J. 271, 305–06 (1979).

ovaries remained capable of producing eggs, however, and the couple eventually considered surrogacy. In 1989 Anna Johnson heard about Crispina's plight from a coworker and offered to serve as a surrogate for the Calverts.

On January 15, 1990, Mark, Crispina, and Anna signed a contract providing that an embryo created by the sperm of Mark and the egg of Crispina would be implanted in Anna and the child born would be taken into Mark and Crispina's home "as their child." Anna agreed she would relinquish "all parental rights" to the child in favor of Mark and Crispina. In return, Mark and Crispina would pay Anna $10,000 in a series of installments, the last to be paid six weeks after the child's birth. Mark and Crispina were also to pay for a $200,000 life insurance policy on Anna's life.[4]

The zygote was implanted on January 19, 1990. Less than a month later, an ultrasound test confirmed Anna was pregnant.

Unfortunately, relations deteriorated between the two sides. Mark learned that Anna had not disclosed she had suffered several stillbirths and miscarriages. Anna felt Mark and Crispina did not do enough to obtain the required insurance policy. She also felt abandoned during an onset of premature labor in June.

In July 1990, Anna sent Mark and Crispina a letter demanding the balance of the payments due her or else she would refuse to give up the child. The following month, Mark and Crispina responded with a lawsuit, seeking a declaration they were the legal parents of the unborn child. Anna filed her own action to be declared the mother of the child, and the two cases were eventually consolidated. The parties agreed to an independent guardian ad litem for the purposes of the suit.

The child was born on September 19, 1990, and blood samples were obtained from both Anna and the child for analysis. The blood test results excluded Anna as the genetic mother. The parties agreed to a court order providing that the child would remain with Mark and Crispina on a temporary basis with visits by Anna.

At trial in October 1990, the parties stipulated that Mark and Crispina were the child's genetic parents. After hearing evidence and arguments, the trial court ruled that Mark and Crispina were the child's "genetic, biological and natural" father and mother, that Anna had no "parental" rights to the child, and that the surrogacy contract was legal and enforceable against Anna's claims. The court also terminated the order allowing visitation. Anna appealed from the trial court's judgment. The Court of Appeal for the Fourth District, Division Three, affirmed. We granted review.

DISCUSSION

Determining Maternity Under the Uniform Parentage Act

The Uniform Parentage Act (the Act) was part of a package of legislation introduced in 1975 as Senate Bill No. 347. The legislation's

4. At the time of the agreement, Anna already had a daughter, Erica, born in 1987.

purpose was to eliminate the legal distinction between legitimate and illegitimate children.

* * *

Civil Code sections 7001 and 7002 replace the distinction between legitimate and illegitimate children with the concept of the "parent and child relationship." The "parent and child relationship" means "the legal relationship existing between a child and his natural or adoptive parents incident to which the law confers or imposes rights, privileges, duties, and obligations. It includes the mother and child relationship and the father and child relationship." (Civ.Code, § 7001.) "The parent and child relationship extends equally to every child and to every parent, regardless of the marital status of the parents." (Civ.Code, § 7002.) The "parent and child relationship" is thus a legal relationship encompassing two kinds of parents, "natural" and "adoptive."

Passage of the Act clearly was not motivated by the need to resolve surrogacy disputes, which were virtually unknown in 1975. Yet it facially applies to any parentage determination, including the rare case in which a child's maternity is in issue. We are invited to disregard the Act and decide this case according to other criteria, including constitutional precepts and our sense of the demands of public policy. We feel constrained, however, to decline the invitation. Not uncommonly, courts must construe statutes in factual settings not contemplated by the enacting legislature. * * *

[[T]he parties'] contentions are readily summarized. Anna, of course, predicates her claim of maternity on the fact that she gave birth to the child. The Calverts contend that Crispina's genetic relationship to the child establishes that she is his mother. Counsel for the minor joins in that contention and argues, in addition, that several of the presumptions created by the Act dictate the same result. As will appear, we conclude that presentation of blood test evidence is one means of establishing maternity, as is proof of having given birth, but that the presumptions cited by minor's counsel do not apply to this case.

* * *

Disregarding the presumptions of paternity that have no application to this case, then, we are left with the undisputed evidence that Anna, not Crispina, gave birth to the child and that Crispina, not Anna, is genetically related to him. Both women thus have adduced evidence of a mother and child relationship as contemplated by the Act. (Civ.Code, §§ 7003, subd. (1), 7004, subd. (a), 7015; Evid.Code, §§ 621, 892.) Yet for any child California law recognizes only one natural mother, despite advances in reproductive technology rendering a different outcome biologically possible.

* * *

Because two women each have presented acceptable proof of maternity, we do not believe this case can be decided without enquiring into the parties' intentions as manifested in the surrogacy agreement. Mark and Crispina are a couple who desired to have a child of their own genetic stock but are physically unable to do so without the help of reproductive technology. They affirmatively intended the birth of the child, and took the steps necessary to effect in vitro fertilization. But for their acted-on intention, the child would not exist. Anna agreed to facilitate the procreation of Mark's and Crispina's child. The parties' aim was to bring Mark's and Crispina's child into the world, not for Mark and Crispina to donate a zygote to Anna. Crispina from the outset intended to be the child's mother. Although the gestative function Anna performed was necessary to bring about the child's birth, it is safe to say that Anna would not have been given the opportunity to gestate or deliver the child had she, prior to implantation of the zygote, manifested her own intent to be the child's mother. No reason appears why Anna's later change of heart should vitiate the determination that Crispina is the child's natural mother.

We conclude that although the Act recognizes both genetic consanguinity and giving birth as means of establishing a mother and child relationship, when the two means do not coincide in one woman, she who intended to procreate the child—that is, she who intended to bring about the birth of a child that she intended to raise as her own—is the natural mother under California law.[10]

Our conclusion finds support in the writings of several legal commentators. (See Hill, What Does It Mean to Be a "Parent"? The Claims of Biology As the Basis for Parental Rights, supra, 66 N.Y.U.L.Rev. 353; Shultz, Reproductive Technology and Intent–Based Parenthood: An Opportunity for Gender Neutrality (1990) Wis.L.Rev. 297 [Shultz]; Note, Redefining Mother: A Legal Matrix for New Reproductive Technologies (1986) 96 Yale L.J. 187, 197–202 [note].) Professor Hill, arguing that the genetic relationship per se should not be accorded priority in the determination of the parent-child relationship in the surrogacy context, notes that "while all of the players in the procreative arrangement are necessary in bringing a child into the world, the child would not have been born but for the efforts of the intended parents * * *. [P] * * * [T]he intended parents are the first cause, or the prime movers, of the procreative relationship." (Hill, op. cit. supra, at p. 415, emphasis in original.)

Similarly, Professor Shultz observes that recent developments in the field of reproductive technology "dramatically extend affirmative intention-

10. Thus, under our analysis, in a true "egg donation" situation, where a woman gestates and gives birth to a child formed from the egg of another woman with the intent to raise the child as her own, the birth mother is the natural mother under California law. The dissent would decide parentage based on the best interests of the child. Such an approach raises the repugnant specter of governmental interference in matters implicating our most fundamental notions of privacy, and confuses concepts of parentage and custody. Logically, the determination of parentage must precede, and should not be dictated by, eventual custody decisions. The implicit assumption of the dissent is that a recognition of the genetic intending mother as the natural mother may sometimes harm the child. This assumption overlooks California's dependency laws, which are designed to protect all children irrespective of the manner of birth or conception. Moreover, the best interest standard poorly serves the child in the present situation: it fosters instability during litigation and, if applied to recognize the gestator as natural mother, results in a split of custody between the natural father and the gestator, an outcome not likely to benefit the child. Further, it may be argued that, by voluntarily contracting away any rights to the child, the gestator has, in effect, conceded the best interest of the child is not with her.

ality * * *. Steps can be taken to bring into being a child who would not otherwise have existed." (Shultz, op. cit. supra, p. 309.) "Within the context of artificial reproductive techniques," Professor Shultz argues, "intentions that are voluntarily chosen, deliberate, express and bargained-for ought presumptively to determine legal parenthood." (Id., at p. 323, fn. omitted.)

Another commentator has cogently suggested, in connection with reproductive technology, that "[t]he mental concept of the child is a controlling factor of its creation, and the originators of that concept merit full credit as conceivers. The mental concept must be recognized as independently valuable; it creates expectations in the initiating parents of a child, and it creates expectations in society for adequate performance on the part of the initiators as parents of the child." (Note, op. cit. supra, 96 Yale L.J. at p. 196.)

* * *

In deciding the issue of maternity under the Act we have felt free to take into account the parties' intentions, as expressed in the surrogacy contract, because in our view the agreement is not, on its face, inconsistent with public policy.

Preliminarily, Mark and Crispina urge us to interpret the Legislature's 1992 passage of a bill that would have regulated surrogacy as an expression of this state's public policy despite the fact that Governor Wilson's veto prevented the bill from becoming law. Senate Bill No. 937 contained a finding that surrogate contracts are not against sound public and social policy. (Sen.Bill No. 937 (1991–1992 Reg.Sess.).) Had Senate Bill No. 937 become law, there would be no room for argument to the contrary. The veto, however, raises a question whether the legislative declaration truly expresses California's public policy.

* * *

Anna urges that surrogacy contracts violate several social policies. Relying on her contention that she is the child's legal, natural mother, she cites the public policy embodied in Penal Code section 273, prohibiting the payment for consent to adoption of a child. She argues further that the policies underlying the adoption laws of this state are violated by the surrogacy contract because it in effect constitutes a prebirth waiver of her parental rights.

We disagree. Gestational surrogacy differs in crucial respects from adoption and so is not subject to the adoption statutes. The parties voluntarily agreed to participate in in vitro fertilization and related medical procedures before the child was conceived; at the time when Anna entered into the contract, therefore, she was not vulnerable to financial inducements to part with her own expected offspring. As discussed above, Anna was not the genetic mother of the child. The payments to Anna under the contract were meant to compensate her for her services in gestating the fetus and undergoing labor, rather than for giving up "parental" rights to the child. Payments were due both during the pregnancy and after the child's birth. We are, accordingly, unpersuaded that the contract used in this case violates the public policies embodied in Penal Code section 273 and the adoption statutes. For the same reasons, we conclude these contracts do not implicate the policies underlying the statutes governing termination of parental rights. (See Welf. & Inst.Code, § 202.)

It has been suggested that gestational surrogacy may run afoul of prohibitions on involuntary servitude. (See U.S. Const., Amend. XIII; Cal.Const., art. I, § 6; Pen.Code, § 181.) Involuntary servitude has been recognized in cases of criminal punishment for refusal to work. (Pollock v. Williams (1944) 322 U.S. 4, 18, 64 S.Ct. 792, 799, 88 L.Ed. 1095, 1104; see, generally, 7 Witkin, Summary of Cal.Law (9th ed. 1988) Constitutional Law, §§ 411–414, pp. 591–596.) We see no potential for that evil in the contract at issue here, and extrinsic evidence of coercion or duress is utterly lacking. We note that although at one point the contract purports to give Mark and Crispina the sole right to determine whether to abort the pregnancy, at another point it acknowledges: "All parties understand that a pregnant woman has the absolute right to abort or not abort any fetus she is carrying. Any promise to the contrary is unenforceable." We therefore need not determine the validity of a surrogacy contract purporting to deprive the gestator of her freedom to terminate the pregnancy.

Finally, Anna and some commentators have expressed concern that surrogacy contracts tend to exploit or dehumanize women, especially women of lower economic status. Anna's objections center around the psychological harm she asserts may result from the gestator's relinquishing the child to whom she has given birth. Some have also cautioned that the practice of surrogacy may encourage society to view children as commodities, subject to trade at their parents' will.

We are all too aware that the proper forum for resolution of this issue is the Legislature, where empirical data, largely lacking from this record, can be studied and rules of general applicability developed. However, in light of our responsibility to decide this case, we have considered as best we can its possible consequences.

We are unpersuaded that gestational surrogacy arrangements are so likely to cause the untoward results Anna cites as to demand their invalidation on public policy grounds. Although common sense suggests that women of lesser means serve as surrogate mothers more often than do wealthy women, there has been no proof that surrogacy contracts exploit poor women to any greater degree than economic necessity in general exploits them by inducing them to accept lower-paid or otherwise undesirable employment. We are likewise unpersuaded by the claim that surrogacy will foster the attitude that children are mere commodities; no evidence is offered to support it. The limited data available seem to reflect an absence of significant adverse effects of surrogacy on all participants.

The argument that a woman cannot knowingly and intelligently agree to gestate and deliver a baby for intending parents carries overtones of the reasoning that for centuries prevented women from attaining equal economic rights and professional status under the law. To resurrect this view is both to foreclose a personal and economic choice on the part of the surrogate mother, and to deny intending parents what may be their only means of procreating a child of their own genetic stock. Certainly in the present case it cannot seriously be argued that Anna, a licensed vocational nurse who had done well in school and who had previously borne a child, lacked the intellectual wherewithal or life experience necessary to make an informed decision to enter into the surrogacy contract.

Constitutionality of the Determination That Anna Johnson Is Not the Natural Mother

Anna argues at length that her right to the continued companionship of the child is protected under the federal Constitution.

* * *

Anna relies mainly on theories of substantive due process, privacy, and procreative freedom, citing a number of decisions recognizing the fundamental liberty interest of natural parents in the custody and care of their children. (See, e.g., Santosky v. Kramer (1982) 455 U.S. 745, 768, 102 S.Ct. 1388, 1402, 71 L.Ed.2d 599; Lassiter v. Department of Social Services (1981) 452 U.S. 18, 27, 101 S.Ct. 2153, 2159, 68 L.Ed.2d 640; Smith v. Organization of Foster Families (1977) 431 U.S. 816, 842, 97 S.Ct. 2094, 2108, 53 L.Ed.2d 14; Stanley v. Illinois (1972) 405 U.S. 645, 651, 92 S.Ct. 1208, 1212, 31 L.Ed.2d 551.) Most of the cases Anna cites deal with the rights of unwed fathers in the face of attempts to terminate their parental relationship to their children. (See, e.g., Stanley v. Illinois, supra, 405 U.S. at pp. 658–659, 92 S.Ct. at pp. 1216–1217; Quilloin v. Walcott (1978) 434 U.S. 246, 247–248, 98 S.Ct. 549, 550–551, 54 L.Ed.2d 511; Caban v. Mohammed (1979) 441 U.S. 380, 99 S.Ct. 1760, 60 L.Ed.2d 297; Lehr v. Robertson (1983) 463 U.S. 248, 103 S.Ct. 2985, 77 L.Ed.2d 614.) These cases do not support recognition of parental rights for a gestational surrogate. Although Anna quotes language stressing the primacy of a developed parent-child relationship in assessing unwed fathers' rights (see Lehr v. Robertson, supra, 463 U.S. at pp. 260–262, 103 S.Ct. at pp. 2992–2994), certain language in the cases reinforces the importance of genetic parents' rights. (Lehr v. Robertson, supra, 463 U.S. at p. 262, 103 S.Ct. at p. 2993 ["The significance of the biological connection is that it offers the natural father an opportunity that no other male possesses to develop a relationship with his offspring. If he grasps that opportunity and accepts some measure of responsibility for the child's future, he may enjoy the blessings of the parent-child relationship and make uniquely valuable contributions to the child's development."]; see also Adoption of Kelsey S. (1992) 1 Cal.4th 816, 838, 4 Cal.Rptr.2d 615, 823 P.2d 1216 ["The biological connection between father and child is unique and worthy of constitutional protection if the father grasps the opportunity to develop that biological connection into a full and enduring relationship."].)

Anna's argument depends on a prior determination that she is indeed the child's mother. Since Crispina is the child's mother under California law because she, not Anna, provided the ovum for the in vitro fertilization procedure, intending to raise the child as her own, it follows that any constitutional interests Anna possesses in this situation are something less than those of a mother. As counsel for the minor points out, the issue in this case is not whether Anna's asserted rights as a natural mother were unconstitutionally violated, but rather whether the determination that she is not the legal natural mother at all is constitutional.

Anna relies principally on the decision of the United States Supreme Court in Michael H. v. Gerald D. (1989) 491 U.S. 110, 109 S.Ct. 2333, 105 L.Ed.2d 91, to support her claim to a constitutionally protected liberty interest in the companionship of the child, based on her status as "birth mother." In that case, a plurality of the court held that a state may constitutionally deny a man parental rights with respect to a child he fathered during a liaison with the wife of another man, since it is the marital family that traditionally has been accorded a protected liberty interest, as reflected in the historic presumption of legitimacy of a child born into such a family. (491 U.S. at pp. 124–125, 109 S.Ct. at pp. 2342–2343 (plur. opn. by Scalia, J.).) The reasoning of the plurality in Michael H. does not assist Anna. Society has not traditionally protected the right of a woman who gestates and delivers a baby pursuant to an agreement with a couple who supply the zygote from which the baby develops and who intend to raise the child as their own; such arrangements are of too recent an origin to claim the protection of tradition. To the extent that tradition has a bearing on the present case, we believe it supports the claim of the couple who exercise their right to procreate in order to form a family of their own, albeit through novel medical procedures.

Moreover, if we were to conclude that Anna enjoys some sort of liberty interest in the companionship of the child, then the liberty interests of Mark and Crispina, the child's natural parents, in their procreative choices and their relationship with the child would perforce be infringed. Any parental rights Anna might successfully assert could come only at Crispina's expense. As we have seen, Anna has no parental rights to the child under California law, and she fails to persuade us that sufficiently strong policy reasons exist to accord her a protected liberty interest in the companionship of the child when such an interest would necessarily detract from or impair the parental bond enjoyed by Mark and Crispina.

Amicus curiae ACLU urges that Anna's right of privacy, embodied in the California Constitution (Cal.Const., art. I, § 1), requires recognition and protection of her status as "birth mother." We cannot agree. Certainly it is true that our state Constitution has been construed to provide California citizens with privacy protections encompassing procreative decisionmaking—broader, indeed, than those recognized by the federal Constitution. (Compare Committee to Defend Reproductive Rights v. Myers (1981) 29 Cal.3d 252, 263, 172 Cal.Rptr. 866, 625 P.2d 779 with Harris v. McRae (1980) 448 U.S. 297, 315–318, 100 S.Ct. 2671, 65 L.Ed.2d 784 [reaching opposing results on the question of whether state and federal Constitutions, respectively, permit legislative denial of funding for abortions for indigent women].) However, amicus curiae fails to articulate persuasively how Anna's claim falls within even the broad parameters of the state right of privacy. Amicus curiae appears to assume that the choice to gestate and deliver a baby to its genetic parents pursuant to a surrogacy agreement is the equivalent, in constitutional weight, of the decision whether to bear a child of one's own. We disagree. A woman who enters into a gestational surrogacy arrangement is not exercising her own right to make procreative choices; she is agreeing to provide a necessary and profoundly important service without (by definition) any expectation that she will raise the resulting child as her own.

The judgment of the Court of Appeal is affirmed.

LUCAS, C.J., and MOSK, BAXTER and GEORGE, JJ., concur.

ARABIAN, JUSTICE, concurring to opinion by PANELLI, JUSTICE.

I concur in the decision to find under the Uniform Parentage Act that Crispina Calvert is the natural mother of the child she at all times intended to parent and raise as her own with her husband Mark, the child's natural father. That determination answers the question on which this court granted review, and in my view sufficiently resolves the controversy between the parties to warrant no further analysis. I therefore decline to subscribe to the dictum in which the majority find surrogacy contracts "not * * * inconsistent with public policy." (Maj. opn., ante, pp. 501–503 of 19 Cal.Rptr.2d, pp. 783–785 of 851 P.2d.)

Surrogacy contracts touch upon one of the, if not the most, sensitive subjects of human endeavor. Not only does the birth of a new generation perpetuate our species, it allows every parent to contribute, both genetically and socially, to our collective understanding of what it means to be human. Every child also offers the opportunity of a unique lifetime relationship, potentially more satisfying and fulfilling than any other pursuit. (See Adoption of Kelsey S. (1992) 1 Cal.4th 816, 837, 4 Cal. Rptr.2d 615, 823 P.2d 1216.)

The multiplicity of considerations at issue in a surrogacy situation plainly transcend traditional principles of contract law and require careful, nonadversarial analysis. For this reason, I do not think it wise for this court to venture unnecessarily into terrain more appropriately cleared by the Legislature in the first instance. In this regard, the Florida Supreme Court made the following pertinent observations; although the factual context obviously differs, socially and morally it compares in the most profound respects: "Because the issue with all its ramifications is fraught with complexity and encompasses the interests of the law, both civil and criminal, medical ethics and social morality, it is not one which is well-suited for resolution in an adversary judicial proceeding. It is the type [of] issue which is more suitably addressed in the legislative forum, where fact finding can be less confined and the viewpoints of all interest institutions and disciplines can be presented and synthesized. In this manner only can the subject be dealt with comprehensively and the interests of all institutions and individuals be properly accommodated." (Satz v. Perlmutter (Fla.1980) 379 So.2d 359, 360, affg. (Fla.Dist.Ct.App.1978) 362 So.2d 160.) The New Jersey Supreme Court echoed similar cautionary tones in Matter of Conroy (1985) 98 N.J. 321, 486 A.2d 1209: "As an elected body, the Legislature is better able than any other single institution to reflect the social values at stake. In addition, it has the resources and ability to synthesize vast quantities of data and opinions from a variety of fields and to formulate general guidelines that may be applicable to a broad range of situations." (Id., 486 A.2d at pp. 1220–1221; accord, Matter of Guardianship of Hamlin (1984) 102 Wash.2d 810, 821–822, 689 P.2d 1372, 1378–1379.)

* * *

KENNARD, JUSTICE, dissenting.

When a woman who wants to have a child provides her fertilized ovum to another woman who carries it through pregnancy and gives birth to a child, who is the child's legal mother? Unlike the majority, I do not agree that the determinative consideration should be the intent to have the child that originated with the woman who contributed the ovum. In my view, the woman who provided the fertilized ovum and the woman who gave birth to the child both have substantial claims to legal motherhood. Pregnancy entails a unique commitment, both psychological and emotional, to an unborn child. No less substantial, however, is the contribution of the woman from whose egg the child developed and without whose desire the child would not exist.

For each child, California law accords the legal rights and responsibilities of parenthood to only one "natural mother." When, as here, the female reproductive role is divided between two women, California law requires courts to make a decision as to which woman is the child's natural mother, but provides no standards by which to make that decision. The majority's resort to "intent" to break the "tie" between the genetic and gestational mothers is unsupported by statute, and in the absence of appropriate protections in the law to guard against abuse of surrogacy arrangements, it is ill-advised. To determine who is the legal mother of a child born of a gestational surrogacy arrangement, I would apply the standard most protective of child welfare—the best interests of the child.

* * *

The determination of a question of parental rights to a child born of a surrogacy arrangement was before the New Jersey Supreme Court in Matter of Baby M. (1988) 109 N.J. 396, 537 A.2d 1227, a case that received worldwide attention. But in the surrogacy arrangement at issue there the woman who gave birth to the child, Marybeth Whitehead, had been impregnated by artificial insemination with the sperm of the intending father, William Stern. Whitehead thus provided the genetic material and carried the fetus to term. This case is different, because here those two aspects of the female role in reproduction were divided between two women. This process is known as "gestational" surrogacy, to distinguish it from the surrogacy arrangement involved in Baby M.[1]

1. The terms "surrogacy" and "surrogate" have been criticized as being inaccurate, particularly when applied to the type of arrangement involved in Baby M., in which the child a woman bears, intending to relinquish the child at birth, was formed from her own egg. (See Capron & Radin, Choosing Family Law Over Contract Law as a Paradigm for Surrogate Motherhood, in Surrogate Motherhood (Gostin edit. 1990) p. 72, fn. 2; Annas, Fairy Tales Surrogate Mothers Tell, in Surrogate Motherhood, supra, at p. 46 [suggesting that the phrase "surrogate mother" derives from Harlow's monkey studies, in which the responses of newborn monkeys were tested by isolating them in cages with cloth or wire "surrogate mothers."].) Because "gestational surrogacy" is now widely used to describe the situation in which one woman agrees to be impregnated with an embryo formed from another woman's ferti-

* * *

The ethical, moral and legal implications of using gestational surrogacy for human reproduction have engendered substantial debate. A review of the scholarly literature that addresses gestational surrogacy reveals little consensus on the desirability of surrogacy arrangements, particularly those involving paid surrogacy, or on how best to decide questions of the parentage of children born of such arrangements.

Surrogacy proponents generally contend that gestational surrogacy, like the other reproductive technologies that extend the ability to procreate to persons who might not otherwise be able to have children, enhances "individual freedom, fulfillment and responsibility." (Shultz, Reproductive Technology, supra, 1990 Wis.L.Rev. 297, 303.) Under this view, women capable of bearing children should be allowed to freely agree to be paid to do so by infertile couples desiring to form a family. (Shalev, Birth Power: The Case for Surrogacy, supra, at p. 145 [arguing for a "free market in reproduction" in which the "reproducing woman" operates as an "autonomous moral and economic agent"]; see also Posner, Economic Analysis of Law (3 ed. 1986) p. 139; Landes & Posner, The Economics of the Baby Shortage (1978) 7 J. Legal Stud. 323 [proposing a "market in babies"].) The "surrogate mother" is expected "to weigh the prospective investment in her birthing labor" before entering into the arrangement, and if her "autonomous reproductive decision" is "voluntary," she should be held responsible for it so as "to fulfill the expectations of the other parties * * *." (Shalev, Birth Power: The Case for Surrogacy, supra, at p. 96.)

One constitutional law scholar argues that the use of techniques such as gestational surrogacy is constitutionally protected and should be restricted only on a showing of a compelling state interest. (Robertson, Procreative Liberty and the Control of Conception, Pregnancy, and Childbirth (1983) 69 Va.L.Rev. 405; Robertson, Procreative Liberty and the State's Burden of Proof in Regulating Noncoital Reproduction, in Surrogate Motherhood, supra, pp. 24–26, 35; Robertson, Embryos, Families, and Procreative Liberty: The Legal Structure of the New Reproduction (1986) 59 So.Cal.L.Rev. 939, 960.) Professor Robertson reasons that procreation is itself protected under decisions of the United States Supreme Court that affirm the basic civil right to marry and raise children. (Robertson, Procreative Liberty and the Control of Conception, Pregnancy, and Childbirth, supra, 69 Va.L.Rev. at p. 414, fns. 22, 23, citing Meyer v. Nebraska (1923) 262 U.S. 390, 399, 43 S.Ct. 625, 626, 67 L.Ed. 1042 ["right * * * to marry, establish a home and bring up children" protected by the Fourteenth Amendment]; Skinner v. Oklahoma (1942) 316 U.S. 535, 541, 62 S.Ct. 1110, 1113, 86 L.Ed. 1655 [describing marriage and procreation as basic human civil rights]; Stanley v. Illinois (1972) 405 U.S. 645, 651, 92 S.Ct. 1208, 1212, 31 L.Ed.2d 551 [emphasizing the importance of the rights "to conceive and raise one's children"].) From this premise, he argues that the right to procreate should extend to persons who cannot conceive or bear children. (Robertson, Procreative Liberty and the Control of Concep-

lized egg, I use the phrase throughout this opinion and occasionally also refer to the woman who gestates the fetus as the "surrogate."

tion, Pregnancy and Childbirth, supra, 69 Va.L.Rev. at p. 411 ["Sterility bars one from conceiving or bearing only to the extent that medicine or society cannot overcome the particular cause of infertility"]; Robertson, Embryos, Families, and Procreative Liberty: The Legal Structure of the New Reproduction, supra, 59 So.Cal.L.Rev. at p. 960 ["The use of noncoital techniques * * * should * * * also be protected."].)

Professor Robertson's thesis of broad application of the right of privacy for all procreational techniques has been questioned, however, in light of recent United States Supreme Court jurisprudence. See Medical Technology, supra, 103 Harv.L.Rev. 1519, 1530, citing Michael H. v. Gerald D. (1989) 491 U.S. 110, 109 S.Ct. 2333, 105 L.Ed.2d 91 as evidence of the high court's reluctance "to extend the right of privacy to new relationships and activities" that the court has not perceived to merit "traditional protection."

Surrogacy critics, however, maintain that the payment of money for the gestation and relinquishment of a child threatens the economic exploitation of poor women who may be induced to engage in commercial surrogacy arrangements out of financial need. (Capron & Radin, Choosing Family Law Over Contract Law as a Paradigm for Surrogate Motherhood, in Surrogate Motherhood, supra, p. 62.) Some fear the development of a "breeder" class of poor women who will be regularly employed to bear children for the economically advantaged. (See Women and Children Used in Systems of Surrogacy: Position Statement of the Institute on Women and Technology, in Surrogate Motherhood, supra, at p. 322; and Corea, Junk Liberty, testimony before Cal. Assem. Judiciary Com., April 5, 1988, in Surrogate Motherhood, supra, at pp. 325, 335.) Others suggest that women who enter into surrogacy arrangements may underestimate the psychological impact of relinquishing a child they have nurtured in their bodies for nine months. (See Macklin, Artificial Means of Reproduction and Our Understanding of the Family, supra, 21 Hastings Center Rep. 5, 10.)

Gestational surrogacy is also said to be "dehumanizing" (Capron & Radin, Choosing Family Law Over Contract Law as a Paradigm for Surrogate Motherhood, in Surrogate Motherhood, supra, at p. 62) and to "commodify" women and children by treating the female reproductive capacity and the children born of gestational surrogacy arrangements as products that can be bought and sold (Radin, Market–Inalienability (1987) 100 Harv.L.Rev. 1849, 1930–1932). The commodification of women and children, it is feared, will reinforce oppressive gender stereotypes and threaten the well-being of all children. (Medical Technology, supra, 103 Harv.L.Rev. 1519, 1550; Annas, Fairy Tales Surrogate Mothers Tell, in Surrogate Motherhood, supra, p. 50.) Some critics foresee promotion of an ever-expanding "business of surrogacy brokerage." (E.g., Goodwin, Determination of Legal Parentage, supra, 26 Fam.L.Q. at p. 283.)

Whether surrogacy contracts are viewed as personal service agreements or agreements for the sale of the child born as the result of the agreement, commentators critical of contractual surrogacy view these contracts as contrary to public policy and thus not enforceable. (Radin,

Market–Inalienability, supra, 100 Harv.L.Rev. at p. 1924, fn. 261; Capron & Radin, Choosing Family Law Over Contract Law as a Paradigm for Surrogate Motherhood, supra, in Surrogate Motherhood, at pp. 62–63; see also Krimmel, Can Surrogate Parenting Be Stopped? An Inspection of the Constitutional and Pragmatic Aspects of Outlawing Surrogate Mother Arrangements (1992) 27 Val.U.L.Rev. 1, 4–5.)

Organizations representing diverse viewpoints share many of the concerns highlighted by the legal commentators. For example, the American Medical Association considers the conception of a child for relinquishment after birth to pose grave ethical problems. (Rep. of the Judicial Council, in Surrogate Motherhood, supra, at p. 304.) Likewise, the official position of the Catholic Church is that surrogacy arrangements are " 'contrary to the unity of marriage and to the dignity of the procreation of the human person.' " (Magisterium of the Catholic Church, Instruction on Respect for Human Life in Its Origin and on the Dignity of Procreation: Replies to Certain Questions of the Day 25 (Feb. 22, 1987), cited in Radin, Market–Inalienability, supra, 100 Harv.L.Rev. 1849, 1928, fn. 271.)

The policy statement of the New York State Task Force on Life and the Law sums up the broad range of ethical problems that commercial surrogacy arrangements are viewed to present: "The gestation of children as a service for others in exchange for a fee is a radical departure from the way in which society understands and values pregnancy. It substitutes commercial values for the web of social, affective and moral meanings associated with human reproduction * * *. This transformation has profound implications for childbearing, for women, and for the relationship between parents and the children they bring into the world. [P] * * * [P] Surrogate parenting allows the genetic, gestational and social components of parenthood to be fragmented, creating unprecedented relationships among people bound together by contractual obligation rather than by the bonds of kinship and caring * * *. [P] * * * [P] * * * Surrogate parenting alters deep-rooted social and moral assumptions about the relationship between parents and children * * *. [P] * * * [It] is premised on the ability and willingness of women to abdicate [their parental] responsibility without moral compunction or regret [and] makes the obligations that accompany parenthood alienable and negotiable." (New York State Task Force on Life and the Law, Surrogate Parenting: Analysis and Recommendations for Public Policy (May 1988) in Surrogate Motherhood, supra, at pp. 317–318.)

Proponents and critics of gestational surrogacy propose widely differing approaches for deciding who should be the legal mother of a child born of a gestational surrogacy arrangement. Surrogacy advocates propose to enforce pre-conception contracts in which gestational mothers have agreed to relinquish parental rights, and, thus, would make "bargained-for intentions determinative of legal parenthood." (Shultz, Reproductive Technology, supra, 1990 Wis.L.Rev. at p. 323.) Professor Robertson, for instance, contends that "The right to noncoital, collaborative reproduction also includes the right of the parties to agree how they should allocate their obligations and entitlements with respect to the child. Legal presumptions of paternity and maternity would be overridden by this agreement of the parties." (Robertson, Procreative Liberty and the Control of Conception, Pregnancy, and Childbirth, supra, 69 Va.L.Rev. 405, 436; see also Shalev, Birth Power: The Case for Surrogacy, supra, at p. 141 [arguing for enforcing the parties' legal expectations].)

Surrogacy critics, on the other hand, consider the unique female role in human reproduction as the determinative factor of questions of legal parentage. They reason that although males and females both contribute genetic material for the child, the act of gestating the fetus falls only on the female. (See Radin, Market–Inalienability, supra, 100 Harv.L.Rev. 1849, 1932, fn. 285 [pointing out the "asymmetrical" interests of males and females in human reproduction].) Accordingly, in their view, a woman who, as the result of gestational surrogacy, is not genetically related to the child she bears is like any other woman who gives birth to a child. In either situation the woman giving birth is the child's mother. (See Capron & Radin, Choosing Family Law Over Contract Law as a Paradigm for Surrogate Motherhood, in Surrogate Motherhood, supra, at pp. 64–65.) Under this approach, the laws governing adoption should govern the parental rights to a child born of gestational surrogacy. Upon the birth of the child, the gestational mother can decide whether or not to relinquish her parental rights in favor of the genetic mother. (Ibid.)

* * *

The debate over whom the law should recognize as the legal mother of a child born of a gestational surrogacy arrangement prompted the National Conference of Commissioners on Uniform State Laws to propose the Uniform Status of Children of Assisted Conception Act. (9B West's U.Laws Ann. (1992 Supp.) Uniform Status of Children of Assisted Conception Act (1988 Act) pp. 122–137 [hereafter USCACA].) This model legislation addresses many of the concerns discussed above.

The commissioners gave careful consideration to the competing interests of the various participants in assisted conception arrangements, and sought to accommodate those interests in the model legislation. Their overriding concern, however, was the well-being of children born of gestational surrogacy and other types of assisted conception. As the foreword to the model legislation notes, the extraordinary circumstances of these children's births deprive them of parentage in the traditional sense. (9B West's U.Laws Ann. (1992 Supp.) USCACA, supra, at p. 123.) Thus, the intent of the proposed legislation was to define with precision the legal status of these children as well as to codify the rights of the other participants in a surrogacy arrangement. The commissioners proposed alternative versions of the USCACA: one that would disallow gestational surrogacy and another that would permit it only under court supervision.

In its key components, the proposed legislation provides that "a woman who gives birth to a child is the child's mother" (USCACA, § 2) unless a court has approved a surrogacy agreement before conception (USCACA, §§ 5, 6). In the absence of such court approval, any surrogacy agreement would be void. (USCACA, § 5, subd. (b).) If, however, the arrangement for gestational surrogacy has court approval, "the intended parents are the parents of the child." (USCACA, § 8, subd. (a)(1).)

To obtain court approval, the parties to the surrogacy arrangement must file a petition. (USCACA, § 6, subd. (a).) The model legislation provides for the court to appoint a guardian ad litem for the intended child and legal counsel for the surrogate mother. (Ibid.) Before approving a surrogacy arrangement, the trial court must conduct a hearing and enter detailed findings, including the following: medical evidence shows the intended mother's inability to bear a child or that for her to do so poses an unreasonable risk to the unborn child or to the physical or mental health of the intended mother; all parties to the surrogacy agreement (including the surrogate's husband if she has one) meet the standards of fitness of adoptive parents; the agreement was voluntary and all parties understand its terms; the surrogate mother has undergone at least one successful pregnancy and medical evidence shows that another pregnancy will not endanger her physical or mental health or pose an unreasonable risk to the unborn child; and all parties have received professional mental health counseling pertaining to the effect of the surrogacy arrangement. (USCACA, § 6, subd. (b).) These provisions serve to minimize the potential for overreaching and to ensure that all parties to a surrogacy arrangement understand their respective roles and obligations.

The USCACA offers predictability in delineating the parentage of children born of gestational surrogacy arrangements. Under the model legislation, if enacted, there would never be a question as to who has the legal responsibility for a child born of a gestational surrogacy arrangement: If the couple who initiated the surrogacy had complied with the provisions of the legislation, they would be the child's legal parents. If they had not, the rights and responsibilities of parenthood would go to the woman who gave birth to the child and her spouse.

Because California Legislature has not enacted the Uniform Status of Children of Assisted Conception Act, its provisions were not followed in this case.

* * *

Faced with the failure of current statutory law to adequately address the issue of who is a child's natural mother when two women qualify under the UPA, the majority breaks the "tie" by resort to a criterion not found in the UPA—the "intent" of the genetic mother to be the child's mother.

This case presents a difficult issue. The majority's resolution of that issue deserves serious consideration. Ultimately, however, I cannot agree that "intent" is the appropriate test for resolving this case.

* * *

[I]n making the intent of the genetic mother who wants to have a child the dispositive factor, the majority renders a certain result preordained and inflexible in every such case: as between an intending genetic mother and a gestational mother, the genetic mother will, under the majority's analysis, always prevail. The majority recognizes no meaningful contribution by a woman who agrees to carry a fetus to term for the genetic mother beyond that of mere employment to perform a specified biological function.

The majority's approach entirely devalues the substantial claims of motherhood by a gestational mother such as Anna. True, a woman who enters into a surrogacy arrangement intending to raise the child has by her intent manifested an assumption of parental responsibility in addition to her biological contribution of providing the genetic material. (See Adoption of Kelsey S., supra, 1 Cal.4th at pp. 838, 849, 4 Cal.Rptr.2d 615, 823 P.2d 1216.) But the gestational mother's biological contribution of carrying a child for nine months and giving birth is likewise an assumption of parental responsibility. (See Dolgin, Just a Gene: Judicial Assumptions About Parenthood (1993) 40 UCLA L.Rev. 637, 659.) A pregnant woman's commitment to the unborn child she carries is not just physical; it is psychological and emotional as well. * * *

To summarize, the woman who carried the fetus to term and brought a child into the world has, like the genetic mother, a substantial claim to be the natural mother of the child. The gestational mother has made an indispensable and unique biological contribution, and has also gone beyond biology in an intangible respect that, though difficult to label, cannot be denied. Accordingly, I cannot agree with the majority's devaluation of the role of the gestational mother.

I find the majority's reliance on "intent" unsatisfactory for yet another reason. By making intent determinative of parental rights to a child born of a gestational surrogacy arrangement, the majority would permit enforcement of a gestational surrogacy agreement without requiring any of the protections that would be afforded by the USCACA. Under that act, the granting of parental rights to a couple that initiates a gestational surrogacy arrangement would be conditioned upon compliance with the legislation's other provisions. They include court oversight of the gestational surrogacy arrangement before conception, legal counsel for the woman who agrees to gestate the child, a showing of need for the surrogacy, medical and mental health evaluations, and a requirement that all parties meet the standards of fitness of adoptive parents. (USCACA, §§ 5, 6.)

In my view, protective requirements such as those set forth in the USCACA are necessary to minimize any possibility in gestational surrogacy arrangements for overreaching or abuse by a party with economic advantage. As the New Jersey Supreme Court recognized, it will be a rare instance when a low income infertile couple can employ an upper income surrogate. (Matter of Baby M., supra, 109 N.J. 396, 537 A.2d 1227, 1249.) The model act's carefully drafted provisions would assure that the surrogacy arrangement is a matter of medical necessity on the part of the intending parents, and not merely the product of a desire to avoid the inconveniences of pregnancy, together with the financial ability to do so. Also, by requiring both pre-conception psychological counseling for all parties and judicial approval, the model act would assure that parties enter into a surrogacy arrangement only if they are legally and psychologically capable of doing so and fully understand all the risks involved, and that the surrogacy arrangement would not be substantially detrimental to the interests of any individual. Moreover, by requiring judicial approval, the model act would significantly discourage the rapid expansion of commercial surrogacy brokerage and the resulting commodification of the products of pregnancy. In contrast, here the majority's grant of parental rights to the intending mother contains no provisions for the procedural protections suggested by the commissioners who drafted the model act. The majority opinion is a sweeping endorsement of unregulated gestational surrogacy.

* * *

As I have discussed, in California the existing statutory law applicable to this case is the UPA, which was never designed to govern the new reproductive technology of gestational surrogacy. Under the UPA, both the genetic mother and the gestational mother have equal rights to be the child's natural mother. But the UPA allows one natural mother for each child, and thus this court is required to make a choice. To break this "tie" between the genetic mother and the gestational mother, the majority uses the legal concept of intent. In so doing, the majority has articulated a rationale for using the concept of intent that is grounded in principles of tort, intellectual property and commercial contract law.

But, as I have pointed out, we are not deciding a case involving the commission of a tort, the ownership of intellectual property, or the delivery of goods under a commercial contract; we are deciding the fate of a child. In the absence of legislation that is designed to address the unique problems of gestational surrogacy, this court should look not to tort, property or contract law, but to family law, as the governing paradigm and source of a rule of decision.

The allocation of parental rights and responsibilities necessarily impacts the welfare of a minor child. And in issues of child welfare, the standard that courts frequently apply is the best interests of the child. (See §§ 222.20, 222.36, 224.64 [matters relating to adoption and temporary placement], 4600 [child custody], 4601 [visitation].) Indeed it is highly significant that the UPA itself looks to a child's best interests in deciding another question of parental rights. (§ 7017, subd. (d)(2).) This "best interests" standard serves to assure that in the judicial resolution of disputes affecting a child's well-being, protection of the minor child is the foremost consideration. Consequently, I would apply "the best interests of the child" standard to determine who can best assume the social and legal responsibilities of motherhood for a child born of a gestational surrogacy arrangement.

* * *

Here, the child born of the gestational surrogacy arrangement between Anna Johnson and Mark and Crispina Calvert has lived continuously with Mark and Crispina since his birth in September 1990. The trial court awarded parental rights to Mark and Crispina, concluding that as a matter of law they were the child's "genetic, biological and natural" parents. In reaching that conclusion, the trial court did not treat Anna's statutory claim to be the child's legal mother as equal to Crispina's, nor did the trial court consider the child's best interests in deciding between those two equal statutory claims. Accordingly, I would remand the matter to the trial court to undertake that evaluation.

Notes

The *Johnson* court holds that a gestational surrogacy contract "is not on its face inconsistent with public policy." Does this mean that California courts must specifically enforce such contracts? Suppose the contract in *Johnson* had been silent about abortion. Or suppose that it gave the Calverts a right to veto any abortion decision made by Ms. Johnson. Would a court have enjoined Ms. Johnson from obtaining an abortion? Conversely, suppose, after genetic testing, it was discovered that the fetus carried by Ms. Johnson had severe abnormalities, but Ms. Johnson refused to have an abortion. Would a court under any circumstances compel her to have an abortion?

Reconsider the traditional concerns that courts often utilize to deny specific performance of personal services contracts. To what extent are they relevant in the surrogate parenting context? In any event, are they applicable when the child has already been born? On the other hand, suppose the surrogacy contract prohibits an abortion except with the consent of all of the parties. Would a court ever compel the surrogate to carry the fetus to term?

SECTION 5. ARBITRATION

Arbitration is a private method of adjudication whereby parties voluntarily submit disputes to a neutral third person for a final determination based on evidence and arguments presented in a hearing before the arbitrator. *See* M. Domke, Commercial Arbitration § 1:01 (Rev.Ed.1984). There are normally two types of arbitration agreements: (1) an agreement to arbitrate future disputes; and (2) an agreement to arbitrate an existing dispute, or a submission agreement.

The arbitrator may be selected by several methods. Often the parties agree in advance on a single arbitrator or, at least, agree to allow some independent group, such as the American Arbitration Association, to select the arbitrator. This frequently results in the arbitrator being an expert in the subject matter of the dispute. Under a second selection method, each party selects one arbitrator and the two so selected then appoint a third, if necessary.

Arbitration is preferred to judicial adjudication for a number of reasons. Speed is probably the main advantage of arbitration. This can be especially important in complex commercial arrangements, such as construction contracts. A prompt decision may also very well reduce the turmoil and bitterness that frequently are associated with protracted judicial proceedings. This is especially important when the parties value a future commercial relationship. Arbitration proceedings are private, which can be advantageous when confidential matters are involved. Further, the arbitration process permits greater remedial flexibility than judicial adjudication. As Professor Dobbs has pointed out, "law courts tend to grant all-or-nothing remedies at least in theory. They tend to make broad rules to cover many cases and to worry very little about particular cases. Arbitration tends, on the contrary, to ignore rules in many situations and to concentrate on working out a pragmatic solution, though of course the arbitrator may be bound by contractual terms or procedures provided by the parties." D. Dobbs, Handbook on the Law of Remedies 936 (1973).

At times, arbitration's advantages become its disadvantages. The flexibility referred to above may result in an undesirable lack of predictability. Because arbitration opinions often are not published, there is no precedent to guide the decision-maker. Consequently, when substantial sums or issues are at stake, parties sometimes prefer what they perceive to be the greater certainty of the judicial process.*

SIMPSON, SPECIFIC ENFORCEMENT OF ARBITRATION CONTRACTS, 83 U.Pa.L.Rev. 160, 161–164 (1934): ** "The refusal of courts of equity specifically to enforce arbitration contracts in spite of the manifest inadequacy of the legal remedy for their breach has been rested on various grounds. It has been said that if the court were to order the defendant to name an arbitrator, it could not compel the execution of its decree; that even if the appointment of arbitrators could be enforced, the arbitrators so appointed could not be compelled to act as such or to agree; and that if the court were to appoint arbitrators, it would 'bind the Parties contrary to their Agreement.' None of these grounds seems sufficient. The ordinary processes of a court of equity will be adequate in the usual case to compel the defendant to appoint an arbitrator; if the arbitrator so appointed refuses to act (and to act in good faith), the court can compel the defendant to appoint another; and, moreover, there would seem to be no objection to an appointment by the court where the defendant has refused to appoint in accordance with his agreement, since it may well be said that he must be taken to have waived his right of selection. More substantial, perhaps, is the argument that, since lay arbitration tribunals do not have the facilities for investigation nor the knowledge of applicable legal principles which the courts possess, a court of equity should not compel a party to submit the determination of his rights to such a tribunal. In reply to this argument it may be said: (1) This is just what the parties have agreed to do, and, unless there exists some public policy against extrajudicial settlement of controversies, that agreement should be respected and enforced. (2) In a considerable number of jurisdictions, general arbitration statutes now authorize compulsory process to obtain evidence in common law arbitrations, and thus eliminate the difficulty in part.

"The sound ground for the accepted equity doctrine that courts of chancery will not specifically enforce contracts to arbitrate is to be found in the common law character and effect of such contracts. A contract to arbitrate, although valid at common law, is 'revocable'. In other words, either party to the contract is regarded as having a power to break it, although rendering himself liable (in nominal damages at least) for so

* For further consideration of the law of commercial arbitration, see M. Domke, The Law and Practice of Commercial Arbitration (1968); R. Rodman, Commercial Arbitration (1985). For a consideration of the obstacles to effective enforcement of arbitration agreements in states without modern statutes, see McBeth, Commercial Arbitration: A Need for Reform, 36 Mo.L.Rev. 343 (1971). As to the interrelationship between common law and statutory arbitration and its effect on enforcement remedies, see Sturges and Reckson, Common Law and Statutory Arbitration: Problems Arising From Their Coexistence, 46 Minn.L.Rev. 819 (1962). For a comprehensive review of alternative methods of dispute resolution, see Alternative Dispute Resolution: A Symposium, 29 Vill.L.Rev. 1219 (1984).

doing. This power of revocation has two important effects at law: (1) if a party 'revokes' (i.e., breaks) his contract to arbitrate, even after arbitrators have been appointed, no valid award can be made. (2) The breach of an agreement to arbitrate cannot be pleaded as a defense to an action brought by the party who has broken ('revoked') that agreement. This characteristic of 'revocability' exists at common law even though the parties have expressly contracted not to revoke the agreement to arbitrate.

* * *

"In consequence of the common law rule of the revocability of arbitration contracts, a court of equity which is asked to enforce specifically an agreement to arbitrate finds itself in this position: If it grants the relief sought by the plaintiff and compels the defendant to appoint arbitrators, the defendant can render the decree nugatory forthwith by revoking the arbitrators' authority. If the equity court should enjoin such revocation of authority, it would be refusing to follow the law in a case in its concurrent jurisdiction and would be setting up a special equity rule as to the character and effect of arbitration agreements—a thoroughly undesirable result. And if the court should appoint arbitrators for the defendant, it again would be refusing to follow the law, and would, in a sense, 'bind the Parties contrary to their Agreement'. Following the law, therefore, courts of equity, if they attempted specifically to enforce arbitration agreements, would be in the same position as if they were to attempt specifically to enforce any other contract which the defendant had a power immediately to terminate. The defendant could render nugatory the court's decree as soon as it was rendered; and it has long been an established doctrine of equity that specific performance will not be granted under such circumstances. In other words, specific performance of arbitration contracts is refused because 'the court will * * * refuse to interfere in any case where, if it were to do so, one of the parties might nullify its action through the exercise of a discretion which the contract or law invests him with'. This is not to say that courts of equity, in denying specific performance of contracts to arbitrate, have not in the past been influenced by old ideas of public policy as to 'ousting the jurisdiction of the court'; but rather that, even though this ghost be laid, there is nevertheless a sound ground for the refusal of equity specifically to enforce such contracts in view of their 'revocability' at law.

"The real difficulty in specifically enforcing agreements to arbitrate is thus not on the equity side of the courts at all. Granted a change in the common law rule, there is nothing (except the numbing effect of precedent) to prevent equity from enforcing specific performance of arbitration agreements on the ground of inadequacy of the legal remedy for the breach thereof, subject, of course, to the exercise of the chancellor's judicial discretion in accordance with the principles applied in other specific performance cases.

"The common law rule of 'revocability' of arbitration agreements is so entrenched in the cases that it can be changed only by legislation; but modern legislation has gone far to change it. Moreover, that legislation in some instances has purported to impose upon the courts a mandatory duty of specifically enforcing arbitration contracts. In order to understand the present state of the law as to the specific enforcement of such contracts, an analysis of the character and an appraisal of the effect of this legislation is therefore necessary."

A majority of states have enacted "modern" arbitration legislation. Such legislation is so designated if it provides for the enforcement of agreements to arbitrate future, as well as existing, disputes. Normally such legislation also authorizes both direct and indirect means of specific enforcement of the arbitration agreement. Direct specific performance is a court order compelling a party to arbitrate. Indirect specific performance can consist of the following: (1) an order staying any court action instituted in violation of the arbitration agreement; (2) a court order appointing arbitrators with the power to act.

Under the United States Arbitration Act, originally enacted in 1925 and revised in 1947, 9 U.S.C.A. ch. 1 §§ 1–14, a contract to arbitrate future or existing disputes is deemed irrevocable and specifically enforceable under federal law if the contract relates to a maritime transaction or to a "transaction involving" interstate commerce. The Act excludes certain "contracts of employment." The Act provides for all of the direct and indirect enforcement remedies referred to above. The United States Supreme Court has given a broad interpretation to the enforcement remedies of the Act. *See* Prima Paint Corp. v. Flood & Conklin Mfg. Co., 388 U.S. 395, 87 S.Ct. 1801, 18 L.Ed.2d 1270 (1967); Guinness–Harp Corp. v. Jos. Schlitz Brewing Co., 613 F.2d 468 (2d Cir.1980) (granting preliminary mandatory injunction against termination of distributorship pending arbitration); Aksen, Prima Paint v. Flood & Conklin—What Does it Mean?, 43 St. Johns L.Rev. 1 (1968); *see also* Vaughn, Jurisdiction of the Federal Courts Under the U.S. Arbitration Act, 27 Tex.L.Rev. 218 (1948); Sturges and Murphy, Some Confusing Matters Relating to Arbitration Under the U.S. Arbitration Act, 17 Law & Contemp.Probs. 580 (1952). Indeed, to the extent that state law requires a judicial resolution of an issue that would otherwise be subject to arbitration under the Act, it is preempted under the Supremacy Clause of the United States Constitution. *See* Southland Corp. v. Keating, 465 U.S. 1 (1984) (parties agreed to submit disputes arising under a franchise agreement to arbitration and agreed that the arbitration agreement would be otherwise enforceable under the Act; California Franchise Investment Law, which required a judicial determination of such disputes, held preempted).

A substantial number of states have adopted the Uniform Arbitration Act. The Act, proposed in 1955 and amended in 1956, applies both to existing and future disputes and provides for both direct and indirect enforcement.*

* Jurisdictions that have adopted the Uniform Arbitration Act in whole, or substantial part, include Alaska, Arizona, Arkansas, Colorado, Delaware, District of Columbia, Idaho, Illinois, Indiana, Kansas, Maine, Maryland, Massachusetts, Michigan, Minnesota, Missouri, Nebraska, Nevada, New Mexico, Pennsylvania, South Dakota, Tennessee, Texas, Vermont, and Wyoming. The text of the Act may be found in 7 Uniform Laws Annotated

Several other states have enacted legislation that differs from the Uniform Act, but nevertheless contains all of the attributes of "modern" legislation referred to above. Such legislation often antedates the Uniform Act. Indeed, New York's legislation, derived from the New York Arbitration Act of 1920, was the pioneer "modern" legislation on which many states modelled their statutes. *See* McKinney's N.Y.Civ.Prac.Law § 7501. *See also* West's Ann.Cal.Civ.Proc.Code Ann. § 1280.

Other states have legislation that lacks "modern" attributes in one or more particulars. Many of these statutes, for example, provide for specific enforcement of arbitration contracts only for those disputes existing at the time the contract was executed. *See, e.g.,* Utah Code Ann. 1953, 78–31–1.

Labor arbitration has tended to develop as a special arbitration area. Not only do some states provide special legislation for dealing with labor disputes, but labor arbitration has largely been subsumed by federal labor law. In this connection, agreements to arbitrate disputes arising out of labor-management contracts are specifically enforceable under a judicial interpretation of section 301 of the Taft Hartley Act, 29 U.S.C.A. § 185. *See* Textile Workers Union v. Lincoln Mills, 353 U.S. 448, 77 S.Ct. 912, 1 L.Ed.2d 972 (1957); D. Dobbs, Handbook on the Law of Remedies 938 (1973).

It is important to distinguish between arbitration and appraisal. Unlike arbitration, "appraisal simply involves valuation of property, which may be regarded as something referable to independent standards, more a matter of pricing items than of adjudicating disputes." D. Dobbs, Handbook on the Law of Remedies 937 (1973). Traditionally, many courts that have denied direct or indirect specific enforcement of arbitration agreements have been more inclined to grant at least the indirect equivalent of such equitable relief in cases involving agreements for appraisal. *See, e.g.,* School Dist. No. 1 of Silver Bow County v. Globe & Republic Ins. Co. of America, 146 Mont. 208, 404 P.2d 889 (1965). Some courts, for example, have granted indirect specific performance of appraisal agreements in insurance policies by making consent to appraisal a condition precedent to a suit by an insured to collect on the policy. *See, e.g.,* Dworkin v. Caledonian Ins. Co., 285 Mo. 342, 226 S.W. 846 (1920). One of the reasons for this difference in approach is based on a judicial belief that arbitrators "act like judges" in making "legal" determinations, whereas the process of appraisal is simply a means of determining the value of property or services. Moreover, some courts emphasize that arbitration awards are reducible to judgment and thus "oust" a court of jurisdiction, while an appraisal determination simply results in evidence and does not result in an independent cause of action. *See* McBeth, Commercial Arbitration: The Need for Reform, 36 Mo.L.Rev. 343, 346 (1971).

1 (1978); Handbook, National Conference of Commissioners on Uniform State Laws 162 (1955), 292 (1956). For a discussion of the Act, see Pirsig, Some Comments on Arbitration Legislation and the Uniform Act, 10 Vand.L.Rev. 685 (1957).

3 D. DOBBS, LAW OF REMEDIES

Practitioner Treatise Series, Vol. 3.
510–513 (2d ed. 1993).*

The Arbitrator's Remedies

Compensatory damages. What remedies may arbitrators award? The power to award remedies is like the other powers of the arbitrator; it is determined by the parties' agreement. In the absence of restriction, the arbitrator usually has a free hand so long as the remedies do not violate the court's conception of public policy.[54] The arbitrator certainly may award money compensation, including unliquidated sums.[55]

Equitable or non-monetary relief. Reinstatement in a job or to job status or privileges is a common kind of award when employment is in issue.[56] At least some courts have held that arbitrators may exercise what might be called equity powers and have approved arbitration awards of specific performance [57] and injunctive orders.[58] One court upheld an award by an arbitration panel which required the defendant to post a substantial bond to secure future arbitration orders against the defendant.[59] Michigan, however, has taken a narrower view, holding that if an arbitrator is to have equity powers, the parties must explicitly confer them.[60]

Relief courts would refuse. Can the arbitrator award equitable remedies which the courts themselves would refuse? Some important cases have said so. In *Staklinski v. Pyramid Elec. Co.,*[61] an arbitrator ordered reinstatement of an employee as a production manager for a utility company at a large salary and percentage of the profits. Personal services contracts are not traditionally enforced, so the court's approval of the award suggests that arbitrators can go further than courts. It is possible that the case merely signals increasing doubt about the personal services rule where an employee seeks to retain a job.[62] But other cases in other areas also approve arbitral relief that courts have traditionally denied.[63] In addition, the Uniform Act specifically provides that the arbitrator's award is not to be vacated merely because it affords relief not available in law or equity.[64]

* Reprinted with permission of West Publishing Co.

54. See Garrity v. Lyle Stuart, Inc., 40 N.Y.2d 354, 386 N.Y.S.2d 831, 353 N.E.2d 793, 83 A.L.R.3d 1024 (1976) (stating the rule, but insisting that the award of punitive damages by an arbitrator violated public policy).

55. E.g., Bankers & Shippers Ins. Co. v. Gonzalez, 234 So.2d 693 (Fla.App.1970) (uninsured motorist arbitration, award of $7300).

56. E.g., Local Union 560, I.B.T. v. Eazor Express Inc., 95 N.J.Super. 219, 230 A.2d 521 (1967).

57. Staklinski v. Pyramid Elec. Co., 6 N.Y.2d 159, 188 N.Y.S.2d 541, 160 N.E.2d 78 (1959).

58. Ruppert v. Egelhofer, 3 N.Y.2d 576, 170 N.Y.S.2d 785, 148 N.E.2d 129, 70 A.L.R.2d 1048 (1958) (injunction against slowdown as part of arbitrator's award was proper, though the contract did not mention remedies at all).

59. Compania Chilena De Navegacion Interoceanica, S.A. v. Norton, Lilly & Co., Inc., 652 F.Supp. 1512, 1516–1517 (S.D.N.Y.1987).

60. Carr v. Kalamazoo Vegetable Parchment Co., 354 Mich. 327, 92 N.W.2d 295 (1958) ("The arbitrator is not a chancellor. He possesses no equitable power excepting as the submission may expressly grant such").

61. Staklinski v. Pyramid Elec. Co., 6 N.Y.2d 159, 188 N.Y.S.2d 541, 160 N.E.2d 78 (1959).

62. See § 12.20(3) above.

63. Matter of Grayson–Robinson Stores, Inc. v. Iris Const. Corp., 8 N.Y.2d 133, 202 N.Y.S.2d 303, 168 N.E.2d 377 (1960) (building contract, award of specific performance).

64. Uniform Arbitration Act § 12(a).

* * *

Punitive damages. Under the best of circumstances feelings run high about punitive damages. In a leading New York decision, *Garrity v. Lyle Stuart, Inc.,*[68] the court said that punitive damages could not be awarded by arbitrators, even though arbitrators otherwise had a free hand with remedies and even though the parties might have given the arbitrator power to make such an award.[69] The court thought that punitive damages was "a sanction reserved to the State," and that it would be "barbaric" to permit "redress by private punitive measures." [70] Some other decisions reach the same ultimate result.[71] Even so, a number of other courts [72] and arbitrators [73] have been dissatisfied with *Garrity* and have insisted that arbitrators could indeed award punitive damages where authorized to do so by the parties. Commentators have suggested that in fact arbitrators are increas-

68. 40 N.Y.2d 354, 386 N.Y.S.2d 831, 353 N.E.2d 793, 83 A.L.R.3d 1024 (1976).

69. The court concluded that "An arbitrator has no power to award punitive damages, even if agreed upon by the parties." Later it announced that

> The freedom of contract does not embrace the freedom to punish, even by contract. On this view, there was no power to waive the limitations on privately assessed punitive damages and, of course, no power to agree to them by the failure to object to the demand for arbitration * * *.

Garrity v. Lyle Stuart, Inc., 40 N.Y.2d 354, 359, 386 N.Y.S.2d 831, 834, 353 N.E.2d 793, 797, 83 A.L.R.3d 1024, 1031 (1976).

70. The court said:

> In a highly developed commercial and economic society the use of private force is not the danger, but the uncontrolled use of coercive economic sanctions in private arrangements. For centuries the power to punish has been a monopoly of the State, and not that of any private individual * * *. The day is long past since barbaric man achieved redress by private punitive measures.

Garrity v. Lyle Stuart, Inc., 40 N.Y.2d 354, 359, 386 N.Y.S.2d 831, 834, 353 N.E.2d 793, 797, 83 A.L.R.3d 1024, 1030 (1976).

71. Pierson v. Dean, Witter, Reynolds, Inc., 742 F.2d 334 (7th Cir.1984) (New York Law as was required by the contract).

72. Raytheon Company v. Automated Business Systems, Inc., 882 F.2d 6 (1st Cir. 1989); Willoughby Roofing & Supply Co. v. Kajima Intern., Inc., 598 F.Supp. 353 (N.D.Ala.1984), aff'd, 776 F.2d 269 (11th Cir. 1985) (construction contract dispute; federal law has no policy against arbitrator's award of punitive damages); Baker v. Sadick, 162 Cal.App.3d 618, 208 Cal.Rptr. 676 (1984) (medical malpractice arbitration, arbitrators can award punitive damages if arbitration agreement is broad enough to permit such award); see Willis v. Shearson/American Express, Inc., 569 F.Supp. 821 (M.D.N.C.1983) (investor's dispute with investment broker over account, federal law governs and permits punitive award by arbitrator); In re Costa and Head (Atrium), Ltd. v. Duncan, Inc., 486 So.2d 1272 (Ala.1986) ("there is authority that supports the submission of both fraud and punitive damages claims to arbitration if the arbitration agreement is broad enough to allow it;" semble, that authority is approved); Rodgers Builders, Inc. v. McQueen, 76 N.C.App. 16, 331 S.E.2d 726 (1985) (Whichard, J.: punitive damages claims were subject to arbitration and hence plaintiff barred from suit by *res judicata* effect of earlier arbitration). Cf. Communications Workers of America Local 7400 v. Abrahamson, 228 Neb. 335, 422 N.W.2d 547 (1988) (enforcement of fines levied by union against members who crossed picket line; a contractual right with punitive and deterrent effects). An intermediate position might be that arbitrators could make punitive awards only where courts could do so. This position would, however, conflict with the usual view that the arbitrator's remedies are more flexible than those of the courts. A restrictive position of this sort would also create some practical problems. See Note, 64 N.C.L.Rev. 1145, 1155 (1986). See also Note, Punitive Damages in Arbitration: The Search for a Workable Rule, 63 Corn.L.Rev. 272, 295 (1978).

73. See Robins, Punitive Damages in Securities Arbitration Proceedings (January 1991) (Westlaw TP–All Database) (reporting that a number of arbitrators were making punitive awards and predicting that they would be legally permitted to do so in New York in the near future).

ingly making punitive awards.[74]

74. Frankhauser & Gardner, An Up-to-Date Review of Judicial, Legislative, and Regulatory Developments in Arbitration with Financial Institutions, 46 W. & L.L.Rev. 583, 607 (1989).

Chapter 8

RESTITUTION AS THE ONLY REMEDY

BEN LOMOND, INC. v. ALLEN

Supreme Court of Alaska, 1988.
758 P.2d 92.

OPINION

MOORE, JUSTICE.

Judith Allen entered into a contract with the defendant builders to purchase a home. As a down payment on the home, Allen conveyed to the builders a lot which she owned in Kotzebue. After Allen breached the contract, she sued Jomax, Inc. and Ben Lomond, Inc. for restitution. The jury returned a special verdict making the following findings of fact: (A) the fair market value of the lot conveyed to the builders was $12,000 and (B) the total amount of consequential damages sustained by the builders was $458.40. This ultimately resulted in an award for Allen of $26,206.21. Ben Lomond, Inc. and Jomax, Inc. appeal. We reverse in part on the ground that the evidence does not support the portion of the jury verdict concerning the builders' consequential damages.

* * *

II.

Restitution is available to a defaulting party to a contract to the extent that the benefit retained by the non-breaching party exceeds the amount of damages incurred by that same party as a consequence of the breach. *See Freedman v. Rector,* 37 Cal.2d 16, 230 P.2d 629 (1951); *see also* D. Dobbs, *Remedies* 863 (1973); Restatement (Second) of Contracts § 374 (1979).[2]

2. The Restatement states the rule as follows:

(1) Subject to the rule stated in Subsection (2), if a party justifiably refuses to perform on the ground that his remaining duties of performance have been discharged by the other party's breach, the party in breach is entitled to restitution for any benefit that he has conferred by way of part performance or reliance in excess of the loss that he has caused by his own breach.

(2) To the extent that, under the manifested assent of the parties, a party's performance is to be retained in the case of breach, that party is not entitled to restitution if the value of the performance as liquidated damages is reasonable in the light of the anticipated or actual loss

We adopt the majority rule which places the burden of proof on the defaulting buyer to prove the amount by which the benefits exceed the damages.[3] *See* I G. Palmer, *The Law of Restitution,* § 5.4, at 583–85 (1978). It is difficult to rationalize placing the burden of proof on the non-breaching party, who is the defendant in such restitution actions.[4]

Applying that rule, Allen is entitled to restitution damages measured by the value of the lot conveyed to the builders less the consequential damages incurred by the builders. Allen has the burden to prove the value of the lot and the amount of the builders' damages.

The builders argue that the trial court erred in failing to grant their motion for a new trial on the ground that the jury verdict was against the clear weight of the evidence. In reviewing the trial court's denial of a motion for new trial, "we must examine the record and determine whether 'the evidence to support the verdict was completely lacking or was so slight and unconvincing as to make the verdict plainly unreasonable and unjust.'" *Sloan v. Atlantic Richfield Co.,* 541 P.2d 717, 724 (Alaska 1975) (quoting *Ahlstrom v. Cummings,* 388 P.2d 261, 262 (Alaska 1964)). If there is an "evidentiary basis for the jury's decision," we must affirm the denial of a new trial. *Olson v. McRae,* 389 P.2d 576, 577 (Alaska 1964). In this case, we find that the jury verdict with respect to the builders' damages is contrary to the clear weight of the evidence.

The jury concluded that the builders incurred consequential damages in the sum of $458.40. A review of the record provides no basis upon which this verdict can rest. The builders offered detailed evidence on several specific items of consequential damages incurred by them. John Ringstad, who handled the mortgage loan applications for Alaska Bank of the North in Kotzebue, testified at trial as to the losses incurred by the builders as a consequence of Allen's breach. Specifically, Ringstad testified as to the following expenses which were definitely paid by the builders: $53.38 for a credit report on Allen and a $402.50 commitment fee to Alaska Housing Finance Corp. for processing the loan. Mr. Ringstad also testified that a loan origination fee of $805 was probably paid to the bank by the builders. Additionally, the cost of heating the home between August and when the home was resold in April of the following year was between $750 and $1,000.

Finally and most significantly, the builders incurred $9,940.16 in finance charges from August 4, 1980, the date the contract was breached, until April 20, 1981, the date the home was ultimately sold. Given the ordinary delays in reselling a home, including finding a buyer and allowing

caused by the breach and the difficulties of proof of loss.

Restatement (Second) of Contracts § 374 (1979). [Numbered footnotes by the Court.]

3. A defaulting buyer does not meet this burden merely by proving that some benefit was transferred to the seller. To prevail, the defaulting buyer must prove the amount of damages suffered by the seller. I G. Palmer, *The Law of Restitution,* § 5.4, at 585 (1978). Failure to offer any proof by the defaulting buyer would result in a judgment for the non-breaching seller. *See Kitchin v. Mori,* 84 Nev. 181, 437 P.2d 865, 867 (1968).

4. The result of placing the burden of proof on the defaulting buyer is that the non-breaching seller will derive the benefit of doubt if the buyer fails in its burden of proof. *See* I G. Palmer, *The Law of Restitution,* § 5.4, at 587 (1978).

the buyer time to conduct a new title search, inspection, and acquire financing, we find that at least some portion of these finance charges was a foreseeable consequence of Allen's breach, and should have been included in the jury award.[5]

In sum, no matter how conservatively one arrives at the number representing the builders' consequential damages, that number would exceed the one arrived at by the jury. Since the jury's verdict as to the amount of consequential damages incurred by the builders is contrary to the clear weight of the evidence, the trial court should have granted the builders' motion for a new trial on this issue. *See* Alaska R.Civ.P. 59(a).

As for the jury's verdict of $12,000 for the value of the lot, we affirm. We believe that the evidence presented on this issue could have led to a lower verdict than that returned by the jury. However, we are not convinced that the jury's verdict was against the *clear* weight of the evidence. Thus, the superior court did not err in denying the builders' motion for new trial on this issue.

* * *

The judgment of the superior court is AFFIRMED in part [and] REVERSED in part * * *

Notes

1. Perhaps the leading case awarding quasi-contract relief to the party in breach is Vines v. Orchard Hills, Inc., 181 Conn. 501, 435 A.2d 1022 (1980). The policy justification for such relief was stated as follows (435 A.2d, at pp. 1025–6):

> "The right of a contracting party, despite his default, to seek restitution for benefits conferred and allegedly unjustly retained has been much disputed in the legal literature and in the case law. *See* 5A Corbin, Contracts §§ 1122–1135 (1964); Dobbs, Remedies § 12.14 (1973); I G. Palmer, Restitution, c. 5 (1978); 12 Williston, Contracts §§ 1473 through 1478 (3d Ed.1970); 5 Williston, Contracts § 791 (3d Ed.1961); Lee, 'The Plaintiff in Default,' 19 Vand.L.Rev. 1023 (1965–66); Talbott, 'Restitution for the Defaulting Buyer,' 9 W.Res.L.Rev. 445 (1958); annot., 'Vendee's Recovery of Purchase Money,' 31 A.L.R.2d, pp. 8–131 (1953). Although earlier cases often refused to permit a party to bring an action that could be said to be based on his own breach; many of the more recent cases support restitution in order to prevent unjust enrichment and to avoid forfeiture. * * *
>
> "A variety of considerations, some practical and some theoretical, underlie this shift in attitude toward the plaintiff in breach. As Professor Corbin pointed out in his seminal article, 'The Right of a Defaulting Vendee to the Restitution of Instalments Paid,' 40 Yale L.J. 1013 (1931),

5. The builders argue that the damage defenses of mitigation and foreseeability do not apply in restitution actions brought by a defaulting buyer. We disagree. Corbin, discussing the measurement of recovery by a defaulting plaintiff in a restitution action, states that "[t]he amount of the defendant's injury will be measured in accordance with the usual rules for determining damages for a breach." 5A A. Corbin, *Corbin on Contracts,* § 1124 at 13 (1964). Accordingly, the damage defenses of foreseeability and mitigation are available in restitution actions brought by a defaulting buyer.

the anomalous result of denying any remedy to the plaintiff in breach is to punish more severely the person who has partially performed, often in good faith, than the person who has entirely disregarded his contractual obligations from the outset. Only partial performance triggers a claim for restitution, and partial performance will not, in the ordinary course of events, have been more injurious to the innocent party than total nonperformance. Recognition of a claim in restitution is, furthermore, consistent with the economic functions that the law of contracts is designed to serve. *See* Kessler & Gilmore, Contracts, pp. 4–6 (1970). The principal purpose of remedies for the breach of contract is to provide compensation for loss; *see* Restatement (Second), Contracts, c. 16, Introductory Note (Tent.Draft No. 14, 1979); Farnsworth, 'Legal Remedies for Breach of Contract,' 70 Colum.L.Rev. 1145 (1970); and therefore a party injured by breach of contract is entitled to retain nothing in excess of that sum which compensates him for the loss of his bargain. Indeed, there are those who argue that repudiation of contractual obligations is socially desirable, and should be encouraged, whenever gain to the party in breach exceeds loss to the party injured by breach. Birmingham, 'Breach of Contract, Damage Measures, and Economic Efficiency,' 24 Rut.L.Rev. 273, 284 (1970); Posner, Economic Analysis of Law § 4.9, pp. 89–90 (2d Ed.1977). To assign such primacy to inferences drawn from economic models requires great confidence that the person injured by breach will encounter no substantial difficulties in establishing the losses for which he is entitled to be compensated. It is not necessary to push the principle of compensatory damages that far, or to disregard entirely the desirability of maintaining some incentives for the performance of promises. A claim in restitution, although legal in form, is equitable in nature, and permits a trial court to balance the equities, to take into account a variety of competing principles to determine whether the defendant has been unjustly enriched. 'Even though we adhere to the rule that only compensatory damages are to be awarded, there are other important questions of policy to be considered. One is whether aid is to be given to one who breaches his contract, particularly when the breach is deliberate and without moral justification. Another is whether restitution can be administered without leaving the innocent party with uncompensated damages.' I G. Palmer, Restitution § 5.1, p. 574 (1978)."

See, also, Truly v. Austin, 744 S.W.2d 934 (Tex.1988) in which quasi-contractual relief was denied to an investor in a joint venture who was obligated under the venture agreement to supervise the construction work and did so for twenty-four months but "voluntarily" refused to sign a note for financing the venture and thereby breached the agreement, "thus precipitating the failure of the project." (*Id.,* at 938). As a consequence "Truly [the plaintiff] by his course of conduct, has violated the reasonable expectations and value that permeate business transactions, * * * [and] may not recover in quantum meruit."

2. The Restatement of Contracts § 374 (1981), contrary to the original Restatement and considerable case law authority, does not deny quasi-contract relief to the buyer because his breach was "wilful and deliberate." It does, however, state in the comments that the quality of the breach may be of such a nature as to make it "officious," and therefore a basis for denying relief to the plaintiff. This approach is criticized in I G. Palmer, The Law of Restitution

(1978) § 5.1 (Supp.1982). The burden of proof to show benefit in excess of the damages suffered, is, however, on the plaintiff, who thus bears the loss in case of doubt. *Id.* A useful discussion of the manner in which the law has evolved in this area, especially as it relates to a buyer of goods who is in default, is to be found in Amtorg Trading Corp. v. Miehle Press & Mfg. Co., 206 F.2d 103 (2d Cir.1953).

3. The situation of the buyer in default under the U.C.C. is considered in Nordstrom, Restitution on Default and Article Two of the Uniform Commercial Code, 19 Vand.L.Rev. 1143, 1168–72 (1966): *

> "Nevertheless, a substantial number of courts—probably the majority—denied the buyer in default any recovery for benefits conferred prior to breach. Allowing recovery for these benefits was viewed as a 'dangerous precedent' which 'would tend to demoralize the whole country.'
>
> > '[T]he establishment of such a principle would have a tendency to encourage the violation of contracts—to diminish, in the minds of contracting parties, a sense of the obligation which rests upon them to perform their agreements. Any principle which would have such an effect, ought not to be recognized as sound law. It is the duty of courts to enforce the performance of contracts, not to encourage their violation.'
>
> "Those cases which denied the defaulting buyer any possibility of restitution recovery are now repudiated by the Code. Further, under the Code, a contract clause providing for forfeiture of payments made by a buyer prior to his breach will not be enforced unless the clause meets the tests of section 2–718(1). The draftsmen of the Code refused, however, to go as far as those pre-Code cases which freely awarded protection of the restitution interest of the defaulting buyer. The Code seller is allowed to retain from any payments made (either in money or goods) 500 dollars or 20 per cent of the value of buyer's total performance, whichever amount is the smaller. This may be a recognition that a seller has been injured in an amount which cannot accurately be measured under any of the existing damage formulas, and that an award of up to 20 per cent on small sales or 500 dollars on larger ones is a rough estimate of that injury. 'Rough' justice may be done by such a formula, but it would be preferable to define more carefully the elements of a seller's damage and to allow restitution of *all* amounts over that damage than to continue any part of the prior practice of letting the extent of performance determine the ultimate financial position of the parties."

4. There are a variety of situations in which a plaintiff in material breach may seek restitution to prevent an unfair enrichment of the defendant. As Professor Palmer has made clear, the cases follow no conceptually consistent pattern, even within a single jurisdiction. Nor do they, in many situations, show an appreciation of whether or not the plaintiff's default was "intentional and deliberate."

There is general agreement that under any circumstances the recovery by a defaulting party must be limited to the defendant's enrichment in excess of the amount of any damage suffered as a result of plaintiff's breach, and arguably should not exceed the contract price or a ratable proportion of it. 5 A. Corbin, Contracts § 1124 (1964); I G. Palmer, The Law of Restitution (1978) § 5.3.

The contexts in which this problem has arisen, and the pattern of the holdings as noted by Professor Palmer, are as follows:

(a) Defaulting buyer of land [as in the *Allen* case].

Traditionally, courts have denied restitution to the party in default unless the sum paid to the seller, if not recovered in part, would amount to a "penalty." *Id.* at 596, 614. A provision in the agreement that the sums paid are to be "forfeited" as "liquidated damages," usually called a "forfeiture clause", should not prevent examination to determine whether the benefit so greatly exceeds the damage suffered due to the breach that it is, in reality, a "penalty."

More recent cases have allowed recovery by a defaulting buyer. There are citations to these cases in *Vines.* For example, California allows recovery without regard to the nature of the buyer's breach unless the seller can show loss due to a decrease in market value. This approach has been criticized as unfair to the seller in many instances. *Id.* at 601.

(b) Defaulting employee under personal service contract.

Virtually all of the older cases deny quasi-contract relief to the employee who quits without cause, and many courts continue to take this position. But there are a substantial number of courts which disagree. *Id.* at 649–52. The more recent cases usually involve more sophisticated forms of compensation, such as bonus plan benefits. Where the discharge is for "cause," recovery is denied unless there is a showing that the employee's conduct was not blameworthy and that he or she was honestly attempting to do the job. *Id.* at 665.

(c) Defaulting seller of personal property.

Almost all cases in this area allow quasi-contract recovery by the seller, as does the U.C.C. § 2–607(1). *Id.* at 628–29 (criticizing in part the U.C.C. measure of benefit).

(d) Defaulting buyer of personal property (discussed above in Notes 2 and 3).

(e) Defaulting party under contract to build or repair structures.

Most courts grant quasi-contract relief, although a few deny it where the breach was in bad faith. *Id.* at 668.

FORDICE CONSTRUCTION COMPANY v. CENTRAL STATES DREDGING COMPANY

United States District Court, Southern District of Mississippi, 1986.
631 F.Supp. 1536.

* * *

Facts

On November 18, 1983, the Army Corps of Engineers, Vicksburg, Mississippi District, solicited bids from small business concerns and/or "entering manufacturers" for the manufacture of 200,000 squares of articulated concrete mattresses for Contract No. DACW38–84–B–001 at Delta,

Louisiana. Both Central States and Fordice submitted bids on the basis that they were small businesses. Central States was the low bidder and was awarded the contract.

Shortly after the bid opening, Fordice, the second low bidder, filed protests with the SBA and the Department of Labor, challenging Central States' self-certification as a small business and its status as an "entering manufacturer" under the Walsh–Healey Act. Fordice claimed that although Central States was a small business, it was ineligible for the procurement because of its alleged joint venture relationship with APAC, a large business ineligible for the contract and Central States' subcontractor.

[The Court found that there was a triable issue of fact as to whether the defendants were ineligible to bid on the project in question.]

* * *

LAW

Defendants move for summary judgment on the basis that: (1) Fordice has no remedies under state law; (2) there was no joint venture between them and, therefore, Fordice has no claim against them for unjust enrichment and fraud; and (3) Fordice is estopped to pursue its claims against them. Fordice asserts the contrary.

With regard to Defendants' contention that Fordice has no state law remedies, this Court previously addressed a portion of this issue in its Memorandum Opinion and Order of April 10, 1985, where it was determined that federal law does not pre-empt state law claims, following *Tectonics, Inc. of Florida v. Castle Construction Company,* 753 F.2d 957 (11th Cir.1985).[2] Specifically, this Court stated that:

> * * * If the plaintiff is able to prove that the two defendants are indeed joint venturers and submitted the bid in an effort to obtain a contract for which they were ineligible under federal law, then allowing the action based on a state law claim would further the goal sought to be achieved by Congress in enacting legislation rather than conflict with them.

Opinion at 1538. The Court did not address "[t]he question of whether or not a state law claim for that which [Fordice] seeks is available under Mississippi law." That portion of the issue is now before the Court.

With regard to Fordice's claim for unjust enrichment, Mississippi law provides that, in an action for unjust enrichment, "the plaintiff need only allege and show that the defendant holds money which in equity and good conscience belongs to the plaintiff." *Dorsey Mississippi Sales, Inc. v.*

2. *See also, Iconco v. Jensen Construction Company,* 622 F.2d 1291 (8th Cir.1980). *Cf. Ferguson–Williams, Inc. v. Bamsi, Inc.,* 782 F.2d 940 (11th Cir.1986), where the Eleventh Circuit reiterated that "although Congress did not intend to provide a civil private cause of action to the second lowest bidder of a federal contract when the lowest bidder has misrepresented itself as a small business, it had not expressly nor impliedly preempted a state remedy for fraud, unjust enrichment or interference with a business relationship based on such misrepresentation." The court further stated that the "key" to such a case would be whether the successful low bidder was, indeed, ineligible to receive the contract.

* * *

Newell, 251 Miss. 77, 168 So.2d 645, 651 (1964). *See also Magnolia Federal Savings and Loan Association v. Randal Craft Realty Company, Inc.,* 342 So.2d 1308 (Miss.1977). The requirements of proof of unjust enrichment are neither technical nor complicated and, Fordice can state a claim against Defendants on the basis that Central States and APAC were unjustly enriched because they received the profits from the performance of a government contract which, under the standards created by the SBA, they should not have been permitted to perform. By engrafting the standards created by the SBA onto a state law claim for unjust enrichment, Fordice has an available remedy under Mississippi law.[4] *See Iconco,* 622 F.2d at 1296–99. Of course, to prevail on its claim for unjust enrichment, Fordice must not only prove that Defendants were unjustly enriched by the award of the contract but also that it was entitled to the award of the contract.

With regard to the claim of Fordice based on allegations of fraud, Fordice need not be a party to the fraud as Central States claims. The right to recover for fraud is not restricted to the parties to the transaction, but extends to third parties injured thereby. 37 Am.Jur.2d *Fraud and Deceit* § 307, p. 408. *See also* 37 Am.Jur.2d *Fraud and Deceit,* §§ 189, 190, 244. In this case, the question of whether false representations were made by Defendants constitutes a genuine issue of material fact which cannot be resolved on motion for summary judgment.

Accordingly, Defendants argument that Fordice cannot pursue its state law claims is not well taken.

Defendants next argue that since there was no joint venture between them, there are no state law remedies. Despite the affidavits, deposition testimony and other documents submitted to the Court by Defendants in support of their position that no joint venture existed, the Court finds that the question of whether a joint venture existed between Defendants presents a genuine issue of material fact which cannot be resolved on motion for summary judgment. *See, e.g., Putt v. Ray Sewell Company, Inc.,* 481 So.2d 785 (Miss.1985); *Hults v. Tillman,* 480 So.2d 1134 (Miss.1985).

Finally, Defendants argue that Fordice is estopped to pursue this action and that Fordice has waived any claims it may have against Defendants. The Court finds that the defenses of estoppel and waiver present genuine issues of material fact which may not be resolved on motion for summary judgment.

Accordingly, Defendants' Motion for Summary Judgment is hereby denied.

4. In *Iconco,* 622 F.2d at 1299, the Eleventh Circuit also considered whether the Supreme Court of Iowa would use the Act as a standard, if the case were pending before it, in determining whether a claim for unjust enrichment had been stated. *See also, Tectonics,* 753 F.2d at 964. The Eleventh Circuit found no authority to indicate the Iowa Supreme Court would not use the Act as a standard and did not disturb the district court's affirmative ruling on this point. We, too, have researched Mississippi law and find no case to indicate the Mississippi Supreme Court would reject consideration of the Act as a standard. Indeed, there is every indication that the Mississippi Supreme Court would refer to federal law as a guidepost in formulating state law. *See, e.g.,* Ron A. Yarbrough, *Rights and Remedies under Mississippi's New Public Construction Bond Statute,* 51 M.L.J. 351 (1980).

Note

1. To the same effect is Iconco v. Jensen Construction Co., 622 F.2d 1291 (8th Cir.1980) which is relied upon by the court in *Fordice,* and Service Engineering Co. v. Southwest Marine, Inc., 719 F.Supp. 1500 (N.D.Cal.1989) (applying California law). Contra, John C. Holland Enter. v. J.P. Mascaro & Sons, Inc., 653 F.Supp. 1242 (E.D.Va.1987), aff'd w/o op., 829 F.2d 1120 (1987) (relying upon Virginia law which provided an express remedy to the unsuccessful bidder in such a situation). *See also,* Della Construction, Inc. v. The Lane Construction Company, 42 Conn.Sup. 202, 612 A.2d 147 (1991) (unsuccessful bidder can sue successful bidder, who allegedly submitted a fraudulent bid, on the theory of tortious interference with prospective contract and business relationship).

MAGNOLIA FEDERAL SAVINGS & LOAN ASSOCIATION v. RANDAL CRAFT REALTY COMPANY, INC.

Supreme Court of Mississippi, 1977.
342 So.2d 1308.

INZER, PRESIDING JUSTICE, for the Court:

This is an appeal by Magnolia Federal Savings & Loan Association from a decree of the Chancery Court of the First Judicial District of Hinds County awarding appellee Randal Craft Realty Co., Inc., $11,500 as a real estate commission. Appellee cross appeals contending that it was entitled to a larger sum.

The record reveals that in 1972 Magnolia Federal Savings & Loan Association, hereinafter referred to as Magnolia, was the owner of a building and lot in north Jackson under lease to Franchise Realty Interstate Corporation and occupied by McDonald's, a nationally known hamburger chain. This lease provided, among other things, that in the event the lessor had an offer from someone to purchase the premises, which it desired to accept, notice of such offer would be submitted to the lessee, and that the lessee would have the first option to purchase the property "by giving notice to the lessor of its intention to purchase within the thirty day period at the same price and the same terms of any such offer." This lease had been arranged by Terry Hairston, a real estate agent, and he was to receive as his commission six percent of the lease payments each year until the expiration of the lease. However, there was nothing in writing relative to these payments until after this controversy arose.

In the early part of 1972, Magnolia was advised by the Federal Home Loan Bank that its investment in this property was unauthorized and it would have to dispose of the property. Magnolia then tried to sell the property to its lessee, Franchise, but Franchise did not display an interest in buying the property. Magnolia then contacted some real estate agents in an attempt to sell the property. On or about August 10, 1972, Craft learned that the property was for sale and acquired listing information from Magnolia. The listing information given to Craft was a gross price of $307,000, with a real estate broker's commission of six percent on the first $50,000 and five percent on the balance. Craft was also instructed that a prospective purchaser would have to assume the payments of the lease commission to Hairston. The listing with Craft was not an exclusive listing.

Craft set about to try to find a buyer for the property. One of the people contacted was David E. Crawley of Kosciusko, who expressed an interest in buying the property as agent for his son and daughter. Craft then prepared certain analysis and appraisal of the property for the prospective purchasers in an attempt to show the Crawleys that the property was a good investment. This required considerable time and effort on the part of Craft.

On August 21, 1972, Craft was advised by Magnolia that it had reduced its purchase price and would sell the property for $275,000 net to Magnolia. Craft then contacted Crawley who agreed to purchase the property at a price of $292,500. This price included a $17,500 broker's fee.

As soon as the agreement was reached, Craft prepared a contract on the standard form for the sale and purchase of real estate. The contract was immediately carried to Magnolia where it was signed by Crawley, Craft and Phillip H. Payment, president of Magnolia. This contract had the following special provisions:

> Purchasers and sellers recognize that Franchise Realty Interstate Corporation has an option to purchase herein described property within thirty days from date of notice *upon the same terms and conditions set forth herein.* If this option is not exercised by Franchise Realty Interstate Corporation, then the contract will then be in full force and effect and this sale shall be closed within 45 days from date of this contract. (Emphasis added).

The contract did not mention the fact that Crawley was assuming the payment of the lease commissions to Hairston, but Crawley understood that he was to assume this payment.

On August 23, Magnolia notified Franchise by letter that it had sold its McDonald's location. The letter stated, "We are enclosing herewith a copy of the contract, so that all of the terms and conditions of the sale will be known to you." The purpose of the letter was to comply with the terms of the lease with reference to the option of Franchise to purchase the property. Nothing was stated in the letter relative to the fact that Hairston was entitled to a commission under the lease. Two days later Magnolia acknowledged by letter to Hairston that he was entitled to a commission under the lease.

On September 4, 1972, Franchise, much to the surprise of all parties, by letter advised Magnolia of its intention to purchase the property in accordance with the purchase and sale agreement. Apparently, there was some discussion between Franchise and Magnolia relative to whether Franchise was required to pay the real estate commission as part of the purchase price. The minutes of Magnolia reflect that the gross price of the property was $292,500 with the association to pay the fee necessary. Thereafter, Payment advised Franchise that the $292,500 was the purchase price that it was obligated to pay under the terms of the lease and contract for sale and that the broker's commission was a matter of contract between the association and Randal Craft and the association would be responsible for any obligation to that broker only. Thereafter, the sale to Franchise was finally closed on December 13, 1972. The minutes of Magnolia of December 13 reflect the following:

> President Payment next reported that the sale of McDonald's had been consummated and we had received a gross check in the amount of $288,000, and that the Association should net approximately $275,000 from the sale proceeds. President Payment was instructed to settle the transaction on McDonalds to Terry Hairston, who was the leasing agent, and with Randal Craft, who was a realtor involved in the sale transaction. President Payment was instructed to report back to the Executive Committee as to his transactions in dealing with Mr. Hairston and Mr. Craft.

It seems clear at this point that Magnolia recognized that the sale of the property was due to the efforts of Craft and it recognized its obligation to pay Craft. However, Mr. Payment made no attempt to settle with Craft but did settle with Hairston. On December 27, 1972, Payment reported to the Board of Directors that he had settled with Hairston and paid him $12,000 but that Craft was not due any commission.

Thereafter, Craft filed this suit. A general demurrer was sustained to the original bill of complaint. Craft then filed an amended bill of complaint which sought recovery on the theory of the resulting or constructive trust. Magnolia answered and incorporated a general demurrer in this answer. This demurrer was overruled. The answer denied that Craft was entitled to recover any amount as a real estate commission.

The chancellor found from the evidence that Craft was entitled to a commission of $17,500, less $6,000 being one-half of the amount paid to Hairston by Magnolia. It was the opinion of the chancellor that Craft was at fault in failing to include in the purchase and sales contract the condition that the purchaser was required to assume the lease commission payable to Hairston. He also found that Magnolia apparently did not carefully examine the contract for sale and purchase before sending it to Franchise and was at fault in failing to see that Franchise was fully advised of the terms that it was required to meet. It was the chancellor's opinion that the disagreement and litigation was brought about by the failure of the parties to see that the full terms and conditions were included in the contract and a decree was entered awarding Craft a money judgment for $11,500, hence this appeal.

On direct appeal Magnolia contends that the chancellor was in error in finding from the facts in this case that Craft was entitled to a commission. Appellant urges that Craft failed to prove a constructive or resulting trust and that the chancellor should have dismissed the bill of complaint. We find no merit in the contention that the chancellor should have dismissed the bill of complaint. The bill prayed for general relief and the chancellor in making a decision was required to determine from the facts and the law whether Craft was entitled to the commission. The chancellor found that Craft was entitled to a commission and in deciding the case we must consider the facts in the light most favorable to Craft, together with all reasonable inferences that may be drawn therefrom. While the proof of this case does not establish a constructive trust, it does establish a quasi-contract or constructive contract. A quasi-contractual obligation closely resembles a constructive trust, one difference being that an action to enforce a contractual obligation seeks to establish personal liability of the defendant to pay over a sum of money, while an action to enforce a constructive trust seeks to recover specific property. A quasi-contract, or constructive contract, is based on the equitable principle that a person shall not be allowed to enrich himself unjustly at the expense of another. In this respect the terms "unjust enrichment" and "restitution" are modern designation for the doctrine of "quasi-contracts" and the basis for an action for "unjust enrichment" lies in a promise, which is implied in law, that one will pay to the person entitled thereto which in equity and good conscience is his. 17 C.J.S. Contracts § 6.

In Old Men's Home, Inc. v. Lee's Estate, 191 Miss. 669, 2 So.2d 791 (1941), we pointed out that a quasi or constructive contract rests on the equitable principle that a person shall not be allowed to enrich himself unjustly at the expense of another. It is an obligation created by law, in the absence of any agreement, when and because the acts of the parties or others have placed in the possession of one person money under circumstances that in equity and good conscience he ought not to retain and which in justice and fairness belongs to another.

Furthermore, in Cooke v. Adams, 183 So.2d 925 (Miss.1966), we held that any conduct of one party from which the other party may draw the inference of a promise is effective as such and the conduct of the parties is viewed as a reasonable man would to determine the existence or not of the contract implied in fact. We also stated:

> A promise which is implied in fact is merely a tacit promise, one which is inferred in whole or in part from the expressions other than words by the promisor, and a promise implied in law is one in which neither the words nor the conduct of the party involved are promissory in form or justify an inference of a promise, and the term is used to indicate that the party is under a legally enforceable duty as he would have been, if he had in fact made a promise. Ferrous Products Co. v. Gulf States Trading Co., Tex.Civ.App., 323 S.W.2d 292, affirmed 160 Tex. 399, 332 S.W.2d 310 (1960).
>
> (183 So.2d at 927).

In spite of the foregoing facts, Magnolia argues that Craft was not entitled to a commission as a matter of law because he had knowledge of Franchise's right of first refusal and the right to first refusal prevented the sale to the purchaser procured by Craft. It is argued that this right of refusal constituted an impediment or defect in the title of Magnolia and the sale to Crawley failed on account of this defect. Magnolia contends that there was no agreement that Craft would be paid a fee if Franchise exercised its option. Magnolia relies on the rule of law announced in Best v. Kelley, 22 Wash.2d 257, 155 P.2d 794 (1945), wherein that Court adopted a rule announced in Renick v. Mann, 194 Ky. 251, 238 S.W. 763, where the Kentucky Court of Appeals stated:

> The general rule is that a broker is entitled to his commission, who, acting in good faith, procures a purchaser willing, able and ready to take the property upon the terms offered by the principal, and this is true notwithstanding the sale fails because of a defect in the principal's title of which the broker had no notice. But if the broker, at the time he makes the contract with the owner, knows of the defect in his employer's title or knows facts sufficient to put a reasonably prudent person on inquiry, which, if followed with reasonable diligence, would bring to him such knowledge, he is not entitled to recover where the sale fails because of such defect, unless it was the intention of the parties that the employer should subsequently perfect his title in order to perform the contract of sale.
>
> (155 P.2d at 799).

Magnolia points out that this Court adopted this rule and cites Shireman v. Wildberger, 125 Miss. 199, 87 So. 131 (1921) and Stewart v. Harrison, 210 Miss. 750, 50 So.2d 624 (1951). While it is true that this Court has adopted a rule substantially the same as announced by the Washington Court, we are of the opinion, under the facts and circumstances of this case, the rule is not applicable and does not prevent recovery under the theory of a quasi-contract established by the facts in this case.

It is true that Craft was aware that Franchise had the first right of refusal under the terms of its lease, but the lease stated that Franchise had the right to purchase at the same price and under the same terms of the offer. Magnolia advised Craft that it would accept $275,000 net to Magnolia and that Craft would have to adjust the price to include any real estate commission he desired to earn. Craft then secured the contract with Crawley whereby Crawley agreed to purchase the property for $292,500. Included in the purchase price was a real estate commission of $17,500. Magnolia agreed and submitted the same to Franchise. Franchise noticed that included in the sales price was the real estate commission. Since Franchise was exercising its option to buy at the same price as the property was offered to Crawley, it was only natural for it to inquire about the real estate commission. If one was to be paid Franchise wanted it to go to its broker. After inquiry Magnolia advised Franchise by letter, dated September 29, 1972, which reads in part as follows:

> In view of our several telephone conferences held with regard to the decision of Franchise Realty Interstate Corporation to exercise its option to purchase described in Article 27 of the lease, there are two material items of the transaction which should be brought to your attention, so as to avoid any misunderstanding later.
>
> First, the purchase price to the Crawleys as stated in the August 22, 1972, contract of sale is $292,500. I have discussed the matter of possible reduction with our Board of Directors and the Board has concluded that $292,500 is the purchase price which Franchise Realty Interstate Corporation is obligated to pay under the terms of both the lease and the contract of sale.

> Next, there is the matter of the broker's commission which has also been discussed with the Board. The broker's commission is a matter of contract between Magnolia Federal Savings and Loan Association and Randall Craft, and the Association will be responsible for any obligations to that broker only. Therefore, no part of the purchase price is to be withheld for the payment of any brokerage fee connected with the transaction.

At this point, the chancellor was certainly justified in finding that Magnolia recognized that Craft was entitled to a commission. Especially is this true since Magnolia admits that the purchase agreement secured by Craft from Crawley was the sole cause of the sale to Franchise and Magnolia collected from Franchise the commission called for in the contract. Under the facts and circumstances of this case, the acts of the parties placed in the hands of Magnolia $17,500 which in equity, good conscience, justice and fairness belongs to Craft. To allow Magnolia to retain the money would allow it to unjustly enrich itself at the expense of Craft, whose efforts Magnolia admits were the sole cause of the sale to Franchise.

We have carefully considered the other errors assigned and find them to be without merit. For the reasons stated we are of the opinion that this case should be affirmed on direct appeal.

CROSS APPEAL

On cross appeal, Craft contends that the chancellor was in error in holding the amount which he was entitled to recover should be reduced to $11,500 because of his failure to put into the contract for sale executed by Crawley and Magnolia the stipulation that Hairston was entitled to a commission under the terms of the lease. This stipulation would have increased the purchase price by the amount of the commission due Hairston. As heretofore pointed out the chancellor was of the opinion that both parties were negligent in failing to put into the contract the stipulation that the purchaser would be liable for the commission due Hairston. It is apparent that the chancellor in holding that Craft and Magnolia were both responsible for this oversight was simply doing equity. Craft having sought equity was required to do equity, and we cannot say the chancellor was manifestly wrong in adjusting the equities. Consequently, we are of the opinion that this case should be affirmed on cross appeal.

This case was considered by the Judges en banc.

Affirmed on Direct and Cross Appeals.

All Justices concur, except SUGG, J., who took no part.

HARPER v. ADAMETZ

Supreme Court of Errors of Connecticut, 1955.
142 Conn. 218, 113 A.2d 136.

BALDWIN, ASSOCIATE JUSTICE. This action, based upon fraud, was brought by the plaintiff against the named defendant and his son Walter Adametz. The court rendered judgment for the defendants and the plaintiff has appealed.

The facts found, which are not subject to correction, are as follows: Joseph B. Tesar was conservator of the estate of his father, William Tesar, an incompetent, who owned eighty acres of land and the buildings thereon in the town of Haddam. The defendant Jere Adametz, a real estate agent, hereinafter referred to as Jere, was acting as agent for the sale of Tesar's property. Jere advertised a portion of it, consisting of five acres and an old colonial house, for $6200, and the advertisement, in a New Haven newspaper, came to the attention of the plaintiff. On December 6, 1948, the plaintiff wrote to Jere expressing an interest in the property advertised. Jere acknowledged this letter on December 8. On December 12, Jere showed the plaintiff the eighty-acre farm and told him that the seller was asking $8500 for it but that the buildings and a smaller acreage could be bought for less. The plaintiff made no offer but showed an interest in purchasing the smaller acreage. On the following day, December 13, Jere wrote to Joseph Tesar, the conservator, stating that he had a client who had offered $6500 cash for the farm (meaning eighty acres) and asked for an immediate reply. On December 15, the attorney for Tesar wrote to Jere stating that Tesar would accept the offer for the entire farm subject to the approval of the Probate Court and asking that a written offer with at least a 10 per cent deposit be sent to him.

The plaintiff visited the property on December 19 and 26, and on one of those dates he made an offer to Jere of $7000 for the entire farm. Jere promised to convey this offer to Tesar, but he did not do so. Instead, he sent his own check for $500 to Tesar on December 29 as a deposit on the purported offer of $6500. Jere told Fred Mazanek, a relative of the Tesars, that the plaintiff wanted to purchase only a small portion of the acreage and that he, Jere, would like to obtain the rest for his son but that he did not want to lose his commission. He prevailed upon Mazanek and John Hibbard, a friend of the family, to act as a medium for the passing of title to the farm. On or about January 2, 1949, Jere told the plaintiff that his offer had been rejected because Tesar desired to keep a major portion of the farm in the family and that certain relatives of the Tesars wished to buy most of the acreage, but that he Jere, could arrange for the plaintiff to buy the buildings and part of the land. The plaintiff then made an offer of $6000 for seventeen acres, including the buildings, and Jere accepted the offer. The plaintiff was satisfied with his purchase.

On January 4 Joseph Tesar signed a contract to sell the entire farm of eighty acres to Mazanek and Hibbard for $6500. The sale was approved by the Probate Court, and a conservator's deed dated January 26, was delivered on February 8 to Mazanek and Hibbard. At the same time, on February 8, they executed and delivered a deed for seventeen acres, including the buildings, to the plaintiff, who paid $6000. On March 11, Mazanek and Hibbard conveyed sixty-three acres, the balance of the farm, to the defendant Walter Adametz, Jere's son. Mazanek and Hibbard were mere "go betweens" who paid nothing when they "bought" the farm and received nothing when they "sold" it to the plaintiff and Walter. Walter paid nothing for the sixty-three acres he acquired. Tesar did not know of the plaintiff's offer of $7000 for the entire farm, and the plaintiff did not know that this offer had not been transmitted to Tesar. The representation by Jere to Tesar on December 13 that he had a $6500 offer for the farm was false. At the time he sent his own check for $500 to Tesar on the purported offer of $6500, the only offer he had was the plaintiff's offer of $7000. Jere engineered the transactions herein related to obtain sixty-three acres of the farm for himself and Walter at the price of $500 and at the same time collect a commission of $325 for the sale.

On these facts, the court concluded that Jere was the agent for Tesar and not for the plaintiff, that there was no contract between Tesar and the plaintiff for the purchase of any property other than the buildings and seventeen acres of land, that the plaintiff sustained no loss by reason of any misrepresentation made by Jere, and that therefore the plaintiff had failed to prove actionable fraud.

It is the general rule that in an action at law for fraud the plaintiff, to recover, must prove that he has been injured. In the ordinary case, this means that the plaintiff must sustain a substantial pecuniary loss. *See* Prosser, Torts, p. 768; Harper, Torts, p. 470. The plaintiff in this action did receive what he paid for. *See* Gilfillen v. Moorhead, 73 Conn. 710, 714, 49 A. 196. He did not, however, because of Jere's fraud, obtain what he was seeking. While acting as an agent for Tesar but with the intent of making a secret profit for himself, Jere told his principal that he had a cash offer of $6500 for the entire farm. This statement was false, and in making it Jere violated his trust. His conduct was a fraud upon Tesar.

Jere was not the agent of the plaintiff. Nevertheless, he could not deliberately deceive him. It was Jere's advertisement in the newspaper which had aroused the interest of the plaintiff in the property and had brought him to Haddam to inspect it. Jere told the plaintiff at that time that the entire farm was for sale for $8500. When the plaintiff later made an offer of $7000 for it, Jere said nothing about having submitted a bogus offer of $6500, and he promised to submit the plaintiff's offer to Tesar. He failed to do so and later lied to the plaintiff by telling him that Tesar had rejected it. It was not until after this that the plaintiff offered $6000 for seventeen acres and the buildings. It can be claimed that when the plaintiff made his $7000 offer Tesar had already signified his willingness to accept the purported offer of $6500 made by Jere in behalf of a fictitious client and that the plaintiff's offer came too late. But the $6500 offer was a fraud and Tesar was not bound to accept it. He could have revoked Jere's authority. * * * Thereafter, he could have sold the property to the plaintiff. Jere's false statements, his concealment of the facts, his promise to submit the plaintiff's offer to Tesar when everything indicates that he had no intention of doing so, worked a fraud upon the plaintiff. * * * As a result, the plaintiff has been denied the right to have his bona fide offer of $7000 submitted to Tesar. In short, the plaintiff has been deprived of his bargain. Jere and Walter, by their fraud, have acquired sixty-three acres of land for $175.

This is an action in equity as well as at law. Equity is a system of positive jurisprudence founded upon established principles which can be adapted to new circumstances where a court of law is powerless to give relief. 1 Pomeroy, Equity Jurisprudence (5th Ed.) p. 78. In equity, as in law, misrepresentation, to constitute fraud, must be material. 3 *Id.,* § 876; Bogert, 3 Trusts & Trustees, § 473. That is to say, the representation must prejudice the party relying upon it. He must suffer some injury or pecuniary loss. Some courts have held that the pecuniary loss need be only slight. 3 Pomeroy, *op. cit.,* pp. 535, 536, and cases cited n. 8. Others have held that mere lack of pecuniary injury or loss does not prevent the granting of relief by way of rescission and restitution. 3 *id.,* p. 537, and cases cited n. 10. * * *

The plaintiff had a clear right to have his offer for the farm transmitted to Tesar. Having been invited by Jere's advertisement to bid for the property, he had a right to assume that Jere would deal honestly with him and be faithful to his principal. Instead, Jere withheld the offer, later lied to the plaintiff about it and, by using the plaintiff's willingness to accept seventeen acres, acquired the farm for himself for less than the plaintiff had offered for it. He induced the plaintiff to make an offer and then used that offer, and the plaintiff's money, to make a secret profit. By his fraudulent misrepresentations, he deprived the plaintiff of his bargain and obtained for himself some of the land which the plaintiff had offered to buy. "If one acquires property by means of a fraudulent misrepresentation of a material fact, equity will assist the defrauded person by fastening a constructive trust on the property." * Bogert, 3 Trusts & Trustees, p. 20; 3 Scott, Trusts, § 462.2; Restatement Restitution, § 133, comment a, §§ 160, 169; 4 Pomeroy, Equity Jurisprudence (5th Ed.) § 1044 * * *. It is true that this rule is most often applied in situations where the relationship between the plaintiff and the defendant is one which equity clearly recognizes as fiduciary. But equity has carefully refrained from defining a fiduciary relationship in precise detail and in such a manner as to exclude new situations. It has left the bars down for situations in which there is a justifiable trust confided on one side and a resulting superiority and influence on the other. 3 Pomeroy, *op. cit.,* § 956a.

Equity will not permit these defendants to keep a benefit which came to them by reason of Jere's fraudulent conduct. It is true that Tesar has not acted to right the wrong done to him. Had he done so, it is probable that the plaintiff could have had the farm. This should not prevent the plaintiff, in his own right, from having a remedy for the wrong done to him. The plaintiff has proffered $1000, which represents the balance of the amount of his original offer over and above the purchase price he paid for the seventeen acres. Upon the payment of this sum into court, to await further order, an order should enter directing the defendant Walter to convey the sixty-three acres to the plaintiff.

There is error, the judgment is set aside and the case is remanded to the Superior Court for proceedings in accordance with this opinion.**

O'SULLIVAN, ASSOCIATE JUSTICE, filed a dissenting opinion, omitted here. [Ed.]

* *See* G. Dawson, Unjust Enrichment 26–33 (1951). [Footnote by the Court.]

** This case is discussed in Notes, 35 B.U.L.Rev. 604 (1955) and 54 Mich.L.Rev. 714 (1956).

Notes

1. *Accord,* Sawyer Realty Group, Inc. v. Jarvis Corp., 89 Ill.2d 379, 59 Ill.Dec. 905, 432 N.E.2d 849 (1982) (the policy underlying the Illinois licensing act relating to real estate brokers justifies recognition of a private cause of action on behalf of a purchaser who was misled by the broker; "Real estate brokers occupy a position of trust with respect to the purchasers with whom they are negotiating." (*Id.,* 432 N.E.2d at 852)). *See, also,* Moore and Company v. T–A–L–L, Inc., 792 P.2d 794 (Colo.1990) (a real estate broker who violates the fiduciary duty owed to the client by failing to disclose relevant information may be liable in quasi-contract for the commission received even where the violation has resulted in no actual monetary loss to the client).

2. Professor Palmer describes the *Harper* case as one involving restitution to protect unrealized contract expectations. I G. Palmer, Law of Restitution (1978) § 3.18.

3. In the *Harper* case the court emphasizes that the defendant's conduct arguably might not constitute tortious misrepresentation because in any event the plaintiff got all he bargained for. If the trade were induced by a misrepresentation it was necessarily an "immaterial" one. A somewhat similar situation was presented in Ward v. Taggart, 51 Cal.2d 736, 336 P.2d 534 (1959) where a real estate agent, Taggart, stated to a potential purchaser, Ward, that he had a listing on certain premises which in fact had not been listed with him. Ward gave Taggart an offer on the property. Taggart told Ward it was not adequate and Ward increased his offer. Taggart, meanwhile, bought the property himself, and resold it to Ward at a large mark-up per acre. Having learned the true facts, Ward sued Taggart. Because Ward got all he bargained for, the court stated that there could be no recovery in tort. He was, however, allowed recovery of damages in quasi-contract, together with punitive damages. The court explained its approval of damages in these terms:

> "Even though Taggart was not plaintiff's agent, the public policy of this state does not permit one to 'take advantage of his own wrong' (Civ.Code, § 3517), and the law provides a quasi-contractual remedy to prevent one from being unjustly enriched at the expense of another. * * *
>
> * * *
>
> "Taggart contends that if recovery is based on the theory of unjust enrichment, the judgment for exemplary damages must be reversed. The argument runs that under this theory the law implies a promise to return the money wrongfully obtained, that the plaintiff waives the tort and sues in assumpsit on an implied contract, and that since such an action is 'contractual' in nature, it does not admit of the exemplary damages allowed under section 3294 of the Civil Code. That section authorizes exemplary damages 'in an action for the breach of an obligation not arising from contract, where the defendant has been guilty of oppression, fraud, or malice * * *.' The word 'contract' is used in this section in its ordinary sense to mean an agreement between the parties, not an obligation imposed by law despite the absence of any such agreement. Taggart's obligation does not arise from any agreement between him and plaintiffs. It arises from his fraud and violation of statutory duties. His fraud is not waived, for it is the very foundation of the implied-in-law promise to disgorge. *See* Corbin, Waiver of Tort and Suit in Assumpsit, 19 Yale L.J.

221, 243–246. The promise is purely fictitious and unintentional, originally implied to circumvent rigid common-law pleading. It was invoked not to deny a remedy, but to create one 'for the purpose of bringing about justice without reference to the intention of the parties.' * * *

"Courts award exemplary damages to discourage oppression, fraud, or malice by punishing the wrongdoer. *See* McCormick, Damages, § 79; Morris, Punitive Damages in Tort Cases, 44 Harv.L.Rev. 1173, 1185–1188. Such damages are appropriate in cases like the present one, where restitution would have little or no deterrent effect, for wrongdoers would run no risk of liability to their victims beyond that of returning what they wrongfully obtained. * * * The record herein discloses no abuse of discretion in the award of exemplary damages. * * *." *

LIPSON v. LIPSON

Supreme Court of Mississippi, 1966.
183 So.2d 900.

INZER, JUSTICE. Appellee, David Lipson, filed suit in the Chancery Court of Quitman County against Harry M. Lipson, Sr., individually, and as executor of the Estate of Morris Lipson, Deceased, and against Alma Lipson, Miriam Lipson and Harry M. Lipson, Jr., seeking to require the executor to make discovery of the assets of the Estate of Morris Lipson, and to set aside certain transactions between Morris Lipson and the defendants.

The bill of complaint alleged that David Lipson was the oldest child of Morris Lipson, Deceased, and that he was one of the beneficiaries under the will of Morris Lipson, and that the will had been duly probated in the Chancery Court of Quitman County. The defendant, Harry M. Lipson, Sr., was the only other child of Morris Lipson, Deceased, and he was named as executor of the last will and testament of Morris Lipson to serve without bond and without accounting to the court for his actions. The bill further charged that the will was executed in 1951, and its contents were known to Harry M. Lipson, Sr., and that thereafter he set about to make the bequest to David Lipson ineffective. The bill charged that a confidential and fiduciary relationship existed between the decedent and Harry M. Lipson, Sr. and Harry M. Lipson, Jr., son and grandson of decedent, and by undue influence, domination and control, that the parties so maneuvered Morris Lipson during his lifetime to cause him to pass title to his property in joint tenancy with the right of survivorship to the defendants; that because of undue influence and because of decedent's mental incapacities, the *inter vivos* gifts to the various defendants were void. The bill of complaint also charged that Harry M. Lipson, Sr. had probated a claim against the estate for $12,000; that his claim was allegedly based upon a promissory note; and that the claim had not been probated in accordance with the statutes. The prayer of the bill was that a temporary injunction be issued restraining the defendants from disposing of any of the property in question; and that the executor be required to post bond and file an inventory of the assets;

* This case is discussed in Notes, 48 Calif.L.Rev. 342 (1960); 57 Mich.L.Rev. 1249 (1959); 12 Stan.L.Rev. 270 (1959); 13 Vand. L.Rev. 390 (1959) (discussing exemplary damages in quasi-contract).

that the title of the defendants to the property in question be vacated and annulled; and the property be declared to be the property of the estate; further, that the probated claim of Harry M. Lipson, Sr. be disallowed and that complainant be awarded a decree for his interest in the assets of the estate.

The defendants, appellants here, answered and denied the material allegations of the bill relative to the undue influence and mental incapacity. The answer of Harry M. Lipson, Sr. exhibited an inventory of all the gifts made by the decedent in his lifetime and all of the property held in joint tenancy with the right of survivorship. The answers of the various defendants also set up demurrers to the bill of complaint. These demurrers were properly overruled.

* * *

A trial was had upon the issue involved, and after taking the matter under advisement, the chancellor rendered a written opinion which is part of the record in this case. The chancellor found that the decedent was mentally competent during all times material to the issues involved; however, he did find that a confidential and fiduciary relationship existed. His finding in this regard is as follows:

> "The facts and circumstances in this case clearly make out a fiduciary or confidential relationship, as that relationship is defined in the cases hereinafter referred to. There was a close family relationship, it appearing that M. Lipson had considerable affection for his son Harry and Harry's wife, children and grandchildren. The 1951 will favored Harry, referring to the 'love, affection and generosity of my son Harry M. Lipson, Senior.' During the period of time in question, M. Lipson lived on the same lot with his son, in a house provided by his son, and apparently ate most of his meals with the son and his family. Harry M. Lipson was named executor of the 1951 will, without bond or accounting. The alternate executor named was Harry M. Lipson, Jr., also without bond or accounting.
>
> "At the time of M. Lipson's death, most of his funds were invested in common stocks. Harry Lipson recommended stock purchases to be made, ordered all of them, instructed the broker as to form of registration, and paid for them. Apparently most of the purchases were made from the proceeds of checks payable to Harry Lipson himself. When a store building was purchased in 1959, in the name of M. Lipson and Harry Lipson as joint tenants, Harry Lipson carried on the negotiations and gave all instructions to the attorney for preparation of the deed. Prior to his death, M. Lipson converted both of his bank accounts to joint accounts with Harry M. Lipson, Jr. Harry Lipson looked after the insurance on M. Lipson's stocks and bonds in his safe. Harry Lipson, Jr., handled the rental transaction by which a part of the store of M. Lipson was rented for a jewelry business. The 1951 will was kept in Harry Lipson's safe from a time soon after its execution until the death of M. Lipson; the Answer of Harry M. Lipson filed September 28, 1962, admits that he knew of the execution of said will and of its contents. Harry Lipson kept all of M. Lipson's stock

and bonds in his safe for at least two years prior to the death of M. Lipson. All of M. Lipson's mail came through Harry Lipson's post office box. Harry Lipson opened and recorded all dividend checks received by M. Lipson, and kept a record of them for income tax purposes.

"The recorded cases present a wide range of facts and circumstances which have been held to constitute or not constitute fiduciary relations, or confidential relations as they are sometimes called. Each case of course must be decided on its own facts. However, it seems to me that we have facts here which would satisfy any definition of fiduciary relationship. The decedent was substantially dependent upon Harry M. Lipson, and to a lesser degree on Harry M. Lipson, Jr., in his personal life, in his business affairs, and particularly in connection with the investment of his savings. He apparently had the utmost confidence in both Harry M. Lipson and Harry M. Lipson, Jr. Quoting the *Wofford* case [Wofford v. Wofford, 244 Miss. 442, 142 So.2d 188], cited below, 'it was a relation in which confidence was reposed, by one, and the influence which naturally grows out of such confidence was possessed by the other.'

"Clearly the confidential relationships with Harry M. Lipson and with Harry M. Lipson, Jr. would affect the gifts to other members of their family. Roper v. Lenois [243 Ala. 583], 11 So. (2) 361, (Alabama, 1943); Annotation, 96 A.L.R. 613."

This finding indicates that the chancellor was of the opinion that the evidence established that Harry M. Lipson, Sr. and Harry M. Lipson, Jr. were the dominant parties in their relationship with Morris Lipson; having so found, the chancellor was correct in applying the law announced.

The chancellor then held that since a fiduciary relationship existed, that the burden of proof was upon the appellants to show that the transactions were free from undue influence. He found that there was no evidence to show that the decedent had the benefit of any independent advice. He then made the following finding relative to the independent consent and action of the decedent:

"Assuming, as I do, that a showing of independent advice is not absolutely essential, what other 'clear evidence of good faith, full knowledge, and independent consent and action' do we have in this case? I have considered M. Lipson's independent spirit; his unquestioned competency during most of the period in question; his reasons for favoring Harry's family; the possible reasons for David being in disfavor; the long period of time over which these events occurred, during which time the donor was not confined or sheltered from contacts with third persons; his statements to third persons as to stock purchases for the benefit of the grandchildren. All these circumstances tend to support the gifts in question, but after considering them and all of the other evidence offered, I cannot say that the evidence is clear (1) that M. Lipson knew and clearly understoof (sic) the legal effect of the joint tenancies being created; or (2) that he realized and intended that practically all of his property was being converted into such form of ownership, and that the son David was being completely disinherited; or (3) that he formed such intention independently, and not as a result of any influence, suggestion, encouragement or information coming from Harry M. Lipson or Harry M. Lipson, Jr."

The chancellor then determined the items in question that were to be included as assets of the estate. His finding is as follows:

"The items hereinafter set our (sic) are held to have been owned by M. Lipson at the time of his death, and are a part of the estate passing under the residuary clause of his will:

"(a) An undivided one-half interest in the store building purchased in 1959, the other one-half being owned by Harry Lipson. Harry Lipson shall make a complete accounting of all funds of each owner which have gone into the purchase and maintenance of said building, and of all income received from the building.

"(b) All stocks listed in Exhibits C, D and E to the Amendment to Answer of Harry M. Lipson; also any other stocks and bonds purchased with funds of M. Lipson from and after February 19, 1951.

"(c) The two bank accounts in Citizens Bank & Trust Co.

"(d) The M. Lipson stock of merchandise, as inventoried in Exhibit G to the Amendment of Harry M. Lipson.

"In addition to the above items, Harry M. Lipson shall make an accounting of the checks which were made payable to him out of the M. Lipson savings account, and reconcile such accounting with the purchases of stocks for M. Lipson. Also, he shall make an accounting of the checks upon said account payable to Kohlmeyer & Company. As Executor he will of course account for any and all other property of M. Lipson which has come into his hands or of which he has knowledge.

"There were checks from the savings account in favor of Harry M. Lipson, Jr. in the total amount of $7500.00 and in favor of Miriam Inez Lipson in the amount of $4000.00. Also four refund checks from DuPont & Co., in the amounts of $2500.00 each, were indorsed respectively to Harry A. Lipson, Miriam Inez Lipson, Dorothy K. Lipson, and Harry M. Lipson, Jr. Apparently all of these checks were intended as gifts, were either signed or indorsed by the deceased himself, and were paid and delivered to the recipients. Although there is some difficulty in clearly distinguishing between these and the items first listed above, it is my opinion that they should be treated as completed gifts, and not included in the decedent's estate. It might be noted that two of the recipients of the DuPont checks are not parties to this suit.

"The probated claim of Harry Lipson upon the note executed by M. Lipson will be disallowed, both because a certified copy of the note was not filed upon withdrawing the original, and because this transaction is affected by the fiduciary relationship discussed above."

A decree was entered in accordance with this opinion. From this decree, appellants have prosecuted this appeal. Appellee, David Lipson, has cross-appealed from that part of the decree which held that certain transactions constituted valid and complete gifts by Morris Lipson during his lifetime.

* * *

[With respect to appellant's direct appeal on the merits, the Supreme Court accepted the Chancellor's findings as to the existence of a confidential relationship and his statement of the governing law, but reversed for error in refusing to admit certain evidence.]

* * *

On cross-appeal appellee and cross-appellant contends that the chancellor was in error in holding that the gifts by Morris Lipson, Deceased, to Harry M. Lipson, Jr. in the amount of $7,500 and to Miriam Lipson in the sum of $4,000, together with checks of $2,500 to each of them, were completed gifts by Morris Lipson in his lifetime. We have carefully examined the evidence relative to this finding of the chancellor, and we are of the opinion that it is supported by the evidence. The record shows that Morris Lipson was fully mentally competent at the time these gifts were made, and he had the right to make them so long as they were freely and voluntarily made. The chancellor found from the evidence that they were completed gifts and were not affected by the fiduciary relationship. It is true that there is some difficulty in clearly distinguishing between these gifts and the other gifts involved; however, the chancellor was able to do so, and we cannot say that he was in error in so doing. For this reason, this case should be affirmed on cross-appeal.

Motion to dismiss overruled; affirmed in part and reversed and remanded for a new trial on direct appeal; and affirmed on cross-appeal.

GILLESPIE, P.J., and RODGERS, BRADY and SMITH, JJ., concur.*

Notes

1. Unfair exploitation of the trust and confidence relationship produces different reactions from those caused by duress. In the latter, one acts as one would not otherwise act to avoid the feared consequences of the threatened conduct. In the case of trust and confidence, the exploited state of mind differs. Here one has been lulled into allowing another party to influence one's decisions, including a decision to transfer something of value which would not have been transferred in an atmosphere free of the influence in question. Such trust is reposed in the other that the transferor has ceased to use natural and usual judgment in managing his or her affairs and protecting his or her own interests.

The "trust and confidence" and "undue influence" concepts have a common basis and the former may be said to be an example of the latter. "Undue influence" is the term used in the earlier equity cases, and may more readily lend itself, semantically, to situations with which it has been traditionally concerned, such as "undue" religious, sexual, and occult influences, physical

* This case is discussed in Note, 38 Miss. L.Rev. 156 (1966).

and mental weaknesses, and the like. *See* Notes, p. 329, *supra*; IV G. Palmer, The Law of Restitution § 19.2(b) (1978).

Once the required relationship is shown to have been present, the burden of proof shifts to the defendant to explain and justify any enrichment acquired during the existence of that relationship.*

2. In Ruebsamen v. Maddocks, 340 A.2d 31 (Me.1975) the Supreme Court of Maine affirmed a finding of violation of a relationship of trust and confidence justifying restitution in the form of a constructive trust, where a father had furnished funds to his potential son-in-law to buy property and, following marriage, paid for improvements. A divorce followed. In discussing the nature of the trust and confidence relationship the court stated:

> "We cannot overthrow the findings of the trial court simply because the parties were mature individuals in full possession of their faculties. Confidential relations can, and do, exist between such people. When we consider the family setting, it is only natural that the father-in-law should contribute to such a hopeful enterprise as marriage, and to the future prosperity and happiness of all within the domestic circle. The family relations of father-in-law and son-in-law here augment the confidential relations of the parties in business dealings and sustain the legal consequences that arise from defendant's benefiting from the confidential relations. *See* Wood v. White, 123 Me. 139, 143, 122 A. 177, 179 (1923). Given proper findings of plaintiffs' inexperience, defendant's larger acquaintance with business affairs, and defendant's consequent influence and superiority, a finding of confidential relations on this record is tenable as a matter of law. *See* Tribou v. Tribou, 96 Me. 305, 308, 52 A. 795, 796 (1902).
>
> * * *
>
> "* * * Here, the Superior Court found as fact that the purchase and eventual merger of the Maddocks and Ruebsamen lands were part of the same transaction and flowed from the same relations of confidence between the plaintiffs and defendant. We cannot impeach that finding of fact simply because a legal instrument such as a joint tenancy deed was used to accomplish the transaction. So long as defendant cannot in fact refute the presumption that his benefits are tainted by the confidential relation, he will not be allowed to retain the benefits derived from the advantage of his influence. * * * This principle extends to every case in which a confidential relation exists as a fact, in which there is a confidence reposed on one side and a resulting superiority of influence on the other. *Id.*

* A number of courts, and notably the Supreme Court of Michigan, have gone to considerable trouble to set out guidelines for trial courts in giving the plaintiff the advantages of such a presumption, especially in those situations where, due to statutory provision or otherwise, the case is to be tried to a jury. *See In re* Estate of Wood, 374 Mich. 278, 132 N.W.2d 35 (1965). Undue influence cases usually invoke equity jurisdiction because "equitable fraud" is present; also, complete relief often requires setting aside a will or gift, or cancellation of deeds. Where appropriate, however, relief may be had in quasi-contract. Eldridge v. May, 129 Me. 112, 150 A. 378 (1930); Woodbury v. Woodbury, 141 Mass. 329, 5 N.E. 275 (1886).

Serious ethical problems may arise where an attorney is a beneficiary under a will drawn by him or her for a client. *See* State v. Collentine, 39 Wis.2d 325, 159 N.W.2d 50 (1968), discussed in Note, 18 Cath.Am.L.Rev. 227 (1968). In this situation, especially, counsel is well advised to be able to establish that the testator (or donor) also received "independent advice" in planning the dispositions.

"Plaintiffs' action sounded in equity and sought to impress a constructive trust on defendant's interest in the joint tenancy. The Superior Court impressed the trust, ordering the defendant to release to plaintiffs by proper deed any and all interest in the joint tenancy property. The constructive trust remedy is well-founded in this case."

3. Conduct amounting to "duress," like that constituting intentional misrepresentation, is clearly "wrongful." In some jurisdictions conduct amounting to duress is also a tort. II G. Palmer, The Law of Restitution (1978), §§ 9.3, 9.5; Note, 53 Iowa L.Rev. 892 (1968). The approach of the courts regarding the allowable measure of damages for duress reflects the wrongful nature of the conduct. The remedies available to one who has conferred a benefit as a result of actionable duress are the same as those for fraud. Restatement of Restitution § 70 (1937).

HERRMANN v. GLEASON

United States Court of Appeals, Sixth Circuit, 1942.
126 F.2d 936.

Suit commenced in the circuit court of Michigan by Marie Herrmann and another, as executors of the estate of Katherine Schreiber, deceased, against Joseph W. Gleason, receiver of the Capital National Bank, a federal banking corporation, to recover interest on rentals paid by receiver for premises leased from plaintiffs. Suit removed to United States District Court on the ground that it involved matters concerning the winding up of a national bank. From an adverse judgment, plaintiffs appeal.

* * *

McAllister, Circuit Judge. Appellants' premises were leased in 1919 for 99 years by the City National Bank of Lansing, Michigan. For the period ending April 1, 1927, a fixed rental was prescribed, payable quarterly in advance. The lease provided that for each ten year term thereafter, the rental should be agreed upon by the parties, and, in case of failure so to agree, it should be determined by referees. The parties agreed on rentals of $600 per month, payable quarterly in advance, for the period from April 1, 1927, to March 31, 1937, and these sums were accordingly paid during that time, by the City National Bank, until it was taken over by the Capital National Bank. Thereafter, a receiver was appointed for this bank, and the same rentals were paid by the receiver for three years after his appointment until the expiration of such ten year period.

Appellants and the receiver, however, were unable to agree on rentals for the new ten year period, beginning on April 1, 1937, and referees were appointed, in accordance with the lease provisions, to determine the rentals to be paid.

After the expiration of 20 months from the time of the last payment of the agreed rentals, the referees rendered an award determining that the fair rental for the period beginning April 1, 1937, and ending March 31, 1947, "is $725.00 per month, payable quarterly in advance." The award was dated September 1, 1939.

On October 12, 1939, the receiver paid appellants a sum equivalent to the rentals up to and including that date, and for the ensuing quarter. Appellants demanded interest on the payments for the period of twenty months during which no rental had been paid, and, upon the receiver's refusal, brought suit therefor in the Circuit Court for Ingham County, State of Michigan, which was removed to the District Court, on the ground that it involved matters concerning the winding up of a national bank.

The District Court held that interest is allowable only when provided for by contract, express or implied; or by statute; or when, as damages, it becomes due after a default by the person liable to pay; that appellants had established no right to interest by express or implied contract; or by statute; and since the receiver could not be in default until the amount of rental was ascertained, interest could not be allowed prior to the award.

* * *

The foregoing cases do not persuade us to the conclusion that, according to the law as expressed by the courts of Michigan, the allowance of interest is confined to cases of wrongful detention of property or money, nor that it is denied on the ground that damages suffered, are unliquidated. At the same time our attention is not directed to any case of that jurisdiction, which holds that interest is allowable, in cases where the party sought to be charged therewith was guiltless of such wrongful nonpayment or detention, or some tortious conduct resulting in loss to a claimant. But we are of the opinion that it is not necessary for a claimant to rely upon tort or wrongful conduct in order that he recover interest, as, under the circumstances of this case, there is implied in law, an agreement to make such payment.

Appellants count upon indebitatus assumpsit. This action, while legal in form, is equitable to the core. Where one has in his hands money which, according to the rules of equity and good conscience, ought to be paid to another, assumpsit is the proper form of remedy; and if, at the time of commencement of action, a party holds money which, ex aequo et bono, he ought not to have retained from plaintiffs, they are entitled to recovery. Beardslee v. Horton, 3 Mich. 560. In Moore v. Mandlebaum, 8 Mich. 433, it was said: "We understand the law to be well settled, that the action of assumpsit for money had and received is essentially an equitable action, founded upon all the equitable circumstances of the case between the parties; and if it appear, from the whole case, that the defendant has in his hands money which, according to the rules of equity and good conscience, belongs, or ought to be paid, to the plaintiff, he is entitled to recover." A contract implied in law is quasi or constructive, and does not require a meeting of minds, but is imposed by fiction of law to enable justice to be accomplished, even where no contract was intended. Cascaden v. Magryta, 247 Mich. 267, 225 N.W. 511. "Assumpsit for money had and received is an equitable action to recover back money which the defendant in justice ought not to retain, and it may be said that it lies in most, if not all, cases where the defendant has moneys of the plaintiff which, ex aequo et bono, he ought to refund." Nash v. Towne, 5 Wall. 689, 702, 72 U.S. 689, 18 L.Ed. 527. The action resembles a bill in equity and lies when money had been received by one person which, in justice and equity, belongs to another; and, in such a case, a promise is implied because natural justice requires it in consequence of some benefit received. Osborn v. Bell, 5 Denio 370, 49 Am.Dec. 275. An action for money had and received, though brought at law, is in its nature a substitute for a suit in equity, and it is to be determined by the application of equitable principles. "In other words, the rights of the parties are to be determined as they would be upon a bill in equity." Myers v. Hurley Motor Co., 273 U.S. 18, 47 S.Ct. 277, 278, 71 L.Ed. 515, 50 A.L.R. 1181. Recovery in such an action is based on the law of quasi contracts, and is ordinarily permitted only when there has been an "unjust enrichment."

The essential elements of a quasi contractual obligation, upon which a recovery may be had, are the receipt of a benefit by a defendant from a plaintiff, which benefit it is inequitable that the defendant retain. Ever since an action for money had and received has been maintainable, it has been employed as a remedy to prevent the unjust enrichment of one at the expense of another, or to prevent one from retaining a benefit conferred upon him by another which would be, under all of the circumstances of the case, unjust or inequitable. Richland County Bank v. Joint School Dist. No. 2, 213 Wis. 178, 250 N.W. 407. It is said that the action is equitable to the degree that it is based on a moral obligation to make restitution which rests upon a person who has received a benefit which, if retained by him, would result in inequity and injustice. Hummel v. Hummel, 133 Ohio St. 520, 14 N.E.2d 923. Under the doctrine of unjust enrichment, a defendant has something of value at the plaintiff's expense under circumstances which impose a legal duty of restitution. American University v. Forbes, 88 N.H. 17, 183 A. 860. *See* Wilson Cypress Co. v. Atlantic Coast Line R. Co., 5 Cir., 109 F.2d 623; Ames' Lectures on Legal History, pages, 149–166; Holdsworth's History of English Law, Vol. 8, page 92 et seq.; Lawrence on Equity Jurisprudence, § 738. A person is enriched if he has received a benefit; and when he has been unjustly enriched at the expense of another, he is required to make restitution. *See* Restatement of the Law, Restitution § 1.

Applying the law to the facts in this case, appellee retained and used the premises for a period of 20 months, while arbitration proceedings were under way to establish an agreed fair rental therefor. During this period, appellants were deprived of the receipt of rental and appellee had the use of the premises, as well as the use of the money representing the fair rental value. When the referees determined such rental value, it expressly dated back to the beginning of the period during which the rentals had remained unpaid. Equity and fairness require that appellants have restitution, by way of interest, on the rentals unpaid during that period. Otherwise, appellee would receive the benefit of the value of the use of such money, to the disadvantage of appellants, and his retention thereof would result in inequity and unjust enrichment at their expense. It is our conclusion that appellants are entitled to the interest claimed. Other questions raised are not sufficiently pertinent to require discussion.

The judgment is reversed and the case remanded to the District Court for entry of judgment in accordance herewith.*

MESSERSMITH v. G.T. MURRAY & CO.

Supreme Court of Wyoming, 1983.
667 P.2d 655.

Before ROONEY, C.J., and THOMAS, ROSE, BROWN and CARDINE, JJ.

BROWN, JUSTICE.

Appellee G.T. Murray and Company filed suit to recover monies it had received from the sale of stock and mistakenly paid the appellants, Daniel and Frances Messersmith. Following a trial to the court, the judge found in appellee's favor and ordered the money returned. From the judgment, appellants raise three issues on appeal. First, they argue the mistake was a unilateral one upon the part of appellee's agent, and therefore it was insufficient to justify the rescission of the contract. Second, they claim that since appellee, as a stockbrokerage firm, had considerably more knowledge, information, and expertise, it should suffer the consequences of its mistake. Finally, they assert that, because to their detriment they changed their position in reliance upon appellee's mistake, justice demands that they not be forced to return the money to appellee.

We affirm.

At about 9:00 a.m. on July 28, 1982, Frances Messersmith called the offices of G.T. Murray and Company. She talked with James King, a stockbroker, about the possibility of selling some stock. She stated she had no idea what it was worth but wanted to find out. When asked the name of the stock, she read off what appeared on the stock certificate. "Western Preferred." King looked up the name and discovered that Western Preferred was selling for approximately $46 per share. Frances Messersmith expressed some surprise but indicated she had 200 shares and would like to sell them. King told her he would take care of the sale and asked her to bring the stock certificate to his office. By the time she arrived at 10:00 a.m., the sale was completed; the stock had been sold for $47 per share.

After the necessary paperwork was completed and some ten days had passed, the Messersmiths received a check in the amount of $9,260.70. This represented the net proceeds from the sale of 200 shares of Western Preferred at $47 per share.

On October 1, 1982, King received a phone call from appellee's parent company, Bache. He was informed that an error had been made in the sale of the Messersmiths' stock. It turned out that that stock had been subject to a reverse stock split two years before. At that time holders of the stock had been directed to return their stock certificates in order to receive new stock issued as a result of a merger with another company. One share of the new stock had been issued for every 40 shares turned in. Though the Messersmiths never responded to the notification, their 200 shares of the

* *See* Thurston, Recent Developments in Restitution, 45 Mich.L.Rev. 935, 937 (1947). *Compare* Crown Industries, Inc. v. Boyertown Burial Casket Co., 300 F.2d 809 (6th Cir. 1962).

old stock actually equalled five shares of the new stock valued at $47 per share, and had a gross value of $235.

After being informed of the problem, King called the Messersmiths. He told them that they had been overpaid by about $9,000. He was advised that $8,000 had been used as a down payment on a house and the rest had been spent.

On October 8, 1982, appellee initiated this lawsuit in order to recover the overpayment. The trial court found in its favor and ordered the appellants to pay appellee $8,810.70.

Appellants first challenge the trial court's determination that a mutual mistake of fact occurred. They contend the mistake was unilateral.

In Ohio Co. v. Rosemeier, 32 Ohio App.2d 116, 61 Op.2d 105, 288 N.E.2d 326 (1972), a stockbroker was asked by Rosemeier if her stock, Santa Fe International, was selling for $36 per share. After the broker checked a stock exchange listing and discovered a Santa Fe International selling at $36 per share, he confirmed that it was. She then told him to sell the 500 shares she believed she owned. However, it turned out that the stock listed was a California corporation and the stock she owned was a Colorado corporation worth 80 cents a share. The appellate court concluded "the parties were mutually mistaken as to the identity of defendant's stock when sold," and thus allowed recovery. *Ohio Co. v. Rosemeier, supra,* 288 N.E.2d at 328.

In the present case, it appears that the mistake was mutual also. Neither party knew the true value of the stock; they were both mistaken. Further, as pointed out in *Ohio Co. v. Rosemeier, supra,* it does not matter that the broker may have negligently induced his client's mistaken belief.

Generally, other courts are in accord with the result reached in *Ohio Co. v. Rosemeier, supra.* However, most courts have not found it necessary to distinguish between mutual and unilateral mistakes with respect to mistaken sale of securities. The courts have proceeded upon the principle that money paid under a mistake of fact, which would not otherwise have been paid, may be recovered unless the payee has changed his position to the extent that it would be unjust to require a refund. Akerson v. Gupta, 458 F.Supp. 189 (E.D.Mo.1978). *See also,* Annot., 48 A.L.R.3d 513, 516 (1973). So long as the parties can be returned to the status quo, courts should strive to achieve such a result. However, if the payees suffer damage as a result of a mistake made by the broker, recovery by the broker may be barred to the extent of the damage.

Second, appellants claim that since appellee was in a better position to discover the mistake, it should suffer the loss. Case law, however, fails to support appellants.

In Westamerica Securities, Inc. v. Cornelius, 214 Kan. 301, 520 P.2d 1262 (1974), the court considered whether a stockbroker's failure to exercise due care could bar it from recovering funds mistakenly paid to a customer. The court concluded it did not and quoted Restatement of the Law, Restitution, § 59, p. 232:

" 'A person who has conferred a benefit upon another by mistake is not precluded from maintaining an action for restitution by the fact that the mistake was due to his lack of care.' "

Also see Board of Education of the City of Chicago v. Holt, 41 Ill.App.3d 625, 354 N.E.2d 534 (1976); and *Ohio Co. v. Rosemeier, supra.*

Lack of due care will not serve to bar an action for restitution of funds mistakenly paid where no damage to the payee has resulted.

Finally, appellants contend that they changed their position as a result of the overpayment and that it would be unjust to force them to return the money. Normally, payees will not be required to return the overpayment where they have changed their position such that demanding a refund would be unfair. *Akerson v. Gupta, supra;* and *Ohio Co. v. Rosemeier, supra.* To constitute such a change, the burden is on the payee to establish that the change has been detrimental to the payee and that it was material and irrevocable such that the payee cannot be returned to the status quo. *Westamerica Securities, Inc. v. Cornelius, supra.* However, a mere change in the form of the proceeds does not qualify when the payee has retained the value. *Akerson v. Gupta, supra. Also see,* 66 Am.Jur.2d, Restitution and Implied Contracts § 136 (1973). In other words, the payor can recover the proceeds only to the extent that the payee will not be damaged.

Here, appellants spent approximately $1,200 on bills. In *Ohio Co. v. Rosemeier, supra,* 288 N.E.2d at 329, the payee used the money to pay off a mortgage. The court there said: "Since the value of the original payment was retained by the defendant, she has not detrimentally changed her position by liquidating her mortgage." Accordingly, to the extent the Messersmiths paid off debts there was no loss of value.

Appellants applied the remaining $8,000 of the overpayment towards the purchase of a house. Though the briefs both make reference to the fact that the money was placed in escrow and subject to forfeiture, no evidence of such was produced at trial. The only competent evidence in the record is Frances Messersmith's statement that she had put $8,000 on a home. Such evidence is insufficient to establish that appellants did not retain the value. Merely putting money down on a house is just a change of form. Since the burden of proof was upon appellants to establish a loss of value and they failed to introduce any evidence to prove that they have not retained the value of the overpayment, we must affirm the trial court's finding. No change of circumstances was established.

Affirmed.

RABBIT EAR CATTLE COMPANY v. FRIEZE

Supreme Court of New Mexico, 1969.
80 N.M. 203, 453 P.2d 373.

OPINION

COMPTON, JUSTICE.

Plaintiff brought this action to recover $832.00 alleged to have been mistakenly overpaid to the defendant for pasturage. The defendant denied any mistake of fact and, at a hearing, the trial court found for the plaintiff. Judgment was entered accordingly, and the defendant appeals.

The question on appeal is whether there is sufficient evidence to support the trial court's finding that the plaintiff mistakenly paid the defendant a balance of $4,160.00 for pasturage of plaintiff's cattle for the 1965 season when the claimed true balance owing by plaintiff was $3,328.00.

Both parties agree that where findings of the trial court are challenged on appeal, ground rules for review are well settled. An appellate court, on appeal, will examine the record only to determine whether the evidence when viewed in its most favorable aspect supports the court's findings. Crumpacker v. Adams, 77 N.M. 633, 426 P.2d 781.

The appellant first contends that the court erred in finding that plaintiff mistakenly overpaid defendant $832.00, the difference between $4,160.00 and $3,328.00, because there was no substantial evidence of mistake. Accordingly, we review the evidence bearing on the issue of mistake. It appears that sometime in May, 1965, the plaintiff and defendant entered into an oral agreement whereby the defendant agreed to pasture 416 head of yearlings for the agreed sum of $16.00 per head for the grazing season beginning on or about June 1, 1965, the pasturage fee payable one half at the time the yearlings were to be placed on pasture and one half to be paid at the time the yearlings were to be taken out of pasture. The cattle were removed from the defendant's pasture October 19, 1965. The next day, the parties met in a cafe in Clayton to settle the account. What took place on this occasion becomes very material here. At that time a controversy arose as to the terms of the agreement and as to the amount due the defendant. The plaintiff was represented by its president, Ted Harris, and secretary, Mrs. Ted Harris. The defendant was represented by her father, W.J. Sink. The plaintiff contended that the grazing season lasted until November 1, 1965. The defendant, on the other hand, contended that plaintiff agreed to remove the cattle not later than October 5, 1965, and demanded $832.00 for a pasturage of 416 head at $2.00 per head for the extra two weeks, October 5th to October 19th. Both parties knew the position of the other, nevertheless, the plaintiff paid the additional amount claimed by the defendant, as Mr. Harris said, so as to avoid an argument in a public cafe. The record indicates that there were no customers in the cafe at the time.

The general rule is that payments made as a result of a material mistake of fact are regarded as involuntary and are recoverable. Elgin v. Gross–Kelly & Co., 20 N.M. 450, 150 P.2d 922, L.R.A. 1916A, 711. Mistake of fact is frequently founded in "unconscious ignorance" or forgetfulness of facts which could have been remedied by the exercise of due care. Sawyer v. Mid–Continent Petroleum Corporation, 236 F.2d 518 (10th Cir.1956). *See also* Smith v. Noble Drilling Co., 272 F.Supp. 321 (E.D.La.1967); Central National Bank of Houston v. Martin Mortg. Co., 396 S.W.2d 218 (Tex.Civ.App.). It is also a well established rule that payments voluntarily made with full knowledge of all material facts cannot be recovered back in absence of fraud or duress. Runcie v. Runcie, 407 S.W.2d 861 (Tex.Civ.

App.); Employers Cas. Co. v. Universal Underwriters Ins. Co., 404 S.W.2d 954 (Tex.Civ.App.); MacGregor v. Millar, 166 Kan. 657, 203 P.2d 137. A person paying money on a controverted or disputed claim while conscious of his want of knowledge of material facts and where the facts are disputed and the disputed facts are specifically brought to his attention, such payment is not payment under "mistake of fact" as to allow recovery of the payments so made. *MacGregor v. Millar, supra.*

On the record before us the finding that the payment was made under a mistake of fact is not factually supported. The evidence is all the other way; the payment was made voluntarily in settlement of a disputed claim. The appellant also asserts another point for reversal of the judgment, but we need not discuss this point as the appellant's first point is determinative of the appeal.

The judgment should be reversed with direction to dismiss the action.

It is so ordered.

NOBLE, C.J., and MOISE, J., concur.

Notes

1. A mutual or unilateral mistake may result in the conferring of a benefit where the mistake is in the performance of a contract as well as in its formation. In either situation, restitution may be appropriate. There are, however, situations in which restitution for either mistake of law or fact may be especially inappropriate, even though later events show that the party paying would easily have prevailed had there been a trial on the merits. This may occur where there is an active dispute as to the existence and extent of the obligations of one party to the other, or by each to the other, and one party pays the other or gives something of value. The parties "decide to settle it." Here there may be no "mistake" at all. Conscious ignorance or doubt as to one's rights and obligations necessarily precludes a contention that the action in question was induced by a mistaken assumption. It is the difference between thinking "I know I know" and acting mistakenly and thinking "I know I don't know" but acting anyway. Moreover, the strong social policy encouraging compromise and settlement of disputes suggests that it is unwise to undo settlements. Even so, and perhaps in recognition of the vagaries of "doubt," relief has been awarded in some instances where the evidence showed "some doubt" by a party paying before litigation is begun. *See* III G. Palmer, The Law of Restitution § 14.7 (1978).

2. In Nebraska State Bank v. Sherlock, 180 Neb. 772, 145 N.W.2d 573 (1966) the plaintiff Bank's employee mistakenly credited certain funds to the defendant's account in the Bank because of a misunderstanding as to the instructions received from the party supplying the funds to the Bank (Glass). The defendant claimed that the law afforded the plaintiff no right to recover "money paid under a mistake of law * * * [where, as here, a party such as the Bank seeks to recover] money voluntarily paid on a claim of right." In holding that the defendant factually had not brought himself within this rule, and ordering the return of the funds, the Court stated:

> " 'The reason of the rule that money voluntarily paid with full knowledge of the facts can never be recovered and its propriety are quite obvious when applied to a case of payment on a mere demand of money unaccom-

panied with any power or authority to enforce such demand, except by suit at law. In such case, if the party would resist an unjust demand, he must do so at the threshold. The parties treat with each other on equal terms, and if litigation is intended by the one of whom the money is demanded, it should precede payment. When the person making the payment can only be reached by a proceeding at law, he is bound to make his defense in the first instance, and he cannot postpone the litigation by paying the demand in silence and afterward suing to recover the amount paid.' 21 R.C.L., sec. 166, p. 143. In the case before us, the defendant made no demand and asserted no claim of right to the payment. Any error of the Bank as to the law arose from a misconception of the legal sufficiency of the instructions obtained from Glass as to the transfer of the credit. There is no suggestion that the plaintiff considered any obligation of it to the defendant motivated the transfer. Any mistake of law made by the Bank did not relate to rights between the defendant and the Bank, but between it and Glass. The rules cited with respect to the denial of recovery of a payment made under a mistake of law has no application to the case before us."

3. Payment by a party in response to a demand is sometimes said to be the act of a "volunteer." *See* Employers Cas. Co. v. Universal Underwriters Ins. Co., 404 S.W.2d 954 (Tex.Ct.App.1966) (insurer who paid claim without investigation or litigation and now claims its liability was only that of an "excess carrier" was a "volunteer" and quasi-contract relief denied); *compare* Phoenix Indemnity Co. v. Steiden Stores, Inc., 267 S.W.2d 733 (Ky.1954) discussed in Note, 40 Cornell L.Q. 618 (1955) (payment in response to demand despite knowledge by insurer that there might be no liability because the theft might be an "inside job," did not prevent quasi-contract relief where the amount of insurance benefits paid showed no intent to compromise). The term "volunteer" also appears in the "officious intermeddler" cases which are discussed at page 342, *supra*. One who pays taxes without "protest" where the tax law was not valid may be said to have been a "volunteer." *See* Mercury Mach. Importing Corp. v. City of New York, 3 N.Y.2d 418, 165 N.Y.S.2d 517, 144 N.E.2d 400 (1957) (quasi-contract relief denied; taxes paid "without protest" may not later be recovered even if the underlying tax law has been declared unconstitutional).

CITY OF BARNSDALL v. CURNUTT

Supreme Court of Oklahoma, 1946.
198 Okl. 3, 174 P.2d 596.

DAVISON, JUSTICE. This is an appeal from the District Court of Osage County wherein the defendant in error, Mabel Curnutt, administratrix of the estate of H.M. Curnutt, deceased, hereinafter called intervenor, obtained a judgment against the plaintiff in error, hereafter called plaintiff, enforcing an attorney's lien.

We find from the record that on January 25, 1941 the plaintiff by written contract employed H.M. Curnutt as its attorney to investigate and determine who was polluting the water supply of plaintiff and bring action for damages and to restrain further pollution. For his services H.M. Curnutt was to receive 40% of the sum recovered either by compromise or prosecution of action to conclusion.

H.M. Curnutt commenced investigation and in August, 1941, the Cities Service Oil Company made a tentative offer of $25,000 in settlement, which was declined by plaintiff. On September 8, 1941 H.M. Curnutt filed petition for damage for plaintiff against Cities Service Oil Company and two of its employees for $253,000 damages, endorsed with his name and "Attorney's Lien Claimed". On September 21, 1941 Curnutt died. On October 7, 1941 the intervenor and her attorney appeared before the city council of the plaintiff and requested that the employment contract be completed by her attorney. On October 13, 1941 the intervenor addressed a letter to the plaintiff reciting the prior visit, the purpose thereof, and that $10,000 was claimed as an attorney's fee for services under the contract. By letter of same date the plaintiff advised intervenor that other attorneys had been procured and to turn over all exhibits, files and evidence. This was done. The claim of intervenor was denied by plaintiff.

The attorneys employed to succeed Curnutt in the litigation are the same attorneys now representing the plaintiff in the present contest.

On May 25, 1943 the action was settled for $35,000, paid by Cities Service Oil Company and Cities Service Gas Company and that amount, by agreement of plaintiff and defendants and by order of the court, was paid to the court clerk to be held for the plaintiff subject to the attorney's lien claims of McCoy, Craig and Pearson, attorneys for plaintiff and of the personal representative of H.M. Curnutt, deceased, and the cause dismissed with prejudice. The court clerk disbursed $10,500 to plaintiff's attorneys, held $10,000 to await the order of the court, and paid the balance to the plaintiff.

On June 11, 1943 the intervenor filed petition in intervention in the case substantially alleging the above facts and further stating $25,000 of the amount secured was the result of the efforts of H.M. Curnutt prior to his decease and that $10,000 was a fair, just and reasonable fee under the contract. The intervenor prayed that the court direct the court clerk to disburse the $10,000 to intervenor for the purpose of discharging the "lien claim of the said H.M. Curnutt upon the funds realized from the settlement of said cause."

* * * Plaintiff filed its answer alleging H.M. Curnutt failed to properly protect the plaintiff's interest by investigation, securing of evidence and preparation and filing of petition; that the employment contract was thereby breached, and was terminated by death; that plaintiff had to employ other attorneys to complete the litigation and pay 30% of the recovery or $10,500 to these attorneys; that the petition had to be amended and further investigation made; that intervenor was entitled to a reasonable fee of $1,000 for the services of H.M. Curnutt. * * *

The court on application of the intervenor and over the objection of the plaintiff found that the matter was an equity case to be tried to the court without the intervention of a jury. Upon the trial of the cause evidence of the parties was heard and the trial court determined the issues in favor of the intervenor, finding that H.M. Curnutt prior to his death had earned the sum of $10,000 under the contract of employment and directing the court clerk to pay to intervenor the $10,000 being held by him. From this judgment plaintiff has appealed.

The plaintiff complains of the trial court's refusal to submit the issues to a jury.

Title 5 O.S.1941 § 6 reads as follows: "From the commencement of an action, or from the filing of an answer containing a counterclaim, the attorney who represents the party in whose behalf such pleading is filed shall, to the extent hereinafter specified have a lien upon his client's cause of action or counterclaim, and same shall attach to any verdict, report, decision, finding or judgment in his client's favor; and the proceeds thereof, wherever found, shall be subject to such lien, and no settlement between the parties without the approval of the attorney shall affect or destroy such lien, provided such attorney serves notice upon the defendant or defendants, or proposed defendant or defendants, in which he shall set forth the nature of the lien he claims and the extent thereof; and said lien shall take effect from and after the service of such notice, but such notice shall not be necessary provided such attorney has filed such pleading in a court of record, and endorsed thereon his name, together with the words 'Lien claimed.' "

In the present case intervenor does not ask a personal judgment against the plaintiff but seeks under the above statute the enforcement of a lien upon the fund remaining in the court clerk's hands from the proceeds of the settlement of the cause of action of plaintiff.

* * *

The plaintiff complains that the theory upon which the case was tried and judgment rendered was erroneous.

The contract of employment had been made and H.M. Curnutt had performed services at the time of his death. A contract of this kind is one of personal trust and confidence requiring personal services and upon death of the attorney the contract is terminated. The recovery permitted in such event is the reasonable value of the services rendered under the contract. 7 C.J.S., Attorney and Client, § 171, p. 1032.

The parties to this appeal agree that a reasonable fee should be recovered. In the case before us the plaintiff's cause of action which was the subject of the employment contract was settled subsequent to the death of H.M. Curnutt and the cause of action filed by him thereon dismissed. Nothing further remains to be done with reference to the action. In Roe v. Sears, Roebuck & Co., 7 Cir., 132 F.2d 829, 832, it is said: "We are, however, convinced that the decisions are well nigh unanimous in holding that recovery may be had in contingent fee cases if the client ultimately recovers on its claim and the attorney rendered service in respect thereto, but dies before the client recovered. The theory seems to be that death terminates the contract of employment but the attorney having rendered services of value to his client, his estate may recover the fair value of the services rendered pursuant to the contract." *See, also,* cases cited therein.

The case of Morton v. Forsee, 249 Mo. 409, 155 S.W. 765, 767, Ann.Cas. 1914D, 197, is cited and relied upon by both parties to this appeal. In that case the estate of a deceased lawyer sought to recover an attorney's fee for services performed by the attorney who died prior to the conclusion of the suit in which he was employed. In upholding recovery the court said:

> "The courts are not uniform in the wording of the rule. Some place it squarely upon the doctrine of proportioning the fee according to the service rendered, taking the contract price as the basis, whilst others denominate it a quantum meruit action, with the contract price fixing the value of all the services, which contract price should be lessened in the recovery by what damages the other party has sustained by the failure of full performance. The damages would be such as would be occasioned by getting another to complete the service and matters incident thereto. Slightly different theories are advanced by other courts.
>
> * * *
>
> "To my mind the sounder rule is that, in a case where there has been no other consequential damages to the surviving party than the employment of other counsel to continue the work, the executor of the deceased lawyer should be entitled to recover on the basis of the contract price for the services actually performed. Death does not put a party in default in matters of contract. The contract is still of value in determining the price of the services. This rule necessarily calls for the proportioning of the fee as to work performed and work not performed at the date of death. It would also allow the direct and consequential damages occasioned by the stopping of the work. Such would cover what the party had been forced to pay out and expend in money and trouble in having the remainder of the work done." *See* cases in annotation in 143 A.L.R. 723.

From an examination of the record this court is of the opinion intervenor proceeded on the theory and sought to recover what was contended to be a reasonable attorney fee earned by H.M. Curnutt in his employment prior to his death. In determining the right to recover and the amount of recovery the contract of employment establishes employment and may be taken into consideration with other elements in determining the amount of the fee and is evidence of what parties considered a reasonable charge. The termination of the contract by death does not invalidate it for all purposes. The trial judge had before him evidence of the work and investigation of H.M. Curnutt and also testimony of several outstanding attorneys of the locality as to the amount and value of the services rendered, measured by the terms of the contract, and all of them stated $10,000 was a proper fee. We think it proper that the court, sitting as a court of equitable cognizance, received evidence of the $25,000 tentative offer of settlement in view of the ultimate $35,000 recovery by settlement when determining the reasonable value of attorney's services prior to his death.

* * *

The judgment of the trial court is affirmed.

RILEY and BAYLESS, JJ., dissent.*

Notes

1. Where "impossibility" renders the agreement unenforceable, usually neither party is at fault. The damages recoverable by the party who has conferred a benefit in performing ordinarily are the fair market value of the performance. However, it has been suggested that the contract price should be used to measure the recoverable "benefit" to the extent the contract has been performed. *See* II G. Palmer, The Law of Restitution (1978) § 7.5. *Compare* 6 A. Corbin, Contracts § 1370 (1962). *See also* M. Ahern Co. v. John Bowen Co., 334 Mass. 36, 133 N.E.2d 484 (1956) (impossibility of performance was the result of the defendant's own misconduct and, as a consequence, the plaintiff could recover in quasi-contract damages based upon the contract price even though the defendant received no actual benefit from the plaintiff's part performance.)

2. The ABA "Code of Professional Responsibility" (1982) states that every fee must be "reasonable." Special rules apply where a fee is shared with lawyers not in the same firm. DR 2–106, 2–107. *See also* ABA "Model Rules of Professional Conduct" Rule 1.5 (1983). The reasoning in the principal case seems difficult to justify in terms of the "reasonableness" of the total fees paid from the viewpoint of the client.

BLACK v. HESSE

United States Court of Appeals, Eighth Circuit, 1989.
869 F.2d 420.

ARNOLD, CIRCUIT JUDGE.

This diversity case arises from a dispute between Donald Black's widow, Janet Black, and his former business associate, Edward Hesse, over the proceeds of Donald Black's $50,000 life insurance policy. The District Court entered judgment for Mrs. Black, after the jury answered each of the special interrogatories submitted at the close of the evidence in favor of Mrs. Black's position. Hesse appeals, claiming that there was insufficient evidence to support the jury's answers to the interrogatories, and that, in any case, the facts found by the jury do not establish Mrs. Black's entitlement to the proceeds as a matter of law. We affirm.

We review the evidence at trial in the light most favorable to the jury's conclusions. In particular, we assume that the jury resolved any direct factual conflicts in Mrs. Black's favor, and that everything this evidence tended to prove is true. See *Brown v. Missouri Pacific Railroad,* 703 F.2d 1050, 1052 (8th Cir.1983).

On his retirement in January 1984, Donald Black decided to open a pizza restaurant in Bellevue, Nebraska. Black initially planned to go into business in partnership with Edward Hesse, an old friend from his service in the Marine Corps. At about this time, the Blacks filled out an application for life insurance, and mailed it along with a handwritten note from

* This case is discussed in Note, 46 Mich. L.Rev. 401 (1948). *See* 6 A. Corbin, Contracts §§ 1367-72 (1962).

Mr. Black, dated February 18, 1984, which named Hesse as his beneficiary. Responding to the insurance company's investigation of the application, Mr. Black wrote a second note to the company explaining that:

> Ed Hesse and I are business partners and we intend to carry life insurance policies on each other to protect our mutual financial interests.

Janet Black testified that her husband had told her several times that he and Hesse intended to take out insurance policies to enable the surviving partner to buy out the other partner's interest in the event of his death. Before the insurance policy issued in June 1984, the partnership between Black and Hesse had been abandoned because of Hesse's failure to contribute capital to the pizza restaurant. Hesse conceded that he never made Mr. Black a beneficiary on any life insurance policy of his own.

The jury was asked whether Mrs. Black had "established by a preponderance of the evidence that the designation was conditional and was only to take effect when Hesse performed certain obligations," Interrogatory No. 2, and, if so, whether Mrs. Black had "established by a preponderance of the evidence that Hesse did not perform the necessary obligations," Interrogatory No. 2(a). We agree with the District Court that there was sufficient evidence to support the jury's answers in the affirmative. It is true, as Hesse argues, that Mrs. Black's evidence regarding the partnership agreement was hearsay, and the District Court properly upheld the objection of Hesse's counsel to Mrs. Black's testimony on direct examination concerning what her husband told her. On cross-examination, however, Hesse's counsel asked Mrs. Black what grounds she had for her belief that a partnership agreement existed. When she answered by repeating her hearsay testimony, Hesse's counsel did not object. We cannot find error in the admission of evidence which Hesse's counsel solicited without objection, see Fed.R.Evid. 103(a)(1). Furthermore, Mr. Black's response to the insurance company's investigation of his application fully corroborates Mrs. Black's report of her husband's expressed intent. Although Hesse's testimony contradicts Mrs. Black's story, the jury was entitled to disbelieve him.

Hesse argues that the jury's finding of Mr. Black's intent is insufficient as a matter of law to make out the existence of a contract between Mr. Black and Hesse. Hesse argues that the requisite written memorandum of mutual intent between Mr. Black and himself is absent, and so there is no contract to enforce. It may be true that rules of contract law, like the statute of frauds, would bar enforcement of Mr. Black's oral agreement with Hesse. However, Mrs. Black's action is not a claim for damages resulting from a breach of an enforceable contract, nor does she seek to compel Hesse to perform his end of the abortive bargain with her deceased husband. Far from enforcing the bargain, she is merely seeking restitution of Mr. Black's performance from Hesse. At common law, where a party to an unenforceable contract fails to perform, the other party may suspend performance, and has a cause of action for the value of the performance rendered before the suspension. See *Restatement of Contracts* (2d) § 141(2). Rules like the statute of frauds, which make certain agreements unenforceable, do not bar claims in restitution resulting from such agreements, and evidence of an unenforceable agreement remains admissible for any purpose other than the enforcement of the agreement itself. See *Restatement of Contracts* (2d) §§ 375 and 143. Here, Mrs. Black proved to the satisfaction of the jury that Mr. Black's designation of Hesse as a beneficiary was a partial performance of a partnership agreement, which Hesse failed to perform. We have no reason to question the District Court's conclusion that Mrs. Black has a remedy under Iowa law for restitution of the benefit conferred on Hesse.

The jury also found for Mrs. Black on her theories that Hesse had never been made a beneficiary to begin with, and that Hesse was estopped to assert his claim by virtue of an oral promise to release the proceeds to her. Because the judgment below is independently supported under Mrs. Black's restitution theory, we do not need to discuss these alternative theories.

Affirmed.

Notes

1. In the usual case the defendant raises the statute of frauds as a defense (a tactic alluded to in the principal case) to justify a refusal to perform the oral agreement which is the basis of suit. Here, if there has been part performance by the plaintiff, quasi-contract relief is appropriate because otherwise the plaintiff is without any relief and the defendant is the beneficiary of his or her own refusal to perform. However, where it is the *plaintiff* who relies upon the statute and on that ground refuses to perform, but nonetheless seeks restitution, it is plaintiff's own conduct which prevents performance or other relief based upon the partly performed agreement. It has been suggested that in this situation the plaintiff's rights should be governed by the rules which relate to claims for restitution by a plaintiff who is in material breach of a contract. The unenforceability of the contract, arguably, should not strengthen the defaulting plaintiff's case. Such an approach is consistent with the policy underlying the statute of frauds which is to provide a *defense* against false, and possibly fraudulent, claims in certain types of contract situations. (II G. Palmer, The Law of Restitution (1978) § 6.2.

2. Quasi-contract relief may be available in a variety of situations where the Statute of Frauds renders an oral promise unenforceable. *E.g.,* Grantham v. Grantham, 205 N.C. 363, 171 S.E. 331 (1933) (oral promise to devise); Kemp v. Kemp, 248 Mass. 354, 142 N.E. 779 (1924) (transfer to place property beyond wife's reach; oral promise to reconvey upon request unenforceable because of the Statute of Frauds). The Court in *Grantham* stated the damages rule in such cases as follows:

> "The general rule is that, where services have been performed in consideration of a promise to devise real property, if the contract, as in the pending case, is not enforceable by reason of the Statute of Frauds, an action cannot be maintained on the special contract, but in case of services performed it may be prosecuted on the theory of implied assumpsit or quantum meruit to recover the value of the services rendered. Williston states the guiding principle to be as follows: 'As the defendant has committed no legal wrong in refusing to perform an unenforceable contract, the plaintiff's measure of damages is based, not on the extent of his

loss from the nonperformance of the contract, but on the reasonable value of what he has done. Some cases do indeed allow recovery of the contract price, but the better view is otherwise. * * * The contract price is, however, an admission of value by the defendant and as such should be admitted in evidence, though not treated as conclusive. Decisions which refuse altogether to admit the agreed price in evidence cannot be supported; and it is probable that in some at least of the jurisdictions which have allowed recovery of the contract price as such, the rule may be restricted so far as to involve a recognition of the principle that the plaintiff's recovery is based not on the contract but on an obligation imposed by law because of the benefit received. It is to be observed, however, that the price fixed in the promise is fixed beforehand, and where the amount of the plaintiff's performance is at that time uncertain or contingent it may turn out that the promised price will bear no relation to the value of the plaintiff's actual performance.' 1 Williston on Contracts, § 536." *See also* II G. Palmer, The Law of Restitution (1978) § 6.3(b).

3. The employment agreements of certain categories of professionals such as real estate brokers must be in writing to be enforceable under the Statute of Frauds in several states. For reasons similar to those given in the licensing cases, quasi-contract relief is usually denied in these situations. *See* II G. Palmer, The Law of Restitution (1978) §§ 6.9, 8.3. These are treated in a manner different from the conventional Statute of Frauds situation because it is thought that different treatment is consistent with legislative intent and public policy considerations where special risks to the public are involved. Moreover, since real estate contracts ordinarily provide for a commission after full performance, to allow quasi-contractual recovery for the value of the agent's services often would largely nullify the Statute of Frauds. *Id.*

4. In addition to the Statute of Frauds, most states have statutes rendering unenforceable in their courts the contracts of an out-of-state corporation "doing business" in the state without having complied with certain statutory conditions precedent to the granting of that privilege. A contract which has been partly performed by a corporation in violation of such a statute may afford a basis for quasi-contract relief. Warren Co. v. Neel, 284 F.Supp. 203 (W.D.Ark.1968), *aff'd per curiam,* 406 F.2d 775 (8th Cir.1969) (foreign corporation which was doing business in Arkansas without "qualifying" to do so cannot enforce a conditional sales contract in an action brought in the state, but quasi-contractual relief is nonetheless available.).

FRANK M. HALL & COMPANY v. SOUTHWEST PROPERTIES VENTURE

Colorado Court of Appeals, 1987.
747 P.2d 688.

VAN CISE, JUDGE.

Plaintiff, Frank M. Hall & Company (the contractor), supplied labor and materials (the improvements) on behalf of Horizon Technology, Inc. (tenant) on property leased by the tenant from defendant, Southwest Properties Venture (landlord). When the tenant failed to pay for the improvements, the contractor brought this action against the landlord and others seeking to foreclose a claimed mechanic's lien against the leased premises or, in the alternative, to recover from the landlord for unjust enrichment. From an adverse judgment on both claims, the contractor appeals. We affirm in part and reverse in part.

In October 1982, the landlord and tenant executed a lease for retail space in the landlord's shopping center. This lease provided that the tenant was to perform, at its expense, certain finish work on the premises according to the landlord's specifications. The lease also provided that, upon termination of the lease for any reason, all tenant improvements except trade fixtures would become the property of the landlord.

On December 3, 1982, the landlord posted a notice of nonliability on a stud in front of the premises. In January 1983, the tenant retained the contractor to perform the required finish work. The landlord's notice remained posted until March 3, 1983, when the work was substantially completed and the certificate of occupancy was issued.

After completion of the work, the tenant defaulted under its lease and failed to pay the contractor. The landlord recovered possession and relet the premises to others. The contractor recorded a lien statement for the amount owing for the furnished improvements. It then brought this action.

The trial court found that the landlord had timely and properly posted the notice of nonliability as provided by § 38–22–105(2), C.R.S. (1982 Repl.Vol. 16A), and that its property was therefore not subject to the lien. * * *

* * *

III.

The contractor next contends that the trial court erred in dismissing its claim against the landlord for unjust enrichment premised upon the landlord's retention of the improvements under its lease with the tenant and its alleged subsequent obtaining of benefit from the sales of the improvements upon reletting the premises to other tenants. Under the circumstances, we agree.

We disagree with the trial court's holding that a claim for unjust enrichment may not be asserted as an alternative to an action to foreclose a mechanic's lien. Section 38–22–124, C.R.S. (1982 Repl.Vol. 16A) provides that a mechanic's lien claimant is not prevented from enforcing any other remedy which he otherwise would have had. *See Hayutin v. Gibbons,* 139 Colo. 262, 338 P.2d 1032 (1959); *Tighe v. Kenyon,* 681 P.2d 547 (Colo.App. 1984). Moreover, the unenforceability of a mechanic's lien does not preclude the assertion of a claim premised on unjust enrichment. *See Jordan v. Lone Pines, Ltd.,* 41 Colo.App. 152, 580 P.2d 1273 (1978).

To recover under a theory of unjust enrichment, a plaintiff has the burden to prove (1) that it conferred a benefit on the defendant, (2) that the benefit was "appreciated" by the defendant, and (3) that the benefit was accepted under such circumstances that it would be inequitable for the defendant to retain it without payment of its reasonable value. *Martinez v. Continental Enterprises,* 730 P.2d 308 (Colo.1986); *Jordan v. Lone Pines, Ltd., supra.*

There is no question that here the contractor conferred a benefit on the landlord which it "appreciated." *See Cablevision of Breckenridge, Inc. v. Tannhauser Condominium Ass'n,* 649 P.2d 1093 (Colo.1982); *Restatement of Restitution* § 1, comment b (1937). The issue is thus whether the improvements were accepted under circumstances that make it inequitable for the landlord to retain them without reimbursing the contractor for their reasonable value.

In several similar cases where a contractor has pursued recovery from a landlord, equitable considerations have operated to prevent restitution. *See General Leasing Co. v. Manivest Corp.,* 667 P.2d 596 (Utah 1983) (improvements made without request or permission of landlord); *Coffee Pot Plaza Partnership v. Arrow Air Conditioning & Refrigeration, Inc.,* 412 So.2d 883 (Fla.App.1982) (landlord unable to find new tenant for improved premises); *Jordan v. Lone Pines, Ltd., supra* (mortgage lender had paid for improvements once); *Puttkammer v. Minth,* 83 Wis.2d 686, 266 N.W.2d 361 (1978) (mere knowing acquiescence in improvements insufficient to justify award).

In contrast here, if we accept as true the admissions in the pleadings, the evidence presented at trial, and the additional evidence contained in the contractor's offer of proof, the equitable factors militate in favor of an unjust enrichment recovery. The landlord not only gave its permission for the work but took an active role in its completion. Indeed, the lease required that the improvements be made, and provided that they would revert to the landlord upon termination of the lease. They were made according to the landlord's specifications, and were inspected and approved by it.

Moreover, the offer of proof was that, by the time of trial, the improved leasehold had been relet twice by the lessor, and the improvements at issue had been sold to the new lessees subject to the same reversion provisions. It was claimed that, in the first such lease, the improvements were transferred to the new tenant for $69,000, payable at the rate of $2,500 per month plus 13% interest; the landlord received approximately $12,500 from this tenant. In the next lease, the improvements were sold again, this time for $55,000, $18,500 down and the balance at $1,250 per month.

In such circumstances, if proved, and absent defenses as yet unpled by the landlord in bar or in mitigation, it would be inequitable for it to retain the benefits it received from the contractor's work and materials without compensating the contractor for its reasonable value. *See Restatement of Restitution* § 168(1) comment b (1937). *See also American Investors Life Insurance Co. v. Green Shield Plan, Inc.,* 145 Colo. 188, 358 P.2d 473 (1960); *Fort Lupton State Bank v. Murata,* 626 P.2d 757 (Colo.App.1981); *Restatement of Restitution* § 161 (1937).

The landlord's argument that its posting of a nonliability notice pursuant to § 38–22–105(2) was sufficient to relieve it from liability for unjust enrichment is without merit.

That part of the judgment dismissing the contractor's claim for unjust enrichment is reversed, and the cause is remanded for trial on that claim. In all other respects, the judgment is affirmed.

SMITH and KELLY, JJ., concur.

Chapter 9

LAW AND EQUITY MERGER: JURY TRIAL AND RELATED PROBLEMS

SECTION 1. THE JURY TRIAL PROBLEM

The Seventh Amendment to the United States Constitution guarantees the right to jury trial in the federal courts "in suits at common law, where the value in controversy shall exceed twenty dollars." Although the Seventh Amendment is not now binding on the states, there are similar state constitutional and statutory provisions. Courts often interpret these provisions by using the "historical" approach. In other words, the right to jury trial as to a particular claim depends upon how that claim was tried at the time of the enactment of the constitutional or statutory provision in effect in the jurisdiction in question.

Based on the foregoing, it has normally been accurate, if somewhat oversimplified, to state that traditionally designated common law actions carry a right to jury trial, whereas suits where equity would have taken jurisdiction do not. The procedural merger of law and equity has, for the most part, not significantly altered this situation. As to pure suits in equity, such as a simple suit for specific performance of a contract, there is no jury trial even though it will be tried in the same court as any other action. On the other hand, a tort action for damages, as an action of common law origin, will entail the right to a jury trial.

Nevertheless, this area is not without difficulty. The state courts' adherence to and application of the historical approach even to simple traditionally equitable claims is not without problems and is, at best, in a confusing state of flux. Moreover, state courts often have serious conceptual and analytical problems in this area. Consequently, it is necessary to give significant coverage to jury trial problems in actions where any form of equitable relief is sought.*

* The literature in this area is voluminous. *See generally,* Chesnin & Hazard, Chancery Procedure and the Seventh Amendment: Jury Trial of Issues in Equity Cases Before 1791, 83 Yale L.J. 900 (1974); Fleming, Right to a Jury Trial in Civil Actions, 72 Yale L.J. 646 (1963); Langbein, Fact Finding in the English Court of Chancery: A Rebuttal, 83 Yale L.J. 1620 (1974); Levin, Equitable Clean-up and the Jury: A Suggested Orientation, 100 U.Pa.L.Rev. 320 (1951); Wolfram, The Constitutional History of the Seventh

The most troublesome jury trial questions, however, arise when, as a result of the procedural merger of law and equity, legal and equitable claims are present in the same action. Some of these questions include the following: How should the factual issues be tried in a case where plaintiff joins legal and equitable claims? What effect should the interjection of a legal or equitable defense or counterclaim have on the right to jury trial? How do res judicata concepts complicate such problems? The following material places substantial emphasis on these problems.

A. THE FEDERAL APPROACH: A PREFERENCE FOR JURIES

ROSS v. BERNHARD

Supreme Court of the United States, 1970.
396 U.S. 531, 90 S.Ct. 733, 24 L.Ed.2d 729.

MR. JUSTICE WHITE, delivered the opinion of the Court.

The Seventh Amendment to the Constitution provides that in "[s]uits at common law, where the value in controversy shall exceed twenty dollars, the right of trial by jury shall be preserved." Whether the Amendment guarantees the right to a jury trial in stockholders' derivative actions is the issue now before us.

Petitioners brought this derivative suit in federal court against the directors of their closed-end investment company, the Lehman corporation and the corporation's brokers, Lehman Brothers. They contended that Lehman Brothers controlled the corporation through an illegally large representation on the corporation's board of directors, in violation of the Investment Company Act of 1940, 54 Stat. 789, 15 U.S.C.A. § 80a–1 et seq.,

Amendment, 57 Minn.L.Rev. 639 (1973); Note, the Right to Jury Trial Under Merged Procedures, 65 Harv.L.Rev. 453 (1952).

For particular emphasis on the federal setting, see Jorde, The Seventh Amendment Right to Jury Trial of Antitrust Issues, 69 Calif.L.Rev. 1 (1981); Kane, Civil Jury Trial: The Case for Reasoned Iconoclasm, 28 Hastings L.J. 1 (1976); McCoid, Right to Jury Trial in the Federal Courts, 45 Iowa L.Rev. 726 (1960); McCoid, Procedural Reform and the Right to Jury Trial: A Study of Beacon Theatres, Inc. v. Westover, 116 U.Pa.L.Rev. 1281 (1978); Redish, Seventh Amendment Right to Jury Trial: A Study in the Irrationality of Rational Decision Making, 70 Nw. U.L.Rev. 486 (1975); Ropski, The Federal Trademark Jury Trial—Awakening of a Dormant Constitutional Right, 70 Trade–Mark Rep. 177 (1980); Rothstein, Beacon Theatres and the Constitutional Right to Jury Trial, 61 ABA J. (1965); Comment, Landlord–Tenant—Tenant Can Assert Seventh Amendment Right to Jury Trial in Eviction Proceeding; *Pernell v. Southall Realty*, 24 Cath. U.L.Rev. 155 (1974); Comment, Right to Trial By Jury in Declaratory Judgment Actions, 3 Conn.L.Rev. 564 (1971); Note, The Right to Jury Trial in Complex Civil Litigation, 92 Harv.L.Rev. 898 (1979); Comment, The Seventh Amendment and Civil Rights Statutes: History Adrift in a Maelstrom, 68 Nw. U.L.Rev. 503 (1973); Comment, Ross v. Bernhard: The Uncertain Future of the Seventh Amendment, 81 Yale L.J. 112 (1971).

For an analysis of the problem in state courts, see Bourne, Merger of Law and Equity Under the Revised Maryland Rules: Does It Threaten Trial By Jury? 14 U.Balt.L.Rev. 1 (1984); Clark, Right to Jury Trial in Alabama, 4 Cum–Sam.L.Rev. 315 (1974); Degnan, Right to Civil Jury Trial in Utah: Constitution and Statute, 8 Utah L.Rev. 97 (1962); Erickson, The Right to a Jury Trial in Equitable Cases, 69 N.Dak.L.Rev. 559 (1993); Mayhall, A Note on Recent Cases Discussing Jury Trials in Cases Combining Legal and Equitable Relief, 38 The Ala.Law. 216 (1977); O'Neil, Law or Equity: The Right to Trial by Jury in a Civil Action, 35 Mo.L.Rev. 43 (1970); Sower, "Complicated Issues" v. The Right to a Jury Trial: A Procedural Remnant in Kentucky Law Raises Constitutional Problems, 3 N.Ky.L.Rev. 173 (1976).

and used this control to extract excessive brokerage fees from the corporation. * * * Petitioners requested that the defendants "account for and pay to the Corporation for their profits and gains and its losses." Petitioners also demanded a jury trial on the corporation's claims.

On motion to strike petitioners' jury trial demand, the District Court held that a shareholder's right to a jury on his corporation's cause of action was to be judged as if the corporation were itself the plaintiff. Only the shareholder's initial claim to speak for the corporation had to be tried to the judge. 275 F.Supp. 569. Convinced that "there are substantial grounds for difference of opinion as to this question and * * * an immediate appeal would materially advance the ultimate termination of this litigation," the District Court permitted an interlocutory appeal. 28 U.S.C.A. § 1292(b). The Court of Appeals reversed, holding that a derivative action was entirely equitable in nature, and no jury was available to try any part of it. 403 F.2d 909. It specifically disagreed with DePinto v. Provident Security Life Ins. Co., 323 F.2d 826 (C.A. 9th Cir.1963), cert. denied, 376 U.S. 950, 84 S.Ct. 965, 11 L.Ed.2d 969 (1964), on which the District Court had relied. Because of this conflict, we granted certiorari 394 U.S. 917, 89 S.Ct. 1190, 22 L.Ed.2d 450 (1969).

We reverse the holding of the Court of Appeals that in no event does the right to a jury trial preserved by the Seventh Amendment extend to derivative actions brought by the stockholders of a corporation. We hold that the right to jury trial attaches to those issues in derivative actions as to which the corporation, if it had been suing in its own right, would have been entitled to a jury.

* * *

However difficult it may have been to define with precision the line between actions at law dealing with legal rights and suits in equity dealing with equitable matters, Whitehead v. Shattuck, 138 U.S. 146, 151, 11 S.Ct. 276, 277, 34 L.Ed. 873 (1891), some proceedings were unmistakably actions at law triable to a jury. The Seventh Amendment, for example, entitled the parties to a jury trial in actions for damages to a person or property, for libel and slander, for recovery of land, and for conversion of personal property. Just as clearly, a corporation, although an artificial being, was commonly entitled to sue and be sued in the usual forms of action, at least in its own State. *See* Paul v. Virginia, 8 Wall. 168, 19 L.Ed. 357 (1869). Whether the corporation was viewed as an entity separate from its stockholders or as a device permitting its stockholders to carry on their business and to sue and be sued, a corporation's suit to enforce a legal right was an action at common law carrying the right to jury trial at the time the Seventh Amendment was adopted.

The common law refused, however, to permit stockholders to call corporate managers to account in actions at law. The possibilities for abuse, thus presented, were not ignored by corporate officers and directors. Early in the 19th century, equity provided relief both in this country and in England. * * * The remedy made available in equity was the derivative suit, viewed in this country as a suit to enforce a *corporate* cause of action against officers, directors, and third parties. As elaborated in the cases, one precondition for the suit was a valid claim on which the corporation could have sued; another was that the corporation itself had refused to proceed after suitable demand, unless excused by extraordinary conditions. Thus the dual nature of the stockholder's action: first, the plaintiff's right to sue on behalf of the corporation and, second, the merits of the corporation claim itself.

Derivative suits posed no Seventh Amendment problems where the action against the directors and third parties would have been by a bill in equity had the corporation brought the suit. Our concern is with cases based upon a legal claim of the corporation against directors or third parties. Does the trial of such claims at the suit of a stockholder and without a jury violate the Seventh Amendment?

The question arose in this Court in the context of a derivative suit for treble damages under the antitrust laws. Fleitmann v. Welsbach Street Lighting Co., 240 U.S. 27, 36 S.Ct. 233, 60 L.Ed. 505 (1916). Noting that the bill in equity set up a claim of the corporation alone, Mr. Justice Holmes observed that if the corporation were the plaintiff, "no one can doubt that its only remedy would be at law," and inquired "why the defendants' right to a jury trial should be taken away because the present plaintiff cannot persuade the only party having a cause of action to sue,—how the liability which is the principal matter can be converted into an incident of the plaintiff's domestic difficulties with the company that has been wronged"? *Id.,* at 28, 36 S.Ct., at 234. His answer was that the bill did not state a good cause of action in equity. Agreeing that there were "cases in which the nature of the right asserted for the company, or the failure of the defendants concerned to insist upon their rights, or a different state system, has led to the whole matter being disposed of in equity," he concluded that when the penalty of triple damages is sought, the antitrust statute plainly anticipated a jury trial and should not be read as "attempting to authorize liability to be enforced otherwise than through the verdict of a jury in a court of common law." *Id.,* at 28–29, 36 S.Ct., at 234. Although the decision had obvious Seventh Amendment overtones, its ultimate rationale was grounded in the antitrust laws.

Where penal damages were not involved, however, there was no authoritative parallel to *Fleitmann* in the federal system squarely passing on the applicability of the Seventh Amendment to the trial of a legal claim presented in a premerger derivative suit. What can be gleaned from this Court's opinions is not inconsistent with the general understanding, reflected by the state court decisions and secondary sources, that equity could properly resolve corporate claims of any kind without a jury when properly pleaded in derivative suits complying with the equity rules.

Such was the prevailing opinion when the Federal Rules of Civil Procedure were adopted in 1938. It continued until 1963 when the Court of Appeals for the Ninth Circuit, relying on the Federal Rules as construed and applied in Beacon Theatres Inc. v. Westover, 359 U.S. 500, 79 S.Ct. 948, 3 L.Ed.2d 988 (1959), and Dairy Queen Inc. v. Wood, 369 U.S. 469, 82 S.Ct. 894, 8 L.Ed.2d 44 (1962), required the legal issues in a derivative suit to be tried to a jury. DePinto v. Provident Security Life Ins. Co., 323 F.2d

826. It was this decision that the District Court followed in the case before us and that the Court of Appeals rejected.

Beacon and *Dairy Queen* presaged *DePinto*. Under those cases, where equitable and legal claims are joined in the same action, there is a right to jury trial on the legal claims which must not be infringed either by trying the legal issues as incidental to the equitable ones or by a court trial of a common issue existing between the claims. The Seventh Amendment question depends on the nature of the issue to be tried rather that the character of the overall action.[2] *See* Simler v. Conner, 372 U.S. 221, 83 S.Ct. 609, 9 L.Ed.2d 691 (1963). The principle of these cases bears heavily on derivative actions.

We have noted that the derivative suit has dual aspects: first, the stockholder's right to sue on behalf of the corporation, historically an equitable matter; second, the claim of the corporation against directors or third parties on which, if the corporation had sued and the claim presented legal issues, the company could demand a jury trial. As implied by Mr. Justice Holmes in *Fleitmann,* legal claims are not magically converted into equitable issues by their presentation to a court of equity in a derivative suit. The claim pressed by the stockholder against directors or third parties "is not his own but the corporation's." Koster v. Lumbermens Mut. Cas. Co., 330 U.S. 518, 522, 67 S.Ct. 828, 831 (1947). The corporation is a necessary party to the action; without it the case cannot proceed. Although named a defendant, it is the real party in interest, the stockholder being at best the nominal plaintiff. The proceeds of the action belong to the corporation and it is bound by the result of the suit. The heart of the action is the corporate claim. If it presents a legal issue, one entitling the corporation to a jury trial under the Seventh Amendment, the right to a jury is not forfeited merely because the stockholder's right to sue must first be adjudicated as an equitable issue triable to the court. *Beacon* and *Dairy Queen* require no less.

If under older procedures, now discarded, a court of equity could properly try the legal claims of the corporation presented in a derivative suit, it was because irreparable injury was threatened and no remedy at law existed as long as the stockholder was without standing to sue and the corporation itself refused to pursue its own remedies. Indeed, from 1789 until 1933, the judicial code expressly forbade courts of equity from entertaining any suit for which there was an adequate remedy at law. This provision served "to guard the right of trial by jury preserved by the Seventh Amendment and to that end it should be liberally construed." Schoenthal v. Irving Trust Co., 287 U.S. 92, 94, 53 S.Ct. 50, 51, 77 L.Ed. 185 (1932). If, before 1938, the law had borrowed from equity, as it borrowed other things, the idea that stockholders could litigate for their

2. As our cases indicate, the "legal" nature of an issue is determined by considering, first, the pre-merger custom with reference to such questions; second, the remedy sought; and, third, the practical abilities and limitations of juries. Of these factors, the first, requiring extensive and possibly abstruse historical inquiry, is obviously the most difficult to apply. *See* James, Right to a Jury Trial in Civil Actions, 72 Yale L.J. 655 (1963). [Footnote by the court.]

recalcitrant corporation, the corporate claim, if legal, would undoubtedly have been tried to a jury.

Of course, this did not occur, but the Federal Rules had a similar impact. Actions are no longer brought as actions at law or suits in equity. Under the Rules there is only one action—a "civil action"—in which all claims may be joined and all remedies are available. Purely procedural impediments to the presentation of any issue by any party, based on the difference between law and equity, were destroyed. In a civil action presenting a stockholder's derivative claim, the court after passing upon the plaintiff's right to sue on behalf of the corporation is now able to try the corporate claim for damages with the aid of a jury. Separable claims may be tried separately, Fed.Rule Civ.Proc. 42(b), or legal and equitable issues may be handled in the same trial. Fanchon & Marco, Inc. v. Paramount Pictures, Inc., 202 F.2d 731 (C.A.2d Cir.1953). The historical rule preventing a court of law from entertaining a shareholder's suit on behalf of the corporation is obsolete; it is no longer tenable for a district court, administering both law and equity in the same action, to deny legal remedies to a corporation, merely because the corporation's spokesmen are its shareholders rather than its directors. Under the rules, law and equity are procedurally combined; nothing turns now upon the form of the action or the procedural devices by which the parties happen to come before the court. The "expansion of adequate legal remedies provided by * * * the Federal Rules necessarily affects the scope of equity." Beacon Theatres, Inc. v. Westover, 359 U.S., at 509, 79 S.Ct., at 956.

Thus, for example, before-merger class actions were largely a device of equity, and there was no right to a jury even on issues that might, under other circumstances, have been tried to a jury. 5 J. Moore, Federal Practice ¶ 38.38[2] (2d ed. 1969); 3B id., ¶ 23.02[1]. Although at least one post-merger court held that the device was not available to try legal issues, it now seems settled in the lower federal courts that class action plaintiffs may obtain a jury trial on any legal issues they present. Montgomery Ward & Co. v. Langer, 168 F.2d 182 (C.A. 8th Cir.1948). * * * 2 W. Barron & A. Holtzoff, Federal Practice and Procedure § 571 (Wright ed. 1961).

Derivative suits have been described as one kind of "true" class action. *Id.*, § 562.1. We are inclined to agree with the description, at least to the extent it recognizes that the derivative suit and the class action were both ways of allowing parties to be heard in equity who could not speak at law. 3B J. Moore, Federal Practice ¶¶ 23.02[1], 23.1.16[1] (2d ed. 1969). After adoption of the rules there is no longer any procedural obstacle to the assertion of legal rights before juries, however the party may have acquired standing to assert those rights. Given the availability in a derivative action of both legal and equitable remedies, we think the Seventh Amendment preserves to the parties in a stockholder's suit the same right to a jury trial that historically belonged to the corporation and to those against whom the corporation pressed its legal claims.

In the instant case we have no doubt that the corporation's claim is, at least in part, a legal one. The relief sought is money damages. There are allegations in the complaint of a breach of fiduciary duty, but there are also allegations of ordinary breach of contract and gross negligence. The corporation, had it sued on its own behalf, would have been entitled to a jury's determination, at a minimum, of its damages against its broker under the brokerage contract and of its rights against its own directors because of their negligence. Under these circumstances it is unnecessary to decide whether the corporation's other claims are also properly triable to a jury. Dairy Queen, Inc. v. Wood, 369 U.S. 469, 82 S.Ct. 894, 8 L.Ed.2d 44 (1962). The decision of the Court of Appeals is reversed.

It is so ordered.

Decision of Court of Appeals reversed.

MR. JUSTICE STEWART, with whom THE CHIEF JUSTICE and MR. JUSTICE HARLAN join, dissenting. [Dissenting opinion omitted.]

* * *

Notes

1. *Ross* was given an especially expansive interpretation in Chauffeurs, Teamsters & Helpers, Local 391 v. Terry, 494 U.S. 558, 110 S.Ct. 1339, 108 L.Ed.2d 519 (1990). In that case, Justice Marshall, writing for a plurality of the Court, concluded that employees seeking back pay from their union for the latter's breach of its duty of fair representation were entitled to a jury trial. He stressed that the nature of the issues, rather than the action as a whole, determined whether a jury was required. Even though he conceded that the action resembled a traditional equity suit by a beneficiary against a trustee, he examined the underlying issues and determined that they were more closely similar to a legal action for breach of contract. Moreover, his conclusion was buttressed by the fact that the employees sought a monetary remedy, damages, which typically are characterized as "legal." According to the three judge dissent, however, "[a]lthough we have divided self-standing legal claims from equitable, declaratory, accounting, and derivative procedures, we have never parsed legal elements out of equitable claims absent specific justifications." *Id.*, 494 U.S. at 590, 110 S.Ct. at 1358.

2. The footnote in *Ross* suggests that the "practical ability and limitations of juries" is a relevant factor in determining the "legal" nature of an issue and thus, whether the Seventh Amendment mandates a jury trial. The foregoing language has provided ammunition for the argument that a jury trial is not constitutionally required in a variety of sophisticated and complex civil cases. Consider the following analysis of this argument:

> "The last fifty years have seen a tremendous liberalization of civil procedure and an unprecedented proliferation of new causes of action, which together make it possible for civil litigation to reach a level of complexity exceeding anything imaginable in the common law courts of 1791. Modern securities and antitrust cases, for example, can involve an enormous number of parties and claims, highly technical factual inquiries, tremendous volumes of documentary evidence, and trials lasting several years. Even when confronted with exceedingly complex litigation, some courts have refused to foreclose a jury trial, holding that complexity is not

a constitutionally appropriate ground for denying a jury.[10] Yet other federal courts have denied demands for a jury trial in complex cases, generally resting their decisions on one of two grounds: first, that a trial of such a case to an uncomprehending jury would constitute a denial of due process;[11] and second, that such cases are inherently beyond the understanding of a jury, so that trying them to a jury would constitute an inadequate remedy at law. * * *

"* * * Insofar as analogies based on complexity are appropriate, complex modern litigation bears much closer resemblance to equitable actions in 1791, heard without a jury, than to common law actions. Nonetheless, it would probably also be incorrect to conclude from this fact alone that modern complex litigation, such as one finds in actions brought under the securities or antitrust laws, falls outside the protection afforded the civil jury right by the seventh amendment.

"The defect in the existing analysis of the seventh amendment is that it pays too little attention to the enormous differences between civil litigation in 1791 and civil litigation today. The framers, schooled in the traditions of the British legal system, were undoubtedly aware of the restricted scope of actions at common law, as well as the limited role of the jury. It seems likely that they were also aware of the reasons for the narrow ambit of the common law jury system. By 'preserving' the distinctions between law and equity, they tacitly acknowledged that the right to a jury trial should not extend to those situations where the jury would be an inappropriate fact-finding body. Their conception of a 'Suit[ ] at common law' must have embodied these notions as much as it embodied notions about the types of rights cognizable and remedies available in the common law courts. Under modern rules of pleading and procedure, a case may be brought that bears so little resemblance to anything that could ever have occurred in the common law courts in 1791 that the difference between them is more aptly called a difference in kind, rather than in degree. Submission of such a case to a jury represents a repudiation, rather than an application, of a historical test. One might as easily assert that a jury is appropriate because the litigation is conducted in a courtroom that was in use in 1791.

"In most cases, the current doctrine's focus on the 'substantive' aspects of the case, the remedies and rights, may be appropriate. It is, however, futile to assume that an unwavering line can be drawn between substance and procedure. More importantly, it flies in the face of a claimed reliance on history to conclude that, in an action involving, for example, over 100 parties contesting eighteen consolidated class actions, with cross claims so numerous as to require a five-page chart merely to list them and a trial expected to last two years and involve about 500 witnesses and 24,000 documents, a jury is constitutionally required simply because the plaintiffs seek money damages, a remedy traditionally granted at law. When one considers that the modern rules on class actions, discovery, and joinder of parties and claims are all derived primarily from equity, it is an abandonment, rather than an application, of a historical view of the

10. *See, e.g.,* In re U.S. Fin. Sec. Litig., 609 F.2d 411 (9th Cir.1979), cert. denied, 446 U.S. 929 (1980).

11. *See, e.g.,* Zenith Radio Corp. v. Matsushita Elec. Indus. Co. (In re Japanese Elec. Prods. Antitrust Litig.), 631 F.2d 1069 (3d Cir.1980).

seventh amendment to call such an action a 'Suit[ ] at common law.' Stated differently, even if one accepts the Court's current focus on substantive rights and remedies, there comes a point at which the changes in procedure have been so extensive that there has been a change in the *substantive* character of the action as well. When such a point is reached, an effort to distinguish cases on the basis of the rights asserted and the remedies sought seeks to preserve the right to a jury trial in what can no longer in any realistic sense be called a suit at common law.

"The ultimate question is determining when that point has been reached. As with other constitutional standards, a determination as to the availability of a jury trial should depend on a consideration of the totality of circumstances in light of a number of relevant factors. These include not only the nature of the rights and remedies, but also the number of parties, the relations they bear to one another, the complexity of the legal and factual issues, the number of claims, and the amount and complexity of the evidence that will be adduced to establish those claims. If the case is so complex because of the combination of flexible procedure and intricate substantive inquiries that, except for the remedy sought, it bears no resemblance whatsoever to suits heard in the English common law system, it is simply not an action for which the jury right can be said to be 'preserved.'"

Comment, Complex Civil Litigation and the Seventh Amendment Right to a Jury Trial, 51 U.Chi.L.Rev. 581, 581–82, 611–13 (1984).* Whether the foregoing reasoning ultimately will be adopted by the Supreme Court is, at best, debateable. As one recent commentary observes, in the post–*Ross* period "there has been no indication that the Court is likely to retreat from its expansive interpretation of the Seventh Amendment." J. Friedenthal, M. Kane & A. Miller, Civil Procedure 499 (2d ed. 1993). *Compare* Jorde, The Seventh Amendment Right to Jury Trial of Antitrust Issues, 69 Calif.L.Rev. 1 (1981) (author recommends a nonjury trial on "market structure issues" in antitrust litigation, and a jury trial on all other issues).**

3. Are civil rights cases one type of case in which the Seventh Amendment does not mandate a jury trial? Consider the following discussion of this issue by the United States Supreme Court in Curtis v. Loether, 415 U.S. 189, 94 S.Ct. 1005, 39 L.Ed.2d 260 (1974), an action for compensatory and punitive damages under Title VIII by a black woman (petitioner) who claimed that the white defendants had refused to rent an apartment to her because of her race:

"Title VIII * * * provides that '[t]he court may grant as relief, as it deems appropriate, any permanent or temporary injunction, temporary restraining order, or other order, and may award to the plaintiff actual

* Reprinted with permission of the University of Chicago Law Review.

** For further consideration of the right to jury trial in complex litigation, *see* Arnold, An Historical Inquiry into the Right to Trial by Jury in Complex Civil Litigation, 128 U.Pa. L.Rev. 829 (1980); Campbell and LePoidevin, Complex Cases and Jury Trials: A Reply to Professor Arnold, 128 U.Pa.L.Rev. 986 (1980); Arnold, A Modest Replication to a Lengthy Discourse, 128 U.Pa.L.Rev. 986 (1980); Devlin, Jury Trial of Complex Cases: English Practice at the Time of the Seventh Amendment, 80 Colum.L.Rev. 43 (1980); Kirst, The Jury's Historic Dominance in Complex Cases, 58 Wash.L.Rev. 1 (1982); Lempert, Civil Juries and Complex Cases: Let's Not Rush to Judgment, 80 Mich.L.Rev. 68 (1981); Wilkinson, Zielinski & Curtis, A Bicentennial Tradition: Modern Alternatives To Seventh Amendment Trial in Complex Cases, 37 U.Kan.L.Rev. 61 (1988); Note, The Right to Jury Trial in Complex Civil Litigation, 92 Harv.L.Rev. 898 (1979).

damages and not more than $1,000 punitive damages, together with court costs and reasonable attorney fees * * *.'

* * *

"The legislative history on the jury trial question is sparse, and what little is available is ambiguous. There seems to be some indication that supporters of Title VIII were concerned that the possibility of racial prejudice on juries might reduce the effectiveness of civil rights damages actions. On the other hand, one bit of testimony during committee hearings indicates an awareness that jury trials would have to be afforded in damages actions under Title VIII. Both petitioner and respondents have presented plausible arguments from the wording and construction of § 812. We see no point to giving extended consideration to these arguments, however, for we think it is clear that the Seventh Amendment entitles either party to demand a jury trial in an action for damages in the federal courts under § 812.

"The Seventh Amendment provides that '[i]n suits at common law, where the value in controversy shall exceed twenty dollars, the right of trial by jury shall be preserved.' Although the thrust of the Amendment was to preserve the right to jury trial as it existed in 1791, it has long been settled that the right extends beyond the common-law forms of action recognized at that time. * * *

"Petitioner nevertheless argues that the Amendment is inapplicable to new causes of action created by congressional enactment. As the Court of Appeals observed, however, we have considered the applicability of the constitutional right to jury trial in actions enforcing statutory rights 'as a matter too obvious to be doubted.' 467 F.2d, at 1114. Although the Court has apparently never discussed the issue at any length, we have often found the Seventh Amendment applicable to causes of action based on statutes. *See, e.g.,* Dairy Queen, Inc. v. Wood, 369 U.S. 469, 477, 82 S.Ct. 894, 899, 8 L.Ed.2d 44 (1962) (trademark laws); Hepner v. United States, 213 U.S. 103, 115, 29 S.Ct. 474, 479, 53 L.Ed. 720 (1909) (immigration laws); *cf.* Fleitmann v. Welsbach Street Lighting Co., 240 U.S. 27, 36 S.Ct. 233, 60 L.Ed. 505 (1916) (antitrust laws), and the discussion of *Fleitmann* in Ross v. Bernhard, 396 U.S. 531, 535–536, 90 S.Ct. 733, 736–737, 24 L.Ed.2d 729 (1970). Whatever doubt may have existed should now be dispelled. The Seventh Amendment does apply to actions enforcing statutory rights, and requires a jury trial upon demand, if the statute creates legal rights and remedies, enforceable in an action for damages in the ordinary courts of law.

"NLRB v. Jones & Laughlin Steel Corp., 301 U.S. 1, 57 S.Ct. 615, 81 L.Ed. 893 (1937), relied on by petitioner, lends no support to her statutory-rights argument. The Court there upheld the award of back pay without jury trial in an NLRB unfair labor practice proceeding, rejecting a Seventh Amendment claim on the ground that the case involved a 'statutory proceeding' and 'not a suit at common law or in the nature of such a suit.' *Id.,* at 48, 57 S.Ct. at 629. *Jones & Laughlin* merely stands for the proposition that the Seventh Amendment is generally inapplicable in administrative proceedings, where jury trials would be incompatible with the whole concept of administrative adjudication and would substantially interfere with the NLRB's role in the statutory scheme. * * * These cases uphold congressional power to entrust enforcement of statutory rights to an administrative process or specialized court of equity free from the strictures of the Seventh Amendment. But when Congress provides for enforcement of statutory rights in an ordinary civil action in the district courts, where there is obviously no functional justification for denying the jury trial right, a jury trial must be available if the action involves rights and remedies of the sort typically enforced in an action at law.

"We think it is clear that a damages action under § 812 is an action to enforce 'legal rights' within the meaning of our Seventh Amendment decisions. * * * A damages action under the statute sounds basically in tort—the statute merely defines a new legal duty, and authorizes the courts to compensate a plaintiff for the injury caused by the defendant's wrongful breach. As the Court of Appeals noted, this cause of action is analogous to a number of tort actions recognized at common law. More important, the relief sought here—actual and punitive damages—is the traditional form of relief offered in the courts of law.

"We need not, and do not, go so far as to say that any award of monetary relief must necessarily be 'legal' relief. *See, e.g.,* Mitchell v. Robert DeMario Jewelry, Inc., 361 U.S. 288, 80 S.Ct. 332, 4 L.Ed.2d 323 (1960); Porter v. Warner Holding Co., 328 U.S. 395, 60 S.Ct. 1086, 90 L.Ed. 1332 (1946). A comparison of Title VIII with Title VII of the Civil Rights Act of 1964, where the courts of appeals have held that jury trial is not required in an action for reinstatement and back pay, is instructive, although we of course express no view on the jury trial issue in that context. In Title VII cases the courts of appeals have characterized back pay as an integral part of an equitable remedy, a form of restitution. But the statutory language on which this characterization is based—

> '[T]he court may enjoin the respondent from engaging in such unlawful employment practice, and order such affirmative action as may be appropriate, which may include, but is not limited to, reinstatement or hiring of employees, with or without back pay * * *, or any other equitable relief as the court deems appropriate,' 42 U.S.C.A. § 2000e–5(g) (1970 ed., Supp. II)—

contrasts sharply with § 812's simple authorization of an action for actual and punitive damages. In Title VII cases, also, the courts have relied on the fact that the decision whether to award back pay is committed to the discretion of the trial judge. There is no comparable discretion here: if a plaintiff proves unlawful discrimination and actual damages, he is entitled to judgment for that amount. Nor is there any sense in which the award here can be viewed as requiring the defendant to disgorge funds wrongfully withheld from the plaintiff. Whatever may be the merit of the 'equitable' characterization in Title VII cases, there is surely no basis for characterizing the award of compensatory and punitive damages here as equitable relief.

"We are not oblivious to the force of petitioner's policy arguments. Jury trials may delay to some extent the disposition of Title VIII damages actions. But Title VIII actions seeking only equitable relief will be unaffected, and preliminary injunctive relief remains available without a jury trial even in damages actions. Dairy Queen, Inc. v. Wood, 369 U.S., at 479 n. 20, 82 S.Ct., at 901. Moreover, the statutory requirement of expedition of § 812 actions, 42 U.S.C.A. § 3614 (1970), applies equally to jury and nonjury trials. We recognize, too, the possibility that jury prejudice may deprive a victim of discrimination of the verdict to which he or she is entitled. Of course, the trial judge's power to direct a verdict, to grant judgment notwithstanding the verdict, or to grant a new trial provides substantial protection against this risk, and respondents' suggestion that jury trials will expose a broader segment of the populace to the example of the federal civil rights laws in operation has some force. More fundamentally, however, these considerations are insufficient to overcome the clear command of the Seventh Amendment. The decision of the Court of Appeals must be affirmed."

4. As noted earlier in this volume, the Civil Rights Act of 1991 (the "Act") significantly expanded the remedies available to a Title VII employee. *See* pp. 1066–1067 *supra*. While previously the major remedies under Title VII were back pay and reinstatement, the Act expanded the relief available to include compensatory damages and reinstatement. Id. More important, "if a complaining party seeks compensatory or punitive damages * * * any party may demand a trial by jury * * *." 42 U.S.C.A. § 1981a.

SANTIAGO–NEGRON v. CASTRO–DAVILA

United States Court of Appeals, First Circuit, 1989.
865 F.2d 431.

Before Bownes, Torruella and Selya, Circuit Judges.

Bownes, Circuit Judge.

The lawsuit giving rise to this appeal was an aftermath of the November 1984 elections in Puerto Rico. Prior to that election, the Mayor of the Municipality of Las Piedras and the majority of its Municipal Assembly were members of the New Progressive Party (NPP). As a result of the election, political control of Las Piedras shifted to the Popular Democratic Party (PDP); the newly-elected Mayor and a majority of the Municipal Assembly belonged to the PDP. Animated by the venerable political and military maxim that "to the victor belongs the spoils," the new Mayor and his administration proceeded to replace Municipal employees belonging to the NPP with those whose allegiance was to the PDP. * * *

Hence a 42 U.S.C. § 1983 civil rights action was brought against the Mayor of Las Piedras, its Personnel Officer, and the Director of Public Works, the President of the Municipal Assembly, the Municipality itself, and the Commonwealth of Puerto Rico. All of the city officials were sued individually and in their official capacity. The complaint alleged that the defendants violated the plaintiffs' constitutional rights to due process and freedom of speech either by firing them or by transferring, demoting, and discriminating against them because of their political affiliation.

After a jury trial, all the defendants, except the Municipality were found liable to some or all of the plaintiffs; compensatory damages were assessed against the defendants separately on each claim and three of the plaintiffs were awarded punitive damages. The district court incorporated into the judgment a reinstatement and back pay order for each plaintiff.

The three individual defendants have appealed. * * * [The court's consideration of non-jury trial issues is omitted.]

We now turn to the more difficult question of whether it should be the judge or jury who awards back pay in a section 1983 case based upon an alleged unconstitutional political discharge where a jury will determine liability and compensatory damages. This is a question of first impression in this circuit.

Most of the courts of appeals that have grappled with the problem have focused on the nature of the relief sought: equitable or legal. The Sixth Circuit formulated the classic test in *Hildebrand v. Board of Trustees of Michigan State University,* 607 F.2d 705, 708 (6th Cir.1979) (citation and footnote omitted):

> The above-cited authorities mandate that the chief focus to be made when determining whether a jury trial right exists is the nature of the relief sought. If the remedy sought is injunctive relief and/or back pay, no jury trial right attaches. In the ordinary case, if the relief sought includes compensatory and/or punitive damages, then there does exist a right to trial by jury.

This reasoning was carried to its logical conclusion in *Moore v. Sun Oil Company of Pennsylvania,* 636 F.2d 154 (6th Cir.1980), in which it was held in a 42 U.S.C. § 1981 action that even though reinstatement was not sought, back pay was equitable relief and the parties were not entitled to a jury trial on that issue. The court then went on to hold that since compensatory and punitive damages were legal relief, plaintiff had a right to a jury trial on those claims.

The rule in the Eleventh Circuit also is grounded on the nature of the remedy sought.

> The district court was correct in holding that appellant's claims were equitable and therefore not the proper subject of a jury trial. Appellant seeks reinstatement, backpay and reimbursement for "other lost professional benefits," all of which are equitable whether sought under Title VII or section 1983. *Harkless v. Sweeny Independent School District,* 427 F.2d 319, 323–24 (5th Cir.1970), *cert. denied,* 400 U.S. 991, 91 S.Ct. 451, 27 L.Ed.2d 439 (1971); *Johnson v. Georgia Highway Express, Inc.,* 417 F.2d 1122, 1125 (5th Cir.1969).

Sullivan v. School Board of Pinellas County, 773 F.2d 1182, 1187 (11th Cir.1985) (footnote omitted).

The Ninth Circuit in a combination Title VII and 42 U.S.C. § 1981 case held that section 1981 provides both legal and equitable remedies, and that the legal remedies include compensatory and punitive damages which carry with them the right to a jury trial. Back pay is characterized as "either equitable or as a legal remedy incidental to an equitable cause of action, and accordingly not sufficient to create a right to a jury trial." *Williams v. Owens–Illinois, Inc.,* 665 F.2d 918, 929 (9th Cir.) (footnote omitted), *cert. denied,* 459 U.S. 971, 103 S.Ct. 302, 74 L.Ed.2d 283 (1982).

In *Bertot v. School District No. 1, Albany County,* 613 F.2d 245, 250 (10th Cir.1979), the Tenth Circuit held that back pay was an element of equitable relief and was not precluded by a good faith defense. *But cf. Skinner v. Total Petroleum, Inc.,* 859 F.2d 1439 (10th Cir.1988) (where trial is both to jury and court due to presence of both equitable and legal issues, seventh amendment requires that essential factual issues central to both must first be tried to the jury. In combination Title VII and § 1981 case, jury determination of back pay award in the § 1981 case must be accepted by court in the Title VII case, if supported by the evidence.).

In a political affiliation-discharge case, the Third Circuit held that a "party seeking compensation or other legal relief under 42 U.S.C. § 1983 has a right to a jury trial * * * although the request for back pay under section 1983 seeks only equitable relief." *Laskaris v. Thornburgh,* 733 F.2d 260, 263 (3d Cir.), *cert. denied,* 469 U.S. 886, 105 S.Ct. 260, 83 L.Ed.2d 196 (1984).

The only circuit, as far as we can determine, that has explicitly found back pay to be legal damages is the Eighth. *Setser v. Novack Investment Co.,* 638 F.2d 1137 (8th Cir.), *cert. denied,* 454 U.S. 1064, 102 S.Ct. 615, 70 L.Ed.2d 601 (1981) was a section 1981 case in which the plaintiff sought back pay, other compensatory damages, and punitive damages. Reinstatement was not sought. The issue was whether plaintiff was entitled to a jury trial on the claim of back pay. After a review of the case law, the court held that back pay determinations "are inherently in the nature of legal damages and require a jury trial." *Id.* at 1142.

In contrast to the other circuits, the Seventh Circuit has blithely ignored the problem or decided that none existed. In that circuit, back pay is routinely submitted to the jury in § 1983 cases. And, at least in the cases we have read, there is no discussion of equitable versus legal relief. *See Webb v. City of Chester, Ill.,* 813 F.2d 824, 836 (7th Cir.1987); *Crawford v. Garnier,* 719 F.2d 1317, 1324 (7th Cir.1983); *Nekolny v. Painter,* 653 F.2d 1164, 1166 (7th Cir.1981), *cert. denied,* 455 U.S. 1021, 102 S.Ct. 1719, 72 L.Ed.2d 139 (1982).

Although the Supreme Court has not squarely addressed the question, we find its opinions in the general area instructive.

* * *

[The court's analysis of *Dairy Queen, Beacon Theatres* and *Ross* is omitted.]

The most recent case in this area is *Tull v. United States,* 481 S.Ct. 412, 107 S.Ct. 1831, 95 L.Ed.2d 365 (1987).[9] The question was,

9. We are aware that in *Bowen v. Massachusetts,* — U.S. —, 108 S.Ct. 2722, 2731–32, 101 L.Ed.2d 749 (1988), the Court restated the longstanding principle that an equitable action for specific relief may include an order for reinstatement with back pay. The issue in *Bowen* was whether a district court had jurisdiction to review a final order of the Secretary of Health and Human Services refusing to reimburse a state for a category of expenditures under its Medicaid program. The Court's statement was made as part of its explanation of why there could be judicial review of the Secretary's disallowance decision. The Court pointed out that the complaint sought declaratory and injunctive relief, not money damages. Because of the nature of the action, there could be no jury trial. We do not think that the statement is relevant to the issue before us.

> whether the Seventh Amendment guaranteed petitioner a right to a jury trial on both liability and amount of penalty in an action instituted by the Federal Government seeking civil penalties and injunctive relief under Clean Water Act, 62 Stat. Ch. 758, as amended, 33 U.S.C. § 1251, *et seq.*

Id. 107 S.Ct. at 1833. The Court examined "both nature of the action and the remedy sought." *Id.* at 1835. In the course of determining the nature of the action the Court stated:

> We need not rest our conclusion on what has been called an "abstruse historical" search for the nearest 18th–century analogue. See *Ross v. Bernhard,* 396 U.S., at 538, n. 10, 90 S.Ct., at 738, n. 10. We reiterate our previously expressed view that characterizing the relief sought is "[m]ore important" than finding a precisely analogous common law cause of action in determining whether the Seventh Amendment guarantees a jury trial. *Curtis v. Loether,* 415 U.S. [189], at 196, 94 S.Ct. [1005], at 1009 [39 L.Ed.2d 260 (1974)].

Id. at 1837 (footnote omitted). The Court found that the assessment of civil penalties did not "involve the 'substance of a common-law right to trial by jury', nor a 'fundamental element of a jury trial.' " *Id.* at 1840. In holding that the jury determines liability and the trial court assesses the penalty, the Court noted: "In this case, highly discretionary calculations that take into account multiple factors are necessary in order to set civil penalties under the Clean Water Act. These are the kinds of calculations traditionally performed by judges." *Id.* at 1840 (citation omitted).

Following the teachings of the Court we look to the nature of the action and the relief sought. There can be no doubt that § 1983 actions create tort liability with damages determined under the common law of torts.

> We have repeatedly noted that 42 U.S.C. § 1983 creates " 'a species of tort liability' in favor of persons who are deprived of 'rights, privileges, or immunities secured' to them by the Constitution." *Carey v. Piphus,* 435 U.S. 247, 253 [98 S.Ct. 1042, 1047, 55 L.Ed.2d 252] (1978), quoting *Imbler v. Pachtman,* 424 U.S. 409, 417 [96 S.Ct. 984, 988, 47 L.Ed.2d 128] (1976). See also *Smith v. Wade,* 461 U.S. 30, 34 [103 S.Ct. 1625, 1628, 75 L.Ed.2d 632] (1983); *Newport v. Fact Concerts, Inc.,* 453 U.S. 247, 258–259 [101 S.Ct. 2748, 2755–2756, 69 L.Ed.2d 616] (1981). Accordingly, when § 1983 plaintiffs seek damages for violations of constitutional rights, the level of damages is ordinarily determined according to principles derived from the common law of torts. See *Smith v. Wade, supra* [461 U.S.] at 34 [103 S.Ct. at 1628]; *Carey v. Phiphus, supra* [435 U.S.] at 257–258 [98 S.Ct. at 1049]; cf. *Monroe v. Pape,* 365 U.S. 167, 196, and n. 5 [81 S.Ct. 473, 488, and n. 5, 5 L.Ed.2d 492] (1961) (Harlan, J., concurring).

Memphis Community School District v. Stachura, 477 U.S. 299, 305–06, 106 S.Ct. 2537, 2542, 91 L.Ed.2d 249 (1986) (footnote omitted).

In tort actions for personal injury tried to a jury, lost wages are invariably treated as being part of compensatory damages. Unlike the calculations required to assess the civil penalty in *Tull,* the computation of back pay normally requires only the addition (or multiplication) of a fixed sum. To paraphrase *Tull,* these are the kinds of calculations traditionally performed by juries. *See* 107 S.Ct. at 1840. Our analysis leads us to conclude that the determination of back pay as a factor of compensatory damages involves the substance of a common-law right to a trial by jury. *See Tull,* 107 S.Ct. at 1840.

In addition to the seventh amendment implication, there is also a sound practical reason for having the jury factor in back pay when determining compensatory damages. Submission of the issue of back pay to the jury as a factor to be considered in its award of compensatory damages eliminates the inevitable overlap between compensatory damages and back pay. In most cases of an alleged unconstitutional firing, there will be evidence of the employee's pay. To expect a jury to ignore this is unrealistic, especially where it may constitute the major item of compensatory damages. * * *

Applying the analysis mandated by the Supreme Court, we hold that in a § 1983 case based upon an alleged unconstitutional political firing where the issues of liability and compensatory damages will be determined by a jury, back pay shall be considered by the jury as one of the items of compensatory damages. We are constrained to add that we are not dissolving the traditional legal-equitable dichotomy. Where only reinstatement and back pay are requested or if they are the only issues, in addition to liability, remaining in the case then both reinstatement and back pay shall be for the court. * * *

Affirmed in Part, Reversed in Part. Remanded.

Notes

1. The availability of a jury trial in civil suits against the United States is limited irrespective of the legal or equitable nature of the litigation. Consider, in this regard, the language of the United States Supreme Court in Lehman v. Nakshian, 453 U.S. 156, 161, 101 S.Ct. 2698, 2702, 69 L.Ed.2d 548 (1981) (holding that a civilian employee of the U.S. Navy is not entitled to a jury trial under the Age Discrimination in Employment Act (ADEA) because, even though Congress amended the ADEA to bring the federal government within its coverage, the amendment did not "clearly and unequivocally" grant a jury trial right):

> "It has long been settled that the Seventh Amendment right to trial by jury does not apply in actions against the Federal Government. In Galloway v. United States, 319 U.S. 372, 388–389, 63 S.Ct. 1077, 1086, 87 L.Ed. 1458, the Court observed (footnotes omitted):
>
> > 'The suit is one to enforce a monetary claim against the United States. It hardly can be maintained that under the common law in 1791 jury trial was a matter of right for persons asserting claims against the sovereign. Whatever force the Amendment has therefore is derived because Congress, in the legislation cited, has made it applicable.'
>
> Moreover, the Court has recognized the general principle that 'the United States, as sovereign, "is immune from suit save as it consents to be sued

> * * * and the terms of its consent to be sued in any court define that court's jurisdiction to entertain the suit." ' United States v. Testan, 424 U.S. 392, 399, 96 S.Ct. 948, 953, 47 L.Ed.2d 114; quoting United States v. Sherwood, 312 U.S. 584, 586, 61 S.Ct. 767, 769, 85 L.Ed. 1058. Thus, if Congress waives the Government's immunity from suit, as it has in the ADEA, 29 U.S.C. § 633a (1976 ed. and Supp. III), the plaintiff has a right to a trial by jury only where that right is one of 'the terms of [the Government's] consent to be sued.' *Testan, supra,* at 399, 96 S.Ct., at 953. Like a waiver of immunity itself, which must be 'unequivocally expressed.' United States v. Mitchell, *supra,* at 538, 100 S.Ct., at 1352, quoting United States v. King, 395 U.S. 1, 4, 89 S.Ct. 1501, 1502, 23 L.Ed.2d 52, 'this Court has long decided that limitations and conditions upon which the Government consents to be sued must be strictly observed and exceptions thereto are not to be implied.' Soriano v. United States, 352 U.S. 270, 276, 77 S.Ct. 269, 273, 1 L.Ed.2d 306.
>
> "When Congress has waived the sovereign immunity of the United States, it has almost always conditioned that waiver upon a plaintiff's relinquishing any claim to a jury trial. Jury trials, for example, have not been made available in the Court of Claims for the broad range of cases within its jurisdiction under 28 U.S.C. § 1491—*i.e.,* all claims against the United States 'founded either upon the Constitution, or any Act of Congress, * * * or upon any express or implied contract with the United States, or for liquidated or unliquidated damages in cases not sounding in tort.' *See Glidden Co., supra.* And there is no jury trial right in this same range of cases when the federal district courts have concurrent jurisdiction. *See* 28 U.S.C. §§ 1346(a)(2) and 2402. Finally, in tort actions against the United States, see 28 U.S.C. § 1346(b), Congress has similarly provided that trials shall be to the court without a jury. 28 U.S.C. § 2402."

Note, however, that the availability of a jury trial in suits against states is not similarly limited. *See* Reiner v. New Jersey, 732 F.Supp. 530 (D.N.J.1990) (Seventh Amendment creates right to jury trial when New Jersey is sued in federal court under state anti-discrimination legislation).

2. In Atlas Roofing Co. v. Occupational Safety and Health Review Comm'n., 430 U.S. 442, 97 S.Ct. 1261, 51 L.Ed.2d 464 (1977) the Supreme Court considered a Seventh Amendment challenge to the Occupational Safety and Health Act ("OSHA") enforcement procedure, which is relatively unique. Under most regulatory legislation the government can obtain a court judgment to enforce an administrative penalty only after a *de novo* civil action is conducted in a federal court. Under the OSHA procedure, however, the judicial action is not *de novo* and relitigation of the facts of the violation in federal court is not required.

The *Atlas* petitioners argued that the OSHA procedure violated the Seventh Amendment because it used the federal courts to enforce the administrative imposition of a penalty without also making provision for a right to trial by jury. The Supreme Court sustained the procedure and held that the Seventh Amendment did not invalidate the OSHA procedure because of a newly recognized "public rights" exception to the Seventh Amendment involving "cases in which the Government sues in its sovereign capacity to enforce public rights created by statutes within the power of Congress to enact." 430 U.S. at 450, 97 S.Ct. at 1266. *Accord* Washington Star Co. v. International Typographical

Union Negotiated Pension Plan, 729 F.2d 1502 (D.C.Cir.1984). For an excellent analysis of *Atlas,* see Kirst, Administrative Penalties and the Civil Jury: The Supreme Court's Assault on the Seventh Amendment, 126 U.Pa.L.Rev. 1281 (1978). *See also,* Congressional Delegation of Adjudication Power to Federal Agencies and the Right to Trial by Jury, 1988 Duke L.J. 539.

3. The "equitable clean-up doctrine" which has been repudiated by the United States Supreme Court, has been described as follows:

> "Historically, when a case had both legal and equitable aspects, the chancery courts employed the so-called 'clean-up doctrine.' This meant that once it was determined that equitable jurisdiction over an action existed, the chancellor would decide all aspects of the controversy, both legal and equitable, thereby obviating the need for two proceedings. But the doctrine would be applied only when the legal aspects of the case were subordinate to the equitable issues. Thus, prior to Beacon Theatres, the Seventh Amendment inquiry had focused largely on ascertaining the 'basic nature of the case' to determine whether a sufficiently important legal claim had been presented giving rise to a right to jury trial.
>
> "Judge Kalodner in *Fraser v. Geist*[11] succinctly stated the problem: 'Where the complaint states one cause of action giving rise to alternative remedies in law or in equity, and where the complainant similarly prays for relief in the alternative, what is the rule as respects the right of trial by jury?' His answer illustrates the typical pre-*Beacon* analysis. 'The decision as to whether or not the plaintiff is entitled to jury trial "as of right" must rest upon a prior determination as to whether the action, in its essence, is one at law or in equity.' Under this approach, when an action was classified as 'essentially equitable,' the federal court could dispose of any incidental legal claims without a jury. *Beacon Theatres* expressly overruled this interpretation of the Seventh Amendment and held that no test utilizing traditional equity procedure could interfere with the right to have a jury determine all the factual issues associated with a legal claim."

J. Friedenthal, M. Kane & A. Miller, Civil Procedure 490 (2d ed. 1993).* While equitable clean-up retains continued vitality in a significant number of states, as will be seen later in this chapter, the extent of its federal demise should be considered in the context of the following principal case.

AMOCO OIL COMPANY v. TORCOMIAN

United States Court of Appeals, Third Circuit, 1983.
722 F.2d 1099.

Before ALDISERT, BECKER, CIRCUIT JUDGES and COHILL, DISTRICT JUDGE.

OPINION OF THE COURT

BECKER, CIRCUIT JUDGE.

The question presented by this appeal is whether the district court erred in refusing to afford defendants John Torcomian and Albert Torcomian a jury trial with respect to both the complaint of plaintiff Amoco and the Torcomians' compulsory counterclaim. The basis of the denial was that

11. 1 F.R.D. 267 (E.D.Pa.1940).

the claims, which arose out of the parties' dealings concerning an Amoco service station, were equitable in nature. The district court, following a bench trial, found for Amoco on all issues, and the Torcomians appeal. Because we hold that many components of Amoco's main claim and the Torcomians' counterclaim, as pleaded, presented legal issues and sought legal relief, the district court erred in refusing to grant the defendants a jury trial. * * * Accordingly, the district court's judgment must be vacated and the entire case remanded for further proceedings.

* * *

Amoco originally sought extensive relief including: (1) ejectment of the defendants from the service station; (2) a permanent injunction restraining defendants from continued use, enjoyment and possession of Parkside Amoco; (3) a permanent injunction restraining defendants from use of the Amoco logo, tradename, service mark or trademark; (4) judgment in the amount of $46,675 for profits lost as a result of defendants' wrongful possession and fraudulent misrepresentations; (5) judgment for $12,000 for defendants' mesne profits and wrongful use of the Amoco logo, tradename, service mark or trademark; and (6) attorneys' fees. At the beginning of trial, however, Amoco attempted to orally amend its complaint to delete, as we understand it, portions of its complaint that sought money damages other than for mesne profits so as to eliminate any claims that might be construed as legal and to thereby foreclose the defendants' right to a jury trial. * * * [T]he defendant sought "(1) [an] injunction enjoining plaintiff to comply with its franchise agreement with John Torcomian; (2) [a] judgment against plaintiff in an amount in excess of $100,000.00 for profits lost by John Torcomian as a result of plaintiff's failure to comply with its franchise agreement and for plaintiff's fraudulent misrepresentations; [and] (3) [a] judgment against plaintiff in the amount of defendants reasonable attorneys' fee [sic] and other costs involved in defending this action."

In its bench opinion on the merits, rendered after a two-day trial, the district court concluded that defendants were at most tenants at will, and that there had never been a valid written or oral lease between Amoco and either or both of the defendants that would authorize them to occupy the property. It further concluded that no representative of Amoco having power to do so had ever told John Torcomian he was a dealer, and that John Torcomian, by failing to go to Dealer Development School * * *, had failed to fulfill a condition of his becoming an official dealer. The district court expressly resolved all questions of credibility in favor of Amoco and stated that it disbelieved testimony of John and Albert Torcomian. * * * Accordingly, it ordered the defendants to vacate Parkside Amoco and awarded Amoco $30,000 because it had been prevented from deriving a profit in that amount as a result of defendants' wrongful occupancy of Parkside Amoco.

II. Were the Components of Amoco's Claim Legal or Equitable?

It has long been settled law that neither joinder of an equitable claim with a legal claim nor joinder of a prayer for equitable relief with a claim for legal relief as to a legal claim can defeat an otherwise valid seventh amendment right to a jury trial. *See* Beacon Theatres, Inc. v. Westover, 359 U.S. 500, 79 S.Ct. 948, 3 L.Ed.2d 988 (1959); Dairy Queen, Inc. v. Wood, 369 U.S. 469, 82 S.Ct. 894, 8 L.Ed.2d 44 (1962). Thus, in order to assess the district court's denial of the defendants' demand for a jury trial as to the main claim, we must consider whether it comprised any legal claims seeking legal relief. If we find such claims, we must vacate the judgment, at least as to those claims, unless we are persuaded that Amoco was entitled to a directed verdict on those claims. *See* EEOC v. Corry Jamestown Corp., *supra.*

At the outset, we note that on its surface Amoco's complaint appears to present a number of essentially legal claims. The complaint sought ejectment, a form of action long regarded as legal. *See* Redfield v. Parks, 132 U.S. 239, 244, 10 S.Ct. 83, 84, 33 L.Ed. 327 (1889) ("In the courts of the United States where the distinction between actions at law and suits in equity has always been maintained, the action of ejectment is an action at law * * *."); United States v. King, 44 U.S. (3 How.) 773, 787–88, 11 L.Ed. 824 (1845) (ejectment is legal). It also sought damages, a form of relief usually treated as legal. Plaintiff offers several theories, however, to counter this surface interpretation.

To rebut the normal rule that ejectment is an action at law, plaintiff cites two Pennsylvania cases. Williams v. Bridy, 391 Pa. 1, 8, 136 A.2d 832, 836 (1957); and Fisher v. Knelly, 68 Sch.L.R. 117, 119 (Schuylkill C.P.1972). These cases purportedly hold that, where actual title to property is not in doubt, an action for injunction against defendant's continued possession of property leased to plaintiff is equitable. While our preliminary reading of the cited cases suggests that Amoco's interpretation and conclusions are dubious,* there is a more telling problem with its argument: Pennsylvania's characterization of ejectment is irrelevant. *See* Simler v. Conner, 372 U.S. 221, 222, 83 S.Ct. 609, 610, 9 L.Ed.2d 691 (1963) (per curiam). As the Supreme Court there held, "[i]n diversity cases, of course, the substantive dimension of the claim asserted finds its source in state law * * * but the characterization of that state-created claim as legal or equitable for purposes of whether a right to jury trial is indicated must be made by recourse to federal law." And federal law, as

* The right to jury trial in actions for the common law remedy of "ejectment" and the equitable suit of a "bill to quiet title" are discussed in Marthens v. B & O Railroad Co., 170 W.Va. 33, 289 S.E.2d 706, 712 n. 2 (1982):

"Ejectment is an action for the protection of one with good legal title to the land who is entitled to immediate possession. * * * Historically, West Virginia has always accorded the right to a jury trial in an action for ejectment. *See* W.Va.Code, 55–4–17 [1929]; Davis Colliery Co. v. Westfall, 78 W.Va. 735, 90 S.E. 328 (1916); Garrett v. South Penn Oil Co., 66 W.Va. 587, 66 S.E. 741 (1909).

"Where the title to land is in question, an equitable bill either to quiet title or to remove a cloud is the traditional remedy. Suits to quiet title are appropriate in cases where a deed is imperfect, Austin v. Brown, 37 W.Va. 634, 17 S.E. 207 (1893); has been forged, Andre v. Hoffman, 81 W.Va. 620, 95 S.E. 84 (1918), or in situations where the owner of real estate executes written instruments providing for the sale of his property, which are of record and which are in the hands of the defendant but which were rescinded by the reentry of the grantors after the grantee had defaulted in the performance of specified conditions. Watzman v. Unatin, 101 W.Va. 41, 131 S.E. 874 (1926). The authority of a court of equity to quiet title to land exists independently of any statute. Dolan v. Hardman, 126 W.Va. 480, 29 S.E.2d 8 (1944)."

we have indicated, unequivocally holds actions seeking ejectment to be legal, not equitable.

While apparently conceding that damages for profits lost by dint of the defendants' wrongful occupancy * * * constitute legal relief, Amoco argues that it abandoned that claim in the oral amendment to its complaint and that the remaining remedy of restitution—which we presume refers to the disgorgement of mesne profits—was equitable. While we do not quibble with this characterization, we regard it too as irrelevant. For while restitution may have been what Amoco wanted, restitution is not what Amoco got. The district court was presented with little evidence on the subject during trial, made no factual findings on the matter, and ordered no accounting. More importantly, the district court explicitly said it was awarding damages because "[a]s a result of defendants' occupancy against the will of the plaintiff, plaintiff has been prevented from deriving a profit from the property in the amount of $30,000." Thus, Amoco apparently never effectively retracted its original demand for legal relief.

III. Were the Components of the Defendants' Counterclaim Equitable or Legal?

It is settled law in this Circuit and elsewhere, *see* Eldredge v. Gourley, 505 F.2d 769, 770 (3d Cir.1974) (per curiam); Thermo–Stitch, Inc. v. Chemi–Cord Processing Corp., 294 F.2d 486, 488 (5th Cir.1961), that even an equitable main claim cannot preclude a jury trial on a legal counterclaim, at least when the counterclaim is compulsory. A rule to the contrary would enable the preemptive filing of a complaint by the holder of an equitable claim, coupled with the doctrine of res judicata, to deprive the holder of a legal claim of his seventh amendment right to a jury trial. *See* Great Lakes Rubber Corp. v. Herbert Cooper Co., 286 F.2d 631, 634 (3d Cir.1961) (failure to assert compulsory counterclaim in earlier action bars assertion in subsequent litigation). Accordingly, we must consider whether there was an element present in the counterclaim which would have given rise to a right to jury trial.

Although the defendants did ask for equitable relief in their counterclaim (i.e., fulfillment of Amoco's obligation under the alleged franchise agreement), defendants also sought damages for the past breach of that agreement. A routine claim such as that presented here for damages stemming from breach of contract is legal. *See* Rogers v. Exxon Research & Engineering Co., 550 F.2d 834, 838 (3d Cir.1977). As we have noted in Part II of this opinion, the fact that equitable relief is sought in addition to substantial legal relief does not eliminate a right to a jury trial.

Notes

1. In Parklane Hosiery Co., Inc. v. Shore, 439 U.S. 322, 99 S.Ct. 645, 58 L.Ed.2d 552 (1979), the Supreme Court confronted the question "whether a party who has had issues of fact adjudicated adversely to it in an equitable action may be collaterally estopped from relitigating the same issues before a jury in a subsequent legal action brought against it by a new party." In concluding that the Seventh Amendment did not preclude the use of collateral estoppel in such a setting, the Court stated:

" '[T]he thrust of the [Seventh] Amendment was to preserve the right to jury trial as it existed in 1791.' Curtis v. Loether, 415 U.S. 189, 193, 94 S.Ct. 1005, 1007, 39 L.Ed.2d 260. At common law, a litigant was not entitled to have a jury determine issues that had been previously adjudicated by a chancellor in equity. Hopkins v. Lee, 6 Wheat. 109, 112; Smith v. Kernochen, 7 How. 198, 217–218, 12 L.Ed. 666; Brady v. Daly, 175 U.S. 148, 158–159, 20 S.Ct. 62, 66, 44 L.Ed. 109; Shapiro & Coquillette, The Fetish of Jury Trials in Civil Cases: A Comment on Rachal v. Hill, 85 Harv.L.Rev. 441, 448–458 (1971).

"Recognition that an equitable determination could have collateral estoppel effect in a subsequent legal action was the major premise of this Court's decision in Beacon Theatres v. Westover, 359 U.S. 500, 79 S.Ct. 948, 3 L.Ed.2d 988. In that case the plaintiff sought a declaratory judgment that certain arrangements between it and the defendant were not in violation of the antitrust laws, and asked for an injunction to prevent the defendant from instituting an antitrust action to challenge the arrangements. The defendant denied the allegations and counterclaimed for treble damages under the antitrust laws, requesting a trial by jury of the issues common to both the legal and equitable claims. The Court of Appeals upheld denial of the request, but this Court reversed, stating that:

> '[T]he effect of the action of the District Court could be, as the Court of Appeals believed, "to limit the petitioner's opportunity fully to try to a jury every issue which has a bearing upon its treble damage suit," for determination of the issue of clearances by the judge might "operate either by way of res judicata or collateral estoppel so as to conclude both parties with respect thereto at the subsequent trial of the treble damage claim." ' 359 U.S., at 504, 79 S.Ct., at 953.

"It is thus clear that the Court in the *Beacon Theatres* case thought that if an issue common to both legal and equitable claims was first determined by a judge, relitigation of the issue before a jury might be foreclosed by res judicata or collateral estoppel. To avoid this result, the Court held that when legal and equitable claims are joined in the same action, the trial judge has only limited discretion in determining the sequence of trial and "that discretion * * * must, wherever possible, be exercised to preserve jury trial." Id., at 510, 79 S.Ct., at 956.

"Both the premise of *Beacon Theatres,* and the fact that it enunciated no more than a general prudential rule were confirmed by this Court's decision in Katchen v. Landy, 382 U.S. 323, 86 S.Ct. 467, 15 L.Ed.2d 391. In that case the Court held that a bankruptcy court, sitting as a statutory court of equity, is empowered to adjudicate equitable claims prior to legal claims, even though the factual issues decided in the equity action would have been triable by a jury under the Seventh Amendment if the legal claims had been adjudicated first. The Court stated:

> "Both *Beacon Theatres* and *Dairy Queen* recognized that there might be situations in which the Court would proceed to resolve the equitable claim first even though the results might be dispositive of the issues involved in the legal claim.' 382 U.S., at 339, 86 S.Ct., at 478.

> Thus the Court in *Katchen v. Landy,* recognized that an equitable determination can have collateral estoppel effect in a subsequent legal action, and that this estoppel does not violate the Seventh Amendment."

Id. at 333–35, 86 S.Ct. at 475–76.

Note, however, that the Supreme Court refused "to extend *Parklane Hosiery Co.* * * * to accord collateral-estoppel effect to a district court's determinations of issues common to equitable and legal claims where the court resolved the equitable claims first solely because it erroneously dismissed the legal claims. To hold otherwise would seriously undermine a plaintiff's right to a jury trial under the Seventh Amendment." Lytle v. Household Manufacturing, Inc., 494 U.S. 545, 110 S.Ct. 1331, 108 L.Ed.2d 504 (1990).

2. In Katchen v. Landy, 382 U.S. 323, 86 S.Ct. 467, 15 L.Ed.2d 391 (1966), petitioner claimed that when a creditor who has received an alleged preference files a claim in bankruptcy and the trustee not only objects to its allowance, but in addition demands the surrender of the preference, the Federal Bankruptcy Act does not give the bankruptcy court summary jurisdiction to order the surrender of the preference. To permit such a result, the petitioner argued, would violate the Seventh Amendment jury trial protection. The Supreme Court held that the summary jurisdiction is conferred by the Act and, as to the jury trial argument, stated: "[A]lthough petitioner might be entitled to a jury trial on the issue of preference if he presented no claim in the bankruptcy proceeding and awaited a federal plenary action by the trustee, * * * when the same issue arises as part of the process of allowance and disallowance of claims, it is triable in equity. The Bankruptcy Act, passed pursuant to the power given to Congress by Art. I, § 8, of the Constitution to establish uniform laws on the subject of bankruptcy, converts the creditor's legal claim into an equitable claim to a pro rata share of the *res,* * * * a share which can neither be determined nor allowed until the creditor disgorges the alleged voidable preference he has already received. * * * As bankruptcy courts have summary jurisdiction to adjudicate controversies relating to property over which they have actual or constructive possession, * * * and as the proceedings of bankruptcy courts are inherently proceedings in equity, * * * there is no Seventh Amendment right to a jury trial for determination of objections to claims. * * * " *Id.* at 336–37, 86 S.Ct. at 476–77.

The scope and impact of *Katchen* may be narrower than meets the eye. Consider the language of Matter of Hallahan, 936 F.2d 1496, 1503–05 (7th Cir.1991), describing the post-*Katchen* case law:

> "By placing emphasis on the forum in which the claim arose, *Katchen* seemed to give bankruptcy courts broad discretion to deny jury trials for claims related to the administration or division of the estate. In 1978 the Bankruptcy Reform Act was enacted, eliminating the old summary/plenary distinction and creating 'core' and 'non-core' matters. Though 'core proceedings' were defined significantly more broadly than summary jurisdiction, some courts read the 1978 Bankruptcy Reform Act and *Katchen* together to conclude that there was no right to a jury trial in all 'core' proceedings. See, *e.g.,* In re Chase & Sanborn Corp., 835 F.2d 1341, 1349 (11th Cir.1988), certiorari granted *sub nom.* Granfinanciera, S.A. v. Nordberg, 486 U.S. 1054, 108 S.Ct. 2818, 100 L.Ed.2d 920, reversed, 492 U.S. 33, 109 S.Ct. 2782, 106 L.Ed.2d 26; In re Merrill, 594 F.2d 1064, 1065 (5th Cir.1979).

"Granfinanciera, S.A. v. Nordberg, 492 U.S. 33, 109 S.Ct. 2782, dramatically revived the rights of some creditors in bankruptcy court to demand a jury trial. *Granfinanciera* involved a trustee's attempt to recover an allegedly fraudulent conveyance from the bank Granfinanciera. The bank, for its part, denied receiving any funds before bankruptcy. As an initial matter, the Court criticized the notion that the core/non-core distinction created by Congress was determinative of a party's jury trial rights.

> Congress cannot eliminate a party's Seventh Amendment right to a jury trial merely by relabeling the cause of action to which it attaches and placing exclusive jurisdiction in an administrative agency or a specialized court of equity.

492 U.S. at 61, 109 S.Ct. at 2800. The inquiry must focus on the legal or equitable nature of the cause of action, and not Congress' 'taxonomic change[s].' *Id.* A proper determination of whether the Seventh Amendment confers a right to jury trial for a claim heard in bankruptcy court entails a two-part inquiry:

> First, we compare the statutory action to 18th–century actions brought in the courts of England prior to the merger of the courts of law and equity. Second, we examine the remedy sought and determine whether it is legal or equitable in nature.

492 U.S. at 42, 109 S.Ct. at 2790, citing Tull v. United States, 481 U.S. 412, 417–418, 107 S.Ct. 1831, 1835, 95 L.Ed.2d 365. Applying the test, the Court held that Granfinanciera could obtain a jury trial in spite of the fact that fraudulent conveyance actions are 'core' proceedings under the Act. The Court discussed at some length the fact that actions to recover preferential or fraudulent transfers were brought at law in 18th–century England. It also held that the nature of the relief sought in a fraudulent conveyance action is legal rather than equitable. Because the claim was legal in nature and Congress was without power to change that characterization, Granfinanciera was entitled to a jury under the Seventh Amendment.

"*Granfinanciera* did not overrule *Katchen.* Instead the Court distinguished *Katchen* in a manner relevant to this case. *Granfinanciera* restated the notion set forth in *Katchen* that a bankruptcy court having actual or constructive possession of the bankruptcy estate could adjudicate objections by the trustee and claims against the estate. However, the Court held that in *Katchen* it was the creditor's submission of a claim to the bankruptcy court which triggered the process of 'the allowance and disallowance of claims' and subjected the creditor's otherwise legal claim to the bankruptcy court's equitable power. In *Granfinanciera,* the party seeking the jury trial (Granfinanciera) had never filed a claim against the estate, and thus the trustee had been forced to initiate what amounted to a legal action against the bank to recover a monetary transfer. In these circumstances, the Court held, defendant is entitled to a jury trial. Granfinanciera, 492 U.S. at 57–58, 109 S.Ct. at 2798. The proposition which emerges from a reading of *Katchen* and *Granfinanciera* together, that a creditor's right to a jury trial on a bankruptcy trustee's preference claim depends upon whether the creditor has submitted a claim against the estate, was reaffirmed by the Court last Term in Langenkamp v. Culp, ___ U.S. ___, 111 S.Ct. 330, 112 L.Ed.2d 343."

See generally, Fruehwald, Jury Trials in Bankruptcy Court After *Granfinanciera,* 24 Cumberland L.Rev. 79 (1994).

B. THE STATE APPROACH: CONFLICTING CROSS–CURRENTS

PELFREY v. BANK OF GREER

Supreme Court of South Carolina, 1978.
270 S.C. 691, 244 S.E.2d 315.

LEWIS, CHIEF JUSTICE:

This is a corporate stockholder's derivative action to recover damages on behalf of the corporation resulting from the alleged negligence and breach of fiduciary duty by the appellant Bank in the handling of the corporation's funds. This appeal is from an order of the lower court refusing the appellant Bank's motions (1) for a compulsory reference of the issues and (2) to strike several portions of the complaint.

The first question involves a determination of whether the stockholder's derivative action is one in equity or at law. It is undisputed that, if the action is in equity, it is to be tried by the court; if at law, it is triable by a jury and the lower court would have been correct in refusing a compulsory order of reference.

* * *

In determining the right to a jury trial, the lower court relied upon Ross v. Bernhard, 396 U.S. 531, 90 S.Ct. 733, 24 L.Ed.2d 729, 733, where the United States Supreme Court held: "* * * the right to a jury trial attaches to those issues in derivative actions as to which the corporation, if it had been suing in its own right, would have been entitled to a jury." The lower court apparently concluded that, since the complaint in this action sought the recovery of damages, a legal cause was stated for trial by jury.

Ross was brought under the Seventh Amendment to the United States Constitution, which governs right to trial by jury in Federal courts. This amendment has never been held applicable to the States; and this Court has interpreted Article 1, Section 14, of the South Carolina Constitution, which preserves the right of trial by jury inviolate, to mean that right of jury trial shall be preserved only in those cases in which the parties were entitled to it under the law or practice existing at the time of the adoption of the constitution. State v. Gibbes, 109 S.C. 135, 95 S.E. 346; C.W. Matthews Contracting Company, Inc. v. S.C. Tax Commission, 267 S.C. 548, 230 S.E.2d 223.

Paraphrasing the rule stated in the last cited cases, the pertinent inquiry is whether, at the time of the adoption of the Constitution of 1868, either party to a stockholder's derivative action had the right, under the existing law or practice, to demand a jury trial of the factual issues. The mode of trial was unaffected by statute in this State and the inquiry thus becomes one of determining the common law with reference to the right to a jury trial. We have found no decision of this court dealing with the present question and none has been cited.

We have, however, in discussing a stockholder's derivative action recognized its equitable nature. * * *

Historically the shareholder's derivative suit has always been tried exclusively in equity. "Even where the only relief allowable is a recovery of damages the suit is nevertheless one in equity and not an action at law." * * *

The dissenting opinion in Ross v. Bernhard, 396 U.S. p. 545, 90 S.Ct. p. 742, 24 L.Ed. p. 740, gives a concise statement of the development of the shareholder's derivation action:

> * * * a shareholder's suit was not originally viewed in this country, or in England, as a suit to enforce a *corporate* cause of action. Rather, the shareholder's suit was initially permitted only against the managers of the corporation—not third parties—and it was conceived of as an equitable action to enforce the right of a beneficiary against his trustee. The shareholder was not, therefore, in court to enforce indirectly the corporate right of action, but to enforce directly his own equitable right of action against an unfaithful fiduciary. Later the rights of the shareholder were enlarged to encompass suits against third parties harming the corporation * * *. Indeed the commentators * * * recognize that historically the suit has in practice always been treated as a single cause tried exclusively in equity. They agree that there is therefore no constitutional right to a jury trial even where there might have been one had the corporation itself brought the suit.

Since the shareholder's derivative action has historically been considered as one exclusively in equity, a party is not entitled to a trial by jury as a matter of right. The constitutional provision (Art. 1, Section 14), that the right of jury trial shall remain inviolate, does not apply to cases within the equitable jurisdiction of the court. Collier v. Green, 244 S.C. 367, 137 S.E.2d 277; Lucken v. Wichman, 5 S.C. 411.

The lower court was therefore in error in refusing the motion of appellant for an order of reference and in refusing to strike from the amended complaint the phrase "the plaintiff demands a jury trial."

* * *

The order denying a compulsory reference is accordingly reversed and the cause remanded for further proceedings in accordance with this opinion.

LITTLEJOHN, NESS, RHODES and GREGORY, JJ., concur.*

Notes

1. Where either the underlying cause of action or the remedy sought is traditionally looked upon as equitable, many state courts continue to interpret

* *Accord* Rankin v. Frebank Co., 47 Cal. App.3d 75, 121 Cal.Rptr. 348 (1975) (derivative action); Lanman Lithotech, Inc. v. Gurwitz, 478 So.2d 425 (Fla.App.1985).

their state constitutions so as to deny a jury trial. *See, e.g.,* Strauss v. Summerhays, 157 Cal.App.3d 806, 204 Cal.Rptr. 227 (1984) (quiet title action); Robair v. Dahl, 80 Mich.App. 458, 264 N.W.2d 27 (1978) (constructive trust); State Bank of Lehi v. Woolsey, 565 P.2d 413 (Utah 1977) (mortgage foreclosure). Moreover, the language of a recent New Jersey case is instructive: "In short, the remedies provided in the statute are injunction, restitution and appointment of a receiver, all clearly equitable in nature. No constitutional right exists to a jury trial in equity actions for injunctive relief. If relief provided is equitable rather than legal in nature, the right to jury trial does not attach, even if financial restitution is part of the equitable relief available." Kugler v. Banner Pontiac–Buick, Opel, Inc., 120 N.J.Super. 572, 295 A.2d 385 (1972) (Attorney General action for consumer fraud).

In Karnes Enterprises, Inc. v. Quan, 221 Kan. 596, 561 P.2d 825 (1977), the Kansas Supreme Court stated: "Some of the specific types of actions held to be equitable in nature are the following: quiet title actions, actions for specific performance, cancellation of a lease, creation of a resulting trust with an accounting, actions to determine the priority of mortgages and other liens, for an accounting, and to impress liens on real estate."

2. Declaratory judgment actions have presented difficult jury trial questions. *See generally* Annot., 33 A.L.R.4th 146 (1984). In large measure this is attributable to the fact the remedy did not exist at common law. Consequently,

"Courts have had to determine whether the remedy was sought as a substitute for a remedy traditionally available only in an action at law or bill in equity. The decision whether to honor a jury trial demand hinges upon this prior determination.

"Precisely how the determination is made varies. Opinions of several federal courts of appeals, after *Beacon Theatres, Inc. v. Westover,* [19] are instructive of the federal view. These cases hold that a declaratory judgment will be characterized as legal if, but only if, it appears from the facts that legal type relief would be possible at the time of the lawsuit. Thus, in a school desegregation case, the inclusion of a request for a declaratory remedy does not authorize a jury trial. Similarly, in a suit for a declaratory judgment construing an oil and gas lease, followed by a counterclaim for possession of the property on account of breach of the lease constituting termination, the court treated the action as a reverse equitable bill for cancellation, not as a reverse claim for ejectment. Because the lease itself provided no automatic provisions for termination, the defendant had no immediate right to possession until the court cancelled the lease. Therefore, no jury trial was authorized. * * *

"There is language in *Beacon Theatres, Inc. v. Westover* which suggests that courts must go much further in order to protect trial by jury. *Beacon's* holding—that factual issues common to the claim and counterclaim regarding the reasonableness of the operator's practices should be triable of right to a jury—is itself not radical. But two of the Court's rationales were radical. First, the Court found that the declaratory judgment act provided a *legal* remedy which 'necessarily affects the scope of equity.' [20] Second, it suggested

19. 359 U.S. 500 (1959)

20. *Beacon Theatres,* 359 U.S. at 509. As James and Hazard have pointed out, the logic of this part of *Beacon* would make all declaratory judgment actions triable by jury. F.

that the fact that the jury trial right is constitutional warrants a requirement that judicial discretion, 'wherever possible, be exercised to preserve jury trial.' [21]

"Few decisions since *Beacon* have followed either of these lines of thought. In Alabama, the courts have held that where the underlying facts indicate that a legal remedy may become available to one of the parties, jury trial as of right is available; [22] but these courts have declined to extend the right to cases where the only conceivable alternative relief would be equitable.[23] In Florida, the supreme court has indicated that doubtful questions regarding the distinction between law and equity should be resolved in favor of jury trial because of the fundamental guaranty of the state constitution; [24] but this court has declined to characterize all declaratory judgment actions as inherently legal.[25]

"A few courts are more restrictive than are the federal courts. In *Lazarus v. Village of Northbrook,* [26] the Supreme Court of Illinois was confronted with an action for declaration of invalidity of a zoning ordinance as applied to plaintiff's property. The complaint contained a prayer for injunctive relief but indicated that it was filed at law. The defendant asked for a jury trial. The court stated that, when a declaration alone is sought,

> the right to trial by jury must be determined by an examination of the disputed issues and an appraisal of their predominant characteristics as indicating the appropriateness of legal or equitable relief. But when, as is ordinarily the case, relief in addition to the naked declaration of rights is sought, the nature of that relief determines the right to a trial by jury.

The court therefore denied jury trial. Ohio's courts show a marked willingness to subordinate parallel claims for legal relief to those for equitable relief and thus to deny jury trial rights as to all claims.[27] Ohio refuses to treat defensive actions for declaratory relief of nonliability of an insurance policy as legal unless that claimant has reduced his claim to judgment and is actively seeking payment.[28] Both the Illinois and Ohio approaches risk the loss of jury rights in many actions in which, but for the statute, the right would probably be available."

Bourne & Lynch, Merger of Law and Equity Under the Revised Maryland Rules: Does It Threaten Trial By Jury?, 14 U.Balt.L.Rev. 1, 47–50 (1984).*

James & G. Hazard, Civil Procedure § 8.10, at 385–86 (2d ed. 1977).

21. *Beacon Theatres,* 359 U.S. at 510.

22. *See* Sherer v. Burton, 393 So.2d 991, 991–92 (Ala.1981). *But cf.* Shubin v. United States Dist. Court, 313 F.2d 250 (9th Cir. 1963) (where the federal court declined to treat as legal a future claim as to which no damages had been inflicted or suffered).

23. *See, e.g.,* Burnham v. City of Mobile, 277 Ala. 659, 174 So.2d 301 (1965).

24. Hollywood, Inc. v. City of Hollywood, 321 So.2d 65, 71 (Fla.1975).

25. *See id.* at 73. In *Hollywood,* the court characterized as legal the tax assessor's bill for declaratory and equitable relief against alternative claimants to land. The court explained that the suit sounded in ejectment because it would likely lead to ouster of a party in possession of property. *Id.* at 71–72.

26. 31 Ill.2d 146, 199 N.E.2d 797 (1964).

27. *See, e.g.,* Miles v. N.J. Motors, Inc., 44 Ohio App.2d 351, 338 N.E.2d 784 (1975) (court discharged debtors from a series of cognovit notes and subordinated debtors' requests for declaratory relief to their claim for injunctive relief to compel defendant to comply with debtors' rights and sell repossessed vehicles at public sales).

28. *See, e.g.,* Republic Indem. Co. v. Durell, 105 Ohio App. 153, 151 N.E.2d 687 (1957).

3. Like their federal counterparts, state courts also must determine the extent to which state constitutional jury trial provisions mandate a right to jury trial in statutory causes of action. Consider, in this regard, the language of the Vermont Supreme Court in a recent decision involving that state's Fair Employment Practices Act (FEPA):

> "Defendant argues that the right to a jury under the Vermont Constitution does not apply to statutory actions but only to common-law causes of action. It maintains that because FEPA does not grant a right to jury trial, there is no such right in actions under the Act. The petitioner in *Curtis* [v. Loether] advanced the same argument, but the Court held that '[t]he Seventh Amendment does apply to actions enforcing statutory rights, and requires a jury trial upon demand, if the statute creates legal rights and remedies, enforceable in an action for damages in the ordinary courts of law.' 415 U.S. at 194, 94 S.Ct. at 1008. Similarly, this Court has found that '[t]he [Vermont] [C]onstitution was intended to provide for the future as well as the past, to protect the rights of the people * * * whether those rights then existed by the rules of the common law, or *might from time to time arise out of subsequent legislation.*'
>
> Plimpton, 33 Vt. at 291 (emphasis added). Thus, we conclude that the right to trial by jury under the Vermont Constitution is not limited to causes of action recognized at common law in 1793.
>
> "Defendant also argues that we should adopt the federal rule, under which there was no right to trial by jury in a Title VII action, because FEPA is patterned on Title VII of the Civil Rights Act of 1964, 42 U.S.C. §§ 2000e–2000e–17. See Graff v. Eaton, 157 Vt. 321, 323 n. 2, 598 A.2d 1383, 1384 n. 2 (1991) ('The consensus has been that there is no right to trial by jury under Title VII because the remedy it provides—reinstatement and award of back pay—is essentially equitable.'). The decisions denying trial by jury under the federal employment discrimination law, however, were based on the remedy provided under Title VII prior to its amendment in 1991. See *id.;* Curtis, 415 U.S. at 197, 94 S.Ct. at 1010. Unlike FEPA, Title VII relief was essentially equitable in nature until 1991, when Congress amended Title VII extending the relief available to include compensatory and punitive damages. *See* Civil Rights Act of 1991, Pub.L. No. 102–166, § 102, 105 Stat. 1071, 1072 (1991) (codified at 42 U.S.C. § 1981a). In 1981, the Vermont Legislature extended FEPA remedies to include 'damages' by an amendment in which it provided for private actions under the Act. *See* 21 V.S.A. § 495b(b). Thus, we are not inclined to follow pre–1991 Title VII case law on the jury trial issue. Accordingly, to the extent that factual issues are in dispute, the parties to an action under FEPA are entitled to trial by jury when the plaintiff requests legal damages."

Hodgdon v. Mt. Mansfield Company, Inc., 624 A.2d 1122, 1126 (Vt.1992).

C & K ENGINEERING CONTRACTORS v. AMBER STEEL CO., INC.

Supreme Court of California, 1978.
23 Cal.3d 1, 151 Cal.Rptr. 323, 587 P.2d 1136.

RICHARDSON, JUSTICE.

The issue posed by this case is whether or not defendant was improperly denied its constitutional right to a jury trial. (Cal. Const., art. I, § 16.) We will conclude that because plaintiff's suit for damages for breach of contract was based entirely upon the equitable doctrine of promissory estoppel (*see* Drennan v. Star Paving Co. (1958) 51 Cal.2d 409, 333 P.2d 757), the gist of the action must be deemed equitable in nature and, under well established principles, neither party was entitled to a jury trial as a matter of right.

Plaintiff, a general contractor, solicited bids from defendant and other subcontractors for the installation of reinforcing steel in the construction of a waste water treatment plant in Fresno County. Plaintiff included defendant's bid in its master bid, which was ultimately accepted by the public sanitation district, the proposed owner of the plant. After defendant refused to perform in accordance with its bid on the subcontract, plaintiff brought the present action to recover $102,660 in damages for defendant's alleged breach of contract. (A second cause of action, claiming defendant's negligence in preparing its bid, was dismissed during trial and is not presently at issue.)

The allegations of plaintiff's first cause of action may be summarized: defendant submitted a written bid of $139,511 for the work; defendant gave a subsequent "verbal promise" that the work would be performed for the bid price; plaintiff "reasonably relied" on defendant's bid and promise in submitting its master bid; defendant knew or should have known that plaintiff would submit a master bid based upon defendant's bid; defendant refused to perform in accordance with its bid; plaintiff was required to expend $242,171 to perform the reinforcing steel work; as a result plaintiff was damaged in the amount of $102,660; and "Injustice can be avoided only by enforcement of defendant's promise to perform * * *."

Defendant's answer to the complaint alleged its bid was the result of an "honest mistake" in calculation; plaintiff knew of the mistake but failed to notify defendant or permit it to revise its bid as is customary in the industry; and plaintiff's conduct in this regard should bar it from recovering damages.

Defendant demanded a jury trial. The trial court, deeming the case to be essentially in equity, denied the request but empaneled an advisory jury to consider the sole issue of plaintiff's reasonable reliance on defendant's promise. The jury found that plaintiff reasonably relied to its detriment on defendant's bid. The trial court adopted this finding and entered judgment in plaintiff's favor for $102,620, the approximate amount of its prayer, together with interest and costs. Defendant appeals.

Defendant's primary contention is that it was improperly denied a jury trial of plaintiff's action for damages. In resolving this contention we first review the nature and derivation of the doctrine of promissory estoppel. Thereafter, we discuss certain authorities governing the right to jury trial in this state. As will appear, we have concluded that by reason of the essentially equitable nature of the doctrine and plaintiff's exclusive reliance upon it in the present action, the case was properly triable by the court with an advisory jury.

1. PROMISSORY ESTOPPEL

The elements of the doctrine of promissory estoppel, as described concisely in section 90 of the Restatement of Contracts, are as follows: "A promise which the promisor should reasonably expect to induce action or forbearance of a definite and substantial character on the part of the promisee and which does induce such action or forbearance is binding if injustice can be avoided only by enforcement of the promise." The foregoing rule has been judicially adopted in California and it applies to actions, such as the present case, to enforce a subcontractor's bid. (Drennan v. Star Paving Co., *supra,* 51 Cal.2d 409, 413–415, 333 P.2d 757; Saliba–Kringlen Corp. v. Allen Engineering Co., 15 Cal.App.3d 95, 111, 92 Cal.Rptr. 799 (1971).) * * *

We have recently characterized promissory estoppel as "a doctrine which employs *equitable* principles to satisfy the requirement that consideration must be given in exchange for the promise sought to be enforced. [Citations.]" (Raedeke v. Gibraltar, Sav. & Loan Assn., 10 Cal.3d 665, 672, 111 Cal.Rptr. 693, 697, 517 P.2d 1157, 1161 (1974), italics added. * * *). Many years ago in *Seymour,* we recognized a comparable doctrine in the enforcement of an oral promise to enter into a written contract of employment, where plaintiff had detrimentally relied thereon by surrendering his former position. We observed therein that "The right of *courts of equity* to hold a person estopped to assert the statute of frauds, where such assertion would amount to practicing a fraud, cannot be disputed." (p. 794, 106 P. p. 94, italics added.) We did not find that application of the doctrine of equitable estoppel was barred by the fact that the case involved a *promise* of future action rather than a representation of *fact.* (Pp. 797–800, 106 P. 88, 94.)

Treatise writers and commentators have confirmed the generally *equitable* nature of promissory estoppel in enforcing a promise which otherwise would be unenforceable. (*See* 3 Pomeroy, Equity Jurisprudence (5th ed. 1941) § 808b, at pp. 211–216; 1 Williston, Contracts (3d ed. 1957) § 140, pp. 618–619, fn. 6; Seavey, Reliance Upon Gratuitous Promises or Other Conduct, 64 Harv.L.Rev. 913, 925 (1951); Henderson, Promissory Estoppel and Traditional Contract Doctrine, 78 Yale L.J. 343, 379–380 (1969); Ames, The History of Assumpsit, 2 Harv.L.Rev. 1, 14 (1888).) As expressed by Professor Henderson, "[P]romissory estoppel is *a peculiarly equitable doctrine* designed to deal with situations which, in total impact, necessarily call into play discretionary powers * * *." (78 Yale L.J., supra, at pp. 379–380, italics added.) * * *

The equitable character of promissory estoppel is confirmed by a close scrutiny of the purpose of the doctrine, namely, that "*injustice* can be avoided only by enforcement of the promise." (Rest. Contracts, supra, § 90, italics added.) As expressed by us in a similar subcontractor bid case, once the prerequisites of the doctrine are met, "* * * *it is only fair* that plaintiff should have at least an opportunity to accept defendant's bid after the general contract has been awarded to him." (*Drennan v. Star Paving Co., supra,* 51 Cal.2d at p. 415, 333 P.2d at p. 760, italics added; *see also* Seavey, supra, 64 Harv.L.Rev. at p. 925; Henderson, supra, 78 Yale L.J. at p. 379 ["The specific concern of section 90 with 'injustice', standing alone, contemplates broad judicial discretion to make use of equitable principles"].) We think that it is noteworthy that a proposed addition to section 90 would add the language "The remedy granted for breach may be limited *as justice requires.*" (Rest.2d Contracts (Tent. Drafts Nos. 1–7, 1973) § 90, p. 215, italics added; Swinerton & Walberg Co. v. City of Inglewood—L.A. County Civic Center Authority, 40 Cal.App.3d 98, 103, fn. 7, 114 Cal.Rptr. 834 (1974).)

We conclude, accordingly, that the doctrine of promissory estoppel is essentially equitable in nature, developed to provide a remedy (namely, enforcement of a gratuitous promise) which was not generally available in courts of law prior to 1850. We now move to an examination of the authorities on the subject of the right to a jury trial, to determine whether the equitable nature of plaintiff's action precluded a jury trial as a matter of right.

2. Right to Jury Trial

The right to a jury trial is guaranteed by our Constitution. (Cal. Const., art. I, § 16.) We have long acknowledged that the right so guaranteed, however, is the right as it existed at common law in 1850, when the Constitution was first adopted, "and what that right is, is a purely historical question, a fact which is to be ascertained like any other social, political or legal fact." (People v. One 1941 Chevrolet Coupe, 37 Cal.2d 283, 287, 231 P.2d 832, 835 (1951)) * * *.

As we stated in *People v. One 1941 Chevrolet Coupe, supra,* "If the action has to deal with ordinary common-law rights cognizable in courts of law, it is to that extent an action at law. In determining whether the action was one triable by a jury at common law, the court is not bound by the form of the action but rather by the nature of the rights involved and the facts of the particular case—the *gist* of the action. A jury trial must be granted where the *gist* of the action is legal, where the action is in reality cognizable at law." (p. 299, 231 P.2d p. 843, fn. omitted, italics added.) On the other hand, if the action is essentially one in equity and the relief sought "depends upon the application of equitable doctrines," the parties are not entitled to a jury trial. (*E.g.,* Hartman v. Burford, 242 Cal.App.2d 268, 270, 51 Cal.Rptr. 309, 311 (1966) [enforcement of promise to make a will]; Tibbetts v. Fife, 162 Cal.App.2d 568, 572, 328 P.2d 212 (1958) [establishment of constructive trust].) Although we have said that "the legal or equitable nature of a cause of action ordinarily is determined by the mode of relief to be afforded" (*Raedeke v. Gibraltar Sav. & Loan Assn., supra,* 10 Cal.3d 665, 672, 111 Cal.Rptr. 693, 696, 517 P.2d 1157, 1160), the prayer for relief in a particular case is not conclusive. Thus, "The fact that damages is one of a full range of possible remedies does not guarantee * * * the right to a jury * * *." (*Southern Pac. Transportation Co. v. Superior Court, supra,* 58 Cal.App.3d at p. 437, 129 Cal.Rptr. at p. 915.)

In the present case, the complaint purports to seek recovery of damages for breach of contract, in form an action at law in which a right to jury trial ordinarily would exist. (*Raedeke, supra,* at p. 671, 111 Cal.Rptr. 693, 517 P.2d 1157; *Interinsurance Exchange, supra,* at p. 694, 124 Cal.Rptr. 239; Code Civ.Proc., § 592.) As we have seen, however, the complaint seeks relief which was available only in equity, namely, the enforcement of defendant's gratuitous promise to perform its bid through application of the equitable doctrine of promissory estoppel. Although there is no direct authority on point, several cases have held that an action based upon the analogous principle of equitable estoppel may be tried by the court without a jury. (Jaffe v. Albertson Co., 243 Cal.App.2d 592, 607–608, 53 Cal.Rptr. 25 (1966) [estoppel to bar reliance on statute of frauds]; Moss v. Bluemm, 229 Cal.App.2d 70, 72–73, 40 Cal.Rptr. 50 (1964) [estoppel to bar statute of limitations defense]; Richard v. Degan & Brody, Inc., 181 Cal.App.2d 289, 295, 5 Cal.Rptr. 263 (1960) [estoppel as defense to unlawful detainer action]; Ford v. Palisades Corp., 101 Cal.App.2d 491, 498–499, 225 P.2d 545 (1950) [statute of frauds]; *see* Raedeke v. Gibraltar Sav. & Loan Assn., *supra,* 10 Cal.3d 665, 674, and fn. 4, 111 Cal.Rptr. 693, 517 P.2d 1157.)

* * *

* * * Defendant before us has argued that because plaintiff sought to recover damages rather than to compel defendant to perform its bid, plaintiff requested relief which is available at common law. Yet, as we have seen, damages at law were unavailable in actions for breach of a gratuitous promise. The only manner in which damages have been recognized in such cases of gratuitous promises is by application of the equitable doctrine of promissory estoppel which renders such promises legally binding. (*See* Saliba–Kringlen Corp. v. Allen Engineering Co., *supra,* 15 Cal. App.3d 95, 111, 92 Cal.Rptr. 799.) Without the employment of this doctrine, essentially equitable, there was no remedy at all. As illustrated by the express language of section 90 of the Restatement of Contracts, promissory estoppel is used to avoid injustice "by *enforcement* of the promise." (Italics added.)

Furthermore, the addition, in such cases, of a prayer for damages does not convert what is essentially an equitable action into a legal one for which a jury trial would be available. This was demonstrated in a recent case, Southern Pac. Transportation Co. v. Superior Court, *supra,* 58 Cal. App.3d 433, 129 Cal.Rptr. 912, wherein plaintiff sought damages as a good faith improver of land owned by another person. (*See* Code Civ.Proc., § 871.1 et seq.) The appellate court rejected the contention that plaintiff's request for damages necessarily identified the action as one at law. The court first noted that since the good faith improver statute had no counterpart in English common law, "classification of the action as either legal or equitable depends upon characterization of the nature of the relief sought." (p. 437, 129 Cal.Rptr. p. 915.)

The *Southern Pac. Transportation* court properly observed that under the statute, the trial court must "effect such an adjustment of the rights, equities, and interests" of the parties as was consistent with substantial justice. (Code Civ.Proc., § 871.5.) Thus, the action was essentially one calling for the exercise of equitable principles. The court added, "The fact that damages is one of a full range of possible remedies does not guarantee real parties the right to a jury," since "there is no possibility of severing the legal from the equitable. The trier of fact must determine whether to quiet title in the improver on the condition he pay to the landowner the value of the unimproved land, or whether and in what amount, to award damages to the improver, or whether to require a completely different form of relief. * * * Such a determination is not susceptible of division into one component to be resolved by the court and another component to be determined by a jury. Only one decision can be made, and it must make a proper adjustment of the 'rights, equities, and interests' of all the parties involved." (Pp. 437–438, 129 Cal.Rptr. p. 915.) The court concluded that in view of the various equitable considerations involved, it would be "an impossible task" for a jury to resolve the dispute. (p. 438, 129 Cal.Rptr. 912.)

Similarly, in the present case, the trier of fact is called upon to determine whether "Injustice can be avoided only by enforcement of [defendant's] promise." (Rest., Contracts, § 90.) The "gist" of such an action is equitable. Both historically and functionally, the task of weighing such equitable considerations is to be performed by the trial court, not the jury. We conclude that the trial court properly treated the action as equitable in nature, to be tried by the court with or without an advisory jury as the court elected.

* * *

The judgment is affirmed.

TOBRINER, MOSK, CLARK and MANUEL, JJ., concur.

NEWMAN, JUSTICE, dissenting.

I dissent. The Chancery Court in England sometimes created rights, sometimes remedies. When California courts decide whether a jury trial should be assured, I believe that they should focus not on rights but on remedies. A plaintiff who seeks damages should be entitled to a jury. One who seeks specific performance or an injunction or quiet title, etc. (plus supplementary damages or "damages in lieu" that would have been allowed in Chancery) is not entitled to a jury.

The majority opinion here discusses "promissory estoppel", "equitable estoppel", "equitable principles", "equitable doctrine", "equitable nature", and even "injustice". To pretend that words like these enable us to isolate "ordinary common-law rights cognizable in courts of law" or that "the *gist* of the action" governs (quoting from People v. One 1941 Chevrolet Coupe, 37 Cal.2d 283, 299, 231 P.2d 832 (1951)) seems to me to be uninstructive fictionalizing. We are told that courts deal with "a purely historical question, a fact which is to be ascertained like any other social, political or legal fact" (*id.* at p. 287, 231 P.2d at p. 835). Yet how often, I wonder, do (or should) California judges instead decide whether the wisdom of a Corbin, in 1963, outweighs comments by Ames, Seavey, Shattuck, and Williston written during the period from 1888 to 1957?

In fact, most rights that are now enforced via a jury were created not by courts but by legislatures. We look at the *remedy* sought, not at the judicial or legislative history of the *right,* to decide whether the trial is to be "legal" or "equitable". There are troubling borderlines, but the basic rule should be that no jury is required when plaintiff seeks equitable relief rather than "legal" damages. That approach requires no complex, historical research regarding when and by whom certain rights were created. It also requires less reliance on the anomalies of England's unique juridical history. Courts thus may focus on a basic policy concern; that is, the typically more continuing and more personalized involvement of the trial judge in specific performance and injunctive decrees than in mere judgments for damages.

The doctrine of promissory estoppel was not, I suggest, "developed to provide a remedy (namely, enforcement of a gratuitous promise)" as the majority here contend. What it really did was to help create a new right (just as statutes help create new rights) that apparently, but only if we reject what seems to have been Corbin's view, was enforced as of 1850 in Chancery but not at common law.

Plaintiff in this case sought damages for an alleged breach of contract. He did not seek equitable relief. Thus defendant should have been granted the jury trial he requested.*

BIRD, C.J., concurs.

STATE EX REL. WILLMAN v. SLOAN

Supreme Court of Missouri, 1978.
574 S.W.2d 421.

SEILER, JUDGE.

This is an original action in prohibition. Relator asks us to prohibit respondent Sloan from empaneling a jury to determine the damages, if any, petitioner suffered as a result of breach of a covenant not to compete by defendant below.

The case is before Judge Sloan on remand from this court, Willman v. Beheler, 489 S.W.2d 770 (Mo.1973). In *Willman,* this court ruled in favor of relator in his suit to enjoin defendant Beheler from breach of his covenant not to compete with plaintiff Willman, his former medical partner, within a twenty-mile radius of St. Joseph, Missouri for a five-year period. However, because only a few months of the five-year period remained at the time of our decision, we concluded that enforcement of the

* *Accord:* A–C Company, Inc. v. Pacific National Bank, 219 Cal.Rptr. 62, 173 Cal.App.3d 462 (1985). *See* Comment, C & K Engineering Contractors v. Amber Steel Co.: Promissory Estoppel and the Right to Trial by Jury in California, 31 Hastings L.J. 697 (1980).

covenant would not be sufficient or proper equitable relief. Because equity will not permit a wrong to go without a remedy, and because "[o]nce having acquired jurisdiction equity will retain it, under a prayer for general relief (there was such a prayer in this petition), to administer full and complete justice, within the scope of pleadings and evidence, between the parties," *id.* at 778, we remanded for a determination of damages due to the breach. We noted that "[w]hile a court of equity is reluctant to, and ordinarily does not, grant a mere money judgment, it may do so in an appropriate case." *Id.*

After remand a hearing was scheduled for January 16, 1978. On January 12, 1978, defendant requested and respondent granted an order to empanel a jury at law (not merely an advisory jury), to determine the remaining issues of damages. On January 16, 1978, relator filed his petition for a writ of prohibition. On February 22, 1978, our provisional rule issued.

The Missouri constitution provides "[t]hat the right of trial by jury as heretofore enjoyed shall remain inviolate * * * ", Mo. Const. art. I, § 22(a). However, there is no right to trial by jury in a case in equity, State ex rel. Duggan v. Kirkwood, 357 Mo. 325, 208 S.W.2d 257, 262 (banc 1948). Thus, defendant's right to a jury depends on whether the cause is tried at law or in equity. Relator, plaintiff below, contends that his suit began as and remains one in equity, that implicit in this court's opinion in *Willman* was the finding that equity retain jurisdiction in order to grant relator full equitable relief, and that defendant thus does not have a right to a jury at law on the issues of damages. Although damages are usually a legal remedy, a court of equity may decree them where they are the relief necessary in order to do equity. Willman v. Beheler, 449 S.W.2d at 778.

Respondent replies that because the only issue on remand is whether relator sustained damages due to the breach of the restrictive covenant, the case, while originally filed in equity, has been converted into a case in which only the legal issue of damages remains. Since an action is generally considered legal rather than equitable when the only relief sought is money damages, thus entitling a defendant to trial by jury, Jaycox v. Brune, 434 S.W.2d 539, 542–43 (Mo.1968), to deny defendant a jury in this case would deny him his right to trial by jury under Mo. Const. art. I, § 22(a). *See* Attebery v. Attebery, 507 S.W.2d 87, 93 (Mo.App.1974).

The principles cited by respondent are valid, but they do not meet the issue to be resolved in this case. The usual rule, as quoted above from *Willman,* is that equity will retain jurisdiction of a cause once it has acquired it in order to afford full relief. As respondent notes, an important exception to this rule applies "when the *facts* relied on to sustain the equity jurisdiction fail of establishment," *Jaycox,* 434 S.W.2d at 543 (emphasis added), because "a court of equity does not have jurisdiction to render a judgment for a plaintiff on legal issues in the absence of a finding that some equitable right of the plaintiff has also been violated." Krummenacher v. Western Auto Supply Co., 358 Mo. 757, 217 S.W.2d 473, 475 (banc 1949); Shultz v. Kline, 552 S.W.2d 333, 334 (Mo.App.1977). However, this exception applies only where the only relief sought is legal, or where the equitable claims of plaintiff are dismissed or found adversely to him, and thus there remains no equity in the case.

However, this court found in Willman v. Beheler, 499 S.W.2d at 777, that there was merit to relator's claim, and that he was entitled to enforce the covenant in equity. The cases cited by respondent in which equity lost jurisdiction because plaintiff's equitable claims were denied are thus inapposite.

In *Willman,* we * * * cited extensively cases holding that a court of equity may retain jurisdiction of a case to grant damages where equity requires this form of relief in the circumstances. *Id.* at 778. The clear implication was that the court on remand was to retain equity jurisdiction of the cause. As such, defendant would not be entitled to a jury trial. * * * We thus make our provisional rule absolute, prohibiting respondent from empaneling a jury at law for the hearing of the issue on damages in the *Willman v. Beheler* case.

MORGAN, C.J., BARDGETT, FINCH, DONNELLY and RENDLEN, JJ., and SIMEONE, SPECIAL JUDGE, concur.

Notes

1. The equitable clean-up doctrine remains alive and well in Missouri. In Linville v. Wilson, 628 S.W.2d 422 (Mo.App.1982), the plaintiff sued the defendant, an adjoining landowner, for damages and injunctive relief, alleging that the defendant had dammed a stream that crossed both parties' property, thereby causing injury to the plaintiff's property. The trial court denied defendant's request for a jury trial and granted the plaintiff's prayer for injunctive relief as well as actual and punitive damages. On appeal, the Missouri Court of Appeals affirmed the denial of a jury trial and stated:

> "Defendants vigorously assert that they were improperly denied a trial by jury. The crux of this argument is a forthright attack upon the doctrine of 'equitable cleanup.' The trial court denied a jury trial under the recognized rule that, when equitable jurisdiction attaches, the court may determine the legal issues incident to the entire case. Defendants rely on two federal cases, Beacon Theatres, Inc. v. Westover, 359 U.S. 500, 79 S.Ct. 948, 3 L.Ed.2d 988 (1959); Dairy Queen, Inc. v. Wood, 369 U.S. 469, 82 S.Ct. 894, 8 L.Ed.2d 44 (1962), which interpret the Federal Rule of Civil Procedure 38 as eliminating the doctrine of 'equitable cleanup.' Defendants say Federal Rule 38 is identical to Missouri Rule 69.01 and that a similar interpretation should be made. The difficulty with the argument is that the latest controlling authority is to the contrary on the issue of a right to jury trial when equitable jurisdiction has attached. State *ex rel.* Willman v. Sloan, 574 S.W.2d 421 (Mo. banc 1978). The *Willman* case recognizes, applies, and affirms the doctrine of 'equitable cleanup' and is controlling."
>
> *Id.* at 425.

2. When a plaintiff joins legal and equitable causes of action in New York, the courts focus on which party is asserting a right to jury trial. Consider, in this regard, the following passage from John W. Cowper Co. v. Buffalo Hotel Development Venture, 99 A.D.2d 19, 22–23, 471 N.Y.S.2d 913, 915–917 (1984):

"It is hardly necessary to state that the right to trial by jury is zealously protected in our jurisprudence and yields only to the most compelling circumstances. 'Trial by jury in all cases in which it has heretofore been guaranteed by constitutional provision shall remain inviolate forever;' (N.Y. Const., art. I, § 2). That guarantee extends to all causes of action to which the right attached at the time of adoption of the 1894 Constitution (4 Weinstein–Korn–Miller, N.Y.Civ.Prac., pars. 4101.07, 4101.08). Historically, however, actions at law were tried by a jury, matters cognizable in equity were tried by the chancellor. Even though the two systems have merged, vestiges of the law-equity dichotomy remain in the area relating to trial by jury (Siegel, New York Practice, § 4; 4 Weinstein–Korn–Miller, N.Y.Civ.Prac., par. 4103.07). For example, joinder in a complaint of both legal and equitable causes of action arising from the same transaction constitutes a waiver by plaintiff of his right to a trial by jury. Such waiver, of course, applies only to the plaintiff as defendant retains his right to a jury trial on the legal issues (DiMenna v. Cooper & Evans Co., 220 N.Y. 391, 115 N.E. 993; CPLR 4102, subd. [c]). [Otherwise a] plaintiff, simply by joining a single cause of action for lien foreclosure, (which incidently also seeks a money judgment), could effectively deprive defendants of their constitutional right to a jury trial on the contract claim. 'A plaintiff cannot, by artful pleading, deprive a defendant of his constitutionally guaranteed right to a jury trial * * * by characterizing a legal action as equitable (citations omitted)' (Gordon v. Continental Cas. Co., 91 A.D.2d 987, 457 N.Y.S.2d 844). Despite inclusion of the lien foreclosure claim, the lawsuit is essentially one to recover money damages for breach of contract and the 'critical factual issues should be resolved by a jury (Siegel, New York Practice, § 439; 4 Weinstein–Korn–Miller, N.Y.Civ.Prac., par. 4101.39; cf. Solnick v. Whalen, 49 N.Y.2d 224 [425 N.Y.S.2d 68, 401 N.E.2d 190])' (Edwards, Inc. v. Lax, 85 A.D.2d 509, 444 N.Y.S.2d 103).

"Although this principle has not been frequently invoked in New York, it is well established under the Federal Rules. In Dairy Queen, Inc. v. Wood, 369 U.S. 469, 82 S.Ct. 894, 8 L.Ed.2d 44, plaintiff sought injunctive relief and an accounting together with damages for breach of contract. The answer set forth defenses of oral modification, laches and estoppel, and violation of the antitrust laws. Plaintiff sought to preclude defendant from a jury trial, arguing that the action was purely equitable because the complaint was cast in terms of an 'accounting' rather than in terms of an action for 'debt' or 'damages.' Commenting that 'the constitutional right to trial by jury cannot be made to depend upon the choice of words used in the pleadings' (Dairy Queen, Inc. v. Wood, 369 U.S. 469, 477–478, 82 S.Ct. 894, 899–900, 8 L.Ed.2d 44, *supra*), the Court found that, despite the inclusion of equitable claims and defenses, the dispute was essentially over interpretation of a contract and an attempt by each party to collect money damages. Consequently, the Court ruled that defendant was entitled to a jury trial on the legal issues involved (*see, also,* Beacon Theatres, Inc. v. Westover, 359 U.S. 500, 79 S.Ct. 948, 3 L.Ed.2d 988; 5 Moore's Federal Practice [2d ed.], pars. 38.16, 38.17)."

FARMERS BANK & TRUST CO. v. ROSS

Court of Appeals of Indiana, 1980.
401 N.E.2d 74.

ROBERTSON, PRESIDING JUDGE.

Farmers Bank and Trust Co. (Bank) brought action against Bob Ross, his wife and his solely owned corporation J.B. Glenn Construction Co. on unpaid promissory notes and to foreclose a mortgage on certain real estate. Ross counterclaimed for damages, alleging a breach of contract by the bank to loan money to Ross for his excavating business. After the evidence was heard, the trial court gave the case to the jury for decision over the objection of the Bank. The jury granted the Bank's claim in part and granted Ross's counterclaim. The Bank appeals and, because of our determination that reversible error exists, we need decide only one issue. That issue is whether it was error for the trial court to refuse to treat the jury only as an advisory jury.

Ross timely requested a jury trial and our first determination is whether he was entitled to one. We note the Indiana Constitution, Art. 1, § 20, provides, "In all civil cases, the right of trial by jury shall remain inviolate." This phrase, "all civil cases," has been strictly construed as referring to all civil cases which were triable by jury at common law. State ex rel. Gannon v. Lake County Circuit Court, (1945) 223 Ind. 375, 61 N.E.2d 168. The result of this construction is bottomed in the historical fact that actions in equity were not tried before a jury, but those in law were.

This basic dichotomy remains in the judicial construction of Ind.Rules of Procedure, Trial Rule 38. *See* Hiatt v. Yergin, (1972) 152 Ind.App. 497, 284 N.E.2d 834. TR. 38(A) states:

> Causes triable by court and by jury. Issues of law and issues of fact in causes that prior to the eighteenth day of June, 1852, were of exclusive equitable jurisdiction shall be tried by the court; issues of fact in all other causes shall be triable as the same are now triable. In case of the joinder of causes of action or defenses which, prior to said date, were of exclusive equitable jurisdiction with causes of action or defenses which prior to said date were designated as actions at law and triable by jury—the former shall be triable by the court, and the latter by a jury, unless waived; the trial of both may be at the same time or at different times, as the court may direct.

Winney v. Board of Commissioners, (1977) Ind.App., 369 N.E.2d 661, 663, summarizes the interpretation of this section:

> In *Hiatt,* this was interpreted to mean that the right to a jury was dependent upon the claim or cause of action which is stated in the pleadings and that the pleader, for purposes of a jury demand, should keep in mind the traditional distinction between law and equity. The test, then, for deciding the right to a jury in a civil action requires a classification of the claim or cause of action as either sounding in equity or at law. *When this process of classification and analysis leads*

> *to the determination that the claim or cause of action, or any essential part thereof, is of equitable jurisdiction, the entire action is drawn into equity and the right to a jury is extinguished.* Conversely, where the claim or cause of action is not such as to invoke equity jurisdiction, it is to be considered to be an action at law where the right to trial by jury must be provided after a timely demand. [Emphasis added.]

There is no doubt in Indiana that an action on promissory notes and to foreclose a mortgage or lien is essentially equitable. Carmichael v. Adams, (1883) 91 Ind. 526. This is so even though the action on the note is legal. *Carmichael, supra.* It is also clear that once equity has the case, even a counterclaim sounding in law must be tried under the umbrella of equity; in short, there is no right to trial by jury as to the counterclaim. Fish v. Prudential Ins. Co. of America, (1947) 225 Ind. 448, 75 N.E.2d 57; Jones Drilling Corp. v. Rotman, (1964) 245 Ind. 10, 195 N.E.2d 857; Henning v. Reith–Riley Construction Co., Inc., (1967) 141 Ind.App. 99, 226 N.E.2d 350; *Winney, supra.*

In sum, then, there was no right to trial by jury as to any of the claims presented in this case.

We turn, then, to TR. 39(B) which states:

> In any case where there are issues * * * upon which there is no right to trial by jury as of right, the court may submit any or all of such issues to a jury for trial. The verdict *shall be* advisory unless, before the jury retires, the court, with the consent of both parties or their attorneys, orders that the verdict shall have the same effect as if a trial by jury had been a matter of right. [Emphasis added.]

Although we give a presumption to the trial court that it correctly determines the law, Ernst v. Sparacino, (1978) Ind.App., 380 N.E.2d 1271, it is clear from the record that the trial court did not treat the jury as advisory. Also, the Bank specifically objected to trial by non-advisory jury. *See also* TR. 39(C). Thus, the trial court committed error.

* * *

Reversed and remanded for action not inconsistent with this opinion.

Notes

1. To what extent is the following language of the Nebraska Supreme Court in Kuhlman v. Cargile, 200 Neb. 150, 155, 262 N.W.2d 454, 458 (1978) consistent with the approach of the principal case?

"The rule is that when a cause of action for equitable relief is stated, and when the plaintiff prays for equitable relief, a jury trial cannot be demanded as a matter of right by the defendant. Even if the defendant pleads legal defenses or a counterclaim for damages, he is not entitled to a jury trial, as when a court of equity acquires jurisdiction over a cause of action for any purpose it may retain the cause for all purposes and proceed to a final determination on all matters put in issue in the case. It is the general rule that if a court of equity has properly acquired jurisdiction in a suit for equitable relief, it may make complete adjudication of all matters properly presented and involved in the case and grant relief, legal or equitable, as may be required and thus avoid unnecessary litigation."

2. Courts often experience difficulty in determining whether cases involving mixed equitable and legal elements are "primarily equitable or legal." Consider in this regard, the approach suggested by the Court of Appeals of Washington in State v. State Credit Association, Inc., 33 Wash.App.3d 617, 622, 657 P.2d 327, 331 (1983):

> "In such cases trial courts are accorded wide discretion in determining whether the case is primarily equitable or legal, thus meriting a bench or a jury trial. Brown v. Safeway Stores, Inc., 94 Wash.2d 359, 617 P.2d 704 (1980). This judicial discretion should be exercised with reference to the following factors:
>
> > (1) who seeks the equitable relief; (2) is the person seeking the equitable relief also demanding trial of the issues to the jury; (3) are the main issues primarily legal or equitable in their nature; (4) do the equitable issues present complexities in the trial which will affect the orderly determination of such issues by a jury; (5) are the equitable and legal issues easily separable; (6) in the exercise of such discretion, great weight should be given to the constitutional right of trial by jury and if the nature of the action is doubtful, a jury trial should be allowed; (7) the trial court should go beyond the pleadings to ascertain the real issues in dispute before making the determination as to whether or not a jury trial should be granted on all or part of such issues.
>
> *Brown,* at 368, 617 P.2d 704."

3. A significant number of state courts are following the federal approach in deciding jury trial questions in cases involving mixed legal and equitable elements. For examples of cases in which jury trial was required on "legal" counterclaims to equitable causes of action, *see* David Steed & Associates v. Young, 115 Idaho 247, 766 P.2d 717 (1988); Higgins v. Barnes, 310 Md. 532, 530 A.2d 724 (1987); Evans Financial Corp. v. Strasser, 99 N.M. 788, 664 P.2d 986 (1983); Construction Systems and Engineering, Inc. v. Jennings Construction Corp., 413 So.2d 1236 (Fla.App.1982); General Electric Credit Corp. v. Richman, 338 N.W.2d 814 (N.D.1983); Landers v. Goetz, 264 N.W.2d 459 (N.D.1978); State *ex rel.* West Virginia Truck Stops, Inc. v. McHugh, 160 W.Va. 294, 233 S.E.2d 729 (1977).

MILLER v. ST. LOUIS & K.C. RY. CO.

Supreme Court of Missouri, 1901.
162 Mo. 424, 63 S.W. 85.

Plaintiff, by this suit, seeks to recover of defendant compensation for injury to his farm, caused by defendant in entering on his land and appropriating a strip 100 feet wide, upon which it constructed and is maintaining and operating its railroad. Defendant, by its answer, admits all the allegations of the petition, but seeks to avoid liability for the damages claimed because it says it had a right to enter on the plaintiff's land, and appropriate it for the purpose named, by virtue of a written contract, executed by plaintiff, granting the right of way, and authorizing the acts complained of, upon payment of $600, which it had tendered the plaintiff before suit, and plaintiff had refused the same. The answer sets out, in effect, that the written agreement mentioned does not in terms give the defendant for its right of way the 100–foot strip actually taken, but was intended to do so; and it prays a reformation of the written instrument, and a specific performance of the agreement as really intended by both parties. * * * The answer is designed to be, in effect, a bill in equity, and seeks the affirmative relief above mentioned. The reply was a general denial. When the cause came on for trial the plaintiff insisted that it was a suit at law, to be tried with the help of a jury. The defendant contended that it was a suit in equity, to be tried by the court as in chancery. The court ruled that the issues presented by the answer made a case in equity, but that if, upon a trial of those issues, the finding should be for the plaintiff, the question as to plaintiff's damages would be for a jury. Thereupon a trial of the issues under the affirmative averments of the answer was had, and the court found for the plaintiff, and entered a judgment in his favor on those issues, and at the same time ordered that the remaining issues were for trial by jury, and continued the cause to the next term for such trial. Defendant filed a motion for new trial, which was overruled, and filed a bill of exceptions, and took an appeal to this court; but when the record was brought here the appeal was dismissed on the ground that it was premature, there being no final judgment. The circuit court then proceeded to try the remaining issues with the aid of a jury, who found for the plaintiff, and assessed his damages at $1,800 principal and $248 interest, making the total $2,048, for which judgment was rendered, and defendant, after due course, has taken this appeal.

* * *

Appellant contends that its answer converted the whole case into a suit in equity, and that the court erred in submitting any of the issues to a jury. In support of that contention appellant refers to the familiar principle that, where a court of equity has jurisdiction of a case for any purpose, it will not leave it to be sent unfinished to another court, but will dispose of all the issues, even if some of them be such as, if standing alone, are triable only in a court of law. Woodard v. Mastin, 106 Mo. 324; McCollum v. Boughton, 132 Mo. 601, 621, 30 S.W. 1028, 33 S.W. 476, 34 S.W. 480, 35 L.R.A. 480. But there must exist in the facts of the case some equity upon which it exercises its peculiar jurisdiction in part relief. If, when it comes to consider the case, there is found no equity in it, and no equitable relief therefor is granted, a court of equity will not retain the case to try the purely legal issues that may be in it. The principles which distinguish a lawsuit from a suit in equity are to be as clearly regarded and preserved under our Code of Civil Procedure as they were when law and equity were administered in separate tribunals. Under the ancient system, if the defendant, after being brought into a court of law to answer the plaintiff's cause of action, had been advised that its remedy lay in a reformation of its written contract and a specific performance of the same, it would have filed its bill in equity showing the facts, and praying that relief, and praying also that the plaintiff be enjoined from the prosecution of his suit in the law court until the cause could be heard in the court of equity. In such case, if the defendant in the lawsuit prevailed in his suit in equity, he would be entitled not only to the reformation of his contract, and a specific performance of the same, but also to a perpetual injunction against the plaintiff in the lawsuit. And in that way equity would dominate the whole case. But, if the defendant in the lawsuit failed in his equity suit, his bill would be dismissed, and the plaintiff in the lawsuit would be free to proceed to final judgment in the court of law. The uniting of law and equity in one suit, as authorized by our Code, does not confuse the two, but only requires both to be tried in one court; the issues in equity being for trial by the judge as a chancellor, the issues in law by the same judge with a jury. Since, however, the same court has control of the whole case, no injunction is required, either temporary or perpetual. When the answer is filed showing an equitable defense and asking equitable relief, the court merely postpones the trial of the issues tendered by the petition until those tendered by the answer are tried; and, if the equitable defense is sustained, and if it covers the whole case, a final judgment is rendered for the defendant, but, if the equitable defense is not sustained, the plaintiff's cause of action stands for trial as at law. This is the view the circuit judge took of this case, and his view was correct. But, after trying the issues tendered in the answer, and finding the equitable defense not sustained, the court should have only recorded its finding, and withheld its judgment on the same until the rest of the case was tried, and then pronounced judgment on the whole case; for there can be but one final judgment in a case.

Note

The question has been raised as to the effect of the interjection of "non-affirmative" equitable matters, such as laches, estoppel, and unclean hands. *See* O'Neil, Law or Equity, The Right to Trial by Jury in a Civil Action, 35 Mo.L.Rev. 43 (1970).

SECTION 2. PUNITIVE DAMAGES

I.H.P. CORP. v. 210 CENTRAL PARK SOUTH CORP.

Court of Appeals of New York, 1963.
12 N.Y.2d 329, 239 N.Y.S.2d 547, 189 N.E.2d 812.

BURKE, JUDGE. The principal law question on these cross appeals is whether the Supreme Court committed reversible error in awarding exemplary damages as incidental to injunctive relief. * * * The facts alleged were that plaintiff was the lessee in possession of the street level floor in the building of one of the defendants; that all of the defendants caused the premises to be broken into at night on two occasions during which certain damage was done to the leasehold; that each time barriers were placed on the means of access to bar plaintiff from the premises, all with the purpose of harassing plaintiff into surrendering its valuable lease; that similar acts will occur in the future unless restrained by the court. The relief requested was an injunction and treble damages. The note of issue repeated the request for injunction, and "$5,000 plus exemplary damages besides injunction".

Defendants challenge the propriety of the award, not as a matter of the law of damages but rather on the procedural ground that "the function of a court of equity goes no further than to award compensatory damages as incidental to injunctive relief: it may not assess exemplary damages." Defendants' position, aside from the right to a jury trial, which we think is waived here, is based on an erroneous concept of the court system of this State. We have one court of general jurisdiction which administers *all* of New York law, be that law of legal or equitable origin. * * *

No amount of authority in other States should persuade us that Judge Cardozo was wrong when he said in Susquehanna S.S. Co. v. Andersen & Co. (239 N.Y. 285, 294, 146 N.E. 381, 384): "The whole body of principles, whether of law or of equity, bearing on the case, becomes the reservoir to be drawn upon by the court in enlightening its judgment." Maitland expressed the same view when he predicted that "The day will come when lawyers will cease to inquire whether a given rule be a rule of equity or a rule of common law; suffice it that it is a well-established rule administered by the High Court of Justice." (Maitland, Equity [1909], p. 20.) Needless to say, we have accepted Maitland's and Judge Cardozo's understanding of the consequences of the merger.

Of course, we are obliged to preserve inviolate "Trial by jury in all cases in which it has heretofore been guaranteed by constitutional provision" (N.Y. Const., art. I, § 2). It is to this sole remaining jurisdictional distinction between law and equity that we now turn.

Assuming that defendants had a constitutional right to a jury trial of the issues of fact supporting the award of exemplary damages (an assumption which is not free from uncertainty—*see* Lynch v. Metropolitan El. Ry. Co., 129 N.Y. 274, 29 N.E. 315, 15 L.R.A. 287; Jamaica Sav. Bank v. M.S. Investing Co., 274 N.Y. 215, 8 N.E.2d 493, 112 A.L.R. 1485; *but see* Hudson v. Caryl, 44 N.Y. 553; Cogswell v. New York, N.H. & H. Ry. Co., 105 N.Y. 319, 11 N.E. 518; City of Syracuse v. Hogan, 234 N.Y. 457, 138 N.E. 406), it is clear that the failure to move to separately state and number the causes of action or to demand a jury trial constituted a waiver of any such right (Civ.Prac.Act, § 425).

* * *

The judgment should therefore, be affirmed, without costs.

[The dissenting opinion of VAN VOORHIS, J., is omitted.]

Note

In reliance on the principal case, courts increasingly sanction awards of punitive damages in equitable actions. *See* Miller v. Cudahy, *supra* pp. 545–546; Hutchison v. Pyburn, *supra* pp. 890–894, Annot., 67 A.L.R.3d 350 (1975) (allowance of punitive damages in shareholder's derivative actions); Annot., Punitive Damages: Power of Equity Court to Award, 58 A.L.R.4th 844 (1987). For an excellent summary of the trend toward awarding punitive damages in equity, see Capitol Federal Sav. & Loan Ass'n v. Hohman, 9 Kan.App.2d 217, 675 P.2d 384 (1984). However, it should be emphasized that equitable relief must actually be granted in order to sustain such a punitive award. *See, e.g.,* Dotlich v. Dotlich, 475 N.E.2d 331 (Ind.App.1985) (since the defendant, who aided and abetted another's acts, was not held liable in equity, punitive damages could not be awarded against him).

*

Index

References are to Pages

References are to Pages

References are to Pages

References are to Pages

†